Wandermore in Minnesota

Your ultimate guide to the
Land of 10,000 Lakes!

Written by Seth Varner
Published by Wandermore Publishing LLC

Copyright © 2025 Wandermore Publishing LLC

All rights reserved. No part of this publication may be reproduced, distributed, or transmitted in any form or by any means, including photocopying, recording, or other electronic or mechanical methods, without the prior written permission of the publisher, except in the case of brief quotations embodied in critical reviews and certain other noncommercial uses permitted by copyright law. For permission requests, please get in touch with the publisher using the e-mail listed below.

Library of Congress Control Number: Forthcoming; Contact Publisher for Information

ISBN: 978-1-7361368-8-1

Printed by DiggyPOD, Inc., in the United States of America. Distributed from Omaha, Nebraska

First printing edition, December 2025

Wandermore Publishing may be reached at
sethvarner@wandermorepublishing.com
https://www.wandermorepublishing.com

Table of Contents

Content Disclaimer 6
Road Trip Games 7
Road Trip Travel Tips 8
An Introduction 9
Foreword 19
Minnesota County Map 20
Minnesota Highway Map 21
Aitkin County 22
Anoka County 25
Becker County 35
Beltrami County 40
Benton County 45
Big Stone County 53
Blue Earth County 57
Brown County 65
Carlton County 72
Carver County 77
Cass County 90
Chippewa County 97
Chisago County 101
Clay County 106
Clearwater County 113
Cook County 121
Cottonwood County 124
Crow Wing County 128
Dakota County 138
Dodge County 152
Douglas County 160
Faribault County 166
Fillmore County 172
Freeborn County 180
Goodhue County 187
Grant County 200
Hennepin County 203
Houston County 230
Hubbard County 235
Isanti County 238
Itasca County 246
Jackson County 254
Kanabec County 258
Kandiyohi County 259
Kittson County 266
Koochiching County 277
Lac qui Parle County 281
Lake County 285
Lake of the Woods County 289
Le Sueur County 291
Lincoln County 302
Lyon County 306
Mahnomen County 313
Marshall County 314
Martin County 326
McLeod County 332
Meeker County 336
Mille Lacs County 342

Morrison County 345
Mower County 353
Murray County 365
Nicollet County 370
Nobles County 374
Norman County 381
Olmsted County 385
Otter Tail County 395
Pennington County 406
Pine County 408
Pipestone County 415
Polk County 421
Pope County 435
Ramsey County 439
Red Lake County 449
Redwood County 452
Renville County 461
Rice County 475
Rock County 481
Roseau County 485
Saint Louis County 490
Scott County 509
Sherburne County 522
Sibley County 525
Stearns County 529
Steele County 546
Stevens County 549
Swift County 552
Todd County 563
Traverse County 569
Wabasha County 571
Wadena County 577
Waseca County 581
Washington County 584
Watonwan County 605
Wilkin County 610
Winona County 614
Wright County 620
Yellow Medicine County 630
QR Code Tutorial 642
QR Code Photo Albums 643
Minnesota Campgrounds 686
Minnesota Fast Facts 693
Minnesota Governors 694
Minn. Scenic & Historic Byways 695
Sources 697
Acknowledgements 698
Town Index 716
About the Author 721
More by Wandermore Publishing 722

Content Disclaimer

Note that communities are dynamic entities and that town attractions, breweries, campgrounds, distilleries, festivals, golf courses, lodging locations, National Register of Historic Places locations, restaurants, Scenic Byways, wineries, and other similar places of business are subject to change. *Please* do your homework before traveling!

An attempt has been made to provide as accurate travel information as possible, but there is the assured possibility that some addresses, business names, etc., will change over time. Additionally, please note that not every entity in every town (brewery, store, restaurant, museum, golf course, National Register of Historic Places locations, etc.) is included in this guide. If you would like to suggest a new or existing place of interest to be added, please get in touch with the publisher.

Wandermore's QR Code photo albums are subject to the longevity of Google Photos, a photo-sharing and storage service developed by Alphabet Inc. Should the photo albums become defunct, please get in touch with the publisher.

We attempt to update our Wandermore guides at least once per calendar year. The copyright page at the bottom of page 4 shows when your guide was published.

All photographs in this guide are the property of Wandermore Publishing LLC and may not be reproduced or distributed without the express written consent of Wandermore Publishing LLC. We ask that readers enjoy the printed photos and QR code photo albums but not use them for their own works and projects without first receiving permission from the publisher.

Wandermore Publishing may be reached at
sethvarner@wandermorepublsihing.com
https://www.wandermorepublishing.com
(Updated December 2025)

Road Trip Games

Wandermore's My Cows: The objective of this game is to "collect" as many herds as possible before reaching your destination. To play, whenever you see a group of cows (or even a single cow roaming the countryside by its lonesome), say "My Cows" to claim the herd as your own. If two players say "My Cows" simultaneously, they must play rock-paper-scissors to determine the rightful herd owner.

If your caravan comes across a cemetery, the first player to shout, "Dead Cows!" effectively "kills" the herds of all the other players, and their scores are reset to zero. If another player mistakes a group of animals (pigs, sheep, horses, etc.) for a herd of cows, they lose one herd (one point). The game revolves around spotting cattle and cemeteries before the other players in the vehicle.

Wandermore's A-Z Game: Players must agree on a category and then name a noun that fits within it while alternating letters of the alphabet. The game continues until (a) there are no longer nouns that fit the corresponding letter and category, (b) a player repeats a noun that another player has already said. For situation (a), if no players can think of a noun, the letter is skipped, and the following letter is used to continue the game with all players.

Example Category: Minnesota towns
Player 1: "Annandale." Player 2: "Bemidji." Player 3: "Cokato." Player 1: "Dassel." Player 2: "Ely." and so forth.

Wandermore's Music Game: One individual is designated as the "DJ" and will connect to the vehicle AUX. The DJ will play a song from their music library, and all other players in the car must try to guess (1) the name of the song and (2) the name of the main artist. Players who successfully name either (or both) options earn one point per correct guess. If two players simultaneously say the artist's or song name, the DJ determines who the rightful owner of the point is, or the players play rock-paper-scissors.

Wandermore's License Plate Game: Ideal for Interstate travelers, players compete to "collect' as many out-of-state license plates as possible before reaching their destination. Plates are claimed by saying "License Plate Claimed" followed by the state listed on the other vehicle's plate. Once a state or province is claimed, another player cannot claim it as their own again.

Road Trip Travel Tips

(1) The most common public restrooms are at gas stations or state-designated rest areas. However, if you're in a pinch, check out local bars/restaurants or public parks, baseball fields, and recreation areas/public water access points for outhouses.

(2) You can earn cashback on the gas you buy in several ways. Consider checking out an app such as Upside (use referral code 2UR6XH for a bonus) to earn up to 25 cents back per gallon. Many credit cards, grocery chains, and gas-station rewards programs also offer cashback on gas.

(3) Always buy your drinks in bulk. Summer temperatures in the Midwest can be extreme, so always stock up on water by buying a 24-pack at a gas station (typically ranging from $4.00 to $8.00). Even better, please bring a reusable bottle and ask to refill it with water at local gas stations or restaurants.

(4) If you plan to visit several state parks or recreation areas within the same year, purchase an annual Park Entrance License rather than paying for the daily park licenses (https://www.dnr.state.mn.us/state_parks/permit.html).

(5) When visiting small-town bars or restaurants, it is necessary to carry cash. Many establishments outside of cities do not accept credit or debit cards, and withdrawing money from a local ATM will often cost you a hefty fee. Also, *always* call ahead to see if they're open.

(6) Many times, the "sketchier" the exterior of the bar or restaurant, the tastier the food will be. Proceed at your own risk! ☺

(7) Use Apple Maps when using a smartphone or GPS to route from town to town (a general area). Use Google Maps when routing to a particular place, such as a museum (an address).

(8) Your roadside emergency kit should include a spare tire (if possible), extra water, snacks, a sleeping bag, blankets, a first aid kit, jumper cables, a phone charger, a flashlight, a towel, an additional quart of oil, windshield washer fluid, a jack and lug wrench, a portable compressor, a small shovel, hand warmers, a tow strap, and a bag of cat litter (for extra grip on your tires).

An Introduction to "Wandermore"

Who doesn't love a good road trip? While in broader terms, we may typically think of them as a half-country haul to the Grand Canyon or a car ride to the sandy white beaches of Florida, we take our own miniature "road trips" every day. Whether it's a morning cross-city commute, picking up a prescription from the local pharmacy, or driving down to grandma and grandpa's house for the weekend, we're constantly hitting the road to visit somewhere. There are infinite things to see and do across the country. Each of us has specific interests that have led us to unique destinations throughout the United States — often intentionally, but sometimes unintentionally!

I'm a road-tripper myself, but it's safe to say that I take the term to the extreme. Over the years, I've had the privilege of traveling to every incorporated town in Nebraska, Iowa, Kansas, both of the Dakotas, and, as of November 2025, Minnesota! That's about 3,623 communities I've had the pleasure of exploring, despite the constantly changing number of new municipalities and the disincorporation of old railroad and mining or logging towns. Whenever an opportunity arises to hit the road with friends or family, I make an effort to tag along and seek out what makes the region I'm in stand out in its own unique way. 2025 was my busiest travel season yet. Not only did I spend a week on the Maine coast with my wife, Eliese, for our honeymoon (very reminiscent of Minnesota between the bogs, the lighthouses, and the Thomas Dambo trolls!) after getting married in September, but I also took to the wild west for a weekend in Deadwood, South Dakota, for my bachelor party, toured the nation's capital for a week with my dad and brother in Washington D.C. (even going as far out of the way as Charlottesville, VA to tour Thomas Jefferson's *Mon-ti-chell-o*, prounced differently from Minnesota's *Mon-ti-sell-o*), and make some side quest trips to Kansas City, KS/MO, and a took a weekend off with my friends in South Padre Island, TX. Between all those excursions, I also completed my sixth Wandermore project over 94 days, visiting every one of Minnesota's 856 incorporated cities.

I've got a constant travel bug. No matter the occasion, I'm constantly looking for another adventure. It's a blast traveling from city to city to take in historical sites like the monuments of D.C. and the National Civil Rights Museum, or to marvel at the beautiful National Parks of the western U.S. Still, sometimes, I like to put my tourist hat and sunglasses away and travel for a different reason. Something more profound and more meaningful. After traveling to every nook and cranny of Minnesota, I documented every municipality through nearly 115,000 photographs, from the sprawling suburbs of the Twin Cities to the mining towns of the Iron Range to the little farming towns with populations in the single digits. I tried to explore the history, architecture, cuisine, and other quirky attractions that set every town or city apart.

Many people are baffled by how I came up with the idea to visit every town in a state. You'd think it's not exactly the idea that somebody comes up with without some backstory or long-winded explanation. And to that, my friend, you guess correctly! It all started with the COVID-19 pandemic in March of 2020. We all know how that went. Life was good and normal, and within a week, the world came crashing down.

Workplaces, schools, and universities ushered employees and students out the doors, and everyone was sent home as the world struggled to learn how to deal with a modern-day pandemic. At that time, I was a 19-year-old freshman in college at the University of Nebraska at Omaha. I worked for the Omaha Athletics Department, taking stats for the basketball, hockey, and soccer teams, and I attended in-person classes and lived on campus. One day, I was sitting in class learning about volcanoes and watching the NBA on television, and the next, I was told I had to move back in with my parents in my hometown of Wahoo, Nebraska.

For a month or so, I worked at the local Dairy Queen and attended my classes on Zoom. I played basketball and video games with my high school buddy Austin, who had also been sent home from Concordia University in Seward because of pandemic mandates. We were fine for a while, playing games and cruising Main Street Wahoo, but quarantine began to take its toll on us. Boredom started creeping in as we realized there wasn't much to do in a world where businesses were closed, and public gatherings of any degree weren't allowed. In a time where travel was limited, everything was closed, and making connections was next to impossible, I had the urge to make a something-out-of-nothing summer and do something that (to my knowledge then) nobody had done before: "Hey Austin, want to visit every town in Nebraska this summer?"

The idea stemmed from some core memories from my childhood. In 2009, when I was about 9 years old, my father, Dave, began working on a family tree project. In addition to your typical family tree information like birthdays, names, and the like, he wanted to expand his project to include photographs of the headstones of deceased relatives, the churches they had attended, and the homes they lived in. He recruited little ole' me and his mother to accompany him on a series of road trips throughout Butler and Seward County, Nebraska, to take some up-to-date photos of the sites. While he photographed points of family interest, I had an agenda of my own. Equipped with my disposable Wal-Mart camera, I took photos of the things that caught my interest: population signs, water towers, and sites like the Baloney Shop of Malmo or the green Wal-Mart in York. Things that captured the attention of a third-grader, you know, the important stuff! Around the same time, my mother, Leigh, instilled a love of travel in me by taking my brother and me on a trip to the Caribbean, where I first began to understand that there was an entire world to explore beyond my little bubble in Wahoo. We stopped our road trips as my dad finished the family tree project. I remember poring over a map of Nebraska on our way home from one trip and asking Dad, "Can we visit every town in Nebraska?" To which I likely got a chuckle and a "Maybe someday, Seth" response.

The thought of visiting all of Nebraska's communities must've stuck in the back of my mind, but my obsession with traveling, geography, and writing was more profound. In third grade, I started writing books about "Fluffy the Kitten," the adventures of my favorite farm cat, who loved spending time with his friends. One such rendition of the fifteen-book series was "Fluffy the Kitten Travels the World," in which Fluffy flew his plane to all corners of the globe to take in the world's most famous sights. My classmates Eli and Marcela drew the pictures for my books and helped me present them to my classmates. As I continued to see the world through our family vacations, I became more enthralled with geography and travel, and in the fifth grade, I launched my then-second website, "SVGeography." I compiled articles, photos, and videos from around the web, and my teacher, Mrs. Julie Simons, would incorporate them in her lesson plans when applicable. By the time I was fifteen, I was in charge of planning our first actual family road trip to Oklahoma City and Kansas City, a responsibility that I have maintained throughout the years as we've made our way to places like the Great Smoky Mountains of Tennessee, the Wisconsin Dells, Washington D.C., and the Grand Canyon and the American West. All things considered, I think it's easy to see how my childhood interests have influenced my career choice to be a traveler and writer, and how a few little trips around my dad's stomping grounds have turned into the ambition to start the pioneer Wandermore project in Nebraska.

On April 22, 2020, Austin and I began our two-and-a-half-month trek across the Cornhusker State. We didn't travel continuously, though. We'd go out for a day and visit a handful of towns, but return to Wahoo to work at Dairy Queen for the next few. It became a weekly thing: every four to eight days or so, we'd hit the road for the day, then come home to sleep in our own beds. The project wasn't very serious for the first few weeks of traveling. We'd visit the towns, take a selfie with something that displayed the town's name—typically the welcome sign—and continue to the next community. Sometimes we'd stop for fast food or wander the town a bit, but we weren't taking pictures, meeting people (since we didn't know much about COVID), or touring businesses, restaurants, or museums. The point of the trips, then, was solely our own enjoyment of getting out of the house and having a little fun with the welcome signs by making funny poses with our Energizer bunny, a little pink plush rabbit that Austin's mom thought should tag along as our "mascot." At the end of our trip, we planned to hand over the photos to our mothers so they could make a scrapbook of our travels, and that would be that.

I didn't tell my parents about the first few trips. I thought they wouldn't be too pleased with my idea to visit every town in the state amid an ongoing pandemic. However, as Austin and I kept disappearing with our friends for entire days, I eventually broke the news to them about fifty towns in the project. It took a little convincing, but after I insisted that we were playing things safe and mostly keeping to ourselves, they ended up being okay with it. My mom suggested I start sharing my photos on Facebook. I had started an Instagram page for our friends, but she thought we'd reach more people if we shared our travels on the larger platform. Part of me now feels that she just wanted to keep tabs on what exactly her son was doing, gallivanting around in the middle of a pandemic!

Her idea to start a Facebook page was ingenious! Within a couple of weeks of launching "Visit531Nebraska" on social media, we began receiving interview requests from television and radio stations and every small-town newspaper. We couldn't believe it. Within the first month, we gained over 10,000 followers, and comments, likes, and messages poured in. At that moment, I recognized that the project could be much more than just a scrapbook adventure, so I embraced the attention and started incorporating followers' suggestions into trips, and began meeting people.

As the months progressed, we continued to hear stories from locals of their favorite memories of the town and what seeing our few photos (at this time, we only took a few since Instagram, my then-favorite platform, only allowed us to share ten in a single post) meant to them. A theme came to light. No matter how big or small the community, its past and present residents were eager to show their hometown pride and make it known to the world what their community was known for. Austin and I saw this theme unfold as we continued our trek around Nebraska: there's something to do in every town, but you've got to go out and find it. A great example that brings this principle to light is our visit to Monowi, a village with a population of one. It's the smallest incorporated town in the United States, with Elsie being the sole resident, mayor, bartender, and librarian. Even in this community of one, we were able to keep ourselves busy. We ate at the bar and talked with Elsie about her life and her memories of the town that once was. She showed us Rudy's Library, a collection of thousands of books owned by her late husband, and an old church in which she was one of the last people in attendance. What many would hardly consider a dot on the map was a several-hour adventure that took us through the life cycle of a small farming town. Even in a place with a population of 50, 500, or 5,000 people, we discovered that there was always something to learn, do, or explore.

We amassed a following of 21,000 individuals by the conclusion of our trip around Nebraska. We finished our journey in our hometown on July 17, 2020, with a small parade and a celebration. In attendance were *Nebraska Stories*, a public television series that showcased clips and photos from our adventure around Nebraska, two other news stations, and a couple of hundred community members. It was a fantastic sendoff for an incredible accomplishment. As I read through the Facebook comments on our final town post, I saw several people calling for our adventure to be documented in a coffee-table book so people could relive the journey again and again. I gave it some thought and decided to give it a go. I worked day and night throughout the fall of my sophomore year of college to compile a book featuring photos and brief information about every incorporated town in Nebraska. I detailed what my friends and I saw, heard, and tasted throughout our two-and-a-half-month escapade, shared historical facts and tidbits, and created a living photo album feature using QR codes. I knew the feature would come in handy down the road because, as I traveled through Nebraska, I could someday add more photos of community buildings or inside looks at museums and restaurants as I continued my travels. Since then, thousands of images have been added to the living albums, and those who purchased the books in 2020 can see where else I've visited in Nebraska since the conclusion of the Visit531Nebraska project. The book, a complete afterthought of a project intended to avoid boredom during a global pandemic, has evolved over the years into a resource for restaurants, lodging, festivals, recreation areas, museums, and more.

The book "Visit531Nebraska: Our Journey to Every Incorporated Town in the State" was an incredible success. I'll never forget the feeling of having to take loans from my family members and pour my life savings into buying inventory, or the joy I felt when I held a copy of my published work for the very first time that November. After hundreds of hours of planning, writing, and traveling, I self-published a book and completed the project of a lifetime. As most of you readers already know, the adventure didn't end there either. It was only just the beginning.

In March of 2021, I decided to conduct a similar project called "Visit939Iowa" across the Mighty Mo, visiting every one of Iowa's incorporated communities. Austin joined me on these escapades as well, but this time I made it clear to Iowans that I intended to write a book about Iowa at the conclusion of my travels. Much to my surprise, the people of Iowa rallied around the project, and we were met with equal hospitality and support. I took more photos, met more people, ate at more local eateries, and checked out more sites. Towards the end of the journey, I had taken on a somewhat documentary mindset when I realized that people wanted to see *everything* left behind in a town. Instead of focusing solely on notable sites like restaurants, historical markers, and downtown areas, by the end of the project in September, I was trying to capture older buildings or even sites like repair shops and city parks. In September, our travels concluded, and I had the book ready to go by November. After another successful trip, the idea cemented in my mind that these projects could become a full-time career.

As I delved deeper into my business classes in the Fall of 2021, I realized I needed to make the business look more professional if I pursued it full-time. The company was then just called "Visit531Nebraska," but people were confused why a business with that name had visited every town in Iowa and written a book about both states. I needed to change the name. I loved the term wanderlust but found it overused, so I kept working to come up with a play on words that could showcase what I was trying to do. I wondered. And my thoughts wandered. And they wandered some more. Thirty minutes into my first brainstorming session in the shower, it came to me: Wandermore Publishing, a book-publishing company whose guides combine travel with history to encourage people to explore their home states across the Midwest. I revamped the website, set up the company, and printed the business cards; thus, Wandermore Publishing was born.

The "Wandermore's Visit310SouthDakota" project was launched in February of 2022, and this time I would be accompanied by my college friend and, later, the best man at my wedding years down the road, Jack, to every community. This state was the first project in which I embraced the documentation mindset and began to spend extra time on the road to capture more photos per town than I had in Nebraska or Iowa. I took several laps in the smaller cities to ensure I didn't miss churches or other buildings on the outskirts. I focused on capturing as many "big ticket" buildings and attractions as possible in the larger communities. The project lasted about four months, and it was then that I came up with the idea of starting the Wandermore Travel Fund to allow people to contribute funds in exchange for having the names of their friends, family, loved ones, pets, and businesses placed in the back of a book. Still in college at the time, the extra funds allowed Jack and me to spend more time on the road as I put together photos and information for my third book. It was released in August of 2022.

"Wandermore in Kansas," conducted between February and October 2023, was the most comprehensive Wandermore project of the four. After finishing Nebraska and traveling east to Iowa and north to South Dakota, it only made sense to look south and take on the Sunflower State. After 17,000+ miles on the road and over eight months of traveling, writing, and researching, I successfully visited every incorporated community in Kansas. I snapped 50,000+ photos—more than I've taken in any other state by a landslide. It was the first state in which I could focus nearly 100% of my attention because, until then, I had always had to work another job and be in school. I remained proactive in my studies from February through May of 2023, when I graduated with my degree in Business Administration, Marketing, and Management. From then on, I was able to devote my full attention to the project. The extra time and freedom allowed me to meet with hundreds of people from all walks of life: convention and visitors bureaus, chambers of commerce, restaurant owners, attorneys, doctors, and blue- and white-collar workers alike. I ate at nearly 100 local establishments across Kansas and toured over 60 museums. Had it not been for the support I received from the previous three states and from all those who followed the Kansas project and left their tips, history, anecdotes, memories, and kind words, the project would not have reached the level of thoroughness it did.

Things only ramped up with the start of my Wandermore in North Dakota project in 2025. It was my first project where I didn't have to worry about keeping up college grades or working another full-time job while conducting it, and the results showed. After 1,500+ hours of work researching, writing, traveling, and maintaining the Facebook page, what emerged was a collection of photos and history unlike any other ever compiled in North Dakota. And I had SO much fun doing it. The extra time allowed me to shift all of my attention—well, at least most of it, since I got engaged to my best friend Eliese halfway through my travels—to experiencing all that the Peace Garden State had to offer. Upon its October release, it immediately became Wandermore's all-time best-selling book (selling over 2,000 copies in the first two days alone). Its success convinced me that what I was doing was important and that it was feasible to turn it into my full-time career.

It's funny to look back and see how a person's career can develop from their childhood interests in hobbies. For a kid who was writing books about his cat, loved traveling and taking photos at a young age, and always showed an interest in geography and history, it appears Wandermore Publishing would've come to fruition at some point. Maybe it's easy to say that now that COVID is essentially a thing of the past, but without that pandemic, who knows if I would have ever had the intention to "wander more" and learn more about Nebraska, Iowa, Kansas, Minnesota, the Dakotas, and all the little towns and cities of the Midwest.

All that leads us to 2025 and this book you now hold: "Wandermore in Minnesota." From February to November, I thoroughly explored the Land of 10,000 Lakes and shared my travels with the world on my sixth Facebook page. I shared the following excerpt on my page upon finishing the project:

When I started this journey in February, I knew it would be a lot of work. Trying to capture and share the essence of 856 towns and cities in a single year wasn't going to be easy. But I was determined to make this the biggest and best Wandermore project yet. And, after spending nearly 3,500 hours this year researching, writing about, traveling, and responding to your Facebook messages and comments, this is by far the BEST of the six Wandermore projects I've completed to date! With over 115,000 pictures (about 134 per community), all my time and effort have resulted in a collection of historical excerpts and photos unlike any other compiled about Minnesota.

Where can I even begin? All year, I've been making these individual wrap-up posts about the highlights of each leg, detailing my favorite bits and pieces of each region. My first time in Minnesota was back in 2018 on a family road trip, where my dad, brother, and I drove all the way up to Green Bay, Wisconsin, and back down through Minnesota on our way home to Nebraska. We did a lot of the typical touristy stuff that other out-of-staters would do. We took a night to shop at the Mall of America. On the drive up, we took a special interest in Saint Peter's Pearly Gates in St. Peter and the World's Largest Candy Store in Jordan. In Minneapolis, we visited Minnehaha Falls and had lunch at Mickey's Diner in St. Paul, but that was all! We spent a single day in the state, and I did not return until several years later in college to catch some Minnesota Vikings games with my roommates. Heck, even just a year ago in early 2024, my wife Eliese and I spent a whole weekend in Minneapolis/St. Paul and did many of the same things I mentioned above! We had no idea that there was SO much more to Minnesota than just the Twin Cities and the roads leading to and from it.

I hadn't expected Minnesota to be so touristy. I've been telling my friends and family all year that every town I've toured has been full of life and opportunities for visitors. Let's take the "Lakes" region, for example. Giant wooden trolls in Detroit Lakes that pop out of the woods when you least expect them to? Hundreds (if not thousands) of little lakes where you'll find anglers and boaters enjoying the waters? A "big foot" in Vining, amongst an extensive sculpture garden in a town with fewer than six dozen people?! Not to mention the legend of the ancient runestone in Alexandria or all of the other "World's Largest" statues that can be found throughout Otter Tail County!

In a single day, I got free beans at a bean festival in Pequot Lakes, then traveled 20 minutes south to Nisswa to cheer on turtle races. On Labor Day weekend, I found myself sitting and chatting with locals amongst thousands of people in the Stillwater and Hastings area, whilst sipping their drinks and enjoying the sunshine on the St. Croix River. In Stearns and Morrison Counties, I went to church more than a dozen times in three consecutive days because of how many small-town communities had preserved their one-thousand-plus-year-old edifices. Heck, I even went caving on two different occasions in the southeast corner of the state at Niagara Cave near Harmony and Mystery Cave outside of Spring Valley!

Or how about "Up North?" Like, the TRUE north, by Warroad, Roseau, and Baudette? Before this adventure, never would I have guessed that a little surveying error would place the far northern tip of Minnesota in a spot where you literally have to drive an hour through Canada to reach. I'd be lying if I said I had the confidence to drive across the 40-mile ice road that crosses the Lake of the Woods. Even in places so far away that some might consider them part of Canada, I found roadside oddities, fascinating history, and more than a few people eager to tell me about their community and showcase all the little things that make it special. And don't even get me started on the beauty of Grand Marais and Highway 61 between Duluth and the city on the sea. If you had told me that northeast Minnesota was home to a dozen waterfalls and that you didn't have to travel to Cancun/the Bahamas to feel like you were in paradise, I would've said you were bluffing! All this to say, no matter where I traveled in Minnesota–from the small prairie towns of the southwest like Pipestone and Walnut Grove, to the sprawling ancient forests like Northome's Lost 40, and the beautiful rocky topography that makes up the Iron Range of Hibbing, Biwabik, and all the gems in between, Minnesota truly is full of surprises.

Traveling across Minnesota has been so much more than checking towns off a list. It's been a chance for me to step into the stories that helped shape the Land of 10,000 Lakes into what it is today. From the beautiful architecture on old main streets to the multi-generational cafes and mom-and-pop shops, and the small-town museums, lakefronts, grain elevators, and everything in between, it's been so inspiring to discover what makes each of your communities unique and to witness your passion for small-town America firsthand. It didn't matter what the population of the town was-there was always somebody willing to offer a helping hand, whether it was inviting me for a meal at the local bar, or offering up an interesting piece of history and story that only a local would know. I talk about this a lot, but I genuinely believe that "Midwest Nice" and hospitality are very real things. Nebraskans claim to be "Nebraskan Nice," and we take great pride in offering a helping hand to those who need it. But you, Minnesota, went above and beyond!

TENS of thousands of Minnesotans, past and present, reached out over the course of the year! You shared suggestions for the best places to eat, and the neatest things to see and do. Many of you offered meetups to share history or provide access to a museum or local business. Others still contributed monetarily to help me conduct this product and share it with the world. A seemingly endless number of you offered words of encouragement and support via the Facebook comments. For all of that, I thank you. Thank you for your kindness and support, and for believing in me to do justice to your state. There are many folks I never had the chance to meet, but even to you, I have to express my gratitude for taking an interest in my project and for taking time out of your day to interact with me. Your cumulative support and enthusiasm have been the driving force behind this project, allowing it to be the success it is, to the point where the NATIONAL news even picked it up! Who would've thought that Blue Earth and Frost would've been shown off to millions on CBS Mornings when this whole thing started?! Certainly not I!

I saw and did a lot. In the 25,000+ miles I covered this year across 94 days, I snapped over 115,000 pictures, ate at over 200 local eateries and restaurants, toured nearly 70 museums, and visited all but six of the Minnesota State Parks. The gas tank in my 2023 Chevy Equinox—which lost a fuel injector in Montevideo, a fuel pump immediately after returning home from a trip, and a headlight in Itasca State Park when a tree attempted to squash me while driving—was filled 113 times. And, in between all the picture-taking and touring, I still found the time to have a meaningful conversation with 700 Minnesotans. We're not counting gas station clerks or restaurant servers here either. I'm talking about business owners, city officials, town historians, and passionate locals who either caught me randomly on the road or scheduled a time to meet with me! Many of these people are pictured above and are a large part of why this project turned out to be the success that it did. If I'm reading my Facebook analytics correctly, my posts reached 26 MILLION unique people this year!

However, I will also be the first to admit that I didn't see it all. I missed out on museums with one-of-a-kind artifacts. I didn't eat at the best restaurant in every community, nor did I have the chance to discover the beauty of every lake or hike every trail. I skipped out on hundreds of meetings because I couldn't find the time in my itinerary to meet with folks. I never got to see the interior of every church, read every historical marker, or learn the stories of Minnesota's unincorporated communities. And I definitely didn't photograph everything in the state either. There are many hundreds of sites I didn't get to during this project. But you know what? That's okay!! How could I do it all in just a year? How could anyone? Minnesota has SO much to see and do across its regions and communities that it would take many lifetimes to truly experience all the wonder and beauty it has to offer! I've had many wonderful experiences in Minnesota that I'll never forget. And now, it is right here, at this moment, that I call you to follow in my footsteps.

Get out of your comfort zone. We've all heard of the "throw a dart at the map" concept, and I challenge you to take that idea to heart. Explore what Minnesota has to offer! Get together with your best friends, your family, your coworkers, or anybody else you love and say, "I want to wander more around Minnesota with you!" Take that trip to the local county museum that you haven't been to since the fourth grade, and find something on display that resonates with you and your passions—how about the End-O-Line Railroad Park and Museum in Currie? Or the Judy Garland Museum in Grand Rapids? Litchfield even has one of Minnesota's last G.A.R. Halls that you can tour! Drive three hours in a random direction and stop at a random small-town bar for lunch. Ditch the menu and ask the waitress to bring you their house specialty. Maybe you'll end up at Bitton's Roadhouse in Garvin, or at King's Place in Miesville, where you'll have the best burger of your life! Maybe if you're extra lucky, you'll find yourself at Gustaf's on Main in Lindstrom for some authentic Swedish lingonberry pancakes! Tour a haunted hotel in Sauk Centre, like the Palmer House, or better yet, stay at Le Roy's Sweets Hotel! Take a road trip through the Iron Range and learn about mining history, or weave your way through the Driftless area, stopping in Amish country like Harmony and hidden gems like Lanesboro. You'd get a hoot out of visiting Houston, or you might catch a wave from the Jolly Green Giant in Blue Earth! I hear his giant nutcracker friend is just down the road in Lu Verne...

Support a local bakery or flower shop, tour a brewery, check out a book from a historic Carnegie library, and find a nearby lake to read it at, or even find a local to talk to, learn why their town–and specifically, any city in Minnesota–is different from all the rest. If you take nothing else from this Wandermore in Minnesota project, then take this: Every community, no matter rural or urban, population 100 people or 10,000 people, has something to offer. You've just gotta go out and find it. Our towns should be celebrated by our generation and the next for their people and the things that make them one-of-a-kind. Please take the time to "wander more" and explore as much of Minnesota as you possibly can in your lifetime. You never know where the road will take you next!

Thank you, Minnesota, for everything. This project has been an unbelievable and unforgettable journey. I feel blessed to have experienced each of your communities and to have helped preserve them for future generations to admire. My forthcoming Minnesota book will truly serve as a testament to all of the history, communities, and stories that make your state special, as well as a way for folks to find new places to explore and discover for themselves. While I'm heartbroken that my journey in Minnesota has come to an end, I must thank you once again for all the kindness and support you have shown this small-town Nebraska boy throughout 2025. I feel as if I can return to your state at any point and be welcomed with open arms! Goodbye for now, Minnesota, but I promise I'll be back time and time again to "wander more" through your state...Eliese and I are already looking forward to planning our next adventure in the Land of 10,000 Lakes! Thank you, thank you, Thank you for everything. And thank you to my wife, Eliese, for putting up with all the time I spent away from home this year. If it weren't for her never-ending support, I don't think I could have made it to the finish line! Thank you to all 232,000 people who follow my travels on Facebook for helping me expand small-town tourism and generate interest in their storied histories.

Never stop wandering more,

Seth Varner

CEO, Wandermore Publishing

Stay up to date with all things Wandermore on our Facebook pages: Wandermore in Nebraska, Wandermore in Iowa, Wandermore in South Dakota, Wandermore in Kansas, Wandermore in North Dakota, Wandermore in Minnesota, Wandermore in Colorado

Foreword: by Eliese Varner

This year, I got to experience Minnesota in true Wandermore fashion. I got to learn so much about Minnesota history and culture (the 'beg' vs. 'bag' debacle), but one thing really stood out to me about Minnesota. I couldn't help but be amazed by the community infrastructure in every town, no matter how big or small. Truly, Minnesotans should be so proud of the community they have fostered, which has allowed two outsiders like Seth and me to feel welcome far from home. Before this year, I had been to Minnesota once to visit the Mall of America, and at that time, I thought that was perhaps the best thing to do in Minnesota. I (wrongfully) assumed that there would be little to do in the state.

When Seth asked me mid-summer to join him on a trip one day before he was supposed to leave, I dropped everything to go, found emergency coverage at work, and prepared myself for what I thought would be a trip with a couple of lakes and not much else. Imagine my surprise when we arrived at the Iron Range, and all I could see was breathtaking beauty around me. I remember driving Highway 61 at sunset and marveling at the views of Lake Superior and the towering cliff faces. It didn't stop there either. Every part of the North Shore has my heart.

After that trip, Seth and I really discussed my joining Wandermore full-time. I was hesitant at first, worrying about what I would do or what would happen if I messed up, because Wandermore is Seth's baby. Eventually, we decided I would join Wandermore full-time after we got married! What a wild ride it's been on just these last three trips. From being interviewed for national television to seeing the Mississippi Bluffs in the fall, to visiting the many suburbs of the Twin Cities. I may not be able to claim that I have visited all 856 of Minnesota's Incorporated Cities, but the ones I have visited have been so full of life and love that I will never forget them.

I am so grateful to the people of Minnesota for supporting us on his mission to visit every town in Minnesota. The kindness and overflowing generosity are what allow us to do what we love—meeting new people, visiting new towns, and eating delicious cuisine (bar food). Minnesota has been such a behemoth of a state (the largest, most populated state Wandermore has EVER done). Without all the encouraging words, donations, and generosity of Minnesotans, we could never have finished it. I hope you enjoy 'wandering more' with Seth through Minnesota as much as I did.

Never stop wandering more,

Eliese Ueding-Varner

Director of Social Media & Fullfillment, Wandermore Publishing

Minnesota County Map

Source: GISGeography.com

Minnesota Highway Map

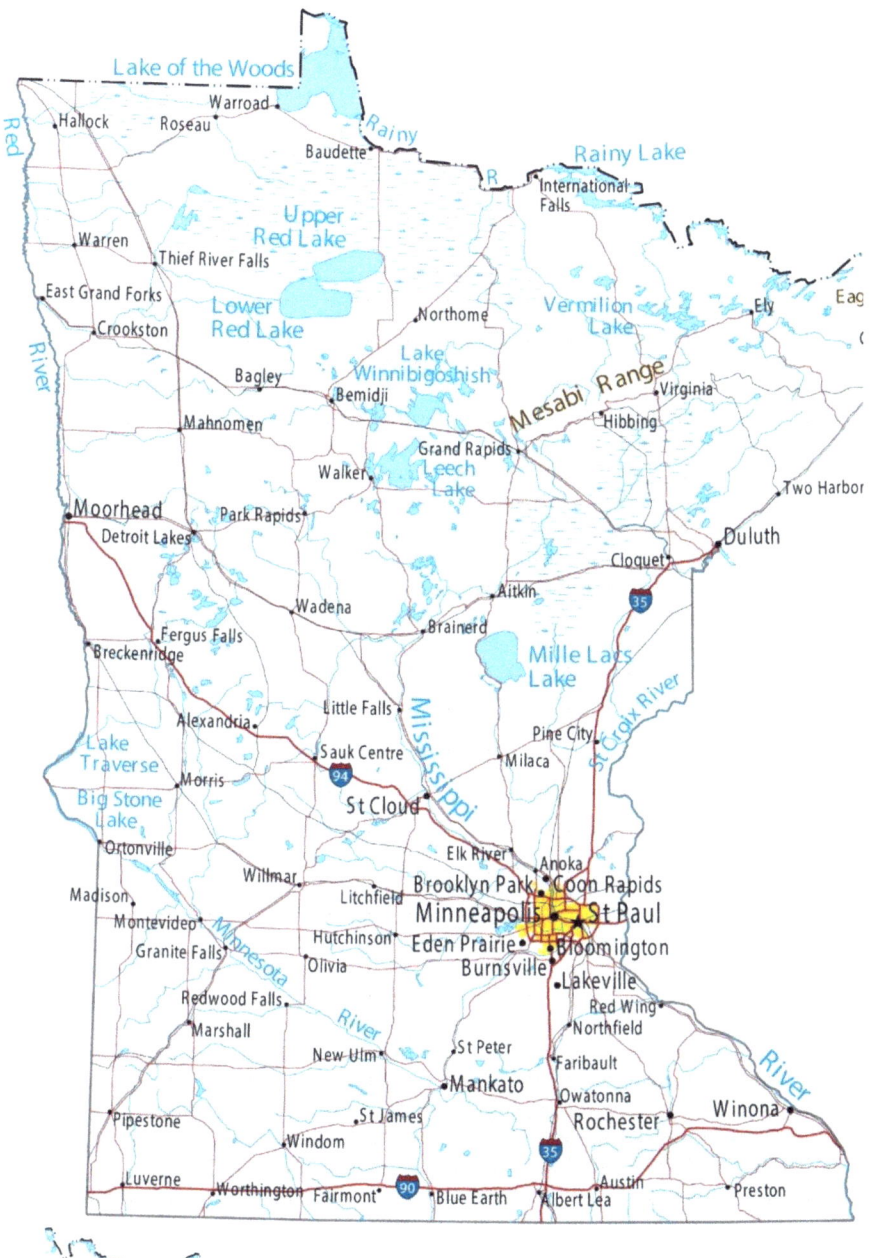

Source: GISGeography.com

★ – Designates County Seats
☆ – Designates County Fairgrounds Location

AITKIN COUNTY
EST. 1857 - POPULATION: 15,697

First established in 1857 as Aiken County, Aitkin's current spelling was adopted in 1872 to honor William Alexander Aitken, who traded furs with the Ojibwe as a member of the American Fur Company.

AITKIN, MN ★☆
POPULATION: 2,168 – CITY 398 OF 856 (7-15-25)
Before there was Aitkin, a town called Lexington had developed near the mouth of the Ripple River, where it connected with the Mississippi. It was annexed by the newly established Aitkin after a Northern Pacific Railroad surveyor, Nathaniel Tibbetts, laid out the present-day townsite circa September 13, 1870. His family settled on a 160-acre claim on the line in 1871 when Tibbetts suspected that the village of Aitkin, so named for the prominent fur trader William Alexander Aitken, would develop into a booming lumber and trade town. He was correct in his assumption, and Aitkin became a substantial riverboat transportation center. The Mississippi Transportation Company, founded by Charles Viebahn and W. F. Puntney, was the most important of these half-dozen-odd companies. Wild success within the industry led to the establishment of new rival trade points further west up the Mississippi, closer to the logging camps, one of which was a small (but now widely recognized) town called Grand Rapids. Aitkin itself became the county seat of the newly established Aitkin County in 1872, the same year that it obtained a post office. As many as seventeen saloons provided thirsty lumberjacks with the liquor they needed to "unwind from the day's activities." Still, as sawmills, churches, schools, and dance halls were built, the town garnered a more favorable reputation: the Minneapolis, St. Paul & Sault Ste. Marie Railroad came to town shortly thereafter. Many of its historic landmarks were built from this point through the end of the 1930s, when the logging industry began to decline. The 1884 Andy Gibson Mississippi River steamboat shipwreck site and the 1897 Swedish-American Bethlehem Lutheran Church are the only two pre-20th-century sites to be listed on the National Register of Historic Places. In 1911, Aitkin was the proud recipient of a Carnegie Library. From 1915 to 1920, a jail and a Beaux-Arts courthouse were built as necessary civic buildings. The Potter/Casey Company Building, formerly a large mercantile business; the 1915-16 Northern Pacific Depot, now home to the Aitkin County Depot Museum; the 1901 Patrick Casey House, built in the Queen Anne/Classical Revival style; and the 1937-38 New Deal Pine-Hickory Lakes Roadside Parking Area. As the local economy has transitioned from logging to agriculture and, more recently, to tourism, numerous resorts and recreational facilities have emerged to accommodate the increasing number of visitors to the area. The Sherwood Forest RV Resort attracts tourists to its campground due to its enormous Robin Hood statue. Thousands of fishermen come to the area in the wintertime to icefish on Lake Mille Lacs and the many other lakes in the vicinity; the day after Thanksgiving, they hold a parade in which their fishhouses and shacks are dragged down Main Street in the "World Famous Fish House Parade." Noteworthy residents from town include Warren William, a 1930s Hollywood actor with a star on the Hollywood Walk of Fame, known for his acting role as Perry Mason; Jonathan Edwards, a country and folk singer-songwriter known for his 1971 hit single "Sunshine"; Robert Kerlan, a pioneer in the world of sports medicine; Jean Keene, the

"Eagle Lady" of the Homer Spit in Alaska, known for feeding and attracting large populations of wild bald eagles, and Francis Lee Jaques, a wildlife painter.

Restaurant Recommendation:
Block North Brew Pub
302 Minnesota Ave N
Aitkin, MN 56431

HILL CITY, MN
POPULATION: 613 – CITY 423 OF 856 (7-18-25)
Docks, pontoon boats, and hydraulic knuckle boom loaders (the first two manufactured by Roll-In Docks, and the latter by Lemco) are the three things that allow Hill City to thrive today as a relatively isolated community in northern Aitkin County. When the Ojibwe's "Poquodenaw mountain," alternatively called *Pikwadina* or *Piquadinaw*, meaning "it is hilly," was selected for a townsite, the Anglicized name Hill City was applied to the plat. The post office opened in 1901 after Al Wandel, James Harper, James Gill, and E.L. Buck began to develop the town on behalf of the Hill City Realty Company. About a decade later, Hill City separated from Hill Lake Township and became an independent municipality. It was fortunate enough to have its own Hill City Railway, a spur line moving westward from the Great Northern Railroad near Jacobson, in addition to three hotels and the National Woodenware Company. The manufacturers of wooden barrels, buckets, and tubs were a subsidiary of Armour & Co. Its headquarters relocated from Itasca, Michigan, to Hill City in 1910, and effectively quadrupled the town's population after they purchased a third of the town's lots and built several residences for their employees. The Superintendent's Residence, built in 1910 during the boom, remains Hill City's sole location on the National Register of Historic Places. After the company's mill closed in 1928, the population dropped from 928 people to 515, a decrease of 44.5%. It is best known today for its recreational activities on Hill Lake and for its annual Fourth of July celebration, which includes turtle races, a street dance, a flea market, and numerous other events. A ten-foot-tall bear statue has welcomed people to the city since 1985.

MCGRATH, MN
POPULATION: 41 – CITY 445 OF 856 (7-19-25)
James E. McGrath established the first of his seventeen logging camps on the Snake River and Chesley Brook in 1895, and in 1907, he willingly donated forty acres of land to be developed into a townsite by the Patterson Land Company. The Soo Line Railroad town was platted as Elmwood, but aptly renamed McGrath in 1908 when the post office was established. As eager loggers and their families moved into the area and constructed their own homes and businesses, the idea was put out that McGrath should seek incorporation. On March 23, 1923, it was incorporated as a village. In 1930, the Census reported a population of 141 people. Leonard Shoen, the founder of the U-Haul moving truck and storage company, was born here in 1916 and moved from McGrath to Oregon when he was only seven years old.

MCGREGOR, MN
POPULATION: 384 – CITY 425 OF 856 (7-18-25)
Long before McGregor existed at the junction of the Northern Pacific and the Minneapolis, St. Paul & Sault Ste. Marie Railroads, trails were being blazed by Native Americans and fur-trading voyageurs about seventeen miles eastward in what is now known as the Savanna Portage. The challenging 6-mile portage connecting Lake

Superior to the Mississippi River watershed has since been developed into the Savanna Portage State Park to preserve its history; the trail itself is now a popular hiking route. Its traffic fell in 1870 when the Northern Pacific Railroad reached McGregor. It was either named for a famous New York hunter and trapper, McGregor, or in honor of Major John G. MacGregor. The post office was established in 1890, and on August 27, 1903, the small village was incorporated, a time when the town featured stores, churches, schools, and all the other typical aspects of a small timber town of the era. As many as 447 people lived in McGregor in the 1980s; today, it is a hotbed for tourist activities.

PALISADE, MN
POPULATION: 162 – CITY 424 OF 856 (7-18-25)
Lee's Hill, appropriately named for early area landowner Mr. Lee, was the name for the hill jutting out far above the surrounding valley before Soo Line Railroad officials changed it to Palisade. The descriptive change was made when they purchased 40 acres of land from Lee and platted a village on a high embankment overlooking the Mississippi River. H. S. McKinley built a store in 1910, the first building in the fledgling town that eventually had hotels, stores, churches, schools, and a post office to serve the needs of its Danish, Swedish, and Finnish settlers. Palisade was incorporated as a village on July 7, 1922, and its population began to decline significantly with the onset of the Great Depression, as the logging industries of northern Minnesota experienced a substantial slowdown. The 1950 flood of the Mississippi River left the town completely cut off from the outside world, accessible only by boat. The event partially contributed to its population decline through the latter half of the 20th century. Jonathan Franzen, known best for his 2001 novel *The Corrections* and his 2010 novel *Freedom*, has ties to the town through his father. Earl T. Franzen grew up in Palisade, and Jonathan used an area surname (the Berglunds, proprietors of the Berglund Park Campground) for the last names of his main characters in the latter novel.

Restaurant Recommendation:
Gabbys Eats and Treats
303 Main St
Palisade, MN 56469

TAMARACK, MN
POPULATION: 62 – CITY 426 OF 856 (7-18-25)
Despite parts of its township burning down entirely in the Great Hinckley Fire of 1894, which torched no less than 200,000 acres of Minnesota forest, and a secondary conflagration in 1918, Tamarack has twice risen from the ashes and the peatlands and tamarack-covered bogs from which it derived its name. Tamaracks are a species of boreal deciduous coniferous larch trees native to parts of Minnesota, Canada, Wisconsin, Michigan, and New England. The town was founded out of necessity when the Northern Pacific Railroad established stations along its route between Duluth and Brainerd. Immigrants (who then called the area Sicottes) had arrived as early as 1874, but a post office was not established until 1898, and incorporation was not achieved until July 26, 1921. In the decade since then, Tamarack has had a low population of 53 people in the 1990s, and a high of 150 in the 1940s. Valuable nickel, copper, and cobalt deposits were discovered in Tamarack as recently as 2020.

Unincorporated/Ghost Towns: Arthyde, Ball Bluff, Bennettville, Cutler, East Lake, Giese, Glen, Glory, Hassman, Haypoint, Jacobson, Kimberly, Lawler, Libby, Malmo, Minnewawa,

Nichols, Rabey, Red Top, Ronald, Rossburg, Sandy Lake, Sheshebee, Shovel Lake, Swatara, Thor, Waukenabo, Wealthwood

National Register of Historic Places:
Aitkin: Aitkin Carnegie Library, Aitkin County Courthouse & Jail, *Andy Gibson* (shipwreck), Bethlehem Lutheran Church, Patrick Casey House, Northern Pacific Depot, Pine-Hickory Lakes Roadside Parking Area, Potter/Casey Company Building
Arthyde: Arthyde Stone House
Hill City: National Woodenware Company Superintendent's Residence
McGrath: Malmo Mounds & Village Site
McGregor: Savanna Portage

Town Celebrations:
Riverboat Heritage Days, Aitkin, MN (1st Weekend in August)
RiverFest, Palisade, MN (2nd Weekend of August)
Tamarack Hey Days, Tamarack, MN (1st Saturday in August)
Wild Rice Days, McGregor, MN (Labor Day Weekend)

ANOKA COUNTY
EST. 1857 - POPULATION: 363,887

Anoka is a Dakota word meaning "on both sides," a reference to the county's jurisdiction on both sides of the Rum River.

ANDOVER, MN
POPULATION: 32,601 – CITY 815 OF 856 (11-11-25)
Round Lake Township was established in 1857 as the first governing body of this area. In 1860, its name was changed to Grow Township in honor of Galusha A. Grow, a strong proponent of the Union and their beliefs just before the outbreak of the Civil War. He had given a speech in Anoka earlier that year that prompted the idea of making the change. Ham Lake Township was partitioned off in 1871. When a north-south line of the Great Northern Railroad came through, they assigned the name Andover Station (after Andover, England) to the local station. Some accounts suggest that the name was derived from a catastrophic event in which a train ran off the tracks and tipped "over and over," but this has been proven false. Grow Township really took its name to heart, starting in the 1960s, when its population grew by 173.2%, from 1,402 to 3,830. By the next Census in 1980, Andover had 9,387 residents, and the village form of government had been adopted. Incorporation was agreed upon in 1972. Since then, Andover has grown exponentially and welcomed several commercial interests—like the Andover Glue Factory, which operated briefly in the 1960s—as well as recreational havens like Anoka County Bunker Hills Regional Park and Bunker Beach Waterpark, and Kelsey Round Lake Park. Its most historic site is the Porter Kelsey House, the 1887 home of an early owner of a brickyard company. Mike Morin, an MLB pitcher for six franchises between 2014 and 2020, and Maddie Rooney, the goaltender for the United States women's national ice hockey team that won gold at the 2018 Winter Olympics, have local ties.

ANOKA, MN ★☆
POPULATION: 17,921 – CITY 823 OF 856 (11-12-25)
Nobody celebrates the spookiest time of year quite like Anoka, the "Halloween Capital of the World," a title given to commemorate its spectacular Halloween activities. The first Halloween celebration/parade in the United States was held here in 1920. Since

then, a large Pumpkin Roundabout mural, a 12-foot-high pumpkin sculpture outside of City Hall, and several other Halloweensque murals have been created to celebrate the holiday. Orrin W. Rice, Neal D. Shaw, and others founded Anoka shortly after many of the first immigrants had arrived in 1844. A school, a general store, and a flour mill were present by the mid-1850s, as were several sawmills, which gathered their logs from loggers who had floated them down the Rum River to Anoka. Postal service began in 1854 once enough people had accumulated. The Minnesota state legislature incorporated the "City of Anoka" on July 29, 1858, and on March 5, 1869, attempts were made to again incorporate it as the "Borough of Anoka." Neither of these formal attempts prevailed, but on May 2, 1878, Anoka finally gained incorporation status through approval of both the township board and the legislature. Its permanent name was derived either from the Ojibwe word *anoki*, meaning 'I work,' in reference to the local sawmills, or from the Dakota word *anoka*, meaning 'on both sides,' because the town straddles the Rum River. When Fort Sumter was attacked on April 12, 1861, Minnesota Governor Alexander Ramsey was in Washington, D.C. He immediately telegraphed former Governor Willis Arnold Gorman and Lieutenant Governor Ignatius L. Donnelly, asking for volunteers to start the Union Army. Ramsey's quick actions have since enabled Anoka to claim it was the first community to provide volunteer soldiers to the Union. In regards to historic sites, Anoka can claim nine National Register of Historic Places locations: the Jackson Hotel, operational from 1884 to 1975; the 1902 Kline Sanitarium hospital building; Colonial Hall and Masonic Lodge No. 30, built in 1904; Windego Park Auditorium, an open air theater built between S. Ferry Street and the Rum River in 1914; the 1916 Georgian Revival Anoka Post Office; the 1929 Anoka-Champlin Mississippi River Bridge, and three historic homes known as the Shaw-Hammons (1852, Greek Revival), and Woodbury (1857, Federal/Greek Revival) Herman L. Ticknor (1867, Gothic Revival) Houses. There are few, if any, pre-1884 buildings in downtown Anoka because of a devastating fire that destroyed 86 businesses. As a result of the conflagration and in an effort to preserve history, the Anoka County Historical Society maintains a downtown museum that houses historical artifacts and documents related to Anoka community history. Many famous persons can claim connections to Anoka, but a few in particular include Larry Constantine, noted for his work in the field of software engineering; Steve Nelson, a three-time Pro Bowl linebacker with the NFL's New England Patriots from 1974 to 1987; Medal of Honor recipient Richard K. Sorenson, who survived throwing himself on a Japanese grenade to save his fellow Marines; Gretchen Carlson, a morning anchor best known for her *The Real Story with Gretchen Carlson* segment on *Fox News* from 2013 to 2016; Michele Bachmann, a Member of the U.S. House of Representatives from Minnesota from 2007 to 2015, and Anna Arnold Hedgeman, the first African-American student and graduate from Saint Paul's Hamline University.

BETHEL, MN
POPULATION: 476 – CITY 818 OF 856 (11-11-25)
One of Anoka County's few remaining small, authentic towns is Bethel, which Rice Price and O. Evans first discovered in the fall of 1855. These two men and other Quaker families were the first to move into the area, but they ultimately decided to relocate elsewhere. Regardless, new immigrants replaced them, and a post office was established in 1865. It took the name "Bethel," suggested by Moses Twitchell of Bethel, Maine. H. Newbert was postmaster; he ran the post office out of his general store. Bethel Township originally spanned all of modern-day Bethel and East Bethel, and parts of Linwood. In 1913, formal city limits were established when this 1.04-square-mile town opted for incorporation following the arrival of the Great Northern

Railroad. Since its first Census in 1910, its highest-ever population has been 476 people, as of the 2020 Census.

BLAINE, MN
POPULATION: 70,222 – CITY 813 OF 856 (11-11-25)
Philip Laddy of Ireland was the first European to come here circa 1862, where he settled on a lake that now bears his name. George Townsend was one of the next to arrive; he was followed by Green Chambers, who took over his claim after his emancipation following the Civil War. Until 1877, this area was considered part of the City of Anoka, but Blaine Township was separated to form its own township. It was named in honor of James Gillespie Blaine, the 28th & 31st United States Secretary of State and a three-time presidential candidate. Villas City was another potential name for the town, but it was forgotten by 1887. Agriculture was not Blaine's strong suit, as it lacked the fertile soils that other Minnesotan towns enjoyed, so growth was slow. Agricultural reports from 1880 showed that only 3,385 bushels of corn and 2,337 bushels of wheat were produced, although over 4,180 pounds of butter had been churned out. Through the 1930s, Blaine never recorded more than 550 permanent residents, though post-World War II, the population began to grow rapidly. By 1950, it had 3,604 citizens, and by 1970, that number had grown to 20,573. Blaine was incorporated as a city on January 29, 1954. Aveda Corporation, a cosmetics company, employs more residents than any other business in the town, although Blaine is most famous for being the site of the National Sports Center. Opened in 1990, the 600-acre facility has 50 regulation-size soccer fields, an eight-sheet ice rink, a soccer stadium, and Victory Links Golf Course. Minnesota United FC, a club team in Major League Soccer since 2017, used to play its games here before moving to St. Paul's Allianz Field. Multiple National and World Championship events in soccer, hockey, rugby, lacrosse, figure skating, and other sports have been held here over the decades.

Restaurant Recommendation:
Stone Pho
10340 Baltimore St NE #170
Blaine, MN 55449

CENTERVILLE, MN
POPULATION: 3,896 – CITY 802 OF 856 (11-10-25)
Centrally located between the Mississippi and the St. Croix Rivers is the City of Centerville, which was platted in the spring of 1854 after several French and German settlers moved to the area. The French lived in the area that is now downtown Centerville, whereas the Germans lived in the western part of the township, now owned by the City of Lino Lakes. Charles Peltier built one of the town's first businesses on Clearwater Creek, a sawmill, in 1854, making it the first in Anoka County. School started that year in the kitchen of a local home. Two years later, the Columbus post office was organized, before changing its name to Centreville from 1863 to 1893. The spelling was Americanized from 1893 to 1905, when the post office was discontinued. As recently as 1950, Centerville's population was only 209 persons, but it began to grow steadily over the next several decades as an enclave of Lino Lakes and a distant suburb of the Twin Cities. From 1980 to 1990, its numbers doubled from 734 people to 1,633; by 2000, they had doubled again to 3,202.

CIRCLE PINES, MN
POPULATION: 5,025 – CITY 805 OF 856 (11-10-25)
Some intellectuals credit shower thoughts as their source of inspiration, but for V.S. Petersen, it was post-swim clarity that prompted him to propose starting a planned cooperative community. He recruited Thomas Ellerbe, an engineer and architect, and Paul Steenberg, the other of the Steenberg Construction Company, and established what is now known as the City of Circle Pines. To grow their community, the idea was to sell equal shares to cooperative homeowners, who, in association with the other homeowners, would help develop the community. Minimum housing costs were set at $4,000, $6,000, and $8,000, depending on the area of town, whereas the maximum house price was $20,000. Each person within the cooperative was required to own at least $100 in the cooperative. For three years, the community operated under this cooperative system, but a lack of financing and disagreements amongst civic leaders led to its downfall. The cooperative and portions of Blaine and Centerville Townships were unified in incorporation on April 8, 1950. As the cooperative movement grew in the United States in the 1940s, a circle encompassing two pines became the movement's official symbol, hence the name Circle Pines. Kaitlin Young, a mixed martial artist in the Professional Fighters League, and Mary Jo Pehl, an actress known for her roles in the sci-fi comedy television series *Mystery Science Theater 3000*, both claim ties to the community.

COLUMBIA HEIGHTS, MN
POPULATION: 21,973 – CITY 831 OF 856 (11-13-25)
One of Anoka County's earlier communities was Columbia Heights, which was organized on March 14, 1898, immediately after separating from Fridley Township. The Minneapolis Improvement Company was responsible for its development, which was no problem, but they needed a name for their community. Instead of just picking it as an eponym for another community or naming it for a railroad official, they instead published an advertisement in the local paper to hold a naming contest. Two thousand two hundred eighty-one names were submitted, but the chosen winner was the submission of Olive Louise Thornbergh, who suggested Columbia Heights. The name Fairview came in second place, and Hazel Heights was third. Thornbergh received a $150 gold prize for first place, while the second- and third-place winners received $100 and $50, respectively. A post office opened under that name and operated from 1898 to 1913 before it was reorganized into a branch office. On July 21, 1921, Columbia Heights acquired its city charter, and the local population began to grow rapidly. In 1920, it had 2,968 residents, by 1950, it had climbed to 8,175, and in 1970, it peaked at 23,997 people. Businesses, churches, schools, parks, and other parts of the city infrastructure came into being. Still, there was one addition to the town that residents were particularly proud of: Abraham Lincoln's funeral car. Purchased by Thomas Lowry, who restored it first as a sales office and later for use in exhibitions throughout the country. When he passed in 1909, he donated the prized piece of American history to the Minnesota Federation of Women's Clubs. They stored it in Columbia Heights. It was sadly destroyed by fire on March 18, 1911, alongside 10 city blocks. Columbia Heights is a Sister city of Lomianki, Poland, and Galdogob, Somalia, because of its large Polish and Somali populations. Earl Bakken, the inventor of the first "external, battery-operated, wearable artificial pacemaker" and the founder of Medtronic; Medal of Honor Recipient James D. La Belle; John Alt, a two-time Pro Bowl offensive tackle with the NFL's Kansas City Chiefs; Don Carlson, a pioneer NBA player who suited up from 1946 to 1951, and Henry Scholberg, a librarian noted for his work on Indian encyclopedias, can all claim local ties.

COLUMBUS, MN
POPULATION: 4,159 – CITY 803 OF 856 (11-10-25)
When reports surfaced in 2006 that Forest Lake was planning to annex the majority of Columbus Township, named in honor of the famed explorer of 1492, Christopher Columbus, residents responded by incorporating their township into an independent municipality. So, on September 21, 2006, the City of Columbus was born to protect its rural identity. John Kleiner and J. H. Batzle were the first men to live in this area circa 1855; that following year, Captain James Starkey platted it. A number of homes were built, as was a hotel, a carriage works, a blacksmith shop, a general store, and two mills. The steam-powered sawmill was open only from 1856-57 before closing down and succumbing to a fire in 1865. The other was a corn mill and cob crusher, a much smaller enterprise. Attempts were made to secure the Anoka County seat, but after losing out on the St. Paul & Duluth Railway right-of-way, the decision was made to locate it elsewhere. While being the governmental seat was not in the cards for Columbus's future, it did become the site of three camps of The American Grass Twine Company. They harvested nearly 10,000 acres of native wiregrass for carpet-making. Visitors may notice the odd street names that make up much of Columbus, honoring baseball players, world rivers, astronomical bodies, automobiles, and famous colleges and universities. Roland Anderson, Anoka County's surveyor from 1958 to 1987, is credited with naming the streets. Columbus is best known for the Running Aces Casino & Racetrack, which opened on April 11, 2008. It boasts a ⅝-mile agricultural lime and a stone dust racetrack.

COON RAPIDS, MN
POPULATION: 63,599 – CITY 814 OF 856 (11-11-25)
Being one of only sixteen Minnesota cities with a population in excess of 60,000 persons as of the 2020 Census, Coon Rapids, whose name was derived from the Coon Creek Rapids on the Upper Mississippi River near the mouth of Coon Creek, is one of the most recognizable cities in the Twin Cities. It began as part of Anoka Township on July 30, 1867, and has since retained all of its boundaries, except those taken by the City of Anoka upon its incorporation. Significant developments came later that century when D. C. Dunham established the Anoka Pressed Brick and Terra Cotta Company in 1881, the first non-agricultural related business in Coon Rapids. Lines of the Great Northern and Northern Pacific Railroads were built during this era of growth and improvements. In 1898, plans were underway to design the Mississippi Power Company's dam, although construction did not begin until 1912. Forty-two thousand cubic yards of concrete and over 1,000 laborers were needed to complete the project. The dam served as a hydroelectric power-generating facility under the Northern States Power Company until 1969, when it was converted into the Coon Rapids Dam Regional Park in 1978. In July 1948, a vote failed to incorporate Anoka Township as the village of Coon Rapids, but in October 1952, the motion was passed. Anoka-Ramsey Community College began in 1965 as a public community college and is now part of the Minnesota State Colleges and Universities System.

EAST BETHEL, MN
POPULATION: 11,786 – CITY 817 OF 856 (11-11-25)
East Bethel is the larger sister city to the much smaller town of Bethel, although both share the same name. Quakers first settled at Bethel in 1856, where they established a school and church. High tensions during the Dakota War of 1862 forced their removal from Anoka County, and they never again returned. However, the name they gave the area, which literally translates to "House of God," remained. Although the

town of Bethel was incorporated in 1913, the rest of Bethel Township operated under the township form of government until June 7, 1957, when its 47.69 square miles were incorporated into an independent municipality called East Bethel. The Anoka County Board of Commissioners ratified the motion by a 232-161 vote, but the Minnesota Supreme Court and the Minnesota Legislature had to approve the decision. Their approval was given on April 27, 1959.

FRIDLEY, MN
POPULATION: 29,590 – CITY 828 OF 856 (11-12-25)
What Minnesotans now know as Fridley was once its own county. The first settler to come here was John Banfill, who had arrived ten years earlier and established the Banfill Tavern. Currently serving as the North Suburban Center for the Arts, the building stands within Manomin County Park and exemplifies Greek Revival architecture in its windows, pilasters, and chimney. Banfill platted a town called Manomin in 1851, the same year that Abram McCormick Fridley arrived. A general store and a sawmill were erected on Rice Creek, and by 1853, the earliest variation of the Fridley post office had begun. Manomin County, named after the abundant wild rice found throughout the state, was established by an act of the legislature on May 23, 1857, at the same time as Anoka County. For about a dozen years, it was the smallest county in the United States by area at only 16 square miles, before it merged with Anoka County in 1869 (shortly after the Saint Paul and Pacific Railroad was built through) and became Manomin Township. Its name was changed in 1879 to honor Mr. Fridley; it stuck even when the village was incorporated on June 18, 1949. For its first year as a municipality, the town relied entirely on funds generated from its municipal liquor store while a lawsuit with Northern Pump was ongoing. The factory opposed Fridley's incorporation as a village, and its lawsuit temporarily froze village funds. Growth accelerated from 1950 onwards, as by 1960 Fridley's population had risen to 15,173 from 3,796 only a decade prior. Growth was excellent until several natural disasters plagued the community in the spring of 1865. First, the Upper Mississippi River flooded, sending record-breaking crests over lower-lying parts of the village. Just as cleanup was underway for that catastrophe, a pair of E-F4 tornadoes ripped through town on May 6, 1965, destroying or damaging one out of every four households in the community. Residents rebounded, and other improvements were brought to the city, such as the 127-acre Springbrook Nature Center, still in operation with nearly 150,000 annual visitors, and the Totino's frozen pizza factory, which operated here from 1970 until Totino's sale to Pillsbury. Columbia Arena was the filming site of the third installment in the *Mighty Ducks* sports comedy-drama film before its destruction in 2016 to build a new City Hall complex. Medtronic, one of the largest medical device companies in the world with nearly $30 billion in annual revenues, has its executive headquarters here. Five of its most noteworthy residents of past and present have been Cory Wong, a songwriter and record producer; Brooke Elliott, an actress known for her roles in the national *Wicked* and *Beauty and the Beast* musical tours; Chris Dahlquist, an NHL hockey player from 1985 to 1996; Mikey Anderson, a defenseman with the NHL's Los Angeles Kings from 2019 to 2025, and MLB pitcher Sean Hjelle, the tallest player in MLB history at 6 feet 11 inches.

HAM LAKE, MN
POPULATION: 16,464 – CITY 816 OF 856 (11-11-25)
A town named Glen Carey was platted in 1856 on the shores of Ham Lake, so named because of the shape of the lake. Things looked promising for its first year of development as homes began to rise from the prairie, but a devastating fire in 1857 brought all progress to a screeching halt. Settlers gave up and moved elsewhere.

Scandinavian families replaced them in the 1860s, who, being unable to pronounce the Scottish name Glen Carey, refused to name the area until the county commissioners named it after the lake. In 1871, Ham Lake Township split off from Andover/Grow Township, and the following year, a grand Swedish Evangelical Lutheran Church was built to serve the growing community's religious needs. It still stands in the countryside, far from the modern developments of the City of Ham Lake. By the late 1890s, local farmers worked together to form the Ham Lake Co-operative Creamery, which brought about the establishment of Soderquist's, C. M. Norquist's, and Ryberg's general stores. In the 1920s, a hamburger-and-root-beer stand, a tavern, a grocery store, and a confectionery were added to the lineup of local businesses. Sodding was another critical industry, and at one point, Ham Lake was considered to be the "Sod Capital of Minnesota." It became Minnesota's newest incorporated city on January 8, 1974. Twenty-five parks are within city limits.

Restaurant Recommendation:
Acapulco Mexican Restaurant
18015 Ulysses St NE Ste 1000
Ham Lake, MN 55304

HILLTOP, MN
POPULATION: 958 – CITY 830 OF 856 (11-12-25)
A dairy farm encompassed the entirety of Hilltop, back when it was an unincorporated section of the much larger Fridley Township. Later developed into a golf course, then the Oak Grove Riding Academy and Stables, and finally as the Trailer City/Sunnyside trailer parks, the decision to incorporate the trailer-park hamlet came when Columbia Heights refused to annex Hilltop into their city. Les Johnson, owner of the Trailer City Park, led the negotiations, but to no avail. Thinking that their affordable low-cost housing would be removed in favor of strip malls and more expensive properties, Hilltop residents instead voted to incorporate as an independent city. The final vote was 137 to 34 in favor of incorporation, and its name was taken from a nearby drive-in movie theatre. Hilltop's new status took effect on May 4, 1956. Columbia Heights annexed all the land surrounding Hilltop and even removed its water and sewer service. In retaliation, Hilltop worked with Fridley to contract for fire protection, and the two established their own police department that operated independently until 1972. A water tower was erected to avoid contracting with Columbia Heights. Eventually, the mayors of the two cities met to set aside their differences, and the rivalry that once was is no longer. Columbia Heights provided fire and police services to the sixteen-block community, whereas Hilltop has its own sewer and water services. It is one of two trailer-park cities in the Twin Cities, the other being Landfall in Washington County.

LEXINGTON, MN
POPULATION: 2,248 – CITY 806 OF 856 (11-10-25)
An early variation of Lexington was laid out on the Rum River circa 1855, but it would take another ninety-five years for the present-day city to come to fruition. Blaine Township was first settled by Phillip Laddy, whose name is still commemorated by a lake in the locality. He arrived in 1862. By 1900, the township's population was still less than 400, until suburban sprawl eventually spread from the Twin Cities into Anoka County. On May 5, 1950, 93 of 154 locals voted to incorporate Lexington to preserve its small-town feel and identity. Leo Ryan gave it the name "The First Pioneer Infantry Regiment" after the Boston, Massachusetts, unit that served in the Battle of Lexington

during the American Revolution. Recent population estimates suggest that the town's population may have grown by as much as 36% between 2020 and 2022.

Restaurant Recommendation:
Boulevard Bar & Grille
3800 Restwood Rd #3737
Circle Pines, MN 55014

LINO LAKES, MN
POPULATION: 21,399 – CITY 804 OF 856 (11-10-25)
Lino Lakes surrounds the City of Centerville, although it, too, was once part of Centerville Township. When Circle Pines became incorporated and annexed 120 acres of the township, resident Arnold Kelling formulated a plan to make the township an independent city of its own. Other citizens opposed the idea until 1955, when the township refused to allocate any funding to fix the dirt roads in the Lakeview area. At that point, it was decided that becoming a municipal corporation was not only advisable but also necessary for those wishing to travel through the area. Paul Schmidt proposed Centerville Township Village, but Kelling and other residents insisted it would be confused with the already-established town of Centerville. Dolor Nadeau mentioned Line' O Oakes, the name of a local tavern, which prompted Kelling to remember Line O' Lakes, Land O' Lakes, Wisconsin. Harry Proulx objected to the length of the name, and so the committee settled on the shortened, abbreviated name of Lino Lakes. Anoka also had a post office in the vicinity called Lino from 1894 to 1904, which operated in Vernum B. Park's general store. Other early institutions of that early township era were the local creamery and Catholic church. Between 2000 and 2010, Lino Lakes grew from 11,791 people to 20,216. Tyler Pitlick, who grew up here, has played in the NHL since 2013-14 for nine different franchises.

NOWTHEN, MN
POPULATION: 4,536 – CITY 820 OF 856 (11-11-25)
James U. Hare, formerly the postmaster within Burns Township, had a bad habit of saying "Now then" in everyday conversation. He used the term so frequently that the post office adopted it from 1897 to 1905 (before it was discontinued), and ultimately, the newly established City of Nowthen adopted it in June 2008. "Burns" should have been the permanent name of the office (as it was from 1876 to 1894 in Anoka County), but another entity with that name already existed in southern Minnesota. Burns Township had broken off from St. Francis Township in 1869, and, out of fear of annexation by a neighboring community, residents proposed incorporating the township into a city at their annual meeting in March 2007. Every year, the Nowthen Threshing Show brings in farm equipment enthusiasts to watch tractor pulls, blacksmithing, and threshing machines hard at work. The grounds also contain an old one-room schoolhouse, depot, church, general store, log cabin, and log barn.

OAK GROVE, MN
POPULATION: 8,929 – CITY 819 OF 856 (11-11-25)
Officially incorporated in 1993, the City of Oak Grove, named by early settlers for its copious oak trees throughout the township, welcomed its first settlers in 1855. David Rogers, Moses S. Seelye Sr., Jarvis Nutter, John M. McKenzie, and Gilbert Leathers were the first of these men. It took two years to create the township, but its small village boasted a post office from 1857 to 1901, along with a select number of churches, schools, and stores. Significant growth in the northwest part of Anoka County led to

its incorporation in the 1990s, when the population surpassed 5,000. Sean Sherk, a former UFC Lightweight Champion with a career record of 36-4-1, claimed Oak Grove as his "fighting out of "town. *Animation Domination High-Def*, a late-night animated programming block on Fox from July 2013 to March 2016, started in Oak Grove, Minnesota, in a roundabout way. One of its shows was *Golan the Insatiable*, an original series that followed a demigod warlord who got trapped in the town after being summoned by a young girl.

RAMSEY, MN
POPULATION: 27,646 – CITY 821 OF 856 (11-11-25)

Thomas A. Holmes and James Beatty built a trading post on this site in 1849, which served as the nucleus of an early Minnesota village called Itasca. Named by Governor Alexander Ramsey for Lake Itasca, the name was also adopted by the Northern Pacific Railroad for its depot. A hotel, a barn, and the first post office in Anoka County, founded in 1852 and run by John C. Bowers, were some of its initial landmarks. When the Winnebago tribe was removed from the area and a township was organized, it was named Watertown. Dover was another alternate name for the site before it was finally renamed Ramsey in honor of the territorial governor. Many permanent settlers arrived on a steamboat named "The Governor Ramsey." With a population of only 670 people in 1950, Ramsey was an authentic small town until the 1970s, when its population exploded by 298% from 2,536 citizens to 10,093 by the time the 1980 Census was conducted. It was incorporated on November 12, 1974. Remnants of the original village and buildings are hard to come by; the 1892 District No. 28 School, later used as the Ramsey Town Hall, remains.

SPRING LAKE PARK, MN
POPULATION: 7,188 – CITY 829 OF 856 (11-12-25)

Often confused with the City of Spring Park, located on Lake Minnetonka in Hennepin County, the City of Spring Lake Park is located almost entirely within Anoka County and is home to five times as many people. Originally a part of Manomin County, which was annexed by Anoka County in 1870, Spring Lake Park was established by the Bronson-Erickson real estate agency in 1936. After 17 years of developing housing developments and welcoming commercial interests, the young village was incorporated on December 31, 1953. A post office branch operated from 1961 to 1978, according to Jim Forte's postal history. A couple of famous people with city ties are David Backes, an NHL ice hockey forward with nearly 1,000 career games and a 2010 Olympic silver medal in the sport, and Troy Merritt, a two-time PGA Tour winning golfer at the 2015 Quicken Loans National and 2018 Barbasol Championship.

Restaurant Recommendation:
Grandpa Joe's Candy Shop
1626 County Hwy 10
Spring Lake Park, MN 55432

ST. FRANCIS, MN
POPULATION: 8,142 – CITY 587 OF 856 (9-3-25)

George Armsby, Ezra Randall, and E. Fowler are largely considered the first settlers of St. Francis, circa 1855. However, Dwight Woodbury is credited with constructing a dam, grist mill, and residence that served as the initial foundations of what is now known as the City of St. Francis. Father Louis Hennepin originally referred to the Rum River as "the St. Francis River" during his 1680 travels, in honor of St. Francis of Assisi, the Catholic patron saint of animals. Alternative names for the area and its post office included Old Jonathan, St. Jonathan, and Otona; however, the postal service adopted St. Francis as the permanent name in 1857. Development of the township was expedited when Mr. Woodbury established the Saint Francis Flour Milling Company in 1888. Other storeowners and entrepreneurs took note of the mill's success. They established their own meat markets, blacksmith shops, drugstores, general stores, and even larger enterprises, including corn-canning and potato-starch factories. Among all the early firms, one of the most unique was Blanchette's Sample Room Beer Parlour, which opened in the early 1890s. It was later converted into an ice cream parlor, before closing in 1933, the same year the iconic mill burned down and the city's dam was destroyed. Despite the test of time, Woodbury's 1860 home still stands as the only surviving building from St. Francis's lumber boomtown era. It was converted into a hotel in 1891, and in recent decades, it has undergone remodeling to become the historic Rum River Inn. It was added to the National Register of Historic Places on December 26, 1979, the same day that H. G. Leathers' Victorian-style home joined the Registry. St. Francis residents sought to incorporate the village in 1962, an honor achieved on May 16 of that year. It has grown extensively since then, doubling in population between 1960 and 1980 and passing the five-thousand-resident mark in the early 2000s. Dakotah Popehn, one of the fastest U.S. marathoners of all-time and a 2024 Paris Olympics long-distance runner; Sean Sherk, a former UFC Lightweight Champion in the mid-2000s, and Kiana Eide, a competitor in the 2016 Rio Olympic Games as a rhythmic gymnast, are three noted athletes with St. Francis ties.

Unincorporated/Ghost Towns: Cedar, Linwood, Martin Lake

National Register of Historic Places:
Anoka: Anoka Post Office, Anoka-Champlin Mississippi River Bridge, Colonial Hall & Masonic Lodge No. 30, Heman L. Ticknor House, Jackson Hotel, Kline Sanatarium, Shaw-Hammons House, Windego Park Auditorium/Open Air Theater, Woodbury House
Andover: Porter Kelsey House
Columbus: Carlos Avery Game Farm
Fridley: Banfill Tavern
Ham Lake: Swedish Evangelical Lutheran Church
Martin Lake: Crescent Grange Hall No. 512
Nowthen: Sparre Barn
Ramsey: District No.28 School
St. Francis: H. G. Leathers House, Riverside Hotel

Golf Courses:
Bunker Hills Golf Club, Municipal (Coon Rapids, MN)
Green Haven Golf Course, Municipal (Anoka, MN)
Hidden Haven Golf Club, Daily Fee (Cedar, MN)
Majestic Oaks Golf Club – Crossroads, Daily Fee (Ham Lake, MN)
Majestic Oaks Golf Club – Executive 9, Daily Fee (Ham Lake, MN)
Majestic Oaks Golf Club – Signature, Daily Fee (Ham Lake, MN)
Rum River Hills Golf Club, Daily Fee (Ramsey, MN)
The Links at Northfork, Daily Fee (Ramsey, MN)
The Ponds Golf Course, Daily Fee (St. Francis, MN)
The Refuge Golf Club, Daily Fee (Oak Grove, MN)
TPC Twin Cities, Private (Blaine, MN)
Victory Links Golf Course – Tournament Putting Greens, Municipal (Blaine, MN)
Victory Links Golf Course, Municipal (Blaine, MN)
Viking Meadows Golf Club, Daily Fee (East Bethel, MN)

Breweries/Wineries/Distilleries:
10k Brewing (Anoka, MN)
Alloy Brewing Company (Coon Rapids, MN)
Forgotten Star Brewing Company (Fridley, MN)
Garphish Brewing Company (East Bethel, MN)
Invictus Brewing Company (Blaine, MN)
Rail Werks Brewing Depot (Columbia Heights, MN)
Willow Tree Winery (Ham Lake, MN)

Town Celebrations:
Blaine Festival, Blaine, MN (Last Weekend in June)
Blue Heron Days, Lino Lakes, MN (3rd Weekend in August)
Game Fair, Ramsey, MN (First Two Weekends in August)
Halloween Parades & Events, Anoka, MN (All October)
Happy Days Festival, Ramsey, MN (Early September)
Nowthen Heritage Festival, Nowthen, MN (Last Saturday in September)
Nowthen Threshing Show, Nowthen, MN (3rd Full Weekend in August)

BECKER COUNTY
EST. 1858 - POPULATION: 35,183

George Loomis Becker was elected to Congress when Minnesota became a state in 1858. Because the state was allowed to send only two delegates, he offered to stay behind in exchange for a county named in his honor.

AUDUBON, MN
POPULATION: 560 – CITY 215 OF 856 (5-5-25)
Windom, Colfax, and Oak Lake were early variants of the township's name, but the village was named Audubon at the request of the niece of John J. Audubon, the great American ornithologist. She was a member of the August 1871 Northern Pacific Railroad surveying party searching for places to establish stations. One such stop was established at Audubon Lake, also so named for the bird-loving man and the numerous waterfowl and birds that lived on its waters. When the streets were laid out, officials continued with the bird theme. They named the horizontal streets on the plat after various species: Robin, Plover, Martin, Lark, Hawk, Falcon, Eagle, Crane, Swan, and Pelican. Pioneers migrated to the town and then built their own "nests" to live and grow on the townsite. L. S. Cravath was responsible for selling off the lands. B. B. Anderson opened the first general goods store in 1872, and another proprietor opened a hotel. Later, O. J. Johnson brought in his own stock of goods. Frank Lacross established his storefront in June 1873, and in the fall of that year, P. P. and O. G. Wall started The Audubon Journal to report on local news. Next were two saloons, a blacksmith shop, a meat market, three attorneys, and a physician's office. On February 23, 1881, Audubon was incorporated as a village. With another fifty years of development, it had expanded to include many more businesses, like a wagon factory, a jewelry store, a music store, a funeral supply store, the depot, a public school, and three churches (two of which were the Congregational and the Norwegian Lutheran congregations) by 1929. The 2005 independent period drama *Sweet Land* is set in Audubon, Minnesota, during the 1920s, but it was filmed in Montevideo, Uruguay. "Home Run Joe" Marshall, who made brief appearances in the MLB between September 1903 and August 1906, hails from Audubon. Ironically, he never hit a home run in the major leagues, but he hit 25 homers while batting for the San Francisco Pirates of the Pacific National League in 1903, a league-high. Minnesota's Largest

Purple Martin (a type of bird) House is a quirky attraction in the parking lot of the Audubon Liquors store.

CALLAWAY, MN
POPULATION: 178 – CITY 217 OF 856 (5-5-25)

Callaway (pop. 178) was platted as Baxter. Its name was changed to honor William R. Callaway, the general passenger agent of the Minneapolis, St. Paul, and Sault Ste. Marie Railroad. The agricultural hamlet saw the laying of the railroad tracks through its townsite by Independence Day, 1904. That same month, N. A. Granquist built a structure for the Bovy Shute Lumber Company, and Andrew Eide opened Callaway's first general store. Later came J. P. and John Ernester's bank in 1906, the *Callaway Tomahawk* newspaper, multiple hotels, grain elevators, Henning Londeen's flour and feed mill, and the Land-O-Lakes Cooperative Creamery building. School District No. 96 was organized in 1906. It was one of several headliner points of interest on a 1929 plat map alongside the Catholic church, the Standard Oil Company filling station, the Callaway Oil Company station, the Fairview Hotel, the Wilcox Lumber Yard, a theatre, a City Hall building, the Congregational church, and several other lines ranging from meat markets and garages to restaurants, grocery stores, and hardware and implement dealerships. In the 1920s, Paul Johnson sparked a buzz in the community by helping establish Callaway's honey industry with his 6,000+ hives. Three hundred and twenty-five residents called Callaway home during that decade, more people than at any other time in its history.

DETROIT LAKES, MN ★☆
POPULATION: 9,869 – CITY 218 OF 856 (5-5-25)

This lakeside paradise sees its population grow by the thousands every summer when seasonal residents and tourists flock to the Becker County seat to take advantage of the picturesque 3,067-acre Detroit Lake and its sister lakes. Fishing, boating, jet skiing, river tubing, horseback riding, golfing, swimming, and other primarily water-related recreational activities are amongst the favorite pastimes of its summer visitors, but snowmobiling, ice fishing, snowboarding, and cross-country and downhill skiing are enjoyed at the Detroit Mountain Recreation Area in the winter months as well. Its historical roots run deep as well. In the early days, the town was called "Detroit" before the 'Lakes' was added in September 1926 to avoid confusion with Detroit, Michigan. It came from the French word *détroit*, meaning "a narrow place in a lake," given by a French Catholic priest who camped on the north shore of the lake. When a long sandbar between Little and Big Detroit Lakes began to shimmer across the body of water, he exclaimed, "What a beautiful detroit!" and the name stuck. Maps dating back to 1860 marked the area, but the township was not settled until 1868. The first settler was Donald McDonald, who built a home circa 1854 at the confluence of the Pelican River and Detroit Lake. In 1871, the city's first beginnings were established by Colonel George Johnston with the arrival of the Northern Pacific Railroad. A small settlement called Tyler Town (later called Johnstonville before it was absorbed into Detroit) existed at that time, and it was from that hamlet that Detroit's new settlers began their village. County commissioners named it the judicial seat in 1877 over its rivals, Frazee, Lake Park, and Audubon, and it was incorporated in 1881. Within three years, it already had an opera house, a bank, a newspaper, the courthouse building, and two hotels: the Lakes Hotel and Hotel Minnesota. In 1892, the Church of the Holy Rosary (a Catholic edifice) was completed; it is now one of thirteen church congregations in town. From 1890 to 1920, Detroit's population grew from 1,510 to 3,426, and by 1940, it surpassed 5,000 residents for the first time. Listing all its infrastructure components would be extensive. Still, according to a 1929 plat map, Detroit Lakes had a dance pavilion and a grandstand near the lakeshore, lumber companies, elevators, and oil stations on its two railroads (the Soo Line had recently arrived and connected with the Northern Pacific), a library, a hospital, the Canfield Hatchery, the Detroit Ice Cream Company, schools, and Congregational, First Lutheran, Episcopal, Methodist Episcopal, Baptist, and Catholic churches. The Art Deco Holmes Theatre was built later. Seven of its most historic buildings have been nominated for the National Register of Historic Places: the 1885 Queen Anne summer home of Homer E. Sargent; the 1892 Holmes Block commercial building; the 1908 Northern Pacific Passenger Depot, which is still used as an Amtrak station; architect Claude and Strack's 1913 Prairie School Carnegie library; the 1916-17 Graystone Hotel structure; two Edgewater Beach Resort cottages built in 1937, and Detroit Lakes City Park, which has always played a key role in the economic and tourism development of the city. In addition to its dance pavilion, athletic fields, and swimming beach, the park is home to the incredible giant wooden trolls of Thomas Dambo. Although only a few are in Minnesota, hundreds of recycled wood material trolls live across five continents. At the Becker County Museum, historians can admire exhibits on the World's Smallest Gas Station (a functional 3.5 by 4 feet filling station that was functional until 1951), a taxidermied two-headed calf, Minnesota's largest meteorite, and even a haunted parrot. As one of the largest towns in northwestern Minnesota, Detroit Lakes has numerous ties to pop culture and famous individuals. The community was briefly mentioned in an opening credit postcard in the 1983 comedy road film *National Lampoon's Vacation*. In 1960, it was mentioned in John Steinbeck's 1962 travelogue *Travels with Charley*. MSNBC's *The Ed Show*, hosted by anchor Ed Schultz, was broadcast live from a Detroit Lakes studio off and on between 2009 and 2015. Noted figures with communal ties also include Adam Thielen, an active wide receiver in the NFL who made Pro Bowls in 2017 and 2018 and holds the NFL record for most consecutive 100-year receiving games with eight; Jessica Lange, a two-time Academy Award, five-time Golden Globe, three-time Primetime Emmy, and one-time Tony Award-winning actress best known for her roles in *King Kong* (1976), *Grey Gardens* (2009), and *American Horror Story* (2011-2015); Dick Beardsley, the third-fastest American-born male marathon runner; Jason Blake, a forward in the National Hockey League from 1999 to 2012; Dave Reichert, a U.S. Congressman from Washington between January 2005 and January 2019; Collin Peterson, a Member of U.S. House of Representatives from Minnesota from 1991 to 2021; Tillie Anderson, once known as the best woman cyclist in the world, and Phil Hansen, a defensive end with the NFL's Buffalo Bills from 1991 to 2001.

Restaurant Recommendation:
Lakeside Tavern & Brewery
200 W Lake Dr
Detroit Lakes, MN 56501

Lodging Recommendation:
BWPr: The Lodge on Lake Detroit
1200 E Shore Dr
Detroit Lakes, MN 56501

FRAZEE, MN
POPULATION: 1,335 – CITY 220 OF 856 (5-5-25)
Frazee's turkey industry is honored by the presence of Big Tom, the World's Largest Turkey, which has had two renditions (both of which can still be found in different

locations in town). The first 22-foot-tall statue of Tom was built in 1984-86. After he was accidentally roasted while undergoing repairs in July 1998, a new statue was commissioned later that year to be a more permanent replacement. The bigger and better turkey weighs over 2.5 tons and measures 20 feet tall by 17 feet wide. He sits in Lions Park on a hilltop, and his smaller counterpart sits on a pedestal at a local gas station. The turkey-loving town was first called Detroit and then Third Crossing before it was named Frazee for Randolph Lafayette Frazee, a prominent sawmill owner. Detroit village was formally established in July 1871, although its earliest plat dates to May 27, 1857. A year after the "new" townsite was laid out, a business company consisting of Absalom and Charles M. Campbell and William G. and T. W. Chilton organized the construction of a dam and a sawmill, which was purchased by Mr. Frazee (who already owned a mill in New York Mills and another in far northern Minnesota). He again laid out the townsite in the summer of 1873 with the help of W. C. Darling, and Frazee convinced the Northern Pacific Railroad to establish a depot and run a line through his property. The presence of the railroad, combined with a thriving milling industry, led to the establishment of many more businesses and to Frazee's incorporation as a municipality in 1891. By this point, R. L. Frazee had sold his mill and its accompanying property to A. H. Wilcox, who turned around in January 1897 and sold it to the Commonwealth Lumber Company. Since 1874, the local post office had been called Frazee City, but in 1892, the 'City' was dropped, and the town's name was permanently shortened to just Frazee. Many businesses popped up in the city on the banks of the Otter Tail River, but its most impressive accomplishments (before the Great Depression) were the Otto Hospital, Rosenblum National Bank, the State Bank of Frazee, a creamery, Frazee High School and its athletic field, Sacred Heart Catholic church, a Baptist church, a German Lutheran church, and a third Protestant church. Nowadays, its largest employers are Frazee-Vergas Public Schools, the Frazee Care Center, and the Daggett Truck Line. This eighty-plus-year-old business delivers freight throughout the United States and Canada. Frazee is the hometown of Kieth Engen, an operatic bass member of the Bavarian State Opera in Munich, Germany, for decades. In addition to Big Tom: the World's Largest Turkey, Frazee is one of a few lucky locations to be home to a Thomas Dambo troll. Located at Wannigan Regional Park, the recycled-wood sculpture is one of several in the area, the others around Detroit Lakes. Another point of community pride is Cornerstone Collective, a community, youth, and family resource center. It was initially designed to give Frazee kids a place to "belong," play table games, cook, and do arts and crafts. The center has since been expanded to include a bistro with crepes and coffee, as well as a full performance stage.

LAKE PARK, MN
POPULATION: 728 – CITY 214 OF 856 (5-5-25)

Lake Park was founded in an area once dominated by elk, wolves, and abundant wildlife, flora, and fauna. Daniel McKay and George Osborne, seeking to take advantage of the Homestead Act of 1862, were the first to settle what was initially known as Liberty Township. They left shortly thereafter, but Norwegian immigrants soon arrived and took a liking to Lake Flora and its surrounding chain of lakes. One of these men was Jonas Erickson, who was approached by Thomas Canfield of The Lake Superior and Puget Sound Land Company to purchase land for a right-of-way on behalf of the Northern Pacific Railroad. He sold his property for three thousand dollars, a handsome sum at the time. By February 25, 1881, the village of Lake Park was incorporated. Other names included Lakeside, which the railroad used for a short time, and the post office called it Loring from 1872 to 1873. "Lake Park" was derived from an Ojibwe phrase roughly translated to "the lakes where there are streams, groves, prairies, and a beautiful diversified park country." Ole J. Weston built a shanty to house the railroad section crew during construction of the line, the first building on the site. Next were three stores owned by R. H. Abraham, Elling Carlson and Peter Ebeltoft, and S. B. Pinney and Charles B. Plummer. Hans Hanson served as the first blacksmith, and Charles B. Plummer established the first of several hotels. By 1929, after half a century of development, Lake Park had close to 700 residents and numerous firms. Some of them were the Olson Sporting Goods store, the Nelson Cafe, the newspaper office of the *Lake Park Journal*, a theatre, a mill, elevators and lumber yards, banks, a Ford Garage, the Lake Park Oil Company, the Foss Oil Company, the Standard Oil Company, and Nelson & Knutson's potato operation. Three churches surrounded the school in the western part of Lake Park in Canfield's Addition, and two other churches were located closer to the central business district. At one point, Lake Park boasted some of the country's only lefse factories, which gave it the title of the "Lefse Capital of the World." The factories were highly successful for many years before rail service was eliminated in the city, and the country entered a recession. Lefse is a traditional Norwegian flatbread made from riced potatoes, butter, and the cook's choice of milk, cream, or lard.

OGEMA, MN
POPULATION: 208 – CITY 216 OF 856 (5-5-25)
Once home to as many as 328 people in the 1940s, Ogema is Becker County's northwestmost municipality. Founded in 1905 on the Minneapolis, St. Paul & Sault Ste. Marie Railroad (the Soo Line), its name means "a chief in the Ojibwe language. Two years after its establishment, it was incorporated on October 28, 1907, and had a post office in Theodore Theonnes's feed store. He was the first postmaster. By 1929, it boasted a feed mill, a lumber yard and office, a creamery, two hotels, a bank, a general merchandise store, a meat market, a fire hall, a blacksmith shop, a garage, an oil station, a Lutheran church, a Catholic church, stockyards, the Standard Oil Company, the M. Barren Elevator Company, the Ogema Grain Company Elevator, and a depot. Potato farming was an important industry, as indicated by C. Groth's large potato warehouse in the western part of town.

WOLF LAKE, MN
POPULATION: 71 – CITY 221 OF 856 (5-5-25)
Gamakobimadagakwad, or "Bear Walking on the Ice Lake," was the Chippewa's name for the 1,400-acre lake that provided them with hunting grounds for deer and habitat for bears and wolves long before any white man had entered the area. When the first settlers arrived from Finland, they mistakenly translated part of the word as 'wolf' instead of 'bear,' thus the discrepancy in its modern nomenclature. John Wirkkanen of Champion, Michigan, was the first pioneer to arrive on May 15, 1888, and soon other Scandinavian families began to filter in. The township was organized on April 4, 1896; it would take another fifty-three years for the village of Wolf Lake to incorporate in May 1949. From 1909 to 1911, its post office was called "Wolf," then discontinued and reopened from 1947 to 1993 as "Wolf Lake." The community never had a railroad, so its highest-ever recorded population was 109 in the 1950 Census.

Unincorporated/Ghost Towns: Bucks Mill, Cormorant, Elbow Lake, Goldenrod, Midway, Oak Lake, Osage, Pine Point, Ponsford, Richwood, Rochert, Shoreham, Snellman, Two Inlets, White Earth

National Register of Historic Places:
Detroit Lakes: Detroit Lakes Carnegie Library, Detroit Lakes City Park, Edgewater Beach

Cottages, Graystone Hotel, Holmes Block, Homer E. Sargent House, Northern Pacific Passenger Depot
Park Rapids: Itasca State Park

Golf Courses:
Black Diamond at Forest Hills Forest, Daily Fee (Detroit Lakes, MN)
Frazee Golf Course, Daily Fee (Frazee, MN)
Wildflower at Fair Hills – Executive 9, Daily Fee (Detroit Lakes, MN)
Wildflower at Fair Hills, Daily Fee (Detroit Lakes, MN)

Breweries/Wineries/Distilleries:
Lakeside Tavern (Detroit Lakes, MN)

Town Celebrations:
Cormorant Daze, Cormorant, MN (3rd Weekend in August)
Northwest Water Carnival, Detroit Lakes, MN (10 Days in July, starting 2nd Friday)
Polar Fest, Detroit Lakes, MN (17 days in February; starting 1st Friday)
Pumpkin Fest, Lake Park, MN (Last Saturday in September)
Turkey Days, Frazee, MN (Last Full Weekend in July)
WE Fest Country Music Festival, Detroit Lakes, MN (Early August)

BELTRAMI COUNTY
EST. 1866 - POPULATION: 46,228

Beltrami County is named for Giacomo Beltrami of Bergamo, Italy, an explorer who first traversed the area in the 1820s in search of the source of the Mississippi River.

BEMIDJI, MN ★☆
POPULATION: 14,574 – CITY 296 OF 856 (6-1-25)
The largest city of industry between Grand Forks, North Dakota, and Duluth, Minnesota (a distance of about 246 miles as the crow flies) also serves as a central haven for members of the Red Lake, White Earth, and Leech Lake Indian Reservations. Its unique name was derived from the Ojibwe's *bemijigamaag*, meaning a "lake with crossing waters." The Mississippi River connects to Lake Bemidji near modern-day Brinkman Park. Chief Bemidji was also the white man's name for Shaynowishkung, an Ojibwe elder who was then a part of the Cass Lake Band of Chippewa. He and his family lived on the nearly 7,000-acre lake before homesteaders moved into the area in large numbers circa 1893. Shaynowishkung was the first customer of a local lumber mill. His kindness towards the Europeans led them to name their settlement "Bemidji" in his honor, mistakenly believing the term was his name rather than a descriptive term for the lake and river. "Bermidji" was used as the spelling for both the town and the post office before the '-r' was removed in 1898, two years after the community's incorporation on May 20, 1896. Like other communities in this part of Minnesota, Bemidji's primary industry (following the decline of the fur trade) was logging. Thomas Barlow Walker, Charles Ruggles, John S., and Charles Pillsbury poured millions of dollars into developing sawmills and lumber centers throughout the region starting in 1874. Their drive to secure large swaths of forests for logging was met with enthusiasm by officials of the Great Northern, the Minneapolis, St. Paul & Sault Ste. Marie, and the Minneapolis, Red Lake & Manitoba Railroad. The latter line connected Bemidji with its northern terminus in Redby, a village on the Red Lake Indian Reservation located on the Lower Red Lake. Saloons, newspapers, blacksmith shops, hotels, and businesses of all varieties popped up on the railroads next to many mills, aiding (or sometimes detracting from, in the case of the saloons that were

ultimately shut down by W.E. Johnson when they proved too rowdy) in Bemidji's growth. From 1900 to 1910, Bemidji grew from 2,183 to 5,099; in the next ten years, its population reached 7,086. In 1919, it was selected as the site of Bemidji State Normal, which, over a century of name changes and alterations, has transformed into Bemidji State Teachers College (from 1921 to 1957), Bemidji State College (until 1975), and Bemidji State University. As the Great Depression approached and many other area logging communities switched to agriculture, Bemidji's townspeople doubled down on their primary industry, providing much-needed materials for the Civilian Conservation Corps' New Deal projects. Over 2,000 employees were still put out of work due to sawmill fires, the depletion of forests, and the relocation of Crookston sawmills to the Pacific Northwest. During this era, one of Minnesota's most iconic landmarks, Paul Bunyan and Babe the Blue Ox, was built in 1937 by Cyril M. Dickinson and Jim Payton to welcome tourists to a winter carnival. The 18-foot-tall Bunyan and 23-foot-long Blue statues were reported to be the "second most photographed statues in the United States" by the Kodak Company, behind only Mount Rushmore. They were added to the National Register of Historic Places in March 1988 and are the most unique amongst Bemidji's seven NRHP-designated locations. The others are the 1902 Beaux-Arts Beltrami County Courthouse; the 1909 Bemidji Carnegie Library; the 1913 Great Northern Depot, now serving as the Beltrami County History Center; the 1917 reinforced concrete deck arch bridge over the Mississippi River, called the Nymore Bridge; a rare Minnesotan 1936 Streamline Moderne home, the David Park House, and a couple of properties at Lake Bemidji State Park associated with the National Youth Administration and the Civilian Conservation Corps. The park was established in 1923 to preserve a spruce-tamarack bog and provide ample opportunities for hiking, wildlife viewing, swimming, boating, camping, biking, fishing, and winter sports. Several other recreational areas, parks, and forests, such as the Big Bog State Recreation Area, Itasca State Park, and Chippewa National Forest, are located near Bemidji, and there are over 400 lakes within a 25-mile radius of the city. In the sports world, Bemidji State University etched itself into the history books as a hockey dynasty, reaching the title game eight consecutive years in the late 1980s and early 1990s. The city self-proclaimed itself as the "Curling Capital of the United States," thanks in part to its native curlers Natalie Nicholson, the leader of the U.S. women's curling team at the 2010 Winter Olympics, and Pete Fenson, the captain (skip) of the 2006 Winter Olympics U.S. men's team. Jane Russell, a famous Hollywood actress in the 1940s and 1950s with a star on the Hollywood Walk of Fame; Brian Paulson, a noted record producer and audio engineer; Terry Frost, a Western film actor; Dave Casper, a five-time Pro Bowl tight end with the Oakland Raiders and a 2002 inductee into the Pro Football Hall of Fame; authors Roy C. Booth and Kent Nerburn; Gary Sargent, a defenseman in the National Hockey League between 1975 and 1983; Bryan Hickerson, an MLB pitcher in the early 1990s; and Joe Motzko, an ice hockey forward from 2003 to 2014, are just some of the famous individuals who claim Bemidji ties.

 **Restaurant Recommendation:**
Lazy Jack's
6735 Fairgrounds Rd NW
Bemidji, MN 56601

Restaurant Recommendation:
Minnesota Nice Cafe
315 Irvine Ave NW
Bemidji, MN 56601

BLACKDUCK, MN
POPULATION: 845 – CITY 291 OF 856 (6-1-25)
Three large black duck statues welcome visitors to Blackduck, a community born from the logging industry. Where a prehistoric Sioux village once stood, early Minnesotans from Crookston decided in the fall of 1900 to exploit the area's logging potential. A town was incorporated on December 21, 1900, almost as quickly as it had been organized (on October 19, 1900, by Marcus D. Stoner), and so named because of its proximity to Blackduck Lake. The lake, in turn, was named for the ring-necked duck that once covered the lake. Pine, cedar, and balsam trees were harvested, and many sawmills were built to process the large amounts of timber. Two large companies, The Minneapolis Cedar and Lumber Company (est. 1903) and The Stoner Lath and Lumber Company (est. 1919), specialized in producing ties and cedar posts, and balsam lath, respectively. The logging quality was excellent thanks to Blackduck's location on the Laurentian Divide, which allowed water to drain, preventing soil from retaining much moisture. However, despite a peak population of 942 people at its inaugural 1910 Census, a branch off the Minnesota and International Railroad (later the Northern Pacific), and several other lines of stores, shops, and enterprises, the timber eventually ran out. Blackduck's population dropped by a quarter over the next two decades as the community shifted to an agricultural perspective. Beltrami County's oldest cooperative creamery was started here in 1915. In 1927, a $12,000 brick-and-concrete plant was erected to aid in the annual production of over 400,000 pounds of butter. From 1935 to 1941, the Rabideau CCC Camp was established nearby as temporary housing for New Deal workers. It has since survived as one of the best-preserved examples of what was once one of 2,650 such camps nationwide. It was added to the National Register of Historic Places in June 1976 and designated as a National Historic Landmark on February 17, 2006. The town's other NRHP-listed location, the Minnesota and International Railway Trestle at Blackduck, is a 701-foot-long timber trestle bridge built in 1901-02. It is now a part of the Voyageurs (the Blue Ox) Trail leading to International Falls. Two extensive forests, the Blackduck State Forest (125,529 acres) and the 666,623-acre Chippewa National Forest, are adjacent to the community and offer opportunities to hike, boat, camp, wildlife-watch, and enjoy other recreational activities. One of the earlier-mentioned duck statues is the World's Largest Black Duck Statue in Wayside Park. The other two are (or were) located in downtown Blackduck and at the Drake Motel.

FUNKLEY, MN
POPULATION: 18 – CITY 290 OF 856 (6-1-25)
One of Minnesota's smallest incorporated communities is ironically also one of its fastest-growing municipalities, as its population grew by a whopping 260% from just five residents to eighteen between 2010 and 2020. As many as 50 to 60 people lived in Funkley closer to its establishment in 1903, when it was organized by Matt Fisher and named in honor of Beltrami County attorney Henry Funkley. A post office opened in 1903 and closed in 1967, and the town was once located at a junction of the Minnesota and International Railway. It had briefly been called Hovey Junction before the name was changed. In May 1953, most of Funkley's 28-person population was flown out to New York City by the bedsheet manufacturer Pacific Mills. They did so because the Women's Missionary Society of the Evangelical Free Church had, for years, worked hard to turn old bed sheets into bandages for patients of the American Cancer Society. The party of 33 from the Funkley area toured the Big Apple, including stops at the Empire State Building, the United Nations, and a New York Giants football game. They were even given a police escort on Broadway and flown out to

Washington, D.C. on an added leg of the adventure to meet President Dwight Eisenhower, Vice President Richard Nixon, and John Edgar Hoover, then the first director of the Federal Bureau of Investigation.

KELLIHER, MN
POPULATION: 258 – CITY 289 OF 856 (6-1-25)
This town, known for timbering, is the final resting place for the legendary folk hero Paul Bunyan, who is said to have perished here in 1893. A small stone reading "Here Lies Paul, And That's All" marks where the gargantuan lumberjack was supposedly buried in what is today known as Paul Bunyan Memorial Park. The quirky attraction has attracted thousands of tourists over the years to Kelliher, which was named for A. O. Kelliher, an early lumber company agent. He platted the townsite on behalf of George S. Eddy of the Crookston Lumber Company. A post office was formulated in 1903 to serve the area's needs; it was the first of many other stores, churches, and schools that ultimately adorned the area, first settled by Ulysses (Jess) and John Freestone in 1892. Five hundred fourteen people lived in Kelliher in its 1920s heyday. At that point, it was the terminus of a northbound branch line of the Minnesota and International Railway. Kelliher is associated with Saum Schools, a 1903 one-room log schoolhouse, and a 1912 building erected as Minnesota's first "purpose-built consolidated school." The largest peat bog in the lower 48 states and its scenic boardwalk can be found outside of the nearby unincorporated town of Waskish at Big Bog State Recreation Area's North Unit. A fire tower can be climbed at the South Unit for an overview of Red Lake, the largest lake (444 square miles) located entirely within Minnesota's borders.

Restaurant Recommendation:
Road Runner Drive In
321 Clark Ave S
Kelliher, MN 56650

SOLWAY, MN
POPULATION: 73 – CITY 295 OF 856 (6-1-25)
The Solway Firth, an inlet from the Irish Sea that forms part of the border between England and Scotland, shares its name with this southwestern Beltrami County community. In 1898, the post office was established during the area's logging boom (between 1887 and 1905), which led to the town's founding and the arrival of a Great Northern Railroad line. The Solway Lumber Company was crucial in keeping Solway's economy afloat. By the turn of the century, there were also seven saloons, restaurants, stores, a sawmill, a community hall, a jail, a blacksmith shop, a feed store, a weekly newspaper, and pairs of hotels and livery barns. Unfortunately, many of these locations were destroyed by fires between 1905 and 1910, halving the town's population from 177 in 1900 to just 85 by 1910. The population rebounded slightly to 136 people by the 1940s, but has since halved again.

TENSTRIKE, MN
POPULATION: 186 – CITY 292 OF 856 (6-1-25)
M. R. Brown, mayor of Crookston, Minnesota, established a series of trading posts throughout Beltrami County to capitalize on the abundant trade generated by the Crookston Lumber Company's activities and the broader logging industry. The most profitable of these were found on the east shore of Gull Lake, which Mr. Brown

frequently referred to as his "tenstrike" because of his luck in locating his trading post at such a busy point. "Tenstrike," alluding to the act in bowling in which all ten pins are knocked down for a strike, was used by Almon A. White of St. Paul for the name of the townsite that he platted on behalf of the forthcoming railroad. In the fall of 1901, the railroad arrived, and in came the sawmills (the first of which was owned by Williams Fellows, in operation from the late 1890s to the early 1950s), grocery stores, hotels, banks, churches, meat markets, a box factory, and even thirteen saloons. The Tenstrike Tribune was founded in the early 1900s, when estimates placed the population at 2,000 or more. The 1910 U.S. Decennial Census, the first conducted in Tenstrike by the federal government, reported a permanent population of 250. Tenstrike's final school edifice was constructed in 1903 but eventually consolidated with Blackduck and was razed in the 1960s when it was no longer used. Around the time of its closure and destruction, Babe Fellows (with Norman Gladen) established the Land O' Lakes Wood Preserving Plant, a larger timber-processing facility. He also built the Fellows Family Museum with the intention of preserving local history. Tenstrike was incorporated on March 11, 1901.

TURTLE RIVER, MN
POPULATION: 88 – CITY 293 OF 856 (6-1-25)
Turtle River and the nearby Turtle Lake were named by explorer David Thompson, who thought the area's topography resembled a turtle's shell. Long before Thompson's arrival, there was a Native American fishing camp during the Woodland Period (three to six thousand years ago), where Indigenous people caught white sucker and northern pike. Fred DeSilver began construction of the townsite in 1899, when he opened a hotel and several stores on Simon E. Bright's homestead, only two years before the Northern Pacific Railroad (then the Minnesota and International) passed through. Nels Otterstad became the first postmaster of the 1899 branch office, which closed in 1944 while the town was experiencing its worst loss of residents in its history. A peak population of 109 had lived there in the 1930s, but between 1940 and 1950, its numbers dropped by 36.7%, from 90 to 57. Gary Burger, lead vocalist of the rock band The Monks, served as mayor of Turtle River from 2006 to March 14, 2014.

WILTON, MN
POPULATION: 263 – CITY 294 OF 856 (6-1-25)
Several post offices throughout Minnesota have been called Wilson. The first was in Waseca County, from 1856 to 1881, and the next was the Fillmore County office from 1877 to 1881. In 1903, the name was used for a third time in Eckles Township, Beltrami County, replacing the name "Selkce." Selkce is "Eckles" spelled backwards. Wilton was selected by the Great Northern Railroad because officials knew of other towns of that name in several different states and in Canada. They were joined in the area by the Minneapolis, St. Paul & Sault Ste. Marie Railroad (a couple of miles to the north), not long after they had arrived, which allowed Wilton to grow as one of Beltrami County's many important railroad towns. It was incorporated on May 26, 1906, and became best known for its sawmill. General mercantile stores, grocery stores, blacksmith shops, liveries, and other typical businesses emerged over the next several years, culminating in a 1910s heyday when Wilton had as many as 215 residents. "Wilton Hill" has long been a popular winter spot for sledders, skiers, hockey players, and other cold-weather enthusiasts.

Unincorporated/Ghost Towns: Andrusia, Aure, Carmel, Debs, Four Town, Hines, Jelle, Little Rock, Pennington, Pinewood, Ponemah, Puposky, Quiring, Red Lake, Redby, Saum, Secluded Acres, Shooks, Waskish, Werner

National Register of Historic Places:
Bemidji: Beltrami County Courthouse, Bemidji Carnegie Library, David Park House, Great Northern Depot, Lake Bemidji State Park CCC/NYA/Rustic Style Historic Resources, Nymore Bridge, Paul Bunyan & Babe the Blue Ox
Blackduck: Minnesota & International Railway Trestle at Blackduck, Rabideau CCC Camp
Debs: District No. 132 School
Kelliher: Saum Schools
Port Hope Township: Three Island Park Site
Turtle Lake Township: Buena Vista Archeological Historic District

Golf Courses:
Bemidji Town & Country Club, Daily Fee (Bemidji, MN)

Breweries/Wineries/Distilleries:
Bemidji Brewery (Bemidji, MN)

Town Celebrations:
Dragon Boat Festival, Bemidji, MN (1st Weekend of August)

BENTON COUNTY
EST. 1849 - POPULATION: 41,379

Established in 1849, Benton County is named for Thomas Hart Benton, one of the minds behind "manifest destiny," which encouraged the westward expansion of the United States.

FOLEY, MN ★
POPULATION: 2,711 – CITY 464 OF 856 (7-21-25)

In 2022, Foley, Minnesota, and Colstrip, Montana, became sister cities, and the two communities realized they shared a common thread with John Foley, one of five lumber baron brothers who came to America from Lanark County, Ontario, Canada. He established the town after the Great Northern Railroad was extended to that point in 1882-84, and assisted in bringing a post office to the vicinity in 1883. John's son Thomas served as one of the earliest postmasters. For years, it grew in the shadow of Sauk Rapids, featuring simple lines of enterprise such as saloons, hotels, restaurants, livery stables, and implement stores. Around the turn of the century, Mr. Foley successfully persuaded the county's residents to vote to transfer the judicial seat to a more centralized location within the county. Locals pledged $12,000 to cover the cost of constructing the courthouse, which John Foley fully covered. Foley won the election by a final count of 1,284 votes to Sauk Rapids's 788. With the new status, Foley found success in various industries, including a pickle factory, creameries, a grain elevator, and three mills known as the Wood, Stave, and Heading Mills. They manufactured wood staves for pails and wood boxes. A bank, a newspaper, a pharmacy, and a meat market were also present. "Foleyland" is the nickname for a collection of folk art along MN-23, featuring several sculptures crafted from old farm machinery and vehicles. Brewed Gems Coffee and Crystals was opened in May 2024 as a joint crystal, gemstone, and coffee shop by Carissa Fouquette to raise money for her brother Jaymeson, who was diagnosed with brain cancer in 2023. Crystal sales are directed toward Jaymeson's cancer treatment.

GILMAN, MN
POPULATION: 226 – CITY 465 OF 856 (7-21-25)
Early institutions, such as a creamery and a cheese factory, helped build Gilman's early economy. However, the community is best known for its incredible Beaux-Arts religious edifice, Saints Peter and Paul Church. Polish immigrants built St. Wenceslas church in 1872 from logs, but in the 1880s, it was replaced by St. Casimir's Church, a wood-frame structure. After St. Casimir's burned in 1891, an even larger wooden building was erected. A school was completed in 1909, and by 1930, the large brick structure was completed, and the parish name changed for good. It was listed on the National Register of Historic Places in 1982, not long after Gilman was incorporated as a village on February 11, 1959. George Pappenfus was postmaster when the office began in 1885; he was a storeowner and the manager of one of the local saloons. Charles A. Gilman, for whom the town was named, had a sawmill here and was the 9th Lieutenant Governor of Minnesota from January 10, 1880, to January 4, 1887.

RICE, MN
POPULATION: 1,975 – CITY 466 OF 856 (7-21-25)
Rice, a successor to a village called Langola, began when George T. Rice built a grist and flour mill, as well as the Luther Hotel, to serve as a stop on a stagecoach route. Rice ingeniously selected a spot that saw traffic from the Red River Oxcart Trail and the Military Road, and unbeknownst to him then, a future line of the Northern Pacific Railroad in 1877. As settlers opted to build their homes and businesses next to Rice's establishments, the need for a post office became imminent. Their wish for a mail office was granted in 1879, and in July of the following year, Rice was incorporated. The fledgling community was the unfortunate recipient of the tail end of the April 14, 1886, F4 tornado that destroyed most of Sauk Rapids and would go on to ravage what little there was of Rice at that time. It took the lives of eleven people in a wedding party, including the groom. Rice was rebuilt, and a creamery, a cheese factory, mills, elevators, and a plethora of other businesses came about as the town welcomed hundreds of new residents. Since 2000, Rice's population has nearly tripled, from 711 people at the turn of the 21st century to approximately 2,000 people today.

SAUK RAPIDS, MN ☆
POPULATION: 13,862 – CITY 468 OF 856 (7-21-25)
Groves of basswood, oak, and maple trees lining the Mississippi River make up most of what Zebulon Pike would have seen as he was exploring the area in 1805. He mapped the local tributary of the Mississippi as the Sack River, and called its slight drop in elevation "Big Falls." It would remain largely untouched by Europeans and immigrants until 1851, when W.H. Wood built his home, the Lynden Terrace mansion. A townsite called Washington had been laid out a year prior by J.C. Ramsey and Henry Jackson. Still, it would eventually take on the name "Sauk Rapids" as an amalgamation of the two geographic features that Pike had documented half a century earlier. From 1851 to 1856, it served as the county seat until it was relocated to Watab (now an unincorporated area). In 1859, it returned to Sauk Rapids, which provided the village with the opportunity to grow alongside Saint Cloud as one of the region's premier economic centers. To list all of the business lines would be extensive, but there were general stores, hotels, flour mills, specialty stores, and even an early brewery, cheese factory, and two weekly newspapers. One of the two news publications was the S*auk Rapids Frontiersman*, founded in 1854 as the first newspaper in Minnesota outside of St. Paul. Congregational, Methodist, Episcopalian, and Lutheran groups were the first four religious groups to construct their edifices. All

seemed well until the dreadful night of April 14, 1886, when the deadliest tornado in Minnesota history, an F4 twister, eliminated the entire town and claimed the lives of 87 people. Over three hundred more were injured. Despite the horrifying events that had unfolded in just a few hours, the townspeople worked together to rebuild, and by 1890, the population of Sauk Rapids had doubled from 598 people in 1880 to 1,185. The county seat moved to Foley in 1897, dealing what could have been considered a devastating blow to the community. Again, Sauk Rapids forged onwards, welcoming in lines of the Great Northern and the Northern Pacific Railroads, and the century since losing the seat it has since become home to about a third of Benton County's entire population. Eldon John "Rip" Repulski, a 1956 All-Star outfielder with the MLB's St. Louis Cardinals, and Bridget Jones Nelson, a screenwriter and actor for *Mystery Science Theater 3000*, a science fiction comedy series on Comedy Central in the 1990s, have ties to the community. An early local tale recalls the 1868 discovery of Sasquatch: a nearly 11-foot-tall skeleton with a 5-foot measurement taken around its chest. The Copper Pony, located in downtown Sauk Rapids since 2021, is an area favorite for creative giftware, seasonal home accessories, coffee, a soda bar, and gourmet cookies.

Restaurant Recommendation:
Copper Pony
208 N Benton Dr
Sauk Rapids, MN 56379

Royalton is only partially located in Benton County (see Morrison County), and Sartell and St. Cloud is only partially located in Benton County (see Steams County).

Unincorporated/Ghost Towns: Brennyville, Duelm, Estes Brook, Fruitville, Glendorado, Granite Ledge, Jakeville, Mayhew, Minden, North Benton, Oak Park, Parent, Popple Creek, Ronneby, Rum River, Silver Corners, Watab

National Register of Historic Places:
Gilman: Church of Sts. Peter & Paul-Catholic
Mayhew Lake Township: Esselman Brothers General Store
Sauk Rapids: Leonard Robinson House
St. George Township: Cota Round Barns

Golf Courses:
Oak Hill Golf Club, Daily Fee (Rice, MN)
Stone Creek Golf Club, Daily Fee (Foley, MN)
Wapicada Golf Club, Daily Fee (Sauk Rapids, MN)

Town Celebrations:
Foley Fun Days, Foley, MN (Mid-June)
Gilman Days, Gilman, MN (Last Weekend of July)
Rock the Riverside, Sauk Rapids, MN (Thursday Evenings in the Summer)
Sauk Rapids River Days, Sauk Rapids, MN (4th Weekend in June)

Aitkin County: Rialto Theater (Aitkin), Aitkin County Courthouse & Veteran's Memorial (Aitkin), former Mississippi River showboat at Aitkin County Fairgrounds (Aitkin), former Foley Hotel (Aitkin), mural at Roadside Restaurant (Aitkin), School House Cafe (McGregor), Bog Boardwalk at Savanna Portage State Park (McGregor), former District 53 Schoolhouse (Tamarack)

Anoka County: former Jackson Hotel (Anoka), "Halloween Capital of the World" Pumpkin Sculpture (Anoka), Rum River Dam (Anoka), Veteran's Memorial (Blaine), Northern Lights (Blaine), The Swedish Evangelical Lutheran Church (Ham Lake), Historic Sparre Round Barn (Nowthen), Spring Lake at Lakeside Lions Park (Spring Lake Park)

Becker County: World's Largest Purple Martin House (Audubon), Mural (Callaway), Ronny Funny Face Thomas Dambo Troll (Detroit Lakes), Lake Sallie Dunton Locks County Park (Detroit Lakes), World's Largest Turkey (Frazee), Jacob Everear Thomas Dambo Troll (Frazee), Mural of Downtown (Lake Park), former Jail (Ogema)

Beltrami County: Paul Bunyan & Babe the Blue Ox Statues (Bemidji), Bemidji State University Gateway (Bemidji), former Carnegie Library (Bemidji), Beltrami County Courthouse (Bemidji) Chief Theatre (Bemidji), World's Largest Black Duck Statue (Blackduck), Paul Bunyan's Grave (Kelliher), Big Bog Fire Tower (Waskish)

Benton County: former Brickhouse Cinema (Foley), Foleyland (Foley), Saint John's Catholic Church (Foley), Interior of Sts Peter & Paul Catholic Church (Gilman), The Old Creamery Cafe (Rice), Verso Paper Sartell Mill Memorial (Sartell), The Clearing Music Venue (Sauk Rapids) Copper Pony (Sauk Rapids)

BIG STONE COUNTY
EST. 1862 - POPULATION: 5,166

Big Stone Lake, the source of the Minnesota River and home to 12,610 surface acres of water, is the namesake of this small county of five-thousand-odd residents formally organized in 1874.

BARRY, MN
POPULATION: 16 – CITY 130 OF 856 (4-11-25)
In 1878, James Barry and William Nash claimed the parcel of land that would become the future townsite of Barry. This now-tiny town of 16 residents was first settled by Edmond and William Barry of Lowell, Massachusetts, who arrived on May 10, 1879, in an area without a railroad or many other neighboring settlers. They worked to develop it by establishing businesses, such as a blacksmith shop and a general store, and in 1881, their efforts were rewarded when a post office was established with Miss Maria M. Barry as postmaster. An alternative name for the area before then was Lowell, but the postal service thought it more appropriate to name it for a prominent local family. Irish settlers helped found other lines of enterprise, including a lumberyard (owned by Thomas O'Phalen), an elevator (managed by John McBrady), a hardware store (operated by P. R. Hatney), and even a bowling alley. The Village of Barry was incorporated in 1900; its post office was discontinued in 1981. Its highest-recorded population was 116 people, according to the 1940 Census.

BEARDSLEY, MN
POPULATION: 216 – CITY 131 OF 856 (4-11-25)
William W. Beardsley lived in New York, Pennsylvania, and Wisconsin before he took advantage of the Homestead Act's offer of free, fertile Minnesota land. He picked a spot in Browns Valley Township in April 1878 and formally settled it on May 25, 1878. When the St. Cloud & Lake Traverse Railway Company (later incorporated into the Great Northern Railroad) built a branch line from Morris, Mr. Beardsley opted to plat a townsite to serve as a shipping point for the railroad. He named the town after himself. Henry Stonebraker built the first building on the new site, a saloon, and a coal and lumber firm. A. W. Jones erected the first general merchandise store in June 1881 and was joined in that trade by Jeffrey Spencer, L. P. Burdick (the two of whom worked together), and Jo Shannon by the end of the year. The thriving townsite soon had a representation of every line, from hotels and lumber yards to hardware stores, banks, and elevators. At one point, the Beardsley Grain and Feed Company operated four elevators: the Westfall, the Dittes, the Cargill, and the old Monarch. A post office branch was established on April 11, 1881, with J. A. Shannon as postmaster. Of all the early accomplishments, Beardsley's proudest was most likely its school, which was first built in 1883. Miss Pauline Hammond was the teacher. A new "modern" brick structure was completed in 1908 to house elementary and high school students; in 1954, a new high school was built. The entire district consolidated with Browns Valley in the fall of 1984. Beardsley has been incorporated as a village since 1891.

CLINTON, MN ☆
POPULATION: 386 – CITY 128 OF 856 (4-11-25)
Once home to six elevators, the booming agricultural hamlet of Clinton (alternatively called Central, Batavia, and Rupert by railroad or postal authorities for many years) rose to prominence through the hard work of its wheat, barley, oat, and potato farmers.

Settled primarily by Norwegians in 1877, it was known as Central for its centralized location within Big Stone County. It would be over half a decade before the locals reaped the rewards of having a railroad. The Fargo and Southern Railroad Company had a loading platform built two miles south of town in 1883. In 1885, the Chicago, Milwaukee & St. Paul Railroad moved the station to present-day Clinton (then called Batavia until 1899, when it was changed to Clinton). It is unknown where the town's name came from, though it was likely named after communities of the same name in other states, such as Iowa or New Jersey. It may have also been named for DeWitt Clinton, the 6th Governor of New York. Peter McCormick opened his store in the building that J. M. Finney built, and in it operated the storefront, a lumber yard office, and the town post office. Two hotels emerged, along with a general store, a drug store, a creamery, a plow factory, and several other businesses. Still, the most impressive of them all was the Clinton Milling Company. Built in 1898, the accomplishment of Olaf Erickson and A. E. Anderson marked the start of Clinton's agricultural boom, which brought its population to as high as 718 residents in the 1950s. Clinton has two modern historical points of interest: its Chicago, Milwaukee, St. Paul, and Pacific Railroad depot, first opened on July 2, 1884, and now a museum featuring historical artifacts on Clinton's local history. The railroad line was discontinued on March 1, 1980, due to financial troubles with the Milwaukee Road. Just outside town is St. Pauli Norwegian Evangelical Lutheran Church, an 1896 Gothic Revival-style edifice built on $3,300 of land by Servin and Lisbet Huselid. It was listed on the National Register of Historic Places in 2010. The town is home to the "world's longest-lasting ice golf tournament," a tradition that has taken place on Clinton's adjacent Eli Lake for several decades. The Big Stone County Fair was held in town for the first time in 1907 and is still celebrated annually with live music, carnival rides, car races, 4-H exhibits, and more.

CORRELL, MN
POPULATION: 26 – CITY 125 OF 856 (4-10-25)
Like some of its neighboring municipalities in the county, Correll began as a railroad town — and, more specifically, a way station — on the Chicago, Milwaukee, and St. Paul Railroad. Being on the main line, one would have assumed its long-term success was guaranteed. Although its population has since dwindled to only about two dozen residents, it was home to as many as 176 individuals, according to the 1920 Census. Its heyday was preceded by the survey of David N. Correll of St. Paul in September 1879, whose work was reviewed by the Hastings & Dakota Railroad Company as a resource to convince them to extend railroad tracks through the region. A railroad depot was the only building for numerous years, and development was minimal until Charles F. Woods purchased the townsite from the Thomas F. Kock Land Company in 1893. The Farmers Elevator was raised, and a hardware store and post office were established. Frank Gold built a lumber yard, managed by J. W. Barr, that aided in the construction of several additional homes and businesses before it was incorporated. A pair of early town tales recalls two incidents: in 1902, when two freight trains collided, and in 1908, when the safe at the local bank was blown up by burglars who made off with their loot in the dead of night. Until recently, Correll was home to the District No. 13 School, an octagonal schoolhouse built in 1898 that was one of the first schools in the county. It was removed to the Big Stone County Historical Museum in Ortonville for permanent preservation.

GRACEVILLE, MN
POPULATION: 529 – CITY 129 OF 856 (4-11-25)
The second-largest town in Big Stone County was started as a part of Bishop John Ireland's "Catholic Land Stock Company" project to bring Catholic settlement to a large

region of Minnesota. He purchased 80 acres for a town site and an additional 120 acres for a farm colony in 1878 and named it in honor of Thomas Langdon Grace. He was the second Roman Catholic Bishop of St. Paul from 1859 to 1884. Another etymology account suggests that Graceville was named after the first white child born in the village, Grace, the daughter of M. J. McDonald, the first settler to build a house on the newly established townsite. An immigration house was built to accommodate other immigrants while their homes were being built. Within it was a grocery store, and the structure doubled as a place of worship on Sundays. The Hastings & Dakota Railroad rolled into the vicinity around the same time. Graceville soon "proved up" and became a leading town in the area. As of 1882, it had four general stores, three saloons, a harness shop, a pharmacy, an elevator, a pair of blacksmith shops, and a Catholic Church. The church property expanded to include a parochial school/academy and a convent affiliated with the Sisters of St. Joseph of Carondelet. In 1885, the Convent of Our Lady of the Lake was started as a Native American residential school (previously referred to as an "Indian boarding school") to educate young Native American girls from Sisseton, South Dakota. Seven girls arrived in February 1886, but by 1896, the government funding for the program was cut off, and the girls were sent home. Two years later, the school was destroyed by fire. Aside from its religious history, Graceville boasted an extensive commercial district for several decades. In the early days, there was a cigar factory, a pop factory, elevators, roller mills, and two breweries: the Schlitz Company and the Golblatz Company. Later reports from 1915 documented the presence of two well-off banking institutions, a creamery, and Dwight's Flour Mills, which had a capacity of 500 barrels of flour a day. A seven-thousand-dollar Carnegie Library and a fifteen-thousand-dollar hospital were erected during the same period. Graceville's historic 1902 brick Queen Anne hotel was demolished in 1999, but its 1940-41 WPA marker on a highway wayside has been preserved for its Rustic landscape architecture. The town's population surpassed 1,000 people twice in the 1920s and 1940s. From within its city limits, an impressive number of famous residents have made a name for themselves: Tom Kelly, a two-time World Series champion manager with the Minnesota Twins; Jack Conway, a director renowned for being only one of two people to direct three Best Picture-nominated films but never be nominated for Best Director; Bill Davis, a first baseman in the MLB in the late 1960s; Éamon de Búrc, an Irish storyteller; poet Maureen Owen; Madeleine Bordallo, the 6th Lieutenant Governor of Guam from 1995 to 2003 and a Delegate to the U.S. House of Representatives from Guam from 2003 to 2019; Todd Hendricks, a football player who played for years in the Austrian Football League and the European Football League, and Charlie Ryan, the singer and songwriter of the rockabilly hit single "Hot Rod Lincoln."

JOHNSON, MN
POPULATION: 24 – CITY 135 OF 856 (4-11-25)
Johnson was settled in 1880 and named in honor of one of the Great Northern Railway's prominent section foremen. Early records indicate that its post office was established in 1883, and that early businesses included a cream station, a hotel, a lumber company, a bank, a blacksmith shop, a livery stable, three grain elevators, and multiple general and dry goods stores. It also had a railroad station and a school. Johnson's population peaked at 192 people in the 1910 Census, but within a decade it had decreased to 100 residents. The advent of the 1990s saw its numbers halve again to fewer than 50 people, and as of 2020, it has 24 citizens. The post office branch was discontinued circa 1993.

ODESSA, MN
POPULATION: 103 – CITY 126 OF 856 (4-10-25)
"Odessa" is most likely an eponym for Odesa, Ukraine, a major city and seaport. Still, some historians have suggested that the town was named for A. D. Beardsley's daughter, Dessa. She passed away from diphtheria at three years old, so the account is palpable. Beardsley, an agent with the Milwaukee Road, located the townsite in 1879 and was also responsible for running one of its earliest stores, operating a lumber business, and being its first postmaster. A building went up in November of that year as its first piece of infrastructure. Later came J. R. Meier's blacksmith shop, a second general store owned by Mr. Wildung, a harness shop, Pearson and Englemann's furniture store, William H. Mueller's Odessa House hotel, a flour mill, and elevators. The flour mill was destroyed by fire in the late 1910s. The Menzel Brothers and the Kollitz family ran Odessa's most successful hardware and general merchandise stores for many years. In 1939, the Menzel store went up in flames despite the best efforts of the Odessa Fire Department and local kids to put out the blaze. Since then, the department has remained active through fundraisers and fire protection contracts. Odessa had reached a population of 316 individuals by 1940, but it began to decline post-World War II. The old Odessa Jail building, a little brick building on Main Street, has remained in its spot since 1913.

ORTONVILLE, MN ★
POPULATION: 2,021 – CITY 127 OF 856 (4-10-25)
Cornelius Knute Orton arrived in 1872 to start a settlement on the shores of Big Stone Lake, just above the mouth of the Minnesota River. The Norwegian banker, merchant, real estate mogul, and member of the county commission recruited Alfred Johnson to help him survey a potential townsite to serve as the county seat of Big Stone County. His efforts to attract the seat of government bid were successful, as Ortonville's prime location near water sources and its agricultural and granite-quarrying opportunities made it an attractive place for new immigrants to plant their roots. Orton ran a trading post and traded with the Indigenous tribes for a couple of years before A. W. Lathrop arrived and opened his own store. His experiment lasted for only six months. It would be a couple more years before Shumaker & Woodly established a more permanent store in 1876, not long after Ortonville's post office was established. Several more businesses sprang up, like a blacksmith shop, a meat market, a newspaper, a hardware store, an implement store, and a couple of saloons, to name a few. However, the town's progress halted on April 20, 1879, when a terrible fire destroyed just over half of its twenty-eight buildings. Rebuilding commenced immediately, and with the arrival of the Hastings & Dakota Railroad, Ortonville blossomed into a "stone city" built from only the finest and most durable materials. From 1879 to 1922, much of the commercial district was built with elements of Victorian architecture and purple granite trim, a unique touch that pays tribute to Ortonville's abundant granite deposits. One of these buildings was the Columbian Hotel, which for years served as a community landmark until it, too, had to be razed due to an October 26, 2012, fire. In 1881, the town was incorporated as a village. By then, it already had an engine house, a depot, a water tank, and a spur track for the railroad; an excellent school, a two-story structure completed in January 1882 for $10,000; and church congregations for the Methodists and the Congregationalists. The largest Victorian structure in town, the Big Stone County Courthouse, was completed in 1902 by Ole H. Olsen. In 1915, a Carnegie library was added to its lineup of crucial public infrastructure, and an armory was completed in 1924. The thirties saw the founding of Ortonville's Corn Festival, which, by 1933, was already attracting well over ten thousand visitors each year who flocked

to the village to attend the festivities and enjoy events like a corn-eating contest. At the 1933 event, Ed Kottwitz was dubbed the "King of the World's Corn-Eating Contest" after he devoured fifty ears in a single sitting. Nowadays, recreationists visit Big Stone Lake State Park, just outside town, to admire the headwaters of the Minnesota River and enjoy wildlife viewing, camping, and hiking. At the Big Stone County Historical Museum, visitors can tour a 1900s boat, a church, log cabins, and the museum complex, and see "Paul Bunyan's Anchor." The enormous granite cut is the largest ever cut from the nearby quarries. It is said to have been the only anchor capable of stopping the boat of Minnesota's legendary folk hero, Paul Bunyan. While Bunyan may be the most recognizable of Ortonville's list of famous folks, other noteworthy individuals are Agnes Gardner Eyre, a pianist and composer who studied under Theodor Leschetizky; Dan Jurgens, a comic book writer best known for his work on *The Death of Superman* and for inventing the DC characters Doomsday, Booster Gold, and Hank Henshaw, and Michael Hunt, a linebacker for the NFL's Green Bay Packers between 1978 and 1980.

Restaurant Recommendation:
Ally Cat
620 US-75
Ortonville, MN 56278

Restaurant Recommendation:
Lingonberry's Pastry & Coffee Shop
124 2nd St NW
Ortonville, MN 56278

Unincorporated/Ghost Towns: Artichoke, Big Stone Colony, Bonanza Grove, Foster, Lagoona Beach, Yankeetown

National Register of Historic Places:
Clinton: Chicago, Milwaukee, St. Paul & Pacific Depot, St Pauli Norwegian Evangelical Lutheran Church
Graceville: Graceville Historical Marker
Odessa: Odessa Jail
Ortonville: Big Stone County Courthouse, Ortonville Commercial Historic District, Ortonville Free Library

Golf Courses:
Graceville Golf Club, Daily Fee (Graceville, MN)
Ortonville Municipal Golf Course, Municipal (Ortonville, MN)

Town Celebrations:
Ortonville Cornfest, Ortonville, MN (3rd Weekend of August)

BLUE EARTH COUNTY
EST. 1853 - POPULATION: 69,112

Abundant deposits of blue-green clay once found throughout the banks of the Blue Earth River eventually led to the naming of this county, located in Minnesota's south-central region.

AMBOY, MN
POPULATION: 535 – CITY 633 OF 856 (9-29-25)
Named by its first postmaster, Robert Richardson, after his former hometown of Amboy, Illinois, the word has been roughly translated as "hollow" or "like a bowl." The townsite was platted on October 31, 1879, after local farmers made a push to attract the attention of the St. Paul and Sioux City Railway. This railroad line, later part of the more recognizable Chicago, St. Paul, Minneapolis & Omaha Railroad, initially considered extending through a different village in Shelby Township known as Shelbyville. Located about two miles south of present-day Amboy, it boasted of a church, a schoolhouse, carriage works, a hotel, a mill, a blacksmith shop, and its own post office. For whatever reason, despite the railroad's expressed interest in building through their community, local leaders struck down a proposition to give the railroad a $10,000 grant to build there. So, local farmers elsewhere banded together and donated 40 acres of land to the railroad in exchange for a depot, a grain elevator, and a formal survey of their land into town lots. The railroad obliged, and over the next several years, Shelbyville vanished entirely, and Amboy took on its newfound role as a railroad shipping point. By 1914, there were several business ventures, including stockyards and a bank, a well-off school, and four churches of the German Evangelical, German Lutheran, Methodist Episcopal, and Presbyterian denominations. Several fires, including an April 26, 1909, conflagration that destroyed an early high school, and a January 4, 1940, blaze that gutted a considerable part of the north side of Amboy's commercial district, had plagued the little farm town over the years. Businesses destroyed in the latter blaze included the John Roerig hardware store, the Torgerson drug store, the Paul Youngdahl jewelry store, and the Shultz & Minse pool hall. Thanks to its rural location, the Sterling Congregational Church has survived fires and the elements since its construction in 1867, leading to its listing on the National Register of Historic Places in July 1980.

EAGLE LAKE, MN
POPULATION: 3,278 – CITY 618 OF 856 (9-28-25)
A post office called Spier (alternatively spelled Speier) was established in 1870, named after the German city, but some settlers referred to this point as Burgess Mill. It was not until 1872-73, when the Winona & Saint Peter Railroad came through, that it was changed to Eagle Lake on account of the copious number of bald eagles that could then be seen patrolling the skies above the nearby lake. Freeman A. Cate surveyed a townsite on his farm in 1872, and two years later, Walter L. Breckenridge and James Steward laid out a new townsite just to the east of the original. Both lumbering and farming were critical early industries of the fledgling community. According to an 1882 business directory, there were two steam saw mills, a steam flour mill, a planing mill, a 12,000-bushel capacity grain elevator, a couple of lumber yards, and three churches of various denominations, Later plat maps indicate the existence of a fourth church, a bank, a hardware and general store, and even a little jailhouse on the corner of Le Sueur and Agency Streets. The local school began in 1859, when Miss Hannah Haslip taught 14 pupils in a two-story schoolhouse; the high school ended circa 1969, when it consolidated with District #77 in Mankato. Since 1970, Eagle Lake's population has soared from 839 residents then to 3,278 as of 2020.

GOOD THUNDER, MN
POPULATION: 560 – CITY 631 OF 856 (9-29-25)
One of Minnesota's more uniquely named municipalities commemorates Chief Good Thunder, known to the Ho-Chunk (Winnebago) as Wakuntchapinka. He was a friend

of the white settlers and was a member of the tribe when the area was a part of the early Winnebago Reservation from 1855 to 1859. Although the reservation has since been moved to Thurston County, Nebraska, his name remained and was used for a local ford over the Maple River. From 1871 to 1885, the local post office branch was known as Good Thunder's Ford, and in the mid-1880s, it changed to simply "Good Thunder" to align with the nomenclature of the newly established Chicago, Milwaukee & St. Paul Railroad. The railway village was incorporated on March 2, 1893, and over the years grew to include a pair of grain elevators, a depot, a lumber office, a fire station, a hotel, a bank, a livery, an Adventist church, a Catholic church, and two German Lutheran churches. From 1989 to 1995, the local Zieglers Ford Bridge, having been built in 1904 as a pin-connected Pratt through truss bridge, was listed on the National Register of Historic Places before its removal. In the world of fine arts, Good Thunder is well-known for its incredible 75-foot grain elevator mural, painted by Ta-Coumba Aiken on behalf of the Good Thunder Corporation for $14,000. Outside of town at 56632 177th Lane (located on private property), Arnie Lillo has filled his yard with a replica Eiffel Tower, the "World's Largest Firing Rifle," and other folk art oddities.

LAKE CRYSTAL, MN
POPULATION: 2,539 – CITY 616 OF 856 (9-28-25)
Some accounts place the "Lake Crystal" name as extant in this area as early as 1838-1843, around the time noted explorers John C. Fremont and Joseph N. Nicollet passed through. When a junction point on the Omaha Road was established here in the late 1860s and the townsite was platted in May 1869, General Judson W. Bishop decided to name the new railway village after the nearby lake (known for its crystal purity and brilliancy). He was the chief engineer of the construction of the Chicago, St. Paul, Minneapolis & Omaha Railroad. Even before the Valley Railroad's (the first name for this line) arrival, attempts were made at establishing a town near the shores of Crystal Lake. William Riley Robinson, Lucius O. Hunt, Calvin Webb, and Samuel Thorne all came to the area between 1853 and 1854, and in 1857 an attempt was made to plat Crystal Lake City. Although the original city never came to fruition, after surviving the Dakota War of 1862 by sheltering in Mankato, settlers returned and helped bring prosperity to the new railroad village. A pair of general stores, a hardware store, a hotel, a grain elevator, a schoolhouse, a doctor's office, a cooper shop, and *The People's Journal* newspaper highlighted a few of the earliest establishments, all of which were served by as many as two dozen trains a day at the junction's peak usage. A larger two-story school edifice was built in 1882 and expanded upon in 1895 and 1905. Other improvements were made to the city, like the Lake Crystal Boat Club, a roundhouse, a mill and elevators, and churches for the Methodist Episcopal, Baptist, Lutheran, Catholic, and two other Protestant religious groups. The worst loss in the city's history came on September 20, 1887, when an arsonist torched seven buildings in the business district. David Oppegaard, a novelist known for his young-adult horror fiction novels, has local ties.

Restaurant Recommendation:
Lakes Sports Bar & Grill
151 W Humphrey St
Lake Crystal, MN 56055

MADISON LAKE, MN
POPULATION: 1,247 – CITY 619 OF 856 (9-28-25)
When surveyors began mapping this part of Blue Earth County, they named several area lakes after former United States presidents, specifically Lake Washington, Lake Jefferson, and Lake Madison. Two other nearby bodies of water were named for the large number of German settlers (German Lake) and the overwhelming presence of bald eagles (Eagle Lake), but it was the Madison Lake name that was applied to the railway village in the 1880s. It was first called Barclay's Addition for L.S. Barclay, who was deeded the land in 1881. After the Wisconsin, Minnesota & Pacific Railroad reached Madison Lake from Red Wing in 1884, prominent officials elected to rename it in honor of the nearby lake and the Fourth President of the United States. The Copananing Hotel, the Lake House Hotel, and the Point Pleasant Resort were among the earliest commercial lines in the region, catering specifically to resort-goers. After Lewis and Margaret Fitcher filed the Madison Lake town plat on January 17, 1885, other lines began to fill in. A separate townsite called Point Pleasant joined Madison Lake on January 5, 1892, when the two communities incorporated together as one. In the early days, the Madison Lake school and creamery were located in Barclay's 2nd Addition on west Walnut Street. Like its peer communities, Madison Lake also suffered a devastating catastrophe in the early 20th century, specifically on December 23, 1910, when four blocks of the business district were destroyed by fire. Howard Taft stopped in town on a "whistle stop" during his 1911 Presidential campaign.

MANKATO, MN ★
POPULATION: 44,488 – CITY 614 OF 856 (9-28-25)
Mankato, the hub of south-central Minnesota, was initially called *Mahkato* by the Dakota, who lived there centuries before European settlement began. Mahkato roughly translates to "green-blue earth," which aligns with the county's nomenclature. Mrs. Hinkley, who spoke Sioux, suggested it not long after Parsons King Johnson settled the area in February 1852. On Valentine's Day of that month and year, the Blue Earth Settlement Claim Association was started by Henry Jackson, Colonel D. A. Robertson, P. K. Johnson, and Justus C. Ramsey, amongst others. At this time, the land was not intended for white settlement, but Johnson, Jackson, and Daniel Williams offered a barrel of pork to Chief Sleepy Eye and his tribe if he agreed to ignore the stipulations of the treaty. Supposedly, the chief obliged, and transportation routes along the Minnesota River and a military road connecting Mankato with St. Paul were furnished to accommodate the influx of settlers. General stores, blacksmiths, and liveries were the norm. Within only a few years, Mankato had established itself as the leading settlement of what was then the southern portion of Minnesota Territory. All was well until the Dakota Conflict began on August 17, 1862, and Little Crow and his men began attacking and eliminating settlements throughout the Minnesota River Valley. Over the next forty-odd days, hundreds were killed, and most settlers from smaller communities fled to Mankato in search of refuge. At the conflict's conclusion, the largest mass hanging in United States history was on December 26, 1862, when the United States government hanged 35 of the Santee Sioux and three French/Native American men for their role in the uprising. President Abraham Lincoln pardoned 265 other offenders, but the 38 perpetrators were hanged on the site of what is now the Blue Earth County Public Library. By March 6, 1868, Mankato had acquired its incorporation charter, and later that year it was selected to be the site of Minnesota's second (only to Winona) Normal School. Residents raised $5,000, and an additional $5,000 was raised through bond sales to fund the school, which started classes in 1868. It was renamed the Mankato State Teachers College in 1921 and has since

evolved into Mankato State University, Minnesota's second-largest university, with an annual enrollment of over 15,000 students as of the 2020s. From 1966 to 2018, the Minnesota Vikings hosted their training camp at Minnesota State University's facilities before moving to Eagan. Multiple railroad lines, namely the Chicago, Milwaukee & St. Paul; the Omaha Road; the Wisconsin, Minnesota & Pacific, and the Winona & Saint Peter lines, entered Mankato over the next several years, allowing for the growth of the city to become Minnesota's fourth largest municipality by 1880, with a population of 5,500 people. Despite minor flooding that disrupted the city's growth at the time, many major enterprises, including packing houses, the Mankato Mills, the International Harvest Company of America, Eagle Manufacturing Company, the Hubbard Milling Company, and countless others, made their home there. Naturally, a great number of architecturally stunning commercial buildings, churches, and schools came to fruition to serve the community; sixteen of which are now listed on the National Register of Historic Places. Amongst the more notable sites are the North Front Street Commercial District, a block-and-a-half of the earliest businesses; the Lincoln Park Residential Historic District with its whopping 247 contributing properties built between 1856 and 1930 for upper-and-middle class Mankatoians; the 1896 Chicago & Northwestern Railway Mankato Union Depot, the last surviving depot in all of Blue Earth County; the 1902-03 Mankato Carnegie Library; Old Main at the Mankato State Teachers College, partially built in 1908 and expanded in 1922-24; the First Presbyterian Church of Mankato, erected in 1893-1896 using locally famous Mankato limestone; the 1896 Federal Courthouse and Post Office building, also noted for its use of the limestone material, and the ornate 1886-89 French and Italian Renaissance-style Blue Earth County Courthouse. Two other colleges joined Minnesota State University in later years: Bethany Lutheran College, founded in 1911 as the Bethany Ladies College but acquired by the Norwegian Synod of the American Evangelical Lutheran Church in 1927, and a branch of Rasmussen University, which has 20 campuses across 6 states. Other noteworthy points of interest include the Children's Museum of Southern Minnesota; Good Counsel Hill, the motherhouse for the School Sisters of Notre Dame; River Hills Mall; the Mayo Clinic Health System Event System; the Hubbard House, operated by the Blue Earth County Historical Society, and the last surviving Happy Chef breakfast-style restaurant (and accompanying 36-foot-tall Happy Chef statue) in the world. All of the Happy Chef locations except for Mankato's were sold off despite their success in the 1960s. Some of the statues have been remodeled into other professions, such as the umpire in Ryan, Iowa, at the local ballpark, while others are on display at locations like the A-Z Restaurant Company in Princeton, Minnesota. In more recent history, Mankato was the subject of a 1990s "scam" in which Don Descy created a faux city-mankato(dot)us website to prove that not everything on the internet is factual. Several potential tourists have visited Mankato in search of pristine beaches and "whale watching in the Minnesota River" as a result of the website. In 2016, the monthly *Food & Wine* magazine attributed the first usage of the term "hotdish" to a 1930 recipe submitted by Mrs. C. W. Anderson to a 1930 Mankato Lutheran church cookbook. Ten of Mankato's most famous residents of past and present include Cliff Fagan, a longtime high school basketball referee inducted into the Basketball Hall of Fame in 1984; Milton Hanna, a Medal of Honor recipient; Mike Lindell, the founder of My Pillow, Inc., known for their television infomercials on pillows; Arthur S. Thomas, the Chief of Chaplains of the United States Air Force from 1995 to 1997; Tim Walz, the 41st Governor of Minnesota and the Democratic Nominee for Vice President of the United States in 2024; Julia Sears, who became the first woman to head a college in the United States in 1872 when she took over at the Mankato Normal School; Walter Jackson Bate, a two-time winner of the Pulitzer Prize for Biography or Autobiography in 1964 (John Keats's biography) and 1978 (Samuel

Johnson's biography); Robert Louis Hodapp, the Roman Catholic Bishop of Belize from 1958 to 1983; Maud Hart Lovelace, the author of the *Betsy-Tracy* series of autobiographical novels, and Frederick Russell Burham, the "father of the international scouting movement."

Restaurant Recommendation:
Happy Chef Restaurant
51646 US-169
Mankato, MN 56001

Restaurant Recommendation:
The Dam Store Cafe
609 S Front St
Mankato, MN 56001

Restaurant Recommendation:
Pagliai's Pizza
524 S Front St
Mankato, MN 56001

MAPLETON, MN
POPULATION: 1,710 – CITY 630 OF 856 (9-29-25)

Sherman and Maple River were among the early names used for "The Curling Capital of Southern Minnesota" in southeast Blue Earth County. Still, it was the "Mapleton" name that ultimately prevailed following a series of changes. The Sherman namesake came from either Isaac Sherman or Asa P. Sherman. It lasted only from 1858 to 1861 before township residents chose Maple River in honor of the nearby tributary. Many maple trees stood on its banks. There had been an early village site, laid out in June 1856, but it was superseded when the Southern Minnesota (the Chicago, Milwaukee & St. Paul) Railroad platted a new site on January 21, 1871, on the land of David Smith. Incorporation followed shortly thereafter on February 23, 1878. Sylvester Hawkins served as postmaster from 1863 to 1866, as one of the earliest officers of the 1857 to 1874 Mapleton post office. In 1874, the word "Station" was added, and in 1888, the postal service again shortened the name to simply Mapleton. A block of 1890s Main Street commercial buildings has been preserved on the National Register, as has the Mapleton Public Library, built in 1910 with grant money from philanthropist Andrew Carnegie, and the 1896 Queen Anne home of Lucas Troendle. Mapleton's curling nickname is a nod to the establishment of the Heather Curling Club, the oldest curling club in Minnesota. It was started in 1856-57 by the city's predominantly Scottish settlers in commemoration of the Scottish poet Robert Burns.

PEMBERTON, MN
POPULATION: 229 – CITY 645 OF 856 (10-1-25)

The Pemberton of 1914 was one full of life and business happenings. In the northeast corner of the townsite, the Chicago, Milwaukee & St. Paul Railroad brought with it the means and the men to establish several lines of enterprise on the adjacent Railway Avenue, running parallel to the tracks. There was a livery shed to keep livestock, and the Pemberton State Bank sat on the corner accepting the deposits of local farmers and merchants. Further down Main Street were a second bank, the Farmers State Bank, the post office, and stores selling hardware, groceries, and dry goods, as well as more luxurious products. A church was located near the town's center. Many of these early structures, including the Modern Woodmen fraternal Hall, were moved to the site from Cream, a town bypassed by the railroad in favor of Pemberton when the latter was platted in 1907. Pemberton had existed as early as 1894, but most of the structures burned long before the railroad ever made it to the area. Incorporation did not occur until April 26, 1946, at which point its citizens decided to keep their name, honoring a railroad official. Pemberton's post office was converted to a rural station in 1996, a year after its school district was discontinued following consolidations.

SKYLINE, MN
POPULATION: 288 – CITY 615 OF 856 (9-28-25)
Skyline was incorporated on January 8, 1957, as a southwest suburb and neighborhood community adjacent to the City of Mankato. Home to about 288 residents as of the 2020 Census, the 0.19-square-mile territory is primarily residential, but it does include two locations on the National Register of Historic Places. The first, the Louis Seppman Mill, was constructed in 1863 as one of the very few authentic early windmills in Minnesota. The gristmill, built entirely of stone by the German stonemason, remained in operation through 1890 before a storm ripped off the last of its blades. It is now preserved at nearby Minneopa State Park, renowned for its Upper and Lower Minneopa Falls and meandering bison herds. It is the third-oldest state park in Minnesota, behind only Itasca State Park near Park Rapids and Interstate State Park near Taylors Falls, having been established in 1905. Several of the parks' WPA-era structures are geographically associated with Mankato, but Skyline is also near the Kern Bridge, Minnesota's only bowstring arch truss bridge. It was built in 1873 on Township Road over the Le Sueur River and welcomed vehicular traffic until 1991.

ST. CLAIR, MN
POPULATION: 750 – CITY 617 OF 856 (9-28-25)
Once the site of the Winnebago Agency and Reservation, the earliest European settlement of this vicinity began circa 1854 when Charles Mansefield and Ansen W. Callen settled on the east side of Rice Lake. The following year, both the Reservation and Agency were established, but they were entirely removed by May 1863 in favor of opening the lands to widespread settlement. On August 11, 1865, a man named Aaron Hilton laid out the earliest version of the St. Clair townsite, which was then known as Hilton. In less than a year, there was already a hotel, three general stores, three wagon shops, two saloons, two blacksmith shops, two boot and shoe stores, and a mill that Hilton had erected. It had a capacity of 10,000 feet of lumber and 100 barrels of flour per day. When the postal service took note of the blossoming settlement, they appointed Aaron Hilton postmaster and stationed his office in George and James Brown's General Store. From 1856 to 1886, it was known as the "Winnebago Agency," then changed to St. Clair. General James St. Clair, a Scottish soldier and Whig politician, was honored with the town's naming after officers of the Chicago, Milwaukee & St. Paul Railroad changed it upon completion of their local line. Over the next several decades, several more accomplishments were made, including William Field and Son's feed mill in 1882; two school districts (#70 and #73), which consolidated in August 1887; Grignon and Coughour's creamery in 1891, and four churches by 1895. St. Clair was incorporated as a village by a vote of 40 to 9 on December 20, 1907. From 1855 to 1986, the Federal Winnebago Agency House stood as a reminder of Saint Clair's early beginnings, before it was intentionally demolished.

VERNON CENTER, MN
POPULATION: 328 – CITY 632 OF 856 (9-29-25)

Edgewood was the first name for this town on the banks of the Blue Earth River, so named for its location at the edge of a large grove of trees. From the 1850s to 1873, it was known as Edgewood, but the name was changed to honor George Washington's home in Virginia, Mount Vernon. Another account states that for 10 days, it was also known as Montevideo between April 16, 1858, and April 26, 1858, before adopting the name Vernon. "Center" was added on October 14, 1858. It was during these pioneer years that the townsite was laid out by Colonel Benjamin F. Smith, Benjamin McCracken, and other surveyors of the Blue Earth Company with ties to Mount Vernon, Ohio. Colonel Smith raised a hotel in 1858, and from the same sawmill came the lumber used to fortify the town with a stockade during the Dakota Uprising of 1862. G.W. Doty's sawmill replaced the Smith-Haynes sawmill in 1867. Flour mills, grain elevators, a creamery, and even a sorghum factory spearheaded Vernon Center's earliest commercial interests. However, there were plenty of "typical" lines, such as a Standard Oil station, general stores, and a lumber yard. Catholic, Baptist, and Methodist Episcopal churches were the prevalent religious organizations as of 1914. At one point, there were even two local opera houses–the Barnes Opera House and the Vernon Center Opera House–that concurrently hosted local community events and performances. The Edgewood name was phased out for good during this bygone era, although the Chicago, St. Paul, Minneapolis, and Omaha Railroad reportedly used it through 1885. In the 1970s, Vernon Center was brought into the international limelight when it hosted the 19th World Plowing Contest as a part of Farmfest U.S.A. KRP Distributing Company boasted a line of 28 soft drinks at the time and distributed them throughout the country. On October 25, 2005, Vernon Center was thrust back into the spotlight when the local elevator, loaded with 5,000 metric tons of corn, exploded, sending flames 200 feet into the air. Harvey F. Thew, a screenwriter with the Warner Bros. entertainment and media corporation from the 1910s to 1940s; Benjamin Tibbets Kemerer, the Bishop of the Episcopal Diocese of Duluth from 1933 to 1944, and Edward A. Burdick, the Chief Clerk and Parliamentarian of the Minnesota House of Representatives from 1966 to 2005, have local connections with Vernon Center.

Minnesota Lake is only partially located in Blue Earth County (see Faribault County), and North Mankato is only partially located in Blue Earth County (see Nicollet County).

Unincorporated/Ghost Towns: Cambria, Garden City☆, Marysburg, Perth, Smiths Mill

National Register of Historic Places:
Amboy: Sterling Congregational Church
Cambria Township: Marsh Concrete Rainbow Arch Bridge
Garden City: First Baptist Church
Garden City Township: James P. Gail Farmhouse
Good Thunder: Zieglers Ford Bridge
Judson Township: Jones-Roberts Farmstead
Mankato: Blue Earth County Courthouse, J. R. Brandup House, Charles Chapman House, Lorin Cray House, Adolph O. Eberhart House, Federal Courthouse & Post Office. First National Bank of Mankato, First Presbyterian Church, Rensselaer D. Hubbard House, William Irving House, Lincoln Park Residential Historic District, Mankato Public Library & Reading Room, Mankato Union Depot, Minneopa State Park WPA/Rustic Style Historic Resources, North Front Street Commercial District, Old Main, Mankato State Teachers College
Mapleton: Main Street Commercial Buildings, Mapleton Public Library, Lucas Troendle House
Shelby: Dodd Ford Bridge
Skyline: Kern Bridge, Seppman Mill

Golf Courses:
Terrace View Golf Club, Daily Fee (Mankato, MN)

Breweries/Wineries/Distilleries:
Javens Family Vineyard (Mankato, MN)
LocAle Brewing Company (Mankato, MN)
Mankato Brewery (Mankato, MN)

Town Celebrations:
Amboy Days, Amboy, MN (First Weekend after Labor Day)

BROWN COUNTY
EST. 1855 - POPULATION: 25,912

Established in 1855 in what was then Minnesota Territory, this county was named in honor of Joseph Renshaw Brown. He was involved in Minnesota and Wisconsin politics for over half a century.

COBDEN, MN
POPULATION: 36 – CITY 102 OF 856 (3-28-25)
First called North Branch for its location near Sleepy Eye Creek, the north branch of the larger Cottonwood River, Cobden took on its present name in 1886. Cobden is the surname of the British statesman Richard Cobden, a Member of Parliament for Stockport, Yorkshire, or Rochdale between 1841 and 1865. It was likely assigned by postal officials when an office was established. After being platted on February 16, 1901, by Thomas Peterson and S. C. Frederickson, the Chicago & Northwestern Railway town ultimately had two creameries, two elevators, a flour mill, a bank, a lumber yard, a blacksmith shop, a livery stable, a hardware store, and two grocery stores. I. N. Davis served as a village blacksmith and owned the garage once automobiles became more prominent. J. R. Schweringer was a restaurateur and barbershop owner, and H. J. Zieske sold general goods and farm implements. There were also two schools, two churches, a town hall, and a fire hall. As of 1916, the fire department comprised sixteen members and had a "chemical engine" to help fight early-day conflagrations. The Cobden Jail was built around 1900 and listed on the National Register of Historic Places in 1979. However, it was removed from the Register in August 1991 due to extensive alterations made to preserve it. In 1972, Cobden lost its post office after its population decreased rapidly from a peak of 136 in 1940 to only 72 by 1980. Roman Mathias "Lefty" Bertrand was born here on February 28, 1909. He etched his hometown's name in the MLB history books after he pitched a single game for the Philadelphia Phillies on April 15, 1936.

Restaurant Recommendation:
Crusher's Corner Bar
430 Center St
Cobden, MN 56085

COMFREY, MN
POPULATION: 392 – CITY 55 OF 856 (2-27-25)
Comfrey is primarily located in Brown County, but a small portion of the town extends southward into the northeastern part of Cottonwood County. Jonathan F. Brown and his family came to the area as early as 1857. After they and other families were killed

during the US-Dakota War of 1862, any developments in the township were made with extreme caution and at an extremely slow rate. A post office opened for business in 1877 and was named by its postmaster, A. W. Pederson, after the comfrey plant, Symphytum officinale. The Western Town Lot Company platted it in 1902 on the Chicago & Northwestern Railroad, two years after being incorporated as a village. Early businesses, such as Hotel Comfrey (built in 1899 and destroyed in 1940) and its Comfrey Farmers Creamery Association creamery (operating from 1899 to 1955), were essential to Comfrey's earliest settlers. Business interests as of 1916 included everything from grocery, drug, hardware, and general stores to an automobile garage, barber shop, banks, jewelry store, lumber offices, meat market, the Comfrey Farmers Elevator Company, and the *Comfrey Times* newspaper. At that time, the two banks were the State Bank and the Farmers State Bank. W. R. Hodges, the newspaper's founder, was well known for his two-story building, which featured a stage and entertainment on the second floor. It was referred to as "Hodges Hall." Most of the town was devastated by an F4 tornado on March 29, 1998, but its residents rebuilt quickly. The disaster triggered a minor exodus of residents between 1990 and 2000 when its population dropped from 433 in 1990 to 367 by 2000. Its highest-ever population was 642 residents in the early 1950s. Comfrey is the proud hometown of Glen Taylor, the founder of Taylor Corporation, and the owner of the NBA's Minnesota Timberwolves, WNBA's Minnesota Lynx, and the Star Tribune of Minneapolis. Taylor is Minnesota's wealthiest individual; his private corporation is the sixth-largest graphic communications company in the United States, employing over 10,000 people. Jeffers Petroglyphs Historic Site is sometimes associated with the town, as the site is located about halfway between Comfrey and Jeffers, another city in Cottonwood County.

EVAN, MN
POPULATION: 70 – CITY 103 OF 856 (3-28-25)
Evan is best known for being the hometown of Ruth Taubert Seeger, the first woman athlete to be selected to compete in the 1957 World Games for the Deaf on behalf of the United States. She participated in tennis, volleyball, and track and field. Her hometown was platted in May 1887 by Nels Hanson and initially named Hanson Station, but it was eventually changed to Evan to match the name of the local post office. "Evan" combines Martin Norseth's wife's first name, Eva, and her first married surname initial, 'n.' Businesses were plentiful in Evan, as it was a station on the Redwood (the Winona & St. Peter) branch of the Chicago & Northwestern Railroad. Peter Hanson preempted the town plat in 1885 when he established a grain warehouse, and Martin Norseth started his store. Thirty years later, C. Jenson's hardware and lumber business, A. L. Maden's garage, A. C. Anderson's blacksmith shop, C. B. Nelson's restaurant, the Hansen Brothers implement store, the Evan Co-operative Creamery Company, and the J. C. Foster and Mogensen stores made up its commercial district. Three elevators, a bank, a library, a school, and two churches rounded out its early pieces of infrastructure. Evan incorporated on March 22, 1904, and reached a peak of approximately 153 residents in the 1960s. Its post office was discontinued in 1993.

HANSKA, MN
POPULATION: 382 – CITY 98 OF 856 (3-27-25)
Hanska, the Sioux word for "long" or "tall," was given by the Indigenous to describe the long, narrow lake located to the west of the present-day townsite. The Iowa Minnesota Land & Townsite Company was responsible for bringing the future Minneapolis & St. Louis Railway station to life after circulating a petition in Lake Hanska Township in 1899 to convince a railroad to take an interest in the area.

Seventy-seven signatures were acquired, and before the area's settlers knew it, daily engines were running through their lands. Harry and Anna Jenkins platted the village of Hanska on October 9, 1899, and took its name from the township and the nearby post office (which had been in operation since 1890). Three grain elevators, a roller mill, and the Hanska-Linden Cooperative Creamery were important facets of early Hanska. Its Norwegian settlers also saw that a hardware store, general store, and numerous other firms would be established. J. W. Thompson opened his hardware store as the first place of business in town. Within a decade, Hanska had 310 residents, and according to a 1916 business directory, its commercial district had expanded substantially to include two banks, the Security and State; the S. Hage Lumber Company; the Lampert Lumber Company; the New Ulm Roller Mill Company elevator; the Eagle Milling Company elevator; Fred Jaramo's jewelry store; Midtbruget & Hangen's meat market; *The Hanska Herald* newspaper, and many more. An early library was hosted in the Liberal Union Hall, which served as a community center in Hanska's early days. It was a 1910 project of the Unitarian separatists of the Nora Free Christian Church. Alternatively, it is also known as the Nora Unitarian Universalist Church, a congregation established by Brown County residents whose beliefs did not align with those of the Lutheran Church of Norway. The first church building existed from July 8 to July 21, 1883, after it was destroyed by a tornado, having hosted only two services. A new edifice was built between 1883 and 1884 and has since been listed on the National Register of Historic Places. The church, the Liberal Union Hall, the early Bjorneberg Garage automobile service station built in 1919, the 1912 round Thormodson Barn, and the Synsteby Site preserved within Lake Hanska County Park are Hanska's five locations on the NRHP.

NEW ULM, MN ★☆
POPULATION: 14,120 – CITY 99 OF 856 (3-27-25)

The City of "Charm and Tradition" was conceived by Frederick Beinhorn of Germany, who, along with a group of other German immigrants, founded the Chicago Land Society in 1853. The company's objective was apparent, as in their words, they sought to "procure a home for every German laborer; popish priests and lawyers excepted, in some healthy and productive district, located on some navigable river." The following year, they had their townsite on the bank of the Minnesota River, where steamboats had only recently passed by for the first time. It was named New Ulm after Ulm, Württemberg, Germany, where many of its original settlers hailed from. Twenty of the company's 32 immigrants had relocated by the fall of 1854. They were joined in 1856 by Wilhelm Pfaender and members of the Turner Colonization Society of Cincinnati, another German colony known for combining gymnastics with lectures and debates about the significant issues of that era. Until their arrival, the Chicago group had been struggling for capital. The Turners introduced new ideas, and Christian Prignitz laid out a new city plan in April 1858, which designated areas for the Brown County Courthouse, Turner Hall, and a grand public school. Within only months, the conjoined "German Land Association of Minnesota" had expanded its site to over ninety buildings, including the Eagle Mill; Adolph Seiter and F. Roebecke's storefronts, and four other general stores; a woolen mill, and two blacksmith shops. One unique industry rose to the forefront of the German town's economy and has remained at the heart of its identity: brewing. Anton Friton started New Ulm's first brewery in January 1858, but it was August Schell, the proprietor of The Schell Brewing Company, whose brews brought great fame to New Ulm. Established in January 1861, the plant was capable of producing eighteen thousand barrels of beer annually by 1916. A recent projection puts their capacity closer to 145,000 barrels of beer per year. It is now the second-oldest brewery in the United States, the oldest and largest in Minnesota, and the only surviving example of New Ulm's seven earliest breweries. The others were Friton's earlier-mentioned brewery, later rebranded as The New Ulm Brewing and Malting Company in 1910; H. A. Subilia's 1861 distillery; Betz & Hauenstein's 1865 brewery, and John Hauenstein's 1864 Hauenstein Brewing Company. While the beer was flowing and "the good times" were going, New Ulm came under serious attack during the Dakota War of 1862. On August 19, 1862, the Mdewakanton attempted to overtake the city but were surprised when many of the town's then nine-hundred-odd residents took up arms and drove them back. A much larger force of Dakota returned four days later, but thanks to the strategic planning of Charles Flandrau, they were again repelled. Barricades had been erected to protect the town, but many were burned, and New Ulm had been reduced to just forty-nine buildings. Dozens of settlers had been killed. Fear of a third attack led to a mass exodus of over two thousand settlers (many of whom had fled to New Ulm from other southwest Minnesota farms and villages) to Mankato. When the threat of repeated destruction was quelled, the settlers returned to their homes, and progress resumed. Over the rest of the 19th century, New Ulm's population grew to 5,403, and it welcomed the arrival of both the Winona & Saint Peter and the Minneapolis & St. Louis Railroad. Its commercial district consisted of several unique business ventures, including brick yards, potteries, two stone quarries, five creameries, five breweries, multiple weekly newspapers, cigar factories, soda water factories, a vinegar factory, a pipe organ factory, elevators, and flour and planing mills. Brown County produced more flour than any other county in Minnesota (aside from Hennepin) in 1905; notable players in New Ulm included The Eagle Mills, with a daily capacity of 5,000 barrels, and the Cottonwood Roller Mills. The Catholic, Lutheran, German Methodist, Episcopal, Congregational, Evangelical, and Evangelical Association were the major religious denominations as of 1916. Father Alexander Berghold, the first Catholic priest in New Ulm, established the Loretta Hospital (originally known as St. Alexander's Hospital) in 1884. By 1915, Protestants had added a second hospital, called the Union Hospital, to accommodate New Ulm's ever-growing population. Federal and state officials flooded into New Ulm upon the U.S. entry into World War I. The German population stood strong together, insisting they opposed the war by a vote of 466-19. On July 25, 1917, over ten thousand people gathered to protest the deployment of American soldiers to fight in a foreign war. Noted speakers at the event were Louis Fritsche, mayor of New Ulm, and Albert Pfaender, the city attorney. Governor James Burnquist removed both of them as they sought to stomp out any anti-war opposition. Things returned to some level of normalcy after the war. Still, another tale during the World War II era recalls the time a local German family helped a German prisoner escape from a POW camp located in what is now present-day Flandrau State Park. The park is one of twenty-three locations on the National Register of Historic Places. Amongst some of the other notable sites are the New Ulm Commercial Historic District and its sixty-four contributing properties; the residential South Broadway and South German Street Historic Districts, each with eight distinctive early homes; St Michael's School and Convent, built in 1872 in Italianate-style; the original 1873 Turner Hall structure; the 1884 Old Main building of Dr. Martin Luther College, now a part of the private Martin Luther College (est. 1995); the one-of-a-kind 1909 Renaissance Revival style New Ulm Post Office; the fortresslike 1914 New Ulm Armory; the 1915 New Ulm High School building; a 1903-04 Stations of the Cross group of statues and paths known locally as The Way of the Cross, and the Hermann Monument. The landmark 120-foot-tall monument rises far above New Ulm and was built in the late 1880s by the Sons of Hermann as a tribute to New Ulm's German-American heritage. The 45-foot-high Glockenspiel in Schonlau Park is one of only a few freestanding carillon clock towers in the world. In 1990, New Ulm became home to the Minnesota Music Hall of

Fame, which is located in the former 1936 library and museum building. The Brown County Historical Society claims to be one of Minnesota's largest genealogical archives. Thousands of tourists visit New Ulm each year to experience its rich German history, traditions, and heritage, which are best showcased at the city's Oktoberfest, Bock Fest, and Bavarian Blast festivals. For a short while, New Ulm had the nickname "Polka Capital of the Nation" due to its annual festival, Sudeten German music influence, and the presence of two ballrooms. Famous persons with New Ulm ties include Whoopee John, a renowned Polka artist and member of the International Pola Association Hall of Fame; Terry Steinbach, a three-time MLB All-Star catcher and 1989 World Series champion; Brad Lohaus, a center-power forward in the NBA between 1987 and 1998; John Lind, the 14th Governor of Minnesota; Tippi Hedren, an actress discovered by Alfred Hitchcock who won a Golden Globe for her appearance in the 1963 American natural horror film *The Birds*; Lenore Ulric, a Broadway theatre and Hollywood actress from 1911 to 1947; Ali Bernard, a 2008 Summer Olympic participant in Women's freestyle wrestling; David Rysdahl, famous for his recent role as Donald Hornig in the 2023 biographical thriller film *Oppenheimer*; Marion Downs, an audiologist who pioneered the universal adaptation of newborn hearing screening in the early 1960s, and Wanda Gág, the author and illustrator of the oldest American picture book still in print (since 1928), *Millions of Cats*.

Restaurant Recommendation:
Kaiserhoff New Ulm
221 N Minnesota St
New Ulm, MN 56073

SLEEPY EYE, MN
POPULATION: 3,452 – CITY 100 OF 856 (3-28-25)

"Sleepy" may not be the best word to describe this now-bustling center of commerce closest to the center of Brown County, but it was the white man's name for a kind, compassionate Sisseton Dakota chief. His real name was Ishtakhaba, but his eyelids drooped so significantly that he earned the nickname "Chief Sleepy Eyes" from those he associated with. He was a significant promoter of peace between Europeans and Native American tribes, signing four treaties, including the 1851 Treaty of Traverse des Sioux, which ceded 21 million acres of land to the United States government. He was one of four members of an assembly of Chiefs that met with President James Monroe in Washington, D.C., in 1824 to help achieve peace. The helpful Chief later instructed early traders to establish the site of Mankato away from floodplains. From 1871 to 1872, the post office was located in Prairieville. It was renamed when Thomas Allison and Walter Breckenridge platted the Sleepy Eye townsite on September 18, 1872, and was designated as a Winona & Saint Peter Railroad division point. The branch line splitting off towards Redwood was established in 1877, and the railroad located its roundhouse and machine shops at Sleepy Eye, which marked the beginning of its growth period. Its name changed a few times to Loreno, then Sleepy Eye Lake, until the original nomenclature was settled upon for good. William Robinson opened the first store in the autumn of 1872, and Chris Emery was the proprietor of its initial hotel, the Lake House. By 1880, a thousand other settlers had caught on that Sleepy Eye was destined to become a prominent railroad town, and with their arrival came twelve saloons, eight general stores, six farm implement dealers, six blacksmith shops, four millineries, four physicians, three lumber yards, three restaurants, two each of weekly newspapers, law firms, drug stores, hardware stores, furniture stores, harness shops, shoe shops, wagon shops, meat markets, liveries, barber shops, and grain warehouses, and a singular boot and shoe store, bakery, feed store, cigar store, grain elevator, and brewery. The most lucrative of all its commercial enterprises was the milling industry, which handled millions of dollars' worth of goods, according to a 1916 report. Five thousand barrels of flour could pass through the mill in a single day at that time. The same document showed that the First National Bank of Sleepy Eye, the Farmers and Merchants State Bank, and the State Bank of Sleepy Eye had a combined capital of $103,000, which was frequently used to further development throughout the city. Sleepy Eye's high school and graded school enrollment was then about 410 students, and several churches were in place too: St. Mary's Catholic Church, St. John's German Lutheran church, a Methodist Episcopal church, a German Methodist Episcopal church, All Souls Episcopal Church, a Danish Lutheran congregation, a German Evangelical church, The Union Congregational church, and a Presbyterian congregation. Sleepy Eye naturally cycled through hundreds more businesses and organizations over the decades—including a Catholic seminary and a vegetable-canning factory for a time—before reaching its peak population of 3,694 in the 1990s. In an interesting scenario, members of several local churches (but primarily the Roman Catholic congregation) banded together in the 1990s to petition the city council to ban MTV from its cable networks for its "immorality" and "unethical behavior." Local points of interest include the 1887 Winona and St. Peter Freight Depot; a 1902 Chicago and North Western Depot; C. Berg's luxurious 1899 Hotel, which housed many of the Sleepy Eye Milling Company's (another NRHP location) businesspeople; and the W. W. Smith House. The milling company erected a monument in honor of Chief Sleepy Eye and inscribed it with "Ish-tak-ha-ba, Sleepy Eye, Always a Friend of the Whites. Died 1860." Famous Sleepy Eye births include Helen Fischer, a proponent for Alaska Statehood and a signer of its Constitution; Dana Kiecker, an MLB pitcher for the Boston Red Sox from 1990-91; Scott Jensen, the Republican nominee for Governor of Minnesota in 2022, and Linus Maurer, an American cartoonist was was the inspiration behind Charles M. Schulz's Peanuts comic strip character, Linus Van Pelt. A cartoon statue of the character grasping his iconic blue blankie is on display at the Dyckman Free Library.

 **Restaurant Recommendation:**
Sleepy Eye Coffee Company
121 Main St W
Sleepy Eye, MN 56085

SPRINGFIELD, MN
POPULATION: 2,027 – CITY 101 OF 856 (3-28-25)

H. M. Gamble operated a store in this vicinity as early as 1872, and settlers were sparingly present in the late 1850s. Named after John F. and Daniel Burns, it was not until 1877 that the village of Burns was platted as a new station point on the Winona & St. Peter Railroad. Gamble had other ideas, and when a postal branch opened in his business in 1873, he chose to establish a presence in Springfield. The name could allude to the former presence of a large, nearby spring on the Cottonwood River or in Springfield, Massachusetts. Shortly after its platting, Burns had four stores, a blacksmith shop, a livery, a doctor's office, two churches, a school, and other businesses. Things were looking promising, so in February 1881, the townspeople looked to incorporate and rename their community Springfield to match the post office. By the time 1890 rolled around, the population had grown by an impressive 328.7% decade-over-decade, from 167 people to 716, and by 1900, that number had doubled again. During this initial growth period, many of Springfield's most prominent businesses emerged. Adolph Casimir Ochs founded the Ochs Brick and Tile Company in 1890, and the bricks were used to construct most of the town's iconic landmarks.

The Opera House was built in 1892 to house Turner Club men's gymnastics, traveling shows, and other dances and events. In circa 1911, the Louis Kreitinger Garage, an early car dealership, was constructed with ornamental elements that earned the structure a place on the National Register of Historic Places in 1979. Even the Ochs House, built in 1911 in the Colonial Revival style using his bricks, has stood long enough to be added to the Registry. Five elevators, the Exchange Hotel, the Springfield Milling Company flour mill, K. S. Reasoner's cigar factory, and the Springfield Farmers Association creamery were among the other essential fixtures of pioneer Springfield. In 1930, the Potter Stockyard became the next "big thing" in Springfield's business sector. Part of the farm and its four structures, built between 1898 and 1913, have been preserved for their historical significance; they are most associated with the prototype burnt-clay, iron, and cement "A.C.O." silo, now found throughout the Midwest. The silo was among the first produced by Ochs' brick company. St. John's Hospital was another early noted fixture built using donations from townspeople. It was situated on a hillside overlooking the river. Schools and churches were also present; three Lutheran churches and a Catholic and United Methodist church still meet as of 2025. St. Paul Evangelical Lutheran Church was started in 1870 with Reverend August Kenter as its pastor. Three different buildings have served the congregation since then, with the current structure having been dedicated on June 1, 1924. Three notably famous men have called Springfield home: Glen Taylor, the founder of the Taylor Corporation and the majority/sole owner of the NBA's Minnesota Timberwolves, WNBA's Minnesota Lynx, and MLS's Minnesota United FC teams; Bernie Bierman, a five-time national championship-winning coach of the University of Minnesota Golden Gophers football program between 1934-41, and Marty Seifert, the Minority Leader of the Minnesota House of Representatives from January 2007 to June 2009.

Unincorporated/Ghost Towns: Essig, Godahl, Leavenworth, Searles

National Register of Historic Places:
Essig: Lampert Lumber Company Line Yard
Hanska: Bjorneberg Garage, Liberal Union Hall, Nora Free Christian Church, Synsteby Site, Thormodson Barn
Milford Township: District No. 50 School
New Ulm: August Schell Brewing Company, Bernard Fesenmaier House, Boesch, Hummel, & Maltzahn Block, Chicago & North Western Railroad Depot, Flandrau State Park CCC/WPA/Rustic Style Historic Resources, Frederick W. Kiesling House, Grand Hotel, Gov. John Lind House, Hermann Monument, Melges Bakery, New Ulm Armory, New Ulm Commercial Historic District, New Ulm High School, New Ulm Oil Company Service Station, New Ulm Post Office, Old Main, Dr. Martin Luther College, Otto Schell House, South Broadway Historic District, South German Street Historic District, St. Michael's School & Convent, Turner Hall, The Way of the Cross, Wanda Gág Childhood Home
Sleepy Eye: C. Berg's Hotel, Chicago North Western Depot, Sleepy Eye Milling Company, W. W. Smith House, Winona & St. Peter Freight Depot
Springfield: Bendixon-Schmid House, Kreitinger Garage, Adolph C. Ochs House, Shady Lane Stock Farm

Golf Courses:
New Ulm Country Club, Daily Fee (New Ulm, MN)
Sleepy Eye Golf Club, Daily Fee (Sleepy Eye, MN)
Springfield Golf Course, Daily Fee (Springfield, MN)

Breweries/Wineries/Distilleries:
August Schell Brewing Company (New Ulm, MN)
Morgan Creek Vineyards (New Ulm, MN)

Sleepy Eye Brewing Company (Sleepy Eye, MN)
Snowdrop Winery (New Ulm, MN)

Town Celebrations:
Bavarian Blast, New Ulm, MN (3rd Weekend of July)
Comfrey Community Days, Comfrey, MN (2nd Weekend in June)
Oktoberfest, New Ulm, MN (1st Two Weekends in October)
Riverside Days, Springfield, MN (Last Full Weekend in June)
Schell's Bockfest, New Ulm, MN (Early March)
Sleepy Eye Summerfest, Sleepy Eye, MN (3rd Full Weekend in August)

CARLTON COUNTY
EST. 1857 - POPULATION: 36,207

Carlton County was founded in 1857 and named for Rueben B. Carlton, one of Minnesota's earliest state senators.

BARNUM, MN ☆
POPULATION: 620 – CITY 431 OF 856 (7-18-25)

Home to the Carlton County Fair since 1890, Barnum was named for George G. Barnum, then paymaster of the Lake Superior and Mississippi River Railroad. The first rail line between the Twin Cities and Duluth was a project of financier Jay Cooke, who vouched for the railroad to be the northern terminus. As the Panic of 1873 began to take effect, the railroad was reorganized as the St. Paul and Duluth Railway, which later became part of the Northern Pacific. Barnum's post office opened in 1872, just before the panic, and after seventeen years of growth, it was incorporated on February 5, 1889. Carlton County's most successful creamery was established here in 1904 and became famous for producing butter and eggs. Three retail grocery stores in Duluth brought the pristine eggs to fame, and patrons from miles around enjoyed their milk and butter. Major businesses in 1911 included the State Bank of Barnum, Martin Christensen's Hardware Store, Cain & Dathe's Mercantile, the *Barnum Herald* newspaper, and the Barnum Trading Company. The Methodist Episcopal church came into being as its principal religious organization. Several fraternal organizations (namely the Modern Woodmen of America, the Independent Order of Odd Fellows, the Rebekahs, and the Royal Neighbors of America) were in operation at the height of Barnum's heyday. Its population has gradually increased over the decades. As of the 2020 Census, it has more residents than ever any (620). The Carlton County Historical Society maintains a historic log cabin and a collection of farming implements and machinery at the fairgrounds, and a 25-foot-tall statue of "Big Louie," the Voyageur guides hungry passersby by to the Lazy Bear Grill.

CARLTON, MN ★
POPULATION: 948 – CITY 434 OF 856 (7-19-25)

Before being renamed Carlton in honor of Minnesota state senator Reuben B. Carlton, this place on the St. Louis River was known as Northern Pacific Junction. It was located at the point where the Northern Pacific Railroad's transcontinental line met the former Lake Superior & Mississippi Railroad. The town began in 1870 with a planing mill and St. Joseph and Mary's log cabin church, two of its earliest pieces of infrastructure, before its incorporation in 1881. A post office called Carlton is documented as being in operation from 1882 to 1886, and again from 1891 to the present. However, there are gaps in the history of the mail and parcel center. In 1889, the county seat was relocated from Thomson to here, which had operated as an independent municipality until it voted to consolidate with Carlton in a November 5, 2013, election. Over the next thirty years, Carlton welcomed the arrival of a third railroad line, this one owned by the Great Northern, as well as Carlton High School, the Carlton Library, The First National Bank of Carlton, The Zenith Concrete Gravel Company, the Carlton Mill and Elevator, a two-story brick city hall, and church edifices for the Presbyterians, the Swedish Lutherans, the Methodists, and the Catholics. From 1922-24, Duluth architect Clyde Kelly orchestrated the construction of the Carlton County Courthouse, now one of five Carlton listings on the National Register. The others are the 1894 Henry C. Oldenburg House and a series of CCC/WPA/Rustic Style structures at Jay Cooke State Park. The park, established in 1915, is home to a challenging stretch of the Saint Louis River that connects the Mississippi River to the Great Lakes by water and portages.

CLOQUET, MN
POPULATION: 12,568 – CITY 432 OF 856 (7-19-25)

Over a million feet of white pine lumber were once cut daily at Cloquet's five sawmills and three lumber companies in the 1910s, at a time when the city on the St. Louis River was considered one of Minnesota's foremost lumber centers. While the exact origin of the name "Cloquet" is disputed, it is known that the city began as pre-1880 settlements, including Shaw Town, Nelson Town, and Johnson Town. All three eventually combined to form Knife Falls, so named for a waterfall that cascaded over sharp rocks, which was platted in 1883. The following year, it took on the name Cloquet after the 104-mile-long tributary of the St. Louis, and it was incorporated as a village. Stokes Wilson was elected mayor. Logs were floated down the St. Louis to the sawmills and other trade points, and a paper-making mill was erected. By 1911, it was capable of producing 115 yards of paper per minute, or over 50 tons per day. The mill, employing over 200 people, shipped its product to newspaper and book binderies throughout the country, including the *Duluth Herald* newspaper office. Dr. A. E. Johnson's drug store, Hotel Crescent, the St. Louis Hotel, the Ostland Electric Company, the Barclay Hospital, and the Rathborne-Hair-Ridgeway's box shook factory were just a few of Cloquet's earliest accomplishments. The Great Northern Railroad and Northern Pacific Railroad came into the city from the southeast before the latter split off into the Duluth & Northeastern line towards the general vicinity of Grand Marais. Following the namesake 1918 Cloquet fire, which destroyed much of the village, several new structures were built using fireproof materials and subsequently added to the National Register of Historic Places. The Cloquet-Northern Office Building was raised as the most significant new building in the city in 1919, and the Cloquet City Hall and Shaw Memorial Library were built in 1920. Park Place Historic District and its four substantial Weyerhaeuser executive homes were completed in 1919. When a new Cloquet High School was built in 1969, the old one was gradually converted into an apartment complex called Carlton Lofts. One of Cloquet's sole surviving businesses from the fire, the Northeastern Hotel, was used as a post office, hospital, and lodging in the aftermath of the event. Even through the fire, the Cloquet Cooperative Society (started in 1910) held together as one of the strongest consumer cooperatives in the country and controlled nearly 35% of the town's business by the end of the 1930s. Its holdings and partner stores ranged from a mortuary and an auto repair shop to cooperative stores, a coal yard, and multiple general goods stores. In the 1950s, the R. W. Lindholm Service Station was built for $20,000. Its high price tag was due to its unique design, furnished by the famous architect Frank Lloyd Wright, making it the only Wright-designed gas station ever built in his lifetime. More documentation on Cloquet's history, the fire, its people, and its buildings can be enjoyed at the museum facility of The Carlton County Historical

Society. A 25-feet-tall Voyageur statue at Dunlap Island Park, the Chief Theater building with its quirky "stuck" biplane, the Gordy's Hi-Hat eatery (as seen on Guy Fieri's Diners, Drive-Inns & Dives), and a giant Dala Horse outside of the former Bergquist Gifts store are other noteworthy places to visit around town. Cloquet's most famous daughter is Jessica Lange, born here on April 20, 1949. The renowned actress achieved the Triple Crown of Acting by winning multiple Academy Awards, Primetime Emmy Awards, and Golden Globe Awards throughout her 50-year career. Other famous townspeople include Udert William Hella, the Director of Minnesota State Parks from 1953 to 1973 and a key player in the establishment of Voyageurs National Park; actress Barbara Payton, a film actress famous for being one of the greatest "hot messes" in Hollywood history; Clarence Larson, the commissioner of the U.S. Atomic Energy Commission from 1969 to 1974; and former NHL players Jamie Langenbrunner, Derek Plante, and Corey Millen.

Restaurant Recommendation:
Gordy's Hi-Hat
415 Sunnyside Dr
Cloquet, MN 55720

CROMWELL, MN
POPULATION: 240 – CITY 428 OF 856 (7-18-25)
Island Lake Station was the initial name of this now town of 240 people in northwestern Carlton County when it began in 1872 via the advances of the Northern Pacific Railroad. In 1883, it was changed to Cromwell in honor of James L. Cromwell of Duluth. The post office had opened in 1882 bearing his surname, and the postal service, the railroad, and townspeople alike wanted to ensure that their community would be known by only one name. In 1903, Cromwell was incorporated as a village, and its timber and agricultural sectors blossomed. Three major sawmills were owned in the area by Andrew Parviainen, who shipped over two million feet of box lumber out into the world in 1919. That same year, The Cromwell Co-Operative Creamery (est. 1913) paid out nearly $70,000 to local farmers for their butterfat and eggs. Most deposits were made into the State Bank of Cromwell, of which J. H. Wright was then president; on average, about $90,000 was deposited each year. The Home of the Cardinals has more residents now than ever before; its biggest decade of growth was from 143 people in 2000 to 234 in 2010.

KETTLE RIVER, MN
POPULATION: 166 – CITY 429 OF 856 (7-18-25)
Two earlier post offices operated in Pine County: first, Kettle River Station from 1870 to 1881, and then Kettle River from 1881 to 1892. However, when referring to a Minnesota town today, the City of Kettle River in Carlton County comes to mind. Located on the 83.6-mile-long tributary of the St. Croix River, first called *Akiko Sibi* by the Ojibwe, the original name of the townsite plat was Finland. Early Finnish immigrants wanted to honor their homeland. Still, they instead opted to use the word *kattilajoki*, meaning "kettle river city," for their community. A post office opened in 1910, and Joseph Winquist was dubbed postmaster, operating the branch out of his general store. The Minneapolis, St. Paul & Sault Ste. Marie Railroad brought a lot of new businesses and settlers to town, but it was also some stray sparks from the railroads that burnt large swaths of Carlton County in an October 12, 1918, fire. All of Kettle River was destroyed except for the brick Farmer's State Bank building (now standing

on the west side of State Highway 73). Nevertheless, the town was rebuilt, and in 1921 it achieved incorporation.

MOOSE LAKE, MN
POPULATION: 2,789 – CITY 430 OF 856 (7-18-25)

Foot trails like the "Old Indian Trail," the Mille Lacs Trail, and the Military Road gave Moose Lake a certain level of distinction as a suitable place to establish a town, long before the lines of the Northern Pacific (in 1870) and the Soo Railroad (in 1909) arrived. The town was appropriately named after Moosehead Lake because it was laid out on its northwestern edge between the 1870s and the 1880s. As usual, one of the original establishments was the post office, founded in 1872. The local logging and farming industries attracted approximately 100 people by 1880, and by 1890, the population had grown to 169. Moose Lake joined the ranks of Minnesota's incorporated municipalities on February 15, 1880. When the great Cloquet Fire of 1918 swept through Moose Lake, the town was paralyzed. Nearly half of the fire's 453 casualties occurred not far outside of the community when cars piled up in the smoke and wreckage, and others perished from excessive smoke inhalation. A 27-foot-tall obelisk monument was raised in the modern-day Riverside Cemetery to mark the mass burial site of over 200 of the victims. Moose Lake's Minneapolis, St. Paul & Sault Ste. Marie Railroad Depot, the only location in town listed on the National Register, survived the event and served as emergency housing for many locals left homeless following the great blaze. Over 52,000 homes were destroyed in the area. Now, the depot serves as the Depot and Fires of 1918 Museum, one of Moose Lake's two biggest draws for tourism. The other is Moose Lake State Park, a 1,194-acre area known for Echo Lake, its hiking trails, and the Agate/Geological Interpretive Center, which features exhibits on Lake Superior Agates, Minnesota's state gemstone. The vibrant agates are sought after for their iron-colored orange and red bands; they were formed in basaltic lava flows over 1.1 billion years ago. In 1935, Moose Lake gained statewide recognition when the Minnesota legislature selected it as the site of the fourth state-sponsored hospital. By May 2, 1938, the $2,165,000 "hospital for the insane" welcomed its first patients and began to use hydrotherapy, physiotherapy, electroshock, and insulin therapies. The medical and surgical wards ceased operations in 1966, and nineteen years later, the facility was renamed Moose Lake Regional Treatment Center.

SCANLON, MN
POPULATION: 987 – CITY 433 OF 856 (7-19-25)

Presently home to about one thousand citizens but never more than 1,132 as of the 1970s, the former manufacturing village of Scanlon was named in honor of M. Joseph Scanlon. He was president of the Brooks-Scanlon Company of Minneapolis, Minnesota, which operated from 1901 to 1994 in Minnesota, British Columbia, Florida, Louisiana, and most notably, Bend, Oregon. The company's first sawmill production facility was strategically located in Scanlon Village and could process 600,000 feet of boards per day. In the same year the company was organized, a post office was also established. Although it was discontinued in 1954 in favor of the Cloquet office, Scanlon has maintained its independence as its own city throughout the decades, with the addition of a community center, an assisted living facility, baseball fields, and multiple restaurants.

WRENSHALL, MN
POPULATION: 428 – CITY 435 OF 856 (7-19-25)
Wrenshall's claim to fame is its former six brick factories, which reportedly churned out over 25,000,000 bricks annually, predominantly used in Carlton County, Duluth, and the surrounding areas. The great industry began with Frederick Jacob Habhegger, who moved here with his wife and nine children in 1887 to 160 acres of homestead land that would someday become the Wrenshall townsite. He learned brickmaking in La Crosse, Wisconsin, and brought his talents to Minnesota. Habhegger opened a single brickyard to start, which, on its own, eventually produced 4,000,000 bricks per year. They were used to erect several local edifices, including the First Presbyterian Church and the Brickyard Restaurant. Although the final bricks were produced in 1954, Wrenshall had other business ventures thanks to its prior establishment as a village. Charles Christopher Wrenshall, an engineer with the Northern Pacific Railroad (one of the two railroad companies in town, the other being the Great Northern), had this town and depot named in his honor while he oversaw the construction of the line from Carlton, Minnesota, to Superior, Wisconsin. He also maintained bridge repairs along the Northern Pacific. Wrenshall briefly claimed the World's Largest White Stag from 2010 to 2011, only to have it repainted brown again.

WRIGHT, MN
POPULATION: 168 – CITY 427 OF 856 (7-18-25)
George Burdick Wright, land agent for the Northern Pacific Railroad, secured permission to extend a railroad branch between 1881 and 82 from Wadena to Fergus Falls and Breckenridge. However, the town named in his honor was nowhere near there. Wright, in Carlton County, welcomed its post office in 1892 and slowly but surely added churches, stores, livery stables, and a few firms on its way to incorporation. At the start of the 1940s, the population reached its peak of 201 people. While many communities across Minnesota host small-town annual festivals, Wright's is notable for its unique "Wrong Days in Wright" name. Every third weekend of July, the townspeople get together for street dances, a parade, game tournaments, and a smorgasbord, that is, a Swedish buffet.

Unincorporated/Ghost Towns: Atkinson, Automba, Big Lake, Duesler, Esko, Harney, Holyoke, Iverson, Mahtowa, Nemadji, Otter Creek, Pleasant Valley, Sawyer, Scotts Corner

National Register of Historic Places:
Carlton: Carlton County Courthouse, Henry C. Oldenburg House, Jay Cooke State Park CCC/Rustic Style Historic District, Jay Cooke State Park CCC/Rustic Style Picnic Grounds, Jay Cooke State Park CCC/Rustic Style Service Yard
Cloquet: Cloquet City Hall, Cloquet High School, Cloquet-Northern Office Building, Lindholm Oil Company Service Station, Northeastern Hotel, Park Place Historic District, Shaw Memorial Library
Duluth: Grand Portage of the St. Louis River
Moose Lake: Minneapolis, St. Paul & Sault Ste. Marie Depot
Sawyer: Church of Sts. Joseph & Mary-Catholic

Golf Courses:
Black Bear Golf Course, Resort (Carlton, MN)
Cloquet Country Club, Private (Cloquet, MN)

Town Celebrations:
Agate Days, Moose Lake, MN ($2^{nd}/3^{rd}$ Weekend in July)
Cromwell Harvest Fest, Cromwell, MN (Weekend after Labor Day)

Spring Fever Days, Barnum, MN (2nd Weekend in June)
Wrong Days in Wright, Wright, MN (3rd Weekend in July)

CARVER COUNTY
EST. 1855 - POPULATION: 106,922

From 1766-67, Jonathan Carver explored and documented the northern Mississippi Valley, which ultimately led to him being honored by the naming of this county in 1855.

CARVER, MN
POPULATION: 5,829 – CITY 775 OF 856 (11-6-25)

Carver's history begins with the arrival of Axel Jorgenson at the dawn of the 1850s, who was the first squatter — that is, a settler who used squatters' rights to claim a parcel of land — in this part of the county. John Goodenough was the second settler in 1852. Others arrived over these next few years, but it was in 1857 that Carver's growth really took off when J. S. Halsted platted it on behalf of the Carver Land Company. Former Territorial Governor Alexander Ramsey was a part of this group, as was Levi Griffin, the original sheriff of Carver County. Griffin selected the name Carver to honor Captain Jonathan Carver, although it was labeled as "Odowan R." on Nicollet's historic map from the 1840s. Twenty-five students comprised the first assembly of Minnesota School District #1, which was held in 1855-56 in a small claim shanty. Reverend Springleer of Young America established the German Lutheran Church in 1856, which initially lacked a physical structure until a $1,200, 24x40-foot building was erected in 1869. In 1856, the Carver post office was established; it stood alongside early establishments, including a hotel, a boarding house, a blacksmith, a general store, a tailor, a carpenter, a livery stable, and two shoemakers. In three years, both the size of the river town and its population had grown substantially, and there was a brickyard, six general stores, three hotels, a brewery, a hardware store, a newspaper, and multiple saloons, professional offices, carriage works, and blacksmith shops. When the Minneapolis & St. Louis Railroad came through in 1871 and the Hastings & Dakota division of the Chicago, Milwaukee & St. Paul followed shortly thereafter, Carver's growth stalled as its residents were forced to adapt from being a Minnesota River trading town to a railroad town. Grain elevators, feed, flour, and wool carding mills, as well as two watchmakers, a bakery, a plow factory, and a bank, were later additions by the 1880s. By the 1990s, Carver remained relatively small, with a population that never exceeded 750 residents. Much of the town's infrastructure suffered from neglect and decay, a problem exacerbated by the April 1965 flooding that inundated much of Old Carver. On June 25, 1969, Edith Herman, Mary Lee Dayton, Anne Neils-Doerr, and Helen McNulty formed the Carver-on-the-Minnesota corporation, which, over the years, has worked to save several historic homes and properties. Through their efforts, many landmark places were saved, and the Carver Historic District was added to the National Register of Historic Places in 1980 to help preserve about ninety properties built between 1850 and 1925. That same year, King Oscar's Settlement, the first Swedish settlement in the county, made nearby Carver, was added to the Register. It is most notable for its historic 1866 Swedish Lutheran church and a parish hall that served as the earliest beginnings of Gustavus Adolphus College in St. Peter, Minnesota. William F. Badè, an archaeologist noted for his excavations at Tell en-Nasbeh, which are likely the Biblical City of Mizpah.

CHANHASSEN, MN
POPULATION: 25,947 – CITY 780 OF 856 (11-7-25)
Nothing brings more attention and visitors to Chanhassen than Paisley Park, the former 65,000-square-foot estate of the late musician Prince. Known for pioneering Minneapolis sound with its new wave and synth-pop elements, Prince commissioned the $10 million studio complex in January 1986 and was using it by September 1987. While Paisley Park now serves as a museum, home to his ashes and many of his personal possessions, the city in which it is located has existed for much longer. Joseph, Frank, and August Vogel were the initial pioneers who settled the area in August 1852. Still, it was either Clarissa Cleaveland or Reverend Henry M. Nichols who gave the area the name "Chanhassen." It is a Dakota compound word meaning "sugar maple," combining the words *chan*, meaning tree, and *hassen*, meaning 'huckleberry/blueberry,' which in context gives rise to the meaning "the tree of sweet juice." Schooling for local children began in the fall of 1855, and the county's first schoolhouse was built. Chanhassen's first town meeting was held on May 17, 1858. One of the ordinances established at that time allowed for all animals except for swine to roam the town between April 1 and November 1 freely. Several small businesses were started in those early years, but Chanhassen was not formally organized as an incorporated village until April 25, 1896. The move was made following the extension of the Chicago, Milwaukee & St. Paul Railroad through the area, which led to the establishment of the State Bank of Chanhassen, a lumberyard, a feed store, and Pauly's General Store. Its two National Register of Historic Places locations had also been erected by this point: the 1887 Catholic Church of St. Hubertus, started by a Franciscan brotherhood at that time; and the 1895 Chaska brick Albertine and Fred Heck House. It was not until the 1960s that Chanhassen experienced explosive growth, when it became a target of land developers as a bedroom community for the Twin Cities. From 1960 to 1970, the population increased from 244 to 4,879, an increase of 1899.6%. During the initial boom period, Chanhassen welcomed Herb Bloomberg, a hardware and lumber store owner who would go on to open a 600-seat theater in town in October 1968. Its popularity skyrocketed, and since then, it has evolved into the Chanhassen Dinner Theatres company (the nation's largest professional dinner theatre), which welcomes hundreds of thousands of visitors each year to its performances. Snap Fitness and Life Time, Inc. (another health club chain) are headquartered here, as were Wyndham's AmericInn chain of hotels and a portion of the Supervalu grocery store chains at one time. Chanhassen has continued to expand substantially, reaching an all-time high population of 25,947 citizens as of the 2020 Census. Famous residents of note have included actress Debbie Turner, known for her role as Marta von Trapp in the 1965 musical drama *The Sound of Music*; Jared Allen, a five-time NFL Pro-Bowl defensive end and a 2025 inductee into the Pro Football Hall of Fame; James Denton, the actor who played Mike Delfino on ABC's *Desperate Housewives* from 2004 to 2012; Frank Ragnow, a four-time Pro Bowl center with the NFL's Detroit Lions, Kris Humphries, an NBA player with eight franchises between 2004 and 2017, and Verne Gagne, a former professional wrestler and a ten-time title holder of the AWA World Heavyweight Championship.

CHASKA, MN ★
POPULATION: 27,810 – CITY 774 OF 856 (11-6-25)
Traders on the Minnesota River were the first Europeans to call the Chaska region home circa 1851, but the earliest permanent settlers came two years later. Much of its initial development can be attributed to David L. Fuller, a land speculator who purchased the site for $1,000 from Thomas Holmes, an Indian agent who had been

trading with the local Madahwahkan tribe. By the end of the 1850s, the Shaska Townsite Company had platted the community, and development was well underway. *Shaska*–frequently given by the Sioux to their first-born sons–should have been the name of the town, but it was misspelled in the original company documents when the community was being formed. Nevertheless, the village of Chaska became home to a myriad of German and Swedish immigrants. On October 14, 1856, Chaska was selected as the Carver County seat in a contentious election in which it prevailed over the rival towns of San Francisco and Carver. It won 303 of the 525 votes cast. Brick making took off as the primary industry in 1857, when rich clay deposits were discovered along the river. By the 1880s, Chaska had solidified itself as a prominent brickmaking city thanks to its location on the Minneapolis and St. Louis Railway and the river. Businesses at this point included six general mercantile stores, five brickyards, five blacksmith shops, three elevators, three millinery stores, fifteen saloons, ten hotels, three breweries, two carriage manufacturers, two steam flour mills, and four lawyers' offices. There were 10 brick yards by 1900, all of which produced an incredible 60 million bricks annually. Other institutions formed around the brickmaking industry included the Minnesota Sugar Company (still Minnesota's oldest surviving sugar beet processing plant), the Samuels Brothers and White Canning Company, the W. A. Gedney [Pickle] Company, and the Beyrer Brewery. Although all of these period companies have since folded, several structures from that era are still standing, including several pre-1920 structures known as the Walnut Street Historic District; the 1871 Chaska Herald Block building; the 1875 Brinkhaus saloon Livery Barn; 1888 Simons Building and Livery Barn, the 1938 Chaska Historical Marker, crafted by the Minnesota Department of Highways, and several homes. Until the 1960s, Chaska's population never exceeded 2,500, but it has since grown nearly tenfold, becoming one of several cities in Minnesota's metropolitan area. In 1962, it welcomed the addition of the Hazeltine National Golf Club, which has since hosted the Ryder Cup and two PGA Championships. Its rapid growth and interesting name have lent themselves to a few pop culture references, including Hank Snow's popular 1962 song "I've Been Everywhere." A handful of famous residents of Chaska's past and present include Mike Lindell, the founder and CEO of My Pillow; Jerry Koosman, a two-time MLB All-Star pitcher and a member of the 1969 "Miracle [New York] Mets" World Series champion team; Jay Goede, the voice of Mewtwo in *Pokémon: The First Movie*; Andy Bisek, a Greco-Roman wrestler who participated in the 2016 Rio Olympic Games; Jeff Isaacson, a two-time gold-medalist Olympic curler; Brad Hand, a three-time MLB All-Star pitcher from 2017 to 2019; professional motocross racer Ryan Dungey; Edward Van Sloen, an actor who appeared in the 1931 horror films *Dracula* and *Frankenstein*; Stephen Wolff, a father of the Internet who encouraged its usage beyond just government needs; Mike Reilly, an NHL ice hockey defenseman with over 418 career game appearances, and Erik Paulsen, a U.S. Congressman from Minnesota between 2009 and 2019.

COLOGNE, MN
POPULATION: 2,047 – CITY 755 OF 856 (11-4-25)

Two villages, Benton and Cologne, thrived alongside one another for a decade, between 1881 and 1891, before merging into one. Benton was established on land owned by Casper Kronschnabel and was named for Thomas H. Benton, a United States senator. Adam and Paul Mohrbacher started the village of Cologne and named it after their homeland in Germany. In those early days, the town surveyed by H. J. Cheever had two general stores, a grist mill, an elevator, a wagon shop, a drug store, a furniture store, a blacksmith shop, and a hardware store. Both communities thrived on the Hastings and Dakota Railroad Company's line between Glencoe and

Minneapolis before agreeing to join forces as a joint farming and milling community; this occurred when Benton filed an Act of Repeal to dissolve its incorporation. Bongard & Company's mill was erected in 1880 for $10,000 and was capable of producing up to 100 barrels of flour per day, according to a 1882 business report. Regarding postal history, Benton's post office first started in 1860, moved to Cologne in 1879, returned to Benton from 1881 to 1891, and then finally moved to Cologne for good. Emma Noyes served as the first public schoolteacher in 1857, when a schoolhouse was organized. Religious history in the area began in 1856, when St. Bernard's Catholic Church was founded as a mission church. It later boasted of a parochial school, founded in 1876, and a convent, started in 1880. West Union, known for its 1868 church built by early Swedish Americans, is located in the countryside near Cologne. Many prominent homes from this era are of interest to historic home-lovers, including the 1878 Chaska brick J. Carsten and Margaretha Harms Farmhouse, the 1880 Paul Mohrbacher House, the 1902 Philip Guettler House, and the 1905 John Knotz House. An early organization of note was the Carver County Homeopathic Society, established for locals to share health secrets, concoctions, and remedies. One of only a few amateur works on the National Film Registry is the 1939 film *Cologne: From the Diary of Ray Esther*, which follows the lives of local German Americans before the United States entered the Second World War.

HAMBURG, MN
POPULATION: 566 – CITY 753 OF 856 (11-4-25)
Hamburg (pop. 566) was home to a German immigrant community as early as the 1850s. Yet, it was not adequately developed until 1881, when the Minneapolis & St. Louis Railroad chose to establish a station on the site. J. D. Roeders was the townsite owner, and when he learned that the railroad intended to use his land for its right-of-way, he opted to plat a town. Streets were named after his daughters, Sophia, Maria, Henrietta, and Louisa. The "Wunderbar" city, as it is known today, was almost named Roeders, Siding, Washburn, or Sultan, but Hamburgh won out from all the suggestions. The '-h' was dropped in 1892, and the post office (which had been open since 1881) followed suit. Incorporation came by the end of that decade, when Hamburg had general stores, hardware stores, saloons, blacksmith shops, and more prosperous lines like two creameries, railroad hotels, a grain elevator, and a sawmill. The Jacob Hebeisen Hardware Store, started in 1907 and later a part of a 1919 consumer cooperative that helped provide a stage for the future development of labor unions, is located at the junction of Railroad and Maria Streets. One of Carver County's last authentic rural communities has also had its share of school and church buildings, but baseball has long served as the heart of the community. A "Schafskopf" (meaning sheephead) tournament was held in 1950, the same year the Hamburg Baseball Club was organized; since then, it has hosted several State Amateur Baseball Tournaments in 1983 and 1988. The fifth president of the Missouri Synod of the Lutheran Church, Friedrich Pfotenhauer, served as the local pastor from 1894 to 1911.

MAYER, MN
POPULATION: 2,453 – CITY 757 OF 856 (11-4-25)
Officers of the Great Northern Railroad gave Mayer the name, but the source of it remains a mystery. Initially, the area was called Helvetia (an alternate name for Switzerland) by the Swiss immigrant John Buhler, who laid out the town and owned one of the original general merchandise stores. Modern-day Mayer was moved to its present-day site with the coming of the railroad in the 1880s. Sawmills, flour mills, a sorghum mill, and a creamery emerged as some of the site's most important business lines. In the education sphere, Public School District 73 boasted of its first school

building in 1887. It was replaced in 1916 by a newer building. Despite losing its railroad in 2001, Mayer has grown quickly in recent decades. From 2000 to 2010, its population grew by 215.7%, from 554 to 1,749; until the 1970s, it had never had more than 200 permanent residents.

NEW GERMANY, MN
POPULATION: 464 – CITY 758 OF 856 (11-4-25)
New Germany is located in Camden Township, but it was named for its large German immigrant population. The earliest settlers came in 1850, but no real development occurred until the extension of the Great Northern Railroad to that point in the 1880s. It was platted on Amanda Bury, Christian Wolfrom, and Joseph Paul's land, which at that time had prosperous woodlands that stretched as far as the eye could see. From 1887 to 1895, lumbering was the community's principal industry, but as citizens shifted towards agriculture, the industry gradually declined. During that time, the Purity post office was moved to town. It was only renamed as the New Germany post office in 1902, thirteen years after its move. Several grain elevators were constructed to handle the hauls of local farmers, as were feed mills, sawmills, sorghum mills, and even a canning factory. The First State Bank of New Germany opened its doors for the first time in 1905. In 1908, School District No. 77 was established to serve the community's educational needs, and in 1914, St. Mark's Lutheran Church began to take shape as a local religious center. To ward off anti-German sentiment, residents of New Germany briefly changed the town's name to "Motordale" between 1917 and 1922. *Herman, U.S.A.*, based on the true story of dozens of bachelor farmers from Herman (in Grant County) who campaigned for women to visit the town to find true love, was filmed in New Germany due to a lack of lodging near Herman for the film's staff and crew. Abigail and Brittany Hensel, one of the very few dicephalic parapagus [conjoined] twins to survive to adulthood, were born here on March 7, 1990, and are fifth-grade teachers.

Restaurant Recommendation:
T-Road Tavern
110 Broadway St E
New Germany, MN

NORWOOD YOUNG AMERICA, MN
POPULATION: 3,863 – CITY 754 OF 856 (11-4-25)
Stiftungsfest, Minnesota's oldest celebration, has been held here by German immigrants and their descendants since 1861, and began shortly after Young America Village was surveyed in the fall of 1856 on the land of R.M. Kennedy and James Slocum Jr. Like other communities in Minnesota, such as Elko New Market and Trimont, Norwood Young America began as two separate municipalities that ultimately merged into a single entity. Young America, the first of the two towns, was first settled by James Neal in the fall of 1855. It was located on the Pacific extension of the Minneapolis & St. Louis Railroad and was incorporated on March 4, 1879. Farmington and Florence were earlier names for the community, which was later changed to honor "the vigor and progressiveness of the young people of the United States." In addition to a creamery, a flour mill, a sawmill, a brewery, and grain elevators, it also boasted a boot and shoe store, a wagon shop, a meat market, a harness shop, and pairs of blacksmith shops, general stores, and hardware stores. Norwood started in 1872, just a mile to the southwest of Young America, and was located on the Hastings & Dakota division of the Chicago, Milwaukee & St. Paul Railroad. It had five general stores, three elevators, three implement dealers, two lumber yards, two harness shops, two wagon

shops, two blacksmiths, two hotels, and two boot and shoe stores as of 1882, amongst other places of interest. Both communities had several churches, fraternal organizations, and educational institutions. Slocum named Norwood for either his wife's friend or a relative "back home" in the eastern United States. The two municipalities operated independently until January 1, 1997, when the city governments decided to merge. Before their merger, the 1990 Census reported almost identical populations for both communities: 1,354 people in Young America, and 1,351 in Norwood. Four interesting points of note within the region are the 1870s Johann Schimmelpfennig's Farmstead home, the 1876 Norwood Methodist Episcopal Church, the 1890 Winter Saloon, and the 1909 Young America City Hall. YA (formerly Young America Corporation) is a prominent local marketing services company that receives copious amounts of mail for rebates, loyalty programs, contest entries, and other offers on behalf of companies from around the country. Such enormous amounts of mail are sent to Norwood Young America that the company has over twenty of its own zip codes, one of which is 55555. While significant, NYA's initial "big business" was the Oak Grove Creamery plant, whose bottling operations became one of the largest operations in the United States following its 1936 founding.

 **Restaurant Recommendation:**
Bongards Creameries – Retail Store
13200 County Rd 51
Norwood Young America, MN 55368

VICTORIA, MN
POPULATION: 10,546 – CITY 773 OF 856 (11-6-25)
Twenty-five parks, thirteen lakes, and nearly two thousand acres of reserved land (most of it being located in the Three Rivers Park District's Carver Park Reserve) make up "The City of Lakes and Parks," perhaps more commonly known as the City of Victoria. Named in honor of the local St. Victoria church, Victoria was likely first settled by Michael Diethelm in 1851. He came around the same time as the Treaty of Mendota, signed by the Mdewakanton and Wahpekute bands of Dakota, which forfeited much of their land in present-day southern Minnesota. Dutch, Swiss, and German immigrants moved to the region and began growing wheat, potatoes, and select fruits and vegetables. By 1882, they were connected to the Minneapolis & St. Louis Railroad system. A post office was established the following year, and soon a plethora of entrepreneurs were conducting business throughout Victoria. St. Victoria had a log church and school erected by 1858; the latter was replaced by a two-story structure in 1875. The Chaska brick church was completed by 1870. Laketown Moravian Brethren's Church was completed in 1878 for $2,500, when the congregation numbered 74 members. It was placed on the National Register in 1980. Wendelin Grimm's Farmstead, a 160-acre property located within the Carver Park Reserve, is noted for being the home of the German immigrant who developed the first alfalfa that was able to withstand North America's harsh winter months. Frank Ragnow, a four-time Pro Bowl center with the NFL's Detroit Lions from 2018 to 2014, hails from here.

 **Restaurant Recommendation:**
Ruby's Roost Bakery & Coffee
7924 Victoria Dr #101
Victoria, MN 55386

WACONIA, MN ☆
POPULATION: 13,033 – CITY 756 OF 856 (11-4-25)
Ridgeview Medical Center and Strom Aviation make up a 3,000-person sector of Waconia's workforce, one of several rapidly growing suburbs of Carver County's northeast metropolitan area. Platted in March 1857 by G. W. King and Roswell P. Russell on the shores of Lake Waconia (then also called Clearwater Lake), the area was likely first settled by Ludwig Sudheimer and Michael Scheidnagel. E. Hyde briefly served as the first postmaster of the office named after a Sioux word meaning "lake of the fountain." St. Joseph's Roman Catholic Church also began meeting that year and had an edifice by the next. Within no time, businesses like the Waconia Sorghum Mill, the Waconia Brewery (est. in 1865 by Zahler & Metz), and the Waconia Steam Saw and Flowering Mill came to fruition. Within about twenty-five years, its business interests also included seven general stores, five saloons, three blacksmith shops, two carriage works, and a mix of hardware, furniture, drug, and harness stores. Trinity Evangelical Lutheran Church had also established itself as a counterpart to the Catholic Church, serving as the town's primary gathering place for Protestants. Lines of the Great Northern and Minneapolis & St. Louis Railroads worked through Waconia just as Coney Island, located in the middle of the lake, was seeing a rapid increase in tourism. Nicknamed the "Paradise of the Northwest," it attracted thousands of visitors from around the country each year. Fast-forwarding another half-century to the 1930s, when Waconia had about 1,300 residents, the Waconia Creamery became the target of Minnesota State Attorney General Benson's lawsuit for pollution of the lake. The suit was one of the first environmental lawsuits in Minnesota, filed in 1932. As historic preservation efforts really began to take hold in the 1970s/1980s, several Waconia places were already in line to be placed on the National Register of Historic Places: the 31-acre island mentioned above; the 1863 Zoar Moravian Church; the 1875 Mock Cigar Factory and House; and the 1909 Waconia City Hall were the most important. St. Joseph's Catholic Church and its street served as the filming location for the scene in the 1999 mockumentary *Drop Dead Gorgeous*, in which the swan float explodes during the parade. Don Herbert, best known as the creator of *Watch Mr. Wizard* and *Mr. Wizard's World*, two children's science and technology shows that serve as precursors to the ultra-famous *Bill Nye the Science Guy* shows, was born here on July 10, 1917. Other celebrities with communal ties are Jenn Bostic, a country-Christian music singer-songwriter; Bob Stinson, a founding member and the lead guitarist of the rock band the Replacements; Maxx Williams, an NFL tight end between 2015 and 2022; and Shane Wiskus, a member of Team USA's 2020 Summer Olympic artistic gymnastics squad.

WATERTOWN, MN
POPULATION: 4,659 – CITY 759 OF 856 (11-5-25)
A brewery, a creamery, a plow factory, hotels, and milling facilities for sorghum, flour, and lumber were just some of the early firms that visitors would have found in Watertown in its early days. Named for the township's seemingly never-ending supply of freshwater via the local lakes, Watertown was platted in 1858 but not incorporated until February 26, 1866. Another town, Rapid City, was located in the same area for several years, further up the Crow River. With the help of the Electric Short Line, settlement in these areas increased, and several improvements were made. William P. Buck taught school in Watertown starting in 1857-58. Other structures replaced it as the pupil population grew, including a 1911 high school building. A $1,000 Catholic church was erected in those earlier years. It was eventually joined by the St. Peter's Evangelical [German] Lutheran church, St. Paul Church, the Evangelical Free Church,

Trinity Lutheran Church, and the Community Church of Watertown. Touching back on two of the earliest business implements of the young village, it was in 1870 that the Watertown Plow Company was established and began to churn out about 1,000 plows and 200 cultivators annually. A bell foundry, the only such institution in Minnesota in its early years, starting in 1864, was founded by W. Bleedorn and had the capacity to produce 3,000 to 5,000 bells annually. Actress Marion Ross, a two-time Primetime Emmy award nominee for her role as Marion Cunningham on ABC's sitcom *Happy Days*, and Gordon Paschka, a pioneer NFL running back who played for the 1943 Phil/Pitt "Steagles," are two noteworthy individuals with Watertown ties.

Unincorporated/Ghost Towns: Assumption, Augusta, Bongards, Coney Island, Crown College, Dahlgren, East Union, Gotha, Hazelton, Hollywood, Maple, Oster, San Francisco

National Register of Historic Places:
Carver: Carver Historic District, King Oscar's Settlement
Chanhassen: Albertine & Fred Heck House, Church of St. Hubertus-Catholic
Chaska: Brinkhaus Saloon Livery Barn, Chaska Historical Marker, E. H. Lewis House, Eder-Baer House, Frederick E. DuToit House, Frederick Greiner House, Herald Block, Simons Building & Livery Barn, Walnut Street Historic District
Cologne: John Knotz House, J. Carsten & Magaretha Harms Farmhouse, Paul Mohrbacher House, Philip Guettler House, West Union
Hamburg: Jacob Hebeisen Hardware Store
Norwood Young America: Norwood Methodist Episcopal Church, Winter Saloon, Young America City Hall, Johann Schimmelpfennig Farmstead
San Francisco Township: District No. 22 School, Tukihasaŋ Oyaŋke/Winter Shell Site
Victoria: Laketown Moravian Brethren's Church, Wendelin Grimm Farmstead
Waconia: Andrew Peterson Farmstead, Charles Maiser House, Coney Island of the West, Emile Amblard Guest House, Mock Cigar Factory & House, Waconia City Hall, West Main Street Houses, Zoar Moravian Church

Golf Courses:
Bluff Creek Golf Course, Daily Fee (Chaska, MN)
Dahlgreen Golf Club, Daily Fee (Chaska, MN)
Deer Run Golf Club, Daily Fee (Victoria, MN)
Halla Greens Executive Golf Course and Driving Range, Daily Fee (Chanhassen, MN)
Island View Golf Club, Daily Fee (Waconia, MN)
The Loop at Chaska, Municipal (Chaska, MN)
Timber Creek Golf Course, Daily Fee (Watertown, MN)

Breweries/Wineries/Distilleries:
ENKI Brewing Company (Victoria, MN)
J. Carver Distillery (Waconia, MN)
Parley Lake Winery (Waconia, MN)
Schram Vineyards and Winery (Waconia, MN)
The Winery at Sovereign Estate (Waconia, MN)
Waconia Brewing Company (Waconia, MN)

Town Celebrations:
Nickle Dickle Day, Waconia, MN (2nd Saturday after Labor Day)
Rails to Trails Festival, Watertown, MN (Last Weekend in July)
Stiftungsfest, Norwood Young America, MN (Weekend before Labor Day)

Big Stone County: Local barn (Barry), former St. Mary's Catholic Church (Beardsley), Clinton Depot Museum (Clinton), Holy Rosary Catholic Church (Graceville), Big Stone Lake (Ortonville), Paul Bunyon's Anchor at Big Stone County Museum (Ortonville), Ring-necked Pheasant at Big Stone Lake State Park (Ortonville), First English Lutheran Church (Ortonville)

Blue Earth County: Depot Mercantile and GTA Co-op Grain Elevator & Mill (Amboy), Dodd Ford Historic Bridge (Amboy), Grain Elevator Mural (Good Thunder), Grain Silo Mural (Mankato), Last Happy Chef Restaurant (Mankato), Blue Earth County Courthouse (Mankato), Stokman State Wildlife Management Area (Minnesota Lake), Buffalo Herd at Minneopa State Park (Mankato)

Brown County: Norwegian Stabbur (Hanska), Hermann the German Monument (New Ulm), New Ulm's [Working] Glockenspiel (New Ulm), Turner Hall (New Ulm), Schell's Brewery Taproom (New Ulm), Linus Statue at Dyckman Free Library (Sleepy Eye), Interior of St. Mary's Catholic Church (Sleepy Eye), St. Paul Lutheran Church (Springfield)

Carlton County: 1st Rural Consolidated School in Minnesota Schoolhouse at County Fairgrounds (Barnum), Rusty Sculpture at Carlton Schools (Carlton), Swinging Bridge at Jay Cooke State Park (Carlton), Dala Horse at Welcome Sign (Cloquet), Frank Lloyd Wright Gas Station (Cloquet), Blackberry Shake & Burger from Gordy's Hi-Hat (Cloquet), Minneapolis, St. Paul & Sault Ste. Marie Depot Museum (Moose Lake), Jumping Stag Statue (Wrenshall)

Carver County: Carver Railroad Water Tower (Carver), Chanhassen History Center (Chanhassen), Chanhassen Dinner Theatres (Chanhassen), Emanuel Lutheran Church & Cemetery (Hamburg), Veteran's Memorial (Mayer) Interior of St. John's Lutheran Church (Norwood Young America), Saint Joseph Catholic Church (Waconia), Painted Sailboat Sculptured at Carver County Fairground (Waconia)

CASS COUNTY
EST. 1851 - POPULATION: 30,066

Lewis Cass, the 22nd United States Secretary of State from 1857 to 1860, is the namesake of this 2,414 square mile county. Several parts of it were partitioned off over time to create surrounding counties.

BACKUS, MN
POPULATION: 262 – CITY 346 OF 856 (6-19-25)
The legendary lumber king Edward Wellington Backus, owner of the second-largest sawmills in Minneapolis in 1890 by the time he was thirty years old, will be forever remembered by the name of this Cass County community in central Minnesota. When fires destroyed his mills in two cities, Backus opted to move his operations "Up North" and establish the E.W. Backus Lumber Company in 1898. It was later renamed the Backus and Brooks Lumber Company and did a great deal of business there. A logging camp and the original Backus townsite were established circa 1885 but abandoned in 1902 in favor of a new site on the Northern Pacific Railroad. A post office was established in 1896, and the name Backus was adopted by both the postal service and town officials. While Backus is remembered for its logging history, its unusual claim to fame is "Colonel Cobber," a humanoid cornstalk sculpture created by Ross Olsen in 2006.

BENA, MN
POPULATION: 143 – CITY 410 OF 856 (7-17-25)
On the southern shore of the great Lake Winnibigoshish, the fourth-largest lake in Minnesota, named by the Ojibwe for its brackish water, lies a town called Bena. "Bena" is a type of bird mentioned in Henry Wadsworth Longfellow's poem *The Song of Hiawatha* and is more commonly known as a ruffed grouse, a partridge, or a pheasant. The post office adopted the Bena name when it opened in 1898, and Ernest Flemming established a small store, which contributed to the development of a Great Northern Railroad village. A wooden dam built by the United States Army Corps of Engineers from 1881 to 1884 was replaced in 1899 by a concrete structure to provide a constant flow of water for loggers and merchants downstream at St. Anthony Falls in Minneapolis. In 1901, the United States government opened the Bena Boarding School, one of a series of "Indian Boarding Schools" that forcibly brought Indigenous children into the system to Americanize them. The school shuttered its doors in 1911, but Bena continued to grow nonetheless. By 1950, it had reached a peak population of 331, and its residents had already introduced many unique aspects to the surrounding area. In 1933, the Winnibigoshish Resort, now known as the Big Winnie General Store and RV Park, was constructed in a Bavarian architectural style to attract travelers. It was supposedly designed by the famous architect Frank Lloyd Wright while he was vacationing in the Bena vicinity. Three miles west of town in 1958, "The Big Fish," a sharp-toothed, 65-foot-long muskie, was built by Wayne Kumpula as a drive-in restaurant and roadside attraction. Although the structure did not serve as a restaurant for long, it has since taken on fame as being a favorite building of many roadtrippers—including Charles Kuralt, the beloved host of CBS's *On the Road* program—and even made appearances in movies like the opening credits of *National Lampoon's Vacation* (1983).

BOY RIVER, MN
POPULATION: 26 – CITY 412 OF 856 (7-17-25)
The small municipality of Boy River shares its name with Boy River and Boy Lake, both of which are commemoratively named to honor the legacy of three young Ojibwe boys who perished at the hands of the Sioux while gathering wild rice for their village. The Ojibwe had driven the Sioux southward from Mille Lacs. Their enemy returned with a vengeance only a short time later via the Crow Wing and Gull Rivers. When the Minneapolis, St. Paul & Sault Ste. Marie Railroad built a spur through the region and adhered to its plan to set a depot every seven to ten miles or so. One of these was Boy River, which by 1910 had its own post office. Hotels, general stores, and other shops emerged, and on April 7, 1922, the city was officially incorporated. Only 92 people lived in town at its inaugural 1930 Census, and by the time it lost its post office in 1975, that number had halved. As recently as 2018, residents of Boy River have considered dissolving their municipal corporation and reverting the city to the care and jurisdiction of the Cass County government. Only two of the five votes in the petition presented that year to the State of Minnesota voted in favor of dissolution, keeping the "City of Boy River" alive.

CASS LAKE, MN
POPULATION: 675 – CITY 409 OF 856 (7-17-25)
As the gateway to Chippewa National Forest, a 666,623-acre forest established in 1908, Cass Lake has long been a hub of tourism. It was located in 1898 on the shore of Cass Lake, its namesake, which was, in turn, named to commemorate Lewis Cass. He was the second Governor of the Michigan Territory from 1813 to 1831. During that time, he participated in an 1820 expedition to locate the headwaters of the Mississippi River and meet with local tribes. Cass insisted that Elk Lake was at its head. Another man on his expedition, Henry R. Schoolcraft, thought otherwise and returned twelve years later with his own crew to discover the true headwaters of the Mississippi River at Lake Itasca. An earlier name for the village and its post office was Tuller, after the postmaster's brother-in-law. Officials of the Great Northern Railroad and residents instead wanted to honor the late General Cass. The change was enacted in 1899, and soon, the local timber industry began to boom. The Glenmont Lumber Company erected the first mill in 1898. The Scanlon-Gipson Lumber Company opened its planing mill the following year. In 1900, the Julius Neils Lumber Company erected several mills of its own. A second railroad, the Soo Line, arrived in 1900 as well. Many other firms came and went, like lumberyards, general stores, and hardware stores. Even box crate factories and wood treatment plants were extant, but one organization proved particularly useful to Cass Lake: the Forest Supervisor's Office Headquarters of the Minnesota Forest Reserve. Built in 1935 and affiliated with many New Deal programs like the Civilian Conservation Corps, one of the organization's proudest accomplishments was the establishment of the world's largest pine (the Lydick) nursery by the end of the 1930s. Over 64,000,000 seedlings were supplied annually to the Chippewa National Forest and other nearby forests. In that same decade, the Indian Reorganization Act of 1934 was passed, establishing the Minnesota Chippewa Tribe, which located its headquarters in Cass Lake. The Leech Lake Band of Ojibwe, the residents of the Leech Lake Indian Reservation (of which the City of Cass Lake is entirely located within), is also headquartered here. Leech Lake Tribal College was established in 1990 and is now a public, tribal land-grant community college that serves the higher educational needs of over 250 area students, the majority of whom are Indigenous. Approximately 2,109 people lived in Cass Lake in 1920. Yet, in every subsequent decade since the 1950s, its population has decreased by anywhere from

6.8% to 24% decade over decade. As of 2020, 675 citizens, most of whom are Native American, live in Cass Lake. Noteworthy residents of past and present have included Roland H. Hartley, the 10th Governor of Washington from January 14, 1925, to January 11, 1933; Charlie Munger, former vice chairman of Berkshire Hathaway from 1978 to his passing in November 2023; Alfred O. C. Nier, the physicist behind the advanced development of mass spectrometry; Dick Siebert, a 1943 All-Star first baseman for the Philadelphia Athletics; Alonzo Barnard, a Presbyterian missionary to Native Americans and an abolitionist, and Chief John Smith, a Chippewa man who may have been as old as 137 at the time of his passing in February 1922. Cass Lake is also notable for its proximity to the Heartland State Trail, a 49-mile rail trail between Park Rapids and Cass Lake that features a 1915 Great Northern Railroad Bridge.

CHICKAMAW BEACH, MN
POPULATION: 128 – CITY 344 OF 856 (6-19-25)
Located just a stone's throw from the City of Pine River across Norway Lake, Chickamaw Beach was separated from Barclay Township on November 20, 1950, to become an independent municipality. The move to incorporate was made entirely out of necessity. A single dirt road connected the residents on the east side of Norway Lake to the rest of civilization, but it was rough. Constant snow removal and repairs were needed. Frustrated by Cass County's lack of maintenance, Fred Thompson came up with the idea to incorporate. He spoke with several residents and a Brainerd lawyer, finding that a new municipality in Minnesota needed only 125 residents to meet the act's population requirements. Of course, there were only 124 full-time residents who could be counted, so the town improvised. They counted Lou Yakymi's unborn child as the 125th person, thinking that the baby would be born by the time the paperwork went through. The baby was not born for two weeks, effectively rendering the incorporation void. However, Minnesota and the Secretary of State opted not to redo the entire filing process. Thus, the Village of Chickamaw Beach was born; its name was taken from the Ojibwe word meaning "on the shore." The word 'Beach' was added because of its location on the beaches of Norway Lake. As many as 148 people lived in town, according to the 2000 Census.

EAST GULL LAKE, MN
POPULATION: 986 – CITY 342 OF 856 (6-19-25)
A group of twelve burial mounds dating from 800 B.C. to 200, and from 500 to 900, were discovered in the East Gull Lake region and added to the National Register of Historic Places on May 7, 1973, making them the first such examples of life in what is now a resort area near Brainerd and Baxter. East Gull Lake township was named for its location on Gull Lake, one of seven lakes of that name in Minnesota. This particular Gull Lake is by far the largest in the state and home to nearly twenty resorts and several golf courses, two of which are The Classic at Madden's and Cragun's Resort. Citizens of the area filed to incorporate as a municipality in 1947, which has since turned into a recreational and vacation hub for some celebrities, including Bret Hedican, an NHL player from 1991 to 2009 and a two-time participant in the Olympics, and his wife, Kristi Yamaguchi, the 1992 Olympic gold-medalist champion in ladies' singles figure skating.

FEDERAL DAM, MN
POPULATION: 123 – CITY 411 OF 856 (7-17-25)
The construction of a dam in 1882 by the Army Corps of Engineers (as part of the Mississippi Headwaters Reservoir Project) allowed downstream flour and lumber mills

to expect a steady flow of water at all times, but it also had unintended consequences. Many Ojibwe communities surrounding Leech Lake experienced elevated water levels and a myriad of problems, which led to a series of lawsuits against the federal government. Despite the issues the dam caused for Indigenous peoples, the new railroad division point established in 1910 for trains traveling between Thief River Falls, Minnesota, and Superior, Wisconsin, was aptly named Federal Dam. The arrival of the Soo Line provided the town with the necessary resources to grow and facilitate its incorporation. Three hundred thirty-two people lived in town in the 1920s, and from 1910 to 1994, it had a post office. Most of its early business focused on leasing land on the lake to boat launch services and docks. Starting on July 16, 1955, and extending through the end of the month, the "Leech Lake Muskie Rampage" took the world by storm when over 163 fish ranging from 18 to 421.5 pounds were angled out of Leech Lake. After the event, Federal Dam and Leech Lake were crowned as being the "Muskie Capital of the World."

HACKENSACK, MN
POPULATION: 294 – CITY 347 OF 856 (6-19-25)

The hometown of Paul Bunyan's Sweetheart, Lucette Diana Kensack, came to fame in the 1950s when the wooden sculpture Lucette was claimed to have started dating the logger folk hero. Standing 17 feet tall, Lucette was born on an Iowa farm but was sent to the northern reaches of Minnesota to help her aunt and uncle in the great forests of the North. Before she arrived, her family commissioned the great Paul Bunyan to build her a home, for which he gathered all the materials with a single swoop of his mighty axe. He ran into Lucette several weeks later in the woods, and after dating for some time, the two were married on June 8, 1838. The charming story was the brainchild of local businessman Doad Schroeder, who built the first statue in the early 1950s. She was decapitated by a windstorm in 1991. While a new fiberglass statue was being built, the story was spread far and wide that she was giving birth to a son: Paul Bunyan Jr. The much smaller lumberjack stands proudly at Hackensack's City Hall. Lothrop was the first name for the settlement in the area, located a few miles north of modern-day Hackensack; James Curo operated a general store, grocery store, and post office at the site. More settlers arrived throughout the 1880s, but because of the lack of a railroad, Lothrop remained unincorporated, and its buildings and residents were dispersed. A new settlement called Hackensack, named by Bye Bartlett and Curo for their hometown of Hackensack, New Jersey, was platted in 1902 with the arrival of the Minnesota and International (later the Northern Pacific) Railroad. Stores, hotels, a meat market, a bank, a hospital, and even the Royal Ice Cream Parlor were among the early businesses. In 1936, the Works Progress Administration completed the Hackensack Conservation Building, which was used by the community for various purposes. A 0.3-mile stretch of the Widow Lake segment of the Pine River to Woman Lake and Longville Stagecoach Road, used from 1891 to 1930, still exists today as one of two Hackensack locations on the National Register (albeit the latter is not accessible to the public).

Restaurant Recommendation:
Big Dipper
113 MN-371
Hackensack, MN 56452

LAKE SHORE, MN
POPULATION: 1,056 – CITY 343 OF 856 (6-19-25)
Lake Shore is another one of Cass County's fairly recently incorporated municipalities, having only attained the status on March 19, 1947. The resort city on the northwestern shore of Gull Lake dates back to the time when the Sioux, their rivals among the Ojibwe, and fur trappers dominated the land, but its first significant development came in 1880. Charles Alfred Pillsbury, the inventor of the finest flour in the world, "Pillsbury's Best," built a sawmill in the vicinity around then. By the end of the decade, a narrow-gauge railroad was established to move the vast amounts of white pine and timber from the area; it was later replaced by the Northern Pacific Railroad, which extended a line just north of Gull Lake. Logging subsided as forests were depleted, and resort tourism became the new focus for those living in the area. Between the Great Depression and World War II, as many as thirty-five resorts had opened. Bar Harbor was a famous nightclub, and the Sherwood Forest Lodge Complex (built in 1929 and still in existence today) and its 20-plus cabins were just two of these havens for lake-loving vacationers. It was during this resort boom era that residents decided that the organization of a formal village in 1930 and incorporation as a municipality in 1947 were finally warranted. Most of the shoreline of Lake Shore has since been heavily developed from resorts into privately owned homes. In 2010, it surpassed one thousand permanent residents for the first time.

LONGVILLE, MN
POPULATION: 153 – CITY 348 OF 856 (6-20-25)
Like many other cities in this part of Cass County, Longville was among the crowd that did not seek incorporation until well after the first settlers arrived in the area in the 19th century. Named for its founder, Jim Long, and incorporated on March 1, 1941, the Longville Post Office dates back to 1904. It was then that the logging industry began to pick up in the area, as did fishing on Girl Lake (Boy River) and the surrounding bodies of water. Long Lake, to the north of town, reportedly reaches a depth of nearly 110 feet at its deepest point, a characteristic trait of many area lakes. Churches, a bank, and stores have been opened and closed over the decades. Still, Longville is known more for one event than any of its businesses or resorts: turtle racing. In the summer months, the "Turtle Racing Capital of the World," much like the towns of Perham and Nisswa in other counties, brings people together to watch turtles "race" down the closed-off highway. A heartwarming tribute to another animal in town, Bruno, the Chesapeake-Lab mix, was dedicated in 2015 for the love and affection he would show townspeople every day for years. From 2004 to 2018, the pup would journey four miles down Highway 84 to visit the shopkeepers (or perhaps to reap the benefits of ice cream and meat they would give him) before returning home before nightfall. Levi LaVallee, a snowmobile racer who won seven Winter X Games medals between 2004 and 2014 in various events, has ties to Longville.

PILLAGER, MN ☆
POPULATION: 507 – CITY 341 OF 856 (6-19-25)
"Pillager" refers to the same thing as the Ojibwe's *Makandwewininiwag*, a historical band of the Chippewa who initially lived near the headwaters of the Mississippi River. The Ojibwe word means "pillaging men," a reference to their invasion of the Sioux's lands as they drove their rivals further south. When it came time to establish a post office in this region of modern-day Cass County in 1886, the name was adopted by both the post office and the Northern Pacific Railroad. A general store, a hotel, and a blacksmith shop were among the first businesses to open in Pillager, but logging,

lumber yards, and sawmills comprised its most significant industry. Three historic places relevant to Native American history are listed on the National Register of Historic Places: the 1851 to 1869 Chippewa Agency Historic District, the 1850s Hole-in-the-Day Farmhouse Site, and four Rice Lake Earthlodge rings. The addresses of those three are restricted, but a fourth, Crow Wing State Park, is open to the public. Established in 1959, the park sits where Old Crow Wing, one of Minnesota's most significant towns in the 1850s and 1860s, had a population of approximately 700 people. Interpretive markers tell the story of the village. Visitors to the site also come for camping, boating, canoeing, hiking, snowmobiling, and cross-country skiing. Pillager was incorporated as a village on September 4, 1900.

PINE RIVER, MN
POPULATION: 911 – CITY 345 OF 856 (6-19-25)
The establishment of the Brainerd and Northern Minnesota Railway in the early 1890s led to the birth of Pine River, an important shipping point for the logging industry. Its founding is frequently attributed to George Angus Barclay and Ammarilla Grace Spracklin, the two of whom managed Barclay's Trading Post. Their store, also selected to be the site of the post office in 1877, supplied early foresters and farmers with the basic implements and supplies they needed to help turn Pine River into a bustling young city. Dozens of storefronts and hotels rose from the dirt on Barclay Avenue, as did a creamery, a grain elevator, and even a pickle factory along the railroad line. Just after the turn of the century, a large brick school edifice was constructed, and several additions were made in the decades to follow. Other popular points of interest included The Marlow Theatre and The Damsite Store, which once doubled as an A&W restaurant. The Brainerd and Northern Minnesota-Minnesota and International Railway (both of which were consolidated into the Northern Pacific Railroad System) Depot was built in 1895, fell into disrepair, and was restored to serve as a stop on the Paul Bunyan State Trail between Brainerd and Bemidji. In addition to the Cass County Fairgrounds, Pine River also has a visitor center with "Paul Bunyan's baby booties" and the giant footprints of the larger-than-life lumberjack. The footprints mark where Paul's giant boots once stood before a tornado in 2010 blew them away. Terry Baker, the only man in history to win a Heisman Trophy (1962, Oregon State) and play in the Final Four of the men's collegiate basketball tournament (1963), was born here on May 5, 1941. Baker was the first overall pick of the 1963 NFL Draft and was inducted into the College Football Hall of Fame in 1982.

REMER, MN
POPULATION: 391 – CITY 349 OF 856 (6-20-25)
The mythological creature known as Bigfoot has been spotted so many times in Remer that the town has decided to turn his frequent appearances into a celebration. Bigfoot Days is held each summer and features events such as cook-offs and races. Big Foot Gas & Gifts features exhibits and sells souvenirs relevant to the cultural icon. While the existence of Sasquatch has never been officially proven, Remer was once a vacation home for the infamous gangster Al Capone, who stayed in the 1912 McCleary Cabin during his holiday visits to the Land of 10,000 Lakes. The cabin was built within the first decade of Remer's existence. Founded in 1904, it was named for the brothers William P. and E. N. Remer, its first postmaster and the manager of the Reishus-Remer Land Company of Grand Rapids, respectively. A sawmill was erected to kick-start the local timber industry, and various stores opened to meet the needs of the new settlers. The Soo Line Railroad transported goods to and from town, which reached its peak population of 492 in 1960, a year after the railroad had terminated passenger rail service. Cafés, banks, garages, grocery stores, and a municipality-owned liquor

store were just a few of the businesses open at that time. While the railroad and its depot no longer serve as the hub for local activity, the circa-1910 depot has been preserved. The Remer District Ranger Station of the United States Forest Service, active from 1936 to 1972, was built by the CCC and helped oversee the management of Chippewa National Forest. A giant ten-foot-tall eagle, possibly the Largest Eagle Statue in the World, pays tribute to area veterans, as well as the National Forest's distinction of being the nesting place of more bald eagles in one area than anywhere else in the lower United States.

WALKER, MN ★
POPULATION: 966 – CITY 408 OF 856 (7-16-25)
With a full-time population of less than one thousand people, those looking at Walker from a statistical perspective alone might expect to find a quiet town nestled in the heart of woodsy Central Minnesota. In reality, the judicial seat of Cass County has long been an important hub of trade, logging, and tourism. There were bands of the Dakota-Sioux and the Ojibwe, and an Indian mission that sought to convert them to Christianity. Thomas Barlow Walker arrived in Minnesota in 1862. Six years later, he purchased a parcel of land with a dense pine forest and platted it on behalf of the Leech Lake Land Company and the St. Paul and Duluth Railway. Until 1896, the area was not more than just forests and camps of men and companies set up to cut them. Patrick McGarry decided that it was time to establish a townsite. Although it was named in honor of Mr. Walker, he took his business to Akeley because his wife objected to the "dirtiness" of Walker's bars and brothels. Four other logging companies, instead, spurred the newly incorporated town of Park Rapids and Leech Lake Railroad towards prosperity. The Great Northern took over the line by 1899, and the Minnesota and International (Northern Pacific) and the Brainerd & Northern Minnesota lines followed shortly thereafter. Walker had its fair share of stores, churches, and schools; Fort Walker, manned by Lieutenant A. B. Downworth circa 1900; and even later still (in 1923), a creamery. But, in 1907, it welcomed the Ah-Gwah-Ching Center. Curing tuberculosis was the primary goal of The Minnesota State Sanatorium for Consumptives (an alternative name for the facility), which strived to do so for nearly 14,000 patients until it was turned into a psychiatric nursing home in 1962. Eventually, a lack of patients forced the center to close in 2008, and by the end of 2010, the complex had been demolished. A pair of other noted buildings were built not long after (in terms of Walker's general history) the hospital: the first-class Chase Hotel in 1922 and a Conservation Building erected between 1934-36 as a municipal facility with a visitor center, museum, rock garden, and office space used by New Deal program employees and organizations. At the Cass County Museum, thirteen bronze statues stand in a circular formation, representing six different eras of human history in northern Minnesota. The Northland Lodge, located a few miles northeast of Walker proper, dubs itself "Paul Bunyan's Guest House" due to one of its rental cabins' tree-stump shape and the giant ax adjacent to it, supposedly one used by Bunyan to clear the forests of the area. Three noteworthy Walkerites include Berit Dybing, an indie-pop singer-songwriter of TikTok fame; Jimmy Darts, another TikToker with millions of TikTok followers and YouTube subscribers; and Mary Welsh Hemingway, a journalist and the fourth wife of Ernest Hemingway, the 1954 Nobel Prize in Literature winner.

Restaurant Recommendation:
Bayside Bar & Grill
412 Minnesota Ave W
Walker, MN 56484

Motley is only partially located in Cass County (see Morrison County).

Unincorporated/Ghost Towns: Ah-gwah-ching, Brevik, Bridgeman, Casino, Ellis, Esterdy, Graff, Inguadona, Leader, Leech Lake, Mae, Mildred, Onigum, Oshawa, Outing, Pontoria, Raboin, Ryan Village, Schley, Sylvan, Tobique, Wabedo, Whipholt, Wilkinson

National Register of Historic Places:
Bena: Winnibigoshish Lake Dam, Winnibigoshish Resort
Cass Lake: Great Northern Railway Company Bridge, South Pike Bay Site, Supervisor's Office Headquarters
East Gull Lake: Gull Lake Mounds Site
Hackensack: Hackensack Conservation Building
Lake Shore: Sherwood Forest Lodge Complex
Leech Lake Indian Reservation: Battle Point (21CA12)
Pillager: Crow Wing State Park,
Pine River: Brainerd & Northern Minnesota-Minnesota & International Railway Depot
Remer: Soo Line Depot, United Forest Service, Remer District Ranger Station
Walker: Chase Hotel, Conservation Building

Golf Courses:
Cragun's Legacy Courses – Dutch 27, Resort (East Gull Lake, MN)
Cragun's Legacy Courses – Lehman 18, Resort (East Gull Lake, MN)
Cragun's Legacy Courses – NICE9, Resort (East Gull Lake, MN)
Long Bow Golf Club, Daily Fee (Walker, MN)
Sandtrap Golf Course, Daily Fee (Cass Lake, MN)
Tianna Country Club, Daily Fee (Walker, MN)

Breweries/Wineries/Distilleries:
Portage Brewing Company (Walker, MN)
Rendezvous Brewing (Hackensack, MN)

Town Celebrations:
Back to Hack, Hackensack, MN (Martin Luther King Jr. Weekend)
Bigfoot Days, Remer, MN (2nd Weekend in July)
Cornfest, Backus, MN (2nd Weekend in August)
Hackensack Chainsaw Event, Hackensack, MN (Last Weekend in September)
Hobo Day, Boy River, MN (Saturday of Labor Day Weekend)
Longville Turtle Races, Longville, MN (Summertime; Wednesday Afternoons)
Pine River Summerfest, Pine River, MN (Last Saturday in June)
Pine River Wefelmeyer Picklefest, Pine River, MN (3rd Weekend in August)
Star Spangled Celebration, Longville, MN (4th of July)
Sweetheart Days, Hackensack, MN (2nd Wednesday in July through next Tuesday)

CHIPPEWA COUNTY
EST. 1870 - POPULATION: 12,598

First organized in March 1868, and reorganized two years later after separating from Swift County, Chippewa County was named after its Chippewa River, which, in turn, was named after the Ojibwe people.

CLARA CITY, MN
POPULATION: 1,423 – CITY 116 OF 856 (3-29-25)

Platted on the Willmar & Sioux Falls Railway in 1887-88, Clara City was named in honor of Clara Koch, the wife of land speculator Theodore F. Koch. He and Martin W. Prins enticed the railroad to build through their property with the promise of free right-of-way land if the railroad company agreed to locate a townsite on it. They obliged, and thus, the newest Chippewa County town of Clara City was born. A depot, a water tank, and a windmill were among the first structures to be erected. In 1888, Jacob Meyering began hosting a post office in his store. When the "Empire Builder" James J. Hill and his Great Northern Railroad acquired the railroad line, its interstate connection brought its growth to new heights. Clara City was incorporated on September 2, 1891, and in 1900, it had an inaugural Census population of 465. Facilities on the tracks included three elevators, a sawmill, a lumber shed, a lumber office, two coal sheds, stockyards, and an implement shed. On the northern part of the tracks, a commercial district developed. Visitors would have counted at least three hotels, a bank, two blacksmith shops, a feed mill, a creamery, a print office, and two liveries, in addition to a post office, a jail, a town hall, a school, a fire department, a German Catholic church, an American Reformed church, a German Reformed church, and a German Lutheran church. A tow mill on Hawk Creek was its southernmost point of interest then, on the land of C. B. Enkema. In the 1980s, Clara City reached its highest population of 1,574; as of the 2020s, it still has four active churches within its city limits, just as it did a century ago.

MAYNARD, MN
POPULATION: 319 – CITY 117 OF 856 (3-29-25)
John M. Spicer, superintendent of the Willmar & Sioux Falls division of the Great Northern Railroad, named Maynard for his brother-in-law, A. K. Maynard. The Spicer Land Company surveyed the townsite on J. V. H. Bailey and L. D. Ruddock's land in 1887, and two years later, in 1889, it acquired its post office. Business lines varied in size and importance. In addition to the typical blacksmith shops, livery barns, hotels, professional offices, and general, hardware, and grocery stores that one would have expected to find in any community of that era, Maynard also had plenty of unique establishments. Five grain elevators stood over the railroad tracks, like sentinels on the prairie. A lumberyard, lime and cement works, and a flour mill were clustered together next to the Scandinavian Lutheran church. A sawmill and a feed mill were located on the southwestmost section of the town plat, and an opera house, town hall, and jail were located on Sherman Avenue. Public School No. 30 was on a plot of land in Maynard's northwestmost corner. It was incorporated as a village on January 8, 1897. Throughout the 1940s, Maynard's population reached a peak of 580 before declining in subsequent decades. Of all its early establishments, its most historically intact is the Maynard State Bank, which was listed on the National Register of Historic Places on May 29, 2018.

MILAN, MN
POPULATION: 428 – CITY 195 OF 856 (4-16-25)
"Norwegian Capital U.S.A." may be limited to only a couple of square blocks of businesses, but visitors to the primarily Norwegian-settled hamlet are surprised to find its gorgeous historic murals, a replica of the Liberty Bell, and a wood-carved statue that alludes to its earliest visitors: the Vikings. The artwork appropriately depicts a classical Viking, a real-life version of the man who left behind a 13th-century iron hatchet discovered a few miles east of the townsite in 1875. Settlers had only arrived in Kragero Township a few years prior, in 1868. In 1879, the Hastings & Dakota Railway located Milan village and named it after Milan, Italy. An alternate tale suggests that Milan originated in a conversation between two early homesteaders arguing over land ownership, both claiming it was "my land." A post office was organized that year at the Thorbjorn Anderson Department Store. The townsite was platted in 1880, and by 1882, there was a second general store, a grain warehouse, and a blacksmith shop.

Thorbjorn sold his store to A. Anderson at a later date, and the second Anderson expanded it to the point that he began calling it the largest and best-stocked store between Minneapolis, Minnesota, and Aberdeen, South Dakota. From its 1880 platting, when it had 28 people, to 1900, the population had grown to 396, thanks to the Chicago, Milwaukee & St. Paul Railroad. By 1905, it had grown to include five grain elevators, three restaurants, a feed mill, a creamery, a newspaper, a bank, a hotel, and several other businesses. The public school was in the western part of Milan, and the Norwegian Lutheran Church was its place of worship. It first held services in 1872 at James Olson's home, with Reverend L. Markus as the minister. Milan had as many as 624 residents in the 1940s and was the final destination in Robert Bly's poem *Driving Toward the Lac qui Parle River*. One interesting point of note is the Norwegian Stabbur House east of Milan on Hwy 40. It was built in Norway circa 1987 by Halvard Pettersen to replicate the traditional storage shed/sleeping quarters found throughout his country, then shipped to Minnesota and reassembled on the farm.

MONTEVIDEO, MN ★☆
POPULATION: 5,398 – CITY 196 OF 856 (4-17-25)

It would have been surprising if settlers had not stumbled upon the fertile valley between the confluence of the Minnesota and Chippewa Rivers, as it is, by all accounts, a perfect situation for a town to grow upon. The milling and agricultural center was platted on May 25, 1870, and named by Cornelius J. Nelson of New York. He was one of the earliest settlers and an essential figure in Montevideo's early development. Montevideo is Latin for "from the mountain, I see," a reference to the beautiful valleys visible from the higher points in that vicinity. The name was first given to Uruguay's capital, and Nelson later recalled it when discussions were underway over what to call the new townsite. As a result of Nelson's name choice, the South American and Minnesota cities have become sister cities. In 1905, the mayor of each town sent their nation's flag to one another as a symbol of friendship, and forty-four years later, Uruguay presented a 2,000-pound bronze statue of José Artigas, the father of Uruguayan Independence, to the community. While Montevideo has since become a melting pot of nationalities with the recent arrival of many Latino and Micronesian families, the first ethnic groups to arrive were primarily Norwegian, Swedish, Dutch, Irish, and German. The groups banded together to establish businesses and build religious and educational facilities. By the end of 1870, they had whisked away the county seat title from the now non-existent Chippewa City. It had been located just across the Chippewa River opposite Montevideo. Residents of that community moved over the blacksmith shop, mill, drug store, and general stores. Montevideo made substantial strides in its growth as a division headquarters for the Chicago, Milwaukee & St. Paul Railroad. An engine house kept several railroad families in the area, bringing many crews and officials on business trips. According to a 1900 North West Publishing Company map, Montevideo at that time had four grain elevators, a flour mill, the Montevideo Creamery Association, the C. Betcher Lumber Company, an I.O.O.F. Hall, city hall, courthouse, public school, grounds and a racetrack for the Chippewa County Driving Park & Fair Association, and churches for the Baptists, Lutherans, Congregationalists, Methodist Episcopalians, Episcopalians, and Roman Catholics. The decade following this map saw the construction of its four most historic structures, all of which are now listed on the National Register: the Chippewa County Bank, built in 1900 as Montevideo's first bank in the Romanesque Revival style; the 1901 Chicago, Milwaukee & St. Paul Depot that now serves as a community museum; a 1906 Carnegie Library, and the Charles H. Budd House, built in 1909 for a prominent local banker and politician. Budd was famous in his own right, but Montevideo also has ties to Wayne Brabender, named one of FIBA's 50 Greatest

Players in 1991 for his twenty-eight combined championship wins across the Spanish League, Spanish Cup, FIBA Intercontinental Cup, and Euroleague leagues and competitions; Paul Gruchow, an author noted for his work on supporting rural communities, particularly those in Chippewa County; Molly Schuyler, a professional eater with All Pro Eating, Emily Temple-Wood, a prominent board member of Wikimedia DC known for her work on expanding articles on women scientists on Wikipedia, and David Minge, a Member of the U.S. House of Representatives from Minnesota between January 1993 and January 2001.

Restaurant Recommendation:
Dairy Freeze
1307 Black Oak Ave
Montevideo, MN 56265

WATSON, MN
POPULATION: 182 – CITY 194 OF 856 (4-16-25)

Chippewa County's oldest history can be found near Watson, Minnesota, at Fort Renville and the Lac qui Parle Mission. The fort, first called First Adam, was the first of the two establishments. The Columbia Fur Company used it as a trading post on the Lac qui Parle, which was later expanded in 1939 when the Works Progress Administration dammed the Minnesota River. The Minnesota Historical Society discovered the foundations of four buildings and a watchtower in the 1960s, but the site itself is not open to the public. Visitors can, however, view the reconstructed version of the Lac qui Parle Mission, which began in June 1835 under the watchful eye of Thomas Smith Williamson and Alexander Huggins. It was abandoned in 1854 after missionaries spent twenty years teaching the faith to the local bands of Sioux. The WPA rebuilt the mission in 1942, not long after completing its dam project. The development of the town closest to these historic sites, Myers, began in August 1879, when the Chicago, Milwaukee & St. Paul Railroad Company platted a townsite. Rasmus Adamson was its first permanent resident and business owner; he was a blacksmith. It was renamed Watson for the Watson Farmers Elevator, which, according to the Minnesota Historical Society, may have been the first cooperative elevator in the United States when it was built in 1886. Unfortunately, the structure was burned down in 1993 by the Watson Fire Department, which deemed it structurally unsound. At the turn of the century, Watson also had four elevators, a depot, two lumber sheds, a stockyard, a hotel, an implement tool business, a town hall, three schools, a post office (est. 1879), and some storefronts. It was incorporated as a village on May 24, 1883. Lac qui Parle State Park, home to the aforementioned fort and mission sites, welcomes so many thousands of Canadian geese and waterfowl each year that Watson was dubbed "The Goose Capital of the USA."

Granite Falls is only partially located in Chippewa County (see Yellow Medicine County)

Unincorporated/Ghost Towns: Asbury, Big Bend City, Bunde, Churchill, Gluek, Gracelock, Hagan, Louriston, Wegdahl

National Register of Historic Places:
Granite Falls: Julian A. Weaver House, Olof Swensson Farmstead
Maynard: Maynard State Bank
Montevideo: Charles H. Budd House, Chicago, Milwaukee & St. Paul Depot, Chippewa County Bank, Lac qui Parle Mission Archeological Historic District, Montevideo Carnegie Library
Watson: Henry Gippe Farmstead

Golf Courses:
River Crest Public Golf Course, Daily Fee (Montevideo, MN)

Breweries/Wineries/Distilleries:
Talking Waters Brewing Company (Montevideo, MN)

CHISAGO COUNTY
EST. 1851 - POPULATION: 56,621

Chisago County is named after Chisago Lake, which was originally spelled "Ki-chi-Saga." *Kichi* means 'large', and *saga* means 'lovely' in the Ojibwe language.

CENTER CITY, MN ★
POPULATION: 629 – CITY 577 OF 856 (9-2-25)
At the heart of Chisago County lies Center City, the first permanent Swedish settlement in the State of Minnesota. First spelled "Centre City" and named for its central location between Chisago City and Taylors Falls, Andes Swenson established the community in 1851 and oversaw its platting in May 1857. The following year, the post office was established. It was renamed Chisago Lake from 1863 to 1877, then Centre City until 1893, when the spelling of "Center" was Americanized. During this period, a couple of stores, public and private schools, and churches, such as the Chisago Lake Swedish Evangelical Lutheran Church, came into being. A courthouse was erected early on after the village was dubbed the Chisago County judicial seat in 1875; the Northern Pacific Railroad arrived shortly thereafter in 1881. A collection of nineteen historic Swedish residences and the church has been preserved on the National Register of Historic Places since 1980. The church was used for the wedding scene of the 1993 comedy *Grumpy Old Men*. In addition to the church, the Sister City of Hassela, Sweden, was long known for the Cheese-N-Bison Munchables Store with its giant mouse and bison statue and herd. Center City also serves as the setting for Vilhelm Moberg's series of four novels, starting with *The Emigrants*, published between 1949 and 1959, and adapted into Swedish films in the early 1970s.

CHISAGO CITY, MN
POPULATION: 5,558 – CITY 579 OF 856 (9-2-25)
With almost 4,500 lake acres, it's no surprise the Ojibwe named the region *Chisago*, meaning "large" and "beautiful." One of the largest lakes is Chisago Lake, on which the town of Chisago City was founded in May 1857 by Swedish immigrant Anders Swenson, and platted on June 20, 1857, by Isaac Bernheimer. The decision to lay out the townsite only came after several dozen Swedes from Krontobeg County, Sweden, came to call the region home. Initially, it included 58 blocks of plats between Green Lake and Chisago Lake, but it was reduced to 15 blocks only a year later. A Swedish Lutheran Church was established at its center, as were homes and businesses. When the St. Paul & Duluth branch of the Northern Pacific Railroad bypassed the original town in 1880, a new plat was laid out on October 17, 1882, again by Isaac Bernheimer. A steam stave factory was its prized business. It is now the southwesternmost part of Chisago City's modern commercial district. Deer Garden was another nearby hamlet that was incorporated into Chisago City proper after August 1906, when Chisago City was incorporated. The city has experienced double-digit population growth in every decade except the 1920s and the 1950s; in recent years, it became a sister city of Algutsboda, Sweden.

HARRIS, MN
POPULATION: 1,111 – CITY 583 OF 856 (9-2-25)
Potatoes and the Harris Starch Factory, built in 1904 by Mr. Began, served as the base cash crop for Harris's economy from 1880 to 1930. Settlers arrived much earlier in 1873, when the town was platted and named in honor of Philip S. Harris of the St. Paul and Duluth Railroad Company. A post office bearing that name entered service the following year. In the 1880s, Harris was incorporated, when two hotels, a livery, a Village Hall, a church, a school, and several storefronts were in operation. Louis LeRoy Griggs built the first flour mill on his farm on Goose Creek, just to the northwest of town. The Harris & Fish Lake Shipping Association started to move livestock–as many as three train carloads at a time–and over the years, thousands of heads of cattle were shipped to provide a slight economic boost to local farmers. The Sayer House, known locally as the George Flanders House, was built circa 1875 in the Italianate style and added to the National Register of Historic Places in 1980. Lonnie Hammargren, the 31st Lieutenant Governor of Nevada from Jan. 1995 to Jan. 1999, hails from Harris.

LINDSTRÖM, MN
POPULATION: 4,888 – CITY 578 OF 856 (9-2-25)
America's Little Sweden, best known for its Swedish coffee-pot water tower, is Lindström, Minnesota. Settled primarily by the Swedes and a handful of Norwegians, Daniel Lindstrom selected the site in 1853 as the home for his family. He was attracted by the area's many lakes, which provided ample water and food resources for his kin, and other settlers arrived around the same time. Two of these men were Daniel's half-brother, Joris Per Anderson, and Eric Norelius, whose personal journals were used to formulate much of Vilhelm Moberg's famous novel series, *The Emigrants*. When Lindstrom sold the majority of his farm in 1878 in anticipation of a new Northern Pacific Railroad (then the St. Paul and Duluth), Lindstrom's development was greatly expedited; it was platted in 1880, and the post office was opened that same year. The city was incorporated on August 28, 1894. Within another ten years, it had two hotels, a grain elevator, a flour mill, and three newspapers, one of which was entirely printed in Swedish. Many tourists and recreationists flocked to the lakes over the decades, and in 1948, an annual local water carnival began, which has since been renamed Karl Oskar Days. The King and Queen of Sweden visited the city in 1996, at which point the official spelling of the town was changed from Lindstrom to Lindström. No other city in the state has an official umlaut (the two little dots above the ö in the city's name) in its name that is required by state law to be printed on official Minnesota Department of Transportation city limit signs. Technically, umlauts are used only in German and Hungary, and the letter ö is one of three additional letters in Swedish that do not exist in English. Similar to its neighboring Chisago County communities, Lindström has a sister city in Sweden: Tingsryd. A "sister city" relationship is a social agreement between two geographic entities to promote each other's cultures or commercial interests. Three local homes, an 1879 Italianate formerly owned by Gustaf Anderson (now home to the locally famous Gustaf's on Main Eatery, known for its authentic Swedish meatballs and healthy homemade dishes), Frank A. Larson's 1898 home, and the 1905 Charles A. Victor house, are located on the National Register of Historic Places.

Restaurant Recommendation:
Gustaf's On Main Eatery
13045 Lake Blvd
Lindstrom, MN 55045

NORTH BRANCH, MN
POPULATION: 10,787 – CITY 582 OF 856 (9-2-25)

The name "North Branch" was given to this town because of its location on the north branch of the Sunrise River. The area began as a township in 1861, and a village was platted in January 1870 under the same name. John Elmgren was the first permanent resident, here before even the building of G. M. Flanders's store in 1868, and the future home of the post office when it was organized in 1889. Development was strong during this time, as it had been before the turn of the century, when North Branch welcomed the St. Paul and Duluth Railroad. J. F. Swanson built a flour mill and saloon on the line in 1874, and three years later, Lem Quillan arrived with a circus act. He ended up adoring the town and its residents, and he stayed to open his own store and an early opera house. An 1888 plat map indicated the existence of two hotels, a blacksmith shop, School No. 32, and churches for the Congregationalists, Lutherans, and Methodist Episcopalians. The North Branch Milling Company, one of the community's largest businesses, arrived in 1899. North Branch was incorporated as a village on November 19, 1881. At thirty-six square miles, the village-township form of government covered a large swath of land until it was divided in 1901. One square mile of the township broke off into North Branch village, and the rest of the thirty-five square miles became Branch township. Years down the road, it too adopted the municipal village form of government, making North Branch village an enclave of Branch village. Talks of a merger began in 1974, when Minnesota required all incorporated municipalities to adopt the "city" title. Measures to consolidate the two entities failed in 1984, but ultimately passed in a second referendum in September 1994. On November 14, 1994, the two cities became The City of North Branch, now home to over 10,000 residents, according to the 2020 Census. In addition to being the hometown of the fictional character Tulip Olsen in Cartoon Network's sci-fi animated series *Infinity Train*, noteworthy folks with ties to North Branch are Becky Pearson, a professional golfer on the LPGA Tour who won the 1986 Chrysler-Plymouth Classic; Jon Lucivansky, an NFL official from 2009 to 2018; Maynard W. Tollberg, the namesake of the USS Tollberg United States Navy high-speed transport boat; Richard Warren Sears, the co-founder of the Sears, Roebuck and Co. chain of department stores, and Doug Mahnke, a comic book artist known for his work with DC Comics.

RUSH CITY, MN ☆
POPULATION: 3,228 – CITY 584 OF 856 (9-2-25)

A great wealth of bulrushes (wetland-like plants; primarily cattails) gave Rush City its name. Located just miles away from the St. Croix River, the village was surveyed and platted in January 1870 by Benjamin W. Brunson. Growth was rapid due to its location on the St. Paul and Duluth Railroad. By March 7, 1873, the town was incorporated. A post office had been in operation for three years. As a junction point on the railroad, where one line continued northward towards Duluth and the other as far east as Grantsburg, Wisconsin, extensive developments were in place within Rush City's first fifteen years of existence. An 1888 atlas points out church edifices for the Swedish Lutherans, German Lutherans, Episcopalians, Catholics, and a Missionary group. Closer to downtown were grain elevators, hotels, liveries, a printing office, and a roller mill, and just west of a Catholic church, an early brewery was extant. The Grant House hotel, which opened eight years after the directory's creation, has remained, since 1896, one of the city's most historically intact points of interest. A stunning 1899 Queen Anne designed by Augustus F. Gauger and owned by early entrepreneur J. C. Carlson is another local historic landmark. Until the record was broken in 1996 at Tower, the lowest temperature in Minnesota history, -59°F, documented at Pokegama Dam, had stood since February 16, 1903. In February 2000, the Rush City Correctional Facility was completed as one of several state prisons on the far eastern side of the state. Clayton Tonnemaker, a College Football Hall of Fame member and a 1953 Pro Bowl center and linebacker with the Green Bay Packers, and Ruth Duccini, the last-surviving Munchkin from the 1939 musical fantasy film *The Wizard of Oz*, have connections to Rush City. A one-ton Walleye statue on Rush Lake Road, allegedly caught by the great lumberjack folk hero Paul Bunyan, sits (swims?) tall as the "World's Largest Walleye" in the "Walleye Capital of the World," two of several such claims made throughout North Dakota and Minnesota.

SHAFER, MN
POPULATION: 1,142 – CITY 576 OF 856 (9-2-25)
Early Shafer enjoyed the fruits of being on the railroad line between Taylor's Falls and the Twin Cities, a luxury brought to early Swedish settlers who came here as early as 1853. Colonists initially called their town Taylor's Falls, but it was renamed Shafer in 1873 in honor of local farmer Jacob Shafer. Why the village was named in his honor is a story mostly shrouded in mystery, as he had lived in the area for only a quarter-century before disappearing. The post office was established in 1881, and several early firms, like a creamery, a feed mill, a general store, automobile dealerships, saloons, and restaurants, made up the early business interests of the early 20th century. Shafer was formally incorporated on March 14, 1922. From 2000 to 2010, the population grew by 204.7% from 343 people to 1,045.

STACY, MN
POPULATION: 1,703 – CITY 581 OF 856 (9-2-25)
Dr. Stacy B. Collins, a very early resident of Stacy, is the city's namesake. The first settlers of the St. Paul and Duluth Railroad town came in 1870. After enough of them had accumulated, the United States Postal Service authorized the establishment of the Stacy post office in 1873. Two years later, the townsite was laid out, and on April 13, 1923, it was incorporated. Minimal businesses and infrastructure were in place until the 1970s, when Stacy was targeted for development as a distant Twin Cities suburb. Between 1970 and 1980, the population grew from 278 to 996 people, and as of the 2020 Census, that number had expanded to 1,703. Effective December 29, 2023, the City of Stacy annexed the entirety of Lent Township, significantly expanding its boundaries. The 2021 International Federation of Arm Wrestling world champion, Jeff Dabe, and Hunter Miska, a goaltender who has appeared in the American and National Hockey Leagues, are two noteworthy individuals from the Stacy area.

TAYLORS FALLS, MN
POPULATION: 1,055 – CITY 575 OF 856 (9-2-25)
Best known for its picturesque Dalles on the St. Croix River, the village of Taylor's Falls was located at the head of these Dalles and served as an early gateway for Swedish settlers entering Minnesota. Once the Chisago County seat (until that honor was removed to Chisago City in 1865), it was named for Jesse Taylor, who arrived in 1838. He sold his claim to Joshua L. Taylor in 1846, and five years later, the town was finally platted. Until that point, it had been called Baker's Falls, then Taylor Place, and later still, Taylor's Falls. The falls were far more prevalent in the early days thanks to a large rock that shifted the current, creating a noticeable waterfall. Nathan C. D. Taylor served as postmaster, and thereafter, a significant influx of Swedish families began arriving on April 23, 1851. Schools, churches, and businesses were plentiful. Storefronts and shops lined the streets of a localized commercial district, and men and

women helped operate everything from blacksmith shops to milliners. What brought Taylor's Falls its first glimpse of fame was its logging industry, sparked by the 1886 St. Croix River log jam, which drew reporters and tourists from around the country. Robert Davidson dynamited the Clam River dam due to its "interference with his meadow lands", leading to an increase in the St. Croix River. As a result, dams on the Kettle and Snake Rivers had to be opened to release excess water. Rainstorms happened to come in at the same time, and in a perfect storm, logs that had been resting on the dry riverbed of the St. Croix began to float and move downstream in enormous numbers. Over 125 million board feet of pine logs jammed up over a two-mile stretch, and four hundred men were employed to clear the logs sent downstream by over one hundred milling companies from upstream Minnesota and Wisconsin communities. Dynamite was used as a last resort when other measures to clear the jam failed, and after spending the entire summer fixing the jam, most of the cleanup was done by that fall. The $250,000 Nevers Dam was completed in 1890, eleven miles upstream from St. Croix Falls, Wisconsin, and no log jam was ever reported again. Five years after the dam's construction, Interstate Park was jointly founded by Minnesota and Wisconsin to help preserve the Dalles of the St. Croix River and the region's glacial potholes. A historic neighborhood district of twenty-eight properties called the Angel Hill District was formed circa April 1972 to help preserve a collection of New England-style Greek Revival homes, including the stately historic home museum of W.H.C. Folsom. A pair of other homes, the John Daubney and the Munch-Roos; the Taylor Falls Public Library; Minnesota's oldest schoolhouse, built in 1852; the 1861 United Methodist Church, the second oldest operating church in Minnesota, and WPA/New Deal properties at Interstate State Park are some of the sites that make up the town's rich ongoing history. The Drive In restaurant, a 1950s-style drive-in, features a rotating Frostop Root Beer mug that draws visitors from MN-95 and US-8. In Vilhelm Moberg's famed Swedish novel *The Emigrants*, Taylors Falls is the home of the main characters.

Restaurant Recommendation:
The Drive In Restaurant
572 Bench St
Taylors Falls, MN 55084

WYOMING, MN
POPULATION: 8,032 – CITY 580 OF 856 (9-2-25)
Not to be confused with "the Cowboy State" out west, this stately town was platted in 1869 when the St. Paul and Duluth Railroad was built through the vicinity. A post office named Wyoming, a word derived from the Delaware language meaning "large plains" or "extensive meadows," began in 1856. Swedish settlers had moved in many years earlier and enjoyed the benefits of the West Branch of the Sunrise River to water their crops and livestock. Stores and hotels were already in existence even before a second railroad line was built in 1879, connecting Wyoming with Taylors Falls. By 1888, the Hotel Wyoming House, a joint post office and store, a second general store, and Catholic and Methodist Episcopal churches were the most significant pieces of infrastructure on the townsite. A patent medicine manufacturer also arrived later. Wyoming's early years were very similar to those of other railroad towns throughout Minnesota for an extended period, until it became the subject of a June 1933 kidnapping situation. William Hamm of Hamm's Brewing, a brewery based in Saint Paul, Minnesota, was the victim. He was taken by the Barker-Karpis gang and only released after a $100,000 payment (the equivalent of $2.48 million in 2025) was made. At Lenfer Automotive & Transmission, tourists can find a replica of Tow Mater and Sheriff from the Pixar movie *Cars* (2006). Until the late 1970s, Wyoming's population

remained under one thousand persons until Interstate-35 was completed, connecting it to the Minneapolis-Saint Paul metropolitan area.

Unincorporated/Ghost Towns: Almelund, Franconia, Palmdale, Rush Point, Stark, Sunrise

National Register of Historic Places:
Amador Township: Point Douglas to Superior Military Road: Deer Creek Section
Center City: Center City Historic District
Chisago Lake Township: Moody Barn
Franconia: Franconia Historic District, Paul Munch House
Harris: Sayer House
Lindström: Charles A. Victor House, Frank A. Larson House, Gustaf Anderson House
Rush City: J.C. Carlson House, Grant House
Taylors Falls: Angel's Hill Historic District, Interstate State Park CCC/WPA/Rustic Style Campground, Interstate State Park WPA/Rustic Style Historic District, John Daubney House, Munch-Roos House, Taylors Falls Public Library

Golf Courses:
Bulrush Golf Club, Daily Fee (Rush City, MN)
Chisago Lakes Golf Course, Daily Fee (Lindstrom, MN)
Falcon Ridge Golf Course – Executive 9, Daily Fee (Stacy, MN)
Falcon Ridge Golf Course, Daily Fee (Stacy, MN)
North Branch Golf Course, Municipal (North Branch, MN)

Breweries/Wineries/Distilleries:
James Perry Vineyards (Rush City, MN)
North Folk Winery (Harris, MN)
Uncommon Loon Brewing Company (Chisago City, MN)
Wild Mountain Winery (Taylors Falls, MN)
WineHaven Winery (Chisago City, MN)

Town Celebrations:
Almelund Threshing Show, Almelund, MN (2nd Weekend in August)
Celebration of the Lakes, Lindstrom, MN (2nd Weekend in February)
Fika Festival, Lindstrom, MN (4th Weekend in September)
Karl Oskar Days, Lindstrom, MN (2nd Weekend of July)
MidSommar Festival, Lindstrom, MN (3rd Full Weekend in June)
Rockin' Rush City Car Show, Rush City, MN (3rd Saturday in August)

CLAY COUNTY
EST. 1862 - POPULATION: 65,318

Clay County is one of several counties in the United States that are named in honor of Henry Clay, the 9th United States Secretary of State. The county was initially known as Breckinridge County for John C. Breckinridge, until he joined the Confederate Army in March 1862.

BARNESVILLE, MN ☆
POPULATION: 2,759 – CITY 204 OF 856 (5-3-25)
Situated in the Red River Valley, Barnesville's fertile soils proved beneficial to immigrant farmers who came to grow wheat and potatoes (specifically Ohio seed potatoes, starting in 1908). Its agricultural-based economy took off when James J. Hill extended the Great Northern Railroad through the valley in 1877, three years after

George S. Barnes had established the village townsite. As well as being the town's first store owner, he founded the Northern Pacific Elevator Company, which worked with the railroad to erect grain elevators along the line between St. Paul, Minnesota, and Tacoma, Washington. Interestingly, his namesake community never boasted a line of the Northern Pacific, but the Great Northern did share part of its tracks with the St. Paul, Minneapolis & Manitoba Railroad (eventually a part of the Soo Line system). The town was formally platted in 1882 by Peter E. Thompson, although it briefly split into two sites–the other being New Barnesville, officially a village between 1886 and 1889–before the rival towns were reunited. There were Great Northern repair shops and a roundhouse until 1907, when they were moved to Devils Lake, North Dakota. At the turn of the century, Barnesville still retained numerous stores, a City Hall (which also served as a fire station and theater; listed on the National Register of Historic Places in May 1980), an Opera House (built in 1891), two breweries, five hotels, five churches, newspapers, theaters, and schools. A private school was the first institution to teach the community's youth starting in 1870, but a public school system was started shortly thereafter. In 1901, the progressive city became the first municipality to install a municipal telephone system. Barnesville's men formed the Clay County Fair and Agricultural Association in 1914 and hosted the first fair that November, but the potato-loving community is just as well-known today for its Potato Day Festival, started on June 17, 1938, by townspeople who wanted to celebrate the success of the cash crop. David Moe, the head coach of Dakota State women's basketball since 2017 and a five-time NSAA regular season champion between 2021 and 2025, and Alta King, a Ziegfeld girl on Broadway, are Barnesville's most famous son and daughter. Two noteworthy homes of interest on the National Register are the 1898-1900 Queen Anne fieldstone Patterson-Hernandez House and the 1903 Neoclassical home designed for Hannah C. and Peter E. Thompson.

Restaurant Recommendation:
Purple Goose Eatery & Drinkery
310 Front St S
Barnesville, MN 56514

COMSTOCK, MN
POPULATION: 100 – CITY 203 OF 856 (5-3-25)
In southwestern Clay County, Comstock was named in honor of Solomon Gilman Comstock of Moorhead. He co-founded the First National Bank of Moorhead, was a leading figure of the Moorhead Foundry, Car and Agricultural Works, and was a friend of the "Empire Builder" James J. Hill. He and Hill were responsible for locating stations of the St. Paul, Minneapolis & Manitoba Railroad throughout the county. David Askegaard was chiefly responsible for building up the site after its establishment. He moved his grain warehouse to Comstock Village in 1889 and organized a store in 1891. Later, he established a creamery, a lumber yard, and a potato warehouse. Askegaard was also the postmaster when the Comstock post office opened in 1890. Businesses were plentiful in Comstock's heyday, but no other structure has withstood the test of time better than the Comstock Public School. It was constructed between 1909 and 1911 and listed on the National Register on May 7, 1980. The 1870 Bernard Bernhardson House is another local point of interest on County Road 59 outside town.

DILWORTH, MN
POPULATION: 4,612 – CITY 207 OF 856 (5-4-25)
If not for the relocation of the Northern Pacific's divisional terminal facilities, Dilworth likely would have never been considered much of a town, let alone the second-largest municipality in Clay County that it is today. The move was made out of necessity due to overcrowding in Fargo. So in July 1906, the railroad purchased 500 acres of land surrounding its Dilworth siding to build facilities, primarily a roundhouse and a turntable. Long before the construction boom, Dilworth had been established as a siding in 1883, named for Joseph Dilworth, a railroad stockholder and director, and the owner of 4,000 acres of land in the vicinity. It had two elevators and a small number of residents then. By 1910, it had over 500 citizens, many of them Italian. That number doubled by the 1940s; by 1960, it had crossed 2,000 individuals. The post office was established in 1907. Early businesses included the Ballord-Trimble Lumber Company, Olaus Anderson's general store, Rasmus Haugsted's general store, two hotels, two restaurants, a bank, a creamery, a grocery store, a meat market, a barber shop, and a bakery. Dilworth Presbyterian Church was dedicated on August 11, 1907. In September 1910, St. Elizabeth's Catholic Church joined it as the second religious institution in town. An earlier name for Dilworth was Richardson.

FELTON, MN
POPULATION: 177 – CITY 210 OF 856 (5-4-25)
Felton was most likely named in honor of Samuel Morse Felton, a manager within the hierarchy of the Great Northern Railroad. The first settlers came from Augusta, Wisconsin, in 1879, the same year the post office was established. Michael Shea was named postmaster. The tracks were originally laid in 1872. However, after the St. Paul and Duluth Railroad platted the village in 1880, the entire town was moved in 1883. It would not be incorporated until March 7, 1901. By the end of its first decade in the 20th century, Felton was home to grain elevators, stockyards, a school, a Catholic church, and a small commercial district. As many as 264 people called the village home in the 1980s.

GEORGETOWN, MN
POPULATION: 86 – CITY 208 OF 856 (5-4-25)
In 1859, near the confluence of the Red and Buffalo Rivers, the Hudson's Bay Company established a trading post to trade furs and other goods up and down the Red. The post was first called Selkirk, for Lord Selkirk, but was renamed shortly thereafter to Georgetown for Sir George Simpson. The company built a fur warehouse, a boat landing, and a store. They were abandoned in September 1862 out of fear that the Dakota War of 1862 would lead to their demise and an unnecessary loss of life. Settlers returned to the area in 1864, and as the company's business and influence in the region grew, the Georgetown post added a hotel, a dwelling house, a guardhouse, and defense sheds. Randolph M. Probstfield was postmaster of what is now known as Old Georgetown, so-called "old" because the entire townsite was moved two miles southeast by the Moorhead Northern branch of the Northern Pacific Railroad in 1883. The new site was platted by Soloman G. Comstock and Almond A. White, and the post office was hosted in C. B. Hill's store. By the end of 1909, Georgetown had fewer than two hundred residents. Yet, it boasted three grain elevators, a depot, a livery, a hotel, a bank, a creamery, a school, and a Catholic church. The John Olness House, built in 1902 in the Queen Anne and Classical Revival styles, is located in the Georgetown vicinity and is listed on the National Register of Historic Places.

GLYNDON, MN
POPULATION: 1,306 – CITY 209 OF 856 (5-4-25)
Clay County's oldest formal village dates to 1872, when officials of the Northern Pacific Railroad platted it, but it was only in recent decades that Glyndon's population grew as its role as a bedroom community for Moorhead came to fruition. Since 1960, the population has grown from 489 people to 1,049 by the 21st century. The earliest settlers of the site came prepared to wait in tents as they eagerly awaited the arrival of the railroad tracks, and once the line was in place, homes were built in place of the tent town. When deciding on a name, "Glyndon" was agreed upon to honor Howard Glyndon (a pseudonym for Laura Catherine Redden Searing), a writer for the Atlantic Hearth and Home. A post office was established in S. Campbell's store, and Stiles R. Nettleton was named the postmaster. Later, the Great Northern Railroad was built perpendicular to the Northern Pacific tracks, and the junction town welcomed in a slew of businesses, including four hotels, churches, and schools. Glyndon was incorporated as a village on Valentine's Day 1881. In modern times, most visitors travel from the Fargo-Moorhead metropolitan area through Glyndon to reach Buffalo River State Park. Established in 1937, the 1,068-acre park boasts multiple Works Progress Administration buildings, 200 species of birds, 40 species of mammals, and 250 species of grasses and wildflowers. Camping, fishing, hiking, cross-country skiing, and birdwatching opportunities highlight the park's popular activities; many bird enthusiasts flock here to witness the competitive lek mating ritual of the greater prairie chicken. As visitors make their way to the park, they may notice the large cement "Boardwalk Kennels" husky dog statue on Highway 10.

HAWLEY, MN
POPULATION: 2,219 – CITY 213 OF 856 (5-4-25)
No town in Minnesota has undergone more name changes than Hawley, a community first settled by Scandinavians and later a colony from Yeovil, Somerset, England, in 1871-72. Its present name honors the memory of Thomas Hawley Cawfield, a surveyor and official within the ranks of the Northern Pacific Railroad. In conjunction with the Lake Superior and Puget Sound Company, the other names at different points were Bethel/New Bethel, Reno's Camp, Buffalo Crossing, Muskoday, and Yeovil/New Yeovil. The Yeovil Colony gave the latter name. Many of those colonists moved shortly after their arrival due to a harsh blizzard, the lack of infrastructure for skilled merchants and artisans, and the Panic of 1873, which temporarily halted construction of the Northern Pacific Railroad. The constant changing of the name caused great confusion amongst those attempting to survey the town and market the settlement. Still, they succeeded in attracting new immigrants. In 1873, the Hawley post office opened for business, and general stores, blacksmith shops, livery stables, and similar pioneer commercial establishments followed. As General George Armstrong Custer was working toward the western frontier by train in 1876, the year of his peril, he chose to stop in Hawley. Several elevators, lumber yards, churches, and schools were erected as key pieces of the infrastructure of the Buffalo River town. Its most famous construction came in the early 1970s at the Leslie Welter Potato Warehouse. Here, Robert Asp, a Moorhead junior high school counselor and avid Viking ship enthusiast, constructed the Hjemkomst. The replica ship was based on the 950 A.D. Gokstad vessel unearthed in Oslo, Norway, some years prior. After developing leukemia, the project appeared in peril until the local Chamber of Commerce and several local rallied with Asp to help fund the ship's completion. On July 17, 1980, the Hjemko was publicly displayed to a large crowd of supporters who had gathered in H and it then set sail for Duluth on its maiden voyage around Lake Superior

as New York City. Later, after Asp's passing, his children arranged for the ship to sail to Norway, where the king greeted the crew and climbed aboard for a while. The vessel is now on display at the Heritage Hjemkomst Center in Moorhead.

Restaurant Recommendation:
Minnesota Slice
112 15th Ave N
Hawley, MN 56549

HITTERDAL, MN
POPULATION: 199 – CITY 212 OF 856 (5-4-25)
Hitterdal's name is an eponym for the valley and lake of the same name in southern Norway. Several of the Minnesota community's earliest settlers used it as their surname, including Bendt O. Hitterdal, the original owner of the townsite before the advent of the Northern Pacific Railroad. A post office branch was opened in 1887. The townsite was platted in 1896, and on the first lot sold, M. J. Solum built a hardware store. Later came a bank, some homes and stores, and a public school, all before it was incorporated as a village on April 1, 1918. Its population has remained relatively constant over the last century, dropping to a low of 198 in 1930 and rising to a peak of 268 in the following decade.

MOORHEAD, MN ★
POPULATION: 44,505 – CITY 206 OF 856 (5-4-25)
Thousands of years ago, the great glacial Lake Agassiz covered the entire area encompassing Moorhead, Minnesota, and its neighboring metropolis of Fargo, North Dakota. Once larger than the cumulative surface area of all of the Great Lakes, the lake slowly drained into Hudson Bay and left behind some of the flattest and richest land in the world. This basin is now referred to as the Red River Valley. It was here in 1871 that William Galloway Moorhead, a director of the Northern Pacific Railroad, and his brother-in-law Jay Cooke chose to establish a townsite on the Red River of the North. From the get-go, it was known that Moorhead would be the county seat because of its strategic location on the river, which served as a conduit for the transfer of goods and people between Winnipeg, Manitoba, Minneapolis, and St. Paul. Moorhead got off the ground relatively quickly thanks to the river and railroad, achieving a population of 1,500 residents by its inaugural Census in 1880. However, not all of its businesses were considered to be positive contributors to the community. Throughout the 1880s, Moorhead became home to over 100 saloons (since neighboring Fargo did not permit alcohol sales). The settlement was given the nickname "Sin City" for its rampant crime and illicit activities. It took many decades for the town to clean itself up. As public utilities were developed and the town incorporated as a city on February 24, 1881, more prominent institutions emerged besides the bars. The Grand Pacific Hotel was built in 1881 (and demolished in 1996) and boasted 140 rooms for incoming railroad traffic. By 1915, the Great Northern and Northern Pacific Railroads, along with their branch lines, ran into and out of the city from eight directions. A streetcar system was developed to connect Fargo, Moorhead, and the nearby town of Dilworth, where the Northern Pacific Railway Company had headquartered its shops and roundhouse. The Great Northern had its grounds in the southern portion of Moorhead. Hundreds of businesses of every imaginable size and variety sprouted from Moorhead's "fertile soils," so to speak, but amongst its proudest accomplishments were a state-of-the-art post office building, a public library, the Trinity Norwegian Lutheran Church, a Catholic church, eight other congregations, and five primary and secondary school buildings.

Park Elementary School, Moorhead's oldest still-standing school building, built in 1900, is one of ten local sites on the National Register of Historic Places. Others include the 1898-99 Shingle Style St. John the Divine Episcopal Church; the former 1915 Neoclassical Federal Courthouse and Post Office building, now the Rourke Art Museum; the 1923 Fairmont Creamery building; the 1879 false front Frank Burnham Building; John B. Bergquist's 1870 log cabin, and the Solomon Gilman Comstock House, a gorgeous Queen Anne/Eastlake home that was built in 1882-83 or the influential Moorhead figure. It is now a museum affiliated with the Cultural Society of Clay County and the Minnesota Historical Society. The Main Building of Concordia College, erected in 1906 shortly after the local Norwegians established the private liberal arts college in 1891, is the only building from Moorhead's four colleges to be listed on the Register. The other schools are Rasmussen University, a national multi-state-and-campus university started in 1900, a branch of the Minnesota State Community and Technical College, and Minnesota State University Moorhead, formerly known as the Moorhead Normal School (1888 to 1921), Moorhead State Teachers College (1921 to 1957), Moorhead State College (1957 to 1975), and Moorhead State University (1975 to 2000). Other noteworthy points of interest include the Clay County Museum and Archives, known for their collection of 30,000-plus artifacts; the Bluestem Amphitheater, a 3,000-seat outdoor Amphitheater that has hosted the likes of Weezer, the Goo Goo Dolls, and The Beach Boys; the Hjemkomst Center, known for its Viking Ship replica and Norwegian-style Hopperstad Stave Church; and the local Dairy Queen. Moorhead's Dairy Queen was the birthplace of the famous Dilly Bar treat in 1955 and is one of a select few franchises that sell store-specific treats like Chipper Sandwiches, Monkey Tails, and Mr. Maltie's that cannot be found elsewhere. A 12-foot-tall Dilly Bar was erected in 2018 to pay tribute to its unique claim to fame. Moorhead and Beardsley share the state record for the highest temperature in Minnesota history, 115°F; Moorhead's occurred on July 6, 1936. Several dozens of famous people have ties to Moorhead, a few of whom include Karl Truesdell, a major general in both World Wars; Mark Ladwig, a figure skater who participated in the 2010 Winter Olympics; Warren Magnuson, a former member of the U.S. House and a United States Senator from Washington between December 1944 and January 1981; Becky Gulsvig, a Broadway actress off and on between 2002 and 2019; Annella Zervas, a Catholic religious sister with the Benedictines and a candidate for canonization in the Catholic Church; Leslie Stefanson, an actress most famous for her role as Captain Elisabeth Campbell in the 1999 film *The General's Daughter*; brothers Adoph and Olaus Murie, ecologists respectively known for being the first to study wolves in their natural habitat and for being the "father of modern elk management;" and NHL players Will Borgen, defenseman, since 2018; Brian Lee, the 9th overall pick in the 2005 NHL Draft; Matt Cullen, a 21-year veteran center from 1997 to 2019, and Chris VandeVelde, who had stints with the Edmonton Oilers and Philadelphia Flyers.

Restaurant Recommendation:
Twenty Below Coffee Co. Moorhead
608 8th St S
Moorhead, MN 56560

Restaurant Recommendation:
Dairy Queen (Treat)
24 8th St S
Moorhead, MN 56560

SABIN, MN
POPULATION: 619 – CITY 205 OF 856 (5-4-25)
A German immigrant named Frank A. Scheel started a little hardware and general merchandise store here in 1902 called "Scheel's Hardware Store." He harvested three hundred dollars' worth of potatoes to finance his storefront, which then, unbeknownst to him, would ultimately develop into the 34-store sporting goods chain now found across sixteen states. Mr. Scheel is arguably Sabin's most famous son, Dwight May Sabin, a former car, engine, and machinery manufacturer and a U.S. Senator who was honored by the naming of this Great Northern Railway town. Homesteaders arrived in the 1870s, but when the St. Paul, Minneapolis, and Manitoba Railroad Company was built through the vicinity in 1880, its arrival spurred the construction of Sabin's first hotel, blacksmith shop, harness shop, lumber yards, general store, and school. Sabin was platted on the land of Mr. Almy. It eventually added two more general stores, two elevators, a bank, a meat market, another hotel, a confectionery, and a barber shop before its incorporation as a village on August 30, 1929. The Sabin post office opened in 1881. Since 1950, the town's population has grown threefold due to its proximity to Moorhead, a major industrial center. The Wulf C. Krabbenhoft Farmstead and its five structures, built between 1890 and 1905, are an excellent example of a pioneer Red River Valley farm.

ULEN, MN
POPULATION: 476 – CITY 211 OF 856 (5-4-25)
The earliest proof of Scandinavian visitation to this heavily Norwegian region of Minnesota may be the Ulen "Viking" Sword, which Hans O. Hansen found on April 20, 1911. As he was plowing his field, its blades unexpectedly unearthed the artifact, a 16-inch blade with a soldier on one side and a breastplate with a dagger and crossed axes on the other. Some experts believe the sword is an authentic Viking artifact. In contrast, others argue that it was likely a 19th-century German military sword. Regardless of its origins, the sword remains an essential artifact of the Ulen Museum today. When the town was founded in the 1880s, it was named after Ole Ulen, the first man to settle there permanently. A post office was opened in 1884, shortly after some of the first roads were built. Due to a lack of tax funding, township officials issued an ordinance that required all able-bodied men in the area to contribute two working days a year, specifically to the construction of Ulen's roads. A year after the post office's establishment, its name was changed to Odneland in honor of Ole Odneland, a local postmaster and general store owner. His store was moved when the Duluth and Manitoba Railway Company (an affiliate of the Northern Pacific Railroad) needed his property for their right-of-way. For unknown reasons, the post office closed in 1885 before being reorganized in 1887 under the name Ulen again. Ole Christian Melbye, a grocer and the first man to have a home in the village, became the postmaster. Plat maps indicate that development went well over the next several decades, as Ulen added elevators, a depot, a school, churches, and eventually Northwestern Bank, which arrived in 1941. With a population ranging from 438 to 590 people (its 1920 peak) since the 1910s, Ulen's communities have maintained a sense of pride and allude to their Norwegian heritage through several local businesses, such as The Nordic Lounge and the Viking Manor Nursing Home. Ulen and its famous sword were featured in an episode of A&E Network's *America Unearthed* series in 2013.

Unincorporated/Ghost Towns: Averill, Baker, Dale, Downer, Kragnes, Manitoba Junction, Muskoda, Oakport, Rollag, Rustad, Tansem, Winnipeg Junction

National Register of Historic Places:
Barnesville: Barnesville City Hall & Jail, Hannah C. & Peter E. Thompson House, Patterson-Hernandez House
Comstock: Bernard Bernhardson House, Comstock Public School
Georgetown: John Olness House
Glyndon: Buffalo River State Park WPA/Rustic Style Historic Resources
Moorhead: Burnham Building, Fairmont Creamery, Federal Courthouse & Post Office, John Bergquist House, Lew A. Huntoon House, Main Building, Concordia College, Moorhead Storage & Transfer Company Warehouse, Park Elementary School, Solomon Gilman Comstock House, St. John the Divine Episcopal Church, Randolph M. Probstfield House
Parke Township: District No. 3 School
Sabin: Wulf C. Krabbenhoft Farmstead

Golf Courses:
Hawley Golf & Country Club, Municipal (Hawley, MN)
Meadows Golf Course, Municipal (Moorhead, MN)
Moorhead Country Club, Private (Moorhead, MN)
Village Green Golf Club, Municipal (Moorhead, MN)
Willow Creek Municipal Golf Course, Municipal (Barnesville, MN)

Town Celebrations:
Potato Days, Barnesville, MN (4th Full Weekend in August)

CLEARWATER COUNTY
EST. 1902 - POPULATION: 8,524

Clearwater Lake, River, and County are all named in honor of the Ojibwe's early name for the land home to Lake Itasca, the source of the Mississippi River.

BAGLEY, MN ★☆
POPULATION: 1,285 – CITY 305 OF 856 (6-2-25)
Four years before it was declared the Clearwater County seat, Bagley was established on the banks of the Clearwater River in 1898 and named in honor of the lumberman Sumner C. Bagley. Loggers had made camp in the area as early as 1894. Still, the community's development did not begin until the Great Northern Railroad was extended to that point. Schools, churches, and businesses of all shapes and sizes came and went over the years. Some institutions have left a mighty legacy for the community. In 1918, 236 members of the Nonpartisan League and the Farmer-Labor Party joined forces to found the Farmers Publishing Company. They purchased the Bagley Independent and *People's Defenders* newspaper and changed its name to the *Farmers Independent*, citing it as a newspaper "of the farmer, by the farmer, for the farmer." To this day, it remains in publication as the only cooperatively owned newspaper in the state. In the religious sphere, early Norwegian immigrant Ole Eneberg contributed to the town in 1897 by building the Gran Evangelical Lutheran Church. The county's first church congregation met in a small log cabin until 1953, when it merged with Our Savior's Lutheran Church in Ebro, Minnesota. On May 19, 1988, the lonely structure was listed on the National Register of Historic Places. Between 1937-38, the Clearwater County Courthouse was built by the Works Progress Administration for $90,358, $29,250 of which was gifted to the project by the Public Works Administration. In keeping with the hockey history of northern Minnesota, the 1996 Bagley High School varsity hockey team was the last Minnesota State High School League school to play its games outdoors.

CLEARBROOK, MN
POPULATION: 464 – CITY 303 OF 856 (6-2-25)
Clearbrook has the distinction of being the hometown and final resting place of Wes Westrum, a two-time MLB All-Star (1952, 1953) and 1954 World Series champion with the MLB's New York Giants. He was one of two athletes featured in the first-ever edition of Sports Illustrated, published on August 16, 1954. One of the first structures in the community, named by Edward Rydeen after the small local brook, was a creamery built atop a hill. Around that enterprise grew a town called Shanty Town, which had a school, a store, a blacksmith shop, and several crude tents that served as homes. Peter Peterson, a homesteader in the area since 1896, decided to purchase the townsites of Shanty Town and Clearbrook with the foresight that the Soo Line Railroad might soon be extending its line through that vicinity. He was correct: Clearbrook Village was formally laid out in 1910. Henry Lewis welcomed railroad travelers to his hotel, the First State Bank of Clearbrook held the deposits of those who stayed, and Andrew Walle supplied the hardware needed to build up many of the town's earliest structures. Peter Peterson owned the first store, Randahl Nelson Grocery. The largest business of them all was Jack Johnson's box and sash factory. Clearbrook was incorporated as a village on June 15, 1918, and reached an all-time high population of 650 in the 1960s. It is now the site of a significant oil pipeline junction between the Enbridge Pipeline System, the North Dakota Pipeline Company, and the Minnesota Pipe Line. Fans of the indie rock band Low, formed in 1993 by Alan Sparhawk and Mimi Parker, may be surprised to learn that the two met as classmates at Clearbrook's elementary schools.

GONVICK, MN
POPULATION: 263 – CITY 304 OF 856 (6-2-25)
Wildwood, the original name of this town, started on the Lost River on Peter A. Monsrud's homestead. He erected a sawmill around 1896, which led to businesses like The Pine Lake Creamery Association and a blacksmith shop with a dance and meeting hall. Other stores opened as well, but the entire town shut down when the Soo Line bypassed it in 1910 in favor of nearby Gonvick. That nearby settlement was established after the United States government opened part of the Red Lake Reservation to homesteaders, after the arrival of the Minneapolis, St. Paul & Sault Ste. Marie Gonvick was retained as the local name in honor of Martin O. Gonvick, the oldest living man in the vicinity. It may have been named for Emma Gonvick Monsrud, the wife of the earlier-mentioned sawmill owner. Gonvick's school building was eventually decommissioned as an educational institution when Gonvick consolidated with nearby Clearbrook in 1992. Elementary students attended Gonvick until 2004. The spacious building is now being used as the Clearwater Life Center. Ed Widseth, a member of the College Football Hall of Fame and a 1938 NFL champion and All-Star with the New York Giants, was born here on January 5, 1910.

LEONARD, MN
POPULATION: 41 – CITY 302 OF 856 (6-2-25)
Less than four dozen Minnesotans call Leonard home nowadays, but in the 1930s and 40s, it had over 100 residents and a station on the Soo Line Railroad. When Dudley Township opened for settlement on May 15, 1896, George H. French established a log-house trading post that also served as the first post office. He called it Leonard, after his first child, and for years, his business was the only commercial structure until the railroad arrived in 1911. A small selection of storefronts was opened in the town on the shore of Four-legged Lake, and the residents of Leonard decided to organize

as a municipal corporation on June 12, 1922. Nels Strand was the head of the village council, and C. O. (Oscar) Lundmark served as the city clerk. As time passed, residents moved away, seeking better job opportunities and amenities in larger communities. In 1991, Leonard lost its post office.

SHEVLIN, MN
POPULATION: 137 – CITY 301 OF 856 (6-2-25)
Minnesota's Logging Championships were once held in Shevlin, a logging camp historically known for hosting loggers who competed in the log toss, speed cutting, power saw, axe throw, standing block chop, and Jack and Jill Crosscut competition, amongst other events. It was part of the Sawdust Dayz celebration, started in 1987, to improve the lives of Shevlin residents and bring fun to the community. Thomas Henry Shevlin, a logging mogul from Minneapolis, had this town named in his honor after he helped kick-start the local industry. Residents were confident they would win the county seat when Clearwater County was partitioned from its neighboring jurisdictions. When Bagley instead took the crown, they settled for being a shipping point on the Great Northern Railroad. Shevlin was platted on 160 acres of Peter Burstad's land, and Andrew L. Gordon took over as postmaster. The office was in his store, the first building on the townsite. Hotels, stores, saloons, and livery stables opened their doors for business at the turn of the century. A creamery, box factory, meat market, sawmill, newspaper, cooperative oil station, and professional offices (as did over a dozen "traditional" era businesses) took their place after mighty fires destroyed the town first in 1904, and then again in 1911. From 1911 to 1991, Shevlin had its own school district, but it eventually closed, and students were sent to the school in Bagley. The Ojibwe call the town *Gwaaba'andaawangaakwa'igaang*, meaning, "where one shovels sand."

Unincorporated/Ghost Towns: Alida, Big Bear Landing, Bonga Landing, Bush Landing, Elbow Lake, Lake Itasca, Mallard, Ponsford Landing, Rice Lake, Roy Lake, South End, Vern, Weme, Zerkel

National Register of Historic Places:
Bagley: Gran Evangelical Lutheran Church
Park Rapids: Itasca Bison Site, Itasca State Park

Golf Courses:
Twin Pines Golf Course, Municipal (Bagley, MN)

Cass County: The Big Fish Supper Club & Resort (Bena), Big Winnie Resort and General Store (Bena), Paul & Babe Statues at Cragun's Resort (East Gull Lake), Leech Lake Dam (Federal Dam), Birch Lake (Hackensack), Paul Bunyan's Girlfriend Lucette Statue (Hackensack), former Soo Line Depot (Remer), Circle of Time at Cass County Museum (Walker)

Chippewa County: Old Barn (Clara City), Norwegian Stabbur (Milan), Mural (Milan), Liberty Bell Recreation (Milan), Pioneer Mural (Milan), former Chippewa County Bank (Montevideo), Art's Dairy Freeze (Montevideo), Lac qui Parle Mission (Churchill)

Chisago County: Chisago Lake Lutheran Church from *Grumpy Old Men* (Center City), Big Chair (Center City), Mural (Lindstrom), Gustaf's On Main Eatery in Gustaf Anderson House (Lindstrom), World's Largest Walleye (Rush City), Old Barn with Barn Quilt (Taylors Falls), The Drive in Restaurant (Taylors Falls), Tow Mater at Lenfer Automotive & Transmission (Wyoming)

Clay County: former 1909 Public School (Comstock), Northern Pacific Caboose at Whistle Stop Park (Dilworth), Georgetown Ravine Bridge over the Red River (Georgetown), Buffalo River State Park (Glyndon), Riverbend Park and the Buffalo River (Hawley), Salem Lutheran Church (Hitterdal), Norwegian Gokstad ship at the Hjemkomst Center (Moorhead), World's Largest Dilly Bar at Dairy Queen (Moorhead)

Clearwater County: Clearwater County Courthouse (Bagley), Dairyland (Bagley), Gran Evangelical Lutheran Church (Bagley), Veterans Memorial (Clearwater), former Railroad Depot (Clearwater), Wild Turkey (Leonard), Clearwater County History Center (Shevlin), La Salle Lake State Recreation Area (Coffee Pot Landing)

COOK COUNTY
EST. 1874 - POPULATION: 5,600

Home to just a single incorporated municipality in Grand Marais, Minnesota's northeasternmost county was named after Major Michael Cook, an early Minnesota State and Territorial legislator.

GRAND MARAIS, MN ★
POPULATION: 1,337 – CITY 387 OF 856 (6-24-25)

Cook County's lone municipality, Grand Marais, on the shores of Lake Superior, has long been treasured by Minnesotans as one of the state's most beautiful and unique cities. For millennia, the natural twin harbors of the site were called "Gitchi-Bitobig" (now Artist's Point) by the Indigenous. French Canadian Voyagers and fur traders arrived in the 1700s. They called their discovery "Grand Marais," meaning "great marsh," a reference to a twenty-acre marsh that has long since disappeared. Small bays and rock outcroppings came together to offer a naturally protected safe harbor, which is why a town was established here in the first place. Geologist J. G. Norwood discovered iron ore in the Gunflint Range to the north circa 1850, which inspired others to visit this part of Minnesota Territory. From 1856 to 1857, the post office operated in Superior County, Wisconsin, before changing its name to Hiawatha in 1857-58 and finally to Grand Marais in 1873. The office was started after Edward W. Wakelin purchased property on the bay in 1872 alongside Henry Mayhew and Samuel F. Howenstein. Cook County was established, and Grand Marais was declared the county seat the following year. From then on, the town developed as a trade point. The east breakwater of the harbor was built in 1884 to improve harbor safety; in 1885, the first lighthouse was constructed. The west harbor wall was completed in 1900. Despite not being accessible by automobile until the 1920s (the only way to reach the small fishing village was by boat, horse, or dogsled), many of Grand Marais's most historical buildings were completed before the first road was built. Amongst these were the 1895 [Catholic] Church of St. Francis Xavier, built as a mission in the now-defunct Ojibwe town of Chippewa City; an 1896 Lightkeeper's House, now the Cook County History Museum; Jim Scott's Fishhouse, once an important commercial fishing location; the Bally Blacksmith Shop, initially built in 1911; and the 1911-12 Neoclassical Cook County Courthouse. The Grand Marais Light, an operational light tower built in 1922 to help guide ships from Lake Superior into the harbor; Clearwater Lodge, erected in 1925-26 to serve as guest accommodations in the Gunflint Trail area; and the Naniboujou Club Lodge, completed in 1928 and noted for its elaborate Art Deco and colorful Cree-inspired interior design. Its interior murals were painted by a French artist when the building served as a gentleman's club before it was repurposed as a lodge and restaurant. Despite losing some of its buildings in an April 13, 2020, fire, Grand Marais has retained its status as one of Minnesota's finest tourist areas with its restaurants, activities, resorts, natural beauty, and access to numerous State Parks. The Gunflint Trail starts in Grand Marais and leads into the largely unpopulated stretches of northwest Cook County known as the Boundary Waters.

Restaurant Recommendation:
The Fisherman's Daughter
418 MN-61
Grand Marais, MN 55604

Lodging Recommendation:
The Naniboujou Lodge & Restaurant
20 Naniboujou Trail
Grand Marais, MN 55604

GRAND PORTAGE, MN
POPULATION: 616 – UNINCORPORATED (6-24-25)

An unincorporated town in Minnesota, by definition, is a region of the state that is not governed by a local municipal corporation–i.e., a municipality. Unincorporated towns include everything from ghost towns (Taconite Harbor/Radium) to some neighborhoods in major metropolitan areas to Census-designated places (Esko, Red Lake). Therefore, unincorporated communities encompass a wide variety of town types. Some are nothing more than empty fields, as there have been no residents or structures for over a century. However, others may still retain a church, an eating establishment, or perhaps even a handful of businesses. Unlike specifically ghost towns, many unincorporated communities may still have activities or attractions for visitors to enjoy.

Depending on the area's population, some unincorporated towns may even retain a post office, as the postal service's system of assigning ZIP codes and mailing addresses aims to maximize efficiency rather than necessarily recognizing precise jurisdictions or boundaries. For example, Birchdale, an unincorporated town in Koochiching County, has retained a zip code of 55629, even though residents are technically supposed to use Baudette's (56623) zip code. They have a post office, but the area is unincorporated. Angle Inlet in Lake of the Woods County has its own zip code, 56711, but its mail also goes through Baudette. On the contrary, some towns have no physical post office buildings but remain incorporated with their own unique zip codes, like Barry (56210) in Big Stone County or Kenneth (56147) in Rock County. It is a common misconception that a town is incorporated if it has a post office, but that is incorrect. The Census maintains a similar practice to the post office regarding unincorporated towns. They may continue to record the population of a specific area (typically an unincorporated town) solely for statistical purposes. These places are known as "Census-Designated Places." One such example is Esko, an unincorporated community in Carlton County, which recorded a population of 2,082 individuals as of the 2020 Census. A town is incorporated only if it has a local government, typically composed of a mayor and a city council. They must meet to establish ordinances, collect local and state taxes, and create municipal road plans to secure funding for items such as street lamps.

There are situations in which, once a population has decreased so dramatically, the residents and/or the city council vote on whether to retain incorporation status. In the case of Tenney, which had a population of only five people as of 2010, the townspeople agreed to dissolve their city by a vote of 2-1 in the June 2011 elections. At that moment, their municipality ceased to exist, as there was no longer an official mayor or a city council. Any services provided to the city are now strictly the responsibility of Campbell Township and Wilkin County, as there is no longer a local government. Until the vote, Tenney had been mentioned alongside Funkley as the smallest incorporated city in Minnesota.

Grand Portage is unincorporated but was once the principal trading point and meeting place for voyageurs between Lake Superior and the Pigeon River. A "grand" nine-mile portage greeted fur traders traveling by canoe, where they would then carry their canoes to alternate waterways. By 1731, French traders had established a cabin, a fur and goods warehouse, and a blacksmith shop. The North West Company established its regional headquarters here, which became known as the "commercial" emporium of the northwestern fur trade; it even rivaled Great Britain's impressive ports at Fort Niagara, New York, and Detroit, Michigan. An American victory in the War of 1812 brought these territories under U.S. control. In 1856, the Grand Portage village was established, two years after the Grand Portage (Ojibwe) Indian Reservation. Various post offices operated under the Grand Portage name from 1856 to 1860 and from 1864 to 1871 before remaining open continuously since 1878. The Dawes Act of 1887 and the Nelson Act of 1889 allowed speculators to take much of this land for themselves. With the help of Alton Bramer, following the Indian Reorganization Act of 1934, the Grand Portage band of Ojibwe and the Minnesota Chippewa Tribe were able to reclaim some of their lost property. Grand Portage National Historic Site was established in 1951 and re-dedicated as a National Monument on September 2, 1958. It has sought to preserve Anishinaabeg Ojibwe heritage and the area's crucial fur-trading history through its 710 acres, which include buildings and exhibits. The old portage trail still exists as an 8.5-mile hike. Other activities for visitors include the Grand Portage Lodge and Casino, as well as Grand Portage State Park, which is notable for its High Falls and for being the only State Park in the country managed by both a state and a Native American tribal organization. Ferries take curious wanderers to the secluded Isle Royale National Park in Michigan, the largest natural island in Lake Superior at 206.73 square miles.

There are many unincorporated communities throughout Minnesota. The parameters of this project were set to enable me to focus on documenting all 856 of Minnesota's incorporated municipalities and showcase the specific aspects that each municipality entails today. A project documenting unincorporated towns would take on an entirely different meaning, as many of the towns have been reduced to not much more than a single grain elevator or an empty field (a heartbreaking reality, but true). However, as seen in examples such as Grand Portage, Angle Inlet, Red Lake, Lutsen, and others, there are indeed unincorporated communities that still have much to offer. This post seeks to honor the few unincorporated towns that are holding on with a church, a restaurant, or a store, and the many hundreds of others that have sadly been entirely abandoned.

Don't count out unincorporated towns when planning your road trips around Minnesota. Although I excluded them from my project to set parameters for myself, they deserve all the love in the world, just like their incorporated counterparts!

Unincorporated/Ghost Towns: Croftville, Grand Portage, Hovland, Lutsen, Maple Hill, Martin Landing, Mineral Center, Pigeon River, Schroeder, Taconite Harbor, Tofte

National Register of Historic Places:
Cascade River State Park: Cascade River Wayside
Grand Marais: Bally Blacksmith Shop, Cook County Courthouse, Jim Scott Fishhouse, Lightkeeper's House, Church of St. Francis Xavier-Catholic, Clearwater Lounge, Height of Land, Naniboujou Club Lodge
Grand Portage: Grand Portage National Monument
Schroeder: *Amboy & George Spencer* Shipwreck Sites, Schroeder Lumber Company Bunkhouse
West Cook: Chik Wauk Lodge

Golf Courses:
Gunflint Hills Golf Course, Municipal (Grand Marais, MN)
Superior National at Lutsen, Municipal (Lutsen, MN)

Breweries/Wineries/Distilleries:
North Shore Winery (Lutsen, MN)
Voyageur Brewing Company (Grand Marais, MN)

Town Celebrations:
The Fisherman's Picnic, Grand Marais, MN (1st Weekend in August)
Rendezvous Days, Grand Portage, MN (2nd Weekend in August)

COTTONWOOD COUNTY
EST. 1857 - POPULATION: 11,517

The organization of Cottonwood County was completed on July 29, 1870, by which point it had been decided to name it after the Cottonwood River, home to many cottonwood trees.

BINGHAM LAKE, MN
POPULATION: 137 – CITY 57 OF 856 (2-27-25)
Named after the lake on which it sits, both the body of water and the City of Bingham were named in honor of Kinsley S. Bingham, a U.S. Senator and later the 11th Governor of Michigan. It was platted by the St. Paul & Sioux City Railroad Company on July 28, 1875, but had its post office four years prior. Daniel C. Davis and Rufus P. Mathews were two of the first permanent settlers. Accounts differ on who the first genuine postmaster was, but the post office was located in Davis's general store. Davis had a generous spirit and was instrumental in assisting early settlers of the townsite who lost everything to the grasshopper plagues of 1872. He gave away significant portions of his general stock but was never repaid. Between 1880 and 1900, the population grew from 44 people to a peak of 311, and by 1916, it had expanded to include fifteen businesses. The most important of these were the First State Bank, John Henderson's brick plant, the St. John Grain Company, the Liam Elevators, Henry Wessel's meat market, and the S. L. Rogers Lumber Company. At one point, the town was proud to host a tile factory. Under John Henderson's direction, it could produce between 6,000 and 8,000 tiles per day. Bingham Lake was incorporated on July 28, 1875, and enjoyed having a local post office branch until its dissolution in 1992.

JEFFERS, MN
POPULATION: 349 – CITY 22 OF 856 (2-23-25)
The Jeffers Petroglyphs offer a glimpse into what life was like in Minnesota long before the state, the United States, or even the ancient civilizations of Greece and Rome existed. Measuring 150-by-650 feet, the Sioux Quartzite outcropping in the rural, prairie-covered countryside features over 5,000 examples of Native American rock art, ranging from human figures to thunderbirds, bison, and turtles, some of which are estimated to be 7,000 to 9,000 years old. W. R. Jeffers Jr., a descendant of town namesake and founder George Jeffers, sold the site to the Minnesota Historical Society in 1966 so it could be preserved and added to the U.S. National Register of Historic Places. George was the principal owner of the land on which Frank H. Peavey and the Inter-State Land Company organized the Jeffers townsite on September 19, 1899, when the Currie branch of the Chicago, Milwaukee, St. Paul & Omaha Railroad was extended to that point. It was incorporated nine days later, and its first depot was

located in a spare boxcar. The streets were named in honor of the Peary Elevator employees. One was dubbed "Courthouse Avenue" because early settlers were confident that Jeffers would be the judicial seat of Cottonwood County. To their surprise, the seat was instead placed in the southern part of the county at Windom, but the street name remained unchanged. Despite not being the county's capital, Jeffers still prospered on its rail line, welcoming first A. A. Faust's general store and other necessary facilities like a bank, a lumber yard, and a drug store, to name a few. The post office was established in the Faust store in 1900. In a 1916 business directory, notable additions to its commercial district included two hotels, The Jeffers and The Leader; H. E. Nimtz's creamery, with the ability to produce one hundred pounds of butter fat per month; the elevators of the Benson Grain Company and the Farmers Co-operative Elevator Company; L. J. Bastian's confectionery; F. J. Armantrout's jewelry store; M. B. Fish's "moving picture show," and *The Review* newspaper, of which E. F. Schmotzer was the proprietor. Six hundred forty-eight people lived in Jeffers in its heyday in the 1940s.

MOUNTAIN LAKE, MN
POPULATION: 1,999 – CITY 56 OF 856 (2-27-25)

William Mason conceived a descriptive name for the lake, which was later used for the village. He first called it "Twin Mountain Lake" because there was neither a mountain nor a lake within a hundred miles of his farmstead (clearly a fallacy, considering that he lived amid The Land of 10,000 Lakes). Mason only renamed it when he discovered the now-dried Mountain Lake. The lake had an island in the middle that rose nearly 40 feet above the water, making it a "mountain." Mountain Lake village was platted on May 25, 1872, and the post office was established the year before. Improvements were not made until the St. Paul & Sioux City Railroad (later the Chicago, St. Paul, Minneapolis & Omaha) came through. They wanted to rename it "Midway" because of its location between St. Paul & Sioux City, but the change never occurred. Most of the community's growth can be attributed to the nearly 300 Mennonite families who came to the site at William Seeger's recommendation, then with the Minnesota State Board of Immigration. Mennonites, particularly those from the Molotschna Colony near present-day Melitopol, Ukraine, were admired by many for their work ethic and were tasked with building up the settlement. They did, and by 1900, nearly fifteen additional subdivisions and out-lots had been added to the original townsite to account for its rapid growth. Early businesses varied in their size, stature, and importance. The first three lines were the general stores of S. J. Soule, J. Lynch, and Paul Seeger, circa 1871. It was at Seeger's where the post office had been established. Grain elevators were raised with the railroad's coming, and David Hiebert started a flour mill in 1875. Its capacity of 120 barrels per day helped it serve as a cornerstone of the local economy for numerous years. By 1916, Mountain Lake enjoyed the fruits of the labor provided by four creamery organizations: the Farmers Co-operative Association, the Fairmount Creamery Company, the Hansford Creamery Company, and the Worthington Creamery Company; the Mountain Lake Roller Milling Company; the North Star Telephone Company; J. J. Vogt's "The Pleasant Corner" confectionery; The Commercial Hotel; and the Schaefer Brothers, Hubbard & Palmer, F. Schroeder, and Farmers Elevator Company elevator in addition to all of the other traditional businesses of the era. There were at least five Mennonite churches at one point, each contributing to the construction of the Mennonite Hospital of Mountain Lake circa 1905. Although it struggled in its earliest years, after becoming a branch of the Bethel Deaconess Home of Newton, Kansas, it became a vital fixture in improving the health of those living in the region. Also relating to Mennonite history, it was in Mountain Lake where the Fellowship of Evangelical Bible Churches (then called the *Konferenz der*

Vereinigten Mennoniten-Brueder von Nord America) was founded on October 14, 1889, by Isaac Peters of Henderson, Nebraska, and Aaron Wall of Mountain Lake's Brudertaler Church. The conference sought to emphasize specific Mennonite doctrines within the coalition of churches across North America. Modern-day Mountain Lake remembers its Native American history with the active preservation of the Mountain Lake Site (listed on the National Register of Historic Places in 1977), now the Mountain County Park. A myriad of Native American villages and settlements called the island in the city-namesake lake home for millennia, long before the arrival of any Europeans to Minnesota. A quirkier attraction is the Papa, Mama, Teen, and Baby Burger collection of A&W figurines at the restaurant, one of the very few remaining complete sets of the family that debuted in the 1960s to showcase the offerings of the prominent fast-food chain. The Isaac Bargen House, a Queen Anne-style home, was built for Isaac A. Bargen, who was locally famed for promoting secular public education and government service. Other noteworthy residents of the community have been Samuel J. Schultz, an Old Testament scholar; Chuck Loewen, an offensive lineman for the NFL's San Diego Chargers in the early 1980s; Neva Pilgrim, a talented soprano in the realm of contemporary classical music, and Larry Buhler, an NFL champion fullback in the pioneer days of the National Football League with the Green Bay Packers. Commercial sunflower seeds were invented here around the turn of the century by a man who called them "George's Solflora Nuts."

STORDEN, MN
POPULATION: 225 – CITY 21 OF 856 (2-23-25)
First called Norsk for its large number of Norwegian immigrants, "Storden" was later the name given to this Cottonwood County settlement at the suggestion of John Fitcha. He wanted to honor the first settler of them all, Nels Storden. An alternative account suggests that the name was derived from the island of Stord, near Bergen, and adopted on March 30, 1875. Settlers influenced the postal service to establish an office branch on the farm of Ole Christopherson that same year, before it was relocated to Copenhagen. The office relocated once more to Storden, once it was certain that Storden would grow as a village under the watchful eye of the Chicago, St. Paul, Minneapolis & Omaha Railroad. As one of several towns on the Currie branch, businessmen like C. H. Shaner (general store and grocer), John Skovley (livery), A. M. Gark (hardware store), A. P. Frederickson (hotel), Roy Egger (blacksmith shop), Henry Peterson (drayman), L. Dolliff (lumber company), and St. John (elevator) ensured their family's futures by establishing lines of enterprise that would prove both profitable and necessary to the continued prosperity of their settlement. The town's two churches, the Storden Baptist Church and the Amo Lutheran Church, were established in 1879 and 1887. Actions to incorporate as a village were not completed until June 7, 1921, but the town was platted nearly eighteen years earlier by the Interstate Land Company on the land of John Sorenson.

WESTBROOK, MN
POPULATION: 758 – CITY 20 OF 856 (2-23-25)
Joseph F. Bean and George B. Walker were among the first settlers to return to Cottonwood County after the aftermath of the Dakota War of 1862. When a sufficient number of immigrants had settled in the immediate area of the township, they sought to establish a post office, which began fulfilling its duties for the first time in 1873 under the name "West Brook." The name comes from its proximity to the west branch of the local Highwater Creek. From 1887 to 1888, the name was briefly changed to Highwater before reverting to a more condensed name, Westbrook. The town was platted on June 8, 1900, by the Inter-State Land Company on the Currie branch of the

Omaha Railroad. Sivert Noreem quickly built his boarding house, the first building on the site, but the L. P. Dolliff Lumber Company and the Laird-Norton lumberyards were the earliest to conduct business. Later came the Sleepy Eye Milling Company, the First National Bank, and a multitude of other professional offices, stores, icehouses, elevators, and more. The Dixie motion-picture show, the *Sentinel* newspaper, and T. F. Leavitt's photography gallery were amongst the most progressive lines as of July 1916. Old Westbrook Lutheran Church, the first Lutheran parish in Minnesota west of New Ulm, was started by Reverend John C. Jacobson in Morton Engebretson's cabin on May 12, 1870. It was then known as the Westbrook Norse Lutheran Congregation. In June 1986, the Chicago, St. Paul, Minneapolis & Omaha Railroad depot in Westbrook was added to the National Register; it now houses the Westbrook Heritage House Museum, featuring artifacts, genealogy information, and local indoor and outdoor history exhibits.

Restaurant Recommendation:
Bonnie & Clyde's II
101 1st Ave
Westbrook, MN 56183

WINDOM, MN ★☆
POPULATION: 4,798 – CITY 58 OF 856 (2-27-25)

While Windom was the name of a post office in Fillmore County from 1862 to 1865, General Judson W. Bishop of the Sioux City & St. Paul Railroad is credited with suggesting the name for the flourishing modern city that has served as the Cottonwood County seat since the early 1870s. It honors the legacy of William Windom, a U.S. Senator from Minnesota who would later serve the nation as the 33rd and 39th United States Secretary of the Treasury. Platted on June 20, 1871, on the Des Moines River by A. L. Beach, a dozen lots were sold for $100 a piece on Windom's principal day of existence. A. P. Lukens, S. C. Highly, and others had premeditated the site a week earlier and already started erecting buildings, some of which by August 1871 likely housed the goods of Windom's two dry goods stores, two bakeries, a meat market, a hotel, a general store, a grocery store, a saloon, a print shop, and a hardware store. Samuel M. Espey became postmaster. Although the railroad laid out all its towns along the line in the same manner —a center square surrounded by businesses —Windom was the only village that followed the blueprints to the letter. The decision may have helped it secure the county seat, which was initially expected to be located nearly twenty miles to the north in another community called Jeffers. The title and its incorporation as a village in 1875 propelled Windom to achieve unbelievable growth. At the 1880 Census, it had 443 residents; by 1890, that number nearly doubled to 835, and by 1900, it had climbed to 1,944, an increase of 132.8% over the previous decade. There were hundreds of businesses, but several stood out as unique to Windom. D. Patten & Company raised the first of several elevators in Windom and the first on the Sioux City & St. Paul Railroad in August 1873. E. F. Drake and Samuel Collins established the flouring mills in 1878 and used a dam to power them with the force of the river's current through 1882. For many years, the Windom Manufacturing Company provided early farmers with state-of-the-art self-feeders for threshing machines and other implements. Walter Brown was the mind behind the local tile factory, and O. S. Skillingstad started the Cigar Factory No. 194 circa 1905. The sweetest manufacturing plant of them all was the Windom Ice Cream Factory of H. E. Hakes, who, in the fall of 1915, brought his ice cream plant from Bingham Lake and began to churn out hundreds of gallons of the treat every day to those living on the Currie branch of the railroad and the surrounding communities. Churches and schools were prevalent in early Windom. Still, the Ruse Hospital, the Windom Library, and the Cottonwood County Courthouse ranked among the most-frequented pieces of infrastructure. County commissioners served far and wide across four states before hiring the Norwegian architects Diedrik A. Omeyer and Martin P. Thori to build the modern structure. For the contemporary equivalent cost of about 3.5 million dollars, the Neoclassical and Renaissance Revival piece of architecture was completed between 1904-05 with the help of Jacob B. Nelson and his crew. The largest employer in the town of 4,798 residents is The Toro Company, a lawn mower, snow blower, and irrigation system company based in Bloomington. On the south edge of town, visitors are invited to marvel at Curt's Aluminum Statues, a collection of folk-and-junk art statues. Several interesting people have ties to Windom, most notably Maria Schneider, a multi-Grammy Award-winning jazz composer and orchestra leader, and Johnny Olson, the longtime game show host of classics like *Match Game*, *The Price Is Right*, *To Tell the Truth*, and *What's My Line?*; Aaron Horkey, an artist known for his work on primarily band concert posters, and Leland Bartlett "Shorty" Elness, the quarterback for the NFL's Chicago Bears in 1929.

**Restaurant Recommendation:
Bergen Bar & Grill
89982 540th Ave
Windom, MN 56101**

Comfrey is only partially located in Cottonwood County (see Brown County)

Unincorporated/Ghost Towns: Delft

National Register of Historic Places:
Jeffers: Jeffers Petroglyphs Site
Mountain Lake: Isaac Bargen House, Mountain Lake Site
Westbrook: Chicago, St. Paul, Minneapolis & Omaha Depot
Windom: Cottonwood County Courthouse

Golf Courses:
Rolling Hills Golf Club, Daily Fee (Westbrook, MN)
Windom Country Club, Daily Fee (Windom, MN)

Town Celebrations:
Storden Town Day, Storden, MN (Last Weekend in July)
Westbrook Fun Days, Westbrook, MN (4th Weekend in June)

CROW WING COUNTY
EST. 1857 - POPULATION: 66,123

Minnesota's Crow Wing County is one of several named after a waterway that meanders through its boundaries; the river was called Crow Wing for a wing-shaped island at its mouth.

BAXTER, MN
POPULATION: 8,612 – CITY 508 OF 856 (8-11-25)
A former railroad tie-treating plant, built by the Northern Pacific Railroad in 1907, marks the beginning of modern-day Baxter, now a 21.11-square-mile municipality that borders the west side of Brainerd. Located near the geographical center of Minnesota,

it was named for Luther Loren Baxter, the former attorney of the railroad company and a member of the Minnesota Legislature. Tie-treating (until 1985) and farming enabled Baxter's incorporation on May 25, 1939, making it one of Minnesota's relatively newest municipalities. At its first Census in 1930, its population was 169, and it has since increased by double-digit percentages in every subsequent decade. The most significant increase in the citizen population occurred between 2000 and 2010, when the population grew from 5,555 to 7,610. Aside from the iconic Elvis [Babe] the Blue Ox statue, Crow Wing State Park (see the Brainerd post) is the town's main driver of tourism. One of Minnesota's oldest communities, Old Crow Wing, was once located nearby. The park is also noted for an intact 1.5-mile section of the historic Red River Trail system. Northland Arboretum, founded in 1972 on 400 acres of a reclaimed former landfill, is another popular spot for visitors to connect with nature through interpretive hiking trails and a visitor center.

Restaurant Recommendation:
371 Diner
14901 Edgewood Dr N
Baxter, MN 56425

BRAINERD, MN ★☆
POPULATION: 14,395 – CITY 507 OF 856 (8-11-25)

As Europeans began to encroach on the Ojibwe's territory, the two groups had to find ways to coexist without further escalating tensions over land or resources. However, being what human nature is, eventually fingers were pointed, and settlers of the area blamed the Ojibwe for the disappearance of a local girl. Two Ojibwe were arrested based on an assumption alone and subsequently killed when an angry mob forced its way through law enforcement officers. When a small group of Ojibwe showed up a short time later, reinforcements were called in from the nearby Fort Ripley to protect the settlement in what was assumed to be an "attack of reprisals." In reality, the Ojibwe were a friendly bunch and wished to sell blueberries to the settlers. The near-catastrophe has since been referred to as the "Blueberry War of 1872." The events took place in the same period that Brainerd came into being when the Northern Pacific Railroad decided to complete a line through the area. They had wanted to bridge the Mississippi River at Crow Wing, on the land of Clem Beaulieu. Still, after repeatedly asking for too much money and accusing the railroad company of bluffing that they would build elsewhere, they did just that. A bridge was completed in 1871, seven miles to the north at Omamagua, otherwise known as The Crossing, and it was named by John Gregory Smith (President of the N.P.R.R.) for his wife, Eliza Brainerd Smith. Much of the early development was spurred by Lyman Smith, an agent of the Lake Superior and Puget Sound Land Company who platted the town, served as mayor and city councilman, and helped organize Brainerd's school district and the First National Bank of Brainerd. As the site of the Northern Pacific's headquarters, Brainerd's development came quickly. By 1873, there were already 21 stores, 18 hotels, and 15 saloons, and every other imaginable line of enterprise and railroad facilities to serve the needs of the townspeople. The offices moved to St. Paul, and Brainerd lapsed in progress for a few years. However, it retained its railroad identity when, in 1882, the Northern Pacific began building a railroad shop district, now listed on the National Register as the Northern Pacific Railroad Shops Historic District. The Brainerd Lumber Company's sawmill and paper mill, along with its proximity to the Cuyuna Iron Range and the Brainerd-Cuyuna Mine, provided residents with additional employment opportunities. However, 90% of its residents still depended on the railroad for work. It was incorporated as a village in 1896, at a time when the population was estimated to be between 5,703 (as recorded by the 1890 Census) and 7,524 (as reported by the 1900 Census). Noted fixtures of improvement built throughout the 20th century included the first municipal water tower in the United States (locally nicknamed as Paul Bunyan's flashlight) to be constructed entirely out of concrete, between 1918 and 1921; Brainerd's 1904 Carnegie Public Library; a 1916 jail and accompanying 1919-20 Beaux-Arts courthouse; the 1932 Franklin Junior High School, now the Franklin Arts Center; Central Lakes College, established in 1938 following a merger of three smaller community colleges and technical institutes, and a giant talking, blinking, animatronic Paul Bunyan statue at Paul Bunyan Land and This Old Farm Pioneer Village. On October 27, 1933, the local First National Bank of Brainerd was robbed of $32,000 by the notorious Baby Face Nelson and his gang of vigilantes. Nelson left behind only bullet holes and the story, but several other Brainerd men and women have brought recognition to the resort community. Amongst the most notable are Leslie Ambrose "Bullet Joe" Bush, an MLB pitcher credited with inventing the forkball pitch and noted for winning three World Series in 1913, 1918, and 1923, including the New York Yankees' first; Charles Marohn, an author and the founder of Strong Towns; Rick Nolan, a U.S. Congressman in the House of Representatives from Minnesota from January 2013 to January 2019; Roger Awsumb, a television show host locally remembered for his *Lunch with Casey* children's show that aired from 1954 to 1973; renowned painter and artist John Carlton Atherton; Joe Haeg, a former offensive tackle in the NFL and a champion of Super Bowl LV with the Tampa Bay Buccaneers; MMA and UFC fighter Brock Larson, and Chief Bender, a Native American pitcher who won three World Series with the Philadelphia Athletics between 1910 and 1913, and was inducted into the National Baseball Hall of Fame in 1953. Parts of the famous 1996 black comedy crime film *Fargo* were set in Brainerd, but no scenes were shot there. The Crow Wing County Historical Society Museum provides visitors with an orientation to local railroad, logging, and 19th-century Brainerd history. Crow Wing State Park serves as the town's main driver of tourism. One of Minnesota's oldest communities, Old Crow Wing, was once located nearby. The park is also noted for an intact 1.5-mile section of the historic Red River Trail system.

BREEZY POINT, MN
POPULATION: 2,574 – CITY 404 OF 856 (7-16-25)

Wilford "Captain Billy" Hamilton Fawcett, the famous creator of Fawcett Publications and the *Whiz Bang* magazine with its quirky cartoons and jokes, purchased 80 acres of land on Big Pelican Lake in 1921. He ordered the construction of several cabins, as well as the Breezy Point Lodge, which featured a casino, bowling alley, pool hall, and even a ballroom. Mr. Fawcett, who also competed in the 1924 Summer Olympics as a trap shooter, lived just long enough (until February 7, 1940) to see his little resort paradise incorporated as the Village of Pelican Lakes in 1939. The resort closed for several years before reopening to the public, but it was destroyed by fire in 1959. Ginny Simms, the Hollywood singer and film actress, rebuilt it and made her own improvements. When a large shipment of furniture intended for the resort was mistakenly shipped to Pelican Rapids, some hundred miles away, the decision was made to rename the small city. Over fifty names were submitted at an October 1969 meeting, but one stood out from all the others: Breezy Point, in honor of the lodge. By January 5, 1970, the name change was in effect, and the Village of Pelican Lakes no longer existed. In another ten years, the Wilford H. Fawcett House, built in the mid-1920s using elements of rustic architecture, was listed on the National Register of Historic Places for permanent preservation. Jeff Kreitz and Creative Steel Works are recognized in the area for their steel fabrication products, particularly a life-size moose located outside the shop.

CROSBY, MN
POPULATION: 2,360 – CITY 396 OF 856 (7-15-25)

Only one city in the United States has ever elected a Communist mayor: the mining town of Crosby, Minnesota. Karl Emil Nygard won the 1932 mayoral election by 170 votes over the incumbent F. H. Kraus. From January 3, 1933, to January 2, 1934, he held the office in the then-town of about 3,400 citizens. Named after George H. Crosby of Duluth, an iron mine manager, Crosby was platted on his behalf on October 5, 1909, and located on the lines of both the Soo Line and the Northern Pacific Railroad. A post office was established in 1910, and the city was incorporated on July 6 of the same year. Things looked promising for the young mining hamlet in its early days. The manganese-content iron ore was plentiful, and the abundant resource allowed Crosby to afford graded streets, cement sidewalks, multiple schools, a public library, two hospitals, and church edifices for the local Catholic, Lutheran, Methodist, and Presbyterian congregations. There were two banks, a multitude of stores, and a newspaper called the *Crosby Courier*. All was well until February 5, 1924, when disaster struck. Forty-one miners lost their lives in what is now referred to as the Milford Mine disaster, when a new mining tunnel was blasted far too close to Foley Lake. Water rushed into the mine, trapping the workers in 15 to 20 feet of water and mud. Only seven of the men survived. Milford Mine Memorial Park (see the Cuyuna post) was named in honor of the fallen men, who left behind over eighty children and thirty-eight widows. It was listed as the Milford Mine Historic District on the National Register in 2011, joining a historic 1910s water tower, the Soo Line Depot, and the Ironton Sintering Plant Complex, built in 1924 by the Hanna Mining Company as the second prominent beneficiation plant ever constructed in the United States on the highly-held list. A large fiberglass serpent statue, perhaps having slithered out of Serpent Lake long ago, protects its shores at Franklin Park. Interesting former residents of Crosby include Thomas W. Simons Jr., the former U.S. Ambassador to Poland from 1990 to 1993 and Pakistan from 1996 to 1998; Nick Anderson, an MLB pitcher from 2019 to 2024 and a member of the 2020 All-MLB First Team; Anthony Bonsante, a professional boxer and former contestant on The Contender, and Robert A Good, the first physician to successfully transplant human bone marrow between patients that were not identical twins. On August 19, 1957, Major David G. Simons launched from the Portsmouth Mine Pit Lake (then without water) in a large stratospheric balloon as the second part of the United States Air Force's Project Manhigh. He was sent to an altitude of 102,000 feet in an experiment to help the country achieve its space exploration aspirations.

CROSSLAKE, MN
POPULATION: 2,394 – CITY 403 OF 856 (7-16-25)

The logging industry here, spearheaded by the Crosslake Lumber Company and its nearly 1,400 men, flourished due to the presence of tens of millions of Norway and White pines. Logs were floated down the Pine River, and millions more were transported via the railroad. Watertown Township (as it was then called) became a part of Crow Wing County in 1887. In 1959 and 1964, its northern and southern portions were respectively incorporated into Crosslake Village and North Crosslake Village. The two consolidated in 1972, bringing the city's conjoined population to 1,064 by the 1980s. Early milestone years of the community also include the formation of a post office branch in 1894 and the construction of the first Pine River Dam in 1899. "The Beauty Spot of Minnesota" derived its name from the crossing currents of two rivers, which resemble a cross from the air. At a visitor center on the Paul Bunyan

Scenic Byway, visitors can compare their shoe size to that of the legendary folk hero Paul Bunyan, whose giant footsteps are marked by concrete.

Restaurant Recommendation:
Moonlite Bay Family Restaurant
37627 Co Rd 66
Crosslake, MN 56442

CUYUNA, MN
POPULATION: 296 – CITY 399 OF 856 (7-16-25)

Wood-tick racing–that's what Cuyuna, Minnesota, the town located within its namesake Cuyuna Range, has come to be known for in the modern day. For a few bucks, spectators can enter the annual race on the second Saturday of June that seeks to determine which wood tick is the best at escaping its table compound. Providing your own tick is free, or the bar sells the pesky parasites for a dollar a pop. While it's unclear whether one can keep their tick as a souvenir, tick-racers may willingly hunt for one of their own anyway at the Cuyuna Country Recreation Area. One of Minnesota's premier mountain biking destinations was established in the mining pits first brought to life by early investors. After George H. Crosby convinced men to move into the vicinity, the village of Cuyuna was laid out a mile west of the Kennedy Mine in 1906. Two years later, on November 14, 1908, it was platted and named for Cuyler Adams and his dog, Una. The duo traversed the area for long periods, seeking out only the most potentially profitable deposits for mining companies to extract ore from. The first shipments from the Cuyuna Range went out between 1910 and 1912, and within five years, production had exceeded 1.1 million tons. Residents voted to incorporate in 1910, and the Soo Line Railroad was completed shortly thereafter in response to a rush request. The First State Bank of Cuyuna (now the Cuyuna Village Hall), the *Cuyuna Miner* newspaper, a hospital, a church, two grocery stores, a waterworks, a sewer system, electricity, and a historic 1912 water tower were among the town's proud early accomplishments. A schoolhouse was built between the Kennedy mine and Rabbit Lake as one of the earliest educational facilities for the miners' children; it was replaced by the Cuyuna High School building in 1910. Iron ore production peaked at 3.71 million tons in 1953, but strangely, the local post office branch closed just a year later. It had stopped altogether by 1977. Milford Mine Memorial Park (see the Crosby post) is a nearby park paying tribute to a disastrous mining accident (Minnesota's worst on record) on February 5, 1924.

DEERWOOD, MN
POPULATION: 526 – CITY 397 OF 856 (7-15-25)

Withington was the first name given to this town in the Cuyuna Iron Range, either in honor of the wife of a railroad official or in recognition of J. S. Withington, a member of the Northern Pacific Railroad's board of directors. From 1871 to 1881, it bore this name, but the post office required it to be changed due to its close spelling and pronunciation to "Worthington" in Nobles County. Under its new name, Deerwood, given on account of the copious numbers of deer found in the woods, the town flourished as the iron range came to life. By 1913, over one hundred businesses of varying kinds, sizes, and importance were conducting trade within Deerwood's city limits. One of several "elevated metal water tanks" was raised in 1914 and later added to the National Register alongside its nearly identical peers. From 1935 to 37, the Deerwood Auditorium was built as Minnesota's most significant project by the State Emergency Relief Administration. It was designed by Carl H. Johnston Jr. and built using 800 tons of native fieldstone. A giant deer statue, appropriately leaping over a log, serves as the town's must-see roadside attraction.

EMILY, MN
POPULATION: 843 – CITY 400 OF 856 (7-16-25)
The City of Emily shares its name with Emily Township and Emily Lake, one of four lakes in the township that bear feminine names (the others being Anna, Ruth, and Mary). Ernest Andrews, George Stirewalt, and a Mr. John "Lambert" Morris settled on the west shore of the lake in the spring of 1899, less than a year before the post office was established on February 20, 1900. The latter gentleman took over postmaster duties. He and his wife, Amelia Lambert, platted the site on November 22, 1905. After five decades of growth and development, the site attained incorporation on March 7, 1957. Since the start of the 20th century, Emily's population has remained relatively stable, ranging from 813 in 2010 to 847 in 2000. A City Park, a baseball field, a branch of the Pine River State Bank, and three churches—St. Emily's Catholic Church, Emily United Methodist Church, and Emily Wesleyan Church highlight their modern pieces of infrastructure.

FIFTY LAKES, MN
POPULATION: 443 – CITY 401 OF 856 (7-16-25)
For centuries, the Sioux lived in this region of Minnesota until the rivaling Ojibwe forced their removal to the Dakotas circa 1730. Various treaties and skirmishes with the United States federal government also led to their relocation, allowing the lands to be sold for profit to prospective homesteaders and businesspeople. Several one-mile-square sections were platted in 1863 and sold to men like W. W. Allen, Nathan Corwith, and Charles Sanborn, each of whom acquired parcels for investment purposes. When a post office was finally established in the Fifty Lakes grocery store in 1926 due to extensive population growth in the area, Robert Dudley suggested that it be named "Fifty Lakes" because he could count no less than fifty lakes within a five-mile radius of his store. On May 10, 1949, the community shifted towards a permanent municipal form of government.

FORT RIPLEY, MN
POPULATION: 84 – CITY 509 OF 856 (8-11-25)
In 1848, the United States Army constructed an outpost on land that would become the second central military reservation of the lands that eventually entered statehood as "Minnesota." It was initially called Fort Marcy, but it was renamed Fort Gaines from 1849 to 1851, when John H. McKinney became postmaster. The name was changed again by the end of 1851, when Charles H. Oakes took over and named it in commemoration of Eleazer W. Ripley, a brigadier general noted for his service in the War of 1812. After helping spur immigration in the region for almost three decades, the fort was decommissioned in 1877. A Northern Pacific Railroad town grew on the opposite side of the Mississippi River and survived far longer than the frontier fort ever did; it was incorporated on March 19, 1927, and had a peak population of 126 people in the 1940s. One historic building from the old fortress remains, but the land was revitalized into Camp Ripley, used by the federal government as a military training facility starting in 1929.

GARRISON, MN
POPULATION: 194 – CITY 446 OF 856 (7-19-25)
Much like its neighbor about 400 miles to the west in Garrison, North Dakota, this similarly-named town in Crow Wing County also claims to be the "Walleye Capital of the World." And, just like the North Dakota town, they back it up with an enormous walleye statue–although this one was supposedly caught by the great Paul Bunyan and fished out of Lake Mille Lacs by Babe the Blue Ox. The vast body of water covers 132,516 acres and was reportedly home to some of the earliest human settlements in Minnesota. The small city dates to the early 1880s, when Oscar E. Garrison (also the founder of Wayzata, in Hennepin County) homesteaded the area. Midland and Rowe were among its early variant names, but when the post office opened in 1884, Oscar's wife, Mary J. Garrison, had it named in honor of her and her husband. Of all its earliest businesses, two sawmills and another mill were the most important. Fishing was another critical industry; in May 1889, an impressive 25,000 pounds of fish were shipped to Brainerd and then on to Minneapolis via the hauls of local Garrison fishermen. In the 1930s, Garrison saw significant improvements (and incorporation on May 3, 1937) when the Civilian Conservation Corps established a camp there with over 200 residents. They helped build many New Deal-era projects in the immediate vicinity, four of which remain on the National Register of Historic Places today: the Garrison Concourse roadside park on the lakeshore built between 1936 and 1939; a 1938 bridge built on U.S. Route 169 near Mille Lacs Lake; the 1939 Kenney Lake Overlook wayside, and St. Alban's Bay Culvert at Mille Lacs Lake, constructed between 1938-39. The four sites are incredibly unique for avid historians seeking multiple examples of New Deal work and stone masonry in a close geographical area. Fast-food enthusiasts frequently visit the local McDonald's as a bucket-list stop, as Garrison is the world's smallest city to have a McDonald's franchise. The Mermaid Lady of the North Shore, located at 43716 Conifer Street (on private property), was carved from a 12-foot-tall tree trunk to serve as an icon of the community.

IRONTON, MN
POPULATION: 576 – CITY 394 OF 856 (7-15-25)
Crosby's twin city of Ironton was platted on September 6, 1910, by Agnes Lamb and Carrie and John Hill. Like many other high-achieving entrepreneurs of that time, Ironton was born out of necessity as a hub and home for miners who ventured deep into the newly established Cuyuna Iron Range: a post office and lines of the Minneapolis, St. Paul & Sault Ste. Marie and the Northern Pacific Railroads moved in to accommodate the transportation of goods and people to and from the townsite. On June 5, 1911, Ironton was incorporated, and by the end of the decade, it already had a population of 1,165. Unexpectedly high tax revenues led to the creation of some luxurious structures for that era, including the 1913 Spina Hotel, a 100 by 75-foot two-story brick building with multiple commercial interests; the 1913 Ironton water tower (now demolished), and the stunning 1917 Ironton City Hall, built using elements of American Craftsman and Colonial Revival architecture. The building was once home to a library, jail, auditorium, and city offices.

JENKINS, MN
POPULATION: 490 – CITY 407 OF 856 (7-16-25)
First incorporated as a village in 1904 and then as a city in 1969, five years before Minnesota Statutes 413.02 required that all municipalities (villages, towns, etc.) formally reorganize as cities on January 1, 1974. George W. and Isabella Jenkins, a lumber family, platted the townsite after the government granted them a supply depot

in 1883. Twelve years later, the Northern Pacific Railroad arrived and began operating twice-daily and twice-nightly services through the community. A formal school district was established in 1904, but was replaced in 1920 by a two-story brick building that could better accommodate the town's young pupils. It consolidated in 1964 with nearby Pequot Lakes. Business lines included lumber yards, hotels, saloons, and grocery stores, as well as specialized firms such as boat works, a confectionery, an ironing board factory, and multiple restaurants. After the railroad discontinued passenger service in 1963 and the line was abandoned entirely in 1983, the railbed was converted into the multi-purpose Paul Bunyan State [Recreational] Trail.

MANHATTAN BEACH, MN
POPULATION: 61 – CITY 402 OF 856 (7-16-25)
Not much meets the eye for those who visit the City of Manhattan Beach on Big Trout Lake, with its population of 61, but much of its history lies with a nearly century-old resort called the Manhattan Beach Lodge. Built in 1929 as a vacationer's paradise for the wealthy elite from Chicago and the Twin Cities, the lodge was first known for its dining, horseback riding, boating, swimming, tennis, and gambling. A private band even played every night after dinner. Hollywood stars like Bob Hope, who starred in over 50 feature films during his career between 1922 and 1999, made a point of frequenting the lodge, as did more infamous figures like John Dillinger. Over the decades, the clientele shifted to families and middle-class vacationers, and it evolved into a fine-dining establishment with a total of nineteen guest rooms. The 1.53-square-mile city itself was incorporated on June 24, 1941, a couple of years after its post office (now closed as of 1994) had opened. Manhattan Beach has never had more than 86 full-time residents, according to the 1940 Census. Former names for the area were "Shore Acres" and "Potencia" until John and Stewart Merrill renamed it after a popular resort in New York.

NISSWA, MN
POPULATION: 1,967 – CITY 406 OF 856 (7-16-25)
Hundreds of avid turtle-racing lovers flock–or perhaps more appropriately, crawl–into Nisswa every Wednesday afternoon during the summertime to watch turtles compete against one another in the town that dubs itself as "The Original Home of Minnesota's Turtle Races." Community members, curious about why so many other towns were copying the event, conducted a research project that determined their annual tradition, which began in 1963, actually started far earlier than any other races in the state. While the turtles (which can be raced by anybody for a small entry fee of five dollars), shopping districts, and numerous lakes attract tourism today, the first people to visit the area arrived via the Northern Pacific Railroad. Ernest Smiley was an early homesteader and was responsible for bringing the first post office and a railroad stop to his property, which he labeled as "Smiley." When Leon E. Lum of Brainerd ordered the land to be surveyed into lots, he convinced the residents to change their name to Nisswa, a corruption of the Ojibwe word *nessawae*, meaning "in the middle." The change was effective in 1908, and Nisswa quickly saw its population rise by double-digit percentage points in every decade of the 20th century except one (between 1980 and 1990, when it dropped by 16 residents from 1,407 people to 1,391). Nisswa was incorporated on December 4, 1946, and at present has five major local historical points of interest: the Nisswa Area Historical Society, the Minnewawa Lodge, an early resort established between the 1890s and the 1920s using wood as a primary construction material; the historic two-part Grand View Lodge, built in 1918 and the mid-1920s respectively; the St. Columba Mission Site, in use from 1852 to 1862 as an Episcopal mission to the Ojibwe, and the Minnesota and International Railroad Freight House

and Shelter Shed, more popularly known as the Lake Hubert Depot on the Paul Bunyan State Trail. Adrianne Lenker, the lead musician of the indie-folk band Big Thief and a 2025 Grammy Award nominee for Best Folk Album (Bright Future, 2024), briefly lived in Nisswa while her family relocated across the country. In a freak accident, the five-year-old Lenker nearly perished when a railroad spike fell out of the family's makeshift treehouse at their Nisswa home and lodged itself in her skull.

PEQUOT LAKES, MN
POPULATION: 2,395 – CITY 405 OF 856 (7-16-25)
Famous for its fishing-bobber water tower (once used as Paul Bunyan's personal bobber), Pequot Lakes was originally known as Sibley and Frogtown before a postal official changed it. The postmaster did not dislike the name of the former logger whose name it honored, but there was already another Sibley elsewhere in southwestern Minnesota. A change had to be made. He wanted to honor Native Americans by naming the community after one of their tribes. The first word that came to mind was "Pequot," a former Algonquian tribe that lived in eastern Connecticut. It is the only instance of the name being used for a geographic location in the country. In 1896, the post office opened using the name "Pequot," and in 1900, Walter and Flora Brown filed the town plat once the Northern Pacific Railroad had completed its northward line from Brainerd. The "Lakes" was added later, but the post office did not add the suffixed noun until 1940. This change was made shortly after the start of the town's inaugural Bean Hole Days festival, which began in 1938 to commemorate the tradition of cooking beans in cast-iron kettles dug into the ground. Beans are baked in six big kettles named Thor, Big Bertha, Ole, Sven, Lena, and Baby Olga overnight, and then served to a couple of thousand festival-goers the following day. The beans and a roll are free, but dozens of vendors sell their goods in City Park. The Shawano House, listed on the Register as the H. H. Broach House, was built in the mid-1920s as a summer estate. It, a 1935 fire lookout tower, and the A.L. Cole Memorial Building, built in 1937 as a New Deal project and now utilized as a museum and senior center, are Pequot Lakes's three most historic structures. Slightly less than 1,000 people lived in Pequot Lakes in 2000, but following the annexation of Sibley Township on June 4, 2002, the population more than doubled to 2,162 people.

RIVERTON, MN
POPULATION: 118 – CITY 393 OF 856 (7-15-25)
Riverton was established in 1912 as a mining village adjacent to Little Rabbit Lake, near where the Rabbit River meets the Mississippi River. The 0.90 square mile townsite is located on the historic Rabbit Lake Indian Reservation, which had been set aside in 1855 for the Rabbit Lake Band of Mississippi Chippewa before they were moved elsewhere. Riverton's post office was organized in 1913 under the direction of the United States Postal Service but closed in 1965 as mining operations on the Cuyuna Iron Range slowed. In 1920, the area's population reached a peak of 398 people when it had both stations of the Soo Line and the Northern Pacific Railroad.

TROMMALD, MN
POPULATION: 99 – CITY 395 OF 856 (7-15-25)
One of the last towns to be established on the Cuyuna iron range was Trommald, named for A. G. Trommald. He was the Crow Wing County registrar of deeds from 1904 to 1930. It was laid out and incorporated in 1917, the second event happening on August 9, and a post office also entered service that same year. The forty-acre site was destined for greatness, as it was served by both the Northern Pacific and the

Minneapolis, St. Paul & Sault Ste. Marie Railroads, but it had multiple mines to kickstart its economy. Amongst these were the Merritt No. 1, the Joan No. 4, the Algoma, and the Ferro. A grand school, a bank, a lumber yard, a hotel, and numerous general mercantile firms were prominent in its early days. Mining operations ceased in the range for good in 1984 due to lackluster profits (compared to mining activities in the Mesabi Range), and several of the pits naturally filled with water, becoming the Cuyuna Country State Recreation Area. A 1918 metal water tower, built as one of five between Crosby, Cuyuna, Deerwood, Ironton, and Trommald thanks to sky-high mining profits, was added to the National Register of Historic Places in 1980.

Unincorporated/Ghost Towns: Barrows, Bay Lake, Crosby Beach, Crow Wing, Ideal Corners, Iron Hub, Klondyke, Lake Hubert, Legionville, Little Pine, Loerch, Merrifield, Mission, Old Crow Wing, Pine Center, Saint Mathias, Shephard, Swanburg, Wolford, Woodrow

National Register of Historic Places:
Baxter: Crow Wing State Park, Red River Trail: Crow Wing Section
Brainerd: Brainerd Public Library, Brainerd Water Tower, Crow Wing County Courthouse & Jail, Franklin Junior High School, Northern Pacific Railroad Shops Historic District, Parker Building, Werner Hemstead House
Breezy Point: Wilford H. Fawcett House
Crosby: Elevated Metal Water Tank, Crosby, Ironton Sintering Plant Complex, Soo Line Depot
Cuyuna: Cuyuna Village Hall, Elevated Metal Water Tank, Cuyana
Deerwood: Deerwood Auditorium, Elevated Metal Water Tank, Deerwood
Garrison: Bridge No.5265- Garrison, Garrison Concourse, Kenney Lake Overlook, St. Alban's Bay Culvert at Mille Lacs Lake
Ironton: Elevated Metal Water Tank, Ironton, Ironton City Hall, Spina Hotel
Nisswa: Grand View Lodge, Minnewawa Lodge, Minnesota & International Railroad Freight House & Shelter Shed
Pequot Lakes: A. L. Cole Memorial Building, H. H. Broach House, Pequot Fire Lookout Tower
Trommald: Elevated Metal Water Tank, Trommald
Wolford: Milford Mine Historic District

Golf Courses:
Breezy Point Resort – Traditional, Resort (Breezy Point, MN)
Breezy Point Resort – White Birch, Resort (Breezy Point, MN)
Crosswoods Golf Course, Daily Fee (Crosslake, MN)
Cuyuna Rolling Hills, Daily Fee (Deerwood, MN)
Deacon's Lodge, Resort (Breezy Point, MN)
Emily Greens Golf Course, Daily Fee (Emily, MN)
Golden Eagle Golf Club, Daily Fee (Fifty Lakes, MN)
Gravel Pit Golf and Event Center, Daily Fee (Brainerd, MN)
Northwood Hills Golf Course, Daily Fee (Garrison, MN)
Whitefish Golf Club, Daily Fee (Pequot Lakes, MN)

Breweries/Wineries/Distilleries:
14 Lakes Brewery (Crosslake, MN)
Big Axe Brewing Company (Nisswa, MN)
Cuyuna Brewing Company (Crosby, MN)
Jack Pine Brewery (Baxter, MN)
Roundhouse Brewery (Brainerd, MN)
Roundhouse Brewery (Nisswa, MN)
Snarky Loon Brewing Co. (Jenkins, MN)

Town Celebrations:
Beanhole Days, Pequot Lakes, MN (3rd Tuesday & Wednesday of July)
Celebrate Emily Day, Emily, MN (3rd Saturday in July)
Crosby Heritage Days, Crosby, MN (3rd Weekend in August)

Deerwood Days, Deerwood, MN (2nd Weekend in August)
Festival of Lights, Nisswa, MN (Black Friday; Day after Thanksgiving)
Fifty Lakes Day, Fifty Lakes, MN (3rd Saturday in June)
Garrison Play Days Festival, Garrison, MN (3rd Weekend of July)
Independence Day Celebration, Nisswa, MN (July 3rd)
Nisswa Turtle Races, Nisswa, MN (Summertime; Wednesday Afternoons)
Santa's Bobbin into Town, Pequot Lakes, MN (2nd Saturday in December)

DAKOTA COUNTY
EST. 1849 - POPULATION: 439,882

Until 1851, "Dakotah" was the name of Minnesota's third most populous county, until the '-h' was dropped. The Dakota Sioux lived in the region long before Europeans arrived in the Mendota area.

APPLE VALLEY, MN
POPULATION: 56,374 – CITY 611 OF 856 (9-5-25)
For a century, Lebanon Township was nothing more than a quiet rural area down the road from the bustling metropolis of the Twin Cities to the north. No downtown existed, nor did a railroad. Commercial interests were few and far between. It was not until the mid-1950s, long after the Township's 1859 establishment, that several residential developments began to appear. The first subdivision started by Orrin Thompson had only nineteen homes, but by 1960, there were another 124 homes and 585 people. An additional 1,500 were added by 1968, and by the time the 1970 Census was conducted, the region's population had grown by a whopping 1,353.3% to 8,502. The Village of Apple Valley was born, with an official incorporation date of January 1, 1969. The name "Apple Valley" was derived from Apple Valley, California, the location of the firm that selected the land for the next great residential suburb of the Twin Cities, starting with a nineteen-home subdivision. Lebanon Valley was also proposed as a name, but it lost the vote by 757 to 1,376. In 1980, Apple Valley's population surpassed 20,000 for the first time; by then, it had become home to the Minnesota Zoological Garden (opened May 22, 1978). Now known as The Minnesota Zoo, the 485-acre zoo boasts roughly 4,500 animals and 500 different species. Famous Apple Valleyians are Coleen Rowley, *Time Magazine*'s 2002 Person of the Year for her service as an FBI special agent and 9/11 whistleblower; Lindsey Vonn, a 2010 Olympic gold medalist in the women's downhill skiing event; Tre and Tyus Jones, two brothers who have played in the NBA since 2020 and 2015, respectively; Gary Trent Jr., another NBA player with ties to Apple Valley High School; Gable Steveson, a 2020 Summer Olympic gold medalist in freestyle wrestling; film actor and director Erik Jensen; Brianna Brown, an actress noted for her role as Lisa Niles in ABC's soap opera *General Hospital*; John Harvatine IV, an animator with the stop-motion animated comedy show *Robot Chicken* on Cartoon Network's Adult Swim; Vincent Kartheiser, famous for playing Pete Campbel on AMC's drama series *Mad Men*; Mark Hall, a multi-time world champion freestyle wrestler in the World Cup, Pan American Championships, and NCAA Division I championships, and Maria Thayer, an actress known for her role as Tammi Littlenut in the sitcom *Strangers with Candy*.

BURNSVILLE, MN
POPULATION: 64,317 – CITY 612 OF 856 (9-5-25)
About 250 Mdewakanton Dakota lived between Black Dog Lake and the Minnesota River in the mid-1700s, about a century before Burnsville's namesake, William Byrne, arrived from Hamilton, Ontario, Canada, with his family. He founded the town of

Hamilton (now Savage), donating land for a church, a school, and a cemetery. In 1858, the Dakota County Board of Commissioners decided to name one of the original Dakota County townships Byrnesville in his honor. Irish and Scottish settlers came in droves and brought with them their traditions and religions, leaving behind many legacy Catholic, Protestant, and Presbyterian congregations that still exist today. When rail access was achieved in 1864, Byrnesville transformed into a resort town, but remained a small town through the 1950s. The 1950 Census reported a population of only 583, but as new housing developments emerged and Interstate 35W was completed in 1960, the population grew substantially to 2,716. Residents warded off an annexation attempt by the City of Bloomington in 1964 and instead incorporated themselves as the Burnsville village that same year. This alternative spelling had been used since the town's inception, and was listed on the official incorporation papers, thus doing away with the Byrnesville variation. City status was awarded on June 18, 1969. Several shopping centers were established throughout the community, among the first being Burnsville Center in 1977. It is a 1,275,703-square-foot mall. On December 31, 1979, Burnsville welcomed the addition of its first and only property to the National Register, the Minneapolis, Saint Paul, Rochester & Dubuque Electric Traction Company Depot. It was built in 1910 on the Dan Patch Line, which connected Northfield with Minneapolis. Recreationists enjoy the sights, smells, and activities of the 1,400-acre Black Dog Preserve unit of the Minnesota Valley National Wildlife Refuge, as well as the 280-acre Crystal Lake and Lac Lavon Lake Park. The Ames Performing Arts Center hosts theaters, concerts, and other acts, whereas "The Garage" was completed as a multi-purpose community center, nonprofit music club, and teen center. Having grown so rapidly over the past century, Burnsville has boasted of an extensive number of famous men and women with communal ties: Doron Jensen, a restauranteur who founded Timber Lodge Steakhouse and Old Country Buffett; Ernie Hudson, renowned for his role as Winston Zeddemore in the *Ghostbusters* supernatural comedy series; Laura Osnes, a Tony Award-winning actress for her role as Bonnie Parker in the Broadway musical *Bonnie and Clyde*; Randy Scheunemann, a presidential campaign adviser with John McCain in 2008; Nicolas Euugene Walsh, the auxiliary bishop of the Roman Catholic Archdiocese of Seattle, Washington from 1976 to 1983; Cedric Yarbrough, an actor in *Reno911!* and ABC's sitcom *Speechless*; Melissa Peterman, an actress known for playing Barbra Jean in Reba and Brenda Sparks in the sitcom *Young Sheldon*; Cole Aldrich, an NBA player between 2010 and 2018; Alex Call, an outfielder with the MLB's Los Angeles Dodgers; contemporary Chrisitan singer Sara Groves; the rock band Dropping Daylight, and NHL players J.T. Brown, Brock Boeser, and Todd Okerlund.

COATES, MN
POPULATION: 147 – CITY 561 OF 856 (8-31-25)
Famous amongst the cityfolk for its "House of Coates" burger restaurant, open since 1962, Coates enjoys its status as one of Dakota County's smallest municipalities, with a population of fewer than 200 people. From 1904 to 1920, the little town on the Chicago Great Western Railway served as a rural post office hub, before local addresses were assigned to the City of Rosemount. The "Coates" name was given in honor of Civil War Captain Henry C. Coates of the 1st Minnesota Volunteer Infantry. It was incorporated as a village on April 7, 1953. Industry in the area is relatively quiet, but there are several metal art sculptures on display–including one of the famous Tasmanian Devil from Looney Tunes–outside of a local trucking company.

Restaurant Recommendation:
House of Coates
16300 Clayton Ave E
Rosemount, MN 55068

EAGAN, MN
POPULATION: 68,855 – CITY 609 OF 856 (9-5-25)

Most famous amongst metropolitan residents for being the site of the Twin Cities Orthopedics Performance Center, home of the NFL's Minnesota Vikings Training Facility, those who first lived in Eagan never would have imagined that their stretch of prairie wilderness would someday be the training grounds for a multi-billion-dollar sports franchise. Once called Montgomery, Eagan Township was established in the early 1860s and named in honor of the early settler Patrick Eagan. He arrived in 1853 with his wife Margaret Twohy, Edward Barry, Robert O' Neil, and Fanning, Thos, and James Wescott. He later served as the town board of supervisors' first chairman. Catholic church services were held at local homes, and the first school was started in Thos Fanning's house. A grocery store, a saloon, a tavern, and a blacksmith shop were among the first businesses to be established. When the Milwaukee, St. Paul & Minneapolis Railroad came through, more entrepreneurs started firms at a railroad station called Wescott. The Eagantown post office operated from 1860-62, but eventually the "town" part of its name was dropped. Irish farmers served as the backbone of the local economy for the first 80 years of its existence. At one point, so many onions were being grown and shipped from the area that it was nicknamed the "Onion Capital of the United States." In early 1950, only 1,185 people lived in town, but the extension of interstates and highways through the vicinity brought immense change to the former rural hamlet. By 1970, Eagan had over 10,000 citizens, a number that doubled in ten years to 20,700 by 1980, and then doubled again by the time the 1990 Census was conducted. West, a branch of Thomson Reuters and one of the largest printers of legal materials in the United States; Scantron, an assessment-creating technology company used in 98% of school districts around the country; Regional Elite Airline Services, affiliated with Delta Air Lines; Universal Cooperatives, an influential agricultural supply cooperative federation, and Blue Cross Blue Shield of Minnesota are five of Eagan's most important current and historical firms that have cumulatively employed thousands of locals and added tens of millions of dollars to Minnesota. Northwest Airlines, an independent airline from 1926 to 2010, was headquartered in Eagan before it merged with Delta Air Lines in 2010. At that point, it had been the world's sixth-largest airline in passenger miles flown and a Fortune 500 company. In addition to the Twin Cities Orthopedics Performance Center, the Minnesota Vikings' headquarters (home to the the Vikings Museum and the Vikings Locker Room merchandise store), Eagan's other prominent point of interest is the Holz Family Farmstead. Built in 1893, the living farm museum is the last remnant of Eagan's once-prosperous agricultural economy. Minnesota Aurora FC, a pre-professional women's soccer club, has been based in Eagan since 2022; it plays at the local TCO Stadium. A few noteworthy Eagan residents include Ken Martin, the chair of the Democratic National Committee since February 1, 2025; Tim Pawlenty, the 39th Governor of Minnesota; Natalie Darwitz, a three-time participant in the Olympic games between 2002 and 2010 with the U.S. women's hockey team; Zach Zenner, an NFL running back from 2015 to 2019; Nicholas David, a finalist on season three of NBC's *The Voice*; Angie Craig, a U.S. Congresswoman from Minnesota since January 2019; Tim Vakoc, the first U.S. Army chaplain to be injured in the Iraq War; Caroline

Innerbichler, an actress known for her role as Anna in the *Frozen* musical tour, and Mike Schneider, a professional poker player.

EMPIRE, MN
POPULATION: 3,177 – CITY 660 OF 856 (10-2-25)
One of Minnesota's newest incorporated cities is the City of Empire, formally incorporated on February 28, 2023. Despite its newness to the municipal scene, the "Empire" name has been used in Dakota County since the 1850s, as evidenced by postal records indicating the existence of a 1856 post office. C. A. Rollins and the Amidon brothers settled near the present site in 1854 on the Vermillion River, within the boundaries of what is now nearby Farmington. Stores and hotels were opened in the locality, and by 1858, the town was organized as Empire City. Most of its early history is better aligned with Farmington's, one of three cities (the others being Lakeville and Rosemount) that forced Empire to incorporate to establish its border and prevent any further annexation of the township's lands. On railroad maps, Empire is marked as the crossroads of the Chicago Great Western Railway and the Chicago, Milwaukee & St. Paul Railroad. Passersby on Highway 50 may notice the Watt Munisotaram, the only Cambodian Buddhist Temple in Minnesota. Decorated in gold, flowers, and Buddha statues, the impressive temple was completed in 2007 as the centerpiece of a forty-acre campus where Buddhist monks and priests live year-round.

FARMINGTON, MN ☆
POPULATION: 23,632 – CITY 661 OF 856 (10-2-25)
The Farmington of 1868 was one of Minnesota's most well-developed communities, albeit its population then (less than six hundred residents) was just a small fraction of what it is today. Seven general and dry goods stores, five saloons, three blacksmith shops, a wagon shop, a hotel, a harness shop, a furniture store, a shoemaker, and a hardware store are just a few of the businesses a wanderer of that era would have encountered, in addition to an $8,000 school building, churches, and lodges for the Grand Masons and the Good Templars. Farmingtonanians (as they had come to call themselves) sought incorporation as a village, but not without opposition. A man named James Donaldson, an early postmaster of the Farmington post office, attempted to stop the bill that had been unanimously passed by both the House and the Senate. Donaldson had close ties with Governor William Rainey Marshall, a major proponent and founder of the Republican Party in Minnesota. Not wanting to pay extra taxes towards an incorporated entity, Donaldson convinced Marshall not to sign Farmington's incorporation into law, against the wishes of the majority of the community and the entire legislature. It was not until after January 7, 1870, when power shifted to Horace Austin (another Republican, not friends with Donaldson), that Farmington was able to take the steps leading to its permanent incorporation on February 12, 1872. Significant events throughout the rest of that century included the moving of the Dakota County Fair to Farmington from Hastings in 1869, the Great Fire of November 22, 1879, that eradicated numerous homes and businesses in present-day downtown when a firework cart was inadvertently tipped over, the graduation of the first pupils from Farmington High School in 1884, and the start of free rural mail delivery in 1897. Farmington was one of the country's first post offices to offer the service. Three railroad lines affiliated with the Chicago, Milwaukee & St. Paul Railroad met at the site, aiding in early development. The Church of the Advent, built in the Carpenter Gothic architectural style under the direction of Episcopal Bishop Henry Benjamin Whipple in 1872, the towering 1880 Exchange Bank Building in downtown Farmington, and the Daniel F. Akin Farmhouse, completed in 1856 for one of the

earliest meteorologists in Minnesota, are just three of its most historical points of interest. An impressive county fair hall, originally built in 1918 and listed on the Register in 1979, was demolished in 1988, but its dome was preserved and placed on the fairgrounds as a gazebo and a testament to the old structure. Being the second-oldest community in Dakota County, second only to Hastings, Farmington has largely retained its original identity and is laid out very differently from the typical township-cities of the county.

Restaurant Recommendation:
Farmington Steak House
329 3rd St
Farmington, MN 55024

HAMPTON, MN
POPULATION: 744 – CITY 659 OF 856 (10-2-25)
Nathaniel Martin suggested the name "Hampton" in honor of his birthplace, Hartford, Connecticut; it won out over the alternate suggestions of Holden and Bellville, names of early area settlers. Although he is credited with giving the city its name, it was actually John M. Bell who first claimed land and settled in the vicinity in 1854. Several additional farmers, namely Michael Kranz, John J. Fox, Isaac N. Holton, and Peter and Nicholas Duffing, arrived that following year. Over the next fourteen years, the most notable developments were two public school buildings, a Catholic church and school (taught entirely in German), and a German Methodist church. James Archer owned the first hotel circa 1856, the same year that a post office was organized, and Peter Meis established the original Hampton grocery store and saloon in 1866. After much deliberation amongst the settlers and the arrival of the Chicago Great Western Railway, Hampton was incorporated on July 13, 1896. Down the road from Hampton at Tom Eilen and Sons Trucking is a collection of large, quirky statues, namely a Viking and a beachgoer.

HASTINGS, MN ★
POPULATION: 22,154 – CITY 562 OF 856 (8-31-25)
Strategically located at the confluence of the St. Croix and the Vermillion Rivers with the "Big Muddy," Hastings has long served as one of Minnesota's earliest and most critical shipping points, and as Dakota County's most important town of commerce despite its far-eastern location. Circa 1820, Lieutenant William G. Oliver and his troops camped on the Mississippi to guard a shipment of supplies en route to Fort Saint Anthony in modern-day Minneapolis. In 1833, Joseph R. Brown became the first settler of the town, then called Oliver's Grove, and seven years later, it became the county seat of St. Croix County, Wisconsin Territory. Developments during that decade by Congressman Henry Hastings Sibley to create the Minnesota Territory brought the village back into modern-day Minnesota on March 3, 1849. Hastings as we know it today was platted in 1853, and its name (honoring the second name of Congressman Sibley, later Minnesota's first governor) was drawn out of a bucket of suggestions submitted by the town founders. No time was wasted building the townsite, as businessmen knew the opportunities the town could offer, given its location on the river's reliable waterpower from Vermillion Falls. Lumber, milling, and railroads were the early industry leaders, as their developments led to the construction of Harrison Graham's (the inventor of the graham cracker) mill in 1854; LeDuc and Stowell's sawmill in 1855; the Pringle Hardware Store, likely the oldest in Minnesota; the *Dakota Weekly Journal* newspaper; the First National Bank of Hastings, Minnesota's second-

oldest national bank, and the St. Luke's Episcopal, First Presbyterian, and Guardian Angels Catholic churches. All of these places existed within the first three years of Hastings's platting, and numerous additional elevators, mills, businesses, churches, and schools emerged over the following decades. The Hastings and Dakota Railway Company was founded in 1867 by William LeDuc, John Meloy, E.D. Allen, P. Van Auken, and Stephen Gardner to connect Hastings with cities as far west as the Pacific Ocean. Although the company never achieved that feat on its own, it did reach Ortonville, Minnesota, before it was annexed into the Chicago, Milwaukee & St. Paul Railroad system. A branch line between Stillwater and Hastings was built in 1880 to move goods between the two river cities for nearly a century before it was abandoned in 1979. Much of Hastings's history has been preserved through listings on the National Register. Thirty-five properties built between 1860 and 1900 are listed as the East Second Street Commercial Historic District, as are thirteen homes constructed between 1850 and 1890 as the West Second Street Residential Historic District. Seven homes are listed separately as the Ignatius Eckert (Italian Villa), William G. LeDuc (Gothic Revival), Byron Howes (Italianate), MacDonald-Todd (Greek Revival), Rudolph Latto (Italianate and Eastlake), Thompson-Fasbender (Second Empire), and VanDyke-Libby (Second Empire) homes. Ramsey Mill and Old Mill Park honor the legacies of Alexander Ramsey and Dr. Thomas Foster, a four-story gristmill that once produced as many as 125 barrels per day before it was burned down on December 22, 1894. Hastings was also home to the Hudson Manufacturing Company Factory from 1914 to 1946, which was one of the nation's largest manufacturers of farm equipment at the time. Two churches, the Hastings Methodist Episcopal Church erected in 1861 and The First Presbyterian Church of Hastings built between 1875 and 1881; the Hastings Foundry-Star Iron Works, a very early industrial building raised in 1859, and the Dakota County Courthouse, one of the state's oldest courthouse buildings having been built from 1869 to 1871, round out most of its historic (registered) landmarks. A unique spiral bridge on the Mississippi directed horse-drawn traffic to street level from 1895 to 1951, before it was no longer able to accommodate modern vehicles. Lock and Dam No. 2 was completed by the Army Corps of Engineers in 1930, and in the 1950s, Frank Lloyd Wright contributed to the cityscape with his Fasbender Clinic. Listing all of the famous men and women who have "put Hastings on the map" over the years would be impossible. Nevertheless, some of them include Craig Kilborn, an anchor of ESPN's Sportscenter from 1993 to 1996 and the first host of Comedy Central's *The Daily Show* from 1996 to 1998; Gil Dobie, a Member of the College Football Hall of Fame since 1951 inducted for his head coaching contributions to several college programs; MaryJanice Davidson, the author and mind behind the *Undead* paranormal romance series; Clara Mairs, an early painter and printmaker, and NHL players Derek Stepan, Jeff Taffe, Dean Talafous, and Taylor Chorney.

INVER GROVE HEIGHTS, MN
POPULATION: 35,801 – CITY 607 OF 856 (9-5-25)
German and Irish settlers located on the Pine Bend on the western side of the Mississippi River starting in 1852, in an area that became known as "Inver Grove." "Inver" referred to an Irish fishing village, and "Grove" was a descriptive word for the motherland of the Germans. The two groups lived in harmony with one another as they worked to establish twenty-dozen farmsteads, four churches, and four schools over the first thirty years of the township's existence. One of these homes was owned by Reuben Freeman, who built an eight-gabled, coursed fieldstone home circa 1875 that has since been added to the National Register of Historic Places. Around the time that the town plat of Pine Bend was made by H.G.O. Morrison, Robert Foster, William A. Bissell, and A.A. Lovejoy, several area businesses were operational, including flouring

and sawmills, stores, and hotels. Although Pine Bend failed as a community, the churches and schools survived, which allowed for other lines of commerce to emerge in Inver Grove Township over the decades. A village called Inver Grove was incorporated on July 12, 1909, after the Chicago Great Western Railway and the Chicago, Rock Island & Pacific Railroads extended their lines through the area, following the natural course of the Mississippi. The City of Inver Grove Heights was founded in 1965 after the construction of highways allowed for land developers to come in and lay out large subdivisions. From 1950 to 1960, the population grew by 159% from 2,419 to 6,266, and by 1970, it had doubled again to 12,148. A small plaque and boulder mark the site where a Cold War-era B-52D bomber en route from Loring Air Force Base, Limestone, Maine, crashed and killed seven men onboard. Nine others were injured, including the one survivor from the plane and eight members of a family on the ground. A Rock Island swinging bridge built in 1894 to serve rail cars on the top deck and horse-drawn carriages on the bottom deck was nearly demolished in 2009. Its decks and remaining structure (those parts which did not naturally decay and fall apart) were refurbished for $2,300,000 into a park. Gertens Greenhouses, one of the largest garden centers in the country, is located here, as is Inver Hills Community College, a public community college established in 1970.

Restaurant Recommendation:
B-52 Burgers & Brew
5639 Bishop Ave
Inver Grove Heights, MN 55076

LAKEVILLE, MN
POPULATION: 69,490 – CITY 613 OF 856 (9-6-25)
One of the largest outer-ring suburbs of the Twin Cities is the City of Lakeville, started in the mid-to-late 1850s by lumber baron J. J. Brackett and G. Phelps as a halfway point between Saint Paul and Saint Peter. He named the lake there Prairie Lake (now Lake Marion), and George Fagan opened a hotel there in 1855. Stores, a blacksmith shop, a school, and other typical establishments were built. However, it was the arrival of the Hastings and Dakota subdivision of the Chicago, Milwaukee & St. Paul Railroad in 1869 that brought about a new semi-permanent village called Fairfield. Because it was located in Lakeville Township and the post office had been using the name Lakeville since 1854, when it came time for the village to incorporate on March 28, 1878, it adopted that name over Fairfield. Cartographers Warner & Foote published a village map the following year that showed the existence of School No. 106, a depot, a post office, a grange hall, All Saints Catholic Church, and a small business district. When Colonel Marion Willis Savage constructed the famous Antlers Amusement Park in 1910, a new short line railroad was built to bring in visitors from throughout the region and connect Savage's farm in Northfield to the Twin Cities. The Minneapolis, St. Paul, Rochester, and Dubuque Electric Traction Company was nicknamed the Dan Patch Railroad Line after the unbeatable horse of the same name; he was the most dominant harness-racing competitor of the time. The Standardbred pacer set the world speed records at least fourteen times in the early 1900s. In 1918, the Dan Patch Lines were taken over by the 87-mile Minneapolis, Northfield and Southern Railway. That same year, the Emil J. Oberhoffer House, built for the founder and first conductor of the Minneapolis Symphony Orchestra, was constructed. It is now Lakeville's only historic property listed on the National Register. Danes, Scots, Irish, and English settlers continued to trickle into the region until the 1960s, when the population exploded by 717.7% from 924 people in 1960 to 7,556 by 1970. Like its neighbors, those numbers doubled by 1980, and in the decades since, Lakeville has grown to

become Minnesota's 10th-largest incorporated city by population. Airlake Industrial Park is located here and is home to over two hundred companies. However, the largest of them all is Post Consumer Brands, a packaged goods food manufacturer best known for producing Honey Bunches of Oats cereal, Peter Pan Peanut Butter, and 9Lives cat food. Hot Sam's Antiques, a famous roadside stop for its all-for-sale folk art pieces built by Bobbie Jake Hood, and a rare F-86H Korean Sabre Jet at Aronson Park are a couple of offbeat tourist attractions in the Lakeville area. Some of the city's most noted people include Paul Krause, a member of the Pro Football Hall of Fame, an 8-time Pro Bowler, and one of the greatest safeties ever to play the game; Regan Smith, a two-time gold medalist in the 2024 Paris Olympic Games in the women's 4x100m medley and 4x100m mixed medley events; Jeff Braun, a mixing engineer who has mixed eighteen #1 songs and won a CMA Award for his work; Rachel Banham, a WNBA player since 2016, and professional ice hockey players Brady Skjei (691+ game appearances), Ryan Poehling (283+ career matches), Jake Oettinger (251+ game appearances), Jordan Schroeder (165 career games), Charlie Lindgren (149+ career appearances).

Restaurant Recommendation:
Taqueria Los Compadres
11276 210th St W #102
Lakeville, MN 55044

LILYDALE, MN
POPULATION: 809 – CITY 605 OF 856 (9-4-25)
Tucked away in the far northwest corner of Dakota County is Lilydale, a town named for the copious amount of lily pads in Pickerel Lake. Initially platted as Lilly Dale in 1886 and incorporated in 1901, the Chicago, Milwaukee & St. Paul Railroad town was susceptible to constant flooding early on because of its location in the river flats of the Mississippi River. Citizens eventually moved and rebuilt their town on top of the bluffs. Lilydale achieved a new all-time high population of 809 people as of 2020.

MENDOTA, MN
POPULATION: 183 – CITY 606 OF 856 (9-4-25)
Some of Minnesota's oldest history took place at Mendota, which bills itself as "Minnesota's First City" because of its early impact on the region. First settled by the Dakota, who called the place *Ohe-ya-wa-he*, for a sacred burial place, it was not until 1805-06 that Europeans—Zebulon Pike and his expedition—made their way up the Minnesota River. The area was noted in his logs, and by the 1820s, Duncan Campbell had established St. Peter's fur trading post. It was a rendezvous point for French fur traders. Fort Saint Anthony (renamed Fort Snelling in 1825) was built opposite the trading post on the western side of the river as a pioneer fortification of the United States government on the frontier of the West. Permanent settlement began closer to 1834, at which point two of Minnesota's oldest stone structures were built: the Henry H. Sibley House, completed in 1836 and now preserved as the Sibley Historic Site, home to Minnesota's oldest private residence; and the Jean-Baptiste Faribault House, part of the same site and the Mendota Historic District on the National Register of Historic Places. In 1837, the settlement was renamed Mendota, a derivation of the term bdóte, meaning "junction of one river with another," which is appropriate given its location at the confluence of the Minnesota and Mississippi Rivers. Trade between Mendota and Fort Snelling began when the Mendota Ferry entered service in 1842, and by 1844, Mendota was incorporated as a town following Congress's passage of

the Town Site Act. Minnesota Territory was introduced in 1849 when Henry Sibley was elected to Congress, and Senator Stephen Douglas of Illinois, the sponsor of the Minnesota bill, suggested that Mendota be designated as the territorial capital because of the grandeur and beauty of Pilot Knob Park. Interestingly, Sibley proposed that the capital be placed in St. Paul rather than at his home, and Mendota was no longer under consideration. It was, however, the site of the 1851 Treaty of Mendota, which relocated the Mdewakanton and Wahpekute to the Lower Sioux Agency in present-day Morton, Minnesota, after they relinquished all their territory in Iowa and the Minnesota Territory. Minnesota's alleged oldest church, The Church of St. Peter, was erected in 1853 using native limestone and funds donated by Sibley and Faribault. From 1854 to 1857, it served as the second county seat of Dakota County. Stores, schools, a creamery, and lines of the Chicago, Milwaukee & St. Paul Railroad and the "Omaha Road" came to town. As the years passed, Mendota remained small yet remembered for its critical early contributions to Minnesota history. In 1925-26, an architectural marvel was completed when the world's largest (now formerly) continuous concrete arch bridge, at 4,119 feet, connected Mendota with Fort Snelling. Aside from Sibley, Minnesota's first Governor from May 24, 1858, and January 2, 1860, and the famed fur trader Faribault, noted Mendota figures include Joseph Godfrey, who fought on behalf of the Dakota during the Dakota War of 1862 as the only African-American combatant; Timothy J. Corbett, the first Roman Catholic Bishop of Crookston, Minnesota from 1910 to 1938, and Hypolite Dupuis, a French Canadian fur trader who owned the first general store in town.

MENDOTA HEIGHTS, MN
POPULATION: 11,744 – CITY 608 OF 856 (9-5-25)

Much of Mendota Heights' history is tied to the nearby City of Mendota. This much larger, eastern neighbor of Minnesota's historic first city was incorporated on February 12, 1956, as the Village of Mendota Heights. Formed out of Mendota Township, the first of twenty Dakota County townships organized in 1858, Mendota Heights is best known for the Oheyawahi-Pilot Knob. The scenic overlook has long been a sacred gathering place and burial ground for the Dakota. In later years, steamboats used it as a landmark to help them navigate the Minnesota River Valley. Stephen Douglas, the famed United States Senator from Illinois, heavily promoted placing the state capital atop the hill, but Henry Hastings Sibley swayed opinion to put it in St. Paul instead. The Treaty of Mendota was signed at a sacred site in 1851, ceding over 25 million acres of Dakota land to the United States government. Trucking and dairy farming were the city's primary industries until the 1950s, when incorporation occurred and the population began to rise rapidly (from 2,107 people in 1950 to 5,028 by 1960). Justin Morneau, a four-time All-Star baseman for the Minnesota Twins and the 2006 AL MVP; Matt Birk, a six-time Pro Bowl center with the Minnesota Vikings from 1998 to 2008; and Robert and Kathleen Ridder. All have communal ties to Mendota Heights.. Mr. Ridder founded the Minnesota Amateur Hockey Association and the Minnesota North Stars NHL hockey franchise, and Mrs. Ridder advocated for women's athletic programs at the University of Minnesota and greatly assisted the women's ice hockey program there.

MIESVILLE, MN
POPULATION: 138 – CITY 558 OF 856 (8-31-25)

Miesville was named in honor of John Mies, who established a saloon, restaurant, and boarding house at the site in 1874. He started the townsite shortly after the Saint Joseph Catholic Church of Douglas congregation began conducting services here. Knowing that German and Irish parishioners would need businesses to accompany their homes, he established the companies mentioned above and encouraged other entrepreneurs to join him in his endeavors. Very few people moved into the village because it had no railroad, but the postal service did establish an office at Trout Brook, which operated from 1878 to 1884. Its name was changed to Miesville in '84 before it was ultimately discontinued in 1903. Miesville was incorporated as a village on August 1, 1951, and is best known today for being the site of King's Place burgers and the Miesville Ravine Park Preserve and its wood-laden hiking trails and trout-fishing stream.

Restaurant Recommendation:
King's Place Bar & Grill
14460 240th St E
Hastings, MN 55033

NEW TRIER, MN
POPULATION: 86 – CITY 559 OF 856 (8-31-25)

At the heart of New Trier is the Church of Saint Mary's, a Catholic congregation founded in 1855-56 when droves of German Catholics moved to the area. Their parish officially began on May 8, 1856, with Father Keller from Saint Paul, and the first Mass was celebrated in Fred Fuchs's shanty. A log church was furnished in 1857, a stone replacement in 1864, and in 1909, the beautiful Beaux-Arts style bright-red brick edifice was completed atop a local hill. When it came time for the townspeople to incorporate and formally name their community, they deliberated between New Luxemburg and New Trier. Many early settlers had come from Luxemberg and Trier, Germany. New Trier was selected. Five saloons, five feed barns, three blacksmith shops, three general stores, two shoemakers, a harness shop, a hardware store, a cheese factory, a doctor's office, and a dance hall were early businesses and points of interest in addition to the church, convent, and a parochial school. When the Chicago Great Western Railroad surpassed the hamlet in favor of Hampton, just to the west, many residents left in search of greener pastures. The local post office branch was discontinued in 1933, after serving the town since 1867. Since then, New Trier has boasted a population as high as 153 in the 1970s and as low as 73 in the 1950s.

RANDOLPH, MN
POPULATION: 466 – CITY 658 OF 856 (10-2-25)

First called Richmond for John Richmond, the town's first settler, the community's name was changed to Randolph after it was discovered that another Richmond already existed in Stearns County. D.B. Hurlburt suggested the new name to honor John Randolph of Roanoke, a Virginia statesman who served in Congress off and on between 1825 and 1833. Richmond arrived in 1854 and was joined by Richard Morrill, William Fowler, Charles Kern, and Mr. Hurlburt, amongst other hopeful pioneers, the following year. Randolph was incorporated as a village on May 23, 1857, but it did not receive a post office until 1886, around the time several railroads passed through the townsite. The Wisconsin, Minnesota & Pacific and the Chicago Milwaukee & St. Paul Railroads ran parallel to one another, and the Chicago Great Western Railway crossed them at a junction. Railroading ended in the 1970s and 1980s when the final tracks were abandoned by the Chicago & Northwestern Railroad. In addition to businesses and schools, Randolph once had three church congregations: the 1889 Methodist church, now serving as the Randolph Area Historical Society Museum; the 1925 Baptist church, demolished in 1987, and Saint Mark's Lutheran Church, located in the old public school building from 1945 to 1994 before that structure was razed.

ROSEMOUNT, MN
POPULATION: 25,650 – CITY 610 OF 856 (9-5-25)

Saratoga was only briefly considered as this town's potential name, as the alternative "Rosemount" was far more popular with the area's large population of Irish settlers. Hugh Derham and Andrew Keegan, both from the village of Rosemount in Ireland, suggested the name circa 1855, when the United States Postal Service established the post office. Keegan was the original postmaster, and the region had briefly been alluded to as Keegan's Lake because his farm adjoined the townsite. Early business development took place on Dodd Road, named for Captain William B. Dodd, who helped to lay the path that would connect Mendota with St. Peter. When landowners demanded that the Iowa & Minnesota Division of the Chicago, Milwaukee & St. Paul pay too much to build their right-of-way along the Dodd, they instead laid their tracks a mile to the east, bringing many of the early lines of commerce with them. A depot, a 40,000-bushel-capacity grain elevator, the post office, the Rosemount Town Hall, a Methodist church, a Catholic parsonage, and Temperance Hall were recorded on a very early plat map as essential points of interest in 1879. Incorporation had been achieved only a few years before the map's drawing, specifically on February 16, 1875. There was another town in the vicinity called Rich Valley, which from 1858 to 1935 had its own post office and a Chicago Great Western Railway depot. By the mid-twentieth century, Rosemount had a population of fewer than 1,000 persons. Still, it did attract large manufacturers like the Gopher Ordnance Works, a World War II era gunpowder plant that manufactured smokeless rifle and cannon powder, and the Pine Bend Refinery, built in 1955 by the Great Northern Oil Company. Rosemount's now-largest employer is the largest refinery in the United States in a state without any oil wells. Dakota County Technical College was established shortly afterwards in 1970 as the area's public technical college. Between 1970 and 1980, Rosemount experienced its "boomtown" period, during which it grew from 1,337 residents to 5,083. By the turn of the century, that number had nearly tripled. The town is most famous in the metropolitan area for being home to the Rosemont High School Marching Band. This prestigious band has performed at the Macy's Thanksgiving Day Parade, the Tournament of Roses New Year's Day Parade, and other major national events. Bernie Leadon, the founding member of the Eagles and a member of the Rock and Roll Hall of Fame; Kirk Cousins, an NFL quarterback since 2012 best known for his 2018 to 2023 tenure with the Minnesota Vikings; Pierce Butler, an Associate Justice of the United States Supreme Court from January 1923 to November 1939; Mike Morris, a long snapper in the NFL from 1986 to 1999; Lona Williams, an early writing assistant with Fox's *The Simpsons*; Mike Richman, a mixed martial artist; Tom Compton, an NFL offensive tackle from 2012 to 2022, and Tom Preissing, who played 326 games in the NHL, all have had connections to Rosemount at some point.

Restaurant Recommendation:
Malekü Coffee
15059 Crestone Ave
Rosemount, MN 55068

SOUTH SAINT PAUL, MN
POPULATION: 20,759 – CITY 602 OF 856 (9-4-25)

Once one of America's largest meatpacking centers, South St. Paul developed an identity of its own as a blue-collar town, distinct from its neighbors to the north, Minneapolis and St. Paul. Clearly named for its geographic relation to its sister cities, this point on the Mississippi River was originally called Kaposia. This Native American village was established in 1826 by Dakota Chief Big Thunder, Little Crow IV; it was moved in 1853 to a reservation after various treaties with the United States government forced their removal from the area. In that same year, settlers began to make their claims, and the new Village of Kaposia was named the judicial seat of Dakota County. This honor lasted only a year before the seat was moved to Mendota. Additionally, the local post office only retained the name Kaposia from 1853 to 1854, before the area was organized into West St. Paul Township. The City of South St. Paul arose in 1887 out of necessity to provide services to farmers and those working at the then-newly established stockyards. A grand Stockyards Exchange building, designed using elements of Romanesque architecture by Charles A. Reed, was erected by the Union Stock Yards Company of Omaha. The building was also the site of South St. Paul's first bank, city offices, and the city post office for some time. With such a large operation occurring on a point served by the Chicago Great Western Railway and the Mississippi River, four major meat packing plants opted to establish themselves nearby. Two of these were Swift & Company in 1887, now a part of JBS USA (which purchased the firm in 2007), and the Armour and Company plant that once dominated Omaha, Nebraska, and Chicago, Illinois's meatpacking industries for decades before selling out to ConAgra Foods. South St. Paul lost part of its land in February 1889 to the newly-established West St. Paul, and later that year, Inver Grove Township annexed some of its southern lands. In 1960, South St. Paul reclaimed some acreage from Inver Grove Township, and as of 2020, it measures 6.07 square miles and has a population of 20,759. Four interesting points of interest separate from the Stockyards Exchange Building are the 1923-24 Serbian Home community building; the 1924 Saint Stefan's Romanian Orthodox Church, an eye-catching mid-century modern office building called the Farmers Union Central Exchange Second Headquarters Building, and Luther Memorial Church, one of Minnesota's newest locations on the National Register of Historic Places as of August 2025. A few of the city's most noteworthy persons of interest include Marguerite Cole, the first woman to vote in the United States (in an August 27, 1920 election in South Saint Paul, a day after the Nineteenth Amendment was ratified); Mike Farrell, noted for his role as Captain B.J. Hunnicutt in CBS's war comedy drama television series *M*A*S*H*; Doug Woog, a member of the United States Hockey Hall of Fame for his contributions to coaching and broadcasting within the sport; Jim Carter, a linebacker with the NFL's Green Bay Packers from 1970 to 1978; Sunisa Lee, a two-time Olympic gold-medalist gymnast in the 2020 Tokyo and 2024 Paris Games; Grant Hart, former drummer for the punk rock band Hüsker Dü; Justin Faulk, a long-time NHL defenseman with nearly one-thousand game appearances; Betty McCollum, a U.S. Congressman from Minnesota since January 3, 2001, and James Patrick Shannon, who briefly served as the Roman Catholic Bishop of the Roman Catholic Archdiocese of Saint Paul and Minneapolis before becoming the first and only Bishop to leave the priesthood post-Vatican II.

SUNFISH LAKE, MN
POPULATION: 522 – CITY 603 OF 856 (9-4-25)

One of America's wealthiest towns, Sunfish Lake, was incorporated as a village on June 12, 1958, separate from Inver Grove Township. The median home price in the neighborhood exceeds one million dollars, and all of its services are provided by neighboring communities (fire service, Mendota Heights; police, West Saint Paul; snow removal, Inver Grove Heights; city planning, Minneapolis). As a result of its grandeur, many famous athletes have called Sunfish Lake home over the years, including T.J. Hockenson, an NFL tight end with the Detroit Lions or Minnesota Vikings since 2019; Joe Mauer, a six-time All-Star, 2009 AL MVP, five-time Silver Slugger Award winner, and three-time Gold Glove Award winner with the MLB's Minnesota

Twins; Linval Joseph, a two-time Pro Bowl defensive tackle with the Vikings in 2016 and 2017, and Corbin Lacina, an Emmy Award-winning sports broadcaster who played as an offensive lineman in the NFL from 1993 to 2003. Ann Bancroft, the first woman to reach the Antarctic and Arctic on multiple occasions, and Vince Flynn, the original author of the *Mitch Rapp* political thriller novels, also have communal ties with the city.

VERMILLION, MN
POPULATION: 441 – CITY 560 OF 856 (8-31-25)

Unlike many of its Dakota County counterparts, not much has changed in Vermillion (size-wise, as it has been untouched by the urban sprawl seen in the northwest portion of the county) since its early days. European inhabitants Moses Cole, Andrew Warsop, R.J. Smith, Samuel Brown, and William Cole, amongst others, decided that the banks of the Vermillion River offered a fruitful opportunity to start anew. Enough people had accumulated by 1855 to warrant the establishment of a post office, which later changed its name to Castle Rock before closing in 1895. In 1874, a second office was started, again using the name Vermillion. The decision to reopen the second Vermillion office was likely made after the Chicago, Milwaukee & St. Paul Railroad was extended to that point, and several businesses were established along the line. Some of these firms would have included blacksmiths, livery barns, elevators, and stores supplying hardware, dry goods, and other essential supplies settlers would have needed to survive during that era. Vermillion was incorporated as a village on February 23, 1881. Since then, Vermillion has attained a peak population (in 1990) of 510 people.

WEST ST. PAUL, MN
POPULATION: 20,615 – CITY 604 OF 856 (9-4-25)

West Saint Paul, which is actually located directly south of Minnesota's capital city, came to fruition when the city split off from the City of South Saint Paul in 1889. The confusing name was not meant to be a descriptor of its geographical location to Saint Paul, but rather for its location on the west bank of the Mississippi River. It was actually a separate legal entity using the "West St. Paul" name that existed at that time in an area now called Saint Paul's lower West Side neighborhood, now one of the largest Hispanic communities in the Twin Cities. This original hamlet was laid out in the fall of 1857 and had ambitious plans to serve as the railroad terminus for lines such as the Minnesota and West St. Paul Railroad, operated via the Cedar Valley Railroad Company. The plan never prevailed, despite the village having numerous hardware, dry goods, and grocery stores, blacksmith shops, a wagon maker, multiple churches, and a schoolhouse. Five years after it was platted, the original West St. Paul reverted to township status, and St. Paul annexed the land in 1874. The new West St. Paul began following the meatpacking and stockyards boom of the late 1880s, and since then it has grown into one of the many highly populated suburbs of the Twin Cities. A 2.5-mile-long retail strip was established along Robert Street to provide commercial opportunities for residents and entrepreneurs alike. Joan Kroc, the third wife of McDonald's CEO and founder Ray Kroc; Tom Gibis, the voice actor of Shikamaru Nara in *Naruto*, and Harold Stassen, the 25th Governor of Minnesota and a former front-runner Republican nominee for United States President in the 1948 election, are West St. Paul's three most famous persons of past and present. The city also claims to have the "Smallest Dedicated Park in the United States," thanks to a recognition obtained from R.L. Ripley's "Believe It or Not." The George W. Wentworth House, a 1887 Queen Anne that housed the man who organized the City of South Saint Paul, was added to the National Register of Historic Places in 1979.

Northfield is only partially located in Dakota County (see Rice County).

Unincorporated/Ghost Towns: Castle Rock, Etter, Lewiston, Nininger, Waterford

National Register of Historic Places:
Burnsville: Minneapolis Saint Paul Rochester & Dubuque Electric Traction Company Depot
Eagan: Holz Family Farmstead
Eureka Township: Christiania Lutheran Free Church
Farmington: Church of the Advent, Daniel F. Akin House, Exchange Bank Building
Fort Snelling: Fort Snelling
Hastings: Byron Howes House, Dakota County Courthouse, East Second Street Commercial Historic District, Fasbender Clinic, First Presbyterian Church, Hastings, Hastings Foundry-Star Iron Works, Hastings Methodist Episcopal Church, Hudson Manufacturing Company Factory, Ignatius Eckert House, MacDonald-Todd House, Ramsey Mill & Old Mill Park, Rudolph Latto House, Thompson-Fasbender House, VanDyke-Libby House, West Second Street Residential Historic District, William G. LeDuc House
Inner Grove Heights: Reuben Freeman House
Lakeville: Emil J. Oberhoffer House
Mendota: Fort Snelling-Mendota Bridge, Henry H. Sibley House, Mendota Historic District
Mendota Heights: Oheyawahi Pilot Knob
New Trier: Church of Saint Mary's- Catholic
South St. Paul: Farmers Union Central Exchange Headquarters Building, Luther Memorial Church, Saint Stefan's Romanian Orthodox Church, Serbian Home, Stockyards Exchange
Waterford Township: District No. 72 School, Waterford Bridge
West St. Paul: George W. Wentworth House

Golf Courses:
Bellwood Oaks Golf Course, Daily Fee (Hastings, MN)
Birnamwood Public Colf Course, Municipal (Burnsville, MN)
Brackett's Crossing Country Club, Private (Lakeville, MN)
Crystal Lake Golf Club, Daily Fee (Lakeville, MN)
Emerald Greens Golf Club, Daily Fee (Hastings, MN)
Hastings Golf Club, Daily Fee (Hastings, MN)
Heritage Links Golf Club, Daily Fee (Lakeville, MN)
Hidden Greens Golf Course, Daily Fee (Hastings, MN)
Inver Grove Golf Course – Executive 9, Short Course (Inver Grove Heights, MN)
Inver Wood Golf Course, Municipal (Inver Grove Heights, MN)
Lost Spur Golf Course, Daily Fee (Eagan, MN)
Mendota Heights Par-3 Golf Course, Municipal (Mendota Heights, MN)
Somerset Country Club, Private (Mendota Heights, MN)
Southern Hills Golf Club, Daily Fee (Farmington, MN)
Southview Country Club, Private (West St. Paul, MN)
Valleywood Golf Course, Municipal (Apple Valley, MN)

Breweries/Wineries/Distilleries:
Alexis Bailly Vineyard (Hastings, MN)
Angry Inch Brewing (Lakeville, MN)
Bald Man Brewing (Eagan, MN)
Hawk Meadow Winery (Hastings, MN)
Lakeville Brewing (Inver Grove Heights, MN)
Lakeville Brewing Company (Lakeville, MN)
North 20 Brewing Co. (Rosemount, MN)
Spiral Brewing (Hastings, MN)
Trove Brewing (Burnsville, MN)

Town Celebrations:
Hastings River Town Days, Hastings, MN (3rd Weekend in July)
Kaposia Days, South St. Paul, MN (Last Full Weekend in June)
Leprechaun Days, Rosemount, MN (3rd through the 4th Saturday of July)
Pioneer Village Antique Power Show, Hastings, MN (4th Weekend in July)

DODGE COUNTY
EST. 1855 - POPULATION: 20,867

Henry Dodge, the 1st/4th Governor of the Wisconsin Territory and the namesake of this jurisdiction, was created from parts of Rice County and unorganized territory in 1855.

CLAREMONT, MN
POPULATION: 513 – CITY 738 OF 856 (10-20-25)
Claremont was named after Claremont, Sullivan County, New Hampshire, and was once an essential agricultural stop on the Chicago & North Western Railway. George Hitchcock was postmaster in 1856 when a branch of the postal service was established; there was also an "East Claremont" post office from 1872 to 1879. After its incorporation on March 22, 1878, Claremont's industry focused primarily on butter, eggs, and other agricultural products. The economy bolstered the town's ability to welcome more residents, thereby opening more businesses and attracting more organizations, a few of which by 1905 included two elevators, lumber yards, stockyards, a feed mill, a creamery, a hotel, a bank, and Catholic and Methodist Episcopal churches. As many as 620 people lived in Claremont at one time (in 2000), according to U.S. Decennial Census records.

DODGE CENTER, MN
POPULATION: 2,844 – CITY 733 OF 856 (10-19-25)
Named for its centralized location within the county, which D. C. Fairbank named for Henry Dodge, the 1st and 4th Governor of Wisconsin Territory, Dodge Center welcomed its first train engine on July 13, 1866, via the Winona & St. Peter Railroad, and was soon platted as Minnesota's newest village in 1867. Some locals disliked the name and instead wanted to name it Silas, but despite submitting a bill to the legislature in 1870, the Dodge Center nomenclature remained intact. D. L. Tyler owned the first general store, but by 1870, there was also the Kinney House hotel and two grain elevators. An opera house, the *Dodge Center Press* newspaper, the Windsor Hotel, the Hartley House hotel, and a three-story roller mill were among the significant business developments of the city as it grew following the arrival of a second railway, the Chicago & Great Western (then the Minnesota & Northwestern) in 1870. Flour from the mill won first prize at the Chicago World Fair in 1893. Religion was also of the utmost importance to the townspeople of that era; by 1905, there were Congregational, Methodist Episcopal, German Lutheran, Seventh-Day Adventist, and Seventh-Day Baptist church edifices. Dodge Center's stature and importance only continued to grow over the decades, as it surpassed the one-thousand-citizen mark in the 1940s and two-thousand persons by the start of the 20th century. In 1990, the schools in Claremont, West Concord, and Dodge Center combined to form Triton Public Schools. Astronomer Milton L. Humason was born in Dodge Center in 1891 and worked with Edwin Hubble to help provide evidence of the expansion of the universe. Perry Greeley Holden, the first professor of agronomy in the U.S. from 1896 to 1900 at the University of Illinois at Urbana-Champaign, also hails from here, as does Shirley Ardell Mason, a woman with dissociative identity disorder whose life was described in the 1973 book *Sybil: The True Story of a Woman Possessed by 16 Separate Personalities*.

HAYFIELD, MN
POPULATION: 1,364 – CITY 732 OF 856 (10-19-25)
Just south of Hayfield, the Mason City & Fort Dodge and the Chicago Great Western Railroad lines converged, helping bring the little farming community into being as one

of Dodge County's premier agricultural shipping points in its early days. Home to the oldest farmer-owned creamery in Minnesota, the Vernon Co-operative Creamery (est. 1884, around the same time as the Rock Dell Zumbro Creamery), Hayfield Township was once a part of Vernon until it separated on March 30, 1872, and took on its name from Hayfield Township in Crawford County, Pennsylvania. In 1885, a post office opened with that name, and on January 7, 1896, the City of Hayfield was incorporated. Hayfield's creamery was shown on a 1905 plat map, as was the local depot, two elevators, a stockyard, a schoolhouse, and two churches. The organizer of the "Kiddy Car Airlift" during the Korean War, Russell L. Blaisdell, graduated from Hayfield High in 1927. The famous December 20, 1950, event rescued 964 orphans and 80 orphanage staff as the Chinese were closing in on Seoul, South Korea.

KASSON, MN ☆
POPULATION: 6,851 – CITY 735 OF 856 (10-20-25)
When the Winona & Saint Peter (Chicago & Northwestern) Railroad was built south of Mantorville rather than through it, landowner Jabez Hyde Kasson allowed the establishment of a new town on his land, bearing his surname. On October 13, 1865, the plat was filed, and by November, trains were already running up and down the line, servicing the village. Postal service commenced in 1866, and on February 24, 1870, Kasson was incorporated. The Dodge County Republican was published in Kasson for the first time on May 3, 1867. Over the next several decades, new and impressive structures like the Eureka Hotel (1894), Kasson Municipal Building (1917), and the Kasson Public School, the local elementary and high school from December 5, 1918, to 1954, were erected. Kasson's iconic limestone water tower was built in 1895 and has since served as a beacon among the city's local landmarks. Other noteworthy places in early 20th-century Kasson included its electric light plant, town hall, a mill, an Episcopal church, a Methodist Episcopal church, a Presbyterian church, a Baptist church, a Lutheran church, and three grain elevators. Peg Lynch, widely regarded as "the woman who invented sitcom" for her work on over 11,000 television and radio scripts and for creating *Ethel and Albert* and *The Couple Next Door*, was born in Lincoln, Nebraska, but grew up in Kasson.

Restaurant Recommendation:
Tammy's Place
111 W Main St
Kasson, MN 55944

MANTORVILLE, MN ★
POPULATION: 1,111 – CITY 736 OF 856 (10-20-25)
Nothing says Mantorville more than its iconic, unique export, Mantorville limestone, which has been used in buildings such as Rochester's St. Mary's Hospital and the Dodge County Courthouse, and in others throughout the country. When Peter, Riley, and Frank Mantor settled here in 1853, they became the namesake of the community, which on March 26, 1856, was platted by Peter, H. A. Pratt, and others. When the Civil War broke out, Peter established Company C of the Second Minnesota Regiment. Nearly every one of the local men was killed, which left Mantorville with a plethora of widows and orphans. Its remaining residents forged onwards, and a sawmill and gristmill were amongst the original establishments. As Mantorville grew in population with the arrival of the Chicago & Northwestern Railway and became the Dodge County seat, many other places naturally sprang up. Two dozen buildings constructed between 1854 and 1918, including the 1856-57 Hubbell House hotel and the 1865

Dodge County Courthouse, Minnesota's oldest continuously operating courthouse, have since been listed as the Mantorville Historic District on the National Register of Historic Places. It was surpassed by the Winona & Saint Peter Railroad in favor of the Kasson area, but eventually it was connected to both that line and the Chicago & Great Western Railway via spurs. The population of Mantorville varied between 381 and 602 residents between the 1880s and 1970s, until it began to rise as automobile commuters to Rochester settled there. Its most famous son is Edwin Osgood Grover, a publisher renowned for his work at Rollins College in Winter Park, Florida.

Restaurant Recommendation:
County Seat Coffeehouse
1 5th St W
Mantorville, MN 55955

WEST CONCORD, MN
POPULATION: 861 – CITY 737 OF 856 (10-20-25)
Formerly the home of the West Concord Cardinals, the historic 1902 West Concord High School, expanded in 1914 and 1936, has since become the West Concord Historical Society & Community Center. The organization seeks to preserve the extensive history of West Concord, which was platted on June 1, 1885, and incorporated for the first time on February 19, 1894. It was named after Concord, New Hampshire. A post office opened in 1885, and within twenty years the community boasted of several elevators, an engine house, a jail, a mill, a creamery, a depot, two hotels, a Methodist Episcopal church, an Episcopalian church, and two schools. The Chicago & Great Western Railroad was responsible for its semi-large (for a small town) population of 635 people in 1900, which eventually grew to 871 in the 1990s. Aside from the public school, only the early-1870s Italianate farmhouse of Perry Nelson is listed on the National Register of Historic Places.

Blooming Prairie is only partially located in Dodge County (see Steele County).

Unincorporated/Ghost Towns: Berne, Concord, Danesville, Eden, Oslo, Rice Lake, Wasioja

National Register of Historic Places:
Kasson: Eureka Hotel, Jacob Leuthold Jr. House, Kasson Municipal Building, Kasson Public School, Kasson Water Tower
Mantorville: Mantorville & Red Wing Stage Road-Mantorville Section, Mantorville Historic District
Wasioja: Wasioja Historic District
West Concord: Perry Nelson House, West Concord High School

Golf Courses:
Dodge Country Club, Daily Fee (Dodge Center, MN)
Oaks Golf Club, Daily Fee (Hayfield, MN)

Town Celebrations:
Marigold Days, Mantorville, MN (Weekend after Labor Day)

Cook County: Grand Marais Lighthouse & Lower Range Light Beacon Station (Grand Marais), Walleye from The Fisherman's Daughter (Grand Marais), The Naniboujou Lodge (Grand Marais), Entrance to the Gunflint Trail (Grand Marais), Lake Superior at Temperance River State Park (Schroeder), Fish at Beaver House Inc. (Grand Marais), High Falls on the Pigeon River (Grand Portage), Grand Portage National Monument (Grand Portage)

Cottonwood County: former Bingham Lake First Methodist Episcopal Church (Bingham Lake), Jeffers Petroglyphs State Historic Site (Comfrey), former Pete Falk's Old Gas Station (Mountain Lake), Papa & Mama Burger Statues at A&W (Mountain Lake), Country School at Heritage Village (Mountain Lake), Westbrook Heritage House [Depot] Museum (Westbrook), Veteran's Memorial (Westbrook), Cottonwood County Courthouse (Windom)

Crow Wing County: Paul Bunyan's Footprints (Baxter), Northern Pacific Railroad Shops Historic District (Brainerd), Babe the Blue Ox at Paul Bunyan Land Amusement Park (Brainerd), Sea Serpent Statue (Crosby), Tank Display at Camp Ripley Military Base (Camp Ripley), Mille Lacs Lake (Garrison), Summer Turtle Races (Nisswa), Fire Tower at Paul M. Thiede Fire Tower Park (Pequot Lakes)

Dakota County: Fire Department Mural (Burnsville), Minnesota Vikings Museum (Eagan), Watt Munisotaram Pagoda (Empire), Vermillion Falls (Hastings), Historic Rock Island Swing Bridge over the Mississippi River (Inver Grove Heights), Water Tower at Sunset (Lakeville), Sibley Historic Site (Mendota), Stockyards Exchange Building (South St. Paul)

Dodge County: Kasson Stone Water Tower (Kasson), Minnesota's First Freedom Rock (Kasson), Minnesota's Oldest [Dodge County] Courthouse Still in Use (Mantorville), The Hubbell House (Mantorville), Mantorville Brewery Ruins (Mantorville), Zumbro River at Riverside Park (Mantorville), former First Baptist Church (West Concord), West Concord Historical Society Public School Museum (West Concord)

DOUGLAS COUNTY
EST. 1858 - POPULATION: 39,006

Organized by the territorial legislature on March 8, 1858, Douglas County's name honors the legacy of Stephen A. Douglas, the famed United States Senator from Illinois at that time.

ALEXANDRIA, MN ★☆
POPULATION: 14,335 – CITY 153 OF 856 (4-13-25)

With its notoriety as the host site of the famous Kensington Runestone, the City of Alexandria has dubbed itself the "Birthplace of America." A twenty-eight-foot-tall Viking named Big Ole (created in 1965 for the New York City World's Fair) stands guard over the Douglas County seat and welcomes visitors to the resort town and its surrounding forty-two named lakes. The earliest beginnings of Alexandria occurred in 1858, when brothers Alexander and William Kinkead arrived, intending to establish a flourishing settlement on the shores of Lake Agnes. They settled on a spot just south of the lake and called it "Alexandria" after Alexander. The spelling was changed to match that of the great city in Egypt of the same nomenclature. A post office was organized, and Charles Cook served as postmaster. He was replaced shortly after by Alexander Kincaid, who sorted the mail at his cabin until J. H. Van Dyke built his general store circa 1865. Thomas F. Cowing also brought in a stock of general merchandise and established his store. The two stores were an excellent early basis for settlers traveling to and through the townsite via the J. C. Burbank stage line. Growth was slow due to the townsite's strategic positioning as a stockade/Fort Alexandria for the U. S. Army. Fear of attack remained high following the recent Dakota War of 1862. It was not until 1868 that W. E. Hicks purchased the site and helped bring Alexandria to new levels of prosperity. While Alexandria was already the county seat, it had no courthouse. So, Hicks donated land to build one. That gesture alone was greatly appreciated. However, Hicks had a vision for his newest investment. In addition to providing property for a courthouse, he donated land for Methodist and Congregational churches and a jail, established a mill, a hotel, and a store, and founded the first newspaper. In 1868-69, a government land office was located in Alexandria, and throughout the following decade, it attracted hundreds of new settlers. On February 20, 1877, Alexandria was incorporated. The first railroad reached the town on November 5, 1878. At the junction of the Great Northern Railroad and the Minneapolis, St. Paul & Sault Ste. Marie, Alexandria saw the establishment of hundreds of businesses. By 1910, the population had surpassed three thousand residents. Notable active firms during that decade included the Baker Weedless Fish Hook Company, the Alexandria Soda-Water Works, the Eagle Clothing Company, the Alexandria Milling Company, the Alexandria Confectionery Company, the St. Anthony and Dakota Elevator Company, the Atlantic Elevator Company, the Alexandria Boat Works, the Wegener Brewing Company, the Alexandria Potato Warehouse Association, a cement works, and countless others. At least six churches and two large schools were also active at that time. Nine early Alexandria locations have been preserved via the National Register of Historic Places: the Alexandria Public Library, a 1903 Carnegie Library built in the Beaux-Arts architectural style; the 1895 Victorian-style Douglas County Courthouse; the Great Northern Passenger Depot, one of the line's finest stations in all of Minnesota; the 1910 Renaissance Revival U.S. Post Office building; the Alexandria Residential Historic District, and the historic Knute Nelson (1872), Thomas F. Cowing (1875), and Noah P. Ward (1903) homes. At the Kensington Runestone Museum, tourists can admire the museum's namesake runestone, discovered in 1898 by Olof Ohman, and other strange artifacts like Spotty, the taxidermied fox terrier, who waits for his 1970s owners to return. Ohman, a Swedish immigrant, brought much excitement to the area in 1898 when he claimed he had found a 202-pound greywacke stone covered with a series of ancient Nordic runes. While clearing land, he is said to have stumbled across the stone between the roots of a poplar tree, which he called an "Indian almanac." He brought the artifact to a nearby Scandinavian artifact, which dated its ancient inscription–discussing a party of Norse explorers and their journey to the area–to 1362. Extensive scientific research has been conducted on the stone, which was labeled a hoax due to the lack of weathering over 500 years and the absence of linguistic and grammatical similarities to Old Swedish. However, modern-day historians have discovered the use of these linguistic features in other writings of the era and have attested that the "experts" who initially "studied" the runestone never actually saw it in person. Ohman, who only had three months of formal education, likely would have been unable to replicate and pass off such a substantial artifact. Hoax or not, the stone has become synonymous with Alexandria and the nearby hamlet of Kensington, and thus it is known as the Kensington Runestone. The actual stone is displayed in the aforementioned museum. An 18-ton replica runestone was erected east of downtown on August 12, 1951. For those interested in maritime history, the Legacy of the Lakes Museum has many rare examples of wooden boats, exhibits on Lake Superior shipwrecks, and more. Alexandria Technical and Community College was established in 1961 as part of the University State Colleges and Universities system to serve as the educational option for the area's residents. The population of the resort town has doubled since the 2000 Census, as it then had only 8,820 residents. The list of famous Alexandrians is extensive, but particularly noted individuals with ties to the community include Peter Krause, a multi-time Primetime Emmy and Golden Globe nominee for his role as Nate Fisher on HBO's drama series *Six Feet Under*; Edward Hanson, the Governor of American Samoa from June 1938 to July 1940; John Hammergren, the CEO of McKesson Corporation (a pharmaceutical distributor and health information and technology company) from 1999 to 2019; Bruce Smith, the 1941 Heisman Trophy winner and two-time National champion with the Minnesota Gophers football team; Tom Lehman, the only golfer to ever be awarded the Player of the Year across all three PGA Tours; John Hawkes, an Academy Award, Primetime Emmy, and Golden Globe Award nominee best known for his role in the 2012 drama film *The Sessions*; Dave Dalby, a three-time Super Bowl champion and 1977 Pro-Bowl center with the NFL's Oakland/Los Angeles Raiders; Cliff Sterrett, the creator of the Polly and Her Pals comic strip published from 1912 to 1958; Jed Johnson, one of "The World's 20 Greatest [Interior] Designers of All Time, and Brock Lesnar, the only human to have ever won the heavyweight championships in the WWE, UFC, NCAA, NJPW, and the IGF.

BRANDON, MN
POPULATION: 501 – CITY 147 OF 856 (4-12-25)

Before Brandon was established, there was a settlement called "Chippewa," which had various names, including Fort Chippewa, Chippewa Station, and Chippewa Lake City. It was first settled in 1860 and named after the nearby bodies of water that share that name. The Chippewa Lake post office was open from 1861 to 1869. On the Burbank stage route between St. Cloud, Minnesota, and the Red River Valley on the present-day border with North Dakota, the settlement centered around Henry Gager's hotel until the site was ultimately abandoned. In August 1879, the new town of Brandon came to light two miles south of Chippewa with the development of the Great Northern Railroad. It was laid out by Lieutenant George A. Freudenreich, the original owner of the townsite, and named for Brandon, Vermont. The county awarded the village municipal status on November 22, 1881. Within thirty years, it had grown to about 276 residents (per the 1910 Census). Three grain elevators, a mill, and a depot lined the railroad tracks in 1912. On Front Street, visitors from the tracks would have seen the Brandon Bank, the Farmers' State Bank, a hotel, the post office, a harness shop, and other businesses. Brandon's school block was located in its northwestern lot, and a Protestant and St. Anne's Catholic Church served as its religious centers. Brandon has been designated as the site of Minnesota's most creative Works Public Administration project: the Brandon Auditorium and Fire Hall. Although it now serves as a community center and the Brandon History Center, the 1935-36 fieldstone building was established as a combination gymnasium, auditorium, fire hall, and city hall. It boasts a balcony, a movie projection booth, and a large mural painted by Elsa Laubach Jemne in its interior; on the exterior, an athlete and a musician welcome visitors through the main entrance. The unique piece of architecture was placed on the National Register of Historic Places in August 1985.

CARLOS, MN
POPULATION: 497 – CITY 150 OF 856 (4-12-25)
Lake Carlos, home to beaver, deer, grebes, and other waterfowl, got its name in 1860 when Glendy King named it after one of his friends in an eastern state. While the lake has been present for many centuries, European settlement did not begin until 1863. A nearby post office was organized in 1881 as one of the first noted pieces of infrastructure, and the Minneapolis, St. Paul & Sault Ste. Marie Railroad was the impetus for its further development. In 1903, the first lots were sold. Within two years, there were general stores owned by the Reuter Brothers, Schoener & Kuhne, Albert Kohler, and Frank & Casper; O. D. Franzen's lumber yard; Frank Sticka's Fairview Motel; Anton Sticka's livery stable; Mrs. Haskel's drug store and millinery; Dr. Haskel's physician's office; August Kohlhass's hardware store; The First State Bank, The Atlantic and The Woodsmith Elevators, and four saloons. In 1906, the two-room schoolhouse building was built in the northern part of town. By 1912, there was a creamery, an engine house, a depot, a town hall, stockyards, and a church, as well. Since its first Census in 1910, Carlos has steadily grown from 167 to a recent all-time high of 502 people in 2010. Lake Carlos State Park was established in 1937 to serve as a recreational hub among the lakes of west-central Minnesota. Several park facilities were erected between 1938 and 1942 as New Deal federal work relief projects. They have been listed on the National Register of Historic Places as the Lake Carlos State Park WPA/Rustic Style Historic District and Group Camp.

EVANSVILLE, MN
POPULATION: 603 – CITY 146 OF 856 (4-12-25)
Evan Evanson, the first rural mail carrier in this vicinity, was honored with the naming of this town when it was platted in 1879 by Lorentz Johnson with the coming of the Great Northern Railroad. Evanson's shanty served as the stage station on the J. C. Burbank & Company stage line, following his mail route between St. Cloud, Minnesota, and Fort Abercrombie in North Dakota. Gustav Willius laid out another adjacent community called East Evansville, but the two settlements ultimately merged into one. With the railroad came significant numbers of immigrants, approximately 452 by the 1890 Census, many of whom established businesses. In 1912, Evansville was an enterprising town with two hotels, a livery, four stores, two hardware stores, a bank, an implement store, a printing office, an elevator, three mills, two churches, and a public school. *The Evansville Enterprise* newspaper began circulation on October 5, 1882. The community's population has increased more recently; in 2010, the Census reported an all-time high of 612 people. The Evansville Historical Foundation's several

historic properties, including a landmark city water fountain built by Otto Moody in 1903, are among its most notable attractions.

Restaurant Recommendation:
Schatzi's
109 Railroad St
Evansville, MN 56326

FORADA, MN
POPULATION: 170 – CITY 154 OF 856 (4-13-25)
Cyrus A. Campbell, a prominent Douglas County landowner from Parker's Prairie, platted his town in July 1903 and worked with the Soo Line Railroad to establish a station there. He first named it Ada in honor of his wife, but because there was another bustling town called Ada in Norman County, he was asked to change it. He still wanted to name it "for Ada," and his solution was to prefix her name with the word "for." The name stuck, and Forada became one of the eventual eleven municipalities in the county. Only 66 people lived in town in 1910, but their hamlet still boasted a depot, a section house, two elevators, two stores, a post office, and a church. The post office operated from 1904 to 1954 before it was discontinued. On May 30, 2022, Forada made state headlines when an EF2 tornado tore through a large section of the community, causing significant damage.

GARFIELD, MN
POPULATION: 349 – CITY 148 OF 856 (4-12-25)
Not so named for the lasagna-loving cartoon cat, but rather for the 20th President of the United States, James A. Garfield, one can trace the history of Garfield to 1868. This year, Alex Richardson and Andrew Sanstead were granted a section of land that would eventually welcome the Great Northern Railroad in 1879 and a post office in 1880. It was platted on February 17, 1882, and incorporated as a village in September 1905. With incorporation papers in hand, city officials such as Torgel Knutson (the first mayor and a local barber and hardware store owner) helped further the town's growth and made significant improvements to its infrastructure. Circa 1905, a two-story frame school building was raised in the city's northeast corner and used to educate Garfield's youth until 1916 (when a new brick edifice was built for the same purpose). Garfield also had a bank and several stores. The entire length of its main street (State Street) was engulfed in flames in 1928, except for the solid brick bank structure. Like its neighbors, Garfield has become a commuter city and bedroom community for nearby Alexandria, leading to a recent increase in its population figures: an all-time high of 354 people in the 2010 Census.

KENSINGTON, MN
POPULATION: 266 – CITY 167 OF 856 (4-14-25)
A Swedish immigrant named Olof Ohman brought great excitement to the village of Kensington in 1898 when he claimed to have found a 202-pound greywacke stone covered with a series of ancient Nordic runes. While clearing land, he is said to have stumbled across the stone between the roots of a poplar tree, which he called an "Indian almanac." He brought the artifact to a nearby Scandinavian artifact, which dated its ancient inscription–discussing a party of Norse explorers and their journey to the area–to 1362. Extensive scientific research has been conducted on the stone, which was labeled a hoax due to the lack of weathering over 500 years and the absence of linguistic and grammatical similarities to Old Swedish. However, modern-

day historians have discovered the use of these linguistic features in other writings of the era and have attested that the "experts" who initially "studied" the runestone never actually saw it in person. Ohman, who only had three months of formal education, likely would have been unable to replicate and pass off such a substantial artifact. Hoax or not, the stone has become synonymous with Kensington and is dubbed the Kensington Runestone. The actual stone is displayed in an Alexandria museum, but a replica can be seen at Kensington's Runestone County Park. It was erected in 1969 by the Kensington Lions Club. The town's history began in March 1887 with the coming of the Minneapolis, St. Paul & Sault Ste. Marie Railroad. William D. Washburn platted it; the post office was also established that year. Incorporation status came in 1891. Over the next twenty years, its two hundred-plus residents worked diligently to contribute to and improve their hamlet. By 1912, it had a public school, a city hall, a fire department, a Swedish Lutheran church, a second church, and a depot; its business district included three elevators, a flour mill, a creamery, a bank, a hardware store, and five general stores.

MILLERVILLE, MN
POPULATION: 100 – CITY 145 OF 856 (4-12-25)
The inland town of Millerville, named after the early German settler John Miller, was pieced together haphazardly due to the lack of a railroad. Businesses were located seemingly at random throughout the town, which was incorporated on September 2, 1903. According to Geo. A. Ogle & Co.'s 1912 atlas, a store and a hotel were the southernmost businesses in town. Two blacksmith shops, one of which doubled as a saloon, a creamery (still open today as the Millerville Cooperative Creamery), a village hall, and a second saloon, were located on what could be considered a "main drag." In the northern reaches of town, there was a general store, a drug store, and a church. Several lots owned by A. J. & J. P. Larsung, E. Schriber, Haen & Lister, L. Marlaing, M. Pinnowski, and U. N. Krott were laid out in a splintered fashion, stretching out in long triangular or rectangular shapes rather than the typical clean square lots. Millerville's post office operated from 1869 to 1907. In the countryside near Millerville, travelers on Lady of the Hills Road will find a 22-foot-tall concrete statue of Mary, the Virgin Mother. It was built in 1993 by Allen Bakke and other locals after he was miraculously cured of cancer following prayers.

Restaurant Recommendation:
Millerville Co-op Creamery
16523 County Rd 7 NW
Brandon, MN 56315

MILTONA, MN
POPULATION: 431 – CITY 149 OF 856 (4-12-25)
Spruce Hill Village and Spruce Center were two early area towns, each with its own stores, blacksmith shops, and mills, which were ultimately replaced by Miltona when the Soo Line Railroad came through in 1902. It was located a couple of miles southwest of the Spruce settlements. Many families moved their livelihoods when it became clear that Miltona would be the township's prominent settlement. It was first on the northeast side of Lake Irene, but later moved to its present location when founder John Hintzen agreed to have the depot built elsewhere. The town was named after Lake Miltona, which was, in turn, named in honor of early settler Florence Miltona Roadruck. From 1873 to 1875, 1891 to 1905, and from 1911 onwards, the post office delivered letters and parcels to the locals. Several other businesses, churches, and

schools were also established. Miltona's fate was almost sealed on July 18, 1970, when a tornado knocked out a dozen homes, several farms, and fifteen businesses, including the depot, a grain elevator, a gas station, a lumber yard, and the café. Since 1990, its population has grown rapidly. In the nineties, it had 181 people; by the 2000 Census, 279 people (a 54.1% increase); and by the 2010 Census, 424 people (an additional 52% increase).

Restaurant Recommendation:
Miltona Custom Meats & Sausage
242 2nd Ave
Miltona, MN 56354

NELSON, MN
POPULATION: 182– CITY 151 OF 856 (4-12-25)
The local post office and village were first called Dent for Richard Dent, an early settler. The town began around 1875, and the post office in 1880, but both entities changed their name in 1881 to Nelson to honor Senator Knute Nelson. He was a noted politician who served as the 12th Governor of Minnesota from January 1893 to January 1895 and, more famously, as a U.S. Senator from Minnesota between March 1895 and April 1923. His namesake community flourished throughout his tenure as a Congressman. With the help of the Great Northern Railroad, Nelson could claim its place as a grain shipping point. In the 1910s, it had two elevators, a depot, a section house, and a carhouse used to store and service railway cars located on its tracks. The post office, a hotel, a general store, a church, a Norwegian church, and the Nelson Creamery were other notable places in town at that time. Since its first Census in 1910 and its most recent in 2020, Nelson has had a low population of 147 people in the 1930s and a high of 209 in the 1980s. Frederick M. "Freddie" Lund, a stunt flyer, the 1930 World Aerobatic Champion, and a member of the Minnesota Aviation Hall of Fame, grew up attending school in Nelson.

OSAKIS, MN
POPULATION: X – CITY 152 OF 856 (4-12-25)
As early as 1859, there were reports of settlement at this stage station on the way to Fort Abercrombie, but they were driven out of the area out of fear that the events of the Dakota War of 1862 would spread to them. Only two years later, though, the Osakis post office branch was established in Douglas County (a reincarnation of the Todd County branch, which existed from 1859 to 1863). Another two passed before the town began to take shape on the southern shore of Lake Osakis. The body of water was called "O-Za-Tee" by the Dakota and *Ozaagi-zaaga'igan* by the Ojibwe. However, the town's etymology is most closely associated with the story of a brave man who nearly drowned in the lake's narrows and shouted, "Oh, save us!" His tribe's camp was called 'Sakis,' meaning "danger." The first Great Northern Railroad engine came through town on November 1, 1878, bringing many new settlers, materials, and ideas. Osakis was incorporated on February 18, 1881. By 1912, it had a creamery, two feed mills, a flouring mill, an ice house, the Idlewilde Hotel and the Linwood Hotel, lumberyards, liveries, banks, churches, schools, and stores selling general goods, pharmaceuticals, farm implements, and more. The population of Osakis had grown to nearly 1,500 people by this point, so the business lines were numerous. Its chief milling industry was dominated by The Osakis Milling Company, whose mill had a capacity of 400 barrels. The mill's structures stood until 1990, when the Minnesota Department of Natural Resources ordered them razed for a public access point to Lake Osakis.

Otherwise, the Farmers' Co-Operative Creamery was equally important, reporting approximately $104,000 in payments in 1913. Two noteworthy Osakis locations that remain today are the John B. Johnson House, a historic 1886 home noted for its steep rooflines, which earned it the nickname "the Cyclone House," and the City Hall building, built in 1936 as a Works Progress Administration federal work relief project. The home was listed on the National Register in December 1977. Noteworthy persons with ties to the lake city include Leif Enger, the author of the 2001 novel *Peace Like a River*; boxers Tommy and Mike Gibbons, the two of whom owned a summer home on the lake; and Gar Wood, a world-record holder for water speed and the first man to travel over one hundred miles per hour on water. He is also credited with inventing the hydraulic-lift dump truck and, at one point in his life, holding more US patents than any other living citizen of the United States.

Restaurant Recommendation:
Tip Top Dairy Bar
22 W Nokomis St
Osakis, MN 56360

Osakis is only partially located in Todd County (see Douglas County).

Unincorporated/Ghost Towns: Belle River, Holmes City, Leaf Valley, Rose City

National Register of Historic Places:
Alexandria: Alexandria Public Library, Alexandria Residential Historic District, Douglas County Courthouse, Great Northern Passenger Depot, Knute Nelson House, Noah P. Ward House, Thomas F. Cowing House, U.S. Post Office- Alexandria
Brandon: Brandon Auditorium & Fire Hall
Carlos: August Tonn Farmstead, Lake Carlos State Park WPA/Rustic Style Group Camp, Lake Carlos State Park WPA/Rustic Style Historic District
Osakis: John B. Johnson House

Golf Courses:
Alexandria Golf Club, Daily Fee (Alexandria, MN)
Atikwa Golf Club at Arrowwood Resort, Resort (Alexandria, MN)
Geneva Golf Club, Daily Fee (Alexandria, MN)
Lake Miltona Golf Club, Daily Fee (Alexandria, MN)
Osakis Country Club, Daily Fee (Osakis, MN)
Pine Ridge Golf Course, Daily Fee (Evansville, MN)

Breweries/Wineries/Distilleries:
68 & Vine Veterans Winery (Miltona, MN)
Burr Vineyards (Brandon, MN)
Carlos Creek Winery (Alexandria, MN)
Copper Trail Brewing Company (Alexandria, MN)

Town Celebrations:
Runestone Days, Kensington, MN (Father's Day Weekend)

FARIBAULT COUNTY
EST. 1855 - POPULATION: 13,921

Partitioned off from Blue Earth County in 1855, Faribault County derived its name from the early French settler and fur trader Jean-Baptiste Faribault.

BLUE EARTH, MN ★★
POPULATION: 3,174 – CITY 637 OF 856 (9-30-25)
Visitors to Blue Earth cannot help but stand in awe of the 55-foot fiberglass statue of a giant green man, aptly dubbed "the Jolly Green Giant." Placed in 1978-79 after the local KBEW radio station owner and broadcaster, Paul Hedberg, conceived the idea, the eye-catching statue pays tribute to the mascot of the local Green Giant company, known for its lines of frozen and canned vegetables. Hedberg was instrumental in bringing Interstate 90 closer to the City of Blue Earth as it was nearing completion. To celebrate the completion of the nation's first transcontinental freeway, two pieces of "golden stripes" were painted on the shoulders of I-90 at the westbound and eastbound stops, as a ceremonial nod to the golden spike placed at Promontory Summit, Utah, when the first transcontinental railroad was completed on May 10, 1869. In addition to these sites, the Southern Minnesota Museum of Natural History and the Giant Welcome Center and Museum, noted for Lowell Steen's collection of thousands of Green Giant memorabilia, Blue Earth has long served as a vital civic center for Faribault County, serving as its seat of government. Laid out in 1856 by H.P. Carstans and J.B. Wakefield, the town was named for the Blue Earth River and the bluish hue of the copper-laden clay on its banks. The Blue Earth City post office was established in 1856 and operated under that name until 1902, when the "City" portion was dropped. Several impressive developments were made, many of which remain visible today. A sprawling commercial district developed, and in December 1892, C. A. Dunham's Richardsonian Romanesque courthouse structure was completed for a little over $70,000. Another essential civic structure, the Etta C. Ross Memorial Library, opened its doors to the public in 1904 and has since been converted into a museum. The Episcopal Church of the Good Shepherd was completed in 1872, featuring elements of Gothic Revival architecture, during a time when the local Episcopal Bishop, Henry Benjamin Whipple, was campaigning to expand the church's presence throughout the area. The First Presbyterian Church was completed in 1897 at a final cost of $12,622.75, featuring a combination of Romanesque Revival and Gothic Revival elements. James Wakefield, the 8th Lieutenant Governor of Minnesota from January 1876 to January 1880, had his 1868 home preserved and added to another local history museum. All of these places were completed in the same era as Blue Earth, which upgraded its incorporation status from village to city in 1899. In addition to its giant claim to fame and appearances on Season 45 of CBS's *Survivor* series, HGTV's 2022 *Ugliest House in America* event, and other series, several men and women have brought notoriety to Blue Earth over the decades. Amongst the more famous are the industrial designer Donald Deskey, *New York Times* music critic William Zakariasen, and former U.S. Congressmen from Minnesota, Tom Hagedorn and his son Jim.

Restaurant Recommendation:
Cedar Inn Drive-In
324 N Grove St
Blue Earth, MN 56013

BRICELYN, MN
POPULATION: 348 – CITY 639 OF 856 (9-30-25)
On the morning of Wednesday, September 27, 1899, the hamlet of Bricelyn came to life when the first lots were auctioned off following the advances of the Chicago & North Western Railroad. Eager businessmen and women opened storefronts selling everything from groceries and farming implements to dry goods and items forged at

the local blacksmith shop. Later joined by a line of the Chicago, Rock Island & Pacific, Bricelyn's population saw steady growth through the 1950s, reaching a peak of 639 residents. Its name was derived from William E. Brice, the original owner of the townsite. When deciding on the town's name, postmaster K.O. Sandum mistakenly assumed John's wife's name was "Evelyn," when in reality it was "Minnie." As a result, the suffix '-lyn' was forever attached to Brice's surname, and it was never corrected. Other accounts suggest that Mr. Brice's name was "John." Bricelyn entered the ranks of Minnesota's incorporated municipalities on July 15, 1903.

Restaurant Recommendation:
Buds Cafe
Main Street
Bricelyn, MN 56014

DELAVAN, MN
POPULATION: 172 – CITY 635 OF 856 (9-29-25)

Guthrie was an alternate name for this town (for pioneer settler Sterrit Guthrie) until May 1, 1872, when the decision was made to match the village's name with that of the recently established Southern Minnesota Railroad. Better known as the Chicago, Milwaukee & St. Paul in its formative years, the new, permanent name was given to honor the legacy of Oren Delavan Brown, a coworker of Henry W. Holley, chief engineer of the Southern Minnesota line. Holley's wife suggested to her husband that they name it after his friend and acquaintance. The townsite was platted on October 11, 1870, and by December of that year, it was welcoming its first passenger trains. Incorporation followed on February 7, 1877, and in 1885, the post office finally shortened its name from Delavan Station to simply "Delavan." Numerous businesses, educational institutions, and religious organizations have emerged over the decades. Still, only one building – an Italianate farmhouse – has been deemed worthy enough to be listed on the National Register of Historic Places. The Adams H. Bullis was listed because of Bullis's scientific contributions to cattle breeding and his role as a prominent early Faribault County farmer. Harland G. Wood, born here in September 1907, is hailed as Delavan's most famous son for his 1935 discovery that animals, humans, and bacteria fix carbon from carbon dioxide to succinate.

Restaurant Recommendation:
Blu Bair
100 S Main St
Delavan, MN 56023

EASTON, MN
POPULATION: 177 – CITY 642 OF 856 (9-30-25)

"The Agri-Heart of Southern Minnesota" was aptly named for its extensive agricultural capabilities and rich farming history. Started in the early 1870s when the Southern Minnesota Railroad was being built between Winnebago and the Mississippi River, Easton was named for Jason Clark Easton, one of the original proprietors of the townsite. The first building on the site was known as "the old harness shop" and was nothing more than a shack used by railroad workers. It had been moved in from a place called Walnut Lake. Another town called Wesner's Grove predated Easton and was located to the southwest, but, like Walnut Lake, it dissolved when the railroad bypassed it. Conrad Ruff and Karl Rath donated farmland to be converted into town lots, and several businessmen, including David Grice (owner of the first carriage works), immediately began to develop a small commercial district. Lura Station was the name of the town for a short time because of its location in Lura Township, Faribault County.

ELMORE, MN
POPULATION: 549 – CITY 636 OF 856 (9-30-25)
Walter C. Mondale, the 42nd Vice President of the United States under President Jimmy Carter from January 1977 to January 1981 and the Democratic nominee for President shortly after, moved to Elmore with his family when he was just nine years old in 1937. Long before Mr. Mondale called this town on the Iowa border his home, it was known as "Dobson" to those who settled here first, circa 1858. Some of the initial area settlers had that surname, but it lasted for only about five years before the name was changed to Elmore in honor of Judge Andrew E. Elmore. Marvin Hughitt, President of the Chicago, St. Paul, Minneapolis & Omaha Railway, selected it because of Elmore's contributions to the formulation of the State of Wisconsin and its Constitution. As for the town of Elmore, its post office was organized in 1863, and it eventually became well-known by railroaders for its roundhouse. Trains coming from the Twin Cities in the north would turn around just before reaching the Iowa border, and just across the invisible line, trains from Omaha, Nebraska, would reverse course just before entering Minnesota. This critical designation brought Elmore's population to 924 people by 1900, with a peak of 1,078 in the 1960s. Saloons, several grocery stores, two grain elevators, two banks, furniture and hardware stores, and even a newspaper called the *Elmore Eye* (in circulation from 1892 to 1991) were all extant throughout these periods of prosperity. Additionally, a local high school operated from 1917 to 1990 before consolidating with Blue Earth. By 1997, Elmore's elementary school had also closed. The Elmore Area Historical Society conducts its local preservation efforts at the former Elmore Methodist Episcopal church edifice.

FROST, MN
POPULATION: 215 – CITY 638 OF 856 (9-30-25)
Not to be confused with the Minnesota Frost of the Professional Women's Hockey League, one of the six charter franchises of the league started in 2023-24, the City of Frost in Faribault County came about circa 1899 when the Minnesota and North Western Railway made its way through the south central portion of the state. Its name commemorates the architect Charles Sumner Frost, best known for designing Chicago, Illinois's famous Navy Pier. As a post office, a public school, churches, and select stores and lines of enterprise were established, Frost's residents sought incorporation as a village. They achieved that feat on November 28, 1903, and experienced a general population increase through the 1960s, reaching a high of 381 people. Lon Clark, a stage actor on Broadway and a familiar network radio voice, was born in Frost in January 1912. The local volunteer Frost fire department is famed for its yellow firetrucks and its friendly jab: "Red firetrucks are for parades, and yellow trucks are for work." Local collector Roger Buckey Legried was featured in the *Guinness Book of World Records* for amassing an impressive collection of 82,792 different ball caps from around the world.

KIESTER, MN
POPULATION: 488 – CITY 640 OF 856 (9-30-25)
Kiester became known by millions of people throughout 2016, albeit in an incredibly unorthodox manner. When a Pfizer marketing team discovered that a town in Minnesota closely resembled "Keister," an alternative name for "buttocks," they knew

it would be the perfect filming location for a Preparation H commercial. Actors showcased the hemorrhoid treatment in front of local Kiester landmarks, such as the Kee Theatre, and locals welcomed the national attention for their then-small town of about five hundred residents. Like other communities in the vicinity, Kiester experienced its most significant growth in the 1960s, when its population peaked at 741. It was established primarily to serve as a railroad stop on the Iowa, Minnesota, and Northwestern line. At the time of its naming in 1882, Kiester was not colloquially named for the body part, but rather in honor of Judge Jacob Armel Kiester. He moved to Blue Earth in 1857 and served as a county surveyor, state senator, and judge for nearly 50 years before his passing. At the turn of the century, local businesses included a newspaper, a state bank, hardware and implement stores, a pair of blacksmith shops, a dray line, and multiple general stores. Geographically speaking, Kiester has been well known for generations as the site of the 1,432-foot-tall Kiester Hills, part of the Algona Glacial Moraine, the fourth of twelve terminal moraines found in Minnesota.

MINNESOTA LAKE, MN
POPULATION: 661 – CITY 644 OF 856 (10-1-25)

The Land of 10,000 Lakes would not be complete without boasting of both a town and an accompanying lake bearing the state's own name: Minnesota Lake. The body of water was named even before the state itself, from a Dakota word meaning "slightly whitish water." Upon its platting in October 1866, the village adopted the lake's name, and it soon became one of a series of railroad stations established by the Chicago, Milwaukee & St. Paul Railroad. Chauncey Barber and family, and Nicholas J., John, and John P. Kremer were among the site's first settlers; the first family was responsible for building the first hotel in the vicinity, when the town was actually called Marples for Charles Marples. The name was officially changed on February 23, 1866, only months before it was platted. Incorporation was achieved on February 14, 1876. For only about a year, the post office was known as Franklintown between 1857 and 1858. Fast-forwarding to about a century later, Minnesota Lake saw its population reach about 700 residents in the 1960s, a number that it has since retained through the following six Censuses. In the early 1900s, local civic leader Peter Kremer erected an ornate Queen Anne-style home for himself and his wife, Millie, that would ultimately be listed on the National Register of Historic Places. It now functions as the Minnesota Lake Public Library and the local history center.

WALTERS, MN
POPULATION: 69 – CITY 641 OF 856 (9-30-25)

Thomas H. Brown filed the plat for Walters on August 15, 1900. With a bit of love, some elbow grease, and the help of other area settlers, within only a few years, a small village had popped up that was worthy of becoming a stop on the Burlington, Cedar Rapids & Northern Railway (alternatively the Chicago, Rock Island & Pacific R.R.). At the time it was incorporated in 1903, the town had a bank, a general store, a post office, an elevator, a lumber yard, a livery stable, a saloon, and a restaurant. School and church edifices soon followed, as did additional stores and saloons. Of all its earliest infrastructure, the Walters Jail, built between 1906 and 1909 for $685 using brick, remains its most historic site to this day. The post office, established in 1901, was discontinued in 1996 due to significant population declines following the 1970s.

WELLS, MN
POPULATION: 2,410 – CITY 643 OF 856 (9-30-25)

The Founding Father of Wells was Colonel Clark W. Thompson, a member of the 6th Minnesota Territorial Legislature in 1855, and later one of the leading men behind the company that constructed the Southern Minnesota Railroad. As a landowner with over 9,000 acres, he graciously deeded some of his land to the railroad company in exchange for naming rights. He elected to call it Wells for the maiden name of his wife, Clark W. Thompson, and her father, J.W. Wells. In January 1870, the railroad arrived, bringing the fledgling village the opportunity to grow and flourish with a wide range of businesses, fraternal organizations, church groups, and schools. Thompson himself furnished the town with its first mill, a creamery, and factories for producing vinegar, barrels, and cheese. On March 6, 1871, Wells was incorporated, and a second line of the Chicago, Milwaukee & St. Paul reached Wells from Mankato in 1874. A water and electric plant was established in 1894 through a local bond issue, and around the same time, Mr. Thompson donated 53 acres of land for use as a sprawling city park. An artificial lake was created, and a race track was added to the park for beautification and economic purposes. Several interesting laws and ordinances came into effect in the years to follow, including a 1899 order that fined any person riding a bicycle on Wells sidewalks. In 1904, a law was passed stating that "any horses left unblanketed in the cold for a long period of time can be fined between $10 and $100." The Muret N. Leland House, built in 1883 for local politician and merchant Muret N. Leland; the Chicago, Milwaukee, St. Paul & Pacific Depot and Lunchroom building, constructed in 1903; and the District No. 40 "Pink" Schoolhouse, operational from 1896 to 1952, are three important historical points of interest. Frederic Warde, a noted twentieth-century book and typography designer, and Larry Buendorf, the Secret Service Agent who thwarted Lynette "Squeaky" Fromme's attempt on President Gerald Ford's life in 1975, both hail from Wells.

Restaurant Recommendation:
Loma Azul Mexican Restaurant
34 1st St SE
Wells, MN 56097

WINNEBAGO, MN
POPULATION: 1,391 – CITY 634 OF 856 (9-29-25)

Dr. Charles H. Parker, Andrew Dunn, Elija Barritt, Warren Dunham, and James Sherlock comprised the townsite company formed in September 1856, which sought to establish a new townsite just off the eastern banks of the Blue Earth River. Due to the recent relocation of the Winnebago (Ho-Chunk) tribe from Long Prairie to a reservation in the vicinity, they chose to name the site "Winnebago City." The name Middleton had been considered an eponym for the town of Middleton, Connecticut, because the new town was located halfway between Blue Earth City and Shelbyville. However, they abandoned the idea when they discovered that another Middleton already existed in Minnesota. Accounts vary from source to source, but it is thought that the Winnebago name comes from the word *ouinepego*, meaning "people of the stinking water." Development of the town came quickly. In January 1857, the area was platted, and it was incorporated the following month. A post office was established under the name Winnebago City that year as well; it differed from the Winnebago Agency in nearby Blue Earth County, which operated from 1856 to 1886. The "City" part of the town's name remained until 1905, when it was dropped for good. Between 1871 and 1878, Winnebago enjoyed serving as the western terminus of the Southern

Minnesota Railroad until it continued westward. In 1879, that line was crossed by the St. Paul and Sioux City Railroad as it worked its way southward towards Iowa. Business lines were numerous at this time. A steam mill was its most important business. There were also seven machine yards, seven warehouses, five dry goods stores, four harness shops, four blacksmith shops, four grocery stores, three hotels, two lumber yards, two drug stores, two millinery stores, two clothing stores, two newspapers, and multiple lawyers' and insurance agents' offices. On October 5, 1859, a very early rendition of the Faribault County Fair was held in Winnebago, although it was also held in Blue Earth City, Wells, and Delavan in subsequent years. The fair, as well as the existence of Parker College from 1888 to 1924 as a local institution of higher learning, were two of Winnebago's earliest and proudest accomplishments. A pair of early structures from this period have been listed on the NRHP for their significant historic attributes: the Andrew C. Dunn House, built in 1901, and the First National Bank of Winnebago building, built from 1916-17 in a Neoclassical style. The Winnebago Area Museum encompasses several downtown buildings and preserves the stories and artifacts of this once dual-railroad town. Winnebago's population peaked at 2,127 according to the 1950 Census. Some of its famous persons of interest include William Knight, born here in 1909 and later the father of Phil Knight, the co-founder of Nike; John E. Grotberg, a U.S. Congressman from Illinois between 1985 and 1986; and Allen Waler Read, an etymologist who discovered the origin of the commonly used phrase, "OK."

Unincorporated/Ghost Towns: Baroda, Brush Creek, Clayton, Dell, Guckeen, Homedahl, Huntley, Marna, Pilot Grove

National Register of Historic Places:
Blue Earth: Church of the Good Shepherd-Episcopal, Faribault County Courthouse, James B. Wakefield House, Memorial Library
Delavan: Adams H. Bullis House
Minnesota Lake: Peter Kremer House
Walters: Walters Jail
Wells: Chicago, Milwaukee, St. Paul & Pacific Depot & Lunchroom, District No. 40 School, Muret N. Leland House
Winnebago: Andrew C. Dunn House, Center Creek Archeological District, First National Bank

Golf Courses:
Minn-Iowa Golf Club, Daily Fee (Elmore, MN)
Riverside Town & Country Club, Daily Fee (Winnebago, MN)
Wells Golf Club, Municipal (Wells, MN)

Breweries/Wineries/Distilleries:
Lost Saint Brewing Company (Blue Earth, MN)

Town Celebrations:
Blue Earth Giant Days, Blue Earth, MN (2nd Weekend in July)
Festag Days, Minnesota Lake, MN (2nd Weekend in July)
Wells Kernel Days, Wells, MN (2nd Weekend of August)

FILLMORE COUNTY
EST. 1853 - POPULATION: 21,228

Originally Minnesota's most populous county in 1860, Fillmore County, named for the 13th President of the United States, Millard Fillmore, was officially established in 1853.

CANTON, MN
POPULATION: 310 – CITY 673 OF 856 (10-14-25)
A significant dispute broke out amongst early settlers of this area over what to call Frank Adams's new railroad town on the Preston-Reno division of the Chicago, Milwaukee & St. Paul Railroad, one that lasted for many months and prevented the townspeople from reaching an agreement. E. P. Eddy proposed the term "Elyria," which was strongly supported by one faction of the town, while Fred Flor suggested "Canton," which was supported by another faction. Elyria was used in select town records through the 1860s, but eventually Canton (selected after an ancient place in China) won out. It was formally platted in 1879, the same year that the United States Postal Service organized the Boomer post office. For three years, it used that name because of the town's "booming" population and business lines, before postmaster James Manuel changed it to Canton. The first two firms in town were the boarding houses of John Meyers and Abraham Wiltse, but by 1896, there were multiple stores and hotels, a lumberyard, a bank, and two elevators. A Town Hall, a public school, and two churches were other notable institutions. The Canton Historical Society has restored Canton's historic 1879 railroad depot to its era-correct state, as well as the Mitson Home Museum on Main Street. A large Amish population began settling north of Canton in 1974; since their arrival, U.S. Hwy 52 between Prosper and Preston has been designated as an "Amish Buggy Byway."

CHATFIELD, MN
POPULATION: 2,997 – CITY 690 OF 856 (10-16-25)
2.59 square miles of Chatfield is split almost equally between Fillmore and Olmsted counties, and is located on the North Branch of the Root River. Pioneers established the townsite on a plateau about forty feet above the river. They named it in honor of Judge Andrew Gould Chatfield, the first United States judge of Minnesota Territory. Thomas B. Twiford was the first permanent settler, and G. W. Willis became the first business owner when he established a log tavern. For its first two years of existence, between 1854 and 1855, it served as the Fillmore County seat, before that title was transferred to Carimona. Eventually, the hamlet was met by a spur line of the Winona & Saint Peter Railroad, and the community that once had not much more than Samuel T. Dickson's flour mill and several general stores ultimately boasted of lumber and sawmill, two banks, the *Chatfield Democrat* newspaper, and a commercial club to promote local interests. Chatfield residents achieved incorporation on February 19, 1887, during a strange period of Census history. The 1880 Census reported a population of 9,001 residents, but by 1890, that number had supposedly dropped by 85.2% to 1,335 persons. It did not cross the two-thousand-citizen threshold again until the 1980s. Three historic homes and a 1915 Prairie School-style Carnegie Library make up Chatfield's four properties on the NRHP. It is also home to The Chatfield Center for the Arts, the Pope & Young Museum of Bowhunting, and the Chatfield Brass Band Music Lending Library. Josef Fahrenholtz, a 2019 graduate of Chatfield High School, now plays professional basketball in Norway for the Nidaros Jets club of the Basketligaen Norge.

Restaurant Recommendation:
Carly Mae's Bakery & Cafe
209 Main St S
Chatfield, MN 55923

FOUNTAIN, MN
POPULATION: 409 – CITY 689 OF 856 (10-16-25)
So named for the "fountain spring" that once provided the Southern Minnesota division of the CM&StP Railroad with a water source, the City of Fountain was once a sprawling town with dozens of business lines. According to George A. Ogle & Company's 1896 plat book, there were at least five general stores, two saloons, two hotels, two elevators, and one each of a livery, blacksmith shop, barber shop, furniture store, harness shop, meat market, implement store, and hardware store. In another sixteen years, there were more hotels, restaurants, grocery stores, and three churches. It was incorporated as an act of the legislature on March 3, 1876. While many of these places have faded over time, Fountain still attracts visitors from around the world for its unique karst topography, characterized by limestone formations with sinkholes, caves, and intriguing drainage systems. The "Sinkhole Capital of the United States" also claims the Fillmore County History Center, famed for its two-headed half and Bernard Pietenpol's home-built flying machine, and a designation as the western terminus of the Root River State Trail. The 60-mile rail trail runs through southeast Minnesota and is a favorite among cyclists in the summertime and cross-country skiers in the winter.

HARMONY, MN
POPULATION: 1,043 – CITY 672 OF 856 (10-14-25)
Home to Minnesota's largest Amish community, with nearly 1,000 people, Harmony's history begins with a village called Greenfield. The small settlement, located just south of modern-day Harmony, had a post office, a church, a school, and a selection of businesses. It was abandoned when the Chicago, Milwaukee & St. Paul Railroad instead opted to build elsewhere. Arguments arose amongst the townspeople on what to call their town, until one man attempted to quell the fighting by shouting out, "Let's have harmony here!" Thus, the name was selected, and in just a few short years, it became home to mills, banks, general stores, elevators, churches, and a unique business called the Harmony Novelty Works. F. M. Trogstad opened Harmony's first business, a general merchandise store, in 1879. The McMichael Grain Elevator still stands today as a reminder of the wooden crib-framed structure's importance in the town's early agricultural market days. Other features as of 1912 included two other grain elevators, a Woodmen Hall, a marble shop, a photograph gallery, and four restaurants. Harmony's post office was first located at Peterson, then moved to the Harmony area in 1862 and was called Windom, and ultimately renamed Harmony. In 1924, three boys discovered Niagara Cave by accident, and eight years later, local businessmen developed it into a tourist attraction. A 60-foot-high waterfall and an underground chapel, where hundreds of couples have been married, are the key features of the cave, as is an 18-hole mini-golf course. The local Swartzentruber Amish population arrived in 1974 from Wayne County, Ohio, in search of cheap land, good soil, and a quiet, less-populated area in which to live out their lives. Many stores sell Amish furniture, quilts, and baked goods. Author Tami Hoag, whose romance and thriller novels have been circulated over 20 million times, was raised here.

Restaurant Recommendation:
Oak Meadow Meats
50 9th St NE
Harmony, MN 55939

LANESBORO, MN
POPULATION: 724 – CITY 687 OF 856 (10-15-25)

Over one thousand people called Lanesboro home in the 1880s, many decades before the community established itself as one of the best "small art towns" in the nation. The "Magical Hamlet" of Bluff Country was settled in 1856 and has transformed from a once-simple Chicago, Milwaukee & St. Paul Railroad village into a place rich in heritage and beauty. Lanesboro's name was most likely taken from F. A. Lane, a stockholder of the Lanesboro Townsite Company. Its location on the South Branch of the Root River made it an excellent place for both the railroad company and immigrants to set up shop as evident by a 1912 gazette that listed it as having a roller mill, an elevator, a lumber yard, two banks, two hotels, a creamery, a canning factory, a newspaper, a school, and four churches. Despite its relatively small size, 36 of Lanesboro's original 19th-century buildings from its milling era have been preserved in the Lanesboro Historic District. Other points of interest include the Root River Recreational Trail; its 1934-37 Inspiration Point Wayside Rest, the only Civilian Conservation Corps erosion-control camp wayside rest still in existence; the 1892 Queen Anne Michael Scanlan House; and the area-famous Commonweal Theatre Company. The professional company began in 1989 under the direction of Eric Bunge, Scott Olson, and Scott Putnam, and hosts four to six plays each year at the Commonweal, a 191-seat facility. Next door are the Lanesboro Arts gallery building and St. Mane Theater, which, along with the Commonweal, gave Lanesboro its very own theatre and arts district, recognized by many from around the world. In 2008, Lanesboro added another designation to its list when Minnesota Governor Tim Pawlenty declared it the "Rhubarb Capital of Minnesota." Lanesborough was the spelling of the local post office from 1868 to 1883. A few noted locals from over the years include Arthur B. Langlie, the 12th and 14th Governor of Washington; Katherine M. Cook, a pioneer in rural education and the former Chief of that division at the U.S. Bureau of Education; Duane Benson, a linebacker in the AFL/NFL from 1967 to 1976; and Edwin Vincent O'Hara, the Roman Catholic Bishop of Great Falls, Montana from 1930 to 1939, and Kansas City, Missouri, from 1939 to 1956.

MABEL, MN
POPULATION: 716 – CITY 674 OF 856 (10-14-25)

Situated amongst Minnesota's bluff country is the town of Mabel, whose name honors the memory of the daughter of railroad engineer Frank Adams, who passed away as a young child. Mr. Adams was the chief engineer of the Reno-Preston division of the Chicago, Milwaukee & St. Paul Railroad in southern Minnesota; he purchased land from William Loomis and C. D. Taber for the townsite. Loomis was the first formal settler in 1853, but it was E. L. Tollefson who opened the first general store. He moved his business from Riceford when he learned that Mabel would be on the railroad line, and later founded The First National Bank of Mabel after his accumulated wealth warranted the backing of such an institution. Two whole blocks' worth of business lines were established, including The Bolland Opera House, the Gem Theater, the Mabel Telephone Exchange Company, and other hardware, general, and implement institutions, to name a few. Two Lutheran churches and a Methodist church were the three prominent church groups of that era. From 1855 to 1880, the post office was called Bellville, with Wilson Bell as postmaster, until it was finally changed to match the railroad's nomenclature. Douglas K. Amdahl, the Chief Justice of the Minnesota Supreme Court from 1981 to 1989, grew up in Mabel.

OSTRANDER, MN
POPULATION: 231 – CITY 719 OF 856 (10-18-25)
Home to as few as 151 citizens in the 1930s but as many as 293 in the 1980s, Ostrander got its start when the Winona & Southwestern Railroad was extended westward through Fillmore County. William Ostrander, a local in this area, offered the railroad several acres for their line if they agreed to build a depot between Spring Valley and Le Roy. The railroad obliged, and thus the town was born. Ostrander was honored with its naming. A railroad station was erected immediately, as were Hans Hanson and L. E. Lundby's store and a pair of grain elevators. A school, a church, and a post office (established in 1891 after being moved from Hurdal) were among the improvements. At one point during World War II, Ostrander became the site of a low-grade iron mining operation. It was incorporated as a village in 1918.

PETERSON, MN
POPULATION: 234 – CITY 685 OF 856 (10-15-25)
Peterson (pop. 234) was established by its namesake founder, Peter Peterson Haslerud, in July 1853. The first post office using this name in Minnesota opened in 1855, but it was opened and closed intermittently until 1870. For fourteen years, Peterson's town plat sat largely empty until he talked the railroad company into building through Rushford Township in 1867. He willingly forked over fifteen acres of land and $800 (some of which was fundraised by other area citizens). Milling began on the Root River when a flour mill was established. More additions were made to Peterson as its population grew. By 1876, it reportedly had the Peterson Hotel, the Northwestern Bar, two general stores, a blacksmith shop, a livery, a steam mill, a hardware store, and a pharmacy. The Quickstad Farm Implement Company was an essential early agricultural manufacturing facility in the area; two of its structures, erected in 1875 and 1901, are now listed in the National Register of Historic Places. As the population grew to 331 persons by the 1940s, other improvements were made, including a casket factory, a creamery, a wagon shop, a feed mill, and a Modern Woodmen of America hall. Peterson Station Museum and Visitor Center has been open since 1974 as a haven for local artifacts and archives.

PRESTON, MN ★☆
POPULATION: 1,322 – CITY 688 OF 856 (10-15-25)
When Fillmore County was established in the mid-1850s, Chatfield and Carimona served as the first two judicial seats, but Preston was chosen in 1856 for its central location. John Kaercher platted the site in 1855 near his mill and named it in honor of his millwright, Luther Preston, who also served as the first postmaster. Despite being located on the banks of the Root River and owning the county seat title, Preston never attracted a direct line of the Chicago, Milwaukee & St. Paul Railroad. It instead had a spur line splitting off to the west of the section between Lanesboro and Harmony. The line that ran directly to flour mills on the South Branch of the Root River also had a wagon works, foundry, lumberyard, elevators, warehouses, an ice house, a roundhouse and turntable, and the Preston Brewery. Over the decades, multiple blocks' worth of hotels, blacksmiths, saloons, stores, banks, and specialty businesses sprang up, and by the time the 1990s rolled around, Preston had reached its all-time population peak of 1,530 people. The Preston Overlook was constructed in 1937-38 as a WPA New Deal project on the highest bluffs above the Root River, and is now one of five localities on the Register in addition to the 1869-1870 Fillmore County Jail (and 1900 carriage house), the bright red 1902 Milwaukee Elevator, the 1899 Allis Barn, and the 1859 Preston Brewery. Like several other nearby communities, Preston

has also designated itself as a "capital" of something, particularly as "America's Trout Capital." A 20-foot chainsaw-carved trout created for Preston Trout Days seeks to prove the town's claim and is one of a few local oddities, along with a double-headed 1950s Oldsmobile and the cave system at Forestville-Mystery Cave State Park. Minnesota's most extensive cave system, discovered in 1937, boasts over 13 miles of passageways and is open to public tours. Preston claims the site, but the State Park is geographically closest to Wykoff and Spring Valley.

Restaurant Recommendation:
Branding Iron Restaurant
1100 Circle Heights Dr
Preston, MN 55965

Lodging Recommendation:
JailHouse Historic Inn
109 Houston St NW
Preston, MN 55965

RUSHFORD, MN
POPULATION: 1,860 – CITY 683 OF 856 (10-15-25)
The larger of Minnesota's two "Rushfords" is the City of Rushford, which was named on Christmas Day, 1854, when its populace unanimously voted to honor Rush Creek. It and the surrounding township were named concurrently, and the Rushford post office opened in 1856. Twenty log houses were amongst the first structures to be raised. With another decade of development under its belt, it attracted the Southern Minnesota Railroad, which made it its western terminus. An incredible 35 stores, 18 saloons, seven churches, five hotels, and two breweries were built that year, amongst a total of 150 buildings, which immediately propelled it towards incorporation as a city in 1868. Growth slowed significantly when the railroad expanded westward. By 1896, other manufacturing interests, such as a woolen factory, a cooper shop, and a marble shop, had opened, as had a couple of factories. Reports from an 1899 edition of the *Rushford Star* newspapers report that the depot that year handled 30,300 pounds of butter and thirty-four rail cars of livestock. Over a century later, some early remnants of Rushford's heyday remain, including the two-story 1867 Southern Minnesota depot, now a visitor center and museum; the Rush Wagon and Carriage Company factory building, built in 1872; the 1875 Rushford City Mill; the 1859-61 Walker and Valentine House, and the 1870s Norway Township Stone House. Sometimes called "Trail City" because of its intersection with seven Native American trails, the town is now part of the Root River State Trail, built on the old railroad grade. Steve Heiden, the offensive line coach for the NFL's New York Jets as of 2025 and a former tight end with the San Diego Chargers and Cleveland Browns, was born here on September 21, 1976.

Restaurant Recommendation:
Creamery Pizza & Ice Cream
407 S Mill St
Rushford, MN 55971

RUSHFORD VILLAGE, MN
POPULATION: 790 – CITY 684 OF 856 (10-15-25)
The counterpart to the City of Rushford is the City of Rushford Village, a 33.73-square-mile municipality that, strangely, surrounds both Peterson and Rushford. What started

as a township in 1858 eventually became an independent municipality on July 18, 1885, when local farmers feared that the rapidly growing city would ultimately annex their land. To protect their property, they incorporated the entirety of Rushford Township as the Village of Rushford. However, in 1975, it was forced to become an incorporated city at the same time as every other municipality in Minnesota. Ripley's Believe It or Not discussed the odd situation in a 1938 column of their now-famous syndicated newspaper. The village had a peak Census population of 1,064 people in 1900, but it quickly dropped by 35.5% to 686 the very next decade.

SPRING VALLEY, MN
POPULATION: 2,447 – CITY 717 OF 856 (10-18-25)

Almanzo Wilder, the husband of Laura Ingalls Wilder, featured prominently in her 1933 novel *Farmer Boy* and lived in Spring Valley between 1870 and 1879 before moving to De Smet, South Dakota, where he met Laura. Before Almanzo moved, he and Richard Warren Sears, the founder of the department store Sears, Roebuck and Company, were friends, as they both lived in the community at the same time. The concurrent existence of these two men in Spring Valley alone is enough to warrant an impressive level of fame, but the start of Spring Valley dates to even before the arrival of these two men in the village. Named for large local springs, it was laid out in 1855. It was later located at the intersection of the Chicago & Great Western Railway and the Southern Minnesota division of the Chicago, Milwaukee & St. Paul Railway. I. N. Cummings was the first proprietor of a store in 1855, and Myron Conklin established the original Spring Valley hotel that same year. The Spring Valley Flour Mills, the Spring Valley Creamery, and the Farmers' Co-operative Buyers and Shippers' Association were three of the city's most important businesses by the 1910s. By that point, it also had a cigar factory, a broom factory, a steel neckyoke factory, marble and monumental works, six dressmakers, six boot and shoe stores, five grocery stores, and four each paint shops, wagon shops, hardware stores, dry goods stores, grain warehouses, real estate dealers, and job printing offices. Pairs of jewelry stores, banks, newspapers, bicycle shops, veterinarians, and baseball clubs were prevalent, as were seven churches, three school buildings, and even two different long-distance rural telephone companies. From 1942 to 1967, the Hanna Mining Company operated a low-grade iron ore mining operation. Some of these now-historic places (and others nearby have been preserved on the National Register despite decades of wear and tear of the structures, thanks to the hard work of locals to keep them operational: the 1874 Commercial House Hotel, the 1871 Tunnel Mill, the 1876-78 Victorian Gothic Methodist Episcopal Church edifice, the 1904 Spring Valley Carnegie Library, and a 1913-14 Spring Valley Mausoleum located in the local Spring Valley Cemetery. A pair of local homes, the 1877 Victorian Gothic residence of Ephraim Steffens and the 1879 Second Empire home of William Strong, are also regarded as important local historic sites. The Methodist Episcopal Church houses two floors of artifacts related to Spring Valley and the Wilder family.

WHALAN, MN
POPULATION: 67 – CITY 686 OF 856 (10-15-25)

Whaalahan was the original spelling of this town, as it was initially established on land owned by John Whaalahan. Eventually, the name and the spelling were simplified by settlers to their present form, at least as of 1869, according to postal records. George Dyer had a store as early as 1866, and J. D. Cameron opened a hotel in 1868 before transforming it into a grain warehouse. His business was succeeded by Carr & Smith's general store, Canfield & Crowl's hotel, a hardware store, a restaurant, a grocery store, a photograph gallery, and a handful of other businesses. Whalan was incorporated on

February 17, 1876, after the Chicago, Milwaukee & St. Paul Railroad came through town. Two grain elevators, a school, and a Norwegian Lutheran church rounded out the significant infrastructure at the turn of the century. By 1940, the population reached an all-time high of 190. The post office was not discontinued until 1993, when the population dipped below 100. Nowadays, Whalan is famous for its local pie stops and its "Stand Still Parade," in which one block's worth of parade floats and vehicles is lined up in the center of town, and locals can walk around the parade to inspect it.

WYKOFF, MN
POPULATION: 432 – CITY 718 OF 856 (10-18-25)
Not one, not two, but six grain warehouses stood along the Chicago, Milwaukee & St. Paul's Southern Minnesota division back in 1896. These structures were joined in importance by two grain elevators, a flour mill, a lumber yard, a farm machinery store, a hotel, a livery, a saloon, a general store, a Public Hall, three churches, and two schools at that time. However, it later had as many as five elevators, five general stores, four churches, and other institutions like two banks, a newspaper, and a creamery. F. H. Barlett was the first settler of the area in June 1856, and H. W. Holley platted the community alongside Barlett circa 1871. They named it for Cyrus G. Wykoff, a surveyor of the railway and an original owner of the townsite. Its incorporation was approved by a special act of the legislature in March 1876. Like some of its neighboring communities, Wykoff boasts a small historic district, colloquially known as the Wykoff Commercial Historic District on the NRHP, due to its seventeen [mostly] 1890s structures. Bartlett's 1876 Second Empire home is a secondary local historic site, as are two major attractions: Ed's Museum and the Jailhouse Bed & Breakfast. Ed Krueger collected large amounts of junk and Wykoff memorabilia at his Jack Sprat grocery store for over sixty-three years, never throwing anything away, until he passed, and the city reorganized his collections into a museum. The Jail Haus Bed & Breakfast was built in 1913 and was only converted into a lodging option in the 1990s, complete with bars on the windows and two bunk beds in a jail cell (alongside a much more comfortable queen bed). Minnesota's most extensive cave system, discovered in 1937 and now known as Forestville-Mystery Cave State Park, boasts over 13 miles of passageways and is open to public tours.

Lodging Recommendation:
Wykoff Jail Haus B&B
217 N Main St
Wykoff, MN 55990

Unincorporated/Ghost Towns: Bratsberg, Carimona, Cherry Grove, Clear Grit, Elliota, Etna, Fillmore, Forestville, Granger, Greenleafton, Hamilton, Henrytown, Highland, Lenora, Newburg, Prosper, York

National Register of Historic Places:
Canton: Chicago, Milwaukee, St. Paul & Pacific Railroad Depot
Carimona Township: William Strong House
Carrollton Township: Allis Barn
Chatfield: Chatfield Public Library, Ellen M. Lovell House, George H. Haven House, Samuel Thompson Dickson House
Cherry Grove: Bernard H. Pietenpol Workshop & Garage
Forestville Township: Forestville Townsite- Meighan Store
Fountain: Bridge No. L4770
Harmony: Daniel Dayton House, McMichael Grain Elevator
Lanesboro: Inspiration Point Wayside Rest, Lanesboro Historic District, Michael Scanlan House
Lenora: Lenora Methodist Episcopal Church

Peterson: Quickstand Farm Implement Company
Preston: Fillmore County Jail & Carriage House, Milwaukee Elevator, Preston Brewery, Preston Overlook
Rushford: Norway Township Stone House, Rushford City Mill, Rushford Wagon & Carriage Company, Southern Minnesota Depot, Walker & Valentine House
Spring Valley: Bridge No. 5722, Commercial House Hotel, Ephraim Steffens House, Parsons Block & Hall, Spring Valley Carnegie Library, Spring Valley Mausoleum, Spring Valley Methodist Episcopal Church, Tunnel Mill, William Strong House
Wykoff: Francis H. Bartlett House, Wykoff Commercial Historic District

Golf Courses:
Chosen Valley Golf Club, Daily Fee (Chatfield, MN)
Ferndale Golf Course, Daily Fee (Rushford, MN)
Harmony Golf Club, Daily Fee (Harmony, MN)
Rivers Bend, Daily Fee (Preston, MN)

Breweries/Wineries/Distilleries:
Four Daughters Vineyard & Winery (Spring Valley, MN)
Karst Brewing (Fountain, MN)
Sylvan Brewing (Lanesboro, MN)

Town Celebrations:
Buffalo Bill Days, Lanesboro, MN (1st Weekend of August)
Hesper-Mabel Steam Engine Days, Mabel, MN (Weekend after Labor Day)
Rhuburb Festival, Lanesboro, MN (1st Saturday of June)
Trout Days, Preston, MN (3rd Weekend of May)

FREEBORN COUNTY
EST. 1855 - POPULATION: 30,895

Created on February 20, 1855, alongside twelve other Minnesota counties, Freeborn County was named in honor of William S. Freeborn, then a member of the Minnesota Territorial Legislature.

ALBERT LEA, MN ★☆
POPULATION: 18,492 – CITY 745 OF 856 (10-21-25)
One of southern Minnesota's earliest major rail centers was located at Albert Lea, the county seat of Freeborn County and a modern-day city at the crossroads of Interstate 90 and Interstate 35. The town of 18,492 residents was named for Albert Lea Lake, which was in turn named for Albert Miller Lea, a topographer who worked with Companies B, H, and I of the United States Dragoons on an 1835 expedition to explore the region. One of his scouts was Captain Nathan Boone, son of Kentucky's famous frontiersman Daniel Boone. Twenty years after the party came through, a small settlement began on the lake when Lorenzo Merry built a cabin. George Ruble came in July 1855, a month after Merry, and located a dam and mill site here, which formed the nucleus of the village. A stage line began running through Albert Lea in 1856, and after Julius Clark established the first store, Charles C. Colby platted the townsite on October 29. Identifying features of his plat were a courthouse site, a designated City Park, and a college site. While a college never came to fruition at that spot, Albert Lea did acquire the Freeborn County seat after another plat was filed with those county commissioners, and from then on, its growth was expedited. Its population in 1895 sat somewhere between 3,305 and 4,500 individuals, and by then, several railroads had built through: the Burlington, Cedar Rapids & Northern, the Minneapolis & St. Louis, and the Chicago, Milwaukee & St. Paul. Listing every one of its development of that

time would be nearly impossible, but amongst the more recognizable sites were the Hall House, Morin Brick & Tile Works, an opera house, two ice houses, marbleworks, two beer depots, four mills, the National Hotel, the Freeborn County Courthouse, the Huron Manufacturing Company, a brickyard, a Catholic church, Norwegian Lutheran Trinity Church, a Swedish Baptist church, a Methodist church, First Baptist Church, a Presbyterian Church, a second Norwegian Lutheran church, a Universal church, two public schools, Luther Academy, a cooper shop, and a packing house on the shores of Lake Albert Lea. That latter industry would prove crucial to Albert Lea's manufacturing development, as the city would ultimately host Wilson & Company's meatpacking plant. In 1959, it was the subject of a 109-day strike by the United Packinghouse Workers of America due to unfair overtime requirements. Violence erupted. Governor Orville Freeman declared martial law on December 11 of that year and forced the plant to shut down. On December 23, a federal district court in Minneapolis ruled that his actions were invalid, and Wilson & Company regained control of the plant and retained its title as one of the country's "Big Four" meatpacking firms. Local historians banded together in the 1980s to assist in listing five locations throughout Albert Lea on the National Register of Historic Places, namely the Albert Lea Commercial Historic District and its three-block collection of historic 1874 to 1928 buildings; the 1903 Albert Lea City Hall; the 1914 Chicago, Milwaukee, St. Paul & Pacific Railroad Depot; the 1880 Dr. Albert C. Wedge House, and the 1898 H. A. Paine Queen Anne House. Other local points of interest are John L. Christensen's Itasca Rock Garden northwest of town, the Freeborn County fairgrounds, the iconic mermaid at New Denmark Park, and the Marion Ross Performing Arts Center. Ross rose to prominence in the 1970s, portraying Marion Cunningham on the ABC sitcom *Happy Days*. Other famous locals include Vinny Cerrato, a former ESPN analyst and General Manager of the NFL's Washington Redskins; renowned muralist Alexander Grinager; Richard Carlson, a television and film director with a star on the Hollywood Walk of Fame; William B. Sieglaff, a double navy Cross recipient; Al Franken, a United States Senator from Minnesota between July 2009 and January 2018 and a performer and writer with NBC's *Saturday Night Live*; underground comix artist Robert Crumb; operatic soprano Beatrice Gjertsen Bessesen; rock and roll artist Eddie Cochran, and Jodi Jill, an author who spent thirteen years of her childhood living in a 10-by-20 foot storage facility at Loveland Self Storage in Colorado.

Restaurant Recommendation:
Jake's Pizza
126 W Clark St
Albert Lea, MN 56007

ALDEN, MN
POPULATION: 583 – CITY 749 OF 856 (10-21-25)
A post office called Alden first commenced operations in 1866, the same year that the town was organized. Three years later, it became one of a line of stops on the Chicago, Milwaukee & St. Paul Railroad, with the tracks being officially completed on January 1, 1870. William Morin and H.W. Holley laid out the townsite, and A.G. Hall erected the first building. Two blacksmith shops, general stores, and a depot were the original structures put up. By 1895, there was a Farmers Co-op Creamery, a stockyard, an elevator, a mill, two hotels, a bank, a town hall, an I.O.O.F. Hall, a Methodist Episcopal church, a Presbyterian church, a Danish Baptist church, and a public school. There were also other businesses, such as the *Alden Advance* newspaper office, a bakery, and a drugstore. However, these places, along with the Methodist church, the bank, and others, were destroyed by a fire that ravaged a significant part of the business

district on September 19, 1896. Alden was incorporated by a special act of the legislature in 1879 and reincorporated in 1908 following challenges to the legality of its initial incorporation. It is unknown why Alden took its present name, but it is shared with seven communities in other states. Home to as many as 713 people in the 1970s, Alden's most significant population increase (by 130.4%) occurred between 1890 and 1900, when the population grew from 276 to 636. The Alden Heritage Center houses a collection of more than 7,000 local artifacts and archival materials related to the town's history.

CLARKS GROVE, MN
POPULATION: 694 – CITY 741 OF 856 (10-20-25)
Occasionally referred to as "James" by the Chicago and Northwestern Railway for several years, the City of Clarks Grove took its current name from John Mead Clark, an early pioneer farmer. He and his wife, Lucy, moved to the area in 1855 to till land near a grove of oak trees. Naturally, the area came to be known as "Clark's Grove," and as the Clark family expanded, so too did the village as more people moved in. More Danish immigrants moved to Minnesota than to any other state, and together, they created the first commercially successful cooperative creamery. It was located on the northwest corner of the P.C. Christianson farm. Dairying became the primary driver of the local economy, and soon the area was home to many dairy farms, three grocery stores, blacksmith shops, barber shops, garages, meat markets, a hotel, a bank, a hardware store, a school, and the First Baptist Church of Clarks Grove. By 1895, the original creamery building was joined only by a post office, a store, and a shop. The third creamery building, built in 1927 and complete with a second-floor meeting hall, still stands tall as the community's most historic institution and is part of the National Register of Historic Places. Theophilus Levi Haecker, a dairy science professor from the University of Minnesota, toured an early version of the creamery in 1892, which served as the cooperative dairying model for establishing over 550 more creameries throughout the state over the next ten years. After Clarks Grove attracted the attention of the Chicago, Rock Island & Pacific Railroad in 1900, its business lines expanded to include a feed mill, an ice cream parlor, and a confectionery store, amongst others.

CONGER, MN
POPULATION: 153 – CITY 750 OF 856 (10-21-25)
Officers of the Chicago, Rock Island & Pacific Railway may have named Conger for a place in China, or for Congressman Edwin Hurd Conger of Des Moines, Iowa, who was the United States Minister to China between July 8, 1898, and April 4, 1905. A branch of the postal office was established in the locality under that name in 1901, and the village was founded on farmland once owned by Fred Miller and Albert Krueger. Stockyards were established, and Pete Flesch remodeled an old granary into a general store. E. A. Brown erected a grain elevator, and by 1903, the creamery building was furnished. A larger brick creamery building was completed in 1941, seven years after Conger's residents finally opted for incorporation. Conger became most famous for the Conger Meat Market, started by Czechoslovakians Ray and Mabel Bajonek on May 1, 1935, and still open today. The former Conger creamery building was purchased in 2015 by Jeremy and Darcy Johnson to expand the operational and retail areas of the meat market business. The John Niebuhr Farmhouse, located outside of town, was listed on the National Register of Historic Places from March 20, 1986, to June 22, 1998. It had been built in 1873 but burned down in 1997.

Restaurant Recommendation:
Conger Meat Market
100 William Ave
Conger, MN 56020

EMMONS, MN
POPULATION: 367 – CITY 752 OF 856 (10-21-25)
Henry G. Emmons of Norway arrived at this point on the Minnesota-Iowa border in 1856, and for fifteen years, he served as the postmaster of the State Line post office from 1864 to 1879. In 1880, his son founded a store on the present townsite. However, when it was discovered that the Minneapolis & St. Louis Railroad was not willing to build to it, the store was relocated a mile south to Norman, Iowa. That now-defunct Iowa town boasted a railroad depot thanks to promises from Winnebago County, but when Emmons grew into a thriving village and Norman did not materialize, the railroad relocated the depot to Emmons on September 24, 1904. The railroad had already been extended to the Minnesota town, but the addition of the depot brought a new influx of stores and residents. Some of the earliest institutions of Emmons were the North Star Creamery, a saw mill, an elevator, a stock yard, a lumber yard, a hardware store, a general store, two blacksmith shops, and the Emmons post office, of which Henry was the first postmaster. By 1910, the commercial district had expanded to include an auto company, a pool hall, a meat market, a shoe and repair shop, a drug store, a harness shop, and a millinery store. An early fun fact about Emmons was that at times, when a long train would stop there, it could be located in Freeborn County, Minnesota, and in Iowa's Worth and Winnebago counties simultaneously.

FREEBORN, MN
POPULATION: 264 – CITY 748 OF 856 (10-21-25)
When the Freeborn County seat election was held on October 13, 1857, the freshly platted village of Freeborn acquired a whopping one vote in an election that favored Albert Lea over the likes of Bancroft, St. Nicholas, and Shell Rock. While its hopes for a judicial seat were doomed, the town founded by Edward S. Dunn in June 1857 would survive as one of Freeborn County's most prosperous farming communities on the shores of Freeborn Lake. Named in honor of William Freeborn, a Minnesota Territorial legislator, Dunn and George F. Rickard owned the first cabin on the townsite, and Lafayette T. Scott's hotel hosted the post office; Ludwig T. Carlson was postmaster just before the post office was moved there. A couple of stores were opened, as was a wind-powered flourmill, the first in Freeborn County, alongside a creamery, a broom factory, carriage works, a shoemaker, and a blacksmith shop. The townspeople opted to incorporate on August 12, 1858, but the status briefly reverted to unincorporated before Freeborn reincorporated on March 27, 1949. School No. 13 and the Congregational and Methodist churches were located near the center of the town plat along Fifth Street. The first church edifice was built in 1867 by a Baptist congregation, which later sold out to the Congregationalists in 1880. Later, when a bank opened, it would make the headlines of local newspapers twice when it was robbed first March 26, 1938, and then again on November 3, 2003. The only Freeborn in the U.S. is best known for being the birthplace of FFA Corn Drives for Camp Courage (now called True Friends). The Freeborn High School FFA chapter started the first drive in 1964 and raised $87 after collecting several acres worth of corn left behind by farm machinery from that year's harvest.

GENEVA, MN
POPULATION: 508 – CITY 739 OF 856 (10-20-25)
Settled between 1855-56 and platted in the winter of 1856-57 by James F. Jones and James Robson, Geneva was named by Edwin C. Stacy in honor of Geneva, New York. He was the town's first postmaster when it opened in 1856 in the O. G. Goodnature home. Jones and Robson opened two of the village's first commercial lines, a store and a hotel, and soon there was also a blacksmith shop, a wagon shop, and a saloon. Schools, lines, and other businesses also came into being, but the most important of all was likely the Geneva Creamery Association. It was formed in 1891 and opened that year with T. F. Linehan at the helm as chief buttermaker. It was located across the street from a blacksmith shop, one of two in operation in the mid-1890s. There were also two stores, a Union Church, a Methodist Episcopal church, and the School No. 4 district. Although it never formally had a railroad, the Chicago, Rock Island & Pacific Railroad ran through the area to the west of Geneva, providing local farmers with an outlet and the opportunity to trade with outside communities. Geneva was the birthplace of Lawrence B. Anderson, the leader of the School of Architecture at the Massachusetts Institute of Technology from 1947 to 1965. Geneva achieved its highest-ever population of 555 people at the 2010 Census.

GLENVILLE, MN
POPULATION: 568 – CITY 744 OF 856 (10-20-25)
Men named Bartlett, Ellswart, and Phillips founded a townsite company in 1856 that brought life to a new village called Shell Rock, located on the western bank of the Shell Rock River. Bartlett had been surveying the area in July 1856 in search of a site for his mill. When he could not convince others in St. Nicholas and Northwood to sell their interests, he opted instead to start his own community on land formerly owned by John Smith and Frederick Cutler. His sawmill was one of the first buildings to be erected on the river, but once all the timber in the area was harvested, it was purchased and relocated to Albert Lea. Around the same time, E.P. Skinner reportedly had established a village of his own in the vicinity of the sawmill, which was likely the original site bearing the "Shell Rock" name. Skinner's town had a general store and a post office, both of which were moved to Bartlett's village when the two began negotiations. A couple of other storefronts came and went, but the town's real development began in 1870 with the arrival of the Burlington, Cedar Rapids, and Northern Railroad. The railroad company called it Glenville from the get-go, but the Shell Rock post office did not change its name to match until 1879. Over the next couple of decades, Glenville grew to a population of over 300 people. The Glenville Creamery was located right along the river, and major businesses on Main Street included lumber yards, hotels, and storefronts. On the Minneapolis & St. Louis Railroad (more popularly known as the Chicago, Rock Island & Pacific), there was a mill, an elevator, a depot, a warehouse, a coal shed, and livestock yards. United Brethren, Methodist Episcopal, and Free Methodist Episcopal church congregations were all administering weekly religious services at this time. School No. 40 was the town's educational stronghold, located on the western side of the Public Square in the center of town. Later, Glenville also served as a western terminus of a line of the Illinois Central Railroad, which helped bring its population to 851 citizens in the 1980s.

HARTLAND, MN
POPULATION: 321 – CITY 747 OF 856 (10-21-25)
There was once a lake in the vicinity of Hartland known to the Dakota as Le Seuer Lake (using that alternate spelling) and to the settlers as Mule Lake. A small settlement

was made, and several stores and a schoolhouse were built circa 1860. When the Minneapolis & St. Louis Railroad bypassed the little hamlet, the town mostly disappeared. Years later, a new village called Hartland, named for the Hartland in Windsor County, Vermont, was established on Torger Samuelson's land. In 1877, the railroad came through, and A. Johnson platted it into town lots. The first building was moved in from Manchester and used as an early boarding house. A Congregational religious society was formed that year in School No. 8, but later acquired a storefront downtown to hold services. Within twenty years, Hartland had grown into a handsome village complete with a creamery (est. 1891), a mill, a lumber yard, a stockyard, three hotels, a livery, a community hall, a post office, a school, and a Norwegian Lutheran church. It was incorporated on August 31, 1893.

HAYWARD, MN
POPULATION: 252 – CITY 742 OF 856 (10-20-25)

In 1930, Hayward's postmaster and the local Chicago, Milwaukee & St. Paul Railroad station agent played the longest-ever recorded game of horseshoes at five months and four days. The postmaster reportedly won by a score of 25,000 to 24,949, meaning that each day the two men averaged about 324 points before calling it quits until their next meeting. Long before the legendary game, Hayward was organized in April 1859 and named for the early settler David Hayward. A post office began operating under that name in 1864, and in 1869, the town entity formally took shape when H. C. Lacy platted it on behalf of the railroad company. A railroad depot, a store, and a warehouse were among the first structures to be built. Still, by the end of the 19th century, Hayward also had an elevator, a hotel, a Norwegian Lutheran church, and School No. 34. Many of the structures were painted a brilliant white, which gave the community the nickname "The White City." In 1909, the Lodge Zare Zapadu No. 44 meeting hall of the Z.C.B.J. (Zapadni Ceska Bratrska Jednota) fraternal society was completed to serve the local Czech population; it was added to the National Register in March 1986. Since its incorporation on June 4, 1924, Hayward's highest population was 294 in 1980. Hayward was featured on a December 2008 episode of *Extreme Makeover: Home Edition*.

HOLLANDALE, MN
POPULATION: 308 – CITY 740 OF 856 (10-20-25)

Hollandale's development began in 1918, when George H. Payne of the Payne Investment Company, in conjunction with the Albert Lea Farms Company, cleared about 15,000 acres of swampland with the hope of transforming it into a "vegetable wonderland" for Dutch immigrants and farmers. Over $2.5 million was spent to drain the swamps and make the land suitable for agricultural activities. Six inches of water once covered the peat beds and silt deposits, but after they were exposed, the call went out to 400 Dutch farming families to settle the land. It was called Maple Island by the Chicago, Rock Island & Pacific Railroad, which ran through, but the name "Hollandale" eventually prevailed in favor of Dutch heritage. The CRI&P line branched off from a main line at Clarks Grove. When the Chicago, Milwaukee & St. Paul Railroad learned of the new farming enterprise, they established a spur line from Hollandale Junction directly to Hollandale (passing through unincorporated areas known as Twin Grove, South Hollandale, and Muckland). Celery, onions, potatoes, and other green vegetables grew prosperously until flooding and early frosts brought development of the village to a screeching halt between 1926 and 1929. A new investment company, Maple Island Farms Company, acquired 7,000 acres of land, and after significant improvements to the local drainage ditches, the Hollandale community was back on its feet. It was incorporated in the 1930s and had as many as 363 citizens during its population heyday in the 1960s. Hollandale's Heritage Huis Museum showcases local history and artifacts, with a particular focus on the area's agricultural history.

MANCHESTER, MN
POPULATION: 52 – CITY 746 OF 856 (10-21-25)
Briefly known as Buckeye and then as Liberty, it was Mathias Anderson who suggested the name Manchester in 1858 as an eponym of a township in Illinois. The name stuck for the modern-day town of 52 residents, which experienced its heyday as a railroad station on the Minneapolis & St. Louis Railroad. Ole Peterson platted the first townsite in 1882 at a time when it had Cosgan & White's elevator, Anton Anderson's blacksmith shop, and a dry goods store owned by H. R. Fossum and E. H. Stensrud. By 1895, the Manchester Creamery Association, a second store, and stock pens had been established. H. W. Fish replatted the townsite in 1898, laying it out into more formally recognized lots, on which a Lutheran School organization and a hardware store owner added their institutions to the town's directory. On October 6, 1947, it was incorporated. Manchester's post office operated from 1878 to 1974, then was reorganized into a rural station, which served until 2000.

MYRTLE, MN
POPULATION: 47 – CITY 743 OF 856 (10-20-25)
Postmistress Myrtle Lane operated the local post office using her name from 1887 to 1900, so when it came time for the Illinois Central Railroad to build through, they had no issue with adopting the name for their station. The town was platted in 1900 following the completion of the railroad to that point through the H. N. Lane farm. Over the next several decades, Myrtle was the site of the Myrtle Cooperative Creamery, the Myrtle State Bank, a grain elevator, a dance hall and community center, lumber yards, blacksmith shops, hardware stores, general stores, harness shops, livery stables, hotels, saloons, shoe repair shops, cafes, and even a concrete block factory and candy shop from 1916 to 1919 and 1920 to 1925, respectively. Charlie Sweet operated both lines, which were amongst the most unique of Myrtle's then-sprawling commercial district. After its incorporation as a village on May 8, 1937, Myrtle reported a peak population of 136 citizens in the 1950s. It lost its post office in 1993 when the population fell below 70 residents.

TWIN LAKES, MN
POPULATION: 134 – CITY 751 OF 856 (10-21-25)
After a waterpower sawmill was built in 1857, William Banning platted a townsite and attempted to start a village around the structure. Much to his disappointment, nothing developed, and his lands reverted to farmland. Twelve years later, a new plat was laid out on William Wilson and J. M. Tanner's land near a flour mill and a blacksmith shop. More improvements, such as the addition of a store and a hotel, were made, and in 1877-78, the Minneapolis & St. Louis agreed to lay its tracks through the vicinity. The Nunda post office, which had been operational since 1859, changed its name to Twin Lakes in 1881. An elevator, creamery, and stockyards were built on the line, and a wagon shop, the blacksmith shop, the mill, and St. James Church thrived downtown. The two bodies of water to the northwest of town are still referred to as "Upper Twin Lake" and "Lower Twin Lake."

Unincorporated/Ghost Towns: Armstrong, Corning, Gordonsville, Mansfield, Maple Island, Moscow, Oakland, Petran

National Register of Historic Places:
Albert Lea: Albert Lea City Hall, Albert Lea Commercial Historic District, Chicago, Milwaukee, St. Paul & Pacific Railroad Depot, Dr. Albert C. Wedge House, H. A. Paine House
Clarks Grove: Clarks Grove Cooperative Creamery
Hayward: Lodge Zare Zapadu No.44

Golf Courses:
Green Lea Golf Course, Daily Fee (Albert Lea, MN)
Oak View Golf Course, Daily Fee (Alden, MN)
Wedgewood Cove Golf Club, Daily Fee (Albert Lea, MN)

Breweries/Wineries/Distilleries:
Three Oaks Wines (Albert Lea, MN)

GOODHUE COUNTY
EST. 1853 - POPULATION: 47,582

Minnesota's first newspaper publisher, James Madison Goodhue, who published *The Minnesota Pioneer*, is the namesake of this county, which was split off from Wabasha County in March 1853.

BELLECHESTER, MN
POPULATION: 176 – CITY 555 OF 856 (8-30-25)
Bellechester's name is a portmanteau of the two townships in which it was established: Belvidere Township in Goodhue County and Chester Township in Wabasha County. As many as fifty families entered the area between the mid-1850s and the mid-1860s, many of whom were Catholic. Mr. Frenier donated 40 acres of land for a church and parochial school, and around these developments, an excellent village developed. Nicholas Heberin founded his general store and saloon in 1871, the first commercial entity in the community. A townsite was laid out in 1877, and the local post office opened in 1879. When the Wisconsin, Minnesota & Pacific Railroad (succeeded by the Chicago Great Western R.R. in 1920) split off a branch line to Bellechester, it allowed for the hamlet to trade–primarily pottery clay–with the neighboring communities throughout Goodhue County and beyond. The Red Wing Sewer Pipe Company owned the land where clay was mined, and a smaller, adjacent community to Bellechester called "New Bellechester" came into existence. Electricity was not installed until 1924, and incorporation was attained on October 5, 1955, when it had four grocery stores, several saloons, elevators, and stores. Peter William Bartholome, the Roman Catholic Bishop of the Diocese of Saint Cloud, Minnesota, from 1953 to 1968, was born here to Luxembourgian immigrants.

CANNON FALLS, MN ☆
POPULATION: 4,220 – CITY 657 OF 856 (10-2-25)
Very few Minnesota communities can claim two presidential visits, but Cannon Falls (population, 4,220) is one of them. Calvin Coolidge came to town on July 29, 1928, to dedicate a memorial to William J. Colvill, the leader of the 1st Minnesota Volunteer Infantry in the Battle of Gettysburg, at the Cannon Falls Cemetery. Eighty-three years later, on August 15, 2011, Barack Obama met with residents at a town hall meeting in Hannah's Bend Park. With a name like "Cannon" Falls, many would likely assume the community's etymology is closely tied to a former battle fought there. This idea, however, is far from the truth. Native Americans and French fur traders named a local stream off the Mississippi the *Riviere aux Canots*, meaning "river of canoes," because

it was there that they hid their canoes. When future settlers arrived and heard the French saying *canots*, they thought they were saying "cannons," and so the tributary was named the Cannon River. Richard and William Freeborn followed the river to a waterfall, on which they made a land claim where the future development of the City of Cannon Falls would take place. It was platted on August 27, 1855, by the Freeborns and surveyed by S. A. Hart. From 1855 to 1889, the post office was referred to as Cannon River Falls. The "River" part of the name was dropped for good in 1889. Commercially, R. C. Knox & Company erected the first flouring mill in 1857, but there was soon a grist mill, a wool mill, and even an amber cane syrup-producing mill. The ruins of the 1878 Oxford Mill still stand as an early example of these essential buildings that brought about economic prosperity in the Cannon River Valley. Listed on the National Register alongside several area homes formerly owned by John Miller, Marrison Miller, Captain Charles Gellett, and Darwin E. Yale, Cannon Falls has worked hard to preserve many facets of their community. Twenty-four properties make up the Cannon Falls Commercial Historic District, many of which were built as early as the 1880s. The Yale Hardware Store, built in 1887, and the Ellsworth Hotel Livery Stable, started in 1871, are two of the contributing properties. The 1866-67 [Episcopal] Church of the Redeemer, a 1909-10 Pennsylvania truss bridge extending Third Street over the Cannon River; the 1893/1912 Cannon Falls School, and the 1888 Firemen's Hall, now home to the Cannon Falls Historical Museum, round out the NRHP-listed locations of the historical city. Pachyderm Studios, where Nirvana recorded their final studio album, In Utero (1993), has existed in a secluded old-growth forest section of the town since 1988. Singer-songwriter Caitlyn Smith, who has helped pen hit songs such as "Like I'm Gonna Lose You" with Meghan Trainor featuring John Legend (#1 US Adult Top 40), was born here on June 13, 1986.

Restaurant Recommendation:
Dairy Inn
1401 MN-20
Cannon Falls, MN 55009

DENNISON, MN
POPULATION: 223 – CITY 656 OF 856 (10-2-25)
Morris P. Dennison, the original owner of the townsite, is the namesake of this former Minnesota & Northwestern (Chicago Great Western Railway) community. Primarily located in Goodhue County, with a tiny portion extending into Rice County, Dennison was one of a few railroad stops on the "Maple Leaf Route," which connected Minneapolis, Minnesota, Chicago, Illinois, and St. Louis, Missouri. Scandinavian settlers built up the railroad community, contributing businesses such as three general stores, two blacksmith shops, a farmer's elevator, a lumber yard, a milk pasteurization plant, a bank, and a hardware store. A Methodist church provided religious services, and there was a town school for children. From 1978 to 1983, it was the hometown of Albert H. Quie, the 35th Governor of Minnesota. He was one month short of becoming a centenarian, having been born on September 18, 1923, and passing away on August 18, 2023. At the time of his death, Quie was the oldest living former U.S. representative and the oldest living former American governor. In 2006, an Act of Congress was passed to name the local Dennison post office the "Albert H. Quie Post Office" in his honor. It originally opened in 1885 in Gunnar A. Bonhus's general store.

GOODHUE, MN
POPULATION: 1,250 – CITY 554 OF 856 (8-30-25)
Both the City of Goodhue and Goodhue County were named in honor of James M. Goodhue, the first editor of the St. Paul Pioneer Press, then called the Minnesota Pioneer. The famed journalist started the paper only days after the Minnesota Territory was established. Like many other Minnesota towns, it began with the arrival of a railroad, specifically the Duluth, Red Wing & Southern Railroad, which was extended to that point in 1888-89. T.B. Sheldon, president of the railroad, ordered its platting in 106 lots on 30 acres of land between two other pre-existing railroad communities. Incorporation occurred soon afterwards, and by 1909, a number of improvements had been made. German Lutheran, English Lutheran, Methodist, and Catholic churches were present, as were both public and parochial schools. A 250-barrel flouring mill served the village until one year before the 1909 assessment, when it succumbed to fire. Still, there were plentiful other lines of enterprise like the Goodhue Hardware and Implement Company, the First National Bank of Goodhue, the Goodhue Co-operative Company, the *Goodhue Enterprise* newspaper, the Goodhue Hotel, the North Star Lumber Company, the Goodhue County Telephone Company, and other facets like a jewelry store, a meat market, a cigar factory, and a millinery. The post office operated under the name Goodhue from 1882 to 1884, was briefly closed, and then reopened in 1889. In recent years, the population has grown significantly, from 533 people in 1990 to over 1,250 as of the 2020s. Gerald Heaney, the Senior Judge of the United States Court of Appeals for the Eighth Circuit from December 31, 1988, to August 31, 2006, hails from Goodhue.

KENYON, MN
POPULATION: 1,894 – CITY 550 OF 856 (8-30-25)
Kenyon was uniquely named after Kenyon College, a private liberal arts college located in Gambier, Ohio. James M. Le Duc named it for his alma mater. He and A. Hilton, Jay A. Day, and Mr. Howe platted the Kenyon townsite in the summer of 1856, and the following year, a steam sawmill and Stephen A. Bullis's "The Pioneer Hotel" were established as two of the town's earliest businesses. An application for the Kenyon post office was approved in the same year it was platted. After being allowed to develop for 50 years, the community ultimately found itself at the crossroads of the Chicago Great Western and the Chicago, Milwaukee & St. Paul Railways. Two railroads meant twice the opportunity for economic growth, and so by 1909, there were two weekly newspapers, the *Kenyon Leader* and the *Kenyon News*; a canning factory; three grain elevators; three hotels; two banks; a flour mill, and a creamery. Naturally, a fire department came into being to defend these structures against conflagrations. An opera house served as the hub of community entertainment, and five churches stood tall, welcoming their Baptist, Methodist, German Methodist, German Lutheran, and Episcopal parishioners every Sunday. The local school district was accredited by the state in 1896, and a new brick structure was erected in 1918. In addition to a 1895 Queen Anne home in town that once belonged to Martin T. Gunderson, two Kenyon area churches have been added to the National Register of Historic Places: the 1871 Hauge Synod Lutheran Church and the Church of St. Rose of Lima, built in 1879 by Irish Catholics. The Holden Lutheran Church Parsonage was once home to Bernt Julius Muus, who founded Holden Academy as a precursor to St. Olaf College in Northfield, Minnesota. Andrew Volstead, the managing legislator of the National Prohibition Act that outlawed alcoholic beverages in the United States, was born here in 1859. Mark Rein-Hagen, the creator of the *Vampire: The Masquerade* video game; Steve Sviggum, the 55th Speaker of the Minnesota House of Representatives from

1999 to 2007; and Mabel Johnson Leland, noted for translating Arne Garborg's The Lost Father from New Norse to English, also have ties to Kenyon.

Restaurant Recommendation:
Angie's
631 2nd St
Kenyon, MN 55946

PINE ISLAND, MN
POPULATION: 3,769 – CITY 552 OF 856 (8-30-25)

When the Dakota first beheld the thicket of pine trees sticking out of the prairie, they called it *Wa-zee-wee-ta*, which roughly translates to "the island of pines." The large white pine forest was located on an island formed by the middle branch of the Zumbro River, and used by the Dakota during times of intense weather or cold as a shelter. After H. B. Powers and Josiah Haggard kicked off the area's settlement circa 1854, multiple claims were made in succession, and a school and a church congregation began providing services to the people. Moses Jewell suggested the "Pine Island" name, which the United States Postal Service began using in 1856 and later adopted by two railroads: the Winona & Saint Peter and the Wisconsin, Minnesota & Pacific. While most Minnesota communities relied on agriculture or logging to jump-start their local economies, Pine Island was unique in that cheesemaking became its largest early industry. In 1911, eighteen local cheese factories collaborated to create the World's Largest Cheese Wheel. This six-thousand-pound monstrosity was put on display at the Minnesota State Fair to promote the town's dairying industry. Arthur W. Parkin conceived the idea and helped convince area business owners to collect a day's worth of milk from 3,300 cows across 250 farms, or about 35 tons. The Pine Island Area Historical Society houses artifacts from the event as well as scores of archives relating to the town's history, and every year, the Pine Island Cheese Festival is held as a tribute to the industry that put Pine Island on the map decades ago. Two local Queen Anne homes, the 1895 Anna and Samuel Murray Burpee and the 1903 Jacob A. and Mary Finn Bringgold houses, are listed on the National Register of Historic Places. So too are the Pine Island City Hall and Fire Station, built in 1909, and the Bank of Pine Island, Opera House Block, constructed in 1895. Ralph Samuelson, the inventor of water skiing, lived out his later days in the city as a turkey farmer.

RED WING, MN ★
POPULATION: 16,547 – CITY 557 OF 856 (8-31-25)

Telling the story of historic Red Wing, Minnesota, would not be possible without starting with He Mni Can-Barn Bluff, the half-billion-year-old landmark that has long served as a sacred burial mound for the Dakota. The 400-foot-tall bluff rises far above the Mississippi River and is still used by Mdewakanton Sioux members of the Prairie Island Indian Community reservation for religious purposes. It was noted in writing by early visitors to the Red Wing area, including the early explorer Zebulon Pike, who [allegedly, according to some sources] founded a village here called Khenichan, "the place of hill, wood, and water," alongside Chief Tatankamani, or Walking Buffalo. Euro-American settlers called him Chief Red Wing. Two Swiss missionaries from the Evangelical Society of Lausanne, Switzerland, arrived in 1837 to Christianize the Indigenous and introduce them to the white man's customs and culture. By the 1850s, steamers were plowing their way up the Mississippi River, and the site became a port of entry for thousands into the Minnesota Territory. Red Wing was selected as the name for the fledgling European settlement, 1850 post office branch, and new

Goodhue County seat. J. J. Knauer platted the initial townsite on behalf of William Freeborn, Benjamin F. Hoyt, Charles L. Willis, and Alexander Ramsey, the "Founding Fathers" of the river town. Wheat farming became a staple industry, and in 1873, Red Wing area farmers were reportedly producing and selling more wheat than any other county in the country. Well over one hundred businesses existed at this point, ranging from banks and barber shops to grocers, hardware stores, printing offices, planing mills, saw mills, and every other business type in between. German, Irish, and Swedish immigrants were mass-producing pottery, boats, buttons, barrels, bricks, and farming implements, and stone-cutting, lumbering, agricultural, and brewing served as alternative economic sectors to the manufacturing lines. Quarrying was important, too, until residents protested the destruction of He Mni Can-Barn Bluff for limestone extraction. Churches, fraternal organizations, and schools were established, and from 1854 to 1869, Red Wing was home to Minnesota's first institution of higher learning, Hamline University. Two years later, it was reestablished in Saint Paul, where it still operates today. From 1879 to 1932, Red Wing Seminary taught Lutheran pastors studying with the Hauge Norwegian Evangelical Lutheran Synod of America before all its programs ultimately merged into Northfield's St. Olaf College curriculum. Minnesota Elementarskola was yet another educational institution, specifically a Swedish elementary school, that started in 1862 in Red Wing as a precursor to Gustavus Adolphus College in St. Peter. Red Wing Pottery, started in 1861 by John Paul; Red Wing Shoes, a footwear company established in 1905 by Charles H. Beckman; and Riedell Skates, a 1945 project started by former Red Wing Shoes employee Paul Riedell to provide affordable ice skates, are the city's three most recognizable and historic business ventures. These firms and scores of others benefited from Red Wing's positioning on the Chicago, Milwaukee & St. Paul and the Wisconsin, Minnesota & Pacific Railroads. The city enjoyed its best days as a trade port on the Mississippi River up until the railroads connected the rest of Minnesota with the enormous flouring mills at Minneapolis and Saint Anthony Falls. Over thirty Red Wing locations are listed on the NRHP, including the 14-block, 153-property Red Wing Residential Historic District; the 48-property Red Wing Mall Historic District, the He Mni Can-Barn Bluff Historic District, and the Anderson Center at Tower View on the former Alexander P. Anderson Estate. The Aliveo Military Museum, the Anderson Center for the Arts, and the World's Largest Boot, a size 638-D on display at the Riverfront Centre and three important tourist attractions for Red Wing, and the Minnesota Correctional Facility at Red Wing, housed in the 1889 Minnesota State Training School; Lock and Dam No. 3 on the Mississippi River, opened in July 1938, and the 1973 Prairie Island Nuclear Power Plant and three essential civil landmarks of the city. A few noteworthy individuals with city ties include Lauris Norstad, former Commander in Chief of the U.S. European Command from 1956 to 1961; actor Patrick Fleuger, who played Shawn Farrell in the sci-fi television series *The 4400*; Eugenie Anderson, the first woman in United States history appointed as chief of mission at the ambassador level; August Weenaas, the founder and first president of Augsburg University in Minneapolis; Stanley E. Hubbard, the founder of Hubbard Broadcasting; Jacqueline West, the *New York Times* bestselling author behind the *Books of Elsewhere* series; Joseph Francis Busch, the Roman Catholic Bishop of the Diocese of Lead, South Dakota from 1910 to 1915 and Saint Cloud, Minnesota from 1915 to 1953, and Norwegian skiing champions Mikkjel and Torjus Hemmestveit. The two brothers practiced at the Aurora Ski Club in Red Wing in the 1880s, which was one of the first ski clubs in North America. It was here that "Red Wing Style" ski techniques were pioneered based on the Telemark skiing form.

Lodging Recommendation:
Round Barn Farm B&B & Wedding Venue
28650 Wildwood Ln
Red Wing, MN 55066

WANAMINGO, MN
POPULATION: 1,113– CITY 551 OF 856 (8-30-25)

Settlement of Wanamingo began around 1851, when prospective farmers Henry Nelson, Toge Nelson, William Williamson, and Nils Gulbrandson, and others arrived in June of that year. Many other Norwegians followed them, and they soon selected a name for their settlement: Wanamingo. The exact origin of this Native American name remains unknown. It is thought to have been derived from the name of an "Indian heroine from a popular nineteenth-century novel." In 1857, the Wanamingo post office began to distribute letters and parcels for the first time. Homes and businesses were erected as the hamlet grew, but when the Chicago, Milwaukee & St. Paul Railroad was built through, citizens moved their settlement one mile to the east to be located on the tracks. Businesses of all kinds came and went over the decades, but the largest of them all was Broin Companies, established in 1983 on Lowell Broin's farm. The biofuel company is now called POET LLC and produces nearly one-fifth of all ethanol in the United States (over 1 billion gallons annually). The population of Wanamingo crossed 1,000 for the first time at the dawn of the 21st century.

ZUMBROTA, MN ☆
POPULATION: 3,726 – CITY 553 OF 856 (8-30-25)

"The only Zumbrota in the world" got its name from the nearby river, which in turn was named after the Zumbro River. Through gradual mispronunciations and mistranslations, the French name for the river, *Rivière des Embarras* (Obstruction River in English), ultimately changed to Zumbro. Joseph Bailey and D. B. Goddard, members of the Strafford Western Emigration Company alongside Josiah Thompson, Ira Perry, Thomas P. Kellett, and Samuel Chaffee, started the village in 1856. Kellett opened the first store in October 1856 and served as the original Zumbrota postmaster. Ezra Wilder built and managed The Zumbrota House hotel that same month. In 1857, Zumbrota residents built the very first rendition of its claim to fame, the Zumbrota Covered Bridge. While not the "only" covered bridge in Minnesota (see Holdingford, Stearns County, and the Lake Wobegon Trail), this architectural masterpiece was built over the North Branch of the Zumbro River in the late 1850s, then underwent renovations in 1863, 1865, and 1869 due to flooding. The last rendition has remained intact as Minnesota's only remaining "original" functioning covered bridge; the 116-foot-long, 15-foot-wide bridge was relocated to the fairgrounds in 1932 and then moved to the 64-acre Covered Bridge Park in 1997, less than a football field away (120 yards) from its original location. Zumbrota also had a "second covered bridge" built in 1905, half a mile up the river, that was used by the Duluth, Red Wing, and Southern Railroad as a railroad bridge. A 1909 city directory listed numerous improvements to the village, which at that time had a little over 1,000 residents. A clay manufacturing company, a cement block plant, a fur factory, a cigar factory, a carriage works, three grain elevators, two lumber yards, a mill, six general stores, five saloons, four milliners, a creamery, and multiple other businesses lined the streets to help bring economic prominence to the city. There was an outstanding high school building for that time, a Carnegie Library, a Lutheran hospital, about a dozen professional offices, and three fraternity halls. Churches ranged from Catholic, Methodist, and Episcopal to

German Lutheran, United Norwegian Lutheran, English Lutheran, and other Protestant congregations. One of these early churches, one of the oldest standing churches in southeast Minnesota, was built in 1862: the First Congregational Church of Zumbrota. It and the Zumbrota Covered Bridge are recorded on the National Register of Historic Places. Charles Clarence Beck, the artist behind DC Comic's Shazam (formerly called Captain Marvel, not to be confused with the Marvel Comics hero) superhero artwork; Gus Bradley, an NFL coach with several franchises since 2006, most recently with the San Francisco 49ers as an assistant coach, and Kenneth O. Chilstrom, the first United States Air Force pilot to fly the XP-86 Sabre (the Sabrejet) and a pilot for eighty combat missions during World War II, hail from Zumbrota.

Lake City is only partially located in Goodhue County (see Wabasha County).

Unincorporated/Ghost Towns: Belle Creek, Belvidere Mills, Bombay, Central Point Township, Claybank, Fairpoint, Florence, Forest Mills, Frontenac, Hader, Hay Creek, Roscoe, Ryan, Skyberg, Sogn, Stanton, Thoten, Vasa, Wacouta, Wangs, Wastedo, Welch, White Rock

National Register of Historic Places:
Cannon Falls: Cannon Falls Commercial Historic District, Cannon Falls School, Capt. Charles Gellett House, Church of the Redeemer- Episcopal, Darwin E. Yale House, Ellsworth Hotel Livery Stable, Fireman's Hall, Third Street Bridge, Yale Hardware Store, Harrison Miller Farmhouse, John Miller Farmhouse, Oxford Mill Ruin
Florence Township: Old Frontenac Historic District
Frontenac: Florence Town Hall
Hay Creek: District No.20 School, Immanuel Lutheran Church
Holden and Warsaw Townships: Nansen Agricultural Historic District
Kenyon: Martin T. Gunderson House, Church of St. Rose of Lima, Hauge Lutheran Church, Holden Lutheran Church Parsonage
Pine Island: Anna and Samuel Murry Burpee House, Bank of Pine Island, Opera House Block, Jacob A. and Mary Finn Bringgold House, Pine Island City Hall and Fire Station, George Baslington Farmhouse
Red Wing: Alexander P. Anderson Estate-Tower View, Chicago Great Western Depot, Dr. Charles Hewitt Laboratory, E. S. Hoyt House, G. A. Carlson Lime Kiln, Gladstone Building, He Mni Can-Barn Bluff Historic District, James L. Lawther House, Kappel Wagon Works, Keystone Building, Mendota to Wabasha Military Road: Cannon River Section, Minnesota State Training School, Minnesota Stoneware Company, Oakwood Cemetery, Pratt-Tabor House, Red Wing City Hall, Red Wing Iron Works, Red Wing Mall Historic District, Red Wing Residential Historic District, Red Wing Waterworks, St. James Hotel, T. B. Sheldon Memorial Auditorium, Theodore B. Sheldon House, Towne-Akenson House, Barton Site, Bridge No.12, Dammon Round Barn, E. J. Fryk Barn, Fred Wallauer Farmhouse
Roscoe: Roscoe Butter and Cheese Factory
Stanton: Carleton Airport
Vasa: Vasa Historic District
Welch: Cross of Christ Lutheran Church
Zumbrota: First Congregational Church of Zumbrota, Zumbrota Covered Bridge

Golf Courses:
Cannon Golf Club, Daily Fee (Cannon Falls, MN)
Gopher Hills Golf Course – Lynx Executive, Daily Fee (Cannon Falls, MN)
Gopher Hills Golf Course – The Heath & The Glen, Daily Fee (Cannon Falls, MN)
Kenyon Country Club, Daily Fee (Kenyon, MN)
Mississippi National Golf Links – Highlands, Municipal (Red Wing, MN)
Mississippi National Golf Links – Lowlands, Municipal (Red Wing, MN)
Mount Frontenac Golf Course, Daily Fee (Frontenac, MN)
Pine Island Golf Course, Daily Fee (Pine Island, MN)
Red Wing Golf Course, Daily Fee (Red Wing, MN)
Summit Golf Club, Daily Fee (Cannon Falls, MN)

Zumbrota Golf Club, Daily Fee (Zumbrota, MN)

Breweries/Wineries/Distilleries:
Cannon River Winery (Cannon Falls, MN)
South x SouthEast Brewing Company (Pine Island, MN)
Tilion Brewing Company (Cannon Falls, MN)

Town Celebrations:
River City Days, Red Wing, MN (1st Full Weekend of August)
Goodhue Volksfest, Goodhue, MN (2nd Weekend of June)
Zumbrota Covered Bridge Festival, Zumbrota, MN (3rd Weekend of September)
Pine Island Cheese Festival, Pine Island, MN (1st Full Weekend of June)
Syttende Mai, Wanamingo, MN (Weekend Closest to May 17th)

Douglas County: Big Ole, the Tallest Viking in America (Alexandria), Douglas County Courthouse (Alexandria) Runestone Museum (Alexandria), WPA Brandon Auditorium and Fire Hall (Brandon), Millerville Butter at Millerville Co-op Creamery (Millerville), Lake Osakis (Osakis), Tip Top Dairy Inn (Osakis), Crooked Willow Wedding Venue & Event Center (Osakis)

Faribault County: Green Giant Statue (Blue Earth), Faribault County Courthouse (Blue Earth), Church of the Good Shepherd Episcopal Church (Blue Earth), American Flag Mural at American Legion (Bricelyn), Main Street Elmore at Sunrise (Elmore), Kee Civic Theatre (Kiester), Walters Jail (Walters), Faribault County Pink Schoolhouse (Wells)

Fillmore County: Amish Horse & Buggy (Canton), Niagara Cave (Harmony), Lanesboro Stone Dam (Lanesboro), View from Church Hill (Lanesboro), Hesper-Mabel Area Historical Society Museum (Mabel), Historic Milwaukee Elevator Company & Milwaukee Road Boxcar (Preston), Spring Valley Methodist Church Museum & Laura Ingalls Wilder Site (Spring Valley), Forestville/Mystery Cave State Park (Spring Valley)

Freeborn County: Itasca Rock Garden (Albert Lea), Soldier Memorial at Freeborn County Courthouse (Albert Lea), Fountain Lake Mermaid (Albert Lea), Old Town Mural (Alden), Clarks Grove [The First] Cooperative Creamery [in Minnesota] (Clarks Grove), Freeborn Cemetery Flag Display (Freeborn), Main Street Windmill (Hollandale), Z.C.B.J. Lodge Zare Zapadu No. 44 (Myrtle)

Goodhue County: Oxford Mill Ruins (Cannon Falls), First Congregational Church (Cannons Falls), The Goodhue Depot (Goodhue), Veteran's Memorial (Goodhue), World's Largest Boot in the Red Wing Shoe Store (Red Wing), Round Barn Farm Bed and Breakfast & Wedding Venue (Red Wing), Wanamingo Veterans Memorial (Wanamingo), Historic Zumbrota Covered Bridge (Zumbrota)

GRANT COUNTY
EST. 1868 - POPULATION: 6,074

One of nearly a dozen counties in the United States named for Ulysses S. Grant, the country's 18th President and the commanding officer of the Union Army in the American Civil War, was organized on March 6, 1868.

ASHBY, MN
POPULATION: 469 – CITY 144 OF 856 (4-12-25)
"You'll Like Ashby" is the official motto of this town of 469 people in northeast Grant County, where, in 1879, this Great Northern Railroad town was platted on the land of Simon Larson. The new station was briefly called Grant after the county, then Brighton, and finally Ashby after officials realized there was already a New Brighton further down the line. Ashby's name was most likely derived from Gunder Ash, an early Norwegian settler east of the townsite who personally knew the "Empire Builder," James J. Hill. It may have also been named for Ashby, England. A post office was opened in 1880. By its inaugural Census in 1890, Ashby reported a population of 231. In 1900, it had all the makings of a thriving community with its depot, hotel, school, two churches, and a small selection of storefronts. Nowadays, the town is best known for its annual Coots Unlimited banquet, a fundraiser for the local sportsmen's club. "Coot," a species of duck-like bird, was once served at dinner. The birds live primarily in the American Southwest, but their breeding grounds are in Minnesota. A large coot statue was erected in Ashby's Boe Park to pay tribute to the town's headliner event. Ashby is also the closest incorporated town to the Fort Pomme de Terre Site, where an early 1859 stagecoach station was converted into a U.S. Army fort during the 1862 Dakota War skirmishes. Ashby was officially incorporated on March 7, 1884.

BARRETT, MN
POPULATION: 366 – CITY 165 OF 856 (4-14-25)
Located on the Pomme De Terre River in 1887 by the Minneapolis, St. Paul & Sault Ste. Marie Railroad, Barrett's first post office, was called Friedhem, a Swedish word meaning "home of peace," before being renamed in honor of local farmer and Civil War veteran General Theodore Harvey Barrett. The post office opened as the first significant piece of infrastructure on the townsite near the adjacent Barrett Lake, now known for its ample fishing opportunities and Historic Barrett Lakeside Pavilion. Schools, churches, stores, and many businesses sprang up throughout Barrett's early days, but one structure has a history and stories spanning several generations: Roosevelt Hall. The centerpiece of the community's social and cultural life was built in 1934 by the Civil Works Administration. This New Deal agency carried out public works projects throughout the United States. Over the years, it has been used as an auditorium, a gymnasium, a bowling alley, an insulation manufacturing facility, and the Prairie Wind Players community theater group. Barrett's incorporation day was December 11, 1889. In 1949, the Setterlund "Elbow Lake" Runestone brought great fame to Barrett and nearby Elbow Lake after a traveling salesman was shown the stone and began making a great deal about it. Experts Johan A. Holvik of Moorhead, Minnesota, and Hjalmar A. Holand of Ephriam, Wisconsin, were called in to verify its authenticity; they interpreted it as having been carved in 1776 and 1362, respectively. In a surprising twist of events, when the stone's discoverer, Victor Setterlund, was asked if he had carved the stone himself, he admitted to doing so. He was a strong proponent of the Kensington Runestone's authenticity. He was convinced that he could fabricate a more historically accurate fake.

ELBOW LAKE, MN ★
POPULATION: 1,276 – CITY 143 OF 856 (4-12-25)
Elbow Lake's name is an eponym for the nearby lake, which is shaped like an elbow. The idea for the name dates back to 1849, when Captain John Pope and Major Samuel Woods crossed the lake during their expedition. When Grant County was organized in 1873, the decision was made by the county commissioners, Henry Sanford, S. S. Frogner, and K. N. Melby, to plat a new townsite somewhere between Herman, in the southwest portion of the county, and Pomme de Terre, located in the northeast corner. A parcel of land was selected not far from Sanford's homestead, and a new community was born out of necessity. In 1878, a courthouse was built amongst the few dwellings and the local post office, which was open from 1873-84, 1986-83, and then from 1883 onwards. A short-lived plot to steal the seat of government from Elbow Lake was foiled in 1881, despite Herman's best efforts to remove the honor from their thriving railroad community. The legislature initially agreed with Herman and had the capital moved there, prompting a raid on the Elbow Lake courthouse in the middle of the night. All county records were transferred to the new courthouse edifice in Herman, but Elbow Lake residents raided them after the vote was overturned. It had been determined that Herman had cheated by failing to count any ballots from Erdahl Township, admitting excess votes from Logan Township, and using workers from the Twin Cities, youth, and non-American citizens to sway the vote in their favor. By the end of 1886, with lines of the Soo Line and the Great Northern Railroad, the city's prosperity was guaranteed. The first commercial establishment was the Elbow Lake House, a joint boarding house and saloon venture established in 1884. A general store followed it. By 1900, there was the Elbow Lake Roller Mill, the F. A. Johnson Lumber Company, the John Berger wood and coal mill, a creamery, an elevator, the Park Hotel, the Elbow Lake Bank, the First National Bank, a blacksmith shop, a jewelry store, a meat market, a harness shop, and various others. Three churches and a courthouse square were also present. The architectural firm of Bell & Detweiler, known for their work on multiple courthouses throughout multiple states and the South Dakota State Capitol, worked with The Prince Construction Company of Minneapolis to erect a grand Beaux-Arts and Renaissance-style courthouse in 1905. That structure, along with the 1933-34 Anna J. Scofield Memorial Auditorium and Harold E. Thorson Memorial Library, widely regarded as one of the defining architectural accomplishments of the Public Works Administration, is Elbow Lake's other National Register of Historic Places location. On Highway 4 outside northeastern Elbow Lake, grassroots art enthusiasts may admire Allen Bakke's collection of large Jesus, troll, and eagle sculptures. Elbow Lake's sister city is Flekkefjord, Norway; an annual festival called Flekkefest pays tribute to this relationship and the community's deep Scandinavian roots.

HERMAN, MN ☆
POPULATION: 384 – CITY 139 OF 856 (4-11-25)
Herman, simply put, is a town of flattery–but that noun needs context to support its proper weight regarding this community of 384 residents. Platted in September 1875 and incorporated for the first time on February 17, 1881, Herman became the first railroad village of the county when the Great Northern Railroad was extended through the vicinity. Its post office was established in 1872 at Sven S. Frogner's general store and named for Herman Trott, then the land agent for the St. Paul and Pacific Railroad Company. Like many other towns in Minnesota, it was located on a lake — specifically Pullman Lake — and was home to several noteworthy businesses by the 20th century. Amongst these were the Herman Roller Mill, the C. E. Wood Prop., the Cargill Elevator, the N. W. Elevator, the Duluth Elevator, a depot and an engine house, Hotel Pullman,

the Grant County Bank, Wieger & Woodman's "Big Store," the H. W. Ross Lumber Company, liveries, stores, and more. Despite losing an early election to Elbow Lake for the county seat title, its ability to sustain so many lines of enterprise, in addition to schools and churches, bolstered its reputation as an outstanding community in which to live and grow. With over 600 residents and all these facets in place, Herman caught the attention of the State Municipal League. In 1914, they named the town the "model town" of Minnesota. They began an experiment to install new state-of-the-art waterworks, electrical, and sewer utility systems, improve the local roads and bridges, and turn every street into a gorgeous boulevard with parks. Plans were even put in place to erect a sign stating, "This is Herman, the Model Village." Throughout the 1960s, the town's population reached an all-time high of 764 residents. As it began to subside amid forthcoming farm crises, a new plan was put in place to save its population: Bachelormania. This viral 1994 event encouraged women to visit Herman and meet any of its 78 eligible bachelors, many of whom were single because the town's men outnumbered its women by 8:1. Thousands of women flocked to the town in search of love. Some men were featured on Leeza Gibbons and Oprah Winfrey's talk shows. At a minimum, seven of the bachelors were married, and over sixty new residents moved into the area. A 2001 movie called *Herman U.S.A.* was written and directed by Bill Semans regarding the event. It was filmed in Carver County's New Germany because Herman had no nearby lodging. Noted residents from the town include Mabel Seeley, a mystery writer known for writing The Chuckling Fingers (1941); Theodore H. Barrett, the Union General who commanded forces at the Battle of Palmito Ranch, the final battle of the American Civil War; and Dorothy Houston Jacobson, the Assistant Secretary for International Affairs at the United States Department of Agriculture in the mid-to-late 1960s. Iron castings throughout Herman pay homage to the Herman Iron Pour, once an event at the Grant County Fair that allowed visitors to mold and cast iron art.

HOFFMAN, MN
POPULATION: 698 – CITY 166 OF 856 (4-14-25)
Described as being at the "prairie's edge," Hoffman was founded on the Chippewa River near large swaths of both prairie and hardwood forests in April 1887 with the arrival of the Minneapolis and Pacific Railroad (later known simply as the "Soo Line"). It was named after Robert C. Hoffman, the Soo's chief engineer for several years. The post office predated the town by four years, starting in 1883 as Wanberg, then moved to the Louis Peterson farm in 1884, and finally to the platted village in 1887. Hoffman was laid out on Andres Lindberg's land, which initially had a depot, a hotel, a grain elevator, and several stores. It later welcomed a pair of churches and a school. Hoffman today has more residents than any other recorded Census in its history: 698 people as of 2020. Harley Refsal, an internationally renowned Scandinavian flat-plane woodcarving expert, was born on a farm near Hoffman on Christmas Day, 1944.

NORCROSS, MN
POPULATION: 52 – CITY 140 OF 856 (4-11-25)
"Norcross" is an amalgamated name that honors both Henry Allyn Norton and Judson Newell Cross, the original townsite owners before the arrival of the Great Northern Railroad circa December 1881. Initially, the railroad wanted to place a depot at Gorton, two miles north. Local rancher N. F. Griswold and Mr. Cross convinced them that more business would be conducted at their ranch. They obliged, and the town plat was completed shortly thereafter. Norton and Cross donated the land for the railroad's right-of-way, depot, and grain elevators, so the town was named for them. The town's main street was called "Griswold Avenue." The post office opened in 1881 (and closed

in October 2019). Over the decades, Norcross sported everything from a creamery, a general store, a liquor store, and a bank (run by Lund and Sellseth from 1909 to 1931) to a town hall, schools, and three churches: Our Savior's Lutheran Church (1901 to the 1990s), St. Mary's Catholic Church (1905 to 1923), and The Faith United Methodist Church (from 1952 to 2007). The Amundson School hosted the Methodist congregation's first services starting in 1919. In 1970-71, the Norcross Elementary School consolidated with Herman, but Norcross students had been attending high school in Herman for much longer than that. The aforementioned town hall building served Norcross from the 1920s to 1997 as a venue for public events, dances, roller skating, and basketball games, before it was razed due to structural failure.

WENDELL, MN
POPULATION: 166 – CITY 142 OF 856 (4-11-25)
Platted in July 1889 and incorporated on March 3, 1904, Wendell was most likely named in honor of Joseph H. Wendell, a Wright County judge. Alternatively, it could have been named by early settlers after the town in Massachusetts or North Carolina. A post office was established in 1887 with John A. Beck as postmaster; by 1900, the Minneapolis, St. Paul & Sault Ste. Marie Railroad had brought in a depot and elevators. A plat map from that era records the existence of the Bigarals Veterinary Hospital, a school, and a proposed site for the Wendell Cheese Factory. At one point, there was a Farmers Co-operative Creamery Company that churned out butter and sold the farmers' products throughout the area. Wendell's highest-ever recorded population was 284 people in the 1950s.

Unincorporated/Ghost Towns: Charlesville, Erdahl, Hereford, Pomme de Terre, Thorsborg

National Register of Historic Places:
Ashby: Fort Pomme de Terre Site
Barrett: Roosevelt Hall
Elbow Lake: Anna J. Scofield Memorial Auditorium & Harold E. Thorson Memorial Library, Grant County Courthouse

Golf Courses:
Tipsinah Mounds Golf Course, Daily Fee (Elbow Lake, MN)

Town Celebrations:
Flekkefest, Elbow Lake, MN (First Full Weekend of August)

HENNEPIN COUNTY
EST. 1852 - POPULATION: 1,281,565

Minnesota's most populous county, with nearly 1.3 million people, was established on March 6, 1852, and named in honor of Father Louis Hennepin. He was responsible for naming Saint Anthony Falls, which gave rise to the world's largest flour mills here.

BLOOMINGTON, MN
POPULATION: 89,987 – CITY 777 OF 856 (11-6-25)
Minnesota's fourth-largest city, named for Bloomington, Illinois, had a population of only 1,000 by the turn of the 20th century. Since then, its population has grown exponentially, beginning in the 1950s, when planning committees decided that it should be the site of Minneapolis-St. Paul's principal post-World War II housing boom

suburb of choice. Between 1950 and 1960, Bloomington grew from 9,902 people to 50,498, and then to 81,971 by the dawn of the 1970s. Settlers who arrived circa 1843 could never have imagined such rapid growth at that time. When Reverend Gideon W. Pond came here, the region was not much more than lakes and prairies. Pond's home served as a joint house and mission school that produced an alphabet and dictionary for the Dakota language. The mission operated from 1843 to 1852, before the Dakota were moved to a different part of the Minnesota River following the passage and signing of the Treaty of Traverse des Sioux. Pond founded Oak Grove Presbyterian Church in the area where Bloomington Cemetery now stands; it is historically known as the First Presbyterian Church of Oak Grove Cemetery and is now listed as one of only three Bloomington locations on the National Register of Historic Places, alongside Pond's home and the 5,100-plus-foot-long Cedar Avenue Bridge over the Minnesota River. It is Minnesota's longest through-truss bridge, built in 1920. From 1961 to 1981, Bloomington hosted the MLB's Minnesota Twins and the NFL's Minnesota Vikings at Metropolitan Stadium. The outdoor sports stadium opened on April 24, 1956, and hosted thousands of events before being replaced in the early 1980s by alternative facilities. Demolition began in January 1985, and for several years, the lot sat empty as officials pondered what to do with the land. Triple Five Group worked with the Ghermezian brothers and the DLR Group design firm on proposals for a shopping mall that would become the iconic Mall of America. America's (and the Western Hemisphere's) largest shopping mall by area — 5.6 million square feet — is a shopaholic and tourist paradise that boasts over 500 unique vendors and upwards of 40,000,000 annual visitors. The mall's anchors are L.L. Bean, Nordstrom, Macy's, and the Crayola Experience, although Nickelodeon Universe at the mall's center is often considered its most significant and most exciting draw. In the heart of the amusement park is a bronze plaque that marks the home plate of Metropolitan Stadium, and on the wall above the Log Flume ride is a red chair that marks where Twins player Harmon Killebrew sent his record-breaking 522-foot home run in 1967. Sea Life Minnesota Aquarium is another staple of the facility that invites guests to walk through a 300-foot-long, 1.3-million-gallon aquarium tunnel to observe sharks, stingrays, and over 4,500 sea creatures. Hyland Lake Park Reserve and its skiing area, the Minnesota Valley National Wildlife Refuge, the Bloomington History Museum at the old town hall, the Northwest Airlines History Museum, and the Bloomington Center for the Arts are worthwhile points of interest to explore outside of the Mall of America. Education-wise, Bloomington has Normandale Community College, founded in 1968 as part of the MnSCU system, and the private Northwestern Health Sciences University, founded in 1941 to focus on alternative health care. From 1995 to 2003, Bloomington Public Schools offered the first online public high school program in the United States. Because of its sheer size and proximity to the Twin Cities, Bloomington has also been selected to be the headquarters of Dairy Queen (a fast food chain known for its ice cream), Holiday Stationstores (a gasoline and convenience store chain), Great Clips (a hair salon chain), Toro (a manufacturer of lawn mowers and snow blowers amongst other items), and Dayforce (a human resources software company), amongst other corporations like the Donaldson Company and HealthPartners. A few of Bloomington's most famous personalities with local ties are Pete Docter, the chief creative officer of Pixar and a nine-time Academy Award nominee, best known for his work on Up (2009), Inside Out (2015), and Soul (2020); Tom Burnett, a hero on Flight 93 who thwarted hijackers' plans on September 11, 2001 to crash the plane in Washington D.C. by rushing the cabin with three other passengers; Bud Grant, the beloved former head coach of the Minneapolis Vikings and Minneapolis Lakers and a member of the Pro Football and Canadian Football Hall(s) of Fame; Kelly Carlson, an actress known for her role as Kimber Henry in the

FX drama *Nip/Tuck*, and Scott Weiland, the lead vocalist of the rock band Stone Temple Pilots from 1989 to 2003 and 2008 to 2013, known for using megaphones during his concerts.

Restaurant Recommendation:
Bubba Gump Shrimp Co.
396 South Avenue 3rd Floor
Bloomington, MN 55425

Restaurant Recommendation:
Rainforest Café
396 South Avenue 3rd Floor
Bloomington, MN 55425

BROOKLYN CENTER, MN
POPULATION: 33,782 – CITY 832 OF 856 (11-13-25)
What started as a large farming area on Minneapolis's northwest corner has since become Minnesota's most ethnically diverse community. From 1893 to 1907, it had a post office, but only a tiny handful of stores opened, alongside a school, a meeting hall, and Baptist and Methodist churches on Osseo Road. Market gardening was the main driver of its economy well into the Great Depression, after which widespread development began. From 1940 to 1950, Brooklyn Center gained about 2,400 residents, but it was during the 1950s that the population grew by an incredible 468.5%, from 4,284 to 24,356 by the decade's end. During that time, it welcomed Brookdale, a shopping center developed by the people behind Dayton's department store. Hennepin County's Board of Commissioners accepted the townspeople's incorporation request in January 1911; the following month, on February 18, it was officially incorporated. It was elevated to city status on October 20, 1966. Marcus Harris, who was awarded the Fred Biletnikoff Award as the nation's best college receiver in 1996, and Dannie Gordon, a film and television director known for her work on the 2004 teen comedy-drama *New York Minute* and the 2001 adventure-comedy *Joe Dirt*, can both claim local ties.

BROOKLYN PARK, MN
POPULATION: 86,478 – CITY 827 OF 856 (11-12-25)
Brooklyn Township was settled in 1852 and formally organized on May 11, 1858, taking its name from Brooklyn, Michigan, the hometown of the people who created the township and first settled there. Primarily an agricultural community for many decades through the 1940s, modern-day Brooklyn Park comprises the area left over when Brooklyn Center and Crystal Lake became independent entities. When the split occurred in 1911, Brooklyn Center immediately incorporated as a village, whereas the Village of Brooklyn Park was not incorporated until 1954. Now serving as Minnesota's 6th-largest incorporated community, the city first surpassed 10,000 residents in the early 1960s, but has recently been home to as many as 86,478 persons according to the 2020 Census. Eldem Homestead, a 19-acre living history potato farm that attracts elementary school students from around the metro, has been in existence since the 1900s. A few of the community's famous persons include Jesse Ventura, the former professional wrestler turned Minnesota State Governor from 1999 to 2003; Tim Laudner, an 1988 All-Star catcher with the MLB's Minnesota Twins; Pat Neshek, a two-time MLB All-Star pitcher who played for seven different franchises between 2006 and 2019; Kirby Puckett, a ten-time All-Star and six-time Gold Glove and Silver

Slugger Award winner with his hometown Minnesota Towns; Ramon Humber, a linebacker in the NFL from 2009 to 2018; Tim Jackman, an NHL player from 2003 to 2016, and Dave Brat, a U.S. Congressman from Virginia from November 2014 to January 2019.

CHAMPLIN, MN
POPULATION: 23,919 – CITY 824 OF 856 (11-12-25)
Located opposite the Anoka County seat on the southern side of the "Big Muddy" is the City of Champlin, the only such city in the United States by that name. It was derived either from Stephen Champlin, an officer in the United States Navy during the War of 1812, or from Ezra T. Champlin, who served in the Third Minnesota Regiment in the American Civil War and served as a Minnesota state legislator. Homesteaders came to Champlin in search of new land, but because the Great Northern and Northern Pacific Railroad tracks were on the northern part of the river, ferry service became common starting in 1855. Growth was so slow and subtle that no Censuses were recorded in Champlin between 1890 and 1950. The 1950 Census was conducted only after Champlin was incorporated in 1946. In the 1960s, the population reached 1,000. By 1990, there were 16,849 citizens. As recently as 2023, Champlin has been in joint talks with Dayton to secede from Hennepin County into Anoka County for tax purposes. The District No. 99 School, also known as the Dunning School, operated from 1876 to 1947 and is listed on the National Register of Historic Places. The Anoka-Champlin Mississippi River Bridge, developed in 1929 as one of many spandrel concrete arch bridges in the Twin Cities area, is also on the list. An authentic 1950s full-service gas station is the first site drivers see as they cross the bridge from Anoka into Champlin; it is known for its iconic green dinosaur, which owner Diana Merkl dresses up on special occasions.

CORCORAN, MN ☆
POPULATION: 6,185 – CITY 838 OF 856 (11-13-25)
When western Hennepin County was opened for settlement in 1855, the Irishman Patrick B. Corcoran knew he had to act fast to claim land for his family. He ended up acquiring 640 acres of farmland, some of which would eventually be used to establish the townsite of Corcoran. In the winter of 1857, he built a schoolhouse and began educating the area's youth, hoping that someday they would become essential businessmen and women and contribute to the town. His endeavors continued with the construction of several general stores, and he also served as postmaster when the office opened in 1863. It was discontinued in 1903, but by that point, Corcoran was already a handsome village with many establishments. The town was organized on May 11, 1858. Ninety years later, it was incorporated on December 4, 1948. One location on the National Register of Historic Places is the Burschville School, part of District No. 107, which was built in 1894 and listed in 2018.

CRYSTAL, MN
POPULATION: 23,330 – CITY 834 OF 856 (11-13-25)
Crystal's landscape changed seemingly in the blink of an eye between 1950 and 1960, when its population grew from 5,713 to 24,283. The area that began as Crystal Township in 1860 has undergone significant change over the years. Minneapolis annexed a large part of the city over the next 30 years, and in 1886, the City of Golden Valley was formed, further reducing the amount of training land. With brick yards, general stores, a blacksmith shop, a hotel, and a post office of its own, Crystal Township residents feared losing their identity altogether. So, on January 11, 1887,

Crystal Village was incorporated following approval from the county commissioners and the state legislature. The town retained the name Crystal Lake, which was ironically assumed under the control of Robbinsdale when that village incorporated in 1893. Nevertheless, the Twin Lakes are still located on the town's eastern border alongside Brooklyn Center. More land was taken by Minneapolis in 1887, and in 1936, New Hope Township was formed, splitting Crystal Township once again. More minor adjustments have been made since then, but it will likely retain the 5.87 square miles that it now encompasses. The most prominent landmark of the city is Crystal Airport, a 430-acre facility that opened in 1948. Todd and Travis Richards, a pair of former NHL players, hail from Crystal.

DAYTON, MN
POPULATION: 7,262 – CITY 822 OF 856 (11-11-25)
Hennepin County's northernmost city, Dayton, which also extends slightly into Wright County, was platted in 1855 and named in honor of Lyman Dayton. Not to be confused with John Geisse and Douglas Dayton, who established the first Target store in nearby Roseville in 1962, Lyman lived a century prior and was responsible for bringing the Lake Superior and Mississippi Railroad into Minnesota. He served as its president and oversaw its operations before it was ultimately folded into the Northern Pacific Railway. Paul Godine of France was likely its first settler, as he arrived in 1851 and stayed until 1853 to trade with the Native Americans. Godine, John Veine, E. H. Robinson, Marcellus Bonlee, and Benjamin Leveillier are the first five recorded men to have lived here. Modern population estimates suggest that Dayton reached 10,000 residents as recently as 2023. The landmark point of interest in the far northwest corner of town is St. John the Baptist Catholic Church, erected in 1904.

DEEPHAVEN, MN
POPULATION: 3,899 – CITY 785 OF 856 (11-7-25)
Founded circa 1880 and named for its harbor, Deephaven Park owes its existence to Charles S. Gibson, an attorney from Saint Louis, Missouri. He purchased the land in 1870 from Warren Chapman and built a summer home called "Northome" there in 1877. He was a strong advocate for the construction of Hotel Saint Louis, a 150-room, three-story luxury hotel that soon brought large numbers of vacationers to the area via the Minneapolis and Saint Louis Railway. 108.55 acres of Gibson's property were platted into lots for more homes. From 1892 to 1914, a post office called Deephaven operated, but by the time it closed, Deephaven had already lost its greatest assets. The hotel was torn down in 1907 due to the advent of trolley service to this part of the metro area. Three years prior, the Minnetonka Ice Yacht Club had burned down after serving area tourists since 1882. One of its co-founders, Hazen Burton, commissioned Arthur Dyer to build a new type of sailboat called a racing scow. Called the "Onawa," the prototype was disqualified after winning every regatta it entered. The rules were later changed to allow for racing scows, and nowadays, the boat can be found at the Excelsior-Lake Minnetonka Historical Society Museum in Excelsior. Despite early struggles to retain its principal points of interest, Deephaven has grown to a population of about 3,900 and is now home to six public beaches and two city marinas. Marisa Coughlan, known for her role as Officer Ursula Hanson in the 2001 comedy *Super Troopers*; Jake Gardiner, an NHL defenseman with 645 game appearances; Jeffrey Hatcher, the playwright behind the 2004 romantic period drama *Stage Beauty*; Mike Plant, a single-handed yachtsman known for setting the world record for fastest circumnavigation [of the world] by an American in 135 days; Max McGee, the first player in NFL history to score a touchdown in the Super Bowl with the Green Bay Packers; Tim Herron, a four-time winner on the PGA Tour; Dean Phillips, the runner-

up to Joe Biden in the 2024 Democratic National Convention with four delegates and a former CEO of his family's Phillips Distilling Company, and Walter Donald Douglas, a co-founder of the Quaker Oats Company, a former Deephaven summertime resident, and a victim of the Titanic disaster in April 1912.

EDEN PRAIRIE, MN
POPULATION: 64,198 – CITY 779 OF 856 (11-7-25)
Home to 1,000 people in the 1930s, 7,000 by the 1970s, and now well over 64,000 people as of the 2020s, Eden Prairie has never reported a negative population increase since its first Census in 1860. As one of several of the Twin Cities' outer suburbs, it has since grown to become one of the largest cities in all of Minnesota as the site of the headquarters of several major firms including Winnebago Industries (a motorhome and RV manufacturer), SuperValu (a grocery store retail chain), Starkey Hearing Technologies (one of the world's largest hearing aid manufacturers), and MTS Systems Corporation (a supplier of test and simulation systems), amongst others. The now-bustling hub of major corporations and manufacturers had to start somewhere, however. Elizabeth Fries Ellet came here from the East Coast in the community's early days and nicknamed it "the garden spot of [Minnesota] territory," which gave rise to the name "Eden Prairie." Some of the very first settlers came in the 1850s to this natural prairie, the same decade that the town board met for the first time at a local log cabin schoolhouse on May 11, 1858. A post office began in 1855 and has been nearly continuously operational, except for brief service interruptions in 1886 and between 1902-03. Large numbers of storefronts, shops, churches, schools, fraternal organizations and halls, and other pieces of city infrastructure came and went over the decades. Still, a couple of sites have been listed on the NRHP for their historic significance. The John R. Cummins Farmhouse is one of southern Hennepin County's last surviving farmhouses, built in 1879. From 1925 to 1950, the place now known as Camp Eden Wood was the Glen Lake Children's Camp, one of a small handful of summer camps dedicated to children with tuberculosis. Although Eden Prairie lost its title of being the site of the NFL's Minnesota Vikings practice facility in the early 2010s, it is still home to some points of interest, like the Eden Prairie Center mall, a $500,000-plus community-funded veteran's memorial, 2,250-plus acres of parks, and 170 miles of multi-use trails like the Minnesota River Bluffs Regional Trail. Eden Prairie has had its share of TV-time in movies like the 1995 buddy comedy film *Mallrats* and the 1999 satirical mockumentary *Drop Dead Gorgeous*, but other persons have brought notoriety to the city over the years as well such as David Baszucki, the CEO and co-founder of Roblox; Sheila Escovedo, a singer-songwriter known as the "Queen of Percussion;" Allison Pottinger, the USA female curling athlete of the year in 2008; Dan Gladden, a two-time World Series champion in 1987 and 1991; Adam Bartley, an actor known for playing Archie Ferguson on the neo-Western crime drama television series *Longmire*, and several professional athletes.

Restaurant Recommendation:
Lions Tap
16180 Flying Cloud Dr
Eden Prairie, MN 55347

EDINA, MN
POPULATION: 53,494 – CITY 790 OF 856 (11-8-25)
While Edina is home to the nation's first fully enclosed, climate-controlled shopping mall, Southdale Center (built in 1956 at nearly 1.3 million square feet and now home

to over 100 tenants), its notorious shopping center was nowhere to be found at the dawn of its existence. Founded as a milling community on Minnehaha Creek in the 1860s, the then-farming village of Edina Mills was split off from Richfield and named after the flouring mill of Andrew and John Craik. They purchased the mill in 1869 and named it after their childhood home of Edinburgh, Scotland. The decision to split off from Richfield Township and become an independent village was made at the local Minnehaha Grange Hall circa 1888, when locals suggested the names Hennepin, Westfield, Park, and Edina. Westfield was nearly the chosen name until a heated debate among the town councilmen prompted them to delay the vote until the next meeting, once things had "cooled down." The name Edina won out by a vote of 47 to 42. From 1888 to 1942, the Minnehaha Grange Hall served as the Edina Village Hall. A 1864 one-room schoolhouse now referred to as the Cahill School, which was used as a theater, community center, school, and church through 1958 before closing. It is the oldest building in Edina. In the 1920s, the Country Club Historic District, noted for its Period Revival architecture, was created as one of Minnesota's first comprehensive planned communities and as a prototype for Edina's many housing developments. The Minnehaha Grange Hall and the Cahill School are both operated by the Edina Historical Society. Like its neighbors, Edina's growth began slowly in the 1930s but accelerated rapidly between 1950 and 1960. During that period, it grew from 9,744 persons to 30,482, then to 44,031 by 1970. With so many citizens in recent decades, many "notable" persons can claim connections to the city, including Paige Bueckers, the 2025 WNBA Rookie of the Year with the Dallas Wings; David W. Anderson, the founder of the Famous Dave's chain of barbecue restaurants; Ron Johnson, the former CEO of JCPenney and the inventor of Apple's retail store concept and the Genius Bar; Doug Risebrough, a retired General Manager for the NHL's Calgary Flames from 1991 to 1995 and the Minnesota Wild from 1999 to 2003; Robert Ulrich, the longtime CEO of Target Corporation; David Bloom, a former journalist known for co-anchoring NBC's weekend *Today* series; Brian Burke, the Executive Director of the Professional Women's Hockey League Players Association; Andrew Zimmern, a restauranter, chef, and television personality known for several television series on the Travel Channel and Food Network; ten-time MLB All-Star baseball player Kirby Puckett; Carl Pohlad, the owner of the Minnesota Twins MLB franchise from 1984 to 2009; P. J. Fleck, the head coach of the University of Minnesota Gophers football program since 2017, and Win Neuger, the former CEO of American International.

EXCELSIOR, MN
POPULATION: 2,414 – CITY 781 OF 856 (11-7-25)
Excelsior owes its name to Henry Wadsworth Longfellow's short poem *Excelsior*, adopted by the Excelsior Pioneer Association of New York City, which sent a colony here in the summer of 1853. George M. Bertram led the group, which was among the first to live in the Lake Minnetonka region of Minnesota. Bertram described the area for its fertile soils, scenery, and fishing and foraging opportunities. In 1877, Excelsior was incorporated, and soon Bertram's description was replaced by summer homes and cottages, hotels and resorts, and docking stations for luxury excursion steamboats. Several businesses, including the Lyman Lumber Company and others downtown (in a 32-property region known as the Excelsior Commercial Historic District), opened to serve the essential needs of more permanent residents. From 1899 to 1901, the city's landmark public school building was erected. In 1925, the Excelsior Amusement Park opened its doors for the first time, and by the mid-1960s, its "Danceland" ballroom had hosted everyone from Lawrence Welk and Tommy Dorsey to the Beach Boys and the Rolling Stones. When Mick Jagger of the Rolling Stones went to the local Bacon Drugstore earlier that day to pick up a prescription, he

had an encounter with Jimmy Hutmaker, who was more or less an ambassador for Excelsior. Jimmy complained to Jagger that he received a Cherry Coke instead of a regular Coke, and finished his sentence with, "You can't always get what you want." Jagger later used the iconic phrase in his 1969 hit song of the same name, which has since been included in *Rolling Stone* magazine's list of the "500 Greatest Songs of All Time." Sadly, both the amusement park and the ballroom where the Stones played have long since disappeared, having closed in 1973. A little bench on Water Street honors "Mr. Jimmy" Hutmaker for his contributions to the community. The Excelsior Streetcar Line, a heritage streetcar, opened in 1999 on the old Minneapolis and Saint Louis Railway right-of-way and is a part of the Minnesota Streetcar Museum. John Berkey, the artist behind the sci-fi post art for the *Star Wars* trilogy and the 1976 *King Kong* remake film; Don Shelby, a distinguished multi-award-winning journalist best known by Minnesotans for his time spent on WCCO-TV; Brent Sass, a dogmusher and one of only six persons in history to have won both the Iditarod and Yukon Quest sled dog races are all worthy of mention when talking about Excelsior's celebrities, but the most famous of them all is Liberty. Born on February 8, 1974, the golden retriever was given to President Gerald Ford and his wife, Betty, by their daughter, Susan, and White House photographer David Hume Kennerly. They bought the pup from Excelsior resident Avis Friberg.

Restaurant Recommendation:
Maynards
685 Excelsior Blvd
Excelsior, MN 55331

Lodging Recommendation:
The Guest House
371 Water St
Excelsior, MN 55331

GOLDEN VALLEY, MN
POPULATION: 22,552 – CITY 836 OF 856 (11-13-25)

Golden Valley is best known as the home of General Mills, a multinational manufacturer of food products with brands including Betty Crocker, Pillsbury, and Nature Valley, as well as nationally recognizable cereal brands such as Wheaties, Cheerios, Cocoa Puffs, and Lucky Charms. UnitedHealth Group (a health insurance and healthcare company), Pentair (a water treatment company), and Honeywell (a conglomerate best known by consumers for its household appliances) are other major corporations that employ heavy numbers of the citizens of the town named for the amber waves of golden wheat that once adorned it. William Varner, one of Golden Valley's first settlers, arrived at St. Anthony Falls in 1854 and began looking for a claim westward on which to make his land claim. As the story goes, he climbed a large hill and, looking down upon the fields, said to himself, "This is my valley, my Golden Valley." This iteration was literally the first usage of the term later used for the city. The Varners were beaten in their settlement only by the Moser clan, but within no time, settlers from Ireland, Germany, and other European nations began to arrive by the hundreds. Golden Valley was incorporated on December 17, 1886. The Lutheran Bible Institute, founded in 1919 in St. Paul, was moved here in 1961 and renamed Golden Valley Lutheran College. Although closed in 1985, the campus was revitalized into the Perpich Center for Arts Education high school. Flip Saunders, the acclaimed NBA coach, began his coaching career here in 1977 before eventually taking over for the Minnesota Timberwolves from 1995 to 2005. Jordan Leopold of NHL fame, from 2002 to 2015; Kelly Lynch, best known for her appearances in the 1989 films *Road House* and *Cocktail*, and Aaron Sele, a two-time MLB All-Star pitcher in 1998 and 2000, are just three of Golden Valley's famous persons of note.

Restaurant Recommendation:
Good Day Café
5410 Wayzata Blvd
Golden Valley, MN 55416

GREENFIELD, MN
POPULATION: 2,903 – CITY 762 OF 856 (11-5-25)

The City of Greenfield, Minnesota, did not exist until March 14, 1958, the date of its incorporation. Before this point, it was part of Greenwood Township, which derived its name from an earlier village of the same name established in the vicinity. Thomas A. Holmes and others laid it out in 1856, but any hope of its prosperity was diminished by its proximity to Rockford. From 1857 to 1875, its post office operated, when Greenwood was best known for Art Mielke's ice-making business on the banks of Lake Sarah. He employed several of the township's farmers during the winter months, when they were unable to till the land or grow crops. Citizens with German and Norwegian heritage make up over half of the modern population.

GREENWOOD, MN
POPULATION: 726 – CITY 784 OF 856 (11-7-25)

Incorporated in 1956 from Excelsior Township to protect its rural identity and to prevent any further annexations by the City of Deephaven and the City of Excelsior, the name "Greenwood" actually dates to the 1850s. Thomas A. Holmes used the name for a townsite platted in Hennepin County in the winter of 1856-57, which ultimately proved a failure, as Rockford in Wright County became the important trade point of that immediate vicinity. The local forests were a bright green at the start of summer, which is why they are called that. From 1857 to 1875, Hennepin County had a Greenwood post office, which was discontinued following Rockford's rise. Until 2024, the former Old Log Theatre (affiliated with both Greenwood and Excelsior) claimed to be the "oldest continuously operating professional theater in the United States," having welcomed over 6 million guests since it began in 1940 in Greenwood. The new theater was built next door to the original in modern-day Excelsior by Herb Bloomberg, the same Chanhassen construction man who later founded Chanhassen Dinner Theatres.

HOPKINS, MN
POPULATION: 19,079 – CITY 791 OF 856 (11-8-25)

Home to the World's Largest Raspberry, a one-thousand-pound fiberglass fruit that dangles from a twenty-two-foot vine, the City of Hopkins is nestled between the city boundaries of Edina, Minnetonka, and Saint Louis Park. Yankees and Bohemians arrived in droves in the early 1850s to take advantage of the fertile farmland and raise livestock. Until 1871, this was the principal use for land in the area, until three railroads–the Great Northern, the Minneapolis & St Louis, and the Chicago, Milwaukee & St. Paul–were built through the region over the next ten years. In 1887, the Minneapolis Threshing Machine Company, better known as the Minneapolis-Moline Company, set up shop here and eventually became the largest employer in western Hennepin County. With so many railroads and such a significant manufacturing presence, residents petitioned for incorporation and independence from Minnetonka and Richfield Townships in 1893. Their request was granted, and the village was called West Minneapolis until a 1928 name change was announced to honor Harley H. Hopkins, an early resident and the town's first postmaster. Streetcars were a preferred mode of transportation from 1899 until the widespread adoption of automobiles, which by 1951 did away with large portions of the citywide transportation system. Fifty streetcars went through Main Street every day at their peak use, right through an area now designated as the 32-property Hopkins Commercial Historic District. Businesses at that time ranged from an opera house and lodges to lumber yards, livery stables, banks, restaurants, and other enterprises. Hopkins' ties to its annual raspberry festival (always held the third weekend of July) began in 1934-35, when local businesspeople established it during peak raspberry season to drum up business amid the Great Depression. Aaron Brown, the founding host of ABC's *World News Now* program; Daniel Grodnik, a film producer/writer primarily known for his work on *National Lampoon's Christmas Vacation* (1989); Samantha Harris, co-host of *Dancing with the Stars* with Tom Bergeron from seasons two through nine; Walter Bush, a major proponent of the growth of ice hockey at both the amateur and professional levels; Ann Bancroft, the first woman to finish multiple expeditions to the Arctic and Antarctic; Nate Berkus, a television personality best known for his TLC series *Nate & Jeremiah By Design*, and Peyton Manning, a Member of the Pro Football Hall of Fame and a two-time Super Bowl champion and five-time NFL Most Valuable Player quarterback, are just a few of the celebrities with connections to Hopkins. Manning, the most surprising individual on the list, attended Tanglen Elementary School for a brief time in the early 1980s, when his father, Archie Manning, was the quarterback of the Minnesota Vikings.

INDEPENDENCE, MN
POPULATION: 3,755 – CITY 764 OF 856 (11-5-25)
This patriotic little city was named for America's favorite holiday, the 4th of July, also known as Independence Day. First settled between 1854 and 1855, the largest lake in the township was named Independence by Kelsey Hinman, one of several early area residents who greatly enjoyed celebrating the national holiday on its shores. Lots of tourists continued to come to the lake for the holiday from far and wide, but permanent residents settled into a routine of farming in the summertime and hunkering down for the wintertime. Independence Township was not incorporated as a village until 1957, around the time that its population numbered about 1,200. From 1979 to 2025, Marvin Johnson served as the city's mayor, making him the longest-serving mayor in Minnesota history. Independence has never had a local post office, but Wabasha County (from 1856 to 1862) and Saint Louis County (from 1890 to 1916) had offices of the Independence name at one point.

LONG LAKE, MN
POPULATION: 1,741 – CITY 767 OF 856 (11-5-25)
The Great Northern Railway village of Long Lake almost had its first residents in the spring of 1855, when a group of Nova Scotians walked the land, but they chose to settle in modern-day Orono instead. While they passed on deciding on the shores of Long Lake, the Fleming Family and George Knettles came just a few weeks later and established a saw mill, a general store, and a schoolhouse. Cumberland Town was named for its ties to Cumberland County, Pennsylvania. A significant presence of tamarack swamps lent their name to the first community post office, Tamarack, established in 1856. In 1869, it was renamed Long Lake, a name approved only by the post office after Faribault County's Long Lake post office (open from 1867 to 1869) ceased operations. After the railroad came to town, other businesses like a flour mill and a hotel were built, as were a Freethinkers Hall and a school district. At the 1880

Census, Long Lake had only 150 residents, but by the next century, the town had grown tenfold to 1,747 people. Mark Dayton, the 40th Governor of Minnesota; Marilyn Carlson Nelson, the former CEO of Carlson, which was known for its holdings in Radisson Hotels and TGI Fridays; and Jon Leuer, an NBA player from 2011 to 2019, are associated with Long Lake.

LORETTO, MN
POPULATION: 646 – CITY 763 OF 856 (11-5-25)

When driving through Medina, Minnesota, travelers may stumble across a small, 0.26-square-mile enclave called Loretto. Settled by German and Dutch immigrants and founded in 1886 as a Soo Line railway village, Loretto opted to incorporate as an independent municipality in 1940, fifteen years before Medina Township did the same. The town's name comes from Loreto, Marche, Italy. This popular Catholic pilgrimage site shares its name with a Jesuit mission near Quebec City, Canada, and the village of Loretto, Kentucky. Being on the railroad, early residents of Loretto enjoyed the perks of being connected to a primary trade route. Sts. Peter and Paul Catholic Church was erected in 1903, along with a convent. Businesses ranged in importance. Major firms would have included the State Bank of Loretto, Loretto Feed and Seed Company, Fullerton Lumber, and The Dutch Mill Dairy. Smaller businesses were Murphy's blacksmith shop, Weidner and Pettit's bars, Koch's meat market, Van Beusekom's general store, and the Standard and Conoco Oil filling stations. The post office opened in 1887. When local college student Kent Koch was elected mayor in 2010, he became the only college student to serve as mayor in the United States. He was then also a student-athlete on the St. Cloud State University baseball.

MAPLE GROVE, MN
POPULATION: 70,253 – CITY 826 OF 856 (11-12-25)

"Retail" has become synonymous with Maple Grove, which has more retail square footage than any other community in Minnesota (except Bloomington, home to the Mall of America). Over six million square feet of commercial development has been recorded within city limits, far more than any early settler would have been able to imagine. The first men to hold land here in 1851, Louis Gervais and Pierre Bottineau, certainly knew nothing about the mega-mall centers that would someday take over their claims. In the early 1850s, W. E. Evans, Patrick Defer, O. R. Champlin, and Harvey Abel also staked their own claims. Many of their families sold their properties as Maple Grove grew into one of Minnesota's largest cities. Maple Grove Township was organized in 1868 and named on account of its large groves of maple trees. From 1866 to 1895, the original post office operated before it was converted to a branch station. The local government erected a town hall in 1877, which was used until 1939, when a new structure was built. Between 1970 and 1990, Maple Grove grew from 6,275 residents to 38,736, making it one of the fastest-growing communities in the state. As a result of this impressive net growth, many famous persons have local connections, including Jesse Ventura, the 38th Governor of Minnesota, Sisqó, born Mark Althavan Andrews, an artist known for his role with the R&B group Dru Hill; Brock Faber, a NHL defenseman with the Minnesota Wild since 2022, and Isaac Collins, a left fielder with the MLB's Milwaukee Brewers since 2024.

Restaurant Recommendation:
Daily Dose Café and Espresso
15517 Grove Cir N
Maple Grove, MN 55369

MAPLE PLAIN, MN
POPULATION: 1,743 – CITY 765 OF 856 (11-5-25)
An abundance of sugar maple trees in local forests gave this sweet name to Maple Plain, a St. Paul, Pacific & Manitoba Railroad village started in Independence Township. Settlers began arriving in 1854, but a post office (est. 1871) and widespread development did not really start until the arrival of the railroad in the late 1860s. Mr. Yokley was the first railroad agent, having formerly served as the first postmaster. Armstrong, another nearby settlement, boasted its own depot and general store, but as Maple Plain grew, the community fell out of favor with locals. The cordwood (firewood) market flourished thanks to abundant forests. Early Maple Plain's business interests included harness and shoe repair shops, feed stores, grocery stores, milliners, and a creamery, first known as the Maple Plain Creamery Company. Frank V. Halogen purchased the creamery on March 1, 1910, from C. D. Ingersoll, and eventually welcomed his son, Adrian V., and his grandson, Bruce F., into the picture in 1928 and 1953, respectively. Brock Lesnar lived in Maple Plain from 2003 to 2014; he is widely regarded as the most prolific "combat sport" athlete in the world for his time spent in the WWE, UFC, and other wrestling and mixed martial arts leagues.

Restaurant Recommendation:
McGarry's Pub
5189 Main St E
Maple Plain, MN 55359

MEDICINE LAKE, MN
POPULATION: 337 – CITY 793 OF 856 (11-8-25)
Predictably located on a peninsula extending into the 902-acre Medicine Lake, this neighborhood-city began as a subdivision of Plymouth, Minnesota, before ultimately becoming its own independent municipality in 1944. Jacob Barge platted the town in July 1887 as a place for cityfolk to relax on the lake "where water meets the sky." His thought was that the Minneapolis Rapid Transit Company would eventually enter the community and spur its growth. Yet, the only public transportation to arrive was the Luce Electric Line, which began on January 18, 1914. Through the 1940s, Medicine Lake was a "snowbird" community, housing its residents primarily in the summer months. With the rise of the automobile, many of these people decided they wanted to stay year-round. So, on April 14, 1944, talks began to discuss the neighborhood's potential removal from Plymouth Township. In an effort spearheaded by Les Johantgen, Ernest Ertl, and Charles Brudigan, the townspeople got what they wanted, and Medicine Lake became the newest incorporated town of Hennepin County. Lois McMaster Bujold, a four-time Hugo Award-winning speculative fiction writer known for her *Vorkosigan Saga*, the *World of the Five Gods*, and the *Sharing Knife* series, and Terry Gilliam, a filmmaker and actor known for being a part of the *Monty Python* comedy troupe, claim local ties.

MEDINA, MN
POPULATION: 6,837 – CITY 788 OF 856 (11-7-25)
With a population of 6,837 as of the 2020 Census, the rural city of Medina has grown significantly in recent years (typically by double-digit percentages) due to its proximity to other Minneapolis suburbs. In 1855, its first settlers began to arrive, most of them German, Irish, and French-Canadian, and on April 10, 1858, the area was officially dubbed Hamburg Township. Only a month later, the name was changed to Medina after the City of Medina, Saudi Arabia, which had made news headlines that year.

From thereon, the development of commercial enterprises began, and Medina's modern borders began to take shape. In 1868, many Excelsior Township residents voted to join Medina to enjoy a more accessible town hall. Twenty-one years later, George A. Brackett partitioned off parts of southern Medina to form Orono, not long after the Minneapolis, St. Paul & Sault Ste. Marie Railroad had been extended to that point. Other attempts were made to incorporate the City of Hamel (or the City of Lenz, for the local millowner Leander Lenzen) into Medina. Still, these efforts failed because of the city's odd potential location between Medina and Plymouth. As other townships throughout Hennepin County were incorporated in the mid-21st century, so too did Medina, which became an official municipality on May 26, 1955. It has since become the corporate headquarters of Polaris, an automotive manufacturer with roots in Roseau, Minnesota. In addition to comedy writer Pat Croft, known for his work on *Scary Movie[s] 3, 4,* and *5* and the *Naked Gun* films, and actress Karen Philipp, known for her role as Lt. Dish in *M*A*S*H*, several athletes have ties to Medina including John Randle, Pro Football Hall of Fame defensive tackle with the Minnesota Vikings and Seattle Seahawks; Greg LeMond, a three-time winner of the Tour de France road cycling race (the only American to ever win the race); Steve Hutchinson, a Pro Football Hall of Fame guard who played from 2001 to 2012; Corey Koskie, a third baseman who played in the MLB from 1998 to 2006 but also made the Canadian Baseball of Fame; Flip Saunders, the former head coach of the NBA's Minnesota Timberwolves, Detroit Pistons, and Washington Wizards between 1995 and 2015, and his son Ryan Saunders, an assistant or head coach in the NBA since 2009.

MINNEAPOLIS, MN ★
POPULATION: 429,954 – CITY 855 OF 856 (11-8-25)

"Mill City," the Flour Mill Capital of the World, was home to the Mdewakanton band of the Dakota long before the first European, Father Louis Hennepin, wandered into the area in the 1680s. Hennepin discovered and named Saint Anthony Falls, the only natural waterfall on the Mississippi River. Although he could not have known it at the time, his discovery of the falls, then a place of spirituality and cultural importance for the Indigenous, would ultimately lead to the creation of one of the largest industrial hubs in Minnesota and United States history. Two settlements were located on either side of the falls: St. Anthony, on the east side, founded in 1848, and Minneapolis, laid out on the west side in the early 1850s. Colonel John H. Stevens built the first house on the Mississippi River in 1849-50, and by May 11, 1858, a township had been created shortly after Stevens designed the town plat. The power of the falls drove the city's growth. St. Anthony Falls Waterpower Company was founded in 1856 to enforce regulations governing the falls, enabling the supervised construction of several dozen sawmills. Lumber was floated down the Mississippi and connecting tributaries from the logging country up north in enormous quantities, making Minneapolis the Logging Capital of the World long before its flour milling industry even took hold. That title came in the 1880s, after enormous milling complexes like the Washburn "A" Mill (once the largest flour mill in the world) and the Pillsbury "A" Mill were built in 1874 and 1881, respectively. Charles Alfred and John Sargent Pillsbury were the masterminds behind the creation of five mills and of working with railroaders like James J. Hill to bring the Great Northern (then the St. Paul & Pacific) Railroad, the Northern Pacific, and the Chicago, Milwaukee & St. Paul Railroads into existence. Cadwallader C. Washburn and John Crosby founded Washburn-Crosby, which ultimately became General Mills. An explosion on May 2, 1878, caused by flour dust, killed 18 workers and effectively eliminated half of Minneapolis's milling capacity. A new mill was built atop the old building in 1880 and remained operational until 1965, then sat empty for 26 years before succumbing to a great fire in 1991. Milling made Minneapolis, the "city of water," famous, but other businesses were abundant as well. There were railroad machine shops, woolen mills, iron works, and additional mills and factories for paper, sashes, and cotton, amongst other products. Religion and social organization were important, too. The First Congregational Church of Minneapolis got its start in 1851, as did the Plymouth Congregational Church in 1857. By 1859, there was already a city library, the Minneapolis Athenaeum. Seven years before Minnesota became a state, the University of Minnesota was founded in 1851, and in 1862, it became a public land-grant university. It is now one of the ten largest universities in the United States by student body, with an enrollment surpassing 55,000 students. Well over one-hundred historic locations have been selected for preservation on the Federal Register of Historic Places, but amongst those most interesting to tourists would be landmarks like the 1913 "Witch Hat" Water Tower at Prospect/Tower Hill Park; the Pillsbury A. Mill within the St. Anthony Historic District, the world's largest flour mill for about four decades; the 1889 Minnehaha Historic District, home to Minnehaha Falls; Minneapolis's tallest skyscraper, the 1927-29 Foshay Tower office building, and the 1907-14 Basilica of St. Mary, the first Catholic basilica in the United States. The Minneapolis Institute of Art, one of the country's largest art museums, the Minneapolis Sculpture Garden, known for its Spoonbridge and Cherry; the American Swedish Institute; the Hennepin History Museum; the 1963 Guthrie Theater, and the Mill City Museum, the pride and joy of the Minnesota Historical Society, located next to the ruins of the Washburn "A" Mill and famous for its working flour mill Flour Tower exhibit, are other noteworthy stops in a sea of potential tourism sites. Sports fanatics can catch an NFL game at U.S. Bank Stadium, home of the Minnesota Vikings; Target Field, home of the MLB's Minnesota Twins; or the Target Center, where the NBA's Minnesota Timberwolves have played since 1990 and the WNBA's Minnesota Lynx have played since 1999. A couple of offbeat sites include the Quietest Place on Earth at Orfield Laboratories, where guests can hear their own blood running through their heads in the anechoic chamber because of its absolute quiet, and Lakewood Cemetery, the final resting place of career circus performer Tiny Tim and Vice President Hubert Humphrey. Listing every one of the city's one-thousand-plus successful persons would be impossible, but Prince Rogers Nelson, the acclaimed musician who pioneered the Minneapolis sound funk rock genre of music; Charles M. Schulz, the creator of the Peanuts comic strip and iconic characters like Charlie Brown and Snoopy; James Hong, an actor in over 400 films like the *Kung Fu Panda* animated franchise and the 2022 film *Everything Everywhere All at Once*; Winona Ryder, known for her roles in iconic pieces of cinematography like *Beetlejuice* (1988), *Heathers* (1989), and Netflix's *Stranger Things* franchise; George Dayton, the founder of the retail giant Target Corporation, are amongst the most recognizable names.

Restaurant Recommendation:
Normandy Kitchen
405 S 8th St
Minneapolis, MN 55404

Restaurant Recommendation:
Fogo de Chão Brazilian Steakhouse
645 Hennepin Ave
Minneapolis, MN 55403

 Restaurant Recommendation:
Victor's 1959 Cafe
3756 Grand Ave S
Minneapolis, MN 55409

Lodging Recommendation:
300 Clifton Bed and Breakfast
300 Clifton Ave
Minneapolis, MN 55403

MINNETONKA, MN
POPULATION: 53,781 – CITY 792 OF 856 (11-8-25)

Likely first explored by Joseph R. Brown and William Joseph Snelling, the series of "succeeding bays and peninsulas" that make up Lake Minnetonka was named by Governor Ramsey. Both *minne* and *tanka* are Dakota Sioux words translating to "big or great." Their use in a compound word was not recorded until Alexander Ramsey, then the 1st Governor of Minnesota Territory, coined the term. A sawmill was likely the first commercial venture developed; it was the first privately operated mill in Minnesota west of the Mississippi River. The Minnetonka post office opened in 1855, and in those years that followed, large numbers of New Englanders, Scandinavians, and Czechs poured into the region. It was the Czechs who introduced other settlers to fruitful raspberry-growing techniques that were used here and in nearby Hopkins to produce impressive yields. In 1876, the Minnetonka Milling Company was established here by Charles H. Burwell, which gave rise to a localized settlement called Minnetonka Mills. Other smaller settlements, such as Oak Knoll, Glen Lake, and Groveland, each came into being with their own stores, shops, and schoolhouses, along with other improvements. However, the area as a whole was still referred to as Minnetonka Township. After several annexations by St. Louis Park, Hopkins, Deephaven, and Wayzata, Minnetonka residents decided to switch to a municipal form of government, which culminated in its 1956 incorporation. Those involved with the process at that time recall a "race to the courthouse" in which one group presented a proposal to incorporate all of Minnetonka Township into a municipal corporation. In contrast, the other proposal, brought into the courthouse only moments later by a different group of residents, would have split the township into Minnetonka and Burwell. The split would have been made at Minnetonka Boulevard. Burwell's 1883 Carpenter Gothic/stick-style home still exists as a house museum operated by the Minnetonka Historical Society, as does the 1906-07 Neoclassical Minnetonka Town Hall. After growing from 6,466 people in 1940 to 35,776 by 1970, and then 51,301 by 2000, Minnetonka has established itself amongst the behemoths of Minneapolis's sprawling suburbs. Since those periods of rapid growth, the city has become home to UnitedHealth Group, Minnesota's largest publicly owned company with annual revenues exceeding $400 billion, and Cargill, the largest privately held company in the United States, with annual revenues exceeding $165 billion. Tom Petters, the former CEO of Petters Group Worldwide, known for a $2 billion Ponzi scheme; Wesley So, the fifth-highest-rated chess player in history with an Elo rating of over 2800; Ryan McCartan, a noted Broadway actor most recently (in 2025) acclaimed for his role as Jay Gatsby in *The Great Gatsby*; Al Quie, the 35th Governor of Minnesota, and Mike Ramsey, an NHL defenseman with 1,070 regular season game appearances, are just a few people with localized ties.

MINNETONKA BEACH, MN
POPULATION: 546 – CITY 768 OF 856 (11-5-25)
"The Beach," on the shores of Lake Minnetonka, was formerly part of Excelsior Township and later Medina Township, but in 1894, it was incorporated as a village. Those who came to the community in 1882 would have likely stayed at the Hotel Lafayette, an impressive lodging accommodation established by the Minneapolis, Saint Paul & Manitoba Railway. It was a project of James J. Hill, who had invested copious sums of money into the land to build the railroad's first-ever luxury summer resort. Dances were held at its ballroom, and military band concerts were held on the property. There were also tennis courts, a feature reminiscent of many modern-day private country clubs. Other summer hotels and homes, like the 1887 Thompson Summer House, were built en masse as Minnetonka Beach developed around the tourism industry. Hotel Lafayette sadly succumbed to a 1897 fire, but the city survived and continued to grow as a place where people could live permanently. The Minnetonka Beach Water Tower, erected in 1928 as the municipal water supply system, was one of the first of these structures to allow more than just temporary residents to stay in the city.

MINNETRISTA, MN
POPULATION: 8,262 – CITY 771 OF 856 (11-5-25)
German heritage prevails in Minnetrista, in a township once named German Home by the county commissioners when it was formally organized in 1859. It was almost immediately changed by settlers to Minnetrista, meaning "crooked/twisting waters," a reference to the many crooked lakes in the area. After enough immigrants had congregated, the United States Postal Service established an office in 1860, which remained operational for 34 years before it was discontinued. Mound and Saint Bonifacius became independent municipalities outside Minnetrista Township before the City of Minnetrista was incorporated in 1970. Between 2000 and 2020, the population increased from 4,358 to 8,262, although the community has remained largely rural across its 31.05-square-mile domain. Two local sites on the National Register of Historic Places are the ruins of the 1876 Schmid Farmhouse within the confines of Lake Minnetonka Regional Park, and the Crane Island Historic District, noted for its collection of fourteen turn-of-the-century summer cottages built around 1900. Big Stone Mini Golf is another local point of interest known for its 14-hole miniature golf course and Bruce Stillman's abstract metal sculptures.

Restaurant Recommendation:
The Table at Everly Farms
6480 Co Rd #26
Minnetrista, MN 55364

MOUND, MN
POPULATION: 9,398 – CITY 770 OF 856 (11-5-25)
Over one hundred unique Native American mounds, built by those who came long before the Dakota between 300 BC and 100 AD, were mapped before 1920, when the municipality of Mound participated in its first United States Census. It then had just 393 people and was known as Mound City. A business district, consisting of general stores, blacksmith shops, and everything in between, was located on the shore of Cooks Bay. When the Great Northern Railroad was built through, all the businesses moved northward. One of these was Mound Metalcraft, a gardening tools company that opened in 1946 when Lynn Everett Baker, Avery F. Crounse, and Alvin F. Tesch

joined forces and purchased an old schoolhouse formerly owned by the Streater Company. That company's owner, E. C. Streater, had no desire to sell toys, and so he sold the idea and patents to the three men. What resulted was Tonka Toys Incorporated, a now-famous manufacturer of steel construction trucks and machinery toys. The "tonka" name was derived from nearby Lake Minnetonka. Although the company's headquarters moved from Mound to Minneapolis in 1968, the City of Mound remained, with its population surpassing 7,500 people by the start of the 1970s. In 1960, the municipalities of Island Park and Mound merged. A few notable people from Mound include Kris Humphries, an NBA player from 2004 to 2017 who once even beat 28-time Olympic champion swimmer Michael Phelps in youth swimming events when they were kids; Dennis Frederiksen, the former lead singer of the bands Trillion, Angel, LeRoux, and Toto; Christopher O'Malley, the CEO of LogRhythm, the security software company; Kevin Sorbo, an actor known for playing Hercules in the fantasy television series *Hercules*: The Legendary Journeys between 1995 and 1999; Henning Linden, a U.S. Army Brigadier General during World War II, and The Andrews Sisters close harmony swing and boogie-woogie singing group. LaVerne Sophia, Maxene Anglyn, and Patricia Marie sold over eighty million records during their tenure.

NEW HOPE, MN
POPULATION: 21,986 – CITY 835 OF 856 (11-13-25)
After Crystal was incorporated as a municipality in 1936, the western portion of Crystal Township was split off to form a new township for farmers who had no interest in contributing tax dollars toward street lights, sewers, and other public works projects. They called their township "New Hope," believing they could continue to prosper under the township form of government. They stuck to their plan for just seventeen years before rapid population growth across the Twin Cities region forced it to become the very thing its residents had tried to avoid. This rapid population increase, coupled with large pockets of New Hope residents who intentionally moved yards from the Crystal-New Hope town line to enjoy modern amenities and conveniences, led to New Hope's incorporation in 1953. Their little township of 691 residents in 1950 grew substantially to 23,180 people by 1970, the largest population ever recorded in its history. New Hope never had its own post office, but there was an office by that name in Meeker County from 1882 to 1888. Mariana Cress, a sprinter who competed in the 2016 Rio Olympic Games, Lance Pitlick, an NHL player who played 393 games between 1994 and 2002, and Rashard Vaughn, an NBA player who played for three franchises between 2015 and 2018, attended local schools here while growing up.

ORONO, MN
POPULATION: 8,315 – CITY 766 OF 856 (11-5-25)
Formerly the southern part of Medina Township and the northern part of Excelsior Township, Orono Township was partitioned off on April 9, 1889. Major George Brackett suggested the name Orono for his hometown of Orono, Maine; he named Brackett's Point to differentiate the area from the surrounding townships. Orono has always remained predominantly rural. A testament to its continued rurality is the Noerenberg Estate Barn, built in 1912 by one of Lake Minnetonka's many wealthy estate owners on his working farm. Several "trades" in land have been made between the primarily residential City of Orono and the communities of Mound (1963), Minnetrista (1980), Long Lake (1993), and Wayzata (1994) in recent years. Recently recorded as being home to 8,315 people as of the 2020 Census, a few of Orono's famous residents have been Gregg Steinhafel and Bruce Dayton, both former CEOs of Target Corporation (Although under Dayton it was known as the Dayton Hudson Corporation); Kevin Garnett, a 15-time NBA All-Star, 2004 NBA Most Valuable Player,

and a member of the Basketball Hall of Fame; Whitney MacMillan, a billionaire and the former CEO of Cargill from 1976 to 1995; Carlos Correa, the first overall pick of the 2012 MLB draft and a three-time All-Star shortstop and baseman; William Hood Dunwoody, an early partner of General Mills and Northwestern National Bank, now known as Wells Fargo; Irwin L. Jacobs. A serial CEO also known for founding the Cable Value Network; William W. McGuire, the former CEO of UnitedHealth Group from 1991 to 2006, and the owner of the Minnesota United FC professional soccer club; and Charles Alfred Pillsbury, a co-founder of the Pillsbury Company.

OSSEO, MN
POPULATION: 2,688 – CITY 825 OF 856 (11-12-25)
When driving between Brooklyn Park and Maple Grove on Minnesota Highway 81, drivers will briefly pass through the City of Osseo, a word made famous by Henry Wadsworth Longfellow in his poem *The Song of Hiawatha*. "Osseo" is likely a corruption of the Ojibwe word *Waaseyaa*, meaning "Son of the Evening Star." The land that made up Osseo was claimed in July 1852 by Pierre Bottineau, a frontiersman who founded cities throughout Minnesota and North Dakota, including Osseo, Breckenridge, and Maple Grove, Minnesota, and Wahpeton, North Dakota. Bottineau, North Dakota, was named in his honor. Osseo was platted in 1856, the same year its post office was established. The region known as "Bottineau Prairie" was settled by several men and their families in those early years. Warren Sampson opened a general merchandise store and worked with Isaac Labissonniere to file the initial plat. By 1873, there was a blacksmith shop, a tin shop, a shoe shop, three hotels, a school, a Catholic church, and two post offices. The strange anomaly occurred when A. B. Chafee platted a town of his own called "Attraction" on the southeast corner of Osseo, forcing the two municipalities to grow together. Attraction was absorbed into Osseo, as having two small independent villages so close to one another was not beneficial. The area operated using the township form of government before it was incorporated as a village on March 17, 1875. James J. Hill's Great Northern Railroad came through in 1882, and soon there were Lutheran and Methodist churches, a large Osseo High School building, and dozens of additional businesses. In 1915, Osseo's iconic water tower (now listed on the National Register) was constructed, and the Osseo Light and Water Carnival, "The Greatest Municipal Prosperity and Improvement Celebration in the History of Northern Hennepin County," was enjoyed by people from miles around. James Martinez, a Bronze medalist in the 1984 Los Angeles Greco-Roman wrestling event, and Caleb Truax, the IBF super middleweight boxing titleholder from 2017-18, are a pair of famous athletes who hail from Osseo.

PLYMOUTH, MN
POPULATION: 81,026 – CITY 837 OF 856 (11-13-25)
Smack dab in the middle of Hennepin County is the 7th-largest incorporated city in Minnesota, Plymouth, with a population of 81,026. While its present name is an eponym for Plymouth, Massachusetts, home of the iconic Plymouth Rock, it was initially called Parker's Lake for its location on the northwest shore of the lake of the same name. A gristmill was built there in 1855, as were several homes. The mill was moved only two years later to Wayzata when the lake flooded, inundating the fledgling village. Other businesses began to emerge, and the township was named "Plymouth" by the Hennepin County Board of Commissioners. An attempt was made to rename it Medicine Lake (now a separate municipality that is an enclave of Plymouth), but the effort failed. Plymouth's post office opened in 1865, and from 1864 to 1866, a second office, known as South Plymouth, operated. Schools, churches, hotels, general stores, livery stables, blacksmith shops, and other pieces of infrastructure sprouted during this

era. In 1885, a town hall was erected after the town board instructed Clem Mengelkoch and Tom Ditter to build one. Built for $2,625, it now serves as the Plymouth History Center. Plymouth finally incorporated as a village on May 18, 1955, a century after the first Europeans arrived. A few celebrities with links to Plymouth include Amy Klobuchar, a United States Senator from Minnesota since 2007; Marion Barber III, a 2007 Pro Bowl running back with the NFL's Dallas Cowboys; James Laurinaitis, a former NFL linebacker who led the league in solo tackles (117) in 2012; Mark Parrish, an All-Star right winger in the NHL who played from 1997 to 2012; Dani Cameranesi, a 2018 Olympic gold medalist winner in women's ice hockey; Rudy Boschwitz, a United States Senator from December 1978 to January 1991, and Blake Wheeler, an NHL player from 2008 to 2024 with nearly 1,200 in-game appearances.

Restaurant Recommendation:
Sunshine Factory Bar & Grill
4100 Vinewood Ln N
Plymouth, MN 55442

RICHFIELD, MN
POPULATION: 36,994 – CITY 778 OF 856 (11-7-25)

Abundant, rich soils gave Richland its name, which was later changed to Richfield by a vote of the settlers. Founded in the 1850s, "Minnesota's oldest suburb" grew for its connections to Fort Snelling, Minnesota's pioneer fortification that overlooked the confluence of the Minnesota and the Mississippi Rivers. Much of the modern-day City of Richfield was split off from former lands that were a part of the military reservation. Riley Lucas Bartholomew (whose home still stands as a local museum and historic site) was one of the first recorded men to live in Richfield. However, it was James Dunsmoor of Harmony, Maine, who was responsible for convincing others to live here. He served as postmaster when the Harmony post office opened in 1854, and by the 1860s, seven out of twenty locals reportedly had originated from Maine. Hotels, general stores, blacksmith shops, and businesses of all kinds opened their doors as Richfield's agricultural output proved it worthy of incorporation. It became a village in 1908, after parts of the township borders were partitioned off to create St. Louis Park in 1886 and Edina in 1889. Fort Snelling and the Minneapolis-St. Paul International Airport took other chunks of its initial 63-square-mile borders in subsequent years; the city's current area is just 6.92 square miles. Hints of significant growth began to show themselves in the 1930s, when the population grew from 1,301 to 3,778. Then, in the 1940s, despite the start of the Second World War, Richfield went from 3,778 people to 17,502. By the 1960 Census, it had a population of 42,523. One of the most considerable changes to Richfield's business sector came in 2003, when the consumer electronics retailer Best Buy moved its corporate headquarters here. Sixty million dollars were invested in bringing the campus to Richfield, much of which was used to demolish 100 homes and three car dealerships to pave the way for the city's now-largest and most important employer. Famous persons of interest with connections to Richfield include Richard Kruger, the CEO of Suncor Energy and a former behemoth within the ExxonMobil administration; Larry Fitzgerald, one of the greatest receivers in NFL history with the Arizona Cardinals from 2004 to 2020; Chad Smith, a drummer with the Red Hot Chili Peppers from 1988 to the present day (2025); Will Steger, the first man to journey to the North Pole by dogsled without resupplying; Steve Christoff, a member of the 1980 gold-medalist "Miracle on Ice" Lake Placid U.S. Olympic men's hockey team; Donald Gleason, the pathologist who invented the "Gleason score" used to evaluate the prognosis of patients with prostate cancer, and

Charles W. Lindberg, a World War II United States Marine Corps corporal who helped to raise the U.S. flag at the Battle of Iwo Jima.

ROBBINSDALE, MN
POPULATION: 14,646 – CITY 833 OF 856 (11-13-25)

Crystal Lake Township, which was later incorporated as the Village of Crystal, lost about 90 acres of its boundaries when real estate developer Andrew Bonney Robbins purchased 90 acres to establish the Robbinsdale Park subdivision. Being the youngest member of the Minnesota Senate when he was elected in 1875 (at 30), Robbins was already well known throughout the state for his political career. So, when he organized his town, he had no issues in attracting manufacturing interests, the Great Northern Railroad, and organizations like a Lutheran seminary. The post office opened in 1890. Robbins himself worked to establish the Hubbard Specialty Manufacturing Company, which focused on the manufacturing of chairs and wheelbarrows. Fawcett Publications was started here in 1919 with the publication of Captain Billy's Whiz Bang, the first in a line of magazines that included *True Confessions*, *Family Circle*, and *Mechanix Illustrated*, an early competitor to Popular Mechanics. In 1950, it ventured into paperback publishing, launching Gold Medal Books, which revolutionized the industry with dozens of titles. Shazam, formerly known as Captain Marvel, first appeared in Whiz Comics #2 before ultimately becoming a DC Comics superhero. During the same general area, in the 1940s, the three-story Victory Hospital was built by Samuel Samuelson; it has since grown into the North Memorial Medical Center, a 518-bed facility that also serves as a Level 1 trauma center. Two modern points of interest for tourists are Graesar Park and the Robbinsdale Historical Society Museum, housed in the 1925 Robbinsdale Library. It was built for about $9,000 using funds raised by the Robbinsdale Library Club. In addition to Steve Zahn, an actor known for his roles in the 1996 film *That Thing You Do!*, the 2003 picture *National Security*, and the *Diary of a Wimpy Kid* film series; The Jets, a Tongan-American band with platinum-selling records and several top-10 hits on the Billboard Hot 100; Tim Vakoc, the first U.S. military chaplain to die in the Iraq War; actor Bee Vang, known for his role as Thao Vang Lor in the 2008 drama *Gran Torino*; John Kundla, a five-time NBA champion head coach of the Minneapolis Lakers between 1947 and 1959, over a dozen professional wrestlers have also hailed from Robbinsdale. Three of the most famous are Curt "Mr. Perfect" Hennig, Verne Gagne, and Brady "Battle Kat" Boone. The greatest interview in the history of professional wrestling, Gene Okerlund, bills himself in the ring as being from Robbinsdale as well.

ROGERS, MN
POPULATION: 13,295 – CITY 840 OF 856 (11-14-25)

Rural Rogers was once part of the "Big Woods" of east-central Minnesota, nearly all of which has since been destroyed in favor of farmland. Hassan Township had settlements like St. Walburga (later Fletcher) and Hassan, which had churches, schools, and/or homes of their own, but it was the village of Rogers that prevailed as the most important. Thomas Rogers, for whom the community is named, sold an acre of his land to the Great Northern Railroad for a singular dollar so that they could furnish a train depot. Around said depot, area Catholics established the Church of St. Martin. Rogers Mill was built as well, and soon residents had worked together to organize a creamery, general stores, hardware stores, grocery stores, the Rogers State Bank, filling stations, cafes, and dozens of other specialty lines as time wore on. In 1855, the Hagel Family Farm began as one of several immigrant farmsteads in this part of Minnesota, and many of their 1890s properties (18 in total) have since been listed on the National Register of Historic Places. On January 1, 2012, Hassan Township, the last fully intact township in Hennepin County, was fully annexed into the Rogers city limits. The gradual annexation phases over the first part of the 21st century brought Rogers's population from 698 in 1990 to 3,588 in 2000, and then to 13,295 by 2020.

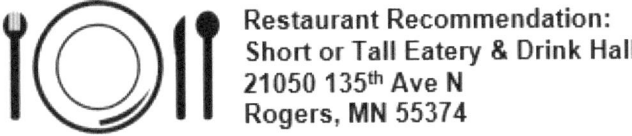

Restaurant Recommendation:
Short or Tall Eatery & Drink Hall
21050 135th Ave N
Rogers, MN 55374

SAINT ANTHONY VILLAGE, MN
POPULATION: 9,257 – CITY 812 OF 856 (11-10-25)
In 1838, Franklin Steele, then a storekeeper at Fort Snelling, claimed land just to the east of the all-powerful Saint Anthony Falls of the Mississippi River. No genuine attempts to develop it were made until 1847-48, when he, Robert Rantoul Jr., and Caleb Cushing built mills to match those in neighboring Minneapolis. Many homes were subsequently built, and businesses of all varieties were established. St. Anthony Township was organized in 1858 to bring some level of order to the region. By the mid-1860s, there were flouring and paper mills, a woolen mill, door and blind factories, foundries and machine shops, and an agricultural implement factory. R. P. Russell and Samuel J. Findley ran the first mercantile establishments. When the City of Minneapolis needed more land, it annexed the entire township, except for 1,087 acres, most of which was used for farming and hog-raising. Following World War II, land developer Al Forsythe saw the potential of St. Anthony Boulevard as a new housing development. He submitted a petition to annex the remainder of the township into Minneapolis, but he didn't anticipate the backlash from the residents already living there. They submitted a petition to incorporate as an independent village, a motion that was granted and carried out after a 167 to 57 vote in favor of incorporation. The State of Minnesota attempted to challenge and repeal the vote because the area was so rural, but the Minnesota Supreme Court upheld the election. From thereon, St. Anthony Village remained independent. The first strip mall in Minnesota, the St. Anthony Shopping Center, was built in the 1950s and owned by the Fulgencio Batista family from Cuba. St. Anthony is a sister city of Salo, Finland; Salo Park commemorates the friendship between the two communities.

SHOREWOOD, MN
POPULATION: 7,779 – CITY 783 OF 856 (11-7-25)
Shorewood was incorporated in 1956 from Excelsior Township to avoid annexation by neighboring municipalities, such as Excelsior and Tonka Bay. Historical population counts for the town, named for its location just outside Lake Minnetonka's shores, date back to the 1860 Census, when 317 people lived there. Since then, those numbers have ballooned to as high as 7,779 as of the 2020 Census. Shorewood's present city limits once included a line of the Minneapolis & St. Louis Railroad. Although it also has affiliations with the City of Tonka Bay, the Peter Gideon Farmhouse, home to the horticulturist who introduced the Wealthy (named for his wife, Wealthy) apple to Minnesota's harsh climate, is listed in NRHP records as being in Shorewood. The Wealthy apple was the earliest cultivar to survive Minnesota's winters.

SPRING PARK, MN
POPULATION: 1,734 – CITY 769 OF 856 (11-5-25)
Hotel Del Otero, one of a series of James J. Hill and the Great Northern Railroad's luxury hotel resorts on Minnetonka Lake, was the first real development made in what

is now the City of Spring Park. William Byers owned 156.24 acres of land in 1850, giving his name to Byers Bay (now Spring Park Bay), and John Carmen owned another part of the region that became Spring Park. After the hotel was built in 1892, over fifteen trains a day rolled into the local station to drop off local tourists. G. F. Hopkins ran the hotel's operations. Other nearby places of interest then were the Del Otero cottages, the Casino, a baseball park, and a dance pavilion. Although the large resort destination burned down in 1945, Spring Park residents chose to incorporate as a village in 1951. Its post office has remained operational since 1949. Tonka Toys Inc., famous for manufacturing steel toy construction trucks and machinery, was headquartered in Spring Park from 1946 to 1991 before being purchased by Hasbro.

ST. BONIFACIUS, MN
POPULATION: 2,307 – CITY 772 OF 856 (11-6-25)

One of the many "Saints" of Minnesota is St. Bonifacius, which was settled by immigrants from Germany in the 1850s. These settlers were devout Catholics, and so one of their first orders of business was to establish a Catholic parish. They selected the name "St. Boniface," a Martyr known as "the Apostle to the Germans." The name was slightly altered to St. Bonifacius when the village was named (inc. 1858), and, starting in 1861, it put itself on the map when a branch of the U.S.P.S. was established. Until the 1950s, the town never had more than 400 residents. Firms in those early 20th-century years included a lumberyard, a canning factory, a grain elevator, multiple banks, general stores, hardware and implement stores, and other businesses. As Cold War tensions with Russia rose, the small rural town was selected as the Minneapolis-St. Paul's western Nike Hercules battery host site. It was one of four locations chosen by the United States government to help protect the city from potential Soviet bombing attacks. In the city park, the remains of one of these deactivated missiles are still on display. The neighborhoods and subdivisions that make up much of St. Bonifacius today began to go up in the mid-1990s; by 2000, the population was 1,873. Milt Bruhn, the head coach of the University of Wisconsin-Madison football program from 1956 to 1966, responsible for Wisconsin's highest-ever season-ending ranking of #2 overall in 1962, was born here on July 28, 1912.

ST. LOUIS PARK, MN
POPULATION: 50,010 – CITY 789 OF 856 (11-8-25)

One of Hennepin County's 50,000-odd populated municipalities is St. Louis Park, known for housing the Twin Cities' largest Jewish and Russian populations. With surveys dating back to the 1850s, the origins of "the Park" can be traced to a time when the prairie lands near St. Anthony Falls and the Mississippi River were still part of Minneapolis Township. Many early pioneers lived in this region then. They worked hard to establish one-room schoolhouses, general stores, and businesses of all varieties, but everything changed when the first railroad, the Great Northern, arrived in 1867. Three years later, the Minneapolis & St. Louis Railroad line came through, and by 1872, a third railroad, the Chicago, Milwaukee & St. Paul Railroad, had arrived as well. With so much potential from the three railroads for businesses to thrive, townspeople in this region opted to incorporate St. Louis Park as a village on October 4, 1886. The name was derived from the Minneapolis & St. Louis Railway, and the word "Park" was suffixed to avoid any confusion with St. Louis, Missouri. Thomas Barlow Walker and other investors helped spur further development of the village starting in 1892, when the Minneapolis Land and Investment Company was established with the interest of converting the open prairies into homes and commercial districts. Progressive thinking was the norm for people in this area of Minnesota. In 1899, the world's first concrete, tubular grain elevator was erected by

Frank Peavey and Charles F. Haglin, who saw it as a potential, widespread alternative to wooden elevators, which were frequently destroyed by fire at the time. After it was demonstrated that the elevator could efficiently retain and disperse grain, the design revolutionized grain storage throughout the Midwest. It led to many of the large, concrete, sentinel-like structures that stand tall in small towns across the country. The original water tower still stands today at the Nordic Ware (the inventors of the Bundt cake, circa 1950) factory complex as St. Louis Park's most historic structure, aside from the St. Louis Park Historical Society's Chicago, Milwaukee, St. Paul & Pacific Railroad Depot. Minnesota's first shopping center, the 30,000-square-foot Lilac Way, was built here in 1935. Other points of interest are the former B'nai Emet Synagogue, a restored 1940s Sinclair gas station on Broadway Avenue, and the Pavek Museum of Broadcasting, home to one of the world's most unique collections of early radio and television equipment. Charles Foley, a co-inventor of the game Twister; Owen Husney, the man who discovered and subsequently managed the artist Prince starting in 1977 with Warner Bros. Records; Al Franken, a United States Senator from Minnesota from 2009 to 2018 and a former writer for NBC's *Saturday Night Live*; Thomas L. Friedman, a three-time Pulitzer Prize winner and a modern columnist with *The New York Times*; three-time Canadian Grey Cup champion coach Marc Trestman; Peggy Flanagan, the 50th Lieutenant Governor of Minnesota; and Joel and Ethan Coen, a filmmaking duo known for works like *Fargo* (1996) and *The Big Lebowski* (1998), claim affiliation with St. Louis Park.

Restaurant Recommendation:
Hazelwood Food & Drink
4450 Excelsior Blvd Suite #120
St. Louis Park, MN 55416

Restaurant Recommendation:
Kip's Irish Pub & Restaurant
9970 Wayzata Blvd
St. Louis Park, MN 55426

TONKA BAY, MN
POPULATION: 1,442 – CITY 782 OF 856 (11-7-25)
At 2.11 square miles (1.17 of that being water), Tonka Bay is one of the smallest incorporated communities in the Twin Cities. The first claims in the vicinity were staked in 1853, but it was not until 1879 that the first hotel — the Lake Park Hotel — was built on Echo Bay to accommodate its newfound tourism designation. Chautauquas were held here regularly. In 1887, John Finley Wilcox planted hundreds of acres of orchards and built a house known as the "Old Orchard House." When discussions of incorporating the summer resort area came to the fore in 1901, residents chose the name "Tonka" as an abbreviation of Minnetonka, the lake's name. Tourism declined, but Tonka Bay has remained a small, independent residential community. One thousand five hundred forty-seven Minnesotans called it home at its peak, according to the 2000 Census.

WAYZATA, MN
POPULATION: 4,434 – CITY 787 OF 856 (11-7-25)
"Wayzata" was derived from the Dakota word *waziyata*, meaning "at the pines" or "north shore." Platted in 1854 by Oscar E. Garrison, within its first year of development, Wayzata had a sawmill, a hotel, and a blacksmith shop. Agriculture became its primary

industry, but following the arrival of the Saint Paul and Pacific Railroad (later annexed by the Great Northern), its resort and tourism industries began to take off. Many hotels were built along the shores of Lake Minnetonka to accommodate visitors. A post office opened around the same time in 1866. Wayzata was incorporated as a village in 1883. One of the council's first orders of business was to reroute the railroad tracks north of town. They ordered the "Empire Builder" James J. Hill to relocate the tracks, although he completely ignored the request. They double-downed by taking the matter to court, an action to which Hill reacted extremely poorly. He demolished Wayzata's depot on Broadway Avenue and ordered the construction of a new station at a town to the east called "Holdridge." He was quoted as saying that residents could "walk a mile for the next twenty years" to catch the train. His pettiness did not end with that one action, however. He rerouted the railroad tracks closer to Lake Minnetonka rather than farther north, and to really voice his displeasure, he purchased Wayzata's Arlington Hotel and intentionally never reopened it. His actions nearly wiped Wayzata off the map. Years later, a new village council passed the "Reconciliation Ordinance" to make amends with Hill. This friendlier version of Hill, not feeling threatened into adapting his empire by force, responded by building a gorgeous new train depot near downtown Wayzata, which still exists today as a museum. Further down Lake Street is the Wayzata Section House, a two-story structure erected in 1902 and expanded in 1944 to house railroad employees. While the railroad helped move visitors travel more quickly and efficiently by land, the Twin City Rapid Transit Company established a new form of water transportation called "streetcar boats." They transported residents between Wayzata, Excelsior, Deephaven, and Tonka Bay until 1926, when the rise of the automobile industry made streetcar boats unprofitable. From 1950 to 1960, Wayzata's population nearly doubled from 1,791 to 3,219 as city-goers opted to live in the suburbs surrounding the Twin Cities, and as of 2020, it has more residents than ever before. A few persons who have called "The Gateway to Lake Minnetonka" home at different points include Douglas Dayton, Target Corporation's first president; James Ford Bell, the first president of General Mills; David Bromstad, the host of several HGTV home renovation shows; James Laurinaitis, an NFL linebacker from 2009 to 2016 who won several outstanding player award trophies as a college athlete with the Ohio State University; Kimberly Elise, famous for her role in the 1998 Gothic psychological horror drama *Beloved*; Amy Klobuchar, a United States Senator from Minnesota since 2007; Jim Ramstad, a Member of the U.S. House of Representatives from Minnesota between 1991 and 2009; Dick Beardsley, the winner of the 1981 London Marathon;, and Marchette Chute, a biographer who made works on William Shakespeare and Geoffrey Chaucer amongst others. In the sci-fi adventure drama series *Lost*, the fictional character Ben Linus assumes the pseudonym Henry Gale to trick the protagonists, claiming to be from Wayzata, Minnesota. The city has also been mentioned or used as a filming location for *Beverly Hills, 90210*, *Fargo*, and *Drop Dead Gorgeous*.

 Restaurant Recommendation:
6Smith
294 Grove Ln E
Wayzata, MN 55391

WOODLAND, MN
POPULATION: 384 – CITY 786 OF 856 (11-7-25)
Historical accounts show that European visitors to Lake Minnetonka and Wayzata Bay began as early as the 1850s, but two specific developments led to Woodland's incorporation as an independent city. The first of these was Maplewoods, a temporary

residence area platted in 1882 for use by Minneapolis families as a place to relax during the summer months. By the end of that decade, the entire shoreline was adorned with residences, and by the mid-1930s, many of these temporary visitors began to make the shift towards living in Woodland full-time. In 1902, the second area of modern-day Woodland started as the Methodist Lakeside Assembly. Better known as the "Groveland Homeowners Association," the organization was established by Methodists to improve religion, morals, literature, and social culture as a whole. In December 1948, the Village of Maplewoods was jointly established by these two groups, and a year later, it adopted the name "Woodland" by combining parts of the names "Maplewoods" and "Groveland."

Chanhassen is only partially located in Hennepin County (see Carver County); Hanover & Rockford are only partially located in Hennepin County (see Wright County). Additionally, Saint Anthony Village in Hennepin & Ramsey County is different from St. Anthony in Stearns County.

Unincorporated/Ghost Towns: Fort Snelling

National Register of Historic Places:
Bloomington: First Presbyterian Church of Oak Grove Cemetery, Gideon H. Pond House, Long Meadow Bridge
Champlin: Anoka-Champlin Mississippi River Bridge, District No.99 School
Corcoran: District No. 107 School
Eden Prairie: Glen Lake Children's Camp, John R. Cummins Farmhouse
Edina: Bridge No. 90646, Cahill School, Country Club Historic District, George W. Baird House, Hendrik & Marrigje (Marri) Oskam House, Jonathan Taylor Grimes House, Minnehaha Grange Hall
Excelsior: Allemarinda & James Wyer House, Excelsior Commercial Historic District, Excelsior Public School, *Minnehaha* (steamboat)
Hanover: Hanover Bridge
Hopkins: Hopkins Commercial Historic District
Minneapolis: Aaron Carlson Corporation Factory, Abbott Hospital, Advance Thresher/Emerson Newton Implement Company, Alano Society of Minneapolis Clubhouse, Amos B. Coe House, Anne C. & Frank B. Semple House, Architects & Engineers Building, Arthur & Edith Lee House, B. O. Cutter House, Bardwell-Ferrant House, Basilica of St. Mary, Bennett-McBride House, Butler Brothers Company, Buzza Company Building, Calhoun Beach Club, Calvary Baptist Church, Calvary Lutheran Church, Cameron Transfer & Storage Company Building, Cappelen Memorial Bridge, Cedar Avenue Bridge, Cedar Square West, Chamber of Commerce Building, Charles & Grace Parker House, Charles J. Martin House, Chicago, Milwaukee & St. Paul Railroad Grade Separation, Chicago, Milwaukee, St. Paul & Pacific Depot Freight House & Train Shed, Christ Church Lutheran, Church of St. Stephen (Catholic), Church of the Incarnation & Rectory, Coliseum Building & Hall, Como-Harriet Streetcar Line & Trolley, Dayton's Department Store, Dr. Oscar Owre House, East Lake Branch Library, Edwin H. Hewitt House, Eitel Hospital, Elbert L. Carpenter House, Elisha Lizzie Morse Jr. House, Elizabeth C. Quinlan House, Eugene J. Carpenter House, Farmers & Mechanics Savings Bank, Farmers & Mechanics Savings Bank, Fire Station No.19, First Congregational Church, First National Bank-Soo Line Building, Flour Exchange Building, Floyd B. Olson House, Fort Snelling, Fort Snelling-Mendota Bridge, Foshay Tower, Fowler Methodist Episcopal Church, Franklin Branch Library, Fredrika Bremer Intermediate School, Frieda & Henry J. Neils House, George R. Newell House, George W. & Nancy B. Van Dusen House, Gethsemane Episcopal Church, Grace Evangelical Lutheran Church, Grain Belt Beer Sign, Great Northern Implement Company, H. Alden Smith House, Harry F. Legg House, Harry W. Jones House, Healy Block Residential Historic District, Hennepin Theatre, Hiawatha Golf Course, Hinkle Murphy House, Hollywood Theater, Horatio P. Van Cleve House, Intercity Bridge, Interlachen Bridge, J. I. Case Building, John G. & Minnie Gluek House & Carriage House, John Lohmar House, Lake Harriet Methodist Episcopal Church, Lake Street Sash & Door Company, Lakewood Cemetery Memorial Chapel, Laurel Apartments, Lawrence A. & Mary Fournier House, Lena O. Smith House, Lincoln Bank Building, Linden Hills Branch Library, Little Sisters of the Poor Home for the Aged, Lock & Dam No.2, Loren L. Chadwick

Cottages, Lumber Exchange Building, Malcolm Willey House, Masonic Temple, Maternity Hospital, McLeod & Smith Inc. Headquarters, Milwaukee Avenue Historic District, Minneapolis Armory, Minneapolis Brewing Company, Minneapolis City Hall-Hennepin County Courthouse, Minneapolis Pioneers & Soldiers Memorial Cemetery, Minneapolis Public Library, North Branch, Minneapolis Warehouse Historic District, Minneapolis YMCA Central Building, Minnehaha Historic District, Minnesota Bridge 2440, Minnesota Linseed Oil Company, Minnesota Soldiers' Home Historic District, Moline, Milburn & Stoddard Company, New Main Augsburg Seminary, Nokomis Knoll Residential Historic District, North East Neighborhood House, Northrop Mall Historic District, Northrup, King & Company Complex, Northstar Center, Northwestern Knitting Company Factory, Northwestern National Life Insurance Company Home Office, Ogden Apartment Hotel, Peavey Plaza, Pence Automobile Company Building, Phi Gamma Delta Fraternity House, Pillsbury A Mill, Plymouth Building, Prospect Park Residential Historic District, Prospect Park Water Tower & Tower Hill Park, Queen Avenue Bridge, Rand Tower, Roosevelt Branch Library, Sam S. Shubert Theatre, Sear, Roebuck & Company Mail-Order Warehouse & Retail Store, St. Anthony's Falls Historic District, St. Olafs Norwegian Lutheran Church, Station 13 Minneapolis Fire Department, Station 28 Minneapolis Fire Department, Stevens Square, Stewart Memorial Presbyterian Church, Strutwear Knitting Company Building, Studio 80, Sumner Branch Library, Swan Turnblad House, Swinford Townhouses & Apartments, The Woman's Club of Minneapolis, Theodore Wirth House Administration Building, Thirty-sixth Street Branch Library, Thompson Flats, Tifereth B'nai Jacob Synagogue- First Church of God in Christ, Twin City Rapid Transit Company Steam Power Plant, United States Post Office, University of Minnesota Old Campus Historic District, Walker Branch Library, Washburn A Mill Complex, Washburn Park Water Tower, Washburn-Fair Oaks Mansion District, Wesley Methodist Episcopal Church, Westminster Presbyterian Church, White Castle Building No. 8, William Gray Purcell House, Woodbury Fisk House, Zinmaster Baking Company Building
Minnetonka: Charles H. Burwell House, Minnetonka Town Hall
Minnetonka Beach: Minnetonka Beach Water Tower, Thompson Summer House
Minnetrista: Crane Island Historic District, Schmid Farmhouse Ruin
Orono: Noerenberg Estate Barn
Osseo: Osseo Water Tower
Richfield: Riley Lucas Bartholomew House
Robbinsdale: Hennepin County Library
Rockford: Ames-Florida House
Rogers: Hagel Family Farm
Shorewood: Peter Gideon Farmhouse
St. Louis Park: Chicago, Milwaukee, St. Paul & Pacific Depot, Peavey-Haglin Experimental Concrete Grain Elevator
Wayzata: Great Northern Railroad Depot, Wayzata Section House

Golf Courses:
Baker National Golf Course – Evergreen, Short Course (Medina, MN)
Baker National Golf Course, Municipal (Medina, MN)
Bearpath Golf & Country Club, Private (Eden Prairie, MN)
Bent Creek Golf Club, Private (Eden Prairie, MN)
Braemar Golf Course – Academy 9, Short Course (Edina, MN)
Braemar Golf Course, Municipal (Edina, MN)
Braemar Golf Dome, Municipal (Edina, MN)
Brookland Golf Park, Municipal (Brooklyn Park, MN)
Brookview Golf Course – Executive 9, Short Course (Golden Valley, MN)
Brookview Golf Course & Lawn Bowling, Municipal (Golden Valley, MN)
Burl Oaks Golf Club, Private (Minnetrista, MN)
Centerbrook Golf Course, Short Course (Brooklyn Center, MN)
Daytona Golf Club, Daily Fee (Dayton, MN)
Eagle Lake Youth Golf Center, Municipal (Plymouth, MN)
Edina Country Club, Private (Edina, MN)
Edinburgh USA, Municipal (Brooklyn Park, MN)
Fort Snelling Public Golf Course, Municipal (Fort Snelling, MN)
Francis A. Gross Golf Club, Municipal (Minneapolis, MN)
Glen Lake Golf and Practice Center, Short Course (Minnetonka, MN)

Hiawatha Golf Club, Municipal (Minneapolis, MN)
Hyland Greens Golf, Short Course (Bloomington, MN)
Mac Nine Par Three Course, Short Course (Maple Grove, MN)
Meadowbrook Golf Club, Municipal (Hopkins, MN)
Oak Ridge Country Club, Private (Hopkins, MN)
Olympic Hills Golf Club, Private (Eden Prairie, MN)
Pheasant Acres Golf Club, Daily Fee (Rogers, MN)
Pioneer Creek Golf Course, Daily Fee (Maple Plain, MN)
Rush Creek Golf Club, Daily Fee (Maple Grove, MN)
Shamrock Golf Club, Daily Fee (Corcoran, MN)
Spring Hill Golf Club, Private (Wayzata, MN)
Sundance Golf Club, Daily Fee (Maple Grove, MN)
The Club at Golden Valley, Private (Golden Valley, MN)
The Minikahda Club, Private (Minneapolis, MN)
Theodore Wirth Golf Club – Par 3, Municipal (Golden Valley, MN)
Theodore Wirth Golf Club, Municipal (Golden Valley, MN)
Wayzata Country Club, Private (Wayzata, MN)
Windsong Farm Golf Club, Private (Independence, MN)
Woodhill Country Club, Private (Wayzata, MN)

Breweries/Wineries/Distilleries:
56 Brewing (Minneapolis, MN)
Arbeiter Brewing Company (Minneapolis, MN)
Back Channel Brewing Collective (Spring Park, MN)
Bauhaus Brew Labs (Minneapolis, MN)
Bear Cave Brewing (Hopkins, MN)
Birch's on the Lake Brewhouse (Long Lake, MN)
Blue Wolf Brewing Company (Brooklyn Park, MN)
Boom Island Brewing Company (Minnetonka, MN)
Broken Clock Brewing (Minneapolis, MN)
Brother Justus Whiskey Company (Minneapolis, MN)
Brühaven Craft Company (Minneapolis, MN)
Copperwing Distillery (St. Louis Park, MN)
Crooked Water Spirits (Minneapolis, MN)
Dampfwerk Distillery (Minneapolis, MN)
Day Block Brewing Company (Minneapolis, MN)
Du Nord Social Spirits (Minneapolis, MN)
Eastlake Craft Brewery (Minneapolis, MN)
Elm Creek Brewing (Champlin, MN)
Excelsior Brewing Company (Excelsior, MN)
Fair State Brewing Cooperative (Minneapolis, MN)
Falling Knife Brewing Company (Minneapolis, MN)
Fat Pants Brewing Company (Eden Prairie, MN)
Finnegans Brew Company (Minneapolis, MN)
Fulton Beer (Minneapolis, MN)
GLUEK BEER (St. Louis Park, MN)
Haggard Barrel Brewing Company (St. Louis Park, MN)
HeadFlyer Brewing (Minneapolis, MN)
Heavy Rotation Brewing Company (Brooklyn Park, MN)
Inbound BrewCo (Minneapolis, MN)
Indeed Brewing Company (Minneapolis, MN)
Insight Brewing (Minneapolis, MN)
Iron Exchange Tavern and Brewing (Maple Plain, MN)
Lawless Distilling Company (Minneapolis, MN)
LTD Brewing (Hopkins, MN)
Luce Line Brewing Co. (Plymouth, MN)
LynLake Brewery (Minneapolis, MN)
Miller and Saints Distillery (St. Louis Park, MN)
Modist Brewing Company (Minneapolis, MN)

Nine Mile Brewing Company (Bloomington, MN)
Northbound Smokehouse & Brewpub (Minneapolis, MN)
Nouvelle Brewing by Travail (Robbinsdale, MN)
OMNI Brewing Company (Maple Grove, MN)
O'Shaughnessy Distillery Co. (Minneapolis, MN)
Padraigs (Minneapolis, MN)
Phillips Distilling Company (Minneapolis, MN)
Pryes Brewing Company (Minneapolis, MN)
Ripple Effect Brewing Company (Rogers, MN)
Rock Bottom Restaurant & Brewery (Minneapolis, MN)
Royal Foundry Craft Spirits (Minneapolis, MN)
Sisyphus Brewing Company (Minneapolis, MN)
Skaalvenn Distillery (Minneapolis, MN)
Sociable Cider Works (Minneapolis, MN)
Surly Brewing Company (Minneapolis, MN)
Tattersall Distilling (Minneapolis, MN)
The Freehouse (Minneapolis, MN)
Town Hall Brewing (Minneapolis, MN)
Twin Spirits Distillery (Minneapolis, MN)
Ullsperger Brewing (St. Louis Park, MN)
Under Pressure Brewing (Golden Valley, MN)
Unmapped Brewing Company (Minnetonka, MN)
Urban Forage Winery and Cider House (Minneapolis, MN)
Utepils Brewing (Minneapolis, MN)
Venn Brewing Company (Minneapolis, MN)
Wander North Distillery (Minneapolis, MN)
Warehouse Winery (Minneapolis, MN)
Wicked Wort Brewing Company (Robbinsdale, MN)
Wooden Hill Brewing Company (Edina, MN)
Wooden Ship Brewing Company (Minneapolis, MN)

Town Celebrations:
Corcoran County Daze, Corcoran, MN (Mid-August)
Father Hennepin Festival, Champlin, MN (2nd Weekend in June)
Hopkins Raspberry Fesitval, Hopkins, MN (3rd Weekend of July)
James J. Hills Days, Wayzata, MN (Weekend after Labor Day)
Maple Grove Days, Maple Grove, MN (3rd Wednesday through Sunday of July)
Twin Cities Con, Minneapolis, MN (Early-to-mid November)

HOUSTON COUNTY
EST. 1854 - POPULATION: 18,843

Initially a part of Wisconsin Territory's St. Croix County circa 1839, this area became Wabashaw County before being split again into Fillmore and Houston Counties in February 1854. It was named after Sam Houston, the 1st and 3rd President of Texas in the early 1840s.

BROWNSVILLE, MN
POPULATION: 566 – CITY 680 OF 856 (10-15-25)
The first established town in Minnesota Territory was none other than Brownsville, named in honor of brothers Job and Charles Brown. They came to the area from New York in November 1848, and six years later, Brownsville was formally platted. Its post office opened in 1852, and in 1854, it was selected as the first county seat of Houston County. Grand Fourth of July celebrations were held, including one that featured barbecuing an ox, hosting dances, and shooting fireworks. By 1870, the river town had grown substantially to 625 people thanks to all the steamboat traffic on the Mississippi

River, and it had over fifty businesses, including lumber offices, a sawmill, and Gluik and Schartzhoff's brewery. Others listed in an 1869 business directory included C. J. Cusic's implement store, Mark Percival's bookstore and stationary store, George Lambert's brick manufactory, Phillip Shuller's flour and grist mill, the Craine Brothers jewelry store, John Juland's planing mill, the Bennett House and the Selfridge House hotels, and many other blacksmiths, doctors, saloon owners, and storeowners. At that point, its four churches were Catholic, Lutheran, Methodist Episcopal, and Presbyterian. One of those four edifices, the Episcopal Church of the Holy Comforter, was built in 1855 and has since withstood the test of time as a town hall and school, among other uses. When the Chicago, Milwaukee & St. Paul Railroad was built through Brownsville, its importance diminished as traders abandoned the river and steamboats in favor of railroads. Its losses were hastened by a fire in October 1920 that caused $75,000 in damage and destroyed nine buildings, including the railroad depot. Post-conflagration, Brownsville had a population of only 274 people, but it has since doubled. Peter Pernin, a survivor of the deadliest wildfire in recorded history—the Peshtigo, Wisconsin, fire of October 1871—served as the Catholic church's pastor in Brownsville from 1886 to 1894. William Kauber, one of the original Keystone Cops actors from the 1912 to 1917 silent film series, was born here on May 20, 1891.

CALEDONIA, MN ★☆
POPULATION: 2,847 – CITY 677 OF 856 (10-14-25)

"The Wild Turkey Capital of Minnesota" was home to far more than birds during the late 1870s. Having been platted in 1854-55 on Badger Creek (a tributary of the Root River) and named by Colonel Samuel McPhail for the Roman word for Scotland, "Caledonia," the then-town of 800-odd residents had grown considerably since its inception. It had been incorporated as a village on February 25, 1870, and the Chicago, Milwaukee, St. Paul and Pacific Railroad had expanded the local wheat and pork industry. With that increased trade, four hotels, brick yards, a bank, general stores, drug stores, and even jewelry stores had come about. It boasted of two different Catholic churches —somewhat of a rarity even to this day — in addition to a Presbyterian, a Methodist, and an Episcopal church. In 1875, a sheriff's residence and jail, along with an accompanying 1883 courthouse, were built in the Italianate and Romanesque Revival styles. These structures, as well as the 1870s Spafford Williams Hotel, the 1875-76 Schech Mill, the only one of Minnesota's gristmills to retain its original millstones, and the Caledonia Commercial Historic District, consisting of ten properties built between 1872 and 1906, are all a part of the National Register of Historic Places. An early town tale recalls the time when Jacob Webster of New England came to the area and intentionally sowed thousands of dandelion seeds to "provide greens to eat" for local livestock. Unbeknownst to him, his actions would result in the overgrowth of the obnoxious weed throughout this part of Minnesota and far beyond. The Houston County Historical Society was formed at the Caledonia courthouse on May 1, 1948, to preserve the community's history, artifacts, and archives through a local museum. Ken Nelson of Capitol Records and a member of the Country Music Hall of Fame; Karl Klug, a defensive end with the Tennessee Titans from 2011 to 2017; Al Sheehan, a vital radio host and producer with Minneapolis's WCCO Radio; William F. Dunbar, the first Minnesota State Auditor from 1858 to 1861; and Isaac Fruechte, who made a brief appearance with the NFL's Minnesota Vikings in 2016, all have communal ties.

EITZEN, MN
POPULATION: 279 – CITY 676 OF 856 (10-14-25)
Settlement throughout Eitzen, named for a place in Germany by Christian Bunge Jr., started slowly as its closest railroad station was in New Albin, Iowa. John Ross settled Jefferson Township in 1847, but it was Freeman Graves who staked the first land claim the following year. It took another two decades before the Eitzen post office was established by the United States Postal Service, shortly after Bunge built a log grocery store. He upgraded his storefront in 1890 with stone, and it has since remained the oldest commercial building within Eitzen's city limits. It hosts the Eitzen Museum. In the vicinity of the community are the rural 1876 Portland Prairie Methodist Episcopal Church, and the 1877 Johnson Mill, one of Minnesota's last surviving water-powered gristmills. Other places on an 1878 business directory list H. F. Bucoltz's general store, H. Gartner's shoe shop, W. Kruse's shoe shop, and C. Laufer's hotel and saloon. Modern incorporation of Eitzen came on May 17, 1947.

HOKAH, MN
POPULATION: 553 – CITY 681 OF 856 (10-15-25)
Nestled between the Root River and the historic Lake Como is Hokah, which on August 19, 2007, became the recipient of the largest amount of rain in 24 hours in recorded Minnesota history. 15.10 inches fell on the Houston County community during a 2007 supersystem that caused massive flooding throughout the Midwest. With 23.86 total inches of rain that month, Hokah also set the record for the most rainfall in any month in Minnesota state history. While the constant downpour did not refill Lake Como, exhibited on a 1878 plat map, the Hokah of that era had many other points of interest. Platted in March 1855, it was named after Chief Wecheschatope Hokah of the Dakota, who took his surname from his people's word for "root." He shared it with the nearby river of the same name, which boasts the sacred Como Falls. Edward Thompson first settled the vicinity in 1852. Thompson built a sawmill that year, then a flour mill in 1853, and a dam in 1866 to allow for the Southern Minnesota Railroad (eventually a part of the Chicago, Milwaukee & St. Paul system) to build through. Minnesota allowed for Hokah to incorporate on March 2, 1871. The Root River Valley Railroad between La Crescent and Rochester made the community an essential part of the local rail system; at its peak, it may have employed as many as 500 workers. Manufacturing practices flourished due to its railroad importance, and early gazetteers list a plow factory, a furniture factory, cooper shops, six general stores, three hotels, three flouring mills, and the *Hokah Blade* newspaper office among the firms. Methodist, Presbyterian, and German Methodist churches existed in 1878. During the WPA period of the 1930s, an Art Deco-style municipal building was completed as Hokah's now lone NRHP-registered location. It was during the 1930s that the 90-acre, 20-foot deep artificial Lake Como, created by the dam built on Thompson Creek, was filled in due to contour plowing. The site has since served as a community park; in August 2018, the falls were destroyed by eight inches of rainfall in less than 24 hours. They were artificially rebuilt to allow for continued enjoyment of the park. William Henry Harries, a Member of the U.S. House of Representatives from Minnesota between March 1891 and March 1893, served as a local attorney for many years before he became a Congressman.

HOUSTON, MN
POPULATION: 997 – CITY 682 OF 856 (10-15-25)
Houston's annual "International Festival of Owls" brings together owl enthusiasts from around the world to the International Owl Center. The all-weekend event invites visitors

to enjoy live owl programs and owl crafts, or to participate in a kids' owl-calling contest. Visitors may also enjoy programs with live owls and the exhibits of the International Owl Center outside of the festival as well. Twelve owl sculptures are located throughout the municipality, which was founded in 1852 when William McSpadden platted the original townsite. He named it in honor of Sam Houston, of Mexican-American War fame, and within a couple of years, several homes and businesses sprang up on what had previously been empty land just outside the Driftless Area. Houston's post office entered service in 1856, with Ole Knutson at the helm. The office was hosted in his store. Mons Anderson contributed land to the Southern Minnesota Railroad's right-of-way in 1866, and by 1878, Houston had established itself as a major exporter of wheat, flour, and pork. About a dozen general stores were operational, as were four hotels, a flouring mill, and a handful of factories. Presbyterian, Episcopalian, and Catholic churches made up Houston's religious sphere. In 1949, a 300-foot-long cantilever bridge, then the longest in the state at the time of its completion, was built over the south fork of the Root River. Francis Martin Kelly, the Catholic Bishop of the Diocese of Winona, Minnesota, from 1928 to 1949, was born in Houston in 1886.

Restaurant Recommendation:
J T's Corner Bar & Grill
125 E Cedar St
Houston, MN 55943

LA CRESCENT, MN
POPULATION: 5,276 – CITY 678 OF 856 (10-15-25)
Peter and Emma Cameron came to this place in 1851 with grand visions for what it could become. Naming it "Camerons" in their own honor, Peter attempted to hand-dig a canal that would force the Mississippi River to reroute itself closer to their town instead of La Crosse, Wisconsin. Sadly, he passed away only weeks before it was set to be completed, and the canal that could have forever changed the course of history (and the river) was never completed. While the Camerons were doing their thing, William and Harvet Gillett started a place called Manton. That name was used for only a brief time (even by the post office, beginning in 1856) before the Kentucky Land Company adopted "La Crescent" as an allusion to the river's curvature. They employed marketing tactics to use the town's name to attract more settlers, of which there were about 380 by La Crescent's inaugural 1870 Census. During this time, the great horticulturist John S. Harris came to town and planted thousands of apple trees and varieties to prove that the fruit trees could survive the harsh Minnesota winters. As a result of his experiments, La Crescent has retained many large apple orchards and even coined the phrase "Apple Capital of Minnesota." The Chicago, Milwaukee, St. Paul & Pacific Railroad served as the impetus for a line of businesses along the Mississippi, including two grist mills, a woolen factory, hotels, carriage works, blacksmith shops, meat markets, and storefronts selling a wide variety of goods. Public schools were operational at that time, as were Catholic, Methodist, and Presbyterian churches. An Italianate home built by Daniel Cameron (Peter's brother) in 1871 was listed on the NRHP in April 1982 as La Crescent's lone nationally-recognized historic property. Eriah Hayes, who played with the NHL's San Jose Sharks in 19 games between 2013 and 2015; Sheldon Jackson, a Presbyterian missionary who reportedly traveled over one million miles during his lifetime (May 1834 to May 1909) establishing churches on the Western frontier, and Siri Carpenter, a science journalist whose work has appeared in the Science academic journal and APA Monitor publications, have La Crescent connections.

 Restaurant Recommendation:
TimeOut Tavern
444 N Chestnut St
La Crescent, MN 55947

SPRING GROVE, MN
POPULATION: 1,256 – CITY 675 OF 856 (10-14-25)
Minnesota's first Norwegian settlement had residents as early as 1852, but it was in 1855 that the Spring Grove post office was started at the home of James Smith, its first settler. He opened a store here in 1853, becoming the first of several businesspeople to set up shop in the fledgling village. Named for its location beside a spring and a grove, the community was platted on William J. Flemming's land during the same period. The Chicago, Milwaukee & St. Paul Railroad served as the community's principal trade route as its population steadily grew to about 750 people in the 1920s. At that time, it had pairs of grain elevators, feed mills, and banks (the Quendahl Savings Bank and the State Bank of Spring Grove), in addition to Ristey's opera house, the Hovey Co-operative Creamery Company, the Spring Grove Lumber Company, a Norwegian Lutheran Church, and the *Spring Grove Herald* newspaper. Spring Grove's Ballard hotel, built in 1893 as one of the city's most impressive commercial properties, now serves as the Giants of the Earth Heritage Center. Near the museum is a collection of Norwegian Viking and troll statues. A few men who have brought recognition to Spring Grove include Robert E. A. Lee, the former head producer of the Lutheran Church's film production team, known for their 1966 Oscar-nominated documentary *A Time for Burning*; John Stewart Socha, a radio broadcaster who focuses on technology, and Carlton C. Qualey, a historian noted for his work on Norwegian-American immigration.

Lodging Recommendation:
The Bespoke Inn
108 2nd Ave SE
Spring Grove, MN 55974

Unincorporated/Ghost Towns: Bee, Black Hammer, Freeburg, Jefferson, Mayville, Money Creek, Newhouse, Pine Creek, Reno, River Junction, Sheldon, Willington Grove, Wilmington, Yucatan

National Register of Historic Places:
Brownsville: Church of the Holy Comforter- Episcopal
Caledonia: Caledonia Commercial Historic District, David R. & Ellsworth A. Sprague Houses, Houston County Courthouse & Jail, Spafford Williams Hotel, Schech Mill
Eitzen: Christian Bunge, Jr. Store, Johnson Mill, Portland Prairie Methodist Episcopal Church
Hokah: Hokah Municipal Building
Houston: Bridge No. 6679
Jefferson Township: Jefferson Grain Warehouse
La Crescent: Daniel Cameron House
Spring Grove: Ballard Hotel, Bridge No. L4013

Golf Courses:
Ma Cal Grove Country Club, Daily Fee (Caledonia, MN)
Valley High Golf Club, Daily Fee (Houston, MN)

Breweries/Wineries/Distilleries:
River View Vineyard and Winery (La Crescent, MN)

Town Celebrations:
Houston Hoedown Days, Houston, MN (Last Full Weekend in July)
International Festival of Owls, Houston, MN (1st Weekend in March)
La Crescent Applefest, La Crescent, MN (3rd Full Weekend in September)
Syttende Mai, Spring Grove, MN (3rd Weekend in May)
Uffda Fest, Spring Grove, MN (1st Weekend in October)

HUBBARD COUNTY
EST. 1883 - POPULATION: 21,344

Lucius Frederick Hubbard, Minnesota's ninth governor, is the namesake of this county whose boundaries have never been altered.

AKELEY, MN
POPULATION: 404 – CITY 298 OF 856 (6-2-25)
Giant lumberjack and folk hero Paul Bunyan can trace his origins to his rightful home in Akeley, Minnesota, where he and Babe the Blue Ox were said to have logged the area and created Minnesota's ten thousand lakes with their giant footprints. William B. Laughead heavily popularized the fabled superhuman woodsman in a 1916 pamphlet advertising the Red River Lumber Company, Akeley's primary business in its heyday. Thomas B. Walker and Healy C. Akeley teamed up in 1893 to create their logging company and log the heavily timbered lands that Walker had surveyed as early as 1876. Settlement began in 1895, and by the end of the century, the Great Northern Railroad had the foresight to establish a depot here. Their decision paid significant dividends, as the presence of the railroad and the establishment of Minnesota's largest sawmill in 1902 by Mr. Walker (and other sawmills) caused Akeley's population to reach as high as 3,500 throughout the 1910s. There was a post office, a brickyard, and stores and hotels galore. It seemed as though Akeley was destined to become one of Minnesota's most significant industrial centers until some men realized that the timber was running out. Overlogging had greatly diminished the supply of lumber in the region. By 1916, Akeley's sawmills had closed, and the Red River Lumber Company moved its operations to California. The mill's loss sent shockwaves through the area and prompted a mass exodus of settlers. Dairying became the new primary industry as the population dropped from 855 in 1920 to 514 in 1930, and Akeley took on a more traditional small-town role, with its collection of churches, schools, and businesses. Since 1984, the World's Largest Paul Bunyan (built by the Krotzer family) has encouraged visitors to step onto his hand for a photo-op. He stands 25 feet tall and is one of three major local attractions, the others being Paul Bunyan Days (held since the 1940s/50s) and the Akeley Paul Bunyan Historical Museum.

LAPORTE, MN
POPULATION: 134 – CITY 297 OF 856 (6-2-25)
Laporte began as a settlement circa 1901 and was incorporated as a village on May 4, 1908. It was predated only by a post office called Ann. From 1899 to 1901, it operated under this name, given by Nelson Daughters in honor of his late wife when he became postmaster. In a bizarre event, the Daughters perished in a gunfight with the local sheriff's department after he escaped arrest. He had been taken into custody after a group of Native Americans went to him asking for whiskey; when they were denied, they turned him in for liquor trafficking. Daughters was being taken to Walker when he escaped. A new office began in 1900 under the name Lake Port. Because of its similarity to Lake Park, it was renamed by the new postmaster's (J. C. Stuart) wife after Laporte, Iowa, where she was married. Throughout its early years, Laporte also

had a hotel, a pickle factory, a bank, a general store, and a blacksmith shop, amongst other businesses, although many of them succumbed to a series of fires or explosions between May 11, 1911 (the worst fire in Laporte's history) or one of four blazes between 1930 and 1936. Laporte's railroad of note was the Northern Pacific. A branch of The Brainerd and Northern Railway split off from the line just north of Laporte towards modern-day Paul Bunyan State Forest.

NEVIS, MN
POPULATION: 377 – CITY 299 OF 856 (6-2-25)
Once home to over a dozen resorts in the 1930s, Nevis dates to roughly 1899 when a post office was established under the name. The precise origins of the town's name are unknown, but it is thought to have come from the "Ben Nevis," a large mountain in Great Britain, or an island in the West Indies. With the help of the Great Northern Railroad, early residents of Nevis were able to establish themselves as an essential trade point on the railroad. Agriculture was prominent, but F. B. Cannada, an early businessman, wanted to capitalize on the area's forests by erecting a sawmill: the Nevis Lumber Company. Surrounding the mill were the Nevis Mercantile Company, a furniture and jewelry store; Fred Giesel's Star Theater; John Bender's meat market; and many other businesses that contributed to the everyday lives of Nevis residents. Its first incorporation as a village came on February 4, 1902, and its second time was in 1921. With all its tourism traffic, in 1948, the town sought to erect an attraction to set it apart from other area communities. The Chamber of Commerce wished to erect a log cabin as a testament to the area's forests, but Warren Perry Ballard had another idea: the World's Largest Tiger Muskie. He designed the 31-foot-long statue and placed it in what ultimately became a town park. On August 22, 1950, Minnesota Governor Luther Youngdahl formally dedicated the fish, and the town celebrated by changing their Eddie Lof Days festival to "Muskie Days" beginning that same year. The annual festival is held every July. Other claims to fame include the Louis J. Moser House, a 1907 homesteader's cabin that began as a fishing resort and eventually became the office of Fremont's Point Resort, and the Heart of Minnesota Emu Ranch, where visitors learn about the inner workings and products of an emu ranch.

PARK RAPIDS, MN ★☆
POPULATION: 4,142 – CITY 300 OF 856 (6-2-25)
Logging, dairying, and wheat farming helped the earliest version of Park Rapids survive, but no early settlers could have foreseen the tourist hub it would become thanks to its location near Itasca State Park, home to the headwaters of the Mississippi River. The 32,690-acre park annually attracts over half a million visitors who primarily enjoy hiking, fishing, birding, skiing, and snowboarding. Established on April 20, 1891, by the Minnesota Legislature, Itasca is the second-oldest state park in the United States, behind only Niagara Falls State Park (established in 1885 in New York); it has since been designated a National Natural Landmark and added to the National Register of Historic Places because of its 72 park facilities built between 1905 and 1942. Wallowing in the Big Muddy is a favorite pastime for tourists and Park Rapids residents, but the town's rise began with the logging camps. It was designated as the supply center for this new, booming industry, and civil engineers ensured Park Rapids could accommodate that title. An extra-wide Main Street was built to allow four-and-six-horse teams to transport goods through the hub of the village. The town plat was filed in 1882 by Joseph Sombs, who accepted the name "Park Rapids" at the suggestion of Frank C. Rice, the town proprietor. He suggested the name for the now-gone rapids of the Fish Hook River and the gorgeous park-worthy fauna that adorned

the riverfront. Frank and his brother Gilbert (the first postmaster when the post office opened in 1881) opened a sawmill and a gristmill, which encouraged Robert F. Shields to found the first general store that same year. In 1883, Park Rapids was designated the judicial seat when Hubbard County was established. With the additional arrival of the Wadena and Park Rapids line in July 1891, its distinction as the best town in the county was affirmed. The Park Rapids and Leech Lake Railway Company, a subsidiary of the Great Northern, extended another line eastward to Cass Lake in 1899 (although the line eventually was abandoned and became the popular 49-mile Heartland State Trail). At its inaugural Census in 1900, the town's population was 1,313. In that decade, Milton Earl Beebe designed the Neoclassical Hubbard County Courthouse, which served as the county's government building from 1900 through the 1970s, before becoming the Hubbard County Historical Museum and Nemeth Art Center. An adjacent jail, now called the Park Rapids Jail, was completed in 1901 and is one of the city's three National Register-listed locations. At that time, six churches, a public library, several schools, and a community hall were other significant points of interest. The Carnegie library building is now home to the Giiwedinong Treaty Rights and Culture Museum, which in 2023 became the first museum in Minnesota to be managed by Indigenous peoples and focus on Anishinaabe culture and treaty rights. By the 1940s, the population had doubled; it has since grown in every subsequent decade except for the 1960s and the 1980s. With so many residents over the years, Park Rapids has claimed several famous individuals: Aaron Pike, a U.S. Paralympian in Nordic skiing and wheelchair racing; Naathan Aseng, an author with more than 130 works, including *Farm Team* and *Hard Ball*; and Will Weaver, whose *Red Earth, White Earth* novel was turned into a CBS-TV movie in 1989.

Restaurant Recommendation:
Great Northern Cafe
218 1st St E
Park Rapids, MN 56470

Lodging Recommendation:
Douglas Lodge
Douglas Lodge Dr
Laporte, MN 56461

Unincorporated/Ghost Towns: Badoura, Becida, Benedict, Chamberlain, Dorset, Emmaville, Hubbard, Kabekona, Lake George, Nary

National Register of Historic Places:
Nary: Consolidated School District No. 22
Park Rapids: Hubbard County Courthouse, Park Rapids Jail, Itasca State Park
Thorpe Township: Louis J. Moser House

Golf Courses:
Bears Den Golf Course, Resort (Park Rapids, MN)
Headwaters Golf Club, Daily Fee (Park Rapids, MN)

Breweries/Wineries/Distilleries:
Forestedge Winery (Laporte, MN)

Town Celebrations:
Nevis Muskie Days, Nevis, MN (3rd Weekend of July)
Paul Bunyan Days, Akeley, MN (Last Weekend of June)

ISANTI COUNTY
EST. 1857 - POPULATION: 41,135

The Isáŋyathi (the Santee Sioux) gave this county its name when it was formed in 1857. *Isanti* roughly translates to 'knife,' a reference to the county's Knife Lake.

BRAHAM, MN
POPULATION: 1,769 – CITY 455 OF 856 (7-20-25)
"The Homemade Pie Capital of Minnesota" rose to fame in the 1930s and 1940s when the local Park Cafe became a must-stop for Minnesotans traveling between the Twin Cities and Duluth. The pies were so scrumptious and well-remembered that in 1990, Rudy Perpich, then the 36th Governor of Minnesota, declared the then-town of about eleven hundred residents to be the official "Pie Capital of Minnesota." Since then, Pie Day has been celebrated every year as a family-friendly celebration with music, games, street and food vendors, and of course, all the pie one could desire. The Braham post office was established in 1891, and the town was founded in 1899 with the arrival of the Great Northern Railroad. It was named, possibly, after an early settler or a railroad official. It was incorporated on March 5, 1901, at a time when it had sufficient business lines to satisfy the needs of its citizens. The Swedish Methodist Episcopal Church was the first religious edifice to be built in 1899, and three years later, Braham had its first school. Many of the businesses on Main Street were destroyed in a 1908 St. Patrick's Day fire, but Braham has since rebuilt and steadily grown over the decades to a modern population of 1,769. The sister city of Yuasa, Japan, is also the hometown of Marlene Johnson, the 42nd lieutenant governor of Minnesota and the first woman to hold the position. Noah Dahlman, a professional basketball player who found success overseas as the 2014 Bulgarian League MVP and Balkan League Player of the Year, was born here.

CAMBRIDGE, MN ★☆
POPULATION: 9,611 – CITY 585 OF 856 (9-2-25)
Home to the highest percentage (more than 50% of its 9,611-person population) of Swedish Americans of any city in the United States, Cambridge was organized on Rum River and the Great Northern Railroad line connecting Minneapolis and Duluth. The initial townsite was platted in 1856 by John Owens and R. F. Slaughter and named by New England settlers for Cambridge University in England. A post office opened that same year. Thirteen years later, most of the townsite had moved to a new plat filed by Ira Conger and D. G. Miller. This new site was located on the railroad, closer to where Jebediah Kimball had established a boarding house in 1859. County residents chose Cambridge as the seat of government over Old Isanti, and with that decision, many important businesses came to fruition. Amongst the most significant were a wool carding and spinning mill, a 1,301-barrel flour mill, a potato starch factory, and several more storefronts, shops, and professional offices of all varieties. Cambridge was incorporated as a village on February 26, 1876; nowadays, its two most historic points of interest are the former Isanti County Courthouse, erected in 1887, and the West Riverside School, a one-room schoolhouse built in 1898. From the start of the 21st century to 2025, Cambridge has seen a population increase of nearly 5,000 people. Todd Hallowell, the Executive Producer behind films like *Apollo 13* (1995), *How The Grinch Stole Christmas* (2000), *A Beautiful Mind* (2001), and *A Minecraft Movie* (2025); Julia Hart, a professional wrestler most recently signed with All Elite Wrestling; Grace McCallum, a silver medalist gymnast at the 2020 Tokyo

Olympics, and Kerri Hoskins, a video game actress noted for portraying Sonya Blade in the *Mortal Kombat* series, have communal ties.

ISANTI, MN
POPULATION: 6,804 – CITY 586 OF 856 (9-3-25)

"Isanti" is an amalgamation of two Santee Sioux words, *isan* meaning "knife," and *ati* meaning "camp." They were the first people to inhabit the lands of Isanti County before explorers and fur traders began to arrive regularly throughout the 1800s. In 1865, the Isanti post office started in the home of Peter Norelius; the following year, there was a school, a church, a collection of gristmills, and a joint store and hotel owned by George Nesbitt. This original townsite, located about three miles north of modern-day Isanti, is now called "Old Isanti." It was moved in 1899 to the railroad line when the Great Northern Railway was extended through the county. Edward and Albert Norelius were recorded as being among the first entrepreneurs to move their store, and Wilfred D. Oleson came to the new site to establish his own stock. St. John's Lutheran Church was one of several early churches built by German immigrants to provide a religious haven for practicing their faith. Located in 1882 in rural Isanti, it was added to the National Register of Historic Places on July 24, 1980, alongside the Edward Erickson potato farmstead. New Isanti was incorporated on February 27, 1901, and has since grown to a population of 6,804 people as of the 2020 Census. Until the 1990s, the City of Isanti had fewer than one thousand residents. Blake Bjorklund, a professional stock car racer in the 2007 NASCAR Craftsman Truck Series, hails from Isanti.

Restaurant Recommendation:
WinterGreens
306 Credit Union Drive Northeast
Isanti, MN 55040

St. Francis is only partially located in Isanti County (see Anoka County).

Unincorporated/Ghost Towns: Andree, Athens, Blomford, Bodum, Bradford, Carmody, Crown, Dalbo, Day, Edgewood, Elm Park, Grandy, Oxlip, Pine Brook, Spencer Brook, Spring Lake, Springvale, Stanchfield, Stanchfield Corner, Stanford, Stanley, Walbo, Weber, West Point, Wyanett

National Register of Historic Places:
Braham: Oscar Olson House
Cambridge: Isanti County Courthouse, West Riverside School
Isanti Township: Linden Barn
Isanti: Edward Erickson Farmstead, St. John's Lutheran Church
Maple Ridge Township: Svenska Mission Kyrka I Sodre Maple Ridge
Spencer Brook: District No.1 School

Golf Courses:
Purple Hawk Country Club, Daily Fee (Cambridge, MN)

Breweries/Wineries/Distilleries:
Isanti Spirits (Isanti, MN)

Town Celebrations:
Braham Pie Day, Braham, MN (First Friday of August)
Isanti Rodeo & Jubilee Days, Isanti, MN (2nd Weekend in July)

Grant County: "The Good Life" Mural (Ashby), World's Largest Coot Statue (Ashby), Grant County Courthouse (Elbow Lake), Niemackl Lake Park (Herman), Grant County Fairgrounds (Herman), Former Art Deco Public School (Norcross), Sunset on the Soo Line Railroad (Wendell), Veteran's Memorial (Wendell)

Hennepin County: Normandale Japanese Garden (Bloomington), Mall of America (Bloomington), Heritage Center of Brooklyn Center (Brooklyn Center), Historic Champlin Sinclair (Champlin), The Historic Flying Red Horse Sign (Eden Prairie), former Excelsior Public School (Excelsior), Port of Excelsior Sign & Former Ticketbooth for Streetcar Boats (Excelsior), World's Largest Raspberry (Hopkins)

Hennepin County: Prospect Park "Witch's Hat" Water Tower (Minneapolis), *Spoonbridge and Cherry* at Minneapolis Sculpture Garden (Minneapolis), Prince Mural (Minneapolis), Hennepin County Courthouse (Minneapolis), Charles H. Burwell House (Minnetonka), St. Bonifacius Public Library (St. Bonifacius), Peavey-Haglin Experimental Concrete Grain Elevator (St. Louis Park), Model Railroad Display at Wayzata Depot Museum (Wayzata)

Houston County: Episcopal Church of the Holy Comforter (Brownsville), Fall-Themed Welcome Sign (Caledonia), Houston County Historical Society (Caledonia), Houston County Courthouse (Caledonia), Como Falls (Hokah), Eastern Screen Owl at the International Owl Center (Houston), Giants of the Earth Heritage Center (Spring Grove), Veteran's Memorial (Spring Grove)

Hubbard County: World's Largest Paul Bunyan Statue (Akeley), Little Free Library (Laporte), former Jailhouse (Laporte), World's Largest Tiger Muskie (Nevis), Mural (Nevis), The Park Theatre (Park Rapids), Downtown Mural (Park Rapids), Headwaters of the Mississippi River at Itasca State Park (Lake Itasca)

Isanti County: Braham Merchandise Mart Sign (Braham), Gardening Club Mannequin (Braham), Stone Turtle on Bench (Braham), West Riverside School (Cambridge), 1888 Historic Isanti County Courthouse (Cambridge), 1872 Mattson Norberg Cabin (Cambridge), Rendezvous Coffee (Isanti), Mural (Isanti)

ITASCA COUNTY
EST. 1849 - POPULATION: 45,014

"Itasca" is a name derived from the Latin phrase *veritas caput*, which literally translates to "truth" and "head." Henry Rowe Schoolcraft determined the true source of the Mississippi River to be Lake Itasca in 1832, although the lake is actually in Clearwater County.

BIGFORK, MN
POPULATION: 400 – CITY 355 OF 856 (6-20-25)
Damase "Uncle Tom" Neveaux squatted on the land at the big fork of the Rice and Big Fork Rivers from 1887 to 1900, until a legal notice was issued allowing widespread settlement of the territory. His cabin was the first structure built, and it served as a place for him to rest after finishing the day's logging. Other loggers and timbermen moved into the "Edge of the Wilderness" with time. In 1902, the Bigfork post office was established as the population grew to a level that warranted its existence. By the time the Minneapolis and Rainy River Railway was built in 1906, the area had undergone significant developments. On January 17, 1907, the new railroad town was incorporated. The Rajala Milling Company and Potlach Milling were major employers. Between 1920 and 1930, its population nearly doubled from 160 to 295. The growth encouraged the Works Progress Administration to build a Fieldstone municipal hall in 1936, one of several in Minnesota, to serve as a local government and community center. It was erected shortly after several park structures and facilities were built in nearby Scenic State Park using elements of the National Park Service's rustic architecture. Pine forests surround Sandwich and Coon Lakes and provide ample opportunities for hiking, fishing, camping, canoeing, and swimming, amongst other recreational activities. Other minor developments in the town's tourism include the wood-carved lumberjack at City Hall, a statue honoring Chief Busticogan of the Ojibwe, and the Uncle Dan Campbell lumberjack statue on US-71.

BOVEY, MN
POPULATION: 829 – CITY 416 OF 856 (7-17-25)
Grace: This town on the western end of the Mesabi Range is most famous for it. Minnesota's official state photograph of Charles Wilden was taken by Swedish-American photographer Eric Enstrom sometime between 1917 and 1920 in a sod house in Bovey; it depicts an elderly Wilden saying a prayer of thanks over a Bible and his meal. Wilden would have been one of many relatively early residents of Bovey village, incorporated on July 21, 1904. It was named for Charles A. Bovey by the merchants who wanted to capitalize on the extensive logging and mining activities in the area. Three hardware stores, one of which was the Bovey Mercantile (now Annabella's Antique Mall, home to thirty-plus small business owners and a former underground speakeasy and escape tunnel), grocery stores, general stores, a blacksmith shop, and as many as two dozen saloons once dominated the commercial establishments of the mining district. When the Canisteo Mine was opened after the Oliver Iron Mining Company found success in ore washing, the Orwell Mine followed. With the success came the Duluth, Missabe & Northern and the Great Northern lines. They intertwined near here and in Coleraine, Bovey's sister city to the west. In 1906, the Bovey School was built for $40,000; in 1919, it underwent remodeling. *The Bovey Record* newspaper was established. Further growth of the community warranted the construction of Bovey Village Hall in 1934-35, one of the first Public Works Administration projects in all of Minnesota. It and the Hartley Sugar Camp, a maple

syrup hobby farm constructed between 1904-09, are the town's two locations listed on the National Register. When the Canisteo Mine Pit (in reality, a series of 19 different mines) closed in 1985, it began to fill with water rapidly. Bovey, Coleraine, and Taconite have implemented drainage projects to prevent flooding in their communities, which is now exacerbated by the 4.8-mile-long lake. Richard Hongisto, a police chief for San Francisco, California, and Cleveland, Ohio, at different times in the 1970s, was born here in 1936.

CALUMET, MN
POPULATION: 334 – CITY 419 OF 856 (7-17-25)

Calumet is a French word derived from the Latin *calamus*, meaning "a reed." They attributed the name to Native American ceremonial pipes used to celebrate the end of wars or the signing of treaties. A post office bearing that name did not open until 1908, nor did the railroad town exist. However, multiple logging companies were present in the 1880s. The first of Calumet's men worked in this industry to provide for their families, but the real boom of Calumet came after the Hill Annex Mine was established. Oliver Iron Mining Company drilled here from 1901 to 1907. They opted to forfeit their lease to its holder, the Arthur Iron Mining Company. The Powers Improvement Company platted 480 acres of land adjacent to the mine, believing that a town would eventually form as a central meeting place for the social and economic needs of people in the area. They were correct in their assumption. The Duluth, Missabe, and Northern Railroad, built in 1906, two years before the plat was filed, brought significant resources and people. A cigar factory, a sauna, a blacksmith shop, a livery barn, an ice house, a butcher shop, and stores selling general goods, hardware, and even women's clothing (similar to a modern-day boutique) were established. The Hill Annex Mine grew with the city and produced 63 million tons of iron ore until its closure in 1978. A 1930s office building, maintenance shop, laboratory, and an even earlier truck repair shop and wooden water tower remained on the site, and the community club building was turned into a museum. It was listed on the National Register of Historic Places in 1986, designated as the Hill-Annex Mine State Park, and underwent several rehabilitation projects over the years. However, in June 2024, it was decided to resume mining operations at the site. Mike Antonovich, a professional hockey player who made appearances in 87 National Hockey League games, hails from Calumet.

COHASSET, MN
POPULATION: 2,689 – CITY 413 OF 856 (7-17-25)

Cohasset is a tale of two cities: one is itself, the other Bass Brook Township. Noted geographer Henry Gannett described the term "Cohasset," the eponymous name of Cohasset, Massachusetts, as meaning "place of pines." In 1892, a post office acquired the name, and when the Great Northern Railway village sought to separate from the township, they, too, called their newly incorporated village Cohasset. Incorporation took place on February 20, 1902; in 1916, Cohasset separated from Bass Brook Township and established its own government. In later years, specifically in 1957, the two reunited, and in 1975, they split. Seventeen years later, the two jointly incorporated as Cohasset. Aside from legal matters, the western suburb of Grand Rapids has grown substantially over the years. In 1970, the city had a population of only about 536 people, but by 2020, it had quintupled to 2,689 people. It is best known for Tioga Beach and its reclaimed-mine mountain biking trails, as well as swimming and fishing opportunities.

Restaurant Recommendation:
Florio's Grill and Tavern
105 NW Main St
Cohasset, MN 55721

COLERAINE, MN
POPULATION: 2,006 – CITY 415 OF 856 (7-17-25)

Thomas F. Cole, the President of the Oliver Mining Company, had the privilege of having this town named for him, thanks to his role in making the town the gem city of the Mesabi Iron Range. He chose to appoint John Campbell Greenway as general superintendent of the Mesabi Canisteo District and Mine, who convinced the directors of the U.S. Steel Corporation that a new town–separate from Bovey–should be organized. As a company-sponsored town, Coleraine flourished. Streets were designed to be wide and paved with curbs, and town lots were enormous. Many structurally firm businesses, churches, and schools were built from stone to ensure they would last. Potential residents were screened to ensure the town remained clean and free from illicit activities. With the arrival of branches of the Great Northern and the Duluth, Missabe & Northern Railroads and its incorporation as a village on April 20, 1909, the future of the town was secured. It already had 1,613 residents according to the 1910 U.S. Decennial Census, a number not again achieved until 2010. Five of its most historic structures were built within a half-decade of its incorporation: one of the largest churches on the Mesabi Range, the 1908-09 Coleraine Methodist Episcopal Church; the Church of the Good Shepherd, built in 1908 by U.S. Steel from logs; the 1910 Coleraine City Hall; the 1911 General Superintendent's House, built for managers of the mining company, and the 1912 Neoclassical style Coleraine Carnegie Library. The 1908 General Office of the Canisteo District was the sixth National Register of Historic Places (NRHP) location until its demolition in 2013. Traditional mining of Coleraine's beloved Canisteo Mine ceased in 1980, when economic conditions deteriorated and operations there became unprofitable. A hidden gem of the region lies within Ravenstone Abbey (the old Methodist Church), where lords and ladies can enjoy potent elixirs—that is, coffee and booze—and axe throwing in a Renaissance-style environment.

DEER RIVER, MN
POPULATION: 909 – CITY 350 OF 856 (6-20-25)

Hundreds, if not thousands, of loggers dominated Itasca County and its heavily timbered lands long before Deer River was so much as a thought. John Richardson may have been the first European to traverse present-day Deer River in 1861. Still, it would be another fifteen years before any surveys were made. August A. Chase, Mike J. Deering, Thomas R. Armstrong, and dozens of others homesteaded and filed claims. Just after the turn of the century, Deer River was at the junction of the Great Northern and the Minneapolis & Rainy River Railroads. The post office had arrived in 1893, and on January 22, 1898, the town was incorporated. There were at least three hotels, three stores, a depot, restaurants, and a school at the time, but surprisingly, no churches. Thirty-five million feet of logs were being exported annually. Rough and rowdy was the name and the game of its foremost citizens. Several saloons were in operation, and in 1898, Kelly's Saloon hosted a fight between Tom Murray and Jack Cross, to which residents could pay a dollar to attend. Governor David Marston Clough put an end to the activities. Despite an epidemic of pneumonia and failed plans for a large stockyard, Deer River found a way to prosper after moving the townsite from a swamp to the junction of the railroads. By the 1920s, the *Itasca News* newspaper, a creamery, a hospital, and pairs of banks and sawmills had been established. At this point, the population surpassed one thousand residents for the first time. Deer River was later the site of a World War II prisoner-of-war camp, where inmates were forced to log the forests. From April 1982 to the early 2010s, Deer River's most historically significant point of interest was the Itasca Lumber Company Superintendent's House, the employee residence of the region's largest lumber company. A large muskie greets fishermen and travelers alike on Main Street, Deer River.

EFFIE, MN
POPULATION: 109 – CITY 356 OF 856 (6-20-25)
Effie was one of a few towns established on the Minneapolis and Rainy River Railway between Deer River and Littlefork, not far from International Falls. When the United States Postal Service established a branch office here in 1903, it allowed Postmaster Eva R. Wenaus to choose its name. Because the post office was hosted in her husband's (O. R.'s) store, the two decided to name it in honor of their daughter, Effie Wenaus. Stores, a sawmill, and potato warehouses allowed Effie to incorporate on June 10, 1940. Still, its post office was eventually discontinued in 1991 and replaced with a rural station. A six-foot mosquito statue was placed on Hwy 38 to make travelers do a double-take as they passed through little Effie, home to the annual "Effie North Star Stampede" rodeo held annually the last weekend of July. Little American Falls is a nearby point of interest located on the Big Fork River.

GRAND RAPIDS, MN ★☆
POPULATION: 11,126 – CITY 422 OF 856 (7-18-25)
In a county dominated by the mining industry and "The Range," one would expect the establishment of the largest town in Itasca County to be largely intertwined with its most notable features. However, a mining company did not establish Grand Rapids, nor was it founded because of its large taconite reserves. Instead, it began as a logging community, with its industries focusing mainly on the production of paper and wood products. Established on the 3.5-mile rapids of the Mississippi River, now hidden beneath the Blandin Paper Mill's dam, the City of Grand Rapids has always been an essential shipping point for Minnesota's logging industry as a whole. It was founded in 1877 (three years after the establishment of its post office, headed by the town's first hotel owner, Lowe G. Seavey) and incorporated in 1881. Eleven years later, it won the county seat war over neighboring La Prairie, becoming the county's leading town. Its significant victory can largely be attributed to the extension of the Duluth and Winnipeg Railroad (later taken over by the Great Northern) through the townsite. The success of Grand Rapids as a trade center gave its city council the confidence to fund the construction of the Richardsonian Romanesque Central School building in 1895, one of the very first high schools in northern Minnesota and the city's only site listed on the National Register of Historic Places. It closed in 1972 as a school but was restored in 1984 for alternative commerce uses. Charles K. Blandin's paper mill opened in 1910 as a successor to another mill. Blandin's enterprise played a significant role in bringing extensive improvements to Grand Rapids. By the 1920s, there were at least six churches, two creameries, two banks, bath, shingle, and copper supply mills, a machine shop, a hospital, a Carnegie library, several storefronts, and three newspapers called *The Grand Rapids Herald-Review* (est. 1894), the *Itasca County Budget* (in 1902), and the *Farm Bureau News* (in 1921). Itasca Community College was founded as a local institution of higher learning in 1922 and was later renamed Minnesota North College-Itasca. That same year saw the birth of Judy Garland (whose

birthplace home can still be toured as a museum), the internationally renowned actress best known for her portrayal of Dorothy Gale in the 1939 classic film *The Wizard of Oz*. Garland has brought great fame to Grand Rapids alongside many other individuals: Hugh Beaumont, the actor noted for his role as Ward Cleaver *in Leave It to Beaver*; Granville Van Dusen, the voice actor of Race Bannon in *The New Adventures of Jonny Quest* and other similar Hanna-Barbera Productions; Norman Ornstein, a political scientist; Lois Hall, a long-term actress active from 1948 to 2006; Bill Baker, a gold-medalist hockey defenseman in the 1980 Lake Placid Olympic Games; Jon Casey, an NHL goaltender with 425 game appearances; Alex Goligoski, an NHL defenseman from 2007 to 2024 with over one-thousand game appearances; Trent Klatt, an NHL right winger from 1992 to 2004 with 782 game appearances; Janelle Pierzina, a reality show contestant on four seasons of *Big Brother*; Jeff Nielsen, an NHL right winger, and Don Lucia, a two-time NCAA national champion head coach or the University of Minnesota's men's ice hockey team. The Myles Reif Performing Arts Center, the Judy Garland Museum, and Birthplace Home, a reconstructed logging camp at The Forest History Center (a living history museum complete with era-correct interpreters), and Paul Bunyan's Adirondack Chair, amongst countless lakes, parks, and recreational activities, bring tens of thousands of visitors to the town every year. The Judy Garland Museum is most famous for being the site of the infamous 2005 heist of Garland's ruby-red slippers, although in modern times it also tells the extensive story of her career and features artifacts from her life. It is attached to the Children's Discovery Museum, which has worked with the local Ojibwe tribe, SuperiorChoice Credit Union, and the Judy Garland Museum to bring unique, hands-on exhibits (many with a "Wizard of Oz" or logging theme) to visiting children and families. At the Forest History Center, visitors can take a pontoon ride on the Mississippi River in the summertime, a horse-drawn sled ride through the snowy forests in the winter, or marvel at the logging camp and accompanying exhibits at the museum.

Restaurant Recommendation:
Rapids Brewing Company
214 Pokegama Ave
Grand Rapids, MN 55744

Restaurant Recommendation:
Tikes Trophy Sausage & Fresh Meats
19457 US-169 S
Grand Rapids, MN 55744

KEEWATIN, MN
POPULATION: 984 – CITY 421 OF 856 (7-17-25)
When the National Steel Pellet Taconite plant (owned by U.S. Steel since May 2003 and renamed Keewatin Taconite, a.k.a. Keetac) was completed in 1974 following a joint investment of several mining companies, it solidified Keewatin as the site of one of the largest taconite steel pellet mining operations in the world. Like other towns in the region, it was the forests that initially attracted the first workers; however, it was the mining interests of the Pillsbury, Longyear, and Bennett families that enabled its permanent existence. They, particularly the Pillsbury Family (through the Sargent Land Company), helped to incorporate the village near the railroad. The St. Paul Mine began operations in 1905, and the following year, Keewatin was established. Apollo was chosen as its first name, but it was decided that the name "Keewatin" was more appropriate. It is Ojibwe for "the north wind." Next came the Bray, the Mississippi, and the Bennett Mines, which were the earliest exporters of ore on the newly laid Great

Northern Railroad (which arrived in 1909). The Mesabi Chief Iron Mine was opened in 1927. It ultimately became the largest of all Keewatin-based mines, shipping over 6.5 million tons of iron ore by 1940. Keewatin then boasted a population of nearly 2,000 residents, almost double its current numbers. Two significant points of interest at the time were the *Keewatin Chronicle* newspaper and a public library with well over 6,000 books. Gino "Mr. Patriot" Cappelletti, a five-time All-Star, five-time AFL scoring leader, and the 1964 American Football League MVP, attended Keewatin High School and grew up in the community. The former head baseball coach of the University of Minnesota from 1982 to 2024, John Anderson, also has ties to Keewatin.

LA PRAIRIE, MN
POPULATION: 653 – CITY 414 OF 856 (7-17-25)
La Prairie was most likely named after the Prairie River, a tributary of the Mississippi, which is best known for the 1991 Enbridge Line 3 pipeline spill that released 1.7 million gallons of oil into the ecosystem. It was the worst inland oil spill in U.S. history. Incorporated on December 29, 1890, the Village of La Prairie's post office operated for less than thirty years between 1890 and the 1910s, but it had surviving businesses on and off for much longer. The little Duluth and Winnipeg Railroad logging community was called Nealsville for Neal Carr, the operator of a steamboat landing before it was renamed Saginaw, then La Prairie. On November 19, 1892, it lost the county seat election to Grand Rapids despite having some railroad facilities and even a hospital. Until the 1950s, La Prairie had a population of only double digits, then grew rapidly to 243 in 1960, 413 by 1970, and 665 by 2010, becoming an eastern suburb of Grand Rapids. The Frank Gran Farmstead is an excellent example of an agricultural farm that paid significant dividends for its Finnish immigrant owner after the local logging industry mostly came to a halt.

MARBLE, MN
POPULATION: 610 – CITY 418 OF 856 (7-17-25)
One of many mining towns on the Iron Range, Marble reached its largest recorded population of 887 in 1910, shortly after its incorporation as a village on April 20, 1909. The Duluth, Missabe & Northern Railroad, along with the founding of the Canisteo, Walker, Holman, and Hill mines, drove the town's early growth. Still, its first homesteader was Albert F. Gross of Duluth in 1888. His property was bought up by the Gross-Marble Mining Company, of which one of the proprietors was R. N. Marble. With the help of John C. Greenway of the Oliver Mining Company, a company town was established between 1907-08 and named in honor of Mr. Marble. Construction on homes and businesses began, and the tent town was replaced by a handsome community that even included 20 acres for a public park. Another piece of lodging, the Oliver Boarding House, built in 1909, remains an NRHP-listed property, reminding people of the impact the Oliver Iron Mining Company had on developing the town.

NASHWAUK, MN
POPULATION: 970 – CITY 420 OF 856 (7-17-25)
NASA's first director of the Manned Spacecraft Center (now known as the Lyndon B. Johnson Space Center), Robert R. Gilruth, spent the first ten years of his life in the mining community of Nashwauk. Located about halfway between Hibbing and Grand Rapids, Nashwauk was established as the very first mining town in Itasca County when the Hawkins Mine began shipping ore in 1902. The Mississippi Land Company gave forty acres to the Nashwauk Realty Company for its platting, and a year later, in 1903, it was incorporated. Its name was taken from the Nashwaak River and the

accompanying village near Fredericton, New Brunswick, Canada. The river's name was, in turn, derived from an Algonquin word meaning "land between." Lines of the Great Northern Railroad, board sidewalks, waterworks, electric street lights, and a state-of-the-art sewer system were all in place by 1910. In two decades, Nashwauk's population grew to 2,555. Unfortunately, the Hawkins Mine ceased operations in 1962, and with its closure, the village's primary industry began to dissolve. Early records indicate that Nashwauk's first ordinance, passed by the city council, regulated the sale and consumption of liquor in the town's then twenty-one saloons.

SQUAW LAKE, MN
POPULATION: 98 – CITY 352 OF 856 (6-20-25)
One of Itasca County's smallest communities welcomed its post office in 1923 and incorporation as a village on December 17, 1940. The Ojibwe were the first people to live here before Europeans took over the region. Still, when fur traders and loggers came in, it was deemed necessary to start a town on what was then called Squaw Lake. *Squaw*, widely considered a derogatory term in Ojibwe, was not considered a slur when the post office was named a century ago. However, in 1995, the adjacent Squaw Lake was renamed Nature's Lake by the Minnesota Legislature after two students from Cass Lake-Bena High School led the effort to rename nineteen geographical locations throughout Minnesota. Despite a 1999 meeting with the Squaw Lake City Council that led to an attempt to petition for a name change, the movement did not advance. Squaw Lake is remembered for its early CCC camps and for the Old Cut Foot Sioux Ranger Station (on Hatchery Road in the Chippewa National Forest), built in 1904. A large Canadian Goose was dedicated on Hwy 46 in 1992 on behalf of Geese Unlimited Inc. This nonprofit organization was founded here.

TACONITE, MN
POPULATION: 651 – CITY 417 OF 856 (7-17-25)
With all the mining activity in the Iron Range of Minnesota, it would be surprising if there were not at least one town in the region named in honor of the low-grade iron ore: Taconite. Taconite, as a mineral, is a sedimentary rock made up of at least 15% iron and primarily magnetite, hematite, and chert. The experimental Diamond Mine and a corresponding washing plant (the first of its kind in the western part of the Mesabi Range) were early developments, but it was the Oliver Mining Company's Holman Mine that warranted the founding of the town. They laid out the townsite near the 1906 post office and ensured its incorporation by April 20, 1909, so that it could prosper as one of several trade points on the Great Northern and the Duluth, Missabe & Northern Railroads. Two railroads gave Taconite the nickname "Hub of the Nation" for their importance in sending the ore on its way to the Twin Cities or the harbors on the North Shore. When mining operations ceased, several of them were consolidated into what is now called the Cannisteo Mine pit. James "Slim Troumbly," a hockey legend and participant in the 1950 Men's World Championships with Team USA, was born here.

WARBA, MN
POPULATION: 168 – CITY 392 OF 856 (6-25-25)
The southeasternmost of Itasca County's incorporated towns is Warba, which underwent several name changes from 1891 to 1911. Siding No. 8 and Dickson's Spur (or the lumberjack Mr. Dickson) were the first names for the Great Northern Railroad's logging site from 1891 to 1898, before it was changed to Verna. A second village, called Feeley, was named after Thomas J. Feeley, a sawmill owner, and was a neighboring community. Its post office was the precursor to the "Warba" office. Still, it

was not called that until 1910 when the postal service began to confuse Feeley for Foley, the seat of government of Benton County. A. A. Hall suggested the Ojibwe name *warbasibi*, likely meaning "soon." The name was corrupted into Warba, which stuck with both the post office and the railroad. Warba was incorporated in the 1920s and recorded its peak population of 183 people at the dawn of the 21st century.

ZEMPLE, MN
POPULATION: 78 – CITY 351 OF 856 (6-20-25)
Practically nothing remains of Zemple, a town named for village president R. T. Zempel, which was the former site of the roundhouse of the Minneapolis & Rainy River Railway. A store, a church, a school, a planing mill, a veneer mill, a box mill, and a sawmill all flourished in its early days. Lumber extraction activities accounted for most of Zemple's early industries. The mill was first owned by the Pillsbury-Watkins Company in 1903, then by the Joyce-Pillsbury Company in 1904, the Deer River Lumber Company in 1906, and ultimately by the Itasca Lumber Company, which operated it until its closure in 1921. The school closed in 1928 as well, and just as Zemple had started, it began to succumb to the overwhelming capabilities of its immediate neighbor to the north, Deer River. Its population dropped from 284 in 1920 to 164 in 1930, and then to just 87 by 1950.

Unincorporated/Ghost Towns: Alvwood, Ball Club, Bass Lake, Bear River, Bergville, Blackberry, Bowstring, Dora Lake, Dunbar, Goodland, Grattan, Gunn, Houpt, Inger, Jessie Lake, Mack, Marcell, Martin, Max, Orth, Pengilly, Pomroy, Rosy, Spring Lake, Suomi, Swan River, Talmoon, Togo, Wawina, Wirt

National Register of Historic Places:
Bigfork: Bigfork Village Hall, Scenic State Park CCC/Rustic Style Service Yard, Scenic State Park CCC/WPA/Rustic Style Historic Resources
Bovey: Bovey Village Hall, Hartley Sugar Camp
Calumet: Hill Annex Mine
Coleraine: Canisteo District General Office Building, Church of the Good Shepherd, Coleraine Carnegie Library, Coleraine City Hall, Coleraine Methodist Episcopal Church, General Superintendent's House
Grand Rapids: Central School
Inger: Winnibigoshish Lake Dam
La Prairie: Frank Gran Farmstead
Marble: Oliver Boarding House
Marcell Township: Marcell Ranger Station
Squaw Lake: Old Cut Foot Sioux Ranger Station

Golf Courses:
Blueberry Hills Golf Course, Daily Fee (Deer River, MN)
Eagle Ridge Golf Course, Municipal (Coleraine, MN)
Pokegama Golf Course, Municipal (Grand Rapids, MN)
Swan Lake Country Club, Daily Fee (Pengilly, MN)

Breweries/Wineries/Distilleries:
Klockow Brewing Company (Grand Rapids, MN)
Rapids Brewing Company (Grand Rapids, MN)

Town Celebrations:
Farmers' Day, Bovey, MN (Labor Day Weekend)
Judy Garland Festival, Grand Rapids, MN (3rd Full Weekend of June)
Kids and Cars in the Park Car Show, Calumet, MN (4th Saturday in August)
St. Urho's Day, Squaw Lake, MN (Weekend Closest to March 16th)

JACKSON COUNTY
EST. 1857 - POPULATION: 9,989

Not named for President Andrew Jackson as many would expect, this county of 10,000 residents was named for Henry Jackson, the first merchant in St. Paul in modern-day Ramsey County.

ALPHA, MN
POPULATION: 97 – CITY 77 OF 856 (3-25-25)
This town of 97 residents on the eastern border of Jackson County was platted on the Chicago, Milwaukee, St. Paul & Pacific Railroad in 1895 in Wisconsin Township. It was called Wisconsin, Earl, and Irwin before it was named Alpha. "Alpha" was named after the letter A in the Greek alphabet. Ironically, its name does not accurately reflect its current status as the second-smallest municipality in the county. The post office under that name was established in 1895, but an earlier mail stop was in operation as early as 1878 when the Southern Minnesota Railroad was built through the vicinity. After a short period of growth in which it saw the construction of an elevator, a lumberyard, a church, a schoolhouse, and two general stores, it was incorporated on July 3, 1899. Its peak population was 261 in the 1920s.

HERON LAKE, MN
POPULATION: 602 – CITY 81 OF 856 (3-25-25)
Many Austrians and Germans came to Heron Lake in the early 1870s, which was named by surveyors of the Sioux City & St. Paul Railroad for the vast populations of black-crowned night herons and great blue herons that nested on the shores of the nearby lake. The tracks were laid in the fall of 1871, and that following spring, the townsite was platted by Alex L. Beach. Many settlers had preemptively made their claims where they speculated the right-of-way would come through, but John T. Smith and C. H. Carroll were the lucky winners who became the first to establish a general store on the first lot sold in the town. Up went the Heron Lake depot, Dr. R. R. Foster's drug store, John Robson's Pioneer Hotel, and the Crocker Brothers & Lamoreaux lumberyard, and thus Heron Lake's status as a future blooming railway village would be confirmed. Several dozen more business interests were organized, and eventually, Heron Lake became a division point for the Omaha Railroad's (later ultimately owned by the Chicago & Northwestern) main line and Black Hills branch line. It was incorporated as a village on November 17, 1881. As of 1887, the accomplishments of Heron Lake were as follows: to the south of the tracks, a tow mill, a lumber yard, four general merchandise stores, a hotel, a bank, a drug store, a meat market, a saloon, the La Grosse House hotel, a blacksmith shop, a barber shop, a public school, a creamery, a Methodist Episcopal church, and the post office; on the right-of-way, the depot, coal sheds, and a hay press; and to north of the line, the Hoffman House hotel, the Chapman House hotel, a livery, and a Catholic Church. The latter church was replaced by a much grander edifice in 1920-21, the $150,000 Neoclassical and Baroque Revival-style Sacred Heart Catholic Church. It was designed by Albert E. Parkinson and Bernard J. Dockendorff and placed on the National Register of Historic Places on March 20, 1989. From 1870 to 1895, the post office branch was called Heron Lake; from 1895 to 1899, it was called just Heron; and from 1899 to 1900, it was called Heron Lake again. Garland Buckeye, who played professional football for various pioneer leagues and baseball in the MLB between 1918 and 1928, hails from Heron Lake. From 1934 to 1937, it was the childhood home of the 42nd Vice President of the United States, Walter F. Mondale.

Restaurant Recommendation:
Nenas Bar and Grill
1011 1st St
Heron Lake, MN 56137

JACKSON, MN ★☆
POPULATION: 3,323 – CITY 78 OF 856 (3-25-25)
In July 1856, William, George, and Charles Wood established a log trading post on the west side of the Des Moines River and named it "Springfield" after three dozen additional settlers staked their claims nearby. Growth was minimal due to a disastrous winter, and those who stayed through the cold did not fare well when spring arrived. On March 26, 1857, they were ambushed by Inkpaduta, the Chief of the Wahpekute Dakota, and his band. Seven people perished, and those who remained fled to avoid exposure to a potential second attack. Two months later, the Minnesota legislature elected to organize the territory as Jackson County and renamed it from Springfield to Jackson in honor of Henry Jackson (the first merchant in St. Paul). It was named the county seat, and a post office was relocated here from Pisa, Brown County, in 1858. Continued attacks by the indigenous and the advent of the American Civil War left Jackson and the surrounding area desolate until the conclusion of both wars. Jackson was finally platted in 1866 and incorporated on April 19, 1881, at which point it had a population of over five hundred residents. The Chicago, Milwaukee & St. Paul Railway built a small branch line off their main line extending into B. W. Ashley's land (as of 1887) to assist with trade in the area. Lumber yards, hotels, livery stables, banks, hardware stores, and numerous business houses were prevalent at this point, and within 30 years, Jackson had a population of about 2,000 people. As of 1915, the county seat had good schools, plentiful churches, flour and town mills, three grain elevators, creameries, three banks, a hospital, an opera house, a public library, a feed mill, and brick, tile, and cement block works. Thirty-one properties, most of which hosted early Jackson businesses, built between 1880 and 1928, were grouped for preservation as the Jackson Commercial Historic District and listed on the National Register in December 1987. Other community landmarks are the District No. 92 School, built in 1906 and one of two octagonal schoolhouses left in Minnesota, and the Jackson County Courthouse, a structure completed by Charles Skooglun in the Neoclassical architecture style between 1908-09. The Bedford limestone Beaux-Arts building cost $117,435 to complete. Fort Belmont welcomes visitors to explore an 1873 log cabin and stockade, a blacksmith shop and home, the 1902 Delafield Lutheran Church, and an accompanying museum. Ashley Park is the site of Jackson County's oldest structure, the Olson-Slaabakken cabin, the Jackson County Fair Village, its historic home, church, and business houses. Minnesota West Community and Technical College has one of its five campuses in Jackson, with the others in Canby, Granite Falls, Pipestone, and Worthington. Notable people who hail from the city include Stephen Censky, the 13th United States Deputy Secretary of Agriculture from October 2017 to November 2020; Milton C. Portmann, a pioneer professional football player and World War I veteran; Jeffrey Bullock, the president of the University of Dubuque since 1998; playwright and author Gary Amdahl; decorated chemist Willis H. Flygare, the inventor of the Fourier-transform microwave spectrometer; Walter Halloran, an assistant in the exorcism of Roland Doe in 1949 that inspired William Peter Blatty to write the 1971 horror novel *The Exorcist*, and David Ellefson, the bassist and backing vocalist for the band Megadeth off and on since 1982. From April 2017 to

July 2018, Ellefson hosted the Museum of Deth at the Ellefson Coffee Company, which displayed walls of memorabilia of the band.

LAKEFIELD, MN
POPULATION: 1,735 – CITY 79 OF 856 (3-25-25)

A state with the nickname "Land of 10,000 Lakes" would not be complete without a town that approximately reflects what Minnesota is: a field of lakes, or "Lakefield." Anders R. Kilen gave the lake a proud name, which has since been subdivided into four basins: Duck Lake, North Heron, South Heron, and North Marsh. Kilen was the progressive Norwegian immigrant who located, platted, and purchased the initial townsite from the St. Paul and Sioux City Railroad Company for $420. For years, he had thought the area would be perfect for a town because of its numerous natural resources and high elevation, and so in the summer of 1879, he set out to fulfill that dream. From his purchase on July 1 to September of that year, he convinced the Southern Minnesota Railroad to build on the land, had it surveyed into lots by James E. Palmer, and welcomed oodles of settlers to their new home. The post office began in 1880 in the general store of Martin A. Foss. By the end of the first year, he was joined by a lumber yard, Barney Foelinger's saloon, John Kilen's hotel, the Chesterson Brothers general store, and Larud and Morland and Company's hardware stores. On September 1, 1887, it was incorporated. In that year, its lines extended to have a bank, two drug stores, a harness shop, a millinery store, two hardware stores, three general stores, a grocery store, two farm implement stores, a saloon, a barber shop, a blacksmith shop, a butcher shop, a lumber yard, the Lakefield Hotel, the Grand Central Hotel, and the *Lakefield Standard* newspaper. A public school was located in the public square at the northern end of Main Street. Lakefield's most famous hotel, the Winter Hotel, was built in 1895 by Grant Winter, listed on the National Register in September 1988, and unfortunately razed only two years after its nomination. Several Catholic and Protestant churches were located in the Lakefield area in its pioneer days, the first of which was the Belmont Lutheran Church of Belmont Township (1867), followed by the Bethlehem Lutheran Church of Lakefield (1870), and the Delafield Evangelical Lutheran Church of Delafield Township (1873). Despite fires in 1900 and 1904, Lakefield grew from 1,000 residents in 1910 to 2,000 in 1920 and has enjoyed a relatively stable population since the 1940s. It had a population of 1,651 in 1950 and as many as 1,845 in 1980. Lakefield is home to the Jackson County Historical Society and Museum, which seeks to preserve local history.

OKABENA, MN
POPULATION: 203 – CITY 80 OF 856 (3-25-25)

Okabena is a Dakota-Sioux word meaning "the nesting places of herons," an etymology consistent with several other communities near Heron Lake. Located in September 1879 in West Heron Township on the Chicago, Milwaukee & St. Paul (then the Southern Minnesota) Railroad, the name was put into use by both the railroad and the postal service (the following year), nearly eight years after the "Okabena" of Nobles County had changed its name to "Worthington." The Okabena post office operated from 1880 to 1884, closed for nearly a decade, and reopened in 1892, once it was clear the area's settlers needed that mail service. K. C. Jackson was the initial postmaster. Until 1897, it was essentially just the railroad station and the post office until Henry J. Schumacher purchased the townsite and invested substantially in its infrastructure and promotion. He built an 18-room hotel, and over the next several years, the lumberyard, blacksmith shop, stores, A. S. Hyde & Company elevator, the Okabena Creamery, and a brick and tile company, amongst others, followed. Five years before it was incorporated on July 30, 1938, the most significant single event in

Okabena history occurred when the Okabena Bank was robbed on May 19, 1933. The burglars, first thought to be Tony, Floyd, and Mildred Strain, unloaded machine-gun rounds into local businesses and homes as they made off with $2,500 in cash (then a relatively large amount, as it was then the Great Depression Era). They were apprehended and sent to rot in prison until the mid-1940s, when they were released following extensive investigations that proved them innocent. To the shock of many, the real perpetrators were the notorious outlaws Bonnie & Clyde, who were exposed when their family members ghost-wrote a book about the duo's escapades and specifically mentioned the Okabena robbery by name.

WILDER, MN
POPULATION: 62 – CITY 82 OF 856 (3-25-25)
Amherst Holcomb Wilder, a philanthropist and wealthy businessman who was instrumental in connecting Minnesota with other states via a system of railways and who had several engagements in the transportation industry as a whole, was honored in 1885 when D. G. Gunn named this town for him. Some accounts report that the city was established as early as November 1871, but was not platted until 1885, when the Sioux City & St. Paul Railroad arrived. A post office, a shoe shop, an elevator, a hay depot, and a passenger depot were some of the initial places of note around Wilder, but it was most interestingly designated as the site of the Breck School in 1886. The college for farm kids was strategically designed to serve as an alternative to public school education at a low cost of $110 per school year. The campus grounds were enormous, taking up over thirty large lots, or the equivalent of 360 individual building lots. As of 1887, the only campus building was the college in the southeastern corner. Wilder had a maximum population of 174 at its inaugural Census in 1900, most likely due to the college's operations. When the school closed in 1909, Wilder's population halved by the 1910 Census (to 95 residents, a decrease of -45.4%). It was moved to Saint Paul in 1916, and as of January 2025, the Episcopal Church-affiliated college-prep school still welcomes students in Golden Valley, Minnesota. Its most famous attendee was Franklin Clarence Mars from 1899 to 1900, who would go on to found the Mars Candy Company, now best known for its Snickers Bar, Milky Way, and line of M&M's candies. It is the fourth-largest privately owned company in the country.

Unincorporated/Ghost Towns: Bergen, Fish Lake, Miloma, Petersburg, Rost, Sioux Valley, Spafford

National Register of Historic Places:
Heron Lake: Church of the Sacred Heart (Catholic)
Jackson: District No.92 School, George M. Moore Farmstead, Jackson Commercial Historic District, Jackson County Courthouse

Golf Courses:
Jackson Golf Club, Daily Fee (Jackson, MN)
Loon Lake Golf Course, Daily Fee (Jackson, MN)
Valley Brook Golf Course, Daily Fee (Lakefield, MN)

Town Celebrations:
Blue Heron Days, Heron Lake, MN (Last Weekend in June)
Independence Day Celebration, Okabena, MN (4th of July)
Lakefield Summerfest, Lakefield, MN (3rd Weekend in June)

KANABEC COUNTY
EST. 1858 - POPULATION: 16,032

After being partitioned from Pine County on March 13, 1858, the Ojibwe name for the Snake River, *Kanabecosippi*, was adopted for the new territory.

GRASSTON, MN
POPULATION: 154 – CITY 456 OF 856 (7-20-25)
Grasston, home to as many as 239 people in the 1920s and as few as 105 in the 2000s, shares its name with Grass Lake township and the tall, shallow marsh grass found in the vicinity of Grass Lake (the body of water). The Great Northern Railway played a crucial role in helping to grow the community and bring in essential infrastructure, including a two-story brick schoolhouse, a bank, a confectionery, a feed mill and elevator, the Swan Hotel, and a post office, which arrived in 1899. Annie Swan was the postmaster. It was platted on June 6, 1899, and was almost named Swanville for its principal landowner, John A. Swan. When he was told that another Swanville already existed in Morrison County, he suggested the name Oxenville, but the railroad chose Grasston instead. Grasston became incorporated on October 21, 1907.

MORA, MN ★☆
POPULATION: 3,665 – CITY 458 OF 856 (7-20-25)
It would be hard for anyone to miss Mora's 22-foot-tall Dalecarlian horse, a significant symbol of the pride local settlers still hold for their Swedish ancestry. Mora also boasts of a Mora clock, a type of grandfather clock specific to Mora, Sweden, the town's namesake. Platted in May 1882 by Myron R. Kent (also the first postmaster) and named by Israel Israelson for his hometown, the community was explicitly established to succeed Brunswick as the county seat. Alvin J. Conger had a trading post nearby as early as 1859 at Spring Brook Hill, located two miles southeast of the present-day townsite; it was abandoned in 1861. He returned two decades later to build a hotel upon learning of Mora's newfound importance within Kanabec County. The Great Northern Railroad sent its first construction locomotive into town on October 27, 1882; it was the first of many engines that would go through the area after Mora was connected to the railroad's Hinckley branch off the Minneapolis-St. Cloud main line. In 1894, architects Buechner and Jacobson designed the Romanesque-style Kanabec County Courthouse, featuring a prominent four-story center tower. A pair of other noteworthy sites in the vicinity are the Ann River Logging Company Farm, established in 1880 as part of a significant area logging operation, and the C. E. Williams House, a 1902 Queen Anne home. Vasaloppet USA, the largest annual cross-country skiing event in Minnesota, is held on the first Saturday of February as the town's premier event. Alice Frost, an actress known for her participation in Orson Welles's Mercury Theatre in New York City; Gladys Nordenstrom, a well-known contemporary classical composer; and Henry Rines, the 15th Minnesota State Treasurer have ties to Mora.

OGILVIE, MN
POPULATION: 388 – CITY 459 OF 856 (7-20-25)
One of Minnesota's most commonly misspelled town names (as was the subject of many articles in July 2023, when the Minnesota Department of Transportation mistakenly flipped the first 'i' with the 'l'), Ogilvie, got its unique nomenclature from Oric Ogilvie Whited. He purchased the land and filed a town plat on July 18, 1889, changing the name from Groundhouse to Ogilvie. The Hersey Lumber Company owned the

rights to the land for logging starting in 1854, and in the 1880s, it became well-known throughout the region for Noah Adams's sawmill and store. A post office called Fisk was established in 1889 but closed that same year; it was succeeded by an office called Groundhouse from 1895 to 1899, and then renamed Ogilvie on the turn of the century, January 1, 1900. Various early businesses of note also included the Nelson Brothers Store, Congers Drug Store, Holgrem's Hardware Store, and the Farmers and Merchants Bank. One of Minnesota's earliest surviving reinforced concrete towers, built in 1918, stands tall as a sentinel over the small city, serving as its lone NRHP-designated location. Ogilvie Raceway, a ⅜-mile dirt-clay oval race track, opened in 2009; the Ogilvie Museum and Elmer Laitala's ten-foot-tall, fire-breathing dragon sculpture, nicknamed "Rusty," highlight other points of interest. The 1980 College Football Hall of Fame inductee Clayton Tonnemaker, who also made the 1953 NFL Pro Bowl as a member of the Green Bay Packers, was born here on June 8, 1928.

QUAMBA, MN
POPULATION: 107 – CITY 450 OF 856 (7-20-25)
Famous for being the only city in Minnesota to start with the letter 'Q,' Quamba acquired its unique name from officials of the Great Northern Railroad. It was derived from the Ottawa word *zhashkwiimbaakmigaa*, meaning "mudhole." The more localized Ojibwe tribe called it *Basa'igani-ziibiwishenying*, which translates to "by the creek to square Cedar timbers." European settlers named the creek that the railroad tracks crossed Mud Creek because it was often muddy. Oric Ogilvie Whited platted the little community in 1901, and a post office arrived that year. Andrew J. Edstrom was the postmaster. It operated until 1903, then reopened in 1906, closed again in 1916, and reopened once more between 1917 and 1966. At that point, it was converted into a rural station. A school, the Quamba Baptist Church, a lumber yard, a blacksmith shop, a hardware store, a hotel and pool room, the Farmers Co-op Creamery, the Quamba Auto Company, and the Quamba State Bank were all operational by the early 1920s during the heyday of the community. Quamba was incorporated as a village in 1952.

Braham is only partially located in Kanabec County (see Isanti County).

Unincorporated/Ghost Towns: Bronson, Brunswick, Coin, Fisk, Grass Lake, Heiden, Hillman, Kroschel, Lewis Lake, Mull, Raritan, Riverdale, Warman, Woodland

National Register of Historic Places:
Mora: C. E. Williams House, Kanabec County Courthouse, Ann River Logging Company Farm
Ogilvie: Ogilvie Water Tower

Golf Courses:
Spring Brook Golf Course, Daily Fee (Mora, MN)

Breweries/Wineries/Distilleries:
BeerClub Brewing (Mora, MN)
Northern Hollow Winery (Grasston, MN)

KANDIYOHI COUNTY
EST. 1858 - POPULATION: 43,732

Kandiyohi County's name comes from a Dakota Sioux phrase that very roughly translates to "for where the buffalo fish come through."

ATWATER, MN
POPULATION: 1,124 – CITY 184 OF 856 (4-15-25)
Summit Lake, Gennissee Station, and Stockholm were various names for this community before "Atwater" was settled upon by the St. Paul and Pacific Railroad to honor E. D. Atwater, the secretary of the land department of that company. Atwater and its commercial district began in 1869 when railroad contractor Christopher L. Peterson started his store. Within two years, G. B. Dahl had set up shop as town blacksmith, Louis LaFoe opened a hotel, McKinney and DeTar stocked a store with hardware, Salter established a lumber yard, and two additional general stores owned by Mr. Pullen and Mark Piper. Both the Immanuel and Trondhjem Lutheran churches were also conducting services by this point. As more German and Scandinavian settlers poured in, Atwater found itself among Minnesota's incorporated villages, incorporated on February 17, 1876. As a railroad town, Atwater found its niche as a grain storage and milling center for the immediate area. An 1886 business directory shows that it had a pair of elevators, a lumber office, a bank, a stockyard, saloons, hotels, feed stables, and shops for harnesses, flour, feed, groceries, hardware, and the *Atwater Press* newspaper. One of its most impressive accomplishments, Hotel Water, was built in 1904 to attract additional commerce to the young community and to house frequent travelers and immigrants who had not yet built their homes. The savior of the headquarters of the Mississippi River at Itasca State Park, Mary Gibbs; the 32nd Governor of Minnesota, Harold LeVander; Mike Kingery, an MLB outfielder off and on between 1986 and 1996, and James Rosenquist, best remembered for his work in the pop art movement concerning advertising in society, have ties to Atwater. The Atwater Area Historical Society was formed to preserve local historic sites.

BLOMKEST, MN
POPULATION: 145 – CITY 113 OF 856 (3-29-25)
Blomkest was one of a few select railroad towns located exclusively on the Electric Short Line Railway, also known as the Luce Line Railroad. Despite its allusion to the word "electric," the Luce family's railroad never operated electric locomotives. A need for refueling, mail delivery, and passenger drop-off led to the establishment of the town of Blomkest in an area initially called Kester and Kesterville for C. E. Kester. He was then the mayor of Hutchinson. The change in nomenclature came when Ole Blomquist platted the town in October 1926, and his and Kester's surnames were combined to create an amalgamation. Blomkest's post office was organized in 1928, and several businesses and homes were established by optimistic settlers looking to capitalize on the opportunities offered by the new line. Approximately two hundred people lived in Blomkest at its peak in the 1980s.

KANDIYOHI, MN
POPULATION: 569 – CITY 183 OF 856 (4-15-25)
Kandiyohi's namesake community was named after a Dakota word meaning "where the buffalo fish come." Early town promoters had incredibly high aspirations for the site, as when the Kandiyohi Townsite Company laid out the first townsite in October 1856, they designated large swaths of land for the construction of the newly established Kandiyohi County courthouse, in addition to the Minnesota state capitol building. The area was called "Capitol Square" and was located atop a large hill reminiscent of the Capitol Building in Madison, Wisconsin. In a shocking March 1869 vote, the legislature passed a bill to move the capital to a brand-new Kandiyohi townsite (moved because of the railroad's arrival) from Saint Paul. It was vetoed by William Rainsey Marshall because "the treeless districts surrounding most of the site

placed it too far from Minnesota's most likely population center." He was correct in his assumptions: the Twin Cities thrived as a regional trading center with the establishment of several railroads, whereas Kandiyohi was forced to settle for a single branch of the St. Paul, Minneapolis & Manitoba Railway (which was annexed by the Great Northern in March 1878). To make matters worse, Kandiyohi lost the county seat to nearby Willmar in 1871 by a vote of 709 to 538, and was again denied its wish to become the Minnesota capital that year by the state government. Repeated attempts were made in 1891 and 1893, but to no avail, and in 1901, the decision was finally made to eliminate 'Capitol Square' and turn it into farmland. As of 1886, the town had one to two hundred residents and two blacksmith shops, two general merchandise stores, two elevators, a drug store, a hotel, a billiard hall, stockyards, a depot, a school, and a Catholic church. The post office was moved several times with the townsite; the first office was in Meeker County from 1857 to 1858, the second was located in Kandiyohi County from 1867 to 1871, the third started in 1870 and remained in operation until 1894 as Kandiyohi Station, before the fourth change came with the dropping of "Station" from the name that year.

LAKE LILLIAN, MN
POPULATION: 246 – CITY 112 OF 856 (3-29-25)
Lake Lillian Township came to fruition on January 23, 1872, but it would be another fifty years before the town was formed when the Luce Line Railroad appeared in southern Kandiyohi County. Its name is a tribute to the wife of Edwin Whitefield, who thoroughly explored the area in the summer of 1856 and helped to name several local bodies of water. A post office opened in the mid-1860s because of the area's popularity amongst very early Minnesota pioneers, but it closed in 1906 due to the lack of a railroad. The arrival of the new line rebirthed a branch in 1923. Lake Lillian was incorporated on February 15, 1926, and experienced a minor boom in the 1950s (when its population was 358) when Axel Lundquist discovered a small oil pocket beneath his restaurant. What he thought was oil was closer to pure gasoline, but several wells were produced adjacent to his property, regardless. When the Great Depression hit the Midwest, the Farmers' Holiday Association was founded in May 1932 by Milo Reno, local John Bosch, and others who protested the rich by withholding their agricultural products from the market. The Bosch Farmstead, with its seven buildings built between 1885 and 1936, was added to the National Register in April 1987. Jake Nordin, a tight end who made a brief appearance for the NFL's Detroit Lions in 2009 in four games, hails from Lake Lillian.

NEW LONDON, MN
POPULATION: 1,252 – CITY 175 OF 856 (4-14-25)
New London, the county seat of Monongalia County from 1866 to 1870, before it merged with neighboring Kandiyohi County, can trace its beginnings to 1860, when Louis Larson discovered a waterfall and proposed establishing a mill at the site. His dream came to fruition in 1861, when he took up a homestead in that vicinity and established a townsite called New London, a reference to his former hometown of New London, Wisconsin. Larson thought the landscapes of the two communities were comparable. He, John Cavanough, Mr. Stoner, and C.J. and A. H. Sperry worked on the sawmill and dam at the juncture of Mill Pond and the Crow River throughout 1862, but they had to abandon their work when the skirmishes of the Dakota War of 1862 proved too dangerous for any future improvements to be made. When the war subsided, settlers cautiously returned to the area. They helped grow the townsite by establishing businesses, namely the grist and sawmill, W.W. Pinney's general store, Samuel Adams and A.S. Lybe's storefronts, a post office, and a blacksmith shop.

Attempts were made to save the county seat by preventing Monongàlia County's annexation by Kandiyohi County, but despite efforts to secure permanent title by printing tickets in St. Cloud that read, "For county seat at New London; Against territory attached," the battle was lost. Settlement throughout western Minnesota and New London did not slow after the election, and from 1880 to 1890, the community's population nearly quadrupled. A schoolhouse, a Scandinavian Lutheran Church, a wagon shop, a saloon, three blacksmith shops, three general stores, a harness shop, a hotel, a flouring mill, a feed and carding mill, a hardware store, and a tannery (where animal hides would be tanned and turned into workable leather) were present as of 1886. It was incorporated on April 8, 1889. New London is the closest community to Sibley State Park, a favorite amongst swimmers, campers, and wildlife enthusiasts. The property was purchased by the federal government in 1938 for use as a fish hatchery. Near the state park is Timber Lake Road, which has been dubbed "Minnesota's Most Haunted Road" for its general creepiness and sightings of a mother ghost who wanders the forest at night searching for the unknown perpetrator who took the lives of her children. Every year, antique car enthusiasts with their automobiles from pre-1908 (or one or two-cylinder vehicles dated as late as 1915) gather at New London every August to start a 120-mile "race" to New Brighton, Minnesota, in Ramsey County. Since 1987, the event and its termini have paid tribute to the London to Brighton Veteran Car Run in the United Kingdom.

PENNOCK, MN
POPULATION: 479 – CITY 181 OF 856 (4-15-25)

The St. Johns townsite was laid out and surveyed circa 1856-57, but the Panic of 1857 (primarily caused by the excessive lending of money from bankers to railroad magnates and companies) delayed its development until 1870-71, when the economy rebounded, and the St. Paul, Minneapolis & Manitoba Railroad was built through. Under the name St. John/St. Johns, a pair of general stores, a grocery store, a saloon, an elevator, a depot, and a section house were completed. The first saloon owner of the community, Louis Wilson, was the subject of several news headlines starting in July 1874 when he mysteriously disappeared. He had been killed by Andrew Roos, a man who had stayed with him at the section house the night before. Roos was disposed of and sent to prison, and St. John residents returned to a quieter life on the prairie. In 1891, the Great Northern Railroad, after buying out the previous line, suggested changing the name to Pennock for George Pennock of Willmar. Pennock was the superintendent of the railroad division, so his name was selected after it was discovered that another town called St. Johns was on the same line. E.G. Berlund (local hardware store owner alongside his brother, C.J.) served as postmaster from 1891 to 1935, after which his daughter, Emma, served until 1972. As of 2010, Pennock had more residents (508) than at any other point in its history.

PRINSBURG, MN
POPULATION: 520 – CITY 114 OF 856 (3-29-25)

Incorporated on June 25, 1952, Prinsburg has retained its identity as a religious Dutch community (as evidenced by its welcome sign featuring a windmill and the "The Lord is my Shepherd" motto) since its establishment in the mid-1880s. Martin W. Prins Jr., a member of the real estate firm Prins and Zwanenburg from Groningen, the Netherlands, and his partner, Theodore F. Koch, first offered land for sale in 1885. They stipulated that if at least twenty Dutch families agreed to purchase lots and live there, they would furnish half of the funds for a church edifice. Double the number of needed sales to fulfill the agreement were sold within only months, and so a town was platted and later called Prinsburg for Mr. Prins, who passed away in 1887 shortly after its founding. The early village consisted mainly of wood-frame homes and a couple of stores (the first of which housed the post office from 1887 to 1889) until the Luce Line Railroad was completed in 1927. With the arrival of the railroad, Prinsburg grew rapidly; at its first Census in 1960, it had 462 residents.

RAYMOND, MN
POPULATION: 782 – CITY 115 OF 856 (3-29-25)
Without Raymond, there likely would be no Cool Whip, Jell-O, Tang, or Pop Rocks, as it was the birthplace of the food chemist William A. Mitchell, who invented all four famous foods. He was born on October 21, 1911, in the then-town of 300-odd citizens and worked at the local American Sugar Beet Company factory as a teenager. When Mitchell was born, the community had been around for only a quarter of a century. It was platted in 1887 as "Raymond Station" and named for Raymond Spicer, the son of John M. Spicer, the founder of the neighboring village of the same name. The post office's start was turbulent: the first iteration existed from February to July 1889, with Charles S. Squire as postmaster. It closed for a few weeks until a new office, Croydon, moved in, and William H. Harris took over the duties. Throughout the years, Raymond saw its livery stables turn into filling stations and garages, its railroad hotels come and go, and its commercial district shift as the Great Northern Railroad lost its influence on the local economy. Eventually, the Burlington Northern and Santa Fe Railway took over the line. On March 30, 2023, a significant disaster occurred when several cars carrying ethanol ignited after derailing. That event and other snippets of information and artifacts regarding the town's history are on display at the Raymond Area Museum, which opened in March 2024 in the Raymond Event Center (the former Raymond school and gym).

REGAL, MN
POPULATION: 43 – CITY 174 OF 856 (4-14-25)
Regal, the home of the Eagles, was established on the North Fork of the Crow River and named after the automotive brand that produced vehicles from 1907 to 1918. It was suggested by George Weidner, who also proposed "Ford" for his friend's automobile brand and "Harvard" after the Ivy League university, when the Minneapolis, St. Paul, and Sault Ste. Marie Railroad requested a change from the name Linton. The change was ordered because another town, Linton, was on the same line. "Lintonville" was an alternative proposed name, but the post office department declined to use it for unknown reasons, despite the local branch being called that from 1887 to 1915. The little farm town did not attain incorporation until April 25, 1940; its highest recorded population was only 64 people in the following decade. Regal is most proud of its baseball history, as in 1991, the local team was state champions, and in 1997, they were runner-ups. Michelle Fischbach, the 49th Lieutenant Governor of Minnesota from January 2018 to January 2019 and a current member of the House of Representatives from Minnesota (since January 2021), has ties to Regal.

SPICER, MN
POPULATION: 1,112 – CITY 182 OF 856 (4-15-25)
Before Spicer, there was Columbia, the dream of E. T. Woodcock, J. M. Ayers, and V. L. Forsythe, who had hoped that their townsite on the southwest side of Green Lake would someday become a bustling metropolis. They were so confident that its beauty and prime location would make it the perfect candidate for Monongalia County's seat of government that they platted a "courthouse square." A fierce battle of persuasion broke out between proponents of Columbia and the rival townsites of Irving and

Norway Lake, from which Columbia emerged victorious. It welcomed Arnold's store, a mill, and a post office as three of its early institutions, but despite the townspeople's best attempts to retain their title, they lost it to the town of New London in the 1860s. Columbia faded into obscurity, but the beautiful site on the lake was transformed into the new Spicer townsite in 1886 when the St. Cloud and Sioux Falls Railroad came through. Its proprietor was John M. Spicer, for whom the new town and post office were named. The postal branch was opened in William Olson's general store, and Burton B. Swetland was postmaster. Later came the schools, churches, and business houses that would make Spicer a formal community, and as of modern times, Spicer has set itself apart from other nearby towns with its thriving lines of antique stores, gift shops, and parks, of which the most famous is Spicer City Park on Green Lake. Spicer crossed the one-thousand-resident mark between 1980 and 1990 and reported a peak population of 1,167 people to the Census Bureau as of 2010. The John M. Spicer Summer House and Farm, built in 1895 by town founder John Spicer, operated for nearly twenty years as the Spicer Castle Inn & Restaurant. The castle was put up for sale in 2018 and was razed shortly thereafter due to major structural problems. It was the last resort on Green Lake when it was sold by owners Mary and Allen Latham

Restaurant Recommendation:
Zorbaz
159 Lake Ave S
Spicer, MN 56288

SUNBURG, MN
POPULATION: 94 – CITY 176 OF 856 (4-14-25)
Established circa 1871 and incorporated on September 8, 1951, the Norwegian settlement of Sunburgh was named after the Norse word *sund*, meaning "straits." It was suggested by the postal worker Jon Sandvigen, who worked alongside Ole Eliason to deliver mail to the earliest settlers. From 1871 to 1894, the town's name was spelled with the '-h' before it was Americanized. The inland village never had a railroad, so its growth was relatively limited. At its first census in 1960, it had a peak population of 161 people, and as of today, Sunburg has a handful of stores and several Protestant churches nearby. In 1918, state senator P. A. Gandrud, a Republican, convinced his party to hold their 1918 kickoff campaign in his hometown. On that day, the town likely had more visitors than at any other point in its history. One of Minnesota's smallest state parks, the 346-acre Monson Lake State Park, was established in 1937 to serve as a memorial to thirteen local Swedish-Americans killed in the Dakota War of 1862. Some of its structures were furnished in the 1930s as part of New Deal projects.

WILLMAR, MN ★☆
POPULATION: 21,015 – CITY 185 OF 856 (4-15-25)
Kandiyohi County's regional center for business, healthcare, and progress was chiefly built up by Scandinavian settlers who arrived in 1869-70, when the St. Paul & Pacific Railroad was completed on the shores of Foot Lake. In this area where Elijah Woodcock, Lars and Guri Endreson, and other early settlers had called their home in the 1850s before the Dakota War of 1862, the railroad decided to make a new town called Willmar their division point. It was named by George F. Becker, the railroad president, after Leon Chadwick Willmar. Willmar was a railroad agent and bondholder with the railroad company that owned the title to the townsite. The townsite was platted in 1869, and two years later, it was named the judicial seat of Kandiyohi County. This

honor, coupled with its location on the railroad, launched Willmar into a period of prosperity that culminated in its incorporation as a village on January 16, 1874, and in a population exceeding 1,000 residents by its first Census in 1880. During that decade, Willmar saw the founding of well over one hundred business houses and establishments of all shapes, sizes, and varieties, of which some of the most interesting were the Willmar Roller Mills, the town hall, a roller rink, a gun shop, an art gallery, multiple wagon shops, elevators and hotels, an engine house, a Presbyterian church, two Baptist churches, two Norwegian Lutheran churches, an Episcopal church, a Catholic church, a courthouse and jail, a schoolhouse, and the Kandiyohi County Agricultural Society grounds. Its growth was less boom-and-bust and more gradual as it became a handsome city (and was incorporated as such in 1901), and it reached and surpassed population milestones of five thousand residents in the 1910s, ten thousand in the 1950s, and twenty thousand in the 2010s. Much of its modern growth can be directly attributed to the Jennie-O turkey plant, which has welcomed immigrant workers from around the world. Nine structures in the Willmar vicinity have since been selected for preservation in the National Register of Historic Places, highlighting Willmar's most significant accomplishments: the Lars and Guri Endreson House, an 1858 log cabin that predates the establishment of Willmar village; the A. Larson & Co, Building, erected in 1876 using elements of Italianate architecture; the historic 1893 Victorian era home of Albert H. and Jennie C. Sperry; District No. 55 (Svea) School, built in 1907 and used as a meeting place for the Farmers' Holiday Association during the Great Depression; the Willmar Hospital Farm for Inebriates Historic District, a collection of twenty-two buildings completed between 1912-33 (now a part of the MinnWest Technology Campus); the 1927 Lakeland Hotel building; the Willmar Tribune Building, home to the local newspaper from 1920 to 1980; the Willmar Municipal Airport, built up in the 1930s as a federal work relief project, and the Willmar Auditorium, a secondary work relief project during the same period. Other points of interest are the Kandiyohi County Courthouse and its 17-foot-tall gold Kandiyohi statue built in 1956; the Kandiyohi County Historical Society Museum, grounds, and Great Northern P-2 Mountain (4-8-2) #2523 locomotive, and Ridgewater College, which was established in 1996 when Willmar Community College and Hutchinson-Willmar Regional Technical College combined. Two significant events in Willmar's history highlight the local banks. In 1930, the Bank of Willmar was robbed of $70,000 (the modern equivalent of well over a million dollars) by Machine Gun Kelly. Nearly fifty years later, Willmar became the focus of national attention when the Willmar 8 went on strike in negative-70-degree wind-chill weather on December 16, 1977. They were picketing against sex discrimination at the Citizens National Bank. Numerous famous folks have connections to Willmar: Earl B. Olson, the founder of the Jennie-O Turkey Company; Curt Swan, a comic book artist noted for his work on *Superman* comics from the 1950s to the 1980s; Bonnie Henrickson, a former women's college basketball coach for Virginia Tech, Kansas, and UC Santa Barbara; George "Pinky" Nelson, a NASA astronaut who spent 17 days in space; Jim Pederson, an NFL player in the early 1930s; Rick "The King of the Iditarod" Swenson, a dog musher who won the 1,000-plus mile race across Alaska on five occasions; Henrik Shipstead, a United States Senator from Minnesota from March 1923 to January 1947; Kenneth L. Olson, a Medal of Honor recipient; Alec G. Olson, a politician best remembered for being the 40th Lieutenant Governor of Minnesota in the late 1970s; Bradley Joseph, a contemporary instrumental music artist and producer, and Olof Hanson, the first deaf American architect. Per Sister Cities International, Willmar, Minnesota's sister cities are Vilelyka, Belarus, and Yakutsk, Russia.

Restaurant Recommendation:
B's Chocolates
1707 Technology Dr NE #101
Willmar, MN 56201

Restaurant Recommendation:
Ruff's Wings & Sports Bar
2100 US-12
Willmar, MN 56201

Unincorporated/Ghost Towns: Hawick, Norway Lake, Priam, Roseland, Svea

National Register of Historic Places:
Atwater: Hotel Atwater
Kandiyohi: Andreas, Johanna, Anna & Frank E. Broman Farmstead, Kasota Lake Site
Lake Lillian: John Bosch Farmstead
New London: Sibley State Park CCC/Rustic Style Historic District
Spicer: John M. Spicer Summer House & Farm
Willmar: A. Larson & Co. Building, Albert H. & Jennie C. Sperry House, Lakeland Hotel, Willmar Auditorium, Willmar Hospital Farm for Inebriates Historic District, Willmar Municipal Airport, Willmar Tribune Building, District No.55 School, Lars & Guri Endreson House

Golf Courses:
Eagle Creek Golf Club, Daily Fee (Willmar, MN)
Hawk Creek Country Club, Municipal (Raymond, MN)
Island Pine Golf Club, Daily Fee (Atwater, MN)
Little Crow Golf Resort, Daily Fee (Spicer, MN)

Breweries/Wineries/Distilleries:
Foxhole Brewhouse (Willmar, MN)
Goat Ridge Brewing (New London, MN)
Intuition Brewing (Willmar, MN)

Town Celebrations:
Lake Lillian Fun Days, Lake Lillian, MN (Last Saturday of July into Early August)
Willmar Fests, Willmar, MN (Last Weekend in June)
Raymond Harvest Festival, Raymond, MN (4th Weekend of August)
Syttende Mai Day, Sunburg, MN (Weekend closest to May 17th)

KITTSON COUNTY
EST. 1879 - POPULATION: 4,207

The northwesternmost county in Minnesota, bordering Canada, was appropriately named in honor of one of its earliest fur traders, Norman W. Kittson.

DONALDSON, MN
POPULATION: 20 – CITY 325 OF 856 (6-4-25)
As of the 2020 Census, only twenty people lived in Donaldson, a far cry from its 1920s heyday, when it boasted no less than 167 citizens. While a gradual rural-to-urban shift has quite literally left Donaldson in the dust, the town named for Captain Hugh W. Donaldson, a Civil War veteran, farmer, and manager of a large swath of land owned by the Kennedy Land Company, was once a crucial shipping point on the St. Paul,

Minneapolis & Manitoba Railroad. As of 1912, four elevators stood tall on the railroad tracks, conducting business with farmers from far and wide. Two churches, a school, and a town hall were located in the eastern sections of the townsite. On Main Street, visitors would have found a general store, a livery, a bank, a hardware store, a butcher's shop, and a post office. Edward Davis, the first storeowner, was appointed postmaster in 1884 after the office's name was changed from Davis to Donaldson.

HALLOCK, MN ★☆
POPULATION: 906 – CITY 323 OF 856 (6-4-25)

The county seat of Kittson County was named after Charles W. Hallock, an author best known for founding the sportsman's magazine Field & Stream. While the town was named in his honor, and he once owned a large sportsman hotel in the area from 1890 to 1892, he was far from the first man to live here. That distinction goes to several Indigenous tribes, namely the Ojibwe, the Lakota, the Cree, and the Assiniboine. Norman W. Kittson, the namesake of the county, worked in this general area and frequently traveled through the Hallock vicinity on his way to St. Paul to conduct business for his company, the American Fur Trade Company. He offered an oxcart hauling service for trappers, enabling them to send their pelts to the big-city markets long before any railroads reached the area. Eventually, when the St. Paul, Minneapolis & Manitoba Railroad arrived, a significant number of businesses were established as Hallock developed into one of the larger regional trade centers. The Ojibwe, also known as the Chippewa, had traded frequently at the Lindegard Brothers store. Their store was followed by myriad others, too many to list in one place; however, elevators, banks, saloons, general merchandise stores, hardware and implement stores, and printing offices were among the regular establishments. A graded school and high school were developed in northeast Hallock, two blocks north of the courthouse. Listed church congregations on a 1912 city directory were the Swedish Mission Church, a Methodist Episcopal church, a Roman Catholic church, a Presbyterian church, and a Congregational church. While its businesses, churches, and schools prospered, residents also had a spark of creative genius when they built Minnesota's first indoor ice rink in 1896. As the population grew from 869 people to 1,353 between 1930 and 1940 (an increase of 55.7%) and then to an all-time high of 1,552 in 1950, new facilities, such as a hospital complex and a modern courthouse were needed to support the community. Some people born during this time may recall the filming of Fargo in Hallock. The lack of snow in Brainerd led production crews to use Hallock as a stand-in for the film's setting. Frederick McKinley Jones, the "Father of Refrigerated Transportation" and the owner of 61 (40 refrigeration technology) patents, moved to Hallock in 1912 to work as a mechanic on one of James J. Hill's farming operations. While Jones was working on the farm, another inventor, Donald Pederson, was born on September 30, 1925, to Oscar Jorgan and Beda Emilia Pederson. He helped design SPICE, a general-purpose, open-source integrated circuit simulator.

Restaurant Recommendation:
Bully Brew Coffee – Hallock
28 2nd St NE SE
Hallock, MN 56728

HALMA, MN
POPULATION: 58 – CITY 318 OF 856 (6-4-25)

A bank, a feed store, a hotel, a restaurant, a livery, a creamery, and pairs of stores and grain elevators made up the bulk of Halma's business lines in the early 1910s, at a time when its population would have been three to five times larger than it is now. Officially incorporated as a village on September 28, 1923, Halma acquired many of its initial settlers and businesses from Beaton. This town was surpassed by the Minneapolis, St. Paul & Sault Ste. Marie Railroad in favor of Halma. Lafgren was the name of the local post office branch in 1902; it was changed in 1904 to Halma, named after the first merchant and postmaster, John Edwin Holm. The post office was discontinued in 2009. T. L. Spilde also had an early business, a department store, which he moved from Beaton. C. E. Braaten operated the feed mill, the Bertram Lumberyard provided materials for early construction projects, and Peter Bjora and Barney Johnson's *Halma Pilot* newspaper reported on the early stories of the times.

HUMBOLDT, MN
POPULATION: 41 – CITY 321 OF 856 (6-4-25)
This 0.11-square-mile town is one of several communities in the United States named in honor of Baron Alexander von Humboldt, the noted German polymath and scientist. A post office had been established earlier in 1899 as Fairview. The name was changed in 1896 once the crews of the St. Paul, Minneapolis & Manitoba Railroad had paved the line through town. Railroad mogul James J. Hill owned about 40,000 acres of land between Northcote and Humboldt, but he chose to sell it to settlers such as Nels Finney, James Diamond, and Charley Clow. Edward and James Florance were directly responsible for much of the development of the little townsite. Edward helped start the First Bank of Humboldt, and James served as a postmaster and a storeowner. The Florance and Nelson Store and the Booker McFadden Store were the largest early stores. Four grain elevators, a lumber yard, a restaurant, the Humboldt United Methodist Church, and a school were contributing to the school's economic, religious, and educational spheres by 1912. Maury Finney, a country music saxophonist best known for his 1977 country single "Coconut Grove," has ties to Humboldt.

KARLSTAD, MN
POPULATION: 710 – CITY 317 OF 856 (6-3-25)
A 14-foot fiberglass moose statue welcomes travelers to "The Moose Capital of the North," perhaps better known to the world as Karlstad, Minnesota. Swedish settler Carl August Carlson homesteaded near here in 1883. After improving the land for over 20 years, he sold it to the Soo Line Railroad for a handsome sum to establish their right-of-way. Many thought the town would be called Clayton or Kingville, but "Karlstad" was selected to honor Mr. Carlson and the Swedish city of Karlstad. The Pearson Hotel was the first business to begin operations at the new railroad site. Others included the Turnwall Mercantile, a lumber mill, a flour mill, an elevator, and two rival lodging options in Nordin's Hotel and Jonas Anderson's Commercial Hotel. Others moved their firms from Pelan, a ghost town incorporated only from 1903 to 1909 because of the lack of a railroad. Two creameries, a lumber office, a bank, and many other general stores and shops were operational, according to Geo A. Ogle & Co.'s 1912 atlas. In the early 1900s, the Wikstrom Telephone Company (Wiktel) was founded by the Wikstrom family as a small venture before expanding into one of the largest providers of phone and internet services for northwestern Minnesota. Karlstad's population reached 934 in the 1980s, during a period when businesses were booming. Its large numbers warranted the opening of a hospital in 1951, which closed in 1995. Mattracks Inc., coincidentally founded by Glen Brazier that same year, is headquartered in Karlstad and specializes in rubber track conversion systems for typically wheeled vehicles. Ned Beatty, the "busiest actor in Hollywood," owned a residence in Karlstad for many years. The Academy and Emmy Award nominee held roles in movies such as *Deliverance* (1972), *Superman* (1978), *Rudy* (1993), and *Toy Story 3* (2010), in

addition to over 160 other films and television series. Other than its moose statue, Karlstad is also known for its Muffler Man statue, Paul Bunyan with a guitar, located at the Kick'n Up Kountry music festival fairgrounds. He lived in Warroad in the 1970s, holding a hockey stick, before vandals sawed off one of his legs, and the statue disappeared for decades. Mr. Bunyan has gone missing once more, but the country music festival still draws thousands of visitors each June.

KENNEDY, MN
POPULATION: 176 – CITY 324 OF 856 (6-4-25)
John Stewart Kennedy, a businessman and philanthropist who was one of only a handful of men to be a part of the Jekyll Island Club (called the Millionaires' Club because of its high-class members like William Rockefeller and J.P. Morgan), had this town named in his honor because of his charity work and affiliation with the railroad industry. The town was platted on December 31, 1880, after the Kennedy Land and Town Company sold the St. Paul, Minneapolis & Manitoba Railroad on the idea of building their line through an already-established townsite. Efforts to bring in the railroad proved successful, and Kennedy assumed its role as one of a line of agricultural shipping points. Its post office was formally organized in 1881. Within thirty years, the town's educational, religious, fraternal, and economic facets had developed to meet its needs. The Kennedy school and a church were located in the southeast part of town, next to the Modern Workmen of America Hall. An Odd Fellows Hall was on the complete opposite side of Kennedy in its northwest faction. Aside from its fire hall, a blacksmith shop, and a pair of other businesses, Kennedy's commercial district, moving from north to south, included a hardware and implement store, a hotel, a real estate office, a drug store, a candy store, a bank, and a second hardware store, amongst a few others. Four hundred eighty people lived in the town at the height of its prosperity in the 1950s.

LAKE BRONSON, MN
POPULATION: 178 – CITY 319 OF 856 (6-4-25)
Called "Bronson" until the word "Lake" was added as a prefix to its name in 1939, this 1904 Soo Line Railroad town was named for Giles Bronson and his family. They were the first settlers of the area in 1882; their homestead was approximately three miles east of the future Lake Bronson townsite. Percy was the name of Mrs. Bronson's post office until it was changed in 1904 by Andrew Vik. When the town was laid out, Swan Olson jumped on the opportunity to profit from the railroad's arrival by erecting a hotel as its first building. A bank, a furniture store, a livery, a blacksmith shop, a creamery, a church, a school, a depot, a Modern Workmen of America Hall, three elevators, and stockyards were just some of the places built up over the next decade. Bronson had a population of 181 in 1920. By 1950, it had increased to 438 with the creation of the artificial Lake Bronson, resulting from the damming of the South Branch Two Rivers. In a county with no natural lakes, a severe drought threatened the survival of its people. The Works Progress Administration sent crews to build a dam (over quicksand, which required some extra creativity in the construction process) and to create a small reservoir, which is today known as Lake Bronson State Park. Fishing, swimming, skiing, and snowmobiling are among visitors' favorite activities. Yet, a 45-foot-tall hexagonal stone water tower serves as the highlight of the park. The park as a whole was listed on the National Register of Historic Places in 1989 for its WPA ties and its 12 contributing properties. It is also the home of the main characters in David L. Robbins' post-apocalyptic novel series, *Endworld*. In addition to its popular State Park, Lake Bronson is home to the Kittson County History Center.

LANCASTER, MN
POPULATION: 364 – CITY 320 OF 856 (6-4-25)

Over a third of the states in the United States have a town or township called Lancaster, named after the county of Lancashire in England. When the Soo Line Railroad was building its line from the junction at Glenwood to the Canadian border, it decided to use "Lancaster" in place of Lanerow, the post office's name. The change was made in 1904 when the tracks were laid on land platted by the Kittson Land Company. By September 30, 1905, Lancaster was the newest incorporated village in Minnesota. Bernard Johnson was the proprietor of Lancaster's first business, a hotel. He was joined in Lancaster's small business world by Charles Ungerth and Charles Peterson, who established The Lancaster Mercantile Company. The Woodworth Company, the Prairie Elevator Company, and the Osborn-McMillen Company owned the three grain elevators. Several other firms, such as the First State Bank of Lancaster and the *Lancaster Herald* newspaper, emerged in the early days. However, the most important of them all was the Lancaster Cooperative Creamery. It was located half a mile out of town. According to a 1912 plat map, there was also a lumber yard, a feed mill, a meat market, a drug store, a barber shop, banks, livery stables, and general stores. The Lancaster-Tolstoi [Manitoba] Border Crossing was established in 1950 as Minnesota's westernmost border crossing point before the closure of the Noyes-Emerson East crossing in 2006.

SAINT VINCENT, MN
POPULATION: 57 – CITY 322 OF 856 (6-4-25)

No town in Minnesota can claim to be more northwestern than St. Vincent. The community of 57 people is situated directly across the Red River of the North from Pembina, North Dakota, only a couple of miles from the Canadian border. Its name was selected by fur trappers circa 1860 in honor of St. Vincent de Paul, a French Catholic priest who founded numerous missions and hospitals in Paris during the 1600s. Peter Grant had a fur trading post here as early as 1793. On March 23, 1857, St. Vincent was incorporated as a village. This action was repeated on March 8, 1881, around the time it began to grow rapidly as the terminus of the St. Paul, Minneapolis & Manitoba Railway (predated by the Saint Paul and Pacific Railroad) and the St. Vincent branch of the Canadian Pacific Railroad. Nearly 500 people lived there at the time. It boasted everything from a brewery, brickyard, and bank to three general stores and a hotel, the *Herald* newspaper, a 90,000-bushel elevator, and a district school and church. Many of the town's earliest landowners were Métis, or people typically born to Indigenous women and French fur trappers. The U.S. Decennial Census reported a high population of only 343 people in 1920, but St. Vincent still had numerous hotels, general stores, churches, and schools. Lot 76 was designated as the site of the courthouse, although Hallock has held the honor since Kittson County was partitioned from Pembina County in the late 1870s. From 1878 to 1986, the post office operated independently as "Saint Vincent" until it was designated as a rural station. A few miles north of Saint Vincent is the unincorporated hamlet of Noyes, where the St. Paul, Minneapolis & Manitoba, and Soo Line Railroads terminated at the border and turned into branches of the Canadian Pacific and the Canadian Northern Railroads. Noyes is also home to a 1931 Colonial Revival Customs station, one of the first land border checkpoint buildings built specifically for that purpose. The crossing was closed in 2006 and listed on the National Register of Historic Places in 2014.

Unincorporated/Ghost Towns: Caribou, Northcote, Noyes, Orleans, Pelan, Robbin

National Register of Historic Places:
Caribou Township: St. Nicholas Orthodox Church
Lake Bronson: Lake Bronson Site, Lake Bronson State Park WPA/Rustic Style Historic Resources
Noyes: U.S. Inspection Station-Noyes, Minnesota

Golf Courses:
Karlstad Golf Course, Daily Fee (Karlstad, MN)

Breweries/Wineries/Distilleries:
Revelation Ale Works (Hallock, MN)

Town Celebrations:
Kick'n Up Kountry Music Festival, Karlstad, MN (2nd Full Weekend of June)

Itasca County: Logger Statue (Bigfork), former Enstrom Studio, home of "Grace" (Bovey), Coleraine Public Library (Coleraine), Ravenstone Abbey (Coleraine), Little American Falls (Craigville), Horses at Forest History Center (Grand Rapids), Hawkins Mine Overlook (Nashwauk), Giant Canada Goose Statue (Squaw Lake)

Jackson County: Rainbow over New Vision Co-op Elevator (Heron Lake), Interior of Sacred Heart Catholic Church (Heron Lake), Jackson County Courthouse (Jackson), former Standard Oil Gas Station (Jackson), Jackson County Massacre Monument and Olson Slaabakken Cabin (Jackson), Fort Belmont (Jackson), former Alpha Railroad Depot at Jackson County Fair Village (Jackson), Bonnie & Clyde's Okabena Bank Getaway Car (Okabena)

Kanabec County: former Public School (Grasston), Kanabec County Courthouse (Mora), Largest Dala Horse in the United States (Mora), Palisade Theatre (Mora), Mora Clock (Mora), former Coin School (Mora), Rusty the Dragon (Ogilvie), Historic Stone Ogilvie Water Tower (Ogilvie)

Kandiyohi County: former Martin Olson Residence & Funeral Home (Atwater), Mural (Lake Millian), Dam at Mill Pond (New London), Windmill & Veterans Memorial (Prinsburg), former Sacred Heart Catholic Church (Raymond), Beach at Green Lake (Spicer), Albert H and Jennie C. Sperry House at Kandiyohi County Historical Society (Willmar), Golden Chief Kandiyohi Statue (Willmar)

Kittson County: Mural (Hallock), former Public School (Halma), Pasture Cow (Halma), former Soo Line Railroad Depot at Kick'n Up Kountry Music Festival (Karlstad), Mural (Kennedy), Wild Black bear at Lake Bronson State Park (Lake Bronson), WPA Water and Observation Tower at Lake Bronson State Park (Lake Bronson), former St. Vincent Elementary School (St. Vincent)

KOOCHICHING COUNTY
EST. 1906 - POPULATION: 12,062

Koochiching is unlike any other name, as it was derived from the Ojibwe word *Gojijiing,* meaning "a place of inlets." The county was founded in 1906, after being partitioned from Itasca County.

BIG FALLS, MN
POPULATION: 175 – CITY 357 OF 856 (6-20-25)
Nestled between Pine Island State Forest and Koochiching State Forest, travelers on Highway 71 will find the hamlet of Big Falls. Given the wooded area, the timber industry naturally emerged as the most critical industry for immigrants who chose to settle at this townsite on the falls of the Big Fork River. Farming became another minor industry after the Big Fork and Northern Railroad (later better known as the Minnesota and International) was built from Northome to Big Falls. Big Falls was incorporated in the early 1900s. In 1906, it received government permission to establish a post office branch. By 1910, it had 325 residents; in 1970, the population reached a peak of 534, and since then, it has dropped considerably. Fishing and camping are favorite pastimes for residents and visitors alike. Uncle Dan Campbell, supposedly a Scottish railroad worker who lived in the vicinity of Big Falls in the late 1870s, greets wanderers at the intersection of Hwy 71 and Hwy 6.

INTERNATIONAL FALLS, MN ★
POPULATION: 5,802 – CITY 359 OF 856 (6-20-25)
International Falls, formerly known as Koochiching Village in its earliest days, is today recognized by many other names: "Frostbite Falls," the "Icebox of the Nation," and the Northern Gateway to Voyageurs National Park. The international port of entry is the second-busiest in North America and home to one of three Foreign-Trade Zones in Minnesota, which provides companies with additional advantages for warehousing and trading goods between the United States and Canada. Long before either country existed, in 1687-88, Jacques de Noyon became the first European to set foot in the area, and other famous explorers, such as Sieur de La Verendrye, followed him circa 1732. No developments were made on the American side of the Rainy River until the late 1810s, when fur trading points began to spring up throughout the Upper Midwest. Alexander Baker squatted on the land in 1870, making it his homestead, which he then sold to H. Winches and C. J. Rockwood of Minneapolis. They foresaw the power of Koochiching Falls and paid Baker a then-hefty sum of $6,000 for his land. L. A. Ogaard platted the village of Koochiching on June 23, 1894. By October 13, a post office opened under the direction of postmaster U.M. Thomas. Many homes and businesses were built, and on August 10, 1901, Koochiching became one of Minnesota's incorporated municipalities. The name was changed two years later to "International Falls" to honor the important falls and rivers that separated the United States from Canada. Early industries varied in scope and size, but amongst the most notable then were the Minnesota and Ontario Paper Company Mill, built in 1904; a dam erected between 1905 and 1908 that raised Rainy Lake to a level that allowed steamboats to enter the city; the Neoclassical-Renaissance Revival Koochiching County courthouse in 1909, three years after International Falls was declared as the county seat; a 1911 Public Library; the Fort Frances International Bridge in 1912; the NRHP-designated Alexander Baker School and E.W. Backus Junior High School in 1914 and 1936; and industrialist E. W. Backus's Insulite Mill, created to reprocess pulp waste from the paper mills into new products. The Minnesota and Ontario Paper Company mill and

corresponding dam, furnished by Backus, were sold to Boise Cascade Corporation in 1965, then to a separate party in 2003, and, most recently, to Packaging Corporation of America in 2013. It is the largest employer in the city, with a population of nearly 5,802; this population size is roughly the average of International Falls' population between 1930 and the 2020s. More recent developments of the city include the 26-foot-tall Smokey Bear, erected on October 13, 1954, as a nod to the local forests and logging and milling industries. One of the world's largest thermometers, at 22 feet, was dedicated in January 1988, next to Smokey, not long afterward. The Bronko Nagurski Museum, dedicated to the legacy of International Falls's most famous World Heavyweight Champion and three-time NFL champion, also brings in some tourists. Still, the crown jewel of the community's tourism industry—Voyageurs National Park—boasts over 250,000 visitors per year. It is among the most unique of America's National Parks, as it is primarily accessible by water. Boating, canoeing, and kayaking are the park's main activities. They are the only methods to truly experience the park as its namesake voyageurs did long before the widespread settlement of Minnesota in the 19th century. Voyageurs N.P. was established on April 8, 1975, on a 218,200-acre sector of wilderness adjacent to the 1,090,000-acre Boundary Waters Canoe Area Wilderness and its pristine forests and glacial lakes within Superior National Forest. Alluding back to two of the early-mentioned nicknames, International Falls holds the "Icebox of the Nation" title due to its freezing temperatures (32°F) for approximately 30% (109.4/365.25 days) of each calendar year. For years, it fought with Fraser, Colorado, for rights to the trademark. In 1986, International Falls paid Fraser $2,000 to permanently resolve the claim. When the federal trademark lapsed in 1996, Fraser jumped at the opportunity to take it for themselves. Years of legal battles culminated in a January 29, 2008, decision by the United States Patent and Trademark Office to register the slogan with International Falls for good. As if to approve the decision herself, Mother Nature brought the city to a blistering -40°F only days after the victory. The lesser-known Frostbite Falls nickname was given by *The Rocky and Bullwinkle Show* (aired from November 19, 1959, to June 27, 1964), which turned International Falls into the fictional hometown of its main characters. Rocket "Rocky" J. Squirrel and Bullwinkle J. Moose are famous in their own right, but so are several other "characters" of the city, including Bronko Nagurski Jr., son of the legendary Bronko Nagurski and a Canadian Football League All-Star offensive tackle in 1962 and 1965; Frank Youso, an offensive tackle in the NFL between 1958 and 1965; Bill Borcher, the head coach of Oregon Men's basketball from 1951 to 1956; Tammy Faye Messner, the co-founder of The PTL Club televangelist program that was widely popular in the 1970s and 1980s; Dean Blais, a former NHL player and head coach for the University of North Dakota from 1994 to 2004 and the University of Nebraska Omaha from 2009 to 2017; long-time hockey coach Kevin Constantine; and multiple other hockey Olympians and professionals like Larry Ross, Richard Dougherty, Mike Curran, Kevin Christiansen, Bob Mason, Gary Sampson, Timothy Sheehy, and Neil Sheehy.

Restaurant Recommendation:
Sammy's Pizza Restaurant & Tavern
301 3rd Ave
International Falls, MN 56649

Lodging Recommendation:
Kettle Falls Hotel
12977 Chippewa Trail
Kabetogama, MN 56669

LITTLEFORK, MN
POPULATION: 553 – CITY 358 OF 856 (6-20-25)
William Slingerland filed for his homestead claim in May 1898 on the banks of the Little Fork River. The river, which joins the Rainy River near International Falls, provided Slingerland, Francis White, and other early settlers with a pristine water source that helped them survive in the dense woodlands of northern Minnesota. Many of them were loggers of the Backus International Lumber Company, who floated their cuts down the river to other trade points. Still, the makings of a permanent town were evident as early as 1905. A post office came even earlier in 1902, but as trees were felled and more area was cleared for farming, the Big Fork and Northern Railroad took note of the little town. They established a station at Littlefork, and with time, it had all the makings of an enterprising community. High schools and elementary schools, churches, and fraternal organizations were established to cover the educational, religious, and social aspects of day-to-day life. Francis White's 1901 log cabin and homestead served as the Forsythe Post Office from 1904 to 1922. They were listed on the NRHP in January 1983. When Littlefork residents wanted to get in on all the lumberjack roadside oddity action, a small Jack Pine Savage statue was constructed and placed on Main Street. The 16th Governor of Montana from 1962 to 1969, Tim Babcock, was born here on October 27, 1919.

MIZPAH, MN
POPULATION: 58 – CITY 354 OF 856 (6-20-25)
On June 4, 1935, residents of Mizpah were surprised when snow–and measurable snowfall, at that–began to fall and accumulate only a week after Memorial Day Weekend. An inch-and-a-half of snow covered their town, setting a still-standing state record for the latest measurable snowfall in Minnesota. Perhaps the snow was a celebratory gesture sent from above for the town's 30th anniversary, as it had only become an incorporated village on January 2, 1905. "Mizpah" is Hebrew for "a watchtower" and a reference to Genesis 31:49 in the Bible. The three Potter brothers, Will, Walter, and Sam, were the first men to live in Mizpah, arriving in 1900. Walter was the first postmaster, and Will was the man responsible for the town's early sawmill. The Minnesota and International Railroad, the precursor line to the Northern Pacific, brought the town's population to a peak of 212 by the 1920s.

NORTHOME, MN ☆
POPULATION: 155 – CITY 353 OF 856 (6-20-25)
The "Big Bear Capital of Minnesota" is a nickname for Northome, given to the area for the abundance of black bears frequently seen throughout the region. New Bridgie (derived from Bridget Moore, who established a post office nearby in 1895) was the name of the site settled by Claude Fish and C. W. Fields initially, before it was changed to Phena in 1902 when a new, separate post office was established. The postal service was unimpressed with the name and requested a change. Harris Richardson selected North Home for Norwegian immigrants as an anglicized version of "Norheim," which literally means "north home." North Home was contracted to Northome in August 1903 at the request of the Big Fork and Northern Railroad. Chris P. Ellingson established a large sawmill and the Island Lake Lumber Company in 1912 to help process white pine, cedar, basswood, and several other trees in the area. By 1920, the forests had been depleted by unsustainable logging practices, and residents turned to tilling the black loam soils of Northome to earn a living. Improvements were made to multiple buildings around town in that decade, the most notable being a $50,000 fireproof addition to The Northome Consolidated School. Upwards of 351 people lived here in

the town's heyday in 1970, which strangely came a decade after passenger service on the railroad had been discontinued. Today, the Koochiching County Fair is held annually during the second weekend of August at the Northome Fairgrounds. From 1905 to 2007, Northome embraced its longstanding newspaper, the *Northome Record*. The Scenic Hotel was another essential fixture in town history, but it was demolished in 1996 after being abandoned in 1921. It had been listed on the National Register from January 1983 to June 1998. In downtown Northome, a slender, 20-foot-tall bear carved from wood gazes into the distance in search of his next meal (perhaps looking for Bartlett or Island Lake, popular swimming and fishing destinations). Northome and Mizpah are the closest incorporated communities to the Lost 40 "old growth" forest, where hikers can walk among towering 250+-year-old pine trees. The trees survived the extensive logging of the 1880s (and beyond then) when Josiah A. King and his three-person surveying crew mistakenly platted Coddington Lake a half mile further northwest than where it actually lies.

Restaurant Recommendation:
Shining Light Cafe
12079 Main St
Northome, MN 56661

RANIER, MN
POPULATION: 569 – CITY 360 OF 856 (6-20-25)
"Big Vic," a large fiberglass voyageur statue, welcomes travelers to this small community on the shores of Rainy Lake across from Canada. John Acey Holler settled in the vicinity in 1898. He served as a U.S. customs officer at Koochiching before selling his claim to the Cook and O'Brien Company several years later. By 1907, the Duluth, Rainy Lake & Winnipeg Railway (later renamed the Duluth, Winnipeg & Pacific) was in operation, and the once-deserted grounds became a bustling site of activity. A post office, hotels, general and grocery stores, and region-specific businesses like Finstad's Auto Marine Shop (built in 1911 and still listed on the National Register of Historic Places) came into being, but so too did the bootlegging industry. Ranier had its share of saloons, but bootleggers used the little lakeport village as a home base for smuggling booze to and from Canada across Rainy Lake. Both federal governments ultimately cracked down on the activity, and Ranier was allowed to remain peacefully as a small suburb of International Falls. Between 1910 and 2010, its population fluctuated only between a low of 145 (in 2010) and a high of 262 people (in 1960). However, by 2020, it had grown exponentially to 569 people, representing a 292.4% increase over the decade. In addition to the auto marine repair shop, Ranier has two other locations on the National Register of Historic Places: the 1939 WPA Ranier Community Building and the twelve contributing properties of the Ernest C. Oberholtzer Rainy Lake Islands Historic District built between 1919 and 1944.

Restaurant Recommendation:
Tara's Wharf Ice Cream Shop
2065 Spruce St
Ranier, MN 56668

Unincorporated/Ghost Towns: Birchdale, Border, Bramble, Central, Craigville, Ericsburg, Fairfield, Falls Junction, Forest Grove, Frontier, Gates Corner, Gemmell, Grand Falls, Indus, Island View, Jameson, Laurel, Lindford, Loman, Manitou, Margie, Nakoda, Nett Lake, Pelland, Pinestop, Rainy Lake City, Rauch, Ray, Ridge, Silverdale, The Pines, Wayland, Wildwood

National Register of Historic Places:
Bramble: Sts. Peter & Paul Russian Orthodox Church
Clementson: Williams Township School
International Falls: Alexander Baker School & E.W. Backus Junior High School, Koochiching County Courthouse
Island View: Gold Mine Sites, Little American Mine
Little Fork: Francis White Homestead
Ranier: Finstad's Auto Marine Shop, Ranier Community Building, Ernest C. Oberholtzer Rainy Lake Islands Historic District

Breweries/Wineries/Distilleries:
Cantilever Distillery (Ranier, MN)
Loony's Brew (Ranier, MN)

Town Celebrations:
Diva Days, International Falls, MN (November: Deer Hunting Opening Weekend)
Ice Box Days, International Falls, MN (3rd Weekend in January)
Internat. Falls Bass Championship, International Falls, MN (3rd Weekend in August)

LAC QUI PARLE COUNTY
EST. 1871 - POPULATION: 6,719

Lac qui Parle is named after the French translation of the Dakota phrase *Mde Iyedan*, meaning "lake that speaks."

BELLINGHAM, MN
POPULATION: 148 – CITY 123 OF 856 (4-10-25)
Platted on September 12, 1887, and incorporated on May 5, 1890, the village of Bellingham was laid out by William R. and Mary P. Thomas, Robert, and Phebe (Morse) Bellingham. The town took its name from the Bellingham family, who moved from Dane County, Wisconsin, to the area. As a Great Northern Railroad station, a multitude of business lines were established to meet the needs of its residents as they tilled the land and sent their yields to other shipping points around the company. Early firms would have included elevators, blacksmith shops, general stores, livery stables, hardware and implement stores, and all the other necessary businesses for prosperity. There was even an early newspaper brought to town by Hans M. Hagestead. He served as the first postmaster when an office was established in 1887. By the 1940s, Bellingham had a population of 456, but its population decreased in every subsequent decade (except for a 10.3% gain from 263 to 290 people between 1970 and 1980). Edgar H. Kienholz, best remembered for simultaneously coaching the football, basketball, and baseball teams of Santa Clara University in 1924, hails from here.

BOYD, MN
POPULATION: 141 – CITY 193 OF 856 (4-16-25)
Not only does Boyd claim to have the "Oldest Continuous Celebration in the U.S.A." with its Boyd "Good Time" Days celebration, but it is also the site of the most haunted home in southwestern Minnesota. The Boyd House, as it is called today, was initially built in 1901, but its storied history began twelve years earlier when Charles F. Hatch took his own life on the very land where the house was constructed. The long-term early owners of the home, Fred and Minnie Eckhardt, passed away there and can reportedly be seen wandering the gardens and property at times. Four of their eleven children also perished in the house and have since allegedly refused to leave. Other

tales suggest that some guests have encountered a ghost cat that occasionally knocks things off tables and curls around the ankles of unsuspecting investigators. Paranormal activities aside, the town of Boyd began as a railroad village circa 1884, when it was platted and named by officers of the Minneapolis and St. Louis Railroad. Businesses varied by type, but early reports indicate that it had banks, hotels, restaurants, pharmacies, general stores, a livery stable, a hardware store, churches, and a school at the height of its prosperity. Fred Eckhardt (mentioned above) and his father helped to build the Lutheran church; he was also a volunteer firefighter, a school board member, a city councilman, and the local Justice of the Peace. Five hundred and forty-nine people called Boyd home at its height in the 1920s, only a few decades after its incorporation as a municipality in 1893.

DAWSON, MN
POPULATION: 1,466 – CITY 259 OF 856 (5-9-25)

"Gnometown USA" has established a unique tradition of honoring prominent locals with their own three-foot-tall garden gnomes in an area of town called Gnome Park or at the Dawson Public Library. The first gnome, carved in 1989, honors Theodore Christianson. He was the 21st Governor of Minnesota from 1925 to 1931 and a former editor and publisher of the *Dawson Sentinel* newspaper (initially established in December 1884 by Charles J. Coghlan). Every year since the unveiling of the "Governor Ted" gnome statue, the City of Dawson has produced a new gnome statue to commemorate one of its past residents. They are typically revealed at the annual community festival, Riverfest, which always takes place in late June. The early history of Dawson dates to 1884, when the Scandinavian settlement was platted on the Lac qui Parle River and named in honor of William Dawson, one of three partners of the Dawson Townsite Company and the 20th Mayor of Saint Paul from 1878 to 1881. Dawson's development was rapid, thanks to the Minneapolis and St. Louis Railroad. Coghlan, the earlier-mentioned newspaper publisher, took on postmaster duties. Within only six years, Dawson had 418 residents and many businesses, churches, and schools to accommodate the needs of its people. In 1892, Christopher M. Anderson (another founder of Dawson) commissioned the construction of the Commercial Bank Building. The Richardsonian Romanesque building was the subject of an April 1930 burglary in which two people robbed the bank and forced eight people into the vault at gunpoint. It was locked, and the thieves fled. Unbeknownst to them, the vault was airtight, and the eight people inside quickly ran out of air. Their screams for help were thankfully heard by a customer, who, despite being unable to open the vault themselves, got the other bank president in town to open it and save everyone. Since the event, the bank has been listed on the National Register of Historic Places, turned into a local history museum, and featured on PBS's *Postcards* television series (S11, E12). In 1917-18, Dawson became the lucky recipient of one of Andrew Carnegie's grants to build a library, which was also added to the National Register. In an ironic twist, the Carnegie building is now a law office, and Dawson's third building on the Register, the Dawson Armory and Community Building, is the current public library. The original intention of the latter structure, built in 1923, was to serve as a multipurpose facility for the Minnesota National Guard. Another noteworthy point of interest within the town is the tiny church next to Gnome Park, which can house up to six people. Carrie Tollefson, a 1997 cross country champion and a member of the 2004 Summer Olympic middle-distance running team; Roger Reinert, the incumbent 40th Mayor of Duluth since January 4, 2024; Jeff Nordgaard, a professional overseas basketball player who achieved the first quadruple-double in Minnesota state basketball history in 1991; Theodore Christianson, the son of the honored 21st Governor and an Associate Justice of the Minnesota Supreme Court in the early

1950s; Phyllis Gates, author and wife of Hollywood star Rock Hudson; Edor Nelson, a multi-sport coach for Augsburg University between 1946 and 1979, and James Day Hodgson, the 12th United States Secretary of Labor and the United States Ambassador to Japan in the 1970s, have ties to the community.

LOUISBURG, MN
POPULATION: 31 – CITY 124 OF 856 (4-10-25)

William R. Thomas and Ole Thompson are recorded as having platted the Louisburg townsite on September 12, 1887, about the time the Great Northern Railway was extended through that part of the county. Ole Thompson named Louisburg in honor of his father, Louis Thompson, who had settled in an adjacent section of Lake Shore Township in 1876. Ole's son, Thomas, became the town's first postmaster when the community was awarded a post office in 1888. Throughout its history, Louisburg had few businesses and residents, reaching a peak population of only 99 in the 1920s. Still, one of its most significant accomplishments has remained to this day: the Louisburg School. The brick Victorian-style school building was built in 1911 to educate Louisburg's youth and provide adequate facilities for the teachers.

MADISON, MN ★☆
POPULATION: 1,518 – CITY 120 OF 856 (4-10-25)

Mr. Lou T. Fisk welcomes visitors to Minnesota's "Lake Country" and his city of Madison, which was dubbed the "Lutefisk Capital of the United States" after the idea surfaced at a 1982 city council meeting. Lutefisk is a Nordic delicacy cured in salt brine or lye that locals eat regularly. The dapper thirty-foot cod may be the most recognizable of the town's fifteen-hundred-plus residents, but alas, he had nothing to do with the town's establishment. Settlement began when Jacob F. Jacobson and others came from Iowa in 1875; it is also documented that S. Halverson and O. M. Larson arrived in 1877. When the Minneapolis and St. Louis Railroad came through, some land was purchased from John Anderson by general store owner H. A. Larson around 1884, and a townsite was platted under the name Madison in honor of Claus P. Moe's former hometown, Madison, Wisconsin. The post office was known as True for only a year before it was renamed Madison. As the trains began to arrive, Madison grew quickly, and it and Dawson began to duel for the county seat title. Lac qui Parle Village was the seat of government at that time and the oldest permanent settlement in the county, but its lack of a railroad led to the honor being removed to Madison in 1889. The courthouse building was moved to Madison after they won the election; it was replaced in 1899 by a much larger, distinct structure. The county commissioners and residents wanted the new building to last, so by using the designs of Buechner and Jacobson and the craftsmanship of Olaf Swenson of Saint Paul, a Richardsonian Romanesque structure with a protruding central tower was completed just before the turn of the century for $30,689. It was the first of three of Madison's distinctive civil buildings to go up during that period; the other two were the Madison City Hall (and opera house), built in 1902-03, and the Madison Carnegie Library, finished in 1905-06. All three locations are on the National Register of Historic Places. Charles W. Buechner partnered with Henry W. Orth on the city hall project after his former partner, John Jacobson, died in 1902. Madison adopted its city charter on March 12, 1902, amidst one of its most significant periods of growth. Its population reached 2,380 by the 1960s. The 2005 independent period drama *Sweet Land* was partially recorded here and in nearby Dawson. A pair of famous authors hail from Madison: Robert and Carol Bly. The two were married. Robert led the mythopoetic men's movement and spent 62 weeks atop the *New York Times* Best Seller list with his book *Iron John: A*

Book About Men. Carol was an award-winning short-story and nonfiction writer whose work sought to show how Minnesota women identified and solved crises through empathy. At the Lac qui Parle Museum, visitors can learn more about the county's townships, schools, wildlife, and more through a large museum building and several outdoor exhibits.

Restaurant Recommendation:
The Sticks Bar & Grill
205 8th Ave
Madison, MN 56256

MARIETTA, MN
POPULATION: 116 – CITY 121 OF 856 (4-10-25)
Marietta (population 116 as of the 2020 Census) is most famous for being the site of Minnesota's only alkaline lake, appropriately named Salt Lake. Alkaline soils surrounding the lake runoff into the water, and with no inlet or outlet, the lake's salinity has increased to about one-third that of typical seawater. Avid birdwatchers have identified over 140 species of birds at the lake over the year, ranging from shoveler and canvasback ducks to willets, avocets, and other fowl that feed on brine shrimp and Sago pondweed. Marietta was platted in 1884 and named by its early settlers after their former hometown of Marietta, Ohio. Like other Minnesota communities, it owes its establishment to the advent of a railroad—in this case, the Minneapolis and St. Louis Railroad. A post office was organized in 1884, and the town was incorporated in 1899. Through its 1920s heyday, when it had 413 residents, Marietta featured an array of general merchandise stores, grain elevators, banks, lumber yards, hardware and implement dealers, professional offices, churches, a school, and more. *The Marietta News*, a newspaper, remained in circulation from 1907 to 1952.

NASSAU, MN
POPULATION: 65 – CITY 122 OF 856 (4-10-25)
This little slice of Minnesota paradise was not named for the capital of the Bahamas but rather for a German town in Rhineland-Palatinate with a modern population of about 5,000. The Great Northern Railway village came into being in 1893, when the railroad needed a mail, refueling, and shipping point just before the South Dakota border. A post office was in operation a half-decade before the town's establishment, but it shuttered its doors in 1998 after several years of population decline. It has experienced a decrease in its numbers in every Census since 1940, with its worst loss coming between 1960 and 1970, when the population dropped by 30.8% from 182 residents to 126 that decade. In its prime, Nassau would have met all the needs of its citizens through commercial, fraternal, educational, and religious organizations and institutions, as in neighboring communities.

Unincorporated/Ghost Towns: Cerro Gordo, Haydenville, Lac qui Parle, Providence, Rosen, Williamsburg

National Register of Historic Places:
Dawson: Commercial Bank Building, Dawson Armory & Community Building, Dawson Carnegie Library
Louisburg: Louisburg School
Madison: Lac qui Parle County Courthouse, Madison Carnegie Library, Madison City Hall
Montevideo: Camp Release State Monument, Lac qui Parle Mission Archeological Historic District, Lac qui Parle State Park WPA/Rustic Style Historic District

Golf Courses:
Dawson Golf Course, Daily Fee (Dawson, MN)
Madison Country Club, Daily Fee (Madison, MN)

Town Celebrations:
Riverfest, Dawson, MN (Last Weekend of June)

LAKE COUNTY
EST. 1856 - POPULATION: 10,905

It would be shameful for the Land of 10,000 Lakes not to have its own "Lake County," a jurisdiction in Minnesota's northeast corner that owes its name to its location on the shores of Lake Superior.

BEAVER BAY, MN
POPULATION: 120 – CITY 389 OF 856 (6-24-25)
The oldest continuous European settlement on the North Shore of Lake Superior, Beaver Bay, was platted on June 24, 1856, by Thomas Clark. He and Robert McLean camped at the mouth of the Beaver River in October 1854, shortly after the Treaty of LaPointe had opened up Minnesota's Arrowhead Region for mining prospectors and settlers. The area's beauty gave them the idea that it would be the ideal place to establish a community. On the same day that Clark filed the town plat in Saint Louis County, twenty-five German immigrants (most of whom were the Weiland brothers and their families) arrived by steamer. Over the decades, they developed a substantial townsite. Mining, fishing, and logging were the primary industries of the lake town, which, until 1886, served as the county seat until the honor was removed to Two Harbors. By this time, the Wielands had all passed away or moved their families to the handsome young city of Duluth, and Beaver Bay's growth had stagnated. It still operated as a port city, and in 1905, it became momentarily famous throughout the region when the Madeira Schooner-Barge wrecked during the Mataafa Storm of November 27-28, 1905, which destroyed about two dozen seafaring vessels on Lake Superior. In response to the disaster, the $75,000 54-foot-tall Split Rock Lighthouse (now part of a State Park) was erected between Beaver Bay and Two Harbors to prevent future accidents. On August 5, 1953, members of the township voted to incorporate Beaver Bay as a village. Mayor Art Lorntson was elected that September. Despite losing its school for good the following year, the structure was reused as a church and a municipal liquor store. A fire department was established in 1958. Nowadays, the little hamlet claims to be the home of the John Beargrease Dog Sled Race, a several-hundred-mile race held each January that starts from Billy's Bar in Duluth and continues up the North Shore. Its name pays homage to John Beargrease, the long-time mail carrier between Two Harbors and Grand Portage, who used a dog sled and a rowboat to aid in his deliveries.

SILVER BAY, MN
POPULATION: 1,857 – CITY 388 OF 856 (6-24-25)
When the Northern Land Company and the Lake Superior Land Company began to subtly sell large swaths of land north of Beaver Bay to the Reserve Mining Company in the early 1940s, people became suspicious. The transactions were quietly made in cash, and many speculated that the company was planning to build an epic hotel and resort not far from Peterson's store. This idea was not too far-fetched, but in 1946, the mining company, owned by Armco and Republic Steel, shocked everyone when it

announced it would build a large taconite processing plant on the shores of Lake Superior. Work was outsourced to the Hunkin-Conkey Company of Cleveland, Ohio; the L. E. Dixon Company of San Gabriel, California; and the Arundal Corporation of Baltimore, Maryland, to put up enough housing and infrastructure between Babbitt (where the taconite was mined) and Silver Bay to support at least 3,500 workers and their families. Throughout the 1950s, the plant was developed, and housing was completed in the form of a trailer park and inexpensive homes that cost some workers only $50 a month to rent. On May 1, 1954, the name "Silver Bay" was selected for the new town. The decision was made to incorporate the town as an independent municipality from Lake County and nearby Beaver Bay on October 16, 1956. The C.L. Austin, a laker, made the first shipment of taconite pellets that year, and within only a few more years, Silver Bay was producing six million tons annually. Campton Elementary School, Mary MacDonald Elementary School, and William Kelley High School were established to provide employees' children with a place to study and play while their parents were at work. When it was discovered that the Corporation was dumping its taconite tailings into Lake Superior, the U.S. The Justice Department filed suit against them on February 17, 1972, for violating the Rivers and Harbors Act of 1899. By July 7, 1977, tailings were instead being dumped at Mile Post 7, a tailings storage basin. Only thirty years after the plant opened, it closed on July 31, 1986, having shipped out approximately 219,024,410 tons of pellets from the "Taconite Capital of the World." Cyprus North Shore Mining Company purchased the plant shortly thereafter, thereby saving the town. Cleveland-Cliffs bought them out in 1994. The scrappy Rocky Taconite mascot statue, unveiled in 1964 as a tribute to Silver Bay's mining history, is one of northeast Minnesota's most recognizable roadside figures. Nearby points of interest are Split Rock Lighthouse State Park, famous for its iconic 1910 lighthouse (see Two Harbors); Tettegouche State Park, home to the historic Tettegouche Camp Historic [Resort] District and the highest waterfall in Minnesota, the 60-foot-tall High Falls on the Baptism River; the Hesper Shipwreck Site, a 1905 bulk freight steamship that went down on May 4, 1905, and Black Beach Park, known for its taconite-rich back sands. The unique taconite-lined beaches were opened to the public in 2015 and are among the most distinctive in the state.

TWO HARBORS, MN ★☆
POPULATION: 3,633 – CITY 386 OF 856 (6-23-25)

Two Harbors, the birthplace of the Minnesota Mining and Manufacturing Company (perhaps better known today as 3M, the multinational conglomerate with billions of dollars in annual revenues because of its strong foothold in the consumer goods sector), has an incredible history based on its designation as one of northeast Minnesota's premier lake ports. The town was once two separate communities: Agate Bay, incorporated in 1854, and Burlington, incorporated on May 23, 1857. Both existed before Minnesota achieved statehood on May 11, 1858. For the next quarter-century, those who elected to live in the quiet region enjoyed peace and prosperity until a life-changing discovery was made in Minnesota's Arrowhead Region: iron. In 1884, an iron ore dock was built, and the Duluth, Missabe & Northern (Iron Range) Railroad was completed. Two Harbors–a new, consolidated name given to the two natural bays and towns in 1885–was ready to rock and roll (its train cars of ore to Duluth and Ely) as an essential trade point. Its newfound industries gave it the Lake County seat in 1886, and two years later, it was incorporated as a village. More than thirty logging camps were in operation by the turn of the century. Factories were built by the Two Harbors Cigar Factory for the production and distribution of cigars, by Two Harbors Bottling Works for the production of bottles, and by the aforementioned 3M company for the production of fiberglass products. The five founders of 3M, Henry S. Bryan,

Herman Cable, William McGonagle, J. Danley Budd, and John Dwan, had sought to capitalize on the area's corundum deposits used to make sandpaper. When they shipped the mineral to a company in Chicago and realized it was not genuine corundum, they chose to focus on alternative products. By 1905, they had moved to Duluth, and in 1907 to the Twin Cities. The John Dwan Office Building, built in 1898 as the law office of the attorney who brought the 3M company to reality, has since been preserved as the 3M Birthplace Museum and listed on the National Register of Historic Places. According to the 1910 Census, nearly 5,000 citizens lived in the bustling city. At that point, Two Harbors had reached its heyday peak. The Two Harbors Carnegie Library building was completed in 1909, as was the 1906 Beaux-Arts Lake County Courthouse and Sheriff's Residence, and the 1907 Duluth and Iron Range Railroad Company Depot, now a Depot Museum. The Edna G tugboat, built for the D&IR Railroad in 1896 to guide ships into the harbor from 1898 to 1931 and 1933 to 1981; the Two Harbors Light Station, first lit on April 14, 1892, and noted for being the oldest operating lighthouse in Minnesota; the shipwrecked (in 1896 and 1922, respectively) Samuel P. Ely Topsail schooner and Harriet B. railcar ferry; Split Rock Lighthouse State Park and its iconic 1910 lighthouse, and 88 contributing parties at Gooseberry Falls State Park built from 1933 to 1941 round out its most historical locations. The scenic park is renowned for its Upper, Middle, and Lower Falls, as well as hiking, mountain biking, and camping. Pierre the Pantsless Voyageur at Earthwood Inn, one of Peter Toth's famous carved Indian Heads, located at the Two Harbors Visitor Center, and the Northern Rail Traincar Inn, where tourists can stay overnight in themed railroad boxcars, and worthwhile points of interest as well. Of course, no town can be known for its attractions alone. Several people have put Two Harbors on the map over the years through their work: Lute Olsen, the head coach of the University of Iowa collegiate men's basketball team from 1974 to 1983 and the University of Arizona from 1983 to 2007 and a member of both the Naismith Memorial Basketball Hall of Fame and the National Collegiate Basketball Hall of Fame; Johnny Western, the renowned country singer-songwriter; Leroy Goldsworthy, a forward in the NHL from 1929 to 1939 and the first Minnesotan to have his name engraved on the coveted Stanley Cup; Rhonda Britten, the author of four bestsellers including "Fearless Living"; Esther Rose, a famous oil, watercolor, and silkscreen painter; Don Moen, a Christian worship singer-songwriter, and Philip Berrigan, a Josephite Catholic priest and activist best known for being one of the Catonsville Nine.

Restaurant Recommendation:
Betty's Pies
2019, 1633 MN-61
Two Harbors, MN 55616

Restaurant Recommendation:
McQuade's Pub & Grill
1102 7th Ave
Two Harbors, MN 55616

Restaurant Recommendation:
Russ Kendall's Smoke House
149 Scenic Dr
Knife River, MN 55609

Restaurant Recommendation:
Great! Lakes Candy Kitchen
223 Scenic Dr
Knife River, MN 55609

Lodging Recommendation:
Lighthouse Bed and Breakfast
1 Lighthouse Point Rd
Two Harbors, MN 55616

Lodging Recommendation:
Northern Rail Traincar Inn
1730 Co Hwy 3
Two Harbors, MN 55616

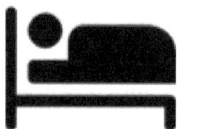

Unincorporated/Ghost Towns: Alger, Avon, Avoy, Beaver, Britton, Buell, Case, Castle Danger, Clark, Cramer, Crystal, Darby Junction, Drummond, East Beaver Bay, Eclfo, Emetta, Fernburg Tower, Finland, Forest Center, Freedom, Green, Greenwood Junction, Highland, Howlett, Illgen City, Isabella, Jordana, Kent, Knife River, Larsmont, Lax Lake, Little Marais, London, Malmota, Maple, Marble Lake, McNair, Moose, Morris, Murfin, Murphy City, Nigadoo, Norshore Junction, North Branch, Riblet, Sawbill Landing, Scott Junction, Section Thirty, Silver, Silver Creek, Splitrock, Stafford, Stewart, Summit, Swift, Thomas, Toimi, Waldo, Wales, Wanless, Westover, Whyte, Wolf, York

National Register of Historic Places:
Beaver Bay: *Madeira* (Schooner-Barge) Shipwreck
East Beaver Bay: Edward & Lisa Mattson House & Fish House
Fall Lake Township: Halfway Ranger Station, Kawishiwi Lodge
Isabella: Isabella Ranger Station
Knife River: *Benjamin Noble* (Shipwreck), *Onoko* (Bulk Freight Steamer) Shipwreck, *Niagara* Shipwreck Site
Larsmont: Larsmont School
Silver Bay: *Hesper* Shipwreck Site, Tettegouche Camp Historic District
Silver Creek Township: Bridge No. 3589-Silver Creek Township
Two Harbors: Duluth & Iron Range Railroad Company Depot, *Edna G* (tugboat), John Dwan Office Building, Lake County Courthouse & Sheriff's Residence, Two Harbors Carnegie Library, Two Harbors Light Station, Gooseberry Falls State Park CCC/WPA/Rustic Style Historic Resources, *Harriet B.* (shipwreck), *Samuel P. Ely* Shipwreck, Split Rock Lighthouse

Golf Courses:
Lakeview National Golf Course, Municipal (Two Harbors, MN)
Silver Bay Golf Course, Municipal (Silver Bay, MN)

Breweries/Wineries/Distilleries:
Castle Danger Brewery (Two Harbors, MN)

Town Celebrations:
Heritage Days, Two Harbors, MN (Thursday through Sunday after the 4th of July)
St. Urho's Day Celebration, Finland, MN (Weekend closest to March 16th)

LAKE OF THE WOODS COUNTY
EST. 1923 - POPULATION: 3,763

Lake of the Woods County, named for the lake with 65,000 miles of shoreline, is unique for not only being the site of the Northernmost Point of the Contiguous United States, but also for being the only county in the nation with four words in its name.

ANGLE INLET, MN
POPULATION: 54 – UNINCORPORATED (5-31-25)

The "Northernmost Point of the Lower 48 States" is at The Northwest Angle and Angle Inlet, the only such place in the United States north of the 49th parallel. The 123.09-square-mile area was inadvertently created due to a mapping error in the 1783 Treaty of Paris, which established the boundaries between British North America (now Canada) and the United States. Benjamin Franklin, the proponent of the treaty, convinced the British to accept that the border extended to the "most northwestmost point" of the Lake of the Woods to the boundary waters. When a south line heading south towards the 49° latitude line was surveyed in 1818, the Northwest Angle and its islands were created. It was then realized that a part of U.S. territory was utterly cut off from the mainland.

While the early history of the Angle's settlement dates back to 1732 when La Vérendrye established Fort Saint Charles, the "functional enclave" is now home to about 54 residents, according to the 2020 U.S. Census. It is the site of the northernmost post office (established in 1936); the northernmost golf course, the Northwest Angle Country Club; the northernmost bar, Jerry's Restaurant & Lounge; the northernmost school, the last-of-its-kind (in Minnesota) one-room Angle Inlet Elementary School, and the northernmost road. As of 2025, Prothero's Post Resort, the Angle Outpost Resort, and Young's Bar Resort operate as some of the options for visiting fishermen to stay, but most visitors come to take pictures with the makeshift buoy reading: "Northernmost Point: Contiguous U.S.A." It is similar to the monument in Key West, Florida, marking the "Southernmost Point" of the lower 48 states. Placing a buoy in the swamp at the actual northernmost point would prove troublesome for sightseers seeking to visit it, so Northwest Angle residents Joseph Laurin, Richard McKeever, and a handful of others elected to establish it on the grounds of Young's Bay Resort.

During the COVID-19 pandemic, a 37-mile ice highway was created across the Lake of the Woods to allow travelers (for $145 to $250 per vehicle) to reach Angle Inlet without passing through Canada. It began at the Springsteel Resort on the southwest corner of the Lake of the Woods and continued northward into the Angle. However, ice does melt, so U.S. citizens typically must travel by boat charter or by road in Manitoba, Canada, to access the point. Drivers usually access the Angle by taking Minnesota State Highway 313 across the Warroad-Sprague Border Crossing, which connects to Manitoba Highway 12. Follow Highway 12 to Provincial Road 308, to Provincial Road 525, which leads into the United States at the Northwest Angle. There is no staff at the border crossing. People instead continue a few miles eastward and use an iPad at "Jim's Corner" to check in with U.S. Customs. When leaving, they use a telephone to notify Canadian Customs of their return to Canadian territory. Upon returning to the mainland, visitors leaving the Northwest Angle and Canada must again stop at the U.S. Border Crossing station. The controversial crossing at Jim's Corner has led some to suggest that Angle Inlet secede from the United States and join Canada. Colin Peterson, a Member of the U.S. House of Representatives from

Minnesota's 7th District from January 1991 to January 2021, proposed legislation in 1997 (using resident Gary Dietzler's mock secession draft) that would have allowed this secession. It drew heavy criticism from the Red Lake Indian Reservation, which owns the majority of the land encompassing the Northwest Angle. Unfair fishing regulations between the United States and Canada led to this idea. Following the incident, the regulations were better synchronized to benefit the local fishing industry.

Restaurant Recommendation:
Jerry's Restaurant & Lounge
7609 Young's Bay Dr NW
Angle Inlet, MN 56711

Lodging Recommendation:
Prothero's Post Resort
17696 Prothero Dr NW
Angle Inlet, MN 56711

BAUDETTE, MN ★☆
POPULATION: 966 – CITY 288 OF 856 (6-1-25)

For nearly 60 years, Willie Walleye welcomed anglers and visitors alike to the "Walleye Capital of the World," an appropriate name given the importance and longevity of the fishing industry there. Willie was demolished in July 2018 after serving for 59 years, and a newer, 40-foot-long fiberglass statue was installed shortly afterward. When the Minnesota and Manitoba (eventually taken over by the Canadian National Railway, whose local depot was listed on the NRHP in August 2005) crossed the Canadian border and the Rainy River, a plan to establish a final United States shipping point on the line was put into motion. It was centralized around the Port Hyland post office, established in 1900 when Daniel Hyland was postmaster. The name was changed to honor Joseph Beaudette, a fur trapper and fisherman who had arrived in the early 1880s. Thomas Cathcart and his family joined him about a decade later. Three hotels and two general stores were established, and plans were enacted to erect a sawmill and roundhouse facilities for the railroad. In 1904, the "twin town" of Spooner was founded just across the river from Baudette and the Shevlin Company Milling Company. Despite losing everything in the Baudette fire of October 1910 that wiped out hundreds of thousands of acres of land and took the lives of about three dozen settlers, Baudette and Spooner, nicknamed "East Baudette," grew in unison with one another. Baudette was designated the judicial seat of Lake of the Woods County, the northernmost county in the United States (since Alaska has no counties), in 1922, when it was partitioned from Beltrami County. Spooner was annexed by Baudette in 1954, and its school was renovated into the new county courthouse. It was demolished in 2001 after a new courthouse was built. Rowell Laboratories, Inc. was a major pharmaceutical manufacturer in Baudette from 1935 to 1986, a period during which Baudette's population reached a high of 1,597 people in the 1960s. The company succeeded when Joe and Theodore H. Rowell discovered that burbot (a type of coldwater ray-finned fish) liver oil was high in vitamins A and D and commercialized it. Frigid winters led to the establishment of Automotive Enviro Testing at Baudette. This company offers its cold-weather test facility to companies like Tesla and Honda. Naturally, hockey has always been an essential piece of the local culture. Keith Ballard, a defenseman in the NHL from 2005 to 2015; Alex Lyon, most recently a goaltender for the NHL's Detroit Red Wings in the 2024-25 season; and Wally Olds, a member of the 1972 Winter Olympics U.S. men's hockey silver-medalist team, hail from here.

WILLIAMS, MN
POPULATION: 157 – CITY 287 OF 856 (6-1-25)

William Mason and George Williams settled in this vicinity circa 1901 after following the railbed of the Minnesota and Manitoba Railroad to this point. When William H. Dure became postmaster in 1903, it was thought appropriate to name the town Williams, as many of its early prominent men had that first or last name. Early Williams likely had only a few residences and businesses, all of which were destroyed in the great Baudette Fire of 1910, which torched no fewer than 300,000 acres of prime logging land. The town was incorporated in 1922, only months before Lake of the Woods County was organized on January 1, 1923. Zippel Bay State Park, located on the sandy southern shore of the Lake of the Woods, was established in 1959. Located closer to Williams than any other incorporated community, it offers prime recreational activities such as fishing, camping, and hiking. Cross-country skiers come to the area in the wintertime. Once home to a peak population of 414 people in the 1950s, Williams hosts an annual "Back Home Days" event during the second weekend of July, when former residents of the town and their families and friends return to celebrate together. In October, the city selects a "Potato Day Queen" at its annual Potato Day Festival.
Roosevelt is only partially located in Lake of the Woods County (see Roseau County).

Unincorporated/Ghost Towns: Angle Inlet, Arnesén, Birch Beach, Carp, Clementson, Faunce, Graceton, Hackett, Long Point, Lude, Oak Island, Penasse, Pitt, Sandy Shores, Wheeler's Point

National Register of Historic Places:
Angle Inlet: Fort St. Charles Archeological Site, Northwest Point
Baudette: Canadian National Railways Depot
Roosevelt: Norris Camp

Town Celebrations:
Williams Potato Day, Williams, MN (1st Weekend in October)

LE SUEUR COUNTY
EST. 1853 - POPULATION: 28,674

Pierre-Charles Le Sueur explored this region circa 1700, about 150 years before it was organized into a county on March 5, 1853.

CLEVELAND, MN
POPULATION: 747 – CITY 627 OF 856 (9-29-25)

Cleveland, Minnesota, is named after Cleveland, Ohio, from which many of its original inhabitants came in the mid-1850s. Others arrived via the privately funded Dodd Road, which connected Mendota and St. Peter as early as 1853, enabling widespread travel in south-central Minnesota. The hamlet was similar to others in its early years, with general stores, blacksmith shops, and livery stables the norm. However, it stood out for one unique rule: temperance. Under the laws of its founders, Cleveland was a temperance town; therefore, no saloons were allowed to operate within its limits. Many settlers enjoyed the peace and tranquility that this rule brought to their community. As the population grew rapidly, Cleveland entered into a rivalry with nearby Le Sueur to secure the coveted county seat. The feud continued for decades. In 1875, Cleveland finally got what it wanted when a militia took the seat by force, causing minor bloodshed. Cleveland held the title for a single year before residents of the county collectively agreed that it should be located in Le Center, at the heart of Le Sueur

County. The Geldner Sawmill was relocated to its present site that year; it has since survived as the county's last remaining early sawmill. Many other business lines also came to fruition once the Omaha Railroad connected Cleveland with other nearby communities. It was incorporated as a village on March 9, 1904.

Restaurant Recommendation:
The Bait Bucket Bar & Grill
114 10th St
Cleveland, MN 56017

ELYSIAN, MN
POPULATION: 708 – CITY 620 OF 856 (9-28-25)
Incorporated on March 2, 1883, and separated from the township on March 20, 1908, Elysian derived its name from the mythical Elysian Fields, the final resting place of Greek heroines. The paradise, alternatively known as Elysium (the name used by the local post office from 1856 to 1858), inspired this town's name due to its quiet, peaceful demeanor and its gently rolling hills and fields. A nearby lake, titled as Okaman Lake on Joseph N. Nicollet's 1843 map, also shares its name with the community. Elysian was platted in 1856 and had a post office by 1859. By the onset of the 20th century, it had approximately 459 residents, a number it would not surpass until the dawn of the 21st century. While many homes, businesses, churches, and the Wisconsin, Minnesota & Pacific Railroad graced the Elysian landscape, the most interesting structure of them all was the 1895 Elysian Public School building. The two-story red brick landmark with its bell tower was constructed for about $5,000, $3,000 of which came from a bond passed by the townspeople. Classes continued in the structure until 1965, when a new school structure was built. It has since been converted into the Le Sueur County Historical Society Museum, serving as a repository of historical and genealogical resources and artifacts for generations.

HEIDELBERG, MN
POPULATION: 137 – CITY 665 OF 856 (10-3-25)
Heidelberg shares its name with Germany's Heidelberg University, one of the world's oldest surviving universities, founded on October 18, 1386. German settlers Frank Heil and Frederick Ihrig suggested the name for this Minnesota town's platting on December 4, 1878, in the same decade that the United States Postal Service established the Heidelberg post office. Unfortunately, the postal branch was closed in 1903 due to Heidelberg's lack of a railroad at the time (the closest was the Minneapolis & St. Louis, located a couple of miles to the east). Yet, its citizens' spirits remained unwavering, and they continued to build. A general store, a shoe shop, and a blacksmith shop were its three primary commercial institutions before the population began to decline. By 1960, Heidelberg had just 44 residents and was well on its way to disincorporation. The small-town lifestyle appealed to many who wanted to live in a rural setting but work in urban areas. So, the town was saved by becoming a distant bedroom community for other nearby cities in Le Sueur County. As of the 2020 Census, Heidelberg recorded a Census population of 137 persons.

KASOTA, MN
POPULATION: 714 – CITY 629 OF 856 (9-29-25)
Located on the southern side of the Minnesota River, across from the former state capital of Saint Peter, Kasota enjoyed service from three major railroads in its heyday: the Winona & Saint Peter, the Chicago, St. Paul, Minneapolis & Omaha, and the

Chicago, Milwaukee & St. Paul. Early records indicate that the oldest inhabitant of the region was Reuben Butters, who found himself on the present townsite in the fall of 1851. A surveyor, either Buell or Folsom, officially laid out the townsite about two years later and named it for an adjacent prairie and a Dakota word meaning "cleared off." As the town developed, an unsuspecting industry emerged as the primary driver of the local economy: stone quarrying. The Babcock Company was founded to quarry the famous Kasota limestone, used to build trestles and culverts, and to decorate people's homes when polished. C.W. Babcock and Tyrrell Swan Wilcox were at the forefront of the company and its marketing efforts, and it was under their direction that tensions arose between the City of Kasota and the company. At one point, Babcock's firm decided to begin blasting within city limits, which led to the creation of the small park now present at County Road 21. When the Babcocks went bankrupt in the 1980s, their firm was acquired by The Vetter Stone Company, a company founded in the 1950s by former Babcock employees who had left to start their own quarrying business. The grandest use of the stone can be found at the National Museum of the American Indian in Washington, D.C., one of several Smithsonian Institution museums in the nation's capital. Aside from quarrying, early Kasota also had two grist mills, a sawmill, a wagon shop, a hotel, a general store, and a blacksmith shop. Some structures built during this early period of development, including the 1888 Kasota Township Hall, the 1898 village hall, and the Shanaska Creek Bridge—the oldest surviving Platt truss bridge, built in 1875—have remained and are listed on the National Register of Historic Places. On July 1, 1892, John Sontag, George Contant, and Chris Evans (not the Captain America we know today) attempted to rob a train traveling between St. Peter and Kasota; their attempt resulted in no spoils of value, but it did attract the attention of Allan Pinkerton, a noted Scottish-American detective. A couple of ships, the Kasota iron ore steamer on the Great Lakes, operational from 1884 until its sinking in 1890; and the 1944 to 1961 USS Kasota naval tugboat, obtained their names from the city. Thrillseekers from around the country come to Kasota to spend a day at Kasota's "Drive A Tank," the only place in the country where civilians can drive real military tanks. Car-crushing, driving through mobile homes, and firing miniguns are just some of the (albeit expensive) activities that visitors can partake in.

KILKENNY, MN
POPULATION: 148 – CITY 625 OF 856 (9-29-25)
Irish emigrants arrived in Minnesota from County Kilkenny and the City of Kilkenny, Ireland, in 1856. The Great Irish Potato Famine of 1845-1852 had just subsided, but excitement was in the air amongst prospective Irish families who wanted a fresh start on American soil. Dennis Doyle built a home and opened a storefront here in the mid-1850s, and from 1857 to 1888, he served as its postmaster. Doyle also served as the first township clerk, one of the first schoolteachers, and as a state legislator, making him one of Kilkenny's most influential figures and a key driver of its early development. When the Minneapolis and St. Louis Railroad came through in 1877, they initially called their station Washburn, but Doyle insisted it be changed to match the pre-existing village. When the depot was removed in the 1960s, approximately one-fifth of Kilkenny's population went with it. In 2013, Kilkenny was "twinned" with its namesake city in Ireland to foster relations and celebrate shared culture.

LE CENTER, MN ★☆
POPULATION: 2,517 – CITY 626 OF 856 (9-29-25)
From its purposeful establishment as the Le Sueur County Seat in 1864 to 1931, this town of 2,500-odd citizens was called "Le Sueur Center" until the name was shortened

to avoid confusion with the nearby town of Le Sueur. It was platted on December 2, 1876, at the geographical center of the county in an area that was once heavily covered by hardwood forests. Several businesspeople, spearheaded by L.Z. Rogers of Waterville, collaborated to acquire 160 acres of land for the townsite and a two-story courthouse building. The modern-day Romanesque courthouse was not completed until 1896, and its equally impressive jail was furnished in 1914. Both locations are listed on the National Register of Historic Places. In 1864, the post office was established on John Chapman's farm under the name Union Centre, but it was replaced by the Lesueur Center office in 1893. As the years passed, the Chicago, St. Paul, Minneapolis, and Omaha Railroad helped convince many store owners to open their shops here, as well as religious organizations to establish their congregations, and educational, civic, and fraternal organizations to flourish.

LE SUEUR, MN
POPULATION: 4,213 – CITY 628 OF 856 (9-29-25)

Le Sueur is best known as the original home of Dr. William Worrall Mayo, who began his practice there and ultimately founded the multi-billion-dollar healthcare company Mayo Clinic with his sons, William and Charles. He arrived only about a decade after early Le Sueur residents selected the name for their townsite to honor Pierre-Charles Le Sueur, a fur trader who was the first European to explore the Minnesota River Valley. Other Frenchmen called the region "Prairie la Fleche," meaning "prairie the arrow." George W. Thompson made his land claim in 1852, and despite Henry McLean's attempts to remove him from the Winnebago Reservation, he, J.M. Farmer, and others were about to lay out a village called Le Sueur. McLean had a government license to work with Native Americans in the area. After evicting Thompson from the land he desired, he worked with John Christy and John Catheart to establish his own community, also called Le Sueur. Unbeknownst to him, Thompson's Le Sueur had already been officially platted, and so he had to change his village's name to Le Sueur City. It was not until 1867 that the Minnesota Legislature remedied the situation by uniting the two communities into a single borough town, thereby allowing for their unified incorporation as a municipality. Some records indicate that Thompson's Le Sueur was incorporated on June 10, 1858, and McLean's Le Sueur City attained incorporation status only seven days later. Until 1875, the joint community was the county seat of government, until its records were stolen by force by a militia from Cleveland. Despite losing the county seat, Le Sueur remained the county's most successful economic center, thanks mainly to its location along a line of the Chicago, St. Paul, Minneapolis & Omaha Railroad. Businesses varied and ranged from a creamery, elevator, and store to more expansive operations, such as vegetable canning. The industry began in 1903 when fourteen merchants banded together to establish the Minnesota Valley Canning Company. They produced 11,750 cases of Evergreen Cream Corn as their first product line; their famous sugar snap peas followed in 1925. As their influence over the region expanded and they acquired over 20,000 acres of land, stakeholders in the company conceived the idea of introducing a company mascot based on the folk hero Paul Bunyan. The result was the Jolly Green Giant, which has since become one of the most recognizable food mascots in the United States. In 1950, the company changed its name to The Green Giant Company, thereby forever associating the giant with its brand. While the company was purchased by Pillsbury in 1979 and the original processing plant was closed in January 1995, there are still some nods to the character around the city, like the 2-D Green Giant on Commerce Street. The Davisco Creamery, the Le Sueur Inc. foundry, and Cambria are now the three largest firms with local operations. Although the 1870 German Evangelical Salem Church, listed on the NRHP in March 1982, is located outside of

Le Sueur city limits, the historic homes of William W. Mayo (1859); Edson Smith/James A. Cosgrove (1878, Second Empire); George W. Taylor (1890, Eastlake movement), and Carson H. Cosgrove (1895), are located in town. The Mayo House has since been restored as a Minnesota Historical Society site.

MONTGOMERY, MN
POPULATION: 3,249 – CITY 664 OF 856 (10-3-25)

At the intersection of the Chicago, Milwaukee & St. Paul and the Minneapolis & St. Louis Railroads lies Montgomery, a Czech settlement that calls itself the "Kolacky Capital of the World." A "kolacky" is a Czech pastry made from puffy yeast dough and typically filled with cherry, apple, or other fruit jam, poppy seeds, or cream cheese. It is traditionally spelled as "kolach" or "koláče." Although rich in Bohemian heritage, as indicated by its annual Kolacky Day celebration (held since October 1, 1929), Kolacky Queen crowning, the Masopust Festival, the Miss-Czech Slovak MN Pageant, and its designation as Minnesota's largest Czech-populated area, the name "Montgomery" honors the British-American military general Richard Montgomery. John and Jane Martin platted the village, townsite on September 5, 1877, shortly after the M&StL Railroad came through. Dense hardwood forests had to be cleared to make way for homes and businesses alike, and Charles L. Lane managed the post office in its proprietary days. Seneca Foods, an American food processor and distributor known for its canned fruit and vegetable brands, now owns and operates the former Green Giant freezing and canning facility at Montgomery. Twenty-nine properties in central Montgomery comprise the Montgomery Commercial Historic District, which was built between 1877 and 1940. The Westerman Lumber Office and House was headquartered in the city in 1889 and built from bricks manufactured in the Minnesota River Valley. Hilltop Hall, another early commercial building constructed in 1892, is located nearby.

Restaurant Recommendation:
Franke's Bakery
200 1st St S
Montgomery, MN 56069

WATERVILLE, MN
POPULATION: 1,750 – CITY 624 OF 856 (9-29-25)

Tourism to Waterville increases significantly in early June during "Bullhead Days," when this town of 1,750 residents comes together to celebrate its community. Named after Waterville, Maine, by E.I. Wright, one of nine New Englanders who platted the village in 1856, Le Sueur County's southeasternmost community grew in conjunction with the establishment of the Wisconsin, Minnesota & Pacific and the Minneapolis & St. Louis Railroad lines by Lake Tetonka and Sakatah Lake. The latter lake, known regionally for its identifying feature, Sakatah Lake State Park, was formed at a natural widening of the Cannon River. Lake Tetonka is known for its fish hatchery. A post office was founded in 1856, and the following year, the first general store and hotel were erected. E. L. Wright replatted the village on behalf of the M&StL Railroad in 1877, and on February 28, 1878, it was incorporated. The Union Hotel, built in 1888 to serve vacationers looking to enjoy the two lakes, still stands as an early reminder of Waterville's very early status as a tourist destination. Famed lithographer Adolf Dehn, noted for contributions to several American art movements, and Major A.B. Rogers, the surveyor who discovered Rogers Pass in British Columbia, Canada, both have communal ties. Waterville's population nearly doubles or triples annually during the summer months as tourists flock to Kamp Dels and other resorts on Sakatah Lake.

Restaurant Recommendation:
Cool Wave Coffee
801 Fremont St E
Waterville, MN 56096

Mankato is only partially located in La Sueur County (see Blue Earth County) and New Prague is only partially located in La Sueur County (see Scott County).

Unincorporated/Ghost Towns: Cordova, Greenland, Henderson Station, Lexington, Marysburg, Okaman, Ottawa, St. Henry, St. Thomas, Union Hill

National Register of Historic Places:
Cleveland & Kilkenny: Dodd Road Discontiguous District
Cleveland: Geldner Sawmill
Elysian: Elysian Public School
Kasota: Bridge No. 4846, John R. Andrews House, Kasota Township Hall, Kasota Village Hall
Le Center: Le Sueur County Courthouse & Jail
Le Sueur: Carson H. Cosgrove House, Dr. William W. Mayo House, George W. Taylor House, Smith-Cosgrove House, German Evangelical Salem Church
Montgomery: Hilltop Hall, Montgomery Commercial Historic District, Westerman Lumber Office & House
New Prague: First National Bank, Hotel Broz
Ottawa: Charles Schwartz House & Barn, John Rinshed House, Methodist Episcopal Church, Needham-Hayes House, Ottawa Township Hall, Trinity Chapel-Episcopal
Ottawa Township: Broadway Bridge
Waterville: Arthur Dehn House, Union Hotel

Golf Courses:
Le Sueur Country Club, Daily Fee (Le Sueur, MN)
Montgomery National Golf Club, Daily Fee (Montgomery, MN)

Breweries/Wineries/Distilleries:
Chankaska Creek Ranch, Winery, and Distillery (Kasota, MN)
Montgomery Brewing Company (Montgomery, MN)
Vintage Escapes Winery (Kilkenny, MN)

Town Celebrations:
Bullhead Days, Waterville, MN (1st Weekend in June)
Giant Days, Le Sueur, MN (1st Weekend in August)
Kolacky Days, Montgomery, MN (Last Full Weekend of July)
Masopust, Montgomery, MN (3rd Sunday in February)
Miss Czech Slovak Minnesota Pageant, Montgomery, MN (Early April)

Koochiching County: Big Falls on the Big Fork River (Big Falls), Koochiching County Courthouse (International Falls), Smokey the Bear Statue (International Falls), Lake Kabetogama Walleye Statue (Kabetogama), Kabetogama Lake in Voyageurs National Park (Kabetogama), The Lost 40 Scientific and Natural Forest (Northome), Rainy River (Ranier), Bic Vic the Voyageur Statue (Ranier)

Lac qui Parle County: Merry-go-round (Bellingham), Gnomes at Dawson Gnome Field (Dawson), Barn Scenery (Dawson), Historic Public School (Louisburg), "The Open Road" on 225th Ave (Louisburg), World's Largest Lutefisk (Madison), Lac qui Parle County Courthouse (Madison), High School Varsity Letter Jacket Display at Lac qui Parle County Museum (Madison)

Lake County: Lake Superior Agate at Beaver Bay Agate Shop (Beaver Bay), Split Rock Lighthouse (Two Harbors), Beaver Falls (Beaver Bay), Rocky Taconite (Silver Bay), Illgen Falls (Illgen City), Two Harbors Pierhead Light and Freighter on Lake Superior (Two Harbors), Two Harbors Lighthouse Museum (Two Harbors), Great! Lakes Candy Kitchen (Knife River)

Lake of the Woods County: The Northernmost Point in the Contiguous 48 States (Angle Inlet), The Northernmost Post Office in the U.S.A. (Angle Inlet), Angle Inlet School, The Northernmost School in the U.S.A. (Angle Inlet), Jim's Corner Bordr Crossing Station (Angle Inlet), Baudette Railroad Depot Museum (Baudette), Willy the Walleye Statue (Baudette), Lake of the Woods International Arena (Baudette), Zippel Bay State Park (Williams)

Le Sueur County: Water Tower (Cleveland), Le Sueur County Museum in former Elysian Public School (Elysian), Mural (Kasota), Le Sueur County Courthouse (Le Center), W.W. Mayo House (Le Sueur), Montgomery Brewing Building (Montgomery), Kolacky Pastries at Franke's Bakery (Montgomery), Sakatah Lake at Sakatah Lake State Park (Waterville)

LINCOLN COUNTY
EST. 1873 - POPULATION: 5,640

Abraham Lincoln, the 16th President of the United States, was always destined to have a Minnesota county named in his honor, per the wishes of the Minnesota legislature. It was created on March 6, 1873, when Lyon County was divided into two.

ARCO, MN
POPULATION: 87 – CITY 36 OF 856 (2-25-25)
Presently home to about 87 people, Arco once had the distinction of being a tourist hotspot because of the work of H. P. Pederson, a rock collector who opened a Texaco gas station in town in 1936. Using pink quartz, volcanic rock, pipestone, and other ores and minerals, Pederson covered his gas station with thousands of stones from his travels and incorporated them into a beautiful design on its facade. In addition to the grassroots art on the station, he also constructed a Liberty Bell, and his son Vernon built a Statue of Liberty. The sculptures were later relocated to Stay Lake Campground, and the station was converted into the private residence of Dave and Liz Herzog. Back when Pederson's filling station was still in operation, families could enjoy his creations. Other business lines in Arco included grain elevators, general stores, restaurants, a Farmers Cooperative creamery, an electric and light plant, and a brick school building. Arco was platted by the Western Town Lot Company in 1900 as "Arcola," after the ancient city in Italy. However, the name was later changed by the Chicago & North Western Railroad due to the existence of a station in Washington County with the same name. The line served the community during Arco's heyday in the 1940s, when it boasted a population of 243 residents. However, it was ultimately abandoned between Tyler, Minnesota, and Astoria, South Dakota, on February 10, 1970. The Arco post office was established in 1900 in the general store of Christian Larsen, who subsequently agreed to serve as postmaster.

HENDRICKS, MN
POPULATION: 616 – CITY 38 OF 856 (2-25-25)
The year was 1884 when the Hendricks post office was established, but it would take sixteen more years before any railroad activity was conducted in the lands located immediately to the east of the picturesque Lake Hendricks. Settlers in the north-central part of Lincoln County had yearned for the establishment of a line through their farmsteads so they would have more accessibility to markets beyond their immediate area. Their prayers were answered in 1900 when the North Western Railroad Company and the Western Town Lot Company decided to build their Tyler-Astoria line. Lots in Hendricks were auctioned off for the first time on April 25, 1900. Within just six months, the area had been transformed into a thriving settlement, complete with grain elevators, stockyards, stores, saloons, temporary homes, and various businesses. Bingham and Hinkel opened the first firm, a restaurant and hotel, which was joined by numerous other business houses by the end of the year: L. A. Larson's general merchandise store; B. F. Raddte's meat market; J. P. Johnson & Son's hardware and tin shop; the Nelson Brothers' lumber yard; J. J. Hill's blacksmith shop; Edward Jacobson's furniture store; Furey and Smoke's creamery; Laird, Norton & Company's lumber yard; Dave Whalen's barber shop; John Muhl's hotel; the Dawson Lumber Company; the Lincoln County State Bank, and the State Bank of Hendricks, to name the most important. The State Bank of Hendricks was headed by O. W. Hagen and had deposits of $6,000 as of November 10, 1900. Trade introduced by the Minnesota division of the Chicago & Northwestern Railroad allowed for the town's

continued growth. From 1910 to 1920, its population nearly doubled, from 406 residents in 1910 to 731 by 1920. In the 1960s, the numbers peaked at 797 people. The town's name is an eponym for the surname of Thomas A. Hendricks, who became the 21st Vice President of the United States in 1884, when the local post office opened its doors. Near the shores of Lake Hendricks is the six-building museum complex of the Lincoln County Historical Society, which aims to preserve historical artifacts from Hendricks and its surrounding towns. Although located in South Dakota, another historical point of interest near Hendricks is the Singsaas Lutheran Church, one of the oldest prairie churches in the United States, which still hosts weekly services. The parish was established on October 26, 1874, to serve the needs of Norwegian settlers, and its edifice was built in 1921, subsequently listed on the National Register in October 2003. Hendricks residents opened The Red Barn Theater in December 2014; the active theater remains rare in modern rural towns.

Restaurant Recommendation:
Wooden Spoons Bakery
108 S Main St
Hendricks, MN 56136

IVANHOE, MN ★

POPULATION: 560 – CITY 37 OF 856 (2-25-25)

"The Storybook Town" and the smallest county seat in Minnesota (pop. 560 as of the 2020 Census), Ivanhoe, was named after Walter Scott's novel. Although the original post office was called Wilno (a corruption of the name of Wilna, in Russia) from 1883 to 1901, when the Chicago & North Western Railroad laid out the town, they wanted to honor the work of Scott and immediately issued the change. Several of Ivanhoe's horizontal streets, specifically Rotherwood, Rowena, and Saxon, were named after protagonists from the tale. Lots were sold at auction in April 1900 on land formerly owned by Mike J. Pukrop. J. G. Lund purchased the first lot, but George Graff had the first permanent residence. It took less than three months for several business houses to be erected and for the first train to arrive on July 2, 1900. Early commercial institutions included S. S. Olson's hardware store, the Dawson Lumber Yard, Goodmundson & Rainson's livery barn, and Geo. W. Jarzyna's elevator, and Mat and Macnikowski's general store, The Ivanhoe Mercantile Company. Most of these early settlers were of Polish descent, having arrived in the early 1880s, long before the railroad arrived. The State Bank of Ivanhoe opened in 1900 and changed its name to "First National" in 1902. Soon after, the Farmers & Merchants National Bank began issuing its own loans and bonds and opening accounts for the townspeople. After Ivanhoe was incorporated as a village in 1901, the county commissioners held a special election to award it the county seat because of its central location. The special election was one, but residents of Lake Benton cried foul and took the matter to the State Supreme Court because proper notices had not been posted to hold the election in the first place. The State sided with Lake Benton, but the town still lost the seat in a formal election on August 5, 1904, in which Ivanhoe secured 57.61% (1,310 of 2,274) of the votes to garner the honor. The Lincoln County Courthouse was not completed until 1920, although it and its jail (built in 1904) were so structurally sound that they have since been listed on the National Register of Historic Places for permanent preservation. Ivanhoe's first annual Polska Kielbasa Days celebration was held in August 1972 as a nod to its rich Polish heritage. Gwen Walz, the 39th First Lady of Minnesota and the wife of 2024 Democratic Party candidate for Vice President of the United States, Tim Walz, grew up in Ivanhoe.

LAKE BENTON, MN
POPULATION: 687 – CITY 35 OF 856 (2-24-25)

"The Original Wind Power Capital of the Midwest" is best known today for being the location of the Buffalo Ridge Rind Farm, one of the largest such farms in the United States. The project began in 1994 following a mandate of the Minnesota legislature to increase the demand for wind power throughout the state. Approximately 283 turbines dot the fields outside the townsite and provide power for hundreds of homes in the immediate area. While its modern energy advancements have helped put Lake Benton on the map as one of the most progressive communities in Minnesota, the early history of the settlement dates to the explorations of Joseph N. Nicollet and John C. Fremont in the summer of 1838. Upon discovering the lake, they named it in honor of Jessie Benton-Fremont, John C. Fremont's wife and the daughter of Thomas Hart Benton, a United States Senator from Missouri from August 1821 to March 1851. Like other communities in Minnesota, the town's name is derived from a geographical feature. The State Legislature incorporated it as a village in 1881, eight years after the United States Postal Service established an office here. From 1882 to 1902, it served as the judicial seat of Lincoln County, first assuming the honor from a now-defunct town called Marshfield before it lost the title in a special election to Ivanhoe. The first business was a feed and flour store owned by J. W. Bush, and the second was Henry Potter's general store. Potter purchased the first lot on the townsite, but it was handed over to Woodford & Gile of Wisconsin for their hardware store. The Chicago & Northwestern Railroad arrived in October 1879, solidifying its viability as a permanent railroad town. An 1898 atlas published by the Northwest Publishing Company shows that the then-county seat was in its prime. Between the establishment of Lake Benton's first businesses and the turn of the century, the population had grown from 184 inhabitants in 1880 to 890 people. A depot, four elevators, stockyards, two coal sheds, a lumberyard, and a turntable were on the railroad tracks. A creamery and waterworks were the two closest pieces of infrastructure (aside from homes) just to the southwest of the lake. Noted places in the commercial district were a mill, a livery, two hotels, a second lumber yard, a bank, an opera house, and the post office; dozens of others accompanied them. Catholic, Episcopal, Methodist Episcopal, Baptist, and Congregational edifices had been raised by this point, and a public school building and the courthouse rounded out the finest of the townspeople's accomplishments. The Lake Benton Opera House and Kimball Building, completed in 1896, was restored to its original splendor in 1970 and added to the National Register of Historic Places later that decade.

Restaurant Recommendation:
Lake Benton Resort
325 Lake Shore Dr
Lake Benton, MN 56149

TYLER, MN ☆
POPULATION: 1,138 – CITY 34 OF 856 (2-24-25)

The City of Tyler has its roots embedded deep in Danish heritage, history, and culture, thus its motto: "Minnesota's Danish Heartland." Platted in 1879 by the Winona and St. Peter Railroad Company and settled by Danish immigrants, the choice to name the community Tyler was made by H. G. Rising in the fall of that year to honor C. B. Tyler. Mr. Tyler was a land agent for Minnesota at the United States Land Office in New Ulm and the former owner and editor of the New Ulm Herald from 1875 to 1878. A post office was established in 1879, and a temporary depot, consisting of nothing more than a boxcar, was located at the present townsite by John Brandt and a team of ten others. Most of its original buildings were brought in from Marshfield and Morse, two towns that could not survive due to the lack of a railroad. Much of Tyler's early development can be attributed to the Grundtvigians, a Danish settlement organization. Its charter members were F. L. Grundtvig, Kristian Anker, Jens C. Kjær, C. Bruhn, and Rasmus Hansen. These men had met at a convention of the Danish Evangelical Lutheran Church in America in Clinton, Iowa, where they conceived the idea to help relocate Danish immigrants from cities to a centralized community in the countryside. They approached the Winona and St. Peter Railroad Company with an offer to purchase 35,000 acres of land, stipulating that the land only be specifically sold to Danes for the first three years of the agreement. Both sides obliged, and by the summer of 1885, at least seventy settlers had congregated at the townsite in a district now referred to as Danebod. The Danebod Folk School opened on December 1, 1888, and the Danebod Lutheran Church was dedicated on June 16, 1895. In 1889, the Danebod Stone Hall was constructed by stonemason Kristian Klink, who used native field rock sourced from local Danish farmers. Sadly, the original school building burned on February 25, 1917, but a new, grander building was erected. Residents were again subjected to tragedy when the fourth-most deadly tornado in Minnesota history, when a large cyclone moved through Lincoln County on August 21, 1918, and took thirty-six lives. Danebrod used the Danish language almost exclusively through the end of the 1940s, and in the 1970s, 79 acres of the district were listed on the National Register. All its buildings survived the tornado and have since withstood the test of time. Other early facets of Tyler were the *Tyler Journal* newspaper (in circulation from 1896 to 1936), the Tyler Roller Mill, three lumber yards, two elevators, a depot, a creamery, a hotel, a bank, a post office, numerous business houses, a public school (constructed) in the Renaissance and Romanesque Revival styles in 1903), a Catholic church, a Congregational church, and the Tyler Race Track, where the bulk of the town's entertainment came from during that period. Late July and August are busy times for Tyler residents in the 21st century. Æbleskiver Days are held annually on the fourth weekend of July, offering guests a variety of Danish food, a parade, and entertainment. The Lincoln County Fair is held every August at the historic Lincoln County Fairgrounds. The fairgrounds have eighteen contributing buildings, built between 1921 and 1945, which are listed on the National Register. Tyler's incorporation as a statutory city came in 1974. Richard Kneip, the 25th Governor of South Dakota from January 1971 to July 1978, and later the 6th United States Ambassador to the Republic of Singapore from August 1978 to September 1980, was born in Tyler.

Porter is only partially located in Lincoln Tail County (see Yellow Medicine County).

Unincorporated/Ghost Towns: Marshfield, Thompsonburg, Verdi, Wilno

National Register of Historic Places:
Drammen Township: Drammen Farmers' Club
Ivanhoe: Lincoln County Courthouse & Jail
Lake Benton: Ernst Osbeck House, Lake Benton Opera House & Kimball Building
Tyler: Danebod, Lincoln County Fairgrounds, Tyler Public School

Golf Courses:
Hendricks Golf Club, Daily Fee (Hendricks, MN)
Tyler Golf Club, Daily Fee (Tyler, MN)

Breweries/Wineries/Distilleries:
Bank Brewing Company (Hendricks, MN)

Town Celebrations:
Aebleskiver Days, Tyler, MN (4th Weekend of July)
Saddle Horse Holiday, Lake Benton, MN (Father's Day Weekend)

LYON COUNTY
EST. 1871 - POPULATION: 25,269

Lyon County took its name from Nathaniel Lyon, the first Union general to be killed in the American Civil War.

BALATON, MN
POPULATION: 595 – CITY 29 OF 856 (2-24-25)
Balaton, the only town in the United States with that name, was most likely named after Hungary's Lake Balaton. It is the largest lake in Central Europe. Other stories suggest that it may have been named after an investor with the Chicago & North Western Railroad or in honor of David Bell as a corruption of "Belltown." He built the first store on the site. Regardless of how its nomenclature came to be, its origins date back to October 1879, when the Winona & St. Peter Railroad Company laid out its tracks on the southwest corner of what was then called Lake Yankton. One of the first orders of business was organizing a post office, which was headed by local hotel owner Ralph E. Town. Many of its early firms varied in importance, but they all collaborated to provide essential goods and services to a prairie town of the era. In 1902, Balaton had the Laird Norton Lumber Yard and the Hayes Lucas Lumber Yard located on the railroad tracks, alongside three grain elevators, two coal sheds, and stockyards. A hotel, a creamery, and a bank were likely the three busiest establishments, aside from the elevators. Religion and education were of the utmost importance to Balaton residents. The town had a public school in the southwest corner, and German Catholic, Methodist Episcopal, and Presbyterian churches were scattered throughout the community. Amongst the thousands of Minnesotans who have called Balaton home since its inception, the most famous has been Harold A. "Barney" Goltz, the President pro tempore of the Washington Senate from January 1983 to January 1987.

COTTONWOOD, MN
POPULATION: 1,149 – CITY 42 OF 856 (2-25-25)
Cottonwood has thrived on the shores of Lake Cottonwood since July 1888, when it was platted in anticipation of the arrival of the Great Northern Railroad. Settlers came to the area in 1871, and their mail was delivered to the Vineland post office in Yellow Medicine County from 1873 to 1888. That office ultimately took the name "Cottonwood," although early records indicate that there was also a brief post office called "Cottonwood Lake" located in Lyon County. The name was given because of the abundance of cotton trees on the lake's shores. After its move, Mrs. Igebor O. Reishus was officially recognized as Cottonwood's first postmaster. Martin Norseth was responsible for starting the community's business sphere. By 1902, the Cottonwood Milling Company and its roller mill were busy processing local farmers' grain, and five elevators stood tall over the line of the Great Northern. Two lumber yards helped to provide the building materials for other firms and infrastructure, of which the most noteworthy at the time were two banks, a hotel, two livery barns, Wellins Big Store, a carriage works, a blacksmith shop, a city hose house (essentially the pioneer equivalent of a modern-day fire department), a jail, the Cottonwood Creamery, a school, a Norwegian Lutheran church, a Norwegian Synod church, and

a Presbyterian church. The Cottonwood Current newspaper remained in circulation from 1892 to 1975, much longer than a typical small-town newspaper would have survived under the same brand name. In March 1982, far into Cottonwood's prominence as a leading town of the county, great care was taken to ensure that Martin Norseth's 1898 Colonial Revival house would be preserved for future generations to admire. Cottonwood made national headlines on February 19, 2008, after a school bus carrying 28 students from Lakeview Public Schools was struck by a minivan, causing the bus to fall onto a pickup truck. Four students lost their lives and have since been immortalized and honored in a memorial garden on school grounds. On June 9, 1921, Cottonwood became the site of the world's first oil cooperative when local farmers agreed to form the Cottonwood Co-op Oil Company.

FLORENCE, MN
POPULATION: 28 – CITY 32 OF 856 (2-24-25)
In its prime, Florence served as one of several little stations on the Great Northern Railroad. The railroad's facilities comprised a pair of elevators, stockyards, lumber yards, two coal sheds, and a depot. On Laine Street, visitors would have been able to stay at a hotel, purchase products from the Florence Creamery Company, or get their mail from the post office. The school was located just a block to the east on Logan Street. It was platted on October 9, 1888, and named in honor of Florence Sherman, the daughter of its founder. The post office entered service the following year but was discontinued in 1992. Mail for its remaining 28 residents (as of the 2020 Census) goes through the Russell post office.

GARVIN, MN
POPULATION: 124 – CITY 28 OF 856 (2-24-25)
This city of 124 people in southern Lyon County underwent a series of name changes in its pioneer days. The Chicago & North Western Railway selected the townsite in 1879, but it would take seven years before any development was underway. Platted as Siding No. 7 on April 30, 1886, by the Winona & St. Peter Railway Company, it was given the name Terry in honor of the Union general Alfred Terry. From 1887 to July 1891, it was known as Kent for the Chicago missionary Father Kent. The post office was called Seefield during this same period, named after the proprietor of a grain elevator. Its final name change honored H. C. Garvin, the traveling freight agent and the son of one of the oldest employees of the Chicago & North Western. With its name finally decided, Garvin residents pushed forward with its development, adding a second elevator, a lumber yard, stockyards, a store, the Garvin Creamery, School No. 47, and the Congregational church to their list of accomplishments. A push for municipality status was not seriously considered and pursued until the 1940s, so Garvin's first formal Census count lists its population at 264. In the 1930s, a 27-acre track of woodland along the Cottonwood River, now known as the Garvin County Park, was developed by H. C. Garvin for recreational purposes. The park featured a swimming pool, a ball diamond, fireplaces, log cabins, and a rock garden when it opened on May 30, 1935. Over 5,000 people attended to enjoy the amenities and the celebration. Sadly, the park was washed away by repeated flooding, but a new committee, established in November 1967, took on the responsibility of making it a viable camping area once again. The Garvin post office closed in the early 2000s. Bitton's Roadhouse, a famous "barstraunt" beloved by many in the Marshall and surrounding rural areas, is renowned for its sweet heat burgers, steaks, and ribs.

Restaurant Recommendation:
Bitton's Roadhouse
101 2nd St
Garvin, MN 56132

GHENT, MN
POPULATION: 376 – CITY 41 OF 856 (2-25-25)
"The Rolle Bolle Capital of the World" was named Grandview (sometimes spelled Grand View) when it was platted by the Winona & St. Peter Railway Company in June 1878. It shared its name with the township and the local post office (established in 1874) until it was formally changed in 1882 in honor of the Belgian city of Ghent. Immigrants from Belgium began arriving in droves after Mr. Angel VanHee, whom Bishop Ireland had sent, found that the soil in this vicinity of Minnesota would prove the most fruitful for his crops and, by association, his family and friends. He hired 20 teams of men to break the land and returned to Flanders, Belgium, to inform his Catholic friends and family of his discovery. Countless deals were struck between the railroad company and the newcomers in the early 1880s. On May 15, 1899, the townspeople asked the county commissioners to grant them incorporation status. By 1902, the Chicago & Northwestern Railroad was the leading railroad of the area; its presence had brought about the construction of four elevators, stockyards, a lumber yard, and a business district boasting a hardware store, a hotel, a livery, a meeting hall, and even a Catholic church, convent, and school. A race track was planned for the southwest corner of the townsite, attracting numerous visitors from throughout the countryside. Its status as the "rolle bolle capital" was given because the "Belgian bowling" game was invented in the Dutch county where many of its sellers came from.

Restaurant Recommendation:
Kb's Bar & Grill
100 E Burlingame St
Ghent, MN 56239

LYND, MN
POPULATION: 436 – CITY 30 OF 856 (2-24-25)
The history of the first permanent settlement in Lyon County is relatively complex, as it involves the establishment and the moving of three separate communities. It all began when James W. Lynd established a trading post in 1855 or 1857. He lived amongst the Sioux and aspired to write a documentary-style novel regarding their language, customs, and traditions. He and both his manuscripts were destroyed at the Indian Massacre at the Lower Sioux Agency, the first event of the Dakota War of 1862. He was the first person killed in the war. The dangerous conflict kept potential settlers away until June 1867, when A. W. Muzzy, James Cummings, and E. B. Langdon took up their claims. In 1869, Lyon County was partitioned from Redwood County through an act of the Minnesota Legislature, and then-Governor William R. Marshall appointed officials to form a county government. They met at Upper Lynd, the first of three communities, on August 12, 1870, in Luman Ticknor's home. It was designated the county seat, but it was not long before Lower Lynd, laid out in June 1870 by A. R. Cummings and A. D. Morgan, took over the honor in 1872, as it had a hotel, a store, and a church. The Kiel and Morgan Hotel, now listed on the National Register of Historic Places, was used as a regular meeting place for county officials, effectively making it the Lyon County Courthouse. Lower Lynd became Old Lynd after the Winona

& St. Peter Railway Company built their line north of town in 1874, and Marshall ultimately became the Lyon County seat. The townsite was largely abandoned until the Great Northern Railway platted modern-day Lynd in November 1888, situated just south of the initial site. As of 1902, it had a depot, two elevators, a coal shed, a Methodist Episcopal church, a hotel, a post office, and a lumber yard. Modern advancements were made during the WPA era, between 1934 and 1938, at Camden State Park, where thirteen park facilities were built using split stone construction techniques. Lynd was incorporated as a village on January 4, 1954, and has since experienced significant population growth due to its proximity to Marshall.

MARSHALL, MN ★☆
POPULATION: 13,628 – CITY 43 OF 856 (2-25-25)

When Charles H. Whitney and C. H. Upton wandered into the Minnesota wilderness in 1869, they considered themselves extremely fortunate when they discovered unclaimed lands on the big bend of the Redwood River. It had rich soil and was close to Lake Marshall, which was named for William R. Marshall, the fifth Governor of Minnesota. Knowing that the Winona and St. Peter Railway Company (commonly referred to as the Chicago & Northwestern Railroad) would soon aid the area's development, the government established the Lake Marshall post office in 1870. Whitney was the postmaster, and in 1872, he requested that it be shortened to just "Marshall." The name Redwood Crossing was briefly considered because it was here that Native Americans and settlers crossed the river to travel between Lynd and Redwood Falls. Development was well underway after the townsite was platted in August 1872, and the first engines began to arrive. D. P. Billings, J. A. Coleman, and Everett & Company each established their general stores. Daniel Farquar took up residence as town blacksmith, W. M. Todd opened a lumberyard, and C. H. Whitney operated the first hotel. Early pioneers of Marshall recall a flurry of activity that was so common that three men would share a bed, and others would sleep on haystacks because of the lack of lodging in Marshall's early days. Progress of any kind was significantly delayed when Mother Nature blew snow drifts across the tracks that winter, but the spring thaw allowed expansion to continue in 1873. According to an excerpt from Samuel Biglari's *The Prairie Schooner*, the first local newspaper, there were over six dozen permanent structures by the end of October. Amid its rapid growth, Marshall was designated the seat of government for the newly established Lyon County after Lincoln County was split off. Marshall was centrally located within the county and the only town with a railroad, so a vote was held to relocate the seat from Lynd. The final vote was 397 in favor of removing Lynd and 99 against. The rest of the decade saw the founding of various enterprises, ranging from Kendall's mill to Blake's cheese factory, H. S. Adam's wagon shop, and A. O. Underhill's confectionery, among many others. Marshall was incorporated on March 18, 1876; from 1880 to 1900, it grew from 961 people to 2,088. As a railroad community at the junction of the Chicago & Northwestern and the Great Northern, opportunities were created to establish structures not commonplace in the average farming town. In 1884, Holy Redeemer Catholic Church was built to introduce competition in the community's religious sector and attract new residents. German Evangelical, German Lutheran, German Methodist, Icelandic, Catholic, Congregational, Presbyterian, and Episcopalian church edifices existed in 1902. In 1913, the Masonic Temple Delta Lodge No. 119 was constructed; it has since been recognized as one of Minnesota's best examples of Egyptian Revival architecture. Seven churches, five hotels, five grain elevators, three banks, The Marshall Milling Company's roller mill, a planing mill, a public library, a courthouse, a high school, and an opera house were among the other accomplishments by 1918. In the 1950s, the Weiner Memorial Hospital was built, and

Schwan's [Food] Company was founded. Marvin Schwan started his company on March 18, 1952, when he came up with the idea to home-deliver his family's homemade ice cream to customers throughout Marshall and the surrounding area. Over the years, he and his employees began to deliver juice concentrates, frozen fish products, and, in modern times, egg rolls and famous frozen pizza lines like Red Baron, Freschetta, and Tony's. Schwan's faced challenges in the 21st-century world of food delivery, and despite rebranding its home delivery service as "Yelloh" in 2022, it ceased operations for good in November 2024. Schwan's corporate headquarters is still located in town and employs many residents. Marshall is also home to Southwest Minnesota State University, which was founded in 1964 as Southwest Minnesota State College. Many famous people have held ties to Marshall over the decades, including Greg Olson, a 1990 All-Star pitcher for the MLB's Atlanta Braves; Isaiah Whitlock Jr., best known as Clay Davis on HBO's The Wire; Lois Quam, the founding CEO of Ovations (a part of UnitedHealth Group) and a three-time member of Fortune's "most influential women leaders in business" list; Steve Zahn, a Primetime Emmy Award nominee and actor; John Ely Burchard, the President of the American Academy of Arts and Sciences from 1954 to 1957; Trey Lance, the third-overall pick in the 2021 NFL Draft and a current quarterback for the NFL's Dallas Cowboys; Randall B. Griepp, a cardiothoracic surgeon who helped to develop the first successful heart transplant procedure in the United States; Carly Gullickson, the 2009 US Open tennis champion in mixed-doubles, and her father Bill Gullickson, a pitcher in the MLB between 1979 and 1994 and the AL wins leader in 1991.

Restaurant Recommendation:
Brau Brothers Brewing Company
1010 E Southview Dr
Marshall, MN 56258

MINNEOTA, MN
POPULATION: 1,366 – CITY 40 OF 856 (2-25-25)

The second-largest Icelandic community in the United States welcomed its first Icelander, Gunninugur Petursson, on Independence Day 1875, when he took up a homestead on the Yellow Medicine River. He was the first of eight hundred of his people to settle across three southwestern Minnesota counties, but they were not the only group to claim parcels of land here. The Norwegians were another prominent group, and once a number of them had accumulated, they decided to call the area Pumpa because there was a railroad water pump there. The Chicago & Northwestern Railroad town was also briefly called Upper Yellow Medicine Crossing, and then Nordland, in honor of Norway, when it was platted by the Winona & St. Peter Railway Company. Its present name, only a single consonant off in nomenclature from "Minnesota," was suggested by either George P. Goodwin or storeowner Thomas D. Seals when the post office moved into Nils Winther Luth Jager's general store. Minneota is derived from the Dakota language and means "much water." Between 1880 and 1890, its population experienced its largest percentage increase (187.6%), rising from 113 to 325. That number more than doubled again by the turn of the century, when the 1900 Decennial Census reported it as 777. Minneota was incorporated on January 21, 1881, and as of 1884, had the following business lines: a feed mill, a meat market, five grocers and/or dry goods stores, two saloons, two blacksmith shops, a shoe store, a harness shop, a hotel, two elevators, a lumber yard, an implement store, a drug store, two hardware and/or furniture stores, a livery, a telegraph office, two doctor's offices, the Bank of Minneota, and Jager's general store. William Davidson was the bank's initial president, established with a capital stock of

$25,000. The Porter elevator and Van Dusen's elevator could hold a combined 275,000 bushels; the latter sold 70,000 pounds of flour in 1883 alone. Laird & Norton's lumber yard sold over a million feet of lumber and half a million shingles in the same year amid the height of the community's growth that decade. In 1901, the O. G. Anderson & Company Store (later known to locals as "The Big Store") was constructed with an upper-floor event space for parties, dances, and meetings. It, along with two other Minnesota buildings, has been listed on the National Register since March 1982. The others are the J. S. Anderson Queen Anne-Colonial Revival house, featuring a three-story rear tower, and St. Paul's Evangelical Lutheran Church & Parsonage. The parsonage was built in 1891, and the church was built in 1895 in the Carpenter Gothic architecture style by early Icelandic immigrants. Other town churches in 1902 included the English Lutheran, Norwegian Lutheran, Baptist, and Catholic churches. Les Josephson, a 1967 Pro Bowl and ten-year running back for the Los Angeles Rams; Bill Holm, a poet and author; and Val Bjornson, the State Treasurer of Minnesota for over two decades, hail from Minneota.

RUSSELL, MN
POPULATION: 348 – CITY 31 OF 856 (2-24-25)
Credit for establishing Russell is owed to Mr. Spicer, who was instrumental in convincing the Great Northern Railroad to run its branch line between Willmar, Minnesota, and Sioux Falls, South Dakota, through this section of the county. He requested that it be named in honor of his son, Russell. The site was platted in 1888 on Redwood River using Spicer's name suggestion, and a branch of the postal service was organized the following year in Ephraim Skyhawk's general store. There had briefly been another post office called Russell in Hennepin County in 1882, but it was deemed acceptable because the name had been unused for seven years. The two other earliest buildings were the railroad section house and an elevator. Twenty years later, it had developed into a thriving hamlet with additional amenities, including a depot, two hotels, a livery, a lumber yard, a bank, a school, and a couple of more elevators. Russell's population peaked at 508 people in the 1950s.

TAUNTON, MN
POPULATION: 136 – CITY 39 OF 856 (2-25-25)
Platted in April 1886 by the Winona & St. Peter Railroad and officially incorporated as a village on March 27, 1900, the name Taunton was given by C. C. Wheeler for Taunton, Massachusetts. The city in the east is one of the oldest towns in the United States, having been founded by members of the Plymouth Colony in 1637. The post office was originally called Lonesome for its location on the seemingly endless prairie, then Ripon, after the town in Wisconsin, and later Taunton. Things were not as barren for very long as the initial settlers of Taunton described. Once the railroad tracks had been laid, workers built four elevators, a lumber yard, a stockyard, a depot, and two coal sheds. Several businesses lined Main Street, amongst the most popular being a blacksmith shop and a hotel. A village hall and a jail were located at its northwestern end, and a school, German Lutheran church, and Polish Catholic church were built in the village's southwestern corridor. All of these places existed as of 1902. The first school was built in 1889, and Sts. Cyril and Methodius Catholic Church was erected in 1895. Its rectory was added in 1905. Beck's Hardware (1903), Taunton State Bank (1905), the Taunton Fire Station (1907), and the H. E. Carstens General Merchandise & Dry Goods store were other notable early accomplishments. Taunton's highest population was in the 1960s, when 233 people called it home.

TRACY, MN

POPULATION: 2,076 – CITY 27 OF 856 (2-24-25)

Nobody could have foreseen the importance that this settlement would hold when it was platted in 1875 by the Winona & St. Peter Railroad, except for the executives of the railroad themselves. Historically referred to as Shetek, Shetek Bend, and Shetek Station, these various names were given in honor of the settlers at Lake Shetek who petitioned for the railroad to be built here, allowing them to be closer to a railroad. Those settlers ultimately got more than they bargained for when the Chicago & Northwestern elected to make it a division point for its lines heading westbound through Garvin, Balaton, and Tyler, to the northwest towards Marshall, and eastward towards New Ulm and St. Peter. Horatio N. Joy hosted the post office in his store, Shetek's first building, and in 1877, it was renamed Tracy in honor of railroad official John F. Tracy. The next building after Joy's was the Commercial Hotel, opened by H. H. Welch. As could have been predicted even by those living in the earliest times of Tracy, numerous more homes, businesses, churches, schools, and fraternal and civic organizations were to follow. Men by the names of Gibbs, Brauns, and Davis founded stores to aid those moving into the community, and a lumber yard, furniture store, livery stable, hardware store, saloon, jewelry store, meat market, wagon shop, and drug store were just a few of the original lines to conduct business there. Tracy's townspeople pushed for incorporation in the early 1880s and attained the honor on February 5, 1881. A brick school building was erected in 1880 for $6,000. At the turn of the century, there were places of worship for the Catholic, German Lutheran, Swedish Mission, Presbyterian, and Methodist congregations. *The Trumpet* newspaper, along with feed mills, liveries, hotels, storefronts, and banks, highlighted the early pieces of infrastructure. One bank in particular, the First National, was built out of Sioux Quartzite in the Romanesque Revival style to serve as the headquarters of Lyon County's oldest bank between 1891 and 1931. On the railroad's property circa 1902, there were machine repair shops, an icehouse, machine shops, and numerous elevators. In 1921, the first annual Box Car Day attracted tens of thousands of railroad enthusiasts and "rail riders" (i.e., hoboes in some contexts); the event is still held every year on Labor Day weekend. On July 18, 2023, the WPA-era Tracy Municipal Building and Armory, constructed to serve as a multipurpose municipal building for the city, was added to the National Register of Historic Places. Seasoned residents of Tracy often refer to the June 13, 1968, F5 tornado as the worst disaster in Tracy's history. The twister took the lives of nine residents and injured 150 others, in addition to leaving a path of destruction in its wake. Tracy rebuilt, although its population declined slowly after the twister. It peaked at 3,085 people in the 1940s; as of 2020, it has about 2,076 residents. Curt Brasket, a FIDE Master and sixteen-time chess champion in the State of Minnesota; Dennis Morgan, a songwriter known for penning hits for country music stars like Faith Hill and Garth Brooks; and Cal Ludeman, the Secretary of the Minnesota Senate since January 2017. The Wheels Across the Prairie Museum boasts an extensive collection of buildings containing artifacts related to Tracy's railroads, military veterans, and local area history.

Unincorporated/Ghost Towns: Amiret, Burchard, Dudley, Green Valley

National Register of Historic Places:
Cottonwood: Martin Norseth House
Lynd: Kiel & Morgan Hotel/Lyon County Courthouse, Camden State Park CCC/WPA/Rustic Style Historic District
Marshall: Bridge No.5083- Marshall, Bridge No.5151- Marshall, Masonic Temple Delta Lodge No.119, William F. Gieske House

Minneota: J. S. Anderson House, O. G. Anderson & Co. Store, St. Paul's Evangelical Lutheran Church & Parsonage
Tracy: First National Bank, Tracy Municipal Building & Armory

Golf Courses:
Balaton Bay Golf Course, Daily Fee (Balaton, MN)
Cottonwood Country Club, Daily Fee (Cottonwood, MN)
Marshall Golf Club, Daily Fee (Marshall, MN)

Breweries/Wineries/Distilleries:
Brau Bros. Brewing Company (Marshall, MN)

Town Celebrations:
Belgian American Days, Ghent, MN (1st Weekend of August)
Box Car Days, Tracy, MN (Labor Day Weekend)
Boxelder Bug Days, Minneota, MN (Weekend after Labor Day)
Cottonwood Coming Home Days, Cottonwood, MN (2nd Weekend in July)
Russell Bandwagon Days, Russell, MN (First Weekend of June)
Sounds of Summer Festival, Marshall, MN (Weekend before Labor Day Weekend)

MAHNOMEN COUNTY
EST. 1906 - POPULATION: 5,411

The Ojibwe use several spellings to describe the wild rice they grow, but *Mahnomen* prevailed when this county was created in 1906. It is the only county in Minnesota located entirely within an Indian Reservation—specifically, the White Earth Indian Reservation.

BEJOU, MN
POPULATION: 84 – CITY 270 OF 856 (5-30-25)

The etymology of Bejou could not be much more welcoming, as its name is derived from the French word *bonjour*, meaning "hello" or "good day." It may have been given in recognition of the presence of French trappers in the area long before widespread settlement. Another account suggests that the town's name came from the Ojibwe word *bizhiw*, meaning lynx, or *boozhoo*, meaning hello. Because it is entirely within the boundaries of the White Earth Indian Reservation, either explanation is plausible. The townsite was formally established in 1904 when the Minneapolis, St. Paul, and Sault Ste. Marie Railroad established it as one of several stations on its line. A post office was organized two years later, and on January 13, 1921, Bejou was incorporated. From 1930 to 1940, its population doubled from 99 to 200, then gradually subsided over the next several decades.

MAHNOMEN, MN ★☆
POPULATION: 1,240 – CITY 269 OF 856 (5-30-25)

The only county seat in Minnesota to be located entirely within the boundaries of a reservation, specifically the White Earth Indian Reservation (established on March 19, 1867), first welcomed the displaced Ojibwe people on June 14, 1868. For years, the region was known as "Wild Rice" for its location north of the Wild Rice River. It was ultimately changed to the Ojibwe noun *manoomin*. Initially, a post office was established in 1874 as Wild Rice. It was relocated in February 1904 to the Wild Rice Church (then a part of the Pembina Mission) and renamed Perrault by Lawrence W. Pettijohn. Not even a year later, Mahnomen was adopted as the office's new and final name. On October 1, 1904, the first railroad engine chugged into town and dropped off its supplies and passengers at the newly established depot, then just a boxcar. A roundhouse was erected to send trains back to where they came from. Around the railroad facilities, general store owners, hotel proprietors, hardware and implement dealers, bankers, and other businesspeople planted their roots, hoping their firms would make it. Sigurd Bernard Olson's hardware store was the first building; it was also the first location of the "Mahnomen" post office. Until 1909, one of the banks rented space for the county courthouse, until architects Kinney & Halden of Minneapolis submitted blueprints for a new Classical Revival edifice to be erected for $10,000. It was the first of Mahnomen's three locations to be added to the National Register of Historic Places, the other two being the Mahnomen City Hall, built in 1937, and eight contributing properties on the Mahnomen County Fairgrounds, constructed between 1936 and 1938. Both the Fairgrounds Historic District and the City Hall structure were Works Progress Administration projects. Nicholas Spaeth, the 27th Attorney General of North Dakota from January 1985 to December 1992, was born here. Approximately 1,464 were reported to be living in Mahnomen its peak years in the 1950s.

WAUBUN, MN
POPULATION: 409 – CITY 268 OF 856 (5-30-25)

The "middle child" of Mahnomen County's incorporated communities, so to speak, welcomed the Minneapolis, St. Paul & Sault Ste. Marie Railroad in 1903-04, and was first called Bement when that area of Minnesota was still under Norman County's control. When the new county was partitioned off in 1906, a name change was ordered by the Soo Line Railroad officials, Thomas Green and Edmund Pennington. They wanted all its stations on the reservation to be named after Native Americans. So in 1906, *Waubun* was adopted in place of Bement. The Ojibwe word roughly translates to "the morning" or "dawn," but residents attest that it means "rising sun." Most of the town's earliest developments occurred in the years immediately following the railroad's arrival. The Luck Land Company had a land office, and the Woodworth Elevator Company raised one of the first elevators to handle the deposits of local farmers. William Bement had a butcher shop, Mr. Dorenkemper operated the lumber yard, the First State Bank opened its doors, and the Golden Rule and Nels Narum's general stores stocked residents with the goods they needed. Waubun was incorporated as a village on December 18, 1907, the same year its new brick school building was built. During construction, some of the community's youth attended classes in the attic above Anderson's Hardware Store.

Unincorporated/Ghost Towns: Beaulieu, Mahkonce, Midway, Naytahwaush, Pine Bend, Riverland, Roy Lake, The Ranch, Twin Lakes, West Roy Lake

National Register of Historic Places:
Mahnomen: Mahnomen City Hall, Mahnomen County Courthouse, Mahnomen County Fairgrounds Historic District

MARSHALL COUNTY
EST. 1879 - POPULATION: 9,040

When the Minnesota legislature split off a parcel of land from the southern half of Kittson County in 1879, they opted to name the new county after William Rainey Marshall, Minnesota's fifth governor.

ALVARADO, MN
POPULATION: 388 – CITY 329 OF 856 (6-4-25)
The Snake post office, located on the Snake River, was the name of the area post office from 1888 to 1905, when it was changed to Alvarado. Alvarado is the name of a Mexican seaport and river about forty miles southeast of Vera Cruz; it was dedicated when the Minneapolis, St. Paul, and Sault Ste. Marie Railroad was built in the area in 1903. Ole Sand was the postmaster of the Snake office, and his son, Martin H. Sand, kept the title in the family when he took over postal duties at the new Alvarado office in 1905. Alvarado's most significant population growth occurred between 1910 and 1920, when its population increased by 182% from 128 to 361. Its facilities were extensive according to a 1928 plat map. On the Soo Line Railroad tracks were three grain elevators, stockyards, two coal sheds, a depot, and an oil storage facility. On Marshall Street, moving from north to south, was a hotel, a lumber yard and office, a garage, the post office, a bank, a hardware store, a meat market, City Hall, a creamery, and a Swedish Lutheran Church at its southern end. A Norwegian Lutheran church was located a block west on Third Avenue, and a Baptist church and school were elsewhere in town. Alvarado attained incorporation status on October 16, 1907.

ARGYLE, MN
POPULATION: 544 – CITY 327 OF 856 (6-4-25)
French-Canadians established the town of Louisa and named it after the famous king, but their settlement was quickly replaced by James J. Hill's Great Northern (earlier called the St. Paul, Minneapolis & Manitoba) Railroad village of Argyle when the line was fully built through in 1879. Louisa had a handful of villages and businesses before Argyle arrived, most of which were moved to the new site. Ferdinand Keye had a store in his log cabin in 1878, the first and only structure on the site for many months. When the railroad arrived on September 8, 1878, it was expected that development would proceed rapidly, but that did not happen. It took another two years for a total of seven lots to be claimed, one of which was Antoine Lafferior's store, and another owned by Sam Connors. He had a saloon called "The Sample Room" where visitors could explore the prototypes of his goods and then place their orders through his catalog. The post office (then known as Middle River) and the village (then called Louisa) were renamed Argyle in 1882 by Solomon G. Comstock, after Argyle, Maine. A general store, a hotel, and a flour mill came to fruition shortly thereafter. On December 13, 1883, the townspeople witnessed the successful conclusion of their petition to the county commissioners for incorporation. A roller skating rink and the Farmers' and Merchants' Bank were the most popular businesses established in the next few years. By March 1, 1894, there were five grain elevators, four hotels, four livery stables, four blacksmith shops, three saloons, pairs of dry goods, grocery, furniture, and hardware stores, a flour mill, a lumber yard, and well over a dozen firms. Three churches, an opera house, and a two-story schoolhouse were also present at the time, when Argyle had recently experienced a significant population increase (an increase of 170.9% from 309 residents in 1890 to 829 by 1900). Two Catholic churches, one noted as a French Catholic institution, and two Protestant churches actively hosted religious services in Argyle's city limits circa 1928. Argyle's primary point of interest in the 21st century is Old Mill State Park, a 406-acre park known for Larson Mill, an NRHP-listed site. The structure was initially constructed in 1889, and its steam engine was rebuilt in 1958 by the state for interpretive and historical purposes. As part of the New Deal work relief projects, eight park facilities were built between 1937 and 1941. Moose, beavers, and marsh hawks are among the rare wildlife visitors to the park, alongside other birds and mammals.

GRYGLA, MN
POPULATION: 180 – CITY 277 OF 856 (5-30-25)
In the summer of 1898, A.O. Flaadeland and Ole Newton established a general store within a half-mile of the modern Grygla townsite. Despite never attracting a railroad, the town did capture the attention of the United States Postal Service, which sent Count Gryglavitch to inspect the townsite and deem it worthy of an office branch. Residents struggled to come up with a new name for the post office, so Mr. Gryglavitch provided the first part of his surname. Alternatively, it could have been named for Frank Grygla, who was then the "Father of the Polish National Alliance." With time, establishments like a Town Hall, a school, a store, a church, a blacksmith shop, a garage, the Brown General Merchandise Store, Citizen State Bank, the Maney Hotel, George Johnson's weekly *Grygla Eagle* newspaper, and the Grygla Co-op Creamery emerged. Because of its distance from other major centers of commerce or infrastructure, the Grygla Hospital was furnished by the townspeople in 1912 and run for many years by Dr. King and Dr. Adkins. Sadly, a 1917 fire destroyed the Willard Hotel, the Ollson Implement and Hardware Company, Louis Bergerson's pool hall, and the Fonnest livery barn as it blazed through the wood-frame buildings. Grygla resident Jeremy Hernandez made national headlines after his heroic actions on August 15, 2007, when he saved several students from a school bus that had been toppled and covered in debris following the collapse of the I-35W Bridge in Minneapolis.

HOLT, MN
POPULATION: 90 – CITY 279 OF 856 (5-30-25)
The hamlet of Holt, located in the heart of Marshall County, was named after the pioneer Norwegian settler Halbor Holte, who shared his name with a Scandinavian word meaning "grove" or "wooded hill." Its post office opened in 1886, merged with the Sandridge office in 1908, and then continued to deliver parcels and letters throughout the area until its closure in 1969. Some of the most noteworthy sites in the Great Northern Railroad town included its general merchandise store, bank, depot, and school. Holt was incorporated on March 16, 1915; it had as many as 232 citizens according to its inaugural 1920 Census.

MIDDLE RIVER, MN
POPULATION: 304 – CITY 280 OF 856 (5-30-25)
Middle River Township was established on October 14, 1879, making it the county's oldest township. Its Great Northern Railway village was first called Breese (as was the post office from 1890 to 1904) before the new "Middle River" was given for its proximity to the tributary of the Snake River. The 96-mile river flows entirely within Marshall County and was named for its location near the midpoint of the Pembina Trail. As settlers poured into northwest Minnesota near the start of the 20th century in search of new opportunities, many elected to start anew at Middle River because of its ample water supply and agricultural opportunities. In 1910, it had 149 residents, but by 1920, that number had grown to 324 people. The "Roaring Twenties" were just that for Middle River and its citizens. Three elevators, one of which was the farmers', a depot, and a pair of oil stations were situated in the southwest region of town near the railroad tracks. South of the river was downtown, where the Central Lumber Company operated, the *Record* published its newspaper, and four garages repaired carriages and early automobiles. A bank, a creamery (now a popular antique/boutique store), and a drug store were in the vicinity, too, as were the Town Hall and the post office buildings. To the north of the river were the Presbyterian and the Lutheran churches,

and a consolidated school. Middle River is located between the wildlife havens of Agassiz National Wildlife Refuge and Thief Lake Wildlife Management Area.

NEWFOLDEN, MN
POPULATION: 352 – CITY 315 OF 856 (6-3-25)
Nicknamed "the Rolling Pin Capital of Minnesota" for being the birthplace of the Lokstad rolling pin, Newfolden was named after Folden, Norway, a now-defunct Norwegian municipality. However, the town was not always located at its current site. A village called New Folden, with a post office and store, had existed since at least 1884 (the post office being called Humboldt from 1884 to 1896), seven years before the arrival of the Soo Line Railroad. Wanting to save money, surveyors and officials of the Soo instead purchased a beautiful $4,800 parcel of land on the Middle River owned by Olaus Larson. It had bountiful forests, but proved too wet to farm. They called it "Baltic" after the brand of grain elevators being established along their line, but the primarily Scandinavian population heavily objected to the name. They instead insisted that it be called "Newfolden," a shortened version of their previous townsite. The Soo Line obliged. By the end of 1905, there were fifteen businesses, including three general merchandise stores, two hotels, a confectionery and tobacco store, a milling company, a soft-drink parlor, a grist mill, and a bank. Its grain elevators and potato warehouses popped up later as agriculture became the dominant industry. Religious services were held at one of three churches through the 1920s, and in western Newfolden, a school was built to educate their youth. In 1974, an updated Marshall County Central High School building was erected. It succumbed to fire only seventeen years later, on November 7, 1991, after a defective switch in a Bunn coffee maker sparked a blaze in the middle of the night. The Minnesota Department of Education insisted that the school would not be rebuilt, but locals campaigned against the decision and overturned the state's decision. By September 1992, the new high school was operational, only 10 months after the fire. Newfolden's primary point of interest in the 21st century is Old Mill State Park, a 406-acre park known for Larson Mill, an NRHP-listed site. The structure was initially constructed in 1889, and its steam engine was rebuilt in 1958 by the state for interpretive and historical purposes. As part of the New Deal work relief projects, eight park facilities were built between 1937 and 1941. Moose, beavers, and marsh hawks are among the rare wildlife visitors to the park, alongside other birds and mammals.

OSLO, MN
POPULATION: 239 – CITY 330 OF 856 (6-4-25)
Not to be confused with the unincorporated ghost town in Dodge County (in southeastern Minnesota), this Norwegian town in the state's northwest corner was, like its counterpart, named for the capital of Norway. At its peak, 440 people lived in Oslo in the 1950s, but the community was well developed long before then. Being located in Minneapolis, St. Paul & Sault Ste. Marie Railroad and pressed against the Red River of the North worked well for Oslo's development. Trade by rail and water made it a significant draw for prospective business owners looking to invest in a new economic center. By 1928, these developments were evident in Oslo's large business district and in its educational and religious facilities. Hotels, banks, garages, filling stations, and general merchandise stores dotted the commercial district surrounding Main Street. The town's school was at the far northern end of Main, and two churches were just off to its west. Three grain elevators stood tall on the Soo Line's right-of-way, guarding the town like sentinels. They were accompanied by stockyards, a depot, and a few oil storage structures. Oslo was incorporated for the first time under its present

name on November 21, 1905, but was briefly renamed Soo City in 1907. The name reverted again in 1908.

STEPHEN, MN
POPULATION: 592 – CITY 326 OF 856 (6-4-25)
It was an ordinary night for Deputy Sheriff Val Johnson. He was patrolling near milepost 68 on southbound Highway 220 when a bright lime green light beam suddenly sped towards him, completely blinding him and sending his squad car a thousand feet down the road before it skidded sideways. Thirty-nine minutes later, just after 2:00 am, he awoke after having been knocked unconscious. Other deputies arrived to his aid and found a shattered windshield, a heavily damaged vehicle, and a very spooked Johnson. The August 27, 1979, event has since been dubbed the "Val Johnson Incident" and discussed as a significant UFO encounter on shows like History Channel's *UFO Files* and Travel Channel's *Mysteries at the Museum*. Stephen, the town of 592 people (per the 2020 Census) near where the event occurred, was briefly thrust into national headlines. Things quieted down after only a couple of months. The town and its post office were established circa 1883 and named for George Stephen. The former president of the Bank of Montreal from 1876 to 1881 and the president of the Canadian Pacific Railway Company from 1881 to 1887 was also a close friend of James J. Hill. An earlier settlement called Tamarack had existed as early as 1878 near the Tamarac River. Half a century after Tamarac's establishment, the entire area had been extensively developed into a Great Northern Railroad town. A mill was located on the river, and four grain elevators handled the agricultural outputs on the right-of-way. Hotels, banks, garages, and stores of all varieties lined both sides of the tracks. In western Stephen, five churches provided religious services to citizens, and the school served as the community's center for education. Stephen peaked at 904 people according to the 1970 U.S. Decennial Census.

STRANDQUIST, MN
POPULATION: 70 – CITY 316 OF 856 (6-3-25)
Strandquist, population 70, was named after the pioneer Swedish general store owner, John Erik Strandquist. He owned the first store near the post office bearing his surname, but moved it in 1904 when the Minneapolis, St. Paul & Sault Ste. Marie Railroad was extended to that point. The railroad village was called Lund because another nearby post office boasted that name. It closed in 1905, leaving behind only the Strandquist name. Growth was slow and steady, and Strandquist residents opted not to formally organize themselves as a municipal corporation until July 31, 1923. When Brock and Company surveyed the town five years later, they found that the hamlet had stockyards, a farmers' elevator, a depot, a bank, three stores, a consolidated school, and most impressively of all, four churches. The largest congregation was Catholic.

VIKING, MN
POPULATION: 79 – CITY 314 OF 856 (6-3-25)
Aside from the National Football League team that has captured the hearts of Minneapolis and fans around the state since 1960, a different "Viking" has been working to conquer the farmlands of northwestern Minnesota for much longer. So named after the seafaring Norsemen who ravaged western and southern Europe for centuries, the small city of Viking was founded in 1884. Then, Reverend Hans P. Hansen, a Norwegian Lutheran minister from Warren, suggested the name for the new Soo Line railroad town. As usual, the post office has remained one of the oldest and

longest-running institutions of the city (since 1890), but Viking was once home to several lines of enterprise. In addition to its school and two churches in the northwest corner of town, downtown Viking in the late 1920s was the site of a lumber office, a bank, and a store; the railroad right-of-way had a creamery, two grain elevators, stockyards, and a loading platform, and a potato house and oil reserve. The town was incorporated on April 12, 1921. Outside Viking at 16928 MN-2, a large blocky farmer made from scrap metal waves hello to passersby.

WARREN, MN ★☆
POPULATION: 1,605 – CITY 328 OF 856 (6-4-25)

Nine grain elevators, six churches, a 100-barrel-capacity flouring mill, a brickyard, and a stunning courthouse once stood tall in The Queen City of the Red River Valley. Located at the junction of the St. Paul, Minneapolis & Manitoba (renamed the Great Northern in 1890) and the Soo Line, coupled with its location in the exceedingly fertile lands of the valley where the glacial lake Lake Agassiz once existed, helped to make Warren the most prosperous town in the county. It was initially platted in 1879 and named Farley, but then quickly renamed for the railroad executive and general passenger agent Charles H. Warren. He was affiliated with the Manitoba line, the first railroad to reach Warren in the summer of 1878, and was responsible for its establishment. Crops were so bountiful in Warren's early years that farmers were required to bring in additional farmhands to help with the harvest. One such instance was when Mr. F. Furlong returned to the country from Scotland with sixty Scotch farmers. Scandinavians, Germans, Irish, and Englishmen made up the majority of the immigrant population, which, by the turn of the century, had exceeded 1,276 people in Warren, according to the Census. With such success, one would have thought Warren would have had no issues retaining the county seat. However, the opposite was found to be true. The Soo Line initially intended to build its branch line from Thief River Falls to Argyle, then westward. Argyle residents believed that if this plan succeeded, their situation as a railroad junction would warrant the removal of the seat from their town. The plan failed. Another attempt was made in 1881 by residents of Argyle and Stephen to move the seat by petition, but the election coincided with a large blizzard that made travel for outsiders to get to Warren impossible. Warren won the election. As recently as 1874, nearly a century after the last contest, residents from eastern Marshall County attempted to move the seat to Newfolden, a more centralized location, via two petitions, both of which also failed. Many businesses were prevalent in Warren, not too far into the 20th century. As of 1928, noteworthy firms included a Buick-Chevrolet Garage, a Ford garage, a foundry, the Sheaf print shop, a formal plumbing-heating business (rarely ever shown on early plat maps), a creamery, the Warren Flouring Mills, the State Bank of Warren, the First National Bank of Warren, brick kilns, two lumber yards, and Warren Hospital. The hospital was tucked away in a bend in the Wake River, across from the Warren City Park and its dance pavilion. Washington School, a High School, a section house on the Great Northern line, the courthouse and jail, and four churches were among the other noteworthy places in Warren. For a short while, the most interesting was North Star College. The short-lived institution was founded in 1908 by Reverend E.O. Chelgren with the Swedish Lutheran Augustana Synod. Despite being called a "college," it was a secondary school. It closed in 1936. Warren's only modern structure listed on the National Register of Historic Places is the Knud J. Taralseth Company building, which was built in 1911. It was once a retail establishment (from 1888 to 1959) that later served as a community center, a Masonic Temple, and a commercial center for Warren. At the Settler's Square Historical Museum, visitors can admire the very police cruiser in which Val Johnson experienced his UFO encounter near Stephen in 1979. Other buildings on the property host exhibits on military and local history. Famous people of wildly varying backgrounds hail from the Marshall County seat: Paul Nelson, a critic and executive with A&R that wrote for publications like Rolling Stone, The Village Voice, and Sing Out!; Gerome Kamrowski, a pioneer artist in surrealism and abstract expressionism; John J. Herrick, the leader of the American watercraft USS Maddox during the Gulf of Tonkin Incident that led to escalated tensions in the Vietnam War, and Carl Panzram, a serial killer suspected of over one-hundred kills who spent time in over one hundred jails and seven prisons during a roughly thirty year stretch between 1903 and 1930.

Unincorporated/Ghost Towns: Big Woods, Englund, Epselie, Florian, Gatzke, Luna, March, Radium, Rosewood

National Register of Historic Places:
Argyle: Larson Mill, Old Mill State Park WPA/Rustic Style Historic Resources
Warren: K. J. Taralseth Company

Lincoln County: Rock-covered Texaco Gas Station; now privately owned (Arco), Anderson Park on Lake Stay (Arco), Mural (Hendricks), Barn at Lincoln County Pioneer Museum (Hendricks), Windmill & Mural (Ivanhoe), Heritage Center (Ivanhoe), Lake Benton (Lake Benton), Interior of Danebod Lutheran Church (Tyler)

Lyon County: former Presbyterian Church (Balaton), Lakeview Public Schools 2008 Bus Crash Memorial (Cottonwood), former Great Northern Railroad through Camden State Park (Lynd), Kiel and Morgan Hotel & first Lyon County Courthouse (Lynd), Interior of The Catholic Church of the Holy Redeemer (Marshall), 9/11 Memorial at Memorial Park (Marshall), Stone Station (Tracy), St. Mary's Catholic Church (Tracy)

McLeod County: former Brownton City Hall (Brownton), Vintage Car at Independent Grain Elevator (Glencoe), Interior of First Lutheran Church (Glencoe), Hutchinson City Library (Hutchinson), Little Crow Statue at Eheim Park (Hutchinson), St. Paul's United Church of Christ (Plato), Veteran's Memorial (Winsted), City Mural in Downtown (Winsted)

Mahnomen County: VFW Post No. 1226 (Bejou), Circa 1910 Grain Elevator (Bejou), Mahnomen County Courthouse (Mahnomen), Painted Canoe Sculpture (Mahnomen), Mural (Mahnomen), Burger Hut (Mahnomen), 1903-05 Prairie Elevator Company & Woodworth Elevator Company (Waubun), St. Ann's Catholic Church (Waubun)

Marshall County: Mural (Argyle), The Old Creamery Antique, Boutique & Gift Shop (Middle River), Ston Holmaas Memorial Park (Newfolden), Suspension Bridge over the Middle River at Old Mill State Park (Argyle), St. Stephen Church (Stephen), Patriotic Rock (Viking), Sky-Vu Drive In Movie Theater (Warren), Val Johnso's UFO Car at the Marshall County Historical Society (Warren)

MARTIN COUNTY
EST. 1857 - POPULATION: 20,025

Some accounts suggest that Martin County was named after an early area businessman named Henry Martin, but it was most likely named for Morgan Lewis Martin, one of the founding fathers of Wisconsin.

CEYLON, MN
POPULATION: 303 – CITY 75 OF 856 (3-25-25)
The Western Town Lot Company platted this townsite as Tenhassen in 1899. Upon discovering that there was already another town of that name, a group of men gathered at Tom Sahr's general store to select a new one. They deliberated for some time before one of the men spotted a box of Ceylon tea on the store's shelves. The tea came from the British island of Ceylon, now Sri Lanka. It was given to the town as a replacement for Tenhassen, and a post office was started that same year. Incorporation status was achieved on October 22, 1900, and in a decade, the Chicago & Northwestern Railroad (formerly the Minnesota and International Railway) town had plentiful businesses and homes. The Ceylon Cement & Tile Company was located on the tracks, as were two elevators, two coal sheds, a depot, old storage, a lumber yard, and stockyards. A third elevator and a livery were allocated on the eastern side of the tracks, but most of its businesses were to their west. A State Bank, a National Bank, the post office, a German church, an Episcopal Lutheran church, a Methodist Episcopal church, and a public school were denoted the most critical institutions of that era on Geo. A. Ogle & Company's 1911 plat map. Walter "Fritz" Mondale, the 42nd Vice President of the United States under President Jimmy Carter, was born here on January 5, 1928, and lived in Ceylon before his family moved to Heron Lake in 1934. Other Ceylon claims to fame include Minnesota's first lighted baseball field, a community museum containing numerous artifacts from the former school, and an annual spring auction. For over 80 years, the auction has attracted visitors from across the Midwest with its large selection of farm equipment, mowers, and implements.

Restaurant Recommendation:
Lake Belt Bar & Grill
103 E Main St
Ceylon, MN 56121

DUNNELL, MN
POPULATION: 133 – CITY 76 OF 856 (3-25-25)
De Sota was started in 1899 when the Minneapolis & St. Louis Railroad came through, but its name was extremely short-lived. It was meant to be a tribute to the famous explorer Hernando de Soto. Because the Spanish-American War had only just concluded in August 1898, pioneers strongly protested having their town's name associated with the Spanish or their language. A request was sent to relocate the entire townsite two miles south and call it Dunnell in honor of Mark H. Dunnell. He was a U.S. Congressman from Minnesota from 1871 to 1883 and 1889 to 1891. De Sota was abandoned entirely. From 1910 to 1920, the population of the settlement grew from 170 to 247, a number not far from its peak of 260 in the 1960 Census. In 1911, Dunnell boasted of a school, a Swedish Lutheran church, a Methodist Episcopal church, a fire department, a post office, a creamery, a hotel, two blacksmith shops, a lumber yard, a livery barn, a depot, and two elevators. The Swedish Lutheran church is now called Immanuel Lutheran Church. It was organized on August 26, 1871, at the

home of John Stenstrom. The building was not raised until 1886, when it had grown to a congregation of four dozen adults and three dozen children. This first edifice was a half-mile north of town, but once it could no longer fit all its members, a new one was built between 1904-05 on Silcox Street.

FAIRMONT, MN ★☆

POPULATION: 10,487 – CITY 91 OF 856 (3-26-25)

Five lakes, twenty-nine parks, and extensive recreational activity options make this city a haven for nature enthusiasts and a great place to establish a townsite. While it's unlikely that E. Banks Hall and William H. Budd chose to settle on the lakes for swimming or waterskiing, they were the first men to build permanent homes in the area. The site would later be known as Fair Mount for its location on a hill overlooking its Central Chain of lakes (George Lake, Lake Sisseton, Budd Lake, Hall Lake, Amber Lake, an unnamed body, and Mud Lake). It was renamed Fairmont after the Des Moines and Watonwan Company platted it in October 1857, and a year later, it welcomed a postal service branch. Williams Budd was the first postmaster. In that era, the law establishing town sites required town companies to build a house on each quarter section of land to "hold" the section. Banks, Budd, and A. L. Sharps erected a building that was to serve as a store, hotel, blacksmith shop, and carpenter shop all in one. Several other sites throughout Martin County were laid out in this manner, but Fairmont was the lucky winner chosen as the seat of government. The title took effect in 1857 despite there being no real town. By 1862, settlement had ramped up but halted during the Sioux Uprising. Fort Fairmont was established that year but abandoned with the resolution of the conflict. After the mid-1870s, the grasshopper plague came and went. Fairmont welcomed the Southern Minnesota Railroad and ushered in a new period of growth and prosperity for its residents. In 1880, it had a population of 541, which doubled to 1,205 by 1890 and increased further to 3,040 by the end of the century. Such growth warranted a city charter in 1902. By 1911, Fairmont had three railroads, the Chicago & Northwestern, the Chicago, Milwaukee & St. Paul, and the Chicago, St. Paul & Minneapolis; a public and high school, a courthouse and county jail; the Martin County Agricultural Society Race Track; The Fairmount Boat Company; the Fairmont Machine Company; Fairmont Railway Motors; the Fairmont Co-stone Company; the Coleman Lumber Company; an Opera House; a creamery; a German Lutheran church; a First Christian Science church; a First Congregational church; a German Evangelical church; a Methodist Episcopal church; a German Methodist church; a Swedish Methodist church, and all the typical banks, hotels, stores, and other establishments of that era. Three of those named locations have since been listed on the National Register of Historic Places, along with three others. The Fairmont Opera House was completed in 1901 after Frank A. Day, the editor of the *Fairmont Sentinel* (founded in 1885 and widely considered Minnesota's most conservative newspaper), encouraged local business people to invest in a theater that could serve as a community meeting place and performance venue. The First Church of Christ, Scientist, was built in 1898 from Sioux quartzite. It was described as "incredibly unusual" because finding a Christian Science church in such a small town so soon after the movement's founding was uncommon. It is now the Red Rock Center for the Arts. A third location on the Register, the Orville P. and Sarah Chubb House, is Fairmont's oldest residence, built in 1867 from brick from the local brickyard. Locals and visitors may be more familiar with the George Wohleter House, a 1899 Queen Anne/Neoclassical architecturally-styled building. The final two historic points of interest are the 1906-07 Martin County Courthouse and the 1926 United States Post Office. At the Martin County Historical Society Pioneer Museum, recently ranked as the "Best County Museum in Minnesota," visitors can admire exhibits on

Linda McCartney's meatless frozen entrees, Southern Minnesota's Hall of Fame bands, pioneer school artifacts, military memorabilia, and much more. One hundred and one painted concrete pigs, located chiefly within city limits, depict local businesses and points of interest and encourage visitors to go "hog wild" as they tour the heart of Minnesota's pork industry. Fairmont's largest employers as of 2020 were Fairmont Foods of Minnesota, a frozen vegetable canning company now associated with the Tony Downs Food Group; Weigh-Tronix Scale Manufacturing, one of the largest suppliers of industrial weighing solutions in the world; and Fairmont Mayo Health Systems, associated with the Fairmont Medical Center. Three famous Minnesotans who hail from Fairmont are Frank A. Day, the 13th Lieutenant Governor of Minnesota; Paul Willson, an actor best known for his role as Paul Krapence on NBC's sitcom *Cheers*; and Jay Maynard, an Internet phenomenon known as "Tron Guy" for his electroluminescent costume based on the 1982 sci-fi film.

Restaurant Recommendation:
Channel Inn
330 W Lair Rd
Fairmont, MN 56031

GRANADA, MN
POPULATION: 291 – CITY 92 OF 856 (3-27-25)
Home to 291 residents as of the 2020 Census, this Martin County community is named after the Moorish city of Granada, Spain. Founded in 1888, it was named for two early settlers, Abner S. and Sally M. Handy. Its post office, managed by postmaster Albert H. Reynolds, operated under that name from 1888 to 1891, until it was renamed Granada with the coming of the Chicago, Milwaukee & St. Paul Railroad. The site was platted in 1890 by Ed Anderson and, by 1911, had a depot, a school, a post office, a bank, a hotel, a livery, and a creamery. Until May 1896, no work was done on the depot. Only months after it was completed, lightning struck it in November 1896. The building survived the strike and continued to serve Granada until its closure circa 1959; it was moved to Voss Park outside of Butterfield in 1977. The Granada Congregational Church started in November 1892 at the local schoolhouse, and in 1894, its edifice was built. Despite mergers with nearby churches, the congregation met for the last time on November 14, 2007, with a pie-and-ice-cream social celebration. When the United Methodist Church of Granada closed in September 2000, the building was donated for use as the Granada Historical Museum.

NORTHROP, MN
POPULATION: 223 – CITY 93 OF 856 (3-27-25)
As a station on the Fairmont branch of the Chicago, St. Paul, Minneapolis & Omaha Railroad, Northrop achieved great success in its development as it could feed off the railroad traffic and bolster its local economy. It began in 1899 when the Inter-State Land Company surveyed the site and named it for Cyrus Northrop, then the 2nd President of the University of Minnesota. He held that honor from 1884 to 1911 and had the famous Minneapolis multi-purpose performance and arts hall named after him. The Northrop post office served Northrop residents from 1900 to 1972, until the Fairmont office took over those duties. According to a 1911 atlas, the town once had an active depot, elevators, a lumber yard, a blacksmith shop, and a general store. Its highest recorded population was 276 people in 1990.

SHERBURN, MN
POPULATION: 1,058 – CITY 89 OF 856 (3-26-25)
When a town is located at a railroad junction, one can only assume its history must be fascinating and extensive. Such is the case for Sherburn, Minnesota, a Minneapolis & St. Louis and Chicago, Milwaukee & St. Paul Railroad town that can trace its early settlement back to the mid-1860s. George Archer lived on Lake Manyaska in a soddie. On his property, a lone cedar tree was a marker for pioneers traversing the otherwise relatively barren terrain between Fairmont and Jackson. Eventually, stage lines were established, as was a post office called Lone Cedar. From 1867 to 1879, the postal service branch was referred to by that name until it was transferred a mile north to the new Sherburn townsite. Platted by the Cargill, Bassett, and Hunting syndicate of La Crosse, Wisconsin, in 1878, it was called Sherburn in honor of Sherburne S. Merrill, the general manager of the Milwaukee Road. Alternate names considered were Lone Cedar, Huntington, and Vestal. "Sherburn" could have also been derived from the name of the wife of an officer of the railroad company living in McGregor, Iowa. By the end of 1879, there were 15 buildings in Sherburn, and over the decades, the number of structures multiplied. Many buildings in its downtown area from 1898 to 1908 remain part of the Sherburn Commercial Historic District. As of 1911, there were also two elevators and a depot on Minneapolis & St. Line Railroad; a depot, elevator, and stockyards on the Milwaukee Road; a Methodist Episcopal church; a Catholic church; a German Lutheran church; a Congregational church; an Adventist church; a Baptist church; the Dan Broth Hall; a school; a hotel; a livery, and a multitude of other businesses. In 1920, many business owners joined forces to create the Fox Lake Park Company. Their mission was to develop the land along Temperance Lake, which they accomplished through the sale of stock. Funds were raised to build a dance pavilion, a bathhouse, grandstands, playground equipment, a diving tower, and fishing piers. Later, the Fox Lake Golf Club was established, and much of the land and amenities for its golf course were bought up when the former company opted to liquidate. The Sherburn Community Building, formerly a municipal theater, was completed in 1940 as the only Art Deco structure in town. Two unforgettable events of Sherburn's history are entirely independent of one another. In October 1896, two brothers robbed the Bank of Sherburn, killing two people. They pedaled away on their bikes with a couple of grand in cash. The first man was "caught" by police and citizens near Elmore, in Faribault County, at a farmhouse. He shot and killed Sheriff William Gallion of Bancroft, Iowa, and then took his own life when he realized he could not outrun the posse. His brother was captured in Lake Mills, Iowa, nearly eighty miles from the bank. The Sherburn Raiders high school basketball team made headlines in 1970 when they defeated the much larger schools of Luverne, Jackson, Melrose, Marshall, and South St. Paul to become the lone victor of the Minnesota State Championship. Noteworthy Sherburnites include Brandon Williamson, a pitcher for the MLB's Cincinnati Reds since 2023; Dale Gardner, a NASA astronaut with two weeks of "in-space" experience; and August Larson, a U.S. Marine Corps Major General who commanded the 22nd Marine Regiment during the Battle of Okinawa in the Pacific Theatre.

TRIMONT, MN
POPULATION: 705 – CITY 88 OF 856 (3-26-25)
Trimont's history is an accurate "tale of twin cities," Triumph and Monterey, that were once competing railroad towns founded by the Minneapolis & St. Louis Railroad and its rival, the Chicago & North Western Railroad. Triumph was the town of the latter railroad company. It was platted in 1899 by the Western Town Lot Company and named by John Steen for the Triumph Creamery Company. The post office, named

by its first postmaster Bertram W. Wetzel, who asserted that his office "[Would] Triumph yet!," dates to 1880: nineteen years before the Monterey office was established at the same time the Minneapolis & St. Louis Railroad established their townsite. It was named after Monterey, Mexico, a place whose name means "king mountain." Both towns grew together, with only a couple of miles separating them. Triumph was incorporated as a village on August 15, 1901; Monterey followed suit on October 14, 1902. A decade later, Triumph had a school, a Methodist Episcopal church, a bank, a drug store, a hotel, and a depot. In contrast, Monterey boasted a depot, a livery, a hotel, a bank, and two churches, one for Catholics and another for Baptists. The Triumph townsite was considerably larger than Monterey's; its Maple Street was the equivalent of its Broadway Street regarding the "main drag" of commercial interests. Strangely enough, despite both towns having banks, only Monterey's were robbed (and twice, at that!). The first burglary was in April 1908, when John H. Arthur and Ralph "Sheeney" Holmes broke into the Peoples State Bank and made off with $1,485 in gold and cash. Arthur was caught in St. Paul, but Holmes was never found. In December 1939, the Farmers State Bank in Monterey was robbed of $700. Its perpetrator was located in Chattanooga, Tennessee, the following year. As railroads became less important with the advent of the automobile and the introduction of cross-country highways and interstates, Triumph and Monterey ultimately decided to put their differences aside and combine into a single municipality called "Trimont." Effective January 1, 1959, the new city was born, its name amalgamating the two former villages. Its extremely long Main Street is noted for its two concentrated business areas, with each center being the heart of the former Monterey in the west or Triumph in the east.

TRUMAN, MN
POPULATION: 1,092 – CITY 94 OF 856 (3-27-25)

The Watonwan Valley Railroad Company was responsible for platting Truman in 1899, but it was the Chicago, St. Paul, Minneapolis & Omaha Railroad (which took over the Watonwan in December 1899) that brought about its chance at prosperity. Like many other towns in southwest Minnesota, Truman was born out of necessity. Local farmers had been tilling the lands of Westford Township as early as 1857, and after decades of being forced to haul their grain twelve to eighteen miles away to the nearest grain shipping points, they pleaded for a new railroad stop to be established. Their calls for help were answered when the W.V.R.C. was incorporated on January 16, 1899, and a new line was built to connect Madelia with Fairmont. Westford was briefly considered for the town's name because of the post office (so named for the ford over Elm Creek) that had been there since 1871, but the name Truman was instead chosen in honor of Truman Clark. He was the son of J. T. Clark, the second vice-president of the railroad. The postal service branch was renamed Truman in 1899, and by June of that year, its first four buildings were under construction: Richard Jones' hardware store, a restaurant, a hotel, and W. A. Hinton's general merchandise store. Trains arrived in October for the first time. About a decade later, Truman's infrastructure directory showed plentiful residences, the depot, a Christian church, a Baptist church, the Truman National Bank, the Truman State Bank, a printing office, a creamery, a hotel, a livery, the School District #77 building, and a cluster of churches, a parsonage, and a school in the northeast corner of town owned by St. Paul's Lutheran Church and the German Evangelical Lutheran Society. The Hubbard and Palmer, the Truman Elevator and Flour Exchange, and the Wolhueter Elevator Company of Fairmont raised the elevators the farmers had desperately wanted for years. Other stores, saloons, and firms emerged over time. In 1920, the two banks merged to form the Truman National Bank, which, in 1946, combined with the Peoples State Bank to become the Peoples

State Bank of Truman until 2003. Truman's peak population was recorded in the 1980 Census: 1,392 citizens. The Truman Historical Museum and the Truman Historical Association continue to document and preserve local history.

WELCOME, MN
POPULATION: 710 – CITY 90 OF 856 (3-26-25)
This welcoming community is hard to say goodbye to, as shown by its resilience in maintaining a population of over 700 people. It was laid out in 1880 by the Southern Minnesota Extension Company on the land of S. K. Campbell and called Campbell's Switch. In July 1881, the post office was established as Lily Creek, but it was changed to Welcome in September after it was discovered that another Lily Creek already existed in Minnesota. Contrary to popular belief, the town is not named for the warm greeting but for early Manyaska Township homesteader Alfred M. Welcome. His farmstead was along the townsite's southwestern side. Early Welcome became a hopping place thanks to the Chicago & Northwestern Railroad in the north and the Chicago, Milwaukee & St. Paul Railroad in the south. Two depots handled train and passenger traffic, and by 1911, four elevators were in place to handle grain shipments. The Chicago & Northwestern Railroad had its own stockyards as well. *The Welcome Times* newspaper office, the Welcome Creamery Company, a bank, and a livery are explicitly listed on early maps of Welcome; these sources also note School District No. 89, a Baptist church, a Lutheran church, and a third church as essential points of infrastructure for the settlement. The newspaper circulated from 1895 to 1969 before merging with the *Sherburn Advance-Standard*. Its school district combined with Sherburn and Trimont in 1988-89 to become the Martin County West School District. Welcome was incorporated as a village on May 7, 1890. One oddity of the community is its 1914 horse-and-human drinking fountain. The water has since been shut off, but horses were meant to drink from the street and humans from the sidewalk.

Restaurant Recommendation:
Welcome Meats
515 Bidwell St
Welcome, MN 56181

Ormsby is only partially located in Martin County (see Watonwan County).

Unincorporated/Ghost Towns: East Chain, Fox Lake, Imogene, Nashville Center, Wilbert

National Register of Historic Places:
Fairmont: Fairmont Opera House, First Church of Christ, Scientist, George Wohlheter House, Martin County Courthouse, Orville P. & Sarah Chubb House, United States Post Office
Sherburn: Sherburn Commercial Historic District, Sherburn Community Building, Fox Lake Site

Golf Courses:
Fox Lake Golf Club, Daily Fee (Sherburn, MN)
Interlaken Golf Club, Daily Fee (Fairmont, MN)
Rose Lake Golf Club, Daily Fee (Fairmont, MN)

MCLEOD COUNTY
EST. 1856 - POPULATION: 36,771

Located in south-central Minnesota, McLeod County was established on March 1, 1856, and named for Martin McLeod. He was a pioneer member of the Minnesota territorial legislature.

BISCAY, MN
POPULATION: 113 – CITY 547 OF 856 (8-14-25)
Six-plus passenger trains made the trek between Hutchinson and Glencoe each day on the formerly operable Chicago, Milwaukee & St. Paul Railroad. Biscay was the lone "stop" between the two larger municipalities; it was established in 1899 and, the following year, became the site of a railroad depot. Named after the Bay of Biscay between Spain and France, the Biscay post office opened in 1888 and remained in operation until 1954, when it became a rural branch before closing in 1965. Biscay's incorporation as a village came in 1949, although the Milwaukee Railroad abandoned its line and allowed for the depot to be moved to Glencoe by the end of the 1950s. Over the last five Censuses, its population has remained at exactly 113 or 114 people, its all-time historical high.

BROWNTON, MN
POPULATION: 731 – CITY 548 OF 856 (8-14-25)
Home to a peak population of 807 people in 2000, Brownton was first marked in 1856 as "Grimshaw's Settlement" in honor of one of its original settlers, Robert E. Grimshaw. When Alonzo L. Brown petitioned for a post office, the postal service awarded one in 1878, and the name "Brownton" was assigned to honor his legacy. Located on Lake Addie, the Brownton post office's location soon gave way to a townsite on October 15, 1877, as well as a line of the Chicago, Milwaukee & St. Paul Railroad. Lines of mercantile establishments, a blacksmith shop, churches, and schools came into being, and within ten years, Brownton was incorporated on February 12, 1886. John Schilling had platted a town called Lake Addie nearby, which grew alongside Brownton for eight years before the two communities merged for good.

GLENCOE, MN ★
POPULATION: 5,744 – CITY 481 OF 856 (8-8-25)
The subject of the 1985 documentary film *God's Country*, directed by the French filmmaker Louis Malle, was Glencoe, Minnesota, then a community of roughly 4,300 residents. Despite the farm crises of that time, the populace of the town has only grown, a trend that has remained consistent throughout Glencoe's history since the time of its first Census in 1880 (except for the 1920 Census, which reported a net loss of 41 residents, the only time in the town's history that its population decreased decade over decade). Founded on June 11, 1855, Martin McLeod of the townsite company suggested the name Glencoe for Glen Coe, Scotland, the modern home of Scottish mountaineering. It was immediately declared to be the McLeod judicial seat, although it has not remained the county's largest municipality. The first piece of infrastructure was its post office, established in 1856. After the Hastings and Dakota Railway was built through in 1872 and the Milwaukee Road (the Chicago, Milwaukee, St. Paul and Pacific Railroad) came later, Glencoe solidified itself as an essential trade center within the region. In 1876, the first version of the McLeod County Courthouse was built, and in 1909, it was heavily renovated to reflect the widespread adoption of Beaux-Arts-

style courthouses throughout Minnesota. When the renovation was made, Glencoe was undergoing several significant changes. For one, its commercial interests had multiplied to encompass several branches unique to towns as large as Glencoe, such as a brewery, two weekly newspapers, a foundry, a creamery, a drain tile factory, three good hotels, three grain elevators, and multiple flour, feed, and saw mills. An opera house and a hospital were amongst its crowning achievements, and a well-off public school system and numerous churches, the largest of which was the Catholic congregation, were noted places as of 1915. In addition to the courthouse building, Glencoe's historic Glencoe Grade and High School, built in 1933 and used as a K-12 school until 1954, is also still standing.

HUTCHINSON, MN ☆
POPULATION: 14,599 – CITY 545 OF 856 (8-14-25)
"Hutch" began on November 19, 1855, when Asa, Judson, and John Hutchinson started it on the South Fork Crow River. The three men weren't just brothers, but rather members of the famous family of singers born in Milford, New Hampshire, known for their patriotic songs of emancipation, temperance, and social songs that brought them nationwide fame throughout the 1840s. A statue of the singing Hutchinson brothers was dedicated in 2005 at the public library for Hutchinson's sesquicentennial (150th) celebration. When they arrived in the region, they settled on a hilltop overlooking the river valley. The beauty of the area spurred them to set aside 15 acres for parkland, making their city park system the second-oldest in the United States, behind only New York City's Central Park. A post office opened in 1856, and for a few years, Hutchinson grew without issue until Little Crow and the Dakota attacked them on September 4, 1862. Several outlying buildings were razed before the settlers were able to repel the attackers from their stockade successfully. The Dakota leader and his 16-year-old son were killed by Nathan and Chauncey Lamson less than a year later, on July 3, while they were picking raspberries in the farmer's territory. $545 was given to the farmer for fulfilling the bounty on Little Crow. As the war subsided and things returned to normalcy, Hutchinson submitted its first Census in 1880, and reported that it had 580 residents. Entrepreneurs started dozens of businesses, ranging from lumber yards and general stores to grain elevators and doctors' offices, and by 1890, the town had 1,414 citizens. By the turn of the century, 2,495 people were living in Hutch, and the numbers only continued to rise as terminal railroad branches of the Great Northern and the Chicago, Milwaukee & St. Paul Railroads greeted the town's commercial district. The Electric Short Line Railroad also ran through the city. The three railroads were abandoned for good in 1956, 1972, and 2001, respectively. Dakota Rail was the final operating railroad entity in the community from 1985 to 2001; it shut down only after failing to turn a profit. Many noted points of interest throughout Hutchinson pertain to its early history, including the 1886 Harry Merrill Hose, the oldest wood-frame structure in Hutchinson; a Neoclassical Carnegie Library erected in 1904; the 1913 Prairie School-design Merton S. Goodnow House; the Komensky School outside of town, active from 1912 to 1959 and noted for serving early Czech American settlers, and the 1942 WPA mural in the town's post office, painted by Elsa Jemne. Ridgewater College has campuses in both Hutch and Willmar that were born out of a 1996 merger of Willmar Community College and Hutchinson-Willmar Regional Technical College. Lindsay Whalen, a five-time WNBA All-Star and a four-time WNBA champion with the Minnesota Lynx; John Jeremiah McRaith, the Roman Catholic Bishop of Owensboro, Kentucky from 1982 to 2009; John W. Foss, a United States Army general and commander of the United States Army Training and Doctrine Command; Kira Sabin, a wildlife painter known for breathing life back into the Federal Duck Stamp contest; Cory Sauter, an NFL quarterback off and on between 1998 and 2003; Carlos Avery,

Minnesota's first Commissioner of the Game and Fish Commission; Ancher Nelsen, a U.S. Congressman from Minnesota from 1959 to 1974; Paulette Carlson, a country music singer-songwriter and the lead vocalist of Highway 101, and Les Kouba, the inventor of the Art-O-Graph in 1947 which transferred a photo to a layout via a projector, are some noteworthy persons of interest from Hutchinson's history.

LESTER PRAIRIE, MN
POPULATION: 1,894 – CITY 483 OF 856 (8-8-25)

Lester Prairie was named in honor of John N. Lester and his wife Maria, who was the niece of John Adams, the second President of the United States, and a first cousin of John Quincy Adams, the sixth President of the United States. German settlement began in the 1870s, but it was not until 1886 that the Great Northern Railroad finally reached the area after it was extended to that point. On September 13, 1888, it was incorporated shortly after George Chamber opened his lumberyard, and a general store was established to serve the residents' needs. A post office opened in 1888 at the lumberyard, and Lena McConahy was appointed postmaster. Lester Prairie's most significant population increase occurred between 1890 and 1900, when it grew by 121.2%, from 189 people to 418. Its next big growth spurt was between the end of the 1940s and 1950, when it grew by 56.7% from 423 people to 663. René Clausen, conductor emeritus of The Concordia Choir and a three-time Grammy Award winner, was partially raised in Lester Prairie.

PLATO, MN
POPULATION: 329 – CITY 482 OF 856 (8-8-25)

As stagecoach lines between Shakopee and Glencoe began to experience heavier traffic amid the western expansion and settlement of Minnesota, some pioneers opted to permanently settle on a small body of water called Kennick Lake. Once enough people had accumulated, the petition was sent out to the United States Postal Service to establish a post office circa 1858. The name "Buffalo Creek" was suggested, but was denied. Ironically, a nearby office in Renville County was established under the name "Buffalo Lake," so it is unclear why the initial suggestion was shut down without explanation. Regardless of the reasoning, local Greek historian and enthusiast James Aldersby chose the name Plato for the noted Greek philosopher, and the town was forever named in his honor. The Chicago, Milwaukee & St. Paul Railroad rolled into the village, bringing with it many of its people, blacksmith shops, saloons, grain elevators, and civic and religious institutions. Plato was incorporated as a village on New Year's Day 1889. Unfortunately, one of the elevators and an entire city block succumbed to a September 28, 1896, conflagration, but Plato forged onwards. Kennick Lake was eventually drained.

SILVER LAKE, MN
POPULATION: 866 – CITY 546 OF 856 (8-14-25)

The body of water known as Silver Lake took its name from the Poles and the Czechs who saw it as an excellent place–a pristine one, at that–to build their homes and invest in their futures. Postal history in the area is relatively extensive, with origins at the Fremont office in Hennepin County in 1856. It was reassigned to McLeod County shortly thereafter. A new office called Silver Lake (although not the first Minnesota office to use that name, as a Silver Lake P.O. existed in Waseca County from 1857 to 1862) started in 1867. Still, the general area retained the name Fremont until the construction of a general store in 1881. Silver Lake was platted that year and incorporated by the end of the decade. The Electric Short Line Railway, also known as Luce Electric Lines, operated from 1908 to 1924 and ran through Silver Lake before its closure. Electric locomotives were never used on the railroad, although gasoline-powered electric railcars carried passengers until September 10, 1947. Many businesses called Silver Lake home over the decades, but the town was best known for its "church row" between the 1910s and 1930s (and beyond), where as many as three edifices stood tall right next to one another.

STEWART, MN
POPULATION: 489 – CITY 549 OF 856 (8-14-25)
Doctor Darwin Adelbert Stewart, a physician from Winona born in New Hampshire, is the namesake of this town of 489 on the western border of McLeod County. In 1871, a post office called Collins was established, but its name was changed to Stewart in 1879 to match that of the Chicago, Milwaukee & St. Paul Railroad townsite. A decade's growth allowed Stewart to "prove up" into a handsome young community, bustling with general stores, blacksmith shops, hardware and implement stores, grain elevators, professional offices, schools, churches, general merchandise stores, and all the other lines of enterprise of early Minnesota. One of its most classical lines, a Red Owl grocery store, came to town in 1939 when William Sunde moved to Stewart. The Minnesota-based chain (formerly headquartered in Hopkins but founded in Rochester) became his employer when he was sixteen. He wanted to own a location of his own someday, and Stewart was selected to be the site where he would fulfill his dream. After forty years of serving the community as "Sunde's Red Owl Agency," he sold out to Larry and Virgene Roepke in 1979. By 2001, the grocery store was closed for good, but in recent years, the community has sought to restore the building and turn it into the Stewart and Red Owl Museum.

Restaurant Recommendation:
Cactus Jack's II
260 South St
Stewart, MN 55385

WINSTED, MN
POPULATION: 2,240 – CITY 484 OF 856 (8-8-25)
"Winsted" is an eponym for the incorporated city in Connecticut of the same name, but its name is a portmanteau of two other towns in The Constitution State: Winchester and Barkhamsted. German settlers arrived in droves in the 1850s, and the site was platted on January 2, 1867. Eli F. Lewis is primarily considered the father of the village; he was an early settler and was responsible for much of its early development. He purchased land from Baptiste Campbell, a half-white, half-Sioux man who owned all the land north of Main Avenue. Winsted Lake was once called Lake Eleanor in honor of his wife, but was later renamed to match the railroad station and post office. From 1858 to 1861, the office was called Winsted before being discontinued for five years. In 1866, it reopened under the name "Winsted Lake." The "Lake" was dropped by the postal service in 1886, and Winsted accepted its role as one of the largest communities on the western end of the Electric Short Line (the Luce) Railroad. It was incorporated on August 27, 1887. By the end of its first decade in the 20th century, it had electricity, waterworks, telephone service, a public school, churches, a soap and potash factory, the Winsted Milling Company, the Winsted Roller Mills, and numerous other businesses. St Mary's Home and Hospital was completed in 1959, and in 1962, the City of Winsted wholly owned and operated the Winsted Municipal Airport. The ornate Queen Anne municipal building, built in 1895, Winsted City Hall, was added to

the National Register of Historic Places on August 19, 1982. The Winsted Winter Festival, with its lighted parade, and the Winsted Summer Festival, with its sand volleyball tournament and street dance, are popular events. Still, most Minnesotans know the city for its Winstock Country Music Festival. Started in 1994, the annual festival attracts well over ten thousand concert-goers each day. It has hosted talent such as Luke Combs, Blake Shelton, Tim McGraw, Miranda Lambert, and Reba McEntire, among many others, over the decades.

Restaurant Recommendation:
Blue Note Restaurant
320 3rd St S
Winsted, MN 55395

Unincorporated/Ghost Towns: Fernando, Heatwole, Komensky, Lake Addie, Sherman, South Silver Lake, Sumter

National Register of Historic Places:
Glencoe: Glencoe Grade & High School, McLeod County Courthouse
Hutchinson: Harry Merrill House, Hutchinson Carnegie Library, Merton S. Goodnow House, Komensky School
Winsted: Winsted City Hall

Golf Courses:
Crow River Golf Club, Daily Fee (Hutchinson, MN)
Glencoe Country Club, Daily Fee (Glencoe, MN)
ShadowBrooke Golf Course, Daily Fee (Lester Prairie, MN)

Breweries/Wineries/Distilleries:
Crow River Winery (Hutchinson, MN)

Town Celebrations:
Brownton Days, Brownton, MN (3rd Weekend of July)
Hutchinson Jaycee Water Carnival, Hutchinson, MN (Week leading into Father's Day)
Pola-Czesky Days, Silver Lake, MN (1st Weekend in August)
Prairie Days, Lester Prairie, MN (3rd Weekend in July)
Stewartfest, Stewart, MN (Late August)
Winsted Summer Festival, Winsted, MN (2nd Weekend in August)
Winsted Winter Festival, Winsted, MN (1st Weekend of December)
Winstock Country Music Festival, Winsted, MN (3rd Full Weekend of June)

MEEKER COUNTY
EST. 1856 - POPULATION: 23,400

Bradley B. Meeker, an Associate Justice of the Minnesota Territorial Supreme Court from 1849 to 1853, was honored with the naming of this county upon its creation in February 1856.

CEDAR MILLS, MN
POPULATION: 62 – CITY 544 OF 856 (8-14-25)
The village of Cedar Mills derived its name from the 1,860-acre "Cedar Lake," so named for its abundance of red cedar trees, and the flour and sawmills on the South Fork Crow River. Daniel Avery Cross came to the township in 1856 with his family. Over a dozen more joined them in 1857, including R. J. Brodwell, Elmer Eighmey,

Philander Ball, and O. S. Merriam. C. G. Topping took over the role of postmaster once the United States Postal Service approved the placement of an office in the vicinity, also called Cedar Mills. When the Dakota became hostile and the Dakota War of 1862 began, the office's records and supplies were hidden to protect them from destruction. Some sources place the office's establishment as early as 1858, and others in 1870, the same year that Cedar Mills welcomed its first general store, owned by J. D. Baldwin. Flour mills, blacksmith shops, and a few other businesses came to fruition, but many moons would pass before the City Investment Company finally platted the village in December 1922. The Electric Short Line was the local railroad of note; they reportedly built here because of the lack of trees, which made it easy to lay their right-of-way.

COSMOS, MN
POPULATION: 507 – CITY 543 OF 856 (8-14-25)
No town in Minnesota can claim to be closer to the stars than Cosmos, a small Meeker County community that boasts of a starry water tower, streets named for planets, and an annual Space Festival every third weekend in July. Daniel Jackman of Maine was the first to make Cosmos Township the center of his universe when he made a claim here in 1867, and then brought in his family the following spring. The place was called Nelson for Ole K. Nelson, a Norwegian farmer, before it was changed to Cosmos. Daniel S. Hoyt, another early settler, was the surveyor who suggested the town's unique Greek name, meaning "order" or "harmony." A post office accepted that name in 1870 while it was still in Renville County; in 1872, it was moved to Meeker County. It closed in 1906 and only reopened in 1924, shortly after the Electric Short Line Railway (alternatively, the Minnesota and Western Railroad) was completed through Cosmos. Between September 21-24, 1926, Cosmos gained notoriety as Minnesota's newest incorporated village. The population of Cosmos soared to 610 in 1990; its two most famous residents have been chemist Mary Jane Shultz, noted for her research on clear-water practices, and Shannon Currier, the head coach of the football programs at Concordia University, St. Paul, and Truman State University since 2000.

DARWIN, MN
POPULATION: 348 – CITY 541 OF 856 (8-14-25)
The largest ball of sisal twine built by a single person (Francis A. Johnson) resides in Darwin, Minnesota. It rivals the "biggest ball of twine" claims made by balls in Cawker City, Kansas; Lake Nebagamon, Wisconsin; and Branson, Missouri. Johnson's project held the official *Guinness Book of World Records* title from 1979 to 1994, and, as of its last measurements, stood 12 feet tall and weighed 17,400 pounds. He worked for no less than four hours a day for 29 years to wind the baler twine ball into an unmovable mass; eventually, it was moved to a gazebo with plexiglass next to the Darwin water tower. The classical roadside attraction has put Darwin on the map for decades as a must-stop spot for roadtrippers, but before its existence, early settlers thought that their town would be notable for other reasons. When the settlement was organized in 1857, it was named Rice City in honor of Edmund Rice. In October 1869, its name was changed to honor Electus Darwin Litchfield, a prominent man and stockholder within the St. Paul & Pacific Railroad Company. John Curran and Martin McKenney platted it. There was a village and townsite called Stella City before Rice City, but the railroad depot and post office both adopted the name "Darwin" by the end of the 1860s. Alexander Cairncross, J. F. Low, and C. D. Brown helped raise some of the earliest storefronts and elevators. Still, Darwin would have had the full range of businesses as any other Minnesota prairie town of that era. For years, Darwin fought tooth and nail to become the Meeker County seat so the railroad company would not

move its division point and center of operations elsewhere. The high expectations forced building lot prices to skyrocket, therefore suppressing Darwin's growth, and likely causing them to lose the county seat war with Litchfield. The rail center was moved to Willmar, which later became one of central Minnesota's most significant economic centers. In contrast, Darwin never exceeded a population of 361 residents (in the 1970s). "Weird Al" Yankovic released an album in 1989 with a song titled "The Biggest Ball of Twine in Minnesota," a folk ballad about a family road trip to Darwin's famous ball of twine. In addition to the ball, the Henry Ames House in Darwin Township is a noted area structure that was added to the National Register of Historic Places for its location on Meeker County's former leading industry, a large brickyard.

DASSEL, MN
POPULATION: 1,472 – CITY 539 OF 856 (8-13-25)

Swedes from Västergötland and Värmland, and immigrants from Ohio, Indiana, Kentucky, and Virginia were the first to settle Dassel, a town of 1,472 named in honor of Bernard Dassel. Mr. Dassel was a friend of the Empire Builder James J. Hill, who appointed him as the chief secretary of the St. Paul & Pacific Railroad, later a part of the sprawling Great Northern Railroad system. While settlers arrived as early as 1856, it would not be until the fall of 1866 that the village was organized using the name "Swan Lake," for one of several bodies of water in the vicinity. The Dassel townsite was platted in 1869, the post office was named Dassel Station, and by 1871, the Dassel name was used in place of Swan Lake by all entities. Parker Simons laid out the townsite and was responsible for putting up its first frame building. James and Charles Morris owned the first stock of general merchandise. A hotel opened shortly thereafter, and in time, three grain elevators, a second hotel, a saw mill, a flour mill, a wool mill, a blacksmith shop, tile stove works, and an engine house came to fruition. James H. Morris, Mickel Henderson, and Norgren & Company owned the three stores that followed. Congregationalists, Swedish Lutherans, Swedish Missionaries, and Seventh-Day Adventists were preaching sermons to their parishioners every Sunday. It was on February 13, 1873, that The Gethsemane Swedish Evangelical Lutheran Church was organized; services were held from 1878 to 1886 in an old schoolhouse before they built their edifice for worship. In later decades, Dassel took on the title of the "Ergot Capital of the World" after becoming the first major supplier of the fungi in the United States. It was used in the fabrication of several wartime drugs starting in the mid-1930s, just before the dawn of World War II. Rice Laboratories was founded in 1935, but Lester R. Peel initiated the ergot business and named it Universal Laboratories. The building where it was produced has since been preserved as the Dassel History Center & Ergot Museum and is listed on the National Register of Historic Places as Dassel's sole entry. Other architectural firms of the city include the famous "mushroom building," once a vintage gas station, now used as a "home base" for local Scandinavian dance groups. At the Dassel Cemetery, Hildred Olson's gravestone marks her final resting place and designates her as the shortest munchkin from the 1939 film *The Wizard of Oz*. She was only three feet tall. Red Rooster Days is held every Labor Day Weekend and is accredited throughout Minnesota as the host of the "largest chicken barbecue in the state."

EDEN VALLEY, MN
POPULATION: 1,027 – CITY 535 OF 856 (8-13-25)

Logering, Minnesota, may be no more, but the ghost town had a significant impact on Eden Valley's development. Started in the late 1850s, the little agricultural hamlet was destined to be one of several stations along the Minneapolis & Pacific Railroad. Unfortunately, the citizens of Logering couldn't reach a reasonable agreement with the

Minneapolis, St. Paul & Sault Ste. Marie Railroad, the railroad company, instead moved its station two miles west to Eden Valley, another fledgling hamlet. It was named by railroad surveyors for its beautiful scenery and its likeness to the "Garden of Eden" in the Bible. Silas Cossairt, F. B. Smith, and the railroad company filed the official town plat on May 11, 1887, about a year after the Parker & Cossairt Store began operating as the first general store. Next came Henry Hukreide's blacksmith shop, William Hardy's store, the Mansard House and Pacific House hotels, Hoskins & Reeves elevator, an elevator for the railroad company, and more blacksmith shops, pool halls, and general merchandise shops. The Eden Valley post office opened in 1887 after having been moved from Eden Lake in Stearns County (where it had started in 1872), and on April 25, 1894, it was incorporated. There were Protestant churches, but the most prominent local religious organizations were the German Assumption Catholic Church and the Irish St. Peter's Catholic Church, which was founded later after receiving special approval from the Bishop. The German congregation had a parochial school that closed in the 1970s; it was one of two major institutions in town, the original being the high school building (and its additions) first erected in 1927. At the A-Maze'n Farmyard, visitors can enjoy a range of up-close-and-personal experiences with farm animals at the petting zoo, parakeets, pony rides, giant slides for thrill seekers, a year-round maze, mini golf, and a bounce barn.

GROVE CITY, MN
POPULATION: 624 – CITY 542 OF 856 (8-14-25)
Platted in 1870 and incorporated on Valentine's Day 1878, Grove City was first settled by the likes of Olaf Levander, A. P. Nelson, Swan Hokanson, and five other men. Levander is credited as the original pioneer, since his dwelling was the first to be built on the townsite; Hokanson was the second. The origins of the town's name are a tad complex. The first village was called Swede Grove, and from 1866 to 1879, a post office existed under that name. When the St. Paul and Pacific Railroad opened its station two miles east and one mile south on August 26, 1870, it was called Grove City. "Grove" in Grove City was directly taken from "Swede Grove," and "City" was meant to represent the hustle and bustle of everyday life that would soon take place there. Confusion between the two sites naturally arose because of their etymological similarity, and eventually, the railroad was persuaded to move its station to Swede Grode. The Grove City name was adopted, and the post office changed its name in 1879, a year after Grove City was formally incorporated. Hines, Kimball & Beedy opened the first general merchandise store, and Larson & Dahlquist opened their own mercantile shortly thereafter. The Swede Grove House, five saloons, two blacksmith shops, four filling stations, four grocery stores, two lumberyards, a barrel factory, boot and shoe stores, a flour and feed store, and elevators owned by Dudley & Nelson, the Northwestern Elevator Company, and C. E. Sundberg were just a handful of the other early firms. The Swedish Baptist, Swedish Lutheran, and Norwegian Lutheran congregations had the first churches. Population growth in the community has remained relatively constant over the decades, with a peak of 635 people in 2010.

KINGSTON, MN
POPULATION: 184 – CITY 538 OF 856 (8-13-25)
Once a contender for the Meeker County seat, the railroadless community of Kingston was named after Kingston, Ontario. The Canadian town was the birthplace of J. B. Atkinson, an early settler. A. P. Whitney & Company erected the Kingston Water Power [Grist] Mill between 1856 and 1858, then a booming business alongside Whitney's general store and several others. Whitney teamed up with G. R. Nourse and R. P. Upton, his fellow pioneer settlers, and in 1858, the three joined forces to start a

new store. A wagonmaker, a blacksmith shop, and alternative general merchandisers established their own businesses as well. Within the confines of Kingston's commercial district was a post office branch from 1857 to 1907, which from 1907 to 1910 became a rural branch. For forty-four years, there was no rural station until it reopened in 1954, only to be discontinued for good in 1990. Bridge No. 90980, one of Minnesota's earliest steel truss bridges, built by the Hewett Bridge Company in 1899, is located nearby on 690th Avenue over the North Fork Crow River. Kingston was incorporated as a village in September 1961, but it attempted to disincorporate on March 12, 2013, in a special election. The measure failed by a vote of 23 to 36.

LITCHFIELD, MN ★☆
POPULATION: 6,624 – CITY 540 OF 856 (8-14-25)
Historic Litchfield, the seat of government of Meeker County and home to 23,400 people as of the 2020 Census, was first named Round Lake, then Ripley, and finally Ness for Næs in Buskerud County, Norway. The latter name was assigned on April 5, 1858, shortly after one Ole Halvorson Ness and his Norwegian settler friends had arrived. Growth was quiet for the first few years as the Dakota War of 1862 brought a sudden halt to European expansion and influence in southwestern Minnesota. Nevertheless, the silence was shattered in 1869 when the St. Paul & Pacific Railroad was built and the town was renamed for three railroad financiers: Edbert S., Edwin C., and Elects Bachus Darwin Litchfield. Mrs. E. B. Darwin Litchfield donated substantial funds for Litchfield's original Presbyterian and Episcopal church. The Presbyterian building was completed in 1870 as Litchfield's first, and the Episcopal structure was finally completed in 1871 using the blueprints of the famous New York architect Richard Upjohn. The eccentric Carpenter Gothic-style church edifice was completed in 1871, although its three-story bell tower was added later. At the time of its platting on George B. Waller's land, Litchfield took the judicial seat title from Forest City and quickly became the town's most important community as settlers from miles around came to build their homes and businesses. A post office was amongst the first organizations started in 1869, of which John A. C. Waller was postmaster. After its incorporation on February 29, 1872, the firms multiplied. S. A. Heard and C. D. Ward opened Litchfield's first general store in the fall of 1869. Vanderhorek & King owned the hardware store, and W. S. Brill had the pharmacy. The Litchfield Woolen Mill, The Litchfield Roller Mill, Stevens & Co.'s Bank, The Litchfield Bottling Works, The Litchfield Bailing Company, the William Grono marble works, The Litchfield Brewery, The Litchfield and Meeker County Nursery, and many grain elevators, hotels, and stores made up the nucleus of the economy in what was then a community of about 1,500 citizens. Many of Litchfield's historic commercial buildings, built between 1882 and 1940, were selected for preservation on the National Register as the Litchfield Commercial Historic District. In 1900, N. P. Franzen orchestrated the construction of the Litchfield Opera House, the town's premier location for entertainment at the turn of the century. However, it could be said that fraternal organizations trumped all other aspects of early life in the community. Civil War Union Veterans worked together to finish a small fortress-like building, their Grand Army of the Republic Hall; Frank Daggett GAR Post No. 35. One of Minnesota's last remaining GAR Halls, the former home of the "Boys of [18]'61" is now the site of the Meeker County Historical Society Museum. Most recently, the Ness Church (built in 1861) and Cemetery, listed on the National Register on May 20, 2025, because of its distinction of being one of Minnesota's oldest surviving historic sites and for being the final resting place of the first five victims of the Dakota War of 1862, has become a focal point of local history. Herbert W. Chilstrom, the Presiding Bishop of the Evangelical Lutheran Church of America from October 1987 to October 1995; Gale Sondergaard, an Academy Award-

winning actress in 1936; Ann D. Montgomery, the Senior Judge of the United States District Court for the District of Minnesota since May 31, 2016; John Carlson, a tight end in the NFL from 2008 to 2014; Michael Shaw, a pioneer of open-heart surgery and the first to use a small, external, portable, battery-powered pacemaker, and William A. Nolen, remembered for his medical advice column in *McCall's* magazine, are noted Litchfieldians.

WATKINS, MN
POPULATION: 991 – CITY 536 OF 856 (8-13-25)
Watkins was laid out on Danville D. Spaulding's land by himself, Alonzo Spaulding, and the Minneapolis & Pacific Railroad, the precursor to the Minneapolis, St. Paul & Sault Ste. Marie Railroad in June 1887. Railroad officials named it for one of their coworkers, Beckers Watkins. In the year it was established, a post office was also formed utilizing the Watkins name. A. D. Spaulding and Joseph Vossen opened a storefront in early 1887. By the end of its first year, Watkins also had a lumberyard and a grain warehouse. A creamery opened in the late 1890s and achieved global recognition in 1938 at the Berlin Exposition when its butter was named the "number one butter in the world." The town was incorporated on May 2, 1893, and, over the years, has experienced net population growth in every decade except for a 3.6% (28-person) drop between 1970 and 1980. A four-time Democratic nominee for President of the United States, Eugene McCarthy, was born in Watkins on March 29, 1916. Despite never winning the Presidency, he served as a United States Senator from January 3, 1959, to January 3, 1971.

Unincorporated/Ghost Towns: Acton, Beckville, Corvuso, Crow River, Forest City, Greenleaf, Jennie, Lamson, Manannah, Rosendale, Strout

National Register of Historic Places:
Collinwood Township: District No. 48 School
Darwin Township: Henry Ames House
Dassel: Universal Laboratories Building
Kingston Township: Bridge No. 90980
Litchfield: Grand Army of the Republic Hall, Litchfield Commercial Historic District, Litchfield Opera House, Trinity Episcopal Church
Litchfield Township: Brightwood Beach Cottage, Ness Lutheran Church & Cemetery

Golf Courses:
Litchfield Golf Club, Municipal (Litchfield, MN)

Breweries/Wineries/Distilleries:
Jomas Hill Vineyard (Darwin, MN)

Town Celebrations:
Cosmos Space Festival, Cosmos, MN (3rd Weekend in July)
Fall'n Into Fun Fest, Litchfield, MN (3rd Saturday of September)
Kraut N' Wurst Days, Watkins, MN (1st Saturday in August)
Litchfield Watercade, Litchfield, MN (2nd Saturday in July)
Red Rooster Days, Dassel, MN (Labor Day Weekend)
Twine Ball Days, Darwin, MN (2nd Saturday in August)
Valley Daze, Eden Valley, MN (4th Weekend of June)
Windmill Days, Grove City, MN (3rd Weekend in August)

MILLE LACS COUNTY
EST. 1857 - POPULATION: 26,459

Mille Lacs translates literally as "thousand lakes" in French, referring to the numerous lakes that make up 16% of the county's land area.

BOCK, MN
POPULATION: 78 – CITY 460 OF 856 (7-20-25)
Bock shares its name with the strong, dark lager enjoyed at German festivals throughout Minnesota, like Schell's Bock Fest in New Ulm. It was not explicitly named for the beer, but rather for the first businessmen of the village, the Bock brothers. They built a sawmill that was eventually sold to Charles W. Burnhelm, who served as the first postmaster when the post office was established in 1892. Tosca was the village's original name when the Great Northern Railroad came through, before it was renamed to honor the two brothers. Other businesses arose thanks to the presence of a major railroad line, and on January 30, 1923, Bock was incorporated as a village.

FORESTON, MN
POPULATION: 559 – CITY 462 OF 856 (7-21-25)
Prime land for timbering spurred the establishment of a town called Bridgman on the west branch of the Rum River. It was named after its first postmaster, Coleman Bridgeman, when the post office began in 1882. Seven years later, it was changed to Foreston because of the extensive hardwood forests surrounding the fledgling community. It was also incorporated on May 9, 1889, as a village of the Great Northern Railroad. At its inaugural 1890 Census, 287 people were living in town, a number that has nearly doubled over the last 130-plus years.

ISLE, MN
POPULATION: 803 – CITY 449 OF 856 (7-20-25)
"The Little City on the Big Lake" was named for the island near its harbor on the southeastern edge of Mille Lacs Lake, the second-largest inland lake in Minnesota after only Red Lake. The island has been known by various names over the years, including Malone Island, Great Island, and Big Island. Homesteaders first arrived in 1891, and the initial business establishment was Charley Malone's general store and hotel, which opened in 1894. He also served as postmaster and owned the island, which he named Ethel after his daughter. Ethel's Island was to be the name of his post office, but the postal service changed it to Isle for simplicity. On November 1, 1913, Isle was incorporated after its population grew by several hundred residents as a result of the Minneapolis, St. Paul & Sault Ste. Marie Railroad. Fishing was by far the Isle's most successful industry. Fishermen on lucky days saw catches as large as one, two, or even as many as nine hundred fish in a single day, according to some accounts. A walleye statue on Main Street pays tribute to Isle as one of Minnesota's many "Walleye Capitals of the World," as do a mean-mugged muskie and walleye statue at Johnson's Liquor. More local history and artifacts from the area are on display at the Mille Lacs Lake Historical Society Museum.

Restaurant Recommendation:
Isle Bakery
210 2nd Ave S
Isle, MN 56342

MILACA, MN ★
POPULATION: 3,021 – CITY 461 OF 856 (7-21-25)

Until 1920, when it became the county seat of Mille Lacs County, Milaca enjoyed a similar early history to many of its counterparts in the now ultra-touristy region surrounding Mille Lacs Lake, its namesake. Lumber companies developed the earliest version of the town around 1882, the year the Great Northern Railroad arrived, and originally called it Oak City because of the abundant forest covering the landscape. That name lasted only six months before the post office changed it. In another decade, it was formally platted, and Milaca had saloons, hotels, and general stores. A pickle factory, a barrel factory, a hospital, and a well-off school district came later. It was incorporated on February 20, 1897. Two noteworthy points of interest worth mentioning are the Mille Lacs County Courthouse, built in 1923 with Renaissance and Classical Revival elements, and the Milaca Municipal Hall, constructed in 1936 by the Works Progress Administration. Fieldstone, brick, and concrete were added to the 1890 fire hall, which eventually became the municipal hall and, most recently, the Milaca Museum. To add a little liveliness to its street corners, Milaca conducted a project in 2014 that repainted over two dozen fire hydrants in the likenesses of famous cartoon characters, such as Mario and the Minions from the *Despicable Me* animated film franchise.

Restaurant Recommendation:
El Jalisco #2
870 Central Ave N
Milaca, MN 56353

ONAMIA, MN
POPULATION: 784 – CITY 447 OF 856 (7-19-25)

Oscar E. Garrison first used the "Onamia" name for the township, but it was later also applied to a nearby lake just south of Mille Lacs Lake. When the Soo Line Railroad was extended to that point, it secured the future of a railroad station, which also bore the same name, derived from the Ojibwe word for vermilion (a synonym for red-orange), *onaman*. It was platted on November 12, 1901. The Ojibwe called the village site *Onamanii-zaaga'iganiing*, and an adjacent town, Ericksonville, *Gibaakwa'igaansing*. Ericksonville, incorporated in 1898, and Onamia, incorporated approximately a decade later, ultimately merged to create a single, conjoined community. In addition to three early Native American habitation sites and villages (Petaga Point, the Cooper Site, and the Saw Mill Site) within Mille Lacs Kathio State Park, Onamia is home to a fourth location on the National Register of Historic Places, the Onamia Municipal Hall. The fieldstone municipal hall, similar to several others constructed throughout Minnesota during the Works Progress Administration era, was completed in 1935-36. In the 1950s, the Crosier Fathers and Brothers of the Catholic Church raised funds from several area communities to build and furnish a twenty-eight-bed hospital that is still open today. Shane Bauer, an investigative reporter best known for his work with *Mother Jones* magazine, hails from Onamia.

PEASE, MN
POPULATION: 238 – CITY 463 OF 856 (7-21-25)

A sawmill, owned by lumber mogul Benjamin Soule, was erected in the vicinity of modern-day Pease in 1882 alongside a hotel. It was called Soule's Crossing for its proprietor and was strategically located on the east branch of the Rum River, making it easy to transport logs downstream. After four years, the Great Northern Railway recognized the economic opportunities the river and its sawmills offered, so they extended their tracks between Princeton and Milaca. Unfortunately, the mills succumbed to the Great Hinckley Fire of 1894, but the weeping and despair of residents was short-lived after a large colony of Dutch settlers moved in. They prompted the establishment of a post office, called Pease for Granville S. Pease of Anoka. It could have also been a misspelling of the word "peace" on the town plat. In 1994, the post office converted into a rural station. At Dick Baas Memorial Park, visitors can enjoy a 1937 Dutch Windmill, most recently renovated in 2006 by Baas Construction. The windmill was built in the late 1930s, when it was designed to serve as a gas station and car service garage.

PRINCETON, MN ☆
POPULATION: 4,819 – CITY 487 OF 856 (8-9-25)
Primarily located in Mille Lacs County, with a portion in the northern reaches of Sherburne County, Princeton was first explored in the late 1840s by Daniel Stanchfield. Still, it was not widely settled until the following decade. John S. Prince of St. Paul, the town's namesake, platted it in 1855 alongside Samuel Ross, James W. Gillam, Richard Chute, and Dorilius Morrison; they submitted it to the land office for recording on April 19, 1856. The local lumberman established three sawmills between then and 1867. During that time, the post office, four blacksmith shops, three large general merchandise stores, two large hotels, two shoe shops, carriage works, and a station of the Great Northern Railway were organized. When Mille Lacs County was established, Princeton was designated as the county seat, a title it retained until 1920. The lumber industry was the main driver for Princeton's economy, but it also later became known for its potatoes at the turn of the century. From 1901 to 1902, it had one of the largest potato markets in the region, and the Princeton Potato Starch Company was established as the local potato starch factory. Brickmaking took off two miles north of Princeton proper in 1889 in an area known as Brickton, where over 20 million bricks were being furnished every year. Millions of bricks continued to be shipped out through the 1920s by a collective of brick yards, although the industry eventually declined. Princeton's industries have evolved over the decades, encompassing everything from injection molding factories to distilleries. Even the federal government took note of its prime location in 1987, when the Federal Aviation Administration chose to relocate its flight service station there as its hub for providing pilots with flight plans and weather information. On November 23, 1977, the Great Northern Depot (built in 1902 and now a museum) was listed on the National Register of Historic Places; nearly eight years later, it was joined by the historic 1872 Gothic Revival Ephraim C. Gile House and the 1902 Colonial Revival Robert C. Dunn House. An A-Z Happy Chef mascot, formerly part of a restaurant chain spanning 65 locations throughout the Midwest, still stands outside a local restaurant supply company. In May 2011, a world record attempt for the "most simultaneously erupting Coke geysers," spearheaded by The Princeton High School Council, was successful when 3,051 bottles of Coke and Mentos were launched simultaneously. Sadly, the attempt was not formally recognized by the *Guinness Book of World Records* as no official was present. Princeton has been brought into the world's limelight through its people over the decades, with the help of former residents like Bob Backlund, a member of the WWE Hall of Fame and the second-longest reigning champion in the history of the sport at 2,135 days; Kevin Odegard, a guitarist on Bob Dylan's "Blood on the Tracks" album; Paul Sather, the head coach of the University of North Dakota men's basketball team since 2019, and Rod Grams, a United States Senator from Minnesota between January 1995 and January 2001.

WAHKON, MN
POPULATION: 235 – CITY 448 OF 856 (7-20-25)
The oldest European settlement in the vicinity of Mille Lacs Lake started in 1885, but it was not until 1907 that Wahkon was platted as a Soo Line Railroad town. Previously known as "Potts Town" from 1885 to 1891, it adopted the name "Lawrence" upon the establishment of a postal service branch. T. E. Potts wanted a town with his name to succeed, so he surveyed a second Pottstown next to Lawrence in 1901. His attempt failed, and Wahkon, backed by the railroad company's extensive capital reserves, emerged as the area's principal "boom town." It was incorporated on November 6, 1912, only a few years after its founding, thanks to the extensive trade generated by the railroad and its strategic location as a docking point for steamships on the lake. One local 42-foot fishing boat, the Ellen Ruth, served a local resort starting in 1933 and became Wahkon's lone NRHP-designated location in August 1985. However, it was removed on June 21, 1990, after being relocated in 1989 to the south end of town.

Unincorporated/Ghost Towns: Bayview, Brickton, Burnhelm Siding, Cove, Estes Brook, Esteville, Freer, Johnsdale, Long Siding, Opstead, Page, Soule's Crossing, Stirling, Vineland, Woodward Brook

National Register of Historic Places:
Kathio Township: Bridge No. 3355 Kathio Township
Milaca: Milaca Municipal Hall, Mille Lacs County Courthouse
Onamia: Onamia Municipal Hall, Cooper Site, Petaga Point, Saw Mill Site
Princeton: Ephraim C. Gile House, Great Northern Depot, Robert C. Dunn House
Vineland: Kathio Site, Vineland Bay Site

Golf Courses:
Izatys Resort – Black Brook, Resort (Onamia, MN)
Princeton Golf Course, Daily Fee (Princeton, MN)
Stones Throw Golf Course, Daily Fee (Milaca, MN)

Breweries/Wineries/Distilleries:
United States Distilled Products (Princeton, MN)

Town Celebrations:
Isle Days, Isle, MN (2nd Weekend of July)
Onamia Days, Onamia, MN (2nd Full Weekend in June)
Run Rimer Festival, Princeton, MN (First Weekend in June)

MORRISON COUNTY
EST. 1856 - POPULATION: 34,010

Brothers William and Allan Morrison, a pair of Canadian-American fur traders, gave their surname to this county when it was broken off from Benton County in 1856.

BOWLUS, MN
POPULATION: 279 – CITY 515 OF 856 (8-12-25)
The first homesteader on the land that would become Bowlus was John Gross, who filed for the plat in 1866 before giving it to his son, Philip, in 1873. Several decades would pass without any significant developments until the Tri-State Land Company and C. A. Campbell purchased the parcel from Martin Czech. In June 1907, the town of Bowlus was born, and it began to serve the Minneapolis, St. Paul & Sault Ste. Marie Railroad is one of several shipping points throughout Morrison County. Early settlers

came from all around, but the largest ethnic group was overwhelmingly Poles from Silesia. They used the abundant trees in the area to center the town's economy on lumbering, which led to the establishment of a sawmill, a lumberyard, and a barrel factory, among other enterprises, including a broom factory, the Gedney Pickle Factory, and the Bowlus Brick & Tile Company. One hundred sixty-five citizens were reported as living in town in 1915; by then, the railroad donated land for a prominent two-story public brick school, and the Bank of Bowlus, the town's premier business outside of logging, was erected in 1911. St. Stanislaus Kostka Catholic Church was completed around the same time (and dedicated on May 8, 1910) for $12,475; it too was built on land donated by the Soo Line. The local Polish farmers donated the stone for its walls and foundation.

BUCKMAN, MN
POPULATION: 307 – CITY 501 OF 856 (8-11-25)
Clarence Bennett Buckman, a Member of the U.S. House of Representatives from Minnesota between March 4, 1903, and March 3, 1907, had this little hamlet named in his honor long before he ever ascended to Congressman status. He was one of many early settlers of the township, but the original five owners of the site were Peter Müller, Peter Kunz, John Sitzman, Michael Oestreich, and Jacob Hohn. Buckman, then a major player in the lumber industry, later acquired 1,400 acres of farmland just northwest of the townsite, which by the turn of the century was one of the most profitable agricultural businesses in all of Minnesota. Near his farm a small village began to develop, taking his name, and offering a multitude of business lines to its citizens like Joe Hortsch and John Schmolke's grocery store, a hardware and general store, a creamery, a bank, a hotel, and later still harness shops, Joseph A. Janson's blacksmith shop, Lawrence Billig's saloon, a livery, a second general store, and a Ford garage. German Catholics made up the bulk of the early population. So, alongside their businesses, they constructed a general meeting place and a place of worship in communion with one another: St. Michael's Catholic Church. It was first established circa 1881, but the more magnificent brick edifice was completed in 1902. School No. 17 was recorded on an 1892 plat map as serving the educational needs of the village.

ELMDALE, MN
POPULATION: 114 – CITY 516 OF 856 (8-12-25)
Elmdale, home to 114 people as of the 2020 Census, was founded by Knute Hans Gunderson in the 1870s. He came to the area in 1871 and built a store in 1878 that would catalyze growth in the fledgling village. He and another Danish man, Jens Hansen, who surveyed the village, are widely regarded as the fathers of the town. From 1878 to 1907, it had its own post office before nearby Bowlus took over mail-delivery duties. A blacksmith shop, a creamery, a sawmill, a second store, and School No. 15 were early fixtures of Elmdale, as were two churches: St. Edward Catholic Church and a Danish Lutheran Church that has since been abandoned. The congregation began on May 1, 1871, and its original edifice served the local Danish Protestant population for many years before it burned in 1918. The new structure was erected the following year and continued to provide services until 1958.

FLENSBURG, MN
POPULATION: 216 – CITY 512 OF 856 (8-12-25)
Flensburg could have been named for the German town of the same name located in Germany's Schleswig-Holstein state, but it was most likely derived from "Flynn's Landing," the Polish name for the site of the mill and depot furnished by the Little Falls

and Dakota Railroad in 1882. J. C. Flynn of Little Falls worked for the Northern Pacific Railroad and had the station named in his honor upon its completion. Eight years later, Olaf and Dagmar Searle formally platted the village of Flensburg. However, it did not receive its name until 1892-93, according to articles from the Little Falls Weekly Tribune, the Little Falls Herald, and the Little Falls Transcript. Around that time, a post office was established using the same name, and by June 17, 1911, it was incorporated as Minnesota's newest municipality. Since its first Census in 1920, when 210 people were recorded as living in town, Flensburg's numbers have hardly changed over the last century. Its peak population of 281 came in the 1950s.

GENOLA, MN
POPULATION: 70 – CITY 502 OF 856 (8-11-25)
Upon its platting in August 1908 on the Soo Line Railroad, this town was called New Pierz, following the same logic that led to the naming of settlements like New London in Kandiyohi County. Another Pierz had already existed in Morrison County a decade prior (just to the north by a mile or two), thus the "New" prefix. Growth was steady, and business lines like Handy Litke's saloon, the First State Bank of Genola, the New Pierz Grain Company, Peter Bekka's blacksmith shop, F. O. Bolster's general merchandise store, and Peter Kelgenberg and Harsch & Grell's hardware and grocery stores came to fruition. When it came time to incorporate the village on April 15, 1915, the name "Grainville" was submitted to the state. Almost immediately, it was changed once again to Genola, after the Italian commune. The United States Postal Service used the name New Pierz from 1912 to 1915, then switched to Genola, which it used until 1951. At that time, the post office began as a rural station and retained the same name until it, too, was discontinued in 1976.

HARDING, MN
POPULATION: 123 – CITY 506 OF 856 (8-11-25)
Located just east of the Platte River, the City of Harding was most likely named in commemoration of Warren G. Harding, the 29th President of the United States. While the White House Historical Association insists that the naming of the community cannot be definitively confirmed, Harding's passing on August 2, 1923, and the establishment of the Harding, Minnesota, post office that same year align in a manner that suggests some truth to the claim. Fifteen years after the organization of a post office in the locality of the Church of the Holy Cross, the town was incorporated as a village on March 15, 1938. Its post office closed in 1953, was discontinued until 1966, reopened as a rural station, and then was closed again in 1975. Harding never had a railroad, but the local lumber industry enabled its population to rise to just above 120; its actual peak came in 2010, when 125 were reported living in the city limits.

HILLMAN, MN
POPULATION: 23 – CITY 504 OF 856 (8-11-25)
Less than two dozen people remain in Hillman, a German village platted in July 1908, shortly after the Minneapolis, St. Paul & Sault Ste. Marie Railroad had been extended to that point. Although the township was named for its founder, Osmer Leigh, and the post office was first managed by Ethel A. Leigh, the municipality was called "Hillman" after the nearby Hillman Creek. The post office operated as usual from 1913 to 1994, before converting into a rural station. Hillman's population peaked at 110 people in 1940, shortly after its incorporation on November 7, 1938.

LASTRUP, MN
POPULATION: 120 – CITY 505 OF 856 (8-11-25)
Measuring only 0.38 square miles, Lastrup is one of several tiny cities located throughout Morrison County with ties to German heritage. Its first settlers were from Schnelten, near Lastrup in Lower Saxony, Germany. In the early days, Lastrup was split between Buh and Granite Townships. East Lastrup came about in 1892 in Granite Township and was best known for its creamery and a saloon, whereas West Lastrup had Vincent Dombovy's blacksmith shop and a post office first manned by William Hoheisel. Archie Decent was the local mail carrier. From 1898 to 1907, the post office operated seamlessly before it closed for sixteen years and then reopened in 1923. In 1992, it was converted into a rural station, much like many of its neighboring offices. Other early facets of Lastrup were St. John's Catholic Church, the Lastrup Farmers' Creamery, and the Brinkman Brothers General Store.

Restaurant Recommendation:
Fisch House Bar & Grill
19248 MN-27
Lastrup, MN 56344

LITTLE FALLS, MN ★☆
POPULATION: 9,140 – CITY 511 OF 856 (8-12-25)
The hometown of the world-renowned aviator Charles Lindbergh, best known for making the first-ever solo transatlantic flight across the pond (then a world record distance of 2,000 miles) from New York to Paris, has a history rooted deep in the waters of another body of water: the Mississippi River. Starting with the Ojibwe who called it *kakabikans*, the "little squarely cut-off rock," the falls at this point on the river were later documented by the explorers Zebulon Pike in 1805, Joseph Nicollet in 1837, Henry Schoolcraft, and Giacomo Beltrami. Permanent European settlement began in 1848 with the arrival of James Green, who built a saw mill. A plat was filed for the site for the first time in 1855. When the Dakota War of 1862 brought uncertainty, death, and fear to settlers throughout southwestern and central Minnesota, those living in the Little Falls area teamed up with Chief Mou-zoo-mau-nee of the Ojibwe, and Little Falls was brought under Ojibwe protection with the help of 150 warriors. As the war progressed and a certain level of normalcy returned, Little Falls continued to grow, and on February 25, 1879, it was incorporated. When it achieved city status in 1889, it was only the third community in Minnesota to have received cityhood. Business lines were expansive and plentiful. James Fergus (the namesake of Fergus Falls) and Calvin A. Tuttle established the Little Falls Company, the first milling company in the area, which owned two thousand acres of land. It merged into the Little Falls Manufacturing Company, a joint-stock company, in 1855, which was responsible for constructing the first of several dams on the "little falls" of the Mississippi. The Pine Tree Lumber Company, where more than sixty million feet of northern pine was cut into lumber annually in the mid-1910s, the Hennepin Paper Company, the Jacob Kiewel Brewing Company, a sash and door factory, a horseshoe factory, brickworks, Little Falls Iron Works, cigar factories, and two large flour mills highlighted some of the largest businesses that set up shop on the banks of the most important trade route in Minnesota, which was rivaled by several lines of the Northern Pacific Railroad Company that helped the city to further its economic reach and influence across the region. It retained its judicial seat status from 1855 onwards as the most important community in the county, and in recent decades, local historians have worked hard to preserve its rich history. Over a dozen locations are listed on the National Register of

Historic Places, including the 1890-91 Richardsonian Romanesque Morrison County Courthouse; the Pine Tree Lumber Company Office Building, formerly one of the state's largest employers; the Northern Pacific's Railway Depot, built just before the turn of the century using architect Cass Gilbert's plans; the Charles A. Weyerhaeuser and Musser Houses, built in 1898 and now preserved as the Linden Hill Historic Estate; the Neoclassical Burton-Rosenmeier House, built in 1900 and now host to the Little Falls Convention and Visitors Bureau; the [Episcopal] Church of Our Savior, built in 1903 in the Tudor Revival style; the 1905 Little Falls Carnegie Library; the Charles A. Lindberg House and Park and its accompanying WPA/Rustic Style Historic structures, of which there are six; and the Little Falls Commercial Historic District, home to 32 contributing properties built between 1887 and 1936. Charles A. Lindbergh State Park was established on the former homestead of the famous aviator and is named for his father. Their historic 1906 restored home was designated a National Historic Landmark on December 8, 1976; it is one facet of the park, along with a museum and a 1938 WPA water tower, that draws visitors for its rich history. While many of the early-mentioned Little Falls enterprises have since subsided with time, new manufacturing interests, including Wabash National, a refrigerated trailer company; Little Falls Machine, a plow manufacturer; Lakemaster, a lake mapping software company; and Hoonuit, an international software company, among many others, have taken their places. The Minnesota Fishing Museum, the Pine Grove Primeval Park and Zoo, the Paul Larson Memorial [boat, motor, and trailer] Museum, Little Falls Granite Works and its inuksuk rock-man "Traveler" statue, and St. Francis Convent and Campus are other mention-worthy sites for tourists and history-lovers located throughout town. The latter location was established in 1891 by the Franciscan Settlers of the Immaculate Conception. Noted figures of the town's history aside from the Lindberghs include Fred Zollner, the founder of the NBA's Detroit (then Fort Wayne Zollner) Pistons; Brian Kobilka, the recipient of the 2012 Nobel Prize in Chemistry; Gale Gillingham, a five-time Pro Bowl offensive guard with the NFL's Green Bay Packers between 1966 and 1976; Duane Bobick, a world champion amateur heavyweight boxer who went 38-0 between 1973 and 1977; Louise Erdrich, the winner of the Pulitzer Prize for Fiction in 2021 and the National Book Award for Fiction in 2012; Frances Eliza Babbitt, a pioneer woman archaeologist who contributed to research on the Paleolithic Era in North America; Ben Hanowski, a professional hockey player with 16 NHL appearances between 2012 and 2014, and Joe Brinkman, a Major League Baseball umpire for 35 years from 1972 to 2006.

MOTLEY, MN
POPULATION: 680 – CITY 340 OF 856 (6-19-25)
Motley, established on a branch line of the Northern Pacific Railroad, first had a post office in 1873, before the townsite itself was laid out in 1874. Records indicate that the Lake Superior and Puget Sound Company laid out the site in 1870, but it was not recorded until 1879. At that time, the local lumber and agricultural industries were booming. H. B. Morrison's lumber mill employed over one hundred men, and two elevators had been erected by Chandler, Fisher & Waite of Long Prairie, and Barnes & McGill. Curtis & Lawrence established a second mill in 1881, allowing an additional 25,000 feet of lumber to be cut each day. Three grand general merchandise stores, a pair of hotels, a livery stable, Lutheran, Methodist, and Catholic churches, two schools, a 20-by-40-foot passenger station, and a 24-by-60-foot freight depot rounded out the noted early firms and infrastructure that made Motley one of the most well-off towns in the region by the 1890s, with its population of 525 people. In the next three decades, Motley had added more specialized firms, including the Central Minnesota Farmers' Co-operative Shipping Association, The First National Bank of Motley, the

Defenbaugh Drug Company, the Dower Lumber Company, the Timber Land Company, the Motley Telephone Company, and *The Mercury* newspaper, to name a few. The very first Motley Fair was held in 1910 and has since continued as one of the oldest continuously running fairs in Minnesota. Almond A. White's House and its four-story tower (listed on the National Register of Historic Places) were built in 1902 in the Queen Anne style.

PIERZ, MN
POPULATION: 1,418 – CITY 503 OF 856 (8-11-25)
German immigrants, ministered to by Francis Xavier Pierz as early as 1865, even back when it was known as Rich Prairie, were so inspired by Pierz's teachings that they opted to build their entire settlement around St. Joseph's Catholic Church. Mass was held in a log church building starting in 1869, and after Pierz served as pastor there for a couple of years, the town's name was changed to honor him. From 1886 to 1888, a new Gothic Revival church was erected between the northern and southern portions of Pierz. In the north, as of 1892, were primarily homesteads and farms, but to the south of the church, convent, and School No. 14 was the town's commercial district, with its post office (est. 1870 in Frank Konen's home), Town Hall, store, hotel, and blacksmith shop. Pierz was incorporated on August 17, 1894, and with the help of the Soo Line Railroad, over the next twenty years it added on enterprises like the Model Clothing Company, owned by Joe Ries; Frank Faust's opera house; the German State Bank, of which A.R. Davidson was president; the *Pierz Journal* newspaper, published by E. H. Kerkhoff; the Columbia Hotel; the Pierz Mercantile Company, and the Rich Prairie Milling Company. Since 1940, the population of Pierz has nearly doubled from 714 people to 1,418. John Stumpf, the former CEO of Wells Fargo from June 2007 to October 2016, was born here on September 15, 1953, and grew up attending the local Catholic church and making bread in the Pierz bakery. Former NFL safety Joey Browner, who played for the Minnesota Vikings from 1983 to 1991, and Mary Kiffmeyer, the 20th Secretary of State of Minnesota, also have ties to the heavily German community. Oktoberfest is celebrated during the last weekend of August each year, featuring live music, games, a parade, and other festivities.

RANDALL, MN
POPULATION: 607 – CITY 510 OF 856 (8-11-25)
Incorporated on August 14, 1900, Randall was established so that trains would not have to take the "long route" through Brainerd to travel between Motley and Staples. It was platted on March 10, 1890, by H.S. Clyde under the direction of Daniel and Alice K. Merrill and named in honor of railroad official John H. Randall. The St. Paul & Northern Pacific Railroad brought many German, Polish, English, Irish, and French settlers, all of whom combined their resources and talents to build a great railroad community. The depot was an important "community center" of sorts for Randall, and the Randall Cooperative Creamery was its most significant business. Two hotels, a blacksmith shop, and a post office (opened in 1889) were among its other major firms during that era. Clough Township Hall, built in 1922 in the Classical Revival style, was added to the National Register of Historic Places in 1985 as Randall's first entry, but it was moved in 2001 and subsequently removed from the list in 2004. The second-highest one-day rainfall ever recorded in Minnesota occurred in Randall during July 21-22, 1972, when over thirteen inches of rain fell. Due to the heavy precipitation, the Little Elk River was heavily flooded, leaving downtown Randall impassable to typical vehicle traffic for several weeks.

ROYALTON, MN
POPULATION: 1,281 – CITY 467 OF 856 (7-21-25)
P. A. Green platted the village of Royalton on his land in 1878, a little over twenty years after its original 1854 to 1857 post office (managed by R. D. Kinney) closed down after transferring to Langola. It returned to Morrison County in 1878 under the name Royalton, after the town of Royalton, Vermont, a hometown of one of the earliest settlers. Green's plat of the village was never formally recorded, so in 1879, J. D. Logan purchased part of the original site and filed a plat of his own using the name. Green tacked his "addition" onto Logan's, and thus was born the newest town in Minnesota. The J. D. Logan & Company sawmill was erected that year on the Platte River; it served as the spearhead of a business district that included two flouring mills, three hotels, two blacksmith shops, an engine house for the Northern Pacific Railroad, the Minnesota Creamery Company, and an opera house by 1892. Although the population only grew by about one-hundred people over the next three decades, Royalton kept up with the times and added on more lines like the Rudd Lumber Company, the Royalton Farmers Co-operative Association, the Powers Elevator Company, a furniture store, a jewelry store, an ice dealer, meat markets, *The Royalton Banner* newspaper, the Farmers and Merchants State Bank, the First National Bank, and well over a dozen others. Church interests were of the Catholic, Methodist, and Episcopal denominations. William Whipple Warren's 1847 home and trading post still stand in the vicinity of Royalton; it was here where he wrote his famed novel, *History of the Ojibways based upon Traditions and Oral Statements*. The Warren-McDougall Homestead was added to the National Register of Historic Places on December 7, 1974. One of Minnesota's longest-serving state senators, with 10,995 service days, Gordon Rosenmeier, also the creator of the Minnesota Pollution Control Agency, was born here on July 1, 1907. The yodeling duo known as The DeZurik Sisters, famed for their performances on the Grand Ole Opry and the National Barn Dance broadcasts, and Jim Langer, a two-time Super Bowl champion, a six-time Pro Bowl selection with the Miami Dolphins, and a Member of the Pro Football Hall of Fame, also have connections with the Morrison County community. At Treasure City, a local souvenir shop open since 1962, visitors can admire a 200-pound "Maneating Clam," a guillotine, and a selection of other oddities.

SOBIESKI, MN
POPULATION: 210 – CITY 514 OF 856 (8-12-25)
John III Sobieski, the King of Poland whose reign spanned from May 19, 1674, to June 17, 1696, had this heavily Polish community named in his honor by the local Poles who built up the settlement. They developed it on a site where other communities once stood, including Ledoux, which served as a post office in the area from 1875 to 1904. It was named after Frank X. Ledoux, the area's first storeowner and postmaster. The town was also known as Swan River for another area post office that operated from 1854 to 1879, a name that persisted in the nearby town until it was changed in 1918 to Sobieski. St. Stanislaus Bishop & Martyr Catholic Church is the community's long-standing religious organization. Two hundred fifty people lived in Sobieski during its heyday in the 1930s, more than at any other point in its short history.

SWANVILLE, MN
POPULATION: 326 – CITY 513 OF 856 (8-12-25)
Logging, agriculture, and the Little Falls & Dakota Railroad (later acquired by the Northern Pacific) brought life to Swanville, a village named for its location on the Swan River. Land along the 37-mile-long tributary of the Mississippi River was deemed ideal

for settlers. A townsite was platted by John Williams Jr., Henry Albert, and Matilda Rhoda in November 1882, and a post office was established the following year under the name Swanville. A former office had been in the area since 1867, but was called Culdrum. By 1892, Swanville boasted five stores, a hotel, a saloon, a blacksmith shop, a planing and feed mill, a school, and a German Lutheran church, now known as St. Peter's Lutheran Church. Townspeople filed for incorporation on May 24, 1893. The First State Bank, the Peoples State Bank, two restaurants, two blacksmith shops, two barber shops, two cream stations, elevators, a jewelry repair shop, and a sawmill were amongst the most notable pieces of Swanville's 1915 commercial district. Since 1900, Swanville has had as few as 244 residents (at its inaugural Census) and as many as 435 in the 1930s.

UPSALA, MN
POPULATION: 487 – CITY 517 OF 856 (8-12-25)

Named for the ancient city of Uppsala, Sweden, renowned worldwide for its 1477 university, the southwesternmost municipality of Morrison County has a history closely tied to its Swedish heritage. Jurgen (J.J.) Schultz, Ib Hanson Misfeldt, and Knut H. Gunderson, three Danish men, were the first to homestead in the vicinity around the end of the 1860s, but in 1872, John Henry Peterson of Sweden made his claim. After the Northern Pacific Railroad took an interest in the region and began to promote it heavily, the influx of Swedish and Scandinavian settlers led the fledgling village to be named "Swedback's Settlement." Charles Swedback was the town's first storeowner. It was only when the post office was established in 1883 and John Anderson became postmaster that it was renamed Upsala. From thereon, a creamery, a hardware store, a grocery store, dry goods stores, a feed mill, a blacksmith shop, a meat market, a confectionery, the Farmer's State Bank of Upsala, the Elmdale Telephone Company, a movie theater, a billiard hall, and a pharmacy were amongst the most prominent business lines. Businesses kept the town's economy running, but religion kept their spirits high. The Swedish Evangelical Lutheran Congregation (originally the Swedish Lutheran and later Gethsemane Lutheran Church) was organized in 1879 by J.H. Peterson and the Johnson brothers, Andrew and Lewis. The Swedish Mission Church arrived between 1885 and 1888, and in 1891, the First Swedish Baptist Church was established. Olive Missouri Synod Lutheran Church was formed in 1935, and the Word of Life Free Lutheran Church was founded in 1988 as the most recent Protestant denomination. St. Mary's Catholic Church entered the heavily-Protestant town in 1953. Upsala's first consolidated public school building was built in 1922 and served the community until 2004, when it was replaced by a modernized elementary, middle, and high school edifice that now serves as the home of the Cardinals.

Restaurant Recommendation:
Buffy's Bar & Grill
MN-238
Upsala, MN 56384

Unincorporated/Ghost Towns: Belle Prairie, Center Valley, Cushing, Darling, Freedhem, Gregory, Lincoln, Little Rock, Morrill, North Prairie, Platte, Ramey, Shamineau Park, Sullivan, Vawter

National Register of Historic Places:
Belle Prairie Township: Our Lady of the Angels Academy
Brainerd: Crow Wing State Park
Camp Ripley Military Reservation: Fort Ripley

Camp Ripley: Bridge No. 4969
Little Falls: Burton-Rosenmeier House, Charles A. Weyerhaeuser & Musser Houses, Church of Our Savior- Episcopal, Little Falls Carnegie Library, Little Falls Commercial Historic District, Morrison County Courthouse, Northern Pacific Railway Depot, Pine Tree Lumber Company Office Building, Charles A. Lindbergh House & Park, Charles A. Lindbergh State Park WPA/Rustic Style Historic Resources, Fort Duquesne (21-MO-20)
Motley: Almond A. White House
Pierz: St. Joseph's Church-Catholic
Royalton: William Warren Two Rivers House Site & Peter McDougall Farmstead

Golf Courses:
Little Falls Golf Course, Municipal (Little Falls, MN)
Pierz Golf Course, Muncipal (Pierz, MN)

Town Celebrations:
4th of July Parade, Hillman, MN (Independence Day)
Bowlus Fun Day, Bowlus, MN (1st Sunday in July)
Harding Days, Harding, MN (First Weekend after Independence Day)
Harding's Horse'n Around Christmas Parade, Harding, MN (1st Saturday of December)
Heritage Day, Upsala, MN (2nd Weekend in August)
June Fest, Motley, MN (2nd Full Weekend in June)
Little Falls Arts & Crafts Fair, Little Falls, MN (1st Weekend after Labor Day)
Pierz Oktoberfest, Pierz, MN (Last Weekend in August)
Platte River Day, Royalton, MN (Last Saturday of July)
Swanville Midsummer Carnival, Swanville, MN (Weekend before/after 4th of July)

MOWER COUNTY
EST. 1855 - POPULATION: 40,029

John Edward Mower, a member of Minnesota's territorial legislature during its operation in the 1850s, is the namesake of this county.

ADAMS, MN
POPULATION: 683 – CITY 722 OF 856 (10-19-25)
Adams Township was established in May 1858, but its municipality did not come into existence until January 30, 1868, when Selah Chamberlain platted it. The arrival of the Chicago, Milwaukee, St. Paul & Pacific Railroad was the most influential factor in the town's development (other than the establishment of the post office in 1861, of which Harold M. F. Ingens was the initial postmaster), before other institutions began to arise. A two-room public schoolhouse was erected in 1869. After 20 years of development, the town named for the New Yorker, Mr. Adams, had a population of 216 people. This number rapidly expanded by 165.3% to 573 by the turn of the century. The city installed public waterworks in 1897, and the following year, Adams House Company No. 1, one of the area's pioneer fire departments, was established. The two-school schoolhouse (which had been expanded to four rooms due to overcrowding) was joined by a Catholic school in 1903 as a secondary option for pupils seeking an education in a more religious setting. Several other church entities and businesses were founded. In 1917, it was selected as the site for one of the bank buildings designed by architects William Gray Purcell and George Grant Elmslie. The Prairie School-style structure was the defining widespread product of the two pupils of Louis Sullivan (known for his "jewel box" banks in Owatonna, Minnesota, and Grinnell, Iowa). However, very few of the buildings remain in Minnesota. Adams's structure, now the Adams Area History Center, was added to the National Register of Historic Places on

March 20, 1986. Hubert H. Peavey, a Member of the U.S. House of Representatives from Wisconsin between March 1933 and January 1935, was born here in 1881.

AUSTIN, MN ★☆
POPULATION: 26,174 – CITY 725 OF 856 (10-19-25)

"SPAM Town USA" is well-known for being home to Hormel's corporate headquarters and the factory responsible for most of America's canned pork and ham products, but the town's history dates back much further to the days of fur trapper Austin R. Nichols. He built a log cabin in the vicinity in the 1850s, at a time when a couple of dozen other families were also arriving to establish their claims and build homes on the Cedar River. Nichols sold his claim to Chauncey Leverich only a year later. Wagon trains traversing the old Territorial Trail brought with them an impetus for new settlement, allowing for the formation of Mower County. Frankfort was named the seat of government, but the newly founded town of Austin took over the honor in 1857. The name was given to honor Austin, the settlement's first citizen. Many businesses emerged, including J.H. McKinley's hotel, the *Mower County Mirror* newspaper, and Dr. Ormanzo Allen's physician's office; however, the most significant developments were those in milling and meat processing. Leverich erected a sawmill in 1854-55, and in 1858, the Truesdell brothers raised the first grist mill in the community. W.A. Woodson started his pork processing business between the construction of the two mills, circa 1856. His activities would later inspire George A. Hormel and Company to establish its own meat processing firm in 1891, which, through national advertising campaigns, made it a household name across the country. It was in that same year that Austin became an incorporated city, although it had been operating as an incorporated village since 1868. By the time George A. Ogle drew up a 1896 plat map, Austin had an electric light plant, six churches, four schools, and plenty of other business enterprises. Lutheran congregations and local doctors joined together that year to form the Austin Hospital Association, which later became St. Olaf Hospital and is now part of the Mayo Clinic Health System. Railroad companies began building through at this point to capitalize on the success of the local mills and meat processors. Two vertically traveling lines of the Chicago, Milwaukee & St. Paul met in the city's southeastern corridor, and the much smaller Mason City & Fort Dodge Railroad line was built much closer to the main commercial district. In 1897, Charles Boostrom opened the Southern Minnesota Normal College, a normal school and business school that called Austin home from 1897 to 1925, alongside the Austin School of Commerce, until it closed due to financial struggles. Despite the failure of its institution of higher education, Austin grew to a population of 10,000 residents by the 1920s and 20,000 by the 1950s, thanks largely to the success of the predecessors of Hormel Foods and Quality Pork Processors, which now cumulatively employ well over 4,000 individuals. The plant nearly folded in the 1980s due to massive wage cuts and a recession, to the point that 1,500 meatpackers went on strike for 10 months and became the subject of the Academy Award-winning 1990 documentary *American Dream*. Modern points of interest include the Jay C. Hormel Nature Center, its 500-acre nature preserve, and the 60-acre Hormel Arboretum, as well as the Riverside Arena, a 2,500-seat multipurpose arena, and four locations listed in the National Register of Historic Places. The First National Bank of Adams, built in 1924 by the students of architect Louis Sullivan, Purcell & Elmslie, serves as the Adams Area History Center. Paramount Theater was erected in 1929 as the county's lone example of Spanish Colonial architecture and a rare atmospheric theater in this portion of the country. The Arthur W. Wright House and the Cook-Hormel House, now the Hormel Historic Home museum for its ties to George A. Hormel, round out the historic points. Horace Austin State Park was a Minnesota State Park from 1913 to 1949, until it was transferred to the city. The present Spam Museum opened its doors on April 22, 2016, with 14,000 square feet of exhibits featuring Spam history, recipes, and interactive exhibits. On the property of Hormel Foods, a 25-foot-tall fork features 20,000 smaller forks, all welded on by Gordon Huether in 2022. A giant Spam can sits five feet tall at the local Spam plant. In addition to all these historic sites, many other persons have brought fame and recognition to the pork-loving community, including John Madden, the namesake of the best-selling American football game franchise and the legendary Oakland Raiders football coach, known for his career record of 103-32-7 (75% winning percentage); Jackie "The Austin Atom" Graves, a professional featherweight boxer with a career record of 82-11-2; Richard Eberhart, a Pulitzer-Prize and National Book Award for Poetry winner; Craig Hutchinson, the director of eighty films created between 1915 and 1928; Bob Motzko, the head coach of the University of Minnesota hockey program since 2018; Bree Walker, the first American television news anchor to broadcast with ectrodactyly (split hand); Sheldon B. Vance, the U.S. Ambassador to Zaire from May 1969 to March 1974; Charlie Parr, a country blues musician; James C. Hormel, the United States Ambassador to Luxembourg from September 1999 to January 2001; Geordie Hormel, the founder of The Village Recorder music studio in Los Angeles, and Philip Brunelle, a conductor and the founder of VocalEssence, amongst other persons of note.

Restaurant Recommendation:
Kenny's Oak Grill
307 W Oakland Ave
Austin, MN 55912

BROWNSDALE, MN
POPULATION: 633 – CITY 729 OF 856 (10-19-25)
"Mower County's Garden Spot" was first settled by three Norwegian families in the spring of 1855, but they didn't stay long. While they moved westward in search of greener pastures, John L. Johnson built a sod shanty that summer and was quick to erect a store and petition the United States government for a branch of the postal service. The following July, Andrew D. and Hosmer A. Brown platted the town of Brownsdale. From then on, other settlers were encouraged to start their own business lines. Thomas Alfred established a shoe store in 1857, and around the same time, a schoolhouse was also erected. Three renditions of the school were built and subsequently destroyed by fires in 1858, 1871, and 1896; however, the two-story, four-room schoolhouse constructed in 1897 managed to survive until 1953, when a new, modern building was furnished. During that time, the local Baptist church was established in 1870, followed by congregations of the Christian, Methodist, English Lutheran, and Catholic churches. The village was incorporated (officially in 1876) under the name Brownsdale, using the Brown name in honor of Andrew's prominence in the lumber industry. Railroad officials with the Chicago, Milwaukee & St. Paul brought Brownsdale to an inaugural population of 346 people at the 1880 Census. Its all-time high number of residents (of 718) was achieved in 2000.

DEXTER, MN
POPULATION: 324 – CITY 728 OF 856 (10-19-25)
Located just outside of the Pleasant Valley Wind Farm is the City of Dexter, a town of 324 people named in honor of Dexter Parritt. He came from Ohio in 1857 with his father, Mahlon, and the two formed the nucleus of the fledgling village. It took 17 years for the town to be platted and for a post office branch to be established. Incorporation

was achieved on February 28, 1878, following the advances of the Chicago, Milwaukee & St. Paul Railroad through the region. Dexter's most significant population growth occurred between 1890 and 1900, when the population increased by 85.3% from 150 to 278. Businesses at that time would have included general stores, hardware stores, and implement stores, as well as livery stables, blacksmith shops, and early variations of churches and school structures.

ELKTON, MN
POPULATION: 130 – CITY 727 OF 856 (10-19-25)

W. E. Richardson and Frank A. Day platted Elkton on January 25, 1887, a date that has since been recognized as the formal founding of the town. Unlike many of the other communities established on the Chicago, Milwaukee & St. Paul Railroad, Elkton's success was due to the Chicago Great Western Railroad, which connected Saint Paul, Minnesota, with its major junction in Oelwein, Iowa. A post office was established in 1887 but discontinued in 2007; other early traditional lines of enterprise, such as storefronts, shops, and lumber offices and warehouses, would have been present in its heyday. It was incorporated in 1906 and, shortly thereafter, saw the construction of its first sidewalks in 1908 and the introduction of electricity in the 1920s. Alvin Baldus, a U.S. Congressman from Wisconsin between January 1975 and January 1981, graduated from Elkton High School in the 1940s.

GRAND MEADOW, MN
POPULATION: 1,127 – CITY 716 OF 856 (10-18-25)

As the story goes, Grand Meadow received its name from an exclamatory phrase uttered by an 1850s pioneer, who said aloud, "What a Grand Meadow!" when he saw the gorgeous open prairie early one morning. The name stuck when Grand Meadow Township was established in 1858, the post office was organized in 1859, and the town was founded on April 20, 1862. From 1858 to 1859, the Grand Meadow post office was known as Gainesville, until Postmaster Cyrus G. Langworthy renamed it to match the village. More settlers arrived with the coming of the Chicago, Milwaukee & St. Paul Railroad in the early 1870s, and businesses and fraternal organizations began to flourish. Two examples of these early town facets are still prevalent today in the 1910 Grand Meadow Exchange State Bank, the first project of architects Purcell and Elmslie in creating early Prairie School style buildings for banking institutions, and the Booth Post No. 130 - Grand Army of the Republic Hall, built in 1891 and one of Minnesota's last remaining G.A.R. Halls. It was initially constructed for use by the Women's Relief Corps in conjunction with the Grand Army of the Republic and was only recently refurbished by the Grand Meadow Girl Scout group. A more recent town development attracting visitor attention is the Grand Meadow Public School, Minnesota's largest monolithic dome school. The domes are lettered A through E and are specifically designed to house different grade levels, athletic or performing arts activities, or administrative offices.

LE ROY, MN
POPULATION: 957 – CITY 720 OF 856 (10-19-25)

Old Town LeRoy, named for Le Roy, New York, was located on the banks of Lake Louise, at a point selected by Lewis Mathews, Daniel Caswell, Martin L. Shook, and Adoniran J. Palmer on April 24, 1857, near Henry Edmond's store and mill (the latter of which was erected in 1855). It was moved entirely when the McGregor & Western Railway laid out a townsite elsewhere for their right-of-way. Stores, schools, hotels, and other essential establishments grew alongside the village. School District No. 79

was initially held in Charles McNeil's home. It was later relocated and expanded over the decades as Le Roy grew into a trade center at the junction of the Chicago, Milwaukee & St. Paul Railroad and the Wisconsin, Minnesota & Pacific Railroad near the Iowa border. The post office spelled its name as Le Roy from 1856 to 1895, then consolidated it to "LeRoy" until 1905, and later added the space for good that year. By the 1960s, Le Roy achieved its highest-ever number of 971 citizens, the same decade that Lake Louise State Park was established on the old townsite by an act of the Minnesota legislature. It boasts of a 25-acre artificial lake created by the Little Iowa River and offers recreational facilities for swimming, camping, and horseback riding. A pair of historic sites also call Le Roy home: the 1914 First State Bank of Le Roy, one of several Prairie School banks in Mower County, and the 1915 Le Roy Public Library, founded through the efforts of a local women's club. Harlan G. Palmer, the former owner of the *Hollywood Citizen* newspaper and the first attorney in Hollywood, California, and George Sitts, the only person to be killed by South Dakota's electric chair for his crimes, hail from Le Roy.

Lodging Recommendation:
Sweets Hotel
128 W Main St
Le Roy, MN 55951

LYLE, MN
POPULATION: 522 – CITY 724 OF 856 (10-19-25)
Three railroad lines–best remembered as the Mason City & Fort Dodge, the Illinois Central, and the Chicago, Milwaukee & St. Paul—once converged at Lyle because of its location less than a mile north of the Iowa border. Because of its importance as a railroad town, its population had already surpassed 500 by the 1910s. Its infrastructure was impressive by this time, but like all other communities, Lyle had humble beginnings as well. One of Mower County's oldest towns was first settled by Orlando Wilder, Eben Merry, William Bean, John Tift, and James Foster in May 1854. Some of them built frame houses, and others began tilling the land to grow corn and potatoes. Robert Lyle arrived in November 1856 and was honored with the town's naming when the first village plat was filed on June 18, 1870. Incorporation occurred five years later, in March 1875, at which point Lyle boasted of general merchandise stores, a hardware store, a grain elevator, and blacksmith shops, among other establishments. An early 1900 business directory listed four elevators, three stockyards, three professional stores, two cream stations, a creamery, a newspaper, a broom factory, a culvert factory, an overall and glove factory, a corn canning factory, and even a bowling alley. Lyle's first schoolhouse was a 16x26 structure built in 1873, but naturally, as the town grew, so too did the subsequent structures in 1877 (with a 1896 addition) and 1906 (with a $530,000 expansion coming in 1957). A new school was built on top of the former facility following a contentious May 24, 2005, election. Religious and fraternal activities were prevalent as well, but residents were most proud of calling themselves the "Croquet Capital of Minnesota" for their then-outstanding croquet court. Regarding postal history, the local office began in 1862 as Lyle, with Nathaniel P. Williams serving as postmaster. It was then called Minnereka from 1870 to 1871 by postmaster William Shelback, and reverted to Lyle/Lyle Center when Thorwald Irgens took over.

MAPLEVIEW, MN
POPULATION: 144 – CITY 726 OF 856 (10-19-25)
Incorporated out of Lansing Township on June 6, 1946, the City of Mapleview was formed on behalf of about one hundred families living near northern Austin who did

not wish to be a part of that municipality. Two years after its incorporation, a municipal liquor store, fire station, pump house, and water tower were erected; in 1954, Hillside Park was established alongside Murphy Creek to provide locals with a recreational area. Four hundred thirty-five people called Mapleview home at its inaugural 1950 Census, but it has since decreased in every decade since then. Mapleview was initially named for a row of maple trees on the west side of town.

RACINE, MN
POPULATION: 458 – CITY 715 OF 856 (10-18-25)
Not to be confused with Wisconsin's fifth-most populous city, the City of Racine, Minnesota, has only recently reached a peak population of 458 people, according to the 2020 Census. The name is derived from the French word for "root," which alludes to the nearby tributaries of the Root River. On October 3, 1890, the town was platted, about a decade after the post office was established. As a station on the Chicago & Great Western (alternatively, the Wisconsin, Minnesota & Pacific), Racine benefited from its railroad's positioning. By 1896, the town had two elevators, a mill, a creamery, a church, a school, and a thriving commercial district with storefronts and shops. On June 30, 1959, Racine entered the ranks of Minnesota's incorporated municipalities, reporting an original population of 180 to the 1960 U.S. Decennial Census. Bearcat Hollow Animal Park, once located outside of town, gained national attention in October 2003 when "Ming," a Bengal tiger born there, was found living in a Harlem, New York City, apartment with his owner, Antoine Yates.

ROSE CREEK, MN
POPULATION: 397 – CITY 723 OF 856 (10-19-25)
Rose Creek, population 397, was named after the nearby Rose Creek, the largest eastern tributary of the Cedar River within Mower County. It began as a flag station in 1868 for the Chicago, Milwaukee & St. Paul Railroad, and boasted of a post office even three years before the advent of that rail line. Sylvester Davis was the first settler in the area, circa 1855. Incorporation occurred on Valentine's Day, 1899. Around that time, the community had a dance hall, a grain elevator, a Standard Oil gas station, a creamery, a bank, a meat market, a feed mill, a restaurant, a blacksmith shop, a hardware store, and a grocery store. An 1896 plat map also indicates the presence of a school and three churches, two of which were located in the northeast corner of town, and one of which was situated in the southwest corner. In March 1982, one of Rose Creek's high school seniors, Todd Nelson, sent an experiment aboard NASA's third Space Shuttle mission to carry his experiment, which aimed to demonstrate how weightlessness affects insects.

SARGEANT, MN
POPULATION: 63 – CITY 730 OF 856 (10-19-25)
In 1896, visitors traveling on the Chicago & Great Western Railroad would have been welcomed first and foremost by the agents at the local depot, which sat just across from Waldron's grain elevator and a pair of nearby grainhouses. Main Street was located just steps away from the depot, as was the post office, a hotel, and several stores. Sargeant's main church was located in the southeast corner. Having been platted only two years prior, the small rural community was named for Harry N. Sargeant, an early area pioneer and the chairman of the September 16, 1873, meeting at his home, which sought to formally organize the community. Sargeant was incorporated as a village on August 25, 1900; at its peak, as many as 138 people lived there during the 1940s.

TAOPI, MN
POPULATION: 61 – CITY 721 OF 856 (10-19-25)
Having been located near the source of the Wapsipinicon River and on two railroad lines — the Chicago & Great Western and the Chicago, Milwaukee & St. Paul — one would have to imagine that Taopi was once a bustling community, ripe with families and businesses of all kinds. To some extent, that fact was true, as the Taopi of 1896 was home to no less than a dozen storefronts, a hotel, a creamery, a stockyard, a church, a school, and three grain elevators, one of which was accompanied by a joint mill. In fact, the flour mill was the largest steam-powered facility in southern Minnesota at its peak. It had a capacity of 300,000 bushels and was the primary driver of the local economy for many decades, contributing to Taopi's peak population of 153 in the 1920s. Unfortunately, residents ultimately moved away in search of other opportunities, and the population dwindled to the point where it is now the smallest incorporated town in Mower County. When the village was platted in 1875 and incorporated on March 6, 1878, it was decided to name it in honor of Taopi, otherwise known as Wounded Man, a leader of a farmer band of the Dakota tribe. He was a good friend of Good Thunder and Wabasha, a Mdewakanton chief, with whom the three established a mission school called the Hazelwood Republic.

WALTHAM, MN
POPULATION: 164 – CITY 731 OF 856 (10-19-25)
The name of this community is an eponym for Waltham, Massachusetts, the hometown of Charles F. Hardy. He was an early county commissioner who participated in the meetings that led to the formation of Waltham Township and its subsequent development into a village. A.J. Burbank platted the first townsite in 1865 about a mile west of the present site, which boasted a three-story hotel and a post office that existed from 1867 to 1874. The Chicago & Great Western Railroad forced the relocation of the village and its residents to its present site in 1885; the new plat was filed on September 8. With its arrival came the construction of a depot, two elevators, and a new post office. Waltham's population has remained relatively consistent since 1900, with a low of 150 in 1900 and a high of 212 in 1950.

Unincorporated/Ghost Towns: Andyville, Corning, Johnsburg, Lansing, Mayville, Nicolville, Ramsey, Renova, Varco

National Register of Historic Places:
Adams: First National Bank of Adams
Austin: Arthur W. Wright House, Cook-Hormel House, Paramount Theater
Grand Meadow: Booth Post No.130- Grand Army of the Republic Hall, Exchange State Bank, Grand Meadow Quarry Archeological District
Johnsburg: Freund Store
Le Roy: First State Bank of Le Roy, LeRoy Public Library
Le Roy Township: Bridge No.5388 (Bridge No. R0529)

Golf Courses:
Austin Country Club, Private (Austin, MN)
Cedar River Golf Course, Daily Fee (Adams, MN)
Meadow Greens Golf Course, Daily Fee (Austin, MN)

Breweries/Wineries/Distilleries:
Angry Hog Brewery (Austin, MN)
Gravity Storm Brewery Cooperative (Austin, MN)

Martin County: Ceylon City Museum (Ceylon), Interior of Immanuel Lutheran Church (Dunnell), Martin County Courthouse (Fairmont), "Going Hog Wild in Martin County" Road Trip Pig Statue (Fairmont), Historic Grain Elevator at Martin County Historical Society Museum (Fairmont), Historic Bandshell (Fairmont), Trimont High School Band Display at Trimont Museum in the former St. Joseph Catholic Church (Trimont), Human and Horse Water Fountain (Welcome)

Meeker County: Galactic Water Tower (Cosmos), Largest Ball of Sisal Twine Built by a Single Person (Darwin), 1931 Mushroom Gas Station (Dassel), Mural (Dassel), Dassel History Center and Ergot Museum (Dassel), A Maze'n Farmyard (Eden Valley), Grove City Windmill (Grove City), Minnesota's Last Surviving Grand Army of the Republic [G.A.R.] Hall (Litchfield)

Mille Lacs County: Mille Lacs Museum (Isle), Mean Muskie Fiberglass Fish (Isle), Mille Lacs Lake at Father Hennepin State Park (Isle), Mural (Milaca), Kathio Observation Tower at Kathio State Park Beach (Vineland), Dick Baas Memorial Park & Windmill (Pease), A-Z Restaurant Equipment Happy Chef Statue (Princeton), *Ellen Ruth* Mille Lacs Lake Excursion Boat (Wahkon)

Morrison County: Interior of St. Stanislaus Catholic Church (Bowlus), St. Michael's Catholic Church (Buckman), Polish Weather Rock/Station (Harding), Morrison County Courthouse (Little Falls), The Falls Theare (Little Falls), Our Lady of Lourdes Catholic Church (Little Falls), St. Stanislaus Catholic Church (Sobieski), Donkey near Pepin Lake (Swanville)

Mower County: Interior of Sacred Heart Catholic Church (Adams), Paramount Theatre (Austin), Tender maid Hamburgers Stand (Austin), SPAM® Museum (Austin), Buffy the Cow at the Mower County Fairgrounds (Austin), "Power of Food" – The Big Fork Sculpture at Hormel Foods (Austin), former Afton School (Le Roy), Resident's Windmill Collection (Le Roy)

MURRAY COUNTY
EST. 1857 - POPULATION: 8,179

Murray County, named after William Pitt Murray, is one of several Minnesota counties named after a local territorial legislator.

AVOCA, MN
POPULATION: 111 – CITY 63 OF 856 (2-27-25)

This Chicago, St. Paul, Minneapolis & Omaha Railroad town was established in 1878, when Archbishop John Ireland and the Catholic Colonization Bureau purchased 50,000 acres of land from the railroad company to attract Catholic settlers and farmers to the region. Its name alludes to the *Sweet Vale of Avoca* in Thomas Moore's poem and a river in County Wicklow, Ireland. A post office branch was established in 1878, followed soon by several business lines. Several fires in 1889, 1907, 1910, and 1952 destroyed several of Avoca's key landmarks, starting with the burning of the original St. Rose of Lima Catholic Church edifice in 1889. Flames devoured parts of its commercial district in 1907 and 1952, from which Avoca would never recover, but its worst loss came on February 12, 1910, when the town's military school for boys was destroyed. The building, formerly a Catholic school for Native American girls between 1882 and 1896, could not be saved because the nearby Lime Lake was completely frozen. A two-story brick school building was erected in 1894 as the first public institution in town, and as of October 1979, it has been listed on the National Register of Historic Places. By 1908, Avoca was home to a Catholic church, a Swedish Lutheran church, and a Norwegian Lutheran church.

CHANDLER, MN
POPULATION: 279 – CITY 14 OF 856 (2-22-25)

Samuel P. Rockey's general store and post office, a creamery, a windmill, a pair of grain elevators, and the depot for the Southern Minnesota Railway were the first pieces of infrastructure to be raised on the Chandler townsite. Platted on June 7, 1886, by G. W. Smith in the Chanarambie Valley, the first European to set foot on the future settlement's land was likely Joseph Nicollet. He came through on June 28, 1838, and noted a "Buffalo Ridge" standing 1900 feet tall. Unbeknownst to him at the time, the ridge was one of the highest points in Minnesota and a division point for the watershed between the Missouri and Mississippi Rivers. All water to the ridge's east eventually drains into the Mississippi, while all rainfall to the west ends up in the Mighty Mo'. The ridge served as a significant religious site for the Sioux, as early documentation reports the presence of one of their cemeteries and a smoke pit at the feature's summit. The railroad came through some forty-odd years later, in 1880, long after Nicollet's expedition, and the "Little Queen of the Hills" was named Chandler in honor of John Alonzo Chandler. He was a railroad official for the Chicago, Milwaukee & St. Paul Railway Company for over forty years, starting in 1856. His company annexed the Southern Minnesota Railway in 1880, only three years after its establishment. Predominantly Scandinavian settlers came to Chandler from Fillmore County, Minnesota, Decorah, Iowa, and New Hampton, Iowa, as well as the Dutch from across the Atlantic. On October 6, 1900, it was incorporated as a village. By 1908, it had a post office (established in 1886), stockyards, a depot, three elevators, an implement store, a lumber yard, a bank, a hotel, and several other lines of enterprise, including a two-room schoolhouse and a Union church. Its peak population of 388 people in the 1960s was spurred by the construction of the Chandler Air Force Station, which served as a radar station from 1951 to 1969. Almost two hundred men served at the base at its peak, so its closure led to a -17.8% decrease in population (according to the 1970 Census). Chandler's numbers dropped further when many residents moved away after the June 16, 1992, Chandler-Lake Wilson F5 tornado leveled half of the community. Monogram Foods Solutions, the small city's largest employer, is known primarily for manufacturing packaged meat and jerky snacks.

CURRIE, MN
POPULATION: 224 – CITY 18 OF 856 (2-23-25)

From 1872 to 1889, Currie served as the seat of government of Murray County. The honor was bestowed upon Slayton, but the "Gateway to Lake Shetek" still experienced a population climb well into the 500s in the 1950s before it began to subside. When Neil Currie and his father Archibald arrived, they were one of only a handful of settlers in Murray County. Fifty-odd early pioneers, who had moved into the area as early as 1855, cleared out following the horrors of the Dakota War of 1862, when the Sisseton Dakota killed fifteen settlers. The site is now known as "Slaughter Slough" and is situated just east of Lake Shetek, the largest lake in southwestern Minnesota and the headwaters of the Des Moines River. At these headwaters, the Scottish-born Curries decided to build their gristmill. Around their mill, a small trade area developed; naturally, more farming families moved to take advantage of it. Neil Currie built the first store, stocked it with dry goods, merchandise, and drugs, and became postmaster when the office was organized in 1872. He retained the role until 1890 and assisted other entrepreneurs in starting their firms, the most notable of which was likely the Murray County Bank in 1874. Lon Cole opened The Farmer's Hotel, and Mr. Finch founded a second boarding house. Mr. Bromwich established the *Murray County Pioneer* newspaper on January 1, 1878, which was later relocated alongside eight other businesses when the county seat was moved circa 1889. Currie seemed destined for failure as an inland town. Nevertheless, officials of the Chicago, St. Paul, Minneapolis & Omaha Railroad had other ideas when they extended a branch line from Bingham Lake to Currie before the start of the new century. The Currie railyards featured a turntable, which is still on display today at the community's impressive "End-O-Line" Railroad Park and Museum. Other complex highlights include the Georgia Northern #102 steam engine, the District No. 1 "Sunrise" School, a Comfrey section house built by the Chicago & Northwestern Railroad, and a HO (1:87) scale model railroad display. Currie's Lake Shetek State Park offers opportunities for water recreation and camping, as well as interpretive displays related to the Dakota War of 1862. Additionally, the park features ten contributing structures built during the WPA era at two National Register of Historic Places sites: the Rustic Style Historic District and the Rustic Style Group Camp.

DOVRAY, MN
POPULATION: 58 – CITY 19 OF 856 (2-23-25)

Norwegians named Dovray after the village of Dovre in Gudbrandsdalen, Norway, and the Dovrefjell plateau. The spellings of both this American community and the former hometown of the settlers in Scandinavia were identical until it was discovered that another township in Kandiyohi County had been given the same name. It was changed accordingly following the discovery, but it would not be the only significant change its residents would be required to make. A cooperative creamery brought several area families together in 1895, approximately one mile north and east of the present townsite. They were forced to move their dwellings and buildings after the Chicago, St. Paul, Minneapolis & Omaha Railroad missed the townsite when laying track in 1899 through Murray County. A new site was platted in 1904, and within four years, it had developed into a thriving community, boasting a community hall, a bank, a livery, a saloon, a hardware store, a blacksmith shop, a lumberyard, an elevator, a depot, stockyards, and a post office (which had been initially established in 1895). It once had both Norwegian and German Lutheran churches until the German congregation was forced to disband due to a lack of membership. Incorporation was not agreed upon by the townspeople for some time and was granted on January 2, 1924. It was done despite a 1916 fire that took a significant portion of the town.

FULDA, MN
POPULATION: 1,371 – CITY 62 OF 856 (2-27-25)
Laid out on November 21, 1881, Fulda, Minnesota, got its start when Benjamin W. Woolstenroft platted it on the shores of Seven Mile Lake. Although its rail line was discontinued permanently in 1980, Fulda owes its existence entirely to the extension of the Milwaukee Road through the southern portion of the county. Before the advent of the railroad, there was a small townsite and post office called Bondin. It operated under this name from 1874 to 1879, before the railroad company decided to rename it "Fulda," after an ancient German city known for its medieval abbey and gorgeous cathedral. The name was suggested by the then-primarily German population, although there were also significant numbers of Irish and Scandinavians in the area. Extensive agricultural trade in the region brought its population to 886 people by 1900. Geo. A. Ogle & Company surveyed the area's lots and businesses in the months leading up to 1908, during which they mapped out many of Fulda's significant accomplishments. These were namely the public school, City Hall, a Presbyterian church, a Lutheran church and parochial school, an Opera House, a hotel, a livery, two banks, the post office, a mill, a creamery, the depot, a Methodist Episcopal church, and, perhaps most appropriately (as if it were a nod to the heritage of the city for which it was named), a Catholic church and accompanying convent. The Chicago, Milwaukee, St. Paul & Pacific Depot (now a local history museum) was built in 1880 and remains an excellent example of Stick style architecture in its second story. In 1919, Fulda's most prominent bank, the First National Bank, was erected in the Beaux-Arts style, featuring significant terracotta detailing. The local Zach Taylor Post No. 42 of the Grand Army of the Republic, a notable early fraternal organization, purchased an authentic Civil War cannon that now resides in Fulda's city park. The purchase was made on June 25, 1892, for $155, which is equivalent to about $5,400 today. Numerous notable persons and groups have connections to the city, the most prominent of which may have been The Continental Co-ets. Founded in 1963, they became the first all-girl rock & roll band to tour the United States. Its members were Nancy Hofmann, her sister MaryJo, Vicki Steinman, Carolyn Behr, and Carol Goins. Other noteworthy residents of Fulda's past include Hilton Smith, a 6x All-Star pitcher and 2001 inductee into the Baseball Hall of Fame; Ted Winter, the Minnesota House Majority Leader from January 1997 to January 1999; Patrick Reusse, a sports personality now affiliated with the *Star Tribune* newspaper of Minneapolis, the seventh-largest circulating newspaper in the United States, and Harold Hotelling, a statistician and economic theorist who came up with Hotelling's law, Hotelling's rule, Hotelling's lemma, and Hotelling's T-squared distribution.

HADLEY, MN
POPULATION: 54 – CITY 17 OF 856 (2-23-25)
Hadley Buttermakers' Baseball has been a favorite pastime of residents of the railway village of Hadley for most of its existence. The team, which now plays its games at Laurie Mahon Memorial Field, reached its peak during the World War II era, advancing to the state tournament on four occasions: 1940, 1941, 1943, and 1945. While baseball serves as the primary driver of entertainment and tourism for the now-town

of 54 residents, Hadley was initially platted in October 1879 as "Summit Lake" to adhere to the needs of the Chicago, St. Paul, Minnesota, and Omaha Railroad. The original name was given due to its location on the namesake body of water. However, it was later changed by the United States Postal Service at the suggestion of L. L. Lucason, who named it for the family of one of his relatives. A general store, an elevator, a livery, and a creamery on the shore of the lake were among its pioneer businesses; they were joined in importance by a Norwegian Lutheran church and a school located in the town's eastern lots. Hadley was granted incorporation as a village on September 1, 1903. Its post office was eliminated in 1993 after its population shrank to less than one hundred residents.

IONA, MN
POPULATION: 166 – CITY 64 OF 856 (2-27-25)
Named after a small island off the coast of Scotland, Iona started when Reverend Martin McDonnell established the Home of the Sacred Heart orphanage. McDonnell strategically platted the village along the Chicago, Milwaukee, St. Paul & Pacific Railroad line so his orphanage would have access to transportation for incoming orphans and to materials for constructing his building. The orphanage was completed in 1882 and joined by a Catholic church and St. Columba parochial school. A post office was established in 1880 with the Reverend at its helm. With more settlers came the establishment of the District No. 49 public school and congregations for the Norwegian Lutherans, the German Lutherans, and the Presbyterians. Businesses as of 1908 varied by importance, but the most notable were the town's mill, a bank, a hotel, and a livery. Iona was incorporated on January 22, 1896, and reached its peak population (365) in the 1920/1940 Censuses.

Restaurant Recommendation:
Town Bar & Grill
390 Parnell St
Iona, MN 56141

LAKE WILSON, MN
POPULATION: 254 – CITY 15 OF 856 (2-22-25)
Three of Lake Wilson's most memorable events are rooted in disaster, two of which almost entirely wiped the community from existence. The first was the fire of 1911, which nearly took out the town's entire commercial district. It was so early in its history that the townspeople were able to rebuild, but disaster would inevitably strike again when an F5 tornado eliminated half of its buildings on June 16, 1992. While the population of Lake Wilson recovered and actually grew by 61.6% decade over decade (from 219 people in 1910 to 354 in 1920) after the 1911 fire, the tornado had the opposite effect. Many of Lake Wilson's residents decided to start anew elsewhere after losing their homes, and between 1990 and 2000, its population declined from 319 residents to 270. On January 12, 2004, the last of Lake Wilson's three major catastrophes occurred when the city's firehall erupted in an explosion, taking out the adjacent elevator as well. Damages totaled $4.2 million, and the blast was reportedly heard and felt as far as thirty miles away. Calamity has plagued the little agricultural community, but the spirit of its residents has remained unwavering. Presently home to over two dozen businesses and organizations, the community's history dates to 1883 when it was platted by the Chicago, St. Paul, Minneapolis & Omaha Railway and named by Jonathan E. Wilson of Chicago, Illinois. He owned seventeen thousand acres of land in the immediate area, including the grounds surrounding the lake, which

he also renamed Lake Wilson, replacing the original name, Sand Lake. It was incorporated in July 1900, and by the end of the decade, it had a City Hall building, a depot, a bank, a hotel, a livery, stores, a Norwegian Lutheran church, and a building for Public School No. 24.

SLAYTON, MN ★☆
POPULATION: 2,013 – CITY 16 OF 856 (2-23-25)

Charles W. Slayton, an agent for what was then the St. Paul and Sioux City Railroad, was honored when this new settlement was platted in 1881 just off the shores of Lake Elsie. The name took effect in 1882 when it was adopted by both the postal service and the railroad. Slayton worked diligently alongside C. E. Dinehart, S. O. Morse, F. D. Weck, W. J. McAlister, and George Woodgate to build up the initial townsite. However, Mr. Slayton relocated to New Mexico after only a couple of years. His peers forged onwards by promoting the lands and encouraging development. Their efforts culminated in success on June 11, 1889, when they successfully removed the county seat from Currie for good, following previous failed attempts (it had held the title briefly from 1886 to 1888). A courthouse was erected in 1892 in the Romanesque Revival style, but it was torn down in 1981, despite attempts in the 1970s to preserve it by listing it on the National Register of Historic Places. The courthouse served the town's residents well throughout its golden years. According to the 1920 Census, it crossed the one-thousand-person threshold for the first time, an outstanding achievement for any young city of that era. It had more paved streets per capita than any other community in Minnesota by the middle of the decade, in addition to a 32-bed hospital, a high school and grade school, a movie theater, two elevators, two lumber yards, a creamery, a bakery, three banks, two churches, and an ever-growing line of stores, professional offices, and community halls used for meeting, recreational, and entertainment purposes. Church edifices for the Catholic, German Lutheran, Mission, Presbyterian, Norwegian Lutheran, and Methodist Episcopal congregations were in place by 1908. More historically significant developments occurred in 1936, when the Works Progress Administration built the community's 4-H Club Building at the Murray County Fairgrounds, and in 1940, when the Slayton Public Library was founded. The most historic home in Slayton was owned by the previously mentioned Christopher E. Dinehart, a charter member of the State Bank of Slayton, and his wife, Flora, who owned the first piano in Murray County. The Murray County Historical Society now operates the Victorian home as a museum. Other notable persons of fame with ties to Slayton include Trevor Winter, who briefly played for the NBA's Minnesota Timberwolves in 1999; Mike Johnson, a two-game pitcher for the MLB's San Diego Padres in 1974; and John Vincent Weber, a Member of the U.S. House of Representatives from Minnesota from January 1981 to January 1993. Kelly James Burnham (professionally known as Alan Roach), the current public address announcer for the NFL's Minnesota Vikings, the NHL's Colorado Avalanche, and the MLS's Colorado Rapids, was born in Slayton on March 29, 1966. He has also served as the official P.A. of the Super Bowl, NFL events worldwide, the Olympic Games, and several All-Star games for the NFL, NHL, and MLB.

Restaurant Recommendation:
Grain Exchange
2022 Maple Ave
Slayton, MN 56172

Unincorporated/Ghost Towns: Current Lake, Lime Creek, Lowville, Owanka, The Lakes, Wirock

National Register of Historic Places:
Avoca: Avoca Public School
Currie: Chicago, St. Paul, Minneapolis, & Omaha Turntable, Lake Shetek State Park WPA/Rustic Style Group Camp, Lake Shetek State Park WPA/Rustic Style Historic District
Fulda: Chicago, Milwaukee, St. Paul & Pacific Depot, First National Bank
Slayton: 4-H Club Building, Murray County Fairgrounds, Dinehart-Holt House

Golf Courses:
Fulda Town & Country Golf Course, Daily Fee (Fulda, MN)
Slayton Country Club, Daily Fee (Slayton, MN)

Breweries/Wineries/Distilleries:
Painted Prairie Vineyard (Currie, MN)

Town Celebrations:
Parade of Lights, Fulda, MN (1st Saturday in December)
Wood Duck Festival, Fulda, MN (Father's Day Weekend)

NICOLLET COUNTY
EST. 1853 - POPULATION: 34,454

Joseph Nicolas Nicollet mapped this area of the country between the 1830s and 1840s, leading to his name being used for this county when it was formed in 1853 out of Dakota County.

COURTLAND, MN
POPULATION: 734 – CITY 472 OF 856 (8-7-25)
From 1856 to 1864, the local post office was known as Hilo, for a bay and town in Hawaii. William Duprey operated it at his home. Most of the other early settlers—Jacob Harmon, John Sidel, Ole Nelson, and Jacob Gfeller, to name a few—came from Germany. Some of them lived in a village called Redstone, surveyed on M. B. Stone's land, but the plat was quickly done away with and the land converted into agricultural use. After a period that saw the establishment of the first Lutheran church in the vicinity and the killing of nine locals during the Dakota War of 1862, the office's name was changed to Cortland for Cortland County, New York. It was respelled as "Courtland" beginning in 1874. The Winona & St. Peter Railroad materialized during that decade, too, which gave rise to the town that remains today. A warehouse and a general store were the first two business-related structures. By 1882, there were three general merchandise stores, two blacksmith shops, a hotel, a creamery, a grain elevator, a harness shop, and carriage works. Courtland broke the 300-resident plane in the 1970s, and in the last fifty years, its population has grown by nearly 150% to 734.

LAFAYETTE, MN
POPULATION: 492 – CITY 471 OF 856 (8-7-25)
Marie-Josesh Pal Yves Roch Gilbert du Motier de La Fayette, Marquis de La Fayette, perhaps better known by his colloquial name "Lafayette," was a French and American Revolutionary War general whose memory was commemorated with the naming of several places throughout the United States. One of these was Lafayette, Minnesota, which was platted as a railroad village on the Minneapolis & St. Louis line on August 22, 1896. John Bush and his family arrived in 1854 and hosted a type of early boarding house for weary travelers; it was there that the first Lafayette post office operated from between 1858 and 1870 before its temporary closure. It returned in 1897 after the

completion of the railroad. A city directory from 1916 reported that the early village consisted of no less than three grain elevators, the Farmers' Elevator Company, the Great Western Grain Company, the Swensen & Carlson Elevator Company; two banks, the Farmers' State and State Bank of Lafayette; three creameries, the Lafayette Co-operative Dairy Association, Lafayette and Bernadotte Creamery Company, and Riverside Creamery Company; the Lafayette House hotel; a harness shop; a feed mill, and the *Lafayette Ledger* newspaper. The Swedish Lutheran and Methodist Episcopal congregations boasted of their church edifices by this time as well. Tippi Hedren, an actress known for her roles in the 1963 horror-thriller film *The Birds* and the 1964 psychological drama *Marnie*, was born in nearby New Ulm but grew up in Lafayette.

NICOLLET, MN
POPULATION: 1,143 – CITY 473 OF 856 (8-7-25)

The City of Nicollet shares its name with Nicollet County, both of which were named for the French explorer Jean Joseph Nicollet. He was most famous for mapping the Upper portion of the Mississippi River in the 1830s and for designating many lakes and landmarks long before widespread European settlement took place throughout Minnesota. The first Nicollet village was laid out in 1856 and was home to the Trinity Lutheran church, a sawmill, a blacksmith shop, a hotel, a stagecoach stop, and a post office called "Eureka" from 1856 to 1858. Eureka village had been established on 500 acres of land selected by the Swan Creek Claim Company and its nine members for a townsite. Although it failed, a second attempt was made by Hiram Saywood to start Eureka. It, too, failed, as did another place called Swan City on the John C. Kettner farm, and yet another village called Dakota City. After several attempts, a more permanent Nicollet took hold once the Winona & St. Peter Railroad established a village called Nicollet Station. James H. Stewart and Walter L. Brackenridge platted it on June 30, 1874, intending to make it a railroad town. The local post office, having used the name Nicollet from 1858 to 1877, co-existed with the Nicollet Station office from 1873 to 1878, before the two merged in 1878 to avoid confusion amongst the settlers and postal employees. By the early 1880s, Nicollet had pairs of hardware stores, general stores, blacksmith shops, harness shops, shoe shops, hotels, and wagon shops, as well as a grain elevator, lumber yard, flour mill, feed mill, meat market, furniture store, and three saloons. Lines like the Nicollet Cream Association and the *Nicollet Leader* newspaper came later. Nicollet has never recorded a decrease in its population. This achievement can likely be attributed to its proximity to Mankato and its newfound designation as a bedroom community for the city. Schmidt's Meat Market, a third-generation family-owned store, is renowned throughout southern Minnesota for its German-style summer sausage, deli meats, and cheese selection.

Restaurant Recommendation:
Schmidt's Meat Market
319 Pine St
Nicollet, MN 56074

NORTH MANKATO, MN
POPULATION: 14,275 – CITY 474 OF 856 (8-7-25)

Despite never having any railroads of its own, North Mankato has become Minnesota's 78th-largest municipality by population thanks to its proximity to its larger southeastern neighbor, Mankato. The "Mahkato", as it was referred to by the Dakota (the Makato Osa Watapa, "the river where blue earth is gathered"), now called the Blue Earth River, was its namesake. The northern counterpart was platted in 1857 and connected to Mankato via two ferry landings; an addition called Le Hillier City was added in 1858. A bridge connecting the two communities was finally erected in 1898. That same year, North Mankato residents incorporated as an independent municipality on December 19, 1898. A. L. Wheeler and O. E. Bennett owned one of the earliest North Mankato commercial lines, a brickyard that gave way to several residences that still exist today. The brickyard closed in 1905 after eighteen years of business. Mr. Bennett's home, listed on the National Register of Historic Places as the William E. Stewart House, was where 127 residents met to incorporate North Mankato. North Mankato Public School, built in 1890 in the Queen Anne style and expanded in 1904, is the most ornate building left from the city's early years. South Central College operates one of its two campuses, the other in Faribault. Taylor Corporation, a print and communications company noted for acquiring over two hundred graphic arts companies since its founding in 1975, is headquartered here. Angie's Kettle Corn, first enjoyed by fans at Minnesota Vikings home games in 2002, originated in Angie and Dan Bastian's North Mankato kitchen but eventually grew so large and popular that it was acquired by Conagra Foods in 2017.

SAINT PETER, MN ★☆
POPULATION: 12,066 – CITY 475 OF 856 (8-8-25)
Fur traders have long used the Traverse de Sioux as an important trade point on the Minnesota River, but in 1851, it was where the Dakota people agreed to cede a large portion of their long-term homeland to the United States government. Losing 24 million acres of land was devastating to the Sioux, who had enjoyed centuries of prosperity free from European involvement. Still, the event served as the catalyst that allowed immigrants to flood into modern-day Iowa, South Dakota, and Minnesota. A town using the name "Traverse de Sioux" was established shortly after the treaty was signed; it had five saloons, two hotels, and many churches, homes, and other structures. It was the county seat of Nicollet County until 1856, when St. Peter took over that role. Captain William Bigelow Dodd settled near Traverse de Sioux in the fall of 1853, but opted to start his own townsite in June 1854, which he named Rock Bend. Daniel L. Turpin surveyed it that year, and after businessmen from St. Paul caught wind of the area's potential, they started the Saint Peter [Townsite] Company, named for the St. Peter (or St. Pierre) River. This name was the French name for what we today call the Minnesota River. The French most likely named it in honor of Pierre Charles Le Sueur, who is also the namesake of Le Sueur County. Interestingly, the company's head was Willis A. Gorman, who was then the 2nd Territorial Governor of Minnesota. Using his gubernatorial powers, he attempted to persuade the Territorial Legislature to move the territorial capital from St. Paul to St. Peter. St. Paul was seen as too far eastward, whereas St. Peter, as a capital, would have placed the government much closer to the center of the territory as a whole. Both houses of the Legislature passed the bill, which, if signed, would have allowed construction of the new Capitol building on land owned by Gorman. The bill did not pass because of the sneaky maneuvering of Joseph J. Rolette, chairman of the Enrolled Bills Committee, who stole the bill and hid in a St. Paul hotel, gambling with his friends. A manhunt ensued, proving fruitless, as Rolette kept himself and the coveted bill hidden until the end of the legislative session. It was too late to sign, so the capital move was never made. Despite the bill's failure, several hundred people had already decided to call St. Peter their new home. It was incorporated on March 2, 1865, and attained city status on January 7, 1873. Two very early institutions have important ties to the overall history of the community: Gustavus Adolphus College, started in 1862 as Minnesota Elementarskola (a name it used from 1862 to 1865) by Swedish Americans and the Evangelical Lutheran Church in

America, and the "Minnesota Asylum for the Insane," started in 1866. The psychiatric hospital was built using the famous Kirkbride Plan. Although much of the original building has been razed, the facility still operates as the St. Peter Regional Treatment Center. Gustavus Adolphus College still exists as a private liberal arts college and enrolls over 2,000 students. Thanks to Winona & Saint Peter Railroad and the Chicago, St. Paul, Minneapolis & Omaha Railroad across the river, an incredible surge of economic growth and prosperity came to St. Peter, and several civic, commercial, and religious improvements were made. Amongst these were the 1870 Gothic Revival Church of the Holy Communion, built from Kasota limestone found on the Minnesota River; the 1871 Eugene Saint Julien Cox House, home of St. Peter's first mayor built using Gothic and Italianate elements; Union Presbyterian Church, built in 1872 in a Gothic Revival style; the Nicollet House Hotel, constructed in 1873 as a hotel for the wealthy; the1875 Italianate Frederick A. Donahower House; the Nicollet County Courthouse constructed in 1880-81; Nicollet County's second oldest bank, the Nicollet County Bank erected in 1887; the St. Peter Carnegie Library, completed in 1904, and the St. Peter Armory, one of the oldest armories in Minnesota built in 1912-13. Over 30 properties on Minnesota Avenue between Broadway Street and Grace Street comprise the St. Peter Commercial Historic District, which contains buildings erected between 1854 and 1930. Several other historic buildings existed until March 29, 1998, when a large tornado destroyed or heavily damaged over 1,000 structures. St. Peter's Catholic Church, St. Peter Evangelical Lutheran Church, Old Central School, Johnson Hall at Gustavus Adolphus College, and the St. Peter Arts and Heritage Center were the five worst losses resulting from the disaster. As with any community with a stature such as St. Peter's, numerous famous people have lived in or have connections to the community, including Anne Martell Denver, the wife of famed country singer John Denver from 1967 to 1982; Paul Granlund, a sculptor whose 650-plus works are displayed throughout the country; Myer "Whitey" Skoog, a potential the inventor of the jump shot during his time with the Minneapolis Lakers; James M. Hinds, the first U.S. Congressman ever to be killed (on October 22, 1868) while serving in office; former NFL players Steve Neils and Earl Witte; and five former Minnesota state governors. Territorial Governor Willis Arnold Gorman was the first, and after Minnesota was admitted to the Union, four more men assumed the role: Henry Adoniram Swift (3rd), Horace Austin (6th), Andrew Ryan McGill (10th), and John A. Johnson (16th). Perhaps after their time on earth, some of these famous men and women passed through "Saint Peter's Pearly Gates," which have been literally manifested at the St. Peter Area Chamber of Commerce for decades. The St. Peter State Hospital Museum and the interpretive center at the Traverse des Sioux are two local museums worth visiting.

 **Restaurant Recommendation:**
3rd Street Tavern
408 S 3rd St #2032
St. Peter, MN 56082

Mankato is only partially located in Nicollet County (see Blue Earth County).

Unincorporated/Ghost Towns: Bernadotte, Klossner, New Sweden, Norseland, North Star, Oshawa, St. George, Traverse, West Newton

National Register of Historic Places:
Norseland: Norseland General Store
North Mankato: North Mankato Public School, William E. Stewart House
Ridgely Township: Fort Ridgely, Fort Ridgely State Park CCC/Rustic Style Historic Resources

St. Peter: Broadway Bridge, Center Building-Minnesota Hospital for the Insane, Church of the Holy Communion, Emily & Stephen Schumacher House, Eugene Saint Julien Cox House, Frederick A. Donahower House, Henry A. Swift House, John A. Johnson House, Nicollet County Bank, Nicollet County Courthouse & Jail, Nicollet House Hotel, Old Main, Gustavus Adolphus College, Sarah & Thomas Montgomery House, St. Peter Armory, St. Peter Carnegie Library, St. Peter Commercial Historic District, Traverse des Sioux, Union Presbyterian Church
West Newton Township: Alexander Harkin Store

Golf Courses:
North Links Golf Course, Daily Fee (North Mankato, MN)
Shoreland Country Club, Daily Fee (St. Peter, MN)
Breweries/Wineries/Distilleries:
Paddlefish Brewing (St. Peter, MN)
Tremendous Brewing Company (St. Peter, MN)

NOBLES COUNTY
EST. 1857 - POPULATION: 22,290

Created on May 23, 1857, but not organized until October 27, 1870, Nobles County was named in honor of one of Minnesota's territorial legislators, William H. Nobles.

ADRIAN, MN
POPULATION: 1,194 – CITY 70 OF 856 (2-28-25)

Officially surveyed in May 1876 by O. D. Brown, Adrian was named in honor of Adrian Iselin, the mother of the St. Paul & Sioux City Railroad's director of the same name. The tracks arrived in August, and a post office was also established. Some of the earliest events on the land that would someday be developed into Adrian began when the Irish-born Bishop John Ireland sent his advisor, Major Ben Thompson, to scout the southwestern Minnesota area for a suitable townsite. By tapping into his extensive personal wealth, Ireland purchased nearly 20,000 acres of land in 1877 and an additional 35,000 acres half a year later. Advertisements were created and promoted via Catholic-based publications. By the end of 1877, Adrian had become a viable settlement with its own hotel, wayside station, and two stores. George H. Carr was the first store owner. When it was reported that over 100,000 bushels of grain were shipped from the station, several more settlers and their families opted to move into the area. In 1880, there were approximately 193 residents. This number more than tripled by 1890, to 671 people, and then practically doubled again by the turn of the century. Its growth was so rampant that in 1893, its residents attempted to split the county in two so they, too, could serve as a seat of government (like Worthington in the eastern portion of Nobles County), but they were unsuccessful. Adrian's first church building, a wood-framed structure, was furnished in 1878 by Bishop John Ireland for $700. Not even a decade later, a new edifice was built from brick and named "St. Adrian Catholic Church," but it sadly succumbed to a fire on Christmas Eve in 1899. Yet another structure was completed in 1900, based on the blueprints of architect Henry Foeller; it was listed in the National Register of Historic Places on May 15, 1980. An adjacent parochial school was established in 1905 but closed its doors for good in July 1973. Two of the community's most notable ex-residents are Lloyd Voss, a 1965 NFL champion with the Green Bay Packers and a first-round draft pick in 1964, and Cedric Adams, one of the most recognizable voices in broadcasting (via WCCO AM radio) from the 1930s to 1950s.

BIGELOW, MN
POPULATION: 227 – CITY 74 OF 856 (2-28-25)
Although it was officially incorporated as a municipality on March 14, 1900, Bigelow was one of Nobles County's earliest communities. Initial surveys of the townsite were made in 1871, but it was the following year that it truly came to fruition, when the St. Paul & Sioux City Railroad began its march across the Minnesota prairie. Like other nearby towns, it was named to honor the legacy of one of the railroad's directors, Charles H. Bigelow. The insurance and lumber businessman never lived in the community but may have visited once to see its progress. Naturally, a post office was one of the first pieces of infrastructure to be instituted into the town's line of businesses and trade, which consisted of a railroad depot, a hardware store, a general merchandise store, a lumber yard, a grain dealer, and a coal business by the conclusion of 1874. By 1880, it had a meager 28 residents and was destined to remain that small until Charles L. Davidson of Hull, Iowa, took a personal interest in the town's prosperity. He bought the entire site in January 1892 and then launched an extensive marketing campaign to encourage prospective settlers to live there. A couple of hundred residents lived there when its status as a municipal corporation took effect eight years later. From 1910 to 2020, Bigelow's population has never been recorded as fewer than 195 (in 1910) and never more than 262 (in 1970). Nicholas Wolterstorff, a well-published author in numerous fields of philosophy, was born to Dutch emigrants in Bigelow on January 21, 1932.

BREWSTER, MN
POPULATION: 506 – CITY 59 OF 856 (2-27-25)
Originally called Hersey, this very first Nobles County community was named after Samuel F. Hersey, a lumber baron (and later a U. S. Congressman) from Maine who held interests in the St. Paul & Sioux City Railroad. The name stuck for many years until, in August 1880, the Chicago, St. Paul, Minneapolis, and Omaha Railroad changed it, having just purchased the previous entity. Because of the prior existence of another Hersey in Wisconsin, the name was discontinued and changed to Brewster by the railroad president, E. F. Drake. He insisted that a man by that surname served as a railroad director, but most sources now attribute the name to Brewster in Barnstable County, Massachusetts. Even before the alteration, the town was a busy place. W. R. Bennett was the first to live there permanently, and T. J. Smith was the first store owner. A hotel, a blacksmith shop, and a lumber yard followed, as did a second store by the end of 1872. A. J. Timlin was named postmaster then, but Peter Geyerman was in charge of the Brewster office when the postal service finally implemented the name change in 1886. His general store, "The Big Store," doubled as the office. An attempt was made in 1873 to relocate the judicial seat to Brewster (then Hersey), but the county's residents voted against the move, 104 to 379. Despite the brutal loss, Brewster blossomed into an essential railroad shipping point and was incorporated on January 9, 1899. Storefronts, banks, professional offices, churches, and schools would soon follow.

DUNDEE, MN
POPULATION: 73 – CITY 61 OF 856 (2-27-25)
Dundee (pop. 73) started as a railroad village in 1879 in Graham Lake Township, only a few miles northeast of Kinbrae. Located on the Heron Lake & Black Hills (otherwise known as the Pipestone) branch of the Sioux City & St. Paul, it was very briefly called Warren in honor of Joseph Warren. He was a Founding Father of the United States who would ultimately perish at the Battle of Bunker Hill while fighting the British in the

American Revolutionary War. When the railroad agent G. Folis moved into the depot in September of that year, he oversaw the initial growth of the settlement. He assisted newcomers in settling into their new homes. The name Warren lasted for only two-and-a-half months; when the post office was organized on November 1, 1879, it was changed to Dundee, an eponym for Dundee, Scotland. The change came about because the Dundee Improvement Company was involved in establishing businesses in nearby Kinbrae, and he hoped it would persuade them to move their operations to Dundee. They did not, but F. D. Lindquist and H. A. Scherlie still built a general store in 1880. It was one of the few firms ever to operate in Dundee's practically nonexistent commercial district. One of its highest-ever recorded populations, 217 citizens, was recorded in 1900 at its initial Census, only two years after it was granted incorporation status by the county commissioners (on January 4, 1898). While most of Dundee's commercial district has been lost to the passage of time, as has its post office (as of 1996), the Sioux City & St. Paul Railroad Section House remains in Dundee. Erected in 1879, it is one of the few unaltered early railroad residences in Minnesota and the first house built in Dundee. It was listed on the National Register in May 1980.

ELLSWORTH, MN
POPULATION: 497 – CITY 69 OF 856 (2-28-25)
Eugene Ellsworth of Cedar Falls, Iowa, is the namesake of this fourth-class Minnesota municipality. Its settlement dates back as early as 1871, when the area was mostly wilderness, with occasional farmsteads dotting the landscape. One of these early farmers was Stillwell, who established a small farm store on his property. Little did he know (as he would move away before it came into existence) that a grand railroad shipping point and an entire village filled with people, homes, and businesses would take over his property starting in 1884. The Cedar Rapids, Iowa & Northwestern Land & Town Lot Company, in conjunction with F. D. Randall, S. L. Dows, and James B. Close, surveyed and platted the site that would ultimately become a division point for a branch line of the Burlington Railroad. The main line crossed the center of Ellsworth from the southeast to the northwest, and the branch line branched off to the southwest, connecting Minnesota communities with Rock Rapids, Iowa. A magnificent depot was erected in addition to a roundhouse and a turntable, which replaced the temporary boxcar depot placed off to the side of the tracks sometime prior. Basic infrastructure, such as stables and general stores, were early facets of the community. They were ultimately joined by banks, lumberyards, elevators, hardware and implement stores, grocers, barber shops, restaurants, churches, and a school. Saint Mary was the first church established in Ellsworth in 1885, and part of its wooden structure was incorporated into the modern edifice. Heavy Catholic influences in this part of Minnesota allowed it to open a three-story parochial school building in 1906 and welcome an impressive 120 pupils in its inaugural year. The church closed in 2018, and its assets were sold off or moved to Luverne and Pipestone. The first storefront— excluding Stillwell's 1870s store — was the general stock of B. Frank Garmer, who doubled as Ellsworth's first postmaster. In 1912, Dr. P. J. Cress moved to Ellsworth and worked to build a hospital where hundreds of future Ellsworth citizens would be born. Its highest population was recorded in the 1920 Census, when 667 citizens were reported living there.

Restaurant Recommendation:
Ellsworth Locker
317 S Broadway St
Ellsworth, MN 56129

KINBRAE, MN
POPULATION: 10 – CITY 60 OF 856 (2-27-25)

Kinbrae, Minnesota's smallest incorporated city, reported a population of just ten residents as of the 2020 Census. The itty-bitty hamlet originated in 1879 on the southern end of Clear Lake when the Southern Minnesota Railroad and the Dundee Land Company of Scotland platted it as a rival community to the Sioux City & St. Paul's town of Warren (later renamed Dundee itself). Kinbrae was then called Airlie in honor of David Ogilvy, the 10th Earl of Airlie (a Scottish nobleman). He was the president of the land company that was quick to erect a three-story hotel, a general store, and a steam elevator with a capacity for roughly 15,000 bushels. Moves were made by the end of the year to rename the community De Forest, although that name was used only by the railroad line, while the post office retained the name Airlie until January 1882. At that point, the two organizations agreed to match their nomenclatures for the community, which was faring only slightly better than its neighbor, a half-mile to the northeast in Dundee. De Forest Station's owners decided to forgo any further improvements to their community following an April 20, 1883, fire that destroyed the elevator. In August 1883, the site was sold to Hanson & Graeger. The name was changed once more by the Chicago, Milwaukee & St. Paul Railroad to Kinbrae, of Scottish origin, but growth remained at a standstill until W. N. Bickley and W. E. Fletcher took a gamble on the site in 1895. Their extensive marketing campaign saved the railroad town from fading entirely into obscurity, as within a year, they had attracted the attention of over one hundred new residents and proprietors who opened a bank, a creamery, a hardware store, a lumber yard, a blacksmith shop, pairs of general stores, and elevators. Religion and educational opportunities were of the utmost importance to these people, so Methodist and Presbyterian edifices were built, along with a public school for the town's youth. Incorporation followed on February 17, 1896, and until the 1940s, its population varied between 107 and 137 permanent residents. Its post office was discontinued in 1971. Disincorporation as a municipality was considered in 2010, after the Census showed Kinbrae's population had dwindled to just 12 people. Nevertheless, it remains a municipal corporation with a mayor and three city council members.

LISMORE, MN
POPULATION: 202 – CITY 66 OF 856 (2-27-25)

Chiefly settled by Irish Catholics in the late 1880s, the name "Lismore" was given by Father C. J. Knauf of Adrian to a village of the same name in County Waterford, Ireland. While these settlers could sustain themselves, the organization of some of their land and skills did not culminate until the Chicago, Burlington & Quincy Railroad began building a spur line between Worthington and Hardwick in the winter of 1899. The blistering cold and weather caused a brief delay in construction, but they finally arrived in present-day Lismore on June 9, 1900, at which point the town was immediately established. The St. Croix Lumber Company entered into business. It began trading its building materials to prospective entrepreneurs like James Beacom, who built a saloon (the very first structure in Lismore), and Ollis B. Bratager, who stocked his building with general goods. Bratager also took on the role of Lismore's postmaster when an office was organized. James Ramage's lumberyard and hardware store and James Montgomery's grain elevator followed soon after, and the race was on to join Lismore's booming commercial district. Traditional firms like a butcher's shop, a livery, a restaurant, and a blacksmith shop were opened by the end of 1900, as was The Bank of Lismore on September 1, which was rare given the town's youth. "The Lismore Leader" began circulating its paper around this time as well, and over the next twenty-odd years, the population of Lismore reached a peak of 350. It was formally incorporated on May 31, 1902.

ROUND LAKE, MN
POPULATION: 377 – CITY 73 OF 856 (2-28-25)
Round Lake is relatively fortunate to exist as a municipality today, as when the town was platted into 100 lots in December 1882, not a single one was sold. The lack of interest in the community can then only be attributed to a complete disregard for marketing it and issues with the original plat. Thankfully, after some quirks were worked out and Edgar Adelbert Tripp took over as station agent of the Burlington Railroad town, specific measures were put in place that enabled it to grow into a necessary agricultural shipping point. When the settlement was founded in the fall of 1882 on the Lake Park, Iowa, to Worthington, Minnesota, branch line of the Burlington, it was named "Indian Lake" because of the presence of Native Americans at the nearby lake when early settlers arrived in 1869. The name lasted for only a brief period before O. H. Roche, the owner of a two-thousand-acre ranch surrounding Round Lake in neighboring Jackson County, donated twenty acres of his land to organize a townsite of the same name in Nobles County. A post office of that name was established in March 1884 following Tripp's arrival. Interestingly, another branch was located in Jackson County under that name from 1872 to 1884. After a new plat was made in 1889, prospective settlers began to show interest in the area. They worked to build it into a handsome community, complete with a bank, a newspaper, general, hardware, and implement stores, elevators, and all the other facets and facilities one would have expected to find in a town of that era. A gorgeous two-story school with a steeple and bell was erected in 1898 for $2,000, the same year that Round Lake found its place amongst Minnesota's municipalities. John Sather, one of the proprietors of the two companies that made up the Farley's & Sathers Candy Company (now a part of the Ferrero Group), started in the candy business as a humble cookie salesman in Round Lake. His company is credited with creating the "hanging bag" method of selling repackaged candy, now seen in retail stores worldwide.

RUSHMORE, MN
POPULATION: 365 – CITY 71 OF 856 (2-28-25)
Land was first broken on the Rushmore townsite in the summer of 1879, after its founders, George I. Seney and S. M. Rushmore, introduced settlers primarily from New York and other eastern states to what was formerly known as Miller Station. The site itself was platted in July 1878, following the completion of the Sioux Falls branch of the Chicago, St. Paul, Minneapolis, and Omaha Railroad, and the station was named in honor of former Governor Stephen Miller. A name change was more or less immediate when a post office was established, and Rushmore was selected to honor Mr. Rushmore and his family because they were the first settlers to establish a storefront on what would ultimately become a prosperous railroad town. Within only a year, the business lines numbered in the double digits, the most noteworthy of which were the general store, a feed mill, a jewelry store, a hardware store, a grocery store, an elevator, a hotel, and a notion store. A notion store, more commonly known as a millinery, is a shop that typically sells thread, needles, pins, and other sewing accessories. Rushmore's numbers reportedly sat around the one-hundred-person mark in 1880. Still, it would take another twenty-plus years of progress for the townspeople to formally accept their incorporation status as a village in March 1900.

WILMONT, MN
POPULATION: 332 – CITY 65 OF 856 (2-27-25)
The etymology of "Wilmont" is more complicated than someone would expect at first glance. The first use of the name dates to 1878, when Willmont Township was organized, and settlers had a dispute over what to call it. Some wanted to call it Willumet, and others Lamont, so a deal was struck to amalgamate (that is, to join together) the two names. On November 22, 1878, the township was born, but it would take two additional decades before the Burlington, Cedar Rapids & Northern Railway decided to extend one of its lines through the area. Thomas H. Brown intentionally dropped an "l" from the name to differentiate the town from the township. On December 16, 1899, settlers began arriving in droves, and the next several months saw the platting of the townsite, the establishment of the post office, and the launch of Wilmont's initial businesses. One of these was Charles William Becker's lumberyard; he also served as the original postmaster. Three saloon owners occupied downtown, as did blacksmiths, doctors, storeowners, pharmacists, and other professionals with their businesses within the year. A Presbyterian and a Catholic edifice would serve the religious needs of its residents by the end of 1900, and the Catholics even later boasted their own parochial school just down the road from the public school (completed by 1902). Wilmont lost its railroad tracks in the 1970s, the same decade its schools closed. What was a town of 473-plus inhabitants in the 1950s and 1960s dropped significantly by 1970, by which point Wilmont had lost 17.5% of its population.

WORTHINGTON, MN ★☆
POPULATION: 13,947 – CITY 72 OF 856 (2-28-25)
The economic hub of Southwestern Minnesota, Worthington, got its start in the summer of 1871 when the National Colony Company fulfilled its promise to populate the large swaths of land it had purchased the previous month with prospective Yankee settlers. The Yankees, so-called because of their ties to New England and upstate New York, were the first immigrants to move to the townsite, then known as Lake Okabena. *Okabena*, a Sioux word meaning "nesting places of the herons," was given to a nearby lake when the French explorer Joseph Nicollet mapped the lands between the Mississippi and the Missouri Rivers in the 1830s. The name stuck because the lake was explicitly marked on Nicollet's map; the herons must have been bountiful on that day of his voyage. The St. Paul & Sioux City Railway Company completed its main road through the area in 1871 to connect those two major cities in Minnesota and Iowa. What the railroad called The Okabena Railway Station was heavily developed, and its path was permanently altered following the actions of the National Colony Company. A. P. Miller and Ransom Humiston, the company's managers, decided that the town should be named to honor the Worthington family of Ohio instead. A. P. Miller's wife's maiden name was Worthington. They declared it would be a village of temperance, where religious Protestants could gather and live in the face of the temptation of alcohol. However, anti-temperance factions of settlers would soon prove too numerous to control forever. An early tale recalls Worthington's first Independence Day celebration when Humiston discovered a keg of beer in the Worthington House Hotel. Furious, he destroyed it with an axe, only to be appalled when several young men in the town gathered its remnants, dug a grave for it behind the hotel, and proceeded to hold a funeral for the wasted beer. They marched to the town icehouse and poured a new keg for themselves and all those who wished to indulge. Despite differences in opinion on temperance, Worthington's growth as a city was unmatched by that of the surrounding towns. By the end of 1872, it had between seven and eight dozen buildings, many of which were storefronts, boarding houses,

and homes. In 1873, the original "crown jewel" of its economy was constructed: the Okabena flour mill. Despite costing $40,000, the mill could produce over one hundred barrels of flour daily, most of which were traded throughout the region for other goods and materials that enabled Worthington to grow rapidly. It was named the seat of government of Nobles County with little contention and incorporated as a village by the end of 1873. A plague of grasshoppers nearly eradicated the community that year, but it survived nevertheless. By 1874, Worthington had added the Union Congregational Church and the Presbyterian Church as its two initial religious edifices. German, Irish, Norwegian, and Swedish settlers moved into Worthington early in the twenty-first century. Its population crossed the two-thousand-person threshold by the 1900 Census, the five-thousand mark by the end of the 1940s, and ten-thousand people by the 1980s. Most of its growth was driven by the arrival of the Chicago & North Western Railway, its prominence as the leading agricultural trade center, its location on highways as automobiles took over, and the emergence of corporate-owned meat packing plants. Noteworthy residents of the community's past and present include George Dayton, the founder of Dayton's department store that would ultimately evolve into Target Corporation, the seventh-largest retailer in the United States as of 2025; Dwayne Andreas, the "Soybean King" and the former CEO of Archer Daniels Midland; Stephen Miller, the fourth Governor of Minnesota; Dudley "Big Tiny" Little Jr., a talented pianist on *The Lawrence Welk Show* in the late 1950s; Lee Nystrom, an offensive lineman in the National Football League in the 1970s; Wendell Butcher, a pioneer player for the NFL's Brooklyn Dodgers from 1938 to 1942; Tim O'Brien, a novelist known for his work on the Vietnam War; Matt Entenza, the Minnesota House Minority Leader from January 2003 to June 2006, and Pete Ludlow, a philosopher noted for his work in the world of generative linguistics and linguistic semantics. Worthington is one of Minnesota's most culturally diverse communities today and a sister city to Crailsheim, Germany. This partnership began in 1947 when Martha (Cashel) McCarthy and her parents held a clothing and food drive to help those displaced in the German city during World War II. Noted points of interest include the George D. Dayton House, built in 1892; Hotel Thompson, one of the largest hotels in southwest Minnesota in the 20th century; and the Worthington Band Shell, the only band shell in the state constructed by the National Youth Administration in 1941. The NYA was a part of the Works Progress Administration from 1935 to 1939.

Restaurant Recommendation:
Lupita's Mexican Restaurant
1906 Oxford St
Worthington, MN 56187

Lodging Recommendation:
Historic Dayton House
1311 4th Ave
Worthington, MN 56187

Unincorporated/Ghost Towns: Leota, Org, Pfingsten, Ransom, Reading, St. Kilian

National Register of Historic Places:
Adrian: Church of St. Adrian- Catholic, Slade Hotel
Dundee: Sioux City & St. Paul Railroad Section House
Ellsworth: Siemer Silo & Barn
St. Kilian: Church of St. Kilian (Catholic)

Worthington: Citizens' National Bank, George D. Dayton House, Hotel Thompson, Dr. E. A. Kilbride Clinic, Nobles County War Memorial Building, Worthington Armory & Community Building, Worthington Band Shell

Golf Courses:
Adrian Country Club, Daily Fee (Adrian, MN)
GreatLIFE Worthington Golf Course, Daily Fee (Worthington, MN)

Breweries/Wineries/Distilleries:
Forbidden Barrel Brewing Company (Worthington, MN)
Round Lake Vineyards & Winery (Round Lake, MN)

Town Celebrations:
Turkey Day, Worthington, MN (2nd Saturday after Labor Day)

NORMAN COUNTY
EST. 1881 - POPULATION: 6,441

Most likely named for Norman Kittson, of fur trade, steamboat, and racehorse fame, some accounts suggest that Norman County could have been named after its large early population of Norwegian and Scandinavian settlers.

ADA, MN ★☆
POPULATION: 1,740 – CITY 263 OF 856 (5-29-25)

The "Loveliest Village of the Plain" was laid out in 1874 on the Wild Rice River and named in honor of a daughter of William H. Fisher, the superintendent of the St. Paul and Pacific Railroad. He brought this branch line through the Red River Valley and was rewarded with the privilege of naming this community. After two years of minimal development, a post office was organized. On February 9, 1881, Ada was formally incorporated as a municipality. Sadly, Fisher's daughter passed away at six years old, the year before the accomplishment. Still, the townspeople were determined to make their community one of Norman County's most prosperous in her honor. It was designated the county seat in a then much larger Norman County, and by 1900 its population had risen to 1,253. Hotel Ada (established in 1877) and a large sawmill (built in 1897) were two of its largest business lines at this point, but a 1903 report also noted the presence of the Ada Cigar Company factory, a creamery, bottling works, a bakery, and planing and flour mills. Five elevators contributed to the economy by moving farmers' grain to faraway lands via the Great Northern Railroad. The First State Bank of Ada was the first in the county. The First National Bank later joined it in safeguarding residents' deposits. Numerous other firms like two newspapers, the One Price clothing house, Amundson & Widen's Northwestern hotel, C. R. Andrews & Company's general merchandise store, C. H. Brown's hardware and implement store, and C. C. Allen & Company's lumber business were also present, to name a few, in addition to five churches, a public school, and a race track and fairgrounds. At that time, Ada was outgrowing its present courthouse. Their nearby rival town of Twin Valley seized the opportunity to take the coveted county seat for itself by building its own courthouse in the early 1900s. Despite their attempts, Ada retained its capital status after a county-wide vote and a series of petitions. Ada's development marched onwards, and three of its most historical buildings (all still standing today and listed on the National Register of Historic Places) were constructed: the 1900 Congregational Church of Ada, dedicated on Christmas Day that year as Ada's first brick church; a multipurpose Village Hall, built in 1904 to serve as a social hall and meeting place through the 1970s, and the Norman County Courthouse, completed in 1904 via

Omeyer & Thori's Romanesque-style architectural plans. Logging remained a significant industry in Ada until 1924, when it was halted after many of the area's forests were depleted. The fairgrounds mentioned above are still used today to host the Norman County Fair annually during the last weekend of June. Next to the grounds is Pioneer Village, a collection of historical museum buildings operated by the Norman County Historical Society. The group seeks to preserve and share the historical and genealogical past of Ada and other area communities.

Restaurant Recommendation:
West Main Pizza
320 E Main St
Ada, MN 56510

BORUP, MN
POPULATION: 96 – CITY 262 OF 856 (5-29-25)
Originally two miles south of its present location, Borup began as a siding of the Great Northern Railroad, complete only with a grain warehouse and a post office. In 1892, it was deemed necessary to move the town since the roads to Hans Olson's 1891 grain elevator were impassable during certain parts of the year. After the move, Borup was platted by Ole Mattison and his wife on January 13, 1899, and in came Peter Melberg, John Anderson, and Ben Peppel, each with aspirations to open a general store. The first two men successfully raised their buildings, but as Peppel was working on his, a fire broke out in Melberg's and destroyed all three structures. Despite the devastating blow to the town's development, storefronts soon sprang up, as did the Security State Bank of Borup on April 6, 1908. It was a reincarnation of the Bank of Borup, initially started in 1898 by E. L. Berg. A hotel, a hardware store, a blacksmith shop, a meat market, and a lumber office were established to meet the community's needs. By 1910, School No. 66 and the Winchester Norwegian Evangelical Lutheran Church were in the eastern part of town. Borup, finally incorporated as a village on February 15, 1951, was named in honor of Charles William Wulff Borup. The Danish man was the first to establish a banking house in Minnesota (near St. Paul) in 1854.

GARY, MN
POPULATION: 227 – CITY 266 OF 856 (5-29-25)
Gary, the Home of the Bulldogs, was established as the Northern Pacific Railroad raced northward to become the dominant rail line before its rivals, the Great Northern Railroad. The town was founded in 1883 in Strand Township and named in honor of Garrett L. Thorpe, the first merchant in the village. It was not developed until the advent of the Northern Pacific about three years later. What came about then was to be expected: a post office was established, specifically, in 1887, and later Gary boasted of a creamery (est. 1896 as The Gary Creamery Association), bank, livery, and general store. Two churches and School No. 59 were marked as essential community staples by a 1910 Alden Publishing Company plat map. In an awful instance of misfortune for the community, nearly the entire town was destroyed by a May 22, 1917, fire that started in the Dewey hotel and destroyed twenty-eight businesses and twenty-five homes. The depot, grain elevators, lumber yards, and a livery barn were all that remained following the blaze. Gary rebuilt despite the loss of firms like the First State Bank and the Farmers State Bank, and in 1920, it peaked at 333 residents. Gary's population began to dwindle with the advent of the Great Depression and the removal of the railroad lines; the tracks were torn up, and the railbed turned into the Agassiz Recreational Trail. Gary is the middle of five towns on the route, the others being Ulen

(the southern terminus), Twin Valley, Fertile, and Crookston (the northern terminus). The trail is approximately 53 miles long and accommodates cyclists, snowmobilers, skiers, ATVs, hikers, and horseback riders.

HALSTAD, MN
POPULATION: 564 – CITY 337 OF 856 (6-5-25)
"You Can't Beet Halstad," a town of 564 beet-loving people located at the heart of Minnesota's sugar beet growing industry. As a tribute to their dominant industry, a 21-foot-tall vegetable, now dubbed "The World's Largest Beet," was installed in 2019 by local artist Josh Porter. Long before giant statues were erected to commemorate the most significant facet of the local economy, Halstad was started for a different purpose: to serve the needs of the Great Northern Railroad. In September 1883, the railroad arrived, and the townsite was platted on behalf of Solomon G. Comstock and Almond A. White. It was named in honor of Ole Halstad, a pioneer farmer from Norway. The post office also took on that name when it was established in 1884, and Erik K. Brandt was named postmaster. Over the next twenty-five years, Halstad grew to a population of nearly 500 people, and its business district blossomed. On the eastern side of the railroad stood four elevators, a mill, and the local high school. Everything else was to the west: the depot, a town hall, the *Halstead Journal* newspaper office, an implement store, two liveries, a hardware store, a general merchandise store, a hotel, a drug store, the post office, the First State Bank, the First National Bank, and Lutheran and Methodist Episcopalian churches. Over the years, the school has undergone several additions. A gym and a stage were built in 1939. Twelve years later, a second addition, also entailing a farm shop, was added, and by 1970, a library, music room, weight room, community rooms, and offices had been completed. It consolidated in May 1982 with Hendrum-Perley to become Norman County West High/Elementary School. Born here in April 1891 was catcher Tony Brottem, who appeared for various MLB teams between 1916 and 1921. Lyle "Skitch" Henderson, a composer and pianist famous for being able to re-sketch any song in a different key, also hails from Halstad.

HENDRUM, MN
POPULATION: 289 – CITY 338 OF 856 (6-5-25)
Hendrum was almost assuredly named after the group of farms in Norway known as the Hindrumgaard. However, some accounts insist that its name honors Olava Hindrum Hagen. She was the wife of Johanas Hagen, a town founder and the first postmaster when the office was organized in 1878. The site was initially located near a Great Northern Railroad bridge, but was moved two miles south shortly after its establishment in the early 1880s. The railroad line was laid in 1883 and was the impetus for the town's growth, helping get home and business construction off the ground. Among the early accomplishments were four elevators, a creamery, a feed mill, an opera house, the *Red River Review* newspaper, a State bank, three churches, a fire department, a school, and a joint confectionery and ice cream parlor. Immanuel Lutheran Church, organized on December 8, 1874, by a group of Norwegian Lutherans, remains the town's oldest parish. The present-day building was built in 1958, but its older structures date back to 1887 and July 1895. Three hundred fifty-five people lived in Hendrum when its first Census was conducted in 1910, a number it has not returned to since. One of the greatest voices and proponents of preserving the history of the Red River Valley, Roy P. Johnson, was born in Hendrum.

Restaurant Recommendation:
Sugar Mama Cafe & Baking
320 Main St E
Hendrum, MN 56550

PERLEY, MN
POPULATION: 113 – CITY 339 OF 856 (6-5-25)

Andrew Aabye was the first recorded merchant in the vicinity that would someday play host to Perley, now a small hamlet in the southwestern corner of Norman County. He established a trading post on the Red River of the North because boats could transport both goods and passengers up and down the channel. His store had enough business to warrant the establishment of a post office in 1885. Not long thereafter, the Great Northern Railroad took an interest in laying its right-of-way through the region, and a 40,000-bushel elevator was erected not long after the town was established. S. G. Comstock named it after his friend George E. Perley, a noted Moorhead attorney. Aabye moved his store to capitalize on all the new customers. Within no time, there was a hardware store, a hotel, a meat market, a drug store, a blacksmith shop, the First State Bank of Perley (organized in 1906 and closed in 1929), and the Lee Cooperative Creamery (established on February 1, 1902, and eventually dissolved in 1961). The school was located in the northwest corner of town, about two blocks north of its two churches. The Sogn (later the Kirkebo) Congregation began circa 1880 in the countryside, but an edifice was raised in town in 1900. Bethlehem Lutheran Church raised its church building in 1902, and the two joined forces in 1910.

Restaurant Recommendation:
Perley's Pub
206 Main St
Perley, MN 56574

SHELLY, MN
POPULATION: 179 – CITY 336 OF 856 (6-5-25)

When Shely Township got its railroad village in 1896 with the extension of the Great Northern from Halstad to Crookston, a second 'l' was added to the village's name to differentiate it from the township. John Shely was an early trapper and homesteader in the vicinity who eventually became an assistant grain inspector in Duluth, Minnesota. With the railroad came a post office around the same time, but Shelly boomed with many interesting lines of commerce in its heyday. That fall, the Caledonia, North Dakota, bank was moved to Shelly and renamed the State Bank of Shelly. Matt Johnson and Peter Herbrandson established the *Shelly Signal* newspaper in 1898, which covered the community's news for eleven years until the Halstad Reporter annexed it. The Shelly Cooperative Creamery opened its doors for the first time in 1911, making it one of several town staples amongst its collection of hotels, general merchandise, and hardware and implement stores. Joe Johnson notably had a soft drink business, a rare establishment for towns of that era. A town hall, a church, and a school rounded out its notable pieces of infrastructure. Three miles east of town is Zion Lutheran Church, an edifice raised in 1883 by local Norwegian immigrants in the Victorian Gothic style. According to the Census, more citizens (approximately 344) resided in Shelly during the 1940s than at any time in its history.

TWIN VALLEY, MN
POPULATION: 723 – CITY 267 OF 856 (5-29-25)
Despite not winning the county seat from Ada in the early 1900s, as they had so greatly desired, Twin Valley has solidified itself as the second-most thriving community in Norman County. Named for its location, where the smaller Mashaug Creek meets the Wild Rice River, this community's history begins with Peter Olsen Skjaeggerud. He searched far and wide for a suitable place to build a flour mill at what is now known as Heiberg Park. Here, he and other settlers erected the mill, bringing notoriety to the area and encouraging other farmers to settle and start their new lives. A post office was organized in 1878, and by 1880, there was also a blacksmith shop, a general store, and a restaurant. The Wilcox Lumber Company is widely regarded as the town's first business. The Northern Pacific Railroad encouraged further growth by connecting farmers and entrepreneurs with surrounding communities. In 1886, they changed Twin Valley's fate forever when they placed their depot about two miles south. Engines were having difficulty tackling the land's slope at the former site, so the line elected to move the depot to a flatter parcel. Between August 24 and 27, 1894, it was incorporated. A population of 356 people was reported in 1900; over the decades, that number grew to 907 in the 1980s. Some of its most noted sites, according to a 1910 directory, were its four grain elevators, a mill, a furniture store, the *Twin Valley Times* newspaper, the First National Bank, District No. 77 School, and two churches.

Unincorporated/Ghost Towns: Betcher, Faith, Flom, Hadler, Lockhart, Ranum, Syre, Waukon

National Register of Historic Places:
Ada: Ada Village Hall, Congregational Church of Ada, Norman County Courthouse
Shelly: Zion Lutheran Church

Town Celebrations:
Shelly Days, Shelly, MN (4th Weekend in July)

OLMSTED COUNTY
EST. 1855 - POPULATION: 162,847

David Olmsted served as the 1st President of the Minnesota Territorial Council before parts of Rice, Wabasha, and Fillmore counties were combined to create his namesake Olmsted County in 1855.

BYRON, MN
POPULATION: 6,312 – CITY 734 OF 856 (10-20-25)
A mountain lion, a wolf, river otters, bison, and white-tailed deer are just a few of the native species that live at the Oxbow Park and Zollman Zoo, a facility founded circa 1967 on 624 acres to help protect at-risk animals. Although it is an Olmsted County Park, it is primarily affiliated with the City of Byron, with a population of 6,312 as of the 2020 Census. Early grain buyer G. W. Van Dusen suggested the name for his home of Port Byron, New York, in place of the former name of Bear Grove (given because of the former presence of black bears here). Village history begins around the fall of 1864, a year before the train cars on the Winona & Saint Peter Railroad started moving through the vicinity, carrying passengers. Byron's post office opened in 1865, and by 1876, significant developments began to take place. A wheat elevator and church were erected; in twenty years, there were three stores, a farm machinery store, a livery, and

a hotel as well. Schmidt Printing, one of Taylor Corporation's more recognizable subsidiaries, is now located in a town that has become one of Rochester's principal suburbs alongside Stewartville. Since the 1960s, its population has grown nearly tenfold, from 660 residents to over 6,312 as of the last Census (2020).

DOVER, MN
POPULATION: 782 – CITY 692 OF 856 (10-16-25)
First called Dover Center for its location in the center of Dover Township, early settlers eventually dropped the "Center" and kept their town's name simple. The name itself was taken from Dover, New Hampshire, the hometown of many early settlers. Dover was platted in the spring of 1869 but not incorporated as a village until December 22, 1908. With the help of the Winona & Saint Peter and the Winona & Western Railroads, Dover by 1896 had three stores, a meat market, a bank, a drug store, a hotel, a blacksmith shop, a lumber yard, and three grain elevators. In the southwest corner of town, Dover had a Methodist Episcopal church and a school. John G. Bush's home, built in 1877, remains today as an excellent early example of Italianate architecture in Olmsted County. Only recently has Dover's population grown rapidly due to its proximity to Rochester; as of 2000, it had only 438 residents.

EYOTA, MN
POPULATION: 2,006 – CITY 691 OF 856 (10-16-25)
Iyotan, meaning "greatest" or "most" in the Dakota language, is also the corrupted name of the Eyota railway village that got its start in 1854 when Benjamin Bear made a land claim. Milo Matteson, the original owner of the townsite, suggested it as a replacement for Springfield, the place's name until 1859. The post office was called Greenfield from 1857 to 1864, until it was changed to Eyota following the arrival of the Winona & Saint Peter Railroad. Samuel E. Everett established the town's first hotel, the Everett House, and Charles P. Russell opened a store. In 1866, the Presbyterian church was organized. Many more places came to fruition in later decades as the population grew, including a creamery, a stockyard, two elevators, a wagon shop, hotels, hardware stores, restaurants, blacksmith shops, the Eyota Hospital, the *Eyota Advertiser* newspaper, three churches, and a school. Until the 1970s, Eyota had a population of fewer than 639 people, but by 1980 it had nearly doubled to 1,244. Local historians of that decade took an interest in preserving two sites, specifically the 1888 Coan Victorian home and the 1924 Period Revival Eyota Farmers Cooperative Creamery Association building.

ORONOCO, MN
POPULATION: 1,802 – CITY 712 OF 856 (10-17-25)
The power of the Middle Branch of the Zumbro River inspired residents (specifically Dr. Hector Galloway) to name this place Oronoco, after the Orinoco River in Venezuela. When the town plat was filed in 1854, it was corrupted to its modern spelling. Leonard B. Hodges, John B. Clark, and Ebenezer S. Collings worked together to establish the community, and M. O. Walker established a stage line between Dubuque, Iowa, and St. Paul, Minnesota, which ran directly through Oronoco. County commissioners met here on August 27, 1855, with the intention of making it the Olmsted County seat. When the state legislature mapped the county lines, Rochester was instead designated the seat for its more centralized location. A mill, a store, and a hotel were the first three businesses, but by 1896, there were four stores, some ice houses, blacksmith shops, a creamery, and other lines. In 1875, Oronoco's Italianate school was erected on the southern bank of the river and used until 1926; in 1980, it

was listed on the National Register of Historic Places. Horace E. Horton, the founder of the Chicago Bridge & Iron Company, began his career in the area and is affiliated with the historic 1895 Frank's Ford Bridge located in the township. Incorporation was achieved on March 6, 1968.

ROCHESTER, MN ★☆
POPULATION: 121,395 – CITY 713 OF 856 (10-18-25)
Minnesota's third-largest city did not begin as a milling community or as part of the Twin Cities, but rather as a simple stagecoach stop on a line between Dubuque, Iowa, and Saint Paul, Minnesota, that followed the Zumbro River. Those traveling on this line would stop in this area to rest and refuel before continuing to their destinations. On July 12, 1854, George Head and his family decided to live here permanently and claim the land that now serves as Rochester's central business district. Head opted to establish a town, naming it after Rochester, New York, his hometown. From 1855 to 1858, the population grew from 50 to 1,500, during which time the legislature designated Olmsted County as the seat of government. In 1863, the "Queen City" acquired one of its two largest growth impetuses in the form of one Dr. William W. Mayo, the examining surgeon for those drafted to serve in the Union Army and fight in the American Civil War. The following year, the Winona and St. Peter Railroad became the first rail line to reach Rochester, and work set out at once to build up the town as one of Minnesota's most important trading points in the southeast. Some of its early school enrollment reports showed that between 905 and 1,174 students enrolled in summer and winter school from 1870 onward. In 1880, the Census reported a population of 5,103, and it appeared that Rochester would continue its exponential growth trend without pause for some time. However, on August 21, 1883, a destructive EF-5 tornado ripped through the heart of Rochester, causing at least 37 deaths and over 200 injuries. The entire town was destroyed. Rochester, lacking a hospital at the time, turned to Rommel Hall as an emergency room. Mayor Samuel Whitten, Doctor Mayo, and his two sons, William and Charles, and the Sisters of St. Francis worked in unison to care for the victims, and as a result of the tragedy, St. Mary's Hospital was built. Mayo aided in establishing the 1889 hospital in a handshake deal with the Sisters. Through the 1890s, the practice expanded into America's first multi-specialty group practices, with the arrival and assistance of Henry Stanley Plummer. As medical technology has advanced, the Mayo Clinic has been at the forefront of innovation, and since 2016, it has been widely recognized as the #1 overall hospital in the United States. From a history and architectural standpoint, many Mayo Clinic-related buildings are listed on the National Register of Historic Places, including the iconic Plummer Building, built in 1928 as an integrated care facility; the 1916-17 W. J. Mayo mansion, serving as the Mayo Foundation house since 1938; the Henry S. Plummer historic Tudor Revival home; the St. Mary's Hospital Dairy Farmstead, erected in 1923 to supply pasteurized milk to patients at the clinic, and the Mayowood Historic District, a 10-acre estate affiliated with C. H. Mayo and his son C. W. Mayo. Rochester's 1915 armory, 1919 Avalon Hotel, 1927 Chateau Dodge [atmospheric] Theatre, the 1936-37 public library, and the 1946 Rochester Art Center also command respect as some of Rochester's most historic places. Seneca Foods is noted for its ear-of-corn water tower, one of Minnesota's most unique. IBM, short for International Business Machines, announced its Rochester campus plans in 1956 and went on to employ over six thousand locals by the late 1970s. Rochester's population surpassed 100,000 persons sometime between 2000 and 2010, making it one of only three Minnesota cities (the others being Minneapolis and St. Paul) to surpass that milestone. With so many residents of past and present, Rochester has yielded many famous persons, a small handful of whom include Lea Thompson, an actress and director known for her

role as Lorraine Baines-McFly in the *Back to the Future* film trilogy; Yung Gravy, a rapper known for songs like "Mr. Clean" and "Betty (Get Money);" Igor Vovkovinskiy, formerly the tallest living person in the United States at 7 feet, 8.3 inches; Johnny Pemberton, an actor known for playing *Son of Zorn* in the Fox sitcom; Warren Skaaren, a scriptwriter with credits on Beetlejuice (1988) and Batman (1989); Robert W. Fleming, a father of the famous 1980 Lake Placid games "Miracle on Ice" U.S. Men's Olympic hockey team; Marshall Burt, the first third-party candidate elected to the Wyoming Legislature in over a century (as a Libertarian in 2021), and four Nobel Prize winners: Albert Szent-Györgyi (Medicine, 1937), Luis Walter Alvarez (Physics, 1968), and Philip Showalter Hench and Edward Calvin Kendall (Medicine; 1950).

Restaurant Recommendation:
Hollandberry Pannekoeken
214 N Broadway Ave
Rochester, MN 55906

STEWARTVILLE, MN
POPULATION: 6,687 – CITY 714 OF 856 (10-18-25)

Charles Stewart of New York arrived here in 1857 to build his milling business, but it was not until 1891 that the Chicago & Great Western Railroad came to town, which warranted the founding of a new village called Stewartville. A post office had operated under that name since 1858. By the time Stewartville's platting was complete, it had grown to encompass two grain elevators, an ice house, a lumber yard, a hotel, a livery barn, two churches, and a school. Wealthy residents lived in a part of town called "Silk Stocking Row," home to the city's physicians, attorneys, and businessmen. Some of these noted Stewartville residents over the years have included David C. Hodge, the president of Miami University in Oxford, Ohio, from 2006 to 2016; John Paul Goode, a crucial American geographer between 1900 and 1940; Jason Hammel, one-half of the husband-wife Indie pop duo Mates of State, and Richard Warren Sears, the founder of the department store chain Sears, Roebuck & Company.

Restaurant Recommendation:
2 Brothers Authentic BBQ
101 10th St NW
Stewartville, MN 55976

Chatfield & Pine Island are only partially located in Olmsted County (see Fillmore County).

Unincorporated/Ghost Towns: Chester, Cummingsville, Danesville, Douglas, Genoa, High Forest, Judge, Marion, Pleasant Grove, Post Town, Potsdam, Predmore, Ringe, Rock Dell, Salem Corners, Shanty Town, Simpson, Viola

National Register of Historic Places:
Chatfield: Milo White House
Dover: John G. Bush House
Dover Township: Christoph Krause Farmstead
Eyota: Coan House, Eyota Farmers Cooperative Creamery Association
Farmington Township: Benike Family Barn
Oronoco: Oronoco School
Oronoco Township: Frank's Ford Bridge
Pleasant Grove: Pleasant Grove Masonic Lodge
Rochester: Avalon Hotel, Dr. Donald C. Balfour House, Chateau Dodge Theatre, Maass & McAndrew Company Building, Mayo Clinic Building, Dr. William J. Mayo House, Mayowood Historic District, Pill Hill Residential Historic District, Henry S. Plummer House, Rochester

Armory, Rochester Public Library, George Stoppel Farmstead, Toogood Barns, Timothy A. Whiting House, St. Mary's Hospital Dairy Farmstead
Viola: Viola Cooperative Creamery

Golf Courses:
Eastwood Golf Club, Municipal (Rochester, MN)
Hadley Creek Golf Learning Center, Municipal (Rochester, MN)
Little Willow's Executive, Short Course (Rochester, MN)
Northern Hills Golf Club, Municipal (Rochester, MN)
Oak Summit Golf Course, Daily Fee (Rochester, MN)
Rochester Golf & Country Club, Private (Rochester, MN)
Soldiers Memorial Field Golf Course, Municipal (Rochester, MN)
Somerby Golf Club, Private (Byron, MN)
Stewartville Golf Club, Daily Fee (Stewartville, MN)
Willow Creek Golf Course, Daily Fee (Rochester, MN)

Breweries/Wineries/Distilleries:
Forager Brewing Company (Rochester, MN)
Grand Rounds Brewing Company (Rochester, MN)
Kinney Creek Brewery (Rochester, MN)
Little Thistle Brewing (Rochester, MN)
LTS Brewing Company (Rochester, MN)
Post Town Winery (Rochester, MN)
Salem Glen Vineyard & Winery (Rochester, MN)

Town Celebrations:
Summerfest, Stewartville, MN (Independence Day)

Murray County: former Avoca Public School (Avoca), "In God We Trust" F5 Tornado Water Tank Memorial (Chandler), Lake Shetek State Monument at Lake Shetek State Park (Currie), Turntable; former First Presbyterian Church at End-O-Line Railroad Park and Museum (Currie), Milwaukee Road Depot Museum (Fulda), Old Soldier at Prairie Hill Cemetery (Fulda), Dinehart-Holt House Museum (Slayton)

Nicollet County: Lions Club Water Fountain (Lafeyette), Schmidt's Meat Market (Nicollet), former North Mankato Public School (North Mankato), Godzilla Sculpture on Mankato Walking Sculpture Tour (North Mankato), Saint Peter's Pearly Gates (St. Peter), Fréy Salon & Spa in the former Carnegie Library (St. Peter), Eugene St. Julien Cox House (St. Peter), Christ Chapel at Gustavus Adolphus College (St. Peter)

Nobles County: St. Adrian Catholic Church (Adrian), former Bigelow Public School (Bigelow), Veteran's Memorial (Brewster), Gymnasium at Ellsworth Public School District (Ellsworth), Saint Anthony's Catholic Church (Lismore), Mural (Lismore), Bandshell at Chautauqua Park (Worthington), Historic Dayton House (Worthington)

Norman County: Norman County Courthouse (Ada), Congregational Church of Ada (Ada), former Syre Depot at Norman County Historical Society (Ada), former One-Room Schoolhouse (Gary), World's Largest Sugar Beet (Halstad), Antique Playground at former Shelly Public School; Red River History Museum (Shelly), Zion Lutheran Church (Shelly), Goodrich Tires Mural (Twin Valley)

Olmsted County: Sculpture at Oxbow Park & Zollman Zoo (Byron), former Dover Public School (Dover), Shack Bar; Bar & Grill (Dover), Mural (Eyota), Chicago & Northwestern Railway Caboose (Eyota), Allis Park & Bridge over the Middle Fork Zumbro River (Oronoco), Mayo Clinic (Rochester), Corn on the Cob Water Tower (Rochester)

OTTER TAIL COUNTY
EST. 1858 - POPULATION: 60,081

With 1,048 lakes to be found within its borders, Otter Tail County, named for Otter Tail Lake and Otter Tail River, can claim more lakes than any other county in the country.

BATTLE LAKE, MN
POPULATION: 857 – CITY 248 OF 856 (5-8-25)
The etymology of Battle Lake dates to a fierce 1795 battle between fifty Ojibwe warriors and a much greater number of Lakota-Sioux, in which over half of the Ojibwe were slain. When a townsite was laid out on the shores of West Battle Lake almost a century later, on Halloween Day, 1881, it was named to commemorate the event. An early post office operated from 1871 to 1874, then was discontinued before being restarted with the establishment of the village. With the help of the Northern Pacific Railroad, the town at the "Heart of 1,001 Lakes" grew to a population of 420 people by the turn of the century. Among the most prominent early firms were four elevators, two cheese factories, two banks, one creamery, a brickyard, the Battle Lake Hotel, and the *Review* newspaper. Other accomplishments included a high school building, a Lutheran church, a Baptist church, and two additional churches. Of all its homes, businesses, and points of interest today, Battle Lake's prized possession is the Prospect House & Civil War Museum. The property was purchased by James Allison "Cap" Colehour in 1882. On it, he erected a 26-room summer resort in a Georgian Revival architectural style. Colehour was a Civil War veteran, and his possessions—amongst them being authentic uniforms with bullet holes—are on display in the Nationally Registered Historic Place. On April 17, 2025, the First Baptist Church was added to the Register as one of three locations (the other being the Morrison Mounds) registered within the city. Giant fish sculptures at the Otter Tail Beach Resort and downtown Battle Lake pay tribute to the area's lake history, and a 23-foot-tall Chief Wenonga Statue remembers the legacy of those who lived on those lakes long before the arrival of European settlers. Glendalough State Park was once owned by the parent company of the Minnesota Star Tribune; it became a State Park on April 22, 1992, near Battle Lake. Camping, fishing, boating, hiking, kayaking, and canoeing are popular activities. Jess Lourey, a young adult and crime novelist, chose Battle Lake to be the setting of her *Murder-by-Month Mysteries* rom-com mystery series.

BLUFFTON, MN
POPULATION: 210 – CITY 229 OF 856 (5-6-25)
The high embankments along the Leaf River led to the naming of this hamlet "Bluffton," with a population of 210 as of the 2020 Census. In 1878, a post office was established to serve the mail needs of the earliest settlers, but it was in March 1880, when the town was platted for the Northern Pacific Railroad, that its growth was assured. A sawmill, a gristmill, and a creamery were some of the first firms to be established. They laid the foundation for a small commercial district with an elevator, shops, and stores. Bluffton was incorporated on February 26, 1903; by 1950, its population had peaked at approximately 239 people.

CLITHERALL, MN
POPULATION: 62 – CITY 249 OF 856 (5-8-25)
Clitherall got its name from the nearby 2,493-acre lake, which was named in honor of Major George B. Clitherall. He was a land agent at Otter Tail City's United States land office from 1858 to 1861. After Brigham Young and his Mormon followers were exiled

from Nauvoo, Illinois, most of them made their way towards modern-day Salt Lake City, Utah, and the Beehive State. As they passed through Iowa, a band of seven families split off from the main group in May 1865 and headed towards Minnesota to launch their own colony. This promising new settlement was Clitherall, which was formally established in 1865, sixteen years before the Northern Pacific Railroad platted a townsite in October 1881. "Old Town" Clitherall was located a couple of miles from the present site; the town and its buildings were moved to the railroad. The Clitherall post office has remained in operation since 1868, while elevators, a creamery, stores, churches, and schools have come and gone. One unique church sect was Clyde Fletcher's True Church of Jesus Christ, founded after a schism with The Church of Jesus Christ (Cutlelrite) in 1953. The Latter Day Saints "spinoff" had fewer than ten members and was disbanded when Fletcher passed away in 1969. Clitherall, aside from Millerville or Urbank, is one of the closest towns geographically to Inspiration Peak. This 310-foot peak offers a 360-degree view of Otter Tail County's Leaf Moraines glacial feature.

DALTON, MN
POPULATION: 215 – CITY 246 OF 856 (5-8-25)
Dalton is synonymous with the Lake Region Pioneer Threshermen's Association. This local group works to restore threshing machines and other farm equipment to working conditions for an annual show every weekend after Labor Day. The Great Northern Railroad town was platted in 1882 by Ole C. Dahl and named for him. A post office entered service that same year. By the time of its first Census in 1910, Dalton was inhabited by at least 175 people. Two grain elevators, a lumber yard, and a depot were located on the northeast side of the Great Northern line. Within the townsite, visitors of that era would have counted three stores, a bank, a livery, a hotel, a school, and a church. The threshing show started in October 1954 when George Melby, Ralph Melby, and Kenneth Bratvold organized the first event.

DEER CREEK, MN
POPULATION: 330 – CITY 231 OF 856 (5-6-25)
Several post offices in Minnesota have wielded the name "Deer Creek" over the years. The first was an office in Fillmore County from 1856 to 1865. Then, in 1879, there was an Otter Tail County office of that etymology until its closure in 1895. It was reopened in 1905 in a town of about 300 pioneer residents in eastern Otter Tail County. It was called Deer Creek after the small stream of the same name that flowed to the Leaf River. Platted in May 1882 by Francis McNamara, the Wadena to Fergus Falls line of the Northern Pacific Railroad served as the impetus for many construction projects that came together to form a unified village. A flour mill, The Farmers Creamery Company, *The Mirror* weekly newspaper, a brick factory, a fire hall, and a grain elevator were among the most important institutions. There were also two hotels, a bank, a store, a blacksmith shop, and Methodist Episcopal and Evangelical churches in place in the early days. Deer Creek was incorporated in December 1899.

DENT, MN
POPULATION: 173 – CITY 239 OF 856 (5-7-25)
Platted on August 19, 1903, and incorporated only about a year later, on September 8, 1904, Dent uniquely took its name from Northwestern Dent Corn. The crop was grown in abundance by the Native Americans long before any European settlers arrived. Early plat maps and business directories indicate Dent was an enterprising town with many unique lines. In 1912, there was a creamery (founded on June 12,

1909, and open as a cooperative firm until 1972), a feed mill, two livery stables, four general merchandise stores, a blacksmith shop, a real estate office, a barber shop, a bank, a meat market, two saloons, a hardware store, two hotels (one of which was John Krekelberg's Park Hotel), stockyards, a barrel heading mill with a dry kiln, and an elevator of the Atlantic Elevator Company. A town hall, fire department, Presbyterian church, post office, depot, and box factory operated by the Dent Box Company were indicated as being important by Geo. A. Ogle & Company. The barrel heading mill, owned by The Stevens Cooperage Company, turned basswood trees into barrel heads to help transport clothing, groceries, dishes, and other goods. After the mill burned down twice, seventeen families who had worked at the mill relocated elsewhere in search of new job opportunities. The loss of the factory put Dent in a bit of a pickle, so naturally, M. A. Gedney & Company established the Dent Pickle factory. As many as 30 barrels of pickles could be sorted and packaged daily. That building, too, succumbed to fire in the late 1930s. Dent's primary railroad was the Minneapolis, St. Paul & Sault Ste. Marie, "the Soo Line."

ELIZABETH, MN
POPULATION: 168 – CITY 243 OF 856 (5-7-25)
The Elizabethtown post office was established in 1871 by the United States Postal Service to serve the early settlers who needed a reliable system for sending and receiving mail from around the country. It retained this name until 1882, when it was shortened to "Elizabeth" at the request of the Northern Pacific Railroad. Elizabeth was the wife of Rudolph Niggler, the first postmaster and a pioneer of the township. On behalf of Herman and Marie Burau, a town plat was recorded on September 18, 1872, and incorporation was granted on November 21, 1884. Thirty years into its existence as a railroad town, Elizabeth had grown to include a variety of businesses. The Maurin elevator handled the grain deposits, and the Pelican River flour mills turned them into fine powder for use in bread products. Three general stores, a millinery, a pool hall, a hotel, a restaurant, a blacksmith shop, a lumber yard, a confectionery, a hardware and implement store, a garage, a bank, and a creamery rounded out the main lines of enterprise then. Religion was prevalent as well. St. Elizabeth's Catholic Church was the first congregation to raise an edifice. It was quickly joined by St. John's [German] Evangelical Lutheran and the Swedish Lutheran churches. The Catholic edifice had an adjacent parsonage. Town and city halls were erected for use by municipality officials, and a two-story brick public school building was constructed in 1905. In February 1984, Elizabeth was granted its first location on the National Register of Historic Places: the Elizabeth Village Hall and Jail. The two-story brick structure and its counterpart were both built in 1898.

ERHARD, MN
POPULATION: 132 – CITY 241 OF 856 (5-7-25)
Alexander E. Erhard, an early settler, became the postmaster of the Erhards Grove post office between 1871-72 and 1874-76. In 1880, the office permanently shortened its name to Erhard. Two years later, the Great Northern Railroad sent workers to extend a branch line between Fergus Falls and Pelican Rapids. A restaurant, a hardware store, a general store, a depot, and the post office were five of the most essential businesses to Erhard through at least 1912. Still, other firms came and went over the decades. The incorporation of Erhard did not occur until October 13, 1949, and at its inaugural Census, it reported a population of 145 people. Hannah Kempfer, who ultimately became Minnesota's first woman speaker of the House on January 28, 1925, spent much of her early life in Erhard.

FERGUS FALLS, MN ★☆
POPULATION: 14,119 – CITY 245 OF 856 (5-7-25)

Otter Tail's principal city was located on former Dakota and Chippewa land in 1857 when the Scottish trapper Joseph Whitford selected a parcel on the Otter Tail River on behalf of land speculator James B. Fergus. Whitford named the site in honor of his employer and because the river's rapids descended over 70 feet as it wove its way through the townsite. Settlement of the area commenced at one, seeing only a brief pause due to the events of the Dakota War of 1862. Whitford perished in the attacks, and Fergus, likely never having visited the settlement for himself, decided to pursue riches during the Montana Gold Rush. The site was repurchased by George B. Wright in 1867 for $100, who had a dream of turning the wooded lake region into a prominent trade center. A post office, administered by H. N. Hannigson, was organized in 1870, and a central dam was erected the following year, creating a pond for milling. Within two years, it had acquired the title of county seat from Otter Tail City. Fergus Falls expanded around the flour and sawmills, reaching 1,635 citizens by 1880 and an incredible 6,072 people by the turn of the century. The Great Northern and the Northern Pacific Railroads had been built to take advantage of the large trade volume, and the business lines numbered well over a hundred. Elevators and mills, an ice cream factory, a creamery, a brewery the Grand Hotel, the First State Bank of Fergus Falls, the Scandia Bank, the Bijou Theater, a library, a police station, Washington School, St. Luke's Hospital, the courthouse and jail, a Lutheran college, Northwestern College, and a dozen churches of Catholic and Protestant and German and Scandinavian faiths adorned the townsite according to a 1912 directory. Vernon Wright and his business partner established the Otter Tail Power Company, which now serves hundreds of towns and serves well over 125,000 customers throughout Minnesota and the Dakotas. The trajectory of Fergus was forever changed only seven years after this survey was conducted, as on June 22, 1919, an F5 tornado destroyed a large part of the city, namely 44 city blocks and 159 homes, the Grand Hotel, the Otter Tail County courthouse and jail, the Northern Pacific Railroad depot, and at least four churches. Fifty-seven people lost their lives, making the event the second-deadliest twister in Minnesota history. About two-thirds of the deceased had been staying at the three-story, 100-room Grand Hotel. The spirit of Fergus remained unwavering despite the catastrophic event. By the 1940s, it had surpassed the ten-thousand-citizen population mark. Fourteen modern locations have been listed on the National Register of Historic Places: the 1881-82 C. J. Wright Stick style house; John W. Mason's 1881 Italianate home; C. C. Clement's Stick style home; Old Main at Park Region Lutheran College, erected in 1901 for a former 1892-1932 college and the home of the Hillcrest Lutheran Academy since 1935; the United States Post Office and courthouse, built in 1904 and now known as the Edward J. Devitt U.S. Courthouse and Federal Building; the last of Fergus Falls' flour mills, the 1915-19 Red River Milling Company; the Northern Pacific Railroad's Depot, built in 1920 to replace the one lost in the tornado; the 1921-22 Beaux-Arts Otter Tail County Courthouse; Fergus Falls City Hall, built in 1928 and designed after Independence Hall in Philadelphia; the 1929 River Inn hotel, which replaced the Hotel Kaddatz (built in 1914-15) as the city's premier hotel; the Barnard Mortuary, unique for its Mission Revival architecture; the Orwell archaeological site, and the Fergus Falls State Hospital Complex. The mental hospital was opened for business in 1890, but closed for good after several name and ownership changes by 2007. It is Minnesota's last surviving example of a former hospital/mental asylum built using the Kirkbride Plan, a design pioneered by psychiatrist Thomas Story Kirkbride. In education, Fergus was the former site of Park Region Lutheran College, which the Norwegian Lutheran Synod closed in 1932 in favor of supporting Concordia College in Moorhead. Northwestern College, a Scandinavian institution, closed that same year but was ultimately acquired by the Lutheran Brethren Seminary as a training center for pastors and missionaries. Minnesota State Community and Technical College, which has multiple campuses throughout this region, came about in 2003 when three campuses of Northwest Technical College and Fergus Falls Community College merged to form a unified institution. Arts and culture are just as important as history and education within the community, as is shown by the presence of the Orpheum Theater, A center for the Arts, and the Kaddatz [Art] Galleries. Quirky art installations are located throughout the city. Eagles Aerie No. 2339 is a nightlife spot modeled after a large ship. Ken Nyberg created the Spartan statue at the local college. Artist Steve Jaenisch is responsible for manifesting the sculptures at the Fergus Falls Fire Station, the Canadian goose at the Otter Tail County Historical Museum, the Continental Divide tripod at Big Chief Cafe, and the famous 40-foot-long Otto the Otter statue at Grotto Park. High school students assisted in Otto's construction in 1972. The ruins of a dam on the Otter Tail River, destroyed by the pressure of natural springs circa 1908, can still be seen at the Broken Down Dam Park. The number of famous persons from Fergus Falls is just as extensive as its points of interest, but amongst the more prominent are Dave Theurer, the game designer behind the Missile Command, Tempest, and I, Robot games for Atari; Richard Edlund, a town-time Academy Award winner for Best Visual Effects for his work on *Star Wars* (1978) and *Raiders of the Lost Ark* (1982); Frank Albertson, an actor best known for his roles in *It's a Wonderful Life* (1946) and *Psycho* (1960); Mary MacLane, a pioneer author in Confessional poetry known for her initial memoir; Mark Olson, a Member of the Federal Reserve Board of Governors from December 2001 to June 2006; Donald Cressey, a genius criminologist who made major contributions towards the study of organized crime, white-collar crime, prisons, criminal law, and criminology en masse; Peter Brandvold, a western fiction author; Marcus Borg, an influential man in spreading Liberal Christianity and a leader of the Jesus Seminar; Chad Daniels, a Billboard-charting comedian with nearly one-billion streams, and Charles Brewster Wheeler, a brigadier general in the United States Army who served from 1887 to 1919.

Restaurant Recommendation:
Outstate Brewing Company
309 S Vine St
Fergus Falls, MN 56537

Lodging Recommendation:
The Hill – Historic Boutique Hotel
309 W Stanton Ave
Fergus Falls, MN 56537

HENNING, MN
POPULATION: 854 – CITY 235 OF 856 (5-6-25)
Henning was once a booming railroad center located at the crossroads of the Northern Pacific and the Minneapolis, St. Paul & Sault Ste. Marie Railroads was one of Minnesota's three most prominent players in the railroad industry. The Northern Pacific arrived first in 1882 when the township was still called East Battle Lake. That name was changed to Henning on August 1, 1884, to mirror the village's name, which was given to commemorate the legacy of one of the earliest druggists in the area: John O. Henning of Hudson, Wisconsin. A post office established in 1881 was the first permanent institution of Henning. Through the decades, it expanded its business interests to include four grain elevators, two lumber yards, stockyards, a mill, and storefronts providing various goods and services. The Soo Line came through in 1902.

A public school and at least four churches were in operation by 1912, although a dozen congregations have called the Henning area home since the inception of its first group, the Peace Prairie congregation, in 1877. No documentation of Henning would be complete without a mention of its two most historic structures: the Trinity Lutheran Church and the Lewis House and Medical Office. The first structure began as a Norwegian Lutheran Free Church in 1898. Its twin spires and Gothic Revival architecture made it unique among the area's churches. After being used by several Lutheran and Catholic church groups, the building ultimately came into the city's hands and was transformed into the Trinity Center, serving the community as an event center. The previously mentioned medical office serves a similar purpose. Constructed in 1914 by Dr. A.J. Lewis to serve as his residence and doctor's office, the Prairie School building has since been converted into the Henning Landmark Center. It hosts meetings, retreats, events, and local groups, and boasts several bedrooms on its second floor. Henning's quirkiest attraction is the large stethoscope, crafted by local artist Ken Nyberg, which sits outside the Astera Health Care Clinic.

Restaurant Recommendation:
The Farmstand
602 2nd St
Henning, MN 56551

Lodging Recommendation:
Henning Landmark Center
415 Douglas Ave
Henning, MN 56551

NEW YORK MILLS, MN
POPULATION: 1,294 – CITY 230 OF 856 (5-6-25)

Copious white pine trees gave way to the large lumber industry in this area, which ultimately led to the founding of New York Mills as one of Otter Tail County's many incorporated communities. While a monument at the Continental Divide commemorates all the countries–France, Spain, England, and America–that have claimed the land that now encompasses the city at one point or another, the Sioux first claimed the timbered forests as their own. As more Europeans moved in by the hundreds, the Sioux were forced out, and the area was transformed into a milling center. The New York Mills Company was established in 1872 by Dr. Van Aernam, Olcot P. Boardman, and George L. Cornwell. The three men spearheaded the marketing efforts that attracted most settlers, primarily Yankees and Finnish families who appreciated the timberland because it reminded them of their mother country. Randolph L. Frazee owned most of the initial townsite and a sawmill, but he sold out to the company in 1873. By 1882, the company had dissolved, but it was too late: the Northern Pacific Railroad had already helped fashion a prosperous settlement focused on Finnish culture and the lumber industry. On May 27, 1884, New York Mills was given the honor of becoming a municipal corporation, just a year after it was formally platted. Noteworthy points of interest per a 1912 atlas were the New York Mills Creamery Association, a fire department, a depot, a livery, and two stores. Several other lines, such as The New York Mills Herald, The New York Mills Journal, and Theissen Pickle Company, arrived later. In 1991, the city invested in the New York Mills Regional Cultural Center as an art gallery, meeting and office space, and community gathering place. The arts have continued to play a critical role in the town's modern identity, as evidenced by the sculpture collection at the New York Mills Sculpture Park. The open-air Finn Creek Museum preserves Finnish culture through its buildings and artifacts, the Finn Creek Store, and its yearly festival in late August. Janet Karvonen, a legendary Minnesota high school girls basketball player who scored over 3,000 points and won three state championships with the local high school from 1977-79, and Peter Hayes, best known for his time with the rock band Black Rebel Motorcycle Club, both hail from New York Mills.

Lodging Recommendation:
Whistle Stop Inn
107 E Nowell St
New York Mills, MN 56567

OTTERTAIL, MN
POPULATION: 629 – CITY 236 OF 856 (5-7-25)

Otter Tail City started in the 1850s as a trading point for fur traders on a trail connecting St. Paul, Crow Wing, and the Red River Valley. Between its early 1858 post office, United States land office, and county seat title, the then-town of fifteen hundred-plus residents had a promising future. But despite having all the assets that made it the county's most dominant economic power, the Northern Pacific and the Soo Line Railroad companies opted to bypass the town in favor of alternate locations. Townsite owners could not agree with the Soo, which would have been the most likely to build through, so they platted a new townsite to the east of the original and named it Ottertail. Otter Tail City was quickly dismantled without a railroad of its own, and its buildings and population moved to the new site. The only remaining trace of the once-prominent seat of government of Otter Tail County (until 1872) is The Saint Paul House, an early hotel. The Minnesota Loan and Trust Company filed the town plat on September 3, 1903, and Ottertail was incorporated on May 5, 1904. The original post office operated under the name Otter Tail City until 1894, when it was changed to Ottertail. It continued until 1931, closed for thirteen years, and reopened in 1944. Stores, elevators, schools, churches, and all kinds of businesses have histories related to Ottertail's development, but visitors to the town today will be most captivated by two of its statues. The first is Ken Nyberg's 14-foot-long otter on Main Street, and the other is Otto the Clown at the local Otter Treat ice cream parlor. Ottertail has enjoyed double-digit population growth every decade since the 1970s, with its highest percentage change between 1990 and 2000, when its population increased by 44.1%, from 313 inhabitants to 451.

PARKERS PRAIRIE, MN
POPULATION: 1,020 – CITY 232 OF 856 (5-6-25)

Parkers Prairie Township was organized under Jasper on January 4, 1870, and named after a mythical Revolutionary War hero. John G. Nelson changed the name in March 1873 to honor "Parker," an early county surveyor who drowned while attempting to cross the Long Prairie River. A town plat was filed as early as August 1880, but it would take another twenty-two years for the Minneapolis, St. Paul & Sault Ste. Railroad to lay its tracks through the townsite. Farmers and townspeople rejoiced as the railroad brought new opportunities to grow their community and export goods far beyond their immediate vicinity. Parkers Prairie was incorporated as a village in 1903 at a new site about one-half mile north of the original settlement. Hotels, stories, liveries, three grain elevators, stockyards, a boat house, a flour mill, a creamery, and the First National Bank of Parkers Prairie were among its earliest businesses, but it also had a rich selection of churches and a public school near the center of town by 1912. Karen Nyberg, a NASA astronaut with 180 days of experience in space; Hugo Magnuson, the founder of Hugo's grocery store chain that still boasts fifteen locations across North Dakota and Minnesota as of 2025; and Donald Maynard Hultstrand, the Ninth Bishop of the Episcopal Diocese of Springfield, Illinois, were all born here.

PELICAN RAPIDS, MN
POPULATION: 2,577 – CITY 240 OF 856 (5-7-25)

Canadian fur trappers from the Northwest Trading Company came to the Pelican Rapids area as early as 1868 to trade with the Ojibwe and other tribes, but it was not until 1882 that the town's development took off with the arrival of the Great Northern Railroad. A post office was organized in 1872, and local storeowner O. A. Edward Blyberg was named postmaster. His 1884 Italianate home remains a city gem and is listed on the National Register of Historic Places. W. G. Tuttle, the man responsible for bringing notoriety to the area in the first place by building its first sawmill and kickstarting the local lumber industry, is widely regarded as its founder. The name Pelican Rapids was taken from the rapids of the Pelican River, an 85.3-mile-long tributary of the Otter Tail River. When the railroad came through a decade later, it was designed to connect Fergus Falls to Detroit Lakes. Tracks were laid through the heart of the townsite, but they were never extended past Pelican Rapids. The sudden pause in their construction effectively made Pelican Rapids the terminus of the branch line, and the community benefited greatly from the unexpected pause. From 1890 to 1900, the population grew by 65.5% to 1,033 people. Dozens of business houses came to fruition. To name them all would be excessive, but mills, hotels, and banks dominated local industry, and by 1912, there were no fewer than five churches. A prosperous high school building stood tall at the corner of Broadway and Hill Streets. When U.S. Highway 59 was being laid in 1931, construction crews unearthed a 10,000-year-old Minnesota Woman skeleton that was then estimated to be the oldest human skeleton ever found on the North American continent. Another quarter-century later, in 1957, residents banded together to raise the 16-foot-tall Pelican Pete statue, which now holds the title of the World's Largest Pelican. Three dozen four-foot pelican statues were hand-painted and scattered throughout the city at local businesses and landmarks for Pete's fiftieth birthday in 2007. Visitors to Maplewood State Park may be lucky enough to spot a real pelican or any one of 150 other species of birds at the park's eight lakes. It is well known for its location in the Leaf Mountains and for its hardwood deciduous trees, including basswood, oak, sugar maple, and American elm. Dave Goltz, a 1981 World Series champion and an MLB pitcher from 1972 to 1983; Tucker Hibbert, a fourteen-time medalist (including ten golds) in the SnoCross event at the Winter X Games, and Buck Paulson, known for his PBS painting TV series *Painting with Paulson*, hail from Pelican Rapids.

Restaurant Recommendation:
Taqueria Chavez1
30 N Broadway
Pelican Rapids, MN 56572

PERHAM, MN ☆
POPULATION: 3,512 – CITY 238 OF 856 (5-7-25)

Josiah Perman, a man with a dream of connecting Lake Superior to the Pacific coast, is credited with helping establish Perham and hundreds of other communities along the Northern Pacific Railroad route. As the first president of the railroad company, it was only right that at least one town along the route was named in his honor. That honor fell to Perham, Minnesota, which was laid out in June 1872 by the Lake Superior and Puget Sound Land Company and formally platted on March 6, 1873. Like other municipalities, a post office was among its first institutions, established in 1872. Henry Kemper was the postmaster. From 1880 to 1890, the town grew rapidly from 269 people to 761 (an increase of 182.9%) as eager entrepreneurs and business owners set up shop, and hundreds of settlers moved in to take advantage of the railroad and its facilities. By 1910, there were 1,376 inhabitants. Visitors traveling along the railroad line would have noted the Perham Milling Company and a freight and passenger depot. If they stepped off the platform to explore the commercial district, they would have been met by three hotels, three general stores, two banks, a drug store, a lodge hall, and a City Hall in the immediately adjoining commercial district. They likely would have been surprised to find two Catholic church edifices, St. James Hospital, and well-off schools in other parts of town. Over a century later, the 1906 City Hall building remains a central landmark in Perham. It was built in 1906 with ten thousand dollars in bond money and designed by Fremont D. Orff to feature a hip roof and an open tower. The Perham City Council began to meet in the structure's council chambers on July 3, 1906. Over time, the structure also served as a jail, a fire station, a community center, a library, extension offices, a municipal liquor store, and storage facilities. With over 3,500 residents today, the growing city has had its fair share of famous citizens: Fritz Hanson, a five-time All-Star halfback in the Canadian Football League and a member of the Canadian Football Hall of Fame; Father John Anthony Kaiser, a Catholic priest who was assassinated while on a mission in Kenya in August 2000; Ray Taylor, a director of 1,599 films between 1926 and 1949; Gabriele Grunewald, a national champion middle-distance runner, and Larry N. Vanderhoef, the Fifth Chancellor of the University of California, Davis from April 1994 to June 2009.

RICHVILLE, MN
POPULATION: 77 – CITY 237 OF 856 (5-7-25)
In its 1920s heyday, Richville had it all. Two hundred eighty-one residents built up a small business district consisting primarily of a creamery, an elevator, and a pickle factory. There was also a general store, a hardware store, and a bank. Charley A. Friberg hosted the post office in his store starting in 1904, three years after the Soo Line arrived in 1901. Richville was platted in 1903, incorporated on October 25, 1904, and named in honor of Watson Wellman Rich. He was a civil engineer for multiple railroads in Minnesota and later the chief consulting engineer of the Imperial Chinese Railway Administration. The nearby unincorporated town of Richdale, located on the Northern Pacific Railroad, was also named in his honor.

UNDERWOOD, MN
POPULATION: 356 – CITY 247 OF 856 (5-8-25)
Heavily wooded areas evoked a sense of safety and opportunity for early pioneers, particularly for those who elected to settle near Bass Lake starting in 1869. Timber was used to erect several early log cabins, the first three of which were built by the Foss, Medjaas, and Seems families. The Ole and Anne Foss Cabin has since been preserved as a Minnesota State Historic Site. Other families came to the area in later years, but in 1876, townspeople grew wary upon hearing of General George A. Custer's defeat at the Battle of the Little Bighorn. Rumors were spread that Indigenous tribes were marching across the frontier and eliminating settlements, including nearby Foxhome and Fergus Falls. Hans Juelson and Berge O. Lee authorized and managed the construction of the 120-by-100-foot Fort Juelson to protect their settlement. Although they heard that the attacks on nearby communities had been falsified, they proceeded with the fort's construction regardless of whether a future attack should occur. It did not, but the settlement—then called Turtle Lake by the postal service—did see the arrival of the Northern Pacific Railroad. They first named it Southvick but then

changed it to Underwood in honor of Adoniram Judson Underwood, then editor of the Weekly Journal at Fergus Falls. A pair of grain elevators, stockyards, a blacksmith shop, a hotel, a bank, the depot, the post office, and the town hall were the town's most prominent points of interest in 1912. From 1939-40, the Works Progress Administration built the District No. 182 [Barnhard] School in the Moderne style. About 10 miles north of Underwood, in an unincorporated area called Phelps, is Phelps Mill. It was built in 1888-89 by William E. Thomas with the capacity of producing as many as 75 barrels of flour per day. By 1939, it had served its purpose, and the mill, 1891 general store, and 1902 miller's house had begun to fall into disrepair. They were saved by the efforts of Geneva Tweten and Otter Tail County, and Phelps Mill Park was established (and eventually listed on the National Register of Historic Places in 1975) to permanently preserve the complex.

URBANK, MN
POPULATION: 52 – CITY 233 OF 856 (5-6-25)
No railroad ever made it as far as Urbank. The closest trade points were eleven miles to the north in Vining, located on the Northern Pacific Railroad, and eleven miles to the east in Parkers Prairie, a Soo Line Railroad community. It briefly had a post office from 1903 to 1906, and despite there being a couple of hundred settlers in the area, Urbank did not incorporate as a village until August 16, 1947. Now home to about four dozen people, the town's all-time high of 177 was recorded during the 1960 U.S. Decennial Census.

VERGAS, MN
POPULATION: 348 – CITY 219 OF 856 (5-5-25)
Vergas has a bit of a "loony" history, including sightings of the Minnesota state bird and even Sasquatch. However, the makings of the small community all began in the fall of 1903 when it was platted as Altona. The post office was called Candor. Both were changed to match the name of the Soo Line station, which had derived the unique name after its series of four sleepers (sleeping cars for railroad passengers) that traveled between Minneapolis, Minnesota, and Winnipeg, Manitoba. The names of the other three railcars were Venlo, Venus, and Viking. The stores, hotels, banks, liveries, saloons, schools, churches, and everything else that comes with being a railroad town arrived with the Soo. As few as 281 people in the 1970s and as many as 361 in the 1920s have lived in Vergas, but one character has remained a constant in its population since 1963: the "World's Largest Loon." The local fire department funded the 20-foot-tall sculpture to honor Edward Krueger, Vergas's third postmaster from 1933 to 1962. It warded off rival loon statues in Mercer, Wisconsin (the World's Largest Talking Loon) and Virginia, Minnesota (the World's Largest Floating Loon) for nearly six decades until 2024, when it finally succumbed to a 90-by-33-foot, 25-ton loon known as The Calling. Artist Andy Scott furnished the enormous statue in St. Paul, Minnesota, on behalf of the McGuire Family Foundation to serve as a centerpiece for the University Sculpture Plaza near Allianz Field. Vergas may have lost its loon title, but it has remained a region of interest for those obsessed with locating the cryptid known as Bigfoot or Sasquatch. The "Vergas Hairy Man" has been spotted several times over the last sixty years. It has reportedly attacked vehicles and chased children who dare wander too far into its territory. One additional point of interest is the 8th Minnesota Freedom Rock painted by Ray "Bubba" Sorensen of Iowa. The state senator from the Hawkeye State has painted a unique rock in each of Iowa's 99 counties, honoring area veterans and county history. He has since expanded his project to paint a Freedom Rock in all fifty states; Minnesota has ten Freedom Rocks as of May 2025.

VINING, MN
POPULATION: 62 – CITY 234 OF 856 (5-6-25)
Like its in-county neighbor of Vergas, Vining has a "big foot" tale to tell. In 1991, visionary artist Ken Nyberg worked to bring the local stories of the cryptid to life, but with a creative twist of his own. At eighteen feet high and 1,200 pounds, the giant human foot with its upturned toenail welcomes visitors to Vining to sit and admire his work. Just down the road, next to Big Foot Gas and Grocery, a giant clothespin, watermelon, cactus plant, and several other sculptures are on display at the Nyberg Sculpture Park. Ken's workshop is a mile-and-a-half down 457th Ave with even more sculptures, like a giant doorknob, a three-prong plug, and a rhinoceros. The roots of the Nyberg family run deep in Vining. Ken's daughter, Karen Nyberg, became the 50th woman to reach space on her inaugural 2008 mission as a NASA Astronaut. Only 62 people live in Vining today, but in the 1900 Census, the number was 249. Pioneers came to Vining in 1882 when it was platted by the Northern Pacific Railroad. Its name replicates that of communities in Georgia, Iowa, and Kansas. Businesses in 1912 included three grain elevators, a lumber yard, a feed mill, a creamery, a hardware store, a blacksmith shop, and a general store. Two churches, a school, a depot, and the post office were prominent early institutions in the town.

Rothsay is only partially located in Otter Tail County (see Wilkin County), and Wadena is only partially located in Otter Tail County (see Wadena County).

Unincorporated/Ghost Towns: Butler, Carlisle, Dunvilla, Heinola, Luce, Parkton, Richdale, Topelius, Wall Lake, Woodland Park, Wrightstown

National Register of Historic Places:
Battle Lake: First Baptist Church, Prospect House
Elizabeth: Elizabeth Village Hall & Jail
Fergus Falls: Barnard Mortuary, C. C. Clement House, Fergus Falls City Hall, Fergus Falls State Hospital Complex, Hotel Kaddatz, John W. Mason House, Northern Pacific Depot, Otter Tail County Courthouse, Park Region Luther College, Red River Milling Company, River Inn, United States Post Office & Courthouse, C. J. Wright House
Henning: Lewis House & Medical Office, Trinity Lutheran Church
Otter Tail Township: Craigie Flour Mill Historical Marker
Pelican Rapids: O. A. E. Blyberg House, Maplewood Site
Perham: Perham Village Hall & Fire Station
Scrambler Township: People's Union Church
Tordenskjold Township: Fort Juelson
Underwood: District No. 182 School, Ole & Anne Foss House, Phelps Mill, Phelps Mill Historic District

Golf Courses:
Balmoral Golf Course, Daily Fee (Battle Lake, MN)
Balmoral North Par 3 & Driving Range, Daily Fee (Battle Lake, MN)
Birchwood Golf Course, Daily Fee (Pelican Rapids, MN)
Lida Greens Golf Course, Daily Fee (Pelican Rapids, MN)
Pebble Lake Golf Course, Municipal (Fergus Falls, MN)
Perham Lakeside Golf Club, Municipal (Perham, MN)
Stalker Lake Golf Course Bar & Grill, Daily Fee (Dalton, MN)

Breweries/Wineries/Distilleries:
ABC Brewing (Battle Lake, MN)
L'Etoile du Nord Vineyard (Parkers Prairie, MN)
Outstate Brewing Company (Fergus Falls, MN)
Thousand Lakes Brewing Company (Parkers Prairie, MN)

Town Celebrations:
Dent Daze, Daze, MN (3rd Saturday in August)
Erhard 4th of July Celebration, Erhard, MN (4th of July)
Finn Creek Summer Folk Festival, New York Mills, MN (2nd Weekend in August)
Lake Region Threshers Show, Dalton, MN (Weekend after Labor Day)
Looney Days, Vergas, MN (End of July/Beginning of August Weekend)
Lun Mania, New York Mills, MN (2nd Weekend in July)
Parkers Prairie Fall Festival, Parkers Prairie, MN (1st Full Weekend of August)
Ronald McDonald House Ride/Great American Think-Off, New York Mills, MN (2nd Saturday in June)
Turtle Fest, Perham, MN (3rd Weekend of June)
Underwood Harvest Festival, Underwood, MN (Labor Day Weekend)
Watermelon Days, Vining, MN (3rd Weekend in August)

PENNINGTON COUNTY
EST. 1910 - POPULATION: 13,992

Pennington County, Minnesota's second-newest, established in 1910, was created out of former Red Lake County lands and named in honor of the former president of the Minneapolis, St. Paul, and Sault Ste. Marie Railway: Edmund Pennington.

GOODRIDGE, MN
POPULATION: 112 – CITY 278 OF 856 (5-30-25)
Pennington County's smallest incorporated community came about in 1914-15 as the eastern terminus of the Minnesota Northwestern Electric Railway. The line and its singular gas-electric interurban car provided passenger and freight service between Thief River Falls and Goodridge, but never beyond. It was designed to continue to International Falls, nowadays a modest 159 miles away by automobile. The Soo Line purchased the line in 1915 and leased it back to Minnesota Northwestern, which operated it until March 15, 1940. Goodridge, named for its location near a broad but low ridge, was incorporated on August 19, 1915, at about the time that the Soo Line made its transaction. Jay Payne was appointed mayor, and his wife, Jennie Noble Payne, served as Goodridge's postmaster from the establishment of the post office in 1915 until 1934. Several other structures businesses came into being, many of which are now on display at the Goodridge Area Historical Society. They include the Garden Valley Telephone Company building, the Woodrow School House, the Goodridge depot, a log house and storage barn, the Brown house, the Tvedt Park gazebo, and a country store and museum. Goodridge never had a population of more than 231 people, as recorded in the 1920 Census.

ST. HILAIRE, MN
POPULATION: 273 – CITY 312 OF 856 (6-3-25)
There are three possibilities for St. Hilaire's etymology, all of which could be potentially true. One account suggests that Arthur Yvernault named it after his hometown in France. Another insists that early settlers would "go to St. Hilaire," a Frenchman who lived near the Red Lake River, for supplies. Frank Ives most likely named it for Jules Barthélemy-Saint-Hilaire, a French Statesman. Ives was a Crookston judge, and his son, Harry Ives, was appointed postmaster in 1882, when the office opened. St. Hilaire was platted as a townsite that year. On July 4, 1883, it celebrated both its incorporation and the arrival of the Crookston-Saint Hilaire branch of the Great Northern Railroad. The town's population skyrocketed to 840 by 1900, an increase of 335.2% decade-over-decade, but nearly halved to 468 by 1910. Despite its losses in numbers, the post

office, two general stores, Pitkins Clothing store, the Merchants State Bank, a hotel, the St. Hilaire Retail Lumber Company, the Crookston Lumber Company planing mill, St. Hilaire Creamery, and the *St. Hilaire Spectator* newspaper were still present circa 1911 as its main commercial interests. The newspaper was published from 1883 to 1942, then sold to the Thief River Falls Times.

THIEF RIVER FALLS, MN ★☆
POPULATION: 8,749 – CITY 313 OF 856 (6-3-25)

The origins of the unique name "Thief River Falls" are directly linked to the falls at the confluence of the Red Lake River and the Thief River. However, the actual story of how that name came to be is much more extensive. As the story goes, the Ojibwe named the Thief after a band of ten Dakota lodges, who were discovered to be secretly hiding and encroaching on their territory. Despite living and hunting in secret and even going so far as to abandon loud guns in favor of bows and arrows, the Dakota were spotted by the Crees and the Assiniboines. They informed their Ojibwian allies, who swiftly dealt with their enemy. Language barriers eventually changed the Ojibwe name for the area, *Gimood-akiwi ziibi*, to "Stealing Earth River," and then, finally, to "Thief River." Frank Russell was the first semi-permanent settler circa 1879, and the town was platted in 1887. A post office called Thief River operated from February to May 1884 while it was part of Polk County, but its long-term post office was relocated from Rockstad in 1891. It was around this time that the town attracted the attention of the Great Northern Railroad and briefly became its terminus. From its first Census in 1890 to the turn of the century, its growth was incredible. The small lumber milling station grew from a population of 191 people to 1,819 by 1900, representing a growth rate of 852.4% over that decade, and then to 3,714 residents by 1910. In the first decade of the 20th century, the Soo Line Railroad also arrived in 1904, and several improvements were made. The city had Hanson & Bargen's O. K. Roller Mill with a capacity of sixty barrels, a lumber mill that could turn out over 40 million feet of lumber per year, four grain elevators, an electric light plant, an $18,000 high school building, two graded schools, an opera house, a fire department, eight churches, an enormous creamery, general stores, banks, hotels, newspapers, and a plentiful array of commercial institutions. After failing to acquire the [Red Lake] county seat from Red Lake Falls, possibly due to foul play in the petition to relocate the seat from Red Lake Falls to Thief River Falls, a new plan was enacted to create Pennington County. On November 23, 1910, the citizens of Thief River Falls got their wish when they were named the seat of government of Minnesota's penultimate "new" county. Cement block works, fairgrounds, an armory, and an Odd Fellows Hall were amongst the other noted places around town at that time. Three places in particular have been handpicked for listing on the National Register of Historic Places: the 1914 American Craftsman in Minneapolis, St. Paul, and Sault Ste. Marie Depot, the former terminus of the Soo Line and the home of a 1912 2-8-2 steam locomotive; the 1914 Thief River Falls Public Library, funded with the help of Andrew Carnegie, and a 1933 Moderne-architecture multipurpose hall listed as the Thief River Falls Auditorium and Municipal Building. Peder Engelstad Pioneer Village, managed by the Pennington County Historical Society, preserves nearly 20 buildings' worth of artifacts, including a 1908 one-room schoolhouse, a 1916 Swedish Lutheran church, five historic storefronts, and two former railroad depots. Joe Wavra's 18+ trolls were installed as a part of a "troll walk" around town. At Red Robe Park, road-trip oddity enthusiasts can find the 1976 statue of Chief Moose Dung, colloquially known as Chief Red Robe to locals. Three modern businesses related to the city's history worth mentioning are Steiger Tractors, invented here in 1957-58 by Douglas and Maurice Steiger; Arctic Cat Inc., a snowmobile and ATV manufacturer established here in 1960 by former Polaris employee Edgar Hetteen; and Digi-Key Electronics, established in 1972 when ham radio enthusiast Ronald Stordahl created a digital electronic keyer kit. Hetteen's invention was eventually marketed worldwide, and Digi-Key has since become one of the largest distributors of electronic components. The three inventors have brought about a certain level of fame to Thief River Falls, but they are far from its only notable residents, others being: Gary Paulsen, the author of over 200 books, most notably *Hatchet*, *The River*, and *Brian's Winter*; Agnes Israelson, the first woman to serve as Minnesota city mayor in 1953; Ralph Engelstad, the former owner of the Imperial Palace casino in Las Vegas, Nevada and the donor of the $104-million-dollar state-of-the-art hockey arena in Grand Forks, North Dakota; Bill Carlson, the longtime anchor of Minneapolis's WCCO station starting in 1951 well into the 21st century; Adam Quesnell, a noted stand-up comedian; Wyatt Smith, an NHL center between 1999 and 2011; Wayne Nordhagen, an outfielder and designated hitter for several MLB teams between 1976 and 1983; Ralph R. Erickson, the Judge of the United States Court of Appeals for the Eighth Circuit since October 12, 2017; Barry "Smash" Darsow, a professional wrestler from 1983 to 2017; Tim Bergland, hockey player with 182 NHL game appearances, and Robert Baker, a member of the 1948 U.S. Olympic Men's hockey team.

Restaurant Recommendation:
Ingram's Candy Store
113 3rd St E
Thief River Falls, MN 56701

Restaurant Recommendation:
Las Ranitas Mexican Restaurant
1845 US-59
Thief River Falls, MN 56701

Unincorporated/Ghost Towns: Dakota Junction, Erie, Hazel, Highlanding, Kratka, Mavie, River Valley

National Register of Historic Places:
Polk Centre Township: Red River Trail: Goose Lake Swamp Section
Thief River Falls: Minneapolis, St. Paul & Sault Ste. Marie Depot, Thief River Falls Auditorium & Municipal Building, Thief River Falls Public Library

Golf Courses:
Thief River Golf Club, Daily Fee (Thief River Falls, MN)

PINE COUNTY
EST. 1856 - POPULATION: 28,876

Seemingly never-ending forests of Eastern White and Red Pine trees made selecting the name of this former Chisago-Ramsey County jurisdiction fairly straightforward when it was organized in 1856.

ASKOV, MN
POPULATION: 331 – CITY 438 OF 856 (7-19-25)
Until the 1970s, Askov was the self-proclaimed "Rutabaga Capital of the World" because of the sheer number of rutabagas it exported. A rutabaga fair and festival still commemorates the town's claim to fame. After the Great Northern Railroad came

through Partridge Township between Hinckley and Superior, a town emerged, complete with multiple lumber companies, a hotel, and a depot. It was destroyed by the Great Hinckley Fire of 1894, like many other area communities, but was rebuilt. Much to the surprise of the Germans and Swedes who had lived there for some time, the entire Partridge townsite and 20,000 additional acres of land were purchased by the Danskfolkesamfund—The Danish People's Society—to start a Danish colony. Immigrants to the colony were mainly Grundvigian Danes from within the United States, who moved here under the direction of Nikolaj Frederik Severin Grundtvig, a prominent Danish Lutheran pastor. Much of the land surrounding the Great Northern Railroad depot was sold to 25 Danish families, and the name "Askov" was chosen as the eponym for Askov, Denmark, the site of one of Grundtvig's largest folk schools. The post office was called Partridge from 1889 to 1909, before changing its name to Askov. It became home to Minnesota's largest concentration of Danish settlers, and on April 25, 1918, the village was incorporated. Several of its finest businesses and structures existed by that point. *The Askov American* Newspaper published its first issue on September 17, 1914, under the direction of Hjalmar Petersen, and once boasted of having the highest circulation of any newspaper in the United States for a town of its size. A merger with the Hinckley News and the Pine County Courier in 2022 formed the North Pine County News. Point of interest in or around Askov are Banning State Park, known for its kayaking and canoeing challenges for diehard sportspeople; the Pine County Museum in the town's former school building, noted for its incredible model railroad, genealogy and research library, antique shop, and multiple rooms of exhibits and two event centers; a Little Mermaid sculpture at the Little Mermaid Cafe within the school building; the 1901 Partridge Township Hall; Peter P. Kilstotfe's 1913 farm and bungalow house, and the 1914-15 Bethlehem Lutheran Church. Services at the church were not regularly conducted in the English language until 1930. Hjalmar Petersen, the 23rd Governor of Minnesota, owned the *Askov American* newspaper from 1914 and served as its village clerk and mayor for some time. Vern Mikkelsen, a six-time NBA All-Star and a four-time NBA champion in the 1950s with the Minneapolis Lakers, was raised in Askov and attended high school here; his father, Michael, was the Lutheran minister at the church.

Restaurant Recommendation:
Little Mermaid Cafe
6333 H C Andersen Alle
Askov, MN 55704

BROOK PARK, MN
POPULATION: 132 – CITY 451 OF 856 (7-20-25)
Doctor Chauncey Almer Kelsey coined the name for the town of Brookpark, within Brook Park Township, which was organized on April 18, 1894. This town would serve as a small resort town with a park-like setting on Pokegama Creek. A lumber camp was established in that vicinity as early as 1874, under the name Pokegama, which served as a precursor to the village laid out by the Kelsey-Markham Land Company. It was located within a couple of miles of a junction point of the Great Northern Railroad. One line of the G.N.R.R. went westward towards St. Cloud, and the other went southward towards Coon Rapids and Minneapolis. After the Great Hinckley Fire of 1894 ravaged the lumber camp and the tiny village (a monument in the local cemetery marks a mass grave for 23 victims), it was rebuilt and renamed Brookpark. Both the town and the post office retained this spelling of the name before the "Brook Park" form was adopted by the postal service on August 1, 1950. Many Jewish families recruited by Dr. Kelsey at the 1893 World's Fair in Chicago began moving into the area

shortly thereafter. Despite the fire, many stayed to help rebuild and give the town a fighting chance at rebounding. Their efforts were successful, and the village, which prided itself on having no saloons, jail, or even a police department, was incorporated on October 1, 1919.

BRUNO, MN
POPULATION: 85 – CITY 437 OF 856 (7-19-25)
The exact origin of Bruno's name is disputed. Formerly known as Mansfield Station, the town platted by Fitzhugh Burns may have been named in honor of an early hotel proprietor or by its Czech population, who may have derived its name from the City of Brno in the Czech Republic (then part of Bohemia). Mansfield was only dropped as a potential name when it was discovered that another Mansfield Township already existed elsewhere in Minnesota. The Eastern Railway Company of Minnesota was the initial proprietor of the Great Northern Railroad station at the site; it was the railroad that enabled Bruno to grow to an initial population of 229 people by the time of the 1910 Census. Its peak population of 234 people came about thirty years later. Bruno's post office entered service in 1896, and it was incorporated on August 29, 1903.

DENHAM, MN
POPULATION: 37 – CITY 444 OF 856 (7-19-25)
Only 37 residents live in Denham today, but it once served as an essential trade point on the Minneapolis, St. Paul & Sault Ste. Marie Railroad. Frank Lind sold part of his homestead to the railroad company circa 1908, at which point the line was extended, and the decision was made to establish Denham. It was named after an employee who assisted with the town plat. Early businesses in Denham included three general stores, a livery barn, a hotel, a blacksmith shop, a barber shop, a sawmill, a restaurant, a creamery, and the Farmers' State Bank of Denham, which opened on July 12, 1910, with Joseph Bocheck serving as president. It closed in 1926 due to a lack of population and depositors. In the late 1920s, a fire destroyed several more stores on Main Street, but Denham residents still managed to attain incorporation by February 1939. The post office branch opened in 1909 but closed in 1974.

FINLAYSON, MN
POPULATION: 295 – CITY 440 OF 856 (7-19-25)
The Oldenburg-Jasberg Land Company, established by John A. Oldenburg (former agent of the St. Paul & Duluth Railroad), brought many of Finlayson's early Finnish settlers to the area in the early-to-mid-1890s. After publishing several articles on Nurmijärvi–an alternative name for the site–numerous Finns moved to the region to take advantage of discounted land prices offered by Oldenburg. Land was set aside for a church, school, and cemetery, and David Finlayson built one of its earliest sawmills. His surname was used by the post office upon its establishment in 1887, before the land company had done any work, and later applied to the townsite in place of Nurmijärvi. With the arrival of the Northern Pacific Railroad, Finlayson's future was secured, and unique lines of enterprise, such as a pickle factory and two potato warehouses, became focal points of the local economy. It was incorporated as a village in August 1905. Within another fifteen years, the business lines had expanded to include four general stores, two hotels, *The Finlayson Register* newspaper, a barber shop, a furniture store, a pool hall, The Finlayson State Bank, and the Finlayson's Farmers' Co-operative Creamery. Finlayson School District #29 was established in July 1898, and its long-standing school building was constructed in 1913. A gymnasium addition was made in 1938. Although the former Finlayson High School

graduated its final class in 1990 and was demolished in 2004, Finlayson has retained a couple of historic buildings on the National Register: the 1896 John A. Oldenburg house, built for the town's founder, and the 1909 Northern Pacific Depot. The Minneapolis-based fashion brand Askov Finlayson, founded by Eric and Andrew Dayton in 2011 to sell men's wear, outdoor gear, and accessories, took its name from the two neighboring Pine County communities.

HENRIETTE, MN
POPULATION: 57 – CITY 457 OF 856 (7-20-25)
Lumber yards, grocery stores, garages, general stores, and a blacksmith shop once made up the commercial district of Henriette. However, the town has quietly shrunk to fewer than 50 permanent residents. Started as Cornell but later renamed Henriette for a local sawmill (due to postal authorities' confusion in distinguishing mail bound for Cornell, Wisconsin, from the Minnesota community), the town primarily grew around the depot of the Eastern Railway Company of Minnesota. It was later a part of the Great Northern Railroad system. Since incorporating as a village on March 13, 1920, Henriette has experienced a high of 148 residents and a low of 57. Yet, its citizens continue to hold events and make improvements to their small city. One of the most recent developments was the construction of a new City Hall in 2009.

HINCKLEY, MN
POPULATION: 1,904 – CITY 452 OF 856 (7-20-25)
Most of Hinckley's history begins with the recounting of the Great Hinckley Fire of 1894, but Europeans had settled in the area as early as 1854. The area was called *Gaa-zhiigwanaabikokaag* by the Ojibwe, meaning "the place abundant with grindstones," because of its location on the 6.7-mile-long Grindstone River. White pine forests provided an opportunity for the logging industry to flourish, so in 1869, the Lake Superior & Mississippi Railroad was built through the area, and the first sawmill in town was constructed. A post office called Hinckley was established in 1870, but the village was named Central Station due to its location at the halfway point between the Twin Cities of Minneapolis and St. Paul, as well as the Twin Ports of Duluth and Superior (Wisconsin). Central Station was incorporated in 1885 and only renamed to Hinckley in 1907 in honor of Isaac Hinckley, a large stockholder in the railroad that was ultimately consolidated into the Northern Pacific Railroad system. It was between these name changes that the firestorm of September 1, 1894, wiped out the entire town and numerous others in its path. Brutally high temperatures and dry conditions allowed the kindling on the forest floor, littered with branches and leaves left behind by years of logging, to catch fire and spread rapidly. Two major fires to the south and numerous smaller ones were burning that morning, and the two larger conflagrations intensified when a vortex of cool air kept the hot gases, heat, and smoke trapped below in the forest. Temperatures rose so high that railcar wheels fused with the railroad tracks, and barrels of nails melted into giant metal balls of ore. Nearly five hundred lives were lost in the disaster, and the town that once called itself "The Town Built of Wood" did away with its nickname as they began to piece their shambled community back together. Many residents survived by taking refuge in a water-filled gravel pit, and others escaped via the railroad. Mass graves of 248 victims have been marked by a large monument in the Lutheran Memorial Cemetery, and the event commemorated by the Great Hinckley Fire Museum at the town's 1895 Northern Pacific Railroad depot. It was built as a replica of the depot lost in the fire and conducted passenger services until January 4, 1967. Farming proved profitable for the locals through the end of the 1990s, thanks to the nutrient-rich soils replenished by the fires, although the town's economy has shifted more towards tourism. Since 1990,

the population of Hinckley has more than doubled from 946 people (in 1990) to 1,904 as of 2020. Saint Croix State Park, the largest in Minnesota at 33,895 acres, is best known for its extensive collection of New Deal projects. One hundred sixty-four structures were built between 1934 and 1943 as part of the Recreational Demonstration Area program. It was designated as a National Historic Landmark on September 25, 1997, only months after its listing on the Federal National Register.

KERRICK, MN
POPULATION: 71 – CITY 436 OF 856 (7-19-25)

Kerrick was the original name of the now-unincorporated town of Duquette, located approximately three miles northeast of modern-day Kerrick. When the decision was made to relocate the Great Northern Railway depot southward to this modern site, the original location was known as Old Kerrick until the establishment of a post office named Duquette, in honor of Frank Duquette, in 1905. The new site, which had been temporarily called New Kerrick, was then shortened to simply Kerrick. The two communities have remained separate ever since. The "Kerrick" name itself was chosen to honor Cassius M. Kerrick, an engineer for the Great Northern Railroad that ran through both communities. Kerrick was incorporated as a village on October 22, 1946. In the early 1890s, a railroad worker named Louis Hultgren discovered a sand pit that he and his family would operate as a molding sand quarry. The sand pit, house, and garage were selected for preservation by the National Register of Historic Places.

PINE CITY, MN ★☆
POPULATION: 3,130 – CITY 453 OF 856 (7-20-25)

When Pine County was formed in 1856, Chengwatana was selected as the county seat – that is, until the city's founders became greedy. They repeatedly denied the railroad the right-of-way it wanted for its line between Lake Superior and the Twin Cities, so the railroad officials scrapped their plans and left, establishing its junction at a new town on the west side of Cross Lake. This place was Pine City, which in 1872 became the judicial seat, only three years after it was platted. The move was partially due to a fire that destroyed the courthouse at Chengwatana. White and red pine trees grew abundantly in the area, thus the name. The Ojibwe called the area *Nezhingwaakokaag*, meaning "on a land-point full of white pines." *Chengwatana*, the early mentioned Ojibwe village, also literally means "Pine Town" in English. Within its first ten years, a stave factory, a shingle mill, two general stores, two hotels, and sawmills arose as Pine City's premier businesses. Business was booming, logs were falling, and residents saw every reason to seek incorporation as a village, which they attained in 1881. Over the decades, Pine City's population grew from 1,258 in 1910 to 2,143 in 1970 and to 3,043 by the turn of the 21st century. MINPACK, Inc. and Atscott Manufacturing are two of the city's largest employers for those who permanently reside there, but visitors to Pine City may take an interest in the Snake River Trading Post, a reconstructed 1804 trading post built initially by John Sayer and the North West Company; one of the town's twelve parks; the Pine Center for the Arts regional arts center; the Pine City Public Library, built in 1978, or a $41,000 wood-carved Voyageur statue at Voyageur statue named Francois. Pine Technical and Community College was established in 1965 as a public community college. Several festivals are held annually in Pine City. In 2005, it made national headlines when it became the first city in rural America to host an annual gay pride event, called East-Central Minnesota Pride. The event is still held annually. In 1978, the first International Polkafest was held at the Pine County Fairgrounds; the event eventually grew so large that it had to be relocated to a larger venue. A recent 2017 article in The Wall Street Journal featured

Pine City's high school boys' basketball team and their innovative three-point shooting strategy. In the same year, on May 14, the Pine City Scrapbooking Company was featured on *CBS News Sunday Morning*. Noted residents of Pine City history have included John Rydberg, one of the best Paralympic athletes in United States history; Rube Walberg, a two-time World Series champion pitcher in 1929 and 1930; Steve Zahn, an actor known for his roles in *Happy, Texas* (1999), the *Stuart Little* film series (1999 to 2002), and the *Dairy of a Wimpy Kid* film series (2010 to 2012); James Adam Bede, a U.S. Congressman from Minnesota between 1903 and 1909; the late professional wrestler Vladimir Petrov, and Anna Dickie Olesen, the first woman to be nominated by a "major" political party for the United States Senate.

Restaurant Recommendation:
Froggy's Bar & Grill
209 5th St SE
Pine City, MN 55063

ROCK CREEK, MN
POPULATION: 1,682 – CITY 454 OF 856 (7-20-25)
Rock Creek Township has existed as an organized entity since March 2, 1874, following the extension of the Lake Superior and Mississippi Railroad through the vicinity in 1870. However, the village's incorporation did not occur until November 4, 1970. The post office was named after the nearby tributary of the St. Croix River and spelled as "Rockcreek" from 1894 to 1950, before its spelling changed to "Rock Creek." In 1985, the postal service converted the branch into a rural station, as most of the city is rural farmland. The city and township's early history is tied to the logging industry, as there were no fewer than five mills in the area in its early days. Rock Creek's population has nearly doubled between 1980 (when the population was 890) and 2020 (when it reached 1,682 people).

RUTLEDGE, MN
POPULATION: 212 – CITY 441 OF 856 (7-19-25)
Indigenous peoples lived on the banks of the Kettle River, a few miles downstream from the modern town of Rutledge. The village, first called Kettle River after the nearby body of water, was renamed Rutledge in 1892 in honor of prominent area businessman and miller Edward Rutledge. It was traversed by travelers on the Government Road between Lake Superior and St. Paul, Minnesota, as early as the 1860s. A stagecoach station was established, and soon weary travelers decided it would be wise to start a more permanent settlement at the site. In 1870, the Lake Superior and Mississippi Railroad was completed through Rutledge. Following the financial Panic of 1873, it reorganized as the St. Paul and Duluth Railroad (later still acquired by the Northern Pacific). The railroad brought with it the necessary means and human resources to establish sawmills, stores, churches, and schools, which warranted Rutledge's incorporation on February 14, 1893. James D. McCormack was elected as the first mayor. Today, Rutledge and the surrounding towns are frequently visited by travelers on the Willard Munger State Trail. The segment running through Rutledge is the fifth-longest paved trail in the United States at 63 miles.

SANDSTONE, MN
POPULATION: 2,462 – CITY 439 OF 856 (7-19-25)
The Village of Fortuna was established in the 1850s, where the Kettle River met the Point Douglas to Superior Military Road. Its strategic positioning helped it grow to a

population of over 200 residents. In June 1887, a second village, called Sandstone, was established and named after the abundant St. Croix sandstone quarried from the bluffs of the Kettle River. Work at the quarries began two years earlier, in August 1885, under the leadership of William Henry Grant Sr. and his son, W. H. Grant Jr., of St. Paul, Minnesota. Junior became postmaster of the Sandstone post office when it opened its doors for the first time in 1887. After the Hinckley Fire of September 1894, the Sandstone townsite was abandoned until James J. Hill and his son-in-law, Samuel Hill, arrived with the financial assistance needed to revitalize it. The Eastern Minnesota Railroad Company, managed by the Hill family, built a line through the railroad community. Their other company, The Minneapolis Trust Company, rebuilt the sandstone quarries and got them back in operation to meet the nation's demand for the ornate building material dubbed by Hill as "Kettle River sandstone." A commercial company building was erected in downtown Sandstone in 1894 and used as the Sandstone State Bank starting in 1906. Nowadays, it serves as the Sandstone History and Art Center and is one of six local properties listed on the National Register of Historic Places. Other locations are the large Kettle River Sandstone Company Quarry, active from 1885 to 1919 but now used as Robinson Park; the Hinckley Fire Relief House, an emergency housing unit built to aid disaster survivors; the 1901 Sandstone School building; the Arnold Schwyzer Summer House and Farmstead, now the Audubon Center of the North Woods, and the 1947-48 deck truss bridge over the Kettle River on Minnesota Highway 123. On April 14, 1920, Fortuna and Sandstone merged to form a single united municipality. Banning State Park and its impressive potholes, ice cave, sandstone rock formations, and Wolf Creek Falls are located just north of town. Yonassan Gershom, an early supporter of the B'nai Or and Jewish Renewal Movements, has ties to Sandstone.

STURGEON LAKE, MN
POPULATION: 436 – CITY 443 OF 856 (7-19-25)
Sharing its name with the large lake in Windemere Township, the village of Sturgeon Lake was born from the minds of the officials of the St. Paul and Duluth Railroad. Consistent with the procedures of the time, a station needed to be established every 7 to 10 miles to serve as a refueling point and for passenger and mail pickup and drop-off. A depot near the lake made sense, and so the townsite was platted on August 14, 1889, twelve days after it had already been granted incorporation status. A post office was established from 1881 to 1882, then closed for a few years before reopening in 1888, just in time for the railroad's arrival. Sturgeon Lake has since grown from a small town with stores and lumber yards to a recreation center for visitors to General C. C. Andrews State Forest and its surrounding lakes and wildlife management areas. Clay Wilson, an ice hockey defenseman who played in 36 NHL games; George Cunningham, a pitcher in the MLB between 1916 and 1921; and Florian Chmielewski, a polka musician and the President of the Minnesota Senate in 1987, were born here.

WILLOW RIVER, MN
POPULATION: 384 – CITY 442 OF 856 (7-19-25)
The Point Douglas to St. Louis River Government Road was built in 1850 to connect Lake Superior with the upper Mississippi River. This vital thoroughfare connected the port cities of Duluth and Superior with St. Paul and Minneapolis. On it, several stations were established, one of which was a changing station for stagecoach horses near where the Willow and the Kettle Rivers meet. Nearly 30 years later, the St. Paul & Duluth Railroad opened for business, enabling widespread development not only in this area but also throughout northern Minnesota. The Fox-Wisdom Lumber Company, founded by Warren D. Fox and John Wisdom, was among the first businesses

established in 1890. A sawmill was erected, and three dams were built on the Willow River to aid in the shipment of logs. Over 125,000 feet of lumber were cut each day at the mill's peak operating capacity. It was at the company store on November 7, 1891, that Willow River was incorporated following a 37 to 18 vote by the townspeople. As many as 10 trains were running through Willow River at its peak, providing its 466 residents (as of 1900) with supplies and passenger transportation. The population had halved by 1910, decreasing by 54.5% to 212 people, due to changing economic conditions. Today, Willow River is proud to host the Willow River Rutabaga Warehouse and Processing Plant, the last facility in Minnesota still standing, built to store and process rutabagas. This hybrid root vegetable falls somewhere between a cabbage and a turnip. The facility was built between 1935 and 1937 and was listed on the National Register of Historic Places on June 21, 1990. Ernie Nevers, a pioneer professional football player who made five All-Pro teams between 1926 and 1931 and set the NFL record for points scored in a game with 40 in 1929, hails from Willow River. He has been inducted into both the Pro and College Football Hall of Fames

Unincorporated/Ghost Towns: Banning, Belden, Beroun, Big Spring, Blomskog, Chengwatana, Clint, Cloverdale, Cloverton, Crooked River, Danewood, Duquette, Duxbury, Eaglehead, Ellson, Friesland, Greeley, Groningen, Harlis, Kingsdale, Lake Lena, Markville, Midway, Milburn, mission Creek, Nickerson, Outflow, Pokegama, Sand River, Tozer Camp, Turpville, Tuxedo, Villstad, Wareham, West Rock

National Register of Historic Places:
Askov: Bethlehem Lutheran Church, Peter P. Kilstofte Farmstead, Partridge Township Hall
Danforth Township: District No. 74 School
Finlayson: Northern Pacific Depot, John A. Oldenburg House
Hinckley: Northern Pacific Depot, St. Croix Recreational Demonstration Area
Kerrick: Louis Hultgren House & Sand Pit
New Dosey Township: Red Clover Land Company Demonstration Farm
Ogema Township: Hinckley State Line Marker
Pine City: North West Company Post
Sandstone: Hinckley Fire Relief House, Kettle River Bridge, Kettle River Sandstone Company Quarry, Minneapolis Trust Company Commercial Building, Sandstone School, Arnold Schwyzer Summer House & Farmstead
Willow River: Willow River Rutabaga Warehouse & Processing Plant, John Doboszenski Farmstead

Golf Courses:
Grand National Golf Club, Daily Fee (Hinckley, MN)
Moose Lake Golf Club, Daily Fee (Sturgeon Lake, MN)
Pine City Country Club, Daily Fee (Pine City, MN)

Breweries/Wineries/Distilleries:
Three Twenty Brewing Company (Pine City, MN)
Town Celebrations:
Quarry Days, Sandstone, MM (2nd Weekend in August)
Rutabaga Days, Askov, MN (4th Weekend in August)
Willow River Area Days, Willow River, MN (Last Full Weekend of July)

PIPESTONE COUNTY
EST. 1857 - POPULATION: 9,424

Formerly called Rock County when it was formed in 1857, the county was renamed Pipestone County in 1862 because of the sacred pipestone quarries in its western corridor, now known as Pipestone National Monument.

EDGERTON, MN
POPULATION: 1,258 – CITY 13 OF 856 (2-22-25)
The 1960 Flying Dutchmen of Edgerton, Minnesota, are arguably one of the most famous high school boys' basketball teams in history. In an era where every school in the state–regardless of its size–competed in the same class at the Minnesota High School Basketball Tournament, this little institution with 94 total students had a legendary run where they defeated the much larger Mankato in their regional tournament, Chisholm and Richfield in the first two rounds, and then finally Austin in the championship game by a score of 72 to 61. With a final record of 27 wins and zero losses, the Flying Dutchmen rivaled even the legacy of the team from the 1986 film *Hoosiers*, which documented the journey of the Milan High School (which then had an enrollment of 161 students, nearly double that of Edgerton's 1960 team) boys team and their 1954 state championship win in Indiana. The proud basketball town owes its existence to the extension of the Southern Minnesota Railroad (later acquired by the Chicago, Milwaukee & St. Paul Railway), which was platted in 1879 and named after Alonzo J. Edgerton. He was a Minnesota politician who served as a United States Senator from the state for a brief eight-month stint in 1881. Its post office was organized in 1879, and Edgerton was incorporated on October 13, 1887. Population growth was rapid during this era, as Edgerton grew from 86 residents in 1880 to 178 by 1890, and then to 450 by the time the 1900 Census was conducted. Noted business institutions in Edgerton as of 1898 were the C. L. Colman Lumber Yard, the Thody & Brady Lumber Yard, a third lumber yard, two elevators, stockyards, a flour mill, a creamery, two hotels, a foundry, a bank, a livery, and a selection of stores. To the west of Edgerton was a race track on the land of William Morrison and C. S. Howard, whose land was used to furnish the plots for the initial townsite. School District No. 2, a Methodist Episcopal Church, a Congregational Church, and a Town Hall rounded out its most notable public infrastructure. As of 2020, Edgerton has 1,258 residents, the highest number ever recorded in its history.

HATFIELD, MN
POPULATION: 53 – CITY 12 OF 856 (2-22-25)
According to local lore, as the workers of the Southern Minnesota Railroad were busy laying the tracks through the future townsite in 1879, a great wind took up and stole the hat of one of the men several times in a short period. After repeatedly leaving his post to retrieve it from the field, the men jokingly laughed that the site should be named "Hatfield." The name stuck, and the little railroad village grew into a relatively small trade center for about one hundred residents. An elevator and stockyards were built on the railroad tracks to serve as holding points for grain and livestock, while a depot facilitated the transportation of goods and people. School No. 13 and the Hatfield post office, established in 1880, were among the other prized community possessions, as per the Title Atlas Company's 1898 plat map. Hatfield was incorporated on September 9, 1919, and its post office was discontinued in 1992. Hatfield's Hollyhock Ballroom was an area center for rock 'n' roll in its heyday. Between 1936 and 1982, it welcomed famous artists like Jerry Lee Lewis, Bobby Vinton, The Everly Brothers, and Conway Twitty. The building no longer stands, but the Hatfield Roadhouse restaurant features various artifacts and a binder full of the ballroom's storied history.

HOLLAND, MN
POPULATION: 178 – CITY 10 OF 856 (2-22-25)
The 13-block Holland townsite was surveyed in May 1888 when the Willmar & Sioux Falls Railway was extended to that point. Built by E. A. Sherman and John M. Spicer

of Willmar under the direction of the "Empire Builder" James J. Hill of the Great Northern Railway, the two men were responsible for platting and naming every one of the sidings along the 149-mile stretch of the railroad. One of these was Holland, whose name was influenced by a large colony of Dutch immigrants living in the area, who had originated from the former province of Holland in the Netherlands. A post office under the same name was established in 1889 in the general store of Janus Huibregtse, whose wife, Clara, had suggested the name to the railroad workers when they passed through the previous year. Upon its incorporation on May 15, 1898, Holland Village had churches for its German Lutheran and Presbyterian congregations, Public School District No. 63, a Modern Woodmen Hall, the Holland Lumber Company, a creamery, two elevators, a store, a hotel, and a post office. The following year, it welcomed the Bank of Holland, a private institution owned by Harris & Jacobs. It was replaced in 1920 by The First National Bank of Holland, which survived a burglary in September 1928 before closing in December 1933 following a second robbery in April 1933. Three hundred and three people lived in Holland at its peak in the 1940s.

IHLEN, MN
POPULATION: 61 – CITY 7 OF 856 (2-22-25)
Ihlen began its life in July 1888, when the Willmar & Sioux Falls Townsite Company platted the town on the land of Carl Ihlen. It was named in his honor, and he volunteered to serve as the settlement's first postmaster. Other pioneers moved in over the next few years, hoping to capitalize on the railroad's success. One of the earliest businesses was the Ihlen Mercantile Company, founded in 1892 and listed on the National Register in 1980 because of its status as southwestern Minnesota's most intact wood-frame commercial building. A blacksmith shop accompanied it, along with the Ihlen post office, an elevator, a coal shed, a depot, and a public school, as of 1898. Most buildings that once housed these places are gone, but a Quartzite arch bridge built between 1937 and 1938 over Split Rock Creek (on County Road 54) remains a significant point of interest for history and architecture buffs. It connects the community to the 1,303-acre Split Rock Creek State Park, located to the south of the community.

JASPER, MN
POPULATION: 610 – CITY 8 OF 856 (2-22-25)
When it was verified that the Willmar & Sioux Falls Railroad would be building its line near the boundary of Eden Township in Pipestone County and Rosedell Township in Rock County, the commissioners of both jurisdictions worked to establish towns along the line. Rock County's version of the community was called Carnegie and later West Jasper; however, it was actually located in Pipestone County. Pipestone County's village of Jasper later annexed it, as it was located on the side of the river where the commercial district was developed. The name Jasper was derived from the rich deposits of the jasper-like mineral mined in the nearby quarries, which were used to construct several buildings in the area. The mineral "jasper" itself is not present in the area, but early settlers confused the red-tinted quartzite stone for it. Jasper was platted by Alfred S. Tee on the Joseph Warren Drew homestead on April 19, 1888, and incorporated as a village only about a year later, in May 1889. Quarrying was the principal industry of the community, as the material was shipped far and wide for use in construction; however, Jasper had an extensive business line of its own. As of 1898, the town on the Split Rock River had banks, hotels, lumber yards, liveries, and stores in addition to more commonplace buildings like a depot, a post office, an engine house (used to store and maintain engines, perhaps or firetrucks or for the steam engines), a public school, and Presbyterian, Norwegian, German Lutheran, and Methodist

Episcopal churches. Selah S. King, the local newspaper publisher, was appointed postmaster when the office opened in 1888. Six early establishments, all built from the gorgeous region-specific Sioux Quartzite, are listed on the National Register of Historic Places as of January 2025: the John M. Poorbaugh Block, a general merchandise establishment called The Quarry Store built in 1889 that now serves as the Jasper Museum; Bauman Hall, a relocated (in 1893) remnant from the ghost town of North Sioux Falls, Minnesota; the Stordahl Building, occupied first in 1894; the John Rowe House, a quartzite bungalow that was purchased by its namesake nomination in 1903 for one-thousand dollars; the Gerber Hospital and Garage, a hospital clinic built in 1913, and the Jasper School Building, which brought education to the community's youth from 1911 to 2001. The Poorbaugh building was the home of the *Jasper Journal* newspaper from 1917 to 1972, before the Jasper Area Historical Society acquired it. On July 8, 1927, local photographer Lucille Handberg captured a famous image of a tornado, which was later used by the American jazz musician Miles Davis and the English bands Deep Purple and Siouxsie and the Banshees on their album covers. Terry Rodman's private collection of four dozen windmills from Brazil, China, the Netherlands, and the United States, among other countries, can be seen from the roadside on 40th Ave.

PIPESTONE, MN ★☆
POPULATION: 4,215 – CITY 9 OF 856 (2-22-25)

Twenty-three tribal nations consider the land that now encompasses the Pipestone National Monument sacred, as it was where differences were set aside for a common need. The ground was declared neutral territory so the tribes could quarry for catlinite, a type of Sioux quartzite used to make ceremonial pipes (thus its nickname, Pipestone). Numerous Plains tribes, most notably the Iowa and the Sioux, lived near and welcomed those who frequented the area for over three thousand years. One of the first documented accounts of a European visitor to the site dates back to 1836, when painter George Catlin visited and sent samples of the stone to his home in Pennsylvania for use as a reference in his work. Explorer Joseph Nicollet toured the site two years later with his party, all of whom inscribed their names alongside rock drawings that dated back to 2000 BCE. Knowing that European settlers would disturb the site and encroach on their territory, the Yankton Dakota tribe attempted to protect the area via a section of the Yankton Treaty signed on April 19, 1858. The government still favored the "rights" of the settlers to live where they pleased. It secured a parcel of the land to construct the Pipestone Indian Training School in 1894, the last of eighteen non-reservation boarding schools operated by the Bureau of Indian Affairs to be closed. It shuttered its doors in 1953 after fifty-nine years of operation. The Minnesota Community and Technical College now utilizes the school building, and the Superintendent's House (listed on the National Register of Historic Places in 1993) is used as storage by the college. After decades of decisive actions by the government and legal cases brought before the United States Supreme Court (and won) by the Yankton Sioux, the quarries were established as the Pipestone National Monument unit of the National Park Service on August 25, 1937, under the authority of Congress. The Upper Midwest Indian Cultural Center, located on the property, serves as the visitor center. It welcomes visitors to explore the craftsmanship of modern Native Americans who still hand-sculpt the stone into pipes, bowls, and other art pieces. Winnewissa Falls and towering Red Quartzite cliffs are among the popular natural attractions located at the site. The founding of Pipestone, a town that would ultimately connect the lines of the Chicago & Northwestern, the Great Northern, the Chicago, Rock Island & Pacific, and the Chicago, Milwaukee & St. Paul Railroads, was conceived by Iowa pharmacist Charles H. Bennett, who arrived here in 1873 and established it as the capital of Pipestone County the following year. He was inspired to visit after reading Henry Wadsworth Longfellow's famous *The Song of Hiawatha* poem, which detailed the area despite Longfellow having never visited it. From 1949 to 2008, Pipestone's The Song of Hiawatha Pageant was held at a natural amphitheater, welcoming thousands of visitors to enjoy performances that showcased Longfellow's vision of Native American culture and customs. Pipestone City was not platted until October 1876. By 1878, it had the Stuart Brothers general merchandise store, Reuben Clark's grocery store, Ralph Wiger's hardware store, S. M. Pasco's lumber office, the harness shop and furniture store of J. A. Phelps & Co., L. H. Hackett's flour and feed store, and A. F. Jackson's blacksmith shop. The first railroad arrived in 1879, and from then on, growth was unstoppable. The town of 222 people in 1880 had grown to 1,232 residents by 1890 and 2,536 people by 1900. The presence of all four major southwestern Minnesota railroads transformed Pipestone into an impressive commercial and industrial center, attracting numerous business interests. Several of the structures that were present in its railroad heyday-era are listed on the National Register of Historic Places: twenty-two properties in the Pipestone Commercial Historic District, home to more Sioux Quartzite buildings in one area than any other location in the state; The Calmet Hotel, located in the said district and built in 1888 in the Richardsonian Romanesque style from light pink jasper quartzite; the Burlington, Cedar Rapids & Northern Railroad (a branch of the Rock Island starting in 1890 depot; the Pipestone County Courthouse, erected in 1900-01 by C. H. Peltier for $45,175 as the most elaborate Sioux Quartzite structure ever created; the Sioux Quartzite Carnegie Library, completed in 1904, and the 132-foot-tall Pipestone Water Tower, only the second such construction to have been built of concrete for use by a municipality in the United States. Raised in 1920, it and a sister water tower in Brainerd, Minnesota, were built by architect L. P. Wolfe. Like other towns of its size, the "Home of the Red Stone Pipe" has had its fair share of famous residents: Donald Petersen, the CEO of Ford Motor Company from 1985 to 1990; Catrina Allen, a two-time PDGA (disc golf) World Champion in 2014 and 2021; Akash Kapur, an author and former writer for the *New York Times*, the Economist, the Atlantic, and other publications; John Lutz, an actor and comedian known for his role as J. D. Lutz on NBC's sitcom *30 Rock*; Hugh Smith, a former news anchor and member of Tampa, Florida's first ever live color telecast and remote broadcast; Vern Ehlers, a Member of the U.S. House of Representatives from Michigan between December 1993 and January 2011; Loran B. Morgan, the ophthalmologist who invented the Morgan Lens, similar to a contact lens; notorious bank robber and Alcatraz inmate Eddie Bentz; Phil Bruns, a television actor best noted for his role in the 1970s soap opera *Mary Hartman, Mary Hartman*; Adelaide George Bennett, a poet who wrote passionately of the pipestone quarry and Native American life, and Sir Harold Rawdon Briggs, a senior officer of the British Indian Army, among others.

Restaurant Recommendation:
8th Avenue Diner
101 8th Ave NE
Pipestone, MN 56164

RUTHTON, MN
POPULATION: 226 – CITY 33 OF 856 (2-24-25)
Tragedy concerning small communities is typically related to natural disasters or famine, but the town of Ruthton suffered its most significant loss on September 29, 1983, when two bankers of Ruthton's Buffalo Ridge State Bank were killed by a man who lost his farm in the 1980s farm crisis. Falling land prices led to a record number

of foreclosures and furthered the rural-to-urban shift of those who grew up on farmsteads to city life. The bank president and loan officer, Rudy Blythe Jr. and Toby Thulin (respectively), were those who were killed and commemorated in *New York Times* reporter Andrew H. Malcolm's book, *Final Harvest: An American Tragedy*. Ruthton village came to fruition in June 1888 when it was platted by the Willmar & Sioux Falls Railroad. Its name honors Ruth, the wife of one of the original townsite owners, W. H. Sherman. It was incorporated on November 2, 1897, and as of 1898, enjoyed the amenities of a post office, stores, two elevators, the depot, a lumber yard, a creamery, a hotel, a livery barn, a blacksmith shop, a bank, a Town Hall, a Public School, and a Methodist Church. According to the Census Bureau, Ruthton had as many as 534 people in 1950, but its population has declined every subsequent decade. Todd Bouman, who suited up for seven different NFL teams as their quarterback between 1997 and 2010, was born in Ruthton on August 1, 1972.

TROSKY, MN
POPULATION: 98 – CITY 6 OF 856 (2-22-25)
Trosky, the only such town in the United States with that name, was platted in September 1884 at the junction of two lines of the Burlington, Cedar Rapids & Northern Railway, which was succeeded by the Chicago, Rock Island & Pacific Railroad starting in 1903. While the origin of the name is unclear, it is known that the post office was established in 1884, and the site's development began when L. P. Kenyon of Rock Rapids, Iowa, invested in it and heavily promoted it to potential settlers. His efforts successfully brought about the arrival of dozens of families, who brought the skills and expertise needed to develop an extensive business district with stores, hotels, livery services, and more. At the western end of the townsite in circa 1898 were the railroad tracks, its lumber yard, three elevators, stockyards, and a depot. The Town Hall was located in one of the northernmost lots, and the Methodist Episcopal Church and School No. 51 were situated in the southeast. It was incorporated on June 10, 1893, in its heyday, and the population (starting in the year 1900) decreased in the following three decades before slightly rebounding in the 1940s. It has since shrunk further, reaching its all-time low at the 2010 Census, when it had only 86 inhabitants.

WOODSTOCK, MN
POPULATION: 110 – CITY 11 OF 856 (2-22-25)
When Granger and Kasson Hickox lived in this area, it was known as "Hickox Prairie" because they were the first pioneers to settle there permanently. Unbeknownst to them at the time, they had chosen a parcel that would soon become the target of a railroad expansion project by the Chicago, St. Paul, Minneapolis & Omaha Railway. They made arrangements to purchase a tract of land for the right-of-way, and by September 1879, a railroad station and the townsite were in order. The name was changed from Hickox to Woodstock, an eponym for the county seat of McHenry County, Illinois. In twenty years, Woodstock had accepted its role as one of several shipping points on the Omaha Road and welcomed several additions to its initial plat. School District No. 32, the depot, and churches for Catholics, Methodists, and Presbyterians were likely among the most frequently utilized fixtures of early Woodstock. Still, it also featured stockyards, stores, a hotel, a bank, a livery stable, an elevator, a lumberyard, and a post office (which was established in 1879 under its current name). *The Woodstock Eagle* newspaper began publishing local news and community events in 1891, although it is unclear when the paper ceased circulation. At one point, the town had five churches; St. Martin's Roman Catholic Church, the oldest Catholic church in Pipestone County, and the Woodstock Community Church, now the only church in

town, are likely the most remembered. Woodstock entered Minnesota's select group of municipality-designated communities on July 11, 1892.

Unincorporated/Ghost Towns: Airlie, Cazenovia, Cresson, Diamond Corner

National Register of Historic Places:
Ihlen: Ilhen Mercantile Company, Split Rock Bridge
Jasper: Bauman Hall, Gerber Hospital & Garage, Jasper School Building, John M. Poorbaugh Block, John Rowe House, Stordahl Building
Pipestone: Burlington Cedar Rapids & Northern Depot, Calumet Hotel, Pipestone Commercial Historic District, Pipestone County Courthouse, Pipestone Indian School Superintendent's House, Pipestone Public Library, Pipestone Water Tower, Cannomok'e- Pipestone National Monument

Town Celebrations:
Water Tower Festival, Pipestone, MN (4th Weekend in June)

POLK COUNTY
EST. 1858 - POPULATION: 31,192

Polk County came into being on July 20, 1858, but it was not formally organized until 1872-73, when it was decided that its permanent name should honor James K. Polk, the former President.

BELTRAMI, MN
POPULATION: 88 – CITY 264 OF 856 (5-29-25)
Minnesota's City of Beltrami and Beltrami County (of which Bemidji is the county seat) were both named in honor of the same Italian jurist and explorer, Giacomo Costantino Beltrami. Known for discovering the headwaters of the Mississippi River in 1823 (although later debunked by Henry Schoolcraft on his 1832 expedition), the famous explorer's name came up in discussions around the turn of the 20th century when the Great Northern Railroad was deciding on what to call their new railroad town in Reis Township, Polk County. The post office was called Edna from 1878 to 1900, in honor of Edna Webb, the wife of the first postmaster, Isaac W. Webb. When the office moved to the new townsite, its name changed. By September 11, 1901, Beltrami was quickly incorporated and ultimately claimed as many as 226 residents in the 1930s. In this era of prosperity, just before the Great Depression took hold and brought a downturn to communities throughout the Midwest, Beltrami was home to only a few stores. The most noted institution was the First State Bank of Beltrami.

CLIMAX, MN
POPULATION: 243 – CITY 334 OF 856 (6-5-25)
"Climax: More than just a feeling" was the slogan this western Polk County community used to celebrate its centennial in the late 1990s, approximately 100 years after it was founded by the Great Northern Railroad. The town's humorous etymology was taken from the Climax Tobacco Company, a popular brand of chew invented by "Climax" [Jim] Rufus Nephew. The first townsite was located on the Steenerson farm about a mile and a half southwest of the present site. Many of its original structures, most notably a flour mill, a bank, a general store, a harness shop, a post office, and a doctor's professional office, were moved when the St. Paul, Minneapolis and Manitoba Railroad (later redubbed as the Great Northern) was extended to that point in 1896. New railroad routes opened new doors for commercial opportunities. Its arrival spurred

the construction of a lumberyard, a stockyard, a roller mill, and three grain elevators: the Farmers, the Monarch, and St. Anthony's. These were the names of the elevators in 1930. At that point, Climax also boasted of a Modern Workmen of America Hall, a joint fire and city mill, the Svenson Insurance Company, a Chevrolet Garage, two hardware stores, a hotel, a general merchandise store, a bank, schools, and even a bandstand next to the Great Northern's loading platform. It is also known that C. C. Knappen was the first publisher of The Climax Chronicle; its first issue came out on June 12, 1897. A later variation of the local newspaper made itself the subject of other newspaper headlines when, after a woman passed away in nearby Fertile, they titled their article about her "Fertile Woman Dies in Climax." James K. Polk, the 11th President of the United States, has a monument dedicated to his legacy and memory located just west of the town.

CROOKSTON, MN ★
POPULATION: 7,482 – CITY 333 OF 856 (6-5-25)

A little fur trading post on the Pembina Trail called Douglas was named the first county seat when Polk County was formed in 1858, when the area was predominantly used as hunting grounds by local tribes. Crookston, named in honor of Colonel William Crooks, the man responsible for locating the St. Paul and Pacific Railroad here, came to fruition after Colonel Crooks convinced the railroad company to extend its St. Vincent branch between Glyndon and Warren. A federal land office was one of the initial institutions that led to its settlement. By 1878, its townspeople had built two sawmills, a flour and grist mill, lumberyards, brickyards, three large mercantile houses, and many other businesses. Over 1,500 people lived in what became known as the "Queen City of the Northwest" by 1880, only a year after its incorporation on February 14, 1879. When Captain Ellerey C. Davis was elected mayor, a movement began to change the name to Davis. A simple coin toss decided that the town would forever be called Crookston in honor of the railroader. German, Scandinavian, and French-Canadian settlers continued to arrive in droves, making Crookston the 14th-largest city in Minnesota by 1915, with nearly 8,000 residents. Over thirty fraternal organizations were meeting at that time, as were over a dozen religious organizations. Seven schools housed Crookston's pupils, its teachers, and its administrative staff. Lines of the Northern Pacific, the Great Northern, and the St. Paul, Minneapolis & Manitoba spurred the creation of countless businesses: The Crookston Bottling Works, the Interstate Power Company, a hospital, a creamery, a greenhouse, Crookston Steam Laundry, the Palace Hall, the City Hotel, Crookston Granite, the Stenshoel Funeral Home, and the Crookston Mercantile Company were just a few of these. Brock & Company's atlas noted other town facilities, such as a library, the Mount St. Benedict Academy and Mother House, athletic facilities at City Park, and even the Crookston Tennis Club building. Most of downtown Crookston, built between 1882 and the 1920s, has withstood the test of time, as 39 contributing structures were selected by the National Register of Historic Places in 1984 and designated as part of the Crookston Commercial Historic District. The district is joined by only three other properties around town that are NRHP-designated, including the 1879-80 Italianate E. C. Davis House, the 1907-08 Neoclassical Crookston Carnegie Public Library, and the Cathedral of the Immaculate Conception. The latter three-spire structure adorns the city skyline as its most stunning edifice. It was designed by architect Burt Keck in the Late Gothic Revival architectural style and built in 1912 to serve as the base of the Roman Catholic Diocese of Crookston. Although still standing, it no longer serves as a church. A new cathedral was dedicated on September 25, 1990, and given the same name. Regarding higher education, the University of Minnesota Crookston began in 1966, when the University of Minnesota Technical Institute opened as a two-year school on the same campus as the previously established Northwest School of Agriculture (a residential, agricultural high school). By 1988, the campus was formally given its present name. Other points of interest include the Polk County Historical Society Museum, where visitors can find the World's Largest Ox Cart, and the Grand Theater, one of several theaters that claim to be the oldest continuously operating movie theater in the United States. It has shown films since 1917. A plethora of noted men and women have ties to Crookston, including Milton Orville Thompson, a NASA research pilot known for his role in the X-15 program; author John Christgau; Ronald Davies, the Senior Judge of the United States District Court for the District of North Dakota from August 1971 to April 1996; Jules Ellingboe, a six-time competitor in the Indianapolis 500 in the 1920s; Joseph H. Ball, a United States Senator from Minnesota in the early 1940s; Dan Anderson, a center in the NBA from 1967 to 1969, and John Noah of the 1952 Winter Olympics silver medalist U.S. men's ice hockey team.

Restaurant Recommendation:
Widmans Candy Shop
116 S Broadway
Crookston, MN 56716

EAST GRAND FORKS, MN
POPULATION: 9,176 – CITY 331 OF 856 (6-4-25)

Polk County's largest municipality and the much smaller counterpart of its westerly neighbor (with a population of 59,166 people compared to this community's 9,176) began as a trading point on the Red River circa 1800. Its positioning at the confluence of the Red Lake River and the Red made it an excellent point for boating merchants to travel down either 'fork' of the waterway. Ox carts stopped here frequently after the American Civil War on their way to or from St. Paul and Winnipeg. As a general influx of settlers accumulated at the site, it was named Nashville in honor of William C. Nash. He was a fur trader and mail carrier who frequently traveled between Pembina, in the far north of North Dakota, and Abercrombie, in the southeast corner. Eventually, Nashville was renamed East Grand Forks as the two cities grew in unison, and the St. Paul, Minneapolis, and Manitoba Railroad established a depot. The Great Northern affiliate operated in the southern part of the city, but the rival Northern Pacific Railroad chose to locate its yards in the northern stretches of the townsite. A roundhouse, a freight depot, and a passenger depot were the N.P.'s most significant assets in the area. With two railroads came two areas of town heavily infiltrated by businessmen and women seeking to profit from the availability of the rail line. Near the Northern Pacific's office (around 1930) were a newspaper office, a laundromat, the Johnson Insurance office, the Linfoot Hardware Store, a Ford garage, a bank, Peoples Service Oil Company, and several other businesses. Five stores, the Red River Potato Company, and a service station were closer to the Great Northern line. Among all the businesses were the public school in the south, a City Hall building, a Presbyterian church, and a Catholic campus, including a church, parsonage, sisters' home, and Sacred Heart school. North Dakota had early prohibition laws, so starting in the 1890s, Hamm's Brewery saw an opportunity to grow its business across the river. In 1890, they built the first of several cold-storage warehouses in East Grand Forks, which was only one of several renditions of structures. Their 1907 warehouse was built directly onto a railroad spur, highlighting the importance of the St. Paul company's "Beer Depot" as it expanded throughout Minnesota. From 1915 to 1947, Polk County also entered an era of prohibition, leading to the temporary demise of large-scale brewing operations in the region. The 1907 structure was added to the National Register of Historic Places on September 20, 1984, as East Grand Forks's only NRHP listing.

Local visionary Edwin "Whitey" Larson did not let prohibition stop him from building the first stainless steel horseshoe bar in the country in 1930, a marvelous Art Deco-style piece still on display at Bernie's. Just as the rivers contributed to the rise of East Grand Forks, one of northwestern Minnesota's premier cities, so too did they nearly destroy the town during extensive flooding in 1997. Numerous neighborhoods were razed, and almost every home in the city was damaged in the destructive $3.5-billion-dollar (in damages) flood. Over 50,000 people were evacuated under a mayoral order; 13.4% of the population moved away after the event. The drop from 8,658 people to 7,501 from 1990 to 2000 is the single-largest decrease in the community's populace since its first inaugural Census in 1890. The Great Grand Forks Greenway and the Red River State Recreation Area were developed as natural ways to combat future flooding. Besides Kurt Knoff, a safety who briefly appeared for NFL teams between 1976 and 1982, Molly Yeh is the most famous personality with ties to East Grand Forks. The restaurateur hosts the Food Network cooking show *Girl Meets Farm* and has written numerous cookbooks. She opened a cafe, Bernie's, in 2022 that blends Midwestern cuisine with Scandinavian and Jewish flair. The city has been home to a branch of Northland Community & Technical College since 1971.

Restaurant Recommendation:
Blue Moose Bar & Grill
507 2nd St NW
East Grand Forks, MN 56721

ERSKINE, MN

POPULATION: 403 – CITY 309 OF 856 (6-3-25)

Erskine is unique in that not only is it located at the junction of two major continental railroads, the Burlington Northern Santa Fe and the Canadian Pacific Kansas City (formerly the Great Northern and the Soo Line), but it is also named for a resident. George Q. Erskine of New Hampshire was the president of the First National Bank of Crookston. He came to Polk County in 1885 and ultimately purchased the homesteads of Martin Rathstock and Daniel Cameron, two early settlers who sold out to Erskine so he could establish a townsite on the Great Northern line. Erskine's post office entered service in 1889, and on March 8, 1897, it was incorporated as a village. Reincorporation happened again in 1917, when it formally separated from its township. More progress brought Erskine's population to 614 in the 1960s, but it tapered off at that point and has since dropped to about 403 as of the 2020 Census. Four grain elevators, a lumber mill, and an ice plant were among its early industries. However, hotels, general stores, blacksmith shops, a lumberyard, a telephone company, a creamery, and the *Erskine Echo* newspaper would also have been prominent businesses. The Erskine Manufacturing Company (now located near Fosston) began manufacturing grain-hitch elevators and snowblowers in 1948. It pivoted to produce skid-steer attachments for the Ingersoll Rand Bobcat Company. Erskine's two novelty roadside attractions are the World's Largest Northern, located on the shore of Cameron Lake, and a 12-foot-tall cement statue near the Win-E-Mac Motel, referred to as the "Indian Lady." Many of Erskine's 300-odd residents today are Russian Old Believers. The followers of the Russian Orthodox Church arrived in droves starting in 1998, when suburban development overtook their land near Woodburn, Oregon.

Restaurant Recommendation:
Ness Cafe
103 Vance Ave S
Erskine, MN 56535

FERTILE, MN ☆
POPULATION: 804 – CITY 265 OF 856 (5-29-25)

Fertile shares its name with Fertile, Iowa, the hometown of many of its original settlers (which boasted fertile soil). Ironically, Fertile's sandy soils make it unsuitable for farming. Its adjacent plots are well-suited to a range of agricultural products. Lars A. Bolstad and his nephews, Knute and Elnar Nelson, were the first to come to the area in May 1879 in search of new homestead claims. Land was issued at the United States Land Office in Crookston, and by May 17, 1879, the Nelsons and their uncle had begun improving their claim. Next came the brothers Askeld Olsen and Anders Olsen Morvig, as well as Jacob Hanson Aldal. The area proved to be a popular one, as on May 25, 1887, James B. and Caroline F. Holms platted a 19-block townsite through which the Duluth, Crookston, and Northern Railroad (active from 1889 to 1898 and succeeded by the Northern Pacific Railway) could extend its right-of-way. A post office had been active since 1881 under the supervision of John S. LaDue, but it was known as LaDue Grove until he moved his grocery store to the Fertile townsite upon its formal surveying. Another early business was owned by Otto Kankel, who also had flour and grist mills in Fergus Falls, Faith, and Elizabeth. He built another on Fertile's Sandhill River, one of the first institutions in a long line of community enterprises. Amongst some of these at the dawn of the 1930s were Eide's Mercantile, the Sims Brick & Tile Company, the Fertile Stock Company, the Fertile Creamery Association, a funeral home, the Pioneer Garage, a Ford service station, the Fertile Oil Company, a branch of the Standard Oil Company, a bank, and three grain elevators. At that time, there were five churches, three of which shared a four-way intersection with the school at Mill Street and Jefferson Avenue, and a large fairgrounds complex with a racetrack, auditorium, and barns operated by the Polk County Agricultural Fair Association. Since 1900, the annual Polk County Fair has been a staple of the town's culture. The Fertile Sand Hills, part of the Agassiz Dunes Scientific and Natural Area, are unlike any other geographical feature in Minnesota. They were created when the sandy deposits of the ancient glacial Lake Agassiz were left behind following its drainage into Hudson Bay.

FISHER, MN
POPULATION: 422 – CITY 332 OF 856 (6-5-25)

Located on a meander of the Red Lake River, Fisher at one time surpassed even Crookston in terms of trade and excellence. It was established in 1875 as a river village where steamboats could deliver goods. Within a few years, it was connected to major metropolitan areas like Winnipeg and Grand Forks via the Great Northern Railroad. From 1875 to 1882, its post office was known as Fisher's Landing, but it was shortened to "Fisher" in honor of William H. Fisher. He was a railroadman who held positions as an attorney, assistant manager, and superintendent for the St. Paul and Pacific Railroad; president and manager of the St. Paul & Duluth Railroad Company; and the general manager and vice president of the Duluth and Winnipeg Railroad Company. Before then, "Shirt Tail Bend" briefly served as the name for the area after a shirt that had been planted on a stick to warn steamboat traffic of an imminent bend in the river's course. After its incorporation as a village on February 9, 1881, Fisher saw its population grow to 481 people by 1890–the largest its numbers would ever be. Crookston accepted its role as the county's judicial seat. While Fisher's growth stagnated, it remained a suitable place to live and grow. Many facilities once adorned its railroad tracks, including elevators for the Fisher Company and the Farmers (as of 1930), and loading platforms or storage sheds for potatoes, sugar beets, and grain. The City Hall building, a hotel, the Knutson & Merrill Garage, and a Standard Oil station accompanied the agricultural structures. Catholic, Lutheran, and Methodist Episcopal churches stood still, proclaiming the faith. Thompson Avenue, the main thoroughfare through Fisher, was the site of the creamery, a feed mill, a bank, a meat market, two cafes, a furniture store, two hardware stores, an implement store, a barber shop, a grocery store, a drug store, two general merchandise stores, a blacksmith shop, and the Fisher Garage.

FOSSTON, MN
POPULATION: 1,434 – CITY 307 OF 856 (6-3-25)

Presently home to 1,434 Minnesotans but once inhabited by as many as 1,704 in the 1960s, Fosston began in 1876 when Charles Adair and his family arrived and claimed a homestead. Several other families followed suit, but all but nine of them were removed by the Chippewa police when eastern Polk County was closed to land claims. It took several years before the lands were reopened on July 4, 1883, to those who wanted to start anew and "prove up" on their claims. Robert Long made $500 in January 1884 when he sold part of his claim to W.J. Hilligoss, who purchased the future Fosston townsite, intending to make it a trade point between Crookston and Walker. Norman Lewis surveyed his project. Hilligoss erected a hotel and worked out a deal with Louis Foss to name the town in his honor if he agreed to move his store and post office there. Foss obliged, and thus, Fosston was given the name in place of Rosebud, the township's name. With the arrival of the Great Northern Railroad came great excitement and the development of all sorts of enterprises. Among these, the more prominent establishments included three grain elevators, four garages, four stores, two filling stations, two banks, a hotel, a hardware store, a creamery, a lumberyard, a doctor's office, a drug store, and a newspaper office. A hospital and a fire hall were located on the far eastern side of Second Street, and the public school building was around the corner heading southward. Another block in that direction was a mill, the third elevator, and a grain storage warehouse. Fairgrounds were established in the southwest corner of Fosston in the Park Addition, and five churches were conducting religious services in the northeastern quadrant of the community. All of these places existed in the early 1930s. Skipping ahead to modern times, Fosston's primary point of interest, a statue of Cordwood Pete and Tamarack, was the brainchild of longtime mayor Arvid Clementson. He wanted to boost tourism in the small city, so he concocted a fake story about Paul Bunyan's younger, much shorter brother, Cordwood Pete. Standing only 4-foot-9, Bunyan's smaller counterpart had his growth stunted when his older brother refused to share food at the table. Not growing to his brother's epic proportions, Pete begrudgingly followed Paul to Minnesota from Bangor, Maine, to make a name for himself. While logging the woods near present-day Fosston one day, he asked to borrow his brother's axe. In one fell swoop, Pete sent the axe spinning through over 100 acres of timber, all of which fell within moments of his swing. He was hired by the railroad to clear the right-of-way, and from that point onward, he and his donkey Tamarack were considered local heroes. Statues of the two characters were erected at the East Polk Heritage Center, which also consists of the historic 1887 L.W. Larson residence, a one-room log cabin, and other historic facilities. A tiny 8-by-12-foot chapel was dedicated to the city in 1975 and placed at the local wayside rest on U.S. Hwy 2. Lily Jo Hanson, a writer known for her work on Smash Cuts, Joe Goes, and current TV, and Francis Stadsvold, the head coach of the University of West Virginia men's basketball program from 1919 to 1933, hail from Fosston.

GULLY, MN
POPULATION: 59 – CITY 276 OF 856 (5-30-25)

It was the highest beach ridge of the Glacial Lake Agassiz, a.k.a. a large gully that served as the inspiration behind the name of this Soo Line Railroad community. Home to as many as 183 people in 1950 but as few as 59 in the modern day, the earliest long-term residents of Gully came around 1896, when the post office was established. A roller mill, a hotel, and a farmers' lumberyard were among the earliest Gully firms. Several others came to fruition in the years to follow. In the 1930s, Gully had a creamery, a Farmers' elevator, a hardware store, a garage, a restaurant, three general merchandise stores, a church, a school, and even a Modern Woodmen of America Hall. The M.W.A. has since evolved into a fraternal benefit society with nearly $20 billion in assets as of the 2020s. Also of note was *The Gully Advance*, a weekly community newspaper published from 1914 to 1936. Gully acquired municipal corporation status on July 16, 1924.

LENGBY, MN
POPULATION: 92 – CITY 306 OF 856 (6-2-25)
"Lindby" should have been the name of this town rather than "Lengby," but the name was distorted by the Great Northern Railroad and the local post office. A Swede named Lindahl was to be honored by the name, and the suffix '-by' meant "village" in their village. Carl Hasselton successfully acquired a post office called Columbia in 1890, which remained in operation under that name until it was renamed Lengby in 1898. Six years later, Lengby was incorporated; at its inaugural Census in 1910, it had approximately 167 residents. The population never rose above forty people beyond that initial figure. Still, the village made do with the available workforce and entrepreneurial spirit that it did have. By 1930, Lengby boasted a creamery, a lumber office, a garage, a bank, the Spring Lake Hotel, two stores, a Baptist church, the Fridhem Swedish Lutheran Church, St. Paul Lutheran Church, a schoolhouse, and an elevator. Accompanying facilities to the grain elevator were a potato warehouse, a coal shed, and a depot. In a bizarre event of luck that can truly only be described as a miracle, local 19-year-old Jean Hilliard survived a 1980 car accident that left her as stiff as a "piece of meat out of a deep freeze." After skidding off the road, she collapsed only feet from a neighbor's door after walking over two miles through the bitter cold. The hospital reported her heartbeat at only twelve beats a minute and a temperature too low to be read by a hospital-grade thermometer. Miraculously, she was revived with heating pads and nursed back to health despite being entirely unable to move for several hours. Her story was later featured on an episode of *Unsolved Mysteries*, putting Lengby and nearby Fosston in the television spotlight.

MCINTOSH, MN
POPULATION: 606 – CITY 308 OF 856 (6-3-25)
The mighty lion of McIntosh has been welcoming visitors to the town of McIntosh, population 606, since 1960. Ernie Konikson sculpted it for use by the local Lions Club in parades, but the King of the Jungle has since retired as a guard at Roholt Park and Campground. Long before the lion was prowling McIntosh's streets, settlers were looking for fruitful lands where they could raise their families. One of these men was Angus J. McIntosh, who erected a store, saloon, and hotel about one-and-a-half miles east of the modern townsite. He petitioned for a post office, and his request was granted on October 14, 1884. Later, when the Great Northern Railroad was surveying its right-of-way, McIntosh's store was overshadowed by Simon P. Johnson, Ole Lee, and Knute Austin's operation to lay out a new townsite closer to the proposed railroad line. The McIntosh post office was moved into town and retained its name, but McIntosh and his family moved to Detroit Lakes to pursue other opportunities. Losing its founder made little difference to the town's development, as by 1901 it had five grain elevators, four blocks of businesses, a fire department, an electric light plant, and a telephone office. Growth continued well into 1940, when McIntosh had 903

residents and amenities such as a hospital, a school, and five churches. The very first of these religious organizations were St. Luke's Norwegian Lutheran Church (1885), St. John's Norwegian Lutheran Church (1887), Salem Swedish Lutheran Church (1887), the New Swedish Baptist Church (1887), and a Congregationalist church. Dozens of firms were operating; a creamery, a Ford garage, a bank, and the *Times* newspaper were its highlights. Several events and economic forces have contributed to a gradual decline in McIntosh's population since its 1940 peak.

MENTOR, MN
POPULATION: 104 – CITY 310 OF 856 (6-3-25)
Located two miles north of Maple Lake and its sugar maple forest, now a popular recreational and fishing lake, Mentor was named after Mentor, Ohio, where President James A. Garfield had recently purchased a farm. The 20th President of the United States passed away on September 19, 1881, two months after being shot. His sudden death, only months into his presidency, led to naming this small Minnesota town and its 1882 post office in honor of his recent acquisition in the Buckeye State. George H. Tripp was the postmaster. Mentor was not platted until September 21, 1892, after the arrival of the Great Northern Railroad, which provided the tools needed to develop the townsite and help it attain incorporation as a village by January 1902. In the 1930s, Mentor had an elevator, three general merchandise stores, two garages, a cream station, a hotel, a school, four churches, and a designated City Park. It saw its largest population of 381 people in the 1960s.

NIELSVILLE, MN
POPULATION: 78 – CITY 335 OF 856 (6-5-25)
One of the smaller towns on the International Historic Highway 75, the "King of Trails," was settled by Nels C. Paulsrud in 1872, less than a mile and a half from the modern-day townsite. His name in Norway had been Nils Olson, so when he became the postmaster in 1883, he suggested it be called Nielsville. The Great Northern Railroad, the precursor to any major highways or roads through the town, was built straight north on its way to the Canadian border. Its facilities were mighty impressive when Brock & Company conducted a general survey of the area circa 1930. In the south were warehouses for Michael Swanson-Brady and the Kolstad Brothers, as well as stockyards. Next in line were more potato warehouses owned by the Spokelie Brothers and by Leonard, Crosset & Riley. J. Daht had a coal shed next to two large elevators, the Crookston Manufacturing Company and the Monarch Elevator. Further north still was a Standard Oil Company filling station, the St. Anthony elevator, and Olendo Danielson's potato warehouses. All these places were on the western side of the track, parallel to F. M. Peerson's Garage, the American Legion Hall, the post office building, a store, and a hotel. A community hall, a rooming house, two cafes, a telephone exchange, a meat market, a garage, a harness shop, a bank, and a general merchandise store comprised the rest of the commercial district on the west side of the tracks, but to the east was the Norwegian Lutheran church and the Nielsville School. George R. Wicker was an agricultural businessman and politician best known as the first CEO of Growmark, Inc., later known as the Illinois Farm Supply Company. The leader of the large agricultural supply cooperative was born here in March 1877.

TRAIL, MN
POPULATION: 40 – CITY 275 OF 856 (5-30-25)
Trail (population 40) has been hanging around since 1910, when it was established as one of the Soo Line Railroad's many stations. Named for its location on a trail that

formerly connected the Red Lake Indian Agency with the Red River Valley, the Trail of its prime would have looked nothing like the town does today in its current state. In the 1930s, it was a busy place. A depot and elevator were on the railroad in the northernmost part of the town, but several businesses adorned its streets. Namely, there were two lumber offices, two garages, a hardware store, a general merchandise store, a restaurant, and a feed store. A church and a school were nestled in its southeast corner. After much debate, Trail was finally incorporated as a village on April 17, 1950. The United States Postal Service opened its Trail office in 1910 but discontinued it in 2011 in favor of keeping the Gully location.

Restaurant Recommendation:
Trails End Bar & Grill
108 North Main St
Trail, MN 56684

WINGER, MN
POPULATION: 174 – CITY 271 OF 856 (5-30-25)

In 1940, Winger was in its prime. Three hundred and one people lived in the Polk County hamlet, and the Soo Line Railroad had brought all the necessary facets to make it a thriving community. Ingebret Messelt moved into the area in 1885 and established the post office in 1886, which was named Winger after a group of farms in central Norway known as the Gudbrandsdal. One of his neighboring settlers was Gullek Overland, on whose land the railroad had agreed to build its right-of-way. He sold out to the Minnesota Land and Trust Company in 1904, and a year later, a full-blown developmental project was in order. The decade leading up to the 1940s was promising. On the railroad tracks was an elevator and a pair of oil stations; the latter structures had been established to accommodate the ever-growing car population of Polk County. A hall, a garage, a bank, two creameries, and Jensen's grocery store were amongst the primary establishments of downtown Winger. There were also three churches and a school in other parts of the community. An early sculpture of a polar bear pinning down a seal, the work of artist Ernie Konikson, welcomes visitors to the busiest intersection of town, between U.S. Highway 59 and County Highway 1.

Unincorporated/Ghost Towns: Benoit, Cisco, Dugdale, Euclid, Greenview, Maple Bay, Olga, Sherack, Tabor

National Register of Historic Places:
Crookston: Cathedral of the Immaculate Conception, Crookston Carnegie Public Library, Crookston Commercial Historic District, E. C. Davis House
East Grand Forks: Hamm Brewing Company Beer Depot
Gentilly Township: Church of St. Peter-Catholic

Golf Courses:
Fosston Golf Club, Municipal (Fosston, MN)
Minakwa Golf Course, Daily Fee (Crookston, MN)
Sandhill River Golf Course, Daily Fee (Fertile, MN)
Valley Golf Course, Daily Fee (East Grand Forks, MN)

Breweries/Wineries/Distilleries:
Grape Mill Vineyard and Winery (East Grand Forks, MN)

Town Celebrations:
Crookston Ox Cart Days, Crookston, MN (3rd Week of August)

Otter Tail County: Prospect House and Civil War Museum (Battle Lake), Fergus Falls Historic State [Kirkbride Plan] Hospital (Fergus Falls), Otto the Otter at Grotto Park (Fergus Falls), World's Largest Pelican (Pelican Rapids), Maplewood State Park (Pelican Rapids), World's Largest Prairie Chicken (Rothsay), World's Second Largest Loon (Vergas), The Big Foot at Nyberg Sculpture Park (Vining)

Pennington County: Woodrow School and Museum (Goodridge), Threshing Machine (Goodrige), Veteran's Memorial Murals (Goodrige), Red Lake River at St. Hilaire City Park (St. Hilaire), Paul Bunyan Statue (St. Hilaire), Mural (Thief River Falls), former Soo Line Railroad Depot (Thief River Falls), former Viking Great Northern Railroad Depot at Engelstad Pioneer Village (Thief River Falls)

Pine County: Bethlehem Lutheran Church (Askov), Interior of Danforth Schoolhouse at the Pine County Historical Society (Askov), Mural at Hinckley Fire Museum (Hinckley), The Great Hinckley Fire State Monument (Hinckley), Mural at American Legion Post (Pine City), Sauser's Hardware Store (Pine City), former Sandstone High School (Sandstone), Phillips 66 Gas Station (Willow River)

Pipestone County: Authentic Dutch Windmill (Edgerton), former Holland Post Office (Holland), Split Rock Creek State Park (Ihlen), Pipestone County Courthouse (Pipestone), World's Largest Peace Pipe (Pipestone), Winnewissa Falls at Pipestone National Monument (Pipestone), Mural (Ruthton), Countryside Barn (Woodstock)

Polk County: Old Cathedral of the Immaculate Conception (Crookston), Blue Moose Bar & Grill (East Grand Forks), "Indian Lady with Papoose" Statue & former Win-E-Mac Motel (Erskine), World's Largest Northern Erskine (Erskine), Mural (Fosston), Cordwood Pete and Tamarack at the East Polk Heritage Center (Fosston), Lion at Roholt Park (McIntosh), former Catholic Church (Winger)

POPE COUNTY
EST. 1862 - POPULATION: 11,308

John Pope, a United States Army general who served during the Dakota War of 1862 and the American Civil War, is the namesake of this county organized in 1866.

CYRUS, MN
POPULATION: 305 – CITY 158 OF 856 (4-13-25)
First laid out as Scandiaville in Pope County's far western New Prairie township by O. H. Dahl and Charles Olson, this town's name was later changed to Cyrus to match the post office. M. Frank Cronquist was its initial postmaster and the first storeowner on the townsite; he named the office following Olson's suggestion. From its founding in the spring of 1882 through its peak population of 386 people in the 1930s, the Northern Pacific Railroad town saw the opening and closure of many businesses. According to a 1910 plat map, significant city attractions and sites included roller mills, a bank, a livery, a school, and two churches. Cyrus was incorporated in March 1899.

FARWELL, MN
POPULATION: 56 – CITY 168 OF 856 (4-14-25)
Started in April 1887 with the arrival of the Minneapolis and Pacific Railway, this future Soo Line community was the brainchild of members of the railroad company who were strategically plotting their stations at intermediate points along the line. William D. Washburn, Peter M. Dahl, Charles D. Hammond, and Frederick D. Underwood were responsible for locating and naming most of the towns on this line. In particular, Mr. Washburn, William Max, and Charles A. Dahlen platted the townsite. There are three accounts of how the small city came to its present name. The first and most likely rendition states that it was named after Washburn's friend and U.S. Congressman Charles B. Farwell of Illinois. The second suggests that it was derived from the Norwegian word *farvsi*, meaning "farewell," an exclamation potentially given by the man in the third account who reportedly stormed out of the meeting room when the railroad men could not agree on a proper name. With its name given, a post office was established, and Ole Irgens was appointed postmaster. He opened the first store in 1890 with Jacob Jacobson, the first of many lines of enterprise in a town that would later boast a depot, a bank, a lumber yard, a hotel, a restaurant, a 1907 Norwegian church, and nearby country schoolhouses. A historic 1886 schoolhouse and the church have been preserved with the help of Ted Irgens and local artist Gloria.

GLENWOOD, MN ★☆
POPULATION: 2,657 – CITY 155 OF 856 (4-13-25)
Glenwood, descriptively named for its positioning within a deep glen (valley) and its abundance of trees, came into existence in September 1866, when Kirk J. Kinney and Alfred W. Lathrop platted the townsite on Kinney's land. The two men established a store together, out of which Lathrop would base his mail operations when he was named postmaster. When the Pope County commissioners saw that the townsite might grow rapidly and become a trade center for their jurisdiction's settlers, they moved the county seat from Stockholm, now unincorporated, to here. Their assumptions were correct: in 1882, the Little Falls branch of the Northern Pacific Railroad arrived, and four years later, the Soo Line. The two lines met, and the Soo took such a liking to Glenwood that they opted to build a branch line. One line went northwest towards Elbow Lake, and the other went north to Alexandria. At its first U.S.

Census in 1890, there were 627 residents; by 1900, 1,116; and by 1910, 2,161. The growth warranted Glenwood's incorporation as a city in 1912, at a time when it had bottling works, four feed and/or livery barns, three hotels, a printing office, a bank, a hardware store, several dozens more stores, a library, a courthouse, a jail, a public school, five churches, the John Gund Brewing Company, the Hamm Brewing Company, county fairgrounds, an Academy Block, and depots for both railroads. Waterworks were in place relatively early, when some townspeople found a spring nearly 200 feet above the townsite, which provided sufficient water pressure to send water through the pipes of many households and seven fire hydrants. Glenwood's 1930 Beaux-Arts Pope County Courthouse; its 1908 Carnegie library; the 1893/1919 Fremad Association Building and its adjacent 1908 Pope County State Bank; the once-popular Sunset Beach Hotel on the southern shore of Lake Minnewaska, and the home of renowned civic leader Ann Bickle are among the town's five most historic locations. They are all listed on the National Register of Historic Places. The recreational haven also sports multiple resorts and campgrounds, golf courses, and opportunities to bike, camp, hunt, fish, and ski. Since 1956, an annual festival called Waterama, held on the last full weekend of July, has paid tribute to Glenwood's watersports scene with boat races, waterski shows, and events for landlubbers, such as parades, craft shows, and sporting events. At the inaugural event, organizers expected a turnout of 5,000 to 10,000 attendees but ended up welcoming over 23,000. Two noted Glenwood residents were Cindy Rarick, a five-time winner on the LPGA Tour, and Ernest O. Wollan, a physician known for his work in health physics and neutron scattering.

Restaurant Recommendation:
Lakeside
180 S Lake Shore Dr North
Glenwood, MN 56334

LONG BEACH, MN
POPULATION: 338 – CITY 156 OF 856 (4-13-25)
Long Beach, the closest municipality to the Minnewaska Golf Club and the Minnewaska Area High School, was incorporated as an independent village on May 18, 1938. The Glenwood suburb lies directly west of the Pope County seat on the northwest shores of Lake Minnewaska. Although it has no post office and little commercial history, the town is best known for its tiny church at Morning Glory Gardens. It was designed to look like a full-scale church. Kaldahl's Long Beach Store, known for selling groceries, meats, and gas to recreationists, is one of its most remembered businesses. As of the 2020 Census, Long Beach recorded its highest population ever: 338. Long Beach is the closest town geographically to Minnewaska Area High School and Minnewaska Golf Club.

LOWRY, MN
POPULATION: 334 – CITY 169 OF 856 (4-14-25)
It could be said that this town's heyday began as early as its establishment, as it was founded as the western terminus of the Minneapolis, St. Paul & Sault Ste. Marie Railroad. A roundhouse and a machine shop were erected. Eventually, Ben Wade– the original name for the community–was destined to become a division point for the line. On the former farms of Hugh Bryce and Thomas Hume, a townsite was platted in 1887 by W. D. Washburn and the latter two gentlemen under the name of Lowry when the railroad arrived. Its name was changed to Lowry in honor of Thomas Lowry, and

John E. Benson became the postmaster of the branch. By 1910, Lowry's residents had established a milling company, Lowry State Bank, a general store, a drug store, a hardware store, a community hall, a depot, a school, and two churches, highlighting the early accomplishments of Lowry's residents. Other accounts allude to John J. Hagstrom's implement dealership, William McIver's general mercantile, and James Simpson's cooperative creamery as staples of the railroad town. A tornado in 1897 (which destroyed the lumber yard, elevator, and depot) and a November 1911 fire (which destroyed the implement store, the mercantile, and the drug store) left the west side of Lowry's main street as wood structures, and the east side as brick. The 1902 Lowry Public School was listed on the National Register of Historic Places on April 1, 1982, but was removed after it was demolished in 1992.

SEDAN, MN
POPULATION: 43 – CITY 172 OF 856 (4-14-25)

W. D. Washburn, alongside Sylvester and Orrin Kipp, laid out Thorson village in May 1887 on the Minneapolis & Pacific Railway. It was almost immediately renamed Fowlds after the early settler Jim Fowlds. Five years later, it was renamed Sedan after the city in France of the same name, where the French and Germans fought each other on September 1-2, 1870. The capture of Emperor Napoleon III at the battle led to the establishment of the French Republic. In 1892, the Fowlds post office, then managed by Charles A. Warner, came under the direction and leadership of John H. Warner at his general store. A blacksmith shop and a railroad depot accompanied his store by 1910, as did a school and two churches. The post office survived until 1996 when it closed due to a decrease in population over the previous four decades. Sedan's largest decrease occurred between 1960 and 1970, when it lost 39.6% of its people in a decade (from 91 to just 55). Visitors may notice the "toaster tree" at 355 Marsh St. within Sedan city limits. The Urjans Iverson House is outside of town. The historic log cabin was built in 1866 and has since been restored and preserved at Fort Lake Johanna Roadside Park.

STARBUCK, MN
POPULATION: 1,365 – CITY 157 OF 856 (4-13-25)

One thing's for sure: Starbuck, Minnesota, was not named for coffee. However, there are at least five conflicting accounts about how it garnered its name. It may have been named for Sidney Starbuck, a Little Falls & Dakota Railroad director who secretly worked with the Northern Pacific Railroad to reach this part of Minnesota and secure a mail office before the Great Northern arrived. Alternatively, it could have been named after William H. Starbuck, who financed Little Falls & Dakota and had other towns in Washington State and Manitoba, Canada, named in his honor. Three different stories still suggest that it may have been derived from the surname "Sagbaken," which was that of an early settler, that it was named for Andrew Hagenson's oxen "Star" and "Buck," who assisted in hauling materials for a railroad bridge, or that its name was given for Stabekk, a residential area near Oslo, Norway. No matter where its name came from, Starbuck was born out of necessity and planted on the western shore of Lake Minnewaska by James D. Poler and Mr. Hagenson in May 1882. The highly covered postal service branch was opened later that year, although an earlier office, White Bear Centre, had existed in the township since 1869. Nels B. Wollan, then postmaster of the White Bear Centre office, became the new Starbuck postmaster upon that office's completion. He moved his store as well. By 1890, there were approximately 224 residents in town, which doubled by 1910. Starbuck then had two banks, a First National and a Security State Bank, a depot, a public school, and plentiful businesses. The business district has evolved as the population has continued to set new record highs every other decade, with the most recent high of 1,365 people in 2020. Recreationists, roadside attraction enthusiasts, and history buffs each have an attraction in Starbuck worth touring. Glacial Lakes State Park, located approximately five miles south of the townsite, was established in 1963 as a 2,423-acre rolling prairie preserve and park for cross-country skiers, snowmobilers, anglers, boaters, and swimmers. Within the town, a hobo pays homage to the early history of rail riders who once used the city as a gathering place to find work. For history buffs, the Little Falls and Dakota Depot remains the only National Register of Historic Places location in town; every year, it is the site of the annual Lefse Dagen festival. The festival has been held since 1987 as a commemorative event to recall the July 1, 1983, centennial celebration, where residents cooked up the World's Largest Lefse, a 9-foot, 8-inch, 70-pound monstrosity, on the depot's grounds. Lefse is a traditional soft Norwegian flatbread typically served with cinnamon, lingonberries, brown sugar, or gomme. Until January 2013, Starbuck had also retained the Minnewaska Hospital building, a clinic built at the turn of the 20th century that, for many years, claimed to be the only hospital between Fargo, North Dakota, and Minneapolis, Minnesota, at the time of its construction between 1899 and 1900.

VILLARD, MN
POPULATION: 225 – CITY 170 OF 856 (4-14-25)
The population of Villard has varied very minimally since its first Census in 1890, when approximately 203 people were recorded as living there. Since then, the number has changed, but the little town on the eastern shore of Lake Villard has never reported a population lower than that or higher than its 1920 peak of 308. It was strategically laid out by John and Calista Williams and surveyed by Charles C. Hinds in August 1882 on behalf of the Northern Pacific Railroad. At that time, its president was Henry Villard, who oversaw the completion of its transcontinental line in 1883. After Villard's incorporation as a village on October 4, 1883, more permanent infrastructure was built. Near its peak, Villard had Catholic, Methodist-Episcopalian, and Adventist churches, a public school, a post office, a bank, and a lumberyard, among other locations. The Villard depot, built in 1882 when the Little Falls and Dakota branch was constructed from Little Falls to Morris, Minnesota, now serves as the eastern terminus of the Villard-Starbuck rail trail. A unique home known as the Daniel Pennie House, located two miles north of Villard, dates to the 1870s or 1880s. It is distinctive for its rare fieldstone-and-grout construction style. On the opposite side of Lake Villard, "Pottyville" encourages bathroom lovers to behold its collection of outhouses.

WESTPORT, MN
POPULATION: 44 – CITY 171 OF 856 (4-14-25)
Now home to less than four dozen people as of the 2020 Census, the first attempts at platting the townsite came in 1866 at the hand (or perhaps quill) of D. M. Durkey. He chose a spot on the Red River trail to build a way station and cabin and advocated for its settlement, but was unsuccessful. His dreams only came to fruition sixteen years later, in October 1882, when the Little Falls and Dakota Railroad crews were racing (so they could beat the Great Northern Railroad) through the area to lay their tracks. Crawford Livingston platted the new site. It was called Belcher from roughly 1883 to 1888, before its name was changed to Westport, an eponym for communities in several other states. The depot, a school, and a post office were among its earliest features, but the post office was discontinued in 1966. Westport boasted a peak population of 102 people per the 1940 Census.

Brooten is only partially located in Pope County (see Stearns County).

Unincorporated/Ghost Towns: Grove Lake, New Prairie, Terrace

National Register of Historic Places:
Glenwood: Ann Bickle House, Fremad Association Building, Glenwood Public Library, Pope County Courthouse, Sunset Beach Hotel
Sedan: Urjans Iverson House
Starbuck: Little Falls & Dakota Depot
Terrace: Terrace Historic District, Terrace Mill Historic District
Villard: Northern Pacific Depot, Daniel Pennie House

Golf Courses:
Minnewaska Golf Club, Daily Fee (Glenwood, MN)

Breweries/Wineries/Distilleries:
Rolling Forks Vineyards (Glenwood, MN)

Town Celebrations:
Cyrus Days, Cyrus, MN (1st Full Weekend in June)
Glenwood Waterama, Glenwood, MN (Last Full Weekend in July)
Heritage Days, Starbuck, MN (1st Weekend of July)
Lefse Dagen Celebration, Starbuck, MN (3rd Saturday in May)

RAMSEY COUNTY
EST. 1849 - POPULATION: 552,352

The first Territorial Governor of Minnesota, Alexander Ramsey, had this county named for his honor when it was created in 1849, using the remnants of St. Croix County, Wisconsin Territory.

ARDEN HILLS, MN
POPULATION: 9,939 – CITY 800 OF 856 (11-9-25)
Land O'Lakes, one of the largest agricultural cooperatives in the country with over 2,500 member-owners and 300,000 dairying producers, was founded in Saint Paul but is headquartered in Arden Hills. Incorporated on February 14, 1951, from lands once comprising Mounds View Township, the city's name was taken from Senator Joseph Hackney's hobby farm: Arden Farms. Eventually, it was broken up and the lands were distributed for alternate use, like in 1941, when the United States government turned 2,530 acres of local farmland into the Twin Cities Army Ammunition Plant. At its peak, its employee numbers tallied 26,000, who worked around the clock to provide the men across the sea with over 4 billion rounds of ammunition. The plant closed at the end of the war, but many people remained. One thousand seven hundred eighty-five acres were set aside for use by the Minnesota Army National Guard and the Army Reserve as a training facility. The remaining land was privatized or turned into public park space. Incorporation was awarded when New Brighton attempted to annex the area for its own usage. Boston Scientific, a biomedical engineering and biotechnology firm traded on the S&P 500, is another large employer in the region, alongside Land O'Lakes. Bethel University, founded in 1871 as the Baptist Union Theological Seminary, and known as Bethel College and Seminary from 1947 to 2004, is located here. Great excitement came to Arden Hills in May 2011 when the Minnesota Vikings and Ramsey County tentatively agreed to build a new stadium atop the former Twin Cities Army Ammunition Plant. The $884 million stadium was set to be jointly funded by the Minnesota Vikings, Ramsey County taxpayers, and general Minnesota taxpayers, about a third each. When it was estimated that fixing roads leading to the

proposed stadium and other infrastructure costs would tack on an additional $350-400 million, Governor Mark Dayton announced that the stadium would instead be built on top of the Metrodome in Minneapolis.

Restaurant Recommendation:
Siam Thai Asian Cuisine
3547 Lexington Ave N
Arden Hills, MN 55126

FALCON HEIGHTS, MN
POPULATION: 5,369 – CITY 810 OF 856 (11-10-25)

A little over five thousand people call Falcon Heights their home at any given time, but come late August, the population of this hamlet grows by the millions during "The Great Minnesota Get-Together." The largest state fair in the United States by daily attendance runs for 12 days leading up to Labor Day and invites event-goers to eat unique fair foods, exhibit art and livestock, and enjoy carnival rides and other entertainment. Rochester, Owatonna, Winona, and the Twin Cities held many of the state's initial State Fairs. On September 7, 1885, the permanent exhibition was chosen to take place on the site of the Ramsey County Poor Farm. While Fairchild, the State Fair Gopher, and the 25-foot-tall pioneer woman greet millions of visitors to the grounds, the City of Falcon Heights itself is much more tame. Stephen Desnoyer was the first to settle in the vicinity near the Mississippi River, but men like Isaac Rose and Heman Gibbs followed shortly thereafter. Gibbs' farm, established in 1859 and home to a 1854 farmhouse and 1910 town, is now listed on the National Register of Historic Places and known as the Gibbs Museum of Pioneer and Dakotah Life. In 1947, a two-building office complex was built for use as the Farmers Union Grain Terminal Association Headquarters, featuring Moderne architectural elements; it, too, was listed on the Register for its historic significance to the area. After parts of Rose Township were incorporated or annexed by larger municipalities such as St. Paul and Roseville, Falcon Heights residents opted to incorporate on April 1, 1949. The State Fairgrounds, the University of Minnesota Campus Golf Course, and the testing fields for the University of Minnesota's St. Paul (a public land-grant research university) make up over two-thirds of the 2.24 square miles of Falcon Heights. Since 1960, its population has never been reported as fewer than 5,291 in the 1980s or more than 5,927 in the 1960s. Parts of the 1996 family comedy film *Jingle All the Way* and the 2001 teen film *Sugar & Spice* were filmed here

GEM LAKE, MN
POPULATION: 528 – CITY 798 OF 856 (11-9-25)

On June 30, 1959, this parcel of White Bear Township joined Vadnais Heights in becoming the second municipality to be partitioned from the township and to become an independent city. Named after its shallow, spring-fed lake known for its extensive wetlands, some of the first Europeans in this area were the Bemis, Bigelow, Daniels, and White families. Many of these early families engaged in outdoor activities offered by the then-vast wilderness, including horseback riding and fox hunting. As more people arrived, the land was tilled for agricultural use, and these activities subsided as Gem Lake took shape as one of the Twin Cities' smaller suburban cities. An early line of the Northern Pacific Railroad extended through city limits, connecting White Bear Lake with Saint Paul.

LAUDERDALE, MN
POPULATION: 2,271 – CITY 811 OF 856 (11-10-25)
Bordering both Minneapolis and St. Paul is a tiny 0.42-square-mile city called Lauderdale, named in honor of William Henry Lauderdale. Mr. Lauderdale was honored for his philanthropic outlook and for donating land to Rose Hill Township for a school and park. Also, once part of Rose Township, like many other communities in Ramsey County, the town was incorporated on January 21, 1949, to avoid annexation by a larger city. Portions of Luther Seminary, the largest seminary of the Evangelical Lutheran Church in America, extend into city limits. It was founded in 1869.

LITTLE CANADA, MN
POPULATION: 10,819 – CITY 796 OF 856 (11-9-25)
Named for its early large French-Canadian population, Little Canada (also known as New Canada township when it was organized in May 1858) was originally home to the Mdewakanton Dakota from Little Crow's Village. In 1844, Benjamin Gervais became the first man of European descent to make a land claim here; the city's Lake Gervais was named after him. He built the first grist mill in Minnesota that was wholly independent from the government. By the end of the 1850s, the 1852 Catholic Church of St. John the Evangelist had been erected, and its adjacent cemetery had been formally organized as the second such organization in all of Minnesota. To protect its identity, the village of Little Canada was incorporated in 1953 to prevent annexation by larger neighbors, primarily Maplewood. The 4.49-square-mile community became sister cities with Thunder Bay, Ontario, now home to over 100,000 residents. Both towns host an annual Canadian Days celebration in early August. Sunisa Lee, a two-time Olympic gold medalist in the 2020 all-around event and the 2024 team event, trained in Little Canada at the Midwest Gymnastics Event.

MAPLEWOOD, MN ☆
POPULATION: 42,088 – CITY 794 OF 856 (11-9-25)
Over 12,000 employees of The 3M Company, originally the Minnesota Mining and Manufacturing Company, contribute to Minneapolis/St. Paul's morning rush hour traffic as they make their way towards the corporate headquarters and main campus of the Fortune 500 Company. The conglomerate produces over 60,000 products ranging from Scotch Tape and Post-it Notes to personal protective equipment and Nexcare adhesive bandages. While these thousands of people make up a considerable percentage of Maplewood's economy and local population, Maplewood, like all other towns, had its humble beginnings. In the 1850s, the Bell, Casey, Conlin, and Vincent families arrived to build up their homes, as did Thomas Carver, whose surname has been commemorated by another nearby county and community. After two decades of improvements, the Lake Superior and Mississippi Railroad (which became part of the Northern Pacific line in 1900) was built through, enhancing trade prospects. In the mid-1880s, Lake Phalen Junction was created when the Wisconsin Central Railroad was built east-west. A formally named settlement called Gladstone took root here, named in honor of the British statesman William Gladstone, and soon St. Paul Plow Works and the St. Paul & Duluth Railroad shops were relocated here. Things were looking pretty good for the locals, but tragedy unfolded shortly thereafter when a fire destroyed the plow works in 1892, forcing its eventual bankruptcy. In 1917, the railroad shops closed, taking with them the bulk of Gladstone's workforce. The surrounding general area up to this time was known as New Canada Township, which was ultimately divided into parts of North St. Paul, St. Paul proper, and Little Canada. The rest of the township was incorporated into Maplewood in 1957, a name suggested by Waldo

Luebben. This decision to incorporate was made to avoid annexation by Saint Paul and to allow 3M to operate on a smaller, village tax base after they had completed their central research laboratory. Warren Berger traced a maple leaf that had fallen in his backyard to serve as the city's official logo. In 1974, the 931,000-square-foot Maplewood Mall opened its doors for the first time. Two women who played in the National Women's Hockey League (later the Premier Hockey Federation), Audra Morrison and Allie Thunstrom, hail from the city.

Restaurant Recommendation:
5-8 Tavern & Grill
2289 Minnehaha Ave E
Maplewood, MN 55119

MOUNDS VIEW, MN
POPULATION: 13,249 – CITY 807 OF 856 (11-10-25)
Mounds View Township began on May 11, 1858, the same day that Minnesota became a state. In search of a better life, many settlers, including H. C. Fridley, Olive Lee, E. F. Lambert, and dozens of others, came to till the land and establish farmsteads here. The occasional trading point, one-room schoolhouses, and even an early post office (est. 1858) could be found throughout the township. It remained primarily rural until the late 1930s, when it began to suburbanize. Several parts of it were divided into communities, such as Arden Hills, whose growth was mainly driven by the creation of the Twin Cities Army Ammunition Plant. In an effort to save the remainder of the township, Mounds View Township was converted into the Village of Mounds View when residents voted 593 to 452 in favor of incorporation. In the mid-1980s, Mounds View was best known for being home to the final Totino's Pizza restaurant, which was then one of the top-selling frozen pizzas in the country at local grocery stores. Its founders and owners, Rose and James Totino, sold their business to Pillsbury for $22 million. Noted firms within city limits in the modern day include Sysco Distributing, a food product and equipment seller and distributor, and Mermaid Entertainment & Event, locally famous for their iconic 38-foot-tall mermaid statue. Amanda Lee, the first female fighter jet pilot to fly with the U.S. Navy Blue Angels Flight Demonstration Squadron, was born here circa 1986.

NEW BRIGHTON, MN
POPULATION: 23,454 – CITY 808 OF 856 (11-10-25)
Accounts differ on who the first settlers in Mounds View Township were, but in New Brighton, the honor is generally attributed to Charles Perry. He purchased 89 acres of land on Lake Johanna in 1849, making him the first in a long line of settlers who called this northern part of the Twin Cities metropolitan area home. Unique to New Brighton (named after Brighton, Massachusetts) in its pioneering days was its cattle industry, as the community long served as a hub for livestock trading. Stockyards were built early on, and the meatpacking business began when the Twin City Packing Company opened here in October 1889. On Independence Day 1892, the Minneapolis Stock Yards and Packing Company was organized in New Brighton, only about a year after the Village of New Brighton was incorporated. Many wealthy entrepreneurs, such as John Sargent Pillsbury, William D. Washburn, and Thomas Lowry, held a stake in the firm. Schools and churches were erected, as were a myriad of businesses, such as blacksmiths, general stores, and liveries, that served the everyday needs of New Brighton residents. From 1889 to 1950, the post office operated independently before converting into a branch office. Visitors to the New Brighton Area Historical Society

can admire a restored Great Northern Railway depot and caboose. The depot, now located in Long Lake Park, was located on the Minnesota Transfer line that connected the Great Northern, the Northern Pacific, and the Soo Lines. Another local point of interest is the Ingeborg and Peder Foss House, a 1896 Victorian home listed on the National Register of Historic Places.

Restaurant Recommendation:
Pho 400
400 Old Hwy 8 NW
New Brighton, MN 55112

NORTH OAKS, MN
POPULATION: 5,272 – CITY 799 OF 856 (11-9-25)

While North Oaks is now a private community managed entirely by homeowners within the North Oaks Home Owners Association, even this gated community has worked to preserve important early facets of its history. Between 1876 and 1880, Charles D. Gilfillan (noted for his namesake estate in Redwood County) purchased over three thousand acres of land in this vicinity with the intention of preserving the lakes that provided St. Paul with freshwater. By 1883, he had sold this land to the railroad mogul James J. Hill for $50,000, who converted it into one of the largest agricultural experimental farms in the United States. It started as a stock farm that sought to breed a hybrid beef-and-dairy cow superior to any other such variation of the animal. The dairying efforts were futile, but the Angus beef was considered among the best available at the time. Hill also built up the property as his country estate and spent thousands of dollars from his personal fortune to keep it pristine. Over forty buildings were erected as a part of the joint farm-estate, but only three remain today: the granary, the blacksmith shop/engine house, and the creamery, now listed on the National Register of Historic Places as James J. Hill's North Oaks Farm, Dairy Building. Louis W. Hill Jr., the great-grandson of James, purchased additional acreage throughout the 1940s and was responsible for developing the plan to convert North Oaks Farm into a private residential community complete with a beach, parkland, and an 18-hole golf course, now known as North Oaks Golf Club. The community had genuine gates for many years, restricting access to outsiders. The aforementioned homeowner's association is responsible for providing services to all residents, as the City of North Oaks itself owns no property; each homeowner's property extends halfway into the middle of the street. Any visitors to the community must be accompanied by a resident, unless visiting the business complex in the southwest corner of town. A few notable individuals with ties to North Oaks include Joe Alt, an offensive tackle with the NFL's Los Angeles Chargers; Paul Moga, a United States Air Force Major General and the host of programs on the American Heroes Channel; and John William Vessey Jr., the tenth chairman of the Joint Chiefs of Staff and a general within the United States Army.

NORTH ST. PAUL, MN
POPULATION: 12,364 – CITY 795 OF 856 (11-9-25)

North Saint Paul was first called Castle in honor of Henry Anson Castle, who arrived in St. Paul in 1868. At only twenty-seven years old, Castle made his mark on Minnesota by serving in the state legislature and founding the St. Paul Dispatch. Knowing that the city would ultimately need to expand outwards, he invested in 520 acres of farmland to the northeast of the state capital. The Wisconsin Central Railroad was extended to that point in 1885, and within two years, the City of North St. Paul was incorporated. By the end of 1888, there were about two dozen retail business lines, a dozen factories, six churches of differing denominations, and a proud brick schoolhouse. One of these places was Neumann's Bar, the oldest continuously operating bar in Minnesota, founded in 1887. Faux-beer products were sold in the bar during Prohibition, and a speakeasy quietly operated in its upstairs quarters. A post office has operated continuously under the North Saint Paul branding since that time, although it underwent reorganization in 1936. Its most significant single-decade increase in population came between 1950 and 1960, when it grew by 100.6% from 4,248 citizens to 8,520. In downtown, visitors may stumble across the 44-foot-tall, 20-ton concrete "World's Largest Stucco Snowman" statue, built in 1974.

ROSEVILLE, MN
POPULATION: 36,254 – CITY 809 OF 856 (11-10-25)

Roseville, Lauderdale, and Falcon Heights once comprised the now-defunct Rose Township, which was established in the 1850s. Named for Isaac Rose, who arrived here in 1843 when he purchased 170 acres of land, some of which was used to erect Macalester College, the "Roseville" settlement has long been documented on Ramsey County maps. Jacob F. True's farmstead was the site of this little farming community, which was platted in a strange parallelogram formation, which offset many future street and neighborhood developments. Roseville's first post office opened in 1857, although it briefly forfeited the name from 1867 to 1887 to a different Roseville office in Kandiyohi County. Until the 1930s, Roseville was primarily farmland, until the arrival of the Northern Pacific Railroad and land developers forced it to restructure itself into an incorporated village in May 1948. Lots of "firsts" for famous corporate and retail chains came to Roseville in the years to follow, including the first McDonald's in Minnesota in 1957, Minnesota's first Dairy Queen, and the first Target store, which opened on May 3, 1962, before being torn down and replaced by a SuperTarget in 2005. Several regional shopping malls, including Rosedale Center and Har Har Mall, have been built in the suburb, and the city also claims to have the "highest number of restaurants per capita" in the metropolitan area. Old Dutch Foods, known for tortilla and potato chips; the Minnesota State Lottery; and Fantasy Flight Games, formerly one of the largest board game businesses in the world, are all headquartered here. In 1993, the Guidant John Rose Minnesota Oval was completed as the largest artificial outdoor skating surface in North America. The only locality on the National Register is the Roselawn Chapel and Administration Building, which serves as a boujee Gothic and Elizabethan Revival entrance to a 1904 cemetery. A few noteworthy residents with ties to Roseville include Peter Krause, best known for his rose as Nate Fisher on HBO's drama series *Six Feet Under*; Mike Muscala, an NBA player from 2014 to 2024; Loni Anderson, the actress who played the receptionist in CBS's sitcom *WKRP in Cincinnati*, and Joey Anderson, an ice hockey forward in the NHL since 2018.

SAINT PAUL, MN ★
POPULATION: 311,527 – CITY 856 OF 856 (11-9-25)

Whereas Minneapolis is known for its milling history, Minnesota's capital city, Saint Paul, is closely associated with the establishment of Fort Snelling and the steamboat trade. The central military and administrative headquarters of the region was built from 1819 to 1825 upon mighty bluffs overlooking the confluence of the Minnesota and Mississippi Rivers. It was called Fort Saint Anthony before being renamed Snelling in honor of Colonel Josiah Snelling, who oversaw its completion. Settling on the grounds of the fort was banned, so traders opted to make their claims and establish their livelihoods downriver. One of these early men was Pierre "Pig's Eye" Parrant, a French

Canadian who arrived in the area in 1838 and opened a tavern. It was called "Pig's Eye Landing" by visitors. Three years later, Father Lucien Galtier of France built Saint Paul's Chapel and decided to rename the region after the church. On November 1, 1849, it was formally organized as a village and declared to be the Minnesota Territorial Capital at that time. That honor was almost lost to Saint Peter in Nicollet County. Territorial legislator Joe Rolette hid the bill for just long enough that the legislative period was over before such a move could be made. Holding onto its title allowed the city to become the principal center of industry for the Upper Mississippi Valley. Within no time, over 1,000 steamboats were moving through Saint Paul annually. Docking stations, warehouses, and endless numbers of riverfront businesses lined the waterways before multiple railroad lines worked their way into the community. At one point, Saint Paul was simultaneously serving the Great Northern, the Northern Pacific, the Chicago, Burlington & Quincy, the Chicago Great Western, the Chicago, St. Paul, Minneapolis & Omaha, and the Minneapolis, St. Paul & Sault Ste. Marie lines. In 1850, the population was only about 1,112, but by the time the 20th century arrived, the city had grown to 163,065. Gaining such a large population in such a short period enabled significant advances in technology and infrastructure, many of which are still evident throughout the community today. One hundred twenty places have been assigned to the National Register of Historic Places for their historical significance, including the Cathedral of Saint Paul, the sixth-largest church in the United States, built in 1915; the Old Federal Courts Building, built in 1901 in the Richardsonian Romanesque/Châteausque style now used as the Landmark Center; Mickey's Diner, a 1939 classic Streamline Moderne diner that still serves food to this day; the 1889 mansion of James J. Hill; the 1928 Highland Park Tower; the 1883 University Hall-Old Main at Hamline University and the 1888 Old Main building at Macalester College, and the Minnesota State Capitol building. This third rendition was completed in 1905, using the Beaux-Arts/American Renaissance blueprints furnished by Cass Gilbert. Fort Snelling State Park, Fort Snelling National Cemetery, and the Capitol and Cathedral buildings highlight the major historic tourism attractions, but other places of interest are the Science Museum of Minnesota, Como Park Zoo & Conservatory (both of which are free, although an amusement park and carousel are also on the grounds), the Wabasha Street Caves (the site of former mobster hideouts and speakeasies) the Minnesota History Center, the Minnesota Transportation Museum, and Grand Casino Arena. The latter entertainment is host to one of the city's two professional sports franchises, the Minnesota Wild of the National Hockey League. Minnesota United FC, the Major League Soccer club for Minneapolis-St. Paul plays its home games at Allianz Field. Many hundreds of famous personalities (including some affiliated with Minneapolis) have called Saint Paul home over the decades, including Francis Scott Key Fitzgerald, best known for his novel *The Great Gatsby*; Josh Hartnett, an actor most recently hailed for his role as Ernest Lawrence in the 2023 biological thriller film *Oppenheimer*; Paul Molitor, a seven-time MLB All-Star and the 1993 World Series Most Valuable Player; Louie Anderson, a stand-up comedian who gained national recognition as the host of Family Feud from 1999 to 2002; Chad Smith, a drummer with the Red Hot Chili Peppers since 1977; George Papandreou, the Prime Minister of Greece from October 2009 to November 2011, and Lindsey Vonn, one of the greatest alpine skiers of all time, noted for her 82 gold medals in World Cup races (mainly in the Downhill and Super-G events).

Restaurant Recommendation:
Mickey's Diner
36 7th St W
St. Paul, MN 55102

 Restaurant Recommendation:
The St. Paul Grill
350 N Market St
St. Paul, MN 55102

Lodging Recommendation:
The Covington Inn
100 Harriet Island Rd
St. Paul, MN 55107

SHOREVIEW, MN
POPULATION: 26,921 – CITY 801 OF 856 (11-10-25)
Three athletes—Sam Hentges, a pitcher with the MLB's Cleveland Guardians from 2021 to 2024; Jesper Horsted, a tight end in the NFL from 2019 to 2024, and Kyra Condie, a 2020 Summer Olympics rock climber—headline some of the more famous residents to come out of Shoreview, population 26,921 as of the 2020 Census. Socrates A. Thompson wandered this area in 1850 in search of good farmland and, after finding success, encouraged others to do the same. Mounds View Township was organized in 1858, and in the 1880s, lines of the Minneapolis, St. Paul & Sault Ste. Marie Railroad began to appear in the area. Named on account of its seven lakes, Shoreview, which also now boasts nine parks, was once visited by Mark Twain. In 1885, he stopped by Shamrock Park while promoting his book, *The Adventures of Huckleberry Finn*. Ronald Reagan made the park one of his campaign stops in the Twin Cities for the 1980 presidential election. After 100 years of progress and population growth, residents of Shoreview voted to incorporate their village. The result was a relatively close 853-748 vote that created Shoreview as Minnesota's newest incorporated municipality on April 23, 1957. The Shoreview Historical Society operates out of the historic Lepak Larson House, located next to the Guerin Family Gas Station, which was built sometime between 1923 and 1926. Locals tout it as the "World's Smallest Texaco Station," although this claim is unverified.

VADNAIS HEIGHTS, MN
POPULATION: 12,912 – CITY 797 OF 856 (11-9-25)
Families bearing the surnames Bibeau, Garceau, Morrisette, and Vadnais were among the first French Canadians to settle this area of Minnesota, which was first part of White Bear Township before becoming an incorporated municipality in 1957. What was once a largely rural area was only comprehensively developed as recently as the 1980s, when municipal plans were introduced to turn County Road E and I-35 East into centers for storefronts, car dealerships, and other businesses. As many as 13,069 people have lived within Vadnais Heights city limits according to the 2000 Census, though that number has not changed much over the last quarter-century.

WHITE BEAR LAKE, MN
POPULATION: 24,883 – CITY 595 OF 856 (9-3-25)
There are several legends about how White Bear Lake got its name, but many of them say the body of water was possessed by the spirit of a white bear killed by a young Ojibwe brave. The gist of the tale suggests that a Sioux maiden fell in love with the brave of the opposite tribe, which would have been strictly forbidden at the time on account of the two parties consistently warring with one another. She warned the brave that her father, the Chief of the Dakota-Sioux, planned to attack the Ojibwe. The brave

entered the Sioux village on his own to seek peace, but the Chief insisted that to avoid conflict, the boy would have to do a brave deed. Later that season, the two lovers were set to meet on Manitou Island when the brave man witnessed the maiden being attacked by a large white bear. He freed her, and upon returning with help, she watched helplessly as the brave killed the bear, and the two perished together. When the white man came in the mid-1800s, the name of White Bear Township was derived from this story. A post office bearing the name existed as early as 1857. The Lake Superior and Mississippi Railroad arrived on September 10, 1868, suddenly bringing a significant influx of new settlers and visitors to one of the largest lakes in what is now the Minneapolis-St. Paul metropolitan area. Because of the lake and its widespread promotion by famous author Mark Twain, several resort features were built in the area, including a dance pavilion, a bowling alley, a ballroom, pool halls, and boating businesses. The hustle and bustle of the resort community faded as the agricultural and timbering industries took hold, and more people elected to live full-time rather than visit. White Bear Lake village was incorporated in 1881, and then reincorporated in 1921 as the City of White Bear Lake. Five properties from this time of growth have been added to the National Register of Historic Places, including the 1921 Neoclassical First National Bank of White Bear; the 1923-1929 National Guard Armory; the 1885 Cyrus B. Cobb House, a Queen Anne; the 1897 E.H. Hobe Victorian [House], and the Charles P. Noyes Cottage. Built in 1869, the Stick style cottage is now operated by the White Bear Lake Historical Society's Fillebrown House museum. The society was formed on September 25, 1970, to collect and preserve the history of White Bear Lake, Birchwood, Dellwood, Mahtomedi, and the greater White Bear Township. The Lakeshore Players Community Theater (est. 1953) and the White Bear Center for the Arts (est. 1968) are significant points of interest; three of its most prominent manufacturers are International Paper, the largest pulp and paper company in the world; Magnepan, a high-end audio loudspeaker manufacturer, and Smart Carte, a travel and leisure company that provides baggage carts to airports around the world. Over a century ago, the local Kohler Mix Company invented soft serve ice cream, a delectable treat now enjoyed by millions at franchises like Dairy Queen and small shops like White Bear Lake's own Cup and Cone. Part of Century College, founded in 1967 as Lakewood State Junior College, shares its campus with neighboring Mahtomedi. Eight of White Bear Lake's most famous citizens have been Moose Goheen, an early NHL player and member of the Professional Hockey Hall of Fame; Josh A. Cassada, a NASA astronaut with over 157 days in space; folk singer Alice Peacock; Paul Miki Nakasone, the 3rd Commander of the United States Cyber Command from May 2018 to February 2024; Brian Bonin, the winner of NCAA Hockey's Hobey Baker Award in 1996; Steve Janaszak, a member of the gold medalist 1980 Lake Placid U.S. men's hockey team; Jacob Volkmann, a professional mixed martial artist from 2007 to 2016; David Tanabe, an NHL defenseman who played from 1999 to 2008, and several other professional athletes and politicians.

 **Restaurant Recommendation:**
Rudy's Redeye Grill
4940 Hwy 61 N
White Bear Lake, MN 55110

Blaine & Spring Lake Park are only partially located in Ramsey County (see Anoka County), and St. Anthony is only partially located in Ramsey County (see Hennepin County).

Unincorporated/Ghost Towns: Bald Eagle, Bellaire

National Register of Historic Places:
Falcon Heights: Farmers Union Grain Terminal Association Headquarters, Herman Gibbs Farmstead
Maplewood: Ramsey County Poor Farm Barn
New Brighton: Foss House
North Oaks: James J. Hill's North Oaks Farm, Dairy Building
Roseville: Roselawn Chapel & Administration Building
Saint Paul: 3M Administration Building, Amhoist Tower, Arlington Hills Library, John M. Armstrong House, Assumption School, Dr. Ward Beebe House, Blair Flats, Bridges No. L 5853 & 92247, Markell & Edward Brooks Sr. House, Benjamin Brunson House, Casiville Bullard House, Burbank-Livingston-Griggs House, Pierce & Walter Butler House, C.S.P.S. Hall, Central Presbyterian Church, Church of St. Agnes- Catholic, Church of St. Bernard-Catholic, Church of St. Casimir-Catholic, Church of the Assumption- Catholic, Colorado Street Bridge, Commerce Building, Como Park Conservatory, William & Catherine Davern Farm House, Degree of Honor Protective Association Building, Derham Hall & Our Lady of Victory Chapel, College of Saint Catherine, Euclid View Flats, Finch, Vanslyck, & McConville Dry Goods Company Building, Fire Station No.19, First Baptist Church of Saint Paul, F. Scott Fitzgerald House, Fitzpatrick Building, Germania Bank Building, Giesen-Hauser House, Henry Hale Memorial Library, Hamline Branch, Hamline Methodist Episcopal Church, Hamm Building, Harriet Island Pavilion, Highland Park Tower, James J. Hill House, Ann Charlotte & Jacob Hinkel House, Historic Hill District, Holman Field Administration Building, Hope Engine Company No. 3, Indian Mounds Park Mound Group, Intercity Bridge, Horace Hills Irvine House, Irvine Park Historic District, Frank B. Kellogg House, Krank Manufacturing Company, Lauer Flats, Olaf Lee House, Lock & Dam No. 2, Lowertown Historic District, David Luckert House, Manhattan Building, Andrew R. McGill House, Mendota Road Bridge, Merchants National Bank, Mickey's Diner, Minnesota Boat Club Boathouse on Raspberry Island, Minnesota Building, Minnesota Historical Society Building, Minnesota Milk Company Building, Minnesota Mutual Life Insurance Company Building, Minnesota State Capitol, Mni Owe Sni/Coldwater Spring, Adolf Muench House, Northern Federal Building, Northern Pacific Railway Company Como Shops Historic District, Norway Lutheran Church, Norwegian Evangelical Lutheran Church, O'Donnell Shoe Company Building, Old Federal Courts Building, Old Main, Macalester College, Osborn Building, Payne Avenue State Bank, Pilgrim Baptist Church, Pioneer & Endicott Buildings, Alexander Ramsey House, Justus Ramsey Stone House, Rau/Strong House, Riverside Hangar, Riverview Branch Library, Robert Street Bridge, Rochat-Louise-Sauerwein Block, St. Agatha's Conservatory of Music & Arts, St. Anthony Park Branch Library, St. Joseph's Academy, St. Joseph's Hospital Nurses Home, St. Matthew's School, St. Paul Casket Company, St. Paul Cathedral-Catholic, St. Paul City Hall & Ramsey County Courthouse, St. Paul, Minneapolis, & Manitoba Railway Company Shops & Historic District, St. Paul Municipal Grain Terminal, St. Paul Public/James J. Hill Reference Library, St. Paul Union Depot, St. Paul Women's City Club, Salvation Army Women's Home & Hospital, Charles W. Schneider House, Schornstein Grocery & Saloon, Seventh Street Improvement Arches, Sam S. Shubert Theatre & Shubert Building, Jacob Schmidt Brewing Company Historic District, Frederick Spangenberg House, Superior Packing Company, Charles Thompson Memorial Hall, Triune Masonic Temple, United Church Seminary, United States Bedding Company, United States Post Office & Custom House, University Hall-Old Main, Hamline University, Vienna & Earl Apartment Buildings, Walsh Building, Dwight H. & Clara M. Watson House, West Summit Avenue Historic District, Woodland Park Baptist Church, Woodland Park District, Anthony Yoerg Sr. House
White Bear Lake: Cyrus B. Cobb House, First National Bank of White Bear, E. H. Hobe House-Solheim, Charles P. Noyes Cottage, White Bear Lake Armory

Golf Courses:
Brightwood Hills Golf Course, Municipal (New Brighton, MN)
Gem Lake Hills Golf Course, Daily Fee (Gem Lake, MN)
Goodrich Golf Course, Municipal (Maplewood, MN)
Highland National Golf Course – Highland Park Nine, Municipal (Saint Paul, MN)
Highland National Golf Course, Municipal (Saint Paul, MN)
Keller Golf Club, Municipal (Maplewood, MN)
Manitou Ridge Golf Club, Municipal (White Bear Lake, MN)
North Oaks Golf Club, Private (North Oaks, MN)
Oneka Ridge Golf Course, Daily Fee (White Bear Lake, MN)

Phalen Park Golf Course, Municipal (Saint Paul, MN)
Town & Country Club, Private (Saint Paul, MN)
University of Minnesota, Les Bolstad Golf Course, Municipal (Saint Paul, MN)
White Bear Yacht Club, Private (White Bear Lake, MN)

Breweries/Wineries/Distilleries:
11 Wells Distillery (Saint Paul, MN)
Bad Weather Brewing (Saint Paul, MN)
Barrel Theory Beer Company (Saint Paul, MN)
Bent Brewstillery (Roseville, MN)
Big Wood Brewery (White Bear Lake, MN)
Black Stack Brewing (Saint Paul, MN)
Burning Brothers (Saint Paul, MN)
Dual Citizen Brewing Company (Saint Paul, MN)
Gambit Brewing Company (Saint Paul, MN)
Joseph Wolf Brewing Company (Saint Paul, MN)
Lake Monster Brewing (Saint Paul, MN)
MetroNOME Brewery (Saint Paul, MN)
Pig's Eye Brewing Company (Saint Paul, MN)
Saint Paul Brewing (Saint Paul, MN)
Summit Brewing Company (Saint Paul, MN)
Wabasha Brewing Company (Saint Paul, MN)
Wandering Leaf Brewing Company (Saint Paul, MN)

Town Celebrations:
Minnesota State Fair, Falcon Heights, MN (Twelve Days leading up to Labor Day)
Rosefest, Roseville, MN (Last Full Week of June)
Saint Paul Winter Carnival, Saint Paul, MN (Late January to Early February)

RED LAKE COUNTY
EST. 1896 - POPULATION: 3,935

This county got its name from the Red Lake River, which begins on the western side of the Lower Red Lake before joining the Red River of the North in East Grand Forks.

BROOKS, MN
POPULATION: 117 – CITY 272 OF 856 (5-30-25)

The "Biggest Little City in the County" started as a Soo Line Railroad station in 1904, as that line was being built between Thief River Falls and Detroit Lakes. Its name was derived from a town in Maine, circa 1883, when the post office was established, and Daniel Little was appointed postmaster. Several stores already existed by the time it was platted. By 1911, it also had a livery barn, a bank, a hardware store, a hotel, and a grain elevator. Union Church was a notable religious organization. In another fifteen years, it also had a blacksmith shop, a meat market, a community hall, a creamery, two saloons, and at least two general stores, although it would have had many more lines if not for a May 1918 fire. The entire western side of Brooks was destroyed (except for the Kienaast garage and the hotel). F. A. Honwaldt's restaurant, Nick Pfeffer's pool hall and barber shop, Edwin Jacobson's harness shop, Paul Leroux's general store, and the Deymonaz Brothers general store were amongst the businesses lost. While the District No. 126 school district, St. Joseph's Catholic Church, and The Brooks Shrine each have their own histories, the story of Brooks would be incomplete without a nod to the Brooks Cheese Factory. The local creamery was purchased in 1926 by Aurelius Parenteau, the former owner of the Terrebonne cheese factory, and renamed the Brooks Cheese Company. His operation reportedly once produced as much as 2,470,716 pounds of cheese and 906,863 pounds of butter from 26,389,286 pounds of milk in 1961. This impressive record would be shattered several more times before the close partner of The Kraft Food Company closed in the 1970s due to heavy competition from major industrial cheese manufacturers. Brooks had a late incorporation date: April 7, 1955.

OKLEE, MN ☆
POPULATION: 413 – CITY 274 OF 856 (5-30-25)

Oklee was named in honor of Ole K. Lee, a Scandinavian settler who sold the townsite to the Tri-State Land Company when they inquired about purchasing the land on behalf of the interests of the Minneapolis, St. Paul & Sault Ste. Marie Railroad. Several other homesteaders had owned land in the vicinity long before Lee, the earliest of which was John C. Fitzgerald on June 22, 1882. He was given the honor due to his willingness to work with the railroad and the land company. He also worked to bring many settlers of Lambert and their businesses to the new townsite. From 1883 to 1912, envelopes and parcels were addressed to the Lambert post office until a new branch, Oklee, was established. Flooding plagued the town for years due to its location on the Lost River. Still, a little bit of civil engineering addressed the issue, allowing Oklee to grow and expand as it desired. Primarily, Frenchmen and Norwegians moved to the area and purchased lots for anywhere between $250 and $300 in the spring of 1910. The Soo Line arrived in September 1910 to find Peter Husby's wooden home and office, K. K. Sannes's hardware store, Mrs. Mary Sannes's restaurant, The First State Bank, and the general store of brothers Ole and Tom Melby. An elevator, a pool hall, a barber shop, a livery stable, and the depot followed, as did several other firms in the years to follow. Oklee Public Schools began in the town in 1915 when a $15,000 structure was erected to educate Oklee's then 87 students. Later known as Consolidated School District No. 1, a new building was constructed in the late 1930s under the direct supervision of the Works Progress Administration. In August 1947, another structure was built to provide additional elementary classrooms. An addition was ratified on March 17, 1952, to expand the facility yet again. St. Francis Xavier Catholic Church and the Zion Lutheran Church had edifices within city limits. Outside of town, the Clearwater [Norwegian] Evangelical Lutheran Church was completed in 1912. The Gothic Revival structure, built by Aslak and Oscar Nesland, was added to the National Register of Historic Places on November 18, 1999. Oklee's population reached its highest-ever level in 1970 and 1980, when 536 people called the community home.

PLUMMER, MN
POPULATION: 276 – CITY 273 OF 856 (5-30-25)

In 1881, Charles A. Plummer organized the construction of a sawmill, feed mill, and trading post on the Clearwater River, which served as the first modern economic development in what is now Plummer. The Soo Line railroad village was platted in 1904, a year after a branch of the post office was organized. Scotland was another proposed name after Erick Iverson's Hotel Scotland. Because of the existence of another Scotland in Fillmore County, the idea was nixed. After the arrival of the first train in September 1904, its business growth was inevitable. The First State Bank of Plummer opened on November 7, 1904. It was joined by Robinson and Company's general store, P. K. Olson's saloon, Louis Seifff's livery and feed stable, the Bowey-Schte Lumber Company, E. Peterson's blacksmith shop, J. A. Rothstein's meat market, J. M. Reed's furniture store and confectionary, and the saloon of W. G. Brown and J. E. Buskirk by the end of the year. On Valentine's Day, 1905, the county commissioners approved its incorporation as a village. The Thief River Falls Milling Company elevator, a second bank, the *Plummer Pioneer* newspaper, and the Ernardville Creamery Association building were built. Religious institutions were both numerous and prevalent: The Plummer Immanuel Lutheran Church, the Redeemer Lutheran Church of Plummer, the First Presbyterian Church of Plummer, and St. Vincent de Paul Catholic Church. Formal education for the children of Plummer began in October 1906, when the District 16 schoolhouse was moved to town. It was replaced by a large brick building in 1918 once enrollment reached sixty-five pupils. Plummer's population has remained relatively consistent since 1920, rising as high as 353 in the 1980s and as low as 270 in the year 2000. Lorie Skjerven Gildea, the Chief Justice of the Minnesota Supreme Court from July 1, 2010, to October 1, 2023, was born here.

RED LAKE FALLS, MN ★
POPULATION: 1,339 – CITY 311 OF 856 (6-3-25)

The confluence of the Red Lake and Clearwater Rivers has always been a strategic location. Jean Baptiste Cadotte, a French-Canadian fur trader, was the first to see the value of the area circa 1798 when he established a Northwest Company trading post in an attempt to ward off the advances of the Hudson's Bay Company into the Red River Valley. Cadotte reportedly provided shelter to the greatest land geographer in the history of the world, David Thompson, during a March 1798 storm. Although the post was abandoned only years later due to the British withdrawal from the North American continent, pioneers a few generations later foresaw the value the two rivers could provide to a settlement. An 1863 treaty ceded Ojibwe lands to the United States, allowing them to be settled in 1876 by French-Americans led by Pierre Bottineau. Earnest Buse and Otto Kankel established a flour mill, marking the first significant development of what would ultimately become Red Lake Falls. Buse became postmaster and platted the townsite, and the Great Northern and the Northern Pacific Railroads decided to extend lines through town. The presence of two of Minnesota's most prominent railroads spurred residents to seek status as a county seat, separate from Polk County and its seat, Crookston. Over the next ten years, legal battles ensued until an election in 1896 led voters to vote for the formation of one of five new counties. The proposed territories of Red Lake, Mills, and Columbia County—all of which had received a majority vote for their formation—overlapped one another. Governor David Marston Clough sorted out the mess and declared Red Lake County the winner. Red Lake Falls was duly named the seat of government, but it was challenged by the much larger Thief River Falls for the title. After years of filibustering by Red Lake Falls, the matter was finally brought to a vote, but the county seat petition, which would have surely given Thief River Falls the victory, was mysteriously lost just before the polling took place. The rival residents opted to instead partition off their own county, Pennington, in 1910. When it was certain that Thief River Falls was no longer a threat to their prosperity, the architects Fremont D. Orff and James Brady were commissioned to design a Beaux Arts-style courthouse. Built for $37,070 and completed by 1911, it was added to the National Register of Historic Places on May 9, 1983. Other notable fixtures of the community at this time included the Red Lake Falls Creamery, a mill, Washington School, LaFayette School, four churches, a Catholic convent, and multiple banks, hotels, elevators, and storefronts. On August 27, 1927, Red Lake Falls welcomed the barnstorming pilot Charles Lindbergh on his adventure through the Upper Midwest. Adrian Baril, an NFL lineman who clocked minutes with the Minneapolis Marines and the Milwaukee Badgers in the 1920s, and Roxy Beaudro, a hockey player from 1896 to 1917 who won the 1907 Stanley Cup with the Kenora [Ontario] Thistles, are two pioneer athletes who hail from town.

Unincorporated/Ghost Towns: Dorothy, Garnes, Huot, Perault, Terrebonne, Wylie

National Register of Historic Places:
Oklee: Clearwater Evangelical Lutheran Church
Red Lake Falls: Red Lake County Courthouse

Town Celebrations:
Blast to Brooks, Brooks, MN (Saturday after Labor Day)
Oklee Market Day, Oklee, MN (2nd Saturday in August)
Summerfest, Red Lake Falls, MN (Last Weekend in July)

REDWOOD COUNTY
EST. 1862 - POPULATION: 15,425

One of several Minnesota counties named after a river, the eastward-flowing Redwood River meets the Minnesota River in this county, established on February 8, 1862.

BELVIEW, MN
POPULATION: 291 – CITY 49 OF 856 (2-26-25)

Belview, one of Redwood County's 15 incorporated communities, was first known as Jones Siding and Rolling Prairie before being renamed Belview with the arrival of the Wisconsin, Minnesota & Pacific branch of the Minneapolis & St. Louis Railroad. The new name means "beautiful view" in French and has been given to several other communities throughout the United States, some of which are spelled differently (i.e., Bellevue). Hibbard F. Jones platted the townsite in 1889, a couple of years after a post office was established. His son, Charles H. Jones, was dubbed its first postmaster. He and his brother, Justin F. Jones, built a general store and a grain warehouse, and F. L. Simpson dedicated an elevator as a storage facility for the harvests reaped by the quickly growing population of farmers. Over the next year, R. L. Seuter established his blacksmith shop, S. O. Kolean brought in a stock of hardware, George Leppman started a grain and lumber business, and John Martin managed a wood and livestock business. On January 3, 1893, the county commissioners approved their residents' resounding request to incorporate as a village. Three early Belview establishments have been placed on the National Register of Historic Places. The first listed was the Odeon Theater, a Queen Anne-style theater hall constructed in 1901. The two other structures, the Minneapolis and St. Louis Railroad Depot and the Gimmestad Land and Loan Office, were completed in 1892 and added to the list on August 11, 1980, thanks mainly to the efforts of the Belview Heritage Preservation Commission.

CLEMENTS, MN
POPULATION: 155 – CITY 53 OF 856 (2-26-25)

As many as 269 people inhabited this community in the 1960s, six decades after it was platted by P. R. Kline and the Western Town Lot Company in 1902. Before the Chicago & Northwestern Railroad was built through the vicinity of Henry Petrie's land, a small trading center named Clements (named after early farmer Peter O. Clements) had existed about one mile north of the present site. It had a post office, established in 1900, in addition to Rongstad & Thorston's general store and the Three Lake Farmers' Co-operative Creamery. All three organizations and their respective proprietors moved to be located on the rail line. They became the first pieces of infrastructure in the small agricultural village that eventually welcomed Gerstmann & Hoffenspringer's hardware store, the Laird-Norton lumber yards, S. G. Peterson's general store, W. P. Schmidt's livery barn, the Wichmann Brothers' blacksmith shop, hotels, saloons, other stores, and elevators owned by the Western Elevator Company, the Sleepy Eye Milling Company, and Schmidt & Anderson. The State Bank of Clements was erected in the same era by a group of men from Springfield, Minnesota, who held commercial interests in the newly founded community. The bank is a cousin to the one in nearby Milroy; both structures were listed on the National Register of Historic Places in August 1980. The District No. 8 School outside of Clements, noted for its accompanying barn and outhouse, still stands on County Road 70. Now home to about 155 citizens, Clements was incorporated on June 29, 1903.

DELHI, MN
POPULATION: 46 – CITY 50 OF 856 (2-26-25)
The first people came to Delhi in 1865, immediately after the conclusion of the American Civil War. However, their settlement was not organized until February 9, 1876, when Alfred M. Cook, the flour mill owner at Redwood Falls, named it after the township in Ohio. In 1884, a local by the name of A. Y. Felton provided the Minneapolis & St. Louis Railroad with large parcels of his land to ensure they would build their right-of-way across his property. They established a station here, which later became known as Delhi. The post office followed suit in its nomenclature and appointed Rodman R. Hurlbut as postmaster. He was also the depot agent. A. H. Anderson and J. L. Borg started a store—the first business in Delhi—and an elevator was erected by the end of the year. Its residents worked extensively over the next two years to earn the right to be a trade point on the railroad by establishing blacksmith shops, hotels, elevators, lumberyards, general stores, and other traditional businesses. A Presbyterian church and a public school were also present in early Delhi. On June 11, 1896, Delhi began to boast of an elevated musical scene when the local band completed the Delhi Coronet Band Hall, which ultimately became the town hall where Delhi residents elected to incorporate their townsite as a municipality on November 25, 1902. It was demolished in 2007 due to extensive damage. The local post office was discontinued in 1979 after Delhi experienced its most significant population drop (-37.7%) between 1970 and 1980, from 154 residents to 96.

LAMBERTON, MN
POPULATION: 792 – CITY 24 OF 856 (2-23-25)
Henry Wilson Lamberton, the president of the Winona Deposit Bank in 1868 and later the president and land commissioner of the Winona & Western Railroad Company in the 1890s, is the namesake of this Minnesota city. Strategically located on the banks of the Big Cottonwood River, Lamberton was initially platted in the late 1870s by surveyor T. G. Carter and incorporated on March 1, 1879. Lamberton enjoyed a long period of prosperity because of its position on the Winona & St. Peter Railroad (which became a part of the Chicago & Northwestern when that company purchased a controlling interest in 1867). A. A. Praxel and Frank Schandera opened the first general store after the brutal winter of 1872-73 had passed. They were joined in business by Charles Bennett and Charles R. Kneeland, who opened boarding houses. Of course, there was also a post office amongst these pioneer businesses, which began in 1873 in Kneeland's general store. According to an 1882 directory, early business interests of the village were as follows: five general stores, three hotels, three lawyer's offices, two blacksmith shops, two saloons, two hardware stores, two butcher shops, two implement stores, one wagonmaker, one drug store and physician's office, one barber shop, one feed store, one furniture store, Horton & Company's lumberyard, Whitten & Judd's grain elevator, and the *Lamberton Commercial* newspaper office. The Methodist and the Congregational churches were the first of Lamberton's eventual six religious organizations, which by 1916 included edifices of the Catholics, German

Lutherans, English Lutherans, English Methodist Episcopalians, German Methodist Episcopalians, and the Congregationalists. A good school was built early on, and nine different fraternal organizations held meetings and events regularly at the height of the community's heyday. Between 1890 and 1900, the population grew by 208.9%, increasing from 202 people to 624. Additionally, between the 1940s and 1950s, Lamberton crossed the one-thousand-resident threshold for the first time. Modern historical points of interest include the City Blacksmith Shop, an era-correct 1898 blacksmith shop operated by the Lamberton Area Historical Society that still retains most of its original equipment, and the former Queen Anne-style home of J. A. Anderson, the best example of that architecture in all of Redwood County.

 **Restaurant Recommendation:**
Ljs on Main
Main Street
Lamberton, MN 56152

LUCAN, MN
POPULATION: 214 – CITY 46 OF 856 (2-26-25)
Lucan was most likely named after Lucan, Ireland, by its earliest inhabitants. A better story suggests that it may have been named by a railroad surveyor who, when asked if he could think of a good name for the new Chicago & Northwestern Railway station, replied: "No, but maybe Lou can." The Lou he was referring to was his coworker, Lou Kartak. From 1890 to 1908, the local post office was called Rock because it was located in Granite Rock Township. Robert Schanberger was appointed as the first postmaster, but Jens Larson changed the name to match the railroad's nomenclature in 1908. Schanberger owned the first store in the area, but it went out of business when the Western Town Lot Company opted to lay out the townsite on the land of George W. Norcutt and Christ Hansen. The early years of Lucan proved fruitful for those who established businesses. Stores, hotels, saloons, and typical lines were organized, but the most notable structures were the elevators of the Springfield Milling Company and the Sleepy Eye Milling Company. A two-story bank building was constructed in 1905 and matched in grandeur only by the Catholic and the Lutheran church edifices. In 1904, the county commissioners established District #108, which began with an enrollment of 48 students before eventually closing its doors in 1981. Strangely, the closure came when Lucan had more residents living there (262) than at any other point in its history, but the school building was saved by the Lucan Lions Club and turned into the Lucan Community Center. The Chicago & Northwestern Depot remains a historic point of interest today.

MILROY, MN
POPULATION: 259 – CITY 44 OF 856 (2-26-25)
The population of Milroy (now 259) has changed very little between the 1940s (then 261) and today. Like its neighboring communities, Milroy was born out of necessity to serve as a shipping point and mail stop for the Chicago & Northwestern Railroad. As businesses developed around the railroad's facilities, it evolved into a passenger stop, which led to the platting of a townsite in March 1902 by the Western Town Lot Company on land originally owned by C. E. Levig and Thomas Murphy. Lots were sold the following month, and by the end of its first year, Milroy had everything from a harness shop, hardware store, barber shop, livery, and saloon to four general stores, a hotel, three elevators, and a pair of lumber yards. Lumber was first obtained from neighboring communities for the first buildings around town. Eventually, the Hayes &

Lucas Lumber Company and the J. H. Queal & Company handled the town's wood supply. The Nelson Brothers, Springfield Milling Company, and Sleepy Eye Milling Company owned the elevators, but two burnt down within only a decade. Several other structures suffered the same fate, including a local schoolhouse. By 1904, the town had its own newspaper, *The Milroy Echo*, Methodist and Norwegian Lutheran churches, and The State Bank of Milroy. Now listed on the National Register of Historic Places, the community bank closed in 1930 but was used for several other purposes. From 1951 to 1989, it was the post office (whose local branch dates to 1902) until a new structure was built to serve that purpose. Afterward, it sat in decay until Sunny Rothschild purchased it in 2009 and renovated it into modern apartments. Milroy was named in honor of Major General Robert H. Milroy, who served in the American Civil War. Another noted soldier, Edwin W. Rawlings, was born in Milroy on September 11, 1904, and became a four-star general of the United States Air Force and the president of General Mills. Today, that company is best known for its popular breakfast cereals, such as Cheerios, Wheaties, and Lucky Charms.

MORGAN, MN
POPULATION: 888 – CITY 52 OF 856 (2-26-25)
"The Father of American Anthropology," Lewis Henry Morgan, had his legacy commemorated when the Sleepy Eye-Redwood Falls branch of the Chicago & Northwestern established a siding. T. G. Holland served as the section boss and the first true resident and postmaster of Morgan, but improvements truly began when he found help from Mel Tolman. A boarding house was established, and Holland put in a grocery store once farmers and their families began moving into the area. The town was formally platted by Arthur Jacobi on August 14, 1878, and incorporated as a village on February 11, 1889, after blacksmiths, general stores, and other dealers put up their business houses. By 1890 Morgan had three blacksmiths, William Miller, Karle Mire, and Harvey Moore; two general stores owned by N. Eischen & Company and Richard Gerdes; Robinson & Teas and Henry Newman's hardware stores; John Marti's and T. F. Lyden's lumber stockpiles; John Hellig's hotel; Joseph Faeber's meat market, and churches for its Catholic, Presbyterian, and German Lutheran religious congregations. Other prominent groups founded during that period included Zion Lutheran Church, the German Methodist Episcopal Church, and St. John's Evangelical Lutheran Church. Its population was 301 people, although it reached 975 in the 1960 and 1980 Censuses. The Gilfillan Estate started in 1882 when Charles Duncan Gilfillan and his son purchased 13,000 acres of land. It once had a grain elevator, a stockyard, tenant homes, and an affluent farmstead. The estate, technically considered its own unincorporated community apart from Morgan, was listed on the National Register of Historic Places on August 11, 1980.

REDWOOD FALLS, MN ★☆
POPULATION: 5,102 – CITY 51 OF 856 (2-26-25)
The history of Redwood Falls is an accurate "tale of two cities," as it and another former city, North Redwood, merged in 1996 to form a single municipality. Redwood Falls was at the forefront of the area's history, as it was where Colonel Sampson R. B. McPhail, John St. George Honner, and several others arrived in the summer of 1864 to build a stockade towards the end of the Dakota conflict. McPhail took lumber from the Dakota reservation to fortify a home with an accompanying eight-foot-tall stockade. Around this structure, more settlers moved in, assuming it was safe to do so. Many of the Native Americans were removed to the Lower Sioux Indian Community, now a tiny 2.69 square mile reservation that was significantly reduced following the Dakota War

of 1862. Life was complicated because of grasshopper plagues and poor crop yields until 1878, when the Minnesota Valley division of the Winona & St. Peter Railroad was completed. The presence of a post office (brought about in 1864 because of Mcphail's stockade) encouraged officials to place a siding there, called Redwood Falls, after the nearby vertical falls and rapids of the Redwood River. In the area where Mr. Honner settled, another office was organized under the name North Redwood, and the two communities grew alongside one another. A third attempt was made to establish a village called Riverside, which at one point had a store, hotel, blacksmith shop, and post office (from 1875 to 1876) of its own (before the buildings were removed to Redwood Falls when boat traffic diminished due to the advent of the railroad). Of the three communities, Redwood Falls was always the most prosperous and well-developed, as the county commissioners designated it as the judicial seat of Redwood County. At its first Census in 1880, it had nearly one thousand residents, and the number of businesses may have exceeded one hundred. To list all of them in a single list would be extensive, but amongst the more interesting lines at this time were the Delhi Flour Mills, operated by A. A. Cook & Company; Werton & Ruter's flour mills; Cuff & Company's flour mill; the Bank of Redwood Falls; the Redwood County Bank; the Bailey House hotel; the Commercial House hotel; the Redwood House hotel; the Exchange Hotel; John Christie's dentistry; George H. Spafford's watches and jewelry store; and a weekly newspaper called the *Redwood Gazette*. William B. Herriott was the editor of the paper. Schools and churches were in order, and the Catholics, Methodists, Presbyterians, Christians, and Episcopalians all had their respective edifices built by 1878. The arrival of a second railroad in 1884 —the Minneapolis & St. Louis —only further spurred the impressive growth of both North Redwood and Redwood Falls. North Redwood was significantly smaller in stature but still grew to include unique businesses such as the North Redwood Roller Mill, owned by Eric Birum and Albert J. Anderson; the Pacific Elevator Company; a stone quarry; John S. G. Honner's hotel; and about a dozen other storefronts. Richard W. Sears, the future founder of Sears, Roebuck & Co., was the first depot agent for North Redwood. He came up with the idea for his store after a local jeweler (perhaps the aforementioned George H. Spafford) refused to accept a shipment of watches he never ordered, which Sears then sold to other railroad agents for a small profit. Two years later, in 1886, the R. W. Sears Watch Company was established in Minneapolis, which, over the decades, transformed into a multi-billion-dollar company before bankruptcy took hold in October 2018. The village, where Mr. Sears once served as an agent, was incorporated in 1903. It remained an independent city for over 90 years before becoming one with its neighbor, Redwood Falls. J. S. G. Honner's home, built in 1872 and later occupied by Thomas Hosken, a local stone quarryman, was listed on the National Register of Historic Places in 1980 as North Redwood's only entry. Honner's North Redwood Granite Works supplied the stone used to pave city streets throughout Minnesota, most notably in St. Paul. Redwood Falls boasts four sites on the list: its 1904 Carnegie Library; the 1925 Scenic City Cooperative Oil Company, whose nickname is a nod to the many parks that the city boasted in its prime; the Redwood Falls Retaining Wall Roadside Development Project constructed between 1934-36 by the Minnesota Department of Highways; and the WPA's Ramsey Park Swayback Bridge, completed in 1938. The Redwood County Courthouse was completed in 1891, but was never listed on the Register due to several additions between 1963 and 1970. Points of interest in Redwood Falls include the largest municipal park in Minnesota, Alexander Ramsey Park, and the Redwood County Museum. The Minnesota Inventors Congress, from 1958 to 2014, was headquartered in Redwood Falls and held an annual exhibition to highlight the state's entrepreneurial spirit and honor inventors' impact on society.

Restaurant Recommendation:
Dari King
711 E Bridge St
Redwood Falls, MN 56283

REVERE, MN
POPULATION: 89 – CITY 25 OF 856 (2-23-25)

"The railroad is coming! The railroad is coming!" must have been exclaimed by at least one or two early settlers when they learned that the Winona and St. Peter Railway Company was planning on founding a townsite in their locality. Platted circa 1886 by John E. Blunt, Revere was named by C. C. Wheeler in honor of the American Revolution patriot Paul Revere, who rode through Boston to warn the Minutemen that the British were on their way. Two boxcars served the young village as its station and freight house until Louis J. Rongstad & Company started a general store, which naturally also became the post office in 1893. The Rongstad store was gone after only a short while. Within five years, Revere had multiple general and hardware stores, blacksmith shops, hotels, and even a confectionery (owned by Arthur Weldon), as well as the Revere Creamery Association, the Parsons Grain Company elevator, and the Standard Lumber Company elevator. After its incorporation as a village on February 21, 1900, *The Revere Record* newspaper was established in May 1901 to report the new developments of the community. Around this time, the Revere Fire Hall was also built. Early records indicate that E. A. Nelson was in charge and had a state-of-the-art "Waterous gasoline engine" used to extinguish fires efficiently. That original building has survived with its bell tower and flagpole intact. Revere had a peak population of 201 people in the 1960s.

Restaurant Recommendation:
Bruiser's Place
155 Main St
Revere, MN 56166

SANBORN, MN
POPULATION: 323 – CITY 23 OF 856 (2-23-25)

Four grain elevators once towered over Sanborn, Minnesota, a rural, agricultural community that started in 1881 when the Winona & St. Peter Railway Company was built on the land of John T. Yager. He named the townsite (noted for being split in two by the tracks) for railroad officer Sherburn Sanborn, who gave many years of his life to the company's benefit. The post office was dedicated on May 17, 1880, and the race to compete with neighboring rail line communities was already ongoing. J. W. Dotson constructed a home that doubled as a storefront, and his son built a warehouse and an abode of his own. According to an 1886 directory published by the Northwestern Gazetteer, Sanborn at that point had already grown to encompass two general stores owned by C. Armstrong and Wells & Schrader; Dr. O. A. Case's drug store; T. A. Murray's harness shop; the carriage works of George Posz; B. L. Bingley's boarding house; John A. Letord's hardware and furniture store; Daniel Wagner's saloon; A. Schellenberger's blacksmith shop, and the lumber stocks of C. F. Waterman and the formerly mentioned Wells & Schrader. By 1916, there were even more businesses, in addition to the towering Sanborn Improvement Company building, which locals heavily used as a theater and a lodge hall for the Modern Brotherhood of America, the International Order of Odd Fellows, and the Masonic and Eastern Star organizations. The four earliest churches were the St. Thomas Catholic Church, the German Evangelical church, the Methodist Episcopal church, and the German Lutheran church. The Sod House on the Prairie, located outside of Sanborn, served for several years as a functional bed & breakfast, where people could dress up in Laura Ingalls Wilder's pioneer attire and spend the night in the utility-less (no running water or electricity) soddie. It is now a small museum that can be self-toured.

SEAFORTH, MN
POPULATION: 82 – CITY 48 OF 856 (2-26-25)

In its heyday, Seaforth was an incredibly prosperous village with all the advantages of being a trade center on a branch line of the Chicago & Northwestern that connected Vesta in the west with Wabasso in the east. Not long after it was incorporated on February 13, 1901, a 1904 assessment by the county newspaper reported that about 30 interests were in operation by then. Amongst the most accomplished were Hotel Drews, of which Gustave Drews and William R. Goudy were the proprietors; the Bank of Seaforth, whose president was H. A. Baldwin; the feed mill of William Ayers; Wilbur R. Johnson's jewelry and drug store; Schmidt & Anderson's elevator; the C. M. Youmans Lumber Company; W. E. Cleveland's creamery, and the *Seaforth Item* newspaper, whose publisher was Glen R. Tuttle. The "Item" circulated from 1901 to 1920 and ceased operations after Seaforth lost 28.5% of its population (from 158 residents to 113) between the 1910 and 1920 Censuses. When the site was platted in the 1890s, it was named Okawa by Harry I. Orwig, an engineer affiliated with the railroad company. *Okawa* translates to "pike" in Ojibwe. The name was changed when a post office called Seaforth, named after Loch Seaforth in Scotland, entered service in 1899. It was discontinued in 1995.

VESTA, MN
POPULATION: 276 – CITY 45 OF 856 (2-26-25)

The western terminus of the Sanborn-Vesta branch of the Chicago & Northwestern Railroad was named by Fred Vail Hotchkiss for his sister, Vesta, whose name was an eponym for the Roman goddess of hearth, home, and family. Platted in 1899-1900 by E. E. Gray of the Western Town Lot Company, Vesta came about out of a need for the farmers of this area to sell their agricultural products. Its post office, organized in 1899, was headed by Timothy L. Crowley and ran out of his home. Ludwig Rosberg sold his land to the townsite company for $32 an acre, and the railroad hastily constructed its station, a roundhouse, and three elevators owned by A. L. Foster, the Bingham Brothers, and the Great Western Elevator Company. August Matz and Herman Schroeder went in together to establish Vesta's first store, and later, all of the implement and hardware storefronts, hotels, saloons, liveries, businesses, and religious and educational organizations came together. It was incorporated on February 6, 1900. By 1902, the primary accomplishments of Vesta included an opera house with regular performances, the C. M. Youmans Lumber Company, the Vesta Creamery Company, the Bank of Vesta, a fire department, a graded school, Lutheran and Presbyterian churches, and the *Vesta Bright Eyes* newspaper owned by Morgan E. Lewis and edited by Fred G. Tuttle. Vesta's population has remained relatively stable over its 125 years; its highest was 360 residents in the 1980s.

WABASSO, MN
POPULATION: 739 – CITY 47 OF 856 (2-26-25)

Wabasso comes from an Ojibwe word meaning "rabbit" or "snowshoe hare," according to Henry Wadsworth Longfellow's poem, *The Song of Hiawatha*. The word's translation into English has historically been spelled 'wabos' and 'waabooz,' but it is pronounced 'wah-bose.' A six-foot-tall namesake white rabbit now welcomes visitors coming into Wabasso from the west on MN-68, but when it was platted by J. C. W. Kline and the Western Town Lot Company in 1899, it was nothing more than prospective farming country. Developed to serve as a meeting point for the Sanborn-Vesta and the Evan-Marshall lines of the Chicago & Northwestern Railroad, the initial lots for prospective entrepreneurs and residents were auctioned off on November 1, 1899. Henry Mayer is recognized as the first settler, but from the land he sought to farm soon arose a bustling village complete with businesses of all shapes and sizes. Half a decade after it had come into existence, Wabasso consisted of Franta & Lockway's flour mill, the Schmid & Anderson Grain Company, C. M. Youmans Lumber Company, the Bingham Brothers grain elevator, the State Bank of Wabasso, the Citizens State Bank, the Wabasso Farmers' Grain & Fuel Company, the Redwood Rural Telephone Company, the *Wabasso Standard* newspaper, five saloons, four blacksmith shops, three general stores, two furniture stores, two grocery stores, two farm implement stores, two attorney's offices, two millineries, a dray line, a joint jewelry store and photographer's office, a barber shop, a construction company, a stonemason, a hardware store, a restaurant, a harness shop, a meat market, a drug store, a livery, a physician's office, and Hotel Wabasso. The Commercial Hotel, a privately funded hotel, opened its doors in 1901 and was listed on the National Register of Historic Places in 1980 before it was demolished circa 2010. Wabasso was incorporated on April 28, 1900, and welcomed its post office that same year in the hardware store of John H. Rahskoph. Folk artist Arnold Kramer has ties to Wabasso.

WALNUT GROVE, MN
POPULATION: 751 – CITY 26 OF 856 (2-24-25)

The childhood home of pioneer author Laura Ingalls Wilder holds a special place in the hearts of fans of the *Little House on the Prairie* book series, as it was here where a young Laura and her family spent a few years between their moves from Burr Oak, Iowa, and to De Smet, South Dakota. Her father, Charles "Pa" Ingalls, served as a butcher and the first justice of the peace when the family returned to Walnut Grove for their second stint before moving to South Dakota in the spring of 1879. They were among the many early residents of the railroad town, which began circa 1872 when Lafayette Bedal settled near the Chicago & Northwestern Railroad's right-of-way and established the Walnut Station post office. While ideas for the post office name were percolating around in his mind, he noted a large grove of black walnut trees on Plum Creek, for which he selected the name because of their rarity in such a northern portion of the country. He was preceded in settlement of the area only by John F. and Daniel Burns, survivors of the Lake Shetek Massacre of 1862, thanks to the warnings of Henry W. Smith and only a select number of others. Bedal's brother Elias filed the Walnut Grove plat on September 10, 1874. By the time it attained village (municipality) status on March 3, 1879, the site had grown considerably due to the railroad's presence. The post office was known as Walnut Station from 1873 to 1881, before it adopted the name Walnut Grove. Some noteworthy points of interest in 1880 Walnut Grove included its hotels, a meat market, a Congregational church, a Methodist Episcopal church, a school, and a steam-powered flour mill. From 1890 to 1900, the commercial district and housing developments expanded rapidly as the population grew from 127 residents to 447 (an increase of 252%), and by 1920, the numbers had increased to 663 people. Two more churches, a cream and egg shipping depot, four grain elevators, a creamery, and a local newspaper were in existence by 1916. The Walnut Grove Creamery Association building, a 1930s cooperative creamery, has survived today as the town's most historically unaltered structure. Wilder enthusiasts can visit the Laura Ingalls Wilder Museum in Walnut Grove, in addition to a small rock with a plaque not far from the original homestead (which has since been eroded to nothing more than a pile of dirt). "Walnut Grove" was the name of the town in the Western historical drama series *Little House on the Prairie*, which aired from September 1974 to March 1983. In the early 21st century, over 250 Hmong immigrants settled in Walnut Grove, significantly shifting the community's racial makeup to approximately one-third Asian. More Hmong communities call Minnesota home than any other state except for California. Aside from the Ingalls family, other notable individuals from the community include Lester Mondale, a Unitarian minister known for writing several books on his religion, and Leo K. Thorsness, who earned the Medal of Honor for his heroic actions during the Vietnam War.

WANDA, MN
POPULATION: 72 – CITY 54 OF 856 (2-26-25)

Twenty-five years before the village of Wanda, there was Mathias E. Eichten, who arrived in 1872 as a homesteader in the relatively new Willow Lake Township. It was here that he put down his roots and farmed the ground for a quarter of a century before the Chicago & Northwestern Railway came through with its line between Sanborn and Wabasso. The townsite was platted in September 1899 by J. C. W. Kline and the Western Town Lot Company, and named Wanda after the Ojibwe word *wanenda*, meaning "forgetfulness." Local historians attest that the town was named after a native girl. Mathias sold forty acres of his land to the railroad company. He then repurchased six lots alongside his brother Valentine to start a lumber yard and a hardware store to supply new settlers with construction materials. It was at their store that the post office was established. Their lumber business was rivaled by C. M. Youmans & Company in the early days. Wanda's two earliest elevators were owned by the Western Elevator Company and the Bingham Brothers; Mathew Jennings ran the general store, Paul Doepke was the proprietor of a hotel and saloon, Herman Wenzel operated a blacksmith shop, and John Drees made "saloon-hopping" within the town available with the construction of a second saloon. More enterprises took hold as the months passed, amongst which the most noteworthy were the State Bank of Wanda, the Commercial Hotel, and the Wanda Creamery Company. A Protestant (German Evangelical Lutheran) and the St. Matias Roman Catholic Church found a home in Wanda by 1904. A two-room schoolhouse was built in 1900 for $2,400, but it was replaced by a larger brick schoolhouse in 1912. Wanda reached a peak population of 185 in 1920, about 20 years after its incorporation as a village on April 12, 1901. Midwest Game Crave is a local, one-of-a-kind wooden board game business that handcrafts UFF-DA, Kubb, Crokinole, Catan, and other legacy game boards.

Unincorporated/Ghost Towns: Gilfillan, Lower Sioux Indian Community, Morton, Rowena

National Register of Historic Places:
Belview: Gimmestad Land & Loan Office, Minneapolis & St. Louis Railroad Depot, Odeon Theater
Clements: Clements State Bank Building, District No.8 School
Lamberton: City Blacksmith Shop, J. A. Anderson House
Lucan: Chicago & North Western Railroad Depot
Milroy: Milroy State Bank Building
Morton: Lower Sioux Agency, Birch Coulee School, St. Cornelia's Episcopal Church
North Redwood: Honner-Hosken House

Redwood Falls: Bank of Redwood Falls Building, H. D. Chollar House, Ramsey Park Swayback Bridge, Redwood Falls Carnegie Library, Redwood Falls Retaining Wall Roadside Development Project, Scenic City Cooperative Oil Company, Gilfillan
Revere: Revere Fire Hall
Walnut Grove: Walnut Grove Creamery Association

Golf Courses:
Farmers Golf & Health Club, Daily Fee (Sanborn, MN)
Redwood Falls Golf Club, Daily Fee (Redwood Falls, MN)

Breweries/Wineries/Distilleries:
Grandview Valley Winery (Belview, MN)

Town Celebrations:
Lamberton Hot Iron Days, Lamberton, MN (Weekend after Labor Day)
Laura Ingalls Wilder Pageant, Walnut Grove, MN (Three Weekends in July)
Old Sod Days, Belview, MN (2nd Saturday after Labor Day)

RENVILLE COUNTY
EST. 1855 - POPULATION: 14,723

Joseph Renville, an interpreter noted for his role in exploring the Louisiana Purchase, gave his name to Renville County when it was created in 1855 from portions of Nicollet, Pierce, and Sibley Counties.

BIRD ISLAND, MN ☆
POPULATION: 1,005 – CITY 107 OF 856 (3-28-25)

Before the ditches were drained and turned into farmland, a six-acre island was once present and surrounded by sloughs on each side. The refuge provided a home for several thousand birds and a large grove of oak, maple, and hackberry trees, and for years it was used as a meeting place for trappers and Native Americans. Eventually, human intervention emptied the sloughs, and the timber was used to build many of the first structures of the new settlement of Bird Island. It was one of several towns platted out on the path of the Hastings & Dakota division of the Chicago, Milwaukee & St. Paul Railroad between Glencoe and Montevideo. Bird Island was platted in July 1878 and rapidly developed as a prized shipping point for the railroad. J. W. Ladd established a store and an elevator, and C. C. Ladd opened the lumber yard. Axel H. Reed, Josiah Richardson, and W. M. Holbrook followed suit with their own store and grain elevator, and by the end of 1879, there was also a hotel, a hardware store, a drug store, two blacksmith shops, two saloons, and the Renville County Bank. These lines and others grow in proportion to the town's population, which reportedly numbered 567 by 1885. At that point, it was larger than Olivia, Renville, and Hector combined. Much of its success was due to its designation as a division point of the railroad, but residents were taken aback when it was moved to nearby Montevideo. That event, coupled with its inability to gain the county seat despite its best efforts to secure it by providing a free courthouse building (later used as a high school and grade school), likely should have discouraged most residents and led to their removal from the town and their families. Despite the challenges, Bird Island's pioneer settlers rose to the occasion. They worked to continue building up their town by building a city hall and auditorium, a new sewer and waterworks system, and numerous clubs and organizations that sought to improve and beautify the community. Of all its businesses, The Bird Island Roller Mills were amongst the most important. The seventy-five-barrel capacity mill began in the 1880s as a two-story flour-milling business. A third story was added when its "Golden Cut" brand became an area favorite. A creamery, two elevators, a school, a Catholic church, and a Baptist church rounded out its notable infrastructure as of 1888. People and businesses have come and gone, but since 1930, Bird Island has maintained a population of at least 1,000 residents. Roger L. Dell, the Chief Justice of the Minnesota Supreme Court from 1953 to 1962, was born here on July 19, 1897. One property on the National Register is the historic Tinnes-Baker House, which was listed on April 26, 2021, thanks to the preservation efforts of the local Cultural Centre.

BUFFALO LAKE, MN
POPULATION: 660 – CITY 109 OF 856 (3-28-25)
Although its little forty-acre namesake lake was drained in the 1920s, Buffalo Lake remains one of Renville County's ten incorporated cities. Some of the earliest reports of Europeans in the area recall the foot traffic of U.S. troops and horse-drawn wagons traveling between Fort Ridgely, Nicollet County, and Hutchinson. Another fort site was present at some point on the modern-day Buffalo Lake townsite. The land was purchased by John C. Riebe in 1880, who had it platted in 1881. He became the postmaster when that facet of the community was established in 1882 and was instrumental in helping locate the county seat in Olivia rather than the now-unincorporated town (and original Renville County seat) of Beaver Falls. Supposedly, the village was only platted with the help of the railroad because of Riebe's role in the county seat war. Monson's Crossing was the drop-off point for the Hastings & Dakota Railway railroad passengers until the depot was finished in 1882. In thirty-four years, Buffalo Lake transformed from open prairie into a business center complete with no less than three grain elevators, three grocery stores, two lumber yards, two general stores, two garages, the State Bank and Farmers' State Bank, two hardware and implement stores, a restaurant, a drug store, a meat market, a harness shop, a furniture store, a photographer's studio, and jeweler, a loathing store, a blacksmith shop, *The Buffalo Lake News* newspaper, Boon Lake Creamery, Buffalo Lake Creamery, an opera house, the Buffalo Lake Motor Company, and a livery feed and flour mill. The mill was established by Green & Dahms in the 1890s. It was a focal point of the town's manufacturing businesses alongside the Buffalo Lake Manufacturing & Supply Company until the latter burned on October 5, 1900. Before its destruction, it was a significant industrial site as a foundry and machine shop. Early churches were Methodist Episcopal, Zion Lutheran, and Evangelical, although it is likely that a German Lutheran building was the first. The population of Buffalo Lake has fluctuated between 637 (in 1940) and 782 (in 1980) people over the last eighty-five years (as of 2025).

DANUBE, MN
POPULATION: 458 – CITY 110 OF 856 (3-29-25)
The first four men to settle the Danube area were John Stange, John Kuether, William Bede, and Henry Henricks from 1876-78. For nearly 20 years, the land between Renville and Area was just that — farmland — but eventually the farmers decided they needed a more accessible market to export their goods more efficiently. A petition was presented to the Chicago, Milwaukee & St. Paul Railroad to establish a station called "Miles" in 1899, and their call to action was granted. A farmers' elevator was ready to go when the townsite was platted. Next came August Sommerfield's post office building, William Terry and H. W. Shoemaker's general stores, Philip Fabel and J. W. Beck's hardware store (later a hotel), Herman Roepke's harness shop, and Thomas Slough's saloon. Bootlegging was a real problem in this general territory between two other major shipping points. So, on November 5, 1902, the county commissioners

removed it from the township and incorporated it as a municipality to better control the situation. At that point, the name was changed from Miles to Danube, supposedly after the European river. As Danube grew, it became the agricultural trade point it was designed to be, welcoming a school (built in 1904 for $4,000), German Evangelical and German Lutheran churches, and the *Danube Herald* newspaper, among several other accomplishments. With a recent peak population of 590 in the 1980s, Danube has retained much of its early history, thanks in part to the care and efforts of the Danube Historical Society. Bob Bruggers, an AFL/NFL linebacker from 1966 to 1968 for the Miami Dolphins and San Diego Chargers, attended Danube High School.

FAIRFAX, MN
POPULATION: 1,250 – CITY 104 OF 856 (3-28-25)

Renville County's southeastern community was platted on August 22, 1882, and named by Eben Ryder, the Minneapolis and St. Louis Railroad Company's president, after the Virginia county where he grew up. The first townsite was originally a half-mile east of its present location on the farmstead of Edmond O'Hara. The railroad moved it because of its poor positioning on a deep slough prone to flooding. Their line on the northern side of the Minnesota River led to the founding of numerous communities, and in most of them, a depot was constructed to aid in moving passengers and freight across the country. Fairfax's depot, a stucco-covered wood-frame building built in 1883, has survived the elements and is now the oldest standing depot in the county. It was listed on the National Register of Historic Places in 1986 and is now host to the local Fairfax museum. When the village was being platted, the name Cairo was suggested after the township. Postal authorities denied it because another town in the state already had that nomenclature. Luke T. Grady became postmaster and the first merchant. Despite its remote location, twenty-plus miles from the closest bank and the county seat of Beaver Falls, many entrepreneurs saw an opportunity to start their businesses in Fairfax. Henry Hauser of Sleepy Eye and John C. Brennescholz moved in to form rival lumber yards, a necessity for those looking for building materials for homes and firms of their own. In came the blacksmith shops and the general stores, and a carriage works was established by Phillip Kipp. By 1888, incorporation was achieved, and several businesses, elevators, and Saint Andrew's Catholic Church were established. Between 1890 and 1900, its population nearly doubled from 351 people to 642, despite a September 17, 1895, fire that destroyed the Methodist parsonage, the J. C. Fullerton mill, and a few other buildings. Drama was at the center point of the town for some years as Grady's store (on First Street) in East Fairfax and the Posen & Anderson store (on Second Street) fought over which district should be the "Main Street." The trivial disputes were so petty that, on one Independence Day, they held two celebrations right next to each other at the same time. Attempts to annex East Fairfax into the city of Fairfax's formal city limits failed several times before the two successfully put aside their differences and merged. The commercial district was extensive. Some interesting pieces of infrastructure within Fairfax as of 1914 were four grain elevators, three banks, a bowling alley, a cigar factory, two orchestras, seven auto dealers, two motorcycle garages and two automobile garages, four churches, two parochial schools, a stone jail, and a 600-barrel mill, amongst many others. Multiple earlier mills, such as Nichols & Hornberg's and the Phoenix Roller Mills, were destroyed by fire; the latter was considered an act of arson. A brick fireproof elevator was likely raised due to these repeated attempts. Fairfax had a peak population of 1,489 people in 1960. It is the closest community to Fort Ridgely State Park, the site of an early battle between the United States government and the Santee Sioux during the Dakota War of 1862. It was attacked on August 20, 1862, by the Sioux, who had just ambushed and defeated the U.S. Forces at the Battle of Redwood Ferry two days prior. They besieged the fort but were driven back on August 27 when Colonel Henry Sibley and 1,400 soldiers arrived from Fort Snelling. The State Park was designated in 1934 and added to the NRHP in October 1989 for the Civilian Conservation Corps Rustic Style buildings that were added to the park between 1934 and 1936. Until September 2016, it was the only Minnesota state park with a 9-hole golf course.

FRANKLIN, MN
POPULATION: 493 – CITY 105 OF 856 (3-28-25)
The Battle of Redwood Ferry took place near present-day Franklin on August 18, 1862, and was the second of several battles in a war now known as the Dakota War of 1862. The first engagement of the day was the Attack at the Lower Sioux Agency in Redwood County, where the Dakota chief, Little Crow, led several bands of Native Americans to raid stores for pork, flour, guns, clothing, and other necessities. In truth, the attacks were in retaliation for the refusal of traders to help Native Americans in a period of famine, in addition to the failure of United States Indian agents to adequately render annuity payments as had been agreed upon in several treaties. Half (24 men) of the forces of Captain John S. Marsh were killed in the ambush, and he drowned in a stream while retreating to Fort Ridgely. Twenty years later, in 1882, long after the war had concluded and peace was restored to southwestern Minnesota, a new townsite called Franklin was platted on Halleck Anderson's land and named in honor of Benjamin Franklin, a polymath and Founding Father of the United States. A post office was established in 1869; its postmaster was Holder Jacobus until 1882. With the Minneapolis and St. Louis Railroad driving the city's early industry and settlement, numerous businesses were established to serve the needs and wants of its initial residents. The Hohle Brothers had a general merchandise store, Nils Anderson owned the first blacksmith shop, and Peter Johnson was the first hotel proprietor. Plat maps show that by 1888, there was a depot, two elevators, a school, the post office, and a mill; these six places would have been the most crucial to the town's success. The Citizens' Milling Company of Franklin operated from 1907 to June 1913, one of the most important businesses, as the agricultural trade was the lifeblood of Franklin's local economy. Later institutions in the 1910s varied in their specialty. Still, some of the more prominent firms of that era were the Franklin Farmers' Co-operative Creamery, the Hauser Lumber Company, the Franklin Produce Company, the Great Western Elevator Company, the Franklin Independent Elevator Company, the Pacific Elevator Company, the Farmers' Elevator Company, the Franklin Automobile Company, the Citizen's State Bank, the State Bank of Franklin, the Farmers' Mutual Fire Insurance Company, and the *Franklin Tribune* newspaper. The paper was published from 1878 to 1969. Franklin residents pucker up at the annual "Kiss the Catfish Contest" during Catfish Derby Days, a yearly celebration held on the 4th weekend of July. The Catfish Capital of Minnesota prides itself on doing just that—awarding a kiss with a catfish to the top fundraisers—during the festivities, as well as a "biggest catch" contest, a street dance, parades, and several tournaments.

HECTOR, MN
POPULATION: 1,012 – CITY 108 OF 856 (3-28-25)
Hector rose to prominence as a Milwaukee Railroad town, but it was a love for flying that brought the community to new heights. At the dawn of World War II, Hector was the "most air-minded city in the country," according to numerous news publications, and for good reason. A whopping 40% of the town's men between the ages of 18 and 40 were pilots or novice fliers, and 10% of the city's population of 1,044 people had taken lessons at some point. Glenn L. Clark started the town's passion for aviation when he purchased a pasture for use as a grassy airfield in the 1920s. As of 2025, the

Hector Municipal Airport has celebrated its one-hundredth anniversary. The town of Hector was formally established on September 14, 1878, with the arrival of the Hastings and Dakota Railway, and its name was changed from Milford because of the supposed existence of another Milford in Minnesota at the time. It was later discovered that the other Milford was in South Dakota, but the name Hector stuck, as many of this community's pioneer settlers hailed from Hector, New York. A couple of businesspeople preceded the actual platting of the town. Charles Lang built a grain warehouse, and M. Abbott moved his store from Lake Preston to the site, intending to be the first merchant. Hogland and Stranberg brought their blacksmith shop in, and the McGregor lumber yard set up as the community's primary lumber dealer. With some of these original businesses in place, Hector was in a prime position to kickstart its development. A post office was located in 1875, a few miles outside of the community, and John Baker was named postmaster. By 1882, only four years after it was founded, the town had five dry goods and grocery stores, four saloons, three hotels, a millinery, a jewelry store, a furniture store, a shoe shop, a harness shop, a livery stable, a lumber yard, and pairs of pharmacies, hardware stores, blacksmith shops, meat markets, and elevators capable of storing 60,000 bushels. Later came the flour mill, the State Bank of Hector, the Merchants' State Bank, the Hector Creamery Company, the *Hector Mirror* newspaper, and several dozen other firms, all contributing to an excellent commercial district in the 1910s. In that same era, religion became an essential part of everyday life. Hector had a Catholic, a German Evangelical, a German Lutheran, a Swedish Lutheran, a Swedish Methodist, and an English Methodist church, according to a 1916 directory, all of which had their own pastors to perform services. An 1888 plat map only shows Catholic, Methodist Episcopal, and Baptist churches. It and its neighboring communities on the same east-west road were connected in the 1910s by the Yellowstone Trail, the first transcontinental highway through the northernmost states of the country, running from Seattle, Washington, to Plymouth, Massachusetts. Hector's most famous daughter was Dorothy Peterson; she appeared in over eighty Hollywood films after making a name for herself on Broadway.

Restaurant Recommendation:
Other Place
540 Main St S
Hector, MN 55342

MORTON, MN
POPULATION: 410 – CITY 106 OF 856 (3-28-25)
The City of Morton is synonymous with Morton Gneiss, the oldest intact continental crust rock in the United States, dating back 3.5 billion years. Since 1884, the "rainbow" stone has been quarried in the area and used first as trackbed material for the Minneapolis & St. Louis Railroad. Several locations in modern Morton, such as the welcome signs and panels on the old high school, showcase the gorgeous stone, but Zion Lutheran Church was built entirely from it. It is present in architecture throughout the country (including fountains at the White House in Washington, D.C., in 1968) and was widely used in the 1920s and 1930s during the Art Deco era. The earliest of Morton's settlers may not have known the actual value of the stone beneath their feet, but their world was rocked on September 2-3, 1862, when their homesteads became the bloodiest battlefield of the Dakota War of 1862. The Battle of Birch Coulee saw the deaths of thirteen soldiers and ninety horses, two Native Americans, and the wounding of over fifty other cavalrymen. Many of the soldiers later died of their wounds. Fatalities were high because the attack had been an ambush, and many of the inexperienced

soldiers were unprepared for such a strong force to descend upon and siege their campsite, beginning in the dead of night. After the war concluded, settlers began to return to the area at least as early as 1867, when the Birch Cooley post office was established. From 1867 to 1894, it was the area's primary office until it was replaced by W. G. Bartley's "Morton" office in 1894. That name was given to the town plat in 1882, when the Minneapolis and St. Louis Railroad employees surveyed it on Buery, Preston, and Bartley's land. His home, or Patrick McGowan's, a railroad contractor, was the first building on the townsite. James Murphy opened a liquor store, and "Bill" Wall started a saloon. As a division point for the railroad, it had a roundhouse and a large eating house that became known for miles around for the delicious cooking of Mrs. Beach. Commerce and spending were plentiful as the railroad brought with it the means and the men to build up a substantial community; as of 1916, it had four hotels, an ice cream factory and creamery, the *Morton Enterprise* newspaper, a farmer's cooperative elevator, two banks, a movie theater, an opera house, and a plethora of other mercantile and commercial interests. Roman Catholic, German Lutheran, Methodist Episcopal, and Protestant Episcopal churches shaped community members' religious beliefs, and local public schools served as educational beacons for their youth. Morton Public School began as School District 55 in a sod shanty, then replaced its "classrooms" with a wooden building in 1883 and a five-room schoolhouse in 1895. The granite quarries were opened by T. Saulpaugh & Company of Mankato, Minnesota, in the early 1880s; they employed hundreds of early residents of Morton. Nowadays, Morton has about 400 residents, a little less than half its peak population of 904 in the 1940s. It is the administrative headquarters of the Lower Sioux Indian Reservation, sometimes known as the Mdewakanton Tribal Reservation, which was established under the Treaty of Traverse des Sioux in 1851. The 70-by-20-mile reservation along the Minnesota River was reduced to just 2.69 square miles following the events of the Dakota War of 1862. Some of the land, approximately 115 acres, was returned to the tribe in February 2021 by the Minnesota government and the Minnesota Historical Society. The Birch Coulee Battlefield has been designated a National Register of Historic Places site; it now features several historical and interpretive markers for visitors interested in learning more about the battle.

OLIVIA, MN ★
POPULATION: 2,343 – CITY 111 OF 856 (3-29-25)

Visitors to Olivia, Minnesota, may first notice the large, looming ear of corn (the world's largest) atop a gazebo at Memorial Park on Highway 212. The ode to the "Corn Capital of the World" was raised as a tribute to Renville County's status as Minnesota's leading corn producer, with its nine seed research facilities and countless communities contributing to its production. The picturesque community originated in September 1878 with the arrival of the Hastings & Dakota Railway Company tracks. It was named in honor of Olive, a female railroad agent in Ortonville, Minnesota, who was a good friend of Albert Bowman Rogers, the line's engineer. Eventually, the name was corrupted into Olivia by its incorporation as a village on March 4, 1881. G. J. DePue was likely the first settler on the site; he founded Olivia's first blacksmith shop and the DePue House hotel for weary travelers passing through the area. Knowing it would likely become a prominent agricultural center, Isaac Lincoln and his brother moved in shortly after and established an elevator and a lumberyard. Isaac was dubbed postmaster. By 1882, there was a hardware store, a wagon shop, a saloon, a shoe shop, a drug store, two elevators, four general stores, and a steam flour mill with an annual capacity of over 30,000 barrels. Protestant and Catholic churches appeared as Olivia developed, as did a public school. Much to the joy of its residents, their town emerged as the victor in the turn-of-the-century county seat war between it and three rival neighboring communities, which saw the removal of the seat of government from Beaver Falls to Olivia. It all began when Bird Island attempted to take over the county seat and build a courthouse in 1889. Olivia joined in on the action in 1894 and won that election, but the Minnesota Supreme Court reversed the decision when other towns called foul. Yet another October 25, 1900, vote gave the honor to Olivia. In the dead of night, four residents stole the county documents from Beaver Falls and brought them to Olivia, where they remain today. An 80-by-120-foot armory, later used as an opera house, roller-skating rink, and community center, was built in 1897 as a point of pride for the community. It was replaced by a newer, slightly smaller building, which started in 1914 and cost $25,000; it served many of the same purposes. The Public Library of Olivia was opened that latter year. Three early fixtures of Olivia that have withstood the test of time are the 1896 Heins Block, built by P. W. Heins to serve as a bank and a hardware store, and the $88,000 Renville County Courthouse and Jail, built in 1902. Its Late Victorian architecture and design were the brainchild of architect Fremont D. Orff of Minneapolis. Paul F. Heard, the executive director of the Protestant Film Commission from 1946 to 1951 and an Academy Award-nominated producer; Kathleen Winsor, the author of the 1944 historical romance novel *Forever Amber*; Tom Ruud, an NFL linebacker between 1975 and 1979, and Blix Donnelly, a 1944 World Series champion with the MLB's St. Louis Cardinals hail from here.

RENVILLE, MN
POPULATION: 1,301 – CITY 186 OF 856 (4-16-25)

Renville County's homonymous community was its first "true" city, established in 1878 when the Hastings & Dakota Division of the Chicago, Milwaukee & St. Paul Railway reached that point. Both the settlement and the town's name honor the French/Dakotaman Joseph Renville. He was the organizer of Fort Renville, a captain in the War of 1812, and the founder of the Columbia Fur Company. That business was founded in 1821 when the North West [Fur Trading] Company and the famous Hudson's Bay Company merged. Renville itself has no relation to those companies. Still, it did boast a plethora of noted early firms that helped shape it into an essential agribusiness unit of the railroad and of southwestern Minnesota. Some of Renville's first settlers were John O'Brien, John Cole, and Thomas Foster, whose land in October 1878 saw the beginnings of Renville's early infrastructure. In addition to stores owned by Samuel T. Rolson, Carl Henning, and Boyd & King, there was also a hotel owned by Dodge & McIntosh and the Griffith & Stevens elevator. Growth was relatively steady over the next several years. In 1880, Renville had 232 residents. That number climbed to 413 according to the 1890 Census, and in another ten years, it had risen to over 1,000 individuals. The growth can be directly attributed to an 1885 investment made by Prins & Koch. This land firm purchased 35,000 acres of land in the Minnesota River Valley, in Winfield Township and nearby Kandiyohi County. Peter Haan acted as their agent, bringing hundreds of eager Dutch, Swedish, and eastern settlers to take advantage of the fertile farmland. Numerous businesses were established to accommodate their needs. Their arrival also led to the establishment of no less than a dozen churches between 1886 and 1896: four Lutheran, three Holland Christian Reformed, one Methodist Episcopal, and pairs of Dutch Reformed and Catholic churches. Fires in November 1891 and February 1893 and a June 27, 1894, tornado caused minor setbacks to Renville's rapid expansion, but the spirit of its residents remained unwavering. A permanent post office organization came about in 1886. Businesses like W. H. Gold & Company's lumber yard, the McGregor Brothers & Company lumber yard, The Renville Roller Mills, Bottge & Hassinger's department store, The Farmers' Elevator, three banks, and *The Star Farmer County* and *The Renville County Independent* newspapers rose to prominence. The Southern

Minnesota Beet Sugar Cooperative, the world's largest sugar beet processing plant, is located just south of Renville. Local Richard Fredrickson is famous for being one of several inventors of the snowmobile (and several other inventions).

SACRED HEART, MN
POPULATION: 510 – CITY 118 OF 856 (3-29-25)

A name like "Sacred Heart" for a town points to an early religious history, which is true for Renville County's westernmost community. As the legend goes, the name was given in 1841 by Father Ravaud. He was a missionary priest traversing the river to spread the gospel. When he became ill, he opted to rest at the fork of two creeks near the modern-day townsite. Upon his recovery, he crafted a cross, inscribed it with the words "Sacred Heart, Ave Marie," and continued his journey. This account is the most widely accepted, although an alternate account states that the Sioux people gave the name to the bearskin hat of Charles Patterson. He owned a trading post on the Minnesota River circa 1783, and the Indigenous people began to call him the "Sacred Hat" man, as the bear was sacred in their culture. That name may have corrupted into "Sacred Heart" over the decades and then applied to the adjacent township. Widespread settlement occurred before the Dakota War of 1862, when numerous European settlers were massacred or taken captive. Joseph R. Brown was one of these early settlers, but he and his twelve children were spared because his wife was of Sisseton descent. The ruins of his home were listed on the National Register of Historic Places in August 1986; they are now known as the Joseph R. Brown State Wayside. As tensions eased, a village called Sacred Heart (whose area post offices were variously called Vicksburg, Minnesota Crossing, and Reishus between 1867 and 1878) was established in 1866 on the Minnesota River. It was moved and replatted in October 1878 by the Hastings & Dakota division of the Milwaukee Road. Like its neighbors, it supported an array of early businesses, churches, and schools. Ole Torbenson owned the first store, and Hans Field owned the first blacksmith shop. A saloon, pairs of elevators, and hardware stores, and numerous additional general stores highlighted its first institutions of trade. As of 1916, it had five elevators, six general stores, two lumber yards, two garages, two banks, three implement stores, a motion-picture theater, a flour and feed mill, a creamery, professional offices, and at least twenty other firms. At that time, there were five churches: the Swedish Evangelical Lutheran, the American Methodist Episcopal, the Free Norwegian Lutheran, the Norwegian Lutheran Synod, and the Norwegian Hauge Lutheran. The sizeable Protestant population is unsurprising, as most Scandinavians are of that faith, yet ironic, given that Sacred Heart's namesake suggests the community would be predominantly Catholic. Henry Paulson was village president when Sacred Heart was incorporated as a village in 1883. In addition to the Brown House, two other notable locations in town have been preserved for their history: the Lars Rudi House, an early 1868 cabin, and Hotel Sacred Heart, a 1914 brick building locally known as the Romborg Hotel. Sadly, the 1901 Sacred Heart Public School was demolished in 2023 despite being a noted community meeting place, auditorium, gymnasium, and early educational institution for several generations of its citizens. Max Ramsland was born in Sacred Heart on January 30, 1882, and interestingly became a member of the Legislative Assembly of Saskatchewan, Canada, in 1917.

Unincorporated/Ghost Towns: Beaver Falls, Bechyn, Churchill, Lakeside, Vicksburg

National Register of Historic Places:
Bird Island: Tinnes-Baker House
Fairfax: Minneapolis & St. Louis Depot

Morton: Birch Coulee
Olivia: Heins Block, Renville County Courthouse & Jail
Sacred Heart: Hotel Sacred Heart, Sacred Heart Public School, Joseph Brown House Ruins, Lars Rudi House

Golf Courses:
Dacotah Ridge Golf Club, Daily Fee (Morton, MN)
Mayflower Golf Club, Daily Fee (Fairfax, MN)
Oakdale Golf Club, Daily Fee (Buffalo Lake, MN)
Olivia Golf Club, Daily Fee (Olivia, MN)

Town Celebrations:
Buffalo Lakes Days, Buffalo Lake, MN (Second to Last Full Weekend in July)
Catfish Derby Days, Franklin, MN (4th Weekend in July)
Corn Capital Days, Olivia, MN (Last Full Week of July)
Fairfax Dayz of Thunder, Fairfax, MN (Last Weekend of June)
Hector Corn Chaff Days, Hector, MN (2nd Week of July)
Island Days, Big Island, MN (Early June)
Sacred Heart Summerfest, Sacred Heart, MN (3rd Weekend of July)

Pope County: former Cyrus Public School (Cyrus), former Standard oil Gas Station (Farwell), Walleye Sandwich at Lakeside Restaurant on Lake Minnewaska (Glenwood), Morning Glory Gardens Chapel (Long Beach), Starbuck Marina Lighthouse (Starbuck), Hobo Statue at Hobo Park (Starbuck), former Northern Pacific Railroad depot (Villard), Outhouse Collection at Pottyville (Villard)

Ramsey County: Mural at Minnesota State Fairgrounds (Falcon Heights), the North St. Paul Snowman (North St. Paul), Central Park Frank Rog Amphitheatre (Roseville), The Quadriga at the Minnesota State Capitol (St. Paul), Mickey's Diner (St. Paul), World's Smallest Texaco Station (Shoreview), Polar Bear Statue at Walser Polar Chevrolet (White Bear Lake), Cup and Cone (White Bear Lake)

Red Lake County: Veteran's Memorial (Oklee), Mural (Oklee), Salem Lutheran Church (Garnes), former Plummer Creamery (Plummer), Mural (Plummer), Red Lake County Courthouse (Red Lake Falls), Confluence of the Red Lake and Clearwater Rivers "The Point" at Sportsman Park (Red Lake Falls), Water Tower (Red Lake Falls)

Redwood County: New Avon Town Hall and former District No. 8 School (Rowena), former Chicago & Northwestern Railroad Depot (Lucan), Reflections Sculpture Park (Vesta), Dari King (Redwood Falls), Ramsey Falls (Redwood Falls), Sod House on the Prairie (Sanborn), White Rabbit Statue (Wabasso), former site of Laura Ingalls Wilder Dugout Home on the Banks of Plum Creek (Walnut Grove)

Renville County: The Prokosh Barn (Bird Island), Central Region Cooperative Grain Elevator (Buffalo Lake), Fort Ridgely State Monument at Fort Ridgely State Park (Fairfax), St. Luke's Lutheran Church (Franklin), Mural (Morton), Renville County Courthouse (Olivia), World's Largest Ear of Corn Gazebo (Olivia), former Hotel Sacred Heart (Sacred Heart)

RICE COUNTY
EST. 1853 - POPULATION: 67,097

Rice County, Minnesota, was named after Henry Mower Rice, a fur trader turned United States Senator when Minnesota became a state on May 11, 1858.

DUNDAS, MN
POPULATION: 1,712 – CITY 653 OF 856 (10-2-25)
Northfield's neighbor to the southwest, Dundas, began in 1857 when George Archibald and his cousins, John Sidney and Edward T. Archibald, settled here and built a series of mills on the Cannon River. Having hailed from Dundas County, Ontario, Canada, they named their new home after their motherland. The first mill was built in 1857, and the second in 1870. The brotherly mills were the first to produce and market patent flour (the type produced universally today) and were among the first to fully convert to a roller mill. The Archibalds were masters of their craft, and their "Dundas Straight" flour soon rose to national fame as the best in the United States and among some of the highest-quality flour products in the world. On New Year's Eve, 1892, both mills were deemed a total loss after a devastating fire. The Archibalds sold out to the local grain elevator proprietors, who rebuilt both structures. By the 1930s, both mills had been partially destroyed again, and to this day, the ruins of the original 1870 structure still stand as a local tourist attraction. While the mills were nationally recognized, Dundas was home to more than just mills. Most of the original business district was on the eastern side of the river until the Minnesota Central Railroad laid its tracks on the western side. According to a 1900 atlas, the Chicago & Great Western Railway and the Chicago, Milwaukee & St. Paul Railroad ran directly through the heart of the local commercial district, which consisted of blacksmith shops, storefronts, hotels, and the aforementioned mills and elevators. Six church congregations existed at that time as well: the German Catholics, the Episcopalians, the Methodists, the Adventists, and a few Protestant churches. One of those churches, the Episcopal Church of the Holy Cross, built in 1868 in the Gothic Revival style, still stands on Second Street. The Ault Store, erected in 1866, is also the last surviving commercial property from the original Dundas commercial district. Mill founder Edward T. Archibald's house, where he lived from 1867 to 1885, is Dundas's most famous home aside from the 1869 Greek Revival/Italianate William Martin House. The growth of Dundas accelerated significantly from 2000 and 2010, during which its population increased by 149.9%.

Restaurant Recommendation:
L & M Bar & Grill & Patio
224 Railway St N
Dundas, MN 55019

FARIBAULT, MN ★☆
POPULATION: 24,453 – CITY 652 OF 856 (10-1-25)
When a town boasts two rivers, the Straight and the Cannon, and multiple railroad lines, the Chicago, Milwaukee & St. Paul, the Chicago, Rock Island & Pacific, and the Wisconsin, Minnesota & Pacific, its development and impact on the immediate region is bound to be profound, and history is destined to be abundant. Such is the case with Faribault, the county seat of Rice County and one of Minnesota's most historic communities, boasting 43 National Register of Historic Places nominations and a history that predates the establishment of the Minnesota Territory itself. Its name

honors Alexander Faribault, the son of the famed French fur trader Jean-Baptiste Faribault, who first established a fur post in the area on the Cannon River in 1826. After eight years of success, it was relocated a mile northward to the confluence of the Straight and Cannon Rivers, where the Faribault townsite began to blossom circa 1854, when a steam-powered sawmill was constructed. Peter Bush and Luke Hulett are widely regarded as some of the original white settlers in the vicinity. Still, Faribault's development occurred so rapidly that within just 15 years, it already had over 3,000 inhabitants and a plethora of homes, businesses, schools, churches, and other essential infrastructure. Alexander Faribault built the first permanent residence around 1853, using elements of Greek Revival architecture. It still stands today and has been historically used as a community civic center and church. After Faribault was designated the Rice County seat in 1858, it was selected for several state institutions and schools – so many, in fact, that it was dubbed the "Athens of the West." The first was the State School for the Deaf, established in 1858; followed by the State School for the Blind in 1864, the State School for the Feeble-Minded in 1879, and the Shattuck and St. James military academies, now known as Shattuck-Saint Mary's School. The Minnesota State Academy for the Deaf still operates today, with over 80 pupils. It was established in Faribault, where townspeople agreed to donate 40 acres of land for the campus, located within two miles of the city center. A memorial marks Dow Hall, a former 1883 structure that served as the Minnesota State School for the Blind. By 1915, there were no less than fourteen churches; flour, feed, planing, and woolen mills; a packing house; a brewery; piano, shoe, furniture, canning, and hand truck factories; a creamery; a hospital; an opera house; St. Mary's Hall Seminary, and many other lines of enterprise. Listing every one of Faribault's historic structures would be difficult, but amongst the more notable (not including those already mentioned above) are the Cathedral of Our Merciful Saviour and Guild House, whose cathedral aspect was completed in 1862 to serve as the center of the Episcopal Church in Minnesota; the 1871 Chapel of the Good Shepherd; the Faribault City Hall, built in 1884; the Thomas Scott Buckham Memorial Library, built in 1930 in the Moderne style; the 1934 Art Deco courthouse and accompanying 1910 brick jail, and the Faribault Historic Commercial District with its nineteen contributing 1870 to 1898 commercial buildings. In 1926, local woodworker Herbert Sellner invented the Tilt-A-Whirl, a popular amusement park ride, in his basement. It debuted at the Minnesota State Fair. Sellner Manufacturing was opened in Faribault to mass-manufacture over one thousand of the rides. Faribault Woolen Mills, open since 1865, is one of only a handful of vertically integrated woolen mills in the country today that take in raw wool and process it into socks, blankets, sheets, and other products. Other noteworthy points of interest include the River Bend Nature Center, the Rice County Historical Society Museum, and the Furball Farm Cat Sanctuary, a nationally famous home for hundreds of feral cats. Of all its famous men and women, ten of the most notable include Tom Lieb, a former head coach for University of Florida football team, as well as Alabama's track and field and Notre Dame's ice hockey programs at different points; Diana E. Murphy, the Senior Judge of the United States Court of Appeals for the Eighth Circuit between November 29, 2016, and May 16, 2018; Henry Benjamin Whipple, the first Episcopal bishop of Minnesota from 1859 to 1901; Raphael Louis Zengel, a Victoria Cross recipient for his actions rendered with the Canadian Expeditionary Force during World War I; Patrick Eaves, an ice hockey forward with 633 NHL game appearances; George Ballis, a photographer and activist noted for documenting César Chávez and his formation of the United Farm Workers; Bruce Smith, the winner of the 1941 Heisman Trophy with the Minnesota Golden Gophers; Elizabeth Strohfus, a pioneer aviator with the Women Airforce Service Pilots during World War II, and Shon "Wendy" Seung-wan, a South Korean singer known for her role in the Korean girl group Red Velvet.

LONSDALE, MN
POPULATION: 4,686 – CITY 663 OF 856 (10-3-25)

Czech and Norwegian settlers began to arrive in this area of Minnesota, known to them as Trondhjem, the name of a city in Norway, in large numbers in 1878. Their Trondhjem Norwegian Lutheran Church was built in present-day Webster Township that year and then rebuilt in 1899, incorporating new Greek Revival and Gothic Revival elements, along with materials from the old church. The church still stands today, but Trondhjem was wiped off the map when a proposed railroad from Mankato to Farmington never came to fruition due to the economic Panic of 1893. About a decade later, the village of Lonsdale was laid out when the Chicago, Milwaukee & St. Paul Railway purchased a right-of-way from Thomas Wilby via the Milwaukee Land Company. The paper town was fully platted by January 1902, and lots were up for sale that summer. Martin Benzik bought several pieces of property and was responsible for Lonsdale's original hotel, livery stable, and saloon. James McFadden established the second saloon, V. Peterka had a butcher shop, and John Gannon owned the hardware store. A 20,000-bushel grain elevator was erected later that year, as were the Skluzacek Brothers and H.E. Westerman lumber yards, and other grocery, hardware, implement, and general stores. Many residents moved out of their homes in Veseli, and essentially the entire Czech community (except for the Catholic Church of the Most Holy Trinity, a landmark edifice built in 1905) moved to be located along the railroad tracks. Lonsdale had its own Catholic Church of the Immaculate Conception, along with a corresponding rectory and Catholic School, built between 1904 and 1912, shortly after its incorporation in 1903. Also during this time, the Lonsdale District No. 76 Public School, now the 3-R Landmark School Museum, was built to serve as the community's educational home for youth. The school, the earlier-mentioned Trondhjem Lutheran Church, and the *Den Svenska Evangeliska Lutherska Christdala Församlingen* [Swedish Lutheran Church], built in 1878, are Lonsdale's primary points of historical interest. Although its exact etymology is disputed, Lonsdale was likely named after a village in Rhode Island. Willoughby was an early variation of its name because of James Wilby's early settlement of the area in 1857.

MORRISTOWN, MN
POPULATION: 949 – CITY 623 OF 856 (9-29-25)

Jonathan Morris, the founder of Morristown, and his son, Walter, were attracted to the area in 1855 when they foresaw the power of the Cannon River for a mill. He platted out the townsite of Morristown and built a sawmill in the autumn of that year, although he sadly passed away in November 1856 due to an illness he developed while assembling the mill. His son, Walter, carried on his legacy, becoming the town's postmaster, and Morristown began to develop as one of Rice County's more successful settlements. Christian Hershey Jr.'s mill replaced the Morris mill in the 1860s, and later still, the Morristown Feed Mill (known for its production of scientifically designed animal feed) was constructed in 1911. To the north of Minnesota and the Cannon River, the Wisconsin, Minnesota & Pacific Railroad served the transportation needs of the communities before the widespread adoption of automobiles. Its presence led to the creation of an elevator, a creamery, a bank, a hotel, two livery stables, three schools, and churches for Baptists, Congregationalists, Methodists, and Episcopalians. Morristown's population has steadily increased over the decades; as of 2010, it had reached a peak of 987. Henry Waldo Coe, a close friend of Theodore Roosevelt and one of the Dakota Territory's pioneer doctors, spent his youth here. The Morristown Feed Mill is now home to the Morristown Historical Society. At Ahlman's Gun Shop, a talking moose welcomes passersby to a western frontier town.

NERSTRAND, MN
POPULATION: 273 – CITY 655 OF 856 (10-2-25)
Nerstrand may be relatively small compared to most Minnesota cities, but this little hamlet is rich in history, starting with the establishment of the townsite by Osmund Osmundson in 1855. He moved to the area from Nedstrand, Tysvær, Norway. In 1877, he strategically built a store on the right-of-way of the Minnesota and Northwestern Railroad, located between Lyle and St. Paul. Many Norwegians lived near Mr. Osmundson, and together they worked to build up the railroad town. Augen H. Brokke became postmaster when the post office opened in 1877 in his store. In twenty-three years, Nerstrand residents had made several significant improvements to their home. On the railroad tracks, visitors would have found the depot, stockyards, a coal shed, and three grain elevators. At the eastern end of Main Street, there was a creamery and an ice house. On the north side of Main Street, a hotel and a few storefronts were located, whereas on the south side, a village hill, a blacksmith shop, a lumber shed, and the post office could be found. School No. 111 and the Norwegian Lutheran Church were located in the far southern part of the town plat, on Osmund Osmundson's property. His 1880 two-story gabled white brick home still stands as a local historic site alongside the 1908 Nerstrand City Hall, the 1875 Bonde Farmhouse, the 1875 Thorstein Veblen Farmstead, and Valley Grove, a pair of adjacent churches built in 1862 from stone and in 1894 in a Gothic Revival style. Veblen was a prominent Progressive Era leader and an economist who strongly criticized capitalism, authoring "The Theory of the Leisure Class," which laid the foundation for institutional economics. His farmstead is a National Historic Landmark and is also noted for being the site of Rice County's first bucket elevator. Nerstrand-Big Woods State Park, home to Hidden Falls on Prairie Creek, was established in 1945 to preserve portions of the expansive contiguous forests that once covered much of southeast Minnesota.

NORTHFIELD, MN
POPULATION: 20,790 – CITY 654 OF 856 (10-2-25)
"Cows, College, and Community" aptly sums up Northfield, renowned for its extensive dairy operations and its two private liberal arts institutions, Carleton College and St. Olaf College. Named in honor of its founder, John Wesley North, who also served in the Minnesota Territorial Legislature and assisted in the formation of the University of Minnesota in Minneapolis, Northfield was platted in 1855 on the Cannon River. With the help of his brother-in-law, George Loomis, North built a sawmill, a gristmill, and a bridge, all of which were purchased in 1859 by Charles Wheaton after the financial panic of 1857 nearly brought the North family to financial ruin. Similar to its neighbors to the southwest in Dundas, the local mill was brought to fame in 1876 by Jesse Ames and sons, who won the "best flour in the United States" award at that year's Centennial Exposition in Philadelphia, Pennsylvania. The mill changed hands again in 1927 when L.G. Campbell purchased the facility and turned it into the Campbell Cereal Company, the inventors of Malt-O-Meal cereal, the only hot cereal product still produced in the country today. Lumber and flour mills emerged as important industries, but Northfield became better known in its early days for its emphasis on higher education. The Minnesota Conference of Congregational Churches was instrumental in establishing Northfield College (now Carleton College) in 1866, located in the northeast corner of Northfield. Charles Augustus Wheaton and Charles Moorehouse Goodsell donated twenty of the campus's 200 acres to help establish the institution. Eight years later, in 1874, Norwegian Lutherans, led by Bernt Julius Muus, founded Saint Olaf's School (now St. Olaf College) to train teachers and preachers in accordance with the doctrines of the Evangelical Lutheran Church of America. The two colleges, which jointly enroll

about 5,000 students, are friendly cross-town rivals. In the midst of Northfield's early growth and the maturing of the two universities, the town experienced an event that would define its tourism draw for several decades to come. On September 7, 1876, the infamous Jesse James and his gang attempted to rob the First National Bank of Northfield. Eight men rode into town that afternoon, three of whom entered the bank. Joseph Lee Heywood, one of the bankers, lost his life when he insisted he could not open the bank vault because it was on a timer. In reality, it was unlocked the entire time. His attempt to waste the burglars' time was successful, as by the time the gang realized that he had tricked them, a large posse had formed. A shootout resulted that made J.S. Allen, A.R. Manning, and Henry Wheeler heroes, but also claimed the life of the non-English speaking Swedish immigrant Nicholas Gustafson. Two of the outlaws were slain in town, and a third was killed near Madelia. The Younger brothers were captured, and only Jesse and Frank James escaped what was then the largest manhunt in United States history when they made it all the way to Missouri. One of the guns used in the shootout is now on display at the Northfield Historical Society Museum. Every year, locals celebrate the heroism of their ancestors with the Defeat of Jesse James Days, held on the weekend after Labor Day. Following the bank robbery, Northfield's growth continued as normal. By 1915, it had four railroad lines: the Chicago, Milwaukee & St. Paul, the Chicago, Rock Island & Pacific, the Chicago Great Western Railway, and the Minneapolis, Northfield & Southern, also known as the Dan Patch Electric Line. Three creameries, three hotels, three banks, two hospitals, two commercial clubs, two grain elevators, an Odd Fellows home, and flour, feed, and knitting mills were just some of the major businesses present at that time. The 1866 Gothic Revival All Saints Episcopal Church, the Northfield Commercial Historic District at Northfield's center, and several historic homes and structures on both college campuses (including Saint Olaf College's Old Main building, Steensland Library, and Carleton College's Goodsell Observatory, Willis Hall, and Skinner Memorial Chapel) are draws for history buffs. Carleton College boasts of an impressive 800-acre arboretum and nature preserve, whereas St. Olaf College owns 430 acres of natural lands, 150 acres of which are restored prairie. Several films based on Jesse James' failed robbery attempt have been released over the years, but a 2016 romantic comedy Christmas movie called *Love Always*, Santa was set in and partially filmed in Northfield. Like other towns of its size and stature, Northfield has well over fifty persons who have risen to fame in one way or another. A few of them include Fredrik Melius Christiansen, an early proponent of a cappella choral arrangements; Ian Barbour, the winner of the 1999 Templeton Prize known for establishing the contemporary field relating science and religion; Alexandra Holden, an actress noted for her roles in several comedy and horror films between 1997 and 2003; Laurence McKinley Gould, the chief scientist on Richard Evelyn Byrd's initial exploration of Antarctica; Kart Fritjof Rolvaag, the 31st Governor of Minnesota and the United States Ambassador to Iceland in the late 1960s; Charles Augustus Wheaton, an earlier mentioned man in this writeup who was a stout abolitionist and assistant of the Underground Railroad; Marilyn Sellars, a country music and gospel singer noted for her 1974 hit "One Day at a Time,"; Peter Agre, a molecular biologist who discovered aquaporin water channels; Ben Wang, a star of the 2025 film *Karate Kid: Legends*, and Lincoln Child, an author noted for the *Agent Pendergast* and *Jeremy Logan* book series, amongst a multitude of others.

**Restaurant Recommendation:
James Gang Coffeehouse & Eatery
2018 Jefferson Rd H
Northfield, MN 55057**

Dennison is only partially located in Rice County (see Goodhue County).

Unincorporated/Ghost Towns: Cannon City, Epsom, Hazelwood, Little Chicago, Millersburg, Moland, Prairieville, Ruskin, Shieldsville, Veseli, Warsaw, Webster, Wheatland

National Register of Historic Places:
Bridgewater Township: Edwin S. Drake Farmhouse
Dundas: Archibald Mill, Edward T. Archibald House, Ault Store, Church of the Holy Cross-Episcopal, William Martin House
Faribault: Administration Building-Girls' Dormitory, Minnesota School for the Deaf, W. Roby Allen Oral home School, Batchelder's Block, Frank A. & Elizabeth Berry House, Cassius Buck House, Thomas Scott Buckham Memorial Library, Louis Carufel & E. LaRose House, Cathedral of Our Merciful Saviour & Guild House, Chapel of the Good Shepherd, Gordon Cole & Kate D. Turner House, Congregational Church of Faribault, John N. & Elizabeth Taylor Clinton Cottrell House, Reverend James Dobbin House, Episcopal Rectory, Faribault City Hall, Faribault Furniture Company, Faribault Historic Commercial District, Faribault Viaduct, Faribault Water Works, Faribault Woolen Mill Company, Alexander Faribault House, Farmer Seed & Nursery Company, M. P. Holman House, Hospital, State School for the Feeble Minded, John Hutchinson House, Johnston Hall-Seabury Divinity School, Vincent & Elizabeth Lieb House, Cormack McCall House, Thomas McCall House, Timothy J. McCarthy Building, Thomas & Bridget Shanahan McMahon House, Noyes Hall, State School for the Deaf, Jonathon L. & Elizabeth H. Wadsworth Noyes House, John Gottlieb Pfeiffer House, Phelps Library, Shattuck School, Rice County Courthouse & Jail, Rock Island Depot, Saint Mary's Hall, Shattuck Historic District, Shumway Hall & Morgan Refectory- Shattuck School, Theopold Mercantile Co. Wholesale Grocery Building, Adam Weyer Wagon Shop, Hudson Wilson House
Lonsdale: Lonsdale Public School, Den Svenska Evangeliska Lutheriska Christdala Forsamlingen, Dodd Road Discontiguous District, Trondhjem Norwegian Lutheran Church
Morristown: Morristown Feed Mill
Nerstrand: Nerstrand City Hall, Osmund Osmundson House, Bonde Farmhouse, Valley Grove, Thorstein Veblen Farmstead
Northfield: All Saints Church-Episcopal, Laura Baker School, Bridge No. 8096, Goodsell Observatory-Carleton College, Drew H. Lord House, Northfield Commercial Historic District, John C. Nutting House, Old Main, Saint Olaf College, O. E. Rolvaag House, Scriver Block Building, Scoville Memorial Library, Skinner Memorial Chapel, Steensland Library-Saint Olaf College, Willis Hall
Veseli: Church of the Most Holy Trinity (Catholic)
Webster Township: Church of the Annunciation

Golf Courses:
Faribault Golf Club, Daily Fee (Faribault, MN)
Legacy Golf, Daily Fee (Faribault, MN)
Northfield Golf Club, Private (Northfield, MN)
Willingers Golf Club, Daily Fee (Northfield, MN)

Breweries/Wineries/Distilleries:
10,000 Drops Craft Distillers (Faribault, MN)
Chapel Brewing (Dundas, MN)
Imminent Brewing (Northfield, MN)
Loon Liquors (Northfield, MN)
Tanzenwald Brewing Company (Northfield, MN)

Town Celebrations:
Defeat of Jesse James Days, Northfield, MN (Weekend after Labor Day)
Lonsdale Community Days, Lonsdale, MN (2nd Saturday in August)

ROCK COUNTY
EST. 1857 - POPULATION: 9,704

Rock County was named Pipestone County from 1857 to 1862, until the legislature swapped the names to reflect their features better. Rock County was named for the Rock River, in turn named for a large outcropping of quartzite that stands in stark contrast to the prairie.

BEAVER CREEK, MN
POPULATION: 280 – CITY 3 OF 856 (2-21-25)

The second-oldest city in Rock County was platted by the O. D. Brown and Worthington & Sioux Falls Railroad in October 1877 on 80 acres of land donated by Charles Williams. His generosity and prominence amongst the earliest pioneers of the area led to him being named the first postmaster of Beaver Creek, a name which had come about in 1873 at the suggestion of James Comar. Beavers were the dominant species of the region long before the arrival of European settlers, and early reports indicate that they numbered in the hundreds. They were hunted for their pelts well into the 1880s, and with time, they were more or less eradicated from the area. While the animals disappeared, a townsite bearing their name rose from the prairie. It briefly served as the terminus of the Chicago, St. Paul, Minneapolis & Omaha line before it was extended westward into South Dakota. The early firms were plentiful, according to an 1886 atlas. A lumber yard, a livery, and the Beaver Creek House were located north of the tracks. Warehouses and a depot dotted the tracks, and in downtown Beaver Creek, there were three general merchandise stores, three blacksmith shops, two saloons, two agricultural implement stores, two drug stores, two printing offices, two wagon shops, a hardware store, a barber shop, a billiard hall, a meat market, a furniture store, a grocery store, a bank, a real estate office, and a hotel. At this point, a feed mill, a schoolhouse, and church buildings for the Presbyterians, Methodists, and Baptists also existed. In 1917, the First National Bank of Beaver Creek was established to meet the financial needs of the local community, and in March 1980, it was added to the National Register. An alternative proposed name for the town was Bishop, in honor of General J. W. Bishop, a railroad executive.

HARDWICK, MN
POPULATION: 189 – CITY 5 OF 856 (2-22-25)

The first hints of Hardwick emerged in the summer of 1885, when residents of Rock County's Denver, Rose Dell, and Mound townships circulated a petition to be presented to the Chicago, Rock Island & Pacific Railroad. They requested that a station be finally placed on Otter Otterson's farm, on a parcel of land that had been previously deeded to the railroad company in 1884. Officials contemplated their request for a few days before sending their townsite agent, E. S. Ellsworth, to consider the potential townsite. He agreed with the locals that they were worthy of a railroad, and in the fall of 1886, the tracks and the station arrived as promised. It was called Hardwick for J. L. Hardwick, who was widely considered the master builder of the Burlington, Cedar Rapids & Northern Railway. John Otterson built the first building, a residence (later a restaurant) on the site, and became postmaster in 1891. Engebret Olson owned the blacksmith shop; he was later rivaled in his profession by William Olson of Larchwood, Iowa. The hamlet was platted as just four blocks by W. N. Davidson in September 1892, the year that its real growth started when general stores, a wagon shop, a hotel, a saloon, a meat market, a livery barn, and a lumber yard were established. Herman Lenz, Thomas Trenhaile, and John H. Dressen competed to hold the largest and most profitable stock of general merchandise and goods. The following year, D. J. Hawley became the manager of a private bank (later the Farmers State Bank in 1907), D. J. Stoakes opened his hardware store, Hauger & Sackett's started a feed mill, and Otter Otterson erected the first of four elevators. Hardwick was incorporated on October 10, 1898, and eventually welcomed a second branch line of the Rock Island from Worthington in 1900. The second line pushed the economy forward, allowing Hardwick to support three other elevators, the First State Bank, a City Hall, and four churches built by the Presbyterians, the German Lutherans Synod, the Independent German Lutherans, and a united Norwegian congregation. Hardwick's school was District #48; it had about one hundred pupils as of 1906 when its four-room structure was built in the eastern part of town.

HILLS, MN
POPULATION: 686 – CITY 2 OF 856 (2-21-25)

The southwesternmost city in Minnesota, Hills, is located just two miles north of the Iowa border and four miles east of the South Dakota border. It was briefly called Oslo, and then Grant, before being named Anderson in honor of local farmer Goodman Anderson. Like the other preceding names, he too only enjoyed being an eponym of the town for a short time before it was renamed for good on March 1, 1890, for Frederick C. Hills. He was the president of the Sioux City and Northern Railway (later acquired by the Great Northern), one of two lines that crisscrossed the site where Hills was platted. The other line, moving horizontally along the southern border of the townsite, was the Illinois Central. It connected Sioux Falls, South Dakota, with Chicago, Illinois, and only barely passed through Minnesota's towns of Steen, Hills, and Bruce (which is unincorporated). The Hills post office began in 1890 when Jacob N. Jacobson and his associate moved their store from Bruce. Other early facets of the community included the Rock County Banking Company (later the First National Bank), established in 1892; *The Hills Crescent* newspaper, launched in August 1893; and a school for the town's youth. It would take another ten years before Hills joined the ranks amongst Minnesota's incorporated communities on November 15, 1904. By 1914, Hills had over four hundred residents and a second bank, two lumberyards, a feed barn, a feed mill, a blacksmith shop, a cement block factory, a creamery, four elevators, stockyards for both railroads, and the Immanuel Norwegian Evangelical Union (Lutheran Synod) Church, Trinity Norwegian Lutheran Free Church, and Union Norwegian Lutheran Church. "The Rez" (reservoir) has been a prominent feature in Hills for over a century and is now home to campsites, playgrounds, and a disc golf course. Visitors can stand on a tri-state marker to the southwest of town and view the Old Iron Post (placed in 1870) that divides Iowa, South Dakota, and Minnesota.

KENNETH, MN
POPULATION: 60 – CITY 67 OF 856 (2-27-25)

The Chicago, Rock Island & Pacific Railroad and W. N. Davidson officially laid out Kenneth on July 30, 1900, and named it for Kenneth Kennicott, the son of J. A. Kennicott. Their family had one of the closest residences to the site where the T. H. Brown & Co. townsite company wanted to place the station on the Burlington's path between Worthington and Hardwick. One of the first businesses was James L. Hogan's general store, so he was appointed postmaster when a post office was established. Five men —Bemis & Howard, Ryan & Berg, and E. A. Brown — worked to erect three elevators. James A. Palmer opened the first saloon for thirsty locals, and a second general store opened when A. D. Parker arrived with the prospect of being the primary supplier of goods in the newly established town. The Trotter family's hardware store and the St. Croix Lumber Company assisted entrepreneurs and residents alike in building their homes and businesses. Many other firms sprouted up in the subsequent year, the most noteworthy of which was the Kenneth State Bank. It was first located in A. D. Parker's building, so he served as the cashier. The Catholics and the Evangelical Lutherans operated Kenneth's two earliest churches; they arrived in 1903 and 1907, respectively. After its incorporation on July 20, 1921, Kenneth enjoyed a period of prosperity that lasted through the 1940s, when it reported a peak population of 148. Since then, most of its buildings and infrastructure have been lost to time, including the original Kenneth School structure. It was built in 1901 shortly after Kenneth was founded, and survived for many years as the only two-story schoolhouse in Rock County. The local post office branch was discontinued in 2011.

LUVERNE, MN ★☆
POPULATION: 4,946 – CITY 4 OF 856 (2-21-25)
More nutcrackers (5,300 as of March 2023) than people presently call Luverne home, thanks to the efforts of the Rock County History Center. What started as Betty Mann's collection of 2,800 nutcrackers has since nearly doubled in size due to generous donations from around the world. During the holiday season, an annual scavenger hunt is held for visitors to find the names of over 130 toothy figures. While Luverne's claim to fame is nothing short of remarkable, the town, once referred to as "the lovely gem of the valley of the rock," has a deep history that dates back to Philo Hawes and a mail route that ran between Blue Earth, MN, and Yankton, SD. Hawes and his family became the first permanent settlers of the site when they built a log cabin to serve as a post office, community center, city hall, and church for the immediate area. In August 1868, it was decided that the post office would be named Luverne in honor of Eva Luverne Hawes, Philo's eldest daughter. Her middle name was likely derived from a book read by Philo's cousin, Lucy Cotter. Throughout the 1870s, new arrivals vigorously pursued their passions and contributed to the community's advancement. In this decade, Luverne was not only platted and incorporated but also declared the seat of Rock County's government by Governor Horace Austin. Schools and churches (the first of which was the Methodist church in 1873) were established, as were countless businesses. According to an 1886 map, Lu Verne then had two branches of the Chicago, St. Paul, Minneapolis & Omaha Railroad, a single branch of the Chicago, Rock Island & Pacific Railroad, and a skating rink, a creamery, the *Rock County Herald* newspaper office, elevators, lumber yards, banks, saloons, hotels, millineries, liveries, and well over twenty different stores selling groceries, hardware, clothing, pharmaceutical goods, dry goods, and general merchandise. To build all these places, the city imported an unfathomable 19.79 million pounds of goods in 1885 and exported 7.6 million pounds of goods made by its residents. The town boasted a concrete company, two brick yards, and the Luverne Automobile Company at different points. Between roughly 1902 and 1904, the Luverne Carnegie Library (now the Carnegie Cultural Center) was constructed using $10,000 in funding from businessman and philanthropist Andrew Carnegie. Another community gem, the 550-seat Palace Theatre, was built using the blueprints of architect W. E. E. Greene and used to show live theater performances and silent films. Several of Greene's other designs were used to build the Carnegie Library, the Maplewood Chapel, the J.W. Gerber House, and the Holy Trinity Episcopal Church, all of which are listed on the National Register of Historic Places. The Gothic Revival church was open from 1891 to 2016 and was built for $6,000 using Sioux Quartzite. A total of fifteen locations in modern-day Luverne are on the NRHP; three other locations worth noting are the historic 1913 Omaha Depot, the Rock County Courthouse and Jail (a pair of Richardsonian Romanesque buildings built between 1887 and 1890), and five contributing WPA/New Deal-era buildings at Blue Mounds State Park. The park hosts an American bison herd

and one of the most significant undisturbed remnants of Minnesota's once-sprawling prairie. Worthwhile points of interest within Luverne include the Verne Drive-in Movie Theater, the Rock County Veterans Memorial, the Herreid Military Museum, the Brandenburg Gallery at the Rock County Veterans Memorial Building, and the Blue Mound Wayside Chapel on US Hwy 75, which features seating for six. In pop culture, Luverne served as the primary setting for the second season of *Fargo*, an FX black comedy, crime drama television series, which aired from October to December 2015. Additionally, Ken Burns' documentary miniseries about World War II premiered at the Palace Theater. Luverne was one of four towns profiled to examine how the war impacted the community and its residents. Luverne has been called home by an extensive number of noteworthy people: Shantel VanSanten, noted for her role as Quinn James in the teen drama series *One Tree Hill*; James Russell Wiggins, the former executive editor of The Washington Post and the 8th United States Ambassador to the United Nations for a brief period in the late 1960s; Jim Brandenburg, a nature photographer for National Geographic who twice won Magazine Photographer of the Year; Monti Ossenfort, the General Manager of the NFL's Arizona Cardinals since 2013 and a four-time Super Bowl champion with the New England Patriots; Quentin C. Aaneson, a World War II-era flying ace; Jerilyn Britz, professional golfer and the winner of the 1979 U.S. Women's Open LPGA Tour event, and Frederick Manfred, an author and the proprietor of the term "Siouxland" used to describe the area where Nebraska, Iowa, South Dakota, and Minnesota meet.

Restaurant Recommendation:
Take 16 Brewing
509 E Main St
Luverne, MN 56156

Lodging Recommendation:
Tipis at Blue Mounds State Park
1410 161st St
Luverne, MN 56156

MAGNOLIA, MN
POPULATION: 196 – CITY 68 OF 856 (2-28-25)

Philo Hawes, the same man who gave the judicial seat in Luverne its name (for his daughter), is behind the naming of this community on the far eastern side of the county. Present-day Magnolia, named for Philo's hometown of Magnolia, Wisconsin, was platted in 1891 when the Sioux City & St. Paul Railway extended its Worthington-Sioux Falls branch. A post office by that name was organized in 1886, but the very first office in the area was in operation possibly as early as 1872 under the name Westside across the county line. There was never a "Drake" post office, but that was the station's original name when the railroad established it. Unfortunately, they had to abandon that station (named in honor of Elias F. Drake, the railroad president) when they could not build side tracks to sort out cars and engines and more effectively distribute grains and agricultural products amongst them. Their mistake at Drake led to the establishment of Magnolia, incorporated on September 4, 1894, which, as of 1914, had three elevators, stockyards, a depot, a school, a post office building, and the Holbert Methodist Episcopal Church. The railroad was known as the "Omaha Road" then, and eventually became part of the Chicago & Northwestern. It is now called the Ellis & Eastern. Magnolia's early two-story schoolhouse was part of the district that ultimately became Magnolia Elementary School. The school closed in 1994.

STEEN, MN
POPULATION: 171 – CITY 1 OF 856 (2-21-25)

Steen (population 171), one of only two Minnesota towns situated on and serviced by the Illinois Central Railroad, was not incorporated as a village until February 5, 1942, well over fifty years after its establishment. The railroad station was founded as Virginia, but it was eventually renamed when the United States Postal Service opted to name it for John P. and Ole P. Steen, two early Norwegian immigrants who donated twenty acres of land for the townsite. J. F. Whalen surveyed it on behalf of the Cherokee & Western Town Lot & Land Company, and the first passenger train came through on June 2, 1888. Christian Clemmetson was dubbed postmaster on August 24, 1888, and the mail originally flowed through his furniture store. A public school went up as early as 1905. Within a decade, Steen's residents had built up an impressive townsite complete with all the necessary facilities a community of their era needed to survive. Amongst these were a general store, a hardware store, a hotel, a lumber yard, a blacksmith shop, a bank, a drug store, a harness shop, a pool hall, a livery barn, a town hall, a pair of elevators, and churches. The German Lutheran and the German Evangelical congregations had built the churches, as most of the town's early residents had come from Germany. Both elevators had to be rebuilt after a fire on February 24, 1900, that destroyed them and resulted in the loss of 20,000 bushels of grain. The last day of Steen's post office came on November 19, 2011, after which all mail was directed to Hills for processing.

Jasper is only partially located in Rock County (see Pipestone County).

Unincorporated/Ghost Towns: Ash Creek, Bruce, Carnegie, Kanaranzi, Manley

National Register of Historic Places:
Beaver Creek: Bridge No. L-4696, First National Bank of Beaver Creek
Hills: Jacob Nuffer Farmstead
Jasper: Bridge No. L-2162, Jasper Stone Company & Quarry
Kenneth: Kenneth School
Luverne: Blue Mounds State Park WPA/Rustic Style Historic Resources, Bridge No. 1482, Bridge No. L-2315, Bridge No. L-2316, J. W. Gerber House, R. B. Hinkly House, Holy Trinity Church- Episcopal, Pierce J. Kniss House, Luverne Carnegie Library, Frederick & Maryanna Manfred House, Maplewood Chapel, Omaha Depot, Palace Theater, Rock County Courthouse & Jail

Golf Courses:
Luverne Country Club, Daily Fee (Luverne, MN)

Breweries/Wineries/Distilleries:
Take 16 Brewing Company (Luverne, MN)

Town Celebrations:
Buffalo Days, Luverne, MN (1st Weekend in June)

ROSEAU COUNTY
EST. 1894 - POPULATION: 15,331

Roseau County, the Roseau River, and Roseau Lake share commonality in that they were named after the French word for reed.

485

BADGER, MN
POPULATION: 429 – CITY 283 OF 856 (5-30-25)
Badger Creek, a tributary of the Roseau River, is the namesake of this community of 429 people. A post office opened in 1889, and five years later, Governor Knute Nelson partitioned off a section of eastern Kittson County to form Roseau County. Eastern settlers had voiced their frustration with being so far from the county seat that it warranted the creation of the new jurisdiction. Roseau was declared the county seat, but residents of Badger contested that honor in 1896. They ordered the county commissioners to hold an election to remove the seat to their town, but the commissioners refused. Despite not getting their wish, Badger grew from 164 residents in 1900 to 395 by 1910. According to a 1913 atlas, the townsite was laid out so that Main Street ran parallel to the Great Northern Railroad tracks until it reached University Avenue. At that point, a visitor would enter downtown Badger, which had four banks, four stores, two livery stables, a lumber yard, a flour mill, and the school.

GREENBUSH, MN
POPULATION: 682 – CITY 282 OF 856 (5-30-25)
When traveling eastward from the Red River Valley, most travelers followed the "ridge road," which ran along a gravel beach ridge of ancient Lake Agassiz almost to Roseau. Along the road were copious spruce trees, called *Sha Ach Wah* by the Ojibwe (sometimes called the Chippewa). The term translates to "spruce tree" or "green bush" in their language. These trees inspired the name given to the old Greenbush townsite by early Scandinavian, Polish, and Bohemian settlers. A site on the Ridge Road in Two Rivers was where residents built their townsite over several years, until the Great Northern Railroad arrived in 1904. They informed citizens that their tracks would not be laid further than a site a couple of miles west of Greenbush. A new site called West Greenbush was laid out at once, and buildings, businesses, and houses were rolled on logs to their new home. Ironically, the Great Northern Railroad decided to expand eastward to Warroad only a couple of years later, with its tracks running directly through Old Greenbush. That site is now marked only by the Hvidso Cemetery on Highway 11. Although the unnecessary move frustrated residents, it did not deter them from building up a grand community complete with numerous lines of enterprise. It was incorporated in 1905 with a population of about 450 people, the lot of whom had built up six grocery stores; four saloons, restaurants, and implement stores; three banks, hardware stores, cream stations, and car dealerships; two each of blacksmith and barber shops, and a general store, print shop, lumber yard, cemetery, and hotel, in addition to several others. Its progress was briefly impeded by a December 27, 1907, fire that began in the Kukowski Block and destroyed two adjacent saloons, the State Bank of Greenbush, and the T. E. Thompson hardware store. Greenbush recovered, and by 1913, more hotels and stores had opened, as had two churches and a school within city limits. Dennis Brazier brought a new industry to Greenbush in 1984 when he founded Central Boiler. This outdoor furnace manufacturer has grown tenfold since its inception.

Restaurant Recommendation:
Remedies
183 Main St N
Greenbush, MN 56726

ROOSEVELT, MN
POPULATION: 153 – CITY 286 OF 856 (6-1-25)
The Canadian National Railroad, established initially as the Canadian Northern, wove its way through modern-day Roseau and Lake of the Woods County in 1904 to help solidify Roosevelt's future as one of the final shipping points of the line before it reached Canada. Roosevelt was named in honor of Theodore Roosevelt, who had recently taken office as the 26th President of the United States. The post office opened in 1901 as its first business unit, but within about 10 years, those lines had expanded to include four stores and a hotel. A church was located at the corner of Third Avenue and Fourth Street, and the school sat by itself northwest of the town plat on the land of Emma Harwood. There was a dedicated city ballpark in the southern part of Roosevelt at the end of Birch Street, perhaps listed on the plat map as a nod to the impact of "America's Game" on small Minnesota towns throughout most of the 20th century. Knutson's Hartz grocery store, best known for its potato sausage, has served Roosevelt as a full-service grocery store for over a century.

ROSEAU, MN ★☆
POPULATION: 2,744 – CITY 284 OF 856 (5-31-25)
"The North Star City," located just a short ten-minute drive from the Canadian border, started in 1822 when the Hudson Bay Fur Trading Company established a trading post to connect it to the rest of Rupert's Land. Rupert's Land was a British territory comprising a large portion of modern-day Canada over which the company held a monopoly from 1670 to 1870. It was not until 1895 that the Roseau post office, one of the first instances of permanent European settlement here, was established when the United States Postal Service decided it was time to open a branch office. *Roseau* comes from the French word for "reed," a name also applied to the 214-mile-long tributary of the Red River of the North that flows through the townsite. The county was formed on December 31, 1894, just before the establishment of the post office, and Roseau village was named the county seat. By 1900, 301 immigrants had opted to take a chance on these far northern homesteads. Twenty years later, the population surpassed one thousand people for the first time. Businesses were plentiful. Two hotels, a general store, a livery, a lumber yard, three banks, a mill, and two grain elevators were among its most notable institutions. Five churches, a courthouse, two schools, two dance halls, and designated grounds for the Roseau County Agricultural Society (complete with a grandstand, barns, and cattle sheds) were in place by 1913. Anton Werner Lignell and Robert Loebeck designed the Roseau County Courthouse, which still stands today as one of two Roseau locations on the National Register of Historic Places, the other being the 1949 Roseau Memorial [Ice Hockey] Arena. Recreation has remained a core part of Roseau's identity. Fishermen, hunters, and outdoor enthusiasts come to the area in droves every year to immerse themselves in the great outdoors. One sport stands head and shoulders, or perhaps track and ski, above all the others: snowmobiling. While Edgar Hetteen was away on a business trip, his brother Allan, David Johnson, Orlen Johnsson, and Paul Knochenmus invented a vehicle that could travel through snow. The prototype was completed in 1954, much to Edgar's frustration: he was angry that his coworkers had wasted so much time on a "silly invention" while he was away. The invention was sold to local lumberyard owner H.F. Peterson for $465 so the company could afford to pay its employees for that payroll period. After giving the invention some thought and making some adjustments, the first "Polaris Sno Travelers" entered the marketplace in 1956. Edgar left the company in June 1960 to start a rival company in Thief River Falls called Polar Manufacturing, which ultimately became Arctic Cat after a 1980s bankruptcy

restructuring. Polaris Inc. eventually produced ATVs (such as RZRs), boats, motorcycles (through its Indian Motorcycle subsidiary), and military vehicles. It is now headquartered in Medina, Minnesota, but the Polaris Experience Center invites visitors to see the beginnings of their company and the changes it has endured over the decades. The Roseau Pioneer Farm and Village has served as the area's general historical research site since 1975. Outside of town is Hayes Lake State Park, a 2,958-acre park established in 1973 that welcomes winter sports enthusiasts, bikers, equestrians, and wildlife enthusiasts hoping to catch a look at black bears, moose, Canadian lynx, timber wolves, minks, bobcats, red fox, or any one of several other species. Over a dozen former professional hockey players hail from Roseau, the most popular of which are Aaron Ness; Paul Broten; Aaron Broten, who played 748 regular season games throughout his career; Neal Broten, the oldest brother of three Brotens mentioned here, and a gold medalist in the 1980 Lake Placid Olympic games with Team USA; Dustin Byfuglien, the first Black American-born player to win the Stanley Cup in 2010; Rube Bjorkman, a member of the 1948 and 1952 U.S. Olympic hockey teams, and Bryan Erickson, whose playing career was between 1979 and 1994. Non-hockey-related persons of note with ties to Roseau also include John Harris, a professional golfer on the PGA and the Champions Tours; actor Garrett Hedlund, known for his roles in *Friday Night Lights* (2004), *Tron: Legacy* (2010), and *The Marsh King's Daughter* (2023); Robert Bergland, the 20th United States Secretary of Agriculture from January 1977 to January 1981 under President Jimmy Carter, Liz Anderson, a singer-songwriter who had more top-50 hits, approximately 26, than any other female songwriter in country music in the 1960s; Phil Bengtson, the head coach of the Green Bay Packers and New England Patriots for short stints in the early 1970s, and sculptor Norman Carlberg.

STRATHCONA, MN
POPULATION: 25 – CITY 281 OF 856 (5-30-25)
Throughout his life, Sir Donald Alexander Smith, 1st Baron Strathcona and Mount Royal, worked with the Hudson's Bay Company, the Canadian Pacific Railway, and James J. Hill and the Great Northern Railway as they built a line through this area. Hill instructed his officials to name the town Strathcona in honor of his friend. Charlie Gunheim built the first store in 1904, and in 1905, Hans Lerum started his 36-year reign as the Strathcona postmaster. A second store, a hotel, a creamery, an elevator, a church, a school, and a depot were the early landmarks of the tiny community, which never grew to a population exceeding 143 in the 1950s. Its population halved by the 1960s to 64 people, a decrease of 55.2%, and then again to 31 people by 1970, an additional 51.6% reduction.

WARROAD, MN
POPULATION: 1,830 – CITY 285 OF 856 (5-31-25)
"Hockeytown USA" is the rightful name for this far-northern Minnesota city, which boasts that no United States men's Olympic hockey team has won a gold medal without a player from Warroad. While incredibly impressive, the first war here was not on the ice but between Ojibwe and the Sioux over the rice fields on the Lake of the Woods. The largest Ojibwe village was once situated on the shores of the expansive lake, which posed problems when the Sioux invaded the land via the Red and Roseau Rivers. The constant power struggle led the early explorer Jonathan Carver to call it the "Road of War" as early as 1766-67. Europeans did not consider making any real significant settlement nearby for another 130 years. A post office opened at Jacob N. Laughlan's trading post, named Warroad, in 1897, taking its name from the township formed two years prior. Warroad village was separated from the township on

November 9, 1901, and it grew in popularity amongst anglers as an excellent commercial fishing location. Designated flight services were eventually established to fly in sportspeople and tourists from around the country. The lumber industry took off around the same time, leading to the inevitable arrival of both the Great Northern Railroad and the Canadian National Railway. The 1914 Canadian depot now serves as the City of Warroad's office and is the lone National Register of Historic Places listing. Of all its stores, banks, and other businesses, the most important was Marvin Windows. George Marvin built his mill in the early 1900s, which would ultimately evolve into Marvin Windows & Doors, one of the largest window manufacturers in North America. The Warroad-Sprague Border Crossing, opened in 1901, is popular for accessing the Northwest Angle. American film actress Sheila Terry and stand-up comedian Robert Baril have ties to Warroad. Still, most of its famous residents have a hockey background. Some of these players include Bill Christian, a 1960 Olympic gold-medalist and member of the United States Hockey Hall of Fame since 1984; his brother Gordon Christian, a 1956 Olympic silver-medalist; a third brother Roger Chrisitan, who was also a member of the 1960 U.S. Olympic gold medalist team and a U.S. Hockey Hall of Fame inductee in 1989; Bill's son Dave Christian, a 1980 Olympic gold-medalist and 15-year NHL veteran forward; Henry Boucha, a U.S. Hockey Hall of Fame inductee and a 1972 Olympic silver medalist; Gigi Marvin, a two-time Silver medal winner in 2010 and 2014 and gold medalist in 2018 with the United States national women's ice hockey team, and NHL players T. J. Oshie (a shootout specialist who won the Stanley Cup with the Washington Capitals in 2018), Brock Nelson (the grandson of hockey legend Bill Christian), and Alan Hangsleben.

Restaurant Recommendation:
Lake of the Woods Brewing Company
104 Main Ave NE
Warroad, MN 56763

Restaurant Recommendation:
Jerry's Restaurant & Lounge
7609 Young's Bay Dr NW
Angle Inlet, MN 56711

Unincorporated/Ghost Towns: Fox, Haug, Mandus, Pelan, Pencer, Pinecreek, Ross, Salol, Skime, Swift, Wannaska, Winner

National Register of Historic Places:
Poplar Grove Township: Lodge Boleslav Jablonsky No.219
Roseau: Roseau County Courthouse, Roseau Memorial Arena
Warroad: Canadian National Depot

Golf Courses:
Oak View Golf Club, Daily Fee (Greenbush, MN)
Oakcrest Golf Course, Municipal (Roseau, MN)
Warroad Estates Golf Course, Daily Fee (Warroad, MN)

Breweries/Wineries/Distilleries:
Lake of the Woods Brewing Company (Warroad, MN)

Town Celebrations:
Badger Fall Festival, Badger, MN (3rd Weekend in September)

SAINT LOUIS COUNTY
EST. 1855 - POPULATION: 200,231

At 6,860 square miles, the massive Saint Louis County is the largest in the United States by area to the east of the Mississippi River. Its name came from the Saint Louis River, the largest river (192 miles) to flow into Lake Superior.

AURORA, MN
POPULATION: 1,678 – CITY 368 OF 856 (6-21-25)
This Duluth and Iron Range Railway mining village dates to about 1898, when the Meadow Mine and its reserves of 300,000 tons of ore were discovered by either David T. Adams, Neil McInnes, Martin Van Buskirk, or some combination of the men on behalf of one another. Buskirk most likely located it. The first townsite was laid out approximately a mile north of the railroad in 1903 and was incorporated that November. However, it was relocated in 1905 to a new plat surveyed by E. J. Longyear. He was the owner of one area mining firm, the Mesabi Land and Improvement Company (proprietors of the Aurora Reserve), which was rivaled by the likes of the Cleveland-Cliffs Iron Company, the Sargent Land Company, the Oliver Iron Mining Company, the Perkins Mining Company, the McKinney Steel Company, and the Pickands Mather brand, to name just a few. Large quantities of iron and taconite ore led to many years of prosperity for the fledgling village, which reached a peak population of 2,809 in 1920 (though that number was almost surpassed at the 1960 Census, when the population was 2,799). When mining activities were temporarily paused, many miners turned to farming and dairying to make ends meet. Aurora High School, Herding High School, and Johnson Grade School were located on a 15-acre campus. They once boasted a grand natural history museum that featured fossils, plants, taxidermied animals, and no fewer than 1,694 insect specimens. The latter two brick buildings, with their shell-pink Kasota stone and Flemish-gray oak finished halls, were listed on the National Register of Historic Places on January 16, 1997, before being demolished only four years later. Aurora means "morning" in Latin, and the Minnesota town bearing this name can claim at least one famous man and woman: Jeno Paulucci, the founder of over 70 companies and the inventor of pizza rolls and Chun King Chinese foods, and Francine York, an actress best known for her roles in the 1962 comedy *It's Only Money* and the 1960s live-action *Batman* television series that starred Adam West. In 1997, Aurora adopted the motto "Minnesota's Star of the North."

 Restaurant Recommendation:
Rudy's Bar & Grill
116 N Main St N
Aurora, MN 55705

BABBITT, MN
POPULATION: 1,397 – CITY 366 OF 856 (6-21-25)
Located on the far eastern end of the Mesabi Iron Range, one of the region's four significant iron range deposits, the town of Babbitt was established in conjunction with Silver Bay (in Lake County) starting in 1944 to connect the mining region with the shore of Lake Superior. The name Babbitt was selected for the post office as early as 1920 to honor the legacy of Judge Kurnal R. Babbitt, who had recently passed away and was a former director of several mining companies. Construction began on a former taconite mine built by AK Steel Holdings Corporation (Armco) and Republic

Steel. Babbitt Village was not incorporated until September 12, 1956, at a time when its population already numbered well into the thousands. Its figures peaked in the 1970 Census with 3,076 residents, one of whom was Buzz Schneider. He was a part of the 1980 US Olympic gold medal hockey team as well as the 1976 squad. Modern-day Babbitt has grown from a mining shanty to a well-off community with multiple churches, a school, a fire department, and a library.

BIWABIK, MN
POPULATION: 961 – CITY 369 OF 856 (6-22-25)
The oldest village in the Mesabi and the Bavarian town of Biwabik have histories that delve deep into the origins of mining in the Arrowhead Region of Minnesota and the legend of mermaids. In the early 1800s, French Canadian fur traders wandered deep into the forests in search of the coveted beaver and other tradable items. When they stumbled upon Embarrass Lake, they claimed to have found a creature unlike any other–a woman-like creature with shimmering auburn hair and a powerful tail that allowed her to navigate the lake seamlessly. While her songs were captured on tape with the advances in technology, there has been no physical proof of her existence otherwise. It is thought that she disappeared when the miners arrived circa 1891, following the discovery of high-grade blue ore that warranted the establishment of the Biwabik Mine. The Cincinnati (part of the Biwabik), Hale, and Kanawha Mines came into existence at about the same time, as did the townsites of Biwabik and Merritt. The villages grew alongside one another for a short time, Merritt proving to be the more successful of the two, but a great fire wiped out all of its advances. The disaster, coupled with the bypassing of Merritt by the Duluth & Iron Range Railroad in favor of Biwabik, solidified the town as the center of population and commerce for this mining area. Its name was derived from an Ojibwe word, *biiwaabik*, meaning "iron." Biwabik was incorporated for the first time on November 10, 1892, and a postal service branch was organized the following year. Its growth accelerated with the arrival of a second railroad, the Duluth, Missabe, and Northern Railway, a precursor to the Duluth, Missabe, and Iron Range Railway and the owner of what were then likely the largest iron ore docks in the world. While its population in modern times is less than half of what it was at its peak in 1920 (2,024 residents), Biwabik has established itself as a nature-centered tourism destination. In the 1980s, the town undertook a renovation project to give its Main Street a Bavarian appearance and welcome visitors to the Giants Ridge Golf and Ski Resort. The golf course is widely regarded as one of the best in the state, and the accompanying gravity mountain bike trails crisscross 9 miles through the Superior National Forest. As a part of its 1980s project, Biwabik residents erected a large statue of "Honk the Moose" on the Mesabi Trail as a testament to a moose that regularly visited during the winter of 1915. Twenty years later, Phil Stong wrote his Newbery Honor children's book *Honk, the Moose*, widely regarded as one of the 100 Best Children's Books of the 20th Century. Around the time Strong brought Biwabik into the national spotlight with his book, Camp Esquaugama was built with prize money won by the local 4-H Club for being the "best county 4-H program in the nation." Formerly known as the St. Louis County 4-H Club Camp, it was constructed as a joint project of the Civilian Conservation Corps and the Works Progress Administration. In geology, Biwabik is notable for being the home of Mary Ellen Jasper, an impure variety of silica that contains fossils of 1.88 billion-year-old stromatolites.

BROOKSTON, MN
POPULATION: 118 – CITY 383 OF 856 (6-23-25)
Brookston, one of three administrative centers of the Fond du Lac Indian Reservation (formerly located at the head of Lake Superior near the mouth of the Saint Louis River),

was platted in 1905 and incorporated as a village on April 13, 1907. In its early years, it was known as Stoney Brook Junction and was located along the Great Northern Railroad. General stores, blacksmith shops, and other era-typical storefronts would have been prevalent in Brookston's early years. The entire town was extinguished in a 1918 fire that also annihilated other area communities, including Cloquet and Moose Lake. Despite the catastrophe, Brookston was rebuilt and reached a population of 180 by the start of the 1950s.

BUHL, MN
POPULATION: 952 – CITY 378 OF 856 (6-22-25)

An ancient glacial aquifer, following some 700 feet below the earth's surface, supplies Buhl with "The Finest Water in America," a motto proudly displayed on the town's water tower. As one of the towns at the heart of the Mesabi Range, Buhl's beginnings relate primarily to the mining industry. However, it was established around 1898, when loggers began moving into the area. Over seven million feet of lumber had been accumulated before the turn of the century. At that point, the Sharon Ore Company platted a forty-acre townsite called Buhl. Frank H. Buhl was its president. He authorized the construction of the well-known Swan D. Olson Hotel for the miners of his company; it took on that name when Olson purchased it on April 1, 1901. The Great Northern Railroad connected its lines to the townsite to take advantage of the newly established iron and taconite mines, and M. A. Nichols was appointed postmaster. Buhl was incorporated on February 25, 1901, when it had eight open-pit mines. One of these was ultimately called the Wabigon, the first mine in the Mesabi Range to be electrified. It also boasts of a shovel with a dipper capacity of an impressive fourteen tons. With a growing population that eventually swelled to over two thousand persons in the 1920s came the establishment of two notable public municipal buildings: the 1913 Beaux-Arts Village Hall and architect Holstead & Sullivan's 1917 public library, both of which are now designated as National Register of Historic Places (NRHP) locations. The Buhl Library is home to a mini-museum showcasing many of Buhl's historic artifacts.

CHISHOLM, MN
POPULATION: 4,775 – CITY 379 OF 856 (6-22-25)

While mining may be a largely bygone era in Chisholm, efforts to revitalize interest in the industry through tourism have proved quite successful for this once town of 9,000-plus residents. Timber was the area's first resource to be extensively "mined.' When iron and gold were discovered at Lake Vermillion in 1865, the Mesabi Range was flooded with prospective miners hoping to strike it rich. As many as forty-five mines opened around Chisholm at the peak of the frenzy, and a grand townsite came into existence at the hands of founder Archibald Mark Chisholm. He had extensive knowledge of the area from years of exploration and was the paymaster of the Chandler and Ely Mines in the Vermillion Range from 1888 to 1894. From its incorporation on July 23, 1901, to 1908, Chisholm's residents erected over 500 buildings. Nearly all of them burned in a September 5, 1908, fire that ravaged the countryside and left the once-bustling city in ashes. New structures were built using fireproof materials, many of which have since survived and have been listed on the National Register of Historic Places as a part of the Chisholm Commercial Historic District. It comprises 55 contributing properties, including civic buildings, two-story commercial buildings, and a park. Most were built between 1908 and 1925, during the same period when the town had three banks, a brook factory, a public library, public school buildings, the *Tribune-Herald* and *Mesaba Miner* newspapers, a Hebrew synagogue, and Saints Peter and Paul Church. The onion-domed Ukrainian church was built by the final major ethnic group to arrive at the Iron Range in search of a new life. The Bruce Mine Headframe, the final standing headframe in the Mesabi Range, was erected in 1925-26 and has since become a popular historical landmark on the Mesabi Trail, the Redhead Mountain Bike Park, and the Chisholm ATV Trail System. Major railroads that once served the community were the Duluth & Grand Rapids division of the Great Northern and the Duluth, Mesaba & Northern Railroad, which had a terminus here. The Minnesota Museum of Mining and its impressive collection of mining equipment and vehicles (including Paul Bunyan's 9,000-pound granite marble), and the Minnesota Discovery Center, one of Minnesota's largest museums (at 660 acres) with exhibits on the iron ore range and Minnesota history, are two major centers for tourism in Chisholm. The Minnesota Discovery Center, which opened in 1977, also features an entertainment venue, a mini-golf course, a research center and library, and a park, and offers interpretive trolley tours of the former Glen Location mining community. The third-largest free-standing memorial in the world, a 36-foot-tall iron miner atop a 50-foot-tall pile of steel known as the Ironman Memorial, pays tribute to the thousands of men who once worked to "earn their keep" in the mines of the 1880s and beyond. In pop culture, Chisholm was featured as a plot point in the 1989 film *Field of Dreams*, as the home of one-game MLB player Archibald "Moonlight" Graham, and in the 2005 drama film *North Country*. Roger Enrico, a longtime CEO of PepsiCo; Philip Falcone, the founder of Harbinger Capital and LightSquared and a billionaire Wall Street investor; Ben Hoberman, the mind behind the all-talk format of radio; Joel Maturi, a former athletic director at the University of Denver, Miami University, and the University of Minnesota; John Blatnik, a member of the U.S. House of Representatives from January 1947 to December 1974; Ann Govednik, an Olympic swimmer in the 1932 and 1936 games; Patricia A. Hajdu, the Minister of Jobs and Families in Canada since May 13, 2025; Jim Oberstar, a U.S. Congressman from Minnesota between January 1975 and January 2011; Cameron Latu, an NFL tight end since 2023; John Schuster, a gold medalist with Team USA's 2018 Winter Olympic curling team; Jason Smith, an Olympic participant curler in the 2010 games; David Tomassoni, President Pro tempore of the Minnesota Senate from January 2021 to August 2022; Shawn Rojeski, a bronze medalist curler in the 2006 Winter Olympic games, and Dan Orlich, a defensive end for the NFL's Green Bay Packers from 1949 to 1951 all have some kind of ties to the community.

Restaurant Recommendation:
Snickers Pizza & Pub
222 W Lake St
Chisholm, MN 55719

COOK, MN
POPULATION: 534 – CITY 362 OF 856 (6-21-25)

Little Fork and Ashawa, meaning "by the river," a reference to this area's distinction as a gateway to Lake Vermillion, were two prior names for the area now known as the City of Cook. Ashawa was the longtime name used by the Indigenous and the first homesteaders until August 1, 1908, when the United States Postal Service requested that it be changed due to its similarity in spelling and pronunciation to Oshawa, a village in Nicollet County. The new name "Cook" was derived from Wirth H. Cook, the owner of the Duluth, Winnipeg & Pacific Railway, built here in 1903-04. Other names for the line included the Duluth, Missabe, and Iron Range Railroad and the Duluth, Rainy Lake, and Winnipeg Railway. Some of Cook's first settlers included John & Martha Olson, Abel & Klara Pearson, and Karl & Ellen Engdall. Charles McGaginnis was responsible for filing the initial town plat of Ashawa, using Engdall's land, before its nomenclature change. Early businesses included August Buboltz's hotel, John & Algot Anderson's store, a saloon, a drug store, a lumber yard, and the *Northland Farmer*, a newspaper started in 1903 by James Garfield. Cook's original bank was established in 1910. Eventually, Cook's residents sought incorporation as a village, which was achieved on May 13, 1926. The Cook Women's Club spearheaded the efforts to build a new Cook Public Library in 1930. A pair of rural locations were added to the NRHP in the 1980s: the Alango School, built in 1927 with the unique inclusion of living quarters for school faculty and staff, and the Flint Creek Farm Historic District, a historic farm from 1915 to 1933 that supplied an area lumber company with food and hay for their camps. Of all of Cook's residents of past and present, of which there were no more than about 800 (in 1980) at any given time, the most famous have been the Ojibwe rock and roll and folk musician Keith Secola and the founder of Wien Alaska Airways, Noel Wien.

Restaurant Recommendation:
Rose Cottage Baking Co.
210 US-53
Cook, MN 55723

DULUTH, MN ★☆
POPULATION: 86,697 – CITY 390 OF 856 (6-25-25)
Duluth was the fastest-growing city in the country from 1869 to 1870, destined to surpass even Chicago as the Midwest's principal metropolis. Its success can be directly attributed to its strategic positioning as the farthest inland freshwater port in North America, which connects it to both the Atlantic and Pacific Oceans. When the French explorers Pierre-Esprit Radisson and Médard Chouart des Groseilliers explored the southern shores of Lake Superior around 1622, they likely could never have foreseen the development of the area into the "Zenith City of the Unsalted Seas," a term coined by Duluth's newspaper editor Thomas Preston Foster in a 1868 Fourth of July celebration. The Northwest Trading Company established a large fur trading post in the vicinity of Duluth in 1794, and it was only after the fur trading boom ended around 1847 that the city began to grow. George E. Nettleton founded his trading post circa 1851, and Robert Emmet Jefferson built the first residence a few years later. Once it was clear that the possibilities for the growth of a booming city were on the horizon, these two men, J. B. Culver, Orrin W. Rice, and William Nettleton, jumped on the opportunity to file a plat for a townsite on May 26, 1856. Several names were proposed, but the winning suggestion was that of Reverend J. G. Wilson of Logansport, Indiana: "Du Luth." The anglicized name was that of Daniel Greysolon, Sieur de Lhut, widely regarded as the first European to visit the modern-day city. Despite an 1857 economic crash and a 1859 scarlet fever epidemic that nearly killed off the fledgling Saint Louis County seat, early settlers forged ahead with the establishment of a sawmill, blacksmith shops, hotels, and numerous other facilities. Two rival towns, called Portland and Rice's Point, had been platted about the same time as Duluth, but all three consolidated as one in 1868. Over the next two years, the Lake Superior and Mississippi branch of the Northern Pacific Railroad arrived from St. Paul after Jay Cooke convinced them to make Duluth their northern terminus. Thousands of hopefuls moved into the area with the railroad's arrival. More came after J. Proctor Knott gave his famous "The Untold Delights of Duluth" speech, which brought significant benefits to the community's growth than he could have anticipated. The first canal was dug in 1871 for ships to access the harbor more easily. An 1873 financial panic caused the city to revert briefly to town status (despite $275,000 in promised county funds to improve the railroad, harbor, and docks, as well as the city's

blast furnace). Still, thankfully, the railroads, in combination with the lumber and mining industries, saved the city. Between 1880 and 1890, the population increased from 3,483 to 33,115, a 850.8% increase. By the turn of the century, it had reached 52,969, and by the 1930s, it had surpassed 100,000 residents. During this period, an unfathomable number of improvements were made to the city, including the Aerial Ferry Bridge. Constructed in 1905 as the first transporter bridge in the country over the Duluth Ship Canal, it could carry 350 people and several vehicles (carriages or automobiles) across the canal in about a minute. A 386-foot-long suspension was added from 1929-30 as a part of the bridge's reconstruction project to handle increasing traffic and tourism demand. It was added to the National Register of Historic Places on May 22, 1973, as one of 44 locations in the city listed. Other entries range from lighthouses (the Minnesota Point Lighthouse, the Duluth South Breakwater Inner Lighthouse, the Duluth Harbor South Breakwater Outer Light, and the Duluth Harbor North Pier Light) to the Duluth Commercial Historic district and its 87 contributing properties; and fixtures, such as the 1915 Duluth Armory; the 1902 Duluth [Carnegie] Public Library; the Fitger Brewing Company and its ten properties built from 1886 to 1920; and two shipwrecks: the Thomas Wilson, an 1892 Whalebank Freighter, and the USS Essex that once served as a U.S. Navy steam sloop. Four churches are on the Register: the 1923-24 St. George Serbian Orthodox Church; St. Mark's African Methodist Episcopal Church, built in 1913 by African Americans for African Americans; the 1922 Gothic Revival United Protestant Church; and the Sacred Heart Cathedral, erected in 1896 to serve as the seat of the Roman Catholic Diocese of Duluth from 1896 to 1957. The Duluth State Normal Historic District was listed in 1985 to save four properties from the original Duluth Normal School campus, now part of the University of Minnesota Duluth. The "Normal School" was known as the Duluth State Teachers College from 1921 to 1947, and it achieved university status shortly after the end of World War II. It is joined by The College of St. Scholastica, a private Benedictine college founded in 1892 as the Sacred Heart Institute, and Lake Superior College, a public community college established in 1995 as one of three local institutions of higher learning. To name all of the notable attractions of Minnesota's share of the "Twin Ports" (the other twin being Superior, Wisconsin) would be difficult. Nevertheless, popular points of interest include Canal Park, a former warehouse district now home to the Lake Superior Maritime Visitor Center, the Great Lakes Aquarium, the William A. Irvin freighter museum, and a lighthouse pier; the Duluth Art Institute; the Tweed Museum of Art; the Karpeles Manuscript Library Museum; the Lake Superior Railroad Museum at the Duluth Union Depot; Leif Erikson Park; Bob Dylan's Boyhood Home at 519 N. 3rd Ave. E., the Lake Superior Zoo, the Enger Tower observation tower, the 20,000-square-foot Glensheen Historic Estate, and the heritage North Shore Scenic Railroad that takes riders between Duluth and Two Harbors. Former attractions and innovations relevant to Duluth's history include the Lark of Duluth (Benoist XIV), the first airline service in the United States between 1913 and 1914; the Lake View Store, the very first indoor shopping mall in the country opened in 1916; the electric elevator doors in 1887 by Alexander Miles, and even pizza rolls, an invention of Jeno Paulucci that he trademarked in 1967. Numerous persons of fame have hailed from Minnesota's 5th-largest city, a handful of whom include Alan Lee and Dale Edward Klapmeier, the founders of the billion-dollar Cirrus Aircraft aerospace company; Albert Woolson, the last soldier of the Union Army to pass away on August 2, 1956; Robert R. Gilruth, the first director of what is now called the Lyndon B. Johnson Space Center; Margaret Culkin Banning, a women's rights activist noted for her best-selling novels; Drew LeBlanc, the winner of the 2013 Hobey Baker Award in men's college hockey; Bob Dylan, the Grammy and Academy Award-winning singer-songwriter; Bill Berry, a drummer for the alternative rock band R.E.M. from 1980 to

1997 and since 2022; Don LaFontaine, the "Voice of God" voice actor who voiced thousands of film trailers and countless more advertisements and trailers from 1962 to 2008 and coined the iconic "In a world" term; Bob Chinn, the owner of the highest-grossing restaurant in the United States in 2022 (Bob Chinn's Crab House; $24+ million in revenue), and Medal of Honor recipient Mike Colalillo.

Restaurant Recommendation:
Fitger's Brewhouse
600 E Superior St
Duluth, MN 55802

Restaurant Recommendation:
Duluth Grill
118 S 27th Ave W
Duluth, MN 55806

ELY, MN
POPULATION: 3,268 – CITY 364 OF 856 (6-21-25)

Gold brought settlers to Ely in 1865 when the valuable mineral was discovered at nearby Lake Vermilion, although it was never found in this vicinity. What prospective miners found instead were high-grade iron ore deposits near the western edge of Miner's Lake, which spurred a small "rush" of immigrants seeking well-paying work. As the population began to increase rapidly, a small town called Florence was established on Lake Shagawa and named after the daughter of Captain Jack Pengilly, a Chandler Mine worker. He was Florence's first major. Larger ore deposits were found further west, not long after its establishment. As a result, the entire town was relocated to be closer to them. It was discovered at that point that "Florence" was already being used as the name of another community in Lyon County, so a motion was made to change the name to "Ely" for Samuel B. Ely. He was a promoter of the Vermillion Range between Tower and Ely, Minnesota. By the end of the 1880s, the Pioneer Hotel had come to fruition, as had McCormick's grocery store, A. J. Fenske's hardware and furniture store, a post office (est. 1888), and numerous other enterprises to provide for miners. In 1888, the same year that the post office was established, the Duluth & Iron Range Railroad arrived. One particularly notable institution that emerged later was the First State Bank of Ely, incorporated on September 30, 1912, and with deposits exceeding $350,000 as of 1915. The 1889 Pioneer Mine, now listed on the National Register of Historic Places since 1978, following its 1967 closing, produced well over 40% of the entire output of the Vermillion Range. It was joined in importance by about a dozen other mines in the area's mining heyday. Still, it is one of two (the other being the Soudan Mine at the State Park) that remain today, with outside structures intact. The buildings have since been converted into the Ely Arts & Heritage Center, one of several points of interest in or around Ely. Historic landmarks include Listening Point, the lakeside cabin retreat of Sigurd F. Olson on Burntside Lake; his "Writing Shack" on Wilson Street; the Burntside Lodge Historic District and its nineteen contributing properties built between 1914 and 1937; the 1936 Streamline Moderne Ely State Theater; the 1938 Public Works Administration Moderne Ely Community Theater building, and the 1901 Tanner's Hospital, built in 1901 as a profitable venture to take advantage of the poor sanitary conditions endured by the laborers of the mines. On the campus of Vermillion Community College is the Ely-Winton History Museum, known for its displays of logging, mining, and Ojibwe culture. Another local museum is the Dorothy Molter Cabin. "Knife Lake Dorothy" was commonly referred to as the "Root Beer Lady," as she lived in the wilderness for 56 years and sold several thousand bottles of homemade root beer to canoeists on their way to the Boundary Waters Canoe Area Wilderness. The most-visited wilderness area in the United States comprises more than a million acres and welcomes over 100,000 visitors per year. Also related to ecology and biodiversity preservation are Ely's North American Bear Center, an educational center first opened in 2007 with four resident black bears, and the International Wolf Center, started by L. David Mech and other biologists in 1985 and featuring onsite "ambassador wolves." On the northeast edge of town, an outcropping of unique 2.7-billion-year-old ellipsoidal lava flow rocks is on display. In addition to promoting its wide variety of attractions, the Ely City Council and Chamber of Commerce have meticulously planned several publicity stunts to market their city to the masses. In 2009, they allegedly made a formal bid to host the 2016 Olympic Games. Before then, they had released a faux story about seceding from the United States to join Canada and asked the public for help in replacing a retiring family by "painting the leaves" of the city's trees in the fall of 2013. Ely was incorporated on March 3, 1891, and reported its highest-ever population of 6,156 in 1930. Jessica Biel, the wife of Justin Timberlake and an actress known for her role as Erin Hardesty in *The Texas Chain Saw Massacre* (2003), was born in Ely on March 3, 1982. The "Jane Goodall of bears," Lynn Rogers; Jim Klobuchar, the father of long-term United States Senator Amy Klobuchar and the first reporter to declare John F. Kennedy's victory over Richard Nixon in the 1960 United States presidential election, and Thomas A. Brown, the infamous corrupt Saint Paul police chief who worked to keep the Dillinger Gang and Barker-Karpis Gang out of legal trouble. Brown was a liquor store owner in Ely at the time of his death in January 1959.

EVELETH, MN
POPULATION: 3,493 – CITY 374 OF 856 (6-22-25)
The three-ton, 107-foot-long World's Largest Free-Standing Hockey Stick welcomes hockey enthusiasts and travelers alike to the "Hockey Capital of the United States" and the United States Hockey Hall of Fame. Since 1973, the museum has worked to preserve our country's ice hockey history, but the town in which it is located has been around for much longer. Eveleth, platted on April 22, 1893, under the primary direction of David T. Adams and named for Erwin Eveleth, a timber company employee working on behalf of Robinson, Flinn, and Fowler, began like many others in the vicinity as a mining camp. Prospective miners began constructing log cabins in 1892. In 1894-95, the "Eveleth Group of Mines" comprised the Adams, Vega, and Fayal Mines. Eveleth was already incorporated by this point, and over the next few years, it grew to encompass a fire department, Archie McComb's hotel, Stetton's store, the *Eveleth Star* newspaper, David T. Adam's sawmill, a school taught first by Florence Kent, and the Methodist Episcopal church. On February 9, 1895, the post office opened, and P. Ellard Dowling, a local drugstore owner, was appointed postmaster. The entire town was moved in 1900 up the hill after the immediate vicinity was mined to the point of exhaustion. It later annexed the unincorporated communities of Alice Mine Station, Fayal, and Genoa as its population climbed to a peak of 7,484 by the start of the 1930s. Significant accomplishments of the time during that stretch included the completion of Hotel Glode, which doubled as a depot on the Mesaba interurban electric Railway from December 24, 1912, to April 16, 1927; the stunning 1905 Queen Anne home of W. Bailey; the 1909 Slovene American Church of the Holy Family, and the Eveleth Recreation Building, constructed in 1918 as a municipal gymnasium but later converted into a shirt factory in 1947. At one point, there were ten churches of various denominations, seven school buildings, three movie theaters, three hotels, and two hospitals and railroads serving the needs of Eveleth's residents, in addition to a well-equipped commercial district. In 1965, the Thunderbird Mine opened and has

since grown to process over 5 million tons of taconite pellets annually. Other historical landmarks of the community have varied over the years, from a replica shrine to Our Lady of Lourdes to "hot" and "cold" water towers that no longer stand. In a saddening event that left citizens throughout the country at a loss for words, Eveleth became the city of national headlines when U.S. Senator Paul Wellstone, his wife, his daughter, and five others perished in a plane crash on October 25, 2002. A memorial was raised in their honor a few miles southeast of Eveleth down US-53, where the eight lost their lives. In addition to being the setting of the 1984 drama film *Wildrose* and the 2005 drama film *North Country*, which covered the landmark Jenson v. Eveleth Taconite Co. lawsuit (filed in 1988), several notable personalities have connections to the mining community. Amongst them are Verner E. Suomi, a Finnish-American scientist and the father of satellite meteorology; Nick Begich Sr., a U.S. Congressman from Alaska who disappeared in October 1972 while in office; Elmer A. Lampe, best known for being the head men's basketball coach at the University of Georgia from 1938 to 1946; writer Kay Nolte Smith; Matt Perushek, a gold medal champion curler in the 2008 World Junior Olympics. James B. Tapp, a World War II flying ace; Myron H. Bright, the Senior Judge of the United States Court of Appeals for the Eighth Circuit from June 1985 to December 2016; and Peter Michael Muhich, the Catholic Bishop of Rapid City, South Dakota, from July 2020 to February 2024. Andre Gambucci, Willard Ikola, John Matchefts, Tom Yurkovich, Mark Pavelich, and John Mayasich were all local hockey players who went on to participate in the Olympic Games; Doug Palazzari, Al Suomi, Pete LoPresti, Sam LoPresti, Frank Brimsek, Rudy Ahlin, John Mariucci, Joe Papike, and Paul Schaeffer were natives (or had ties to Eveleth) who appeared in National Hockey League games.

Restaurant Recommendation:
The Rink Sports Bar & Grill
301 Hat Trick Ave
Eveleth, MN 55734

FLOODWOOD, MN
POPULATION: 517 – CITY 382 OF 856 (6-23-25)

Fur traders used Floodwood as a strategic trade point long before there was any widespread settlement, as it was here where the East Savanna River intersected the Saint Louis River. The Floodwood River, named for the driftwood that would accumulate and cause flooding, met the Saint Louis at the townsite and gave its name to the community. The Savanna Portage (a State Park since 1961) connected the Mississippi River and the Lake Superior watersheds over a six-mile stretch of wilderness that had been used for centuries by the Ojibwe and later by trappers. When it was clear that the Great Northern Railroad would be passing through the area starting in 1889, homesteaders like Bob Sutherland and Jean W. New began to arrive in droves to take advantage of the economic opportunities it would bring. J. C. Campbell initiated logging operations, and not long after, the C. N. Nelson Lumber Company, based in Cloquet, funded a miniature logging railroad. In 1890, the Floodwood post office was established, and by 1899, it had been incorporated as a village. New developments, like a six-room schoolhouse operated by Independent School District No. 19, were made. Many stores came and went, but many went out of business following the October 1918 Cloquet Fire, which torched an estimated 250,000 acres and 38 communities. The logging industry flourished as many lumber companies moved into town; however, by the end of the 1920s, it had stalled and was replaced by dairy operations. Floodwood later dubbed itself "The Catfish Capital of the World" for its annual Catfish Days festival and boasted a large wood-carved catfish in downtown Floodwood until it disappeared in November 2021. John Raymond Ylitalo, the 29th United States Ambassador to Paraguay from August 1969 to September 1972, was born here on December 25, 1916. He and Joe Polo, a 2018 Winter Olympics gold medalist curler, are Floodwood's two most famous sons.

 Restaurant Recommendation:
Savanna Portage Restaurant & Bar
102 E Hwy 6, 6600 Elm St
Floodwood, MN 55736

GILBERT, MN
POPULATION: 1,687 – CITY 371 OF 856 (6-22-25)
Scuba diving is a favorite pastime of visitors to Lake Ore-be-gone, which was once three separate open-pit iron ore mines. Divers can see "ancient" mining relics left behind when the mine shut down for good; swimming, fishing, and camping are other popular activities. In addition to the 1,200-acre Iron Range Off-Highway Vehicle State Recreation Area and its 36 miles of off-road vehicle trails, Gilbert has solidified itself as a haven for recreationists in the Arrowhead Region. But before the mines were abandoned, they were bustling with activity. The first mining location opened around 1892 and eventually developed into the Village of Sparta. It was moved when richer ore deposits were found beneath the foundations of local businesses and homes. The entire Sparta townsite was acquired by the Oliver Mining Company in 1911 to make way for increased mining activities. Residents of this Sparta moved to Gilbert, named after the local Giles Gilbert mine. Gilbert's residents had some incorporation problems only a few years prior. On April 7, 1908, they voted for municipality status. They faced opposition from the Pitt Iron Company, which insisted that the lands to be incorporated were "not conditioned to be subjected to government." Regardless of their attempts to stop the incorporation process, Gilbert acquired municipal corporation status on April 29, 1909, after significantly downsizing the proposed city limits. Gilbert's Village Council's first act was to grant a liquor license. It was served by both the Duluth & Iron Range and the Duluth, Missabe & Northern Railroads, and as the eastern terminus of the state-of-the-art Mesabi Electric Railway between Gilbert and Hibbing. Nearby towns were annexed twice in 1914 and 1975. Of all its early businesses, the First National Bank of Gilbert, built in 1920 in Neoclassical style, remains its most notable historical building. It was raised at a time when Gilbert's population had more than doubled from 1,700 residents in 1910 to 3,510. Bernie Kukar, a National Football League referee from 1984 to 2005, was born and raised here.

HERMANTOWN, MN
POPULATION: 10,221 – CITY 384 OF 856 (6-23-25)
When the City of Duluth announced in 1974 that it planned to annex two-thirds of Herman Township, they were surprised when their proposal was declined because Herman had taken the foresight to apply for incorporation as a city of its own. On February 11, 1975, the decision was made that "Hermantown" would become Minnesota's newest municipality at the end of the calendar year. It would retain its name, "Herman," given by early German settlers after the German hero (the same one honored with a monument in New Ulm). While Native Americans were the first inhabitants of "the land up over the hill," the two earliest homesteaders in the vicinity were August Kohlts and Lambert "Pat" Acker in 1867. While Duluth's population grew rapidly, so too did Herman Township, which retained a mostly rural identity up until the Jackson Project of 1937. This housing project, overseen by the federal government,

built 84 homesteads, each with a brick-veneer farmhouse, a garage-barn combination, five to ten acres, and an animal "stipend" of a cow, a pig, and 35 chickens. Prospective buyers could purchase one of these homesteads for only $2,687.40, plus the interest charged to them by the government. A similar project was conducted in Austin, the only other location selected in Minnesota. From that point onwards, Hermantown began its transition from a rural to an urban area. In 2020, it surpassed the 10,000-resident threshold for the first time. Its population in 1980 was just 6,759.

HIBBING, MN ☆
POPULATION: 16,214 – CITY 380 OF 856 (6-23-25)
"We're Ore and More," claims Hibbing, which is the site of the World's Largest Open Pit Iron Ore Mine and was the home of Bob Dylan, one of the greatest songwriters of all time with over 125 million records sold worldwide; Kevin McHale, a member of the Basketball Hall of Fame and a 7-time All-Star with the NBA's Boston Celtics, and Roger Maris, the MLB single-season home run record holder (for 37 years) with his 61 homers in 1961. Fame and fortune surround the mining community, which began in January 1892 when iron prospector Frank Hibbing "felt in his bones" that his camp was sitting atop one of the richest deposits of iron ore ever discovered in the Americas. His hunch was correct, and soon Hibbing's campsite grew into tents, cabins, and mining camps, and later still into wood-frame structures and extensive infrastructure fit to support the needs of several thousand miners. Mr. Hibbing himself funded the first roads, hotel, sawmill, bank, and water and electric plants. Despite living in Duluth, he stayed in touch with the community that bore his name until his early death on July 30, 1897. Several mines came into being, including the "granddaddy" of them all, now nicknamed the "Grand Canyon of the North": the Hull-Rust-Mahoning Open Pit Iron Mine. Over four dozen mines and an equal number of properties make up the sprawling 3.5-by-1.5-mile pit that sinks deep into the earth at about 535 feet. Leonidas Merritt discovered it. Over 800 million tons of iron ore have been extracted from the mine since 1895, making Minnesota the world's largest steel producer and the country's largest iron ore producer between the two World Wars. However, before acquiring those two lucrative titles, the town of Hibbing had its share of difficulties. Residents knew that the iron deposits continued beneath their feet in their homes and businesses. In 1916, the Oliver Mining Company ordered that the northern part of the town be moved to allow operations to continue. In 1918, 185 homes and 20 businesses were transferred two miles to the south for $16 million, and the company financed a new downtown. Hibbing's population grew substantially over the next few decades, reaching a peak of 21,193 in the 1980s. Throughout that time, about thirty annexations (including that of the towns of Alice and Stuntz) were made. The Hull-Rust Mine was the first (in November 1966) of twelve Hibbing locations to be listed on the National Register of Historic Places, others being the East Howard Street Commercial Historic District and its 34 contributing properties built as promised by the Oliver Iron Mining Company from 1919 to 1925; the 1921 Renaissance Revival Androy Hotel and 1922 commercial Delvic Building, both part of said district; the 1922 Colonial revival Hibbing City Hall; the unbelievably lavish Hibbing School, known as the "school with the golden doorknobs" built from 1920 to 1922 at a modern-day cost of over $300 million; the 1930 Sons of Italy Hall; the 1938-39 Hibbing Disposal [sewage] Plant built by the Public Works Administration; the 1905 Mitchell-Tappan House, used by executives of the Oliver Iron Mining Company; the 1916 Colonial Revival home of Emmett Butler; the 1920 Colonial/Spanish Revival Andrew G. Anderson House, and Mesaba Cooperative Park, established on 160-acres in 1928 to be used as a cooperative retreat for Finnish Americans. Other noteworthy Hibbing accomplishments and points of interest include its Carnegie Library, opened in 1908;

Hibbing Community College, founded in 1916; Hibbing Memorial hockey arena, erected in 1935; the Hibbing Historical Society & Museum; the Paulucci Space Theatre; Bob Dylan's Teenage Home, the Bob Dylan Collection and Exhibit, two golf courses, over thirty parks, and the Greyhound Bus Museum. Carl Wickman and Andrew "Bus Andy" Anderson founded Greyhound Lines, the world's largest bus transportation company, in 1914 to connect Hibbing with Alice, Minnesota, which was absorbed by Hibbing in 1920. Over one hundred famous personalities have ties to Hibbing, a few of whom have already been mentioned. Still, others include Frank Riley, the winner of the Hugo Award for Best Novel (*They'd Rather Be Right*) in 1955; Scott Perunovich, the winner of the 2020 Hobey Baker Award and a defenseman for the NHL's St. Louis Blues; Gus Hall, the General Secretary (leader) of the National Committee of the Communist Party USA from December 1959 to May 2000 and a four-time U.S. presidential candidate; Bruce A. Carlson, a four-star general and the 17th Director of the National Reconnaissance Office from June 2009 to July 2012; Vincent Bugliosi, the prosecutor of Charles Manson, and Frankie Campbell, a professional boxer killed in an August 25, 1930 fight against Max Baer. Bazooka and Tripwire, a pair of fictional characters in the *G.I. Joe* series, claim Hibbing as home.

HOYT LAKES, MN
POPULATION: 2,020 – CITY 367 OF 856 (6-21-25)
Hoyt Lakes came into existence in 1955, when the Erie Mining Company decided it needed to provide a community to house its employees and meet their needs. An enormous trail park housed construction workers who worked day in and day out to complete the townsite, named for the firm's president, Elton Hoyt II, from 1952 to 1955. The Cliffs Erie Railroad opened in 1956 to transport taconite from Hoyt Lakes to Taconite Harbor on the shores of Lake Superior. On April 14, 1957, the first taconite was loaded at Hoyt Lakes. By 1970, Erie Mining had procured 100 million tons, and in 1981, that number had more than doubled. Although Taconite Harbor ultimately became a ghost town after the railroad shut down in 2008, Hoyt Lakes has remained an incorporated municipality with a population of over 2,000 residents. A post office has been in operation since 1955, and today's notable attractions include Fisherman's Point Campground, a 9-hole golf course, hiking and biking trails, a hockey arena, and four baseball fields. The Longyear Drill Site has been registered on the NRHP as the spot where the first core samples of the Mesabi Range were taken in 1890.

IRON JUNCTION, MN
POPULATION: 110 – CITY 372 OF 856 (6-22-25)
Legally still called "Iron Junction" but now called "Iron" by the locals, this Duluth, Missabe, and Iron Range Railroad station was aptly named for its positioning at the junction where two lines of the railroad split off from one another. One line went north in the general direction of Mountain Iron. In contrast, the other went eastbound towards range towns like Gilbert and Biwabik. A post office was established in 1893 under the name Iron Junction, dropping the "Junction" in 1895, and a small number of businesses emerged. 118 people lived there at the time of its inaugural 1900 Census. As many as 187 people resided there at the start of the 1960s. It is a modern-day ghost town that has remained incorporated since 1893.

KINNEY, MN
POPULATION: 152 – CITY 377 OF 856 (6-22-25)
Orrin Day Kinney, one of the initial owners of the Merritt site alongside Judge J.T. Halle and Captain Joseph Sellwood, was the principal founder of this village in 1892 on the

Mesabi Range. For decades, Kinney reaped the benefits of the area's iron mines, achieving incorporation on November 11, 1910, and reaching a peak population of 1,200 in the 1920s. Lines of both the Duluth, Missabe & Northern and the Great Northern Railroads transported ore from Kinney to distant trading points. However, the city's decline was rapid, and Kinney lost over a quarter of its citizens in the following four Censuses. There was a brief rebound from 1960 to 1980, during which the population grew from approximately 240 to 447; however, it has since decreased again to 152 as of 2020. Amid their despair, Kinney decided to make a drastic decision: it seceded from the United States on July 13, 1977, and declared "war" on the United States. The publicity stunt was designed to draw attention to the city's failing water system, which was so outdated that mineral deposits were turning white linens yellow. After a series of unsuccessful attempts to secure funding, Kinney Mayor Mary P. Anderson and her council believed it would be easier to secure foreign aid if they seceded, declared war, and immediately lost. The story went viral. David Brinkley featured it on *NBC Nightly News* on February 7, 1978. Less than a week later, Jeno Paulucci, the founder of Bellisio Foods, recognized Kinney as a sovereign nation and offered a 1974 Ford LTD police squad car and ten cases of Jeno's Sausage Pizza Mix as foreign aid. Between March and April 1978, a couple of thousand "Republic of Kinney" passports were sold at a dollar apiece. Eventually, the Iron Range Resources and Rehabilitation Board stepped in to put an end to the stunt. They approved a $198,000 grant for the town to fix its water system, install fire hydrants, and construct cement runoff basins. Some buttons and t-shirts from the Republic's days are still floating around as souvenirs from the stunt, which was even commemorated on August 1-2, 1987, at a summer festival called Secession Days.

LEONIDAS, MN
POPULATION: 50 – CITY 373 OF 856 (6-22-25)
In a small area of the Mesabi Iron Range west of Eveleth are the unincorporated hamlets of Snowden, De Forest, and Largo, as well as the municipality of Leonidas. It was likely named in honor of Leonidas J. Merritt, whose family was responsible for the establishment of the largest iron mine in the world. Incorporated in the 1910s near where the Duluth, Missabe & Northern, Duluth, Winnipeg & Pacific, and Duluth & Iron Range Railroads met, Leonidas's peak population was 499 in 1930, a far cry from the 50 people who called it home as of the 2020 Census. The Leonidas Overlook offers picturesque views of the surrounding open-pit mines and landscapes.

MCKINLEY, MN
POPULATION: 103 – CITY 370 OF 856 (6-22-25)
McKinley, population 103, is home to the Iron Range Historical Society and its collection of newspapers and 20,000-plus photographs that offer a glimpse into the lives of early miners in Minnesota's premier mining district. The small hamlet was first settled in 1890 and named after the McKinley brothers' mine. Incorporation followed in 1892, the same year a post office was established (although it was discontinued in 1991). The Duluth, Missabe & Iron Range Railroad served McKinley and helped to connect it to the nearby city of Virginia and places beyond. At its peak in the 1910s, 411 people lived in McKinley.

MEADOWLANDS, MN
POPULATION: 134 – CITY 381 OF 856 (6-23-25)
Appropriately named for its highly arable land near the White Face River, Meadowlands was one of the new communities in Saint Louis County that relied more

on farming than it did mining to support its local economy. The Duluth, Missabe & Iron Range Railroad town was incorporated on October 15, 1924. Its township was organized almost a decade earlier, on July 13, 1903. Religion remains prevalent in the Meadowlands today, with its numerous churches of various denominations, but its commercial district is practically nonexistent. There was once a bank, a grocery store, a cheese factory, a movie theater, a farmer's cooperative store, a Ford dealership, and a K-12 school called the Toivola-Meadowlands School. The decline of farming through the 1980s led to the school's permanent closure. Meadowlands is located not far from the Sax-Zim Bog, famous for its Great Gray Owls and winter birdwatching opportunities. It is also the closest municipality to the Western Bohemian Fraternal Association Union Hall, built in 1925 as a meeting palace for the fraternal organization and a venue for Sokol gymnastics.

MOUNTAIN IRON, MN
POPULATION: 2,878 – CITY 376 OF 856 (6-22-25)

The "Taconite Capital of the World" was aptly named Mountain Iron, as it was built on a mountain of iron near the first mine on the Mesabi Range, the largest iron ore deposit ever discovered and extracted in the United States. Leonidas Merritt discovered a high-grade iron boulder, which led him and his six brothers–the "Seven Iron Brothers"– to establish Mountain Iron Mine and the Duluth, Missabe, and Northern Railway in 1892 to connect their mines to Duluth. Naturally, miners needed a place to call home at the end of the day and stores to purchase goods, barber shops to trim beards, blacksmith shops to yield tools of the trade, and grocery stores to supply them and their families with nourishment. Thus came the town of Mountain Iron itself, which began as a mere campsite area before several improvements were made starting in 1912. A two-story city hall building was erected, as were a jail and a fire department. A post office was established in 1913 under the name Mountain Iron, a minor change from its former names, Marfield (1892-1894) and Mount Iron (1894-1913). Even Andrew Carnegie donated funds for the construction of a library, albeit it was a bit ironic. Carnegie had come to control the Merritts' Missabe Railroad from John D. Rockefeller, who, in turn, had acquired all their shares and their small fortune during the financial Panic of 1893, which left them nearly bankrupt. Rockefeller had provided additional financial support for the railroad's construction after the Merritts had approached him for help only months before, a decision that they ultimately deeply regretted. Although their family was ruined, Leonidas's legacy was cemented–literally– when a 10.5-foot-tall concrete and granite statue was unveiled on the grounds of the town's public library. At the Mountain Iron Locomotive Park sits a 1910 Baldwin locomotive and a class S-4 switcher, as well as an overlook of the Mountain Iron Mine. The mine was raised to the level of National Historic Landmark in 1968, in addition to being listed on the Federal Historic Register. Mountain Iron was finally incorporated as a city in 1972, during a decade when its population grew from 1,698 to 4,143 (an increase of 143.5%). Its local mine, Minntac (formerly Pilotac), is a subsidiary of United States Steel Corporation. It processes over 2.2 billion tons of iron ore annually.

ORR, MN
POPULATION: 211 – CITY 361 OF 856 (6-21-25)

A giant bluegill statue built by the same man (Gordon Shumker) who erected Alexandria's "Big Ole" Viking statue and Smokey Bear in International Falls welcomes Highway 53 travelers to Orr, Minnesota, on Pelican Lake. Orr, named for the former postmaster and general store owner William Orr, once had the closest Duluth, Winnipeg & Pacific Railroad station to the Bois Forte Indian Reservation. It began as a timber town with lumber yards and sawmills, but developed into a thriving community with stores, hotels, and all the typical lines of enterprise that one would have expected to find in that era of Minnesota history. Orr is a gateway to Voyageurs National Park, 33 miles away, as well as the 619,287-acre Kabetogama State Forest and its boating, fishing, and canoeing activities. The Orr Roadside Parking Area was built in 1935-38 as a New Deal-funded wayside rest using elements of National Park Service rustic architecture.

Restaurant Recommendation:
T Pattenn Cafe
4557 US-53
Orr, MN 55771

PROCTOR, MN
POPULATION: 3,120 – CITY 391 OF 856 (6-25-25)

When the Duluth, Missabe, and Northern Railroad was built in 1892 between Mountain Iron and Stony Brook to connect the mine's output with the quickly growing town and commercial center of Duluth, it had additional unforeseen effects on the region's development. One of these was the establishment of Proctorknott, which was selected to be the site of the roundhouse, railroad shops, and classification yards. These facilities effectively made it the most significant hub for iron transportation on the planet, and the town experienced a minor boom. Its name honored J. Proctor Knott, who unintentionally brought great fame and attention to Duluth after he satirically belittled the port city during his January 27, 1871, speech now referred to as "The Untold Delights of Duluth." In short, Knott had hoped to fight the extension of a land grant for the newly completed Lake Superior and Mississippi Railroad. His humorous speech knocked down the land-grant proposition, but Duluth grew into an enormous trade hub thanks to its location between the Great Lakes and the iron-rich Arrowhead Region of Minnesota. Proctorknott and its accompanying post office (established in 1894) shortened its name to just Proctor by 1904. While the Proctor post office closed in 1943 due to Duluth's extensive growth, several improvements had been made to the town, including a $102,000 two-story Village Hall finished in 1940, churches, athletic fields, a YMCA, four schools: Proctor High School, the St. Rose of Lima parochial school, Proctor East Side Grade School, and Summit Grade and Junior High School. Between 1960 and 2020, the population fluctuated slightly, ranging from 2,852 people in 2000 to 3,180 in 1980. Later improvements to Proctor included the South Saint Louis County Fairgrounds, the Proctor Speedway, and the Proctor Area Museum, located in a 1927 car shop superintendent's office. Two of its highlighted attractions are its Duluth, Missabe & Iron Range Yellowstone Engine #225 and an F-101 Voodoo Jet that commemorates Captain Sherman Gonyea and James Verville. The two Proctor men perished when their plane crashed during a 1974 exercise out of Duluth Air Base. A Titanic memorial was completed in 2016 by Jason Seguin to honor Anna Salkjelsvik, a Norwegian emigrant who survived the sinking of the famed ship in 1912. She lived at 420 N. Ugstad Rd before Mr. Seguin purchased the home and erected the impressive monument (located on private property).

Restaurant Recommendation:
Proctor Pizza & Sub Shop
204 3rd Ave
Proctor, MN 55810

RICE LAKE, MN
POPULATION: 4,112 – CITY 385 OF 856 (6-23-25)
Fearing that Duluth would someday annex the entire Rice Lake Township, residents began the incorporation process to prevent future annexations of their mostly rural community. On August 20, 2015, Judge Barbara J. Case allowed for the incorporation of the City of Rice Lake. By October of that year, a mayor and a city council had been elected. Both the township and the city derived their names from Wild Rice Lake, called *megwewundjiwmanominikan* by the Ojibwe. Wild rice covered the lake in the days before the settlers arrived in droves, starting in the latter part of the 19th century. The township's population was only 63 in 1880, but after centuries of growth and development, it had reached 3,861.

TOWER, MN
POPULATION: 430 – CITY 363 OF 856 (6-21-25)
The second-oldest city in the Arrowhead Region, behind only Duluth, was incorporated on March 13, 1889, about twenty-four years after some of the first prospective gold miners had arrived at Vermillion Lake in search of the rare earth nuggets. Iron mining began in 1882, when the open-pit Soudan, Minnesota's oldest, deepest, and richest mine, began operations. Two towns developed nearby, one named Tower and the other Soudan. Soudan was established on March 13, 1885, and named as an intentionally ironic contrast to Sudan in Africa for its frigid temperatures. It was never formally incorporated. Tower, on the other hand, was named for Charlemagne Tower, a large investor in the Minnesota Iron Company and the Duluth & Iron Range Railway. Tower's post office opened in 1883, and as the town grew, several notable structures were erected to benefit its residents. In 1895, the Tower Fire Hall was built from brick in a Commercial Queen Anne style. The Duluth and Iron Range Railroad Company Station, built by George Spurbeck in 1916 to provide passenger service until 1951, is now the Tower-Soudan Historical Society Center Museum. Using tamarack logs and scrap metal, at least 143 boathouses were built by miners on Lake Vermillion between 1900 and 1950 to provide housing for themselves and their families in an area now called the Stuntz Bay Boathouse Historic District. The three locations were listed on the National Register, as was the Soudan Iron Mine, now the Lake Vermillion-Soudan Underground Mine State Park (located in unincorporated Soudan). It was active from 1884 to 1962 and has since also been designated as a U.S. National Historic Landmark. The University of Minnesota built a physics laboratory in the old mineshaft in the 1980s, which was used (and open to the public for tours) until 2016. It was considered to be the site of the U.S. Deep Underground Science and Engineering Laboratory. However, the lab was instead located at the Homestake Mine in Lead, South Dakota. Attractions still open to the public today include the Tower Train Museum and the McKinley Monument, dedicated on November 15, 1901, to President William McKinley, who had been assassinated only two months prior. The 18-foot-tall obelisk, which reads "Our Martyred President," was reportedly built for $12,000. On February 2, 1996, Tower entered the history books when the temperature dropped to a bone-chilling -60°F. It and Embarrass Valley are the coldest continuously inhabited locations in the contiguous 48 states.

VIRGINIA, MN
POPULATION: 8,423 – CITY 375 OF 856 (6-22-25)
Virginia, formerly home of the Blue Devils before its consolidation with Eveleth-Gilbert into Rock Ridge High School (now the Wolverines), was a mining city and even earned the nickname "Queen City of the Mesabi Range" for its location at the heart of the

world's great iron-producing region. Any one of several men could have been the "first" to begin extracting ore in the vicinity, whether it was Fred Barrett of Tower, Thomas H. Pressnell of Duluth, David T. Adams, or Captain John G. Cohoe, amongst others. Regardless of who bored the first hole, it is clear that mining activity began in the early 1890s, specifically around March 1892, and that Virginia was established to accommodate the influx of prospectors and their families. A. E. Humphreys' men laid out the townsite on Orrin Day Kinney's land and had hoped to name it in honor of their boss, but Humphreys declined the honor. It was instead named for the "virgin" timber and countryside, as well as Humphreys's home state of Virginia. While they were largely unable to move iron ore and lumber for many years, on June 23, 1892, the idea was suggested to establish the Duluth, Missabe & Northern Railroad between Duluth and Mountain Iron. Incorporation was achieved in November 1892, and by the following year, the populace had grown to a sizable 5,000-plus. A post office was established, and for a short time, Virginia even boasted a courthouse serving as the judicial seat of the northern part of the country. A June 1893 fire destroyed the entire city: saloons, homes, businesses, and all, but Virginia rebuilt. A second conflagration occurred in 1900, destroying the entire business district except for two hotels. Stores and firms were constructed of fireproof materials, and by 1910, the mining and logging city had grown to 10,473. The Duluth & Iron Range, the Great Northern, and the Duluth, Winnipeg & Pacific all found a way to extend their lines into city limits, giving Virginia four railroads in total to move its exports to faraway lands. The City of Franklin, a nearby mining community, was absorbed by the City of Virginia in later years, as the Queen City boasted the largest white pine mill in the world and the largest ore-producing mine at Mesaba Mountain. Nineteen locations have been listed on the National Register of Historic Places, including the Virginia Commercial Historic District and its 78 contributing properties built between 1900 and 1941; the St. Louis County District Courthouse, constructed in 1910 in the Beaux-Arts style to better serve the needs of northern residents of the county; the 1905 Virginia Brewery, a 1912 commercial Finnish Sauna; a 1906 Finnish-American meeting hall called the Valon Tuote Raittiusseura; the 1913 Duluth, Winnipeg & Pacific Depot; the 1924 Polish-American Church of St. John the Baptist; the 1922 Jacobean Revival-style Lincoln School Building; the WPA's Olcott Park Electric Fountain (provided by General Electric) and Rock Garden, built in 1937, and the B'nai Abraham Synagogue, the first purpose-built synagogue built in the region in 1909 that now serves as a Jewish history museum. Noteworthy roadside attractions of Virginia are the World's Largest Floating Loon on Silver Lake at Olcott Park and sculptor Gareth Andrews' 16-by-27-foot bronze eagle, a tribute to veterans. The loon is located near Minnesota North College - Mesabi Range, Virginia, which traces its origins to the 1920s as the town's first and only public community college. The area also features the Virginia Area Historical Society Heritage Museum, the superintendent's residence, a Finnish log house, and a 1930s tourist cabin. Minnesota's tallest bridge, the Thomas Rukavina Memorial Bridge, spans 1,125 feet over the Rouchleau Mine Pit and was opened in 2017 to connect Virginia to southern communities. Virginia's most famous birth by far is that of actor Chris Pratt, one of the highest-grossing film stars of all time, known for his roles as Star-Lord in Marvel's *Guardians of the Galaxy* series, Andy Dwyer in NBC's political satire sitcom *Parks and Recreation*, and as Owen Grady in the *Jurassic World* trilogy. Pratt moved to Alaska as a toddler, but several others have called Virginia home at one point or another: Robert Mondavi, the winemaker and marketer responsible for bringing California's Napa Valley wines to worldwide fame; Leonard C. Ward, former Chief of the Army Division at the National Guard Bureau; Jesuit priest, Vietnam War activist, and pacificist Daniel Berrigan; noted reporter and news anchor Alex Rozier; drag racers Kurt and Warren Johnson, and at least ten professional hockey players. Some hockey legends include Jack "Killer" Carlson; Steve Carlson, one of the three Hanson brothers in the 1977 sports comedy *Slap Shot*; three-time Stanley Cup champion center Matt Cullen; defenseman Matt Niskanen; and John Harrington, a member of the 1980 Lake Placid "gold-medalist U.S. men's Olympic hockey squad.

WINTON, MN
POPULATION: 169 – CITY 365 OF 856 (6-21-25)
William C. Winton, of the Knox Lumber Company of Duluth, was honored by having this logging community named for him after he oversaw the construction of its first sawmill in 1898. The Duluth, Missabe & Iron Range Railroad helped bring Winton's population to a high of 499 people in the 1920s, not long after it had incorporated as a village on July 23, 1901. Stores, lumber yards, and a post office (discontinued in 1996 before becoming a rural station) were among its initial businesses, many of whose histories have been preserved by the Ely-Winton Historical Society at Vermillion Community College in Ely. A 15-foot-tall lumberjack statue welcomes travelers into town at the corner of Hwy 169 and Main Street.

Unincorporated/Ghost Towns: Alborn, Angora, Ash Lake, Bassett, Bear River, Bengal, Brimson, Britt, Burnett, Burntside, Buyck, Canyon, Carson Lake, Celina, Central Lakes, Cherry, Clover Valley, Costin Village, Cotton, Crane Lake, Culver, Cusson, Elcor, Eldes Corner, Elmer, Embarrass, Fairbanks, Fermoy, Florenton, Forbes, Four Corners, French River, Gheen, Gheen Corner, Glendale, Gowan, Greaney, Idington, Independence, Island Lake, Kabetogama, Keenan, Kelsey, Linden Grove, Mahnomen, Makinen, Markham, McComber, Meadow Brook, Melrude, Munger, Nett Lake, Palmers, Palo, Payne, Peary, Petrel, Peyla, Pineville, Prosit, Ramshaw, Robinson, Rollins, Saginaw, Sax, Shaw, Sherman Corner, Side Lake, Silica, Simar, Skibo, Soudan, Spina, Sturgeon, Taft, Toivola, Twig, Vermilion Dam, Wakemup, Whiteface, Wolf, Zim

National Register of Historic Places:
Biwabik Township: St. Louis County 4-H Club Camp
Buhl: Buhl Public Library, Buhl Village Hall
Chisholm: Bruce Mine Headframe, Chisholm Commercial Historic District, Saints Peter & Paul Church- Ukrainian Catholic
Cook: Alango School, Flint Creek Farm Historic District
Cusson: Civilian Conservation Corps Camp
Duluth: Aerial Lift Bridge, Bridge No.5757, Bridge No. L-6007, Bridge No. L6113, Bridge No. L8515, Chester Terrace, Chester & Clara Congdon Estate, DeWitt-Seitz Building, Duluth Armory, Duluth Central High School, Duluth Civic Center Historic District, Duluth Commercial Historic District, Duluth Harbor North Pier Light, Duluth Harbor South Breakwater Outer Light, Duluth Masonic Temple, Duluth Missabe & Iron Range Depot (Endion), Duluth Public Library, Duluth South Breakwater Inner (Duluth Range Rear) Lighthouse, Duluth State Normal School Historic District, Duluth Union Depot, Endion School, Engine House No. 1, Fitger Brewing Company, Hartley Building, Irving School, Kitchi Gammi Club, Lester River Bridge-Bridge No. 5772, Lincoln Branch Library, Minnesota Point Lighthouse, Bergetta Moe Bakery, Munger Terrace, Northland, Sacred heart Cathedral. Sacred Heart School & Christian Brothers Home, St. George Serbian Orthodox Church, St. Mark's African Methodist Episcopal Church, Oliver G. Traphagen House, United Protestant Church, United States Army Corps of Engineers Duluth Vessel Yard, US Fisheries Station, Duluth, *USS Essex* Shipwreck Site, *William A. Irvin* (freighter), Wirth Building, YMCA of Duluth, *Thomas Wilson* (Whaleback Freighter) Shipwreck
Elmer: Church of St. Joseph (Catholic)
Ely: Burntside Lodge Historic District, Ely Community Center, Ely State Theater, Sigurd F. Olson Writing Shack, Pioneer Mine Buildings & "A" Headframe, Tanner's Hospital, Listening Point
Embarrass: Elias & Lisi Aho Historic Farmstead, Finnish Apostolic Lutheran Church of Embarrass, Height of Land Portage, Matt & Emma Hill Historic Farmstead, Erick & Kristina Nelimark Sauna, Anna & Mikko Pyhala Farm, Alex Seitaniemi Housebarn, Waino Tanttari Field Hay Barn

Embarrass Township: Gregorius & Mary Hanka Historic Farmstead, Mike & Mary Matson Historic Farmstead
Eveleth: W. Bailey House, Church of the Holy Family (Catholic), Eveleth Recreation Building, Hotel Glode
Gheen: LeMoine Building
Gilbert: First National Bank of Gilbert
Hibbing: Andrew G. Anderson House, Androy Hotel, Emmett Butler House, Delvic Building, East Howard Street Commercial Historic District, Hibbing City Hall, Hlbbing Disposal Plant, Hibbing High School, Hull-Rust-Mahoning Open Pit Iron Mine, Mitchell-Tappan House, Sons of Italy Hall, Mesaba Co-Operative Park
Hoyt Lakes: E.J. Longyear First Diamond Drill Site
Kabetogama: Kabetogama Ranger Station District
Lester Park: *May Flower* (Shipwreck)
Meadowlands: Western Bohemian Fraternal Union Hall
Morse Township: *Bull-of-the-Woods* Logging Scow
Mountain Iron: Mountain Iron Mine
Orr: Orr Roadside Parking Area
Palmers: *Robert Wallace* (bulk carrier) shipwreck site
Tower: Duluth & Iron Range Railroad Company Passenger Station, Soudan Iron Mine, Tower Fire Hall, Stuntz Bay Boathouse Historic District
Virginia: B'nai Abraham Synagogue, W.T. Bailey House, Church of St. John the Baptist (Catholic), Coates House, Duluth, Winnipeg, & Pacific Depot, Finnish Sauna, Jukola Boardinghouse, LaSalle Apartments, Charles Lenont House, Lincoln School Building, Olcott Park Electric Fountain & Rock Garden, St. Louis County District Courthouse, Calon Tuote Raittiusseura, Virginia Brewery, Virginia City Hall, Virginia Commercial Historic District, Virginia-Rainy Lake Lumber Company Manager's Residence,Virginia-Rainy Lake Lumber Company Office, Virginia Recreation Building
Voyageurs National Park: Jun Fujita Cabin, William Ingersoll Estate, Kettle Falls Historic District, Kettle Falls Hotel, Adolph Levin Cottage, Monson's Hoist Bay Resort, I. W. Stevens Lakeside Cottage

Golf Courses:
Ely Golf Club, Daily Fee (Ely, MN)
Enger Park Golf Course, Municipal (Duluth, MN)
Eshquaguma Country Club, Private (Gilbert, MN)
Eveleth Golf Course, Municipal (Eveleth, MN)
Giants Ridge Golf & Ski Resort – The Legend, Municipal (Biwabik, MN)
Giants Ridge Golf & Ski Resort – The Quarry, Municipal (Biwabik, MN)
Hoyt Lakes Golf Course, Municipal (Hoyt Lakes, MN)
Mesaba Country Club, Daily Fee (Hibbing, MN)
Northland Country Club, Private (Duluth, MN)
Ridgeview Country Club, Private (Duluth, MN)
The Wilderness at Fortune Bay, Daily Fee (Tower, MN)
Virginia Golf Course, Municipal (Virginia, MN)

Breweries/Wineries/Distilleries:
Bent Paddle Brewing Company (Duluth, MN)
Blacklist Artisan Ales (Duluth, MN)
Canal Park Brewing (Duluth, MN)
Fitger's Brewing Company (Duluth, MN)
HammerHeart Brewing Company (Ely, MN)
Hoops Brewing (Duluth, MN)
Lake Superior Brewing Company (Duluth, MN)
Ursa Minor Brewing (Duluth, MN)
Warrior Brewing Company (Duluth, MN)

Town Celebrations:
3rd of July Parade & Celebration, Gilbert, MN (July 3rd)

Floodwood Catfish Days, Floodwood, MN (2nd Weekend of July)
Hoyt Lakes Water Carnival, Hoyt Lakes, MN (4th Weekend of July)
Land of the Loon Festival, Virginia, MN (3rd Third Weekend in June)
Timber Days Festival, Cook, MN (2nd Weekend of June)

SCOTT COUNTY
EST. 1853 - POPULATION: 150,928

Scott County's etymology honors Winfield Scott, the Commanding General of the United States Army from 1841 to 1861. It was formed in 1853 from land that was formerly a part of Dakota County.

BELLE PLAINE, MN
POPULATION: 7,395 – CITY 671 OF 856 (10-3-25)

When E. and E. L. Farnham were asked if their claims could be utilized for a townsite, they happily obliged and allowed J. F. Baldwin to conduct and record a survey in January 1857 for Belle Plaine city. Another 320-acre site was laid out in W. H. Stodder on the land of Judge Andrew G. Chatfield's two years prior; he named it *Belle Plaine* for the French phrase meaning "beautiful prairie." He intentionally located the site halfway between Mendota and Traverse des Sioux, near modern-day Saint Peter, as it was about halfway along the path he used while serving as a Minnesota Territorial Supreme Court Judge. A post office operated under that name from 1854 to 1895, then disappeared until 1936. Edward P. Berry was appointed as the first postmaster. In 1868, it was incorporated as Minnesota's only borough, an administrative division of government similar to that of a city (of which it became in 1974, when all municipalities in Minnesota became cities). By 1882, the hamlet had a population of over 600. Business interests included eight saloons, six general stores, three wagon shops, three shoe shops, three blacksmith shops, three hotels, two millinery stores, two drug stores, two hardware stores, an elevator, a brick yard, a brewery, a harness shop, well-off schools, and no less than five church congregations. The first church was the Episcopal Church of the Transfiguration, organized in 1858 by Reverend J. B. Van Ingren, D.D., and notable for its 1869 edifice, which still stands today as one of two locations on the National Register of Historic Places in Belle Plaine. The other point of interest is the Hooper-Bowler-Hillstrom House, erected in 1871 and now the site of a local house museum that boasts of a two-story outhouse connected to the home via a pioneer skyway. Anton Swingler's 1860 brewery, which burned twice in 1866 and 1877, was one of the city's most popular early business ventures. The Belle Plaine elevator, with its 45,000-bushel capacity, was built in 1866 when the Chicago, St. Paul, Minneapolis & Omaha Railroad came through. Belle Plaine's population has increased in recent decades, most notably between 2000 and 2010, when it grew from 3,789 to 6,661. Some of its more famous residents have been Ryan Dungey, a four-time AMA Motocross and four-time AMA Supercross Champion; actress Beth Riesgraf, known for her role as Parker on the action crime drama television series *Leverage*; and Patrick J. Hessian, the 16th Chief of Chaplains of the United States Army from 1982 to 1986.

Restaurant Recommendation:
Oldenburg Brewing Company
116 W Main St
Belle Plaine, MN 56011

CREDIT RIVER, MN
POPULATION: 5,493 – CITY 669 OF 856 (10-3-25)
Credit River joined Minnesota's municipalities fairly recently, having been incorporated as a city on May 11, 2021. While its status as a city was short-lived, the township of Credit River has been extant since its platting in 1854. John Spratt, William McQuestion, and Fayette Ufford were among the earliest settlers along the Credit River tributary. Several others followed, working their way past the Mississippi River and towards the Minnesota River. The township and community's etymology is heavily disputed. However, it was likely named for either a shopkeeper who gave poor Irish immigrants "credit" on goods from his store, or for the French traders from Mendota who issued credit to Irish families traveling through the vicinity. Another account suggests that the river got its name from Reverend Albert Ostet of Lakeville, who, after being forced to return home due to heavy flooding, was able to see his ailing mother before she passed. He gave the river "credit" for allowing him to spend some final moments with her. The Chicago, Milwaukee & St. Paul Railroad passed through the township's northern stretches and enabled local farmers to send their products to market. The First National Bank of Montgomery v. Jerome Daly court case, also known as the Credit River Case, took place here when Daly argued that the bank had not actually loaned him any real money but had instead created credit on its official books. Credit River's most significant population increase occurred between 1960 and 1970, when it grew by 165.4% from 439 to 1,165.

ELKO NEW MARKET, MN
POPULATION: 4,846 – CITY 662 OF 856 (10-2-25)
Similar to the story of Triumph and Monterey in Martin County, the City of Elko New Market resulted from the consolidation of two rival communities and governments into one unified municipality. However, the development of the two towns could not have been more different. New Market's development dates to the establishment of the township using the New Market name on October 12, 1858, although it was briefly known as Jackson before then. Records of the first church and schoolhouse surfaced during this pioneer area. Still, its most prominent early institutions were a post office opened in November 1867 with P. J. Baltes as postmaster, a blacksmith shop, a hotel, and two stores—most communal activities centered around the German Catholic Church. Business activity eventually faltered due to the presence of nearby Elko, which was established in 1902 by the Chicago, Milwaukee & St. Paul Railroad. Scandinavian Lutherans settled this area in droves, and the town developed as a more traditional railroad community, complete with a commercial district. New Market's schools taught in German and incorporated several religious aspects into their courses, whereas Elko maintained a separation between religion and education. After both towns lost their schools in 1916 (New Market) and in the 1950s (Elko, when Elko consolidated with Lakeville), consideration was given to joining the two communities. This idea only began to come to fruition in October 2005, when officials from both cities met and made a formal public proposal on March 21, 2006, that resulted in an overwhelming 86% vote by residents of both communities to merge the two cities. Nowadays, telling the two communities apart is relatively easy, as most of old New Market is west of Minnesota Highway 91, and Elko is to the road's east. New Market was incorporated as a village on August 28, 1895, whereas Elko achieved incorporation on October 24, 1949. Elko's post office dates to 1907, whereas New Market's came about forty years earlier, as was mentioned previously. The New Market Hotel and Store, built in 1897, is the only surviving early commercial building from New Market's early days. In Elko, the Elko Speedway is $3/8$ miles and hosts events

such as the ARCA Menards Series Shore Lunch 250 and the ASA Midwest Tour. The track also has a drive-in movie theater.

Restaurant Recommendation:
Firehouse Grille
7875 Old Town Rd
Elko New Market, MN 55054

JORDAN, MN ☆
POPULATION: 6,656 – CITY 667 OF 856 (10-3-25)

Many signs tout Jordan as the site of "Minnesota's Largest Candy Store," known for its pop culture displays, enormous selection of sodas and old-fashioned and modern candies, and jigsaw puzzles. While the sweet selection is a favorite amongst motorists entering the Twin Cities from the southwest, the town of Jordan itself had a tumultuous start, particularly over what to call it. Differing accounts suggest that the townsite was platted on the land of William Holmes, perhaps by both him and Thomas A. Holmes, between 1854 and 1855. Thomas brought in a crew from Shakopee to erect a sawmill on the Minnesota River, the first mill in Scott County, circa 1853. William, his brother, named the town Jordan City after the Jordan River in Palestine. The earliest residents suggested multiple other names, but Mr. Holmes's suggestion prevailed, as he was responsible for the earliest developments of the city we know today. A post office was established, and several business owners started era-appropriate firms. In 1860, S. A. Hooper, J. H. Gardner, and R. W. Thomas founded an adjacent rival settlement called Brentwood, which also boasted many of its own businesses. Jordan and Brentwood consolidated on February 26, 1872, into a unified municipality following a special act of the legislature. The Minnesota Valley Railroad, which was part of the larger Omaha Road, was built first, and the Minneapolis & St. Louis line came later. Between 1857 and 1858, John Ninniger, G. B. Clitherall, and Ignatius Donnelly surveyed the Ninniger and Dakota Railroad, intending to connect Ninniger, Minnesota, with the Dakota Territory. However, the death of one of the men also took with it the prospects of carrying out the project. As of 1882, business lines included two large flouring mills with a corresponding roller mill and elevator, a pair of early breweries, a limestone quarry, a factory for lumber, sash, doors, and blinds, and two or more each of meat markets, jewelers, hotels, grocery stores, and more typical lines. *The Scott County Advocate* newspaper began in 1878 under the editorial guidance of Frank Matchett. Naturally, fraternal, educational, and religious organizations emerged as citizens organized themselves; among the earliest were St. John's Catholic Church, a German Lutheran church, a German Methodist church, and a Presbyterian church. For the better part of fifty-seven years, between 1872 and 1929, Jordan residents repeatedly tried to take the county seat from Shakopee, but to no avail. The earliest attempt came in 1873, when Jordan lost by only 92 votes in the county elections. Jordan's economy took a significant hit in 1919 when Prohibition took hold and closed its breweries, which were then among the largest in Minnesota. The ruins of the Jordan Brewery, which operated on and off between 1861 and 1948, are listed on the National Register alongside the Jordan Historic District and its fourteen historic commercial properties, the 1858 sandstone Foss and Wells House, and the 1864 sandstone Abraham Bisson House. The Mudbaden Sulphur Springs Company building, constructed in 1915 as a health resort that promoted sulfur-rich mud paths, lies only a couple of miles northeast of Jordan. Since the 1970s, Jordan has grown considerably, from a population of only about 1,836 persons.

Restaurant Recommendation:
Minnesota's Largest Candy Store
20430 Johnson Memorial Dr
Jordan, MN 55352

NEW PRAGUE, MN
POPULATION: 8,162 – CITY 666 OF 856 (10-3-25)

Despite being chiefly built by Czech immigrants and clearly named after Prague, the capital of Bohemia (now the Czech Republic), the town's first settler was actually a German named Anton Philipp. He arrived at the suggestion of the Catholic Bishop Joseph Cretin and began selling lots in 1856 after he acquired 160 acres of land in Helena Township, Scott County. Forty acres of Philipp's initial 160-acre investment was donated to the Catholic church; his gift was generously accompanied by an additional ten acres (each) from Albert Vrtish, Frank Bruzek, and John Bernas. Mass was held in a simple log building for some time before a log parsonage was built in 1863, which was later replaced by a brick edifice in 1868. Another new church was completed in 1874, and finally, in 1907, the final and present construction of the Church of St. Wenceslaus was finished. It cost over $85,000 to construct the two-tower brick and Kasota limestone Georgian Revival and Romanesque Revival style edifice, which, alongside its 1908 rectory and 1914 school, was listed on the NRHP on February 19, 1982. While the church serves as the centerpiece of the Czech community, New Prague's history extends well beyond just its Catholic faith. Praha was the original name for the settlement, and it was under that name that the town operated as an incorporated village from March 1, 1877, to February 25, 1884. During that period, the Minneapolis & St. Louis Railway arrived in July 1877, the first flour mill and grain elevator were built in 1881 for the "Flour City", and the Le Sueur County side of the settlement came to fruition in 1883. Many businesses came to a head throughout the 1880s, including the Czech-Slovak Protective Society Opera Hall, the New Prague Foundry, and a second public school, among many other improvements. Hotel Broz, the Minnesota & St. Louis Depot, the New Prague Flouring Mill Company, and First National Bank of New Prague were equally important. From 1910 to 1940, the population remained relatively stable, fluctuating between 1,540 and 1,645 persons. Dožínky is held annually in the community as a Czech Harvest Festival. At Fishtail Bar and Grill, a giant fiberglass statue attempts to catch the eye of hungry pescatarians.

Restaurant Recommendation:
Lau's Czech Bakery
121 Main St W
New Prague, MN 56071

PRIOR LAKE, MN
POPULATION: 27,617 – CITY 668 OF 856 (10-3-25)

One of the oldest incorporated cities in RiverSouth, the southwest part of the Twin Cities, began in 1875 when it was surveyed on land owned by Charles H. Prior. It was located on the Hastings & Dakota division of the Chicago, Milwaukee & St. Paul Railway in 1875. It took its name from the preexisting post office established in 1872 under the direction of Malcom McCall, the first postmaster. The village, the lake, and the post office's "Prior Lake" name all honor the legacy of Mr. Prior, who was superintendent of the railroad division. Seven years after it was surveyed, Joseph

Wankey's 1880 flour and feed mill, William B. Reed's general merchandise store, and wheat storage house, a blacksmith shop, and two saloons were reported to be the only commercial establishments in town. Over the next fifty years, its population never surpassed 250 residents, and it was known by very few for its Grainwood Hotel and its lake. Its population steadily increased through the post-World War II era as more citygoers took an interest in the lake, and by the time the 1970s rolled around, the town's numbers had increased dramatically. Over 6,100 new residents moved in during this time, bringing Prior Lake's population to 7,284 by the 1980 Census. Since then, it has nearly quadrupled as Prior Lake has become one of the many suburbs surrounding Minnesota's largest center of population, culture, and economy. Portions of the Shakopee Mdewakanton Sioux Community were annexed by the city in 1972, creating a small area of the town that can legally host a casino. The Mystic Lake Casino, established in 1992 and noted for its teepee-shaped spotlights that reach far into the night sky, has since become a prominent landmark of the community. Prior Lake High School is the subject of Elinor Burkett's book, *Another Planet: A Year in the Life of a Suburban High School*, which sought to study a school similar in demographics to Columbine High School in Columbine, Colorado. Noted persons of interest with ties to Prior Lake are Tiffany Stratton, the current WWE Women's Champion; actress Kylie Bunbury; John Roach, the Roman Catholic Archbishop of Saint Paul and Minneapolis from 1975 to 1995; Thomas Fluharty, an illustrator whose work has been featured in *Time*, *Mad*, and *The New York Times* amongst other publications; Erik Westrum, an NHL center from 2003 and 2007, and Teal Bunbury, a forward for the Nashville SC Major League Soccer club.

SAVAGE, MN
POPULATION: 32,465 – CITY 670 OF 856 (10-3-25)

The Mdewakanton Dakota claimed the area that is now Savage circa 1750, at a point known as Chief Black Dog's camp. For decades, they retained control of the area and enjoyed its abundant natural resources, including a perpetual "boiling" artesian well known as the Maka Yusota. In 1852, a small trading post was established at the confluence of the Credit and Minnesota Rivers, which came to be known as Hamilton Landing, in honor of Alexander Hamilton, a founding father of the United States. The port town grew with the steamboat trade. In October 1865, a railroad line (an early variation of the Chicago, St. Paul, Minneapolis & Omaha Railroad) was extended to Mendota to increase its economic prominence in the region. A post office was established under the Hamilton name, but it was later renamed Glendale in 1894 and then again as Savage in 1904. Marion Willis Savage was the president of the International Stock Food Company. As a wealthy businessman, Savage could afford to participate in high-society activities such as horse racing, for which he became particularly famous due to his racehorse, Dan Patch. A covered half-mile racetrack was built under Savage's direction, and Dan Patch rose to international fame when he set the mile record at one minute, fifty-five seconds in 1906. Between July 11 and 12, 1916, both horse and owner fell ill. They passed away within twenty-four hours of each other, leaving behind their legacy and namesakes to the town of Savage and the "Dan Patch" railroad line that connected Faribault, Northfield, Savage, and Minneapolis. A 1922 conflagration destroyed the legendary stables and racetrack. Exciting times continued into the following year, when a young Charles Lindbergh was forced to make an emergency landing in a swampy area near Savage. Although unknown, several locals helped to pull Lindbergh's plane onto solid ground, and he stayed in the local Savage depot with the railroad agent and Charles F. McCarthy until a replacement propeller came in from Little Falls. During World War II, Savage experienced a significant population increase when Camp Savage was constructed to house the

Military Intelligence School's language school. Attendees were taught Japanese to aid in the war effort. Around the same time, Cargill made its own contributions to the war effort by building ships for the United States Navy. They were dredged down the Minnesota River from Port Cargill (the former site of Hamilton Landing) to the Mississippi River, where they would then be sailed to the points where they were most needed. Savage's most significant population increase occurred between 1980 and 2000, when the population grew over fivefold from 3,954 to 21,115.

SHAKOPEE, MN ★
POPULATION: 43,698 – CITY 776 OF 856 (11-6-25)

"The Village of the Six" was the name given to Chief Shakopee II's Mdewakanton Dakota village on the Minnesota River. This settlement long predated any Europeans who brought their influence to the region. Many Indigenous peoples moved to this village and sought refuge here after ceding incomprehensible amounts of land to the United States government. When Thomas A. Holmes established a trading post here in 1851, this region, too, saw widespread settlement, and in 1854, a village was platted and named for Chief Shakopee II. "Shakopee," alternatively spelled "Zhaagobe," "Jack-O-Pa'," or "Shakpe," is actually a term that was generally passed down from father to son in Dakota tradition. Growth was rapid; by 1857, there was a post office, and on May 23 of that year, Shakopee was incorporated. When the Dakota War of 1862 sent Europeans fleeing elsewhere for safety, the city surrendered its charter, and the town of 1,100-plus people came to a standstill. On March 1, 1866, it reincorporated as a village and did not regain its charter until 1870. Stations of the Chicago, Milwaukee & St. Paul and the Chicago, St. Paul, Minneapolis & Omaha Railroads wove their way through the county. They followed parts of the Minnesota River through Shakopee. When The Irish Standard of Minneapolis surveyed the town's business interests in 1915, the city reportedly had an opera house, a cement plant, a brewery, a creamery, a cooperage, four hotels, two banks, two grain elevators, two weekly newspapers, bottling works, and flour and feed mills. A sanitarium and the Catholic church were considered to be two other vital pieces of infrastructure. Many early residences, including the "Early Shakopee Houses" built in 1865, the 1856 Strunk-Nyssen House, and the 1887 Julius A. Coller House, are still standing as outstanding examples of 19th-century neighborhood homes. The Shakopee Historic District, with its Murphy's Landing and Murphy's Inn, and The Pond Gristmill, highlights area history. At Sever's Corn Maze, fall tourists can enjoy walking through elaborate corn mazes in the shapes of the Titanic or the Egyptian Sphinx (among others). Canterbury Park hosts the Fall Poker Classic annually, as well as thoroughbred horse races. Valleyfair amusement park opened on May 25, 1976, and has since expanded to over seventy-five attractions. Some of its original rides in 1977 were bumper cars, a carousel, a Ferris wheel, and even Minnesota's very own Tilt-A-Whirl and Giant Tilt Ride, the only Super Tilt model 14-car Tilt-A-Whirl ever. In the 1994 family sports film *Little Big League*, many of the park's attractions are visible in the background of the amusement park scene. NBC's *Saturday Night Live* and Comedy Central's *The Daily Show* have both featured the town in various sketches, one of which (on SNL) was about the fact that the local women's prison (started in 1915 as the State Reformatory for Women) had no fence. Some noteworthy folks with Shakopee ties are Andrew Reiner, the executive editor of the video game magazine *Game Informer*; Maurice Stans, the 19th United States Secretary of Commerce; Jack Bergman, a Member of the U.S. House of Representatives from Michigan since 2017; Amy Menke, a professional ice hockey player with the PWHPA; Eleanor Gates, a playwright known for her work *The Poor Little Rich Girl*; Scott Ferrozzo, a mixed martial artist who participated in several UFC events, and Christopher Stauub, a fashion designer whose work has been featured on the Lifetime network.

Restaurant Recommendation:
Wampach's Restaurant
126 1st Ave W
Shakopee, MN 55379

Restaurant Recommendation:
Tommy's Malt Shop
1101 Adams St S
Shakopee, MN 55379

Unincorporated/Ghost Towns: Blakeley, Cedar Lake, Helena, Lydia, Marystown, Mudbaden, Spring Lake, St. Benedict, St. Patrick, Union Hill

National Register of Historic Places:
Belle Plaine: Episcopal Church of The Transfiguration, Hooper-Bowler-Hillstrom House
Elko New Market: New Market Hotel & Store
Jordan: Abraham Bisson House, Foss & Wells House, Jordan Brewery Ruins, Jordan Historic District, Mudbaden Sulphur Springs Company
Marystown: St. Mary's Church of the Purification
New Market Township: Wencl Kajer Farmstead
New Prague: Church of St. Wenceslaus
Savage: Maka Yusota
Shakopee: Julius A. Coller House, Early Shakopee Houses, Holmes Street Bridge, Šákpe Mounds- Pond Mounds Site, Šákpe Mounds- Steele Mounds Site, Herman Schroeder House & Livery, Shakopee Historic District, Strunk-Nyssen House

Golf Courses:
Boulder Pointe Golf Club, Daily Fee (Elko New Market, MN)
Creeksbend Golf Course, Daily Fee (New Prague, MN)
Legends Golf Club, Daily Fee (Credit River, MN)
New Prague Golf Club, Municipal (New Prague, MN)
Ridges at Sand Creek, Daily Fee (Jordan, MN)
Stonebrook Golf Club – Waters Edge, Daily Fee (Shakopee, MN)
Stonebrook Golf Club, Daily Fee (Shakopee, MN)
The Meadows at Mystic Lake, Daily Fee (Prior Lake, MN)
The Wilds Golf Club, Daily Fee (Prior Lake, MN)

Breweries/Wineries/Distilleries:
Badger Hill Brewery (Shakopee, MN)
Boathouse Brothers Brewing Co (Prior Lake, MN)
Giesenbrau Bier Company (New Prague, MN)
Mana Brewing (Shakopee, MN)
Next Chapter Vineyard (New Prague, MN)
Shakopee Brewhall (Shakopee, MN)
The Savage Tap (Savage, MN)

Town Celebrations:
Dozinky Festival, New Prague, MN (3rd Weekend in September)
Heimatfest, Jordan, MN (1st Weekend after Labor Day)
Minnesota Renaissance Festival, Shakopee, MN (Mid-August through September)

Rice County: The Episcopal Church of the Holy Cross (Dundas), Rice County Courthouse (Faribault), Mural (Faribault), Furball Farm Cat Sanctuary (Faribault), Historic 3-R Landmark School (Lonsdale), Historic Morristown Feed Mill (Morristown), Hidden Falls at Nerstrand Big Woods State Park (Nerstrand), Old Main at St. Olaf College (Northfield)

Rock County: former Pettit's Gas Station (Beaver Creek), Car Display outside of Green Lantern Café (Hardwick), Tripoint Border Marker IA/MN/SD (Hills), Rodman Willman Farm (Jasper), World's Largest Collection of Nutcrackers at the Rock County History Center (Luverne), Wild Buffalo at Blue Mounds State Park (Luverne), Verne Drive In Theater (Luverne), Grain Elevator (Magnolia)

Roseau County: Badger Area Community Heritage Wall Mosaic (Badger), Working Telephone Booth (Greenbush), World War I Veteran's Memorial (Roosevelt), Roseau River Spillway at Hayes Lake State Park (Wannaska), Polaris Exhibit at Roseau County Museum (Roseau), Polaris Experience Center (Roseau), former Canadian National [Railroad] Depot (Warroad), Interior of "The Shed" Car Museum (Warroad)

Saint Louis County: "Honk the Moose" Statue (Biwabik), Buhl: The Finest Water in America Water Tower (Buhl), Iron Man Memorial (Chisholm), Bruce Mine Headframe (Chisholm), Lake Superior Maritime Visitor Center & Aerial Lift Bridge (Duluth), Duluth North Pier Lighthouse (Duluth), former Central High School (Duluth), Enger Tower (Duluth)

Saint Louis County: Gray Wolf at International Wolf Center (Ely), World's Largest Hockey Stick (Eveleth), Interior of Hibbing High School (Hibbing), Colby Lake (Hoyt Lakes), Leonidas Overlook (Leonidas), Sax-Zim Bog Boardwalk (The Meadowlands), Giant Bluegill Welcome Sign (Orr), Headframes at Lake Vermilion-Soudan Underground Mine State Park (Soudan)

Scott County: Episcopal Church of the Transfiguration (Belle Plaine), Jordan Brewery Ruins (Jordan), Sand Creek Waterfall at Lagoon Park (Jordan), World's Largest Porta-Potties at Minnesota's Largest Candy Store (Jordan), St. Wenceslaus Catholic Church (New Prague), Mural (New Prague), Mural (Shakopee), Wampach's Restaurant (Shakopee)

SHERBURNE COUNTY
EST. 1856 - POPULATION: 97,183

About 100,000 people called Sherburne County home as of the 2020 Census; it was named for Moses Sherburne, an Associate Justice of the Minnesota Territorial Supreme Court.

BALDWIN, MN
POPULATION: 4,672 – CITY 486 OF 856 (8-9-25)
On July 16, 2024, Sherburne's Baldwin Township formally began the transition into becoming Minnesota's newest incorporated municipality. Two decades of work went into transforming the largely rural township into a municipality to protect its rural landscapes from being annexed by neighboring cities, such as Princeton. The earliest settler of the township was likely Homer Hulett, who located himself on section four in 1854. He was followed by H. P. Burrell in 1855 and C. H. Chadbourne in 1856. The first schoolhouse in town was built in 1862. The latest population count, 4,672 people, was recorded within the township limits in 2000.

BECKER, MN
POPULATION: 4,877 – CITY 488 OF 856 (8-9-25)
Named in honor of George Loomis Becker, Becker Township welcomed its first settler, Mr. Vadnies, in 1855. John A. Wagner, Noble Crawford, John Sadley, and John Curtis recognized the area's potential due to its prime location between the Mississippi and Elk Rivers, and they built their own homes there the following year. With another fifteen years of progress, Becker boasted that there were enough people, businesses, and buildings to warrant surveying and formal platting of the territory into a townsite. The city plat was made on December 5, 1870. The Pleasant Valley post office, in operation since 1866, changed its name to match the town plat. Pleasant Valley Church, whose congregation organized itself on July 21, 1867, followed suit and changed its name to the American Baptist Church. Swedish Baptist and Swedish Lutheran churches were established in the 1870s to accommodate Becker's largely Scandinavian populace. Both the Great Northern Railroad and the Northern Pacific Railroad had stations here, which helped Becker maintain a population of 200-odd residents from its first Census in 1910 through the 1960s. Its growth was exponential from that point onward. Between 1900 and 2000, the population increased from 902 people to 2,673, a 196.3% rise decade-over-decade. By 2010, the city had 4,538 citizens. The rapid growth of the community in such a short period can be partially attributed to the construction of the Sherburne County Generating Station in the 1970s, the largest power plant in Minnesota with a two-unit capacity of 1,704 megawatts. Its operator, Excel Energy, accounts for over two-thirds of the city's tax revenue. However, it is also the single-largest source of carbon dioxide emissions from "air permitted facilities" within the state, leading to the decision to close the plants by the end of the 2020s. A Microsoft data center is expected to be constructed in the vicinity soon and could be powered by the Monticello Nuclear Generating Plant, located a few miles away in Wright County's City of Monticello. Becker is home to the uniquely large 27-hole Pebble Creek Golf Course, nine city parks, and a single location on the National Register of Historic Places: the Herbert M. Fox House, at the Sherburne History Center. The 1876 home is just 21x16 feet and was built with load-bearing vertical planks rather than wall studs.

BIG LAKE, MN
POPULATION: 11,686 – CITY 845 OF 856 (11-14-25)
Ice and potatoes may sound like strange things for a town to be "famous" for, but for the heyday pioneers of the City of Big Lake, those two commodities were irreplaceable in the town's early economy. Joseph Brown arrived in 1846, and James, Eli, and Newell Houghton of Vermont arrived in 1848; they were among the first citizens in the area, which would be platted in 1857 as Liberty. While that "paper town" never actually materialized, the cluster of structures near Big Lake later took on the name Humboldt when it was declared the county seat of Sherburne County. In 1867, the name was changed to "Big Lake" for the large, pristine lake to the town's west that provided the ice for three large, three-story-tall ice houses. Elk River took over the county seat title, but Big Lake's booming ice industry attracted the attention of both the Great Northern Railway and the Northern Pacific Railroad. They allowed for the quick transportation of the product to other communities. The success of the ice industry, along with numerous other businesses like Dickey, Obert & Company's 34 by 44 foot, three-story-high flouring mill, gave Big Lake reason to seek incorporation as a municipality on December 29, 1898. Numerous resorts, a dance hall, a roller rink, and even an amusement park have entertained locals and visitors alike over the decades. Nowadays, Big Lake is best known for its annual "Spud Fest," a celebration of all things potatoes. The potato-loving city has frequently been named one of Minnesota's safest communities. It is also notable for housing the tallest human-made structure in Minnesota, the 1,505-foot-tall KPXM guyed aerial mast tower.

CLEAR LAKE, MN
POPULATION: 641 – CITY 489 OF 856 (8-9-25)
The smallest incorporated town in Sherburne County, located on the Great Northern and Northern Pacific Railroad lines between Saint Cloud and Elk River, was named for the pristine lake two miles west of the village. Several smaller lakes were in the vicinity, but the large Clear Lake was the inspiration for the settlers' name. Mr. White and Isaac Marks thought so highly of the area that, in 1848, they established a trading post at a significant bend in the Mississippi River. Others succeeded them, and many of these individuals sought to establish a formal townsite for the benefit of all. F. E. Baldwin and John H. Stevenson laid out a town with the hopes of garnering the county seat, but when their plan failed, so too did the townsite. It was not until 1867 that Clear Lake Station was established, and in 1879, the modern-day site was surveyed. It was replatted again on March 24, 1882, on Alanson C. Potter's land; he was then the depot agent. The typical general stores, an elevator, a hotel, and a blacksmith shop were started by entrepreneurial spirits, but it was a pickling plant and a canning factory that brought the most prosperity to the fledgling village. A Methodist Episcopal church was the first religious edifice in town. Clear Lake was incorporated on March 13, 1900.

ELK RIVER, MN ★☆
POPULATION: 25,835 – CITY 844 OF 856 (11-14-25)
When Zebulon Pike passed through the area in 1805 while following the Mississippi River, he discovered enormous herds of elk roaming about the valley. Their presence inspired him to name the 84-mile river at the confluence of the Mississippi River the "Elk," a name that would later be used for a city now home to over 25,000 residents as of the 2020s. Forty years after Pike's passage, David Frederic Faribault, the son of fur trader Jean-Baptiste Faribault, built a trading post that was purchased in 1848 by H.M. Rice and S.P. Folsom. Those two men, in turn, sold it to Pierre Bottineau, the namesake of the North Dakota town and county and the proprietor of settlement

parties that gave rise to Osseo, Maple Grove, and Breckenridge, Minnesota. Another one of his projects was the village of Orono, better known as "Upper Town." Orono was established when Silas Lane sold his claim to Ard Godfrey and John C. Jamieson (of Orono, Maine), and they constructed a dam and a sawmill in 1851. Bottineau had already built a hotel here in 1850, and a post office had been organized in 1851. It was platted in May 1855, and in 1865, Elk River, also known as "Lower Town," was established to serve as the county seat. A replatting was in order in 1868 with the arrival of the St. Paul & Pacific Railroad. By 1872, it had finally become the seat of government for good, as its population had grown significantly. Orono and Elk River incorporated under the common Elk River name in 1880-81. The milling industry dominated the town's economy at that time, as it was then home to Mills & Houlton's lumber mill, Mills & Houlton's flouring mill, H. Houlton's "Lower Town" lumber mill, and Thomas S. and W. C. Nickerson's planing mill. Educational, religious, and fraternal organizations grew as the village's population increased, which, as of 1970, still barely totaled over 2,000 persons. In the 1920s, the historic Elk River Water Tower was built, as was Elkhi Stadium, a community-funded and built city and school athletic field. The National Youth Administration made significant improvements to the facility in 1940 as part of a New Deal program. These two sites, in addition to the Oliver H. Kelley Homestead, which was occupied from 1850 to 1870 by the founder of The National Grange of the Order of Patrons of Husbandry (and is now operated as a living history museum by the Minnesota State Historical Society), are listed on the National Register of Historic Places. The Great River Energy plant, the first rural nuclear power plant in the country, was activated here in 1960 but shut down only a few years later, as it was intended only as a testing and demonstration facility. Due to its nearly tenfold population increase over the last half-century, modern-day Elk River now boasts dozens of parks, two golf courses, the ERX Motor Park, several restaurants, and other leisure facilities. A few famous Elk River residents include Dave Mordal, the host of the Discovery Channel's *Wreckreation* Nation travel/reality television show in 2009; Emma Bates, the winner of the USA Marathon Championships in 2018 and one of the world's best marathon runners in the 2020s; Margaret Frazer, noted for her historical and mystery novels; Nancy Mudge, a member of the 1954 AAGPBL (All-American Girls Professional Baseball League) All-Star Team; Michael Kurilla, the 15th Commander of the United States Central Command, and former NHL players Joel Otto (943 games), Paul Martin (870 games), Dan Hinote (503 games), Nate Prosser (360 games). Otto was one of the top defensive centers in the National Hockey League between 1984 and 1998 and a two-time finalist for the Frank J. Selke Trophy, the "MVP" award for defensive forwards.

Restaurant Recommendation:
Tipsy on Main Kitchen & Cocktails
709 Main St NW
Elk River, MN 55330

ZIMMERMAN, MN
POPULATION: 6,189 – CITY 485 OF 856 (8-9-25)
Until 1967, this rural city was known as the Village of Lake Fremont, in honor of John C. Fremont, the noted explorer and associate of Joseph Nicollet, as well as the first Republican nominee for president in 1856. The Great Northern Railroad named their village Lake Fremont, while the post office used the name Zimmerman, after an influential railroadman and an early proprietor of the townsite. The Lake Fremont post office entered service in 1865 and closed in 1902, but the Zimmerman post office, established in 1890, took its place. There were lumber yards, general stores, hardware

and implement stores, churches, a school, and the typical array of pioneer businesses and institutions characteristic of the time. The Village of Lake Fremont ceased to exist in the 1960s when it was renamed as the City of Zimmerman. As the "Gateway to the Sherburne National Wildlife Refuge," one of the last remaining natural oak savannas in the United States, Zimmerman attracts many recreationists seeking the thrill of boating, hunting, camping, sailing, snowmobiling, and numerous other activities.

Restaurant Recommendation:
Zimmerman Cafe Bar Bowl
25920 Gateway Dr
Zimmerman, MN 55398

Princeton is only partially located in Sherburne County (see Mille Lacs County), and St. Cloud is only partially located in Sherburne County (see Stearns County).

Unincorporated/Ghost Towns: Bailey, Briggs Lake, Cable, Orrock, Salida, Santiago

National Register of Historic Places:
Becker: Herbert M. Fox House
Elk River: Elk River Water Tower, Elkhi Stadium, Oliver H. Kelley Homestead
St. Cloud: Minnesota State Reformatory for Men Historic District

Golf Courses:
Elk River Golf Club, Daily Fee (Elk River, MN)
Pebble Creek Golf Club, Municipal (Becker, MN)

Breweries/Wineries/Distilleries:
Aegir Brewing Company (Elk River, MN)
Lupulin Brewery (Big Lake, MN)

Town Celebrations:
Elk RiverFest, Elk River, MN (Last Saturday in July)
Spudfest, Big Lake, MN (Last Full Weekend of June)
Wild West Days, Zimmerman, MN (Memorial Day Weekend)

SIBLEY COUNTY
EST. 1853 - POPULATION: 14,836

Henry Hastings Sibley, Minnesota's First Governor from May 1858 to January 1860, became the namesake of Sibley County upon its establishment on March 5, 1853.

ARLINGTON, MN ☆
POPULATION: 2,247 – CITY 478 OF 856 (8-8-25)
Minnesota's statehood and Arlington's etymology are closely intertwined: on May 11, 1858, Minnesota entered the Union as the 32nd state, and Arlington's name was officially approved. Settled in 1855 and platted in 1856, Arlington experienced steady growth in German settlers and businesses for 25 years before it was moved in 1881 to a location on the Minneapolis & St. Louis Railroad. When its first Census was completed in 1890, Arlington had 417 residents, and the beginnings of its first businesses, churches, schools, and fraternal organizations emerged. A post office entered service in 1857. The population exceeded 1,000 residents for the first time at the dawn of the 1940s, and in 1948, it was incorporated as a "Home Rule Charter"

city. A home rule charter city operates under a self-governing charter, granting it more autonomy than a general-law city. John McGovern, a College Football Hall of Fame member inducted in 1966, was born in Arlington and attended the local high school before becoming the quarterback at the University of Minnesota from 1908 to 1910. Arlington's municipal water tower has been painted to resemble a giant baseball.

Restaurant Recommendation:
Arlington Haus
147 W Main St
Arlington, MN 55307

GAYLORD, MN ★
POPULATION: 2,273 – CITY 479 OF 856 (8-8-25)

When William Washburn authorized the extension of the Minneapolis & St. Louis Railway from his flour mills in Minneapolis to the prairie of South Dakota, he knew that the engines would need to establish several stopping points along the way as refueling points. Many of these stops became bustling railroad towns, one of which was Gaylord, which was formally established in October 1881. Its namesake was Edward W. Gaylord, a prominent railroad official. A post office was established that same year, and Henry A. Boettcher was appointed postmaster. He had the first building on the site, a general store. After its incorporation as a village in 1883, Gaylord enjoyed subtle growth over the next thirty years, reaching a population of around six hundred residents by the time its next impetus for growth arrived. Residents of Sibley County, frustrated by how far east Henderson was from most of their homes and farmsteads, voted to move the county seat to Gaylord because of its central location. It took three popular votes before victory was attained in 1915, which forever reshaped the town's history. The Sibley County Courthouse, Sheriff's Residence, and Jail were built in 1916, using (respectively) elements of Neoclassical and Spanish Colonial Revival architecture. That same year, a dance pavilion was added to Gaylord City Park, which became known for its 1940 bridge and bandshell built by the Works Progress Administration. From 1890 to 2010, Gaylord never experienced a decrease in its population, but from 2010 to 2020, its numbers decreased for the first time, albeit by only 32 people.

GIBBON, MN
POPULATION: 784 – CITY 469 OF 856 (8-7-25)

Formerly home to a large Polka festival for years before the town's ballroom closed its doors in 2011, Gibbon was established as a primarily German and Scandinavian community. After the Minneapolis & St. Louis Railroad came through, Gibbon was incorporated in 1887 and named in honor of General John Gibbon of Civil War fame. He was also an officer at Minneapolis's Fort Snelling in 1878 and from 1880-82. An alternate account argues that it was named for the English historian Edward Gibbon, but it is generally accepted that it was named for the man with military honors. August Peterson was the first to settle here in 1878, and the area was called Peterson's Grove until he donated forty acres of land for the townsite. Peterson owned the first lot, and on the second, Wenzel Friedl built a saloon. More lines of enterprise blossomed, and in 1883, the Gibbon post office was established. A uniquely designed village hall building originated in 1895, when the Romanesque Revival structure was built using architect Charles Webster's blueprints. Other firms near the turn of the century were the Citizens State Bank, the State Bank of Gibbon, a barber shop, the Palace Hotel, a meat market, a city drug store, and mercantile.

GREEN ISLE, MN
POPULATION: 522 – CITY 477 OF 856 (8-8-25)
A high proportion of Irish settlers gave way to the "Green Isle" name for this municipality and township, which alludes to Ireland, "the Emerald Isle." Christopher Dolan suggested the name. The town originated when the Minneapolis & St. Louis Railway completed its line between Morton and Norwood circa 1880; it was platted the following year in August 1881. Immigrants had lived in the area since 1857. They established a considerable number of businesses, including general stores, blacksmith shops, and hardware and implement stores, to cater to the needs of the townspeople. About 200 to 300 people lived in Green Isle between 1890 and 2000, before its population suddenly spiked by 67.4% from 334 residents to 559 in the first decade of the 21st Century.

HENDERSON, MN
POPULATION: 960 – CITY 476 OF 856 (8-8-25)
Sibley County's original seat of government owes its existence to Joseph R. Brown, a prominent area politician who established the town in August 1852 and named it in honor of his aunt's maiden name: Margaret Brown Henderson. By 1855, the village on the Minnesota River had several dozen structures, amongst the most popular of which were a steam sawmill, a hotel, a store, and Brown's home, which doubled as a boarding house. From 1857 to 1861, he published the *Henderson Democrat* newspaper, one of the earliest newspapers in the region. A trade route was forged towards Pembina, North Dakota, and businessmen and women recognized Henderson's potential as the crown jewel of the Minnesota River Valley. The Herman Mattei and Schwartz brick yards forged the dark red building materials that would soon be used in several of Henderson's civic structures and local residences. Mattei's brickyard reportedly produced over a million bricks annually by 1882. H. Poehler & Company operated the original lumberyard. Other businesses of note were Christian Enes's Henderson Brewery, the Henderson broom factory, Herman Mollering's pork packing house, F. Schafer's beer keg factory and cooper shop, B. F. Paul's flour mill, a feed mill, a sawmill, two grain elevators, and three hotels called The Union House, The Minnesota House, and The McClellan House. Using local bricks, a two-story brick building was erected in 1878 and graduating pupils by 1882. Churches were plentiful as well. Catholics, Lutherans, Methodists, and Episcopalians all found a home in Henderson where they could practice their faith. Twelve properties built between 1874 and 1905 have since been jointly listed on the National Register of Historic Places as the Henderson Commercial Historic District, along with the 1884 Queen Anne August F. Poehler House and the 1879 Sibley County Courthouse. Poehler's home is now the site of the Sibley County Historical Society Museum, and the former courthouse structure (used from 1879 to 1915, before the county seat was moved to Gaylord) is the modern-day Henderson Community Building, a senior center, and the Joseph R. Brown Minnesota River Center. Much of Henderson's early success can be attributed to the arrival of the Chicago, St. Paul, Minneapolis & Omaha Railroad, commonly known as the "Omaha Road." Fans of Prince may appreciate the mural tribute to the artist in downtown Henderson, inspired by the 1984 romantic rock musical drama film *Purple Rain*. Many politicians have ties to Henderson, but two of its more unique residents have included Mary L. Mallett, an early temperance advocate and president of the Oregon State Woman's Christian Temperance Union, and Ray Oldenburg, an urban sociologist noted for coining the term "third place," referring to a person's wanting to belong to a third social environment separate from home or their workplace.

NEW AUBURN, MN
POPULATION: 411 – CITY 480 OF 856 (8-8-25)
Neither the Chicago, Milwaukee & St Paul Railroad nor the Minneapolis & St. Louis Railroad thought that New Auburn was a worthwhile place to give a depot to, and so the small city has always remained as an inland town. Despite the lack of a railroad station, New Auburn, briefly called High Island by the United States Postal Service from January to June 1857, adopted its modern name because many of its original settlers were from Auburn, New York. The High Island site was registered as a townsite with the state by Bell and Chapman, who thought that a small general store would serve as the nucleus of a booming settlement. While stores, churches, schools, and other staples of everyday life were present in the early village, its "boom" did not truly begin until the start of the 21st century. From 1990 to 2000, the population grew by 34.4%, from 363 to 488, a number New Auburn has not yet returned to.

WINTHROP, MN
POPULATION: 1,332 – CITY 470 OF 856 (8-7-25)
Situated at a junction of two lines of the Minneapolis & St. Louis Railroad, one heading southbound to New Ulm and the other eastwards towards the Twin Cities, is the City of Winthrop, population 1,332. Before there was Winthrop, there was a post office called Eagle City from 1858 to 1882, first established in Michael Cummings's halfway house on the Old Fort Ridgely Road. Eagle City was an accompanying municipality (incorporated on May 19, 1857) to the post office, which, after a series of moves, eventually landed in a new townsite called Winthrop in 1882. Residents of Winthrop had been petitioning for an office for some time, and Elford Andrew Campbell, then the Eagle City postmaster, jumped at the opportunity to move his office to a town that would be destined to become one of the wealthiest agricultural centers of southern Minnesota. The Winthrop townsite was platted in 1881 on land owned by Erick and Brita Olson. At its first Census in 1890, the population was 488, and in 1910 it had grown to over one thousand residents. The Winthrop of 1915 had over one hundred different lines of businesses, as recorded by a July 25, 1915, article written by The Minneapolis Journal. To list every line would lead to an extensive list, but amongst the more interesting institutions were a sash and door factory, stone and marble works, The First National Bank of Winthrop, the State Bank of Winthrop, *The Winthrop News* newspaper, the Winthrop Canning Factory, the Winthrop Co-operative Creamery Association, the Winthrop Grain & Mill Company, Ostrom's Photo Studio, Winthrop Wagon & Carriage Works, a motion picture theater, an ice and wood business, four grain elevators, three "exclusive" grocery stores, and an exclusive shoe store and exclusive clothing store. Many of these businesses came and went over the years as Winthrop's population fluctuated to as high as 1,391 people in the 1970s.

Le Sueur is only partially located in Sibley County (see Le Sueur County).

Unincorporated/Ghost Towns: Assumption, New Rome, Rush River

National Register of Historic Places:
Gaylord: Gaylord City Park, Sibley County Courthouse & Sheriff's Residence & Jail
Gibbon: Gibbon Village Hall
Henderson: Henderson Commercial Historic District, August F. Poehler House, Sibley County Courthouse-1879
Jessenland Township: Church of St. Thomas

Golf Courses:
Winthrop Golf Club, Daily Fee (Winthrop, MN)

Town Celebrations:
Arli-Dazzle Christmas Light Parade, Arlington, MN (1st Weekend of December)
Eggstravaganza, Gaylord, MN (2nd Weekend in August)
Gibbon Funfest, Gibbon, MN (3rd Weekend in July)
Gibbon Winterfest, Gibbon, MN (3rd Weekend in January)
Henderson Hummingbird Hurrah, Henderson, MN (3rd Saturday in August)
Winthrop Farm City Fun Fest, Winthrop, MN (2nd Weekend in July)

STEARNS COUNTY
EST. 1855 - POPULATION: 158,292

Stearns County was first named after Isaac Ingalls Stevens, the 1st Governor of Washington Territory, but a clerical error led to it being spelled as "Stearns" and instead named for Charles Thomas Stearns, an early Minnesota territorial legislator.

ALBANY, MN
POPULATION: 2,780 – CITY 520 OF 856 (8-12-25)
Albany has always been a happening place. Named after the capital of New York, it was first settled by the Obermiller and Schwinghammer families in 1862. Isador Obermiller married Maria Schwinghammer after the two met on the open range, and they hosted the first post office in their hotel once the United States Postal Service officially opened a branch office there in 1870. At that point, it was called the Schwinghammer Settlement and then the Two River Mission Settlement of Two Rivers, before the Great Northern Railroad arrived in 1871 and opened the Albany depot. A plat was filed in 1872, and Carl Herberger built up the first building on the site, a general store. About twenty years later, on January 20, 1890, Albany was incorporated. The town had grown exponentially, and by 1896, it was home to a stockyard, a bank, a grist mill, a brickyard, a creamery, three hotels, two elevators, a wagon shop, the post office, a fire station, a jail, Public School No. 58, the Catholic church, and a "German church," as listed on Charles M. Foote's 1896 *Plat Book of Stearns County, Minnesota*. Later, the Minneapolis, St. Paul & Sault Ste. Marie Railroad crossed the Great Northern, and Albany continued to grow at a steady pace. Since its first Census was conducted in 1900, there have only been two decades in which its population has decreased (from 1970 to 1980 by 1.9%, and then again the following decade by 1.3%); its most prosperous decade came between 2000 and 2010, when it grew from 1,796 people to 2,561, an increase of 42.6%. James Steven Rausch, the Bishop of the Roman Catholic Diocese of Phoenix from June 17, 1977, to May 18, 1981, was born in Albany in 1928. Albany is one of a handful of towns located on the course of the Lake Wobegon Trail Marathon. The event, started in 2008, is a qualifier for the Boston Marathon using the straight-line Lake Wobegon Trail, formerly the railbed of the Great Northern.

AVON, MN
POPULATION: 1,618 – CITY 496 OF 856 (8-10-25)
The River Avon in Warwickshire, England, was the inspiration for Avon, Minnesota's name, as James J. Hill planned and platted towns along his newly established Great Northern Railway line. It was laid out in 1873, the same year its post office was organized. The Keppers brothers arrived from St. Joseph in the 1860s as the area's first settlers. They selected a spot on the Spunk Lakes, which was once a single lake

separated by several channels. It was on the shores of this lake that Avon was established, and a sawmill was built as one of its earliest businesses. A hotel, a creamery, and a feed barn were listed on an 1896 business directory as being other important institutions within town; in the southern part of town was the post office, a Catholic Church, and Public School No. 60. Avon was incorporated on January 26, 1900, and for decades was held primarily to its original town plat before extending past the spunk lakes in 1992. On July 4, 2009, it was noted as the site of the 35th anniversary broadcast of the *A Prairie Home Companion* weekly radio show, which aired from 1974 to 2016, and was known for its "News from Lake Wobegon" segment hosted by Garrison Keillor. The fictional town of Lake Wobegon was used in Keillor's stories, and he once said that Avon was "about as close to Lake Wobegon as you can get." The Roman Catholic Bishop of Agats, Indonesia, Alphonsus Augustus Sowada, was born in Avon on June 23, 1933.

BELGRADE, MN
POPULATION: 738 – CITY 529 OF 856 (8-13-25)
The World's Largest Black Crow at 20-feet-tall and 3,000 pounds watches over Belgrade from its branch pedestal in Belgrade Centennial Memorial Park. Crows were selected to represent the community because of crows monogamous traits and devotion to their young. Belgrade parents and pioneers alike have been devoted to growing their community since its establishment in 1887, when the Pacific Land Company platted out the site. A post office called Crow Lake had existed since 1871 until it was changed fifteen years later to Belgrade, the capital city of Serbia. Several businesses existed before the advent of the Minneapolis and Pacific Railroad, which later became a part of the Soo Line Railroad system. Otto Christianson built the first home in 1874. Three elevators were erected on the rail line to assist in the transportation of grain from Belgrade to faraway lands, and a grist mill stood just north of the tracks in Borgerding's Addition. To the south of the tracks was a flour mill and downtown Belgrade with its stores and hotels. At least four churches provided religious services throughout the city as of 1896: a Catholic congregation, the Swedish Methodists, the Zion Lutherans, and the United Lutherans. The Christopher Borgerding House was built from 1904 to 1905 in the Colonial Revival style. It was listed on the Federal Historic Register in 1982 as Belgrade's sole property on the list.

Restaurant Recommendation:
Red Onion Drive Inn
610 Wells St
Belgrade, MN 56312

BROOTEN, MN
POPULATION: 626 – CITY 173 OF 856 (4-14-25)
A tiny part of Brooten's city limits extends into Pope County, but it is primarily located in Stearns County. The town in "The Heart of the Bonanza Valley" began in 1886 when the Minneapolis, St. Paul, and Sault Ste. Marie Railroad was being built. It was established on the land of the Scandinavian farmer Reier O. Liabraaten, whose name was corrupted to Brooten when the site was named. Embrick E. Knudson took over postmaster duties, and the town was well on its way to establishing itself as a significant grain shipping point. Irrigation improvements in the valley gave way to large-scale agricultural operations and the establishment of local businesses, such as grist mills and grain elevators. By 1896, only a decade after Brooten's founding, there was also a lumberyard, three hotels, a bank, a blacksmith shop, a Norwegian church, and

Public School No. 145. In 1920, it had a population of 649, which has served as a general baseline for its population over the last century. In 2010, Brooten reached a population of 743 residents. Its incorporation as a village came on February 16, 1892.

Restaurant Recommendation:
Jenniges Meat Processing
10135 Hwy 55
Brooten, MN 56316

COLD SPRING, MN
POPULATION: 4,164 – CITY 494 OF 856 (8-10-25)

Cold Spring was named so on account of the many natural mineral springs that could be found throughout the vicinity. Early companies capitalized on the springs and their "healing properties," reportedly generating well over $20,000 in revenue by selling the water and attracting tourists to the source. Such was the case with many towns across the Midwest that had "Spring" in their names. The earliest rendition of the townsite was platted in 1856, a year before the post office was established under the name Cold Spring City. The "City" part of the Cold Spring City name was dropped when the community was incorporated on June 26, 1889. Yankee Protestants were the first to live on the claim and serve as storekeepers, farmers, and blacksmiths. They were quickly overwhelmed by the influx of German Catholics seeking refuge as immigrants from anti-Catholic oppression in Europe. Francis Xavier Pierz was responsible for bringing them to the area through his newspaper advertisements, such as in the Der Wahrheitsfreund, in which he described a "land flowing with milk and honey" in the Sauk River Valley of Minnesota. Cold Spring became the site of one of nearly 20 parishes in Stearns County formed as a result of Pierz's missionary work. Unbeknownst to the early settlers until an annual pattern began to take shape, there was a common enemy that would significantly impede the area's growth: grasshoppers. They came by the millions each year, devouring everything in their path from crops and hay to clothing and fruit trees. The plagues were so devastating that on April 26, 1877, Governor John S. Pillsbury proclaimed a statewide day of prayer to abolish the grasshoppers. A rainstorm suddenly turned to snow that night, which helped slow the spread of the grasshoppers' devastation, but they returned in the coming weeks with a vengeance. In early July 1877, Father Winter suspected that the plague had continued because the settlers had forgotten about God after becoming too self-sufficient. He arranged for the construction of a small chapel to honor Mary, Help of Christians, in exchange for her intercession with Jesus to end the plague. Almost as soon as the construction of the chapel began, several accounts–including one made by Laura Ingalls Wilder, author of the "Little House on the Prairie" series– were made that the grasshoppers disappeared that month. The chapel was completed for $865 that year, and Masses and pilgrimages have continued since then. There has not been a grasshopper plague in Minnesota or the surrounding Midwest since the chapel was raised and the prayers began. In 1894, a tornado destroyed everything in the chapel except for artist Joseph Ambroziz's wood-carved statue of Mary and Jesus, which had been placed there years before. It stood untouched amongst the wreckage. In 1952, the second chapel was finally completed as a replacement using materials primarily donated by the Cold Spring Granite Company (now called Coldspring, as of 2013). It was one of several early institutions in Cold Spring, having been moved here in 1920 from Rockville by Patrick H. and John Alexander, the sons of founder Henry Nair Alexander. Early places of note before the turn of the century included a grist mill, creamery, lumber yard, beer hall, three hotels, a firehouse, an opera house, a brewery, an elevator, the *Cold Spring Record* newspaper (still in publication since October

1899), a depot, Public School No. 14, and the Catholic church. Three homes built during these early Cold Spring days, all affiliated with the Cold Spring Brewing Company, have since been added to the National Register of Historic Places for their historical significance: the John Olster House, the Ferdinand Peters House, and the Eugene Hermanutz House. The first two were constructed in 1907, and the Hermanutz House in 1912. Alvin Ganzer, a director with Paramount Pictures from the 1940s to 1970s; Justin Stommes, a professional basketball player in Europe from 2011 to 2016; and Eric Decker, a wide receiver in the NFL from 2010 to 2017, hail from Cold Spring.

Restaurant Recommendation:
Side Bar & Grill
15 Red River Ave N
Cold Spring, MN 56320

ELROSA, MN
POPULATION: 213 – CITY 528 OF 856 (8-13-25)
Settled circa 1907 and incorporated on March 1, 1938, Elrosa took its name from two granddaughters of one of its early city council members: Ella and Rose Nichols. Located in Lake George Township, the little Soo Line Railroad village welcomed its post office in 1913. Several firms came to fruition, like general and hardware stores, liveries, and other lines that would have been necessary for the early townspeople of the time. Elrosa's population peaked at 214 individuals in the 1980s.

FREEPORT, MN
POPULATION: 675 – CITY 521 OF 856 (8-12-25)
A smiley-faced water tower greets travelers to "The City with a Smile" via Interstate-94, a symbol of the town since the mid-1970s. It was painted on the town's 1920 water tower and has since served as a civic symbol, even being mentioned in entertainer Garrison Keillor's fictional town of Lake Wobegon. Ten families settled here in the 1860s and called their hamlet Oak Dale. A smiley-faced water tower greets travelers to "The City with a Smile" via Interstate-94, a symbol of the town since the mid-1970s. It was painted on the town's 1920 water tower and has since served as a civic symbol, even being mentioned in entertainer Garrison Keillor's fictional town of Lake Wobegon. Ten families settled here in the 1860s and called their hamlet Oak Dale, which later became Oak Station once the Great Northern Railway established a depot here. Frank Benolken became postmaster of the Oak Station post office in 1875; he was responsible for changing the town's name to Freeport in 1881 after Freeport, Illinois, a village near his former home of Johnsburg, Illinois. The change was likely made because "Oak Station" was just a little too close in spelling to Osakis, which was just down the line. Within fifteen years, several businesses had come to fruition, including a harness shop, a blacksmith shop, a hotel, a wagon shop and foundry, a grain elevator, and stockyards. There was also a Town Hall, a depot, the School No. 102 building, and a Catholic church edifice. At that time, the church structure was the second for Sacred Heart parish. The first was built in 1882 as a 70-by-36-foot wood-frame structure, and in 1896, a new brick-veneered one that was nearly twice as large. It cost $30,000 to construct, but it was destroyed by fire in 1904. At that point, Paul Koshiol and Co. built a much larger edifice for $115,000 between 1905 and 1906, using Gothic and Romanesque Revival Style plans furnished by Parkinson & Dockendorff of La Crosse, Wisconsin. The Church of the Sacred Heart was added to the National Register of Historic Places in 1991. The Freeport Mill and Miller's House—better known as the Swany White Flour Mills—were also listed on the Register before

they burned down on December 27, 2011. For 114 years, the building has stood as a testament to Hubert and Peter Thelen and their family, who still operate the new Swany White [flour] mill today. Its most popular product is Faith's Best, a bleached flour. Janice Ettle, a long-distance runner noted for competing in several Olympic marathon trials and for winning Grandma's Marathon twice on the North Shore and the 1985 Twin Cities Marathon, grew up in the Freeport area.

GREENWALD, MN
POPULATION: 197 – CITY 527 OF 856 (8-13-25)
Wald is a German word meaning "grove," so the literal translation of this predominantly German settlement's name is "green grove." Formally established in 1907, the site welcomed a postal service branch in 1910, and was granted incorporation status on June 10, 1915. The 0.71-square-mile townsite once had storefronts, schools, and churches, like those in its surrounding communities. While many of these community features have since faded away, Greenwald's population has remained relatively constant. Since 1930, the second decade for which the small city's population was counted, the population has wavered between an all-time low of 197 in 2020 and a high of 266 in 1960.

HOLDINGFORD, MN
POPULATION: 743 – CITY 518 OF 856 (8-12-25)
Two early entities combined to form the City of Holdingford as we know it today, the "Gateway to Lake Wobegon." Randolph Holding, an Irish Catholic, settled on the ox cart trail in 1865. He lived on a ford of the South Two River, which gave rise to the name "Holding's Ford" as a descriptive term for travelers through the area. Dr. A. G. Warde purchased and platted land to the east of the ford, which was called "Wardeville." From 1872 to 1894, the post office in the locality was called Holdings Ford until the two words were amalgamated into Holdingford. On October 23, 1896, the settlement of Wardeville and the post office reached an agreement that led to the incorporation of the two into a town called Holdingford. On the river were the post office, located in a general store; a grist mill; a sawmill; two blacksmith shops; a hotel; and Union church. Religion was complicated in the town, as it had many Irish-American and Canadian Gaelic-speaking residents from Nova Scotia. The local Scottish-Canadian community was relatively large, and it was accompanied by a "melting pot" of German and Polish Catholics, Slovaks and Rusyns, and other groups. There were separate Catholic parishes and Protestant and Orthodox denominations to serve the diverse beliefs of the townspeople. The most unique of all these was likely St. Mary's Russian Orthodox Church, built in 1897 and located across the road from the Slovak Congregational Church–a.k.a. The "Country Church"–that still stands to this day. By the time Prohibition ran from 1920 to 1933, Holdingford became less known for its religious differences and more famous as the "Moonshine Capital of Minnesota." Local Polish and German farmers supplied the Twin Cities, Chicago, and Kansas City with Minnesota 13 moonshine, a premium twice-distilled and aged whiskey that brought Stearns County to a level of regional fame. An early tale recalls the time that Clarence "Tuffy" Olson met his end after attempting to steal 85 gallons of the coveted moonshine from the Dzierweczynskis. When liquor became legal again, Holdingford's population continued to grow from 477 residents to 527 by the start of the 1940s, until it entered a new chapter of world history: World War II. Several good men from Holdingford were lost, and residents wanted to honor them with "The Soldier's Shrine." Dedicated on September 6, 1942, three years before the end of the conflict, it was the first memorial in the United States built to honor World War II veterans. Its other most-noted site is its 186-foot-long covered bridge on the Lake

Wobegon Trail, the longest covered bridge in Minnesota. The rural Catholic Church of the Sacred Heart (formerly listed on the NRHP) remained in its country location off County Highway 9 until 1989, when the Stearns County Pioneer Club moved it to their grounds in Albany. Holdingford's most famous son is Kenneth Benkowski, a professional wrestler best known by his ring name Kenny "Sodbuster" Jay.

KIMBALL, MN
POPULATION: 799 – CITY 537 OF 856 (8-13-25)

When a group of pioneers arrived on the Minnesota prairie from Maine, they thought it appropriate to name their brand-new settlement Maine Prairie, as a nod to where they had come from and where they had elected to start anew. There were several churches, a blacksmith shop, and even a cheese factory. All was going well until the Minneapolis, St. Paul & Sault Ste. Marie Railroad issued a devastating death blow to the community: they bypassed the town entirely. They instead opted to build five miles to the south at Kimball Prairie. All of the buildings at Maine Prairie were subsequently moved to Kimball. The once-barren parcel of land gave way to a blossoming railroad station complete with stockyards, elevators, hotels, a creamery, School No. 80 (burned in 1911 before being replaced by a new brick building, which a modernized 1989 elementary school later replaced), and a Methodist church. The Kimball Prairie post office, which had existed only from 1867 to 1870 before being revived with the railroad's arrival, reopened permanently in 1887. Its name was initially derived from Frye Kimball, a pioneer settler. In 1908, Kimball City Hall was built as a grand office building to host the local government, professional offices, a public library, a municipal theater, and the local telephone company. Its importance to Kimball led to its listing on the National Register of Historic Places in the early 1980s.

LAKE HENRY, MN
POPULATION: 72 – CITY 531 OF 856 (8-13-25)

Lake Henry originally got its name from the explorers Woods and Pope, who identified this lake as Lake David or Lake Henry in their early journals and maps. The township bearing the name "Lake Henry" only came about in 1869, fourteen years after the first settler, Xavier Poepping, arrived to plat the town. He patented the platting of the village after he and Michael Kraemer got into a dispute, as he wanted to ensure that his settlement made it beyond "paper town" status. It was located on the shores of the lake on the Ox Cart Trail, and eventually, the Soo Line Railroad would be extended through the area just southwest of the townsite. The Lake Henry post office remained open from 1883 to 1905, but was discontinued before the town was incorporated as a village on October 6, 1913. A Catholic church and parochial school, a hotel, a bank, a garage, a grocery store, and a filling station made up the bulk of Lake Henry's early commercial district.

MEIRE GROVE, MN
POPULATION: 180 – CITY 526 OF 856 (8-13-25)

Meire Grove has gone by many variable names throughout its short history, including Meire's Grove (the name of the post office from 1873 to 1893, Meiregrove, and Meire Grove (the present formatting of its name and the spelling of the post office from 1893 to 1895), but it has also served as a primary city of Grove Township alongside Greenwald. It was named for Herman and Henry Meyer, who arrived here in 1858 and initially lived in dugouts and log cabins. Like its neighbors, early Meire Grove had a Catholic church, a post office, and School No. 103, the three of which served as its principal pieces of infrastructure. Incorporation was achieved on Christmas Eve in

1896, during a period when the Imdieke Brickyard was its principal industry. Father Meinulf Stuckenkemper of the local St. John the Baptist parish inquired about purchasing bricks for his new Gothic Revival-style church, which inspired nearly three other residents to place purchase orders for bricks for their own homes. Business was booming as the brickyard helped to build the town from the ground up. It continued to provide building materials for residents of Meire Grove until its closure in 1915.

MELROSE, MN
POPULATION: 3,602 – CITY 524 OF 856 (8-12-25)

Father Pierz was responsible for bringing most of Melrose's earliest immigrants to the area. Still, it was Edwin Clark who gained notoriety as the "Father of Melrose" after he and his brother William H. Clark platted the townsite in December 1871. The terminus of the Great Northern Railroad line was most likely named by Warren and Napoleon Adley and Robert Wheeler for Melrose, Scotland, their hometown. An alternate account states that Warren Adley named it in honor of Melissa Rose, his kin. Considering the heavy Catholic influence in the area brought about by Pierz's newspaper recruitment ads in Europe, it was almost certainly named for the Irish settlement. The first settlers arrived in the late 1850s, and Mr. Adley and Mr. Wheeler were responsible for establishing a feed mill, flour mill, lumberyard, hardware store, and bank. The post office started in 1859. When a business survey was made just before the turn of the century, it showed that Melrose's primary institutions were a brewery, a foundry, four hotels, an elevator, stockyards, a flour mill, and a sash, door, and blind factory. A train dispatcher's office and a roundhouse were located in the northwest part of town to accommodate its designation as the railroad line terminus from November 18, 1872, to 1878. School No. 48 was located about a block east of the dispatcher's office. Further down the tracks, one could find an Episcopal church, an Irish Catholic church, and a German Catholic church with an accompanying parochial school. In 1899, German immigrants made a significant upgrade when they began construction on a large two-spired Romanesque Revival church and a Queen Anne rectory (the latter completed in 1907). First called the Church of St. Boniface, the grand edifice was later renamed the Church of St. Mary and added to the National Register of Historic Places. Unfortunately, it had to be razed in May 2020 after an arsonist caused significant damage to the structure on March 11, 2016. A new church was built nearby. An impressive number of notable people have ties to Melrose, including Calista Flockhart, an actress best known for her title role in Fox's television series *Ally McBeal* from 1997 to 2002; Matt Herkenhoff, an offensive tackle in the NFL from 1976 to 1985; Amanda Smock, a competitive triple jumper in the 2012 Summer Olympic Games; Blake Elliott, a 2025 inductee into the College Football Hall of Fame because of his multiple NCAA Division III football records; Mitch Clem, the cartoonist behind the web comic Nothing Nice to Say; Bill Daley, an early NFL player and a two-time National champion football player with the Minnesota Golden Gophers; Mark Olberding, an NBA player from 1975 to 1987, and Walter Breuning, the oldest man in the world at the time of his death who lived to be 114 years and 205 days old at the time of his passing on April 14, 2011.

Restaurant Recommendation:
JD's Taphouse
209 E Main St
Melrose, MN 56352

NEW MUNICH, MN
POPULATION: 356 – CITY 523 OF 856 (8-12-25)

A Bavarian hunter from Munich, Bavaria, helped early pioneers of this settlement gain their footing when they arrived circa 1856. So they decided to name the town after his hometown. "New" Munich was formerly called Oak when it was established in 1859, but the name was changed four years later to New Munich. The Soo Line Railroad brought about its development, and the hamlet on the Sauk River soon had a creamery, a blacksmith shop, a hotel, a flour mill, a brewery, a Catholic church, and School No. 23. All these places existed on January 28, 1896, when New Munich was incorporated. The Pitzl Brewing Company, established by the Hungarian immigrant Mathew Pitzl after he took over operations in 1900, rose to prominence as Minnesota's third-largest beer producer by 1910. When Prohibition threatened to destroy all of Pitzl's hard work and that of Minnesota's many other breweries, underground bootlegging operations became the norm. The brewery was busted by federal authorities in 1924. When agent Albert Whitney suffered a fractured skull during one of the raids, Pitzl was able to move his equipment in secret to Estevan, Saskatchewan, Canada, via a northbound Soo Line train. An attempt was made to revive the brewery in 1933, post-Prohibition, but the movement failed. New Munich is one of many communities that inspired content for Garrison Keillor's fictional segment "News from Lake Wobegon" on A Prairie Home Companion, which ran from 1974 to 2016.

PAYNESVILLE, MN
POPULATION: 2,388 – CITY 534 OF 856 (8-13-25)

Fur traders and the Dakota Mdewakanton Sioux boast of the earliest history in the Paynesville vicinity. It was only in 1856 that William B. Reed and his party came to the North Fork Crow River and began to build up their settlement. Two attempts were made at making a formal town, but it was the third attempt in 1857 by the Paynesville Townsite Company that brought it into reality. It was named in honor of Edwin Ebenezer Payne, the surveyor of the site and one of its earliest homesteaders. For five years, a few improvements were made, like a wood-frame hotel building and several soddies, but all progress came to a screeching halt during the Dakota War of 1862 when the entire town was evacuated. Settlers moved to Richmond or St. Cloud for protection, and Little Crow and his men destroyed the whole village. They spared two buildings that European friends of Little Crow owned. When people returned to the rubble, the U.S. Army was contracted to establish a wooden stockade, and Paynesville rose again. However, things got complicated when the Great Northern and the Soo Line Railroads arrived in the area in 1886. A town called North Town/North Paynesville took shape on the Great Northern Railroad line running from St. Cloud to Willmar, and on the Soo Line between Minneapolis and Canada was a town nicknamed Jim Town (est. 1890), now the site of downtown Paynesville. As of 1896, the G.N. town had two grain elevators, a flour mill, a hotel, a store, a jail, a broom factory, a train depot, and School District No. 171. It was much smaller than Jim Town with its two grist mills, three grain elevators, flour mill, carriage works, stockyards, planing mill, foundry, bank, fire station, two hotels, high school, creamery, and churches for the Congregationalists, Methodists, and German Lutherans. The three Paynesvilles, the third being the original reconstruction of the village post-war but pre-railroads, existed concurrently before they all merged as New Paynesville in 1904. The "New" was dropped from its name the following year. There was a general area post office called Paynesville from 1857 to 1904, a second office called New Paynesville from 1891 to 1905, and a current office opened in 1905. Modern Paynesville is known for its good fishing in two nearby lakes, the 3,014-acre Lake Koronis, known for its walleye, bass, and northern pike, and Rice Lake.

RICHMOND, MN
POPULATION: 1,475 – CITY 495 OF 856 (8-10-25)
Pontoon motorboats were invented in Richmond and used for the first time on the Horseshoe Chain of Lakes in 1952, after Ambrose Weeres, a farmer and feed mixer manufacturer, attached a wooden platform to two steel barrels and welded them together. The demand for his invention was unprecedented, and now hundreds of thousands of pontoons can be found throughout the Land of 10,000 Lakes and far beyond. While the invention of pontooning is the city's crowning achievement, its history dates back nearly a century, to when Reuben Richardson platted the seven-by-seven-block parcel of land. For many years, it and the nearby post office were most frequently referred to as Torah (although some plat maps still listed it as Richmond), because Winona County, Minnesota, had a township and its own post office that utilized the name Richmond. In 1896, the Great Northern Railroad community had a population of nearly six hundred residents, a mill, a creamery, three grain elevators, a depot, a village hall, two blacksmith shops, two hotels, a wagon shop, a school, and, in typical Stearns County fashion, a Catholic church. Granite quarries have also been prominent for the better part of a century. Richmond was incorporated as a village on January 18, 1890, and has grown in population in every decade since 1930. As of 2020, it was home to 1,475 people, a new peak.

ROCKVILLE, MN
POPULATION: 2,382 – CITY 493 OF 856 (8-10-25)
Large outcroppings of granite along the Sauk River and Mill Creek gave Rockville, platted in 1856, its rock-solid name (which has not changed since its first settlers arrived). William Capple and Mack explored the region in the fall of 1854, but it was in 1857 that the Rockville post office was established and the dawn of the now-town of 2,382 truly began. Levi Gaylord was postmaster, and Newton Smith replaced him in June 1861. After the Great Northern Railroad connected Rockville with greater Minnesota and beyond, hungry entrepreneurs tried their hand at establishing a myriad of businesses. Two hotels, a blacksmith shop, and a grist mill were the most important firms in 1896; School No. 44 and a train depot also existed at that time. In 1907, the John Clark and John McCormick Quarry started operations. They became the primary source of Rockville Pink granite, a building material used heavily in the construction of one of the most distinctive cathedrals in the United States: the Cathedral of Saint Paul, in the twin city of the same name. John Clark took over the business entirely by 1916, and in 1924, his home was built using granite from the quarry. Both properties were listed on the National Register of Historic Places in 1982, forty years after the John Clark Company sold out to Cold Spring Granite, now Coldspring. Other noteworthy points of interest include an authentic piece of New York City's Twin Towers outside of the Rockville Fire Department building, one of the last to be given to a small town as a memorial of the tragic 2001 event, and the landmark bass statue atop the Rockville Gas & Bait store. Two veterans of the Napoleonic Wars, who fought between 1803 and 1815, are buried in the Jacobs Prairie parish cemetery: Michael Hanson and Herr Pieck. Rockville's incorporated territory grew substantially on June 1, 2002, when it merged with the City of Pleasant Lake and Rockville Township.

ROSCOE, MN
POPULATION: 130 – CITY 533 OF 856 (8-13-25)
Located on the St. Cloud-Willmar line of the Great Northern Railroad, Frogtown was established in 1865, with a post office called Zions that was open until 1914. The town also primarily went by the name Zion before the railway changed it to Roscoe after one of their executives. Three grain elevators handled the loads of grains of farmers from far and wide, and a singular hotel hosted the overnighters only yards away from the railroad tracks. A blacksmith shop, a garage, a lumberyard, a creamery, and St. Agnes Catholic Church (dedicated on October 18, 1898) were other places of note in Roscoe's heyday; it had a maximum population of 202 people during the 1930s. Some of its population growth could be attributed to the town's successful moonshining business, which during Prohibition helped to supplement local farmers' income. Marie Inez Hilger, a Benedictine nun and the very first woman to be enrolled at the Catholic University of America in Washington, D.C., was born here in October 1891. Roscoe's post office was discontinued in 1995, shortly after the railroad tracks were abandoned.

SAINT AUGUSTA, MN
POPULATION: 3,497 – CITY 492 OF 856 (8-10-25)
Berlin and Neenah were the original names for this townsite, which was settled in 1854. It was changed in 1856 to St. Augusta after Father Pierz stumbled upon a stray German holy card in the field where the German congregation wanted to raise a church. The prayer card pictured St. Augustine, but the name was mistakenly corrupted and misprinted as St. Augusta on official town documents. St. Mary Help of Christians Church, the current edifice built by German immigrants in 1873, retains the original holy card. The church and its 1890 rectory stand out as the most significant structures in the rural city, which has since grown to over 3,000 citizens. It was located on the Mississippi River and on one of its tributaries, Johnson Creek, which aided its selection as a Great Northern Railroad station. From 1857 to 1903, the post office operated before the township began relying on nearby offices to meet its mail needs. Like other towns throughout Stearns County, St. Augusta was a "haven" for moonshiners selling Minnesota 13, before feds found the still and blew it up while the townspeople were having a community dance at Schill's Hall. When Saint Augusta Township was incorporated as a city on May 2, 2000, it took on the name Ventura in honor of the then-38th Governor of Minnesota, Jesse Ventura. The townspeople were happy they had avoided annexation by the City of Saint Cloud, but not as pleased about their historic name being changed. On November 7, 2000, voters officially changed the new municipality's name from Ventura to Saint Augusta. St. Boniface Chapel, built in 1877 around the same time as Cold Spring's Assumption Chapel, serves as a symbol of hope and pilgrimage for parishioners of the local church parish and those from nearby Luxemburg. It was constructed during the Rocky Mountain locust plagues of the latter part of the 19th century; the yearly pilgrimage originated as a bid to God to deter any further locust plagues from overtaking the area. The treks ended in 1897, but Father Severin Schwieters restored the chapel in the late 1950s.

SAINT JOSEPH, MN
POPULATION: 7,029 – CITY 497 OF 856 (8-10-25)
Saint Joseph is about as close as a "college town" gets to the truest sense of the term as it is used today, as the focal point of the community is most definitely the College of Saint Benedict and Saint John's University down the road in Collegeville Township. The two Benedictine liberal arts colleges are closely related. They are specifically geared toward women-only studies at the College of Saint Benedict and men-only

studies at Saint John's University in the western township. The women's college, located entirely within Saint Joseph's city limits, began in 1913 with six students under the direction of Saint Benedict's Monastery. The largest Benedictine community of women in the world had as many as 1,278 members at its peak in 1946, and its entire convent, girls' boarding school, and campus are listed on the National Register of Historic Places as the St. Benedict's Convent and College Historic District. Going back to the City of Saint Joseph's earliest years, it was called Clinton by the postal service from 1856 to 1870, during which John Linnemann was the first postmaster, and was first settled by the German immigrant Peter Loso in 1854. The original townsite was platted on his claim and was the early site of a mill, store, and hotel. Loso was postmaster when the post office finally changed its name to match the commonly used "Saint Joseph" among the heavily Catholic German, Polish, and Slovenian settlers. Most of the settlers arrived following the advertisement of Father Francis X. Pierz, the father of settlement in Stearns County. Following its incorporation on January 29, 1890, Charles M. Foote surveyed the town plat and recorded the existence of two flour mills, a hotel, carriage works, a blacksmith, a planing mill, a public school, and a Catholic church, convent, and school complex, located in the southeast corner of the Great Northern Railroad town. He even went so far as to note five cisterns in downtown Saint Joseph: two on Spruce Street and three on Minnesota Street. Construction of the Gothic Revival-style Catholic Church began in 1869, and on June 29, 1871, the structure was consecrated. A 1918 Egyptian Revival style bank building, the First State Bank of St. Joseph, joins the church and the St. Benedict's Convent and College Historic District as the town's three locations on the National Register of Historic Places. Noted folks with connections to Saint Joseph include Joyce Sutphen, Minnesota's second Poet Laureate; Annella Zervas, a designated "Servant of God" well on her way to Canonization as a Saint in the Catholic Church, and Patty Wetterling, the chair of the National Center of Missing and Exploited Children.

SAINT MARTIN, MN
POPULATION: 312 – CITY 532 OF 856 (8-13-25)
Smartin, the colloquial name used for Saint Martin by the locals, had all the makings of a thriving community in its early days despite being in an inland town (that is, a town without a railroad). Settled in 1857 and officially founded in 1866, this community is named for St. Martin, Bishop of Tours. In addition to its Catholic church and School No. 22, Saint Martin at the turn of the century had its own post office, established in 1868 as Leedston but renamed in 1891; two blacksmith shops, and a hotel for voyaging pioneers. From 1905 to 1928, the post office was briefly discontinued due to the sheer number of offices throughout Stearns County. The townspeople sought and achieved incorporation on January 7, 1890. More people live in Saint Martin today (312) than at any other point in its history.

SARTELL, MN
POPULATION: 19,351 – CITY 499 OF 856 (8-11-25)
When French traders voyaged into central Minnesota, they nicknamed this area "The Third Rapids" after encountering their third set of rapids on the Mississippi, just upstream of Minneapolis's ultra-famous St. Anthony Falls. In the same vicinity was Watab Creek, which marked a sort of "no man's land" boundary between the rival Anishinaabe (also called Ojibwe or Chippewa) and Dakota tribes. It was marked by the 1825 Treaty of Prairie du Chien, which was an attempt to separate the warring tribes. Between 1846 and 1848, members of the Ho-Chunk were moved to the demarcation zone to serve as a physical barrier between the Ojibwe and the Dakota-Sioux. However, feeling as if they were in constant danger, they moved southward in

1853 to less hostile lands. While the Indigenous people continued to move from one reservation to another, the millwright Joseph B. Sartell stayed behind and worked at an early sawmill. He reportedly built a sawmill in 1857, according to some sources, opened a flour mill on the Watab River in 1877, and started the Sartell Brothers Lumber Company in 1884. While many businesses sprang up on the grounds surrounding the mills, the crowning achievement of the community was the completion of a dam across the Mississippi River in 1905-07 and the establishment of the Watab Pulp and Paper Company. It was started by loggers from Wisconsin and Michigan on May 10, 1905, and through a series of mergers and acquisitions, became the Verso Paper Sartell Mill. The city's largest employer closed after a May 29, 2012, explosion that put the mill and its nearly two hundred employees out of work for good. Former employee Matt DeZurik left the company in 1925 to start his own company, the DeZurik Valve Company, noted for producing industrial valves for paper mills and large factory plants. From its incorporation in 1907, Sartell (originally named Wengert after a local businessman) had a descendant or relative named "Sartell" on the city council until 1973. Since 1960, the population has grown tremendously due to its proximity to St. Cloud. Only 791 individuals lived in town in 1960, but by 1980, that number had grown to 3,427, by 2000 to 9,641, and as of modern times, nearly 20,000 citizens. For All Those Sleeping was a metalcore band made up of high school classmates Mike Champa, Ethan Trekell, David Volgman-Stevens, and Jerad Pierskalla, formed in 2007 while they were attending Sartell High School. Three noted professional athletes also hail from the community: Craig Sauer, a linebacker in the NFL from 1996 to 2000; his brother Michael Sauer, who appeared in 98 games with the NHL's New York Rangers; and a third brother, Kurt Sauer, who played in 357 career NHL games.

Restaurant Recommendation:
Second Street Coffee House
1091 2nd St S
Sartell, MN 56377

SAUK CENTRE, MN ☆
POPULATION: 4,555 – CITY 525 OF 856 (8-13-25)

Sinclair Lewis, the first American to win the Nobel Prize in Literature, was born on February 7, 1885, in Sauk Centre, a gem of a central Minnesota community that has retained the vast majority of its historic downtown district, built up around the time of Lewis's childhood. The 74-property Original Main Street Historic Street includes commercial and civic buildings, homes, parks, a Sauk River bridge and dam, and the 1901 Palmer House Hotel, now a restaurant, pub, and hotel. First settled in 1856 and platted in 1863, Sauk Centre was named by lottery. Eight town shareholders, all of whom contributed towards putting the village on the map, submitted suggestions for the community and had an equal chance at having their suggestion randomly selected. The exact manner in which this was done is unrecorded, but the winning name was Alexander Moore's suggestion of "Sauk Centre," a nod to the town's central location on the Sauk River between Sauk Rapids and Lake Osakis. From 1857 to 1893, the post office used the spelling "Centre" 1857 1893 before Americanizing it to "Center" from 1893 to 1936. It was only restored to its original archetype after the city challenged the post office's decision in the mid-1930s. Growth in the early days of the settlement was incredible. By the turn of the century, there were several dozen firms in the commercial district, and several advancements had been made in the community's religious, educational, and social spheres. A Lutheran, an Adventist, a Baptist, a Methodist, a Congregationalist, an Episcopal, and two Catholic churches were present as of 1896, and other significant sites included a town hall, a public school, a G.A.R. Hall, and a bandstand in the northeast corner of town. Keller Manufacturing Company, an engine house, a planing mill, stockyards, and two elevators were noted fixtures on the Great Northern Railway. Four hotels and the business district separated the Great Northern's facilities in the south from the Northern Pacific Railroad in the north, and from its two grain elevators, a creamery, a grist mill, and a cooper shop (a craftsman who makes barrels, wooden casks, and other containers). As noted earlier, some of these early fixtures have been preserved by generations of town residents, as have two additional locations now listed on the National Register: the Sinclair Lewis Boyhood House, now a museum because of its ties to the famous novelist from 1885 to 1902, and the Minnesota Home School for Girls Historic District, established in 1911 as Minnesota's first all-female youth detention center. It is now the Eagle's Healing Nest Veteran Care Center. The old Carnegie Library hosts the city's public library and the Sauk Centre Museum. A pair of local oddity sites includes the Viking Altar Rock, a landmark that was falsely claimed to be a Norse artifact when it was discovered in 1943, and the "glowing headstone" of Mr. Boss at Oakdale Cemetery. The holes in the altar rock were, in actuality, drilled by early farmers to potentially blast them apart, although some boulders were left untouched. The phenomenon of the Boss headstone can be explained by its perfect positioning, which allows city lights to reflect off its base at a certain angle, creating a paranormal "glow." In addition to Sinclair Lewis, Sauk Centre has been home to Paul Zehrer, an Emmy Award nominee for Best Director for his work on Nickelodeon's Blue's Clues; his brother Terrence "Lee" Zehrer, the founder of the first online dating service to use pictures, Kiss(dot)com; Frank Eddy, a U.S. Representative from Minnesota between 1895 and 1903; Cory Undlin, a two-time Super Bowl champion NFL coach; Rachael Ellering, a professional wrestler with Ring of Honor and a former WWE wrestler under the name Rachael Evers; Colleen Randall, an abstract painter whose work focuses on abstract expressionism connecting nature and human consciousness, and James Hendryx, a western fiction novelist.

Lodging Recommendation:
Palmer House Hotel & Restaurant
500 Sinclair Lewis Ave
Sauk Centre, MN 56378

SPRING HILL, MN
POPULATION: 68 – CITY 530 OF 856 (8-13-25)
Visitors to the Spring Hill of 1896 would have been immersed in simpler times, as the inland town was far from any railroad line and home to everything that its then-sub-100-person population could have wanted. A Catholic church located on land owned by the Order of Saint Benedict served as the center of community activity. To its north was the joint post office (established in 1867) and general store and School No. 38. In western Spring Hill, there were two hotels, a creamery, and about a dozen plots of land with homes. Several women are listed as landowners on the town plat of the time, including Mary A. Brock, Agnes Wuttke, and Mary Schneider. Spring Hill was incorporated as a village on July 8, 1900, and named for its natural springs and low morainic hills. Spring Hill had 112 citizens during its peak in the 1920s.

ST. ANTHONY, MN
POPULATION: 91 – CITY 519 OF 856 (8-12-25)
Not to be confused with the much larger City of St. Anthony in Hennepin and Ramsey Counties (pop. 9,257), this hamlet in Stearns County is one-one hundredth the size of its counterpart. Settled around 1880 in Krain Township, St. Anthony was named after

the Catholic Saint by Slovene American Catholics attracted to the area by Father Francis Xavier Pierz. A post office called Gates served the area from 1886 to 1899; its name was changed to St. Anthony before it was discontinued in 1905. The hamlet was incorporated on May 31, 1911. A small farmstead formerly owned by Anton Gogala has structures dating back to 1875; it was listed on the National Register of Historic Places on April 15, 1982.

ST. CLOUD, MN ★
POPULATION: 68,881 – CITY 491 OF 856 (8-10-25)

Three towns called "Upper Town, Middle Town, and Lower Town" each uniquely contribute to the history of the City of St. Cloud, the Stearns County Seat, and the dominant agricultural and economic center of a large swath of territory to the north of Minnesota's Twin Cities. After the 1851 Treaty of Traverse des Sioux opened up parts of Minnesota Territory for settlement, the first semi-permanent European settlers arrived in 1851 near two deep ravines that adjoined the Mississippi River. The Norwegian Ole Bergeson is sometimes credited as the earliest settler, but it was John L. Wilson, the "Father of St. Cloud," who purchased his territory in 1854 and gave the settlement its name. His studies on Napoleon inspired him, and he named the site "St. Cloud" after the magnificent palace outside of Paris, France, that was a favorite home of Empress Josephine. Wilson's Middle Town began in 1854 and became the dominant town when Father Pierz's flood of German immigrants settled there and built an extensive commercial district. Lower Town was the brainchild of George Fuller Brott, owner of the St. Cloud Township Company. His two partners, Charles T. Stearns and Joseph Wilson, John's brother, helped to bring in settlers from New England and the mid-Atlantic States. The third community, Upper Town, was first called Acadia when Sylvanus P. Lowry started it. It was later renamed Lowry's Addition when the City of St. Cloud annexed it as an addition to the original plat. Lowry was an enslaver and brought enslaved people with him despite Minnesota Territory's designation as a free territory; he was president of the 1856 town council and heavily criticized for his support of the Confederacy. In that year, St. Mary's Catholic Church and St. Cloud Presbyterian Church were established as rivaling churches, and in 1858, St. Cloud's growth was hastened when a land office was moved here from Sauk Rapids. Steamboat traffic increased heavily, and granite quarrying began in 1868, giving way to the nickname "The Granite City." Over the next forty-odd years, St. Cloud grew to a population of 10,000-plus residents by 1910. Many of the city's fourteen NRHP-designated places came to fruition during this period of growth and prosperity: an early 1884 home owned by Francis Arnold, the owner and operator of an early town gristmill; the gorgeous First National Bank of St. Cloud building, completed in 1889; the Richardsonian Romanesque Foley-Brower-Bohmer House; a Second Empire home built in 1891, known as the Michael Majerus House; the 1893 Queen Anne Nehemiah P. Clarke House; the 1902 Carter Block, an early retail and office space; the 1904 John N. Bensen Queen Anne home; Minnesota's oldest surviving laboratory school building, Model School, now Riverview at St. Cloud State University, built in 1913; the 1916 Chancery Office, built in the Second Renaissance Revival architecture style for the Roman Catholic Bishop of St. Cloud at the time; one of Minnesota's earliest and longest-lived attempts at an automobile manufacturing company from 1917 to 1922, the Pan Motor Company Office and Sheet Metal Works (started by Samuel Pandolfo who thought Pan-Cars would make St. Cloud the new Detroit, Michigan); the Stearns County Courthouse, completed in 1921 using Beaux-Arts elements; the St. Cloud Veterans Administration Hospital Historic District and its 34 properties furnished between 1923 and 1950; a set of six commercial buildings built between 1883 and 1914, now called the Fifth Avenue Commercial Buildings, and a set of 41 buildings in downtown St. Cloud built between 1870 and 1947 and listed as the St. Cloud Commercial Historic District. The Great Northern Railroad held all the cards for trade as the town's primary railway, although the Northern Pacific Railroad was located just across the Mississippi River in Sauk Rapids. St. Cloud State University has long served the region as one of Minnesota's largest institutions of higher learning; it was started as the Third State Normal School in 1869 and later called the State Normal School at St. Cloud from 1873 to 1921, the St. Cloud State Teachers College from 1921 to 1957, and St. Cloud State College until 1975. The men's ice hockey team is touted as the school's most successful athletic program, having reached the 2021 NCAA men's ice hockey championship. St. Cloud Technical and Community College, established in 1948 and a branch of Rasmussen University, with campuses throughout the United States, is St. Cloud's other accredited school. Ninety-five parks, the Cathedral of Saint Mary, built in the 1920s; the Paramount Theatre and Visual Arts Center; the Great River Regional Library and its collection of one million items; the Minnesota Amateur Baseball Hall of Fame; the flower-path filled 14-acre Munsinger Gardens and Clemens Gardens, and the Stearns County Museum, noted for its ultra-rare two-headed pig, each invite visitors to explore their unique contributions to St. Cloud's tourism scene. In popular culture, St. Cloud has ties to numerous films including *Catch Me If You Can*, a 1989 action comedy film both set and filmed in town, Disney's *The Mighty Ducks*, a 1992 sports comedy drama partially filmed at the courthouse; *Juno*, a coming-of-age comedy drama released in 2007 is partially set in St. Cloud, and Marshall Eriksen from CBS's *How I Met Your Mother*, claims the Minnesota city as his hometown. While the actor (Jason Segel) of the fictional character of Marshall is not from St. Cloud, noteworthy individuals with communal ties are Tom Petters, the former CEO of Petters Group Worldwide and the head of a $3.65 billion Ponzi Scheme; Tom Burgmeier, a 1980 All-Star pitcher with the MLB's Boston Red Sox; Lawrence M. Hall, the longest-serving Speaker of the Minnesota House of Representatives from January 1939 to January 1949; June Marlowe, noted for her role as "Miss Crabtree" in the *Our Gang* shorts produced from 1922 to 1944; Anne Schleper, a 2014 Sochi Olympic Games silver-medalist with the 2014 U.S. women's hockey team; Stephen Miller, the 4th Governor of Minnesota; John McMartin, an actor on Broadway for more than fifty years; Gig Young, an Academy Award winning actor for his role in the 1969 psychological drama *They Shoot Horses, Don't They?*, and NFL players Jim Fanhorst (a three-time Super Bowl champion with the San Francisco 49ers) and Keith Fahnhorst (a two-time champion on two 49er Super Bowl champion teams), amongst a plethora of others.

 **Restaurant Recommendation:**
Green Mill Restaurant & Bar
100 4th Ave S
St. Cloud, MN 56301

ST. ROSA, MN
POPULATION: 58 – CITY 522 OF 856 (8-12-25)
One of the smallest municipalities in the St. Cloud Metropolitan Statistical Area, St. Rosa began around 1904 and grew around Saint Rose of Lima Catholic Church. German and Irish immigrants named it after the first person born in the Americas to be canonized as a saint. Since its incorporation on August 9, 1939, St. Rosa has reported a high population of 93 people, according to the 1970 U.S. Decennial Census.

ST. STEPHEN, MN
POPULATION: 797 – CITY 500 OF 856 (8-11-25)
The oldest Slovenian community in the United States is in Saint Stephen, Minnesota, one of a multitude of primarily Roman Catholic settlements in Minnesota's Stearns County. An early town, Brockway, was platted in 1857. Until 1905, it had a post office and an identity of its own, but it was incorporated into the joint City of St. Stephen on May 18, 1914. Slovene immigrants worked tirelessly in 1903 to build the community's most magnificent Romanesque Revival edifice, the Church of St. Stephen, using the architectural plans of John Jager. It was preceded by a 1890 rectory, which was jointly listed with the church on the National Register of Historic Places. The post office did not open until 1957. Outside of Viking Industries, the furniture company advertises its products with a massive roadside bed that changes as nationwide furniture trends change.

WAITE PARK, MN
POPULATION: 8,341 – CITY 498 OF 856 (8-10-25)
Between 1890-91, the Great Northern Railroad set up shop (literally, by building its massive railroad shops) outside St. Cloud, in a place that would be called "Waite Park" upon its incorporation as a village. This canon event took place on March 20, 1893, and the town was named in honor of Henry Chester Waite, St. Cloud's first attorney and an early entrepreneur. The area was nicknamed Waite's Crossing in its earliest days because early pioneers crossed the Sauk River on Waite's land to travel between Breckenridge and St. Paul, but the town came into being when James J. Hill purchased 300 acres for his railroad shops. The community was platted into 60 lots, and in Lot 42, School No. 152 was established to educate the children of railroad workers and employees. A post office was established in 1897 as Waite Park became one of the principal suburbs of St. Cloud, the largest city in central Minnesota. Granite quarrying was its primary industry, and one of its quarries was turned into the 684-acre Stearns County Quarry Park for use by avid scuba divers, swimmers, cliff jumpers, and rock climbers. The growing city has experienced positive growth in every decade since its first Census in 1900, with the most significant percentage increase of 134.7% between 1910 and 1920, when it grew from 406 to 953 citizens. From 1970 to 2017, Waite Park called itself "A City with a Smile," a claim supported by its iconic yellow smiley face water tower. It was repainted in 2018, and the city slogan changed to "Where Minnesota Connects."

Clearwater is only partially located in Stearns County (see Wright County), and Eden Valley is only partially located in Stearns County (see Meeker County). Additionally, St. Anthony in Stearns County is different from Saint Anthony Village in Hennepin & Ramsey County.

Unincorporated/Ghost Towns: Collegeville, Fairhaven, Farming, Five Points, Georgeville, Jacobs Prairie, Marty, Opole, Padua, Saint Anna, Saint Francis, Saint Nicholas, Saint Wendel, St. John's University

National Register of Historic Places:
Belgrade: Christopher Borgerding House
Cold Spring: Eugene Hemanutz House, John Oster House, Ferdinand Peters House
Collegeville: St. John's Abbey & University Historic District
Fairhaven: Fair Haven Flour Mill
Freeport: Church of the Sacred Heart
Kimball: Kimball Prairie Village Hall
Melrose: Church of St. Boniface
Rockville: Clark & McCormack Quarry & House

Sauk Centre: Sinclair Lewis Boyhood Home, Minnesota Home School for Girls Historic District, Original Main Street Historic District, Palmer House Hotel
St. Anna: Church of the Immaculate Conception- Catholic
St. Anthony: Anton Gogala Farmstead
St. Augusta: Church of St. Mary Help of Christians-Catholic
St. Cloud: John N. Bensen House, Bishop's House/Chancery Office, Carter Block, Nehemiah P. Clarke House, Fifth Avenue Commercial buildings, First National Bank, Foley-Brewer-Bohmer House, Michael Majerus House, Model School, Pan Motor Company Office & Sheet Metal Works, St. Cloud Commercial Historic District, St. Cloud Veterans Administration Hospital Historic District, Stearns County Courthouse & Jail, Francis Arnold House
St. Joseph: Church of St. Joseph- Catholic, First State Bank, St. Benedict's Convent & College Historic District
St. Stephen: Church of St. Stephen-Catholic

Golf Courses:
Albany Golf Club, Daily Fee (Albany, MN)
Angushire Golf Club, Daily Fee (St. Cloud, MN)
Blackberry Ridge, Daily Fee (Sartell, MN)
Boulder Ridge Golf Club, Daily Fee (St. Cloud, MN)
Greystone Golf Club, Daily Fee (Sauk Centre, MN)
Kimball Golf Club, Daily Fee (Kimball, MN)
Koronis Hills Golf Course, Daily Fee (Paynesville, MN)
Lynx National Golf Course, Daily Fee (Sauk Centre, MN)
Meadowlark Country Club, Daily Fee (Melrose, MN)
Old Course Sauk Centre, Daily Fee (Sauk Centre, MN)
Prairie View Community Golf Course, Daily Fee (Brooten, MN)
Rich Spring Golf Club, Daily Fee (Cold Spring, MN)
River Oaks Golf Course, Daily Fee (Cold Spring, MN)
St. Cloud Country Club, Private (St. Cloud, MN)
Territory Golf Club, Daily Fee (St. Cloud, MN)
Three Tees Golf & Social, Daily Fee (Sartell, MN)

Breweries/Wineries/Distilleries:
Bad Habit Brewing Company (St. Joseph, MN)
Beaver Island Brewing Company (St. Cloud, MN)
Iron Street Distillery (St. Cloud, MN)
Koronis Brewing Company (Paynesville, MN)
Millner Heritage Winery (Kimball, MN)
Obbink Distilling (St. Joseph, MN)
Pantown Brewing Company (St. Cloud, MN)
Third Street Brewhouse (Cold Spring, MN)

Town Celebrations:
Albany Heritage Day, Albany, MN (1St Saturday in August)
Barley Days, Greenwald, MN (1St Weekend in August)
Belgrade August Fest, Belgrade, MN (2nd Weekend in August)
Bonanza Valley Days, Brooten, MN (Weekend after Independence Day)
Granite City Days, St. Cloud, MN (Last Weekend in June)
Holdingford Daze, Holdingford, MN (2nd Saturday in July)
Joetown Rocks, St. Joseph, MN (July 3/July 4)
Kimball Days, Kimball, MN (2nd Weekend in August)
Melrose Riverfest, Melrose, MN (Last Full Weekend in June)
Pioneers Days, Albany, MN (Second Weekend after Labor Day)
Richmond River Lake Days, Richmond, MN (3rd Weekend in July)
Sinclair Lewis Days, Sauk Centre, MN (3rd Weekend in July)
Spunktacular Days, Avon, MN (3rd Weekend in June)
Summertime by George!, St. Cloud, MN (Wednesdays in the Summertime)
Waite Park Family Fun Fest/Spass Tag, Waite Park, MN (2nd Week of June)

STEELE COUNTY
EST. 1855 - POPULATION: 37,406

Steele County was created on February 20, 1855, using lands once belonging to Rice, Blue Earth, and Le Sueur Counties. It was named in honor of Frank Steele, one of its pioneer residents who would later help develop Saint Anthony Falls in Minneapolis.

BLOOMING PRAIRIE, MN
POPULATION: 1,974 – CITY 649 OF 856 (10-1-25)

While the names and the types of businesses have changed, the buildings that once hosted Blooming Prairie's booming commercial district, a byproduct of the arrival of the Chicago, Milwaukee & St. Paul Railroad, have remained intact and are now collectively known as the Blooming Prairie Commercial Historic District. The collection of 20 properties, built between 1893 and 1932, serves as a reminder of Blooming Prairie's early days, when its population was closer to 1,000 full-time residents. However, in 1856, the townsite was nothing more than what its name now describes: a prairie blooming with flora and fauna. It was then a part of Oak Glen Township in Dodge County, although after being annexed by Steele County, John Blythe settled here and built himself a log cabin. Other settlers trickled in, and by 1867 the town was formally established after serving as a shelter for construction crews of the Minnesota Central Railroad. A flour mill was erected as wheat was chosen to be the principal crop of the region. As the years wore on, general stores, hotels, blacksmith shops, and a cooperative creamery, amongst other establishments, came into existence. Charles W. Gardner was one of the earliest merchants and the first postmaster when the office opened in 1868. The first Blooming Prairie schoolhouse was built for $700 in 1868. After being renovated into a meat market, a second structure, two stories tall, was completed in 1873 for $3,000. Twenty-six more years passed until the final eight-room brick building was completed just before the turn of the century. During this period, locals benefited from an "underground economy" in which unfathomable amounts of liquor were produced in tunnels beneath Main Street businesses and sold to consumers in nearby Mower, Freeborn, and Dodge counties. Steele County was one of only a few "wet" counties in the state, so the town's presence in the far southeast corner of the county allowed it to serve a large radius and, consequently, a large population. Eventually, that industry subsided with the passage and repeal of the Prohibition Act, and with time, the town's population grew to a peak of 2,043 people by 1990. Josh Braaten, an actor who has appeared in *Criminal Minds*, *That 80's Show*, *CSI: Miami*, and *American Horror Story: Hotel*, hails from here.

ELLENDALE, MN
POPULATION: 676 – CITY 648 OF 856 (10-1-25)

Situated about halfway between Owatonna and Albert Lea on the Burlington, Cedar Rapids & Northern Railroad (popularly recognized as the Chicago, Rock Island & Pacific), Ellendale was laid out on Elling Ellingson's farm on land selected by Thomas H. Brown, the townsite agent for the railroad. C.J. Ives was the president, and his wife, Ellen, was honored by the naming of this community upon its platting in the Fall of 1900. Ellen, whose maiden name was "Dale," had passed away a couple of years prior but was fondly remembered by railroad workers for her acts of kindness and generosity. The Ellendale post office opened under that name the following year (although the Cooleysville post office had been in existence since 1858) and was subsequently succeeded by stockyards, a lumberyard, two grain elevators, livery stables, and a meat market. By 1910, the population had surpassed 261, all working diligently to expand the town's housing and business interests. Two hotels, two barber shops, a second lumber yard, two blacksmith shops, a creamery, the *Ellendale Eagle* newspaper, a drugstore, three general stores, a novelty store, and a bank, among other establishments, were in operation at this time. The Berlin and Summit (later the Ellendale) Creamery Association was Ellendale's most important asset. From its organization on January 10, 1891, to 1910, it churned out several million pounds of cream and butter from many more pounds of milk. Its 1910 receipts through July 1, 1910, included 96,237,387 pounds of milk, from which 4,294,040 pounds of butter were made. A brick school building had been erected at this time for $12,000, and four church congregations–the Norwegian Lutherans, the Danish Lutherans, the Baptists, and the Methodists were meeting every Sunday to sing praises. Early fraternal societies included the Royal Neighbors Fraternity, Camp No. 3614; the Modern Woodman of America, Camp No. 9666; the Yeomen; and the Danish Brotherhood, D.B.S. Lodge No. 237. School District No. 67 was established when the village was platted. In 1910, a two-story brick structure was built, and additions were made between 1922 and 1923. Ellendale and Geneva's schools were consolidated in 1961, and in 1993, they merged with New Richland-Hartland to form NRHEG District #2168.

MEDFORD, MN
POPULATION: 1,315 – CITY 651 OF 856 (10-1-25)
Medford's initial settlers arrived in 1853 to a valley that contained the Straight River, on land originally owned by Smith Johnson and platted by Reverend O. A. Thomas. The township itself was organized on August 29, 1855, and its name chosen as an eponym for the ship Medford. It was suggested by William K. Colling, whose son was born on the vessel. A post office was among the first of Medford's permanent establishments. In the early years, a steam sawmill, a gristmill, Albert McKinney's store, Sulley & Francis's *Medford Valley Argus* newspaper, and Howard & Johnson's cheese factory emerged as some of the town's most prominent early businesses. The Chicago, Rock Island & Pacific (formerly the Cedar Rapids, Burlington & Northern) and the Chicago, Milwaukee & St. Paul Railroads served the town, allowing Medford's population to grow steadily and more businesses to emerge. Many structures were destroyed in a December 20, 1883, fire that wiped out five storefronts, a meat market, a doctor's office, and two drug stores. In the vicinity of 1877, the Daniel S. Piper House was established as a New England-style interconnected farm complex. Medford was incorporated on May 22, 1936, and has reported an all-time high population of 1,315 people as of the 2020 Census. Lynn Frazier, the 12th Governor of North Dakota from 1917 to 1921, was born in Medford and became famous for being the first American governor to be successfully recalled from office. After being removed, he went on to become a United States Senator for the Peace Garden State from 1923 to 1941.

OWATONNA, MN ★☆
POPULATION: 26,420 – CITY 650 OF 856 (10-1-25)
The Steele County seat of Owatonna shares its name with the Straight River, which in the Dakota language is known as *Wakpá Owóthaŋna*. When Yankees from New England began to pour in the mid-1850s, one such man, Josef Karel Kaplan of Bohemia, built his home on a 160-acre quarter section of land near the river that soon developed into a bustling settlement with 1,500 inhabitants in its first five years. A mineral springs health resort helped bring in many early settlers and tourists, and in September 1855, Owatonna was formally platted on land owned by A. B. Cornell, W. F. Pettit, and John Abbott. Kaplan was responsible for organizing the local Catholic cemetery and the Bohemian National Cemetery of Owatonna. Incorporation was

achieved on August 9, 1858. Over the next few decades, Owatonna blossomed into a primary railroad hub for southern Minnesota, serving the Chicago, Rock Island & Pacific, Winona & Saint Peter, and Chicago, Milwaukee & St. Paul Railroads. Much of the city's essential development occurred in the 1880s, specifically when it hosted the Minnesota State Fair in 1883 and 1884. In 1885, it was selected to be the site of the State Public School for Dependent and Neglected Children. Over the course of sixty years, the school, now the site of the Minnesota State Public School Orphanage Museum, housed approximately 10,635 children, who lived on the property and were taught "the value of drill, discipline, and labor." Minnesota Academy was founded in 1877, but in 1886, it became the Pillsbury Military Academy. The latter name was used until 1957, when it was changed again to Pillsbury Baptist Bible College. The school closed for good in 2008. In addition to the nineteen contributing buildings and the Administration Building at the Minnesota State Public School for Dependent and Neglected Children, and the Pillsbury Academy Campus Historic District, Owatonna has several other notable locations throughout the city that hold historical significance. Seventy-five properties of downtown Owatonna built between 1871 and the 1950s are a part of the Owatonna Historic District. Louis Sullivan's eyecatching "jewel box" National Farmers' Bank of Owatonna, the 1906-07 Owatonna City and Firemen's Hall, and the 1891 Romanesque Revival Steele County Courthouse are listed individually but included in the district's boundaries. The 1899 Owatonna Free Public Library, the 1860 Ezra Abbott House, and the 1913 Dr. John H. Adair Prairie School-style House are the town's other three NRHP-designated locations. On the Steele County Fairgrounds, the Village of Yesteryear was founded by the Steele County Historical Society in approximately 1962 to serve as a relocation site for historic buildings, museum structures, and artifacts. Cabela's is known for its 53,000-gallon aquarium filled with Minnesota fish and African taxidermy; next door at the Owatonna Municipal Airport, three T-38 jets are frozen midair as a tribute to the United States Air Force. Two films have been at least partially filmed at Owatonna Senior High School: the 1995 coming-of-age comedy movie *Angus*, and the 2014 silent film *The Root of Evil*. Many persons of interest have communal connections, a few of whom include Arthur Fry, the co-creator of the Post-it Note; E. G. Marshall, an actor known for his role as Juror 4 in the legal drama film *12 Angry Men* and as the President of the United States in the 1980 superhero movie *Superman II*; Travis Wiuff, a mixed martial artist in the Heavyweight division with a career record of 78-22-1; Tom Moore, a four-time Super Bowl champion player or coach in 1978, 1979, 2006, and 2020; Adam Young, the lead singer and creator of the electronic music band Owl City; Lillian Colton, a crop artist who earned the nickname "the Andy Warhol of seeds" for her works commonly showcased at the Minnesota State Fair; Don Laughlin, the Founding Father of Laughlin, Nevada, a resort town, and Sean Tillmann-Hauser, better known as Har Mar Superstar, a singer-songwriter and actor.

Restaurant Recommendation:
Torey's Restaurant & Bar
208 N Cedar Ave
Owatonna, MN 55060

Unincorporated/Ghost Towns: Bixby, Clinton Falls, Deerfield, Havana, Hope, Lemond, Litomysl, Meriden, Merton, Moland, Pratt, Rice Lake, Saco, Steele Center

National Register of Historic Places:
Blooming Prairie: Blooming Prairie Commercial Historic District
Clinton Falls Township: Bridge No. L-5573
Medford: Daniel S. Piper House

Owatonna: Ezra Abbott House, Dr. John H. Adair House, Administration Building-Minnesota State Public School for Dependent & Neglected Children, Minnesota State Public School for Dependent & Neglected Children, National Farmers' Bank, Owatonna City & Firemen's Hall, Owatonna Commercial Historic District, Owatonna Free Public Library, Pillsbury Academy Campus Historic District, Steele County Courthouse

Golf Courses:
Blooming Prairie Country Club, Daily Fee (Blooming Prairie, MN)
Brooktree Golf Course, Municipal (Owatonna, MN)
Havana Hills Golf, Range & Event Center, Short Course (Owatonna, MN)
Owatonna Country Club, Private (Owatonna, MN)

Breweries/Wineries/Distilleries:
Mineral Springs Brewery (Owatonna, MN)

Town Celebrations:
Gem Days, Owatonna, MN (Late July/Early August)

STEVENS COUNTY
EST. 1862 - POPULATION: 9,671

When the Minnesota Legislature was establishing new counties in 1862, they did their due diligence (see Stearns County) to ensure that Isaac Ingalls Stevens, an American Civil War hero with the Union Army, had this county named in his commemoration.

ALBERTA, MN
POPULATION: 94 – CITY 137 OF 856 (4-11-25)

When the Great Northern Railroad came through in the early 1880s, the decision to name the town was determined by the surname of the man whose land the first elevator was built upon: Homer D. Wheeler's in 1882. After a couple of years, postal authorities discovered another Wheeler in Minnesota. So, the name was changed to Clearfield. This name stuck from 1884 to 1887 until it was changed one final time from 1896 to "Alberta" for Alberta Hardin, the daughter of then-postmaster Andrew Hardin. An alternate etymology suggests it may have been named for the wife of E. B. Lindsey, a local farmer. As many as three elevators were in operation in Alberta at one point, along with general merchandise stores, the Alberta State Bank (from 1912 to 1942), a dance hall, the Trinity Lutheran Church (dedicated on December 7, 1919), and the Alberta School and Teacher's Manse. Originally, Alberta's young pupils had to travel two-and-a-half miles to District No. 25 daily for their education. It and District No. 19 merged in 1911, one of the first such school consolidations in the state. This unique action prompted the Rockefeller Foundation to launch an experiment by funding what is now known as the Alberta Teachers' House. Listed on the National Register in February 1983, the 21-room abode (dedicated on February 16, 1917) featured several apartments, a model dining room, and even a designated cooking and sewing laboratory, among other features. A model of the structure was shown at the World's Fair in San Francisco. Another fascinating tale of Alberta history recalls the time the heavily guarded bank was successfully robbed on July 21, 1921, by thieves who were never found. They had cut all the telephone wires in town and used tools from the Great Northern Railroad depot to dig their way into the vault.

CHOKIO, MN
POPULATION: 404 – CITY 136 OF 856 (4-11-25)
Chokio is a relatively rare example of a rural community that has maintained much of its population since the railroads reigned supreme. At its first Census in 1900, it had 300 residents, and as of 2020, it has retained a population of 405. Its numbers have fluctuated over the decades, but it reached its peak prosperity in the 1950s, when about 541 people called it home. The town's establishment can be traced back to 1865 when the "Halfway House" was established six miles north of the present-day townsite on the Wadsworth Trail. The trail connected St. Cloud, Minnesota, with Fort Wadsworth in Sisseton, South Dakota. There was a need for a resting spot at the *chokio* point, a Dakota word meaning "halfway." It served primarily as a trading post but also boasted facilities for a grocery store, a saloon, a livery, and a schoolhouse. The trail and the town moved south when the Great Northern Railway laid its tracks in 1880. These primarily German, Irish, and Scandinavian settlers suggested that the railroad allow Grandmother Harmin, a prominent cook at the Halfway House, to name the newly laid town. She called it Chokio after a young Native American boy who shared the name with the term for the trading post's original location on the trail. The local post office was called Chokago from 1878-79, then Cho-ki-o until its closure in 1881, and reopened in 1891 as Chokio. By 1910, it had all the makings of a well-off farm town, including a depot, creamery, cheese factory, two hotels, two banks, a schoolhouse, a Methodist Episcopal church, a Lutheran church, and the *Chokio Review* newspaper. About eight miles southwest of Chokio, on 640th Avenue, are the Frank Schott Stone Barn ruins, a stunning structure of stone and concrete built in 1923 by the German immigrant Frank Schott. The barn roof collapsed in 1993 due to continuous weathering via exposure to the elements.

DONNELLY, MN
POPULATION: 221 – CITY 138 OF 856 (4-11-25)
Home to the Donnelly Threshing Bee since 1965, Douglas was the name of the present-day town of 221 people. Platted on December 8, 1871, and established in 1872 on the Great Northern Railroad, John Gavin Donnelly served as its first depot agent. He clued in his brother, the renowned pseudoscientist, author, and Minnesota Congressman Ignatius L. Donnelly, to purchase farmland in the area and capitalize on the railroad's shipping capabilities. As a result of his influence on Minnesota politics, the brothers' prominence in the area was due to the farm, so the townsite was renamed Donnelly in 1876. The earliest of Donnelly's history is rooted in its stores and saloons. Still, the District No. 11 school established in 1877 was a significant point of pride. It was located in the McGowan Store before being replaced by a wooden schoolhouse and, later, a larger brick structure. The Donnelly school never boasted a high school curriculum and closed its doors for good nearly a century later, circa 1971. Also in 1877, David Huddlestone built the Donnelly Hotel, the cornerstone and gem of its then-booming business district. A 1910 plat map shows that Donnelly still had the Donnelly Creamery Company, a bank, a livery, a lumber yard, and churches for the local Catholic, Presbyterian, and Lutheran congregations.

HANCOCK, MN
POPULATION: 863 – CITY 159 OF 856 (4-13-25)
The second-largest town in Stevens County was most likely named in honor of the Native American missionary Joseph Wood Hancock, when it was founded in 1871-72 by officials of the St. Paul & Pacific Railway Company. A post office was established around that same time, and shortly thereafter, the Great Northern Railroad took over

the line. Its growth was so rampant that T. P. Kerr and A. J. Comstock added additions between December 1879 and January 1880. By the turn of the century, there were over three dozen different lines of business. Amongst the most notable was the Columbia Hotel (better remembered as the Hotel William), established in 1895 by Isaac Lemaster. It had nineteen rooms and welcomed hundreds of businessmen, travelers, and hunters to the Pheasant Capital of Minnesota for many years. Two banks, two hotels, a livery, an elevator, two churches, a school, and the depot were listed as the most significant points of interest in a 1910 directory. School District No. 3 was established on September 9, 1872; its first building was completed in 1883-84 and also served as the site of the first meetings of The First Congregational Church of Hancock. The historic church building, built in 1883, had its final service on December 24, 2019. Since the 1870s, Hancock has hosted an annual Independence Day celebration with parades, street dances, baseball games, and, of course, fireworks.

MORRIS, MN ★☆
POPULATION: 5,105 – CITY 164 OF 856 (4-14-25)

Rich agricultural land drew droves of settlers to the lands surrounding the Pomme de Terre River, and two major railroads, the Great Northern and the Northern Pacific, both connected here, bringing the outputs of Morris's farmers to faraway markets. It was April 1871 when the St. Paul & Pacific Railway (which was annexed by the St. Paul, Minneapolis & Manitoba in 1879 and eventually became the Great Northern in 1889), Minnesota's first active railroad, extended its right-of-way into the region. Morris was immediately established, platted, and named for Charles F. Morris, a chief engineer of the railroad. Henry B. Wolff opened his general store as the first place of trade within the town plat, which sparked the hustle and bustle that would take over the region for the next several decades. The business lines were extensive. In 1910, it had multiple banks, flour mills, liveries, stores, elevators, and a creamery. Two depots, an armory, an engine house, a courthouse, and six churches were significant pieces of infrastructure, but Morris truly stood out in its educational sphere. It had three elementary and/or high school buildings at that time. From 1887 to 1909, it was the site of the Morris Industrial School for Indians. The school had been called the Sacred Heart Indian Mission; the nuns themselves built its buildings. In 1895, it was the largest Indian boarding school in Minnesota, with an enrollment of 103 students. It was managed by Roman Catholic nuns affiliated with the Sisters of Mercy until 1896, when the United States government's Office of Indian Fairs took over that role. In 1909, the school closed for good, but in 1910, it was repurposed by the state as the West Central School of Agriculture. From 1910 to 1963, the institution operated as a residential high school for youth interested in agriculture and home economics. Several additional buildings were built due to the school's success (as it was one of the country's longest-running schools of that type), eleven of which were built between 1899 and 1929 and annexed to the University of Minnesota Morris in September 1960. The final high schoolers graduated in 1963, but the public liberal arts college continues as one of five University of Minnesota System branch campuses. Interestingly, it has been ranked as one of the "greenest" campuses in the United States (per capita) because its biomass gasification plant converts crop residues into steam used to heat and cool campus buildings. The National Register of Historic Places lists many of the historic campus buildings as the West Central School Agriculture and Experiment Station Historic District. Another individual building on campus, the Morris Industrial School for Indians Dormitory, is the last surviving building of the original Indian School. It is now the Multi-Ethnic Resource Center. Two other historic points of interest are the 1881 Lewis H. Stanton House, "The Chimneys," with its eye-catching Stick-Eastlake architecture, and the 1905 Morris Carnegie Library, now host to the Stevens County

Historical Society Museum. The university, healthcare, manufacturing, and agribusiness contribute to the town's economy; two such businesses synonymous with Morris are Superior Industries, with its two steel conveyor and storage tank manufacturing plants, and Riverview LLP, Minnesota's largest dairy milking operation. Every community has endured hardships at different times, but Morris has, strangely, been the site of two of Minnesota's three largest earthquakes of the 20th century. The first was on July 9, 1975, and was rated 4.6; the second was on June 4, 1993, at 4.1. Unsurprisingly, a town like Morris, especially one with such educational capabilities, has ties to several famous people of past and present: Trina Radke, an Olympic swimmer at the 1988 summer games in South Korea; Jim Hall, a computer programmer famous for his work on FreeDOS; Aaron Schock, a U.S. Congressman from Illinois from January 2009 to March 2015, who was notably the youngest member of Congress in 2009 at the age of 27; Paul Zachary Myers, the author of the popular biology-related blog Pharyngula; Mike Morley, a former PGA Tour golfer; Dlck Grace, a stunt pilot whose job was to crash planes for Hollywood films like the 1927 silent war film *Wings*; Sara McMann, the 2004 Olympics silver medalist in women's freestyle wrestling; Erick Rowan, a professional wrestler with the WWE; Rachel Brand, the 18th United States Associate Attorney General from May 2017 to February 2018, and Monti Ossenfort, the general manager of the NFL's Arizona Cardinals since 2023.

Restaurant Recommendation:
Don's Cafe
15 E 5th St
Morris, MN 56267

National Register of Historic Places:
Alberta: Alberta Teachers House
Morris: Morris Carnegie Library, Morris High School, Morris Industrial School for Indians Dormitory, Lewis H. Stanton House, West Central School of Agriculture & Experiment Station Historic District

Golf Courses:
Pomme de Terre Golf Club, Daily Fee (Morris, MN)

Town Celebrations:
Alberta Harvest Fest, Alberta, MN (Early September)
Chokio Community Picnic, Chokio, MN (2nd Weekend in June)
Donnelly Threshing Bee, Donnelly, MN (Weekend before Labor Day)
Independence Day Celebration, Hancock, MN (4th of July)
Prairie Harvest Fest, Morris, MN (4th Weekend in September)

SWIFT COUNTY
EST. 1870 - POPULATION: 9,838

Established in 1870 from former Chippewa County lands, Swift County was named in honor of Henry Adoniram Swift, Minnesota's third governor from 1863 to 1864.

APPLETON, MN ☆
POPULATION: 1,392 – CITY 163 OF 856 (4-13-25)
The "Home of Honored Veterans" is home to more veterans and retirees per capita than most other Minnesota communities, which is why it's nicknamed "Home of Honored Veterans." Patriotism runs deep in the now-town of 1,392 residents, as every

street in Appleton (except for Minnesota Street) honors a fallen veteran who perished in combat. Its original name was Phelps for Addison Phelps and her family, who acquired a parcel of land on the Pomme de Terre River in 1868. A few years later, the Phelps family decided they no longer wanted the settlement to bear their surname, so they changed it to Appleton, an eponym for Appleton, Wisconsin. Around the same time, Civil War veterans and brothers A. W. and W. V. Lathrop built a flour mill, which led to a small impetus of growth and the establishment of a store, hotel, and blacksmith shop before the arrival of the Great Northern Railroad and the Hastings & Dakota division of the Chicago, Milwaukee & St. Paul Railroad. The Episcopalians and the Methodists began conducting their religious services during the 1870s. By the 1880s, Appleton's scope of influence beyond economic accomplishments included an excellent schoolhouse built for $7,000 to house its 125-plus students, two additional religious organizations, the United Brethren and the Norwegian Lutherans, and several fraternal organizations. Over that decade, the population grew by 148.5% from 400 residents to 994, and by 1915, its population numbered well over 1,000. Noted institutions in 1915 included its four grain elevators, two banks, two hotels, a brewery, a creamery, a feed mill, a flour mill, an opera house, a public library, and six churches. One of the church edifices, the Gethsemane Episcopal Church, was built in 1879 in the Gothic Revival and Carpenter Gothic styles. Although it closed in 1991, it was listed on the National Register of Historic Places in 2011. Appleton's other significant building is the old City Hall building, completed in 1895 to serve as a joint building for city offices, the fire department, an auditorium and meeting place, and a jail. One of the City's most significant modern projects was the Prairie Correctional Facility, which opened in 1992 but lasted only through 2010 due to a lack of demand for prisoner housing in a rural setting. Herbert A. Winkelmann, the co-inventor of the first antioxidant AgeRite and the holder of 48 patents in the field of rubber technology; Jerry Koosman, a two-time All-Star and World Series champion pitcher with the New York Mets in 1969; Brad Rheingans, a two-time Pan American Games gold-medalist in the 100kg Greco-Roman wrestling weight class in the mid-to-late 1970s; actor Clinton Sundberg, and Elmer A. Benson, the 24th Governor of Minnesota, have local ties.

BENSON, MN ★
POPULATION: 3,480 – CITY 177 OF 856 (4-15-25)
When Ole Corneiliusen of Norway arrived in 1866, only the Chippewa River and vast swaths of natural land explored almost exclusively by the Indigenous Chippewa and Sioux were there to greet him. Not long after he settled in the area, a village named Benson was surveyed in the spring of 1870 by C. A. F. Morris on behalf of the First Division of the St. Paul & Pacific Railroad Company. The name was given to honor Ben H. Benson, another Norwegian settler who operated an early mercantile in the township. A. W. and W. V. Lathrop, the same brothers who had invested in a flour mill in nearby Appleton, pre-empted the railroad's arrival by establishing a general store on the townsite in 1869. They were joined in their commercial interests by Meldal & Sunde's store, Theodore Hanson's general store, Thomas Knudson's saloon, L. S. William's Central House hotel, and the lumberyard of L. R. Davis and O. N. Barsness. R. Sunde was named postmaster, and after Benson secured the Swift County seat, nothing could stop its growth towards being the region's economic hub. As the terminus of the railroad, it enjoyed being the market center for an area extending over one hundred miles to the north, south, and west (but not to the east because of Minneapolis and St. Paul). Benson's people traded heavily with those in nearby Wahpeton, North Dakota, using the Red River Ox Carts. Benson boomed to a population of half a thousand by 1880, most notably between 1875-76, when a rush of immigrants spurred the construction of several more hotels, stores, elevators, and

other businesses. Its residents petitioned the county commissioners for incorporation status, which was granted on February 14, 1877. When the new century rolled around, it had 1,525 full-time residents, despite significant population losses due to the smallpox epidemic of 1872, the statewide plague of locusts in 1876, and an 1880 fire that started in Joe Fountain's saloon and ultimately destroyed 20 businesses (an entire city block). Benson's Carnegie Library was established in 1911 with a $7,500 donation from the railroad mogul and philanthropist Andrew Carnegie, and in 1912, the Swift County Hospital was completed for $15,000. Out of the several hundreds of buildings that adorn the county seat's streets today, three structures, in particular, stand out for their rich history: the Christ Episcopal Church, an 1879 project of Bishop Henry Benjamin Whipple to expand the Episcopalian religion throughout Minnesota; the Richardsonian Romanesque style Swift County Courthouse built between 1897-98, and The Church of St. Francis Xavier, a Catholic edifice famous for being amongst the grandest in western Minnesota. Just outside Benson is the Christian F. Uytendale Farmstead, dating to 1868, on property sold to the wealthy Danishman by the Norwegian Johannes Torgerson in 1879. Benson has seen no shortage of famous folks over the years, as it has ties to James A. Johnson, the CEO of Fannie Mae (The Federal National Mortgage Association) from 1991 to 1998; David Hazewinkel, a Greco-Roman Olympic wrestler in 1968 and 1972; Edgar Dale, an educator known for his development of the Learning Pyramid theory; Martha Ostenso, a Canadian author best known for her 1925 novel *Wild Geese*; Ernie Wheeler, an early back in the National Football League in 1939 and 1942, and Becca Kufrin, the winner of the 22nd season of ABC's *The Bachelor* and the central star of the 14th season of *The Bachelorette*. Five former members of the U.S. House of Representatives from Minnesota can also claim ties to Benson: Darwin Hall, 1889 to 1891; Saxe J. Froshaug, 1911 to 1915; Ole J. Kvale, 1923 to 1929; his son, Paul J. Kvale, 1929 to 1939; and Mark Kennedy, 2001 to 2007.

Restaurant Recommendation:
Track Bar & Grill
1199-1101 Pacific Ave
Benson, MN 56215

Restaurant Recommendation:
Benson Bakery
1305 Pacific Ave
Benson, MN 56215

CLONTARF, MN
POPULATION: 128 – CITY 160 OF 856 (4-13-25)

The influence of Bishop Ireland's Catholic Colonization Bureau extended well beyond his ventures in southwestern Minnesota; in the mid-1870s, a push for a second colony of Irish Catholics was underway. Platted and then settled in 1876, Clontarf was named after Clontarf, Ireland, now a coastal suburb of Dublin. Lumberyard owner Dominick F. McDermott volunteered to serve as its postmaster when an office was established there that year, and in November 1881, it was incorporated as a village. Two general stores, a hotel, a schoolhouse, a Great Northern depot, and a church were present as of 1882, but its growth was pretty contained. From 1910 to today, its highest population was 230 residents (as of 1940), and its lowest was 128 (as of 2020). Between 1877 and 1898, Clontarf was home to St. Paul's Industrial School, which instructed white orphans and Indigenous children in Catholic teachings, life skills, and academics. St. Malachy Catholic Church celebrated its final Mass on November 7, 2021.

DANVERS, MN
POPULATION: 103 – CITY 161 OF 856 (4-13-25)
This Great Northern Railroad station was born out of necessity when railroad workers needed an additional stop on their new line connecting Benson and Appleton, Minnesota, with Watertown, South Dakota. After being platted in 1886, settlement of the new Danvers townsite began, and in 1887, the first engines arrived. "Danvers" is an eponym for a town in Massachusetts of the same name. Early business directories show that some of the first institutions were the general store of A. N. Matteison and a post office, but by the time the new century rolled around, circa 1900, it had nearly twenty houses, including a blacksmith shop, lumberyards, and dry goods stores. Danvers was incorporated as a village on January 19, 1900, and reached a peak of 253 residents in 1920.

DE GRAFF, MN
POPULATION: 110 – CITY 178 OF 856 (4-15-25)
The Church of St. Bridget has towered over the De Graff city skyline since 1901, when it was built to serve the needs of the first Catholic parish in the region, which Archbishop John Ireland was attempting to populate with Irish Catholics. Built by E. C. Richmond and designed by Edward J. Donahue in a Gothic Revival style, the edifice was a welcome addition to parishioners who had worshipped in De Graff since 1876. This period was the same era in which De Graff was laid out on the Great Northern Railroad, and the townsite came to fruition. A little more than a half-decade of development later, De Graff was home to three general stores, two hotels, a hardware store, a blacksmith shop, an elevator, a meat market, and a pair of churches. Its name honors Andrew De Graff of St. Paul, a chief engineer for the Great Northern Railroad and a vital figurehead in establishing several other lines throughout Minnesota. The post office was established in 1875 with William Clint at its helm; it was closed in 1996.

HOLLOWAY, MN
POPULATION: 87 – CITY 162 OF 856 (4-13-25)
Swift County's smallest municipality was initially called Norton but was renamed in 1887 by officials of the Great Northern Railroad when they platted it in honor of a local farmer. It is known that T. B. Boyle owned the first store in Holloway, and that a post office branch opened in 1889, but early records indicate that the population of Holloway may have been as low as two people in 1900. For whatever reason, seriousness about achieving success or development in Holloway did not come until the mid-1900s, when settlers moved in and established stores, saloons, a bank, and other businesses. Most of these businesses were destroyed in a January 1907 fire, but by 1920, it had grown into a small agricultural village with a population of nearly 300 people. During this time, it welcomed numerous businesses, each of which played an essential role in shaping day-to-day life in the community. In 1912, the *Holloway Herald* was published for the first time before moving to Appleton in 1923 and rebranding as *The Appleton Independent*. Holloway was incorporated in 1903.

KERKHOVEN, MN
POPULATION: 805 – CITY 180 OF 856 (4-15-25)
"Kerk" is the typical slang Minnesotans use for Kerkhoven. This Dutch village got that name on February 17, 1883, when Johannes and Theodores Kerkhoven of the

Kerkhoven Brokerage Company of Amsterdam were given the green light to extend the St. Paul & Pacific Railroad to the townsite. Some of its earliest inhabitants had arrived in Pillsbury township nearly twenty years earlier, after which the town was named when it was platted for the first time in 1870. Before the railroad, these people accomplished many feats and, as of 1882, boasted a commercial district with four general stores, three saloons, a cheese factory, pairs of blacksmith shops, hotels, elevators, a pharmacy, a hardware store, a harness shop, carriage works, and a newspaper. Kerkhoven experienced a massive population increase from 94 residents in 1880 to 299 by 1890 after its tracks were laid and it was connected to other towns.

MURDOCK, MN
POPULATION: 306 – CITY 179 OF 856 (4-15-25)
Sabin S. Murdock is the namesake of this community, which was platted by P. M. Quist in 1878 on a portion of the three thousand acres of land he owned in this region of Minnesota. The former Minnesota railway commissioner was solely responsible for promoting his town. He successfully attracted the Great Northern Railway and a plethora of Irish immigrants to his land, which was organized into a village on January 28, 1881. According to a business directory published the following year, early implements of Murdock were a bank, a hotel, a hardware store, a wagon shop, a saloon, a butcher shop, a harness shop, two grain elevators, two blacksmith shops, and a whopping five general stores selling all the primary goods of an 1880s farm town. The Murdock depot served as Murdock's first place of worship; in the spring of 1878, the Methodist Episcopal minister D. J. Higgins held the first service. The post office started on January 23, 1879, and George Botham was the postmaster. Mr. Murdock's Victorian home has been a staple of the community's architecture since its construction in 1878 and, as of 1985, has been listed in the U.S. National Register of Historic Places. Another noteworthy Murdock resident is Dave Frederickson, who served as Minnesota's Agriculture Commissioner from January 3, 2011, to January 7, 2019. Murdock became the focus of national headlines in June 2020 when the Asatru Folk Assembly purchased the local Calvary Lutheran Church for use as one of four "hofs," or neo-pagan temples, in the United States.

Unincorporated/Ghost Towns: Fairfield, Swift Falls

National Register of Historic Places:
Appleton: Appleton City Hall, Gethsemane Episcopal Church
Benson: Christ Church-Episcopal, Church of St. Francis Xavier-Catholic, Swift County Courthouse, Christian F. Uytendale Farmstead
De Graff: Church of St. Bridget-Catholic
Murdock: Sabin S. Murdock House
Sunburg: Monson Lake State Park CCC/WPA/Rustic Style Historic Resources

Golf Courses:
Appleton Golf Club, Daily Fee (Appleton, MN)
Benson Golf Club, Municipal (Benson, MN)
Kerkhoven Community Golf Course, Daily Fee (Kerkhoven, MN)

Town Celebrations:
Appleton Applefest, Appleton, MN (3rd Weekend of September)
De Graff Labor Day Celebration, De Graff, MN (Labor Day)
Kid Day, Benson, MN (3rd Saturday in July)
Town & Country Days, Kerkhoven, MN (Last Weekend in July)

Sherburne County: Bailey Gas Station at Sherburne History Center (Becker) Mural (Big Lake), former Public School (Big Lake), McDonald's Meats Mural (Clear Lake), St. Marcus Catholic Church (Clear Lake), Storefront Murals (Elk River), Gazebo at Rivers Edge Commons on the Mississippi River (Elk River), Saint Francis River at Sherburne National Wildlife Refuge (Zimmerman)

Sibley County: Baseball Water Tower (Arlington), former Gibbon Village Hall (Gibbon), Main Street (Gibbon), Mural (Gibbon), Prince Mural (Henderson), Ney Nature Center Barn (Henderson), W. W. Mayo House (Le Sueur), The Jolly Green Giant 2-D Plywood Sign (Le Sueur)

Stearns County: World's Largest Crow Statue (Belgrade), Lake Wobegon Trail Covered Bridge (Holdingford), St. Margaret's Catholic Church (Lake Henry), Sauk River/Melrose Lake Dam at Sauk River Park (Melrose), Immaculate Conception Catholic Church (New Munich), Munsinger Gardens (St. Cloud), Saint John's Abbey at Saint John's University (Collegeville), Sinclair Lewis Historic Home (Sauk Centre)

Steele County: Veteran's Memorial (Blooming Prairie), State Bank Mural (Blooming Prairie), Welcome to Ellendale Sign (Ellendale), First Lutheran Church (Ellendale), Owatonna City Hall; former Minnesota State Public School for Dependent and Neglected Children (Owatonna), former Union Depot (Owatonna), former National Farmers' [Jewel Box] Bank of Owatonna (Owatonna), Dunnell House at Village of Yesteryear (Owatonna)

Stevens County: former Great Northern Railroad Tracks and Grain Elevators (Alberta), Frank Schott Old Barn (Chokio), former Donnelly School (Donnelly), Homer Simpson Mural (Donnelly), Morris Theatre (Morris), Don's Cafe (Morris), former Carnegie Library (Morris), Catholic Church of the Assumption of the Blessed Virgin Mary (Morris)

Swift County: Old Swimming House on the Pomme de Terre River (Appleton), Appleton City Hall & Heritage Center (Appleton), Swift County Courthouse (Benson), Whistle Stop Diner (Benson), Benson Bakery in 1900 Bakken Building (Benson), St. Francis Catholic Church (Benson), Danvers Oratory of the Visitation (Danvers), Historic 1878 Samuel S. Murdock House (Murdock)

TODD COUNTY
EST. 1855 - POPULATION: 25,262

Formally organized on January 1, 1867, Todd County was named after John Blair Smith Todd, who was best known for serving as a Union Army general during the American Civil War conflict.

BERTHA, MN
POPULATION: 560 – CITY 251 OF 856 (5-8-25)

John C. Ristau built a log cabin on this site circa 1880 and turned it into both a store and a post office, with the United States Postal Service's permission. When deciding on a name, he chose to honor his wife, Bertha Ristau, the first white woman settler of the townsite. The area's extensive development did not occur until the railroad's arrival nearly a decade later. Either C. A. Germond, Francis M., and Louisa Riggs platted the townsite on August 25, 1891. Six years later, Bertha attained incorporation status. By 1906, it had nearly 300 residents, a designated town hall, a public school, Evangelical and Congregational churches, and a Modern Woodmen of America Hall. A depot, stockyards, and two elevators stood tall over the Great Northern Railroad. In its commercial district, Bertha had all the lines that one would have expected to find during that era: the Eagle Bend Roller Mill, a sawmill, a creamery, a blacksmith shop, a lumber yard, two banks, a hotel, a livery, and a printing office. As "America's Game" took the country by storm as a favorite pastime, Bertha welcomed a semi-pro baseball team in the mid-1920s. The Bertha Fishermen had a pair of famous players during the 1925 season: John Donaldson, a Negro League baseball pitcher who was widely considered to be the greatest pitcher of his era with over 420 wins and 5,221 strikeouts, and Elmer Brandell, a catcher who most notably appeared on the roster of the barnstorming All Nations national team in 1914. Bertha has a local historical society and museum, as well as one of the few remaining round barns in Minnesota.

Restaurant Recommendation:
Buford's Bar & Grill
115 2nd Ave NW
Bertha, MN 56437

BROWERVILLE, MN
POPULATION: 839 – CITY 254 OF 856 (5-8-25)

The birthplace of LaVyrle Spencer, a best-selling romance novelist with over two million sales, and Joseph Kiselewski, a famous sculptor whose works are now found worldwide, has a history deep in religion and the railroad. John Bassett was the first to settle in the vicinity in 1865 on the Long Prairie River. It was called Hartford. Four years later, this pioneer community was moved three miles south to the future site of the Sauk Centre branch of the Great Northern Railroad. It would not be until 1882 that Jacob V. Brower platted out the townsite on his land. Brower, the father of the Minnesota State Park system and Itasca State Park, cemented his legacy and impact on Minnesota with these actions. He was honored by the railroad, which named this town for him. Early business houses included the general stores of D. C. Davis and Perry & Scott; the hardware store of A. M. Jaques and Dr. M. L. Murphy's drug store. The Browerville Creamery Association, lumber yards, hotels, a newspaper office, a roller mill, liveries, banks, garages, public schools, a hospital (purchased by the Traditional Catholic Sisters of the Society of Saint Pius X in 1990 for use as a Novitiate), and a post office (established in 1894) all played a crucial role in making

Browerville one of Todd County's premier communities at the turn of the century. However, its most interesting history lies with its churches. In 1882, Polish and German settlers established St. Joseph's congregation, and in 1893, they erected a building. Only two years after the construction of the $1,500 building, because they could not overcome the language barrier, the parish split into St. Joseph's Polish congregation and St. Peter's German congregation. The Germans invested $60,000 in their edifice, which was erected in 1896. Both churches grew independently of one another, each practicing the same Catholic faith. The Polish church would see tremendous growth despite the Germans' significant investment. Their parochial school opened in 1890 (back when they were still with the Germans). From 1908-09, the large congregation significantly upgraded its church facilities by constructing the Church of St. Joseph (now Christ the King Catholic Church). The gorgeous Baroque Revival edifice with its 70-foot-tall tower and onion dome was designed by the architects Boehme and Cordella and built by Hirr and Zierton of St. Cloud, Minnesota, at a cost of nearly $30,000. It was listed on the National Register of Historic Places in September 1985, the same decade that the Polish and German parishes again merged due to declining membership. United Brethren and Protestant Christian churches naturally came about as well. For some time, there was a third Catholic-related church: the Byzantine Catholic parish church, established by a group of Rusyns in the early 20th century. Their church was called the Holy Trinity Greek Catholic Church (known locally as The Farmer's Church). Most of its parishioners transferred to St. Peter's Church over the years because the parish was unable to find a regular Orthodox pastor. The building was ultimately demolished. In addition to the Church of St. Joseph, the Kahlert Mercantile Store, built in 1883 by William and Ferdinand Kahlert as one of the original general and grocery stores in town, is another local point of pride. Nine miles east of Browerville is the Zion Chapel in the Hills, a former church steeple taken from a 1931 church that was turned into a lovely chapel in 1983. Modern-day Browerville is now home to more residents than ever in its recorded history: 839 people.

Restaurant Recommendation:
Cherry Grove Market
30619 241st Ave
Browerville, MN 56438

BURTRUM, MN
POPULATION: 123 – CITY 256 OF 856 (5-8-25)
Platted as Hansen, this Northern Pacific Railroad village in Burnhamville Township got its start in April 1884 and was eventually renamed Burtrum. Settlement in the vicinity was minimal until it was certain that the Morris and Little Falls branch of the railway would be built through. In 1888, it received its post office, and by March 20, 1894, it stood among Minnesota's incorporated villages. A depot, an elevator, a stockyard, a bank, and some stores were in operation, according to a 1906 business directory. By 1915, there was a fire department, a village hall, Congregational, Free Methodist, and Lutheran churches, and a four-room brick school building that educated the community's youth through the early 1980s. Several area lakes and a Grand Army of the Republic cemetery highlight the modern tourism attractions of the southeastern Todd County hamlet, which saw its heyday in the 1940s (population 297, according to the U.S. Decennial Census).

CLARISSA, MN
POPULATION: 661 – CITY 253 OF 856 (5-8-25)
Home to as many as 681 citizens as recently as 2010, Clarissa started its march towards cityhood in the late 1870s, when it was platted (on July 21, 1879) on the Cass Lake branch of the Great Northern Railroad. George G. Howe did the surveying on behalf of Lewis Bischoffsheim and his wife, Clarisse, who hailed from London, England. George W. Pearmine and Mr. Howe were the first two permanent settlers. After the railroad came through, many businesses came about, like Frank B. Nutting's large general merchandise, hardware, and furniture store, Frank Nutting Sr.'s roller mill, an accompanying sawmill, two elevators, stockyards a bank, a pharmacy, The Eagle Valley Cooperative Creamery Company, *The Todd County Independent* newspaper, hotels, liveries, lumberyards, a box and egg case factory, and numerous other storefronts and shops. The Clarissa post office went into service in 1880, and the town was incorporated in 1897. For a brief period in 1895, some residents rallied to urge the relocation of the Todd County seat from Long Prairie to Clarissa, but the movement failed. Religion was another important facet of early Clarissa. According to a 1906 atlas, Swedish Evangelical and Norwegian Lutheran churches sat beside one another in the far southwestern corner of town, down the street from the public school. The Catholic and the Congregational church edifices were in the northeast corner of Clarissa, across Eagle Creek.

EAGLE BEND, MN
POPULATION: 546 – CITY 252 OF 856 (5-8-25)
Famous for Clarence "Tuffy" Olson and its bootlegging days, the town of Eagle Bend would never have come to fruition without the help of the Great Northern Railroad. The Park Rapids branch (formerly known as the K-Line of the St. Paul, Minneapolis, and Manitoba Railway) of James J. Hill's impressive railroad system boasted numerous towns, one of which was Eagle Bend, noted for its turntable and engine house. Benjamin F. Abbott purchased the Eagle Bend townsite (so named for its location on a bend of Eagle Creek) in 1883. He worked to provide sustainable solutions and new impetuses for growth. Charles G. O'Dell had already welcomed a post office branch to his general store in 1882. After Abbott's investment, Eagle Bend gave way to two banks, two liveries, lumber yards, grain elevators, hotels, a creamery, the *Eagle Bend News* newspaper, a sawmill, and a 125-barrel-capacity flour mill. Five churches were present shortly after the turn of the century: the Methodists, Norwegian Lutherans, Swedish Episcopalians, Catholics, and another Protestant congregation. The Ancient Order of United Workmen, the Yeomen, the Masons, and the Odd Fellows were among the era's fraternal organizations. Early country schoolhouses eventually consolidated into a larger, localized public school structure in western Eagle Bend; its building was rebuilt in 1942 using elements of WPA Moderne architecture. The school and its accompanying 1952 auditorium/gymnasium building were added to the NRHP for preservation on July 25, 2024. It was also notable as the first school in the United States to obtain a license for a low-power educational television station, now locally remembered as "Channel 45." Eagle Bend's "boom period" occurred between the 1930s and 1940s, when the population grew by 18.6% from 575 people to 682. It was in this era that the infamous Prohibition-era bootlegger Tuffy Olson met his demise in nearby Holdingford. He primarily ran his operations out of Eagle Bend. He perished when Joseph and Anthony Dzierweczynski shot him twice in the back with a shotgun when attempting to steal 85 gallons of Minnesota 13 moonshine.

GREY EAGLE, MN
POPULATION: 330 – CITY 257 OF 856 (5-8-25)
Grey Eagle's ultra-specific name can be attributed to A. M. Crowell, a Bemidji judge who shot an eagle here in 1868, about a half-decade before the township was created. The name stuck when the village was platted in September 1882, and the town was introduced to the Northern Pacific Railroad system. A post office (est. 1877) was the first of its enterprising firms. Within thirty-five years, it had a Village Hall, School No. 13, a Congregational church, a German Lutheran church, a United Brethren church, the *Gazette* weekly newspaper, two banks, two hotels, a livery, a lumber yard, an elevator, stockyards, a creamery and a sawmill on the shores of Trace Lake, and most uniquely of them all, a sash and door factory. James Huffman served as Grey Eagle's first postmaster, and his brother James M. was a hotel owner and justice of the peace. As Franklin D. Roosevelt's New Deal programs swept across the nation to help bring America out of the Great Depression, Grey Eagle was dealt a hearty hand of good luck when it was selected as a recipient of a 1934 government office, fire station, and community auditorium. In 1934, the 40-by-90-foot building was erected using fieldstone by the Civil Works Administration (a temporary agency affiliated with the WPA). The structure has also served as a bowling alley, a roller rink, and a manufacturing facility for personal flotation devices. From its inaugural 1900 U.S. Decennial Census to the 2020 Census, Grey Eagle has reported a low population of 313 in 1900 and a high of 428 in the 1940s. Paul Ellering, a professional wrestling manager and a former WWE wrestler known as "The Body Doc" and "Mr. Dot Com," has ties to the community.

HEWITT, MN
POPULATION: 251 – CITY 250 OF 856 (5-8-25)
Henry Hewitt donated the land on which the Great Northern Railroad founded a new townsite. In return, the railroad company named it after him. In April 1891, the site was platted, and lots were auctioned off to prospective settlers seeking an opportunity to start anew in the wilderness of central Minnesota. Initially established in George Hildreth's farmhouse under the name Powell, the Powell post office was moved to Hewitt and accordingly renamed by the end of 1891. Over the next fifteen years, the population grew to exceed three hundred persons, the lot of whom built up a roller mill, a grain elevator, stockyards, a lumber yard, an opera house, a bank, a hotel, a livery, *The Banner* newspaper, a public school, and United Brethren, Adventist, and Methodist Episcopal churches. The roller mill could reportedly churn out seventy-five barrels daily, and the stockyards averaged a car of livestock per week. Hewitt's first larger schoolhouse was erected in 1910-11 for $10,000. From December 1979 through its closure as an educational institution, it hosted first-grade through high school pupils at various times. The incredibly unique Colonial Revival-style building was designed by C. Howard Parsons, built entirely of concrete (a rare feat at that time) by the Medson Brothers as a two-and-a-half-story cruciform building. Post-closure, the property was sold to the City of Hewitt for a dollar, which sought to preserve the structure and revitalize it for use as the Hewitt Museum, a library, and a community center. Much time and effort were put into ensuring its listing on the National Register of Historic Places. Hewitt was incorporated as a village on February 20, 1899.

LONG PRAIRIE, MN ★☆
POPULATION: 3,661 – CITY 255 OF 856 (5-8-25)
So named for the long, narrow stretch of prairie that borders the eastern side of the Long Prairie River for twenty miles, the Todd County seat of Long Prairie was predated

by an 1848 agency for the Ho-Chunk tribe. It was strategically located at that site to buffer the warring Sioux and Chippewa (alternatively, Ojibwe) tribes. The tribe erected an impressive collection of homes, a church, and Francis Vivaldi's mission school. By 1855, the Ho-Chunk were moved to Mankato, the reservation and the agency disbanded, and Todd County was formed. The post office was closed from 1850 to 1854, but reopened in 1857 when the town was established. General Horatia Van Cleve and his wife Charlotte had arrived in 1856; A. J. Gibson joined them in the winter of 1857, and by the spring of 1860, the county had approximately twenty-seven settlers. Long Prairie was finally platted in May 1867. From then on, its duties as the county's principal center of population and economic activity were assured. One of the state's largest creameries emerged in what eventually became known as Minnesota's creamery belt. Not long after the turn of the century, it had four grain elevators, ironworks, a brewery, brickyards, two planing mills (one of which doubled as a sawmill), a flour mill, a silo factory, and the Hansmann Manufacturing Company with its then state-of-the-art corn husking machine. Several smaller yet equally essential firms, including two lumber yards, two hotels, three banks, and many more stores, were in operation by 1906. Long Prairie then also had a top-of-the-line electric light and water powerhouse, a county jail and courthouse, a public library, a fire station, fairgrounds, a "speed ring" (a racetrack), public and parochial schools, and churches for the German Evangelical, Catholic, Baptist, Methodist-Episcopalian, and Presbyterian religious groups. Several of these locations were listed on the National Register in more recent years: the 1883 Italianate Todd County Courthouse and its accompanying Sheriff's House, Jail, and 1938 WPA entryway; the 1902-03 Hotel Reichert, a magnificent 141-by-107-foot Neoclassical building; the 1903 Bank of Long Prairie building, and Dr. George R. Christie's 1901 Neoclassical home, which also served as the home office of Todd County's first licensed physician. The Christie house is now a museum. The Todd County Historical Society and Museum helps preserve Long Prairie's early history, such as the story of George H. Williams, a village marshal who was killed on July 29, 1922, following a botched bank robbery in nearby Hewitt. The Veterans Memorial Park and its helicopter, tank, Statue of Liberty, five-story-tall mural, and Iwo Jima tribute are other local points of interest. Noteworthy Long Prairie residents of past and present include Charles P. Davis, a Medal of Honor recipient for his actions taken during the Philippine-American War in May 1899; Barry Bennett, a defensive tackle in the NFL from 1978 to 1988; and Tom Barnard, the longtime host of *The KQ92 Morning Show* on 92.5 KQRS Minneapolis from 1985 to 2022.

STAPLES, MN
POPULATION: 2,989 – CITY 225 OF 856 (5-6-25)

The story of the City of Staples truly began with the arrival of the loggers Samuel and Isaac Staples, whose family held extensive logging and manufacturing interests in the vicinity. Their sawmill was established not far from the geographical center of Minnesota, and this position, coupled with the proximity to the Crow Wing River, led to the running of the main line of the Northern Pacific Railroad through the townsite. The entire area was incorporated as the village of Presto in 1889, a name it shared with its post office, until both were changed to honor the Staples family. Kate P. Staples was the postmaster when the change was made, although it did not go into effect until 1895. The lumber industry was so profitable here that the Northern Pacific opted to make "Staples Mill" a division point and terminal for three divisions of the railroad. From 1890 to 1910, its population quadrupled from 585 to 2,558, and several improvements were made to its infrastructure, including a municipal electric light plant, a state-of-the-art sewer system, waterworks, and a fire department. Several dozen lines of enterprise were in operation during this era of growth and prosperity, such as banks, hotels, lumber yards, stores, and the like. Some of the more popular firms of the time were a laundry, *The World* newspaper office, a silo-making factory, a wood-pulp processing plant, a creamery, large stockyards, two brickyards, and multiple roller and planing mills. A seven-hundred-seat opera house provided the community with a center for performing arts and gatherings, and there were church edifices for religious services by the Catholic, Episcopalian, Methodist, Baptist, Congregational, and Adventist denominations. The school system reportedly had over 1,000 pupils across the primary and public schools. As the railroad division point, the Northern Pacific installed enough trainage for 1,750 railcars, and built a roundhouse, a repair machine shop, and a three-story office depot that still stands today as the Northern Pacific Railway Depot and Freighthouse, a National Register of Historic Places location. It is one of six Minnesota stops on Amtrak's daily Empire Builder passenger train between Seattle, Washington, and Chicago, Illinois. The city's other NRHP site is the aforementioned opera house, now known as the Batcher Opera House Block. Many famous personalities have ties to the primarily Todd County community: Alfred E. Perlman, once President of the New York Central Railroad and the Western Pacific Railroad; Jon Hassler, a writer noted for his novels on small-town life in rural Minnesota; Dick Bremer, a sports broadcaster primarily known for announcing Minnesota Twins baseball games on television from 1983 to 2023; LaVyrle Spencer, a romance novelist with twelve titles on the *New York Times* bestseller list; Frankie Thorn, an actress known for her role as "The Nun" in the 1992 neo-noir crime film *Bad Lieutenant*, and Dave Joerger, a professional basketball coach who led the NBA's Memphis Grizzlies from 2013 to 2016 and the Sacramento Kings from 2016 to 2019.

WEST UNION, MN
POPULATION: 92 – CITY 258 OF 856 (5-8-25)

Todd County's smallest incorporated town, presently home to 92 people but never home to more than 169 citizens according to the 1920 Census, was platted on Joel Myers's land in June 1881 and incorporated in 1900. The earliest Europeans to traverse the area traveled along the Kandota Section of the Saint Cloud and Red River Valley Stage Road, which enabled pioneers to move from St. Cloud, Minnesota, into the fertile Red River Valley on the state's western border. An 1857 agreement between the Hudson's Bay Company of Canada and the Northwestern Express and Transportation Company established the heavily traveled route, which diminished in 1871 as railroads began to be built. West Union landed itself on the main line of the Great Northern Railway and had its first store, owned by Tony Poplinski, in place by 1880. By the time a 1906 Northwest Publishing Company map was published, West Union had two grain elevators, a depot, stockyards, two stores, two blacksmith shops, a saloon, a hardware store, a creamery, School No. 4, and a German Catholic church, residence, and cemetery. West Union has had three different post office institutions: its 1860 to 1861 office, a secondary, long-running post from 1872 to 1986, and a rural station beginning in 1986. When driving eastbound on Interstate 94, sightseers may notice a thirty-foot limo stuck headfirst into the ground near mile marker 113.

Restaurant Recommendation:
Sidewalks Saloon & Grill
51 Main St
West Union, MN 56389

Swanville is only partially located in Todd County (see Morrison County).

Unincorporated/Ghost Towns: Philbrook, Pillsbury, Ward Springs

National Register of Historic Places:
Browerville: Church of St, Joseph-Catholic, Kahlert Mercantile Store
Eagle Bend: Eagle Bend High School
Germania Township: Germania Hall
Grey Eagle: Grey Eagle Village Hall
Hartford Township: Bridge No. L7075
Hewitt: Hewitt Public School
Kandota Township: Saint Cloud & Red River Valley Stage Road-Kandota Section
Long Prairie: Bank of Long Prairie, Dr. George R. Christie House, Hotel Reichert, Todd County Courthouse, Sheriff's House, & Jail
Staples: Batcher Opera House Block, Northern Pacific Railway Depot & Freighthouse

Golf Courses:
Long Prairie Country Club, Daily Fee (Long Prairie, MN)
The Vintage Golf Club, Daily Fee (Staples, MN)

Breweries/Wineries/Distilleries:
Dragon Willow Winery (Long Prairie, MN)

Town Celebrations:
Bertha Days/Truck & Tractor Pull, Bertha, MN (2nd Saturday in July)
Browerville Heritage Centers, Browerville, MN (Last Full Weekend in June)
Burtrum Bean Bake, Burtrum, MN (Early October)
Hewitt Picklefest, Hewitt, MN (3rd Weekend in July)
Staples Railroad Days, Staples, MN (3rd Weekend of August)

TRAVERSE COUNTY
EST. 1862 - POPULATION: 3,360

Traverse County's name comes from Lake Traverse, an 11,200-acre lake that separates Minnesota and South Dakota. It was established in 1862.

BROWNS VALLEY, MN
POPULATION: 558 – CITY 132 OF 856 (4-11-25)

The first village and original county seat of Traverse County, located in the Traverse Gap that once connected Lake Traverse and Big Stone Lake via a river channel, was initially named Lake Traverse for this unique geographical feature. In rare instances, floodwaters can flow from one drainage basin to another because of the Gap's perfect position along the path of a continental divide. The Brown family invested in one thousand acres of land in the valley when it was made available for settlement. Major Joseph Renshaw Brown became its earliest permanent settler in 1866-67. From 1867 to 1872, the post office kept the name Lake Traverse until the post office and the townsite were renamed Browns Valley upon Joseph's death. His son, Samuel J. Brown, was the postmaster from 1867 to 1878; he lived in the town for over half a century before his passing. His legacy and impact on Browns Valley are remembered today via the Sam Brown Memorial State Wayside and its historic post-and-plank construction, "Fort Wadsworth Agency and Scout Headquarters Building," a name given to it by the National Register of Historic Places in 1986. It was constructed in 1864 at South Dakota's Fort Wadsworth, but used by the Browns as a residence and store. Alongside their Browns, Searles & Downie store were blacksmith shops and real estate offices, Prescott & Company's store, William Cameron's store, and the drug store of A. Cowles, the Larkin & Brothers general store, and eventually lumber yards, elevators, lawyers' offices, The Traverse House hotel, *The Browns Valley Reporter* newspaper (started on May 2, 1880), and other commercial lines. It lost its county seat to Wheaton in 1886 when county residents insisted on a more centralized capital city, but despite the loss, Browns Valley continued to grow. It welcomed the Great Northern Railroad, and by 1902, there were Episcopal, Methodist Episcopal, Presbyterian, and Catholic churches, as well as a public school. In 1915-16, the Browns Valley Carnegie Library was erected as the most architecturally stunning building in the community. As many as 1,117 people lived in the community, according to the 1950 Census. Amongst its most famous residents of past and present are Charles M. Dale, the 66th Governor of New Hampshire; Charles Burnett, the Chief of the Air Staff of the Royal Australian Air Force during World War II; Arthur C. Townley, the founder of the National Non-Partisan League that found itself infiltrating the North Dakota and Minnesota state governments in the 1910s, and Osborne Cowles, a head coach for basketball, football, and baseball teams with multiple college institutions between 1922 and 1959.

DUMONT, MN
POPULATION: 75 – CITY 134 OF 856 (4-11-25)
Dumont was born during the construction of the Fargo and Southern Railroad, whose crews were trekking across the plains and laying the track in 1884. They were met by a French hunter who helped supply the workers with food as they worked; his friendliness and hunting abilities were so much appreciated that the railroad officials named the town in his honor. Steam engines brought with them enough settlers to warrant the establishment of a small business district, and on April 1, 1885, Dumont was platted. A branch office of the postal service arrived the following year. Michael Zemple served as postmaster and was responsible for building the first four buildings on the townsite. District No. 33 school began in the 1890s, and in 1900, the local Catholic community erected a church. Their private parochial school operated from 1918 to 1968. The Chicago, Milwaukee & St. Paul Railroad town peaked at 238 residents in the 1940s, not far from the 236 people it had at its inaugural Census in 1900. The most significant event in the town's history occurred on June 22, 1919, when a tornado swept through, destroying a substantial part of the fledgling village. Dick Bremer, the voice of the Minnesota Twins on television from 1983 to 2023 and a sportscaster for several Minnesota Golden Gophers collegiate programs, spent time in Dumont during his youth.

TINTAH, MN
POPULATION: 67 – CITY 141 OF 856 (4-11-25)
Located in the far northeast corner of Traverse County, little Tintah, population 67, derived its name from a Dakota word meaning "prairie." The *Tintonha* nickname was also given to the tribes because of their rule and dominance over the prairies of southwest Minnesota. The town was established when the Great Northern opened a station in section 3 of the township in 1872. It would be another 15 years before Tintah was platted as an actual townsite, and in 1880, it welcomed a post office, with postmaster Charles Smith at its helm. J. E. Henry was the first to start a business, the Tintah Hotel. Mr. Trumbee and Charles Smith hosted the first store in that building. Although the Great Northern crossed the Minneapolis, St. Paul & Sault Ste. Marie (the Soo Line) Railroad, about a mile north of town, and another branch of the Great Northern connected with Tintah's line running eastbound towards Elbow Lake in Grant County. The population of Tintah never surpassed 249 people in the 1920s. It would have had storefronts and shops, liveries, hotels, a bank (opened in 1901 and shuttered in 1929), St. Gail's Catholic Church, and a Congregational church.

WHEATON, MN ★☆
POPULATION: 1,460 – CITY 133 OF 856 (4-11-25)

The "Wheaton Mallard," one of the largest ducks in the world, has been welcoming visitors to the Traverse County seat since its construction in 1960 under the direction of Robert Bruns and Elmer Olson. But the community dates back much earlier than that, to September 1, 1884, when the Fargo Southern (later the Chicago, Milwaukee & St. Paul Railroad) was being built. Initially, the name was to be Swedenburg in honor of the townsite owners, Swan C. and Ole Odenborg, but they declined the honor. Instead, they thought it should be named after the townsite surveyor, Daniel Thompson Wheaton. The name stuck, and the post office changed from Lake Valley to Wheaton five years after it had been organized. As settlement began to pick up throughout the region, many became frustrated by the long treks required to conduct government business in Browns Valley. The solution to their problem was simple: move the county seat to Wheaton, the most centralized town in their jurisdiction. This action was done in 1886, just two years after its founding. Knowing the importance of holding the seat of government, Browns Valley went so far as to hire a private detective who claimed Wheaton had won the county seat election through "fraudulent voters." A three-fifths majority was needed to carry the removal of the county seat. Wheaton had only 59.06% of the vote (668 for and 463 against). Representatives of the town went to Governor Lucius F. Hubbard to obtain a formal decree recognizing their election victory, and their wish was granted: they were officially designated the judicial seat. For years, the skirmishes continued until 1889, when Wheaton finally acquired the county records and its title for good. Wheaton's population grew rapidly to 883 people by 1890. Its business district was extensive, as entrepreneurs had set up general, drug, hardware, and implement stores; others had blacksmith shops or livery stables; and organizations were established to accommodate the educational, religious, and fraternal/entertainment needs of Wheatonites. The Wheaton Depot, built in 1906, remains one of the best-preserved buildings from the town's early days. It was listed on the National Register of Historic Places on August 23, 1985, a week after Larson's Hunters Resort had acquired the same designation. The historic property was rented as a hunting lodge by Andrew and Bertha Larson, who hosted upwards of 50 to 60 guests at a time in their sizeable 14-room house and eight additional buildings.

Unincorporated/Ghost Towns: Boisberg, Charlesville, Collis, Dakomin

National Register of Historic Places:
Browns Valley: Browns Valley Carnegie Public Library, Fort Wadsworth Agency & Scout Headquarters Building
Taylor Township: District No.44 School
Wheaton: Chicago, Milwaukee, & St. Paul Depot, Larson's Hunters Resort

Golf Courses:
Wheaton Country Club, Daily Fee (Wheaton, MN)

Town Celebrations:
Sam Brown Days, Browns Valley, MN (Last Full Weekend in June)

WABASHA COUNTY
EST. 1849 - POPULATION: 21,387

Wabasha III, former chief of the Mdewakanton Dakota and a firm opponent of the Dakota War of 1862, is the namesake of one of Minnesota's original nine counties.

ELGIN, MN
POPULATION: 1,115 – CITY 707 OF 856 (10-17-25)
Known as the "Butter Capital of the World" in its dairying heyday, Elgin village was named after the Scottish town and was formerly known as West Greenwood. Its founding date is set to November 1878, when the Winona & Saint Peter Railroad branch connecting Eyota and Plainview was completed. Several Vermonters had arrived much earlier in 1855 to live in the area: George and Curtis Bryant, George Farrar, and Henry Atherton. Bryant was postmaster when the post office commenced distributing local letters and parcels in 1857. Miss Gould was Elgin's first teacher when a schoolhouse was built. With many decades of hard work, residents greatly expanded the town's commercial district. In 1896, those moving from south to north would have found a Farmers' elevator, a depot, two additional elevators, a feed mill, a blacksmith shop, and stockyards. A German Lutheran school and church were situated in Elgin's northwest corner, and in the southeast, one could find the school, another church, and a livery. Park Street was full of businesses at this point, including six stores, two saloons, an implement store, a meat market, two hotels, The First State Bank of Elgin, a hardware store, a drug store, a doctor's office, a wagon shop, and a blacksmith shop. More places had existed before, but a November 1889 fire destroyed one of Elgin's banks, a dance hall, and a saloon. A second bank, The Farmers and Merchants State Bank, had opened by 1920, as had the *Elgin Monitor* newspaper office, the Elgin Cheese Factory, the Elgin Ice Company, and the Elgin Co-operative Creamery.

HAMMOND, MN
POPULATION: 130 – CITY 709 OF 856 (10-17-25)
Hammond's name honors Joseph Hammond, the original owner of the townsite, before the Chicago, Milwaukee & St. Paul Railroad established a station in the area. When the post office was organized, it was known as Hammonsford between 1878 and 1881, until the "ford" was dropped from the name. Despite never having a population higher than 252 people (as of 1940), Hammond, in its heyday circa 1896, was the site of School District No. 2, a depot, two churches, the N. Brochures store, the Dale & Arnold hardware store, the Wabasha Lumber Company sheds & office, and J. M. McLaughlin's barn and regent office. While the Zumbro River brought much prosperity to Hammond, it was also the cause of one of the town's most devastating events in its history, when two-thirds of the local homes were severely damaged in historic September 2010 flooding that forced evacuations.

KELLOGG, MN
POPULATION: 415 – CITY 704 OF 856 (10-17-25)
Nestled within the stunning bluffs of the Mississippi River is the little town of Kellogg, which was named out of an act of kindness for L. H. Kellogg, who furnished the signs for the local Chicago, Milwaukee & St. Paul depot. Laid out in 1870 and incorporated in 1877, Kellogg had a similar array of businesses to those one would have expected in that era. The local post office was called Pawselin from 1862 to 1872. By the time a business directory was created by Geo. Ogle & Company in 1896, Kellogg's commercial lines ranged from a creamery, elevator, and stockyard to general stores, saloons, hotels, and blacksmith shops. While these lines are familiar to many, Kellogg has, in recent years, made a name for itself by establishing "the best toy store in Minnesota," Lark Toys. The 20,000-square-foot facility is widely considered one of America's best toy stores for its original handmade toys, antique toy museum, working carousel, blue waterfalls, miniature golf course, ice cream counter, and selection of arts, crafts, games, and puzzles. Just down the road is SVJ Creative Designs, the

brainchild statuary of Shelly and David Speedling that has shipped thousands of statues—from the "Hog Wild" pig statues throughout Martin County, to White Bear Lake's beloved polar bears, and military statues for veteran memorials—throughout Minnesota and the rest of the country. Mississippi River Lock and Dam No. 4 is nearby and has been restraining the waters of The Big Muddy since its opening in May 1935.

LAKE CITY, MN
POPULATION: 5,252 – CITY 556 OF 856 (8-31-25)

"The Birthplace of Waterskiing," Lake City, was originally a part of a 32-by-15-mile tract of land called "The Sioux Half-Breed Reserve on Lake Pepin." This unique area was carved out of Dakota tribal lands by the 1830 Prairie du Chien Treaty to give land to European men and to Dakota women. By 1857, a scrip issued by Henry Rice relinquished the rights provided by the treaty in exchange for 640 acres of unoccupied, unsurveyed land. Over six hundred people were eligible for the scrip, and every eligible person was removed by the end of the decade. Jacob Boody, a land speculator, arrived in 1853. Three years later, men by the surnames Doghtys, Dwelly, and Tibbits platted the town of Lake City in 1855-56, and the race was on to build up the port town on Lake Pepin. The settlers voted to name the village Lake City, and the lake was named for Father Louis Hennepin, who camped on the lakeshore in 1680. Harvey F. Williamson owned the general store in which the first Lake City post office was established. The State Legislature allowed a port market for grain to be established in 1864 because of its prime positioning on the lake. Within two years, the port was reportedly bringing in over $1.5 million, the modern-day (2025) equivalent of about $30.5 million. On February 26, 1872, the city was incorporated in anticipation of the arrival of the Chicago, Milwaukee & St. Paul Railroad. By 1910, there were at least four hotels, five churches, one newspaper, one bank, and several stores in place. Aside from its prominent nursery industry, many of the town's major historical events were centered around its situation on the lake. On July 13, 1890, the Sea Wing was overturned by a strong squall line, killing 98 people in the worst maritime disaster in Minnesota history. The freshwater clam and pearl-button industry took off in the 1880s and continued well into the 1920s. Ralph Samuelson, who experimented with staves from wooden barrels and pine boards, successfully pioneered water skiing in the summer of 1922. His invention led to the annual Water Ski Days celebration, held annually during the last full weekend in June. In addition to the 1868 Greek Revival/Neoclassical William-Russell-Rahilly and the 1872 Carpenter Gothic James C. and Agnes M. Stout homes, the Lake City City Hall, built in 1899, is the city's most historic and architecturally appealing structure. Famous men and women with Lake City ties are Mark McKenzie, a composer who has orchestrated music in movies including *Men in Black* (1997), *Lilo & Stitch* (2002), *The Nightmare Before Christmas* (2003), and *Spider-Man 1* and *2* (2002 and 2004, respectively); Randy Breuer, an NBA center from 1983 to 1994 with four different franchises; Mary Pat Gleason, an Emmy Award-winning writer and the character Jane Hogan in CBS's daytime soap opera *Guiding Light*; John Kobs, the head baseball coach of Michigan State University baseball from 1925 to 1963, and Taylor Heise, a professional ice hockey forward with the Minnesota Frost of the Professional Women's Hockey League.

Restaurant Recommendation:
Lake House on Pepin
1702 N Lakeshore Dr
Lake City, MN 55041

MAZEPPA, MN
POPULATION: 874 – CITY 711 OF 856 (10-17-25)
Joseph Fuller, Enoch Young, I. O. Seely, and C. C. Sleeper were the original four men to call the Mazeppa area home, having arrived in February 1855. Over that next year, John E. Hyde built a store, G. W. Judd became the local blacksmith, O. D. Ford erected a hotel, and a saw and grist mill were raised to harness the power of the Zumbro River. Ivan Mazeppa, a Cossack chief made famous by a Lord Byron poem, became the town's namesake when it came time to name the local post office, and later, the station on the Chicago, Milwaukee & St. Paul line. It was nicknamed the "Bug Line" because of its odd twists and curves as it followed the Zumbro eastward to Hammond and Millville. Over 600 barrels of flour were produced each day at the local mills at their peak, powered by the 26-foot-tall wooden dam and "Mill Pond" that served the community until February 2, 1891, when it was burned. A survey conducted five years later showed that Mazeppa at that time had an elevator, a lumber shed, a stockyard, a public park and bandstand, two churches, and a school, amongst numerous other businesses. A walking bridge for horse-and-buggy traffic over the river was built in 1904, offering spectacular views of the local mill and pond. While many of these original places are now gone, Mazeppa is still home to the historic 1904 Walnut Street Pratt truss bridge and the 1917-1919 Lake Zumbro Hydroelectric Generating Plant on the northern end of Lake Zumbro. Trains stopped running to Mazeppa in 1952, but the new high school building was still completed in 1958. On December 26, 1975, a conflagration nearly destroyed the building (as it did the elementary school). Keith Ramthun and Joseph Liffrig heroically closed the fire doors between the two buildings, allowing the fire department to arrive and extinguish the blaze. Leonard "Stub" Allison, best known for coaching the 1937 national champion University of California football program, was born here in 1892.

MILLVILLE, MN
POPULATION: 151 – CITY 708 OF 856 (10-17-25)
The Millville, Minnesota, of 1896 boasted five stores, two saloons, a blacksmith shop, a Lodge Hall, a church, a lumber office, and stockyards. Interestingly, the town was named for its promising location on the Zumbro River and was expected to host a great grist mill, although no such structure was ever constructed. A post office opened using the Millville name in 1867, but the village itself was not incorporated until June 1899, well after the arrival of the Chicago, Milwaukee & St. Paul Railroad. Charles F. Read, the namesake of Reads Landing, was also Millville's first postmaster. Local Swedish, Norwegian, and German congregations were instrumental in building and using a Swedish Evangelical Lutheran Church; it was built in 1874 and added to the National Register on January 19, 1989.

MINNEISKA, MN
POPULATION: 97 – CITY 703 OF 856 (10-17-25)
Loosely translating to "water white" in the Dakota language, Minneiska was one of a chain of river towns established along the Mississippi River to take advantage of its trade potential. It was platted in 1854 and had a post office by 1856, which briefly changed its name to "Mount Vernon" between April and September of that year before becoming Minneiska for good. It was discontinued in 1985. Once home to as many as 395 citizens in the 1910s, the community had six stores, three elevators, a hotel, a livery barn, a blacksmith shop, a saloon, an ice house, two churches, a school, and a depot. It was incorporated on March 4, 1857, but separated from the township only on May 9, 1921. Seven gas stations, a two-story school, a brewery, a Temperance Hall,

and several more ice houses were later established. Putnam Gray, the inventor of the Ferris wheel, built a towering three-story castle that was a tourist attraction and oddity to those traveling by steamboat from St. Louis, Missouri.

PLAINVIEW, MN
POPULATION: 3,483 – CITY 706 OF 856 (10-17-25)
Once an underdog contender for the Wabasha County seat of government, Plainview was established as Centerville before its name was changed to Plainview in 1856 for its location on a high central prairie. For miles around, the city could be seen "plain as day" from miles away. Platting of town lots was underway in the summer of 1857, the same year that the local post office can trace its origins to. Six hundred thirty-seven people lived in Plainview in 1870, when its first Census was conducted, and by the dawn of the 20th century, it had a population of about 1,000. The Winona & Saint Peter Railroad entered the village during that timeframe and spurred a plethora of developments, including five churches, a depot, a public school, and a creamery. One of the churches was ultimately redeveloped into the Plainview Area History Center. Two miles south of town is Carley State Park, best known for its location in Minnesota's Driftless Area and its bluebell flowers that bloom every spring. Slim Dunlap, a guitarist and singer-songwriter with the Replacements from 1987 to 1991, and author Jon Hassler have Plainview connections.

WABASHA, MN ★☆
POPULATION: 2,559 – CITY 705 OF 856 (10-17-25)
One of Minnesota's oldest communities was forged out of the logging, milling, and clamming industries and was first called Cratte's Landing by a blacksmith who built his shop atop a levee on the Mississippi. In an area that was home to an early British trading post (owned by Augustin Rocque) and Alexis P. Bailly's 1834 trading post, this part of the river always appeared to be destined for widespread settlement. In 1843, an influx of settlers began to arrive, and the Dakota name *Wabashaw*, meaning "red leaf," was given to the Mdewakanton Dakota-Anishinaabe chief. Twenty-five years later, the "w" was dropped. A. S. Hart platted Wabasha in 1855, and in 1857, the 75-mile-long Mendota to Wabasha road was completed. It served as an early predecessor to the same pathway that the Minnesota Central Railroad would later follow to help connect the city with towns and cities far beyond the Mississippi River Valley. From 1860 to 1870, the Wabasha County seat's population boomed by 94.5%, from 894 to 1,739, and many unique places, such as a library, a tuberculosis sanitarium, and a pearl button factory, began to develop. Dozens of businesses came to fruition over the next several decades, including a designated cigar store, a theatre, a paint store, and a gobbler. It is likely that this gobbler, an early turkey processing plant, was one of the first such specialized places in all of Minnesota. By 1915, there were seventeen elevators, a boat yard, a lumber company, the Big Jo Flour Mill, the Wells Fargo Express Company, the Anderson Hotel, a fire department, a health department, two banks, nine lodges, five churches, and two public schools. Wabasha's Commercial Historic District, consisting of 52 properties built between 1856 and 1928, was established in the 1980s to preserve much of Wabasha's earliest settlers' developments. The 1856 Hurd House/Anderson Hotel is one of its most famous contributing properties. Grace Memorial Episcopal Church (known for its famous Tiffany glass window) is another local landmark built in 1900 by architect Cass Gilbert, as is the 1879 Wabasha County Poor House hospital. The Alexander Thoirs House, erected in 1868, is Wabasha's oldest surviving brick house, and is joined on the NRHP by several other local homes, including the 1874 William H. and Alma Downer

Campbell home, the 1878 Lucas Kuehn Italianate house, the 1882 Henry S. and Magdalena Schwedes and Lorenz and Lugerde Ginthner Italianate homes, and the 1888 Italianate Clara and Julius Schmidt House. Although not related to history, Wabasha was selected as the home of the National Eagle Center because of its natural location on prime bald eagle-hunting grounds at the confluence of the Mississippi and Chippewa Rivers, where fish naturally congregate year-round. The 1993 romantic comedy film *Grumpy Old Men* and its 1995 sequel, *Grumpier Old Men*, are both set in Wabasha, though none of the film's scenes were shot there. Noted Wabashians include Larry Brandenburg, an actor with appearances in the 1994 prison drama *The Shawshank Redemption* and the 1994 comedy *The Santa Clause*; Baron von Raschke, a former professional wrestler; John Van Dyke, a U.S. Congressman from New Jersey from 1847 to 1851; Tom Tiffany, a U.S. Congressman since 2020 from Wisconsin, and Mdewakanton Dakota chief Tamaha "Standing Moose."

Restaurant Recommendation:
Silver Star Saloon & Grill
170 Pembroke Ave
Wabasha, MN 55981

Lodging Recommendation:
The Historic Anderson House Hotel
333 Main St W
Wabasha, MN 55981

ZUMBRO FALLS, MN
POPULATION: 155 – CITY 710 OF 856 (10-17-25)

Repeated flooding has caused many problems for this community on the "Riviers des Embarrass," a.k.a. The River of Difficulties. In 1855, a small settlement began when the Tibbetts brothers built homes on either side of the river and operated a ferry between them. They sold it three years later. In 1866, Benjamin Clark built a gristmill and a dam, which formed a small waterfall known to locals as Zumbro Falls. From 1857 to 1858 and 1869 to 1872, a post office used that name intermittently, before deciding to use it for good beginning in 1873. Uriah S. Whaley platted the original townsite, and the Midland Railroad, ultimately part of the Chicago, Milwaukee & St. Paul Railroad system, came through in the late 1870s and helped spur the development of many businesses, churches, and schools. An 1896 plat shows that the original Zumbro Falls site (home to two churches) was located northwest of the present site. The "present" town of that time had a school, a depot, a hotel, a livery barn, and a stockyard. Zumbro Falls was incorporated by the county commissioners on February 28, 1898, after several townspeople petitioned for that designation. Local NRHP sites in the vicinity include the 1874 Bear Valley Grange Hall, the 1937 double-arch Zumbro Parkway Bridge, and the 1938 Works Progress Administration No. 5827 arch bridge. After the September 2010 flood that decimated many local communities, Zumbro Falls experienced decrease in population from 207 residents to 155.

Bellechester is only partially located in Wabasha County (see Goodhue County).

Unincorporated/Ghost Towns: Bear Valley, Camp Lacupolis, Conception, Dumfries, Jarrett, Maple Springs, Oak Center, Reads Landing, South Troy, Theilman, Weaver, West Albany, West Newton

National Register of Historic Places:
Lake City: Lake City City Hall, James C. & Agnes M. Stout House, Williamson-Russel-Rahilly House, Lake City & Rochester Stage Road-Mount Pleasant Section, Patrick H. Rahilly House
Mazeppa: Walnut Street Bridge, Lake Zumbro Hydroelectric Generating Plant
Millville: Swedish Evangelical Lutheran Church
Reads Landing: Reads Landing School, Reads Landing Overlook
Wabasha: William H. & Alma Downer Campbell House, Lorenz & Lugerde Ginthner House, Grace Memorial Episcopal Church Hurd House-Anderson Hotel, Lucas Kuehn House, Clara & Julius Schmidt House, Henry S. & Magdalena Schwedes House, Alexander Thoirs House, Wabasha Commercial Historic District, Wabasha County Poor House
Weaver: Weaver Mercantile Building
Zumbro Falls: Bridge No. 5827-Zumbro Falls, Zumbro Parkway Bridge, Bear Valley Grange Hall

Golf Courses:
Coffee Mill Golf Course, Daily Fee (Wabasha, MN)
Lake City Golf, Daily Fee (Lake City, MN)
Lake Pepin Golf Course, Daily Fee (Lake City, MN)
Piper Hills Golf Course, Daily Fee (Plainview, MN)
The Jewel Golf Club, Daily Fee (Lake City, MN)

Breweries/Wineries/Distilleries:
Reads Landing Brewery (Reads Landing, MN)
Whitewater Wines (Plainview, MN)

Town Celebrations:
Cheese Days, Elgin, MN (Father's Day Weekend)
Corn on the Cob Days, Plainview, MN (3rd Weekend of August)
Grumpy Old Men Festival, Wabasha, MN (Last Weekend in February)
Mazeppa Daze, Mazeppa, MN (2nd Full Weekend in July)
SeptOberfest, Wabasha, MN (Last Weekend in September, First Weekend in October)
Wabasha Riverboat Days, Wabasha, MN (Last Weekend in July)
Water Ski Days, Lake City, MN (Last Full Weekend in June)
Watermelon Festival, Kellogg, MN (Weekend after Labor Day)

WADENA COUNTY
EST. 1858 - POPULATION: 14,065

Parts of Cass County and Todd County were amalgamated together to create Wadena County in 1858, which was most likely named in honor of Chief Wadena of the Ojibwe.

ALDRICH, MN
POPULATION: 35 – CITY 226 OF 856 (5-6-25)
Wadena County's first permanent settlement and post office (first headed by Michael W. Kelly) was established on the banks of the Partridge River circa 1877 and named by the Northern Pacific Railroad Company for Cyrus Aldrich. He was a U.S. Congressman. Within three years, it had a blacksmith shop, carriage works, a saloon, and a pair of general stores. The railroad gave it a growth impetus that also helped to bring a creamery, a hotel, a lumber yard, an elevator, a railroad depot and section house, a one-room schoolhouse (established in 1883), a First Congregational Church, and the first Catholic church in the county. The Congregational church was destroyed by fire in 1961. The former Mother of Sorrows Catholic Church building, built initially in 1870, remains standing. Aldrich's residents sought incorporation as a village in the late 1930s and achieved the feat on March 4, 1938. Its first census recorded an all-time high population of 152 people in 1940. However, it likely had a higher population

closer to its founding. Ted and Gen's BBQ Steakhouse was a community staple for many years. During its tenure, it was known for having the "largest open pit barbecue in Minnesota" and attracting visitors from far beyond the county's borders.

MENAHGA, MN
POPULATION: 1,340 – CITY 222 OF 856 (5-5-25)

"The Gateway to the Pines" and "The Home of St. Urho" derive their names from an Ojibwe word meaning "blueberry." Spelled as Meenahga by Henry W. Longfellow's poem, *The Song of Hiawatha*, this fruit once abundantly grew throughout the region. It was a popularly traded item among native tribes, early Scandinavian (most of them Finnish) immigrants, and European immigrants. The first of these settlers arrived in the 1860s, but it would not be until 1891 that E. Jones laid out a town site on Spirit Lake. Jones with the arrival of the Great Northern Railway. "Uncle" Charles Lane pushed for the community's incorporation, a goal achieved on August 20, 1892. He was responsible for establishing much of Menahga's early infrastructure. Colonel William Crooks, a railroad employee, chose the town's name. By 1906, Menahga had grown to roughly 350 residents. The following lines were in order: three elevators, a flour mill, a stockyard, a hotel, a bank, a lumber yard, a feed barn, and some other stores. Visitors at that time would have also noticed a public school building in the southern part of town, a Methodist Episcopal church, and a section house. The American Grass Company was its most renowned business, a rug and mat manufacturer that used the area's tough wire grass to make its goods. Logging was another critical part of its early economic development, which ties into its primary nickname, given in 1916 when the Louisiana State governor traveled the entirety of the newly-laid Jefferson Highway and declared that he had traveled "from the palms [of the beaches] to the pines [of Minnesota]." The town's other nickname, "The Home of St. Urho," dates to a tale invented by the department store manager, Richard L. Mattson, in 1956. Mattson, a Finn, devised a story about the heroic efforts of the Finnish priest St. Urho, who saved his country by casting a swarm of dog-sized grasshoppers into the sea and killing many more with his giant pitchfork. He first set St. Urho's Day as May 24 but changed it to March 16, a day before St. Patrick's Day, to spite his Irish coworkers. Three statues of the grasshopper vanquisher are on display throughout the city: one at a mausoleum in the Menahga City Cemetery, another at the Menahga Area Museum, and the third in a roadside park. Wallace Wood, a comic book writer and artist best known for establishing the iconic red costume of Marvel's Daredevil superhero and working on early issues of *MAD Magazine* from 1952 to 1964, was born here on June 17, 1927. Don Monson, the head coach of the University of Idaho and the University of Oregon men's basketball programs from 1978 to 1983 and from 1983 to 1992, also hails from Menahga.

NIMROD, MN
POPULATION: 84 – CITY 224 OF 856 (5-6-25)

While a name like "Nimrod" elicits a lot of chuckles in the modern era, the word now meaning "foolish" was initially chosen by its settlers to honor Nimrod, the grandson of Ham in the Bible. He was a mighty hunter and was responsible for the construction of the Tower of Babel. The negative connotation originated in a 1940 *Looney Tunes* episode in which Daffy Duck called Elmer Fudd a "nimrod," and the name stuck. Without a railroad, Nimrod served primarily as a halfway point for merchants traveling the Wheat Trail between Shell City and Verndale. Jake Graba put up a halfway house here, which was later purchased by Paluski Williams in 1885, who turned it into a hotel. His wife, Mary L. Williams, served as postmaster until 1903. The local post office continued until 1916, and then a new rural station was established in 1938. Nimrod's incorporation as a village occurred in 1924, and its highest population was 112 in the 1950s. Dick Stigman, an All-Star pitcher with the MLB's Cleveland Indians in 1960 who played from 1960 to 1966, was born here on January 24, 1936. The town's 90-foot-tall fire tower, built in 1928, has been recognized as a nationally historic lookout.

SEBEKA, MN
POPULATION: 741 – CITY 223 OF 856 (5-6-25)

Colonel William Crooks, the chief engineer of the Manitoba Railway (later annexed by the Great Northern), named Sebeka for the Ojibwe word *sibi*, meaning "the village beside the river." On the Red Eye River, the town plat was made in 1891, the same year a post office branch was established in John Anderson's general store. With the railroad's arrival the following year, immigrants (most of them being Finnish) began to come in droves, and the town's development was well underway. After its incorporation on March 19, 1898, the population nearly doubled from 223 citizens to 428 between 1900 and 1910. Business lines of all varieties were established, from blacksmith shops and hotels to a sawmill, a bank, an elevator, stockyards, and stores. German Catholic and Methodist Episcopal church edifices and the primary and public school buildings stood on East 3rd Street in a centralized religious and educational district. In 1938, the famous New Deal muralist Richard Haines was commissioned to produce a fresco painting using the casein paint process in the Sebeka High School building. Two noted figures of the town's past and present include Patrick Volkerding, the founder of the Slackware Linux distribution, and Kenneth Arnold, the pilot who spotted and reported the first nationally covered modern UFO sighting in June 1947. He reportedly saw nine silver-colored discs flying in sync as he passed near Mount Rainier, Washington. The Sebeka Historical Society hosts the local city museum in a pioneer cabin, with exhibits on the Jefferson Highway and Finnish culture and history.

VERNDALE, MN
POPULATION: 511 – CITY 227 OF 856 (5-6-25)

Named in honor of Helen "Vernie" Smith, the granddaughter of early pioneer settler Lucas W. Smith, the town's first general store owner and postmaster. Verndale sits between a pocket of pine trees to its northwest and a gorgeous prairie on the opposite side, which led to it being called "the most beautiful townsite along the Northern Pacific [Railroad] between Brainerd [Minnesota] and Fargo [North Dakota]." Captain John E. Butler, Charles W. Brown, Charles C. Kelly, and John B. Kelly were the first four men to make claims near the future townsite in July 1877; by 1878, the post office had been organized, and the Northern Pacific Railroad had been laid. Throughout that year and the ones to follow, the Crandall House hotel opened, as did G. H. Clark's hotel, C. C. Parker's store, W. H. Raymond's general supply store, L. W. Farwell's lumber yard, Dr. H. J. Harding's drug store, C. E. Bullard's implement and tool store, E. L. Ingalls blacksmith shop, a second blacksmith shop and lumber yard, a butcher shop, a shoemaker, and a newspaper. A 1906 plat map drawn by the Title Atlas Company shows the presence of an electric light plant, two elevators, stockyards, a depot, a village hall, a bank, a creamery, Public School No. 5, a Methodist church, an Adventist church, and even a bandstand across from the depot on the railroad tracks. Its grist mill was the first of its kind in northern Minnesota. It was built in 1880 by Thomas C. Myers and his crew of 25 men after residents met and decided they needed the firm to advance their growth. It was at this time that Verndale had its peak population of 672 residents, according to the 1900 Census. Those numbers have never been reported as being lower than 504 people (according to the 1980 Census). With its success as a bustling milling center, Verndale sought to gain the attention of Wadena County officials, presenting itself as the county's principal town to secure the coveted seat of government from Wadena. They built a courthouse in 1884 for $9,000 in the Second Empire style and offered it to the county for free if they moved the seat to the new courthouse. The county declined, but in 1886, an election was held that determined the seat should remain in Wadena. Interestingly, there were only about 600 registered voters in the election, yet well over 1,000 ballots were cast, and Wadena won by 474 votes. A Catholic academy briefly opened in the old courthouse from 1892 to 1894. Later, its second floor was used as an opera house until the town's electrical engine caught fire, burning the building to the ground on January 5, 1912. Lesley J. McNair, a lieutenant general posthumously promoted to the rank of general following his death during World War II, hails from Verndale.

WADENA, MN ★☆
POPULATION: 4,325 – CITY 228 OF 856 (5-6-25)

The "Largest Puzzle in the World" throughout the Wadena County seat depicts over a thousand years of Minnesota history and invites visitors to wander about the downtown and admire one of over 100 hand-painted murals that tell the story of the Land of 10,000 Lakes. They were painted by over forty artists who worked in unison to complete the project and tell the story. While the murals focus on the state as a whole, the history of Wadena began early in 1782, when the first of three successive trading posts was established in an area now called Old Wadena County Park. Here, early European fur trappers established contact with the indigenous people and conducted trade for many decades. The first well-known post was Jean-Baptiste Cadotte's 1792 establishment. After the abandonment of that post and a subsequent 1825 post, the Wadena townsite was organized in 1856 by Augustus Aspinwall at the point where the Woods Oxcart Trail crossed the Crow Wing River. He called it Wadena for the Ojibwe chief of the same name. Aspinwall built a general store, hotel, ferry, and post office, but sadly, the townsite failed due to the Panic of 1857 and the events of the Dakota War of 1862. New attempts were made to settle the area in the fall of 1871, and in time, Wadena became a critical junction for the Northern Pacific and the Great Northern Railroads. It was declared the county seat by an act of the legislature on February 21, 1873. Despite the best attempts of Verndale residents to acquire the title, the opposition never succeeded. Over 115,000 bushels of wheat were moving through the Wadena elevators by 1879, and its business district encompassed every imaginable line of enterprise. Methodist, Episcopal, and Congregational churches were in place by 1880. Three Wadena locations have been nominated for the National Register of Historic Places and have thus been preserved with extra care from its early days: the 1885 Commercial Hotel, an early Commercial Queen Anne Style edifice; the 1912 Wadena Fire and City Hall building built by the Harrison Brothers using Kirby T. Snyder's Renaissance Revival architectural style blueprints, and the 1915 Northern Pacific Passenger Depot, now a museum and event venue. The latter two structures, along with two large church edifices and several commercial buildings, were constructed during Wadena's 1910 to 1915 building boom. Until recently, there was a fourth location on the Register, the Peterson-Biddick Seed and Feed Company, which grew into one of Minnesota's most prominent independent agricultural companies. Now home to 4,325 residents, Wadena has persevered through modern trials and tribulations. On June 17, 2010, over a third of the city's homes were razed by an EF-4 tornado, as was the local high school and community center. A new middle-high school building opened in 2012 after students had attended classes for a few semesters at the local branch of the Minnesota State Community and Technical College. In 2015, Wadena made national headlines when the "Freedom From Religion" group threatened legal action against the City of Wadena for displaying a nativity scene in the city park. The city sold the set to a private buyer to avoid the lawsuit. In a humble act of retaliation against the organization, Wadena citizens erected over 1,000 nativity scenes throughout the city. The founder of Mars, Incorporated, Frank C. Mars, and his son Forrest Mars Sr., briefly lived in Wadena around Forrest's birth. Forrest was the mind behind the Milky Way candy bar, the Mars bar, and M&M's candies.

Restaurant Recommendation:
Uptown
224 Jefferson St S
Wadena, MN 56482

Staples is only partially located in Wadena County (see Todd County).

Unincorporated/Ghost Towns: Bluegrass, Huntersville, Leaf River, Oylen, Shell City

National Register of Historic Places:
Staples: Old Wadena Historic District
Wadena: Commercial Hotel, Northern Pacific Passenger Depot, Wadena Fire & City Hall

Golf Courses:
Blueberry Pines Golf Club, Daily Fee (Menahga, MN)
Whitetail Run Golf Course, Municipal (Wadena, MN)

Town Celebrations:
Jubilee Days, Nimrod, MN (Labor Day Weekend)
Midsummer Celebration, Menahga, MN (2nd Weekend of July)

WASECA COUNTY
EST. 1857 - POPULATION: 18,968

The borders of Waseca County have remained unchanged since its founding on February 27, 1857, when it was named for a Dakota word meaning "rich," in reference to its fertile soil.

JANESVILLE, MN
POPULATION: 2,421 – CITY 621 OF 856 (9-28-25)
Old Janesville was located on the west side of Lake Elysian and known as "Empire," but in 1856, J.W. Hosmer platted an addition and had the site renamed in honor of Mrs. Jane Sprague. It was known to early area immigrants as the site of the Ike Terill Trading Post and later as the post office, which began operating in 1858. When the Winona & Saint Peter Railroad was extended through the area about a decade later, a new townsite called East Janesville was laid out in August 1869, located on the line. As a result, ninety-plus percent of the buildings from the old site were moved to the railway village, and Old Janesville was wiped from existence. Janesville was incorporated as a village on May 10, 1870. After twenty-five years of progress, it had developed into a thriving community with four churches, two schools, a town hall, two hotels, three livery stables, a creamery, a bank, a mill, three lumber yards, and three grain elevators. An opera house and the Janesville Free Public Library, erected in 1912 using funds donated by the wealthy businessman and philanthropist Andrew Carnegie, were late additions to downtown Janesville. The town was famous in the early 20th century for its Hofmann Apiaries, one of the leading honey producers in the Upper Midwest, and the Seha Sorghum Mill, Minnesota's last surviving sorghum syrup

mill. It was active from 1904 to 1956. The apiary buildings, built from 1907 to 1933, can still be found at 4661 420th Ave. Folk art enthusiasts get a kick out of a space alien, a metal cowboy, and other quirky statues next to the old railroad depot. A couple of noteworthy individuals from Janesville's history are Albert Henry Woolson, the last surviving member of the United States Union Army, who grew up in Janesville and passed away near Duluth in 1956, and Aaron Sheehan, a classical singer and the 2015 Grammy Award winner for Best Opera Recording.

NEW RICHLAND, MN
POPULATION: 1,229 – CITY 647 OF 856 (10-1-25)

Colonists from Wisconsin and Norwegian immigrants settled in the present-day area of New Richland in June 1856, but the town, named for Richland County, Wisconsin, was not platted until August 1877. The Minneapolis and St. Louis Railroad had arrived four years earlier, and so Henry T. Wells took it upon himself to survey the land and lay out town lots along the tracks. John Larsen's store and post office predated most other earlier institutions in town, having been organized in 1870. Over time, the area was home to multiple meat markets and general stores, three hotels, two banks, two lumber yards, a creamery, a mill, a cheese factory, a poultry and egg factory, a movie theater, a school, and churches for the Catholic, Lutheran, and Congregational religious groups. The Strangers Refuge Lodge No. 74 of the Independent Order of Odd Fellows was built in 1902 and served New Richland's residents as a venue for local events and group meetings through the years. Different store owners began renting out the first floor in 1918, and local businesses operated out of the building until 1986, when the city took possession of the structure. In 2006, it underwent a complete renovation to become the New Richland Public Library. Gerald Gustafson, a recipient of the Air Force Cross and a fighter pilot during the Vietnam War, retired to New Richland in his later years.

Restaurant Recommendation:
Nancy Jane's Bakery
118 Broadway Ave N
New Richland, MN 56072

WALDORF, MN
POPULATION: 201 – CITY 646 OF 856 (10-1-25)

The smallest of Waseca County's four municipalities is Waldorf, which began in 1895 with the construction of the first Plum Valley Creamery building. A joint dry goods/grocery store and hardware store were built nearby, and later joined by a blacksmith shop and a bank. Plum Valley was already a thriving settlement, but when the "Alphabet Railroad," a part of the Chicago, Milwaukee & St. Paul Railroad, came through, they decided to name their village after a town in Waldorf, Maryland. Incorporated on November 22, 1920; it peaked at 285 people in the 1970s.

WASECA, MN ★☆
POPULATION: 9,229 – CITY 622 OF 856 (9-28-25)

J. C. Trowbridge is credited with suggesting the name "Waseca" for the first farming settlement in the area, established in 1855. The Dakota word translates to "rich in provisions" or "fertile," alluding to the fertile soils of Waseca County. Waseca, as we know it today, began in July 1867, when it was platted as a series of railroad stations on the Winona & St. Peter Railroad. Within a year, it had been incorporated on March 2, 1868, and became one of the state's primary wheat shipping hubs. One hundred twenty-nine buildings had been erected, most of them homes, and over 700 people lived in town. Its impressive growth enabled it to overtake Wilton as the Waseca County seat in 1870. By the turn of the century, its population had surpassed 3,000, and it welcomed a second railroad with the arrival of the Minneapolis & St. Louis line. By 1915, a breakfast food factory, a wholesale grocery enterprise, bottling works, and impressive milling facilities were in place. One account suggests that the Chicago & North Western (a successor to the Winona & St. Peter Railroad) paid its resident employees a monthly wage of $20,000, which would be a modern-day (2025) equivalent of approximately $640,000. In 1912, Waseca was selected by the University of Minnesota as the site of the Southeast Station experimental farm, which eventually evolved into the Southern School of Agriculture in 1953 and the University of Minnesota Waseca in 1971. Between the early 1970s and 1992, over twenty thousand students studied at the short-lived institution. The buildings have since been converted into the Federal Correctional Institution at Waseca, which briefly housed former Enron CEO Jeffrey Skilling. Two other major Waseca firms were started in 1923 and 1937, respectively. The first was Edgar F. and Ethel John's E.F. Johnson Company, a heavily surveilled major World War II supplier of defense materials, particularly radio transmission parts; the other was George Herter and his successful Herter's mail-order retailing business, now used by Cabela's and Bass Pro Shops. In addition to four historic homes owned by John W. Aughenbaugh, Philo C. Bailey, Roscoe P. Ward, and William R. Wolf, the Waseca County Courthouse, built in 1897; the W.J. Armstrong Company Wholesale Grocers warehouse, furnished in 1900, and the Waseca Commercial Historic District and its 54 contributing properties are listed on the National Register of Historic Places. Some famous persons from Waseca include Dave Kunst, the first person to walk around the world (14,450 miles) between 1970 and 1974; Leroy Shield, noted for his composition work on the *Our Gang* and *Laurel and Hardy* series; Gene Glynn, an MLB coach with several franchises between 1994 and 2019; Reverend Robert Alden of Little House on the Prairie fame; Tim Penny, a Member of the U.S. House of Representatives from Minnesota between 1983 and 1995; Ray Madden, a Member of the U.S. House of Representatives from Indiana from 1943 to 1977, and George Herter, the founder of the Herter's outdoor goods firm.

Restaurant Recommendation:
Oscar's All American Food & Drinks
1290-1380 State St N
Waseca, MN 56093

Elysian is only partially located in Waseca County (see Le Sueur County).

Unincorporated/Ghost Towns: Alma City, Lake Elysian, Matawan, Otisco, Palmer, Saint Mary, Smiths Mill, Vista, Wilton

National Register of Historic Places:
Janesville: Hofmann Apiaries, Janesville Free Public Library, Seha Sorghum Mill
New Richland: Strangers Refuge Lodge Number 74, IOOF
Otisco: Vista Lutheran Church
Waseca: w. J. Armstrong Company Wholesale Grocers, John W. Aughenbaugh House, Philo C. Bailey House, Roscoe P. Ward House, Waseca Commercial Historic District, Waseca County Courthouse, William R. Wolf House

Golf Courses:
Prairie Ridge Golf Course, Municipal (Janesville, MN)
Riverview Golf Course, Daily Fee (New Richland, MN)
Waseca Lakeside Club, Daily Fee (Waseca, MN)

Breweries/Wineries/Distilleries:
Half Pint Brewing Company (Waseca, MN)
Indian Island Winery (Janesville, MN)

WASHINGTON COUNTY
EST. 1849 - POPULATION: 267,568

Started as one of Minnesota's original nine counties when St. Croix County, Wisconsin Territory, was dissolved, this county's name honors George Washington, the first president of the United States.

AFTON, MN
POPULATION: 2,955 – CITY 563 OF 856 (8-31-25)
On paper, Afton changed overnight between 1970 and 1980, as its population during those ten years was recorded by the Census as growing from 248 individuals to 2,550 by the eighties, a staggering increase of 928.2%. What happened, in reality, was that Afton village and township both incorporated into the City of Afton, making it Minnesota's newest municipality in 1971. The first settler in the township where the Valley Creek empties into the St. Croix River came circa 1837. His name was Gaspare Bruce, a Canadian voyageur who was joined by Joseph Haskell and James S. Morris by the end of that decade. When it came time to give a name to the collection of homes and businesses that made up the area, Mrs. C. S. Getchel offered the name "Afton" for Robert Burns' poem *Afton Water*, with its hills and winding rills. Catfish Bar was an early alternate name for a sandbar in the St. Broix that allowed people and animals to ford during low water. A post office established in 1857 using the name Afton. Local grist mill owned by Lemuel Bolles was postmaster; other early businesses alongside the grist mill were Emil Asp's blacksmith shop, Spreeman's fish market, Charles Getchell's grocery store, the Patterson House hotel, the Cushing House hotel (still extant today as the Afton House Inn), and Selma's ice cream parlor. Churches and educational institutions existed as well, but the most famous of them all was The St. Croix Academy, built in 1868 and operational until 1884 as one of the first coed high schools in Minnesota. Afton's railroad of note was the Chicago, Milwaukee & St. Paul, which brought with it wealthy and famous men like Erastus Bolles and Newington Gilbert, whose historic Greek Revival homes still stand today. Two notable local points of interest are Afton State Park, known for its bluffs and glacial moraine along the St. Croix River, and Afton Alps, the closest ski and snowboard area to the Twin Cities. Jessie Diggins, a gold medalist with the 2018 Olympic U.S. women's team sprint freestyle skiing team, grew up in Afton. Jacob Fahlström, the first Swedish settler in Minnesota, and his wife, Margaret Bonga Fahlström, who was one of the very few free Ojibwe and African women in the vicinity in the 1840s, also have ties to the area.

Restaurant Recommendation:
The Lumberyard Pub
3121 St Croix Trail S
Afton, MN 55001

BAYPORT, MN
POPULATION: 4,024 – CITY 568 OF 856 (9-1-25)
Three smaller settlements on the St. Croix River were consolidated in January 1873 by the St. Croix Railway Improvement Company into "South Stillwater," a southern neighbor to Minnesota's original city, named after the river's calmness. Thirty years

before its establishment, some of the first settlers arrived, the first being François Bruce. Norman Kittson established an early trading post, likely the first instance of commerce on the site, but in 1852, Nelson, Loomis & Company changed the area's future with the establishment of a steam sawmill. Multiple other sawmills were established nearby, as were printing houses, furniture and box factories, a brass foundry, a soap factory, boatyards, and the St. Croix Lake Ice Company, which was shipping over two thousand railcars of ice each year to the Twin Cities and La Crosse, Wisconsin. Many lines of business flourished, but sawmills were the city's main economic driver. One such company, the Andersen Lumber Company, came to town in 1913 before eventually rebranding as Andersen Corporation, the largest window and patio door manufacturer in North America. They have annual revenues of over $3 billion, making them one of the largest privately held companies in the United States. Originally, Andersen came to town to take advantage of Chicago, St. Paul, Minneapolis & Omaha and the Chicago, Milwaukee & St. Paul Railroad lines. An electric streetcar, supposedly the "first of its kind," connected South Stillwater with Bayport from July 1889 to 1892 before shutting down. Streetcars had a resurgence in 1905 and operated until 1932, when South Stillwater was no more. By that point, its name had changed to Bayport (officially in 1922) after railroad and postal authorities deemed it too confusing to have two "Stillwaters" so close in proximity to one another. Bayport's population has steadily grown over the decades, and by the 21st century, it was heavily associated with the Minnesota Correctional Facility - Stillwater. Built from 1910 to 1914 and now listed on the National Register of Historic Places, the prison was built as the American prototype of a central-spine-and-crosstree design derived from Fresnes Prison in France. At the time of its completion, it was considered to be one of the most advanced penal facilities in the country. *The Prison Mirror* is still published as the oldest continuously-operating prison newspaper in the United States.

BIRCHWOOD VILLAGE, MN
POPULATION: 863 – CITY 594 OF 856 (9-3-25)
"Birchwood Village, a City of the Fourth Class," was developed on the shores of White Bear Lake by wealthy residents of Saint Paul looking for a summer getaway on the lake. At the turn of the century, the Lakewood Park and Orchard Homesites developments were furnished after streetcar service was extended between Wildwood Park and White Bear Lake. Advertisements were published in newspapers and shared far and wide, promoting electric railway service, room to grow orchards and vineyards, and plentiful recreational opportunities ranging from sailing and rowing to fishing and even bathing (per official Lakewood Park Association marketing materials). A medley of summer cottages was built in various architectural styles; they served as the first homes of the many residents who would soon choose to live year-round in Birchwood, which was incorporated as a village in 1921. Although the streetcar was abandoned in 1932, a bus was sponsored by the South Shore Transportation Club to move tourists to and from the little hamlet. Birchwood Village achieved a peak population of 1,059 people in the 1980s.

COTTAGE GROVE, MN
POPULATION: 38,839 – CITY 599 OF 856 (9-4-25)
The "New England of the West" was primarily settled and built up by pioneer groups from New England, who brought with them some of the first instances of wheat production and creameries to what would someday become Minnesota. James Sullivan Norris, who arrived in 1842, was the brains behind the development of the community, which saw the likes of the Furber and Watson families in the years that followed. John and Isabella Furber owned an early general store in the region, and by

1849, the post office had been established. In the spring of 1871, the first townsite was platted by John and his brother Joseph; it included a pair of blacksmith shops, carriage works, and a dry goods and grocery store. The township had a second railroad village called Langdon (for Robert Bruce Langdon), platted by J. T. Dodge on behalf of the Chicago, Milwaukee & St. Paul Railroad. It flourished for many years with an elevator and feed mill, a Catholic church, the Langdon Butter and Cheese factory, and a handful of other firms. Still, over time, the railroad village faded into obscurity since it was never formally incorporated. In 1933, the Langdon post office ceased operations, and the Cottage Grove entity remained the township's sole provider of mail handling and delivery. In 1961, an attempt was made to incorporate Cottage Grove and Woodbury into the Village of Washington, but the motion was denied. Residents instead opted to incorporate as an independent municipality in 1965, and by 1970, it numbered 13,149 residents. The 37.52-square-mile suburb has been one of Minnesota's fastest-growing cities over the last half-century, and its population is now likely well over 40,000. Of all its business developments, the 3M production facility, operational since 1947, is among Cottage Grove's most important manufacturing firms. Until 2012, Cottage Grove had one of two drive-in movie theaters in the metro, but it was razed to make room for a Walmart. Popular points of interest include the 515-acre Ravine Regional Park; the 1871 Italianate John P. Furber house; and the Cordenio Severance House, a 26-room mansion now better known as the Cedarhurst event venue. It was built in the 1880s but remodeled between 1911 and 1917 by architect Cass Gilbert, the designer of the United States Supreme Court building in Washington, D.C., the Minnesota State Capitol building, and the Woolworth Building in New York City. Some noteworthy individuals with ties to Cottage Grove include Seth Appert, an assistant head coach of the NHL's Buffalo Sabres franchise; Seann William Scott, an actor best known for his role as Steve Stoifler in the *American Pie* film series released between 1999 and 2012; Sean O' Connell, a former professional mixed marital artist; poet and activist Aurilla Furber, and Kerry Ligtenberg, an MLB pitcher off and on from 1997 to 2005.

Restaurant Recommendation:
Muddy Cow – Cottage Grove
7350 Hardwood Ct
Cottage Grove, MN 55016

DELLWOOD, MN
POPULATION: 1,171 – CITY 590 OF 856 (9-3-25)

On the northeast shores of White Bear Lake is the City of Dellwood, the wealthiest city in Minnesota and one of the ten most affluent (wealthiest) towns in the United States as of 2020, with a median household income of $129,136 according to the Census Bureau. Although it has only been a city since 1993, the first settlers around the lake arrived as early as the 1850s. The Stillwater & St. Paul Railroad, later part of the massive Northern Pacific Railroad system, came to town in 1870 and boosted both population and a select few businesses. It was joined in 1900 by the Minneapolis, St. Paul & Sault Ste. Marie Railroad, eighteen years after it was platted as a primarily summer home hamlet. According to local lore, the famous writer F. Scott Fitzgerald wrote his 1922 novel *The Beautiful and the Damned*, the precursor to his most distinguished work, *The Great Gatsby*, which was published only three years later. Now primarily homes, Dellwood is home to three main businesses: the Pine Tree Apple Orchard, the Dellwood Country Club, and 7 Vines Vineyard and Winery. Legendary hockey coach Herb Brooks, best known for leading the 1980 U.S. Olympic men's hockey team to an upset "Miracle on Ice" victory over the Soviets, lived here for some time, as did Jesse Ventura, the 38th Governor of Minnesota with the Reform Party and a member of the WWE Hall of Fame because of his elite performances and tenure within the organization.

FOREST LAKE, MN
POPULATION: 20,611 – CITY 588 OF 856 (9-3-25)

Named on account of the heavily timbered forests that once stood on the shore of the nearby lake, Forest Lake Township and its subsequent city were amongst the last to be settled in the Washington County area. On August 19, 1825, the Treaty of Prairie du Chien was signed to establish boundaries between the warring Ojibwe and Sioux tribes. The north shore of Forest Lake sat on the boundary line intended to keep the Ojibwe in the north and the Sioux in the south. Stage lines between St. Paul and Duluth developed in the area and aided in wider settlement in the region. Still, it was the Lake Superior & Mississippi River Railroad (later owned by the Northern Pacific) that led to the platting of Forest Lake village in 1868. A train arrived for the first time on December 23, 1868. The Forest Lake post office opened in 1869 with the German Michael Marsh at the helm; he also owned a local resort hotel and an early mercantile. His Marsh House hosted Presidents William McKinley and Grover Cleveland at different points, as well as the wealthy elite of St. Paul. Around the resort, dance pavilions, a bandstand, and tennis courts came to fruition, and more necessary establishments like a cooperative creamery, a roller mill, an elevator, a stockyard, and banks, grocery stores, hardware stores, and more were built up in the town's commercial district. In the 1920s-1930s, resident bootleggers worked with local police and Chicago gangsters like "Ma" Barker to quietly move illegal whiskey to St. Paul and then elsewhere in the country. Forest Lake was incorporated as a village on July 11, 1893, but it did not annex the surrounding township until 2001. At that point, the population grew from 6,856 residents in 2000 to 18,375 by 2010. Many noted persons have lived in the community over the years, a few of whom include Bud Grant, a member of the Pro Football Hall of Fame and a successful head coach with the NFL's Minnesota Vikings and the CFL's Winnipeg Blue Bombers; Walter Mondale, the 42nd Vice President of the United States under Jimmy Carter; Pete Hegseth, the 29th United States Secretary of Defense; Terry Redlin, a famous wildlife artist who rose to fame in the 1990s for his works; Dan Andersson, a prolific Swedish poet whose poems are among the most popular in all of historic Swedish literature; Christopher Sieber, a two time Tony-Award nominated actor in 2005 and 2009; Elmer L. Anderson, the 30th Governor of Minnesota; Nora "Molly Holly" Greenwald, a former WWE world champion pro wrestler; Jack Trudeau, an NFL quarterback from 1986 to 1995; William Rush Merrian, the 11th Governor of Minnesota; Arne Carlson, the 37th Governor of Minnesota; James B. Bullard, the President of the Federal Reserve Bank of St. Louis from April 2008 to August 2023, and Matt Wallner, an outfielder with the Minnesota Twins since 2022.

Restaurant Recommendation:
Grundhofer's Old Fashion Meats
4869 208th St N #102
Forest Lake, MN 55025

GRANT, MN
POPULATION: 3,966 – CITY 572 OF 856 (9-1-25)

Grant Township was originally known as Greenfield Township when it was organized in 1858. After only six years, it took on its present name to commemorate the legacy of Ulysses S. Grant, the commanding general of the United States Union Army during the American Civil War and the 18th President of the United States. The Stillwater & St. Paul Railroad was laid out in the fall of 1870, and later, the Wisconsin Central Railroad crossed it at a nearby location called Duluth Junction. When the Minneapolis & St. Croix Railroad came through in 1883, a small village called Withrow was established, featuring an elevator and feed mill, stockyards, a bank, a creamery, a blacksmith shop, a general store, a lumberyard, and a pool hall. It was denied incorporation in 1947 because it did not have the minimum required population of 50 residents. Aside from that small now-unincorporated community, the township remained largely rural. In 1996, the City of Grant was formed to help preserve its rurality. A post office called Grant operated in Washington County from 1889 to 1904; similar offices existed in Cass, Faribault, and Olmsted counties at different points.

HUGO, MN
POPULATION: 14,767 – CITY 589 OF 856 (9-3-25)
It was primarily French and French Canadians who settled Oneka Township in the 1850s, near the shores of Oneka Lake at the township's center. The Dakota-Sioux word *onakan* means "to strike or knock off," rice into a canoe, a popular harvesting method at that time. In 1856, a plat was filed, and the land was named Washington, but it never developed. Instead, a place called Centerville Station came into being with the extension of the Lake Superior & Mississippi Railroad. Another Centerville existed just down the line in Anoka County, so the post office ordered a name change to avoid any further confusion between the two areas. Michael Houle proposed the name "Houle" for himself, but it was rejected. Instead, the name Hugo was selected to honor either Trevanion William Hugo, the chief engineer of the Consolidated Elevator Company in Duluth, or Victor Hugo, a famous French author. The latter suggestion is likely more accurate, as Trevanion had not yet emigrated from Canada by the time the post office was using "Hugo". Major early industries in Hugo included The Inter-State Lumber Company, opened around the turn of the 20th century, a community bank in 1910, and The Hugo Feed Mill in 1917. The village was incorporated in 1906, and in 1972, Oneka Township was officially incorporated into the City of Hugo.

LAKE ELMO, MN
POPULATION: 11,335 – CITY 571 OF 856 (9-1-25)
Bernard B. "Bun" Cyphers and his wife, Maria, came to the "Lake Elmo" area from Virginia in 1848, becoming the first settlers of what is now a city with over 11,000 residents. They owned the Lake House, which operated as a stage stop, a hotel, and a tavern all-in-one for those traveling between St. Paul and Stillwater and beyond. Eventually, it also became the District 12 schoolhouse and a general community center for a fledgling village named after the nearby lake. Records indicate that a post office opened in 1876 under the name Bass Lake, the lake's original name. Neither the village nor the post office agreed on a euphonious name until 1879, when Alpheus B. Stickney insisted they match after he made a significant investment in the area and constructed a 58-room resort hotel. Thanks to the St. Paul, Stillwater & Taylors Falls Railroad, part of the Chicago, St. Paul, Minneapolis & Omaha Railroad system, many significant developments occurred in the town in the years that followed. Carriage works and blacksmith shops were in full swing. Saloons and general stores were serving the locals. A creamery, grain elevator, a bank, a hospital, and a roller skating rink were established, and by 1925, the commercial district of the township was platted as Lake Elmo Village. Until 1951, Lake Elmo was part of Oakdale Township, which split into Oakdale and East Oakdale; in 1972, East Oakdale Township and the village combined to form the City of Lake Elmo. Rasmussen University, a private for-profit

university with campuses across six states, operates a branch of its college locally in Lake Elmo.

LAKE ST. CROIX BEACH, MN
POPULATION: 1,043 – CITY 566 OF 856 (9-1-25)
Incorporated in 1952, Lake St. Croix Beach dates to the early 1900s, when wealthy firms and individuals began buying up farmland to develop it into a resort area. Demand was high for summer homes and recreational opportunities, and the land adjoining the Saint Croix River offered ample space for new development. One major investor was the *St. Paul Daily News*, which sold lots for $67.50 each to advertise newspaper subscriptions. Within twenty years, cottages lined the shores, as did The Anchorage: George H. Atwood's 30-acre property that from 1908 to 1912 served as the headquarters of the St. Paul Automobile Club. When the club moved to White Bear Lake, the Ford Motor Company briefly considered razing the building to build a factory. They instead chose to build in St. Paul, and the Anchorage site turned into the clubhouse of the Lake St. Croix Beach Property Owners' Association. Lake St. Croix Beach was served by the Milwaukee Road and peaked at 1,176 people in the 1980s.

LAKELAND, MN
POPULATION: 1,710 – CITY 564 OF 856 (9-1-25)
Lakeland, Minnesota, one of 856 incorporated communities in the Land of 10,000 Lakes, was appropriately named for its location on the western shores of Lake St. Croix. Archaeological findings suggest that French Canadians lived on the site in the early 1840s, but written records indicate that Henry W. Crosby was the first settler. Moses Perin opened a ferry that serviced Lakeland and Hudson, Wisconsin; Captain John Oliver operated it from 1850 to 1869. Perin laid out the town plat in 1849, and Mr. Oliver built his Greek Revival-style home that same year. It still stands alongside the 1850 Mitchell Jackson Farmhouse and the 1858 concrete-and-rock Gothic Revival John T. Cyphers House as one of three of Lakeland's homes listed on the National Register of Historic Places. The concrete used in Cyphers' home was made from a mixture of mud, sand, gravel, and lime, a new form of building material. Noted early institutions of Lakeland that went up during the same period as the three homes were several stores and shops, a set of hotels, a blacksmith shop, a saloon, and professional offices for a lawyer and doctor. Several mills came and went, but the most successful of them all were the C. N. Nelson Lumber Company and the R. H. McCoy sawmill. When the St. Paul & Milwaukee Railroad came through in 1880, Lakeland was replatted to accommodate public park space and mill sites. It was ultimately incorporated as a village in 1951, at which point it boasted of only one paved and lighted street: Quinnell Avenue North.

LAKELAND SHORES, MN
POPULATION: 339 – CITY 565 OF 856 (9-1-25)
The Lake St. Croix shoreline community dubs itself "A Special Place To Be," perhaps because it is one of the very few towns in Minnesota that is strictly residential. Presently home to about 339 citizens according to the 2020 Census, the enclave of Lakeland was once the farmstead of William and Mary Jones. Seeing the development of Lakeland on their northern doorstep prompted the family to survey lots on the former Chicago, Milwaukee & St. Paul Railroad line. They filled up quickly, leading to a significant increase in taxes on residents, so they banded together in 1949 to incorporate their own village, Lakeland Shores.

LANDFALL, MN
POPULATION: 843 – CITY 597 OF 856 (9-4-25)
The itty-bitty 0.08-square-mile community of Landfall is unique, as it is entirely made up of manufactured mobile homes. In 1901, it was nothing more than farmland tilled by John Schiltgen, but eventually the land passed into the hands of James and Mitzi Olson. They lived in a tiny cottage there, once supposedly inhabited by the notorious John Dillinger in 1934. Being used to living in smaller homes and understanding that not everybody could afford a standard home, the Olsons did something unprecedented. They developed all of their land into a mobile home park, which became the most affordable community in the Twin Cities. By 1959, their little trailer park village had been incorporated, and at its inaugural Census in 1960, it reported a population of 437. By the 1990s, a developer was seeking to purchase the land for several million dollars to build luxury homes or a shopping mall. Thankfully, the Washington County Housing and Redevelopment Authority rescued the city and sold it in 1997 to the Landfall Housing and Redevelopment Authority for future preservation of the low-income housing development.

MAHTOMEDI, MN
POPULATION: 8,138 – CITY 591 OF 856 (9-3-25)
Mahtomedi was initially platted in July 1883, on the northeast shore of White Bear Lake by the Mahtomedi Assembly of the Chautauqua Association out of Lake Chautauqua, New York. The name Mahtomedi was derived from the Dakota's name for the lake, *mathó* meaning "grey bear," and *mde* meaning "lake." Its establishment was predated by the Lake Superior & Mississippi Railroad in the early 1870s, which helped bring in many of the thousands of Chautauqua event attendees who came for summer assemblies, Sunday school courses, and lecture study groups. Streetcar service was established at the end of the century with the arrival of the Minneapolis & St. Paul Suburban Railroad Company and the Twin City Rail Transit Company. The latter company also established the Wildwood Amusement Park, which offered hot-air balloon rides, a roller coaster, and other unique forms of entertainment related to the lake. Although the park closed in 1932, different activities soon took hold in Mahtomedi. Incorporation was achieved in August 1931 by a vote of 225 to 180. Over the next couple of years, John Dillinger, "Baby Face" Nelson, Kate (Ma) Barker, Al Karpis, and several other Chicago mobsters came and went as they worked to transport prohibited liquor to the railroad hub of St. Paul. These illicit activities subsided with the end of the Prohibition Era, and Mahtomedi was allowed to grow in a more typical fashion. From the 1950s to the early 2000s, the population grew by 24.1% to 57% decade-over-decade. Century College was established in 1967, with half in Mahtomedi and half in White Bear Lake, and has remained the immediate area's primary institution of higher learning. Warren Strelow, the Olympic gold medalist winning goaltending coach with the 1980 Lake Placid U.S. men's hockey team; Nuni Omot, the MVP of The Basketball Africa League in 2023; Justin Pierre, the lead vocalist of the pop punk band Motion City Soundtrack; Mike Baumann, a professional baseball pitcher in the MLB from 2021 to 2024, and Lindsey Weier, a participant in the 2006 Winter Olympic Games as a cross-country skier, all have ties to the community.

MARINE ON ST. CROIX, MN
POPULATION: 664 – CITY 573 OF 856 (9-1-25)
A group of New Englanders based out of Marine, Illinois, set out in 1838 to identify a spot on the St. Croix River that would prove suitable for a steamboat landing and a sawmill. From that group, Lewis Judd and David Hone became the two men who found

the perfect site, and by August 24, 1839, the mill was cutting lumber. Interestingly enough, the land had not even been opened to settlement, as it had been purchased only two years prior in a treaty with the Ojibwe and the Dakota-Sioux, making it the site of Minnesota's first commercial sawmill. A village with homes and other businesses, such as a brewery, a blacksmith shop, a hotel, a general store, and a café, formed around the mills' activities. The colony became known as "Judd's Mills." Eventually, the name changed to Marine Mills in 1853, shortly after a significantly larger structure replaced the original mill. It burned in 1863 and was not replaced until 1866 after the American Civil War had concluded. The Walker, Judd, and Veazie Mill could cut up to 30,000 feet of lumber per day, and by the time it closed in 1895, it had produced nearly 200 million feet of lumber. Orange Walker worked with the company for over forty-five years. He was a highly recognizable name in the area alongside the likes of the Judd family, Asa Parker, William Dibble, and others. Incorporation occurred in 1875, when the township also included May and New Scandia Townships until 1893, and in 1950, the village was reincorporated as Marine on St. Croix. The Marine Mill Site, now just a collection of ruins, has been registered on the National Register of Historic Places and is managed as one of 26 Minnesota Historical Society sites. Much of the city has been preserved by the NRHP as the Marine on St. Croix Historic District, thanks to its distinction as the birthplace of Minnesota's lumber industry. Two miles north of town is William O'Brien State Park, known for its ample recreational opportunities and rolling glacial moraine and oak savanna. A few noted figures with ties to the historic hamlet are Marjorie Edgar, noted for her work in preserving Finnish folk songs; jazz pianist Richard "Butch" Thompson; Ellen Torelle Nagler, a noted science educator; and Walter Kirn, the author of the book *Up in the Air* that was adapted into a 2009 comedy-drama film starring George Clooney.

Restaurant Recommendation:
Marine General Store
101 Judd St
Marine on St. Croix, MN 55047

NEWPORT, MN
POPULATION: 3,797 – CITY 601 OF 856 (9-4-25)
Newport was predated by a town called Red Rock, which John Holton of Pennsylvania first settled in the spring of 1837. He arrived at the same time as Reverend Alfred Brunson, who established a Methodist mission called Kaposia in an attempt to convert the local Dakota to Christianity. Brunson retired from this missionary field only two years later, and his successor, Benjamin T. Kavanaugh, moved the mission across the river onto Holton's claim. It failed by 1844, and ten years later, the Kaposia name was done away with for good when the local post office changed its name to Red Rock. Steam ships came to Red Rock on the Mississippi River. A steamboat landing soon developed, leading to the formation of a few businesses, stores, and a second, localized community called Newport in 1852. Its name, suggested by Mrs. James H. Hugunin, was likely taken after any one of several other communities called Newport throughout the United States. This new town was founded when E. M. Shelton and his brothers erected a steam-powered sawmill in 1857; by the 1870s, it had added a flour mill, a store, and a school. The two settlements were incorporated into the Village of Newport in 1889. From 1940 to 1950, Newport saw its most significant population increase, growing from 872 residents to 1,672 in ten years. Joe Fritz started the Fritz Candy Company during this time; the Farmer's Terminal [Cudahy] Meat Packing Company opened some years prior as one of the city's largest employers.

OAK PARK HEIGHTS, MN
POPULATION: 4,849 – CITY 569 OF 856 (9-1-25)
Oak Park village was platted in May 1857 by John Parker, William Dorr, William M. McCluer, Olive Anderson, and Gold and Mary Curtis as a new community separating Stillwater and South Stillwater (now called Bayport). The earliest commercial development of note came in the 1880s, when a sawmill and barrel-making company were built on the St. Croix Riverfront. Other lines came to fruition when two lines of the Chicago, St. Paul, Minneapolis & Omaha were built to straddle both sides of the community before running parallel with one another through Stillwater. Among all the early events, the most significant contribution to Oak Park's history was the founding of a 1932 restaurant called Log Cabin. This roadhouse served gangsters and automobile owners in what was then a relatively isolated part of Washington County. The once dual eatery and nightclub structure now houses Phil's Tara Hideaway; the building itself was added to the National Register of Historic Places in December 2007. On the same date, the Lake St. Croix Overlook, a wayside rest built in 1938-39 using elements of National Park Service rustic architecture, was also added to the Register. Oak Park was replatted in 1938 into the village of Oak Park Heights, and finally added to the ranks of Minnesota's incorporated municipalities in 1959. Post-incorporation, Oak Park Heights has added a pair of malls, the "new" Stillwater Area High School building, and numerous more stores, restaurants, and lines of commerce.

OAKDALE, MN
POPULATION: 28,303 – CITY 596 OF 856 (9-4-25)
White, black, and burr oak trees were once heavily in Oakdale Township before the first settlers, namely Bernard B. "Bun" Cyphers, arrived circa 1848. He built the Lake House, a hotel for travelers moving across what was then the Minnesota Territory. John Morgan replaced him as the area's primary "man of importance" when he built his own place, The Halfway House, between St. Paul and Stillwater. It was here that the Concord stages of Willoughby & Powers would acquire fresh horses and enjoy dinner before continuing with the latter part of their trek. Between 1870-71, the St. Paul & Stillwater Short Line Railroad and the St. Paul & Taylors Falls Railroad (assimilated into the Chicago, St. Paul, Minneapolis & Omaha Railroad later on) built through, and assisted in Oakdale's development as a suburb to Lake Elmo, which split off in 1926, and Pine Springs, which became a municipality in 1959. Oakdale was incorporated as a city in 1974 from the remaining 11.31 square miles of Washington County's Oakdale and East Oakdale Townships. Imation Corporation, a spinoff of 3M's data storage business, was once headquartered in Oakdale before it rebranded as GlassBridge Enterprises in 2017. Its headquarters were moved to New York City after O-Jin Corporation bought out the company.

PINE SPRINGS, MN
POPULATION: 377 – CITY 593 OF 856 (9-3-25)
Pine Springs (pop. 377) started as a series of summer cottages on the east side of Long Lake. Commercial activity was limited despite the proximity of the Wisconsin Central Railroad, and Pine Springs has instead retained its identity as a small, rural-like residential community. It was incorporated in 1959 from portions of Lincoln and East Oakdale Township after the locals banded together to present a petition to the Washington County Board of Commissioners. Their request was approved, and the 0.92-square-mile city has since retained a population of no more than 436 people, a peak reached in 1990.

SAINT MARY'S POINT, MN
POPULATION: 353 – CITY 567 OF 856 (9-1-25)
Saint Marys Point (officially spelled without an apostrophe), one of five Washington County cities located on the banks of Lake St. Croix, was incorporated in 1951. Now primarily a residential community, the original owners of the 0.392-square-mile townsite were Gaspare Bruce, Henry Sibley, and then Joseph R. Brown. Some of Brown's family members established a farmstead on the site, and it was called "Brown's Farm" for its first few years. Eventually, Lemuel Bolles erected a flour mill in 1845-46, and by 1855, the first rendition of the townsite we know today was platted 1855 by Thomas W. Coleman. He called it St. Mary Village. The plat was redone by Alexander Cathcart and William R. Marshall two years later. Lumbering activities brought some economic prosperity to the region. Because of several neighboring hamlets and mills, the town was little more than a Chicago, Milwaukee & St. Paul Railroad station and some homes. It was saved at the turn of the century by St. Paul investors who turned the struggling town into a collection of summer homes for vacationing Twin Cities families. The mind behind United States Satellite Broadcasting, the precursor to DirecTV, and the CEO of Hubbard Broadcasting, Stanley Hubbard, has ties to St. Mary's Point. So too does Phil Housley, a former NHL defenseman with 1,495 game appearances from 1982 to 2003 and a member of both the Hockey Hall of Fame and the United States Hockey Hall of Fame.

SAINT PAUL PARK, MN
POPULATION: 5,544 – CITY 600 OF 856 (9-4-25)
Located just 5 miles down the Mississippi River from the Minnesota State Capitol, St. Paul Park originated in 1887 as a railway village in Newport and Cottage Grove Townships. Men like Joseph Hugunin, R.S. Snow, and Giles and William Fowler were amongst the first settlers; the latter gentleman sold his land for $80,000 to the St. Paul Park Improvement Company so they could start the townsite. It would be served by the Chicago, Milwaukee & St. Paul and the Chicago, Burlington & Northern (alternatively and earlier still called the Chicago, Rock Island & Pacific) Railroads, enabling over a dozen manufacturing operations to take hold. In addition to factories for sleighs, carriages, terracotta, baby carriages, rattan, sash and doors, brooms, and mattresses, some of the more prominent lines were St. Paul Knitting Works, the Black Hawk Mills, Globe & Engine Boiler Works, and Dewey Harvester Works. The earliest recorded population of the young town was 1,173 in 1890, but in the decades that followed, many of the workers at these plants and factories arrived by rail on the Burlington Motor commuter train from St. Paul. The Panic of 1893 dealt a major setback to St. Paul Park's development, but the city rebounded and soon boasted multiple grocery stores, hotels, livery stables, and professional offices. Schools and churches were built to accommodate the religious and educational needs of the townspeople. In 1936, the Northwestern Refining Company, now known as the St. Paul Park Refinery, owned by Marathon Petroleum, arrived and, at present, produces over 100,000 barrels per day. With its newfound footholds in the oil industry and several successful lines of commerce to promote well-being amongst its citizens, St. Paul Park has since grown to a high population of 5,544 as of the 2020 Census. In 2005, land was annexed from Grey Cloud Island Township to allow for future growth. A pair of famous men with area ties are Dale Arnold, the play-by-play announcer for the NHL's Boston Bruins (and other Boston-area teams) for several decades, and Dallas Holm, a Christian singer-songwriter whose work has circulated since 1965.

SCANDIA, MN
POPULATION: 3,984 – CITY 574 OF 856 (9-1-25)
Dalecarlian horses welcome travelers to Scandia, home of the first Swedish settlers in Minnesota. These three men–Carl A. Fernstrom, Oscar Roos, and August Sandahl–established the base farmstead in October 1850 on Hay Lake that would change hands to Daniel Nilson the following year, and attract other Swedes to settle nearby. For twenty years, development was minimal, until a railroad branch ultimately owned by the Minneapolis, St. Paul & Sault Ste. Marie Railroad was completed through the township. There was a brief town called Vasa, named after the Swedish monarch Gustavus Vasa, but it was obsolete by 1860, despite having a sawmill, store, saloon, hotel, and post office. Copas was the next township community, established in 1886 with the arrival of the Soo, and was primarily home to potato warehouses and a handful of other businesses. By 1963, the depot was moved elsewhere, and the town became a ghost town. Scandia was the only prosperous town to achieve incorporation. Several stores were opened, selling hardware, groceries, and all the necessities that residents of the era would have needed to survive. A creamery was erected in 1894 as a significant industrial hub, and by the end of the 1920s, there was an auto dealer, a bank, and several professional offices. Fearing annexation by the City of Forest Lake, New Scandia Township became the City of Scandia on January 1, 2007. In addition to hosting portions of the 16.4-mile Washington County Barn Quilt Trail, Scandia is best known for being the site of the Hay Lake School, Scandia's first school building, used from 1895 to 1962, and the adjacent Johannes Erickson House, a historic 1868 log cabin known for its distinctive Swedish gambrel roof. Both sites were added to the National Register of Historic Places in the early 1970s and are now a part of the Washington County Historical Society Museum. Parts of season five of the FX television series *Fargo* are set in Scandia.

STILLWATER, MN ★☆
POPULATION: 19,394 – CITY 570 OF 856 (9-1-25)
"The Birthplace of Minnesota" earned its nickname because it was here that a territorial convention was held at the corner of Myrtle and Main Streets to separate Minnesota Territory from Wisconsin Territory in 1849. Before this pivotal turning point in Minnesota's history, the place began as the simple home of Joseph Renshaw Brown, a fur trader who opted to base his operations at the head of Lake St. Croix. His early arrival prompted the establishment of the village of Dacotah, the county seat of St. Croix County, Wisconsin Territory. Advertisements were sent out to attract settlers from eastern lands, and some of Brown's relatives moved in to establish homes of their own. One of these men was Jacob Fisher, who altered his claim so that Browns (then Pine) Creek could provide enough water power to establish a mill. After Captain Stephen B. Hanks, cousin of Abraham Lincoln, took a raft of logs down the St. Croix River, other millwrights took an interest in Fisher's claim so they could start a mill of their own. John McKusick and three other men formed the Stillwater Lumber Company, purchased the land, and began cutting timber by 1844. Alongside their mill on October 26, 1843, they laid out a settlement called "Stillwater," so named by McKusick for the stillness of the river at this site. Dacotah faded into obscurity. On March 4, 1854, Stillwater was incorporated as a municipality, as was Saint Paul some miles to the west. At this point, it was designated as the Washington County seat. Despite Minnesota not becoming a state until 1858, Stillwater was nominated to be the site of one of the three most important territorial institutions of the Minnesota Territory at that time: the Minnesota Territorial Prison. Governor Alexander Ramsey proposed the plans for the prison, and between 1851 and 1853, Jacob Fisher and the

Jesse Taylor Company worked side by side to erect a large complex. Although the prison closed in 1914 and all but one surviving structure (the State Prison Warden's House, now the Warden's House Museum) was razed and ultimately destroyed by arson in September 2002, Stillwater still grew substantially. It became a domineering economic power in the region. By 1890, it had already surpassed 10,000 residents for the first time. Eventually, it served as a railroad connection point for the Northern Pacific, Chicago, Milwaukee & St. Paul, and the Chicago, St. Paul, Minneapolis & Omaha Railroads. Because of the successful lumbering industry, Stillwater became home to a multitude of factories, elevators, and sawmills, and steamboat shipping was heavily used from 1860 to 1890. Eleven blocks and sixty-three properties of Stillwater's central business district, built between 1860 and 1940, still exist today as the Stillwater Commercial Historic District. The Washington County Courthouse, built in 1870 using Italianate elements, was one of Minnesota's longest-serving functional courthouses until a new government center was erected in 1974-75. A little over twenty historic sites in Stillwater proper and the surrounding Stillwater Township have been listed on the National Register of Historic Places, a few of which include the St. Croix Boom Site and its accompanying Company House and Barn, where lumber was stored from 1856 to 1914 at the head of the once-massive St. Croix River's log drives; the St. Croix Lumber Mills-Stillwater Manufacturing Company stone powerhouse, built in 1850; the 1897 Neoclassical and Georgia Revival Nelson School; the historic 1883 Chicago, Milwaukee & St. Paul Freight House; the Moritz Bergstein Shoddy Mill and Warehouse, a Jewish-founded firm that once recycled fabric and manufactured mattresses around the turn of the century; the Soo Line High Bridge and Stillwater Bridge that extend into St. Croix County, Wisconsin, and numerous historic homes, the oldest of which is the 1865 Italianate Mortimer Webster home. Another formidable day in Stillwater history was October 18, 1921, when Charles Strite invented the first automatic pop-up bread toaster. The Toastmaster Company began to sell a slight variation of the toaster later that decade. Extensive numbers of famous folks have once called Stillwater home, a few of whom include James B. Clark, an Oscar-nominated film editor best known for his editing work on the 1941 drama *How Green Was My Valley*; Thomas J. Abercrombie, the first journalist to reach the South Pole; Alpheus Beede Stickey, the first president of the Chicago Great Western Railway; Zach Sobiech, an eighteen year-old boy who passed away from cancer in 2013 but released a single "Clouds" that served as the inspiration of Disney's 2020 musical drama teen film of the same name; Ed Ackerson, a producer of several records and the co-founder of the Susstones record label; Charles Gardner Sullivan, a prolific screenwriter noted for his early contributions to the motion picture industry; Rich Sommer, an actor best known for his role as Harry Crane on AMC's drama series *Mad Men*; Thomas Vanek, an NHL winger with over one-thousand game appearances between 2004 and 2019; Ben Blankenship, a world record holder in the distance medley relay; Glen Perkins, a three-time All-Star pitcher with the MLB's Minnesota Twins from 2013 to 2015; Sam Shepard, a playwright, Academy and Tony Award nominee, and the 1979 Pulitzer Prize for Drama winner; Denis McDonough, the 11th United States Secretary of Veterans Affairs; a two-time Super Bowl champion linebacker Bob Nelson, and Sam Gorski and Niko Pueringer, founders of the production studio Corridor Digital.

 **Restaurant Recommendation:**
Nelson's Ice Cream
920 Olive St W
Stillwater, MN 55082

Restaurant Recommendation:
DJ's Clam Shack
221 Myrtle St E
Stillwater, MN 55082

Lodging Recommendation:
Lora Hotel & Event Center
402 S Main St
Stillwater, MN 55082

Lodging Recommendation:
Aurora Staples Inn
303 4th St N
Stillwater, MN 55082

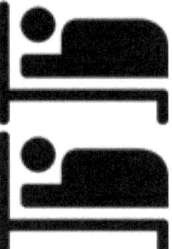

WILLERNIE, MN
POPULATION: 515 – CITY 592 OF 856 (9-3-25)

Nestled within Mahtomedi is the City of Willernie, an enclave of its larger neighbor that was formerly called Wildwood Manor. There were settlers in the region in the latter quarter of the nineteenth century who lived on the Minneapolis & St. Paul Suburban Railroad Company and the Twin City Rapid Transit Company streetcar lines, but it was the Wildwood Park Association that platted the village of Wildwood Manor in 1914 to attract more residents. It was intended to serve as a residential suburb of the nearby Wildwood Amusement Park on White Bear Lake, complete with summer cottages. A grocery store, a car repair garage, and a lodging establishment were constructed. As the tourists began to arrive more frequently, restaurants and taverns were added to the town's commercial lineup. Eventually, many of these business lines were dissolved, and the Village of Willernie was incorporated in 1948. The population peaked at 697 in the 1970s.

WOODBURY, MN
POPULATION: 75,102 – CITY 598 OF 856 (9-4-25)

Minnesota's seventh-most-populous city, Woodbury, was once a rolling prairie with occasional oak groves before decades of development turned it into the sprawling metropolis it is today. Settlement began near Colby Lake when John McHattie arrived in 1841; he was joined by his brother, Alexander, in 1845, and by William Middleton in 1844. Only after Minnesota became a territory did it see a significant increase in population. Minnesota Territory was split into congressional townships, one of which was Red Rock Township. Once it was discovered that another township existed of that name, the name was changed at once to honor Levi Woodbury, the 13th United States Secretary of the Treasury from July 1, 1834, to March 4, 1841, and the Associate Justice of the Supreme Court of the United States between September 23, 1845, and September 4, 1851. German immigrants flooded into the area to start farmsteads, and in 1869, the first Woodbury post office was established. For a long time, the only authentic village of the township was Newport (now the name of a separate municipality to Woodbury's southwest), until Woodbury Heights was established in 1955 to accommodate the ever-growing number of automobiles traveling along Highway 12. Incorporation was proposed in 1963 to provide utility services to newer developments, but the vote failed. The Minnesota Municipal Commission attempted to get Woodbury and Cottage Grove Township to incorporate together as Washington village, but the vote failed by a final count of 662 to 1,284. Cottage Grove was incorporated in 1965 on its own terms, and two years later, on March 7, 1967, the Village of Woodbury came into being after a successful vote. Since then, population growth has been nothing short of rampant. From 1980 to 1990, Woodbury's population doubled from 10,000 people to 20,000. By 2000, the population had exceeded 46,000, and as of 2020, it was reported to have surpassed 75,000. In a community where the highest percentage of residents work for M Health Fairview HealthEast, the South Washington County School District ISD 833, and Target Corporation, Woodbury has still retained its own identity separate from its peers, with its forty-five parks, two golf courses, and the HealthEast Sports Center. Extensive urban development has left only one location in Woodbury listed on the National Register of Historic Places: the Charles Spangenberg Farmstead, noted for its 1871 farmhouse and 1887 barn. The Woodbury Heritage Society operates the Woodbury Heritage House and Garden. A few noteworthy residents of the city's past include Michelle Young, the star of season 18 of ABC's *The Bachelorette*; Joel Johnson, the former head coach of the United States women's national ice hockey team in the 2022 Winter Olympics, Zach Zebrowski, the recipient of the Harlon Hill Trophy (the Division II version of the Heisman Trophy) as a quarterback for the Central Missouri Mules, and Chip Lohmiller, the NFL's 1991 scoring leader and a Pro-Bowler that same year.

Hastings is only partially located in Washington County (see Dakota County), and White Bear Lake is only partially located in Washington County (see Ramsey County).

Unincorporated/Ghost Towns: Arcola, Basswood Grove, Carnelian Junction, Garen, Maple Island, Point Douglas, Siegel

National Register of Historic Places:
Afton: Erastus Bolles House, Cushing Hotel, Newington Gilbert House
Arcola: Johns & Martin Mower House & Arcola Mill Site
Bayport: State Prison Historic District
Copas: John Copas House
Cottage Grove: John P. Furber House, Grey Cloud Lime Kiln, Cordenio Severance House
Denmark Township: District No. 34 School
Lakeland: John T, Cyphers House, Mitchell Jackson Farmhouse, Capt. John Oliver House
Marine on St. Croix: Marine Mill Site, Marine on St. Croix Historic District
May Township: Benjamin B. Sheffield House
Oak Park Heights: Lake St, Croix Overlook, Log Cabin
Scandia: Johannes Erickson House, Hay Lake School
Stillwater: Moritz Bergstein Shoddy Mill & Warehouse, Chicago, Milwaukee, & St. Paul Freight House, Roscoe Hersey House, Capt. Austin Jenks House, Albert Lammers House, Ivory McKusick House, Minnesota Territorial/State Prison Warden's House, Nelson School, St. Croix Lumber Mills-Stillwater Manufacturing Company, William Sauntry House & Recreation Hall, Soo Line High Bridge, Stillwater Bridge, Stillwater Commercial Historic District, Washington County Courthouse, Mortimer Webster House
Stillwater Township: Bridge No. 5721, Pest House, Point Douglas-St. Louis River Road Bridge, St. Croix Boom Company House & Barn, St. Croix Boom Site, Henry Stussi House
Woodbury: Charles Spangenberg Farmstead

Golf Courses:
Applewood Hills Golf Course, Daily Fee (Stillwater, MN)
Dellwood Country Club, Private (Dellwood, MN)
Eagle Valley Golf Course, Municipal (Woodbury, MN)
Forest Hills Golf Club, Private (Forest Lake, MN)
Loggers Trail Golf Course, Daily Fee (Stillwater, MN)
Oak Glen Golf Course – Executive 9, Daily Fee (Stillwater, MN)
Oak Glen Golf Course, Daily Fee (Stillwater, MN)
Oak Marsh Golf Course, Daily Fee (Oakdale, MN)

Prestwick Golf Club, Daily Fee (Woodbury, MN)
River Oaks Municipal Golf Course, Municipal (Cottage Grove, MN)
Royal Golf Club, Private (Lake Elmo, MN)
Stillwater Country Club, Private (Stillwater, MN)
StoneRidge Golf Club, Daily Fee (Stillwater, MN)
Tanners Brook Golf Club, Daily Fee (Forest Lake, MN)

Breweries/Wineries/Distilleries:
3rd Act Brewery (Woodbury, MN)
7 Vines Vineyard (Dellwood, MN)
Lift Bridge Brewing Company (Stillwater, MN)
River Siren Brewing Co. (Stillwater, MN)
Rustic Roots (Scandia, MN)
Saint Croix Vineyards (Stillwater, MN)

Town Celebrations:
Heritage Days, St. Paul Park, MN (3rd Weekend of August)
Midsommardagen, Scandia, MN (Saturday closest to Summer Solstice; June 21)
Strawberry Fest, Cottage Grove, MN (3rd Weekend of June)
Strawberry Festival, Afton, MN (Late June)
Woodbury Days, Woodbury, MN (4th Weekend of August)

Todd County: Christ the King Catholic Church (Browerville), Grey Eagle Village Hall (Grey Eagle), Hewitt Public School Museum (Hewitt), Long Drive-In Theatre (Long Prairie), Veteran's Memorial & Mural (Long Prairie), Historic Riverside Park Ruins (Long Prairie), Staples Theater in 1916 Desmarais Building (Staples), Dower Lake Fishing Pier; The Longest in Minnesota (Staples)

Traverse County: St. Anthony's Catholic Church (Browns Valley), Little Red Schoolhouse & Sam Brown's Cabin at Sam Brown Memorial Park (Browns Valley), St. Gall's Catholic Church (Tintah), World's Largest Mallard (Wheaton), the Gopher Theatre (Wheaton), Mural (Wheaton), Milwaukee Road Railroad Depot Museum (Wheaton)

Wabasha County: Veteran's Statues at SVJ Creative Designs (Kellogg), Carousel at Lark Toys (Kellogg), Lake City City Hall (Lake City), Mural (Lake City), Lake Pepin (Lake City), Old Frontenac Overlook at Frontenac State Park (Frontenac), Plainview Area History Center; former Methodist Church (Plainview), Eagle Statue at the National Eagle Center (Wabasha)

Wadena County: Statue of St. Urho (Menahga), Spirit Lake (Menahga), Sauna at Spirit Lake Resort & Motel at Menahga Beach (Menahga), Fire Tower (Nimrod), Welcome Sign (Nimrod), Mural (Sebeka), Cozy Theatre (Wadena), Interior of St. Ann's Catholic Church (Wadena)

Waseca County: Seha Sorghum Mill (Janesville), Vintage Dairy Queen (Janesville), Cowboy Sculpture & Water Tower (Janesville), Mural (New Richland), Mural (Waldorf), Waseca County Courthouse (Waseca), Grain Bin Mural (Waseca), Sacred Heart Catholic Church (Waseca)

Washington County: St. Croix River (Bayport), St. Croix River at Beanie's Marina (Lakeland), Marine General Store (Marine on St. Croix), Oldest Methodist Building in Minnesota (Newport), Oakdale-Lake Elmo Historical Society District 12 Schoolhouse (Oakdale), Dala Horse (Scandia), Veteran's Memorial (Stillwater), Stillwater Lift Bridge Historic Site (Stillwater)

WATONWAN COUNTY
EST. 1860 - POPULATION: 11,253

Founded in 1860, Watonwan shares its name with the Watonwan River, which was named after the Dakota word *watanwan*, meaning "bountiful fish."

BUTTERFIELD, MN
POPULATION: 601 – CITY 85 OF 856 (3-26-25)
Not so named because its fields runneth over with butter, but rather for William Butterfield, its original townsite owner and settler, Butterfield was platted on September 13, 1880, with the coming of the St. Paul & Sioux City Railroad. E. F. Drake was then president of the railroad company and ordered its establishment. Other accounts insist that the railroad was in place as early as 1871 and that the site was named after James Butterfield, an engineer on the line. Supposedly, he was shunned for years after he ran off with the wife of one of the initial settlers, but his reputation and name (in the township) were restored when he invented the locomotive ash pan. General stores, grocery stores, and lumberyards were among the early establishments of Butterfield. A 1916 directory lists the following firms: the Hubbard & Palmer Company elevator, the Farmers Elevator Company, the Butterfield Hotel, the Butterfield Creamery Company, the Peoples State Bank, the State Bank of Butterfield, the Butterfield Auto Company, the St. James Milling Company, The Butterfield Opera House, *The Butterfield Advocate* newspaper, the Butterfield Mercantile Company, and about twenty others. It had churches and schools by this point as well. In 1895, it was incorporated, and Bern Remple was elected mayor. The post office opened its doors for business in 1879. Most early settlers were Mennonites from Austria-Hungary or Russia who arrived in the 1870s. They could not have predicted that, nearly a century later, their settlement would reach a peak population of 634 people in the 1980s. Butterfield was frequently mentioned during 1979-80. It was then that one of its sons, Bruce Laingen, was being held as the most senior American official during the Iran hostage crisis. Laingen was born on a farm between Butterfield and Odin in 1922 and was the United States Ambassador to Iran from June 16, 1979, to April 7, 1980. Nowadays, Butterfield is best known for its annual Butterfield Steam and Gas Engine Show (established in 1967), which attracts upwards of 15,000 visitors every August.

DARFUR, MN
POPULATION: 84 – CITY 84 OF 856 (3-26-25)
"Why you stop dar fur?" a Norwegian Chicago & Northwestern Railway worker asked when his coworker placed the survey stake a bit farther than he should have. The year was 1899, and the railroad (in conjunction with the Western Town Lot Company) was busy extending its line and platting towns every seven to nine miles to serve as refueling and passenger dropoff points. When the community was surveyed, it was named "Darfur," either because of this memorable expression used by a railroad worker, or because of the region in western Sudan. Its population never rose above 191 people in the 1960s, but Darfur's hardworking settlers built a substantial commercial district in its early days. By 1916, it had approximately thirteen businesses: The State Bank of Darfur, the Darfur Co-operative Creamery Company, the Farmers' Co-operative Elevator Company, Hotel Darfur, the C. M. Youngman Lumber Company, the Darfur Stock Buyers' Association, John Gustafson's auto garage, L. Stoutenberg's barber shop, W. Buche's blacksmith shop, S. Weast's dray line and livery, Englin & Samuelson's hardware and implement store, and Edward Goring and A. Jaeger's general merchandise dealership. Locals attest that there were eventually

two grocery stores, two gas stations, and several more "pairs" of most of its business lines, many of which have since closed. The post office began in 1900 and was initially headed by Jacob D. Heppner, on whose land the townsite was platted. Darfur was incorporated as a village on December 31, 1903.

LA SALLE, MN
POPULATION: 79 – CITY 97 OF 856 (3-27-25)

The French name La Salle is a testament to the legacy of René-Robert Cavalier, Sieur de La Salle, who canoed and then claimed all the lands between the Great Lakes and the Gulf of Mexico and between the Appalachian Mountains and the Rocky Mountains in the name of France. He named the territory "La Louisiane" in honor of King Louis XIV; it later became part of Thomas Jefferson's 1803 Louisiana Purchase. The town of La Salle was one of thousands of future communities that would be established on these lands. It was platted in 1899 as a station on the Minneapolis & St. Louis Railroad and, by 1900, had a post office. John Sundt was the postmaster. By 1916, the Eagle Roller Milling Company and the Great Western Grain Company had elevators to store local farmers' grain, and the La Salle Co-operative Creamery Association was formed to help bring dairy products to market. L. C. Carlson owned the blacksmith shop, and J. Benson was the proprietor of The LaSalle Hotel. There was also a hardware and implement store, lumber yard, two general dealers, and the State Bank of LaSalle. It was robbed on January 12, 1908. In the same decade, the post office was looted twice for $171.39 on April 3, 1904, and $149.52 on November 13, 1909. However, burglars could not steal La Salle's determination to become an incorporated community, which its townspeople achieved in January 1921. The capture site of the Younger Brothers is located a mile south of town.

Restaurant Recommendation:
Village Inn
103 S Broadway
La Salle, MN 56056

Restaurant Recommendation:
La Salle Meats
108 S Broadway
La Salle, MN 56056

LEWISVILLE, MN
POPULATION: 204 – CITY 95 OF 856 (3-27-25)

Lewisville was given its name to honor the legacy of Richard, James, and Nelson Lewis, the sons of the early Irish homesteader Thomas Lewis. All three brothers held stock in the Inter-State Land Company, a partner of the Chicago, St. Paul, Minneapolis & Omaha Railroad. The town was established on May 3, 1899, along a branch line connecting Madelia to Fairmont from north to south. When the post office was established in 1899, Richard Lewis volunteered to be its postmaster. He and his brothers wanted to ensure the prosperity of their new settlement, and they did so alongside many other men who made substantial contributions and improvements to the site. In seventeen years, Lewisville grew to a couple of hundred residents and a couple of dozen businesses that met their needs. Amongst these were an elevator, the Farmers' Elevator Company; a hotel run by Mrs. B. Mueller; John E. Moore's Lewisville Drug & Jewelry Company; Hillesheim & Company's general dealership; Weyerhaeuser & Company's lumber yard, and the Merchants' State Bank, to name a few. James Lewis was the bank's president in its early years. Surrounding the townsite and the railroad's right-of-way was an operation known as Tilney Farms, a large parcel of several thousand acres rented out to farmers by John S. Tilney of New York. An early publication notes that Lewisville was incredibly progressive for its time, as its businessmen and women worked to keep the city 100% debt-free. As of the 2020 Census, Lewisville has unfortunately regressed to a population of 204 residents, about half of what it had at its peak of 375 in the 1960s.

MADELIA, MN
POPULATION: 2,396 – CITY 96 OF 856 (3-27-25)

The original Watonwan County seat from 1860 to 1878 dates to September 10, 1857, when it was originally named Wacapa. That name survived for only a few months before it was changed to Madelia by Mr. Hartshorn, Shepard, and Haire to honor the memory of General Philander Hartshorn's daughter. One of the area's original post offices, Wacapa, was established in Brown County in 1857 but moved to Watonwan County in 1860, at which point its name was also changed. Jonathan and Caleb Leavitt opened a steam sawmill as the first real business in Madelia, and several attempts were made at making permanent business houses. Progress halted when the entire area was abandoned circa 1862 with the Sioux Uprising. Historical markers about Fort Cox, Fort Siocum, and Fort Hill document that era's military history and stories. Fort Cox, alternatively called Camp Willkin, was started by Captain E. St. Julien Cox and his men to defend settlers from attack during the Dakota War of 1862. The hexagonal log fortification served as a garrison until 1865. Madelia enjoyed the fruits of being the county seat during this period. Early firms included a blacksmith shop, a harness shop, a jewelry store, a millinery, a restaurant, a furniture store, a lumber yard, a hotel, a doctor's and a lawyer's offices, and plentiful general, hardware, and implement stores. Catholic, Methodist, and Presbyterian churches were the first to preach the "good news" and bring religion to the community. On September 21, 1876, a seventeen-year-old farmer boy named Asle Oscar Sorbel sounded the alarm that thieves fleeing from a botched robbery in Northfield, Minnesota, were drawing near Madelia. Under the direction of Sheriff James Glispin and Captain W. W. Murphy, 100 Madelia citizens gathered to catch and apprehend the burglars, some of the remaining members of the infamous James-Younger Gang. The gang centered around Jesse and Frank James. For months, the community bragged about their accomplishment (and even commemorated it in an event over a century later called Younger Brothers Day). The celebration was short-lived when a fire on October 31, 1877, started at the Eskstrom Brothers and Brown's store and destroyed a block of buildings. Thankfully, all the owners relocated their businesses to new facilities despite having no insurance. Enterprise was plentiful, and the structures were numerous at this time, but the Flanders' Block commercial building has survived as Madelia's most historic. The 1872 Italianate edifice served as the Watonwan County courthouse until 1878, when the honor was removed to St. James, much to the dismay of Madelia citizens. It also housed an International Order of Odd Fellows lodge, the Watonwan County Bank at different points, and countless commercial establishments. Despite a 594-371 vote that removed the county seat to St. James, Madelia grew as a division point on the Chicago, St. Paul, Minneapolis & Omaha Railroad. As of 2020, it has its highest-ever recorded population of 2,396 people. The last surviving work of Commodore P. Jones, a noted Minnesota bridge builder, is located near Madelia. The Warren truss Bridge is a 1908 steel truss bridge that boasts an early example of riveted joints. At The Watonwan County Historical Society, visitors can browse artifacts, documents, and more stories about Madelia's rise as one of Watonwan County's most significant communities. Knut Hamsum, the 1920 Nobel Prize in Literature winner, lived in

Madelia from 1883 to 1884. Shortly after his departure, Winfield Scott Hammond became the Madelia School Superintendent and later served as the 18th Governor of Minnesota. A relatively recent event in Madelia's history in 2016 mirrored the October 1877 events mentioned above: a devastating fire destroyed a restaurant, a dentist's office, a hair salon, an insurance office, an upholstery, and three other businesses.

ODIN, MN
POPULATION: 123 – CITY 86 OF 856 (3-26-25)
While Norwegian and Swedish settlers were searching for a name for their new Chicago & Northwestern Railroad community, platted in 1899 by the Western Town Lot Company, Sulfest Langeland suggested it be called Odin. The principal Norse god of wisdom, healing, death, and war was called *Woden* by the Anglo-Saxons and is the namesake behind "Wednesday," a.k.a. "Woden's Day." The influential figurehead of Germanic mythology also had Odin, Illinois, named in his honor. The Minnesota town was incorporated on July 17, 1902, and welcomed its post office in 1880. It was initially known as the Aasten's Town post office. As its population approached 200 residents in the mid-1910s, multiple businesses came to fruition: the Great Western Grain Company and Bingham Brothers elevators; the Odin Farmers' Telephone Company; the Odin Opera House; the Odin Co-operative Creamery Association; the Odin State Bank; P. M. Olson's auto garage; O. A. Kabrick's jeweler; Nixon & Son's meat market; J. H. Queal and Company's lumberyard, and several others dealing in general goods, pharmaceutical goods, barber services, furniture and harnesses, and more. Odin is the other community, alongside Butterfield, that claims ties to former United States Ambassador to Malta and later Iran, Bruce Laingen.

ORMSBY, MN
POPULATION: 118 – CITY 87 OF 856 (3-26-25)
Colonel Edwin Samuel Ormsby of Emmetsburg, Iowa, the man behind that community's Methodist Episcopal Church and the Burnham, Ormsby, and Company Bank, is the namesake of this town that splits the Watonwan and Martin county line down its Main Street. He was heavily involved in the business world, so when rumors began to spread that the Minneapolis & St. Louis Railroad planned to connect Fort Dodge, Iowa, and Fort Ridgely in Minnesota, he jumped on the opportunity to invest in the project. A town on the line was named in his honor, and he ensured its prosperity by establishing its Farmers State Bank and serving as president from July 1902 to January 1907. On the Watonwan side of the county line (as of 1916), there was the Stockdale and Dietz Elevator Company, the Tri-state Telephone Company, the A. G. Dushinske's hardware store, the Hans M. Vagstad farm tools and implements store, W. A. Urhback's barber shop, and Christian Jensen's general store. Ormsby's early residents had a preventive mindset. In the year the town was founded, the Ormsby Fire Department was also established. A 300-foot-deep well was bored to the water table north of the city, and pipes were installed to connect five groundwater reservoirs beneath the city's blocks. Investments continued decade after decade, and in August 1985, the fire department began its annual hog roast. A chicken fry fundraising event was held for the first time in April 1986 to help provide funds for the organization.

ST. JAMES, MN ★☆
POPULATION: 4,793 – CITY 83 OF 856 (3-26-25)
In 1867, the directors of the St. Paul and Sioux City Railroad Company met to determine where to establish a major division point between their two namesake cities. After much deliberation, they settled on Watonwan County, Minnesota, and began at

once to plan a townsite in the center of the county to link the cities. One of the men on the board was General Henry Hastings Sibley, the first Governor of Minnesota and a decorated military leader in the Dakota War of 1862. The then-railroad president, Elias F. Drake, permitted him to name the community. Sibley chose a long Dakota name in 1871, but when asked in 1874 to replicate it for formal application to the town plat and map, neither he nor Drake could remember it. Sibley offered to reference his papers at home to remember the name, but Drake suggested they choose a name that could be "more easily remembered." His choice of nomenclature was St. James, which, according to some accounts, is a tribute to James Parrington, the original townsite owner before the advancement of the railroad. St. James became a point of pride and prosperity within the county with its permanent name finally assigned. S. C. Clark selected the first lot on July 18, 1870, as the future hotel site, and J. Dean & Company started a lumber yard that September. The first passenger train rolled into town on November 22, 1870; by 1871, St. James was already incorporated as a village. During that winter, it welcomed several business interests: five general merchandise stores, the St. James Hotel, the Union Hotel, two saloons, Shannon & Skelton's grocery store, the Parker Brothers hardware and drug store, and Herrick & Bacon's store. To spur even more growth, the railroad offered to donate a lot to any religious denomination that wished to erect an edifice. The first such group to capitalize on that offer was the First Baptist Church of St. James, whose building was completed by September 1872. Next were the Methodist Episcopalians in 1872. The Presbyterian congregation opted to split time with the Baptists in their building, and the Catholics completed their structure in 1876. Because its growth was expected to outpace that of Madelia and all other towns within the county, a series of elections was held that ultimately resulted in the permanent removal of the county seat to a significant railroad division point. That event, coupled with the presence of the Chicago, St. Paul, Minneapolis & Omaha, and the Minneapolis & St. Louis Railroads, catapulted St. James to a population of 2,607 residents by the turn of the century. It was chartered as a city on April 27, 1899. All the commercial interests of the town would be far too numerous to list, as there were well over three hundred total buildings in St. James by this point. Some of its proudest accomplishments included three carriage and wagon factories, a cigar factory, a bottling works, an opera house, a flour mill, a creamery, a steam laundry business, four grain elevators, four hotels, eight churches, and seven fraternal lodges. C. T. Crowley and L. Halverson founded the Crowley cigar business in 1899 and produced over 300,000 cigars annually. A second cigar factory started in 1904 by brothers Edward, Frank, and Philip Wermerskirchen could match that production. St. James Bottling Works manufactured unique soft drinks and beer as early as 1887 when Joseph J. Sperl started the business. Just before World War II, St. James had about 3,400 residents, and its business lines had shifted to include 13 filling stations, 11 eating places, 10 grocery stores, and even pairs of jewelry and music stores. Three locations in and around St. James are listed on the National Register of Historic Places; they are Alfred R. Voss's Farmstead, Southern Minnesota's largest private 19th-century farm built between 1893 and 1920; the St. James Opera House, a Queen Anne-style building built from 1891-92 that was an important performance venue and meeting place for the city from 1892 to 1921, and the Watonwan County Courthouse. The large Victorian and Romanesque Revival structure was designed by H. C. Gerlach and built from 1895-96 by Otto Kleinschmidt. The St. James Library started in 1911 and became the official county library in 1943. Since 1947, the Tony Downs Foods Company has been one of the largest employers of St. James and surrounding town residents. Loads of famous folks are connected to the city in one way or another: Winfield Scott Hammond, the 18th Governor of Minnesota; Becky Buller, a bluegrass artist and member of The Becky Buller Band and First Ladies of Bluegrass; Moses K.

Armstrong, a delegate from the U.S. House of Representatives from Dakota Territory from March 1871 to March 1875; Henry N. Graven, the Senior Judge of the United States District for the Northern District of Iowa from August 1961 to February 1970; and MLB players Mike Kingery and Gary Mielke. Kingery played from 1986 to 1996 as an outfielder for multiple franchises, and Mielke was a pitcher for the Texas Rangers in 1987, 1989, and 1990. Theodore S. Mondale, a former pastor of the First Methodist Church of St. James, was the father of Walter Mondale, the 42nd Vice President of the United States.

Restaurant Recommendation:
Plaza Jalisco Mexican Restaurant & Cantina
608 1st Ave S
St. James, MN 56081

Restaurant Recommendation:
Home Town Cafe
403 1st Ave S
St. James, MN 56081

Unincorporated/Ghost Towns: Echols, Godahl, Grogan, South Branch, Sveadahl, Tenmile Corner

National Register of Historic Places:
Godahl: Nelson & Albin Cooperative Mercantile Association Store
Madelia: Flanders' Block, West Bridge
St. James: Grand Opera House, Watonwan County Courthouse, Alfred R. Voss Farmstead

Golf Courses:
Madelia Golf Course, Municipal (Madelia, MN)
St. James Golf Course, Daily Fee (St. James, MN)

Breweries/Wineries/Distilleries:
Lost Sanity Brewing (Madelia, MN)

Town Celebrations:
St. James Railroad Days, St. James, MN (Last Full Week of June)
Butterfield Threshing Bee, Butterfield, MN (3rd Weekend of August)
Butterfield Summer Sizzler, Butterfield, MN (Weekend of July 4th)

WILKIN COUNTY
EST. 1858 - POPULATION: 6,506

Wilkin County (est. 1858) was named for Colonel Alexander Wilkin, a Mexican-American and American Civil War veteran who perished in combat during the 1864 Battle of Tupelo.

BRECKENRIDGE, MN ★☆
POPULATION: 3,430 – CITY 200 OF 856 (5-3-25)
Breckenridge grew along its twin city of Wahpeton, North Dakota, at the confluence of the Bois de Sioux River and the Otter Tail River, where the headquarters of the Red River of the North (the longest North-flowing river in the United States) begins. The riverboat town was opened for settlement in 1851 and platted initially in 1857-58 by

Henry T. Welles. A postal service branch opened at that time, taking the name Breckenridge in honor of John Cabell Breckinridge, who was then the 14th Vice President of the United States under James Buchanan. He later served as the 5th Confederate States Secretary of War and as a Major General in its Army during the American Civil War. A sawmill, a hotel, and some residences were among the town's first businesses. They were destroyed between August 23-24, 1862, during the Dakota War of 1862. Most of the village had been deserted due to the Civil War in the South, but early warnings also caused many of the settlers to flee before the Native Americans arrived. When they did come across the town, they were met in battle by three Breckenridge men, all of whom were killed trying to protect the community. Wilkin County would not see many new settlers until the arrival of the St. Paul and Pacific Railroad in the fall of 1871. The line, eventually backed by the capital of the Great Northern (which established a roundhouse facility), opened new trade opportunities for area farmers and enabled Breckenridge to establish itself as the most important trading point in the county. It was designated the seat of government, and its NRHP-nominated Beaux-Arts-style courthouse was built in 1928-29. Before constructing its historic courthouse, Breckenridge residents had numerous other feats under their belts. A 1903 atlas recorded the presence of an electric light plant, a high school, a Catholic church, a Methodist Episcopal church, a Presbyterian church, a hospital, a fire department, a feed mill, flour mills, grain elevators, lumberyards, four banks, the *Breckenridge Gazette* newspaper office, and myriad other firms. The Northern Pacific Railroad and the Fergus Falls division of the St. Paul, Minneapolis & Manitoba (in 1879) entered Breckenridge later. They helped it grow to a population of 4,335 by the dawn of the 1960s. Some of the community's most famous persons have been Heidi Heitkamp, a United States Senator from North Dakota between January 2013 and January 2019; George Putnam, a Los Angeles talk show host active from 1934 to 2008; Cheryl Tiegs, widely regarded as "America's first supermodel" for her famous appearances in 1970s magazines like the *Sports Illustrated Swimsuit Issue*; Gary Sikorski, a U.S. Congressman with Minnesota from 1983 to 1993; Fritz Scholder, a Native American artist whose works are displayed at numerous prominent art institutions throughout the country, and Dick Enderle, a guard in the National Football League from 1969 to 1976.

 Restaurant Recommendation:
Wilkin Drink & Eatery
508 Minnesota Ave
Breckenridge, MN 56520

CAMPBELL, MN
POPULATION: 164 – CITY 198 OF 856 (5-3-25)

Initially established on the stage route to Fergus Falls, this small town of 164 people began to develop in 1871 when it was laid out by the St. Paul and Pacific Railroad (later the Great Northern) company. Campbell, a name of Scottish origin, was given to the newly minted townsite and the postal branch when they were organized in 1873. Thirty years later, when the Northwest Publishing Company came through to map the area, they reported the presence of three grain elevators, two lumber yards, a depot, two hotels, a bank, a livery, a newspaper office, a roller mill, a German Lutheran church, the Union Congregational Church, and a school. Campbell was incorporated as a village on January 28, 1899; it reached a peak population of 424 in 1920. Errol Man, a placekicker in the NFL from 1968 to 1978 who won Super Bowl XI with the Oakland Raiders, was born in Campbell on June 27, 1941. Thomas D. Schall, a United States Senator from Minnesota, grew up here.

DORAN, MN
POPULATION: 36 – CITY 199 OF 856 (5-3-25)
Once upon a time, this community of three dozen people was one of a series of stations on the Great Northern Railroad that served as a hub for shipping agricultural products and moving passengers across the prairie. The proprietor of the Great Northern, James J. Hill, named this particular town in honor of Michael Doran of St. Paul, Minnesota. He was a Minnesota State Senate politician and an avid businessman. By 1903, Doran had two elevators, a depot, the School District No. 29 building, and a small commercial district. Its post office began in 1892 but was discontinued in 1989 after several years of communal population decline. As many as 137 people lived in Doran in its heyday in the 1930s. Not far from the town's city limits is the Stiklestad United Lutheran Church, a historic 1898 Carpenter Gothic church raised by Norwegian immigrants to practice their faith.

FOXHOME, MN
POPULATION: 126 – CITY 244 OF 856 (5-7-25)
The hay town of Foxhome, named for original townsite owner and real estate dealer Robert A. Fox, once had the capability of producing 400-500 carloads of hay each year for transport via its Northern Pacific Railroad depot and station. The little village was incorporated on January 21, 1902, six years after it welcomed a postal service branch. The 1910s, leading into 1920, were Foxhome's most prosperous decade, when 266 people lived there. As of 1903, a lumberyard, a livery, a newspaper office, a school, and a pair of elevators and hotels were located here. At one point, it also had churches for three congregations: Catholics, Lutherans, and Methodists.

KENT, MN
POPULATION: 65 – CITY 201 OF 856 (5-3-25)
Two hundred thirty-eight citizens lived in Kent at its first Census in 1910, six years after the county commissioners opted to incorporate it on November 22, 1904. When the town was laid out by the Great Northern Railroad, it was named after the county in England. A post office was organized in 1888, and by 1903, the little village had reaped the benefits of the railroad and built up multiple elevators, a lumber yard, a blacksmith shop, a bank, a hotel, and a livery along its Main Street. The public school was located in the northwestern corner of the plat, near Whiskey Creek, much as the parochial school, church, and parsonage were in Kent's southeast corner. Many of its original buildings came from McCauleyville, a now-defunct community. Frederick E. Murphy, a newspaper publisher from Minneapolis, moved to Wilkin County circa 1918 with his family and purchased five farms (about 5,000 acres) on which he grew numerous cash crops and specialized in purebred livestock. One of his prized cows, Lady Pride, reportedly produced 35,626 pounds of milk and 1,483 pounds of butter in a year, nearly eight times that of an average cow. Femco Farms was disbanded and sold off in the 1940s, but its Femco Farm No. 2, built in 1922, has been added to the NRHP.

NASHUA, MN
POPULATION: 67 – CITY 197 OF 856 (5-3-25)
When coming into Nashua from the east or the west circa 1903, travelers along the Minneapolis, St. Paul & Sault Ste. Marie Railroad would have been welcomed by a very tiny town. From west to east, the then-village of a couple of hundred residents (but 271 by 1910) had only stockyards, the depot, an elevator, a lumber yard, a store that doubled as a post office, a hotel, the German Lutheran church, and various residences. The post office began in 1892 under Philip F. Nash, but was discontinued

by 1996. It was named after the Nash family, but the '-ua' was added to match the names of the communities in Iowa and New Hampshire. Nashua was incorporated on April 19, 1902.

ROTHSAY, MN
POPULATION: 498 – CITY 242 OF 856 (5-7-25)

Rothsay was born out of necessity when the Fergus Falls division of the St. Paul, Minneapolis, and Manitoba Railroad was laid through the northeast corner of Wilkin County in 1879. As the tracks were being laid, the employees (named Gilbert Gilbertson) concurrently constructed a shanty saloon, which effectively served as the townsite's first business despite the line not yet being fully finished. Hard liquor was poured out and enjoyed by all until a brawl broke out, destroying the saloon as quickly as it had been erected. Many workers left the skirmish with bruises and broken bones. The mishap put a slight damper on celebrating the railroad's completion. Still, the Rothsay townsite was surveyed on Christen Tanberg's land. He platted the townsite, but officials named it after Rothesay, Scotland, the only such usage of that name in the United States today. Country schoolhouses and churches like the South Immanuel Lutheran Church, Hedemarken Lutheran Church, and the North Friborg Lutheran Church had existed in the area as early as 1872, but the development of Rothsay truly began after the railroad connected it with other nearby communities. Amund A. Baatten and Anders B. Pedersen opened the first two general stores. In 1880, Mr. Pederson became the first postmaster with the arrival of the branch office, and then along came the elevators, a roller mill, a stockyard, a lumber yard, a hotel, a livery, a bank, the *Rothsay Record* newspaper office, and a pair of Norwegian Lutheran churches by 1903. Of all its early accomplishments, one stands out as the town's most intact historic building: the J. A. Johnson Blacksmith Shop. Much of the shop's original equipment is still in place, making it one of Minnesota's most intact early-20th-century renditions of the business. It was listed on the National Register of Historic Places on February 23, 1996. When taking the Interstate-94 Center Street exit for Rothsay, travelers often gape at the 9,000-pound, 13-foot-tall alien-like creature standing on the side of the road: the World's Largest "Booming" Prairie Chicken. Art Fosse built it on behalf of the City of Rothsay for the 1976 Bicentennial. On June 10, 1975, Rothsay was named the "Prairie Chicken Capital of Minnesota."

WOLVERTON, MN
POPULATION: 128 – CITY 202 OF 856 (5-3-25)

Not much remains from Wolverton's heyday, but its Public School building, built in 1906 and closed in 1978, still stands today as the gem of the northwestern Wilkin County town. The first senior class graduated from Wolverton High in 1922, only four years after it first offered a secondary education program. Louis M. Miller had one of the first businesses, a trading post called Miller's Station. The post office operated under that name from 1878 to 1881, then shortened to just Miller in 1881, and then changed to Jacksville from 1881 to 1886. It changed one final time in 1887 to honor the legacy of Dr. William D. Wolverton, an original area landowner and the physician at North Dakota's Fort Abercrombie. His land was purchased by the Great Northern Railroad, which brought with it the means and the men to bring about all kinds of businesses: three grain elevator, a blacksmith shop, a hardware store, a livery stable, a meat market, a hotel, a bank, a creamery, a lumber company, a dentist's office, the *Wolverton Progress* newspaper, and two general stores. Wolverton's population peaked at 222 in 1940.

Unincorporated/Ghost Towns: Brushvale, Childs, Everdell, Lawndale, McCauleyville, Tenney

National Register of Historic Places:
Breckenridge: Wilkin County Courthouse
Doran: Stiklestad United Lutheran Church
Kent: Femco Farm No. 2
Rothsay: J. A. Johnson Blacksmith Shop
Wolverton: Wolverton Public School, David N. Peet Farmstead

Golf Courses:
Bois De Sioux Golf Cub, Daily Fee (Breckenridge, MN)

WINONA COUNTY
EST. 1854 - POPULATION: 49,671

Winona was a fictional Dakota woman who took her own life after jumping off Lake Pepin's "Maiden Rock," because she was set to marry a man she did not love. Winona generally refers to the firstborn female child within a tribal family, per Dakota customs.

ALTURA, MN
POPULATION: 471 – CITY 695 OF 856 (10-16-25)
Altura was named by the Winona & Southwestern Railway in 1889 for a town in Valencia, Spain, although that name had been in use since the first settlers in the vicinity in the 1850s. That railroad, more commonly known as the Wisconsin, Minnesota & Pacific, brought enough settlers and attention to the area that the formation of the Altura post office was warranted in 1891, replacing the former Norton office. It was located in Herman Hilke's store, as he was the postmaster. E. C. Burns platted the Altura townsite on his land in August 1901, and from that point forward, businesses, schools, and churches were established. George Henry Speltz, went on to become the Bishop of the Diocese of St. Cloud, Minnesota, from 1968 to 1987.

DAKOTA, MN
POPULATION: 295 – CITY 679 OF 856 (10-15-25)
Dakota, located on Lake Onalaska and the Mississippi River, primarily grew as a railway village along the Chicago, Milwaukee & St. Paul line. It was laid out in 1855, and Nathan Brown later developed it that decade. He was a stockyard owner and a ferry operator between Minnesota and Wisconsin. Postal service operated between 1855-57, then closed for 18 years before restarting in 1875. Several business lines, such as a sawmill, were operational in 1894, as were School No. 86, a Grand Army of the Republic Hall, and Catholic and Episcopalian churches. Dakota attained incorporation as a village in May 1951, nearly a century after it was initially laid out. The berry and apple industries have long been among its primary economic drivers. Great River Bluffs State Park preserves 3,067 acres of large, steep bluffs along the Mississippi River in an area of southeast Minnesota known as the Driftless Region, which is characterized by deep river valleys and colorful deciduous trees in the fall.

ELBA, MN
POPULATION: 129 – CITY 694 OF 856 (10-16-25)
The inland town of Elba, which is without a railroad, was founded in 1856 and named after the island of Elba in Tuscany, Italy. Chiefly built up by German and

Luxembourgish immigrants, they welcomed their original post office in 1858, which, until 1960, served the community as an independent post office before becoming a rural station. It closed in 1965. Other institutions in the town on the North Branch of the Whitewater River included a flour mill, two blacksmith shops, and two hotels. A pair of 1850s-era homes built in the Whitewater Valley have since been preserved on the National Register of Historic Places as the William Hemmelberg and the Nicholas Marnach Houses. In nearby Whitewater State Park, several New Deal-era structures built between 1934-41 still stand and welcome over 300,000 annual visitors to the park known for its trout fishing and impressive blufflands. The town survived a massive flooding incident on August 18, 2007, when the dikes holding back the Whitewater River failed, inundating the small city. As a result of the flooding, Elba experienced its largest decade-over-decade population loss in its history, with 29% of the town moving away. The population decreased from 214 in 2000 to 152 in 2010.

GOODVIEW, MN
POPULATION: 4,158 – CITY 700 OF 856 (10-16-25)
Winona's northwestern neighbor began as a suburb of the county seat, located only about six blocks west of the Winona City limits. Clarence F. Witt was the original owner of the land that would become this "sister city" located on the bluffs of the scenic Mississippi River Valley. The beauty of the surrounding area prompted many residents to move there and call it "Goodview" for its gorgeous views. After some time, an idea circulated that the subdivision should be incorporated as its own independent municipality. On August 8, 1946, a vote was held, and Goodview's roughly 400 residents voted in favor of independence. Over the last eight decades, its population has grown tenfold, with no negative growth periods decade over decade.

LEWISTON, MN
POPULATION: 1,533 – CITY 697 OF 856 (10-16-25)
Jonathan Smith Lewis is the namesake of this town of 1,533 people near the center of the county. From 1855 to 1872, the post office was called New Boston in honor of postmaster W. H. Dwight's former home in Boston, Massachusetts, but it was changed in 1872 when the office moved from Houston County to Winona County. Unlike so many other towns in southeastern Minnesota, Lewiston's residents did not have to wait long for incorporation. That day came on February 23, 1875, primarily because of the community's designation as the first restocking and rest stop on the Winona-Rochester stagecoach line. Given another 20 years to develop, Lewiston found itself located on the Winona & St. Peter Railroad and the site of several business lines, including a wagon shop, two blacksmith shops, a bank, two hotels, and elevators, to name a few. The northern part of town had a Lutheran church and school, as well as an Evangelical church and school. School No. 22 was located in east Lewiston, and a Catholic church and cemetery could be found in the southern reaches of town, far down Fremont Street. From 1930 to March 2020, the *Lewiston Journal* was an independent newspaper covering the events and stories of Lewiston, until it merged with the St. Charles Press to form the St. Charles Press & Lewiston Journal. Lewiston surpassed one thousand residents for the first time in the 1970s.

MINNESOTA CITY, MN
POPULATION: 202 – CITY 699 OF 856 (10-16-25)
In the early days, some settlers in Minnesota Territory had great confidence that their village, aptly named Minnesota City for its location on the Mississippi River within said territory, would someday serve as the state capital. The site was platted in 1852 on

behalf of the Western Farm and Village Association, a group of colonists from New York City. Robert Pike gave the village its name, hoping it would blossom into Minnesota's most important entity. While those dreams never came to fruition because of its far eastern location, Minnesota City did attract three railroads: the Chicago, Milwaukee & St. Paul, the Winona & St. Peter, and the Winona & Southwestern. A post office predated all other local institutions, having been started in 1852. Minnesota City of the 1890s had a flouring mill, a brewery, School No. 29, hotels, banks, and churches operated by the Methodist Episcopalians, Baptists, and German Lutherans. Since its first Census in 1880 (of 273 people), the population has never been recorded as being fewer than 141 (in the 1920s) or higher than 301 (in the 1970s).

ROLLINGSTONE, MN
POPULATION: 678 – CITY 702 OF 856 (10-17-25)
One of the largest Luxembourg-American communities in the United States is the City of Rollingstone, established by immigrants from the Grand Duchy (a nickname for Luxembourg, the only nation in the world ruled by a Grand Duke or Duchess) in March 1855. They filed land claims at the Winona land office at that time, and over the next half-century, hundreds of farmers from the small European country settled in the region. Interestingly, a different group from New England attempted to colonize the area in 1853 through the Western Farm and Village Association, but they failed due to illness and poor planning. Luxembourg immigrants fared much better, and within no time, the village on the North Branch of Rollingstone Creek had blacksmiths, hotels, stores, School No. 30, and a grand Catholic Church. That original Catholic church structure, called the Church of the Holy Trinity, has served Rollingstone Catholics since 1869 and features heavy elements of the Gothic Revival style. Charles Wender was the architect, and Nicholas Arnoldy was the second architect when it was expanded in 1893 to accommodate significantly more parishioners. The church was later added to the National Register of Historic Places. Rollingstone Village Hall, which served as the local government building from 1900 to 1962, is also on the Register and is now called the Rollingstone Luxembourg Heritage Museum.

SAINT CHARLES, MN ☆
POPULATION: 3,990 – CITY 693 OF 856 (10-16-25)
"The Gladiolus Capital of the World" was named "St. Charles" in honor of Saint Charles Borromeo, the Catholic Archbishop of Milan, Italy, from 1564 to 1584. It was suggested by Lewis H. Springer of St. Charles, Illinois, who arrived in this part of Minnesota circa 1853. He established the first store, boarding house, and post office in town. The village itself began in 1854 on Springer's land and was platted to include 49 blocks and a public park, which helped market the would-be agricultural center to prospective immigrant farmers. Railroad tracks connected St. Charles to Winona in 1864, and soon it became a railroad stop for the Winona & Southwestern and the Winona & St. Peter Railroads. The first line passed right by the Catholic church, storefronts, and a grain elevator through downtown St. Charles, whereas the second line was much larger and boasted of a flour mill and four elevators. By the end of the century, there were also dozens more businesses and storefronts, a jail, a creamery, wagon works, a high school, and churches for the German Lutherans, Methodists, and Baptists. Some of these early structures, built between 1890 and 1901, are preserved in the Whitewater Avenue Commercial Historic District. Saint Charles City Bakery, the last remaining structure of the original St. Charles commercial district, built in 1876, and the Trinity Episcopal Church, constructed in 1874 in the Carpenter Gothic style, also remain. In modern history, residents of the area may recall a scare at North Star Foods when a

fire at the local poultry processing plant threatened to release toxic anhydrous ammonia gas from its tanks. St. Charles was fully evacuated on April 17, 2009, but allowed to return to town only a day later. Local floriculturist Carl H. Fischer, the founder of Noweta Gardens, is renowned for developing over 600 hybrids of the Gladiolus perennial. He is remembered by the name of the city's annual festival, Gladiolus Days, which is always held the weekend before Labor Day. Three other famous men from town included Erastus Milo Cravath, a co-founder of Nashville, Tennessee's Fisk University, and other HBCUs in the South; Arthur Donahue, a pilot with the Royal Air Force in World War II who was killed in action; and Brad Nessler, a sports commentator for CBS Sports.

Restaurant Recommendation:
Genesis Restaurant
331 W 6th St
St. Charles, MN 55972

STOCKTON, MN
POPULATION: 809 – CITY 698 OF 856 (10-16-25)
J. B. Stockton, the original owner of the Stockton townsite alongside William Davidson and William Springer, is the namesake of the community. Development began in the summer of 1856 along Rollingstone Creek and its west branch. A post office opened in 1855 and preempted every other establishment, but H. A. Putnam quickly put up a general merchandise store. A blacksmith shop and wagon shop were amongst the ensuing firms to be established, as were a hotel, a gristmill, and the School No. 18 building. From 1857 to 1875, the 20' x 28' school building hosted the town's young pupils, before a 28' x 50' structure took its place. The second rendition lasted until 1957, when a new brick-and-concrete building went up. It was purchased in 1982 for use as a community center and the Stockton City Hall offices. Other noted places in town as of 1894 were the town's flour mill, a Lutheran church, a Methodist Episcopal church, a hotel, an elevator, and the stockyards. Stockton benefited greatly from the construction of the first eleven miles of the Winona & St. Peter Railroad coming westward from Winona, as in 1862, it was one of only a few select communities in Minnesota to be located on a functional railroad other than the St. Paul & Pacific line between St. Paul and St. Anthony Falls. Trinity Episcopal Church, now the Grace Evangelical Lutheran Church, was built in 1859 and remains standing as an early example of a German-immigrant-led church congregation. Doctor Helen Cordelia Putnam, known for her work in women's and children's health, particularly within schools, was born here on September 14, 1857.

UTICA, MN
POPULATION: 266 – CITY 696 OF 856 (10-16-25)
Conflicting sources credit either John W. Bentley or Austin Raymond with suggesting the name Utica, after Utica, New York, for this town that once served as a stop on both the Winona & Saint Peter and the Wisconsin, Minnesota & Pacific Railroads. Utica was platted in 1866 by Benjamin Ellsworth, about a decade after the post office opened. It was moved into town from the Bentleys' home following the town's platting. Ellsworth gave Utica its first grain elevator, and as the years flew by, it added on a second elevator (this one on the opposite rail line), a creamery, two blacksmith shops, a hotel, a feed mill, a Presbyterian church, and School No. 21. Benjamin Ellsworth's personal Italianate-style home, built in 1873, has survived as Utica's most historic point of interest; it was added to the NRHP in August 1984. Utica is another example of a

community that has retained a similar number of citizens since its first Census in 1900. It has reported a low population of 179 people in the 1940s, but as many as 291 citizens in the 2010s.

WINONA, MN ★
POPULATION: 25,948 – CITY 701 OF 856 (10-17-25)

One of Minnesota's most recognizable railroad towns is Winona, which served as the eastern terminus of the Winona & Saint Peter and the Winona & Southwestern Railroads. It also enjoyed the presence of a line of the Chicago, Milwaukee & St. Paul Railroad, and was the only city in Minnesota to be a part of the Green Bay & Western Railroad line (as its western terminus). While railroading was clearly important in those early days, it was Winona's location on the Mississippi River that brought in its first settlers: the Dakota. They lived at the village of Keoxa, a precursor to the village of Montezuma.. The name selected by Ervin H. Johnson honored the renowned Aztec leader only briefly, but it was quickly changed to a Dakota word meaning "first-born who is a daughter." Alternative spellings have included "Winuŋna," "Wenonah," and "Wynona," whereas other settlers called the area "Wing Prairie," "Wabasha's Prairie," or "The Island City." Winona was designated the county seat in 1854, the same year its first sawmill was built. A flour mill was established in 1856, and in 1857, it was incorporated as a city, despite the meandering of the Mississippi River, which cut a new channel and forced the city's steamboat landing to be moved. One of its largest and earliest accomplishments was the First State Normal School of Minnesota, which opened in 1858 to educate new elementary school teachers. Most of its male students, and even its principal, left in the 1860s to serve in the American Civil War, forcing it to briefly close until both the war and the events of the Dakota War of 1862 in western Minnesota had subsided. Throughout the 1850s, New Englanders, Germans, and eventually Poles came here by the thousands, and by 1860, it had 2,464 citizens. That number grew to 7,192 by 1870 and then nearly 20,000 by the turn of the century, making it one of Minnesota's largest and most important economic centers. A selection of its important places documented on Charles M. Foote's 1894 plat map included facilities of the CM&St.P Railway company, the Winona Manufacturing Company, the Winona Wagon Company, harvester works, a sash, door & blind factory, a furniture factory, a soap factory, a slaughter house, a sawmill, a planing mill, a conservatory, ironworks, an engine house, St. John's Hospital, a high school, the Madison School, the Kosciusko School, the Washington School, the county fairgrounds, multiple churches, and hundreds of other businesses. At least three dozen places and historic districts have been listed in the National Register of Historic Places to help preserve them. The Winona Commercial Historic District encompasses six blocks of downtown and 65 contributing properties, whereas the East Second Street Commercial Historic District focuses on 14 properties primarily built in the late 1860s. Twenty-five properties of an early upper-class Winona neighborhood are preserved as the Windom Park Residential Historic District. Other noteworthy places on the list range from the Lake Park Bandshell, built in 1924, to the 1912 Merchants National Bank, or the 500-foot-high Sugar Loaf river bluff and the historic 1872 to 1969 Sugar Loaf Brewery at its base. Many of the earlier-mentioned schools are still standing, as are the Model School Building and College Hall (Phelps Hall and Somsen Hall) of the Winona Normal School (now Winona State University). A stunning High Victorian Gothic/Richardsonian Romanesque First Congregational Church, built in 1882, and the 1895 Catholic Church of Saint Stanislaus (now known as the Basilica of Saint Stanislaus Kostka), constructed by Minnesota's largest Polish American community, are the two notable historic churches. With over 5,000 Poles, most of them Kashubians, moving into Winona before the turn of the century, Winona earned the nickname "The Kashubian Capital of America." Many modern day businesses deserve recognition for being headquartered in Winona, including Fastenal, an industrial supply company frequently listed in the Fortune 500; Willet Hauser Architectural Glass, Inc., a stained glass firm that has given Winona the title of the "Stained Glass Capital of the United States;" WinCraft Sports, and Watkins Incorporated, a manufacturer of health, baking, and household products, amongst several others. Winona State University adopted its current name and status in 1975, after 117 years of serving primarily as a teacher's college. In 1912, Saint Mary's College (now Saint Mary's University of Minnesota) was established as a private Catholic university. Its sister campus of sorts was the College of Saint Teresa, a Catholic women's college that operated first as a women's seminary and, from 1907 to 1989, as an institution of higher learning under the Sisters of Saint Francis. Many Winonians deserve recognition for their contributions to society. Ten of the most notable men and women are Carol Bartz, the former CEO of Yahoo! and later of Autodesk; James Earle Fraser, noted for his work on multiple Washington D.C. statues and for designing the Buffalo nickel (in circulation from 1913 to 1938); Paul Giel, a 1975 inductee into the College Football Hall of Fame for his time spent with the Minnesota Golden Gophers as a halfback; William D. Mitchell, the 54th United States Attorney General under President Herbert Hooer from March 1929 to March 1933; Joseph Ray Watkins, founder of the direct sales industry as a whole via his Watkins Incorporated company and the first businessman to offer a money back guarantee in the United States; William Windom, the 33rd and 39th United States Secretary of the Treasury under Presidents James A. Garfield and Benjamin Harrison; Tracy Caulkins, a three-time Olympic gold medalist swimmer at the 1984 Los Angeles Olympic Games and a sixty-three time American record-setter in the sport; Bernhard Brenner, the founder of Knitcraft Corporation known for St. Croix luxury knitwear; Eugenia Wheeler Goff, a co-founder of the National Historical Publishing Company, and Paul Breza, a Catholic priest and the founder of the Kashubian Cultural Institute and Polish Museum at Winona. The museum is located in the former Laird-Norton Lumber Company office. It is a facilitator for foreign exchange student programs between Winona and Bytów, Poland, a sister city of Winona.

Restaurant Recommendation:
Bloedow Bakery
451 E Broadway St
Winona, MN 55987

Restaurant Recommendation:
Norvary
1035 Frontenac Dr
Winona, MN 55987

Lodging Recommendation:
Alexander Mansion Historic B&B
274 E Broadway St
Winona, MN 55987

La Crescent is only partially located in Winona County (see Houston County), and Minneiska is only partially located in Winona County (ese Wabasha County).

Unincorporated/Ghost Towns: Ashton, Beaver, Bethany, Centerville, Clyde, Donehower, Dresbach, Enterprise, Fremont, Grover, Homer, Lamoille, Nodine, Oakridge,

Pickwick, Pine Creek, Ridgeway, Saratoga, Troy, Whitewater Falls, Whitman, Wilson, Witoka, Wyattville

National Register of Historic Places:
Elba: William Hemmelberg House, Nicholas Marnarch House, Whitewater State Park CCC/WPA/Rustic Style Historic Resources
Homer: Willard Bunnell House
Pickwick: Pickwick Mill
Rollingstone: Church of the Holy Trinity-Catholic, Rollingstone Village Hall
St. Charles: Saint Charles City Bakery, Trinity Episcopal Church, Whitewater Avenue Commercial Historic District
Stockton: Trinity Episcopal Church
Utica: Benjamin Ellsworth House
Winona: Anger's Block, Central Grade School, Chicago, Milwaukee & St. Paul Railway, Choate Department Store, Church of Saint Stanislaus-Catholic, East Second Street Commercial Historic District, First Congregational Church, Dr. J. W. S. Gallagher House, Grain & Lumber Exchange Building, Abner F. Hodgins House, Huff-Lamberton House, Jefferson School, Kirch/Latch Building, Laird, Norton Company Building, Lake Park Bandshell, Madison School, Merchant's National Bank, Model School Building & College Hall of the Winona Normal School, Schlitz Hotel, Sugar Loaf, Washington-Kosciusko School, J.R. Watkins Medical Company Complex, Paul Watkins House, Windom Park Residential Historic District, Winona & St. Peter Engine House, Winona & St. Peter Railroad Freight House, Winona Athletic Club, Winona City Hall, Winona Commercial Historic District, Winona County Courthouse, Winona Free Public Library, Winona High School & Winona Junior High School, Winona Hotel, Winona Masonic Temple, Winona Savings Bank Building

Golf Courses:
Cedar Valley Golf Course, Daily Fee (Winona, MN)
St. Charles Golf Club, Daily Fee (St. Charles, MN)
The Bridges, Daily Fee (Winona, MN)
Westfield Golf Club, Daily Fee (Winona, MN)

Breweries/Wineries/Distilleries:
Garvin Heights Vineyards (Winona, MN)
Two Fathoms Brewing (Winona, MN)

Town Celebrations:
Gladiolus Days, St. Charles, MN (Weekend before Labor Day)
Winona Steamboat Days, Winona, MN (3rd Week of June)

WRIGHT COUNTY
EST. 1855 - POPULATION: 141,337

Swedish and German settlers made up the initial significant portions of Wright County's population; the county was named after Silas Wright, the 14th Governor of New York from 1945 to 1946.

ALBERTVILLE, MN
POPULATION: 7,896 – CITY 842 OF 856 (11-14-25)
Two earlier names are affiliated with this community of 7,896: Hamburg and St. Michael. Joseph and Josephine Vetsch gave it its Hamburg name, likely after the city in Germany, and later that same year (in 1881), the Minneapolis and Northwestern Railroad Company extended its right-of-way through the vicinity. They reportedly paid $125 for the land and called their station St. Michael after a separate village in the south. Several years later, in 1902, J.P. Eull, Anthony Vetsch, and Theodore Adyt

petitioned the county commissioners to incorporate the township under the name "St Michael's Station," a request that was granted. Albert Zachman donated land for a Catholic church site, and an ordinance was passed to erect a village hall for a cost of $531.95. Mass was held in the village hall basement until the church was finished. Business buildings like the Albert Roller Mill (built in 1909 and demolished in 2006), homes, and schools were built alongside the Church of St. Albert, and in 1909, the decision was made to change the town's name to Albertville in honor of the man who had given the land for the church. The name was legally changed with the county and state on September 24, 1919. Just over eighty years later, Albertville's commerce sector expanded rapidly when the Albertville Premium Outlets mall opened in April 2000, featuring brands like Nike, Puma, and Ralph Lauren. Space Aliens Grill and Bar, an outer-space-themed restaurant known for its extraterrestrial decor, artifacts, and mascot, is among the strangest family restaurants in all of Minnesota.

ANNANDALE, MN
POPULATION: 3,763 – CITY 849 OF 856 (11-15-25)
Fort Harriman (alternatively called Fort Skedaddle) was built on the southwest shore of Pleasant Lake to defend early settlers from Native attacks through the 1860s, at which point white settlers forced the Indigenous out of the area. Many families lived in and stood guard at the fort until it was clear that Chief Little Crow and his Dakota men posed no threat to permanent settlement. Once enough people had reconvened in this area, an application was submitted to the postal service to start an office called "Abbeyville," although there was already an office of that name operating within the state. Several different accounts suggest that Annandale may have been named for a seaport in Scotland or for the showgirl Lizzie Annandale (as indicated by Senator W. D. Washburn). Regardless of its origins, it was adopted by the post office in 1887 (with William H. Towle serving as postmaster) and then by the village on April 17, 1888, when it was incorporated. It was platted in October 1886 by James Pratt. With the help of the Minneapolis and Pacific Railroad, later a part of the Soo Line, schools, hardware stores, a pickle factory, filling stations, West Albion Creamery, Browns Velvet Ice Cream Shop, the State Bank of Annandale, the *Annandale Advocate* newspaper office, and the Thayer Hotel came to fruition as just a few of its people's accomplishments. St. Mark's Episcopal Chapel, a 1871 Gothic Revival style church, has survived as the city's sole church on the National Register of Historic Places. Other religious places of note were St. Ignatius Catholic Church, the Methodist Episcopal Church, and Mt. Herman Lutheran Church. "The Heart of the Lakes" was the nickname given to Annandale because of its proximity to 26 lakes within a 10-mile radius. Dean Barkley is its most famous son, having served briefly as a United States Senator from Minnesota from November 4, 2002, to January 3, 2003.

Restaurant Recommendation:
In Hot Water Coffee Shop
20 Cedar St E
Annandale, MN 55302

BUFFALO, MN ★
POPULATION: 18,168 – CITY 847 OF 856 (11-14-25)
Platted on December 27, 1856, on land owned by Aurasa Ackley, the Wright County seat was incorporated on May 23, 1857, and only garnered the county's seat of government in 1873. For the previous eighteen years, that honor had belonged to Monticello. While most people would assume the city was named for the great

mammal that once roamed the Great Plains in the tens of millions, its name actually came from nearby Buffalo Lake, which was known for its abundance of buffalo fish. Postal service began in 1856, the year of its platting, and after being given 60 years to develop, the Buffalo of 1915 had about 1,300 residents and a portion of the Soo Line running through it. Swedish, Norwegian, German, and French-Canadian immigrants were the most prominent ethnic groups that settled here. Commercial fishing peaked in the 1890s and was an essential part of the town's economy. Other businesses flourished too, including resorts, three hotels, two banks, a box factory, a veneer mill, a flour mill, a saw mill, and a co-operative creamery. Seven churches of the Catholic, German Lutheran, Swedish Lutheran, Presbyterian, Methodist, Free Mission, and Swedish Mission denominations were extant then, as were some of the area's best public schools. Over 425 pupils were enrolled in Buffalo's public high school as of 1915, with more in the grade schools. Until the 1960s, Buffalo never had more than 2,000 recorded residents, but its population has since nearly quadrupled since the 1980 Census (population 4,560). The Wright County Heritage Center hosts over 8,000 square feet of museum exhibits and artifacts, as well as a historic log cabin and town hall. Since 1983, the Buffalo Community Theater has been producing plays for locals to enjoy; since 1995, the fifty-plus-member Buffalo Community Orchestra has entertained thousands of listeners. At Norm's Wayside Saloon, an outdoor sculpture collection includes a rusty T. rex/alligator hybrid and a motorcycle. There is also a 20-foot-tall wooden nickel inscribed with the words "Wooden Nickel - 2018 - Buffalo, Minnesota" located nearby on private property.

Restaurant Recommendation:
Thirsty Buffalo Saloon
904 Commercial Dr
Buffalo, MN 55313

CLEARWATER, MN
POPULATION: 1,922 – CITY 490 OF 856 (8-9-25)
One of Wright County's earliest towns had its name recorded on explorer Joseph Nicollet's map in the 1830s as "Kawakomik" or "Clear Water R," over 20 years before the town was established. The town, platted in 1856, shares its name with the Clearwater River, a 43.4-mile-long tributary of the Mississippi River. Alonzo Boyington and Asa White made land claims in 1854 and hoped to call the area Eldorado. In 1855, Simon Stevens, Horace Webster, and John Farwell arrived. The latter three used their money and influence to rename it Clearwater and put an end to Boyington and White's "El Dorado" nomenclature. A three-inch manila rope, the first ferry cable strung across the Mississippi, was placed the following year. Variations of it have remained as the longest operating ferry at any point on the river. Old-Stock Americans built up the village in a New England fashion, introduced the Burbank Stage Company in 1856, and helped to incorporate the town on February 26, 1857. When the Great Northern Railroad rolled through in later decades, it opened many new economic doors for the townspeople. A community center, a sample room, a planing mill, and a roller mill were located closer to the Clearwater River than any other early institutions. An elevator, a hotel, hardware stores, pharmaceutical stores, mercantile lines, blacksmith shops, professional offices, a public school, and Catholic and Congregationalist churches also existed by 1896. Several newspapers came and went during the early years as well, including the *Clearwater Messenger* (est. 1878), the *Clearwater Review* (est. 1884), and the *Clearwater Advance* (est. 1885). The community post office shortened its name from "Clear Water" to "Clearwater" sometime around 1895 or 1922. Three of Clearwater's "must-see" historical attractions are the First Congregational Church of

Clearwater, erected in 1861 using Greek Revival architecture and a haven for Clearwater residents during the Dakota War of 1862; the 1863 Greek Revival William W. Webster House; and the Clearwater Masonic and Grand Army of the Republic Hall, used by local fraternal organizations following its completion in 1888. Clearwater has recently seen a significant increase in its population, from 858 residents in 2000 to 1,735 in 2010.

Restaurant Recommendation:
Nelson Bros. Restaurant & Bakery
950 MN-24
Clearwater, MN 55320

COKATO, MN
POPULATION: 2,799 – CITY 851 OF 856 (11-15-25)
When the original division of the St. Paul & Pacific Railroad was being built, railroad officials knew that several stops would need to be established westward to ensure their trains could stop and refuel whenever required. Typically located seven to nine miles apart, one of these stops was "Cokato," at the center of a historic geographical region called The Big Woods, which spanned the land between Willmar in Kandiyohi County and the Mississippi River. Cokato is derived from the Dakota word *Cokaya*, meaning "in the midst of," a reference to these once-expansive woodlands. Josiah P. Mooers of Deerfield, New Hampshire, was its earliest resident circa 1858, and the original post office was named Mooers Prairie. Marvin R. Lewis was the postmaster when the name changed to Cokato in 1878; his office was in the railway depot. Hotels, blacksmith shops, liveries, general stores, and saloons were the norm when it came to businesses, but in 1903, something new came to town: August Akerlund's Photographic Studio. The Swedish immigrant purchased the studio from a photographer in another area and later added living quarters to the rear after marrying Esther Hanson. Now listed on the National Register of Historic Places, the studio has been repurposed as the Cokato Museum, which features an early 20th-century scale model of the town, historic newspapers, a full-size, furnished log cabin, and other historical exhibits. In 1904, the Cokato Canning Company, only the second canning factory to open in Minnesota, began operations and was later a part of the Minnesota Valley Canning Company/Green Giant. Northland Canning joined it in 1924 as a second local canning factory, which was bought out by Faribault Foods in 1969. Green Giant's plant was closed in 1978, and the Faribault plant shuttered in 2019. Of course, in addition to business lines, there were also schools, the first of which was built in 1871 before being replaced by a two-story brick building in 1884. Religious and fraternal society organizations were plentiful as well, although the 1896 Cokaton P.R.S. Onnen Tovio Raittiusseura [Clubhouse], used by the local Finnish population, remains the most famous. From 1868 to 1885, Finns used the oldest sauna in North America, before neighbors complained of "too many nude Finns walking about." In a hilarious twist, the neighbors attempted to sue the Finns to shut down the sauna, but they lost the case. Finnish residents counter-sued for damages and then used the funds to build a bigger, better sauna away from the road. A 1899 one-room schoolhouse is also on the site as a part of the Finnish Pioneer Park of the Cokato Finnish American Historical Society. White Front Locker & Market, owned by John Nienaber, is one of a select few butcher shops in Minnesota that do on-farm butchering and custom processing for pigs and cattle. A few persons of interest who have brought fame to Cokato include Sydney Eckman Ahlstrom, the winner of the 1973 National Book Award for Philosophy and Religion for his book *A Religious History of the American People*; Steve Knapp, the 1998 Indianapolis 500 Rookie of the Year and

one of only three drivers to finish the race; David Bromstad, the host of several HGTV shows, and the Aho Family, whose twelve sons played football at Dassel-Cokato High School over a two-decade period. Steve Hartman featured the family on *CBS News Sunday Morning* on December 9, 2012, for the impressive feat.

DELANO, MN
POPULATION: 6,484 – CITY 760 OF 856 (11-5-25)
Edmund Brissett was trading furs on Lake Pulaski as early as 1850, but it was James P. Lyle who claimed land here on June 15, 1855, which would ultimately become part of the City of Delano. James Patten, S. Patten, and J. C. Ellis were amongst his party and were responsible for exploring and laying the earliest foundations of what is now a community of over six thousand citizens. When the railroad arrived in 1868, it served as the impetus to plat a village called Crow River. The name was changed to Delano to honor Francis Roach Delano, a lumber baron in the St. Croix Valley and the first warden of the Minnesota State Prison system. He later joined the railroad company as the superintendent of the St. Paul & Pacific Railroad, which came through this point. A post office opened in 1870 after large numbers of German and Polish people moved in, many of whom worked for the railroad for $1.75 an hour. The Great Northern Hotel was the first central lodging accommodation for these men and others who wished to visit the area. The Epple Brothers erected a large store to sell a variety of goods and general merchandise. John Haffner managed the inventories of the Lucas Brothers hardware store before purchasing it for his own store. Other places over the years included a grist mill, an adjoining saw mill, the *Big Woods Citizen* newspaper, the State Bank of Delano, a cooper shop, a pickle factory, and saloons, amongst many stores. Later, for entertainment, a 4,000-square-foot roller-skating pavilion was erected with gorgeous hard maple floors for theater performances, dances, community gatherings, and, of course, skating. In 1881, the *Big Woods Citizen* became the *Delano Eagle*, and its 1883-85 buildings were ultimately added to the National Register of Historic Places alongside other local features, such as the 1888 Delano Village Hill, the 1893 Queen Anne home of Simon Weldele, and the 1871 District No. 48 Schoolhouse. The *Eagle* is not the only paper published in town; the bimonthly *Kurier Polski*, the only Polish-American newspaper in the Midwest, is also circulated to about 1,500 people. Minnesota's oldest and largest Independence Day celebration has been held since 1857. Tom Emmer, a U.S. Representative from Minnesota since 2015 and the Chair of the National Republican Congressional Committee from 2019 to 2023, served on the Delano city council early in his career. Ben Meyers, most recently a member of the NHL's Seattle Kraken from 2024-25, also hails from here.

HANOVER, MN
POPULATION: 3,548 – CITY 839 OF 856 (11-13-25)
One of several cities in this part of the Gopher State named after its German counterpart by early German immigrants, Hanover, was named after the Vollbrecht brothers. Jacob was the first to live at the spot known as Vollbrecht Mills, and after finding success in Minnesota, he wrote to his brother William in Atlanta, Georgia, to join him in the north. The presence of the mills raised the population in the following years, and several new homes, businesses, churches, a post office, and a school were erected. Incorporation was achieved on October 9, 1891, following a vote of the people. To help make the town more accessible to more people, a pin-connected Pratt truss bridge was built in 1885 near the flour mill to allow for the crossing of the Crow River. Its architects were from the Morse Bridge Company. Exponential growth in Hanover did not begin until the turn of the 21st century, particularly between 2000 and 2010, when the population grew from 1,355 to 2,938. Bob Dylan, one of the greatest

songwriters of all time, with 100 million records sold worldwide, used to own a ranch just outside Hanover, in the Hennepin County portion of the city limits.

HOWARD LAKE, MN ☆
POPULATION: 2,071 – CITY 852 OF 856 (11-15-25)
Howard Lake has experienced consistent population growth in every decade since 1920, and in 2020, it reported an all-time high of 2,071 residents. The town's origins date back to 1855, when Morgan V. Cochran, on behalf of a townsite company, established the village of Lynden. When the company refused to pay him for his services, Cochran took it upon himself to improve the site by building a home that later served as the first school and church. After eight years, he sold his claim to Charles Goodsell, who farmed the land until the Great Northern Railroad built a station here at the end of the 1860s. A new place was platted and named Howard, after the nearby lake named in honor of the noted English prison reformer John Howard. The post office began in John F. Pearson's general store after being transferred from Middlesville; its name did not change to Howard Lake until 1892. In its early heyday, seven churches, four doctors' offices, three law firms, grain elevators, hotels, livery stables, stores, a bank, a lumberyard, and a mill were present. Still, the most impressive structure was the city hall. The original 1891 structure was destroyed by fire, but a new Queen Anne municipal building was built in its place in 1904. It was carefully constructed of red Menominee brick and features elements of Richardsonian Romanesque and Victorian architecture, and initially housed Howard Lake's government offices, public library, fire department, community center, and post office. In recent years, it has been revitalized as an off-sale municipal liquor store and the South Shore Event Center, the latter of which is used for weddings, graduation parties, and other community events.

MAPLE LAKE, MN
POPULATION: 2,159 – CITY 848 OF 856 (11-15-25)
There was briefly a town on the northwest shore of Maple Lake called "Geneva," which was platted in 1857 by C. H. Hackett. The Panic of 1857 led to its failure to develop beyond a paper town, but the following year, a new site called Maple Lake was laid out. Its name was derived from the nearby lake of the same name, known for its abundant sugar maple woodlands. Patrick O'Loughlin Sr. and other Irish immigrants were among the first to arrive; O'Loughlin's son-in-law, James Madigan, platted it in 1886 when the Soo Line Railroad came to town. Schooling began twenty years earlier when District #28 started in a log house. It was reorganized into District #104 in 1882, which called the "new" school building home from 1907 to 1991 before it was demolished and replaced by the new facilities in northeast Maple Lake. Businesses of all trades opened, including the Maple Lake Cooperative Dairy Association, the Jude Hotel, the Security State Bank of Maple Lake, the Maple Lake Garage, a grain elevator, and countless others that a visitor would have expected to find in a town of that era. Maple Lake was incorporated on December 23, 1890. Two of Maple Lake's most famous residents have been James Jude, one of the creators of cardiopulmonary resuscitation (CPR), and William Henry Bullock, the Catholic Bishop of the Diocese of Des Moines, Iowa, from 1987 to 1993, and Madison, Wisconsin, from 1993 to 2003.

MONTICELLO, MN
POPULATION: 14,455 – CITY 846 OF 856 (11-14-25)
Formerly the judicial seat of Wright County, Monticello began as a steamboat landing in the midst of fertile farmland. Settlers began arriving in August 1854 and were subject to only one rule that differed from most other land claim opportunities in Minnesota:

No lot was to be sold to any person who did not agree not to use the lands to furnish saloons, billiard halls, bowling alleys, or casinos. Ferry service started across the Mississippi River in the spring of 1855. Monticello was named by Thomas Creighton for a small hill southeast of the village, and incorporated by an act of the Territorial Legislature on March 1, 1856. A rival town called Moritzious was laid out in September 1854 by Ashley C. Riggs at Moritzious Weissberger opposite Monticello, and was respectively incorporated by the Territorial Legislature on August 13, 1858. Only years later, in 1861, the two merged into a single municipality under the Monticello name when they recognized the benefits of working together rather than against each other. So much timber was being sent down the river from "Up North" that eventually Monticello's steamboats could no longer pass through. So the Great Northern Railroad became the primary mode of transporting people and goods. The Monticello Starch Company, a creamery, a lumberyard, and two mills were amongst the largest of the community's enterprising firms. There were also smaller developments, such as storefronts and blacksmith shops. An early tale recalls the time Hull Hotchkiss opened a tavern in 1858, only to be confronted by early Protestant activists who opposed alcohol. When he refused to close his business, they disguised themselves as Native Americans and obliterated his business, booze, building, and all. Word of the destruction spread quickly, and the event served as a cautionary tale to those in the liquor business that Monticello was not a place of tolerance for alcohol. Between 1870 and 1889, three affluent homes now listed on the federal National Register of Historic Places were built by some of the more wealthy area residents: the 1870 David Hanaford Farmstead, the 1884 Queen Anne of Rufus Rand Summer and its accompanying carriage barn, and the 1889 Queen Anne and Shingle Style Nicherson-Tarbox House, Shed and Barn. Monticello is also known for its 28 city-owned parks, amongst which the most popular are Lake Maria State Park (est. 1963), Montissippi Regional Park, and Swan Park. Every winter, thousands of trumpeter swans descend upon Monticello to nest in the warm waters of the Mississippi River heated by the discharge of the Monticello Nuclear Generating Plant. Built in 1971, the Xcel Energy plant has an annual net output of over 5000 gigawatt-hours. Since the plant's opening and the implementation of conducive plans generated by the city council to promote growth, Monticello has gone from a population of 1,636 people in 1970 to 4,941 by 1990 and 12,759 by 2010. A couple of notable locals are Joel Przybilla, an NBA center who played from 2000 to 2013, and Tobias Mealey, a successful California Gold Rush miner whose 1855 home was also listed on the NRHP.

MONTROSE, MN
POPULATION: 3,775 – CITY 854 OF 856 (11-15-25)

The establishment and platting of Montrose was the result of a joint effort between J. F. Miller, T. S. Gunn, and J. N. Haven to formulate a central trade point on the border of Marysville and Woodland Townships. The three men built a grain house and general store as the first structures on the site that were not private residences. Montrose was platted in 1878 and named after a seaport in Scotland; it was incorporated in 1881. George Wright hosted the post office at his house until it was moved to the Great Northern Railroad station some years later. Businesses of many lines were formulated, but Montrose's pride and joy was the Dr. E. P. Hawkins Clinic, Hospital, and House. The medical practice began in 1897 as a single room in the Hawkins residence, but its popularity soared in those early years to the point that it warranted the construction of a separate, ten-bed hospital building next door by 1903. Yet another structure went up in 1913 and served as a joint clinic and a three-year nursing school known as the Montrose Training School for Nurses. Montrose's commercial district — consisting of places like Onstott's hotel, Eckerman's grocery, and the Lundsten lumber office — was primarily located on Railroad Street until a 1930s conflagration convinced business owners to relocate to U.S. Highway 12. Throughout the 1970s, Montrose's population ranged from 200 to 400, before growing to 762 by 1980. Growth has impressive since 2000, as Montrose has grown from 1,143 permanent residents then to 4,000 now.

Restaurant Recommendation:
Gorton's 12/12 Meats
221 Nelson Blvd
Montrose, MN 55363

OTSEGO, MN
POPULATION: 19,966 – CITY 843 OF 856 (11-14-25)
Named after Otsego County, New York, Wright County's largest city by population has grown alongside its neighbor to the north, Elk River. Surveyed in 1857 on 400 acres of land shortly after the Ho Chunk tribe was removed from the area, many of the first people who lived in Otsego knew the village for Samuel Carrick's ferry service, which allowed people to move across the Mississippi River. David Ingersoll's brick factory was established in 1854 as the city's primary economic driver. Circa 1856, the local post office opened (as Berling, changing its name to Otsego the following year) before closing in 1901. The brickyard was gone by 1890 as well, as there was no railroad to serve the community and help bring the products of local manufacturing interests to a larger market. Since 1970, its population has grown rapidly, from 1,526 to 19,966 by 2020. It was incorporated in 1990.

ROCKFORD, MN
POPULATION: 4,500 – CITY 761 OF 856 (11-5-25)
Two Illinoisans, brothers-in-law George F. Ames and Joel Florida, moved here in 1855, where they founded the townsite of Greenwood, and then William Frazer. Frazer, who was supposedly tired of the large numbers of bugs and mosquitoes, wished to move and eagerly sold his claim to the two men. With the help of Guilford George, a sawmill was erected on the Crow River. A colony of settlers was gathered back east by Ames and Florida that winter, and after the party arrived, they helped to build a road from Minneapolis to Rockford. The Minnesota Territorial Legislature had intended for the road to reach the Greenwood townsite. When Ames-Florida's settlement party inadvertently stumbled upon the construction workers in the wild, they rerouted the path of the road towards their soon-to-be home. The result was Greenwood's failure to develop into a viable community, and the growth of Rockford – named in honor of Cyrus C. Jenks's hometown of Rockford, Illinois – as the area's most important town. Amesville and Big Rock were suggested as alternative names. Growth was typical, though in 1859, the first United States troops ever called to Minnesota were sent to Rockford as a preventive response to the "Wright County War," a period marked by multiple riots. Through all the challenges that come with starting a town on undeveloped land, Rockford residents forged forward and built everything from woolen mills and flour mills to general, hardware, and implement stores. Of course, city buildings were constructed for use by citizens and the local government, and schools and churches came into being for educational and religious purposes. The Rockford School District was established on September 6, 1856, and the first schoolhouse was erected in 1860. Rockford was incorporated as a village in the fall of 1881; five years later, the Soo Line Railroad arrived. Its largest-ever decade-over-decade population increase occurred between 1970 and 1980, when the town grew by 229.9%, from 730 citizens to 2,408. Joel McKinnon Miller, noted for his role as Norm Scully on the Fox

television series *Brooklyn Nine-Nine*, was born here. The Rockford Area Historical Society prides itself on protecting the historical collection of artifacts related to the 1856 household of the Ames, Florida, and Stork families. They claim to have one of Minnesota's largest collections of period clothing from Rockford's early days.

SAINT MICHAEL, MN
POPULATION: 18,235 – CITY 841 OF 856 (11-14-25)

St. Michael essentially began as a missionary outpost of St. John's University (in Collegeville) when Father Francis Xavier Weninger came here to start preaching from a small log church near the city's modern-day Millside Tavern. The new church was raised in September 1856 and named for St. Michael the Archangel, then replaced a decade later by a better structure once early Catholic settlers had had ample time to build homes of their own. From 1866 to 1889, the post office was called St. Michaels, before changing to simply St. Michael. It was also known as St. Michaels Station and St. Michael Station until 1909, when it was discontinued and permanently moved to Albertville. While the community had storefronts, schools, and many other aspects, St. Michael was always best known for its church. In 1876, a Catholic school and convent were opened, but in 1890-92, the grand Gothic Revival Church of St. Michael was constructed with the help of only seventy local families. Parishioners then built it to withstand a peak capacity of 500 persons, but over the next century, the large local German Catholic community outgrew the structure. On December 19, 2004, the fourth church in the parish's history was completed after millions of dollars were pledged to build yet an even larger edifice. The old structure is still used for Mass on Fridays during the school year and was listed on the National Register of Historic Places in December 1979. Corner Bar, established in 1897, was one of Minnesota's oldest drinking establishments before it closed in January 2020. The city, one of several Wright County suburbs, crossed the five-thousand-person threshold in 1990, then the ten-thousand-person threshold sometime in the early 2000s. Some of its favorite residents have included Matt Spaeth, an NFL tight end from 2007 to 2015; Caleb Truax, the IBF super middleweight title holder (in boxing) from 2017 to 2018; Dick Bremer, the television announcer for the Minnesota Twins from 1983 to 2023; Chad "El Grande Americano" Gable, a WWE wrestler, and Paul Marx, a monk who was an activist and Benedictine monk within the Roman Catholic Church.

SOUTH HAVEN, MN
POPULATION: 185 – CITY 850 OF 856 (11-15-25)

Not many communities can say they have a city tree, a city bird, or a city color, but the City of South Haven has all three: the oak tree, the hummingbird, and the color red. Trains began arriving in 1887, and in 1888, it was platted. Its name combines its location in Southside Township, Wright County, and its location directly south of Fair Haven Township, Stearns County. The post office adopted the name for its office in 1887, when Adolph G. Lane began serving as postmaster. Incorporation took place on May 2, 1902, after the railroad had allowed it to grow to include a long line of wood-frame businesses and houses. Unfortunately, two fires in 1910 and 1911 destroyed much of its commercial district, yet its all-time high population of 346 people still came by the 1920 Census.

WAVERLY, MN
POPULATION: 1,900 – CITY 853 OF 856 (11-15-25)

Minnesota has been home to several "Waverly's" over the years in Blue Earth, Martin, and Wright Counties, but it is the Wright County variety that has survived through the decades. It was platted in 1855 after the Minnesota Territorial Legislature permitted its surveying and the allocation of lots to homesteaders who wished to improve upon the land. In 1856, the Colwell brothers named a townsite Waverly after Waverly, Tioga County, New York, and gave that same name to two adjacent lakes, one "Big" and one "Small." A dam, a sawmill, and a gristmill were built here circa 1865 at the outlet of Little Waverly Lake. A store, a log church, and a cemetery were established later, as was a post office, first called Zellingen from 1863 to 1869, then Waverly Mills from 1869 to 1899. The office was also known as Waverly Station for a month, from December 12, 1871, to January 14, 1872, after the Saint Paul and Pacific Railroad was built through the area. Waverly Station was the second rendition of the Waverly townsite and was platted about a mile away from the first site started by the Colwell brothers. "New" Waverly incorporated as a village in 1881, and by 1915, it had a large Catholic church, three grain elevators, two banks, a flour mill, a creamery, a hotel, lumber companies, hardware and general stores, meat markets, livery stables, saloons, a pharmacy, and a weekly newspaper. The "Station" was dropped from the name in 1899. Two historic points of interest today are the 1891 Marysville Swedesburg Lutheran Church and the 1939 New Deal Waverly Village Hall, both built in Moderne architecture. Hubert Humphrey, the 38th Vice President of the United States, lived primarily in Waverly from 1958 to 1978 with his wife, Muriel, before passing away there on January 13, 1978. Reuben G. Soderstrom, an American leader in organized labor history who helped to define policy following the formation of the AFL-CIO in 1955, was born here in March 1888.

Dayton is only partially located in Wright County (see Hennepin County).

Unincorporated/Ghost Towns: Albion Center, Albright, Dickinson, Enfield, French Lake, Hasty, Highland, Knapp, Oster, Rassat, Rice Lake, Silver Creek, Smith Lake, Stockholm, West Albion

National Register of Historic Places:
Annadale: Thayer Hotel, St. Marks Episcopal Church
Clearwater: Clearwater Masonic Lodge-Grand Army of the Republic Hall, First Congregational Church of Clearwater, William W. Webster House
Cokato: August Akerlund Photographic Studio, Cokaton P.R.S. Onnen Tovio Raittiusseura
Delano: Delano Village Hall, District No. 48 School, Eagle Newspaper Office, Simon Weldele House
Hanover: Hanover Bridge
Howard Lake: Howard Lake City Hall
Monticello: David Hanaford Farmstead, Nicherson-Tarbox House, Shed & Barn, Rufus Rand Summer House & Carriage Barn
Montrose: Dr. E.P. Hawkins Clinic Hospital & House
St. Michael: Church of St. Michael-Catholic
Waverly: Marysville Swedesburg Lutheran Church, Waverly Village Hall

Golf Courses:
Albion Ridges Golf Course, Daily Fee (Annandale, MN)
Buffalo Heights Golf Course, Daily Fee (Buffalo, MN)
Cedar Creek Golf Course, Daily Fee (Albertville, MN)
Cokato Town & Country Club, Daily Fee (Cokato, MN)
Fox Hollow Golf Club, Daily Fee (St. Michael, MN)
Monticello Country Club, Daily Fee (Monticello, MN)
Riverwood National Golf Course, Daily Fee (Otsego, MN)
Southbrook Golf Club, Daily Fee (Annandale, MN)
Whispering Pines Golf Course, Daily Fee (Annandale, MN)
Wild Marsh Golf Club, Daily Fee (Buffalo, MN)

Breweries/Wineries/Distilleries:
Buffalo Rock Winery (Buffalo, MN)
Dangerous Man Brewing Company (Maple Lake, MN)
Hayes Public House (Buffalo, MN)
Rustech Brewing Company (Monticello, MN)
Spilled Grain Brewhouse (Annandale, MN)
The Nordic Brewing Company (Monticello, MN)

Town Celebrations:
4th of July Celebration, Delano, MN (4th of July Weekend)
Albertville Friendly City Days, Albertville, MN (2nd Week in June)
Buffalo Days, Buffalo, MN (2nd Saturday in June through Father's Day)
Buffalo Rodeo, Buffalo, MN (Weekend after Father's Day)
Celebrate Montrose, Montrose, MN (3rd Weekend of August)
Cokato Corn Carnival, Cokato, MN (2nd Week of August)
Good Neighbor Days, Howard Lake, MN (4th Weekend in June)
Hanover Harvest Festival, Hanover, MN (1st Saturday in August)
Monticello Riverfest, Monticello, MN (Weekend following 4th of July)
Rockford River Days, Rockford, MN (2nd Full Weekend of August)
Rocktoberfest, Rockford, MN (1st Saturday in October)
St. Michael Daze & Knights Festival, St. Michael, MN (2nd Weekend of August)
St. Patrick's Day Celebration & Parade, Maple Lake, MN (Saturday before March 17th)

YELLOW MEDICINE COUNTY
EST. 1871 - POPULATION: 9,528

Menispermum canadense, the scientific name for the common moonseed plant, is a yellow root used by the Dakota for medicinal purposes. Thus, the name "Yellow Medicine" was applied to this county when it was established in 1871.

CANBY, MN ☆
POPULATION: 1,695 – CITY 119 OF 856 (4-10-25)

Second only to Granite Falls in its importance to the development of Yellow Medicine County, the Canby townsite was home to a single man for two years: John Swenson. He built a claim shanty and, with a bit of foresight about what the area might become because of its location on the Lac qui Parle Creek, he opened a store. In November 1874, he acquired the right to establish the Canby post office, which he named in honor of the admirable General Edward Richard Sprigg Canby. Chief Kintpuash of the Modoc tribe had recently killed him during a peace talk conference amid the Modoc War. Its hasty development began on August 24, 1876, when the Winona & St. Peter Railroad Company platted the townsite in anticipation of extending its line. Lots were sold shortly thereafter. Peter Erickson and A. G. Feldhammer built a second store, the Gerald Brothers started a pharmacy, Gustav Erickson established the first hotel, Jacob Olson began the always-coveted saloon, and O. N. Lund assisted in the development of several additional businesses (namely a dry goods store, a grocery store, a hardware store, and a tin shop, all divided in his 48x60x20 foot building). The Norwegians built up the initial site, which was incorporated as a village in 1879. Things were moving swimmingly; by 1890, it had numerous additional homes and businesses and a population of 470 people. A September 8, 1893, fire in the Odland & Landru meat market forever changed its fate. Supposedly, Mr. Odland and Bernt Nelson had almost extinguished the flames when a third man ran in, jumped onto the blanket covering the fire, and spilled the entire tin of kerosene oil directly onto the embers. The sparks took, the wind picked up, and swaths of Canby were destroyed in mere hours.

In response to $150,000 of destruction that led to the razing of a significant portion of its commercial district, Canby residents decided to rebuild with stone and brick. From 1890 to the 1930s, the historic downtown rose from the ashes. Since 1980, it has been preserved by the National Register of Historic Places as the Canby Commercial Historic District. Aside from commerce, Canby had a strong educational, entertainment, and religious presence. As of 1900, it had churches for the Norwegian Methodist Episcopal, the German Lutheran, the Roman Catholic, the Presbyterian, the Methodist Episcopal, and two Norwegian Lutheran congregations. The public school was on its own, just a couple of blocks off 2nd and Ring Streets, and a large park was in the center of the community. A town hall, an engine house, banks, hotels, elevators, and lumber yards were among the other notable pieces of its infrastructure. When all these things were being mapped, the John G. Lund House was remodeled into a Queen Anne; it is now the Lund-Hoel Museum. A neat English Cottage Revival filling station, built in 1926 using Dipple of Chicago's designs, has survived as Canby's third-most-historic point of interest. At its peak population of 2,173 in the 1950s, the city was estimated to have over 160 businesses. The home of the Yellow Medicine County Fair has also been home to a handful of notable folks of the years: Layton Kor, a pioneer rock climber who was the first to ascend several famous rock spires throughout the Americas; Lee Savold, the most victorious heavyweight champion in boxing history with his 106 victories, and Jerome Clark, a ufologist who has specialized in researching unidentified flying objects and other paranormal subjects in numerous magazines and television networks. He authored the 1992 book *The UFO Encyclopedia: The Phenomenon From The Beginning*.

Restaurant Recommendation:
P K Egans Family Restaurant
115 St Olaf Ave N
Canby, MN 56220

CLARKFIELD, MN
POPULATION: 852 – CITY 192 OF 856 (4-16-25)

As many as 1,171 people lived in Clarkfield at its peak in the 1980s, but the town came from much humbler beginnings. Friendship Township lacked large permanent settlements until 1884, when the Minneapolis & St. Louis Railway began working northwestward through Yellow Medicine County. On October 7, 1884, Charles F. Hatch planned the twenty-seven-block townsite; by November, train traffic was daily. The new village was named for Thomas E. Clark, a railroad official. Henry Monson's farmhouse was the only building on the site until lots were sold, but soon, there was a depot, an elevator, a section house, and a saloon. The five pioneer structures were accompanied by Herman Linstad's grocery store, Peter Anderson's hotel, S. Coleman's general store, and Knute Solberg's blacksmith shop before the year ended. As any modern-day historian or Clarkfield resident at that time could have predicted, that rapid pace of growth continued for some time. Growth was so rampant that in 1886, a petition was presented to the county commissioners to remove the county seat to the community. The movement made it no further than the signatures on the parchment, and no election was ever held. At the 1900 Census, Clarkfield had a population of 437, a sharp increase from the 178 people reported to be living there a decade earlier. The section house and depot, stockyards, three coal sheds, and four grain elevators were on the main railroad tracks. A small spur directed train traffic towards The Clarkfield Roller Mill, a lumber shed, a fifth elevator, and a hotel, the last of which was at the southern point of its business district. There was a Town Hall that doubled as an opera House, the Clarkfield State Bank, and two blacksmith shops that serviced wagons and carriages. On Maple Avenue was the School District No. 43 building, a Methodist Episcopal church (established 1894), and a Norwegian Lutheran church (organized May 26, 1885) within three blocks of one another. "The Heart of the Prairie" is now best known for Clarkfield Outdoors, a store founded in 1983 that specializes in hunting apparel and workwear. Its only structure ever listed on the National Register was the Swede Prairie Progressive Farmers' Club, a 1915 meeting hall more commonly known as Roberg Hall. Harland Svare, a former NFL linebacker from 1953 to 1960 and assistant or head coach from 1960 to 1973, was born here in November 1930, as was Larry Cole, a 1968 to 1980 Dallas Cowboys defensive lineman and two-time Super Bowl champion, in 1946. Clarkfield's most famous daughter is Cecilia H. Hauge, the director of nursing for the U.S. Department of Veterans Affairs from 1954 to 1966.

ECHO, MN
POPULATION: 243 – CITY 188 OF 856 (4-16-25)
The echoes one may expect to find today in this town of 243 lie mainly in the past, but they tell a story of a once-bustling community that began with the arrival of the Minneapolis & St. Louis Railroad in August 1884. Settlement of the township started a bit earlier, around 1869. It was called Empire, then Rose, and then Echo because it seemed to be the only name available for a township that "echoed" back that it had not yet been used elsewhere. The townsite adopted the name when the railroad platted the townsite on September 8, 1884, in conjunction with its arrival. Samuel Mather opened his general store, a typical "first" business establishment for most newborn towns. Through the end of 1885, Echo welcomed R. L. Macklenburg's hotel and saloon, William Giske's blacksmith shop, W. F. Riedell's store and hotel, a town hall, and the general store of Charles Phillips and George Lippman. Rumors that the railroad was considering abandoning the Echo and Wood Lake townsites in favor of a new Sand Lake depot caused a brief stir and pause in Echo's development. Instead, the company shrank the Echo plat to three blocks in 1889. By 1900, the town that had worried them had proved a successful investment. On the tracks were five elevators, a lumber yard and shed, stockyards, a coal shed, and cold storage. A sorghum mill and the Echo Milling Company (established in 1889 by A. F. Koch, Paul Voss, and George Schmidt) structures were nearby. Many of the earlier-mentioned business lines still existed in some capacity in their commercial district around this time. There were also new organizations, such as the private bank of C. D. Griffith and W. W. Smith. They were also the proprietors of the First National Bank of Sleepy Eye. Their "branch" in Echo was incorporated as the State Bank of Echo in 1904. On the eastern end of the main drag, the Methodist Episcopal, German Methodist, and German Lutheran congregations built their church edifices. From 1895 to 1926, Echo's first school building survived Minnesota's harsh winters and blizzards before it was retired; a March fire destroyed the second version of the school. The replacement E.C.H.O. (Every Child Has Opportunities) Charter School building began construction in 1926 and underwent a reorganization in 1997, becoming the school it is today. The Wood Lake Battlefield Historic District is north of Echo.

GRANITE FALLS, MN ★
POPULATION: 2,737 – CITY 187 OF 856 (4-16-25)
Pejuhutazizi Kapi, "the place where they dig for yellow medicine," was the original name given to this general area of Minnesota where the Dakota Oyate lived for thousands of years before the arrival of European settlers. Near present-day Granite Falls, the United States government established the Upper Sioux Agency on the

Minnesota River. From 1854 to 1862, it was the site of a manual labor school, employee housing, and warehouses; most of it was destroyed in the Dakota War of 1862. For ten years after its abandonment, there was little to no development in this country until a post office called Palmers Creek was opened by George W. Daniels in Chippewa County in 1868; two years later, it was moved to Yellow Medicine County and descriptively named "Granite Falls" for the abundant outcroppings of gneiss and granite and the 38-foot drop of the river bed. On May 7, 1872, Daniels surveyed the Granite Falls townsite. The plat was filed by Henry Hill, who, alongside his brother Thomas P. Hill, built some of the first dwellings and established a grist and saw mill. A flurry of activity ensued. A hotel was built, and Fortier & Davidson and H. J. Simpson founded stores. The nearby rival settlements of Yellow Medicine City, the original county seat, and Minnesota Falls had a brief county seat war circa 1874. Granite Falls emerged victorious when it donated the grounds and the buildings for the county offices. A small one-room courthouse went up at once. Coupling the judicial seat title with the presence of the Chicago, Milwaukee & St. Paul, and the Great Northern Railroads (both of which came later) gave Granite Falls all the tools it needed to surpass its rivals and become the chief economic center of the county. It was incorporated in 1879, and in 1889, it joined with East Granite Falls (a smaller settlement across the river with a 1880 population of 174 compared to Granite Falls' 578) to form a single municipality. During that period, religion found its place in the community. The Congregational Church organization was the first permanent one, starting on November 3, 1872. The Norwegian Evangelical Lutheran, Episcopal, and Baptist churches were also raised. By 1905, the city boasted an impressive seven general stores, five grain elevators, five blacksmith shops, four banks, four hardware stores, four hotels, four physician's offices, six lawyers for its six saloons, four real estate offices, three grocery stores, three restaurants, two public schools and high schools, five churches, a 500-person-capacity opera house, a creamery, a flour mill, a produce "factory," a bicycle shop, A. W. Winter's famous horse sale stables, a one-half mile rack track, and even baseball grounds amongst several other accomplishments. Hundreds of other businesses were established and discontinued over the following decades, and the town's population culminated in the 1980s at 3,451 people. A July 25, 2000, F4 tornado caused millions of dollars in damage and prompted some residents to leave, as they did not wish to rebuild. Many interesting sites survived the tornado, making Granite Falls a fun destination for visitors to explore. Just outside the Yellow Medicine County Historical Society is the "World's Oldest Rock," more appropriately 'rocks,' a group of 3.8 billion-year-old Granitic Gneiss stones. The Andrew John Volstead House, a National Historic Landmark now operated by the Granite Falls Historical Society, was the home of the ten-term United States Congressman. As the House Judiciary Committee chairman, he was required to draft the Volstead Act, better known as the National Prohibition Act, which established alcohol prohibition in the United States under the Eighteenth Amendment. Military enthusiasts from around the world travel to Granite Falls to admire three full hangars of operational World War II-era planes and displays at the Fagen Fighters WWII Museum. Visitors can climb a control tower on the grounds, hide in a bunker, and even walk through a D-Day Utah Beach scene. Air shows during the summer use the museum's artifacts. The Upper Sioux Agency was a Minnesota State Park from 1963 to February 2024, but closed due to rapidly deteriorating roads and grounds.

Restaurant Recommendation:
Carl's Bakery
810 Prentice St
Granite Falls, MN 56241

HANLEY FALLS, MN
POPULATION: 243 – CITY 190 OF 856 (4-16-25)
No other town in Minnesota claims a larger collection of agricultural equipment, implements, tools, and exhibits than Hanley Falls does at Minnesota's Machinery Museum. All its artifacts are stored within five large buildings, one of which is a 1939 WPA schoolhouse, on a six-acre site. The town began on August 19, 1884, when the Minneapolis & St. Louis Railroad arrived and named it Cable, then Cleveland, and finally Hanley after their general freight agent, John A. Hanley. The nearby Silliards post office was rebranded as Hanley Falls in 1887, three years after being moved to the site. "Falls" was only added to the name because of its similarity in enunciation and spelling to Hawley, Minnesota, in Clay County. When the townsite was surveyed, the plat map was modeled after Washington, D.C. A park was established at the center, with Riverside Avenue and Prairie Avenue crisscrossing in an "X" pattern to serve as the two main thoroughfares, surrounded by east-west streets and north-south avenues. Hanley Falls flourished, and it was incorporated on January 8, 1892. Its location at the bend of the Yellow Medicine River and at the junction of the Minneapolis & St. Louis and Great Northern Railroads attracted hundreds of new settlers, many of whom founded businesses to capitalize on the economic advantages offered by the two railways. Business lines at the turn of the century were Emil Werden's Roller & Flouring Mill, stockyards, a lumber yard and shed, an elevator, a depot, and bottling works on the M & St. L line; a depot, an elevator, and stockyards on the G. N., the *Hanley Falls Leader* newspaper, The First State Bank of Hanley Falls, the Commercial Hotel, and stores in its commercial district. A public school, town hall, fire station, Methodist church, and Norwegian Lutheran church were also present. Although Hanley Falls has since lost its schools, churches, and businesses, the town has retained a population not far from its peak of 336 in the 1940s. Minnesota's Machinery Museum brings in visitors from around the world to experience Hanley Falls history firsthand—and far more than just machinery—on the grounds of the same park that once served as the community's central point of pride.

HAZEL RUN, MN
POPULATION: 55 – CITY 191 OF 856 (4-16-25)
The quiet little town of Hazel Run was named after the local creek, which ultimately runs into the Minnesota River. Like its neighbors, it was founded in 1884, while the Minneapolis & St. Louis Railroad was busy extending its line and establishing access points for farmers and merchants to trade their goods. When the tracklayers arrived, they discovered that Guttorm Halvorson "Ole" Fostvedt and O. Harris had already established a store here. Fostvedt was named postmaster. B. Langmandsgaard built his store across the way from the pre-existing business. O. P. Berg joined in the mix of general merchandising options, and an elevator was completed by the conclusion of 1885. The Farmers Warehouse Company built a grain warehouse in 1886, the first (alongside the elevator) of multiple structures that dotted the stretch of railroad within Hazel Run by the time the North West Publishing Company mapped the town in 1900. On the map, the company denotes the presence of a coal and wood yard, a cattle yard, two coal sheds, a depot, four elevators, two scales, a lumber office, a section house, and a lumber yard and shed. On Laurel Avenue was a hotel, the post office, and three blacksmith shops, one of which doubled as a feed mill. The School No. 20 building and a Norwegian church were located in the southeast corner of the community, but both have closed over time, as have all the previously mentioned businesses. In 1992, the post office was discontinued. The City of Hazel Run, with all

its ups (1920s; population of 145) and downs (2020s; population of 55), has remained incorporated since May 1902.

PORTER, MN
POPULATION: 166 – CITY 261 OF 856 (5-9-25)
Best known now for its annual Porter Community Auction event that attracts thousands of prospective buyers of farming and implements, tools, and equipment from miles around, the population of Porter itself has never been too large. At most, it had 291 people living there in the 1950s. Initially, there was no need for a town at this point of the Winona & St. Peter Railroad. Yellow Medicine County was still relatively desolate in the mid-1870s, and Canby sufficed as the principal point for grain shipments. A post office called Harstad was established at the home of G. A. Harstad in Lincoln County in 1875 for convenience. Until 1882, the entire area was referred to as Harstad (and briefly as Lone Tree, for a large elm tree removed in 1909 to build a sidewalk adjacent to Main Street), until the railroad deemed it necessary to construct a new depot. In October 1881, the Dalston townsite was platted and named after local storeowner Ole Dahl, but it was renamed Porter in 1882 when the L. C. Porter Milling Company built the first grain warehouse on the site. The Van Dusen Elevator Company later that Fall placed another warehouse, and W. E. Drummond opened his blacksmith shop. By February 1892, there was still no school, church, or even a saloon; only two stores, three warehouses, and the blacksmith shop. Things picked up later that year when the United Norwegian Lutheran Church was erected. School District No. 83 was organized on February 15, 1898, and a school building was put up for $2,500. A second church, the Methodist Church of Porter, held its services in a newly built structure dedicated on December 3, 1899. On November 1, 1900, the State Bank of Porter was open for business, and there was a lumber yard, a stockyard, a harness shop, a meat market and livery barn, a hardware store, a furniture store, and the Farmers' Produce Company. The Scandinavian settlement survived two large floods in 1930 and 2010, but on March 27, 2011, it took a blow when the Porter Elevator Feed Mill was destroyed by fire. It was the last remaining "traditional" elevator still standing in Porter. The aforementioned Porter auction, held every April, has been held for over 90 years. It is locally famous for its homemade pies and sandwiches, served at the Porter Community Hall by Bethel Lutheran Church.

SAINT LEO, MN
POPULATION: 93 – CITY 260 OF 856 (5-9-25)
The story of St. Leo, sometimes spelled "Saint Leo," centers primarily on the Catholic church of the same name, dedicated on June 4, 1896, in front of a crowd of no fewer than 2,000 people. As an inland town (a town without a railroad), establishing St. Leo as a municipality was an effort entirely carried out by the proud homesteaders who lived in Omro and Burton Townships. They first arrived around 1878, and after enough of them had accumulated, the postal service established the rural St. Leo post office in January 1880 on Valentine Lenz's farm. Catholic settlers chose the name to honor Pope Leo the Great. Businesses were started sparingly and served only the needs of the immediate area's population. Frank Antony had a general store in 1885, and Math Braun began another store in Jacob Geib's building in 1890. Henry Schanberg brought in a hardware stock in 1897, which by 1914 doubled as its only general store. Saloons and blacksmith shops were the only other early businesses ever to be started. The post office was moved into the village in 1900, and St. Leo was incorporated on June 6, 1940. Early postcards show that St. Leo's Catholic Church had an accompanying parochial school.

WOOD LAKE, MN
POPULATION: 381 – CITY 189 OF 856 (4-16-25)

Appropriately named after the nearby lake that once had dense timber surrounding it, the history of this town of 381 people is primarily associated with the Battle of Wood Lake. On September 23, 1862, the final battle of the Dakota War of 1862 saw Colonel Henry Hastings Sibley and his men achieve a decisive victory, dispersing the remaining forces of Chief Little Crow. Sibley would give chase to the "hostile" chiefs the following year, but the heavy losses endured by the Dakota effectively ended the conflict. On July 23, 2010, the Wood Lake Battlefield Historic District (located closest to the town of Echo) was placed on the National Register of Historic Places. William Churchill and Samuel Ferguson are widely recognized as the first Wood Lake townsite settlers. They arrived in 1868, but the village of Wood Lake would not be platted until September 8, 1884, with the arrival of the Minneapolis & St. Louis Railroad. Trains arrived the month before, and businessmen who sought to take advantage of the railroad's facilities moved in. At Wood Lake's first Census count in 1900, it had 264 people, and the following businesses were in order: five grain elevators, stockyards, cold storage, a lumber shed, a creamery, a feed mill, two hotels, two blacksmith shops, the State Bank of Wood Lake, and various stores. The School No. 7 building was in the southwest part of town. A joint town hall and opera house venture was located on Second Avenue; a "prison," more likely than not a tiny jail, was on Third, and there were church edifices for the English Methodist Episcopal and German Lutheran congregations. A significant gap in the post office's history shows that the Wood Lake branch was open from 1879 to 1894 and did not reopen until 1951. Its reopening coincides with Wood Lake's highest-ever recorded population of 504/506 people recorded in the 1950 and 1960 Censuses.

Unincorporated/Ghost Towns: Burr, Lorne, Normania, Spring Creek

National Register of Historic Places:
Canby: Canby Commercial Historic District, John G. Lund House, Lundring Service Station
Clarkfield: Swede Prairie Progressive Farmers' Club
Granite Falls: Andrew John Volstead House, Upper Sioux Agency
Sioux Agency Township: Wood Lake Battlefield Historic District

Town Celebrations:
Hat Daze, Canby, MN (Father's Day Weekend)

Watonwan County: Veteran's Memorial (Butterfield), Livery Stable at Voss Park Campground (Butterfield), Capture Site of the Younger Brothers (La Salle), Presbyterian Church (Madelia), The Citizenry of Madelia Mural (Madelia), Watonwan County Courthouse (St. James), Schmidt's Bakery (St. James), Hayloft Barn (St. James)

Wilkin County: Wilkin County Courthouse (Breckenridge), Ox Cart Mural (Breckenridge), Wilkin Drink & Eatery (Breckenridge), Mural (Breckenridge), Stiklestad Lutheran Church (Doran), St. Thomas Catholic Church (Kent), former Wolverton Public School (Wolverton), Swedish Lutheran Church Bell & Gazebo (Wolverton)

Winona County: Papenfuss General Store Vintage Pepsi Advertisement (Dakota), Mississippi River Overlook at Great Rier Bluffs State Park (Dakota), former Holy Trinity Catholic School (Rollingstone), Welcome to Utica Barn (Utica), Winona County Courthouse (Winona), Watkins Museum & Store (Winona), Lake Winona (Winona), St. Stanislaus Basilica (Winona)

Wright County: former Soo Line Railroad depot at Minnesota Pioneer Park; Buffalo Roam Tour Sculpture (Buffalo), St. Francis Xavier Catholic Church (Buffalo), School District No. 131 at Temperance Corner (Cokato), Chicken Statue at Flippin' Bill's Convenience Store (Delano), Hanover Bridge No. 92366 Pratt Through Truss Bridge (Hanover), Historic Howard Lake City Hall (Howard Lake), former St. Michael's Catholic Church (St. Michael).

Yellow Medicine County: Canby Theatre (Canby), Lund Hotel House Museum (Canby), Clarkfield State Bank of Art (Clarkfield), Rock Valle Lutheran Church (Echo), Wood Lake Battlefield Monument (Echo), Interior of Fagen Fighters WWII Museum (Granite Falls), Minnesota's Machinery Museum (Hanley Falls), Downtown Scene (Wood Lake)

QR Code Tutorial

Throughout a Wandermore project, we take tens of thousands of photos of businesses, churches, parks, and other points of interest in each community. Since one book cannot possibly have all the photos in print, Wandermore has created a unique QR code system that enables readers to take a virtual tour of every incorporated community in the state. An online photo album of each town can be accessed by scanning a "QR Code." They're simple to use, and the instructions below will teach you how to use them with ease!

To scan a QR code, follow these instructions:

1) Open the "Camera" app on any mobile device.
2) Position your camera over the pixelated box (as seen above). Ensure your camera can see the entire box, or it won't work!
3) Tap the link or notification bubble that appears at the top of your screen.
4) Voila! You now have access to our pictures and videos from the specified town.
5) Note: Some users may have to download a "QR code reader" app on their smartphone or device to scan the codes. Several varieties of these apps can be found for free in your device's App Store.

If the QR codes become defunct in the distant future, please notify sethvarner@wandermorepublishing.com. We will create new ways to access the photos through our website or social media outlets.

QR Code Photo Albums

Minnesota Campgrounds

Are you looking to enjoy the great outdoors of Minnesota? Campgrounds are available throughout the Land of 10,000 Lakes. Check with online sources to check availability before traveling and to find contact information.

Ada – Norman Motel (502 W Thorpe Ave)
Adrian – Adrian Campground (501 Franklin St)
Aitkin – Aitkin Campground (814 Fourth Ave NW)
Barneveld's Resort (39245 MN-18)
Doc's Harbor (39629 MN-18)
Farm Island Lake Resort & Campground (29551 Pioneer Ave)
Hickory Lake Properties (29510 US-169)
Malmo Bay Campground (22782 327th Pl)
Pete's Retreat Family Campground and RV Park (22337 State Hwy 47)
River View Lodge (701 Minnesota Ave S)
Akeley – Akeley City Campground & Park (14 Crow Wing Lake Dr NE)
Crow Wing Crest Lodge (31159 County 23)
Moore Springs Resort & RV Park (5127 Howard Lake Rd NW)
Stompin' Grounds Lodge and Camping (26993 MN-64)
Albert Lea – Hickory Hills Campground (15694 717th Ave)
Myre – Big Island State Park (19499 780th Ave)
Alexandria – Alexandria Shooting Park (6533 CR-87)
Big Foot Resort (8231 MN-114 SW)
Eden Acres Resort I and II (6153 MN-114)
Scenic View RV Campground (4957 County Rd 91 SW)
Altura – Lazy 'D' Campground & Trail Rides (18748 County Rd 39)
Whitewater State Park (19041 MN-74)
Angle Inlet – Jake's Northwest Angle (9270 Golf Course Rd NW)
Annandale – Schroeder County Park & Campground (9201 Ireland Ave NW)
Apple Valley – Lebanon Hills Campground (12100 Johnny Cake Ridge Road)
Appleton – Appleton Municipal Campground (Cross Roads W Thielke Ave and Minnesota River Valley Scenic Byway)
Argyle – Island Park Municipal Campground (307 E 5th St)
Memorial Park Municipal Campground (Hwy 75)
Old Mill State Park (33489 240th Ave NW)
Ashby – Ashby Resort & Campground (10415 County Hwy 82)
Indian Mounds Resort & Campground (10811 Big Island Rd)
Austin – Adventure Bound Camping at Beaver Trails of Austin (21943 630th Ave)
Oakwood Trails Campground (23614 890th Ave)
Avoca – Lime Lake County Park (1998 Lime Lake Dr)
Babbitt – Birch Lake RV Park & Campground (2015 I lwy G20)
Mattila's Birch Lake Resort (8387 First Ave)
YMCA Northern Lights (9089 Ely-Babbitt Road, Hwy 21 N)
Backus – Bayside Cabins & Resort (206 Rosalind Ave W)
Mountain View Resort (590 Wood St N)
Ruttger's Pine Mountain Camping Resort/Pine Mountain Cottages (5068 State 87 SW)
Sandy Pines Family Resort (2731 Raven Ln NW)
Shell City Horse Campground (Off 199th Ave)
Tuck-a-Way Resort & Campground (70 Lake Hattie Dr NW)
Bagley – Bagley City Park & Campground (Cross Roads Picnic Rd NW and Main Ave N)
Balaton – Swenson Park Campground (2199 MN-91)
Barnesville – Wagner Park Campground (15911 190th St S)
Barnum – Barnum City Park (Cross Roads Main St. and City Pk)
Bent Trout Lake Campground (2928 Bent Trout Lake Rd)
Barrett – Barrett Lake Resort & Campground (427 Co Hwy 7)
Battle Lake – Glendalough State Park (25287 Whitetail Ln)
Holiday Haven Resort & Campground (27333 Holiday Rd)
Twin Lake Resort (34554 Co Hwy 74)
Vacationland Resort (38555 Wagon Trail Loop)
Baudette – Adrian's Resort (3362 Red Oak Rd)
Bayview Lodge (1609 26th Ave NW)
Bugsy's on Bostic (3984 County Rd 8 NW)
Bur Oak Campground (3228 Bur Oak Rd NW)
Ken-Mar-Ke Resort (3147 Ken Mar Kee Dr NW)
Lake of the Woods Campground (2769 CSAH 32)
Morris Point Lake View Lodge (3812 42nd Ave NW)
Rainy River Resort (2811 Riverview Dr NW)
River Bend's Resort (3343 Red Oak Rd NW)
Slim's Resort (3140 MN-172)
Sportsman's Lodge Resort & Campground (3244 Bur Oak Rd NW)
Timber Mill Community Park (1020 Front St NE)
Twin River Resort (1982 Twin River Dr NW)
Wigwam Resort (3502 Four Mile Bay Dr NW)
Beaver Bay – North Shore Camping Co. (4595 MN-61)
Bemidji – Balsam Beach Resort & RV Park (51155 219th Ave)
Bemidji KOA Kampground (510 Brightstar Rd NW)
Dreamers Resort (16585 Wilkey Loop Rd NE)
Fox Lake Campground of Bemidji (2556 Island View Dr NE)
Joe's Lodge (15228 Joes Lodge Dr SE)
Lake Bemidji State Park (3401 State Park Rd NE)
Oak Haven Resort and Campground (14333 Roosevelt Rd SE)
Pimushe Resort (7376 Pimushe Trail NE)
Royal Oaks RV Park (2874 Fenske Farm Ln SE)
Bena – Becker's Resort (17048 Wild Rice Dr NW)
Big Winnie RV Park And Campground (1510 US-2)
Four Seasons Resort (952 River Dr NW)
Iowana Beach Resort (14877 Iowana Beach Rd NW)
McArdles Resort (1014 W Winnie Rd NW)
New Leech Lake Campground (12962 Sunset Beach Rd NW)
Nodak Lodge & Resort (15080 Nodak Dr NE)
Sunset Beach Resort (14703 Portage Rd NE)
Benson – Ambush Park Campground (2400 Atlantic Ave)
Swift Falls County Park (990 70th St NE)
Big Falls – Big Falls Campground & Horse Camp (123 Whispering Pine Dr)
Big Lake – Ann Lake Campground and Day-Use Area (Prairie's Edge Wildlife Dr)
Bigfork – Lost Lake Campground (Lost Lake Trl)
Scenic State Park (56956 Scenic Hwy)
Birchdale – Franz Jevne State Park (MN-11)
Biwabik – Vermilion Trail Park (321 Main St)
Blackduck – Hide Out Resort (6109 Rice Lake Rd NE)
Lost Acres Resort (26772 Birchmont Beach Rd NE)
Scenic Hi-Way Resort (11774 Mud Turtle Rd NE)
Webster Lake Campground (13928 Webster Camp Road NE)
Blooming Prairie – Brookside Campground (52482 320th St)

Brainerd – Crow Wing Lake Campground (2393 Crow Wing Camp Rd)
Crow Wing State Park (3124 State Park Rd, Brainerd, MN 56401)
Eagle Lake Campgrounds & Retreat (17040 Co Rd 102)
Gull Lake Dam Rec Area-ACOE (10867 E Gull Lake Drive)
Hidden Paradise Resort & Campground (20621 HIdden Paradise Dr)
Lum Park (1619 NE, Washington St)
Niemeyer's Rugged River Resort (12241 Stailman Rd)
Paul Bunyan Land Campground (17553 MN-18)
Sullivan's Resort & Campground (7685 County Rd 127 N)
The Harbor On Crescent Bay RV Resort (9799 Lakeside Rd)
Brandon – Chippewa Park (9461 County Rd 108 NW)
Long Lake Lodge, LLC (16021 Long Lake Rd NW)
Breckenridge – Welles Memorial Park & Fairgrounds (101 Nebraska Ave)
Breezy Point – Highview Campground & RV Park (11090 Old Co Rd 39)
Brimson – Indian Lake Campground (Hwy 44)
Britt – Voyageur's Sand Lake Resort (7449 Britt Bypass)
Brownsville – Reno Horse Campground (16728 Hillside Rd)
Wildcat Park & Landing (11011 MN-26)
Brownton – Lake Marion Regional Park (11655 MN-15)
Burtrum – Cedar Lake Memorial Park Campground (1736 Abaca Rd)
Butterfield – Sands Country Cove Campground (39312 680th Ave)
Buyck – Life of Riley Resort (3256 Cedar Rd)
Byron – Oxbow Park and Zollman Zoo (5731 County Rd 105 NW)
Caledonia – Beaver Creek Valley State Park (15954 County Rd 1)
Winnebago Springs (19708 Camp Winnebago Rd)
Cambridge – Fairgrounds Campground (3101 MN-95)
Canby – Canby Triangle Park Campground (1304 St Olaf Ave N)
Lake Sylvan Park (Haarfager Avenue S)
Stonehill Regional Park (1801 County Road 30)
Cannon Falls – Cannon Falls Campground (30365 Oak Ln)
Lake Byllesby Campground (7650 Echo Point Rd)
Carlos – Lake Carlos State Park (2601 County Rd 38 NE)
Carlton – Jay Cooke State Park (780 E Hwy 210)
Cass Lake – Allen's Bay Lodge & Grille and Sunset Cove Resort (4083 Kangas Curve Rd SE)
Birch Ridge Resort on Leech Lake/Sucker Bay (12797 N Shore Ln NW)
Cass Lake Lodge (16293 60th Ave NW)
Chippewa National Forest & Campgrounds (200 Ash Ave NW)
Highland Resort and Seasonal Park (539 Highland Inn Rd NE)
Little Wolf Resort (7159 Little Wolf Rd NW)
Marclay Point Resort & Campground (16636 Marclay Point Lane Southeast)
Norway Beach Recreation Area (2005 Norway Beach Rd)
Oak Point Resort (10583 Oak Point Rd NW)
Stony Point Resort, Trailer Park & Campground (5510 US-2)
Center City – Wild River State Park (39797 Park Trail)
Centerville – Rice Creek Campgrounds (7373 Main St)
Chisholm – Chisholm Iron Trail Campground (115 6th Ave SW)
Clarissa – Clarissa City Park (302 US-71)
Clarkfield – Oraas Park (1963-1977 US-59)
Clearbrook – Clearbrook City Park (Cross Roads Hazel Ave & Main St)
Clearwater – A-J Acres Campgrounds (1300 195th St E)
St Cloud/Clearwater RV Park (2454 Co Rd 143)

Cleveland – Beaver Dam Resort (46115 Beaver Dam Rd)
Clitherall – Silver Sage Guest Ranch (15381 410th Ave)
Cloquet – Big Lake Shores and The Lounge (979 Cary Rd)
Cloquet/Duluth KOA Kampgrounds (1381 Kampground Road)
Spafford Park (401 Main St)
Cohasset – Sugar Bay Campground/Resort (21812 Moose Point Rd)
Cokato – Cokato Lake RV Resort (2945 County Hwy 4 SW)
Collinwood Regional Park & Campground (17251 70th St SW)
Cook – Bass Lake Park (Bass Lake Park Rd)
Hinsdale Island Campsites (7360 Hinsdale Is)
Larson Lake Campground (Off Bass Lake Campground Rd)
Polley's Resort (2434 Polley Rd)
Stony Brook Horse Campground (11207 North Snake Trail State Forest Road)
Thistledew Campground and Day-Use Area (63353 County Road 551)
Togo Horse Campground (Co Rd 551)
Vermilion Motel/RV Park (320 US-53)
Vermilion Sunsets RV Park (2475 Vermilion Dr)
Wakemup Bay Campground and Day-Use Area (2443 Wakely Rd)
Coon Rapids – Bunker Hills Campgrounds (13101 County Pkwy B)
Crosby – Crosby Memorial Park Campground (2 2nd St SW)
Cuyana Range Campground (21704 Dewing Rd)
Greer Lake Campground (17340-17796 Greer Lake Rd)
Red Rider Resort & Campground (23457 Co Rd 31)
True North Basecamp (825 1st St SW)
Crosslake – Cross Lake Recreation Area ACOE (35507 Co Rd 66)
Currie – Lake Shetek State Park (163 State Park Rd)
Schreier's On Shetek Campground (35 Resort Rd)
Cushing – Campfire Bay Resort (31504 Azure Rd)
Fishtrap Camping & RV Resort (30894 Fishtrap Lake Dr)
Dalton – Ten Mile Lake Resort & Steakhouse (12303 Co Rd 35)
Dawson – Dawson City Campground (123 1st St)
Veteran's Park Campground (1000-1098 7th St)
Deer River – Ball Club Lake Lodge (34858 Co Rd 39)
Bowen Lodge (58485 Bowens Rd)
Cottonwood Lake Campground (Cross Roads Cottonwood Rd & Itasca County Rd 248)
Georgene's Haven (50241 Co Rd 35)
High Banks Resort (17645 N Highbanks Rd NE)
Hundred Acre Wood Resort (32228 Co Rd 39)
Jessie View Resort & RV Campground (45756 Co Rd 35)
Little Winnie Resort (55671 Co Rd 9)
Moose Lake Campground (CR 238 1 mi N of CR 19)
Northern Acres Resort & Campground (47292 Bowstring Acc)
Northland Lodge (17207 Winnie Dam Rd NE)
Pines Resort & Campground (5000 17221 Co Hwy 9)
Schoolcraft State Park (9042 Schoolcraft Ln NE)
Snug Harbor Resort and Campground (50351 CR 35)
Starck's Tamarack Lodge (4314 Winnie Dam Ln NE)
Deerwood – Camp Holiday Resort & Campground (27406 Round Lake Rd)
Clearwater Forest (16595 Crooked Lake Rd)
Dent – Abbywood Resort (38034 Co Rd 35)
Bells Resort Bar & Grill (39578 Co Hwy 41)
Heart Beach Resort (38052 Co Rd 35)
Hollywood's Resort (30995 MN-108)
Detroit Lakes – American Legion Family Campground (810 W Lake Dr)
Country Campground (13621 260 Ave)
Forest Hills Golf & Resort (22931 185 St)
Hatfield's Island View Resort (23546 Warbler Way)
Long Lake Campsite (17421 W Long Lake Rd)
The Hideaway Resort (25574 E Island Lake Rd)
Valhalla Resort (24218 E Island Lake Rd)

Dexter – Green Acres RV Park (236 Main St)
Duluth – Boundary Waters Canoe Area Wilderness (2M27+CG Prairie Portage, Minnesota)
Buffalo Valley Camping (2590 Guss Rd)
Eagle's Nest Resort (6103 Lavaque Rd)
Fond du Lac Campground (13404 MN-23)
Hi Banks Resort & Campground (5392 Fish Lake Dam Rd)
Indian Point Campground (7000 Pulaski St, Duluth, MN 55807)
Lakehead Boat Basin (1000 Minnesota Ave)
River Place Campground (9902 Hudson Blvd)
Silver Fox Lodge Resort (7495 Boulder Lake Rd)
Snowflake Camping and Nordic Ski Center (4348 Rice Lake Rd)
Spirit Mountain Ski & Recreation Area (9500 Spirit Mountain Pl)
Superior National Forest (8901 Grand Ave Pl)
Dundee – Talcot Lake County Park (53100 MN-62)
East Grand Forks – Red River State Recreation Area (515 2nd St NW)
Edgerton – Rock River Campground (W. Mill St)
Effie – Button Box Lake Campground and Day-Use Area (Cross Roads Button Box Campground Rd & Button Box Rd)
Owen Lake Campground and Day-Use Area (Owen Lake Campground Rd.)
Elbow Lake – Tipsinah Mounds Park Campground (26527 Tipsinah Mounds Rd)
Ellendale – Crystal Springs RV Resort (15649 SW 35th Ave)
Ely – Bear Head Lake State Park (9301 Bear Head State Park Rd)
Big Lake Wilderness Lodge & Outfitters (3012 Echo Trail)
Boundary Waters Grouse Lodge (638 Kawishiwi Trail)
Canoe Country Outfitters Cabins & Campgrounds (14623 Moose Lake Rd)
Cliff Wold's Campground (339 Fernberg Rd)
Fall Lake Campground (Fall Lk Rd)
Lodge of Whispering Pines (3060 Echo Trail)
Shagawa Inn Resort (1973 W Shagawa Rd)
Silver Rapids Lodge (459 Kawishiwi Trail)
Snowbank Lodge and Outfitters (14564 Snowbank Lodge Rd)
Stony Ridge Resort & Cafe (60 W Lakeview Pl)
YMCA Camp du Nord (3606 N Arm Rd)
Embarrass – Heritage Park & Campground (4789 Salo Rd)
Emily – Lake Emily Resort (21345 Dam Rd)
Little Pine RV Park (39396 MN-6)
Mantrap Lake Campground and Day-Use Area (21517 Papoose Road)
Erskine – 2Annes Lakeside RV Park (400 Park St)
Lake Sarah Farmers Union Park & Campground (38524 200th Ave SE)
Union Lake Sarah Campground (20049 Campground Rd SE)
Esko – Knife Island Campground (234 W State Rte 61)
Eveleth – Eveleth Veterans Park Campground (4392 Miller Trunk Rd)
Excelsior – Camp Fire Minnesota (3300 Tanadoona Dr)
Eyota – Chester Woods County Park (8378 14 Highway Southeast)
Fairbault – Roberds Lake Resort & Campground (18197 Roberds Lake Blvd)
Fairfax – Fort Ridgely State Park (72158 Co Rd 30)
Fairmont – Flying Goose Campground and Resort (2521 115th St)
Faribault – Camp Faribo (21851 Bagley Ave)
Le Mieux Resort (7710 Cedar Lake Blvd)
Winjum's Shady Acres Resort (17759 177th St W)
Farmington – Whitetail Woods Camper Cabins (17100 State Trail)
Federal Dam – Leech Lake Recreation Area (1217 Federal Dam Dr NE)
Machart's Landing (11 2nd Ave)
Sugar Point Resort (10125 Sugar Point Dr NW)

Fergus Falls – Swan Lake Resort & Campground (17463 Co Rd 29)
Fifty Lakes – Up a Creek Campground (16263 Co Rd 1)
Finland – Crooked Lake Resort (9449 Cramer Rd)
Eckbeck Campground and Day-Use Area (Eckbeck Park Rd)
Finland Campground and Day-Use Area (233-1, Co Rd 6)
George H Crosby Manitou State Park (7616 Co Hwy 7)
Wildhurst Lodge & Campground (7344 State Hwy 1)
Finlayson – Waldheim Resort (9096 Waldheim Ln)
Fosston – City of Fosston Campground (224 S Johnson Ave)
Tilberg Park on Cross Lake Timber Mill Community Park (Right on 390th Ave SE to Tilberg-Cross Lake Park)
Frazee – Birchmere Resort & Campground (18346 Birchmere Rd)
Rose Ridge Resort (34568 Co Hwy 4)
Frontenac – Frontenac State Park (29223 County 28 Blvd)
Fulda – Seven Mile Park (900 S Lafayette Ave)
Garden City – Shady Oaks Campground (340 Fairgrounds St)
Garfield – Oak Park Kampground (9561 County Rd 8 NW)
Garrison – Bobber's RV & Mobile Home Park (10116 Carey Ln)
Garrison Bay Resort (9825 US-169)
Wilderness of Minnesota Campground (9923 US-169)
Garvin – Garvin Park Campground (1442 US-59)
Sundquist Park at West Lake Sarah County Park (1410 211st St)
Gilbert – Sherwood Forest Campground (301 Ore-Be-Gone Dr)
West Forty RV Park & Campground (245 MN-37)
Glencoe – Oak Leaf Park Campground (3 Desoto Ave S)
Glenwood – Barsness Park Campground (1022 MN-104)
Lake Reno Resort (10583 MN-29)
Pelican RV Resort (17486 N Pelican Lake Rd)
South Pointe RV Park (21405 S Lakeshore Dr)
Woodlawn Resort & Campgrounds (24050 N Lake Shore Dr)
Glyndon – Buffalo River State Park (565 155th St S)
Graceville – Big Stone County Toqua Park (Toqua Lake Road, 23390 Big Stone County Rd 18)
Graceville Gun Club (1320 MN Hwy 28)
Grand Marais – Devilfish Lake Rustic Campground (Superior Hiking Trail)
East Bearskin Campground (124 E Bearskin Rd)
Esther Lake Rustic Campground (Esther Lake Rd)
Flour Lake Campground (468 Clearwater Rd)
Golden Eagle Lodge-Resort, Campground, & Nordic Ski Center (468 Clearwater Rd)
Grand Marais Recreation Area (114 S 8th Ave W)
Gunflint Pines Resort & Campground (217 S Gunflint Lake Rd)
Hungry Hippie Hostel (401 Co Rd 14)
Hungry Jack Lodge & Campground (372 S Hungry Jack Rd)
Judge C R Magney State Park (4051 MN-61)
Kimball Lake Campground (FR 140)
McFarland Lake Rustic Campground (Arrowhead Trail CR16)
Nor'Wester Lodge & Outfitter (7778 Gunflint Trail)
Pine Mountain Campground (2 Thompson Park Dr)
Poplar Haus Cabins (7890 Gunflint Trail)
Trail's End Campground (12582 Gunflint Trail)
Twin Lakes Campsites (Lima Mtn Rd)
Way of The Wilderness (12582 Gunflint Trail)
Grand Portage – Grand Portage Lodge & Casino (X835+HF, 70 Casino Dr)
Grand Rapids – Camp Fire's Bluewater Lodge (37508 Bluewater Rd)
Fishing Springs Campground (18862 Sherrys Arm Rd)
Jaspers Resort (36418 Hunter Drive)
Pine Acres Resort and RV Park (29604 MN-38)
Pokegama Dam & Rec Area (34385 US-2)

Prairie Lake Campground & RV LLC (30730 Wabana Rd)
WA-GA-THA-KA Resort (36363 Wabana Lake Road)
Winnibigoshish Dam & Rec Area-ACoE (State Hwy 46)
Granite Falls – Prairie's Edge Casino Resort & Campground (5616 Prairies Edge Ln)
Wegdahl Park (Co Road 15 & Highway 212)
Granite Falls Memorial Park (MN-67)
Grasston – Nature Retreats MN (16117 MN-107)
Greenbush – City of Greenbush Legion Park (Cross Roads Waters of the Dancing Sky Scenic Bywy & Forsness Rd)
Hackensack – Hyde-A-Way Bay Resort (3489 Ford Dr NW)
Mascot Resort & Lodge (2517 N Webb Lake Dr NW)
Nies Cabins & Campsite (5003 Woodland Ln NW)
Owl's Nest Motel (218 MN-371)
Pleasant Pines Resort & Campground (3443 Pleasant Pine Dr NW)
Quietwoods Resort (4755 Alder Ln NW)
Tri-Birches Resort & Campground (2186 W 5 Point Lake Rd NW)
Wildwood Beach Resort (4417 Buxton Rd NW)
Hadley – Camp Summit (430 S Main St)
Hallock – Gilbert Olson Campground (716 7th St S)
Horseshoe Campground (31 N Birch Ave)
Hanley Falls – MN Machinery Museum Campground (5th St S)
Hanska – Lake Hanska County Park (11189 County Road 11)
Hastings – Afton State Park (6959 Peller Ave S)
Greenwood Campground (13797 190th St E)
St Croix Bluffs Regional Park (10191 St Croix Trail S)
Hawley – Lee Lake Campground (823 270th St S)
Hendricks – Lake Hendricks Campground (Co. Rd 132)
Henning – Linden Park Resort & Campground (23736 Castle Trail)
Herman – Niemackl Lake Park (25225 105th St)
Hibbing – Mesaba Co-op Park (3827 Mesaba Park Rd)
Hill City – Blue Moon Resort (68584 US-169)
Hill City Park Campground (300 Park Ave)
Trails Inn Quadna Mtn Motel & RV Campground (100 Quadna Mountain Rd)
Hinckley – Boulder Campground and Day-Use Area (Tamarack Forest Rd)
Grand Casino Hotel, RV Resort & Chalets (707-771 Lady Luck Dr)
Kettle River Camping Park (Van Gordon Rd)
St Croix State Park (30065 St Croix Park Rd)
Tamarack Horse Campground and Day-Use Area (Tamarack Forest Rd)
Hines – Pine Tree Park Municipal Campground (20857 N Blackduck Lake Rd NE)
Dunrovin Resort (19262 N Blackduck Lake Rd NE)
Tomahawk Lodge Resort & RV Park (24777 Pass Rd NE)
Holyoke – Gafvert Campground and Day-Use Area (S Net Lake Rd)
Houston – Cushon's Peak Campground (18696 MN-16)
Gilles Family Dairy and Woodland (29246 Hass Rd)
Houston Nature Center (215 W Plum St)
Money Creek Haven Inc. (18502 County Rd 26)
Oak Ridge/Wet Bark Recreation Area (County Rd 13)
Outback Ranch Inc. (7750 Tt Rd)
Howard Lake – Codger's Cove RV Resort (5912 County Rd 6 SW)
Hoyt Lakes – Fisherman's Point Campground (32 Fishermans Point Rd)
Hutchinson – Masonic West River Park (1003 Les Kouba Pkwy NW)
Piepenburg Park (21104 Belle Lake Rd)
International Falls – Rainy Lake RV (2967 MN-11 E)
Voyageurs National Park (360 MN-11)
Voyageurs RV Campground & Cabins (2031 2nd Ave)
Ironton – Cuyana Country State Recreation Area (307 3rd St)
Isanti – Country Camping Tent & RV Park on the Rum River (27437 Palm St NW)
Isle – Agate Bay Resort (19139 328th Ave)

Father Hennepin State Park (41296 Father Hennepin Park Rd)
Fiddlestix RV & Golf Resort (1081 395th St #2691)
Fisher's Resort (32390 212th Ln)
McQuoid's Inn (1325 State Hwy 47)
Nitti's Hunter's Point Resort (5436 479th St)
South Isle Family Campground (39002 State Hwy 47)
Jackson – Anderson Park (71816 475th Ave)
Brown Park South (71693 483rd Ave)
Jackson KOA Kampground (2035 US-71)
Robertson Park (48804 715th St)
Jacobson – Hay Lake Campground and Day-Use Area (657th Lane)
Jacobson Campground (69136 Great River Rd)
Jasper – Split Rock Creek State Park (336 50th Ave)
Jordan – Minneapolis SW KOA/Shakopee/Jordan (3315 W 166th St)
Minnesota Valley State Recreation Area (20550 Park Blvd)
Kabetogama – Arrowhead Lodge (10473 Waltz Rd)
Harmony Beach Resort (10002 Gappa Rd)
Herseths Tomahawk Resort (10078 Gappa Rd)
Pine Aire Resort (9978 Gappa Rd)
Sandy Point Lodge (10606 Gamma Rd)
The Pines of Kabetogama (12443 Burma Rd)
Kandiyohi – Diamond Lake County Park (6903 County Rd 4 NE)
Karlstad – North Star Motor Inn (305 Main St S)
Kasota – Lake Washington Regional Park & Campground (47102 Washington Park Rd)
Kelliher – Rogers Resort & Campground (49670 Rogers Rd NE)
Kellogg – Zumbro Bottoms Horse Campgrounds (T-83 off of Hwy 60)
Kensington – Andes RV Park (4505 Andes Rd SW)
Kerrick – Hoffman's Oak Lake Campground (52777 Hoffman Dr)
Kimball – Loch Nest Resort (10248 Co Rd 8)
Lake Bronson – Lake Bronson State Park (County Rd 28)
Lake City – Camp Lacupolis (71000 US-61)
Hok-Si-La City Park and Campground (2500 US-61)
Lake Pepin Camp Grounds and Trailer Court (1818 N High St)
Lake Crystal – Rapidan Dam Park (54101-54199 Glory Ln)
Lake Elmo – Lake Elmo Park Reserve (1515 Keats Ave N)
Lake Lillian – Big Kandiyohi Lake County Park East (9144 123rd Ave SE)
Big Kandiyohi Lake County Park West (14391 45th St SE)
Lakefield – Kilen Woods State Park & Prairie Bush Clover SNA (50200 860th St)
Sandy Point Park (41699 850th St)
Lamberton – Kuhar Park (13494 County Hwy 6)
Landfall – Landfall Terrace (50 Aspen Way)
Lanesboro – Eagle Cliff Campground (35455 MN-16)
Sylvan Park/Riverview Campground (202 Parkway Ave S)
Laporte – Gulch Lakes Campground and Day-Use Area (E Gulch Forest Road)
Le Center – Clear Lake Park Campground (35194 Clear Lake Ln)
Winjum's Shady Acres of Le Center (35032 Clear Lake Ln)
Le Roy – Lake Louise State Park (12385 766th Ave)
Le Sueur – Peaceful Valley Campground (33952 348th St)
Lindstrom – Hillcrest RV Park (32741 N Lakes Trail)
Litchfield – Lake Ripley Campground (1810 S Ripley Dr)
Spirit of Ripley Campground (25169 CSAH 1)
Little Falls – 37 Acres RV and Campground (21486 Forest Rd)
Charles A Lindbergh State Park (1615 Lindbergh Dr S)
Littlefork – Lofgren Memorial Park Campground (413 4th Ave)
Longville – All Seasons Resort (3539 MN-84)

Deer Trail Resort & Campground (1608 Deer Run Dr NE)
Diamond Crest Resort, LLC (2916 Diamond Crest Rd NE)
Evergreen Lodge (230 County 11 NW)
Little Boy Resort & Campground/Front Porch Tavern (3600 County Rd 54 NE)
Long Birch Lodge (262 Birch Ln)
Longville Campground (1367 Co Rd 5)
Pikedale Lodge (7995 Partridge Point Dr NE)
Lutsen – Cascade River State Park (West, 3481 MN-61)
Luverne – Blue Mounds State Park (1410 161st St)
Luverne Campground (803 W Edgehill St)
River Road Campground (1405 111th St)
Lynd – Camden State Park (1897 Camden Pk Rd)
Madelia – Watona Park & Campground (519 Everett Christensen Dr)
Madison – J.F. Jacobson Park (226 8th Ave)
Madison Lake – Bray County Park (22214 Oriole Rd)
Point Pleasant Resort & Campground Inc. (463 Sheppard Cir)
Sakatah Trail Resort (24102 Greenland Rd)
Magnolia – City of Magnolia Campground (301 Luverne St.)
Mahnomen – Shooting Star Casino, Hotel & Event Center (777 S Casino Rd)
Mahtowa – Park Lake Resort, Eatery & Saloon (2243 County Rd 7)
Mankato – Land of Memories Park (491 Amos Owen Ln)
Minneopa State Park (54497 Gadwall Rd)
Maple Grove – Minneapolis Northwest KOA Campground (10410 Brockton Ln N)
Maple Lake – Olson's Campground (5669 123rd St NW)
Maple Plain – Baker Park Reserve & Campground (2309 Baker Park Rd)
Mapleton – Daly County Park (11056 571st Ln)
Marcell – Cedar Point Resort (38268 Cedar Point Rd)
Spider Lake Resort (43859 Spider Lake Rd)
Marine on St. Croix – William O'Brien State Park (16821 O'Brien Trl N)
Maynard – Lions Club Park (Vardis St)
Mazeppa – Ponderosa Campground (40460 Wabasha County Rd 90)
McGrath – Snake River Campground (10890 MN-65)
McGregor – Aldrich's Aitkin Lake Resort (21607 537th Ln)
MN National RV Park (23247 480th St Suite A)
Sandy Lake Dam & Recreation Area (22205 531st Ln)
Savanna Portage State Park (55626 Lake Pl)
Melrose – Birch Lake Campground and Day-Use Area (Cross Roads Unnamed Road and Birch Lake Rd)
Sauk River Campground (206 5th Ave NE)
Menahga – City of Wolf Lake Campground (16596 Wolf Pack Rd)
Huntersville Forest Landing Campground (35550 Campsite Dr)
Municipal Memorial Forest Park Campground (825 Aspen Ave SE)
Shell City Landing Campground (Off 390th St)
Mentor – Lakeview Resort, Restaurant & Lounge (16233 340th St SE)
Merrifield – Lake Edward Resort (25103 Co Rd 3)
Mission Beach Resort & Campground (26847 Co Rd 19)
PineCrest Resort & Seasonal Campground (13873 Co Rd 109)
Sunset Bay Resort & Campground (26823 Co Rd 19)
Middle River – Middle River Community Club Campground (120 S First St)
Milaca – Recreation Park (435 2nd St NW)
Milan – Milan Beach Resort (18095 MN-40)
Miltona – Lazy Days Campground (10247 County Rd 36 NE)
Smokey Timbers Camp (15567 Smokey Timbers Rd NW)
Minnesota City – Bass Camp Resort (12786 Bass Camp Ln)
Montevideo – Lagoon Park Campground (725 Forest Ave)

Monticello – Bertram Chain of Lakes Regional Park (9910 Briarwood Ave NE)
Lake Maria State Park (11411 Clementa Ave NW)
Moose Lake – Moose Lake City Campground (1 Couillard Ln)
Moose Lake State Park (4252 Co Rd 137)
Red Fox Campground & RV Park (1000, Park Pl Dr)
Mora – Eagles Cove Seasonal Park (764 Fish Lake Dr)
Morgan – Gilfillan Estate Campground (28269 MN-67)
Morristown – Camp Maiden Rock West (24505 Jackson Ave)
Maiden Rock East (9403 Morristown Blvd)
Morton – Beaver Falls County Park (31521 Co Rd 2)
Jackpot Junction Casino Hotel (39375 County Rd 24)
Motley – Auger's Pine View Resort (34052 Auger Dr)
Hardy's Lake in the Woods RV Resort (1788 330th St)
Mountain Iron – West Two River Campground (4988 Campground Rd)
Mountain Lake – Island View Campground (716 Prince Street)
Naytahwaush – Pinehurst Resort (27345 Co Rd 4)
Nerstrand – Nerstrand Big Woods State Park (9700 170th St E)
Nevis – Anderson's Starlight Bay Resort (27155 County 33)
Breezy Pines Resort & Campground (25138 County 2)
Campers' Paradise (19478 Edgewater Dr)
Crow Wing Inn (117 MN-34)
Eagles Landing Resort & RV Park (17592 Daylight Trail)
Nevis – Green Valley Resort (19586 County 13 Blvd)
In-We-Go Resort & Motel (27385 County 33)
Knotty Pines Resort (21396 County 18)
Round Bay Resort & RV Park (23608 MN-87)
Woodson Cabins (24519 Fairwood Ln)
New London – Games Lake County Park (20944 County Rd 5 NW)
Hideaway Campground (11890 199th Ave. NE)
Sibley State Park (800 Sibley Park Rd NE)
New Ulm – Flandrau State Park (1300 Summit Ave)
The Brown County Fairgrounds (1201 N State St)
New York Mills – Olson's Big Pine Get-A-Way (42919 County Hwy 53)
Nisswa – Point Narrows Resort (991 Point Narrows Rd)
Birch Bay RV Resort (1497 Sandy Point Rd SW)
Cozy Bay Resort (23684 Co Rd 4)
Fritz's Resort Campground (26483 MN-371)
Galles' Upper Cullen Resort (28317 Upper Cullen Rd)
North Branch – Kozy Oaks Kamp (8620 277th Ave NE)
Northome – October Ridge Resort (66211 Co Rd 31)
Sleepy Hollow Resort (64264 State Hwy 46)
Norwood Young America – Baylor Regional Park
Bayside Cabins & Resort (10775 County Rd 33)
Ogema – Woodland Trails Resort (33616 Loon Dr)
Ogilvie – The Camps At The Vineyard by Boudreau (1005 205th Ave)
Woodsong RV Resort (2186 Empire St)
Olivia – Memorial Park Campground (1800 West Lincoln Ave West Hwy 212/71)
Onamia – Mille Lacs Kathio State Park (15066 Kathio State Park Rd)
North Star Resort (17106 Walleye Rd)
Rocky Reef Resort (13207 Twilight Rd)
Orr – Ash River Campground; Kabetogama State Forest (9397 Orr-Buyck Rd)
Ash Riviera Resort and RV Campsites (10351 Ash River Trail)
AshKaNam Resort (10209 Ash River Trail)
Aspen Resort & Campground (11023 Slade Rd)
Cabin O' Pines Resort & RV Park (4378 Pelican Road)
Frontier (10141 Ash River Trail)
Sunset Resort & Campground (10294 Ash River Trail)
Trail's End Resort & Campground (6310 Crane Lake Rd)
Ortonville – Big Stone Lake State Park (35889 Meadowbrook State Park Road)
Ortonville – Hilltop Estates RV Park (1141 US-12)
Lakeshore RV Park Inc. (39445 Lake Shore RV Park)
Rustling Elms Resort (74637 Rustling Elms Rd W)
Osage – Breezy Point Resort (54852 MN-34)
Jack Pines Resort & Campground (53014 MN-34)

The Wilds Resort & Campground (45120 Maple Ln)
Osakis – Head of The Lakes Resort (15080 Gardenia Dr)
Idlewilde Resort (811 Lake St E)
Linwood Resort & Campground (17898 Lake St E)
Midway Beach Resort & Campground (1821 Lake St E)
Two – Mile Trailer Park & Campground (451 County Rd 10 SE)
Ottertail – Bladow Beach Resort & Campground (36052 Rush Lake Loop)
Hidden Haven Resort and RV's (36242 Rush Lake Loop)
Shady Grove Resort (35686 Rush Lake Loop)
Thumper Pond Resort (300 Thumper Lodge Rd)
Wild Walleye Resort (46463 Boys Shore Rd)
Outing – Clint Converse Campground and Day-Use Area (5861 Lake Washburn Rd NE)
Owatonna – Hope Oak Knoll Campground (9545 County Rd 3)
Rice Lake State Park (8485 Rose St)
River View Campground (2554 28th St SW)
Palisade – Berglund Park Campground (510 Marconi St)
Gun Lake Family Campground (43016 328th Pl)
Park Rapids – Breeze Camping & RV Resort (25824 County 89)
Cedar Shores Lodge & Resort (17915 Dayspring Dr)
Hungryman Lake Campground and Day-Use Area (Two Inlets State Forest)
Itasca State Park (36750 Main Pk Dr)
Niawa Star Lodge Resort (17777 Jasmine Dr)
Sleeping Fawn Resort & Campground (20097 County 24)
Vagabond Village Campground (23801 Green Pines Rd)
Whippoorwill Resort (21421 County 24)
Wilderness Bay Resort (36701 Wilderness Bay Dr)
Paynesville – Lake Koronis Regional Park (51612 Co Hwy 20)
Pelican Rapids – Cross Point Resort (39870 Cross Point Ln)
Lake Lizzie Shores Resort & Campground (47627 E Lake Lizzie Rd)
Maplewood State Park (39721 Park Entrance Rd)
Pelican Hills RV Park (20098 S Pelican Dr)
Sherin Memorial Park (289 E Mill St)
Pengilly – Swan Lake Campground and Resort (29945 E Shore Dr)
Pennington – Bliss Point Resort (26851 Roadrunner Dr NE)
Chippewa Pines Resort on Cass Lake (27418 Chippewa Paws Ln SE)
Knutson Dam Campground & Boat Landing-Chippewa National Forest (Forest Road 2176)
Red Beard's Resort (30353 Squirrel Way NE)
Pequot Lakes – Rock Lake Campground and Day-Use Area (Orchard Park Ln SW)
Wildwedge Golf & RV Park (32620 Paul Bunyan Trail Drive)
Peterson – Peterson City RV Campground (330 Fillmore St)
Pierz – Pierz Park Campground & Municipal Golf Course (603 Park Ave SE)
Pillager – Shady Hollow Resort & Campground (1009 Shady Hollow Rd)
Walter E. Stark House Campground (11871 Pillsbury Forest Rd SW)
Pine City – Pokegama Lake RV Park & Golf Course (19193 Island Resort Rd)
Snake River Campground (Snake River Campground Dr)
Pine Island – Hidden Meadows RV Park Inc. (6450 120th St NW)
Pine River – River View RV Park & Campground (3040-16th Ave SW)
Pipestone – Pipestone Family Campground (919 N Hiawatha Ave)
Plainview – Carley State Park (50366 Wabasha County Rd 4)
Ponsford – Bad Medicine Resort & Campground (38257 Bad Medicine Resort Rd)

End-of-Trail Resort (48883 Marilou Dr)
Tamarac Resort & Campground LLC (32152 Co Hwy 35)
Veronen's Resort (36916 Sunset Dr)
Whaley's Resort and Campground (35974 Whaley's Rd)
Preston – County Fair Campground (Fairgrounds off Highway 12)
Forestville/Mystery Cave State Park (21071 Co. Rd 118)
Maple Springs Campground Inc. (21606 County Rd 118)
Old Barn Resort (24461 Heron Rd)
Valley View Campground (23750 US-52)
Princeton – Riverside Park (300 N Rum River Dr)
Prior Lake – Dakotah Meadows RV Park (2341 Park Pl NW)
Fish Lake Acres Campground (3000 210th St E)
Ranier – The Lakeview Resort (3485 Poplar St)
Ray – Birch Grove Resort (10466 Waltz Rd)
Woodenfrog Campground and Day-Use Area (Co Rd. 122)
Red Lake Falls – Voyageurs View Campground (18611 105th Ave. SW)
Red Wing – Hay Creek Valley Campground Inc. (31655 MN-58)
Redwood Falls – Ramsey Park (99 E Oak St)
Remer – Baker & White Oak Lake Campsites (Land O'Lakes State Forest Draper Forest Rd)
Balsam Bay Resort (6231 72nd St NE)
Graves Lake Resort (6532 Graves Lake Drive NE)
Remer Motel & Campground (309 W Airport Dr)
Thunder Lake Lodge (5316 Cisco Ln NE)
Timber Trails Resort & Campground (3014 S Boy Lake Dr NE)
Rice – Benton Beach Campground (96 125th St NW)
Richmond – El Rancho Manana Campground & Riding Stable (27302 Ranch Rd)
Morning Star Resort & Campground (22954 Green Acres Dr)
Riverside Resort & Campground (21026 MN-22)
Richville – Northern Lights Resort (35387 Northern Lights Trail)
Sunset Bay Resort (38274 Co Hwy 44)
Walker Lake Preserve with Ottertail Lake access (38493 Preserve Dr)
Rochester – AutumnWoods RV Park (1067 Autumn Woods Cir SW)
Rochester/Marion KOA (5232 65th Ave SE)
Roseau – Hayes Lake State Park (48990 Co Rd 4)
Royalton – Two Rivers Campground & Tubing (5116 145th St NW)
Rushford – Bluffview Campground (30-98 Bluffview Trailer Ct)
Money Creek and Vinegar Ridge (270 Township Rd)
Northend Campground (101 N. Mill St.)
Rushford Village – Trailside Campground (43293 MN-16)
Saginaw – Red Pine Campground (5020 Red Pine Dr)
Sanborn – Sailors & Soldiers Memorial Park and Campground (431 S Main St)
Sandstone – Banning State Park (61101 Banning Park Rd)
Osprey Wilds Campgrounds (54165 Audubon Drive)
Sauk Centre – Sinclair Lewis Campground (826 Park Rd)
Savage – Town & Country Campground and RV Park (12630 Boone Ave)
Schroeder – Lamb's Resort Cabins & Campground (19 Lambs Way)
Temperance River State Park (7620 West MN-61)
Sebeka – Gloege's Northern Sun Canoe Outfitting & Campground (30153 Huntersville Rd)
Sebeka Dept of Parks (W Minnesota Ave)
Shafer – Wildwood RV Park & Campground (20078 Lake Blvd)
Sherburn – Everett Park (334 Kenzie St)
Shevlin – Black Lantern Resort & Campground (26844 320th St)
Long Lake Park & Campground (19141 Heart Lake Rd)
Side Lake – McCarthy Beach State Park (7622 McCarthy Beach Rd)
Silver Bay – Tettegouche State Park (5702 MN-61)

Slayton – Valhalla Island Campground (6 Valhalla Dr)
Sleepy Eye – Sportsman's Park Campground (1000 3rd Ave NW)
Solway – La Salle Lake State Recreation Area (10899 Co Hwy 9)
Soudan – Lake Vermilion-Soudan Underground Mine State Park (1302 McKinley Park Rd)
McKinley Park Campground (5563 Hoodoo Point Rd)
South Haven – BJ's Bait & Tackle LLC Castaways Campground (13155 Bayview Rd)
Clearwater Forest Resort Community (13449 Campfire Cir)
Spicer – Green Lake County Park (12381 N Shore Dr)
Island View Resort (5910 132nd Ave NE)
WestRich RV Park (720 Agnes St)
Spring Lake – Anchor Inn Resort (55960 Co. Road 4)
Edgewater Resort (52001 Edgewater Rd)
Springfield – Springfield Rothenburg Campground (33 South Case Ave.)
Squaw Lake – Bright Star Resort (62563 County Road 149)
Cut Foot Sioux Horse Camp (Forest Rd 2171)
Dixon Lake Resort (49442 Dixon Lake Resort Rd)
Wausota Resort (61493 Wausota Rd)
St. Cloud – St Cloud Campground & RV Park (9447, 2491 2nd St SE)
St. James – Tiell Campground (301 Tiell Dr)
Eagle Nest Park (34239 780th Ave)
St. Peter – Riverside Park Municipal Campground (227 South Front St)
Staples – Dower Lake Recreation Area (26415 Thunder Rd)
Starbuck – Glacial Lakes State Park (25022 Co Rd 41)
Hobo Park Campground & Marina (401 E 1st St)
Stephen – Marshall County Park at Florian (28219 380th St NW)
Northwest Acres Campground (11 Lincoln Ave)
Sturgeon Lake – Timberline RV Resort (9152 Timberline Rd)
Sunburg – Monson Lake State Park (1690 15th St NE)
Talmoon – Loon's Landing LLC (48989 Co Rd 134)
Rising Eagle Resort (47405 Co Rd 135)
Taylors Falls – Camp Waub-o-Jeeg (2185 Chisago St)
Interstate State Park (307 Milltown Rd)
Tenstrike – Birch Haven Resort (11801 Paper Birch Dr NE)
Eagle Ridge Resort (10246 Stallion Ct NE)
Hendricks Haven (6335 Hendricks Haven Rd NE)
Pike Point Resort (10393 S Gull Lake Rd NE)Tenstrike – Summer Haven RV Resort (21588 Gull Lake Loop Rd NE)
Thief River Falls – Tourist Park (701 Oakland Park Road)
Togo – Bear Lake Campground and Day-Use Area (Cross Road Highway 552 and W Bear Lake Forest Rd)
Tower – Fortune Bay Resort Casino (1430 Bois Forte Rd)
Hoodoo Point Campgrounds (Tower Park, 5788 Hoodoo Point Rd)
Trancheff's Cabins (4293 Arrowhead Point Rd)
Tracy – Swift Lake Park Campground (1342 Co. Rd 11)
Trimont – Cedar Hanson Park (691 215th St)
Truman – Perch Lake Park (2163 200th Ave)
Two Harbors – Burlington Bay Campground (Cross Roads Voyageur Hwy & N Shore Scenic Dr)
Gooseberry Falls State Park (3206 MN-61)
Penmarallter Campsite (725 Scenic Dr)
Sullivan Lake Campground (Off CR 15; Forest Hwy 11)
Underwood – Whispering Waters Resort (27921 340th Ave)
Vergas – Loon Lake Resort (32053 Loon Dr)
Loonies Pub & Campground (31870 Co Rd 130)
Lost Valley Resort LLC (49506 Lost Valley Rd)
Spirit Lake Resort (30274 Co Hwy 4)
Victoria – Carver Park Campground (7400 Grimm Rd)
Villard – Canary Beach Resort (17405 Co Rd 28)
Shady Rest Resort & Campground (16953 142nd St)
Wabasha – Bailey Park/RV Community (Cross Roads 10th St. and Pembroke Ave.)

Big River Resort (1110 Hiawatha Dr E)
Kruger Campground and Management Unit (20462 County Rd 81)
Pioneer Campsite (64739 140th Ave)
Wadena – Sunnybrook Campground (217 Harry Rich Dr)
Wahkon – Island View Resort (145 6th St)
Walker – Acorn Hill Resort (4691 Acorn Hill Ln NW)
Agency Bay Lodge (8491 Onigum Rd NW)
Anderson's Cove (11246 Portside Ct NW)
Anderson's Pine Point Resort (9693 Pine Point Rd NW)
Anderson's South Shore Resort (1696 Whipholt Beach Rd)
Andersons Horseshoe Bay Lodge (8098 Hawthorn Trail NW)
Bayside Resort (8039 Onigum Rd NW)
Bluewater Lodge by Chase on the Lake (5203 Ninebark Ct NW)
Hiawatha Beach Resort & Houseboat (10904 Steamboat Loop NW)
In The Woods Campground (7440 Onigum Rd NW)
Mabel Lake National Forest Campground (6715 Mable Lake Road NW)
Shores of Leech Lake Marina, RV Park & Cottages (6166 Morris Point Rd NW)
Stony Point National Forest Campground (3290 Stony Point Camp Road NW)
Trails RV Park (9424 MN-371)
Walnut Grove – Plum Creek County Park Campground (11000 Crown Ave)
Warren – Holiday Park Campground (N 8th St)
Warroad – Bemis Hill Campground (Cross Roads Thompson Forest Road & Stanton Forest Road)
Birch Ridge RV Campground (34352 568TH Ave)
Springsteel Resort & Marina (38004 Beach St)
Warroad City Campground (1101 Lake St NE)
Waseca – Kiesler's Campground & RV Resort (14360 Old Hwy 14)
Waskish – Beacon Harbor Resort (57153 Hudec Resort Rd NE)
Big Bog State Recreation Area (55716 MN-72)
West Wind Resort (54719 MN-72)
Waterville – Best Point Resort (49843 T-20)
Kamp Dels (14842 Sakatah Lake Rd)
Lakeview Resort (14972 Sakatah Lake Rd)
Sakatah Lake State Park (50499 Sakatah Lake St Park Rd)
Watson – Lac qui Parle State Park (14047 20th St NW)
Watson Hunting Camp (13070 10th St NW)
Waubun – Cedar Crest Resort (29783 387 St)
Elk Horn Resort & Campground (2929 293rd St)
Rainbow Resort (36571 Co Hwy 35)
Welch – Treasure Island Resort & Casino (5734 Sturgeon Lake Rd)
Welcome – Welcome Creek Campground (601 N Guide St)
Williams – Blueberry Hill Campgrounds (Highway 11 & MOM's Way)
Williams – Faunce Campground (3684 54th Avenue Northwest)
The Williams City Park & RV Campground (Pine St. & CR 2)
Zippel Bay Resort (6080 39th St NW)
Zippel Bay State Park (3684 54th Ave NW)
Willow River – Bremen Woods Resort (22007 Bremen Wds Ln)
Willow River Campground (Off Frontage Rd of 135W Exit #205)
Winona – Camp Everyday (22718 Little Smokies Ln)
Great River Bluffs State Park (43605 Kipp Dr)
Prairie Island Campground (1120 Prairie Island Rd N)
Wood Lake – Timm Park (T-191)
Worthington – Olson Park Campground (951 N Crailsheim Rd)
Zumbro Falls – Bluff Valley RV Park & Campground Inc (61297 390th Ave)
Zumbrota – Shades of Sherwood (14334 Sherwood Trail)

Minnesota Fast Facts

Minnesota was the 32nd State admitted to the Union on May 11, 1858. Derived from the Dakota language, "Minnesota" can be translated to "cloudy water".

Population: 5,793,151 (22nd as of the 2020 Census)
Area: 86,935 square miles (12th)
Highest Elevation: 2,300 feet (Eagle Mountain, northwest of Grand Marais in the Boundary Waters Canoe Area Wilderness)
Lowest Elevation 600 feet (Lake Superior near Grand Marais)

Bee: Rusty patched bumblebee – *Bombus affinis* (2019)
Beverage: Milk – (1984)
Bird: Common Loon – *Gavia immer* (1961)
Butterfly: Monarch – *Danaus plexippus* (2000)
Constellation: Ursa Minor (2025)
Fish: Walleye – *Sitzostedion vitreum* (1965)
Flower: Pink-and-white lady's slipper – *Cypripedium reginae* (1967)
Fossil: Giant Beaver – *Castoroides ohioensis* (2025)
Fruit: Honeycrisp apple – *Malus pumila* (2006)
Gemstone: Lake Superior agate (1969)
Grain: Wild rice – *Zizania palustris* (1977)
Latin Motto: *L'Étoile du Nord* (1861)
Motto: Star of the North (1861)
Muffin: Blueberry muffin (1988)
Mushroom: Common morel – *Morchella esculenta* (1984)
Nicknames: "Land of 10,000 Lakes," "the Gopher State," "the North Star State"
Photograph: *Grace* (2002)
Soil: Lester (2012)
Song: "Hail! Minnesota" (1945)
Sport: Ice Hockey (2009)
Tree: Norway pine – *Pinus resinosa* (1953)

Minnesota State Flag 1983-2024; Minnesota State Flag 2024-present

Minnesota Governors

Alexander Ramsey, Republican/Whig (06/01/1849-04/01/1853)
Willis A. Gorman, Democrat (04/01/1853-03/13/1857)
Samuel Medary, Democrat (03/13/1857-05/24/1858; until statehood)

Henry Hastings Sibley, Democrat (05/24/1858-01/02/1860)
Alexander Ramsey, Republican (01/02/1860-07/10/1863)
Henry Adoniram Swift, Republican (07/10/1863-01/13/1864)
Stephen Miller, Republican (01/13/1864-01/08/1866)
William Rainey Marshall, Republican (01/08/1866- 01/07/1870)
Horace Austin, Republican (01/07/1870- 01/09/1874)
Cushman K. Davis, Republican (01/09/1874-01/07/1876)
John S. Pillsbury, Republican (01/07/1876-01/09/1882)
Lucius Frederick Hubbard, Republican (01/09/1882-01/05/1887)
Andrew Ryan McGill, Republican (01/05/1887-01/09/1889)
William Rush Merriam, Republican (01/09/1889-01/04/1893)
Knute Nelson, Republican (01/04/1893-01/31/1895)
David Marston Clough, Republican (01/31/1895-01/02/1899)
John Lind, Democrat (01/02/1899-01/07/1901)
Samuel Rinnah Van Sant, Republican (01/07/1901-01/04/1905)
John Albert Johnson, Democrat (01/04/1905-09/21/1909)
Adolph Olson Eberhart, Republican (09/21/1909-01/06/1915)
Winfield Scott Hammond, Democrat (01/06/1915-12/30/1915)
Joseph A. A. Burnquist, Republican (12/30/1915-01/05/1921)
J. A. O. Preus, Republican (01/05/1921-01/07/1925)
Theodore Christianson, Republican (01/07/1925-01/07/1931)
Floyd B. Olson, Farmer-Labor (01/07/1931-08/22/1936)
Hjalmar Peterson, Farmer-Labor (08/22/1936-01/04/1937)
Elmer Austin Benson, Farmer-Labor (01/04/1937-01/03/1939)
Harold Stassen, Republican (01/03/1939-04/27/1943)
Edward John Thye, Republican (04/27/1943-01/08/1947)
Luther Youngdahl, Republican (01/08/1947-09/27/1951)
C. Elmer Anderson, Republican (09/27/1951-01/05/1955)
Orville Freeman, Democratic/Farmer-Labor (01/05/1955-01/04/1961)
Elmer L. Andersen, Republican (01/04/1961-03/25/1963)
Karl Rolvaag, Democratic/Farmer-Labor (03/25/1963-01/02/1967)
Harold LeVander, Republican (01/02/1967-01/04/1971)
Wendell R. Anderson, Democrat/Farmer-Labor (01/04/1971-12/29/1976)
Rudy Perpich, Democrat/Farmer-Labor (12/29/1976-01/01/1979)
Al Quie, Republican (01/01/1979-01/03/1983)
Rudy Perpich, Democrat/Farmer-Labor (01/03/1983-01/07/1991)
Arne Carlson, Independent/Republican (01/07/1991-01/04/1999)
Jesse Ventura, Reform/Independence (01/04/1999-01/06/2003)
Tim Pawlenty, Republican (01/06/2003-01/03/2011)
Mark Dayton, Democrat/Farmer-Labor (01/03/2011-01/07/2019)
Tim Walz, Democrat/Farmer-Labor (01/07/2019-Incumbent)

Minnesota Scenic & Historic Byways

Minnesota's Byways are a great way to traverse much of the state and take in beautiful scenery or a string of historic sites. There are 22 Byways in Minnesota, two of which are also categorized as National Scenic Byways (in **bold**).

Apple Blossom Drive Scenic Byway (17 miles)
- Passes through La Crescent, Dakota, Nodine, Pickwick, Lamoille

Avenue of Pines Scenic Byway (46 miles)
- Passes through Deer River, Squaw Lake, Alvwood, Bergville, Northome

Edge of Wilderness National Scenic Byway (47 miles)
- Passes through Grand Rapids, Marcell, Bigfork, Effie

Glacial Ridge Trail (220-425 miles)
- Passes through Willmar, Spicer, New London, Terrace, Glenwood, Long Beach, Villard, Sauk Centre, Alexandria, Starbuck, Swift Lake

Grand Rounds National Scenic Byway (50 miles)
- Passes through Minneapolis, Saint Anthony, Columbia Heights

Great River Road – MN Segment (565 miles)
- Passes through La Crescent, Dresbach, Dakota, Winona, Goodview, Minnesota City, Minneiska, Weaver, Kellogg, Wabasha, Reads Landing, Camp Lacupolis, Lake City, Frontenac, Wacouta, Red Wing, Harliss, Hastings, Inver Grove Heights, South Saint Paul, Newport, Saint Paul, Lilydale, Mendota Heights, Mendota, Fort Snelling, Minneapolis, Columbia Heights, Fridley, Brooklyn Center, Brooklyn Park, Champlin, Dayton, Otsego, Monticello, Clearwater, Saint Augusta, Saint Cloud, Sauk Rapids, Sartell, Little Falls, Camp Ripley, Fort Ripley, Lennox, Crow Wing, Baxter, Brainerd, Wolford, Crosby, Deerwood, Aitkin, Palisade, Grand Rapids, Cohasset, Ball Club, Bena, Bemidji, Vern, Lake Itasca

Gunflint Trail National Scenic Byway (57 miles)
- Passes through Grand Marais, Maple Hill

Historic Bluff Country National Scenic Byway (88 miles)
- Passes through La Crescent, Hokah, Houston, Rushford Village, Rushford, Peterson, Whalan, Lanesboro, Preston, Fountain, Wykoff, Spring Valley, Grand Meadow, Dexter

Historic Highway 75 "King of Trails" (414 miles)
- Passes through Luverne, Hardwick, Trosky, Pipestone, Lake Benton, Ivanhoe, Canby, Madison, Bellingham, Odessa, Ortonville, Clinton, Graceville, Collis, Dumont, Wheaton, Doran, Breckenridge, Brushvale, Kent, Wolverton, Comstock, Rustad, Moorhead, Kragnes, Georgetown, Perley, Hendrum, Halstad, Shelly, Nielsville, Climax, Eldred, Girard, Wilds, Crookston, Shirley, Euclid, Angus, Roan, Warren, Luna, Argyle, Stephen, Donaldson, Kennedy, Hallock, Northcote, Humboldt, St. Vincent, Noyes

Lady Slipper Scenic Byway (28 miles)
- Passes through Pennington, Blackduck

Lake Country Scenic Byway (88 miles)
- Passes through Detroit Lakes, Snellman, Osage, Park Rapids, Nevis, Akeley, Walker, Arago, Lake Itasca

Lake Mille Lacs Scenic Byway (68 miles)
- Passes through Onamia, Cove, Bayview, Wahkon, Isle, Malmo, Nichols, Garrison, Vineland

Minnesota River Valley National Scenic Byway (287 miles)
- Passes through Browns Valley, Beardsley, Foster, Ortonville, Watson, Montevideo, Granite Falls, Morton, Franklin, New Ulm, Cambria, Judson, Mankato, North Mankato, Kasota, Saint Peter, Le Sueur, Henderson, Jessenland, Belle Plaine

North Shore Scenic Drive (154 miles)
- Passes through Duluth, French River, Palmers, Knife River, Larsmont, Two Harbors, Castle Danger, Beaver Bay, Silver Bay, Illgen City, Kennedy Landing, Bell Harbor, Little Marais, Taconite Harbor, Schroeder, Tofte, Lutsen, Grand Marais, Chippewa City, Colvill, Red Rock, Grand Portage

Otter Trail Scenic Byway (150 miles)
- Passes through Fergus Falls, Erhard, Pelican Rapids, Dent, Perham, Battle Lake, Clitherall, Vining, Urbank, Dalton

Paul Bunyan National Scenic Byway (54 miles)
- Passes through Pequot Lakes, Breezy Point, Crosslake, Ideal Corners, Lakewood Court, Jenkins, Manhattan Beach, Swanburg, Pine River

Saint Croix Scenic Byway (124 miles)
- Passes through Point Douglas, Afton, Saint Mary's Point, Lake Saint Croix Beach, Lakeland Shores, Lakeland, Bayport, Oak Grove Heights, Stillwater, Arcola, Marine on St. Croix, Scandia, Franconia, Shafer, Taylors Falls, Palmdale, Sunrise, Harris, Rush City, Pine City, Beroun, Mission Creek, Hinckley, Friesland, Sandstone

Shooting Star Scenic Byway (32 miles)
- Passes through Le Roy, Taopi, Adams, Rose Creek, Nicolville

Skyline Parkway Scenic Byway (24 miles)
- Passes through Duluth, Proctor, Eldes Corner

Superior National Forest Scenic Byway (80 miles)
- Passes through Silver Bay, Toimi, Bassett, Fairbanks, Hoyt Lakes, Aurora

Veterans Evergreen Memorial Drive (50 miles)
- Passes through Askov, Bruno, Kerrick, Duquette, Nickerson

Waters of the Dancing Sky Scenic Byway (181 miles)
- Passes through Hallock, Lake Bronson, Halma, Karlstad, Greenbush, Badger, Fox, Roseau, Salol, Warroad, Swift, Roosevelt, Williams, Graceton, Pitt, Baudette, Hackett, Wheelers Point, Clementson, Central, Border, Frontier, Birchdale, Manitou, Indus, Loman, Laurel, International Falls

Sources

Parts of the following works and sites were used to help compile figures and historical and travel-related information. Please visit the links below to learn more about the Land of 10,000 Lakes and its towns, history, and people.

*A History of the Origin of the Place Names Connected with the Chicago & North Western...*by Chicago and North Western Railway Company (1908)
https://ia803107.us.archive.org/15/items/historyoforigino00sten_0/historyoforigino00sten_0.pdf

Explore Minnesota: Star of the North – Official State Tourism Site
https://www.exploreminnesota.com/

Jim Forte Postal History – Minnesota
https://www.postalhistory.com/postoffices.asp?task=display&state=MN

National Register of Historic Places – U.S. National Park Service -
https://www.nps.gov/subjects/nationalregister/index.htm

Golf Courses – MNGolf.org
https://mngolf.org/Courses

Minnesota geographic names; their origin and historic significance by Warren Upham (1920)
https://archive.org/details/minnesotageogra00uphagoog

Minnesota Historical Society Archives
https://www.mnhs.org

Minnesota History and Genealogy Research
https://genealogytrails.com/minn/

Rail Guide
https://rail.guide/

Roadside America Minnesota Map - https://www.roadsideamerica.com/map/mn

The Official Northern Pacific Railway Guide: For the Use of Tourists and Travelers... by Northern Pacific Railway Company & Henry Jacob Winser (1897) -
https://books.google.com/books?id=JA5FAQAAMAAJ

The Origin of Certain Place Names in the United States by Henry Gannett (1905) -
https://books.google.com/books?id=9V1IAAAAMAAJ

United States Census Bureau
https://www.census.gov/

University of Minnesota Libraries – Digitized plat maps and atlases
https://www.lib.umn.edu/collections/borchert/digitized-plat-maps-and-atlases

Additional information was sourced from city websites, Convention & Visitor Bureau and Chamber of Commerce materials, city Historical Society sites and materials, assorted news articles, and interpersonal communication.

Acknowledgments

This book is dedicated to the State of Minnesota and the following individuals who helped make the Wandermore in Minnesota project possible. Thank you for your generosity and for allowing us to help others see all the Land of 10,000 Lakes has to offer!

Friends & Family:
To my lovely wife, Eliese Varner <3
Dave & Leigh Varner
Sandy & Norm Girmus
Sofia Brummer

General Minnesota:
10K Construction
Alice & Walter Meissner
Amboy Class of 1967
Amy Arneson
Ana Baldwin
Anita Boeddeker Nikolov
April Soupir
Arnold & Dorothea Wentzel Family
Arvin Olson
Barb Willie Christman
Barry Hultquist
Benjamin Walsvik
Beth Hoffman
Bill Block
Bob Blanshan
Bollig Engineering - Designed for Small Cities.
Bonnie Kjos
Boyle Bunch
Brandi Lillegaard
Brandon Wieling
Brennen Brown
Brett & Lanae Arneson
Brody & Amanda Kirkeby
Brooks Baldwin
Bruce S. Goodrich
Cade & Kiley Ekstrom
Caden Seibert
Caleb Brown
Cam Stutelberg
Carley & Jarret
Carol Norris
Carrie & Ross Wubben
Carson Gardner
Catherine Hengel & Nate Borud
Channing Wubben
Charlotte & Margaret
Chuck & Faye Potrament
Chuck Galli
Cindi Bockwitz
Connect2Mn, *MNConnect.com*
Cory Brown
Dan & Deb Hengel
Daniel & Stacy Balcer

David Meissner
David Messer
David Wieling
Dean Hoffman
Debbie Schneider Welch
Denise & Lon Stutelberg
Dominic Hoffman
Doug Whitlock
Drew Hultquist
Ellie Samborski
Erin Fogerty
Gabby Hoiland
Galli Furniture & Appliance
Gary Gustafson
General Chelberg
Genevieve LaMorie
Grace Rinehart
Grayson Wubben
Hannah, Alex, Tessany, & Troy Levenhagen
Haven Anne (haventureawaits)
Heather Galli
In Honor of Glen Douglas's 13 grandchildren & four great-grandchildren
In Loving Memory of Todd Goskeson
In Memory of Axel & Hilda Carlson
In Memory of Bryan Handyside
In Memory of Carl Galli
In Memory of Christopher Duane Douglas
In Memory of Dennis Krueger
In Memory of Duane Arthur Douglas
In Memory of Dwain & Nancy Tollefson
In Memory of Eric Smith
In Memory of Evelyn McGrand
In Memory of Flora Bockwitz
In Memory of Jennifer Marie Hengel
In Memory of Jerome Huschle
In Memory of Jesse Grimsley

In Memory of Kelly Huschle
In Memory of Leo Crummy
In Memory of Lillian Carr
In Memory of Nancy Hoglund
In Memory of Shelly McGrand
In Memory of Walt & Milli Johnson
In Memory of Wilma Crummy
Inga Olson
Isaac Seibert
Ivan Brown
J&K Properties of Martin County
Jackson Baldwin
Jackson Groskreutz
Jake Eleanor
Jennifer Hoglund
Jerry Olson
Joe Arneso
John Blissenbach
John Decker,
John & Julie Opgrand
Judy O'Brien
Justin & Kaliee
Karina & Michael
Karla Krueger-Moulton
Kelly Brown
Kristophet Hengel
Larry & Dianne Bunjer
Laura Christman White
Laverne Messer
Leah Arneson
Lee Kjosand
Leone Brewer
Lisa Krueger
Logan Baldwin
Lois & Wally Meissner
Lois Olson
Lonnie Flickinger
Lori Wolden
Lynn Dilley Lahd
Mara Arneson
Mark Christ & Colleen Rohloff Christ
Marlys Gustafson
Mary Blissenbach
Mason Husted
Matt Arneson
Matt Blissenbach

McGregor Baking Company
Megan J. Chase
Melanie C. I. Trent
Michelle Marotzke & Matt Savig
Michelle Morris
Michelle Muggli
Mikki Kjelvik
Miranda Flickinger
Morris Vacura
Myriam Madla Sanchez
Nancy (Rakotz) Wieling
Nicole Seibert
Nikki Gustafson
Nikolaus Hengel
Nimue (cat)
Ole H. & Helen Nordin
Olivia Baldwin
Ovidia & Clarence Chelberg
Owen Samborski
Pam Hultquist
Pank 5 Farms
Pat & Greg Anderson
Quinn, Gracen, Cole, Luke, Cora
Raymond & Jan Chelberg
Renee Lutz
Renita Britton Goodrich
Richard Buskirk
Rita & Wallace Buskirk
Rory LaMorie -Flickinger
Rose & Steven Parker
Ruth Block
Ryan Schumacher
S & D Savoie & Family
Sally Behringer
Sandy Gallagher
Scot Zeltwanger
Scott Vacura
Sharon Vacura
Shyla Stradtman
Sigourney Wubben
Suzanne Lynn Everson
Ted Brewer
The Frank & Sarah Srp Family
The Husted Family
The Keith & Patricia Haarstick Family
Tiffany (Breth) Walsvik
To Jorge's favorite travel partners, Macy, Lisa, Megan, Taylor
Treasure Valley Dave
Victor Chelsner
Wayne Wolden
Willy the Cat
Zachary Wieling
Ada:
In Honor of Solveig Kitchell

Adams:
April Horne
Dennis Mullenbach
Denny's Car Wash
Gary Komaniecki
In Memory of Byron Huseby
In Memory of Erwin Mullenbach
In Memory of Helen Huseby
In Memory of Johanna Mullenbach
In Memory of Michael J. Schmitz
Marcia Mullenbach
Mary C. Schmitz
Adrian:
Jerry & Linda Loonan
Aitkin:
Bentley Host
D'Ette Larson
Elaina Host
Erin Host
In Loving Memory of Mike "Murph" Murphy
In Memory of Dale & Carol Larson
In Memory of Harry William Hasskamp
Joshua Host
Lauren Host
Lyndon Host
Tom Larson
William Hartman Hasskamp
Albany:
Clarence Silbernick
In Memory of Agnes Knapp Hondl
In Memory of Anton Hondl
In Memory of Gertrude Michael Gill
In Memory of Thomas Gill Sr.
Kyle Breth
Albert Lea:
Albert Lea Convention & Visitors Bureau
Konrad Hawkinson
Alberta:
Alberta Bar & Grille
In Memory of Ginger, David, & Jodi Hagen
Keri, Trinity, & Tayla Abel
Alden:
Albert & Marjean Jacobs
In Memory of: Edward & Bertha Jacobs
Maria Svedlöf Lexander
Stuart & Cheri Potter
Thomaz Svedlöf

Alexandria:
Blane & Zoë Walberg
Jared, Hannah & Landon Wagner
Altura:
Melanie Bluhm
Alvwood:
Flora Nestberg
Amboy:
Leslie Curry
Linda's Place Bar & Grill
Twyla Curry
Andover:
Gerald Thorp
Annandale:
Amber Lemieux
Glen & Diane Johnson
Jake & Laura Iskierka
Joe Dwenger Jr
Joey Dwenger III
Levi Lemieux
Maddison Dwenger
Margaret Dwenger
Presley Dwenger
Squirrely's Bar & Grill
The Linns
Toby Lemieux
Anoka:
In Memory of Bob Weil
Shanna M Taylor
Apple Valley:
Harper Hechsel
Lainey Hechsel
Appleton:
Appleton Art & Culture
Bobbie Jo Banken
Eric Banken
In Memory of Mary Voorhees
James R. Banken
Melissa Banken
Rod Halvorson
Will Voorhees
Arco:
Jerry Behnke
Argyle:
AHS Class of 1985
David Hangsleben
Denise (Lubarski) Bruggenthies
In Memory of Veronica Lubarski
John Lubarski
Arlington:
Coal Bear Pomplun
In Memory of Henry Blaze Pomplun
Ashby:
Bryce, Brandi & Isla Conklin
Atwater:
Erica Melbie

In Memory of Ronnie
Hedtke
Kaleb Melbie
Audubon:
Kaylee Swenson
Kinsey Swenson
Rylan Swenson
Austin:
Debra Rutledge
Discover Austin, MN
www.AustinMN.com
In Loving Memory of
James W. Lingbeck
In Memory of Mr. & Mrs.
Maynard Enright
Jeanne Poppe
Kevin Hanson
Loni Baldner
Avon:
Garrett Goerger
In Memory of Florence
Maciejewski
In Memory of Jeanette
Maciejewski
In Memory of John A
Maciejewski, Jr,
In Memory of Margaret
Mary Yurczyk
Badger:
VBA Enterprises Inc,
Garten Family
Bagley:
Dale & Jody Bellefy
In Memory of Carol
Tollefson
Joseph & Dorothy Bellefy
Balaton:
Carolyn Lustfield
Orlin Lustfield
Barnesville:
Gus & Judy Frederiksen
Barnum:
Kris & Brady Holmes
Sandy Lake Turkey Farm
Susan Olson
Barrett:
Elaine Ray
In Memory of Dayle Ray
Karen Alvstad
Leslie Alvstad
Phyllis M. (Bollman)
Lehrke
Battle Lake:
Alane Kinn
Cindy & Keith Lillevold
Donald Okeson
Eunice Okeson Lillevold
In Memory of Farris
Okeson
Pearl Okeson Goosen
Baudette:
In Memory of August &
Lydia Frohreich

In Memory of Fred & Betty
Frohreich
In Memory of Richard &
Annie Frohreich
Laurence & Susan
Frohreich
Baxter:
April S. Canfield
Christ Alive Church
Jeff Sparrow - Owner of
371 Diner
Michael S. Higley
Beaver Creek:
Paulette Stempfley
Becker:
In Honor of Vivian Clark
In Memory of Buddy the
Shih Tzu
Bejou:
Jo Ann (McCollum)
Thieling
Michael D. Thieling
Belgrade:
Brad & Theresa
Gulbranson
In Memory of Melvin &
Louise Weisser
James Stiegen
Belle Plaine:
Alexandra Brooks
Colin Schultz
In Memory of Donald
Schultz
In Memory of Lorraine
Schultz
Renee Schultz
Timber the Husky
Timothy James
Belview:
Billy Kissner
Don & Lori Ryer
Geraldine Michaels
In Memory of Michael
Straumann
In Memory of: Mary
Kissner
Bemidji:
Austin, Taylor, & Asher
Storbeck
Breann Johnson
Bryan Tuey
Daltyn Lofstrom
Dave Brooks
In Memory of Daniel Smith
Keith Marek
Rob Johnson
Bena:
Anna Gramke
Iris Gramke
Oliver Gramke
Rick Gramke
Violet Gramke
DB Rentals & Adventures

Big Lake:
Olivia Bond
Averie Ellingson
Case & Griffin Johnson
Evan Pishney
In Memory of Don Orrock
In Memory of Michelle
Carlin (Johnson)
In Memory of Spencer &
Landon
In Memory of Truman
"Pete" Sanford
Josiah Sprung
Katie Lindula
Liam Holland
Lydia Holland
Lynn Adams
Mary Carlin
Michelle (Sanford) Donner
Patrick Carlin
Paxton & Blake Heath
Richard Adams
Shelly Halvorson
Susan Martin
Wyatt Bond
Bigelow:
In Memory of Ailt &
Henrietta Aielts
Bird Island:
Alisha Adams
Chris Adams
David Adams
Matt Adams
Blackduck:
Drake Motel
Vera Tuey
Blaine:
Dennis & Debbie Erickson
Blomkest:
In Memory of Kim Stahl
In Memory of Tracey
Lippert
Blooming Prairie:
Alice Johnson
Kim Johnson Farrand
Bloomington:
Deb & Ron Peters
In Memory of Emily Martin
John Bayard's 3 children
Lisa MacKay Longpre
Mary Dutton
Ryan Bredeson
Scottie Kopnick
Blue Earth:
Blue Earth Area Chamber
of Commerce &
Convention & Visitors
Bureau
Green Giant Welcome
Center & Museum
Life Family Church

Borup:
In Memory of Arlis Claudia Stevenson
Bovey:
Rob Litchke
Boyd:
Philip Bruce Larson
Braham:
Wanda Koehler
Brainerd:
Bernie & Carol Penner
Cheryl & Bill Bailey
Gayle Elaine Johnson
Jeffery Kent Smith
Justin "Pete" Soderman
Kim M Anderson
Roy Johnson
Roy Robert Johnson
The Yerks Family
Brandon:
In Memory of Doyle Walberg
In Memory of Lloyd S., Violet E., & Beverly K. Olson
Mary Pohlmann
Nelson Bus Company
Brewster:
Bradley Altman & Victoria Altman
Sharon Weaver
Brooklyn Center:
In Memory of Persephonee Norma Nefzger Banks
Brooks:
In Memory of Lorna (Mercil) Wicks
In Memory of Lorraine Mercil
Lori (Mercil) Sorenson, Loring Mercil
Lynae (Mercil) Finseth
Lynette (Mercil) Grove
Brooten:
Paul Linn
Sarah Linn
Browerville:
In Loving Memory of Lois Karsnia
Joni Lee (Canfield) Johnstone
Michael George Johnstone
Brownsville:
In Honor of Robert & Debra Mann
Bruno:
MN Connect
Buckman:
Connie Kieffer
Burnsville:
Jenny Phyle

Luke Kopnick
Sandra Cook
Burtrum:
Brock Rocheleau
Burke Rocheleau
Century-old Wunderlich Farm
Heidi Esch
In Memory of Jeanette Barthel
Kalison Rocheleau
Byron:
Daniel McGowan
Michelle McGowan
Caledonia:
Amelia Hoskins
Cooper Hoskins
Kimberly K. Klug
Callaway:
Barbara Modey Scherping
Ed & Rose Schreiner Modey
Gordon & Mary Eidenschinck Modey
Jenny Modey Jenkins
Jim & Carol Zurn Modey
Joel & Caroline Modey
Patricia Modey Sitz
Calumet:
The Zaren Family
Cambridge:
Cash Rosandich
In Memory of Ardis & Rueben Noren
Margaret Nelson
Canby:
Gene Buchholz
Cannon Falls:
Dorothy Quam
Jeff Anderson
Carlton:
Andy & Jan Bailey
Emmie & Claire
Carver:
Lynn Gillies
Cass Lake:
Dannell Savage-Ofanoa
Darci (Savage) Swan
In Memory of Delores & James (Bunny) Broekemeier
In Memory of Martin & Ellen Johnson
In Memory of William (Bill) & Nora Broekemeier
Shawna (Savage) Premo
Centerville:
Matt, Becca, Lily, Izzy & Obi Oldenburg-Downing
Ceylon:
BUKE'S Bar & Grill Memory
Chris Griffin

Howells Community Days
Tyler Strong
Champlin:
Brendan Gormsen
Chance Vang
Claire Vang
Collin Vang
Kai Youngberg
Chaska:
Dave, Amy, Penny, Taylor, Thor, & Kara Pluth
Debbie Meregildo
In Memory of Stanley Shima
Isobel Shima
Julia Zieman
Kathy Nelson
Ron Nelson
Chatfield:
Burnett Family Big Girl Stickers & Stems Chatfield Alliance
In Memory of Carlton & Ellen Denny
James, Andrea, Austin, Abigail, & Aaron Hanson
Kappers' Big Red Barn
Patrick, Beth, & Genevieve Whitney Wall
Chisago City:
John, Lisa, & Mia Maraschiello
Chisholm:
In Loving Memory of Billy & Iris
Chokio:
In Memory of Russell & Donna Larson
Circle Pines:
Janice Ann Nielsen Hier
Ken Moen
Sharon Moen
Clara City:
Marvin & Loretta (Thein) Fuhrmeister
Clarkfield:
Betsy Pardick
Joe Coubal
Tim Pehrson
Clarks Grove:
Daryl Jensen
Dean Jensen
Debra Pirsig
Everett Jensen
Mitch Jensen
Clearwater:
Chris Farber
Climax:
Emily Boyer
Thomas Boyer

Clitherall:
In Memory of Laverne Walberg
Clontarf:
In Memory of Scott Kent
Raymond Cameron
Cloquet:
Arlene (Johnson) Peterson
In Loving Memory of Roland Peterson
Marilyn Hunter Standridge & Charles (Stan) Standridge
Nancy (Johnson) Burry
Nikki & Denny Staton
Cokato:
White Front Locker & Market Inc.
Cold Spring:
Ali Anderson
Bennett Anderson
Blasius & Katherine Jonas Scherer
Bob Bellmont Diann Bellmont
George & Johanna Durr Scherer
Joe Anderson
Joseph & Mary Anna Reiter Jonas
June Anderson
Spencer Anderson
The Degerstrom Family
Coleraine:
Lefty's Tent & Party Rental
The Shaggy Dog (Pawspa) LLC
Cologne:
Alex Nichifor
Alissa Nichifor
Tim & Jessica Dauwalter
Comfrey:
Austin & Brooke Fischer
In Memory of Wendell & Martha Fredins
Linda Wallin
Conger:
Greg Lutteke
Kathy Lutteke
Melford & Arlean Swenson
Cook:
The Blake Family
Coon Rapids:
Brad Bloomquist
Bryan T. Klaes
Chuck R Taylor
In Memory of Elyse Gorham Pevensie
Jake, Jessie, & Jack Harless & Luna
Cosmos:
Fire Chief

In Memory of Bruce Berry
Jon Fruetel & Jody Fruetel
Cottage Grove:
Brady Radke
Brooke Radke
Christian Bettis
Cindi Benjamin
Glenda Benjamin
In Memory of Chuck Momsen
Melissa Benjamin
Roger Benjamin
Sadie Benjamin
Taylor Benjamin
Cottonwood:
The Alm Family
Chase Thompson
Lydia Kan
Crookston:
Advanced Tire & Auto Service
Carol Hennager
In Memory of Donald & Mary Ann Simmons
In Memory of Kathy Umlauf
In Memory of Larry Hennager
Jerome & Heidi Simmons Family
Michael Jobe
Crosby:
Arnold Lahd
In Memory of Brian James Oren
Patrice Parks
Crosslake:
Joe & Kathy Faust
Paul Berthiaume
Crystal:
Cindy Gasparrini
Dave Gasparrini
Culver:
Ahnaleah Anderson
Jadin Merzwski
Renley Merzwski
Currie:
Tim & Kris Rignell
Cyrus:
Glen Kraemer
Dakota:
In Memory of Lester Unnasch
Sandra Unnasch
Dalbo:
Barbara J. Klaes
Daley-Zoerb Family
Danube:
Custom Motors of Danube
Danvers:
Jean Hoffman (b. 1929)
Darfur:
Tricia Roedel

Dawson:
Carla Draack
Rodney Johnson
Deer Creek:
Bonnie Zeise Brown
Gordon C. Zeise
Gwen Hatling Zeise
Jen, AJ, & Abigail Jones
Paul S. Zeise
Deer River:
Cathy Lee Thompson-Guastella
Don Tervo
Erik & Nicole Beissel
In Memory of Beryl Lee
In Memory of Hjalmer & Joy Tervo
In Memory of Linda Tervo Warner
In Memory of Ray & Ellen Tervo
In Memory of Rob Metke
Jon Tervo
Deerwood:
Greg & Shelly Skeim
The Gunderson Family
Delano:
Alex Crotteau
Casey O'Connor
Charlotte Crotteau
Cooper Reuter
Curt Reuter
Evan Crotteau
Heather O'Connor
James O'Connor
Maeve O'Connor
Owen Crotteau
Trent Meyer
Dent:
In Memory of Arthur Wagener
In Memory of Nelda Sonnenberg Erickson
Detroit Lakes:
The Ask Family
Audrey Tovson
In Honor of David & Jeannine Eiesland
In Memory of Elinas Crotnes
In Memory of Emma Anderson Grotnes
In Memory of Evelyn Grotnes Olson
In Memory of Len Grotnes
In Memory of Selah Jensen
Valhalla Resort
Dodge Center:
Alex Schlichting
In Memory of Gustave & Agnes Kuske

Donnelly:
In Memory of Beverly Eisel
In Memory of Robert Eisel
Dovray:
In Memory of Marlowe & Amy Johnson
Duluth:
Charmayne Randall
Douglas McLaughlin
Emma & Rebecca Collier
In Loving Memory of Skip Malone
Judith McLaughlin
Lloyd Carper-Running
Roger Dahl & Cathy Dahl
Stacey & Mitchell
Dumont:
Garis Jacoby
Dundas:
Reed, Ella, Andria, Anthony
Dundee:
In Memory of Mary Schipper
Dunnell:
Lena Ufer
Paul Ufer
Duquette:
In Memory of Orville & Eleanor Koecher
Eagan:
Allie Maas
Anastasia Reece Oberg
East Bethel:
Pam McGovern
Ryan McGovern
Seth Gillies
Tim McGovern
East Grand Forks:
Alli Osborn
Curtis & Betty Amundson
Henry Osborn
In Loving Memory of Kishsa Carnes
Richie Osborn
Echo:
Alec Dirnberger
Darlene Dirnberger
In Loving Memory of Jean Boyum
In Memory of Ethel Dirnberger
In Memory of Jeanette "Red" Dahl
William Keech
Eden Prairie:
Katherine Sakalos
Stoltenberg Family
Tom Gunderson
Trudy Gunderson
Edgerton:
Alyson Gunnink

Breanna Drooger
Codi Gunnink
Gay Lynn Drooger
Lindsey Drooger
Luke Drooger
Max Drooger
Mike Drooger
Mykah Gunnink
Edina:
Albert Donald Becker
Kenneth O'Hara
Lois Jean Holt O'Hara
Lorraine Jane Holt Becker
Elba:
Stanley Ellringer
Elbow Lake:
Elbow Lake Area Chamber of Commerce
Glen Lohse
In Memory of Janet Rosin
Mike & Lyndsay Bruns
Mike Mallow
Orville Lien
Elgin:
In Memory of Ross Lee Grobe
Elk River:
In Memory of Pat Weil
Alice Taylor Weicht
Bill Weicht
Carlee Weicht
Finnegan Demarre
Heidi Weicht Belanger
In Memory of John Weicht
Matt Weicht
Michelle Fisher Weicht
Natalie Weicht
Richard Koehler
Sandy Frederiksen Weicht
Thumbs Up (thumbsupformentalhealth.org)
Wes Belanger
Willy Weicht
Elko New Market:
Alberta's Mexican Restaurant
Elmdale:
Mark & Kaye Nienaber
Elmore:
Jerry Bellecourt
Ely:
Ali Garner Hoffman
Blue Loon Gallery & Boutique
Dale Hegfors
J.L. Hegfors
John Hoffman
Nolan Hoffman's Dragon Biographies
Emmons:
In Memory of Ahziyas Dampha FE2

Erskine:
2Annes Lakeside RV Park
Eveleth:
Dody Evenson
Dylan Lehman
Jen Evenson
Jillian Lehman
True Ranger: Julie Terch
Excelsior:
Adam James Vernes
Judy Rende
Eyota:
Aubrey Koball
Rylie Durdahl
Fairfax:
In Honor of the Dickmeyer & Bleick Families
In Memory of Daniel & Dorothy Borth
River Valley Low Voltage, low voltage electrician
Fairmont:
Brittany Hartman
Charlie & Joell Schaefer
Debi Harens
Esther Holt, Martin Holt
Everett Nutt
In Memory of Corey Eiden
In Memory of Ken & Betty Thate
In Memory of Leroy "Bud" Eiden
In Memory of Marjorie Eiden
In Memory of Thomas Eiden
James W. Marushin
Jeff, Sharon, Glenda J. & Zoe Sauer
Luella Ufer
Martin County Historical Society
Megan Marushin
Nutt Zehms
The Wokasch Family
Visit Fairmont
Wilhelmina Marushin
Farmington:
Frank S. & Ruth E. Phillips
In Memory of Theodore & Elizabeth Phillips
Kory Halterman
Lynne Halterman
The Pilcher Family
Tom Tutewohl
Fergus Falls:
Andrew O. Runningen (1-8-1878)
Cindy Gross
Genevive (Gustafson 5-24-1921) & John W. Sweson (8-28-1920)

Gilford O. Runningen (11-10-1907)
Ida A. (Tollefson) Mohagen (12-9-1893)
In Memory of Dad Ralph Schiesser
In Memory of Donna Koester
In Memory of Erlyce Fosmoe
In Memory of Kaare Fosmoe
Irene E. (Runningen) Bjorklund (10-26-1909)
Joan E. (Mohagen) Runningen (10-6-1929)
John R. Runningen (8-4-1953)
Karen Runningen (1942)
Karen Sophie (Borgos) Runningen (6-25-1882)
Keith J. Lillevold
Lee Runningen (11-23-1948)
Lila (Bergerud) Runningen (10-31-1909)
Marg & Bob Halvorson
Margaret (Bjorklund) Waye (1943)
Mary D. (Runningen) Monsted (4-9-1951)
Oressa (Toots) Runningen (10-24-1916)
Orris M. Runningen (8-24-1906)
Ramona Long
Raymond M. Runningen (10-29-1911)
Richard Runningen (6-18-1944)
Rudolph M. Mohagen (8-28-1897)
Runningen Cafe/Viking Cafe
Vernon Bjorklund (12-8-1898)
Fertile:
The Clifford Bevolden Family
Fifty Lakes:
Becky Strohmeier
Peyton Lind
Fisher:
In Loving Memory of Patrick T. Quigley; love Patricia Quigley Vickers
Floodwood:
In Loving Memory of Robert "Bob" Dressely Tracy Johnson
Foley:
Anthony Perry

Brewed Gems Coffee & Crystals
Carissa Fouquette
Cassidy Muldowney
Dick Kieffer
In Loving Memory of Grandma J. "Lorraine Janson" 1932-2025
In Memory of Vernon Almlie
Jordan Family
Korra Fouquette
Kyson Miller
Laura, Scotty, Ayla, Aidan, Audrey, Bella, Avara, Rae, Belen
The Nathan Lease Family
Forest Lake:
In Loving Memory of Mary Schaeppi
Fort Ripley:
Bill Weidenbach
JoAnne Donna
Fosston:
In Memory of Daryl Foster
In Memory of Laurel Skala
Fountain:
Cory Spratte
Jessica Meyer
Franklin:
Jeff McColley
Pam McColley
Frazee:
Amelia Smith
David Daggett
H.V. Anderson
Helen Daggett
Hugh Smith
Isaiah Smith
Minerva Anderson
Roxann Daggett
Sawyer Smith
Vernon Daggett
Freeborn:
In Memory of Jack Anderson
Freeport:
In Memory of Kade Feldewerd
Fridley:
Miles Overbo Byrne
Sarah L. Byrne
Thomas R (TK) Kelly
Frost:
Frost Class of 1960
Karen Stoll Griffin
Fulda:
In Memory of Bryan Lund
Garrison:
Kevin & Sherri McLaughlin
Garvin:
Jaeda Nelson
Cody Nelson

Cory & Staci Staufacker
Craig & Mary Staufacker
Creed Nelson
Emily Nelson
Hadli Nelson
Hayes Nelson
In Memory of Douglas & Nina West
Gary:
Byron & Lori Thronson
Gaylord:
Eastside Ford Mercury
In Memory of Duane Messner
Gemmel:
Harold & Louise Curb
Ghent:
Dawn Wilmes Wood
In Memory of Dennis Wilmes
Rosemary Wilmes
Vicki Wilmes St. Aubin
Gibbon:
AJ Grewe
Cindy L. Johnson
Connor W. Olson
Ron Swanberg
Gilbert:
Ruby & Zane
Glencoe:
In Memory of Al's Cafe
In Memory of Florence's Gift Shop
Glenville:
In Memory of Marjory Hamersly
In Memory of Winston Hamersly
Glenwood:
Becki Gugisberg Drum
Allie Kelling
Chajez Baker
Garrett Kelling
Hayley Hoiland
In Memory of Douglas & Buzzi Rollins
Peyton Rooney
Sarah Guderjahn
Sean Kelling
Gonvick:
In Memory of Laurel Skala
Larry Skala
Good Thunder:
Anna Johnson
Autumn Johnson
Bradley Johnson
Megan Kilian
Shelley Martin Fahey
Goodhue:
In Memory of Donald & Marcy Jonas
Thomforde Family

Goodland:
Troy Maki's
Goodview:
Pat & Steve
Graceville:
The Popoff Family
Granada:
Jim & Michelle Johnson
Karen (Thate) Green
Grand Marais:
Mary L. Sommerness
Grand Rapids:
Arild Frederiksen
Chris Frederiksen
Davin Luoma
Deb Wilson Bueltel
Denda Wilson Evans
Diane Blondie Glienke
Frederiksen
Faye Randall Sorensen
George Frederiksen
Hannu Family
Hansen Frederiksen
In Loving Memory of
Amanda Dosen-Windorski
In Loving Memory of
Daren Wilson
In Memory of Anne Wills &
Harry (Uncle Harry) Wills
Marie Sorensen Albright
Randall Belanger
Tanner Belanger Askov
Thora Dixen Frederiksen
Koch
Granite Falls:
Cindy Hanka Okubo
Garcia Gray Family
Granite Falls Convention
& Visitors Bureau
In Honor of Grandpa Gary
& Grandma Re
Green Isle:
The Kevin Riley Family
Greenbush:
In Memory of Linn C.
Rigstad
Gust & Bertha Diesen
Joe Dezelar
Selma Rigstad
Greenwald:
In Memory of Asha
Poepping Gregory
In Memory of Karlyann M.
Boecker
Grove City:
Barbara Dilley
In Memory Of Conrad C
Erickson
In Memory of Don & Elsie
(Remmel) Johnson
Jean Silkey
Jeff & Betsy Ammermann
Kris Casey

Grygla:
Grygla Seed & Services
In Memory of Kernal &
Edna Paulson
In Memory of Roy & Ida
Paulson
Oslund Family Farms
Gully:
Irvin, Geraldine, Sonja,
Judy Thoreson
Hackensack:
Audi
Carol & Cliff Thon
Gregory Alan Cain
In Memory of Donald Curo
In Memory of K. Sally
Knight
Jim & Rachel Lyons
Landon Alan Cain
Tisha Marie Cain
Hadash:
Dick & Sharon Hadash
Hadley:
Angela Dahlgren
Dawn & Allan Shumaker
Eric & Sarah Dahlgren
Vanessa Dahlgren
Hallock:
Addie Lindegard
Alex Lindegard
Austin Ricklefs
Blair & Jorja Younggren
Brinley Sang
Cameron Curry
Ceres Grant
Chloe Lindegard
Connor Younggren
Corey & Amanda
Younggren
Dan & Diane Younggren
Darryl Younggren
David Lindegard
Diane M Younggren
Dorothy Cameron
In Loving Memory of Jerry
Lindegard
In Loving Memory of Lois
Lindegard.
In Loving Memory of
Robert Cameron
In Memory of Rose &
Larry Younggren
Isaac Lindegard
Jacob Ingeman
Jake Curry
Janna Curry
Jaya Ingeman
Julie Lindegard
Kailey Younggren
Leanna Lindegard
Mike Lindegard
Rebecca Ingeman
Summer Curry

Halstad:
In Memory of Bjorn Larson
In Memory of William
Larson
Kyle Aasand
Regan Aasand
Hamburg:
Angie Iverson
In Memory of Fredrick
"Fritz" Oelfke
Mike & Elisa Litfin
Susan "Oelfke" Iverson
Hammond:
Phil's A.G. Grocery Store
1970/1976
The Johnson Family
Vern & Phylis Johnson
Family
Hancock:
Elaine Jacoby
Mildred & Wally Erickson
Hanover:
Hanover Historical Society
In Memory of Gracie
Heinz
Michelle Leimer
Hardwick:
In Memory of Don
Weinkauf
Hartland:
Evelyn Bogue
Gina Crumb
Hastings:
Cory Heppes
Geno Halberg
In Memory of Ed Savoie
Mya Beck
William Beck
Hawley:
In Memory of John Young
Jr.
Betty Young
John Young Jr.
Hayfield:
In Memory of Barbara &
Gene Franke
Hazel Run:
Joe Coubal
Hector:
Brenda Peterson
Denise Peterson
Gary S. Ness
Pete's Grill
Roger, Peggy, Denise,
Danette & Brian Horky
Terrylea Meier Ness
Henderson:
In Memory of Dolores
Hagan, founder of
Henderson Feathers, Inc.
Hendricks:
Alivia Gilbertson
Greg Gilbertson

Harlan Gilbertson
MascotDB.com
Henning:
Cade & Jess Strege
Gaby (Moe) Paul
Hedy Moe
In Memory of Harlan Walberg
In Memory of Les Moe
Kristy (Moe) Schuler
Petra (Moe) Ashleman
Herman:
Stanley Harstad
Heron Lake:
Alan Liepold
Chad Knutson
Don & Mary Lou (Haberman) Liepold
George & Karen Mathias Family
In Memory of Jim & Jeanette Hady
Les Knutson
Hewitt:
Al Knutson
Ardy McCallister
City of Hewitt
Dawn Simpson
Hewitt Historical Society
Robert Aldrich
Trinity Gruenberg
Hibbing:
In Memory of John Sordi
In Memory of Peggy Joy (Hendrickson) Palmersheim
In Memory of Robert Avery
In Memory of Sharon Connors Foster
Pamela Avery
The Sandelin Family
Hillman:
Allen Hoskins Family
Joe Faust Family
Hills:
Glenda McGaffee
In Memory of Samuel McGaffee
Hoffman:
Lee Well Drilling
Holdingford:
In Memory of Charles "Chuck" P. Burzlaff-Meyer
In Memory of Cyril & Donna Ebnet
In Memory of George & Hildegard Bieniek
Jane Victoria Bieniek
Litchy
Luke & Lynne Nienaber
Mary Skudlarek

Shane, Jeana, & Dawson Olson
Holland:
Ron & Ramona Cooley
Hollandale:
Mary (DeJong) Kirkpatrick
Sadie (Bremer) DeJong
Holloway:
Cooper Smith
Eric Smith
In Memory of Allen Smith
Stephanie Smith
Hopkins:
Christian Sanchez
Kate Sanchez
Kristiane Sanchez
Leo Sanchez
Houston:
In Honor of Michael & Sharon Frauenkron
In Memory of Donald W. Evenson
Janis Anderson
Michelle Hoskins
Steve Hoskins
Howard Lake:
Eldon & Joyce Glessing
In Memory of David Luhman
Hugo:
Bernice LaCasse
Bob & Gina Bernier
Eugene LaCasse
Jessi, Dan, Joey, Linnea, Stacy, & Karen
Marylee Sallowicz
Humboldt:
Audrey Farol
Hutchinson:
Angie Glieden
Ashley Bell
Cory Klassen
Dave Glieden
Dave Hall, Kathy Hall
Elizabeth Klassen
Gavin Bell
Henrietta Wentworth
John Hess
Kevin Lee
Lukas Liepold
Melvin Wentworth
Michelle Hess
Owen Glieden
Pam Bell
Shaelynn Glieden
Steve, Colleen M.
Wes Bell
International Falls:
In Honor of The Spot Supper Club
Jane Barthell
Jerry Wherley
Melody Ostroot Lueders

The Dick Ostroot Family
Tom Barthell
Inver Grove Heights:
In Memory of Robert Ahlberg
Iona:
Bernice McCormick
Colleen McDonald Toye
Connie McCormick
Dennis McCormick
Dorinda Scheumann
Patrick McCormick
Sharon Powell
Ironton:
Amanda McAllister
Keenan Niemand
Keith Niemand
Isanti:
In Memory of Althea Hechsel
Justin Nelson
Ivanhoe:
Brad Janiszeski
Connie Janiszeski
Heather Bednarek
In Memory of Ruth & Ray Johnson
Kulla Repair & Towing LLC
Randy Janiszeski
Richard Bednarek
Jackson:
In Memory of Thomas Ringkob
In Memory of Esther Ringkob
In Memory of Kent Ringkob
In Memory of Thomas P. Ringkob
Kathleen Ringkob Starrs
Ken Fiala
Marita Ringkob Rouse
Janesville:
Faith Ryan
In Honor of the NRHP-Designated Hofmann Apiaries
Kelly Kennedy Kuhns
Kristin Bartelt
Mark, Vicki, Carley, & Jack Borneke
Paul & Gloria Kennedy
Scott Kennedy
Theo & Taylor West
Jasper:
Jule "Terry" Rodman
Jeffers:
Martin Giese Family
Orin McCloud Family
Russell N. McCloud
Vonna Vee Giese McCloud

Jordan:
In Honor of the Myron & Deb Pauly Family
In Memory of my husband, Myron Pauly
Kasota:
Delores Gens
Earl Gens
Marjorie Van Guilder
Walt Van Guilder Sr.
Kellogg:
David & Shelly Speedling
Business: SVJ Creative Designs, Kellogg, MN
Grandparents to Ashton, Lakelynn, Jett, Aubrey, Sutton, & Ruby
Mother-in-law & Father-in-law to: Adam, Jerrod, & Ashley
Parents of Shauna, Valerie & Jeffrey
Kensington:
Terri Reuter
Kerrick:
The Robert & Joyce Thomsen Family
Kettle River:
Nick & Kelly Crossman
Kiester:
Beth Cody
Gubbs
Ryan Goodman
The Hawk
Kimball:
In Memory of Donald Wimmer
In Memory of LuWanna Misho Lawler
In Memory of Marilyn Wimmer
Neva Linn
Kynji:
Ashley Winter
La Crescent:
In Memory of Carolyn "Tuddy" Thesing
Jim Gross
Nels & Sue Anderson
Paula (Peter) Grendys
Lake Benton:
In Memory of Larry Berger
Lake Bronson:
Greg & Dorinda Anderson
In Memory of Harry & Hazel Anderson
Lake City:
Carrie Cronin
In Memory of Ervin & Florabelle Carsten
In Memory of Gary Carsten
In Memory of Kim Carsten
In Memory of Sandra Carsten
In Memory of Wayne Carsten
Penny Carsten-Linder
Lake Crystal:
Blake, Allie, baby girl, Kira, McKenna, Tracy
Doug Kelley
Nicole Kelley
Roger Luiken
Lake Elmo:
Adam Grode
Lake Park:
Ivan Nienaber
Stephen & Emma Nienaber
Tommy Nienaber
Lake Wilson:
In Memory of Jean Gendron
Lakefield:
In Loving Memory of Verne, Betty, & Roy Voelker
In Memory of Emanuel & Betty Bezdicek
Rene' Rubis Siria
Sarah Voelker-Bradley
Lancaster:
Mason Swenson
Rhett Swenson
Laporte:
Eunice Antonson
In Memory of James (Jim) Antonson
John Dascalos
Le Center:
Gracie Miller
Ky Olson
Le Roy:
Dorothy & Arthur McKenzie
Emma & Marina Crowson
In Memory of Darrell Ruggeberg
John & Kim McKenzie
Kaci McKenzie
Kallie McKenzie & Ryan Crowson
Kayla McKenzie
Kelly McKenzie & Aubree Tagge
Kristine McKenzie
Lorie Crowson
Madison, Bonnie & Ruby Crowson
Maezlyn Holthaus & John McKenzie, Jr.
Marian Ruggeberg
Parker & Jameson Root
Susan Batt
Le Sueur:
In Honor of our Granddaughters, Harlow & Hollyn Latzke
In Loving Memory of Lionel (LA) & Helen Boldthen
In Memory of the Luskey Families
Lengby:
Thomas Joseph Winkelman
Leonard:
In Loving Memory of Matthew Bagley
Lester Prairie:
Danielle Lohse
Stephanie Lohse
Lewiston:
In Memory of Barney Flanaghan
In Memory of Ronald Kessler
Kimberly Flanaghan
Lexington:
Chuck LaClare
Daisy Blakeman
Lindstrom:
In Memory of Gregg Linehan
Lismore:
Harlan & Vicki Groenewold
In Memory of Amos Ivy Krogman
Litchfield:
Brandon Farber
Deana Wheeler
In Memory of Dennis Grotto
Jenni & Jim Dagner
Lakeside Oaks Farm
Larry Jones
Lou Hoffman (b. 1927)
Piper Coughlin
The Adair Rosenow Family
Little Canada:
Anna Rabe
Jeannine Vig
John Buer
Paul "St. Paul" Mangan
Paul Buer
Little Falls:
In Memory of Teresa Darlene Wagner
Brittany Barchus
Elizabeth Tenold
Elliott's Tattoo
Jacob Tenold
John & Suzie Chaika
Johnny C's Sport Bar

Joseph & Susanna
Shyprett Trettel
Lindy Scoop
Ryan Tenold
The Refuge Little Falls
Trish Tenold
Trish Tenold - Central MN Realty
Valerie Tenold
Zoey Barchus
Littlefork:
Emily Fairchild
Hope Fairchild
Long Prairie:
Amanda McGovern
Chase Nordstrom-McGovern
Corbin Nelson
Darrel & Lisa Holmquist
Jeremy Nelson
Rhiannon Nelson
Longville:
Frosty's Ice Cream & Pizza Parlor
In Memory of Bob & Corny Wright & Cindy Collett
In Memory of Ronald Gilsrud
Lonsdale:
James Vosejpka
The Vikla Family
Lowry:
Kristy's Succulent Kreations | All Things Succulents, LLC
The Nohl Family
Luverne:
Brad (& Cate) Willers, class of 2000;
Dr. Nicole (Willers) & Kyle Woodley, both Class of 2005
In Memory of Susan Badger Horton
Jerry & Renae Reu
Karen & Mark Willers
Luverne Monuments
Natalie (Willers) & Robert Golden
Patricia (class of 2002) & Mario Willers-Miranda
Rubi & Jay Peters
Russell, Nancy, Andrew, Adam & Grant Lofthus
Those Blasted Things
Vance & Becky Walgrave
Lyle:
Nelda Lewis
Lynd:
Hughes Family
The Fred & Arlene Kleine Family

Madelia:
Gordon Ufer
Hazel Holt Ufer
Madison:
In Loving Memory of Alan D. Monson
In Loving Memory of Lee & Lorraine Crosby
Paul & Betty Jo DuFrane
Madison Lake:
Pat Weston
Magnolia:
Jim & Gail Rust
Mankato:
Darlene Parks
In Memory of Gordon & Ruth Schultz
In Memory of Priscilla Jane Petrie
Ron Tostenson
Terry & Mary (Hager) Kahl
Mantorville:
Chace Phy
Charlton Phy
Chyanna Douk
In Memory of Nancy Houston
Michael Phy
Sakhann Douk
Maple Grove:
Douglas Knops
Hallie & Eric Anderson
Joni Voit
Larry Weist, Barbara Weist
Tater Tot Wilbur
Mapleton:
In Memory of Campbell & Mildred Ellis
Maplewood:
Bridget was here
In Memory of Warren & Ann Rinehart
Mary Rinehart
Jane Rinehart
Margie:
The Stoltzman Family
Marietta:
Myrtle Harriett Strain
Marshall:
Aubree Hiepler
David Valentin
Deacon Morgan
Dean Valentin
In Memory of David Fiegen
In Memory of Elsie Buysse
In Memory of JoLynn Speidel
Jane Kelley
Jeff Hiepler
Jim & Joanne Valentin
Josh Roles

Kayla Speidel
Kevin & Brenda Elton
Kevin Speidel
Kris Speidel
Maggie Roles
Trina Hiepler
Mayer:
April Tesch
Carl Fred Tesch
Greg Tesch
In Memory of W.A.E. Zastrow
Lillie Tesch
Mazeppa:
Berna Bakken
In Memory of Ivan & Darlene Frank
In Memory of Patrick & Maureen Simmons.
In Memory of The Gahler Hotel
McGregor:
Carol Holland
DC Tast Chiropractic
Dr. Rachel Tast
Fireside Inn Restaurant & Bar
Kathy Twaddle
Ty Twaddle & Corey Holland
Meadowlands:
In Loving Memory of Brenda Yvonne Kortekaas
In Memory of Uno & Mary (Wilhelm) Makitalo
Natasha Caldwell
Medford:
Sean Gilligan
Meire Grove:
In Memory of Erwin & Verona Meyer
Melrose:
The Pearsons
Menahga:
Curtis & Barbara Marjama
Archie & Velma Newhouse
Clyde Makela
Elmer John & Ida Makela
Ervin Makela
Russell Makela
Vern Makela
Milaca:
Adrianna Mach
Carol Bock Sharlow,
Paloma, Bella
David Mach
Frank Sharlow
Milan:
Aslak & Annie's Bed & Breakfast; retired
Bergen Standahl
Bergen's Prairie Market
Nancy Strand

Ray Strand
Winnie Strand
Milroy:
In Loving Memory of Louie
& Aggie Veit
Minneapolis:
Alec Beck
Helen (Wilson) Burry
In Loving Memory of
Christopher Mullenix
In Loving Memory of
Windolyn Melville
In Memory of Carol
Habstritt
In Memory of Janet
Bachleitner
Joan Phillips
Manny Kaminer
Marlene Longpre
Monica Surber
Peter Nils Nordgaard
Phyllis Holt Grube
Robert Grube
Thomas Burry
Timothy Niccum & Annie
D'Ambrosio
Walter Burry
Minneota:
Arthur Jeremiason
Bradley Jeremiason
Bruce Jeremiason
Helen Jeremiason
Mary Jeremiason
Meghan Travis
Minnesota City:
In Memory of Bryce
James "B. J." Gillies
Kevin & Dorothy Ferden
Minnesota Lake:
In Memory of Al & Joan
Rindfleisch
Minnetonka:
James H. Jordal
Loretta Felber
Performance Hub
Revolution Performance
Montevideo:
In Memory of Julene Kill
DeZeeuw
Paul DeZeeuw
Montgomery:
Alena Schweiger
Krista Schweiger
Sophie November
Schweiger (pet)
Tom Eischens
Monticello:
In Memory of Sandee
Kunz
Lynne Fleming
Susan Newman
Moorhead:
Allen & Hailey Antonson

Betty Borgen
Brad Borgen
Cecelia Borgen Schmit
Cindy Antonson-Lillevold
Curt Borgen
Ginna & Josh Nustad
In Memory of Mark
Gunstenson
In Memory of Virginia
Holm Borgen
Jaden Nustad
Jaidyn Borgen
James E. Nelson
Jorren Antonson
Kadence Antonson
Laura & Reuben
Mcgowan
Layla Nustad
Lisa Borgen
Mark Lillevold
Philomena Nelson
Riley Erickson
Taylor Erickson
Moose Lake:
Catch & Release Tumble
& Cheer Club
In Memory of Jack
Wagers
In Memory of Norma
Wagers
The King Family
The Pangerl Family
Mora:
Alan Opatz
Brenda Opatz
Morgan:
In Memory of Jeanette
Fenske
In Memory of Kevin W.
Gegner
In Memory of Sue Gegner
Russell James Hier
Morris:
"Doc" Robert & Betty Lou
Zierke Family
Dick & Lou Burns
In Memory of Robbie D.
Baum
In Memory of Vickie R.
Bratton
Morton:
River Valley Groom &
Spa, pet grooming salon
Mound:
Barbara Jordal Vernes
Mountain Lake:
Brad & Lois Herrig
Debra & Dan
Schoenenberger
Gary & Florence Dunker
Gary Hildebrandt
Greg & Colleen Dunker
Mary J. Classen

Mike Dunker
Nancy & Mike Swenson
Steve Dodge & Marcia
Dunker
The Bryan Rempel Family
Nashwauk:
Corbin's Ink Designs
Hugh Stempfley
Nelson:
Amanda Gilbertson
New Brighton:
Lawrence Schoppe
Lorna Schultz
Robert Schultz
New Germany:
M.J. Iverson
Susan Iverson
New London:
Jasmine Stiegen
Leonard Schmitz
New Prague:
Brentan Carkhuff
Craig Larson
Eric Stradtman
In Memory of Ryan
Carkhuff
In Memory of Tami
Odenthal
Michelle Carkhuff
Rachel Larson
Renee Walden
Steve Walden
New Richland:
Keith & Melisa Leonardo
Keith, Melisa, Jayce,
Mariah, Kenzie, & Reid
Leonardo
Kirtina Anderson-Carter
Panther Power House
New Trier:
In Memory of Lloyd Peine
New Ulm:
"Big Don" Dannheim
(Pioneer Businessman)
Ah Dannheim (Pioneer
Businessman)
In Memory of Dolly
Bassett
In Memory of James
Bassett
In Memory of Kenneth
Bassett
In Memory of Vernon
Rosenau
Mark Dicke
Otto Boock (Pioneer
Businessman)
Ralph "Whitey" Guldan
(One of a Kind)
Randy Tastel (Local
Legend)

New York Mills:
In Honor of the Fraki, Majava, Pajari, & Rattamaa Families
In Loving Memory of Lucille Schik
Lloyd's Lanes (1962-1975)
Newburg Township:
In Memory of Marta Larsdatter
Newfolden:
Michael Waterworth
North Branch:
North Branch American Legion Riders - Post 85
North Mankato:
In Memory of Cathryn L. Johnson
In Memory of Loren Hanel
Jeremy, Kim & Grant Taylor
John A. Johnson
North Saint Paul:
Dean Schwanke
In Memory of Karen L. Merrick (NSP Historical Society)
In Memory of Raymond Reinke
Jane Warzeka Schwanke
Northfield:
In Memory of Dianne Kyte
In Memory of Douglas Herbert Petersen
Northrop:
Heidi Koeritz
Tom Koeritz
Norwood Young America:
Alan & Linnae Paumen
Brett & Samantha Fahey
Nowthen:
The Linn's
Oakdale:
Ireland Cook
Jill Bemis
Michael Bemis
Pamela Grode
Odessa:
Herman Ellingson
Odin:
B&B Specialties
In Memory of Barb Anderson
Ogema:
In Memory of Tracy Mae Jirava
Okabena:
In Honor of Donald & Lula Junker "70th Wedding Anniversary 2025"
Steve DeWall & Connie DeWall

Oklee:
Donna Lee (Jensen) Larson
In Memory of Alvin F Jensen
In Memory of Jack Rindahl
Mary Lou Schmidt
Olivia:
Dorothy Boerboom
Florence Dyrssen
In Memory of Joseph Hronesh
James David Martin
Ruth Martin
Tackle Box Web & Printing
Onamia:
The Depot on 169
Ormsby:
Stacey (Olson) Haldemann
Ortonville:
In Memory of Mom Arlys Schiesser
Joel Koch
Karen Koch
Osakis:
Erickson's Petting Zoo
Hannah Dierks
In Loving Memory of Darlene M Zabel & Melvin D Lamar
Madison & Tyler Stier
Otsego:
In Memory of Grandma Rose Sieberlich
In Memory of Kathe Meyer
In Memory of my dog Waylon
In Memory of Rick Simon
The Cardinal Family
Ottertail:
The Preston Family
Owatonna:
Asher Berge
Edwig Vyncke
Fisher Framing & Finishes, LLC
In Memory of Don & Mary Jane Reigel
James & Jessica Dahlgren
Kent Reigel
Marc Reigel
Nora Sletten
Owatonna Photo News (1956-74)
Pascal Rorive
Soren Dahlgren
Park Rapids:
Adam Thompson
In Memory of Conner Decker
Jill & Kevin Thompson
Mary Garlie

Milton Hanson
Myah Hanson
Vicky Hanson
Parkers Prairie:
Glenn & Mary Cornish
In Memory of Judy & Justin Hemmerlin
Paynesville:
Ardith & David Ampe
Brandon West
Claudia Schmitz
Rachel Ampe
Pelican Rapids:
Bob & Mimi Uhrig
In Memory of Tanner Markgraf
Marilyn Folden
Thomas Albright
Pemberton:
Hella Wendt
In Memory of Otto Wendt
Perham:
Ben & Lisa Kadow Family
Cassie Horn
Devin Meyer
Donna Gill
Eli Schwab
Gabe Schwab
In Memory of Russel P. Kadow
Isaiah Horn
Jacob Berthiaume
Karlie Dombeck
Morgan Dombeck
Sabrina Rottelo
Taylor Dombeck
Zaine Berthiaume
Perley:
In Memory of Marv & Margie Thompson
Peterson:
Boutique Station
In Memory of Jon Haslerud
Pillager:
Mayor Adam Sparrow
Tucker Bunte
Pine City:
DeAnna Skare Vander Vegt
Pine Island:
Beach Family (47)
Bernard Riley
Evan Goplen & Josselyn Lindahl
Hayden Ferguson
Marianne Riley
The Little Hair Salon
Pine River:
Blind Lake Cattle Company
Hanneken Insurance
Pine River DMV

Pipestone:
Catherine Lindstrom
Harold & Marlys Carrow family
In Loving Memory of Eileen & Larry Otter
Julie Carrow
Plainview:
Bailey Sue Sangren
Linda Marie Mulholland
Melissa Sue Sangren
Shelby Elaine Sangren
Steven Raymond Sangren
Thomas James Mulholland
Plummer:
Greenwald Family
Plymouth:
Brandon McClintock
Dale Schlender
Endurium
Erika McClintock
Princeton:
1st Congregational UCC Church
Allan & Catherine Tou
Amy Hoffman (b. 1964)
Clara Olson Lund
Eleeya Estelle (Larson) Palmer
Gary Schultz
In Memory of Douglas Sanford
In Memory of George Sanford
In Memory of Meggie Schultz
In Memory of Ruth (George) Sanford
Jeff Hoffman (b. 1962)
Lindsay Sharon (Larson) Cournia
Meredith Dana (Larson) Kind
Michelle (Sanford) Donner
Nancy A.
Prior Lake:
Marie Hanel
Proctor:
Alan Stingley
Gwen Carroll
In Loving Memory of Dudley Stingley
Piper Ann
Puposky:
Tom & Peggy Arms
Ramsey:
Charlee Heppes
Gavin Heppes
Randall:
In Memory of James W. Schmidt

Rapidan:
Jim Jaycox
Lynn Yunker Jaycox
Raymond:
J.A.C.K Family
Mark Hirman
Red Lake Falls:
Adeline Weiss Beyer
Irving Beyer
Red Wing:
Bitsy Joy
Diane Nordgaard
Jack Nordgaard
Mike, Megan, Selena & Colton Schenach
Redwood Falls:
Cayden Sanchez
Dennis Pendleton
In Memory of Ernie Roller
In Memory of Thomas Amberg
Lilly Pendleton
Melanie & Timothy Frederiksen
Shelley Barker
Silas Berry
The Worsech Family
Willow Berry
Remer:
Don & Paula Justen
Mabel Lake
In Memory of Jordan Perkins
Renville:
Bill Sietsema
Brad Beckendorf
Heidi Beckendorf
In Memory of Aeilt Feldman
In Memory of Gary Beckendorf
In Memory of Lois Beckendorf
In Memory of Tim Feldman
Jennifer Beckendorf
Jessica Beckendorf
Karen Sietsema
Meghan Beckendorf
Natalie Beckendorf
Vicki J. Baxendale
Revere:
Bruce & Jen Starkson
Bruiser's Place
Rice:
Donna Brown
Frank Simon Trutwin married Francis Bernadine Marshik (1924)
In Memory of Doris Trutwin
In Memory of Mike Hunter

In Memory of Nancy Jane Anderson
In Memory of Steve Ablan
Rice Lake:
In Memory of Jeffrey Wayne Mrozik
Richfield:
Ben Kopnick
Joanne & Jerry Mercier
Richmond:
In Memory of Michael Joseph Schreifels
In Memory of Susan Lucas
Richmond Historical Collective
Tom & Terry Niehaus
Robbinsdale:
Bill MacKay
In Memory of James Zukauska
The Gagnon Family
Rochester:
Amanda Staven family
Baril Noel Family
Bonnie Nemoede
Cathy Finken
Charlie & Mackenzie Wallace
Clete & Norma Pollack
Heather Johnson
In Honor of Mike, Sophia, Maja, Olivia, Jessmar, Yasmin Kunze, Quelles, Santiagos, Gamises & Matubises
In Memory of Leia Baril Noel
In Memory of my sister, Jane Pollack
Iossi Family
Jerry Olson
Jim "Jamma" Connell
Ken & Lousette Schultz
Leone Brewer
Marie Barner
Mark, AmyJo, Ashli, Abbi, Marky, Mia Clement
Miss Nimoy Baril Noel (dog)
Sandy Johnson
Stacey Kern
Team Al Nofal
Ted Brewer
Rockford:
Rockford Area Historical Society
The Klatt Family
The Koehler Family
The Loeffler Family
The Mutterer Family

Rogers:
Rollo Pederson
Roscoe:
In Memory of Bella (Spiczka) Leyendecker
Rosemount:
Jason Carlson
Jody Powell
Roseville:
Wayne Groff
Rothsay:
In Memory of Ethelwyn McBain
In Memory of Henry Lillevold
In Memory of Roy McBain
Round Lake:
Barb Markus
Brandi Markus
Cindy M Watson
Dennis Markus
Devin Markus
Gwen L Watson
In Memory of Gwendolyn A Watson
In Memory of Jack D Watson
Jill D Watson
Karen Markus
Rush City:
Cheswick Schuldt
Rushford:
Ayla Hoskins
Creed Hoskins
Ivie Hoskins
Rushmore:
Virgil & Vera Loonan
Russell:
Diane Christopherson
In Memory of Marvin Minett
Patty Minett
Ruthton:
In Memory of Al & Betty Zeinstra
Rutledge:
Blue Sky Electrolysis
Orth Realty
Sacred Heart:
David Grove
Orville & Angie Wolf
Shirley Grove
Stacy Peterson
Saint Anthony Village:
Chris Nogosek
Emilie Nogosek
Joe Nogosek
Kim Nogosek
Max, Buddie, Ellie, Iroh (pets)
Rachel Nogosek
Sam Nogosek
The Nogosek Family

Saint Charles:
Chet Fenske
Fohrman Family
In Memory of Leland & Jeanne Ferden
Page Family
Saint Joseph:
Christian & Mary Fruth Speiser
Elijah Stenman
In Memory of: Michael & Elisabeth Reinert Theisen
Jacob & Anna Maria Hankes Lahr
Jonas Stenman
Joren Stenman
Kari Stenman
Math & Elizabeth Lahr Scherer
Saint Michael:
Ella Kaiser
Rowan Kaiser
Ryan Gleason
Saint Paul:
Loving Memory of Alfred Schaeppi
Don Tofthagen
Dorothy Tutewohl
In Loving Memory of Betty Schaeppi
In Memory of Dean Schafer
In Memory of Duane Demko Sr
In Memory of Muriel Demko
The Soler Family
Todd Tofthagen
Saint Peter:
Gail Dummer
Jonette Havemeier
Saint Vincent:
St. Vincent Memories
https://56755.blogspot.com
Sanford:
Beverly Larson
In Memory of Gilbert Larson
In Memory of William Nathan Irvine
Sargeant:
Luverne, Kristine & Noah Maier
Sartell:
In Memory of Nathaniel Schultz
Lisa Beek
Sauk Centre:
Cindy & Rich LeBrun
The Lisa Rosenow Family
Wayne & Mary Jo Yokiel

Sauk Rapids:
Marcella Deppa
Philip Pederson
Savage:
Kaden Dierke-Heppes
Nick Knoll
The Wroge Family
Sedan:
Vern Rende
Shakopee:
Edna MacKay
Shelly:
Derek Dunham
Sherburn:
Earl Zehms
In Memory of Pat & Woody Hanson (love, your grandkids)
Shevlin:
Mel & Paula Davis
Shoreview:
Bill Rinehart
Kevin & Barb Whelan
Shorewood:
Mike & Molly Keogh
Silver Bay:
Sandra Coffey
Wehrman Family
Slayton:
Brian Byers
Danielle McFarland
Mary Ellen Moline
Sleepy Eye:
In Memory of Nicole Steffl Fuchs
Blanca Dena & Rudy Dena
Borth Memorials
In Memory of Brandon Hoffmann
The Borth Family
The Bruckbauer Family
Wesley Hoffmann
South Saint Paul:
Larry & Robin Ross
Thomas J. Johnson
Spicer:
Cathy Diedrichsen
Spring Grove:
Charles & Nora Beckjord
Spring Valley:
Scott's Auto Works
Brady & Hannah Osterhus
Curt & Barb Osterhus
Kylie Osterhus
Mitch & Dani Osterhus
Scott & JoAnn Osterhus
The Watson Family
Springfield:
24 North Second Story Suite
Alexis Deibele
Connie Helget

Gary & Lois Mattson &
Family
In Memory of Eugene &
Donna Arndt
Jeff & Stacey Weisensel
Jesse Deibele
John Mueller
Katie Mueller
Kelvin & Char Bast
Lisa Arndt Walsh
Lowell Helget
Mia Deibele
Noah Mueller
Oliver Deibele
Steve & Colette Huiras
Wyatt Mueller
Squaw Lake:
A great hunt companion, Belle.
Blayne Tuey
In Memory of Chuck & Joan Clark
St. Cloud:
In Memory of Evelyn "Evy" Koop
In Memory of MaryAnn O'Konek Moog
In Memory of Mildred Hoagland Chapp
In Memory of Valerian "Val" Chapp
St. Francis:
Class of 1994
Earl W. Smith Jr.
In Loving Memory of Jessica Mueller
In Memory of Annie E. Smith
In Memory of Karen (Lindh) Davis
In Memory of Myra (Stroeing) Davis
Lori Burnette
Opp Family Chiropractic
The Stephen Fisher Family
St. Hilaire:
In Honor of the Scott Family & Relatives
St. James:
In Memory of Dennis & Carol Thompson
Jenny Hanen
Kimberly Rosenberg
St. Louis Park:
Performance Ready
Tom & Sandy Olson
St. Paul Park:
Bee & Butter Naturals
Oliver Johnson
Shannon Johnson
St Stephen:
Matthew Nienaber

Staples:
In Memory of Jim & Anne Sadusky
Mary Knoll
Ultra Color Inc.
Starbuck:
Ada Pederson
Harvey Pederson
Heidi Rooney
In Loving Memory of John & Judy Dell
Julian Pederson
Patrick Rooney
Roger Pederson
Stewart:
In Memory of Vicki Switala
Kuttner Seed
Stewartville:
Aaron Martin
Aaron Miller
Karinn Miller
Manette Black
Storden:
Charles Berger
Karen Hildebrandt
Malcolm & Madge Potter
Strandquist:
DeAnn Lofstrom
Lenny Lofstrom
Strasburg:
Tanya Lee Raycroft
Sturgeon Lake:
Michael Minks
Swan River:
In Loving Memory of Bruno Hill
Karen Skorich & Joseph Skorich
Sylvia Hill
Swanville:
Bernd & Käti
In Memory of Joseph & Gladys Oven
Rosemary Nienaber
Tamarack:
In Memory of Arvid "Pete" & Bernice (Geving) Brandt
In Memory of Ruth Tuholski
Taopi:
Angela Kiefer
Talmoon:
The Kanes
Taunton:
In Loving Memory of Barbara M. Carlson
Peter Breyfogle
Tenstrike:
#TeamKalan
Alan & Kelley Pryor
Toivola:
Angela, Jason & June Randall

Tracy:
Connor Towne
Gary Helgemo
In Memory of Brian John Carlson
Joshua Stiegen
Lisa Towne
Stacy Sue Carlson
Trail:
George Reitter
Helen Flateland
Leona Brekke
Maggie Reitter
Travis Christianson
Trimont:
Farmers State Bank of Trimont
In Memory of Douglas Bettin
Joshua & Hayley Ellanson
Tyler Bettin
Trosky:
Arlyn & Shirlene Zylstra
Truman:
Blue Pit Brewing
Gladys Drager Ufer
In Memory of Darrell Urban
In Memory of Edward & Amanda Wessel
Lyle Ufer
Twin Valley:
Chris, Leah, & Trista Lee
Tyler:
Elaine Kraemer
Lena Burckhardt
Opal Jensen
Paula Hansen
Steven Svendsen
Thooft Bros. LLC
Wendell "Pete" Jensen
Underwood:
David Wass
Katrina Wass
Susan Groff
Upsala:
Dan Hovland
Schultz Auctioneers
Urbank:
In Memory of Marvin & Bernice (Jesnowski) Koep
Utica:
Bonnie Denzer
Mardelle & Walter Midler
Vadnais Heights:
Kevin Burke-Bopp
The Swanson Family
Vergas:
Gerald Kratzke
Nellie Kratzke
Thomas, Kelsey & Rousey Varty

Vermillion:
Nancy Halberg
Verndale:
Casey Greer Jr
Eliza Greer
In Memory of Dale Nelson
Nancy Grunau
Sarah Belknap
Vernon Center:
Baarts Storage
Calvin Baarts
Mary Kay Hohenstein
Sue Baarts
Tammi (Looft) Born
Vernon Center Lumber
Vesta:
Deborah Halvorson
Richard Halvorson
SouthWest Pest LLC
Victoria:
Julius, Romani & Esme Meregildo
Viking:
Deborah Waterworth
In Memory of Erv & Vi Melvie
Virginia:
Brian Makela
Don Makela
In Memory of J. Edward Pearsall, Mayor
Troy Makela
True Rangers: Sherrie Nelson
Wabasha:
Doug, Savannah Meyer
In Memory of Bill & Neatsie Glomski
In Memory of Corky & Cracky Kreye
Linda Odden
Michaela & EllieMae Kreye
Rise & Shine Vacation Rental on Pembroke
SVJ Creative Designs
Wabasso:
Carmen Arends
In Loving Memory of Rodney & Sandra Boyum
Kenneth Arends
Teresa & Mark Wagner
Waconia:
Alexis Jade Sennes
Deb Falk Lohse
Dennis & Cindy Niccum
Paige Marie Sennes
Wadena:
David & Deb Wiese
Wahkon:
In Memory of Floyd, Shih Tzu puppy
Teresa Ebnet

Walnut Grove:
In Loving Memory of George, Robert & Suzanne Hahn
Wanda:
Kyle, Samantha, Clancy & LeDoux Prechel
Warba:
Sharon Bulinski
Warren:
Alan Morkassel
Bryan Murphy
Diana Morkassel
In Memory of Jane Amiot Murphy
Jon & Rodney Nicholls
Larry Murphy
Molly Fridstrom
Stacy Navarro
Tammy Knutson
Vyron Morkassel
Warroad:
Aaron & Katie Marvin
Cornel & Rosie Rygh
Franklin Ernst
Hendri & Sarah Ernst
Kristi Rygh Johnson
Lisa Rygh Heppner
Neighbors Chevrolet
Waseca:
Charles Bogue
Charlotte M. Frankenberry
Donald K. Frankenberry, Sr
Dorothea Waite
James (Jamie) Mariner
Watertown:
Autumn Guetzkow
Jenny, Rachelle, Alex Pierson
Lindsay Zumbrunnen
Summer Guetzkow
The Motzko Family Farm
Winter Guetzkow
Waterville:
In Memory of Ron & Tammy Remme
Watkins:
Roger Linn
Waverly:
Carol Borg
In Memory of Elaine (Perra) Luhman
James Borg
John & Rebecca Nienaber
Northline Print Co.
Wayzata:
Mike Dilley
Wells:
Dona Fisher Wilder
In Memory of Ade & Yvonne Yokiel

In Memory of Chick & Shirley Larson
In Memory of Francis Wilder
Lyle & Anthony Doerr-Rodriguez Jr.
Wendell:
Anthony Lien
Don Weigand & Gloria Weigand (the best grandparents in existence)
Elmer Jesness
In Memory of Annie Anderson
In Memory of LeRoy Anderson
In Memory of Lowell Pargman
In Memory of Lyle Anderson
In Memory of Ole Anderson
West Concord:
Kim Christians
Cheryll Eggert
In Memory of August Eggert
In Memory of Verna (Fitzgerald) Eggert
Patti & Mike Krier
West Concord Historical Society
West Cook:
Benita Alleman
West St. Paul:
In Memory of Dixie Mitchell
Jerry & Eileen Langeslag
Westbrook:
Dakotah Danielson
Emmett Danielson
Jeremy Schreier
Kelly Danielson
Maverick Danielson
Michaela Miller-Schreier
Wheaton:
August James
Bella Ann
Colleen Fiala
In Loving Memory of Owen Schultz
Lilly Joy
Oliver Lee
White Bear Lake:
Collins Jane Schmidt
Eldred Luehmann Ufer
In Memory of Donna Whitman
In Memory of Gary Whitman
PMS Hohnstadt
Roland Ufer

White Bear Township:
Jim Rinehart
Willernie:
In Memory of Delores "Jackie" Anderson
Williams:
In Loving Memory of Gertrude Muggli
Willmar:
Healthy Fusion of Willmar
Jerod, Erin, Maura, & Blane Wendt
Rebekah Schmitz
Wilmont:
In Memory of Jack & Carl Slater
In Memory of John & Lue Schipper
In Memory of Ray & Mary Johanning
In Memory of the Deceased Members of the William Slater Family
Windom:
BJ Video Productions
Buckwheat, Sonya, & James Johnson
Cheryl Knutson
Jack & Roxanne Potter
Winnebago:
Gear Head Garage
Jennifer Quintero
Juan Diaz Lujan
Winona:
In Memory of Susan Lettner

Ken Gillies
Winsted:
Alan Wiederholt
Alexis Wiederholt
Amber Wiederholt
Carol Hertel Kluk
Frances (Franny) Hertel Tieman
In Honor of: Mary Jo Hertel Smuda
In Loving Memory: Leo & Genevieve Hertel
In Memory of Mark Wiederholt
In Memory of Ronald James "RJ" Wiederholt
James (Jim) Hertel
Jane Hertel Campbell
Jerome (Jerry) Hertel
John (Jack) Hertel
Lynise Wiederholt
Rosanne Hertel
Shannon Wiederholt
Winthrop:
Dalton Weber
Grayson Weber
In Memory of Jacob William Weber
In Memory of Peter Machaiek
John Weber
Karla Weber
Maggie Margosian
Marianne Machaiek
Matt Machaiek
Morgan Weber

Ryan Weber & Emma, Cody & Zoe
The Lavender Boutique
Troy & Amy Martin
Tyler Weber
Wood Lake:
Hartke Farms
In Loving Memory of Guadalupe Herrera
Kaylee Hartke
Preuss Farms Inc.
The Preuss Family
Woodbury:
Kevin Bloomquist
Worthington:
Gary's Painting & Hardwood Lumber
In Memory of Alieen J Watson
Lara Liepold
Pete & Jeanne Suby
Shelly Kilker
Zimmerman:
Deb Erickson
In Memory of Clifford & Ruby Kreager
LeAnn Marie Kreager
Zumbrota:
Benjamin, Chelsea, Leila, Lucy, Teresa, & Peter Lawson
Thomas Milardo, Shari Christianson

Town Index

Ada 381
Adams 353
Adrian 374
Afton 584
Aitkin 22
Akeley 235
Albany 529
Albert Lea 180
Alberta 549
Albertville 620
Alden 181
Aldrich 577
Alexandria 160
Alpha 254
Altura 614
Alvarado 315
Amboy 58
Andover 25
Angle Inlet 289
Annandale 621
Anoka 25
Apple Valley 138
Appleton 552
Arco 302
Arden Hills 439
Argyle 315
Arlington 525
Ashby 200
Askov 408
Atwater 260
Audubon 35
Aurora 490
Austin 354
Avoca 365
Avon 529
Babbitt 490
Backus 90
Badger 486
Bagley 113
Balaton 306
Baldwin 522
Barnesville 106
Barnum 72
Barrett 200
Barry 53
Battle Lake 395
Baudette 290
Baxter 128
Bayport 584
Beardsley 53
Beaver Bay 285
Beaver Creek 481
Becker 522
Bejou 313
Belgrade 530
Belle Plaine 509

Bellechester 187
Bellingham 281
Beltrami 421
Belview 452
Bemidji 40
Bena 90
Benson 553
Bertha 563
Bethel 26
Big Falls 277
Big Lake 523
Bigelow 375
Bigfork 246
Bingham Lake 124
Birchwood Village 585
Bird Island 461
Biscay 332
Biwabik 491
Blackduck 42
Blaine 27
Blomkest 260
Blooming Prairie 546
Bloomington 203
Blue Earth 167
Bluffton 395
Bock 342
Borup 382
Bovey 246
Bowlus 345
Boy River 91
Boyd 281
Braham 238
Brainerd 129
Brandon 161
Breckenridge 610
Breezy Point 130
Brewster 375
Bricelyn 167
Brook Park 409
Brooklyn Center 205
Brooklyn Park 205
Brooks 449
Brookston 491
Brooten 530
Browerville 563
Browns Valley 569
Brownsdale 355
Brownsville 230
Brownton 332
Bruno 410
Buckman 346
Buffalo 621
Buffalo Lake 462
Buhl 492
Burnsville 138
Burtrum 564

Butterfield 605
Byron 385
Caledonia 231
Callaway 36
Calumet 247
Cambridge 238
Campbell 611
Canby 630
Cannon Falls 187
Canton 173
Carlos 162
Carlton 72
Carver 77
Cass Lake 91
Cedar Mills 336
Center City 101
Centerville 27
Ceylon 326
Champlin 206
Chandler 365
Chanhassen 78
Chaska 78
Chatfield 173
Chickamaw Beach 92
Chisago City 101
Chisholm 492
Chokio 550
Circle Pines 28
Clara City 97
Claremont 152
Clarissa 565
Clarkfield 631
Clarks Grove 182
Clear Lake 523
Clearbrook 114
Clearwater 622
Clements 452
Cleveland 291
Climax 421
Clinton 53
Clitherall 395
Clontarf 554
Cloquet 73
Coates 139
Cobden 65
Cohasset 247
Cokato 623
Cold Spring 531
Coleraine 248
Cologne 79
Columbia Heights 28
Columbus 29
Comfrey 65
Comstock 107
Conger 182
Cook 493

716

Coon Rapids 29
Corcoran 206
Correll 54
Cosmos 337
Cottage Grove 585
Cottonwood 306
Courtland 370
Credit River 510
Cromwell 74
Crookston 422
Crosby 131
Crosslake 131
Crystal 206
Currie 366
Cuyuna 132
Cyrus 435
Dakota 614
Dalton 396
Danube 462
Danvers 555
Darfur 605
Darwin 337
Dassel 338
Dawson 282
Dayton 207
De Graff 555
Deephaven 207
Deer Creek 396
Deer River 248
Deerwood 132
Delano 624
Delavan 168
Delhi 453
Dellwood 586
Denham 410
Dennison 188
Dent 396
Detroit Lakes 36
Dexter 355
Dilworth 108
Dodge Center 152
Donaldson 266
Donnelly 550
Doran 612
Dover 386
Dovray 366
Duluth 494
Dumont 570
Dundas 475
Dundee 375
Dunnell 326
Eagan 140
Eagle Bend 565
Eagle Lake 58
East Bethel 29
East Grand Forks 423
East Gull Lake 92
Easton 168
Echo 632

Eden Prairie 208
Eden Valley 338
Edgerton 416
Edina 208
Effie 249
Eitzen 232
Elba 614
Elbow Lake 201
Elgin 572
Elizabeth 397
Elk River 523
Elko New Market 510
Elkton 356
Ellendale 546
Ellsworth 376
Elmdale 346
Elmore 169
Elrosa 532
Ely 496
Elysian 292
Emily 133
Emmons 183
Empire 141
Erhard 397
Erskine 424
Evan 66
Evansville 162
Eveleth 497
Excelsior 209
Eyota 386
Fairfax 463
Fairmont 327
Falcon Heights 440
Faribault 475
Farmington 141
Farwell 435
Federal Dam 92
Felton 108
Fergus Falls 398
Fertile 425
Fifty Lakes 133
Finlayson 410
Fisher 425
Flensburg 346
Floodwood 498
Florence 307
Foley 45
Forada 163
Forest Lake 587
Foreston 342
Fort Ripley 133
Fosston 426
Fountain 174
Foxhome 612
Franklin 464
Frazee 37
Freeborn 183
Freeport 532
Fridley 30

Frost 169
Fulda 367
Funkley 42
Garfield 163
Garrison 134
Garvin 307
Gary 382
Gaylord 526
Gem Lake 440
Geneva 184
Genola 347
Georgetown 108
Ghent 308
Gibbon 526
Gilbert 499
Gilman 46
Glencoe 332
Glenville 184
Glenwood 435
Glyndon 109
Golden Valley 210
Gonvick 114
Good Thunder 58
Goodhue 189
Goodridge 406
Goodview 615
Graceville 54
Granada 328
Grand Marais 121
Grand Meadow 356
Grand Portage 122
Grand Rapids 249
Granite Falls 632
Grant 587
Grasston 258
Green Isle 527
Greenbush 486
Greenfield 211
Greenwald 533
Greenwood 211
Grey Eagle 566
Grove City 339
Grygla 316
Gully 426
Hackensack 93
Hadley 367
Hallock 267
Halma 267
Halstad 383
Ham Lake 30
Hamburg 80
Hammond 572
Hampton 142
Hancock 550
Hanley Falls 634
Hanover 624
Hanska 66
Harding 347
Hardwick 481

717

Harmony 174
Harris 102
Hartland 184
Hastings 142
Hatfield 416
Hawley 109
Hayfield 152
Hayward 185
Hazel Run 634
Hector 464
Heidelberg 292
Henderson 527
Hendricks 302
Hendrum 383
Henning 399
Henriette 411
Herman 201
Hermantown 499
Heron Lake 254
Hewitt 566
Hibbing 500
Hill City 23
Hillman 347
Hills 482
Hilltop 31
Hinckley 411
Hitterdal 110
Hoffman 202
Hokah 232
Holdingford 533
Holland 416
Hollandale 185
Holloway 555
Holt 316
Hopkins 211
Houston 232
Howard Lake 625
Hoyt Lakes 501
Hugo 588
Humboldt 268
Hutchinson 333
Ihlen 417
Independence 212
International Falls 277
Inver Grove Heights 143
Iona 368
Iron Junction 501
Ironton 134
Isanti 239
Isle 342
Ivanhoe 303
Jackson 255
Janesville 581
Jasper 417
Jeffers 124
Jenkins 134
Johnson 55
Jordan 511
Kandiyohi 260

Karlstad 268
Kasota 292
Kasson 153
Keewatin 250
Kelliher 43
Kellogg 572
Kennedy 269
Kenneth 482
Kensington 163
Kent 612
Kenyon 189
Kerkhoven 555
Kerrick 412
Kettle River 74
Kiester 169
Kilkenny 293
Kimball 534
Kinbrae 377
Kingston 339
Kinney 501
La Crescent 233
La Prairie 251
La Salle 606
Lafayette 370
Lake Benton 304
Lake Bronson 269
Lake City 573
Lake Crystal 59
Lake Elmo 588
Lake Henry 534
Lake Lillian 261
Lake Park 38
Lake Shore 94
Lake St. Croix Beach 589
Lake Wilson 368
Lakefield 256
Lakeland 589
Lakeland Shores 589
Lakeville 144
Lamberton 453
Lancaster 270
Landfall 590
Lanesboro 175
Laporte 235
Lastrup 348
Lauderdale 441
Le Center 293
Le Roy 356
Le Sueur 294
Lengby 427
Leonard 114
Leonidas 502
Lester Prairie 334
Lewiston 615
Lewisville 606
Lexington 31
Lilydale 145
Lindstrom 102

Lino Lakes 32
Lismore 377
Litchfield 340
Little Canada 441
Little Falls 348
Littlefork 279
Long Beach 436
Long Lake 212
Long Prairie 566
Longville 94
Lonsdale 477
Loretto 213
Louisburg 283
Lowry 436
Lucan 454
Luverne 483
Lyle 357
Lynd 308
Mabel 175
Madelia 607
Madison 283
Madison Lake 60
Magnolia 484
Mahnomen 313
Mahtomedi 590
Manchester 186
Manhattan Beach 135
Mankato 60
Mantorville 153
Maple Grove 213
Maple Lake 625
Maple Plain 214
Mapleton 62
Mapleview 357
Maplewood 441
Marble 251
Marietta 284
Marine on St. Croix 590
Marshall 309
Mayer 80
Maynard 98
Mazeppa 574
McGrath 23
McGregor 23
McIntosh 427
McKinley 502
Meadowlands 502
Medford 547
Medicine Lake 214
Medina 214
Meire Grove 534
Melrose 535
Menahga 578
Mendota 145
Mendota Heights 146
Mentor 428
Middle River 316
Miesville 146
Milaca 343

Milan 98
Millerville 164
Millville 574
Milroy 454
Miltona 164
Minneapolis 216
Minneiska 574
Minneota 310
Minnesota City 615
Minnesota Lake 170
Minnetonka 217
Minnetonka Beach 218
Minnetrista 218
Mizpah 279
Montevideo 99
Montgomery 295
Monticello 625
Montrose 626
Moorhead 110
Moose Lake 75
Mora 258
Morgan 455
Morris 551
Morristown 477
Morton 465
Motley 349
Mound 218
Mounds View 442
Mountain Iron 503
Mountain Lake 125
Murdock 556
Myrtle 186
Nashua 612
Nashwauk 251
Nassau 284
Nelson 165
Nerstrand 478
Nevis 236
New Auburn 528
New Brighton 442
New Germany 81
New Hope 219
New London 261
New Munich 536
New Prague 512
New Richland 582
New Trier 147
New Ulm 67
New York Mills 400
Newfolden 317
Newport 591
Nicollet 371
Nielsville 428
Nimrod 578
Nisswa 135
Norcross 202
North Branch 103
North Mankato 371
North Oaks 443

North St. Paul 443
Northfield 478
Northome 279
Northrop 328
Norwood Young America 81
Nowthen 32
Oak Grove 32
Oak Park Heights 592
Oakdale 592
Odessa 56
Odin 608
Ogema 39
Ogilvie 258
Okabena 256
Oklee 450
Olivia 466
Onamia 343
Ormsby 608
Orono 219
Oronoco 386
Orr 503
Ortonville 56
Osakis 165
Oslo 317
Osseo 220
Ostrander 176
Otsego 627
Ottertail 401
Owatonna 547
Palisade 24
Park Rapids 236
Parkers Prairie 401
Paynesville 536
Pease 343
Pelican Rapids 402
Pemberton 62
Pennock 262
Pequot Lakes 136
Perham 402
Perley 384
Peterson 176
Pierz 350
Pillager 94
Pine City 412
Pine Island 190
Pine River 95
Pine Springs 592
Pipestone 418
Plainview 575
Plato 334
Plummer 450
Plymouth 220
Porter 635
Preston 176
Princeton 344
Prinsburg 262
Prior Lake 512
Proctor 504

Quamba 259
Racine 358
Ramsey 33
Randall 350
Randolph 147
Ranier 280
Raymond 263
Red Lake Falls 451
Red Wing 190
Redwood Falls 455
Regal 263
Remer 95
Renville 467
Revere 457
Rice 46
Rice Lake 505
Richfield 221
Richmond 537
Richville 403
Riverton 136
Robbinsdale 222
Rochester 387
Rock Creek 413
Rockford 627
Rockville 537
Rogers 222
Rollingstone 616
Roosevelt 487
Roscoe 538
Rose Creek 358
Roseau 487
Rosemount 148
Roseville 444
Rothsay 613
Round Lake 378
Royalton 351
Rush City 103
Rushford 177
Rushford Village 177
Rushmore 378
Russell 311
Ruthton 419
Rutledge 413
Sabin 112
Sacred Heart 468
Saint Anthony Village 223
Saint Augusta 538
Saint Charles 616
Saint Joseph 538
Saint Leo 635
Saint Martin 539
Saint Mary's Point 593
Saint Michael 628
Saint Paul 444
Saint Paul Park 593
Saint Peter 372
Saint Vincent 270
Sanborn 457

Sandstone 413
Sargeant 358
Sartell 539
Sauk Centre 540
Sauk Rapids 46
Savage 513
Scandia 594
Scanlon 75
Seaforth 458
Sebeka 579
Sedan 437
Shafer 104
Shakopee 514
Shelly 384
Sherburn 329
Shevlin 115
Shoreview 446
Shorewood 223
Silver Bay 285
Silver Lake 334
Skyline 63
Slayton 369
Sleepy Eye 69
Sobieski 351
Solway 43
South Haven 628
South Saint Paul 148
Spicer 263
Spring Grove 234
Spring Hill 541
Spring Lake Park 33
Spring Park 223
Spring Valley 178
Springfield 70
Squaw Lake 252
St. Anthony 541
St. Bonifacius 224
St. Clair 63
St. Cloud 542
St. Francis 33
St. Hilaire 406
St. James 608
St. Louis Park 224
St. Rosa 543
St. Stephen 544
Stacy 104
Staples 567
Starbuck 437
Steen 485
Stephen 318
Stewart 335
Stewartville 388
Stillwater 594
Stockton 617

Storden 126
Strandquist 318
Strathcona 488
Sturgeon Lake 414
Sunburg 264
Sunfish Lake 149
Swanville 351
Taconite 252
Tamarack 24
Taopi 359
Taunton 311
Taylors Falls 104
Tenstrike 43
Thief River Falls 407
Tintah 570
Tonka Bay 225
Tower 505
Tracy 312
Trail 428
Trimont 329
Trommald 136
Trosky 420
Truman 330
Turtle River 44
Twin Lakes 186
Twin Valley 385
Two Harbors 286
Tyler 304
Ulen 112
Underwood 403
Upsala 352
Urbank 404
Utica 617
Vadnais Heights 446
Vergas 404
Vermillion 150
Verndale 579
Vernon Center 64
Vesta 458
Victoria 82
Viking 318
Villard 438
Vining 405
Virginia 505
Wabasha 575
Wabasso 458
Waconia 83
Wadena 580
Wahkon 345
Waite Park 544
Waldorf 582
Walker 96
Walnut Grove 459
Walters 170

Waltham 359
Wanamingo 192
Wanda 460
Warba 252
Warren 319
Warroad 488
Waseca 582
Watertown 83
Waterville 295
Watkins 341
Watson 100
Waubun 314
Waverly 628
Wayzata 225
Welcome 331
Wells 171
Wendell 203
West Concord 154
West St. Paul 150
West Union 568
Westbrook 126
Westport 438
Whalan 178
Wheaton 571
White Bear Lake 446
Wilder 257
Willernie 596
Williams 291
Willmar 264
Willow River 414
Wilmont 379
Wilton 44
Windom 127
Winger 429
Winnebago 171
Winona 618
Winsted 335
Winthrop 528
Winton 507
Wolf Lake 39
Wolverton 613
Wood Lake 636
Woodbury 596
Woodland 226
Woodstock 420
Worthington 379
Wrenshall 76
Wright 76
Wykoff 179
Wyoming 105
Zemple 253
Zimmerman 524
Zumbro Falls 576
Zumbrota 192

About the Author: Seth Varner

Hi! I'm Seth Varner, and this is my lovely wife, Eliese! We're the faces behind Wandermore Publishing, a small travel guide and history book publishing company that strives to document history and promote tourism all throughout the Midwest, in towns big and small.

Having been raised on an acreage near Malmo, Nebraska (pop. ~100) in my early years, grown up in nearby Wahoo, Nebraska (pop. ~5,000) as a teenager, and attended college in Omaha, Nebraska, at the University of Nebraska at Omaha, I can attest that no matter how big or small your town is, there's always something to learn or see! I graduated from UNO as a Maverick in May 2023 with a Bachelor's in Business Administration. Using the skills I learned in university, I turned my passions for travel, writing, history, photography, and social media into a full-time career. While growing my business and serving on campus as a Resident Assistant, I met my wife, Eliese. We married in September 2025 at Omaha's historic Durham Museum, the former Omaha Union Station.

As of November 2025, I have had the pleasure of visiting thirty-three states and eleven foreign countries. Someday, I hope to say that I have visited and documented every incorporated municipality in at least ten states. When I'm not buried in centennial books and plat maps or browsing through thousands of Facebook comments, I look for any excuse to hit the road with my friends and family for some more leisurely trips, like sporting events and country music concerts. Eliese and I are quite the foodies—we love trying new restaurants and experimenting with recipes at home using ingredients we've gathered on the road!

Thank you for supporting our mission to show that every town deserves to be celebrated, as they've all got a story to share. You can get in touch with me about all things travel and Wandermore on Facebook, or at sethvarner@wandermorepublishing.com

Photo courtesy of Margaux Cruz Photography (https://www.margslens.com/)

More by Wandermore Publishing

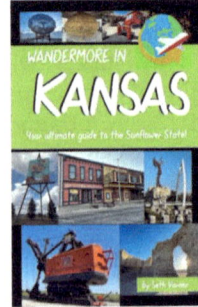
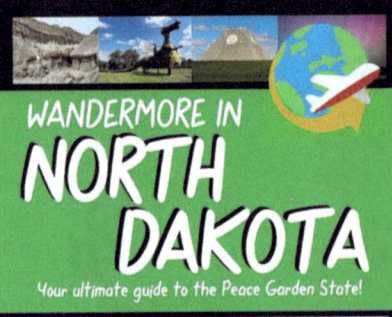

Enjoying your copy of "Wandermore in Minnesota"?

Learn more about town history, travel vicariously through each state via thousands of photos, and explore what Nebraska, Iowa, Kansas, and the Dakotas have to offer with the help of our other five books!

Visit531Nebraska: A Guide to Nebraska's 531 Incorporated Communities

Wandermore in Iowa: Your ultimate guide to the Hawkeye State!

Wandermore in South Dakota: Your ultimate guide to the Mount Rushmore State!

Wandermore in Kansas: Your ultimate guide to the Sunflower State!

Wandermore in North Dakota: Your ultimate guide to the Peace Garden State!

Complete your collection at wandermorepublishing.com/shop!